S0-CEW-485

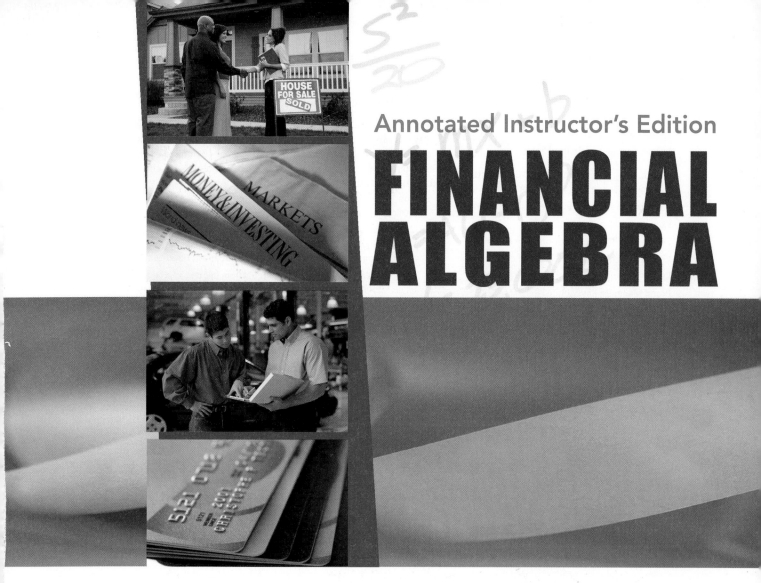

Annotated Instructor's Edition

FINANCIAL ALGEBRA

Advanced Algebra with Financial Applications

Robert Gerver

Richard Sgroi

Australia • Brazil • Japan • Korea • Mexico • Singapore • Spain • United Kingdom • United States

Annotated Instructor's Edition

Financial Algebra: Advanced Algebra with Financial Applications
Robert Gerver and Richard Sgroi

EVP Learning Operations and Development: Sean Wakely

Vice President/Editor-in-Chief: Karen Schmohe

Executive Editor: Eve Lewis

Senior Developmental Editor: Dave Lafferty

Consulting Editor: MATHQueue, Inc.

Senior Editorial Assistant: Debbie Roark

Brand Manager: Kay Stefanski

Market Development Manager: Mark Linton

Marketing Coordinator: Elizabeth Murphy

Art and Cover Direction, Production Management, and Composition: Integra Software Services Pvt., Ltd.

Media Editor: Lysa Kosins

Rights Acquisition Director: Audrey Pettengill

Senior Manufacturing Planner: Kevin Kluck

Cover Images: Getty Images, Media Bakery, iStock

For product information and technology assistance, contact us at
Cengage Learning Customer & Sales Support, 1-800-354-9706
For permission to use material from this text or product,
submit all requests online at www.cengage.com/permissions
Further permissions questions can be emailed to
permissionrequest@cengage.com

Library of Congress Control Number: 2012956435

Student Edition ISBN-13: 978-1-285-44485-7
Student Edition ISBN-10: 1-285-44485-X

Annotated Instructor's Edition ISBN-13: 978-1-285-44753-7
Annotated Instructor's Edition ISBN-10: 1-285-44753-0

South-Western Cengage Learning
5191 Natorp Boulevard
Mason, OH 45040
USA

Cengage Learning products are represented in Canada by Nelson Education, Ltd.

For your course and learning solutions, visit **www.cengage.com/school**

Visit our company website at **www.cengage.com**

Printed in the United States of America
1 2 3 4 5 6 7 8 9 17 16 15 14 13

Financial Algebra Reviewers

Ida Baird
Mathematics Teacher and Co-Department Chair
Richland High School
Richland, Washington

Margaret L. Bartels
Mathematics Teacher
Broward County, Florida

Elaine M. Bell
Mathematics Teacher
Hartland High School
Hartland, Michigan

Kevin R. Bowdler
Mathematics Teacher
Loveland High School
Loveland, Ohio

Sharon Deiling
Math Integration Specialist
Dauphin County Tech School
Harrisburg, Pennsylvania

Lori DeWitt
Mathematics Teacher
Space Coast Jr./Sr. High School
Brevard County, Florida

Robert M. Early
Mathematics Teacher
Cocoa Beach Jr./Sr. High School
Cocoa Beach, Florida

Joshua Folb
Mathematics Teacher
Arlington Public Schools
Arlington, Virginia

Elaine Gottschalk
Mathematics Teacher
Notre Dame Prep School
Towson, Maryland

Katie Gruenwald
Mathematics Teacher
Madison Central High School
Richmond, Kentucky

Marie B. Jump
Mathematics Teacher
Lloyd Memorial High School
Erlanger, Kentucky

Robert Kimball
Consultant
Wake Technical Community College
Raleigh, North Carolina

Sherry M. Larson
Mathematics and Science Teacher
Lennox High School
Lennox, South Dakota

Linda Lebovitz
Mathematics Teacher
Viera High School
Viera, Florida

Greg Malkin
Mathematics Teacher
University School
Cleveland, Ohio

Tara L. McCasland
Mathematics Teacher
Kankakee High School
Kankakee, Illinois

Jodi Meyer
Mathematics Teacher
St. Margaret's School
Tappahannock, Virginia

Ronald G. Noble
State Coordinator, Washington Applied Math Council
Colville High School
Colville, Washington

Cindy Percival
Mathematics Teacher
Roosevelt High School
Des Moines, Iowa

Peter G. Rudowski
Mathematics Teacher
Mason City Schools
Mason, Ohio

Melanie Scott, NBCT
Mathematics Teacher
Madison Central High School
Richmond, Kentucky

Traci L. Stiles
Mathematics Teacher
Merritt Island High School
Merritt Island, Florida

Andy Wait
Math Department Chair
San Luis High School
San Luis, Arizona

Terri L. Wargo
Mathematics Teacher
Palm Bay High School
Melbourne, Florida

Sharon S. Whitehead, PhD
Independent Mathematics Consultant
Arizona State University
Arizona Department of Education
Mesa, Arizona

Matt Wheeler
Math Department Chair
Mesquite High School
Gilbert, Arizona

Robert Gerver, Ph.D. and Richard Sgroi, Ph.D. are well known mathematics teachers, authors, and speakers at mathematics conferences throughout the United States. Over the course of their 30-year careers, they have developed teaching methods to unmask the mysteries of mathematics with applications to music, business, finance, and practical living skills.

Dr. Gerver

Dr. Sgroi

Financial Algebra aligns to the

Common Core State Standards for Mathematical Content

The CCSS provide clear and consistent guidelines so students, teachers, administrators, and parents have an awareness of the mathematics proficiencies expected and how to attain them. The standards are designed to be rigorous and relevant to the real world, reflecting the knowledge and skills that students need for future success.

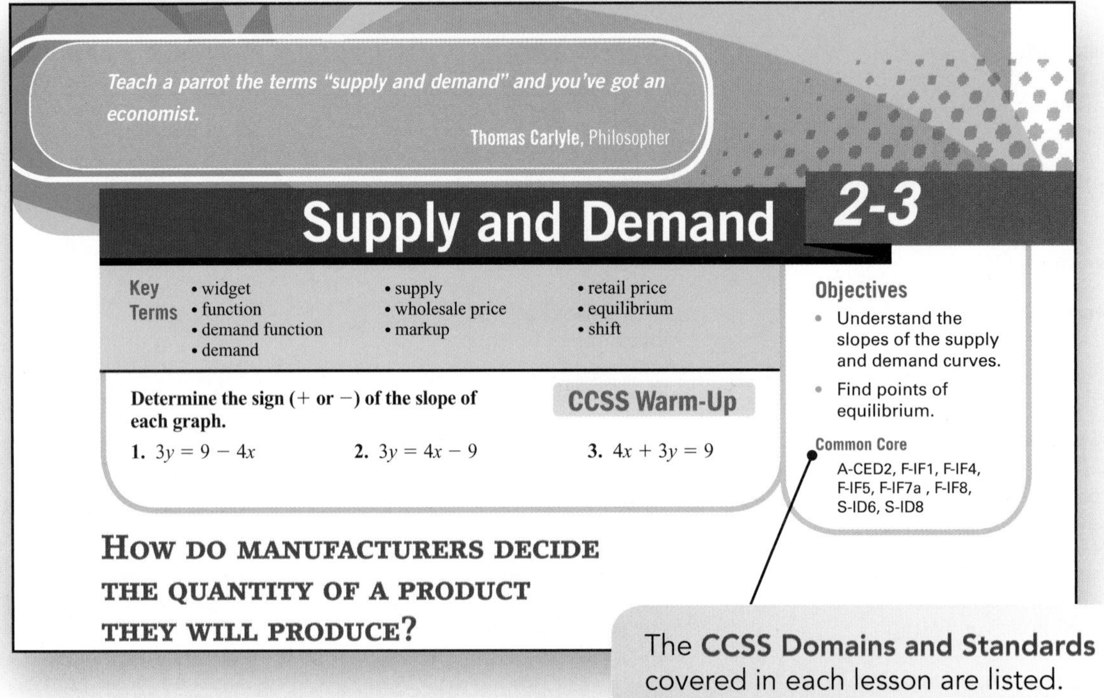

Teach a parrot the terms "supply and demand" and you've got an economist.
Thomas Carlyle, Philosopher
Supply and Demand 2-3
Key Terms • widget • function • demand function • demand • supply • wholesale price • markup • retail price • equilibrium • shift
Objectives
• Understand the slopes of the supply and demand curves.
• Find points of equilibrium.
Common Core
A-CED2, F-IF1, F-IF4, F-IF5, F-IF7a , F-IF8, S-ID6, S-ID8
Determine the sign (+ or −) of the slope of each graph.
CCSS Warm-Up
1. 3y = 9 − 4x
2. 3y = 4x − 9
3. 4x + 3y = 9
HOW DO MANUFACTURERS DECIDE THE QUANTITY OF A PRODUCT THEY WILL PRODUCE?

The **CCSS Domains and Standards** covered in each lesson are listed.

Refresh your memory with CCSS Warm-Ups

The CCSS Domain and Standard are identified to demonstrate that *Financial Algebra* addresses at least one, if not several, core standards in each lesson.

Conceptual Categories

- Number and Quantity
- Algebra
- Modeling
- Functions
- Geometry
- Statistics and Probability

A complete correlation of *Financial Algebra* to the CCSS for Mathematical Content is available on the community website.

www.cengage.com/community/financialalgebra

Common Core State Standards for Mathematical Practice

Engage students as they grow in mathematical maturity and expertise throughout their high school years.

MP 1 Make sense of problems and persevere in solving them.
MP 2 Reason abstractly and quantitatively.
MP 3 Construct viable arguments and critique the reasoning of others.
MP 4 Model with mathematics.
MP 5 Use appropriate tools strategically.
MP 6 Attend to precision.
MP 7 Look for and make use of structure.
MP 8 Look for and express regularity in repeated reasoning.

***Financial Algebra* drives instruction by applying the Common Core State Standards for Mathematical Practice.**

Standards for Mathematical Practice	Examples
Problem solving perseverance (MP 1)	Loan Calculations, Regression, and Credit Cards (Lessons 4-3; 4-4)
Reasoning (MP 2)	Employee Benefits, Social Security and Medicare (Lessons 6-4; 6-5)
Apply and model with mathematics (MP 4)	Graphing Fixed and Variable Expenses (Lessons 2-4; 2-5)
Calculate and communicate with precision (MP 6)	Driving Safety Data and Accident Investigation (Lessons 5-7; 5-8)
Tools are used strategically (MP 5)	Reconcile a checking account using a spreadsheet (Lessons 3-2)
Investigate patterns and structure (MP 7)	Charting a Budget and Cash Flow (Lessons 10-3; 10-4)
Construct arguments and critique reasoning (MP3)	Pensions and Life Insurance (Lessons 9-3; 9-4)
Explore and express regularity in repeated reasoning (MP 8)	Compound Interest Formula (Lessons 3-5; 3-6)

Financial Algebra makes mathematics relevant for college and career.

Contents

Chapter 1 The Stock Market 2

MATH TOPICS

Candlestick charts
Fractions, decimals, and percents
Line graphs
Linear equations
Literal equations
Mean – arithmetic average
Percent increase and decrease
Ratios and proportions
Simple moving averages
Spreadsheets and formulas

COMMON CORE

N-Q Reason quantitatively and use units to solve problems
A-SSE Interpret the structure of expressions
A-CED Create equations that describe numbers or relationships
A-REI Solve equations and inequalities in one variable

Chapter 2 Modeling a Business 62

MATH TOPICS

Causal relationships
Functions - domain and range
Linear equations – slope-intercept form
Linear regression
Parabolas – vertex and axis of symmetry
Quadratic formula
Scatterplots and correlation
Spreadsheets and formulas
Transitive property of dependence

COMMON CORE

N-Q Reason quantitatively and use units to solve problems
A-CED Create equations that describe numbers or relationships
A-REI Understand solving equations as a process of reasoning and explain the reasoning
A-REI Solve equations and inequalities in one variable
A-REI Solve systems of equations
A-REI Represent and solve equations and inequalities graphically
F-IF Understand the concept of a function and use function notation
F-IF Interpret functions that arise in applications in terms of the context
F-IF Analyze functions using different representations
S-ID Summarize, represent, and interpret data on two categorical and quantitative variables
S-ID Interpret linear models

Chapter 3 Banking Services 114

MATH TOPICS

Exponential base (e)
Exponential functions
Exponential growth and decay
Formulas
Limits
Linear equations and inequalities
Order of operations
Recursive and iterative thinking: patterns, growth, decline, compound interest

COMMON CORE

N-RN Extend the properties of exponents to rational numbers
A-SSE Interpret the structure of expressions
A-SSE Write expressions in equivalent forms to solve problems
A-CED Create equations that describe numbers or relationships
F-IF Interpret functions that arise in applications in terms of the context
F-IF Analyze functions using different representations

MATH TOPICS

Cubic regression
Exponential growth and decay
Linear equations and inequalities
Linear regression
Measures of central tendency
Natural logarithms, base e
Percents
Quadratic regression
Spreadsheets and formulas

COMMON CORE

N-Q Reason quantitatively and use units to solve problems
A-SSE Interpret the structure of expressions
A-SSE Write expressions in equivalent forms to solve problems
A-CED Create equations that describe numbers or relationships
F-IF Analyze functions using different representations
F-LE Construct and compare linear, quadratic, and exponential models and solve problems
S-ID Summarize, represent, and interpret data on two categorical and quantitative variables

iStock

MATH TOPICS

Circles (radius, diameter, chord)
Distance Formula
Exponential growth and decay
Linear and exponential functions
Linear equations and inequalities
Measures of central tendency
Metric System
Natural logarithms
Percents and Proportions
Piecewise functions
Quartiles
Range
Read and interpret data: frequency tables, stem-and-leaf plots, box plots
Slope, slope-intercept form
Spreadsheets and formulas
Square root equations
Straight line equations (depreciation)
Systems of linear equations and inequalities in two variables

COMMON CORE

A-SSE Interpret the structure of expressions
A-SSE Write expressions in equivalent forms to solve problems
A-CED Create equations that describe numbers or relationships
A-REI Understand solving equations as a process of reasoning and explain the reasoning
F-IF Understand the concept of a function and use function notation
F-IF Interpret functions that arise in applications in terms of the context
F-IF Analyze functions using different representations
F-LE Construct and compare linear, quadratic, and exponential models and solve problems
G-C Find arc lengths and areas of sectors of circles
S-ID Summarize, represent, and interpret data on a single count or measurement variable
S-ID Summarize, represent, and interpret data on two categorical and quantitative variables
S-ID Interpret linear models

Chapter 6 Employment Basics 288

MATH TOPICS

Cusps
Exponential functions
Graphs
Linear functions
Literal expressions
Measures of central tendency
Percent discount
Piecewise functions
Spreadsheets and formulas

COMMON CORE

A-SSE Interpret the structure of expressions
A-CED Create equations that describe numbers or relationships
A-REI Solve equations and inequalities in one variable
F-IF Understand the concept of a function and use function notation
F-IF Interpret functions that arise in applications in terms of the context
F-IF Analyze functions using different representations
F-BF Build a function that models a relationship between two quantities
F-LE Construct and compare linear, quadratic, and exponential models and solve problems

Chapter 7 Income Taxes 326

MATH TOPICS

Cusps
Domains
Linear equations and inequalities
Literal expressions
Percents
Piecewise functions

COMMON CORE

A-SSE Interpret the structure of expressions
A-CED Create equations that describe numbers or relationships
F-IF Understand the concept of a function and use function notation
F-IF Analyze functions using different representations
F-BF Build a function that models a relationship between two quantities

Chapter 8 Independent Living 382

MATH TOPICS

Area and scale factors
Area of irregular regions
Bar graphs
Exponential regression
Greatest integer functions
Literal expressions
Monte Carlo method
Probability
Rational and exponential equations
Scale drawings
Scatterplots and linear regression
Spreadsheets and formulas
Systems of linear equations and inequalities in two variables

COMMON CORE

A-SSE Interpret the structure of expressions
A-APR Rewrite rational expressions
A-CED Create equations that describe numbers or relationships
F-BF Build a function that models a relationship between two quantities
F-LE Construct and compare linear, quadratic, and exponential models and solve problems
G-C Find arc lengths and areas of sectors of circles
G-MG Apply geometric concepts in modeling situations
S-ID Summarize, represent, and interpret data on two categorical and quantitative variables
S-ID Interpret linear models

Chapter 9 Planning for Retirement 436

MATH TOPICS

Collect, organize, and interpret data
Domains
Expected value
Exponential equations
Greatest integer functions
Histograms
Inequalities
Literal expressions
Measures of central tendency
Percent increase
Probability
Rational equations
Slope-intercept forms
Spreadsheets and formulas

COMMON CORE

A-SSE Interpret the structure of expressions
A-CED Create equations that describe numbers or relationships
F-IF Analyze functions using different representations
F-BF Build a function that models a relationship between two quantities
S-MD Calculate expected values and use them to solve problems

Chapter 10 Prepare a Budget 480

MATH TOPICS

Circle (sectors, central angles)
Cusps
Domains
Fractions, decimals, and ratios
Greatest integer functions
Linear equations and inequalities
Literal expressions
Matrices
Piecewise functions
Proportions
Rational and exponential equations
Read and interpret data: line graphs, bar graphs, circle graphs
Slope and graphing linear functions
Spreadsheets and formulas
Systems of equations
Volume

COMMON CORE

N-Q Reason quantitatively and use units to solve problems
N-VM Perform operations on matrices and use matrices in applications
A-SSE Interpret the structure of expressions
A-REI Represent and solve equations and inequalities graphically
F-IF Interpret functions that arise in applications in terms of the context
F-IF Analyze functions using different representations
F-BF Build a function that models a relationship between two quantities

Inside the Student Edition

CHAPTER 1

The Stock Market

The safe way to double your money is to fold it over once and put it in your pocket.

Frank Hubbard, Journalist

What do you think Frank Hubbard meant in this quote?

In the future, you will incur many expenses, such as a home, automobile, insurance, food, clothing, and health care. Some are major expenses and some are minor, but each costs money. To have money for major expenses, it helps to have your savings grow in value. Investing can help money grow in value.

You need to find a personal balance between risk and reward when you make choices about investments. Investments are never without questions. Did you miss the chance to make more money because you were being overly cautious? Was the investment too risky? Did you risk losing too much money by investing in something that may not have had a sound foundation?

Investors struggle with these questions every day. The stock market is a forum in which the investment risk/reward balance is put to the test. Will the market advance? Will the market decline? No one can be certain. With a strong knowledge of the stock market, you as an investor can make decisions that are based on experience, data, trends, and mathematics.

A **relevant quote** and **chapter introduction** set the stage for the topics covered in the chapter.

"This information is interesting and relevant! Showing real-world relevance is always a good lead into the lesson."

Really?

Most people are familiar with the United States Secret Service as the group that guards the President. Its officers are frequently seen on television surrounding the President as he tends to the affairs of the country.

What most people do not realize is that the Secret Service, established in 1865, was created to help the United States government combat the widespread counterfeiting of U.S. currency at the time. Counterfeiting, one of the oldest crimes in history, had become a national problem. It is estimated that approximately $\frac{1}{3}$ to $\frac{1}{2}$ of the nation's currency in circulation at that time was counterfeit.

The problem, although not as severe, still exists today. Modern printing and scanning equipment makes counterfeiting easier, and the government has instituted changes in currency to make it harder to counterfeit. Although most citizens have no intentions of counterfeiting U.S. currency, Americans have a responsibility to learn about counterfeiting, because they may receive a counterfeit bill one day. If a counterfeit bill is received, try to recall where it was acquired. Contact the nearest Secret Service office. The bill will be taken and no compensation will be returned to you. If a counterfeit bill is deposited in a bank account, you will lose the bill and the credit for the value of the deposit. Go to the Federal Reserve Bank website and read tips for spotting counterfeit currency. The penalty for trying to pass a counterfeit bill is a fine or imprisonment.

Really!

115

Really? Really! captures students' attention by discussing a fascinating real-life topic that relates to the chapter's content.

Structure Puts Math into Context

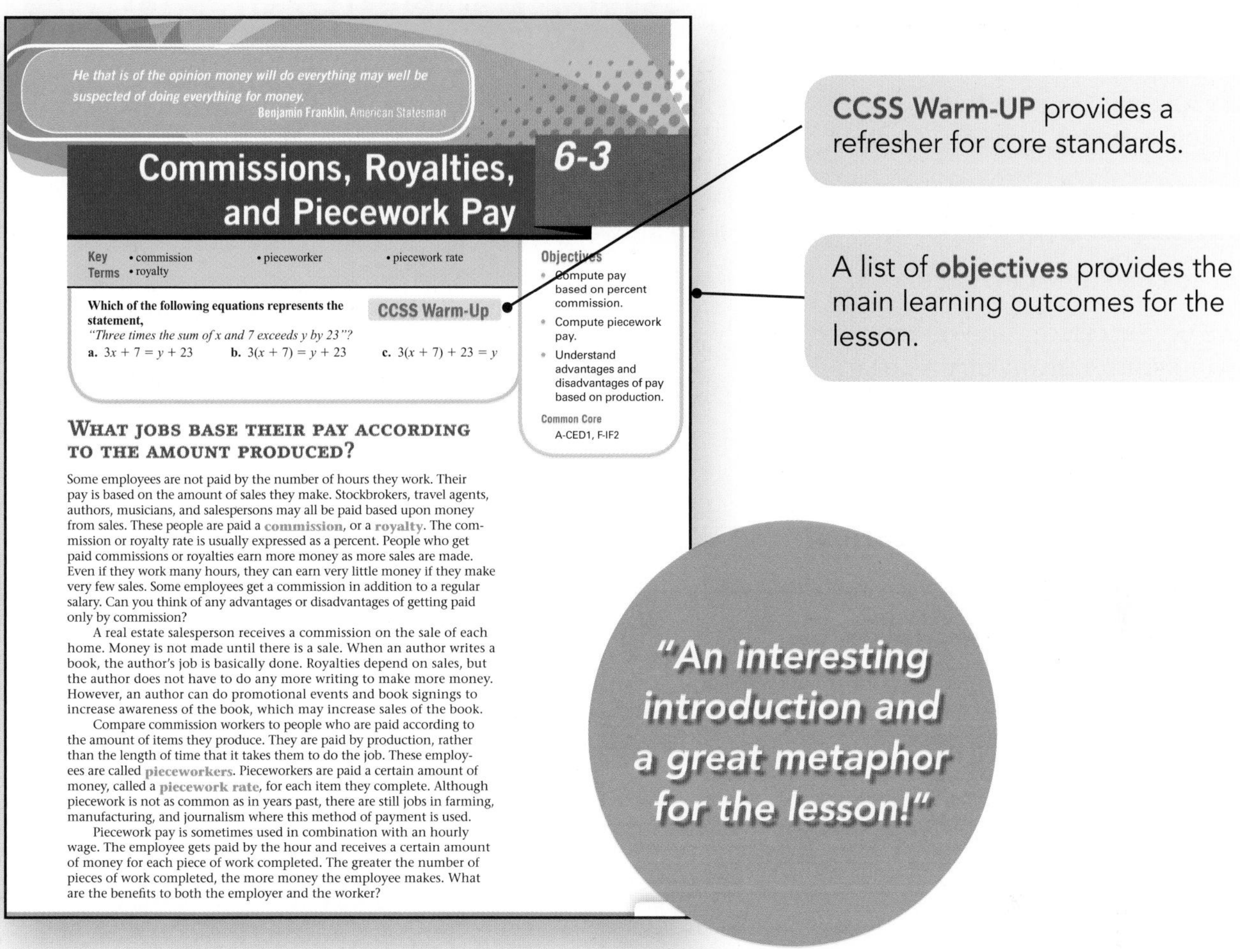

He that is of the opinion money will do everything may well be suspected of doing everything for money.
Benjamin Franklin, American Statesman

Commissions, Royalties, and Piecework Pay 6-3

Key Terms • commission • royalty • pieceworker • piecework rate

Objectives
- Compute pay based on percent commission.
- Compute piecework pay.
- Understand advantages and disadvantages of pay based on production.

Common Core
A-CED1, F-IF2

CCSS Warm-Up

Which of the following equations represents the statement,
"Three times the sum of x and 7 exceeds y by 23"?
a. $3x + 7 = y + 23$ **b.** $3(x + 7) = y + 23$ **c.** $3(x + 7) + 23 = y$

What jobs base their pay according to the amount produced?

Some employees are not paid by the number of hours they work. Their pay is based on the amount of sales they make. Stockbrokers, travel agents, authors, musicians, and salespersons may all be paid based upon money from sales. These people are paid a **commission**, or a **royalty**. The commission or royalty rate is usually expressed as a percent. People who get paid commissions or royalties earn more money as more sales are made. Even if they work many hours, they can earn very little money if they make very few sales. Some employees get a commission in addition to a regular salary. Can you think of any advantages or disadvantages of getting paid only by commission?

A real estate salesperson receives a commission on the sale of each home. Money is not made until there is a sale. When an author writes a book, the author's job is basically done. Royalties depend on sales, but the author does not have to do any more writing to make more money. However, an author can do promotional events and book signings to increase awareness of the book, which may increase sales of the book.

Compare commission workers to people who are paid according to the amount of items they produce. They are paid by production, rather than the length of time that it takes them to do the job. These employees are called **pieceworkers**. Pieceworkers are paid a certain amount of money, called a **piecework rate**, for each item they complete. Although piecework is not as common as in years past, there are still jobs in farming, manufacturing, and journalism where this method of payment is used.

Piecework pay is sometimes used in combination with an hourly wage. The employee gets paid by the hour and receives a certain amount of money for each piece of work completed. The greater the number of pieces of work completed, the more money the employee makes. What are the benefits to both the employer and the worker?

CCSS Warm-UP provides a refresher for core standards.

A list of **objectives** provides the main learning outcomes for the lesson.

"An interesting introduction and a great metaphor for the lesson!"

The best way to deal with credit card debt is to educate yourself.
Mark Rosen, Author

An intriguing **quote** at the beginning of each lesson motivates learning.

Although it's easy to forget sometimes, a share is not a lottery ticket . . . it's part-ownership of a business.
Peter Lynch, American businessman, Investment strategist, and Philanthropist

Nobody ever lost money taking a profit.
Bernard Baruch, Businessman

The Essential Question

helps focus attention on the big idea

What are Social Security and Medicare?

How do people gain access to money they keep in the bank?

What is compound interest?

What information do you need to know before taking out a loan?

What information does a credit card statement give you?

How do revenue and expenses contribute to profit calculation?

The **Essential Question** helps focus attention on the big idea of each lesson. You will be able to answer the question by the end of the lesson.

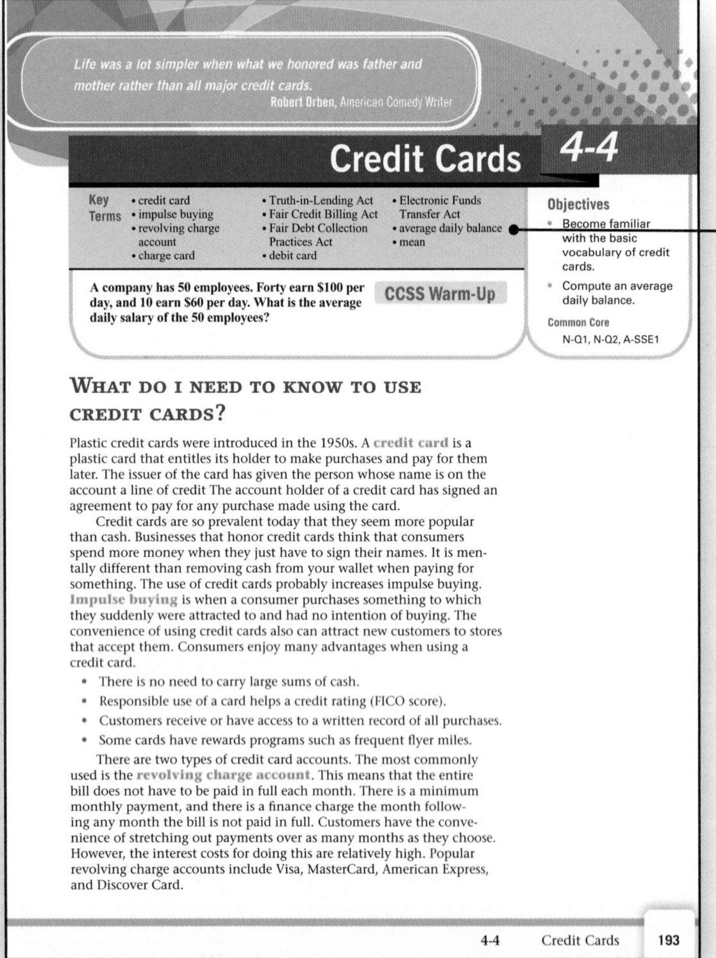

Life was a lot simpler when what we honored was father and mother rather than all major credit cards.
Robert Orben, American Comedy Writer

Credit Cards 4-4

Key Terms
- credit card
- impulse buying
- revolving charge account
- charge card
- Truth-in-Lending Act
- Fair Credit Billing Act
- Fair Debt Collection Practices Act
- debit card
- Electronic Funds Transfer Act
- average daily balance
- mean

Objectives
- Become familiar with the basic vocabulary of credit cards.
- Compute an average daily balance.

Common Core
N-Q1, N-Q2, A-SSE1

CCSS Warm-Up

A company has 50 employees. Forty earn $100 per day, and 10 earn $60 per day. What is the average daily salary of the 50 employees?

What do I need to know to use credit cards?

Plastic credit cards were introduced in the 1950s. A **credit card** is a plastic card that entitles its holder to make purchases and pay for them later. The issuer of the card has given the person whose name is on the account a line of credit The account holder of a credit card has signed an agreement to pay for any purchase made using the card.

Credit cards are so prevalent today that they seem more popular than cash. Businesses that honor credit cards think that consumers spend more money when they just have to sign their names. It is mentally different than removing cash from your wallet when paying for something. The use of credit cards probably increases impulse buying. **Impulse buying** is when a consumer purchases something to which they suddenly were attracted to and had no intention of buying. The convenience of using credit cards also can attract new customers to stores that accept them. Consumers enjoy many advantages when using a credit card.

- There is no need to carry large sums of cash.
- Responsible use of a card helps a credit rating (FICO score).
- Customers receive or have access to a written record of all purchases.
- Some cards have rewards programs such as frequent flyer miles.

There are two types of credit card accounts. The most commonly used is the **revolving charge account**. This means that the entire bill does not have to be paid in full each month. There is a minimum monthly payment, and there is a finance charge the month following any month the bill is not paid in full. Customers have the convenience of stretching out payments over as many months as they choose. However, the interest costs for doing this are relatively high. Popular revolving charge accounts include Visa, MasterCard, American Express, and Discover Card.

4-4 Credit Cards 193

Each lesson begins with a discussion of **terms and concepts** related to the lesson topic.

"This book contains relevant and current information high school students need. The educational focus of today is on standards. This book allows both to be addressed."

When am I ever going to use this in real life?

EXAMPLE 5

Glassman Chevrolet pays commission to its car salespeople. They are paid a percent of the profit the dealership makes on the car, not on the selling price of the car. If the profit is under \$750, the commission rate is 20%. If the profit is at least \$750 and less than or equal to \$1,000, the commission rate is 22% of the profit. If the profit is above \$1,000, the rate is 25% of the profit. If x represents the profit, express the commission $c(x)$ as a piecewise function.

SOLUTION There is a different rule for each of the different domains.

The 20% commission rate is for profits less than \$750.
The 22% commission rate is for profits from \$750 to \$1,000, inclusive.
The 25% commission rate is for profits greater than \$1,000.

Translate the words into algebraic symbols.

$$c(x) = \begin{cases} 0.20x & \text{when } 0 \le x < 750 \\ 0.22x & \text{when } 750 \le x \le 1{,}000 \\ 0.25x & \text{when } x > 1{,}000 \end{cases}$$

CHECK YOUR UNDERSTANDING

Find the difference between the commission paid if a Glassman Chevrolet salesman, from Example 5, sells a car for a \$750 profit compared to selling a car for a \$749 profit.

EXAMPLE 6

Joyce works at Fortunato's Furniture. She is paid on commission. She receives 10% of her first \$900 in sales and 15% of the balance of her sales. Last week she earned \$750. What was the total value of the furniture she sold?

SOLUTION Let x represent the total value of the furniture.

Commission for the first \$900.	$0.10(900)$
Balance of sales after the first \$900.	$x - 900$
Commission for the balance.	$0.15(x - 900)$
Add the two commissions.	$0.10(900) + 0.15(x - 900) = 750$
Simplify.	$90 + 0.15x - 135 = 750$
Combine like terms.	$0.15x - 45 = 750$
Add 45 to each side.	$0.15x = 795$
Divide each side by 0.15.	$x = 5{,}300$

Joyce sold \$5,300 worth of furniture last week.

CHECK YOUR UNDERSTANDING

Lauren is a salesperson at Koslow's Tires. She is paid a monthly commission. She receives 6% of her [...] the balance of her sales. Today she e[...] value of the tires she sold?

In **Skills and Strategies**, the heart of the lesson, math concepts are taught through **worked-out examples**. Examples present each math concept step-by-step.

"I love the emphasis on applications with relevance to the world we live in, not on symbolic manipulation."

Skills and Strategies

Here you will learn about a variety of employee benefits and the mathematics that is needed to get the most out of them.

EXAMPLE 1

Alan works for a printing company. It has been a little over four years since he was hired. He now makes \$54,080 per year. When he was hired, he was told that he had five days of paid vacation time. For each year that he worked at the company, he would gain another two days of paid vacation time to a maximum of 20 days. How many paid vacation days does he now get at the end of four years of employment and how much will he make during the time he is on vacation?

SOLUTION Examine the table. Alan has completed four full years of work for his company. He is in his fifth year of employment and is entitled to 13 paid vacation days. Because he is making \$54,080 per year, you can determine his weekly salary by dividing this amount by 52 weeks.

Number of Years Worked	Number of Paid Vacation Days
0	5
1	5 + 2 = 7
2	5 + 2 + 2 = 9
3	5 + 2 + 2 + 2 = 11
4	5 + 2 + 2 + 2 + 2 = 13

$$54{,}080 \div 52 = 1{,}040$$

Alan makes \$1,040 per week. A typical workweek consists of five business days. Therefore, Alan has two work weeks plus three days of paid vacation coming to him this year. The remaining three vacation days can be expressed as a fractional part of a work week. The fraction $\frac{3}{5}$ can be written as 0.6. Alan gets 2.6 work weeks of paid vacation time.

Weekly salary × 2.6 $\quad 1{,}040 \times 2.6 = 2{,}704$

Alan will make \$2,704 while on vacation this year.

CHECK YOUR UNDERSTANDING

Let x represent the number of the working year and y represent the number of paid vacation days. Based on the table above, write an algebraic equation that models the relationship between these two variables.

All math concepts are taught within **real-life context**. *When am I ever going to use this in real life?* is answered here!

Ongoing Assessment and Review

■ **CHECK YOUR UNDERSTANDING**

Jillian owns 60% of the stock in a private catering corporation. There are 1,200 shares in the entire corporation. How many shares does Jillian own?

EXAMPLE 3

Three partners are investing a total of $900,000 to open a garden and landscaping store. Their investments are in the ratio 2:3:5. How much does the partner that invested the least contribute?

SOLUTION Use the ratio 2:3:5 to write an expression for the amount each partner invested.

Let $2x$ represent the amount invested by the first partner.

Let $3x$ represent the amount invested by the second partner.

Let $5x$ represent the amount invested by the third partner.

Write an equation showing the three investments total $900,000.

$$2x + 3x + 5x = 900,000$$

Combine like terms. $10x = 900,000$

Divide each side of the equation by 10. $x = 90,000$

The partner that invested the least is represented by the expression $2x$.

Substitute $90,000 into the expression. $2(90,000) = 180,000$

The partner who invested the least amount contributed $180,000.

■ **CHECK YOUR UNDERSTANDING**

Two partners are starting a wedding planning business. The total investment is $45,000. Their investments are in the ratio 4:5. How much does each investor contribute?

■ **EXTEND YOUR UNDERSTANDING**

Two partners each invest 35% in a startup business. They need to find another investor for the rest of the money. What percent of the business will that person own? Write a ratio to represent the investments in the business.

Applications

When somebody buys a stock it's because they think it's going to go up and the person who sold it to them thinks it's going to go down. Somebody's wrong.

George Ross, *Television actor*

1. Is it always true that someone sells a stock because they think it is going to go down in price? How do those words apply to what you've learned in this lesson?
2. Zach bought 200 shares of Goshen stock years ago for $21.35 per share. He sold all 200 shares today for $43 per share. What was his gross capital gain?
3. Mitchell bought 600 shares of Centerco two years ago for $34.50 per share. He sold them yesterday for $38.64 per share.
   a. What was the percent increase in the price per share?
   b. What was the total purchase price for the 600 shares?
   c. What was the total selling price for the 600 shares?
   d. What was the percent capital gain for the 600 shares?
   e. How does the percent increase in the price of one share compare to the percent capital gain for all 600 shares?
4. Tori bought x shares of Mattel stock for m dollars per share. She sold all of the shares months later for y dollars per share. Express her capital gain or loss algebraically.
5. Ramon bought x shares of Xerox stock for a total of $40,000. Express the price he paid per share algebraically.
6. In 2004, Joe bought 200 shares in the Nikon corporation for $12.25 per share. In 2007 he sold the shares for $31.27 each.
   a. What was Joe's capital gain?
   b. Express Joe's capital gain as a percent, rounded to the nearest percent.
7. General Motors stock fell from $32 per share in 2006 to $20 per share during 2008.
   a. If you bought and then sold 300 shares at these prices, what was your loss?
   b. Express your loss as a percent of the purchase price. Round to the nearest tenth of a percent.
8. Elliott purchased shares of Microsoft in 2008 for $28 per share. He plans to sell them as soon as the price rises 20%. At what price will he sell his shares?
9. Maria purchased 1,000 shares of stock for $35.50 per share in 2003. She sold them in 2007 for $55.10 per share. Express her capital gain as a percent, rounded to the nearest tenth of a percent.

"I like the immediate check of understanding instead of waiting until the end of the chapter."

Check Your Understanding allows you to immediately practice the concept on your own. The questions are similar to the example and help you gauge your understanding of the skills being taught.

Extend Your Understanding provides an opportunity to solve a more challenging problem.

Carefully developed, proven **applications at the end of each lesson** require you to apply the concepts to a specific question or scenario.

Chapter Assessment provides an opportunity to check your knowledge of the chapter content.

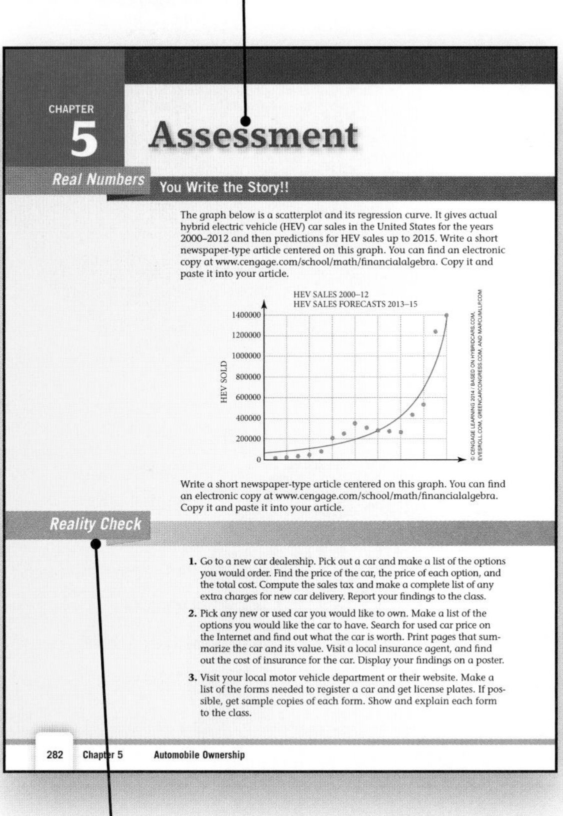
CHAPTER 5

Assessment

Real Numbers You Write the Story!!

The graph below is a scatterplot and its regression curve. It gives actual hybrid electric vehicle (HEV) car sales in the United States for the years 2000–2012 and then predictions for HEV sales up to 2015. Write a short newspaper-type article centered on this graph. You can find an electronic copy at www.cengage.com/school/math/financialalgebra. Copy it and paste it into your article.

Write a short newspaper-type article centered on this graph. You can find an electronic copy at www.cengage.com/school/math/financialalgebra. Copy it and paste it into your article.

Reality Check

1. Go to a new car dealership. Pick out a car and make a list of the options you would order. Find the price of the car, the price of each option, and the total cost. Compute the sales tax and make a complete list of any extra charges for new car delivery. Report your findings to the class.
2. Pick any new or used car you would like to own. Make a list of the options you would like the car to have. Search for used car price on the Internet and find out what the car is worth. Print pages that summarize the car and its value. Visit a local insurance agent, and find out the cost of insurance for the car. Display your findings on a poster.
3. Visit your local motor vehicle department or their website. Make a list of the forms needed to register a car and get license plates. If possible, get sample copies of each form. Show and explain each form to the class.

282 Chapter 5 Automobile Ownership

Real Numbers: You Write the Story! asks you to examine a graph and write a story focused around the graph's information, giving you an opportunity to be creative while at the same time sharpening your graph interpretation skills.

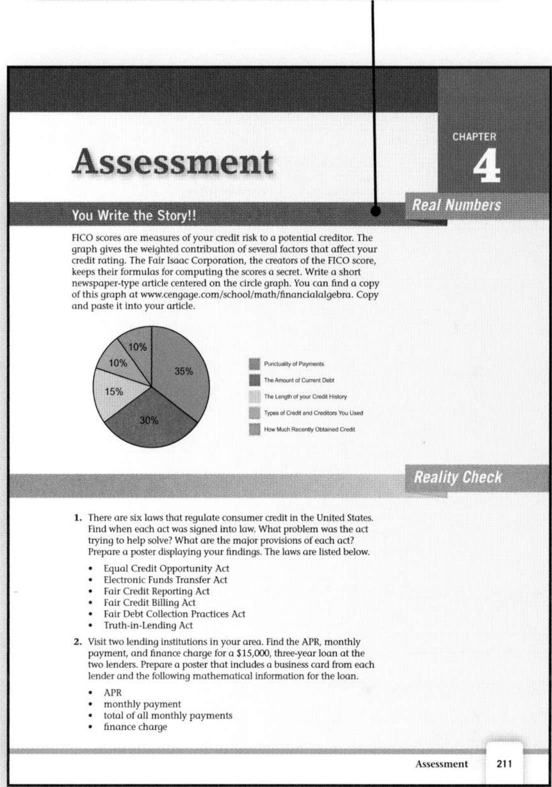
Assessment

CHAPTER 4

Real Numbers You Write the Story!!

FICO scores are measures of your credit risk to a potential creditor. The graph gives the weighted contribution of several factors that affect your credit rating. The Fair Isaac Corporation, the creators of the FICO score, keeps their formulas for computing the scores a secret. Write a short newspaper-type article centered on the circle graph. You can find a copy of this graph at www.cengage.com/school/math/financialalgebra. Copy and paste it into your article.

Reality Check

1. There are six laws that regulate consumer credit in the United States. Find when each act was signed into law. What problem was the act trying to help solve? What are the major provisions of each act? Prepare a poster displaying your findings. The laws are listed below.
   - Equal Credit Opportunity Act
   - Electronic Funds Transfer Act
   - Fair Credit Reporting Act
   - Fair Credit Billing Act
   - Fair Debt Collection Practices Act
   - Truth-in-Lending Act
2. Visit two lending institutions in your area. Find the APR, monthly payment, and finance charge for a $15,000, three-year loan at the two lenders. Prepare a poster that includes a business card from each lender and the following mathematical information for the loan.
   - APR
   - monthly payment
   - total of all monthly payments
   - finance charge

Assessment 211

Reality Check provides specific suggestions for research opportunities, projects, and guest speakers to extend your learning experience.

Dollars and Sense guides you to the companion site where you will find a link to a website containing up-to-date information and activities related to the chapter content.

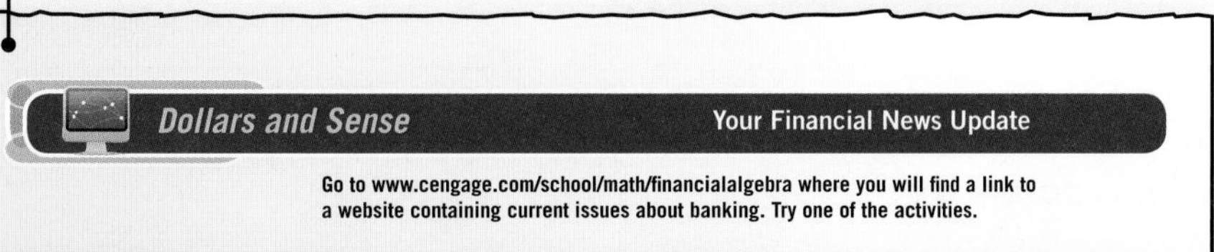
Dollars and Sense Your Financial News Update

Go to www.cengage.com/school/math/financialalgebra where you will find a link to a website containing current issues about banking. Try one of the activities.

"Excellent activities that help connect math to the real world."

Each chapter concludes by **revisiting the Really? Really!** discussion for a cohesive presentation.

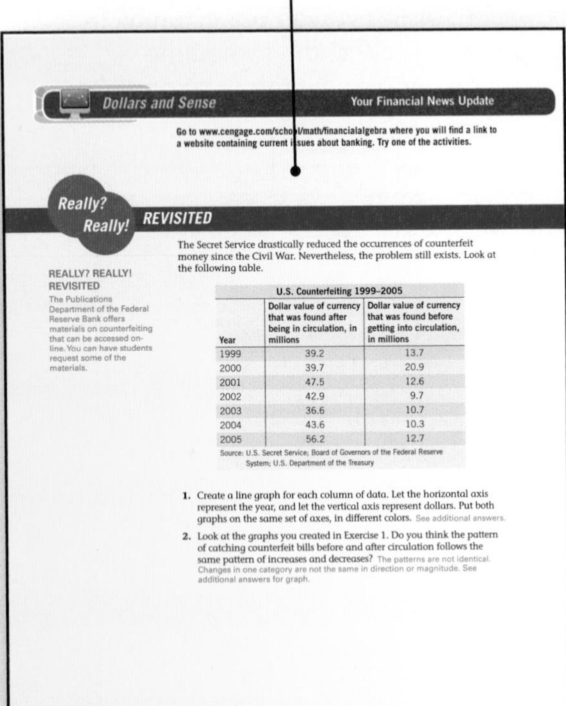

Dollars and Sense — Your Financial News Update

Go to www.cengage.com/school/math/financialalgebra where you will find a link to a website containing current issues about banking. Try one of the activities.

Really? Really! REVISITED

REALLY? REALLY! REVISITED
The Publications Department of the Federal Reserve Bank offers materials on counterfeiting that can be accessed online. You can have students request some of the materials.

The Secret Service drastically reduced the occurrences of counterfeit money since the Civil War. Nevertheless, the problem still exists. Look at the following table.

U.S. Counterfeiting 1999–2005

Year	Dollar value of currency that was found after being in circulation, in millions	Dollar value of currency that was found before getting into circulation, in millions
1999	39.2	13.7
2000	39.7	20.9
2001	47.5	12.6
2002	42.9	9.7
2003	36.6	10.7
2004	43.6	10.3
2005	56.2	12.7

Source: U.S. Secret Service; Board of Governors of the Federal Reserve System; U.S. Department of the Treasury

1. Create a line graph for each column of data. Let the horizontal axis represent the year, and let the vertical axis represent dollars. Put both graphs on the same set of axes, in different colors. See additional answers.
2. Look at the graphs you created in Exercise 1. Do you think the pattern of catching counterfeit bills before and after circulation follows the same pattern of increases and decreases? The patterns are not identical. Changes in one category are not the same in direction or magnitude. See additional answers for graph.

"I love how it is tied to what started the chapter!"

"Great variety of problems that will prepare students for life outside of school!"

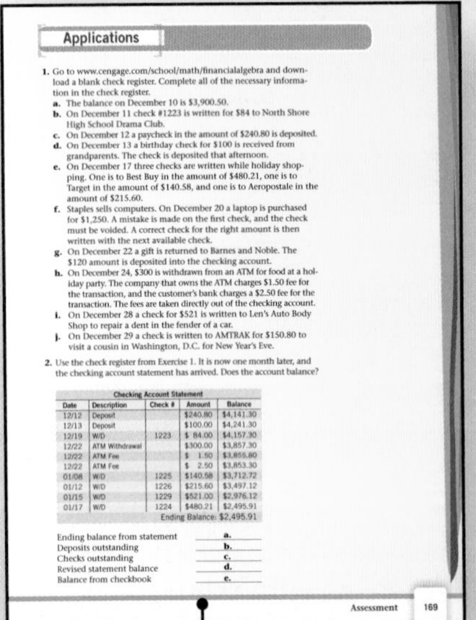

Applications

1. Go to www.cengage.com/school/math/financialalgebra and download a blank check register. Complete all of the necessary information in the check register.
   a. The balance on December 10 is $3,900.50.
   b. On December 11 check #1223 is written for $84 to North Shore High School Drama Club.
   c. On December 12 a paycheck in the amount of $240.80 is deposited.
   d. On December 13 a birthday check for $100 is received from grandparents. The check is deposited that afternoon.
   e. On December 17 three checks are written while holiday shopping. One is to Best Buy in the amount of $480.21, one is to Target in the amount of $140.58, and one is to Aeropostale in the amount of $215.60.
   f. Staples sells computers. On December 20 a laptop is purchased for $1,250. A mistake is made on the first check, and the check must be voided. A correct check for the right amount is then written with the next available check.
   g. On December 22 a gift is returned to Barnes and Noble. The $120 amount is deposited into the checking account.
   h. On December 24, $300 is withdrawn from an ATM for food at a holiday party. The company that owns the ATM charges $1.50 fee for the transaction, and the customer's bank charges a $2.50 fee for the transaction. The fees are taken directly out of the checking account.
   i. On December 28 a check for $521 is written to Len's Auto Body Shop to repair a dent in the fender of a car.
   j. On December 29 a check is written to AMTRAK for $150.80 to visit a cousin in Washington, D.C. for New Year's Eve.
2. Use the check register from Exercise 1. It is now one month later, and the checking account statement has arrived. Does the account balance?

Checking Account Statement

Date	Description	Check #	Amount	Balance
12/12	Deposit		$240.80	$4,141.30
12/13	Deposit		$100.00	$4,241.30
12/19	W/D	1223	$ 84.00	$4,157.30
12/22	ATM Withdrawal		$300.00	$3,857.30
12/22	ATM Fee		$ 1.50	$3,855.80
12/22	ATM Fee		$ 2.50	$3,853.30
01/08	W/D	1225	$140.58	$3,712.72
01/12	W/D	1226	$215.60	$3,497.12
01/15	W/D	1229	$521.00	$2,976.12
01/17	W/D	1224	$480.21	$2,495.91
			Ending Balance:	$2,495.91

Ending balance from statement a.
Deposits outstanding b.
Checks outstanding c.
Revised statement balance d.
Balance from checkbook e.

Assessment 169

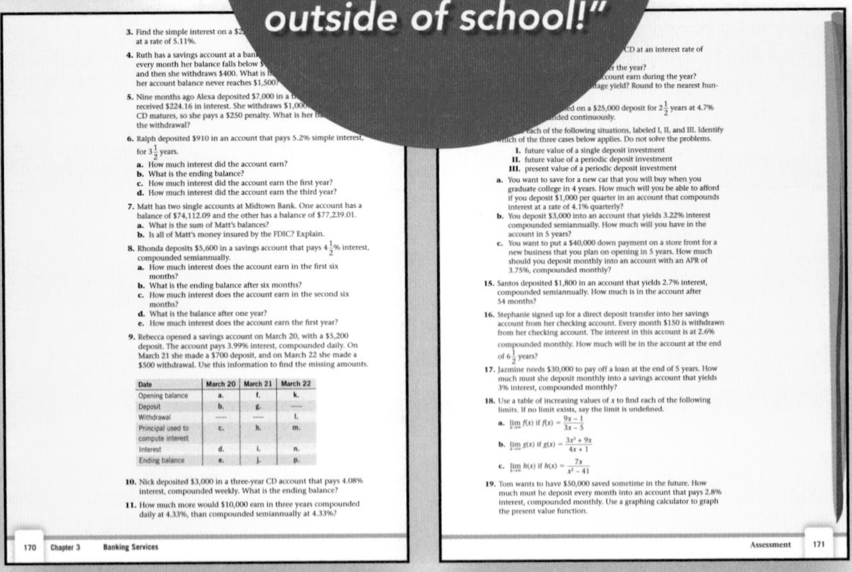

170 Chapter 3 Banking Services

Assessment 171

Meaningful applications at the end of each chapter require you to apply concepts that were taught throughout the chapter.

Comprehensive Teaching and Learning Tools

Annotated Instructor's Edition 9781285447537
The Annotated Instructor's Edition keeps useful teaching and reference notes, helpful suggestions, and ready solutions at your fingertips.

Financial Algebra Instructor's Resource CD 9780538450188

- Lesson plans
- PowerPoint slides for each lesson
- Workbook answers

ExamView Computerized Test Generator 9780538450195
ExamView saves time in effectively assessing your students' understanding of chapter concepts. Simply edit, add, delete, or rearrange questions.

Guided Practice CD 9781111575991
The Guided Practice CD provides print on demand reteaching worksheets. Key concepts are reviewed through guided practice exercises and additional applications. This alternative option to the student workbook will strengthen students' understanding of algebraic concepts and their business and finance applications.

Interactive Whiteboard Presentation CD 9781111573638
The Interactive Whiteboard Presentation CD saves preparation time and enhances your classroom instruction with interactive whiteboard lesson presentations. Presentation CD is compatible with all interactive whiteboards.

Solutions Manual
The solutions manual saves you time with worked out solutions for all end-of-lesson and end-of-chapter applications. The solutions manual is located on the instructor companion site www.cengage.com/school/math/financialalgebra.

Student Workbook 9780538449700
The student workbook offers additional resources for mastering algebraic concepts within a financial context.

Financial Algebra Online Adobe PDF eBook
6 Year Access
Textbook/6 Year Access Bundle 9781285447889

Website – www.cengage.com/school/math/financialalgebra

CHAPTER

1 The Stock Market

The safe way to double your money is to fold it over once and put it in your pocket.

Frank Hubbard, Journalist

What do you think Frank Hubbard meant in this quote?

In the future, you will incur many expenses, such as a home, automobile, insurance, food, clothing, and health care. Some are major expenses and some are minor, but each costs money. To have money for major expenses, it helps to have your savings grow in value. Investing can help money grow in value.

You need to find a personal balance between risk and reward when you make choices about investments. Investments are never without questions. Did you miss the chance to make more money because you were being overly cautious? Was the investment too risky? Did you risk losing too much money by investing in something that may not have had a sound foundation?

Investors struggle with these questions every day. The stock market is a forum in which the investment risk/reward balance is put to the test. Will the market advance? Will the market decline? No one can be certain. With a strong knowledge of the stock market, you as an investor can make decisions that are based on experience, data, trends, and mathematics.

What do you think?

Answers might include that gambling and the stock market can increase or decrease wealth significantly. Bank accounts do increase wealth, and are safe, but interest earned will not make you rich.

TEACHING RESOURCES

Instructor's Resource CD

Exam*View*® CD, Ch. 1

eHomework, Ch. 1

www.cengage.com/school/math/financialalgebra

Really?

Corporations sometimes choose names that are personal, humorous, historical, or psychological. Below are some well-known corporations and how their names were established.

AMAZON.com was originally known as Cadabra.com. The name was changed by its founder Jeff Bezos. He selected Amazon as a corporate name because the Amazon River is known as the biggest volume river in the world. He also wanted a name that began with A so that alphabetically it would appear at the top of a list of similar corporations.

COCA-COLA is a name that has its origins in the flavoring used to make the product—coca leaves and kola nuts. The founder, John Pemberton, changed the "K" in kola to a "C" for appearance purposes.

ADIDAS is taken from the name of the company's founder Adolph (Adi) Dassler.

eBay was created by Pierre Omidyar, who originally wanted to use the name Echo Bay. The name was already taken by a gold mining company, so he shortened it to eBay.

XEROX comes from a Greek expression for "dry writing." The Xerox process was invented in 1937 by law student Chester Carlson.

CHAPTER OVERVIEW

The course begins with an indepth study of the stock market. Most students are familiar with the existence of the market, but are unfamiliar with how it works. The concept of risk and reward is a constant presence. In this chapter, students use mathematics to understand market events and make wise decisions about personal investments.

REALLY? REALLY!

Students are introduced to some of the types of corporations they will be reading about in the chapter. Interesting facts are given about the etymology of a corporate name. As a first night's assignment, have students pick three different companies and research how the company names were developed.

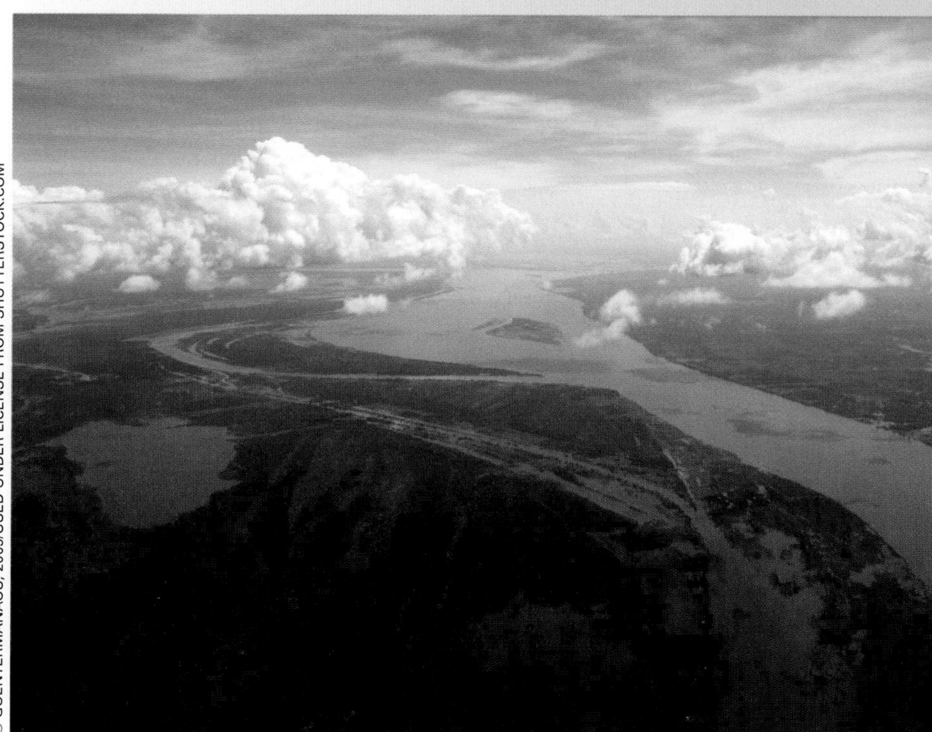

Really!

Genius is 1% inspiration and 99% perspiration. Accordingly a genius is often merely a talented person who has done all of his or her homework.

Thomas Edison, Inventor

1-1 Business Organization

Objectives

- Learn the basic vocabulary of business organizations.
- Compute financial responsibility of business ownership based on ratios and percents.

Common Core

A-CED1, A-REI3

Key Terms

- capital
- sole proprietorship
- profit
- personally liable
- partnership
- corporation
- shares of stock
- shareholders
- limited liability
- public corporation

CCSS Warm-Up

Create and solve an equation in terms of x.

Find two consecutive integers such that the sum of three times the first and twice the second is 27.

$3x + 2(x+1) = 27$; 5, 6

EXAMINE THE QUESTION

One major decision that business owners have to make is about the form of the business. The decision to be a sole proprietorship, partnership, or corporation is based on many aspects, such as profit, liability, and shares of stock.

CLASS DISCUSSION

What are common everyday products that you think sell millions each year?

In which type of business do you think an owner's personal possessions may potentially be taken in the event of a lawsuit or a financial crisis?

If you owned shares of stock in a public corporation, what would that mean to you in terms of profit and personal liability?

How do businesses start?

Think of everything you use on a daily basis, from complex electronic devices to simple items like straws, paper clips, and toothbrushes. Have you ever wondered who invented them, or how each has been improved upon? Some inventions provide an opportunity to build a business, but not all. It takes imagination, money, and effort to create a successful business. The money used to start or expand a business is **capital**.

A business owned by one person is a **sole proprietorship**. The owner, or proprietor, can hire people to help run the business, but these employees are not owners. The owner is responsible for all expenses, including labor and raw materials used in manufacturing a product or providing a service. The money left after all expenses are paid is **profit**. The owner of a sole proprietorship is entitled to all of the profits. However, the owner is responsible, or **personally liable**, for any losses. Even if the business does not make a profit, the owner must still pay all of the bills of the business.

A business that is owned by a group of people, called *partners,* is a **partnership**. Partners share the profits and the responsibility for any losses. The partners are *personally liable* for any losses. Personal liability may require risking personal property. Sole proprietors and partners must consider this possibility when creating a business.

A **corporation** is a business organization that can be owned by one person or a group of people. Each owner who invests money in the corporation receives **shares of stock** in the corporation. The owners are called **shareholders**. *Stock certificates* are used as proof of ownership. Unlike sole proprietorships and partnerships, the shareholders in a corporation have **limited liability**—each owner cannot lose more than the value of his or her share of the business. The number of shareholders in a corporation depends on the structure of the business. When anyone can purchase stock in a corporation, the corporation is a **public corporation**. You might already be familiar with public corporations, such as NIKE, McDonald's, Xerox, and Apple. The prices of shares of stock in public corporations can be found in newspapers, on television business channels, and on the Internet.

Skills and Strategies

When a business is owned by more than one person, the owners do not necessarily own equivalent portions of the business. Ratios and percents can be used to represent the financial responsibility of owners and partners. Recall the relationship between decimals and percents.

To convert a decimal to a percent, multiply the decimal by 100.

To convert a percent to a decimal, divide the percent by 100.

EXAMPLE 1

Michelle invests $15,000 in a partnership that has four other partners. The total investment of all partners is $240,000. What percent of the business does Michelle own?

SOLUTION Represent Michelle's investment as a fraction of the total investment. Convert the fraction to a decimal and write as a percent.

Write as a fraction. $\frac{\text{Michelle's investment}}{\text{Total investment}} = \frac{15{,}000}{240{,}000}$

Divide. $15{,}000 \div 240{,}000 = 0.0625$

Multiply by 100. Write a percent sign. $0.0625 \times 100 = 6.25\%$

Michelle owns 6.25% of the partnership.

■ CHECK YOUR UNDERSTANDING

Kyle invests $20,000 in a partnership that has five other partners. The total investment of the partners is $160,000. What percent of the business is owned by the five other partners?

EXAMPLE 2

The total number of shares of stock in the Bulls Corporation is 650,000. Mike owns 12% of the shares. How many shares of Bulls Corporation stock does he own?

SOLUTION Let x represent the number of shares Mike owns.

Express 12% as a fraction. $12\% = \frac{12}{100}$

Write a proportion. $\frac{12}{100} = \frac{x}{650{,}000}$

Cross multiply. $100x = (12)(650{,}000)$

Find the product. $100x = 7{,}800{,}000$

Divide both sides by 100. $\frac{100x}{100} = \frac{7{,}800{,}000}{100}$

$x = 78{,}000$

Mike owns 78,000 shares of Bulls Corporation.

TEACH

In the study of types of businesses, personal liability, and profit, students use ratios, proportions, and percents to calculate appropriations of ownership, costs, and profits.

EXAMPLE 1

Review percent to decimal conversions using a few examples on the board. Reteach students how to convert fractions with a denominator of 100 to percents and decimals.

CHECK YOUR UNDERSTANDING

Answer 87.5%

Subtract Kyle's $20,000 from the total investment of $160,000. Divide 140,000 by 160,000 and convert to an equivalent decimal. Then multiply the decimal by 100 and insert a percent sign.

EXAMPLE 2

Students can use a proportion or an equation to solve this percent problem. The equation to use is $0.12(650{,}000) = x$.

CHECK YOUR UNDERSTANDING

Answer 720

Find 60% of 1,200 using any method.

EXAMPLE 3

Point out the importance of writing "Let" statements, as students will be using them frequently. Students need to understand that defining the variables and variable expressions, will help them understand better what is given in the problem and what is being asked. Given that you are provided with a ratio, you can think of this problem as looking for the common factor in the amounts that were invested, which in this case is *x*.

CHECK YOUR UNDERSTANDING

Answer $20,000 and $25,000

EXTEND YOUR UNDERSTANDING

Answer 30%; 7:7:6

■ CHECK YOUR UNDERSTANDING

Jillian owns 60% of the stock in a private catering corporation. There are 1,200 shares in the entire corporation. How many shares does Jillian own?

EXAMPLE 3

Three partners are investing a total of $900,000 to open a garden and landscaping store. Their investments are in the ratio 2:3:5. How much does the partner that invested the least contribute?

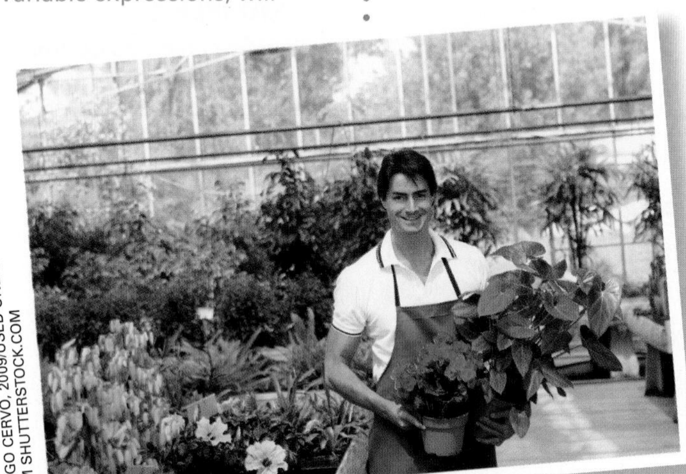

SOLUTION Use the ratio 2:3:5 to write an expression for the amount each partner invested.

Let $2x$ represent the amount invested by the first partner.

Let $3x$ represent the amount invested by the second partner.

Let $5x$ represent the amount invested by the third partner.

Write an equation showing the three investments total $900,000.

$$2x + 3x + 5x = 900{,}000$$

Combine like terms. $\quad 10x = 900{,}000$

Divide each side of the equation by 10. $\quad x = 90{,}000$

The partner that invested the least is represented by the expression $2x$.

Substitute $90,000 into the expression. $\quad 2(90{,}000) = 180{,}000$

The partner who invested the least amount contributed $180,000.

■ CHECK YOUR UNDERSTANDING

Two partners are starting a wedding planning business. The total investment is $45,000. Their investments are in the ratio 4:5. How much does each investor contribute?

■ EXTEND YOUR UNDERSTANDING

Two partners each invest 35% in a startup business. They need to find another investor for the rest of the money. What percent of the business will that person own? Write a ratio to represent the investments in the business.

Applications

Genius is 1% inspiration and 99% perspiration. Accordingly a genius is often merely a talented person who has done all of his or her homework.

Thomas Edison, Inventor

1. What do you think Thomas Edison meant by the word *perspiration*? How do those words apply to what you've learned in this lesson? See margin.

2. Tomika owns $\frac{3}{5}$ of a law partnership. What percent of the partnership does she own? 60%

3. Ryan owns three-eighths of a florist shop worth $76,000. What is the value of Ryan's share of the business? $28,500

4. A corporation issues 1,200,000 shares of stock at its beginning to shareholders. How many shares must a shareholder own to have a majority of the shares? 600,001

5. Elisa owns 28% of the Grudman Corporation. The rest of the shares are owned equally by the remaining six shareholders. What percent of the corporation does each of the other shareholders own? 12%

6. Julie and Kristen are the partners in a local sporting goods shop. They needed $51,000 to start the business. They invested in the ratio 5:12, respectively.
   a. How much money did each invest? Julie, $15,000; Kristen, $36,000
   b. What percent of the business was owned by Kristin? Round to the nearest tenth of a percent. 70.6%
   c. If the business grows to $3,000,000, what percent of it will Julie own? Round to the nearest tenth of a percent. 29.4%

7. Joe, Thea, and Taylor invested in a partnership in the ratio 1:4:7, respectively. Years later, when the partnership was worth $1.6 million, Thea decides to go to graduate school and sells her part of the partnership to Joe.
   a. How much would Joe need to pay Thea to buy her share of the business? Round to the nearest dollar. $533,333
   b. What percent of the business will Joe own after he buys Thea's portion? Round to the nearest tenth of a percent. 41.7%

8. Seventy-two percent of the shareholders in a service corporation are women. If the corporation is owned by 45,600 people, how many of the shareholders are women? 32,832

9. The 120 shareholders of a corporation are voting for a new Board of Directors. Shareholders receive one vote for each share they own. Would it be possible for one shareholder's votes to choose the new Board of Directors? Explain. Yes, if that shareholder has more than 50% of the shares, he can outvote the other 119 shareholders.

10. The top x shareholders in a corporation each own y shares of a certain stock. The corporation's ownership is represented by a total of w shares of stock. Express the percent of the corporation owned by the top x shareholders. $100\frac{xy}{w}$

TEACH

Fractional Parts

Throughout the applications, students will be examining fractional parts of a whole. They will be using percents primarily, and fractions less frequently.

Percents

Because percents always compare a number to the number 100, it is easier to get an intuitive feel for a percent. For example, if a student scored 17 out of 25 on a quiz, he would immediately convert $\frac{17}{25}$ to a percent to see how well he did. You could argue that the equivalent form, $\frac{68}{100}$, is simpler than $\frac{17}{25}$, even though $\frac{17}{25}$ is simplest form.

Exercise 6

Point out to students that if the ratio is 5:12, then Julie owns $\frac{5}{17}$ of the business.

Exercise 8

This can be done using a proportion or an equation.

Exercise 10

Students will frequently need to multiply by 100 to convert decimals to equivalent percents. Look out for students who forget to do this.

ANSWERS

1. Edison is stressing that good ideas are not enough. A strong work ethic is necessary to achieve. The word *perspiration* represents that effort is required.

TEACH

Exercise 15
As the section closes, review the important difference between a corporation and a partnership—the concept of limited liability.

11. A corporation is having a shareholders meeting. Not all shareholders are able to attend. In fact, most usually do not. The ownership of the corporation is represented by 2,351,000 shares of stock owned by 111,273 shareholders.

a. Must all of the shareholders own more than one share of stock? no

b. If 3,411 shareholders attend the meeting, what percent of the shareholders are represented? Round to the nearest percent. 3%

c. If the shareholders who do attend own a combined 1.8 million shares of the corporation, what percent of the shares are represented at the meeting? Round to the nearest percent. 77%

12. A private corporation owned by 35 shareholders is worth $1.7 million. The corporation loses a lawsuit worth $3 million. What is the value of any personal property of the shareholders that can be taken to pay the settlement? Explain. Due to limited liability, the shareholders forfeit $0 in personal property, but would forfeit the shares of stock in the company.

13. A partnership owned equally by 13 partners is worth $1.3 million. The partnership loses a lawsuit worth $3 million. What is the value of any personal property each partner must forfeit to pay the settlement? Explain. $130,769.23 because partners are personally liable.

14. A sole proprietorship is worth w dollars. The owner loses a lawsuit against him for y dollars where y is greater than w. Express algebraically the value of the personal property the owner must forfeit to pay the settlement. $y - w$

15. Six equal partners own a local pizzeria. The partners have made a tremendous profit and bought many personal items such as cars, boats, new homes, and so on. In order to protect their personal possessions, they decide to incorporate the pizzeria, so that the six partners own shares in the corporation and have limited liability. The business is worth $675,000. After an accident, the partners lose a lawsuit and have to pay $1.2 million in damages. How much money will each partner personally lose to pay this lawsuit? Explain.
They will only lose their shares of the business. They are not personally liable.

16. Three people invest in a business. The first two invest in the ratio 2:3, and the third person invests twice as much as the other two combined. The total invested is $30 million.

a. How much did the major investor contribute? $20 million

b. Does the major investor own more than half the business? yes

c. What fraction of the business does the major investor own? $\frac{2}{3}$

17. Ten years ago, Lisa bought a hair salon for x dollars. She built up the business and it is now worth nine times what she paid for it. She decides to sell half of the business to a friend, and they become partners. Express the amount Lisa's friend must pay Lisa to buy half the business. $\frac{9x}{2}$

18. Four people invested in a restaurant. One person invested $100,000. Two others invested in the ratio x:$2x$, and the fourth person invested an amount equal to the other three investors combined.
The total investment was $1,100,000.

a. Write an expression for the amount invested by the fourth person. $100{,}000 + x + 2x$

b. Write an equation that allows you to find the amount invested by each person. $2(100{,}000 + x + 2x) = 1{,}100{,}000$

c. How much did each person invest? $100,000; $150,000; $300,000; $550,000

> *One of the funny things about the stock market is that every time one person buys, another sells, and both think they are astute.*
>
> **William Feather**, Publisher and Author

Stock Market Data 1-2

Key Terms

- stock market
- trades
- NYSE
- NASDAQ
- last
- close
- high
- low
- volume
- sales in 100s
- 52-week high
- 52-week low
- net change
- after-hours trading
- spreadsheet
- cell

Objectives

- Use stock data to follow the daily progress of a corporate stock.
- Write spreadsheet formulas.

Common Core

N-Q1, N-Q2, N-Q3, A-CED1, A-REI3

CCSS Warm-Up

Write an expression in terms of x.

The temperature at noon today was 70°. Yesterday the temperature was x degrees less than today at noon. Write an expression for the temperature yesterday at noon in terms of x.

$70 - x$

WHAT STOCK MARKET DATA IS AVAILABLE ON A DAILY BASIS?

Stock market is a general term for an institution through which stocks are bought and sold. Stock market transactions are known as **trades**. The two most well known stock markets are the **New York Stock Exchange (NYSE)** and the **National Association of Securities Dealers Automated Quotation System (NASDAQ)**. A wise investor in stocks makes data-driven decisions by examining short and long term trends, changes, fluctuations, and consistencies. Investors intend to profit from their investments. You don't need to be a professional stockbroker or a financial analyst to follow the market. What you need is an understanding of trading data. This data can be found in newspapers, online, or on television financial channels. The best source for information is the Internet because it is current and accurate within minutes of a market event. However, you want to be certain that you are using a credible source.

In order to interpret stock market data, you need to know the meaning of the categories used in stock market international charts.

- **Last** is the price per share of the last trade that was made for a particular stock. In a newspaper, the last amount is usually the closing price for the trading day. Online, it is usually the price of the last trade made for one share of the stock.
- **Close** or *closing price* is the last price at which a stock was traded during a regular day's trading session. For most stock markets across the country, the daily sessions run from 9:30 A.M. to 4:00 P.M. Eastern Standard Time.
- **High** is the highest price at which one share of the stock was traded on a given day.
- **Low** is the lowest price at which one share of the stock was traded on a given day.

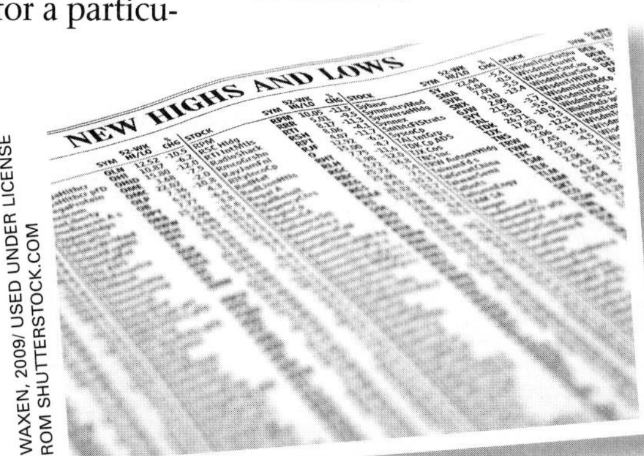

EXAMINE THE QUESTION

To get basic information of volume trades and benchmark prices, you can check financial Internet sites, news websites, television, and newspapers. Obviously, the Internet has a capacity to deliver up-to-the minute data about the day's trading.

CLASS DISCUSSION

Where have you heard the word *trend* used before? How might trends be important when following the stock market?

What makes an Internet site a credible Internet source? Name credible Internet sources that offer financial information.

AT&T 37.70 ↑0.11 (29%) as of 2:11 P.M.	
Last Trade:	37.59
Trade Time:	↑2:03 P.M. ET
Change:	0.08(0.21%)
Prev Close:	37.51
Open:	37.46
Bid:	N/A

- **Volume** is the number of shares that was traded in a given time period. In a newspaper, the volume is usually the day's volume. Online, the volume represents the total number of shares traded within a few minutes of the last trade. Sometimes the volume is listed as **Sales in 100s**. This represents the number of groups of 100 shares that were traded on a given day. Some websites may post the exact volume, while other websites state the volume in hundreds, thousands, or even millions.
- **52-week high** is the highest price at which one share was traded over the last year.
- **52-week low** is the lowest price at which one share was traded over the last year.
- **Chg** or **net change** shows the change between the previous day's closing price and the current day's closing price. This can be a monetary amount or it can be expressed as a percent. The change is positive if the current day's close is greater than the previous day's close and negative if the current day's close is less than the previous day's close.
- **After-hours trading** means that some trades are made after the market closes. A difference between one day's closing price and the next morning's opening price means after-hours trades on that stock occurred.

CLASS DISCUSSION

What is a stock trade? What data is collected when accounting for the number of trades made in a day?

Why do you think that net change is such an important stock statistic?

TEACH

As students examine changes in stock prices over time, they use computations involving subtraction and percents to understand the impact of the price changes.

EXAMPLE 1

Students need to have an understanding of high and low prices as they pertain to the 52-week period and for any given day. The more trades studied, the more likely students will see how the magnitude of the differences in highs and lows can indicate the volatility in price during the trading day.

CHECK YOUR UNDERSTANDING

Answer $0.80

To obtain the difference, subtract the day's low price from the day's high price. 51.40 − 50.60 = 0.80

Skills and Strategies

Examine the data for XYZ Corporation published at the close of two trading days. These categories are used when analyzing data about stock.

XYZ Corporation		XYZ Corporation	
May 5		May 12	
Last	52.20	Last	49.98
Trade Time	4:00PM ET	Trade Time	4:00PM ET
Chg	2.61	Chg	−1.55
Open	50.10	Open	49.90
52-week High	60.45	52-week High	60.45
52-week Low	43.60	52-week Low	43.60
Sales in 100s	28000	Sales in 100s	32000
High	52.60	High	51.40
Low	49.00	Low	50.60

EXAMPLE 1

What was the difference between the high and the low prices on May 5?

SOLUTION The day's high price was $52.60 and the low was $49.00.

Subtract the low from the high. $52.60 – $49.00 = $3.60

The difference in the high and low prices on May 5 was $3.60.

CHECK YOUR UNDERSTANDING

What was the difference between the high and low prices on May 12?

EXAMPLE 2

On May 12, what was the actual volume of XYZ shares posted? Write the volume in thousands.

SOLUTION The data for May 12 does not use the category name volume. Sales in 100s indicates volume. Because volume in 100s is the number of groups of 100 shares traded, 32,000 hundreds is written

$$32{,}000 \times 100, \text{ or } 3{,}200{,}000$$

Sales in 1,000s represent the number of groups of 1,000 shares traded.

Divide by 1,000. $3{,}200{,}000 \div 1{,}000 = 3{,}200$

On May 12, there were 3,200 thousands of shares traded.

CHECK YOUR UNDERSTANDING

On May 5, what was the actual volume of XYZ shares posted? Write the volume in thousands.

EXAMPLE 3

At what price did XYZ Corporation close on May 4?

SOLUTION XYZ Corporation ended the trading day on May 5 with a closing price of $52.20. This reflected a change of $2.61 from the previous day's close. Let x represent the closing price on May 4. Write an equation for the current day's closing price as the previous day's closing price plus the change.

Substitute values from the chart. $x + 2.61 = 52.20$

Subtract 2.61 from each side of the equation. $-2.61 = -2.61$

$x = 49.59$

XYZ Corporation closed at $49.59 on May 4.

CHECK YOUR UNDERSTANDING

At what price did XYZ Corporation close on May 11?

EXAMPLE 4

Use the May 4 closing price from Example 3 and the May 5 opening price to find the difference in prices as a percent increase. Round to the nearest hundredth percent.

SOLUTION The percent increase of one share of stock for these two prices can be calculated by using the following formula.

$$\text{Percent increase} = \frac{\text{Open} - \text{Close}}{\text{Close}} \times 100$$

Substitute values from the chart. $\frac{50.10 - 49.59}{49.59} \times 100$

Simplify the fraction. 0.010284×100

Multiply. Then round. 1.03

There was approximately a 1.03% increase in the price per share of XYZ Corporation due to after-hours trading.

EXAMPLE 2

Volume or sales is often quoted in units other than one. Calculate an actual volume by first converting the stated unit into numbers. The volume is quoted in 100s. Therefore, the sales numbers must be multiplied by 100 in order to report the actual number of sales.

CHECK YOUR UNDERSTANDING

Answer 2,800 thousands

May 5 sales were 28,000 hundreds of shares. This can be reported as 28,000 × 100 or 2,800,000. The question asks students to report the number of sales in thousands. Divide 2,800,000 by 1,000.

EXAMPLE 3

Net change is often counter-intuitive for students. It relies on the working backwards approach for solving the problem. Students need to understand that a positive net change means an increase in the closing price from the previous day's close and a negative net change means a decrease in the closing price from the previous day's close. Students should set up an equation so that they can see how the inverse operations work in the solution.

CHECK YOUR UNDERSTANDING

Answer $51.53

Set up and solve the equation $x - 1.55 = 49.98$, where x represents the closing price on May 11.

EXAMPLE 4

For a percent increase/decrease problem, the numerator is the difference in the before and after amounts. The denominator is the before amount, closing price on May 4. Therefore, this ratio needs to be converted to a percent.

CHECK YOUR UNDERSTANDING

Answer –3.16%

Since this situation represents a decrease in price from May 11 to May 12, the numerator of the fraction is negative.

EXAMPLE 5

Have students identify the numbers to subtract for the numerator and the number to use in the denominator. Students need to understand that the percent change is a change in the May 5 closing price, so the closing price for May 5 is the denominator of the fraction.

CHECK YOUR UNDERSTANDING

Answer –8.5%

Use the percent change formula and the correct substitutions.

$$\frac{45.72 - 49.98}{49.98} \times 100$$

■ **CHECK YOUR UNDERSTANDING**

Use the May 11 closing price from the previous Check Your Understanding and the May 12 opening price to represent the difference as a percent decrease. Round to the nearest hundredth percent.

EXAMPLE 5

On May 6, the XYZ Corporation announced a decrease in earnings. This news caused the price of their stock to drop. It closed at $44.37. Express the net change from May 5 to May 6 as a percent.

SOLUTION You can find the net change using the following formula.

Net change $\frac{\text{May 6 close} - \text{May 5 close}}{\text{May 5 close}} \times 100$

Substitute values from the chart. $\frac{44.37 - 52.20}{52.20} \times 100$

Simplify the fraction. -0.15×100

Multiply. -15%

The net change expressed as a percent is –15%. This means the closing price on May 6 reflects a 15% decrease from the closing price on May 5.

■ **CHECK YOUR UNDERSTANDING**

On May 13, the XYZ Corporation announced another decrease in earnings. The price of their stock dropped to close at $45.72. Express the net change from May 12 to May 13 as a percent, to the nearest tenth.

Spreadsheets

A **spreadsheet** is an electronic worksheet that can be used to keep track of stock information. Spreadsheets allow you to enter data into columns and rows. The intersection of a column and a row is a **cell**. Cells can contain numbers, words, or formulas. While the structure of a formula may differ based on the software, formulas have a fundamental algebraic basis. In spreadsheet formulas you use an * (asterisk) for the multiplication symbol and a / (forward slash) for the division symbol. Do not use spaces around symbols.

Examine the spreadsheet below that contains information on the XYZ Corporation for May 4–May 6. Columns are named using letters of the alphabet, while rows are numbered. Because a cell is the intersection of a column and a row, a cell is named with its column letter and row number.

cell D4

	A	B	C	D	E	F
1	XYZ CORP					
2						
3	Date	High	Low	Close	Change	% Change
4	4-May	50.23	49.34	49.59		
5	5-May	52.60	49.00	52.20		
6	6-May	52.20	40.78	44.37		

The closing price for May 4 is in cell D4. A formula can be stored in cell E5 to calculate the net change. Think of each cell name as a variable. If E5 represents the net change of the closing price from May 4 to May 5, the equation needed is E5 = D5 – D4. You enter the right side of the equation in cell E5 beginning with the = symbol. The formula uses the values in cells D5 and D4 to calculate the net change for May 5 and stores it in cell E5.

	A	B	C	D	E	F
1	XYZ CORP					
2						
3	Date	High	Low	Close	Change	% Change
4	4-May	50.23	49.34	49.59		
5	5-May	52.60	49.00	52.20	2.61	
6	6-May	52.20	40.78	44.37		

=D5–D4

EXAMPLE 6

Write a formula for cell F6 to calculate the percent net change for May 6.

SOLUTION The percent net change from May 5 to May 6 was calculated in Example 5. The formula uses the May 5 and May 6 closing prices. These prices are in cells D5 and D6, respectively. Use the cell names as the variables and multiply by 100 to get a percent.

Substitute cell names into formula. $\frac{D6 - D5}{D5} \times 100$

Convert to a spreadsheet formula. =(D6–D5)/D5*100

	A	B	C	D	E	F
1	XYZ CORP					
2						
3	Date	High	Low	Close	Change	% Change
4	4-May	50.23	49.34	49.59		
5	5-May	52.60	49.00	52.20	2.61	
6	6-May	52.20	40.78	44.37		–15

=(D6–D5)/D5*100

Order of Operations Notice there is only one set of parentheses in the formula. Following the order of operations, division by D5 occurs before multiplication by 100. However, it is necessary to enclose the numerator in parentheses so the difference D6 – D5 is divided by D5. Without those parentheses, the spreadsheet first divides D5 by D5, then multiplies that quotient by 100, and finally subtracts that answer from D6, which results in an incorrect value.

Rounding You can set the number of rounding places for each cell according to the degree of accuracy needed in your calculations. Be aware that the computer retains the entire calculation to many decimal places. In this case, it just shows the value to two decimal places.

■ CHECK YOUR UNDERSTANDING

Write formulas for cells E6 and F5 in the spreadsheet above.

EXAMPLE 6

Have students identify the cell names that contain the numbers needed to calculate the percent change for May 6. After students have written the formula, discuss the order of operations. Students can then determine if there is a need for parenthesis in the formula =D6–D5/D5*100.

As is, the D5/D5 will be calculated first, which is not what is needed. For the subtraction to be computed first, parenthesis must be inserted.

CHECK YOUR UNDERSTANDING

Answer for E6: =D6–D5; for F5: =E5/D4*100

Use the change and percent change formulas.

Applications

One of the funny things about the stock market is that every time one person buys, another sells, and both think they are astute.

William Feather, Publisher and Author

TEACH

Exercise 5
Remind students that a positive net change means that the day's closing price was higher than the previous day's closing price and a negative net change means that the day's closing price was lower than the previous day's closing price. To find the previous day's price, add the opposite of the day's net change to the close, or last price.

ANSWERS

1. Both the buyer and the seller think that their trade has been made at a price which is acceptable. For example, a buyer may want in on a hot stock and sees its growth potential. A seller may want to cash in on the current success of a stock and "take the money and run". Both the buyer and the seller think they have made a smart choice.

1. Why might the buyer and seller of the same stock both think that their trading price was an "astute" decision? How might those words apply to what you have learned? See margin.

Use the following information posted at the end of the trading day on April 22 to answer Exercises 2–7.

52-week High	52-week Low	Symbol	Stock	Last	Change	Sales of 100s	High	Low
151,650	107,200	BRK/A	Berkshire Hathaway Inc	127,200	−1000	4.11	128,600	127,000
120.2	66.39	FCX	Freeport-McMoRan Copper & Gold Inc	118.65	3.51	147,540	120.06	116.64
63.69	46.64	MCD	McDonald's Corporation	58.35	−0.55	106,077	58.77	57.42
266.81	112.11	PTR	PetroChina Company Ltd	137.19	+2.16	16,266	140.92	136.09
39.63	27.51	TXN	Texas Instruments Inc	28.85	−1.74	288,012	29.64	28.38
144.04	92.18	WBK	Westpac Banking Corporation	113.62	2.45	332.7	115.35	113.50

2. What was the difference between the 52-week high and 52-week low price for one share of PetroChina Company Ltd? $154.70
3. What is the difference between the day's high and low prices for McDonald's Corporation? $1.35
4. Determine the volume for each of the following stocks.
   a. Berkshire Hathaway Inc 411
   b. McDonald's Corporation 10,607,700
   c. Texas Instruments Inc 28,801,200
   d. Westpac Banking Corporation 33,270
5. Determine the closing price on April 21 for each of the following stocks.
   a. Texas Instruments Inc $30.59
   b. Freeport-McMoRan Copper & Gold Inc $115.14
6. Use the information from Exercise 5 to determine the percent of net change from April 21 to April 22 for each of the corporations listed in that question. Round answers to the nearest tenth of a percent. a. −5.7% b. 3%
7. On April 22, which stock(s) had a daily high that was approximately 50% lower than the 52-week high? PetroChina Company Ltd
8. If the April net change for Westpac Banking Corporation was –3.03, what was the closing price for that day? $110.59

9. Which of the following is a true statement? Explain your reasoning. See margin.
The 52-week high can never be higher than the day's high.
The day's high can never be higher than the 52-week high.

10. At the end of the trading day on April 25, Texas Instruments Inc closed at $28.84, which was a +5.22% net change from the previous day's close. What was the approximate close on the previous day? $27.41

11. On April 25, Berkshire Hathaway Inc closed at $126,875 per share. One year earlier, one share closed at $108,750. What was an approximate one-year percent change? 16.7%

TEACH

Exercise 10
The information given in the chart for BBW and NTGR contains both the change and the percent change amounts. You might want to show students how to verify that the two amounts are equivalent.

Use the spreadsheet below to answer Exercises 12–16.

	A	B	C	D	E	F	G	H
1	**Symbol**	**Stock**	**April 25 Last**	**Change**	**% Change**	**April 24 Close**	**Volume in 1,000s**	**Volume in 100s**
2	AAPL	Apple Inc	169.73	0.79		168.94	35,445	
3	BBW	Build-A-Bear Workshop Inc	10.15	1.15	12.78%		616	
4	CTB	Cooper Tire & Rubber Co	14.7	−1.82		16.52	2,671	
5	F	Ford Motor Co	7.5	−0.9			227,269	
6	INTC	Intel Corp	22.56		−0.57%		47,604	
7	MSFT	Microsoft Corp	29.83		−6.19%	31.80	145,194	
8	NTGR	NETGEAR Inc	16.76	−3.37	−16.74%		8,085	
9	YHOO	Yahoo! Inc	26.8		−1.83%		50,523	

12. Write a formula that will convert the volume given in 1,000s into a volume given in 100s. Use the left side of the equation to indicate in which cell to store the formula.
   a. Intel Corp H6=1000*G6/100, or H6=10*G6
   b. Yahoo! Inc H9=1000*G9/100, or H9=10*G9

13. Write a formula that will store the exact volume for each stock in column I. Use the left side of the equation to indicate in which cell to store the formula.
   a. Build-A-Bear Workshop Inc I3=1000*G3
   b. NETGEAR Inc I8=1000*G8

14. Write a formula to determine the close on April 24 for each of the following. Use the left side of the equation to indicate in which cell to store the formula.
   a. NETGEAR Inc F8=C8–D8
   b. Ford Motor Co F5=C5–D5

15. Write a formula to determine the percent change for each of the following. Use the left side of the equation to indicate in which cell to store the formula.
   a. Apple Inc E2=(C2–F2)/F2*100 or E2=D2/F2*100
   b. Cooper Tire & Rubber Co E4=(C4–F4)/F4*100 or E4=D4/F4*100

16. Write a formula to determine the net change for each. Use the left side of the equation to indicate in which cell to store the formula.
   a. Microsoft Corp D7=C7–F7
   b. Cooper Tire & Rubber Co D4=C4–F4

ANSWERS

9. The 52-week high is the highest price for a stock over a 52-week period. Therefore, the day's high could be equal to the 52-week high, but can never be greater than it.

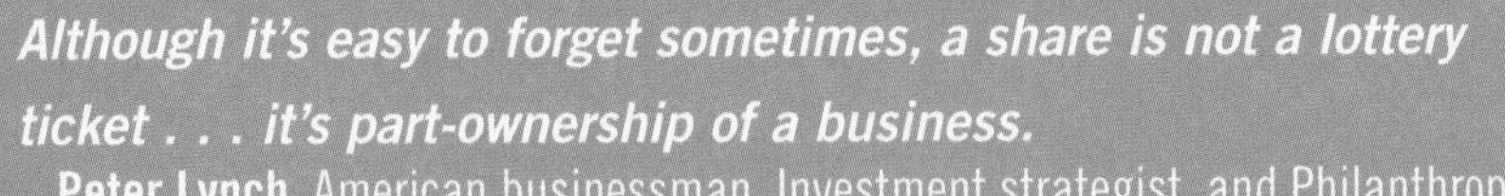

Although it's easy to forget sometimes, a share is not a lottery ticket . . . it's part-ownership of a business.
Peter Lynch, American businessman, Investment strategist, and Philanthropist

1-3 Stock Market Data Charts

Objectives

- Interpret a stock bar chart.
- Create a stock bar chart.
- Interpret a stock candlestick chart.
- Create a stock candlestick chart.

Common Core

N-Q1, N-Q2

Key Terms

- stock chart
- stock bar chart
- candlestick chart

CCSS Warm-Up

An item usually sells for X dollars. It is marked down to Y dollars. Interpret each of the following algebraic expressions in this context.

1. $|Y-X|$
1. The absolute difference in prices.

2. $|Y-X|/X$
2. The fractional part of the original price that is the discount.

3. $100|Y-X|/X$
3. The percent discount or the percent decrease in price.

HOW CAN STOCK DATA BE DISPLAYED?

EXAMINE THE QUESTION

As students think of the numerous types of data displays they have studied, they will likely come to the conclusion that none are a good fit for stock market data. Thus, there is a need to learn how to create and interpret a new type of data display.

CLASS DISCUSSION

Why might an investor be interested in historical information about the trading prices and volumes of a particular stock?

Data can be presented in list form or in graphical form. The graphical form is known as a **stock chart**. These charts offer pictorial information on anything from a day's worth of data to multiyear data trends. Most stock charts present historical information about the trading prices and volumes of a particular stock.

A common stock chart format is the **stock bar chart**. The chart below shows price and volume information for General Electric on April 30.

Notice the chart consists of two graphs. The top portion shows daily information about the day's high, low, open, and close prices. The bottom portion shows the daily volume for that stock.

The top shaded bar is a rectangle formed between the day's low and high. The line segment on the left side of the rectangle is positioned at the day's opening price and the line segment on the right side is positioned at the day's closing price.

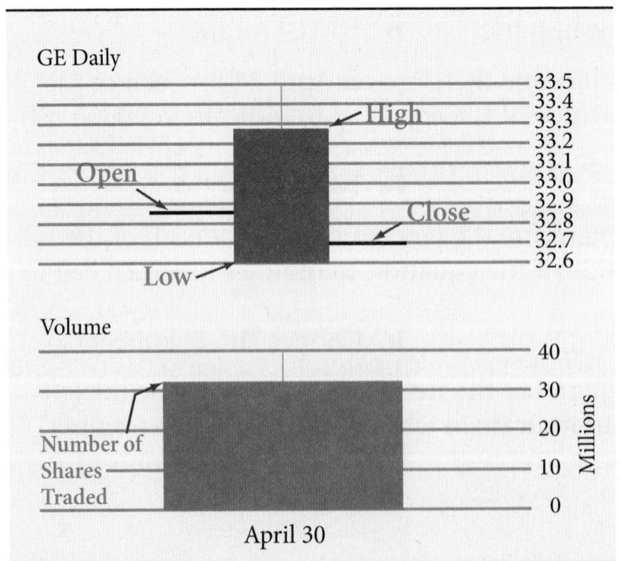

The bottom shaded bar starts at 0 and rises to the approximate number of shares traded on that date. Notice that the scale for this particular portion of the chart is in millions, although it could be in hundreds or thousands depending upon the range in the volume. Stock bar charts can also be used to show the market action on multiple days.

Skills and Strategies

Here you will learn how to interpret and create stock charts. The stock bar chart below presents trading information for the week of April 28 for Ford Motor Company.

TEACH

Distribute graph paper and rulers.

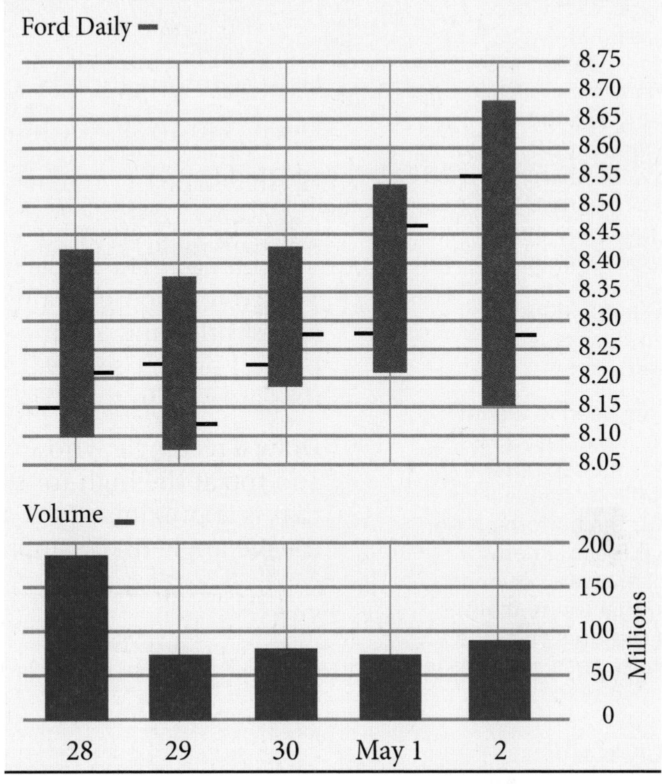

EXAMPLE 1

Which day had the greatest high price? Which day had the least low price?

SOLUTION The top portion of the chart shows the day's trading prices. Because the top of each bar represents the day's high price, the greatest high for the week was on May 2.

The bottom of each bar represents the day's low price, so the lowest low for the week occurred on April 29.

■ CHECK YOUR UNDERSTANDING

Between which two days did after-hours trading appear to have the biggest impact on the difference between the closing price and the following day's opening price?

EXAMPLE 2

Approximately how many shares of Ford Motor Company were traded over the five-day period?

SOLUTION The bottom portion of the chart shows the daily volume of shares traded. The scale is in millions of shares. While it is not possible to give an exact accounting of each day's volume, you can determine approximations of these amounts.

For April 28, the top of the volume bar reaches at a point slightly higher than half the distance between the 150 million and 200 million lines. An approximation of the day's volume is 185 million shares.

For April 29, the volume appears to be slightly above the 50 million line. So an approximation is 60 million shares.

Approximations for the rest of the week's trading volumes are 65 million, 60 million, and 90 million.

Add the five approximations. $185 + 60 + 65 + 60 + 90 = 460$

About 460,000,000 shares of Ford Motor Company were traded during the week of April 28.

EXAMPLE 1

Guide students to realize that a lot of information is available on a stock trend graph. Students can begin to understand the at-a-glance advantage of this type of graph when identifying the greatest high and the least low price for the period of time covered by the graph.

CHECK YOUR UNDERSTANDING

Answer 4/29 and 4/30

EXAMPLE 2

Point out that two different units are used in the graph. The bottom portion of the graph charts amounts in millions of shares traded.

CHECK YOUR UNDERSTANDING

Answer On April 28, one share of Ford Motor Company opened at $8.15. During the day, the shares reached a high of approximately $8.42 per share and a low of $8.10 per share. Ford closed at approximately $8.21 per share. On April 29, one share of Ford Motor Company opened at approximately $8.23. During the day, the shares reached a high of approximately $8.37 per share and a low of $8.07 per share. Ford closed at approximately $8.12 per share on that date.

EXAMPLE 3

Students need to identify the intervals that will be used for the top portion and the units that will be used for the bottom portion. While there are many correct answers, students should make sure that the graph captures all of the necessary price amounts in an easy-to-read display.

CHECK YOUR UNDERSTANDING

Answer If trading is suspended, there are no prices to chart and no volume to report. Therefore, the chart could either show a blank space on that trading day, or a horizontal line (bar with no height) for each portion of the chart.

■ CHECK YOUR UNDERSTANDING

Use the stock bar chart to write a brief financial story of the trading action that occurred for Ford Motor Company on April 28 and April 29. Begin your story with "On April 28, one share of Ford Motor Company opened at $8.15. During the day . . . "

EXAMPLE 3

Use the information below to construct a one-day stock bar chart.

Open: $40.10 Close: $39.79

High: $40.65 Low: $39.39 Volume: 44,500,000

SOLUTION Determine an appropriate interval to use to display the information. The range of the daily prices is from $39.39 to $40.65. Therefore, choose a value to begin the interval that is less than the lowest price and a value to end the interval that is greater than the highest price. Use $39.25 to $40.75. Next, establish interval amounts that are easy to read. Use intervals of $0.25.

Draw a rectangle whose bottom is positioned at the low for the day and top at the high for the day. Draw a line to the left of the rectangle that is approximately at the opening price and a line to the right of the rectangle that is approximately at the closing price.

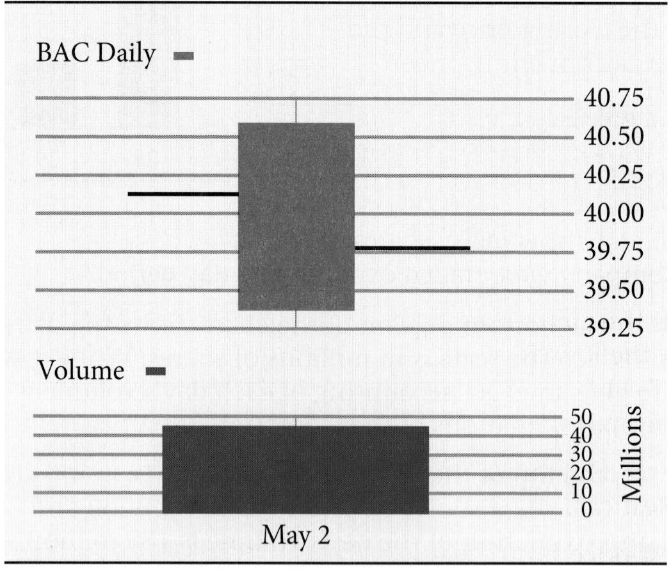

Next construct the volume portion of the chart. Select a suitable interval in millions, in this case 0 to 50. Beginning at 0, construct a bar that rises to the approximate volume for the day.

These two portions form a one-day stock bar chart.

■ CHECK YOUR UNDERSTANDING

Suppose that trading was suspended for one entire day for a corporation. What might the stock bar chart look like?

Candlestick Charts

Another type of chart that is similar to a stock bar chart is a **candlestick chart**. A candlestick chart may be easier to read and contains more information at a glance. The top and bottom of the vertical line indicate the high and low prices over the given time period. The rectangular region is known as the *real body* and is displayed in two different colors depending upon the action for the day on that stock.

the highest price for the day
open or closing price
body is black (or red) if stock closed lower than opening price; body is white (or green) if it closed higher than opening price
open or closing price
the lowest price for the day

The colors used to indicate the changes in the day's prices can be customized. The candlestick chart for Sept. 7–11 depicts market action for a particular stock for five days in September. The green candlestick indicates that the closing price is greater than the opening price. The red candlestick indicates the opposite; the closing price is less than the opening price.

EXAMPLE 4

Explain the difference between the market action on September 8 compared to September 9 shown in the candlestick chart for Sept. 7–11.

SOLUTION The candlestick is green on September 8, which means the closing price for the day was higher than the opening price. The red candlestick on September 9 indicates that the opening price for the day was higher than the closing price.

CHECK YOUR UNDERSTANDING

Interpret a green candlestick that is shown as only a rectangle with no lines at the top or bottom.

Candlestick Chart, Sept. 7–11

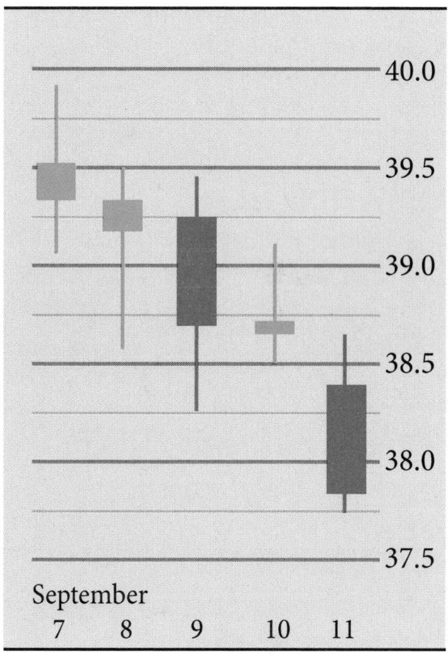

EXAMPLE 5

What was the approximate difference between the highest price and the lowest price for the week shown in the candlestick chart for Sept. 7–11?

SOLUTION The highest price for the week, approximately \$39.90, occurred on September 7 as indicated by the highest portion of any of the candlesticks.

The lowest price for the week, approximately \$37.75, occurred on September 11 as indicated by the lowest portion of any of the candlesticks.

The difference between the week's high and low prices is approximately \$39.90 – \$37.75, or \$2.15.

CHECK YOUR UNDERSTANDING

The lengths of the candlesticks for September 8 and 11 are approximately the same. What does this mean about the trading prices on both of those days?

EXAMPLE 4

Candlestick charts depend on color for interpretation.

CHECK YOUR UNDERSTANDING

Answer The close was higher than the open. Without any lines at the top or bottom, the graph indicates that the closing price was the high for the day and the opening price was the low for the day.

EXAMPLE 5

Have students identify the highs and lows for each of the days.

CHECK YOUR UNDERSTANDING

Answer The differences between each day's high price and low price are about equivalent.

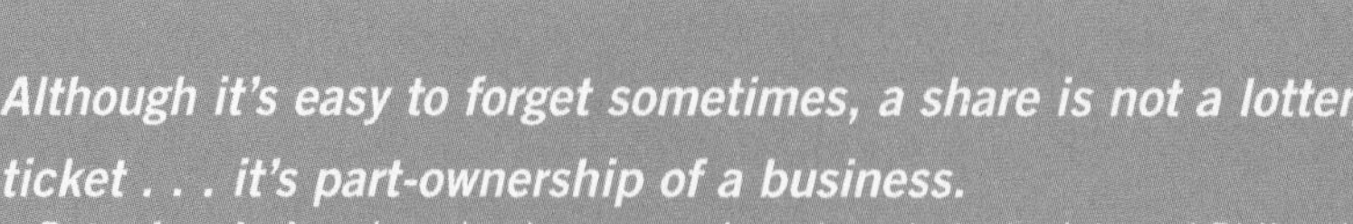

Applications

Although it's easy to forget sometimes, a share is not a lottery ticket . . . it's part-ownership of a business.

Peter Lynch, American businessman, Investment strategist, and Philanthropist

TEACH

Exercises 2–12
When reviewing these problems with the students, you should display the graph using some type of projection device. Have students come to the front of the room to identify the locations that indicate the correct answers to the questions.

ANSWERS

1. The writer indicates that playing the market is not a game. It is not a quick way to make money like a lottery. Rather, it is a way to invest in a corporation by becoming a part owner of the business.

1. How might those words apply to what you have learned? Why is the author warning readers that a share is not a lottery ticket? See margin.

The following stock bar chart depicts the market action for The Washington Post Company during the week of April 28. Use the chart to answer Exercises 2–11.

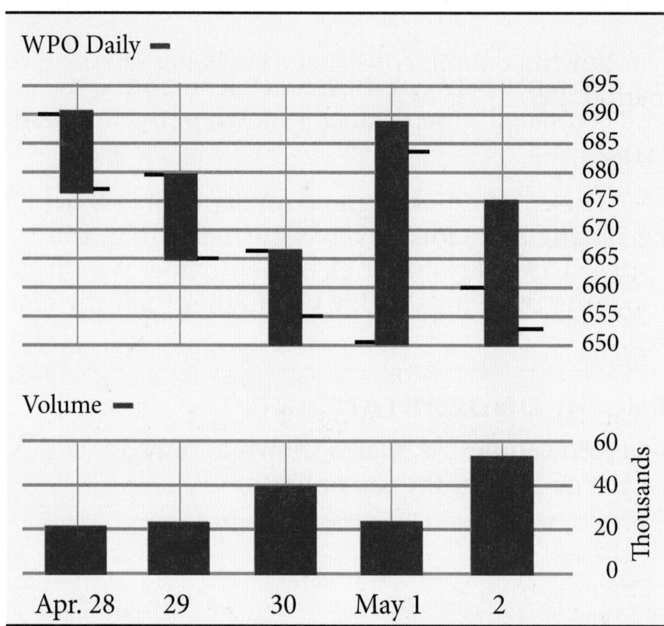

2. On what date did the stock close at a price higher than it opened? May 1

3. What was the day's opening price on the following days?

April 28 approx. 690
April 29 approx. 679
April 30 approx. 667
May 1 approx. 651
May 2 approx. 660

4. What was the day's high price on April 29? $680

5. What was the day's low price on May 1? $650

6. What was the day's close on May 2? approx. $653

7. What was the approximate net change from April 29 to April 30? Express that net change as a monetary amount and as a percent to the nearest tenth. $655 – $665 = –$10; approx. –1.5%

8. What was the approximate net change from April 30 to May 1? Express that net change as a monetary amount and as a percent to the nearest tenth. $684 – $655 = $29; approx. 4.4%

9. Approximately how many shares were traded on April 30? approx. 40,000 shares

10. Approximately how many fewer shares were traded on April 28 than on May 2? approx. 52,000 – 20,000 = 32,000

11. Suppose that the volume numbers had been listed in hundreds on the table. How would that have changed the labels? 0, 200, 400, 600

12. Use the following data to construct a stock bar chart for the 5-day period. See additional answers.

Day	Open	Close	High	Low	Volume
1	20.48	20.24	20.50	20.20	58,000,000
2	20.21	20.25	20.30	20.00	52,000,000
3	20.30	20.10	20.34	20.02	42,000,000
4	20.17	20.44	20.45	20.10	50,000,000
5	20.48	20.61	20.65	20.36	50,000,000

13. Use the following data to construct a stock bar chart for the 5-day period. See additional answers.

Day	Open	Close	High	Low	Volume
1	59.75	59.60	60.00	59.22	7,900,000
2	59.15	60.20	60.50	59.15	8,000,000
3	60.00	59.58	60.61	59.55	8,200,000
4	59.55	60.90	60.90	59.37	7,000,000
5	60.87	60.93	61.25	60.79	7,750,000

14. Use the candlestick chart to answer the questions.

a. On which days were opening prices higher than the closing prices? April 28 and 30

b. On which days were the closing prices higher than the opening prices? April 27, April 29, and May 1

c. What was the approximate closing price on April 28? \$32.45

d. What was the approximate high price on May 1? \$33.45

e. What was the difference between the lowest price and the highest price recorded for this time period? \$33.45 – \$31.95 = \$1.50

f. What does the very short line at the bottom of the May 1 candlestick indicate? See margin.

g. Had the chart used white and black candlesticks, which days would be white and which days would be black? white: 4/27, 4/29, 5/1; black: 4/28, 4/30

h. On which consecutive days was the closing price of the first day higher than the opening price of the second day? 4/28 and 4/29; 4/30 and 5/1

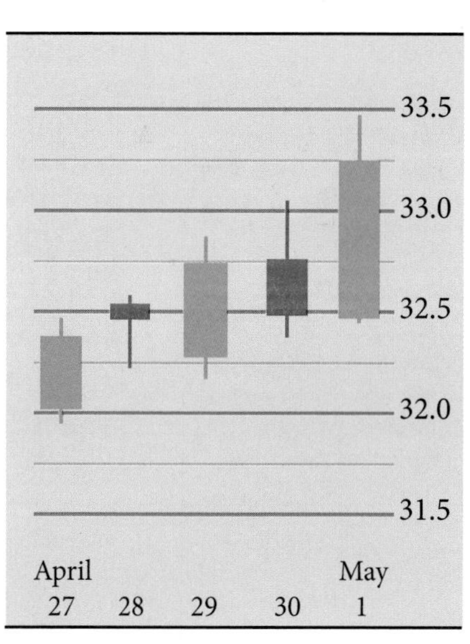

15. Construct a candlestick chart for the information presented in Exercise 12. See additional answers.

16. Construct a candlestick chart for the information presented in Exercise 13. See additional answers.

TEACH

Exercise 11

Alert students to the variety of ways that numbers can be written using numerals and words.

ANSWERS

14f. The opening price for the day was close to the low for the day.

Never try to walk across a river just because it has an average depth of four feet.

Milton Friedman, American economist

1-4 Simple Moving Averages

Objectives

- Understand how data is smoothed.
- Calculate simple moving averages using the arithmetic average formula.
- Calculate simple moving averages using the subtraction and addition method.
- Graph simple moving averages using a spreadsheet.

Common Core

N-Q1, N-Q2

Key Terms

- smoothing techniques
- simple moving average (SMA)
- arithmetic average (mean)
- lagging indicators
- fast moving average
- slow moving average
- crossover

CCSS Warm-Up

Given $A > B > C > D$, which of the following has the greatest value? Explain your reasoning.

1. The average of A, B, C, and D
2. The sum of A, B, C, and D
3. The difference between A and D

The sum, because that will yield a value greater than A, B, C, or D. The average and difference have to be less than the greatest of the four numbers.

How can stock data be smoothed?

Stock market prices can fluctuate greatly from trade to trade based upon a variety of external factors. You have already seen that the high and low for a day may not necessarily be near the day's opening or closing prices. Those differences often make it difficult to spot trends that are occurring over time. **Smoothing techniques** are statistical tools that allow an investor to reduce the impact of price fluctuations and to focus on patterns and trends. One such technique is known as a **simple moving average (SMA)**. Simple moving averages are calculated by determining the **arithmetic average (mean)** closing price over a given period of time.

The graph shows the daily stock closing prices, 5-day SMA and 10-day SMA over a period of 30 trading days. Notice how the closing prices fluctuated from day to day and the moving average graphs smoothed out that data. The longer the moving average time interval, the smoother the graph appears to be.

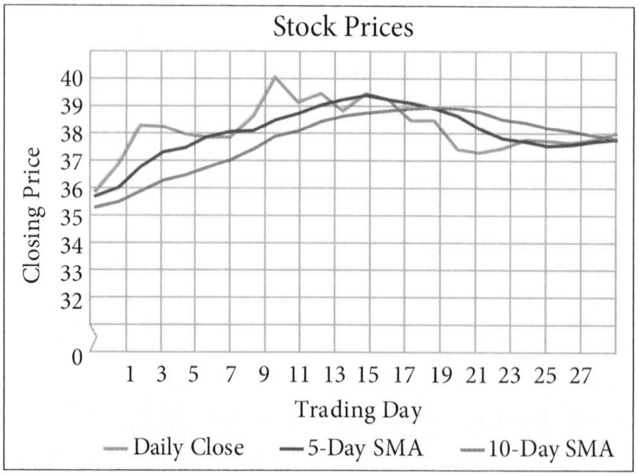

Stock Prices

Closing Price: 0, 32, 33, 34, 35, 36, 37, 38, 39, 40

Trading Day: 1 3 5 7 9 11 13 15 17 19 21 23 25 27

— Daily Close — 5-Day SMA — 10-Day SMA

Moving averages are known as **lagging indicators** because they use past data. Investors use simple moving averages when they want to identify and follow a trend in prices.

EXAMINE THE QUESTION

Stock market professionals and statisticians needed to find a technique that brought prices into a more central range, while still representing the data that is true to the numbers.

The smoothing technique is used to calculate SMA over a variety of time periods. Students will learn to calculate these moving averages and interpret their meanings to the stock market data.

CLASS DISCUSSION

What factors might contribute to the fluctuation of stock market prices?

Skills and Strategies

Recall that the average of a set of numerical data is the sum of the items in that set divided by the number of items. You can determine the average of any number of closing prices, but this gives you little information about trends because you would have nothing to compare the averages to. A better comparison method to use is a simple moving average.

TEACH

Review the concept of an average. Be sure students understand what the average is in relation to the numbers in the data set.

Simple Moving Averages Using the Arithmetic Average Formula

Although simple moving averages can span any length of time, in Example 1 you will find averages by taking closing prices 5 days at a time. Find an average of the prices for each of the 5-day time spans: days 1–5, days 2–6, days 3–7, days 4–8, days 5–9, and days 6–10. Graph the six averages. The graph has a smoother appearance compared to the graph of the closing prices of days 5–10. A moving average graph appears to smooth the fluctuations in closing prices.

EXAMPLE 1

Students use the basic arithmetic average formula repeatedly using closing prices for five consecutive days at a time. Show students that the move occurs by deleting the first day's average and adding the next day's average.

EXAMPLE 1

The closing prices for 10 consecutive trading days for a particular stock are shown. Calculate the 5-day SMA and plot both the closing prices and the averages on a graph.

Day	Closing Price
1	35.02
2	35.01
3	34.65
4	36.09
5	35.32
6	35.50
7	35.03
8	35.79
9	37.07
10	36.05

SOLUTION Find the average of the closing prices in groups of five.

Find the SMA using the closing prices from days 1–5.

$$\frac{35.02 + 35.01 + 34.65 + 36.09 + 35.32}{5} = 35.218 \approx 35.22$$

Days 2–6 $$\frac{35.01 + 34.65 + 36.09 + 35.32 + 35.50}{5} = 35.314 \approx 35.31$$

Days 3–7 $$\frac{34.65 + 36.09 + 35.32 + 35.50 + 35.03}{5} = 35.318 \approx 35.32$$

Days 4–8 $$\frac{36.09 + 35.32 + 35.50 + 35.03 + 35.79}{5} = 35.546 \approx 35.55$$

Days 5–9 $$\frac{35.32 + 35.50 + 35.03 + 35.79 + 37.07}{5}$$

$$= 35.742 \approx 35.74$$

Days 6–10 $$\frac{35.50 + 35.03 + 35.79 + 37.07 + 36.05}{5}$$

$$= 35.888 \approx 35.89$$

The five consecutive 5-day SMA are \$35.22, \$35.31, \$35.32, \$35.55, \$35.74, and \$35.89.

The graph of the closing prices and the simple moving averages for days 5 through 10 are shown. Notice how the moving averages smooth out the data.

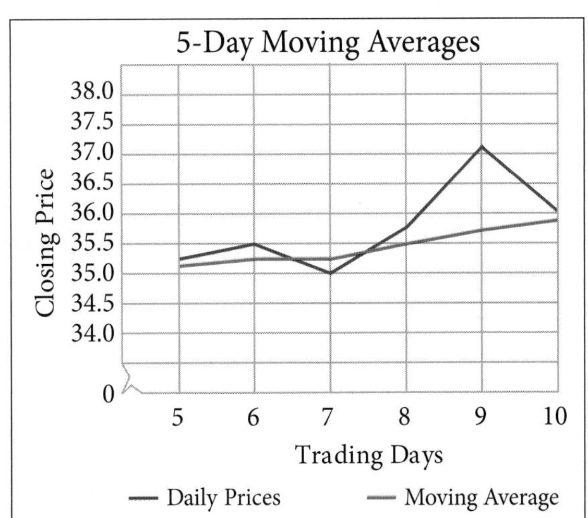

CHECK YOUR UNDERSTANDING

Answer 5-day moving averages are \$53, \$50.40, \$47.40, \$44.20, \$43.20, \$45.

Graph should have a line that connects the points of closing prices and a line that connects the points of the 5-day moving averages.

EXAMPLE 2

The subtraction and addition method is a time saver that requires an understanding of the process. Be sure to work through the explanation with the students.

Students need to understand why to subtract and add a fraction whose denominator is the number of days in the cycle.

■ CHECK YOUR UNDERSTANDING

Closing prices for 10 consecutive trading days were \$55, \$60, \$62, \$48, \$40, \$42, \$45, \$46, \$43, and \$49. Calculate the 5-day SMA. Plot both the closing prices and the averages on a graph.

Simple Moving Averages Using the Subtraction and Addition Method

The calculation of a simple moving average can be tedious because you have to find the average for each time interval. There is an alternate way to compute the moving average that is simpler.

Suppose you want to determine a 3-day simple moving average for 6 trading days. Let the trading prices for the days be represented by *A*, *B*, *C*, *D*, *E*, and *F*. The trading prices for the first three days are *A*, *B*, and *C*. The average of those prices is

$$\frac{A + B + C}{3} = \frac{A}{3} + \frac{B}{3} + \frac{C}{3}$$

Using the method in Example 1, find the average of days 2–4 using *B*, *C*, and *D*. This is the same as subtracting price *A* and adding price *D*, or

$$\frac{A}{3} + \frac{B}{3} + \frac{C}{3} - \frac{A}{3} + \frac{D}{3}$$

Rearranging the terms and simplifying, this process is the same as finding the average for days 2–4.

$$\frac{A}{3} - \frac{A}{3} + \frac{B}{3} + \frac{C}{3} + \frac{D}{3} = \frac{B}{3} + \frac{C}{3} + \frac{D}{3} = \frac{B + C + D}{3}$$

EXAMPLE 2

Use the subtraction and addition method to determine the 4-day SMA for the following closing prices.

\$121, \$122, \$120, \$119, \$124, \$128, \$126

SOLUTION Calculate the average closing prices of days 1–4.

Add the first 4 prices. Divide by 4. $\frac{121 + 122 + 120 + 119}{4} = 120.50$

Use subtraction and addition to determine the averages for days 2–5.

Use previous average, $\frac{A}{4}$, and $\frac{E}{4}$. $120.50 - \frac{121}{4} + \frac{124}{4} = 121.25$

Find the averages for days 3–6 and days 4–7.

Use previous average, $\frac{B}{4}$, and $\frac{F}{4}$. $121.25 - \frac{122}{4} + \frac{128}{4} = 122.75$

Use previous average, $\frac{C}{4}$, and $\frac{G}{4}$. $122.75 - \frac{120}{4} + \frac{126}{4} = 124.25$

The simple moving averages are \$120.50, \$121.25, \$122.75, and \$124.25.

■ **CHECK YOUR UNDERSTANDING**

Use the subtraction and addition method to determine the 3-day SMA for the closing prices $28, $31, $37, $38, and $35.

■ **EXTEND YOUR UNDERSTANDING**

In Example 2, what would the eighth trading day's closing price have to be so that the next moving average remains the same at $124.25?

CHECK YOUR UNDERSTANDING

Answer $32, $35.33, $36.66

EXTEND YOUR UNDERSTANDING

Answer $119

In order that the next cycle of 4 consecutive days has the same SMA as the last cycle, the number subtracted (the 4th day's price) and the number added (the 8th day's price) need to be the same.

Graph Simple Moving Averages Using a Spreadsheet

Simple moving averages are more informative when they are determined over a longer period of time. Often, financial websites and newspapers report long moving average time intervals. These calculations are time consuming if done by hand or even using a calculator. However, if you use a spreadsheet you can get results easily and quickly. The spreadsheet shown lists the closing prices of 30 consecutive days of trading for a particular stock. The 10-day moving averages are calculated in column C and begin on day 10. Cell C11 equals the average of the closing prices on days 1–10.

Most spreadsheets have a sum function, which is used to calculate the sum of amounts in a group of cells. The format for using a sum function varies depending on the spreadsheet software you are using. The format used here is =sum(starting cell:ending cell). The formula in cell C11 that yields the correct average is =sum(B2:B11)/10. The cells have been formatted to show all decimals rounded to two places.

The formula in cell C12 is =sum(B3:B12)/10. Notice that the starting and ending cells in the formula have each shifted down by one cell. Rather than typing this formula repeatedly and changing the cell names used, most spreadsheets have a fill command that recognizes the pattern. To use this command in this spreadsheet select the cells that you want to fill with the formula and apply the fill command. Most spreadsheets allow the user to *fill up, fill down, fill left*, or *fill right*. In this case, you *fill down*. The formula is placed in each selected cell with the cell names automatically adjusted for each row.

	A	B	C
1	**Day**	**Closing Price**	**10-day Moving Average**
2	1	35.02	
3	2	35.01	
4	3	34.65	
5	4	36.09	
6	5	35.32	
7	6	35.5	
8	7	35.03	
9	8	35.79	
10	9	37.07	
11	10	36.05	35.55
12	11	36.85	35.74
13	12	38.03	36.04
14	13	38	36.37
15	14	37.76	36.54
16	15	37.66	36.77
17	16	37.66	36.99
18	17	38.3	37.32
19	18	39.48	37.69
20	19	38.72	37.85
21	20	39.01	38.15
22	21	38.48	38.31
23	22	39.01	38.41
24	23	38.8	38.49
25	24	38.19	38.53
26	25	38.2	38.59
27	26	37.3	38.55
28	27	37.2	38.44
29	28	37.33	38.22
30	29	37.61	38.11
31	30	37.57	37.97

=sum(C2:C11)/10

=sum(C3:C12)/10

CHECK YOUR UNDERSTANDING

Answer D4; =sum(B2:B4)/3

CLASS DISCUSSION

Why is the graph with the shorter time interval "faster" than the graph with the longer time interval?

EXAMPLE 4

Identify the three important portions to the graph: Days 1–26, Day 27, Days 28–29.

CHECK YOUR UNDERSTANDING

Answer Sell; the slow moving graph has overtaken the fast moving graph indicating a reversal of the trend. The buyer might consider selling the stock.

CLASS DISCUSSION

What prices might you see when a crossover is about to occur?

EXAMPLE 3

Use a spreadsheet to calculate the 5-day SMA of the closing prices for 10 consecutive trading days.

SOLUTION Moving averages lag behind the closing prices, so in cell C6 calculate the average of the closing prices for April 28, 29, 30, May 1 and 2. The formula is =sum(B2:B6)/5.

Next, highlight cells C6 through C11 and apply the fill down command to have the 5-day moving averages appear in the appropriate cells as shown in blue.

	A	B	C
1	Day	Close	Moving Average
2	28-Apr	29.39	
3	29-Apr	29.27	
4	30-Apr	29.21	
5	1-May	29.70	
6	2-May	29.08	29.33
7	5-May	29.24	29.30
8	6-May	29.40	29.33
9	7-May	28.52	29.19
10	8-May	28.64	28.98
11	9-May	28.99	28.96

■ CHECK YOUR UNDERSTANDING

Add column D to the spreadsheet to calculate the 3-day SMA. In what cell do you start? What formula do you use?

Crossovers

Sometimes, investors construct stock charts that depict moving averages for two different intervals. The graph with the shorter time interval is known as the **fast moving average** and the graph with the longer time interval is known as the **slow moving average**. As changes in closing prices occur on a day-to-day basis, the fast moving average will reflect those changes quicker than the slow moving average will.

A **crossover** occurs when a one-time interval moving average graph overtakes another. Crossovers signal that a stock trend reversal might be near. Some say that an investor should consider buying when the fast moving average graph overtakes (rises above) the slow moving average graph. Likewise, an investor might consider selling when the fast moving average graph crosses below the slow moving average graph.

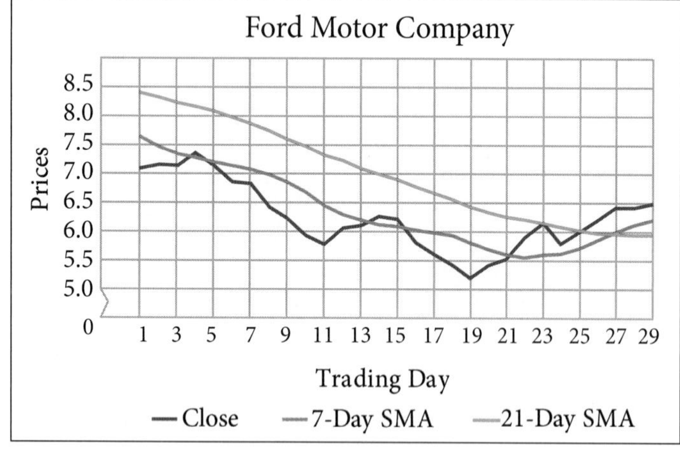

EXAMPLE 4

The graph shows the closing prices for 29 consecutive trading days. It also charts the 7-day and 21-day simple moving averages. What signal might the graphs give an investor?

SOLUTION A crossover occurs on the 27th day. The fast moving average graph rises above the slow moving average graph giving a signal to consider buying the stock.

■ CHECK YOUR UNDERSTANDING

Suppose that on the 35th trading day, the 21-day SMA graph rises above the 7-day graph. What might that indicate?

Applications

Never try to walk across a river just because it has an average depth of four feet.

Milton Friedman, American economist

1. Why might the author be warning readers to be cautious of averages? How might these words apply to what you have learned? See margin.

In Exercises 2–5, use the method illustrated in Example 1 to determine the simple moving averages by repeatedly finding sums. See margin.

2. Determine the 3-day SMA for the ten consecutive day closing prices of Sprint Nextel Corp listed below.
$7.78, $8.08, $7.99, $8.02, $7.89, $8.72, $9.19, $9.16, $8.98, $9.38

3. Determine the 5-day SMA for the ten consecutive day closing prices for MasterCard Inc listed below.
$242.50, $273.98, $278.16, $293.94, $285.04
$290.80, $296.02, $291.01, $293.41, $286.85

4. Determine the 4-day SMA for the ten consecutive day closing prices for Wal-Mart Stores Inc listed below.
$57.35, $58.61, $57.98, $58.07, $57.50
$56.97, $56.35, $56.83, $57.16, $57.18

5. Determine the 6-day SMA for the twelve consecutive day closing prices for Exxon Mobil Corp listed below.
$92.60, $92.46, $92.45, $91.79, $93.07, $89.70
$89.61, $89.51, $90.07, $88.82, $89.93, $88.82

In Exercises 6–9, use the method illustrated in Example 2 to determine moving averages by subtraction and addition. See margin.

6. Determine the 2-day SMA for the ten consecutive day closing prices for Toyota Motor Corp listed below.
$101.96, $101.80, $101.50, $103.07, $104.94
$105.12, $105.66, $104.76, $100.56, $101.31

7. Determine the 3-day SMA for the ten consecutive day closing prices for Procter & Gamble Co listed below.
$66.21, $65.90, $67.05, $67.03, $66.80
$66.65, $66.65, $65.80, $65.92, $65.21

8. Determine the 4-day SMA for the ten consecutive trading day closing prices for International Business Machines Corp listed below.
$121.69, $122.85, $120.70, $123.61, $123.18
$122.03, $122.82, $124.14, $124.92, $124.06

9. Determine the 6-day SMA for the ten consecutive trading day closing prices for Rite Aid Corp listed below.
$2.65, $2.63, $2.70, $2.63, $2.50, $2.65, $2.66, $2.56, $2.52, $2.37

TEACH

Moving Averages
When calculating moving averages, alert students that a calculator error of even a single digit can cause the entire answer to be incorrect.

ANSWERS

1. Conceivably, a river could have an average depth of 4 ft but be 20 ft deep at some point. The writer warns the reader to be careful about averages since they smooth out the data and may cause the reader to lose sight of specific data.
2. $7.95, $8.03, $7.97, $8.21, $8.60, $9.02, $9.11, $9.17
3. $274.72, $284.38, $288.79, $291.36, $291.26, $291.62
4. $58.00, $58.04, $57.63, $57.22, $56.91, $56.83, $56.88
5. $92.01, $91.51, $91.02, $90.63, $90.13, $89.61, $89.46
6. $101.88, $101.65, $102.29, $104.01, $105.03, $105.39, $105.21, $102.66, $100.94
7. $66.39, $66.66, $66.96, $66.83, $66.70, $66.37, $66.12, $65.64
8. $122.21, $122.59, $122.38, $122.91, $123.04, $123.48, $123.99
9. $2.63, $2.63, $2.62, $2.59, $2.54

TEACH

Exercises 10–12

Before assigning these problems show students how to read this chart. They should be reading down columns rather than across rows.

10. Use a spreadsheet to determine the 7-day SMA for Citigroup Inc.
See additional answers.

7-Apr	24.60	14-Apr	22.51	21-Apr	25.03	28-Apr	26.81	5-May	25.75
8-Apr	23.76	15-Apr	22.80	22-Apr	25.12	29-Apr	26.32	6-May	25.87
9-Apr	23.58	16-Apr	23.44	23-Apr	24.63	30-Apr	25.27	7-May	24.48
10-Apr	23.71	17-Apr	24.03	24-Apr	25.76	1-May	25.99	8-May	24.30
11-Apr	23.36	18-Apr	25.11	25-Apr	26.60	2-May	26.39	9-May	23.63

11. Use a spreadsheet to determine the 10-day SMA for Dell Inc.
See additional answers.

31-Mar	19.92	8-Apr	19.00	16-Apr	18.72	24-Apr	19.14	2-May	19.32
1-Apr	20.33	9-Apr	18.69	17-Apr	19.05	25-Apr	19.11	5-May	19.10
2-Apr	19.95	10-Apr	18.77	18-Apr	19.47	28-Apr	18.87	6-May	19.19
3-Apr	20.12	11-Apr	18.50	21-Apr	19.56	29-Apr	18.97	7-May	18.90
4-Apr	19.53	14-Apr	18.24	22-Apr	19.05	30-Apr	18.63	8-May	18.84
7-Apr	19.23	15-Apr	18.28	23-Apr	19.05	1-May	19.08	9-May	19.03

12. Use a spreadsheet to determine the 2-day, 3-day, and 5-day SMA.
See additional answers.

31-Mar	440.47	8-Apr	467.81	16-Apr	455.03	24-Apr	543.04	2-May	581.29
1-Apr	465.71	9-Apr	464.19	17-Apr	449.54	25-Apr	544.06	5-May	594.90
2-Apr	465.70	10-Apr	469.08	18-Apr	539.41	28-Apr	552.12	6-May	586.36
3-Apr	455.12	11-Apr	457.45	21-Apr	537.79	29-Apr	558.47	7-May	579.00
4-Apr	471.09	14-Apr	451.66	22-Apr	555.00	30-Apr	574.29	8-May	583.01
7-Apr	476.82	15-Apr	446.84	23-Apr	546.49	1-May	593.08	9-May	573.20

13. The stock chart shows the 3-day and 10-day SMA for 20 consecutive trading days of Sony Corp stock. Identify the crossovers and discuss the implications. See additional answers.

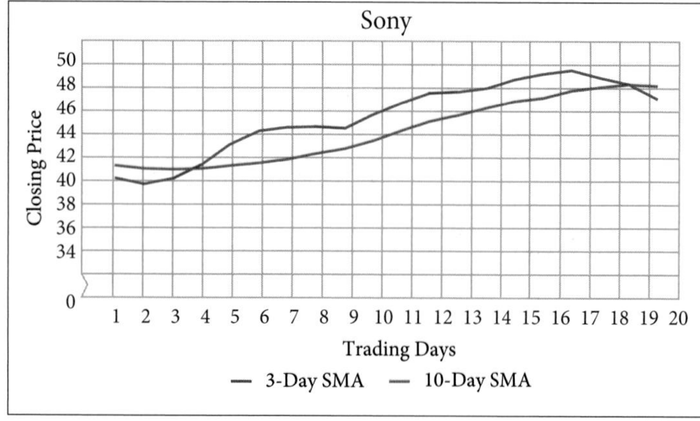

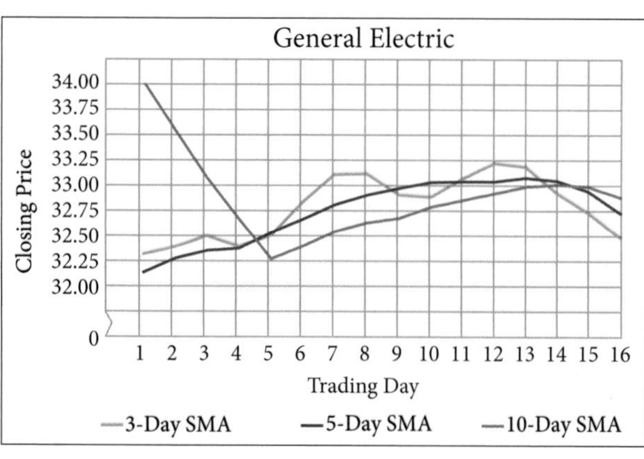

14. The stock chart shows the 3-day, 5-day, and 10-day SMA for 16 consecutive trading days of General Electric Co stock. Examine days 6–16. Identify the crossovers and discuss the implications.
See additional answers.

15. Use a spreadsheet to calculate the 2-day and 5-day SMA for ten consecutive day closing prices of Yahoo! Inc. Graph the closing prices and averages. See additional answers.

21-Apr	28.55	1-May	26.81
22-Apr	28.54	2-May	28.67
23-Apr	28.08	5-May	24.37
24-Apr	27.30	6-May	25.72
25-Apr	26.80	7-May	25.64
28-Apr	26.43	8-May	26.22
29-Apr	27.36	9-May	25.93
30-Apr	27.41		

The average trade of an individual is in the thousands of shares, whereas the institutional trade can be in the millions of shares. Clearly, the bigger the order, the bigger the move in the stock.
Maria Bartiromo, Business news anchor

Stock Market Ticker 1-5

Key Terms
- Dow Jones Industrial Average (DJIA)
- ticker
- stock symbol
- ticker symbol
- trading volume
- trading price
- directional arrow
- total value of a trade
- uptick
- downtick
- money flow
- positive money flow
- negative money flow
- daily money flow
- net money flow

Objectives
- Understand stock market ticker information.
- Determine the total value of a trade from ticker information.
- Determine trade volumes from ticker information.

Common Core
N-Q1, N-Q2

CCSS Warm-Up

Let C be the number of calls per minute, let M be the number of minutes, and let T be the total number of calls.

1. What does CM represent?

2. What does T/C represent?

1. T, the total number of calls

2. M, the number of minutes

How is stock market data transmitted to the investor?

Investors are always interested in how the market is doing. You can refer to a variety of published information systems to track the performance of certain types of stocks. Perhaps the most well-known of these systems is the **Dow Jones Industrial Average (DJIA)**, also known as the Dow. The Dow follows the daily trading action of 30 large public companies. Historically, these were industrial companies, but the corporations included in the Dow have grown to include those in telecommunications, pharmaceuticals, broadcasting, retail, insurance, and more. The Dow is a well-respected average that offers a broad picture of how the market is performing from day to day.

Investors wanting specific information often turn to another source. One of the first stock information transmission machines was invented by Thomas Edison in 1869. It was known as the Universal Stock Ticker and had a printing speed of about one character per second. The machine was known as a **ticker** because of the ticking sound that it made as printed tape came out of it. This *ticker tape machine* replaced the need for handwritten and hand-delivered messages about stock trades. Stock tickers in different buildings were connected by telegraph machines. The printed tape would contain a ticker symbol that was unique to a given company. Once the company was identified by the symbol, the ticker would print information about the number of shares traded, the price of that trade, and any change in the direction of the price of a share of the stock. While actual stock ticker machines are now a thing of the past, the idea of transmitting this important information is not. Ticker machines have been replaced by electronic scrolling information that appears on electronic billboards, computers, and TV screens. Many financial TV programs have stock information scrolling across the bottom of the screen during the trading day.

EXAMINE THE QUESTION

For traders that want basic stock market data and in a timely manner, the stock market ticker is available. If you have seen financial buildings in New York City on television, you may have noticed a ticker scrolling on the face of the building.

Today with the wise spread use of the Internet on laptop computers, cell phones, and PDAs, stock market tickers can easily be located.

For the ticker to have meaning, you need to learn how to interpret the information and how to use that data to calculate trading prices, changes, and volume.

CLASS DISCUSSION

Why might an investor be interested in a ticker?

TEACH

The ticker offers stock market transaction information in an easy read-and-interpret format Students need to know how to convert large numbers expressed using alphabetical symbols into numerals. These numbers represent the size of the individual transaction. They also need to master how to use the net change in determining a previous day's closing price. The ticker requires only basic mathematical skills but yields a great deal of important information.

EXAMPLE 1

The ticker symbol has three important parts: the number of shares traded (usually expressed in condensed form using K, M, or B), the price of each share for that trade (the price is preceded by the symbol @ which translates as "each at"), and finally the change from the previous close (the up arrow indicates that the price per share of the trade is higher than the close, and the down arrow indicates that the price per share is less than the close).

CHECK YOUR UNDERSTANDING

Answer The ticker indicates that 12,000 shares of GE were traded at $73.72 per share which is down $0.55 from the previous closing price.

EXTEND YOUR UNDERSTANDING

Answer upward arrow followed by 13.08

The change indicates that the previous close was 55 cents higher than the price per share, or $74.27. Had the ticker indicated a price per share of $87.35, subtract 87.35 – 74.27 = 13.08. This means the price per share of this trade was $13.08 higher than the previous close.

Stock tickers let you know that a stock transaction (trade) has occurred. The ticker offers the following information in coded format.

- **Stock Symbol** or **Ticker Symbol** The letter or letters used to identify a corporation whose shares are traded on a stock market are *stock symbols* or *ticker symbols*. Stocks that trade on the New York Stock Exchange have 1-, 2-, or 3-letter symbols. Stocks that trade on the NASDAQ had only 4-letter symbols until recently when stocks that transferred to the NASDAQ from the NYSE were allowed to keep their symbols even if fewer than 4 letters.
- **Trading Volume** The *trading volume* is the number of shares traded in a single transaction. Trading volumes are listed on the ticker using a shorthand information system. For example, 10K indicates that 10,000 shares traded, 10M indicates that 10,000,000 shares traded, and 10B means that 10,000,000,000 shares traded (rarely seen).
- **Trading Price** The trading price per share may be displayed on the ticker preceded by the @ symbol, meaning that each share was traded at the specified price. The @ symbol is not always used.
- **Directional Arrows** Arrows indicate whether the traded price of a single share is greater than the previous day's closing price (▲) or less than the previous day's closing price (▼).

Skills and Strategies

The following examples show how to interpret stock ticker information.

EXAMPLE 1

Marcy is following the stock market ticker scrolling across the bottom of her TV screen on cable business station. She had purchased some shares of Visa, Inc. last week and is interested in seeing if there are any current trades. She knows that Visa, Inc. has the ticker symbol V. She saw the following information: V 12K@87.37 ▲ 0.12. What can Marcy learn from this line of symbols?

SOLUTION The letter V indicates that a trade has been made for a certain amount of Visa shares. The next piece of information, 12K, indicates that the volume of the most recent trade was 12 thousand shares. Each of those shares was traded at $87.37. This price was up $0.12 from the previous day's closing price of one share of Visa, Inc.

CHECK YOUR UNDERSTANDING

Kevin knows that General Electric has the ticker symbol GE. What can Kevin learn from the following line of symbols: GE 12K@73.72 ▼ 0.55?

EXTEND YOUR UNDERSTANDING

Had the trading price of this transaction been at $87.35, what number would have appeared after the directional arrow? Explain your answer.

EXAMPLE 2

Tom needed money for graduate school tuition. He called his broker and asked her to sell all 3,000 of his Coca-Cola (KO) shares on Wednesday as soon as the trading price hit $57 per share. Tom knew that Coca-Cola closed at $57.25 on Tuesday. How will his trade appear on the ticker?

SOLUTION Tom is selling 3,000 shares, so the volume is 3K. The sale price of $57 is down from the previous day's close by $0.25. This trade appears as KO 3K@57 ▼ 0.25.

CHECK YOUR UNDERSTANDING

What would be the previous day's close for a share of Coca-Cola if the ticker had read KO 3K@57 ▲ 0.25?

Total Value of a Trade

The **total value of a trade** is determined by multiplying the number of shares traded by the trading price. This value does not include any fees.

EXAMPLE 3

Toni purchased 15,000 shares of stock of Target Corporation at $54.88 per share. Her trade appeared on the stock ticker as TGT 15K@54.88 ▼ 0.17. What was the total value of her trade?

SOLUTION Each of the shares cost Toni $54.88. Multiply the number of shares by the price to find the total value of her trade.

Number of shares × price $\quad 15{,}000 \times 54.88 = 823{,}200$

The total value of her trade was $823,200.

CHECK YOUR UNDERSTANDING

Suppose Toni made her purchase at the previous day's closing price. What would have been the difference between the values of the trades?

Trade Volume

Trade volume can appear in decimal formats on the stock ticker. For example, 2.5K is 2.5 thousand, or 2.5 × 1,000, or 2,500. The volume of 3,890,000 shares can be expressed in ticker notation by using the symbol M to represent millions. To determine the number of millions in 3,890,000, divide by 1,000,000. Moving the decimal left 6 places, 3,890,000 is 3.89 million and is symbolized as 3.89M.

EXAMPLE 4

Grandpa Rich left his three grandchildren: Nicole, Jeff, and Kristen, 8,750 shares of Apple Inc (AAPL) in his will. The grandchildren sold all of the shares at a price of $190.30 on Friday. The closing price of Apple on Thursday was $187.83. How did this trade appear on the stock ticker?

SOLUTION Divide the total number of shares by 1,000. Moving the decimal point 3 places to the left, 8,750 equals 8.75 thousand. The

EXAMPLE 2

Assist students in converting the number of shares into compressed form. Once done, follow the structure of the ticker knowing that $57 is lower than the previous close by $0.25.

CHECK YOUR UNDERSTANDING

Answer $56.75

Had the ticker included a downward arrow before the 0.25, it would have indicated to add 25 cents to the trading price of $57.

EXAMPLE 3

The total value of the trade is the product of the number of shares traded by the price per share. Students can convert the compressed form of the number of shares and then multiply by the price per share. They can also multiply the number in front of the symbol, in this case 15, by the price per share, 54.88 to obtain 823.2. Then, multiply that product by the value that the symbol represents, 823.2 x 1,000 = $823,200.

CHECK YOUR UNDERSTANDING

Answer First, determine the previous day's close, $54.88 + 0.17 = $55.05. Had Toni purchased her 15,000 shares at $55.05, the total value of her trade would be $825,750. The difference between this trade and the one in Example 3 is $2,550.

EXAMPLE 4

There are multiple steps to be completed and students should understand the purpose of each. Write 8,750 in compressed form by dividing by 1,000, which equals 8.75K. Compare the selling price with the previous day's close. The grandchildren sold at a price that was $2.47 more than the previous close.

volume of 8,750 shares is 8.75K on the ticker. Because the shares were sold on Friday at a price that was $2.47 higher than the previous day's close, an upward directional arrow indicates the increase. The trade appeared on the ticker as follows: AAPL 8.75K@190.30 ▲ 2.47.

CHECK YOUR UNDERSTANDING

Express 0.15M shares traded using the K symbol.

CHECK YOUR UNDERSTANDING

Answer 150K

Students are asked to convert from one compressed form to another. It is easiest to convert the first compressed form and then write that in the second compressed form.

Customized Tickers

Some stock traders follow customized tickers that offer trade-to-trade information. The term *tick* is used whenever there is a change in the price of a share from one trade to the next. A trade is an **uptick** if the price is higher than the previous trade. A trade is a **downtick** if the price is lower. These tick changes contribute to a type of market analysis known as **money flow**. When a stock is purchased at an uptick, it is **positive money flow**. When it is purchased at a downtick, it is **negative money flow**.

Daily money flow is a calculated indicator that is the average of a day's high, low, and close, multiplied by the volume for the day. This calculation can be compared with that for the previous trading day and indicates whether there was a positive or negative money flow. If more shares were bought on the uptick than the downtick, **net money flow** is positive because more investors were willing to pay a price above the market price.

CLASS DISCUSSION

Does daily money flow represent an actual monetary occurrence in the market?

EXAMPLE 5

The average of the high, low, and closing price on a particular day is used for comparison purposes when examining money flow. It does not represent the average of the day's trading prices. Multiplying that average by the volume for the day results in a monetary amount, which again can be used for comparison purposes. It indicates the total value of all of the trades during the day when calculating with the comparison average. In Example 5, the money flow for Monday is greater than that for Tuesday. This indicates a negative money flow from Monday to Tuesday.

EXAMPLE 5

Laura is interested in trades of Microsoft (MSFT). She has been following the upticks and downticks for the past two days. She knows that MSFT closed on Tuesday at $20.68, with a high at $21.25 and a low at $20.50. There were 11,902,000 shares traded on that day. She found that Monday's closing price was $21.23. The high was $21.30 and the low was $19.95. The volume for Monday was 16,537,000 shares. Was the net money flow from Monday to Tuesday positive or negative?

SOLUTION Calculate the average of each day's high, low, and close, and then multiply that by the daily volume.

Find Monday's average. $\frac{21.30 + 19.95 + 21.23}{3} \approx 20.83$

Multiply price by volume. $20.83 \times 16{,}537{,}000 = \$344{,}465{,}710$

Find Tuesday's average. $\frac{21.25 + 20.50 + 20.68}{3} = 20.81$

Multiply price by volume. $20.81 \times 11{,}902{,}000 = \$247{,}680{,}620$

There is a negative net money flow from Monday to Tuesday.

CHECK YOUR UNDERSTANDING

Let H represent a day's High, L represent a day's Low, C represent a day's close, and V represent the day's volume. Write a formula that can be used to determine the day's money flow.

CHECK YOUR UNDERSTANDING

Answer $\left(\frac{H + L + C}{3}\right)V$

Applications

The average trade of an individual is in the thousands of shares, whereas the institutional trade can be in the millions of shares. Clearly, the bigger the order, the bigger the move in the stock.
Maria Bartiromo, Business news anchor

1. How might a large trade "move the market"? How might those words apply to what you have learned? See margin.

Use the following ticker information to answer Exercises 2–9. The stock symbols represent the following corporations: HD, Home Depot Inc; S, Sprint Nextel Corporation; VZ, Verizon Communications Inc; and XOM, Exxon Mobil Corp.

HD 32.3M@29.13▲1.13 S 1.1K@9.14▼0.78 VZ 3.32K@38.77▲2.27 XOM 0.66K@92.67▼1.58

2. Jessica put in an order for some shares of Exxon Mobil Corp.
   a. As shown on the ticker, how many shares did Jessica buy? 660
   b. How much did each share cost? $92.67
   c. What was the value of Jessica's trade? $61,162.20
3. Phil sold his shares of Verizon Communications Inc, as indicated on the above ticker.
   a. How many shares did he sell? 3,320
   b. How much did each share sell for? $38.77
   c. What was the total value of all the shares Phil sold? $128,716.40
4. How many shares of Home Depot are indicated on the ticker? 32,300,000
5. What is the total value of all of the Sprint Nextel Corporation shares traded? $10,054
6. How can @29.13 be interpreted? Each share of HD was traded at $29.13.
7. How can XOM .66K be interpreted? 660 shares of Exxon Mobil were traded.
8. How can ▼1.58 be interpreted? The traded price of XOM reflected a $1.58 drop from the previous day's closing price.
9. What was the previous day's closing price for each stock? Home Depot $28; Sprint Nextel $9.92; Verizon $36.50; and Exxon Mobil $94.25

Use the following ticker to answer Exercises 10–17. The stock symbols represent the following corporations: PG, Procter & Gamble Co; BAC, Bank of America Corp; DIS, Walt Disney Co; and K, Kellogg Co.

PG 4.5K@66.75▼0.39 BAC 0.65M@36.17▲0.54 DIS 2.55K @34.90▼1.08 K 0.76K@51.49▲0.04

10. Michele is following the trades of Procter & Gamble Co on the business channel. The result of the latest trade is posted on the ticker above.
    a. How many shares of PG were traded? 4,500
    b. How much did each share cost? $66.75
    c. What was the value of the Procter & Gamble Co trade? $300,375
    d. Suppose that the next PG trade represents a sale of 23,600 shares at a price that is $0.18 higher than the last transaction. What will Michele see scrolling across her screen for this transaction? PG 23.6K@66.93 ▼ 0.21

TEACH

Stock Market Ticker

The numbers presented in the stock market ticker are compressed as they would appear on an actual ticker. Some students may have difficulty separating the information given on one transaction from the next. Suggest they rewrite the information on the single transaction in question so that they can focus on only the data pertaining to that transaction.

ANSWERS

1. Large market trades, whether they are purchases or sales, can have an effect on market upticks and downticks since they carry a great deal of weight in determining future market action for a stock.

TEACH

Exercises 19 and 20

Make sure that you assign Exercise 19 with Exercise 20 because Exercise 19 offers a numerical example. Then, students will be able to apply the work from Exercise 19 to the algebra they will use in Exercise 20.

Exercises 21 and 22

Alert students to the importance of the correct use and placement of parentheses in the money flow formula. Show them how an incorrect placement yields a completely different and incorrect answer.

ANSWERS

21. 5/15 money flow = \$2,190,938,750; 5/16 money flow = \$1,474,805,466; There was a negative money flow from 5/15 to 5/16.
22. 6/6 money flow = \$2,518,114,595; 6/7 money flow = \$2,889,952,100; There was a positive money flow from 6/6 to 6/7.

11. Sarah sold her Disney shares as indicated on the ticker.

- **a.** How many shares did she sell? 2,550
- **b.** How much did each share sell for? \$34.90
- **c.** What was the total value of all the shares Sarah sold? \$88,995
- **d.** Suppose that the next DIS trade that comes across the ticker represents a sale of 7,600 shares at a price that is \$0.98 higher than the last transaction. What will Sarah see scrolling across her screen for this transaction of DIS? DIS 7.6K@35.88 ▼ 0.10

12. How many shares of Kellogg Co. are indicated on the ticker? 760

13. What is the total value of all of the Bank of America shares traded? \$23,510,500

14. How can @36.17 be interpreted? Each share of BAC traded at \$36.17.

15. How can K 0.76K be interpreted? 760 shares of Kellogg Co. were traded.

16. How can ▲0.04 be interpreted? The trading price of Kellogg Co. was \$0.04 higher than the previous day's closing price.

17. What was the previous day's closing price for each stock?

- **a.** Procter & Gamble Co \$67.14
- **b.** Bank of America Corp \$35.63
- **c.** Walt Disney Co \$35.98
- **d.** Kellogg Co \$51.45

18. Write the ticker symbols for each situation.

- **a.** 36,000 shares of ABC at a price of 37.15 which is \$0.72 higher than the previous day's close ABC 36K@37.15 ▲ 0.72
- **b.** 1,240 shares of XYZ at a price of \$9.17, which is \$1.01 lower than the previous day's close XYZ 1.24K@9.17 ▼1.01

19. Maria is a stock broker and has been following transactions for Ford Motor Co (F). On Tuesday, the last trade of the day for Ford was posted on the ticker as \$8.11. On Wednesday, the last trade of the day was \$0.56 higher than Tuesday's close for a purchase of 5,600 shares of Ford. Write the stock ticker symbols that would appear on the scroll for the last trade of the day on Wednesday for Ford. F 5.6K@8.67▲0.56

20. Dorothy purchased x thousand shares of Macy's Inc (M) at y dollars per share. This purchase price reflected a decrease of z dollars from the previous day's close. Express the ticket symbols algebraically. M xK@y ▼z

21. Danielle is examining the change in the money flow for Yahoo! Inc shares on two consecutive dates. The information is given in the table. Do the May 16 numbers reflect a positive or negative money flow? Explain. See margin.

Date	High	Low	Close	Volume
16-May	27.95	27.40	27.66	53,299,800
15-May	27.90	26.85	27.75	79,670,500

22. Isaac follows the market action of Google Inc. He has watched the prices for two consecutive days. The information he collected is given in the table. Do the June 7 numbers reflect a positive or negative money flow? Explain. See margin.

Date	High	Low	Close	Volume
7-June	584.68	578.32	580	4,974,100
6-June	582.95	575.60	581	4,342,700

When somebody buys a stock it's because they think it's going to go up and the person who sold it to them thinks it's going to go down. Somebody's wrong.

George Ross, Television actor

Stock Transactions 1-6

Key Terms
- portfolio
- round lot
- odd lot
- trade
- gross capital gain
- gross capital loss

Objectives
- Learn the basic vocabulary of buying and selling shares of stock.
- Compute gains and losses from stock trades.

Common Core
N-Q1, A-CED1, A-CED4, A-REI3

CCSS Warm-Up

Solve each literal equation for the indicated variable.
Isolate the indicated variable on one side of equation.

1. Solve for x: $2y = (3x - 5)/4$

2. Solve for z: $2y = (3x - 5)/z$

1. $x = (8y + 5)/3$

2. $z = (3x - 5)/(2y)$

What is a stock portfolio?

A **portfolio** is a grouping of all the stocks a person currently owns. A portfolio changes whenever stocks are bought or sold. Stocks are best for long-term goals as over time good stocks tend to grow and become more valuable. There are many reasons that stockholders buy or sell shares.

Stocks can go up or down in value. Because some stocks do not perform as planned, it is best to have a diversified portfolio of stocks of different-sized companies in different industries.

When stock is bought and sold, a **trade** is made with another stockholder. If an investor is buying 600 shares of Xerox Corp, the investor is buying the shares from another shareholder who wants to sell them, not from Xerox Corp. Only the first purchaser of the stock actually bought it from Xerox Corp.

Most shareholders buy and sell stocks in multiples of 100 shares, which are called **round lots**. A purchase of less than 100 shares is called an **odd lot**. When you buy stock, even if its value increases, you will not make a profit until you actually *sell* the stock. If the shares are sold at a higher price than they were purchased for, you make a profit.

The difference between the selling price and the purchase price is a **gross capital gain**. If you sell a stock for less money than you paid for it, you have a **gross capital loss**. You must report capital gains and losses to the Internal Revenue Service because each affects the amount of income taxes owed.

EXAMINE THE QUESTION

Students will likely know the word "portfolio", but will associate it with an artist or a student's portfolio for college. Students should make connections between what they know about portfolios and stock portfolios.

TEACH

In this section, students will examine the difference between selling price and purchase price. Remind students that if the price of a stock they own goes up, they have not made any money until they sell it.

EXAMPLE 1

Remind students that the purchase price is the minuend, and the selling price is the subtrahend. Write the following displays on the board.

Minuend – Subtrahend = Difference
Purchase price – Selling price = Capital gain

The sign of the difference indicates whether there was a gain or a loss.

CHECK YOUR UNDERSTANDING

Answer –$1,567; loss

EXAMPLE 2

Show students that they will get the same result by computing the gain on one share, and then multiplying that result by 300.

$41 – $34.87 = $6.13
$6.13(300) = $1,839

CHECK YOUR UNDERSTANDING

Answer $2,206.25

EXTEND YOUR UNDERSTANDING

Answer $450y - 450x$

Skills and Strategies

Investors should keep careful track of the stock market and the stocks in their portfolio, so they know when to buy new stocks, add to what they already own, sell, or just hold on to what they own. Here you will learn how investors determine their capital gains and losses.

EXAMPLE 1

Several years ago, Marlene purchased stock for $7,241. Last week she sold the stock for $9,219. What was her gross capital gain?

SOLUTION Subtract the purchase price from the selling price to find her capital gain.

Selling price – Purchase price $\qquad$ 9,219 – 7,241 = 1,978

Marlene has a gross capital gain of $1,978. She must report this as income on her income tax return for the year in which she sold the stock.

■ CHECK YOUR UNDERSTANDING

Brett used money he received as a gift for high school graduation to purchase $4,000 worth of shares of stock. After he graduated from college, he needed money to buy a car, so he sold the stock for $2,433. What was his capital gain or loss?

EXAMPLE 2

Five years ago, Jessica bought 300 shares of a cosmetics company's stock for $34.87 per share. Yesterday she sold all of the shares for $41 per share. What was her capital gain?

SOLUTION Multiply to find the purchase price of all 300 shares. Multiply to find the selling price of all 300 shares. Subtract to find the capital gain.

Multiply purchase price by 300.	$34.87 \times 300 = 10{,}461$
Multiply selling price by 300.	$41 \times 300 = 12{,}300$
Subtract.	$12{,}300 - 10{,}461 = 1{,}839$

Jessica's gross capital gain was $1,839.

■ CHECK YOUR UNDERSTANDING

Kelvin bought 125 shares of stock for $68.24 per share. He sold them nine months later for $85.89 per share. What was his capital gain?

■ EXTEND YOUR UNDERSTANDING

Three years ago, Maxine bought 450 shares of stock for x dollars per share. She sold them last week for y dollars per share. Express her capital gain algebraically in terms of x and y.

EXAMPLE 3

Randy paid \$3,450 for shares of a corporation that manufactured cell phones. He sold it for \$6,100. Express his capital gain as a percent of the original purchase price. Round to the nearest tenth of a percent.

SOLUTION Find the amount of capital gain from the sale.

Capital gain = Selling price – Purchase price

Substitute values. Capital gain = 6,100 – 3,450 = 2,650

Think of \$2,650 as part of a whole. The whole is \$3,450. You need to express "what percent of 3,450 is 2,650" as an equation. Let x represent the percent increase, expressed as a decimal.

Write the equation. $(x)(3{,}450) = 2{,}650$

Divide each side of equation by 3,450. $x = \dfrac{2{,}650}{3{,}450}$

Calculate. $x \approx 0.7681$

Randy earned a 76.8% capital gain on his investment.

CHECK YOUR UNDERSTANDING

Allison bought shares in Citigroup Corporation in early 2007 for \$55 per share. She sold them later that year for \$35 per share. Express her loss as a percent of the purchase price. Round to the nearest percent.

EXAMPLE 4

Andy paid w dollars for shares of a corporation that manufactured cell phones. He sold it for y dollars. Express his capital gain as a percent of the original purchase price. Round to the nearest tenth of a percent.

SOLUTION Find the capital gain using variables.

Capital gain = Selling price – Purchase price

Substitute values. Capital gain = $y - w$

Think of $y - w$ as part of a whole. The whole is w. Express "what percent of w is $y - w$" as an equation. Let x represent the percent increase, expressed as a decimal.

Write the equation. Solve for x. $(x)(w) = y - w$

Divide each side of equation by w. $x = \dfrac{y - w}{w}$

Andy earned a capital gain of $100\dfrac{(y - w)}{w}$ percent on his investment.

CHECK YOUR UNDERSTANDING

Linda bought \$800 of stock in a garden equipment corporation. The selling price is x dollars. Express the percent increase of Linda's potential capital gain algebraically.

EXAMPLE 3

Discuss how the length of time of the investment is a factor in deciding if it was a good investment. In this case, if this gain was made over 5 years, it would have been a good investment. If this gain was made over 30 years, it would not have been as good an investment.

CHECK YOUR UNDERSTANDING

Answer 36%

Point out that these were actual prices in 2007, so this loss could have actually happened.

EXAMPLE 4

By not using numbers in this problem, students might forget that they need to convert to a percent. They must remember to multiply by 100.

CHECK YOUR UNDERSTANDING

Answer $\dfrac{x - 800}{800}(100)$

Advise students to write the fraction in stacked form. If they write it without using a stacked fraction, such as [(x – 800)/800]100, they need to enter parentheses correctly.

Applications

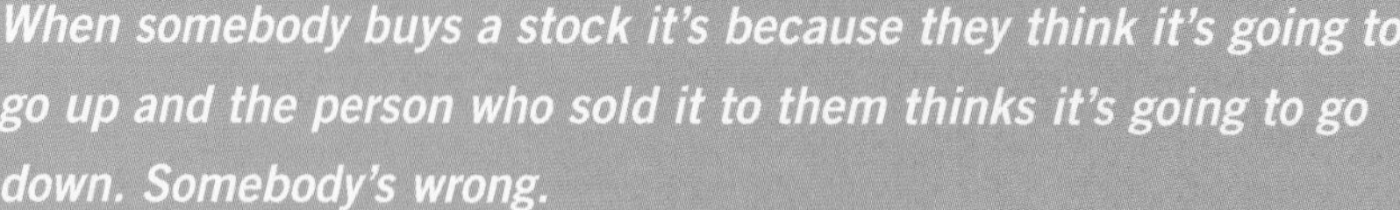

When somebody buys a stock it's because they think it's going to go up and the person who sold it to them thinks it's going to go down. Somebody's wrong.

George Ross, Television actor

TEACH

Percent Increase and Decrease

Throughout the applications, students will be computing gains and losses as raw differences and as percents. Make sure that when students calculate percent increase or decrease, that they are always basing it on the purchase price. The purchase price will be the denominator in these cases.

Exercise 3

After students complete 3e, discuss the example intuitively—if each item increases 12%, the total costs increases 12%. Pose this question: If you bought 3 items and each increased in value by 20%, did the total value of the three items increase by 60%?

Exercise 4

Point out the equivalent form of the answer, which is $(y - x)m$, and ask students to interpret this version. It finds the gain per share, and then multiplies it by m.

ANSWERS

1. People who do research on stocks could come to different conclusions as to what is going to happen to the price of a share. Sometimes people sell stock purely because they want the money for some other purpose; they do not necessarily have to feel that the price is going to go down.

1. Is it always true that someone sells a stock because they think it is going to go down in price? How do those words apply to what you've learned in this lesson? See margin.

2. Zach bought 200 shares of Goshen stock years ago for $21.35 per share. He sold all 200 shares today for $43 per share. What was his gross capital gain? $4,330

3. Mitchell bought 600 shares of Centerco two years ago for $34.50 per share. He sold them yesterday for $38.64 per share.
- **a.** What was the percent increase in the price per share? 12%
- **b.** What was the total purchase price for the 600 shares? $20,700
- **c.** What was the total selling price for the 600 shares? $23,184
- **d.** What was the percent capital gain for the 600 shares? 12%
- **e.** How does the percent increase in the price of one share compare to the percent capital gain for all 600 shares? It is the same.

4. Tori bought x shares of Mattel stock for m dollars per share. She sold all of the shares months later for y dollars per share. Express her capital gain or loss algebraically. $|xy - xm|$

5. Ramon bought x shares of Xerox stock for a total of $40,000. Express the price he paid per share algebraically. $\frac{40{,}000}{x}$

6. In 2004, Joe bought 200 shares in the Nikon corporation for $12.25 per share. In 2007 he sold the shares for $31.27 each.
- **a.** What was Joe's capital gain? $3,804
- **b.** Express Joe's capital gain as a percent, rounded to the nearest percent. 155%

7. General Motors stock fell from $32 per share in 2006 to $20 per share during 2008.
- **a.** If you bought and then sold 300 shares at these prices, what was your loss? $3,600
- **b.** Express your loss as a percent of the purchase price. Round to the nearest tenth of a percent. 37.5%

8. Elliott purchased shares of Microsoft in 2008 for $28 per share. He plans to sell them as soon as the price rises 20%. At what price will he sell his shares? $33.60

9. Maria purchased 1,000 shares of stock for $35.50 per share in 2003. She sold them in 2007 for $55.10 per share. Express her capital gain as a percent, rounded to the nearest tenth of a percent. 55.2%

10. Austin purchased shares of stock for x dollars in 2004. He sold them in 2010 for y dollars per share.

a. Express his capital gain algebraically. $y - x$

b. Express his capital gain as a percent of the purchase price. $\frac{y-x}{x}$

11. During 2003, a share of stock in the Coca-Cola Company sold for \$39. During 2008, the price hit \$56 per share. Express the increase in price as a percent of the price in 2003. Round to the nearest tenth of a percent. 43.6%

12. Alexa purchased 700 shares of Campagna Corporation stock for x dollars per share in 2005. She sold them in 2010 for y dollars per share, where $y < x$.

a. Did Alexa have a gross capital gain or a gross capital loss? Explain. She had a gross capital loss because $y < x$.

b. Alexa used the formula $\frac{700y - 700x}{700x}$ to compute the percent of the loss. Her husband Tom used the formula $\frac{y-x}{x}$ to compute the percent of the loss. She told him he was incorrect because he didn't take into account that she bought 700 shares. He says that his formula is correct, and so is hers. Who is correct, Alexa or Tom? Explain. Tom is correct because both formulas can be used to find percent increase.

13. Zeke bought g shares of stock for w dollars per share. His broker called him and told him to sell the shares when they earn a 40% capital gain.

a. Express the total purchase price of all the shares algebraically. gw

b. Express the capital gain algebraically. $0.4gw$

c. Zeke decides to sell his shares. Express the total selling price of all the shares algebraically. $gw + 0.4gw$, which is equal to $1.4gw$.

14. Jake bought d shares of stock for x dollars per share years ago. His stock rose in price and eventually hit a price that would earn him a 140% capital gain. He decided to sell half of his d shares.

a. Represent half of the d shares algebraically. $0.5d$

b. Represent the capital gain earned on each of the shares that were sold algebraically. $1.4x$

c. Represent the capital gain earned on all of the shares that were sold algebraically. $1.4dx$

d. Represent the total value of the shares that were sold algebraically. $0.5dx + 1.4(0.5)dx$, which is equal to $1.2dx$.

e. Jake keeps the remaining half of the shares for several more years. The company goes bankrupt and those shares become worthless. Jake had a large gain on the shares he sold earlier—and took a loss on the shares that became worthless. Did investing in the d shares result in a capital gain or loss for Jake? Explain using the algebraic expressions you created in parts a–d. See margin.

15. Ahmad sold 125 shares of stock for x dollars that he had purchased for \$32.75 per share.

a. How much did he originally pay for the shares of stock? \$4,093.75

b. Write an inequality that represents an amount such that Ahmad made money from the sale of the stocks. $x > 4{,}093.75$

c. Suppose Ahmad lost money on the stocks. Write an inequality that represents an amount such that Ahmad lost no more than \$1,000 from the sale of the stocks. $3{,}093.75 \le x < 4{,}093.75$

TEACH

Exercise 10

You could compare this actual gain in Coca-Cola stock to investing \$39 in a savings account for 5 years.

Exercise 14

In certain multistep problems, answers to certain parts depend on answers to previous parts. If a student has an incorrect answer, see if it is correct based on the previous answer so you can isolate the part that the student did incorrectly.

ANSWERS

14e. There was a gain, because the selling price of the first half of the shares was $1.2dx$, and the original purchase price of all d shares was dx. $1.2dx - dx = 0.2dx$, which represents a capital gain.

The bad news is time flies. The good news is you're the pilot.
Michael Althsuler, Businessman

1-7 Stock Transaction Fees

Objectives
- Compute the fees involved in buying and selling stocks.
- Become familiar with the basic vocabulary of stock trading.

Common Core
A-CED2

Key Terms
- stockbroker
- broker fee
- commission
- discount broker
- at the market
- limit order
- net proceeds

CCSS Warm-Up

Twice a number x increased by 10 equals 52, and 115 less three times the number also equals 52.

1. Write two equations in terms of x for this situation.
2. Use your equations to determine the number.

1. $2x + 10 = 52$ and $115 - 3x = 52$ 2. $x = 21$

EXAMINE THE QUESTION
Since the first shares of stock were traded on Wall Street in the 1700s, stock trades took place by stockbrokers meeting face to face. The Internet has drastically changed this.

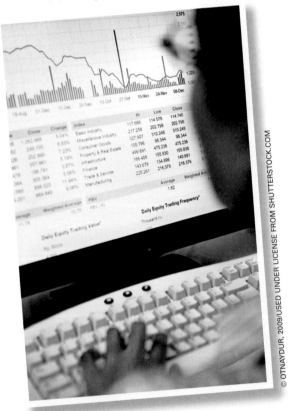

How do you buy and sell stock?

You don't buy stock at a store. Shares of stock can only be purchased through a licensed **stockbroker**. If you decided to sell your shares, you couldn't bring them to school and sell them to someone in the cafeteria. You also cannot walk into a stock exchange to sell your shares. Only stockbrokers buy and sell stocks. They also give advice to investors. For their services, stockbrokers charge a broker fee. The **broker fee** can be a flat fee, which does not depend on the value of the transaction, or a commission, which does depend on the value of the transaction. A **commission** is a percentage of the value of the stock trade.

Some people make their own investment decisions. They read the financial newspapers and websites to learn about new developments in the stock market. They still must buy and sell through brokers, but they may decide to use a discount broker. **Discount brokers** charge low fees. They do not give investment advice. They only make stock transactions. Discount brokers are available online, by phone, and in person. An online trading account is convenient because the investor can access it 24 hours a day.

If you buy or sell **at the market**, you are instructing your broker to get the best available price. You can also place a **limit order**, which specifies the price you want to pay. If you put in a limit order to buy a stock only for a specific price, your broker will not make a purchase for any price higher than the price specified.

The fees you pay brokers when buying or selling stock affect the amount you gain or lose on the trade. Your **net proceeds** represent the amount of money you make after broker fees are subtracted. Make sure you are aware of the broker fees whenever you make a stock trade.

Skills and Strategies

To compute the actual gain or loss for a given stock trade, you need to include the broker fees in your calculations.

EXAMPLE 1

Lee made two trades through his online discount broker, We-Trade. We-Trade charges a fee of $12 per trade. Lee's first purchase was for $3,456 and his second purchase, later in the day, was for $2,000. How much did he spend on the day's purchases, including broker fees?

SOLUTION Lee made two trades. He paid two broker fees.

Fee × Number of trades $(2)(\$12) = 24$

Lee paid $24 in broker fees. Next, find the sum of his purchases.

Add amount of both trades. $3{,}456 + 2{,}000 = 5{,}456$

The purchase price of the stock was $5,456. Find the total spent.

Fee + Total purchase price $5{,}456 + 24 = 5{,}480$

Lee spent $5,480 on the trades using his online discount broker.

CHECK YOUR UNDERSTANDING

Garret made two trades in one day with his discount broker that charges $7 per trade. Garret's first purchase was for $1,790 and his second purchase was for $8,456. How much did he spend including broker fees?

EXAMPLE 2

Adriana purchased $7,000 worth of stock from a broker at Tenser Brokerage. The current value of Adriana's portfolio is $11,567. What broker fee must she pay?

Tenser Brokerage Fee Schedule	Online Trades	Automated Telephone Trades	Trades Using a Broker
Portfolio value less than $250,000	$15 per trade	Online fee plus $9.50	0.5% commission plus online fee
Portfolio value greater than $250,000	$12 per trade	Online fee plus $9.50	0.4% commission plus online fee

SOLUTION Adriana's fees are in the first row because her portfolio is under $250,000. She is using a broker, so use the fees in the last column. First, multiply the percent expressed as an equivalent decimal by the amount of stock and add $15.

$$(0.005)(7{,}000) + 15 = 50$$

The total broker fee is $50.

CHECK YOUR UNDERSTANDING

Jared has a portfolio worth $500,000. He made 10 telephone trades during the past year, buying and selling $50,000 worth of stock. What was his total broker fee for the year? Express his total broker fee algebraically if Jared had made b automated telephone trades.

EXAMPLE 1

An alternative method to calculate the total for the day's purchase is to add the broker fee to each purchase price before adding to find the total.

$3,456 + $12 = $3,468
$2,000 + $12 = $2,012
$3,468 + $2,012 = $5,480

CHECK YOUR UNDERSTANDING

Answer $10,260

The total broker fee is $14 because there were two trades.

EXAMPLE 2

Students often experience difficulty when changing percents that are not whole numbers into decimals. Review this and give examples on the board.

Point out the percent given is a decimal percent. In this case, the percent has been changed to a decimal with three zeros between the decimal point and the non-zero digit. These zeros impact the placement of the decimal point in the product.

CHECK YOUR UNDERSTANDING

Answer $215 and $21.50*b*

EXAMPLE 3

Remind students that you do not have to sell the stock through the same broker with whom you bought it.

CLASS DISSCUSSION

Why might an investor sell a stock using a different broker than the broker from whom it was purchased?

CHECK YOUR UNDERSTANDING

Answer –$811.63

The net proceeds are negative.

EXAMPLE 4

Students may have their answers in different forms. Have students offer different, but equivalent answers. The commutative property shows the following are all acceptable answers.

$y - 35 - 1.02x$
$y - 1.02x - 35$
$-1.02x + y - 35$
$-1.02x - 35 + y$
$-35 - 1.02x + y$
$-35 + y - 1.02x$

CHECK YOUR UNDERSTANDING

Answer $(h - 0.01h) - (p + 40)$
This is equivalent to $0.99h - p - 40$.

EXAMPLE 3

Erin purchased $23,510 worth of stock and paid her broker a 1% broker fee. She sold when the stock price increased to $27,300, and used a discount broker who charged $21 per trade. Compute her net proceeds.

SOLUTION Find the purchase cost.

$$\begin{aligned}\text{Purchase cost} &= \text{Cost of stock} + \text{Broker fee}\\ &= 23{,}510 + (0.01)(23{,}510) = 23{,}745.10\end{aligned}$$

When Erin sold the stock, the broker's fee was deducted from the sale price. Find Erin's sale proceeds.

$$\begin{aligned}\text{Sale proceeds} &= \text{Sale price of stock} - \text{Broker fee}\\ &= 27{,}300 - 21 = 27{,}279\end{aligned}$$

The net proceeds is the difference between the purchase cost and the amount she received from her broker.

$$\begin{aligned}\text{Net proceeds} &= \text{Sale proceeds} - \text{Purchase cost}\\ &= 27{,}279 - 23{,}745.10 = 3{,}533.90\end{aligned}$$

Erin's net proceeds were $3,533.90.

■ CHECK YOUR UNDERSTANDING

Yolanda purchased stock for $7,000 and paid a 1.5% broker fee. She sold it for $6,325 and paid a 0.5% broker fee. Compute her net proceeds.

EXAMPLE 4

Johan purchased stock six years ago for x dollars and paid a 2% broker fee. He sold that stock yesterday for y dollars and paid a discount broker $35 for the sale. Express his net proceeds algebraically.

SOLUTION The purchase cost is the sum of the cost and the broker fee.

$$\begin{aligned}\text{Purchase cost} &= \text{Cost of stock} + \text{Broker fee}\\ &= x + 0.02x\end{aligned}$$

When the stock was sold, the broker fee was $35. The sale proceeds is the difference of the sale price and the broker fee.

$$\begin{aligned}\text{Sale proceeds} &= \text{Sale price of stock} - \text{Broker fee}\\ &= y - 35\end{aligned}$$

The net proceeds is the difference between the purchase cost and the amount spent.

$$\begin{aligned}\text{Net proceeds} &= \text{Sale proceeds} - \text{Purchase cost}\\ &= (y - 35) - (x + 0.02x)\end{aligned}$$

Simplify. The net proceeds are $y - 35 - 1.02x$.

■ CHECK YOUR UNDERSTANDING

Rob purchased stock for p dollars and paid a flat $40 broker fee. Rob needed money for a home improvement so he sold it at a loss, for h dollars, plus a 1% broker fee. Express his net proceeds algebraically.

Applications

The bad news is time flies. The good news is you're the pilot.
Michael Althsuler, Businessman

1. How do those words apply to an investor? How do those words apply to a stockbroker? See margin.

2. Carlos does his online trading with Super Trade. Super Trade's rates are listed in the table below.

Fee Schedule for Super Trade Discount Broker	Online Trades	Automated Telephone Trades	Telephone to a Live Broker
less than 100 trades per year	\$17 per trade	Online fee plus \$11	$\frac{3}{4}$% commission plus online fee
100 or more trades per year	\$17 per trade for the first 100 trades, \$14 per trade for trades over 100	Online fee plus \$11	$\frac{1}{2}$% commission plus online fee

a. If Carlos makes three dozen online trades in a year, what is the total of his broker fees? \$612
b. What is the cost of 99 online trades? \$1,683
c. What is the cost of 120 online trades? \$1,980
d. If he makes t online trades in a year, and $t > 100$, express the total of his broker fees algebraically. $14(t - 100) + 1{,}700$
e. Suppose Carlos made q online trades and t automated telephone trades last year, where $q + t < 100$. Express the cost of all the trades algebraically. $17q + 28t$
f. Suppose Carlos makes 20 trades in a year. If Carlos purchased x shares of stock for y dollars each using a phone call to a live broker, express the total broker fee algebraically. $0.0075xy + 340$

3. The ticker shows trades of stock in Hewlett-Packard (HPQ), Exxon-Mobil (XOM), and Chevron (CVX).

HPQ 6K47.29 ▼ 0.23 XOM 3K92.67 ▲ 0.08 CVX 9K100.38 ▼ 0.22

a. How many shares of Hewlett-Packard were sold? 6,000
b. What was the total value of all the HPQ shares sold? \$283,740
c. Joan bought the shares at this price, and her broker charged her 1% commission. What was the total cost of her investment? \$286,577.40
d. Reggie sold the shares of Exxon-Mobil shown in the above trade, and his broker charged him 1.5% commission. How much money did the broker receive? Round to the nearest cent. \$4,170.15
e. Lisa sold the shares of Chevron indicated above through her discount broker, who charges \$28 per transaction. How much money did Lisa receive from the above sale after the broker took his fee? \$903,392

TEACH

Effect of Fees
Remind students that the fees associated with buying and selling stocks will always reduce the net gain, or increase the loss.

Fractions to Decimals
Look for students who might have difficulty changing fractional percents to equivalent decimals. A classic error is, for example, $\frac{3}{4}\% = 0.75$.

Exercise 2
This problem starts out numerically, and bridges to an algebraic representation. This is common throughout the book, and uses the strategy "solve a simpler, similar problem." It is important for students to realize that they can substitute numbers and think arithmetically to form algebraic expressions.

ANSWERS

1. The investor and the stockbroker are each in control of their decisions. Investors can make a decision to seek the investment advice of a stockbroker, or make their own decisions on which stocks to buy and sell.

TEACH

Exercise 8

Be alert for equivalent forms of the correct expression. You may want to have students put different equivalent forms on the board so students can compare them. Usually, the scenario of the problem is best exemplified by an expression that is not simplified. Often, the simplified version "masks" what actually happened step-by-step.

Exercise 9

You can have students put their answers on the board and show that they satisfy the problem.

ANSWERS

11. Sample answer: $x = 200$, $y = 1$, $p = 100$, $q = 3$; Ron's commission was 1% of $200, or $2. Dave's commission was 3% of $100, or $3.

4. Taylor bought 200 shares of stock for $18.12 per share last year. He paid his broker a flat fee of $30. He sold the stock this morning for $21 per share, and paid his broker 0.5% commission.

a. What were Taylor's net proceeds? $525

b. What was his capital gain? $576

5. Laura bought 55 shares of stock for $3.50 per share last year. She paid her broker a 1% commission. She sold the stock this week for $2 per share, and paid her broker a $10 flat fee.

a. What were Laura's net proceeds? Round to the nearest cent. –$94.43

b. What was her capital gain or loss? –$82.50, a loss

6. Lenny bought x shares of stock for $\$y$ per share last month. He paid his broker a flat fee of $20. He sold the stock this month for $\$p$ per share, and paid his broker a 2% commission. Express Lenny's net proceeds algebraically. $(xp - 0.02xp) - (xy + 20)$

7. Mackin Investing charges its customers a 1% commission. The Ross Group, a discount broker, charges $25 per trade. For what amount of stock would both brokers charge the same commission? $2,500

8. Fierro Brothers, a discount broker, charges their customers a $19 flat fee per trade. The Sondo Investment House charges a 2% commission. For what amount of stock would both brokers charge the same commission? $950

9. Darlene purchases $20,000 worth of stock on her broker's advice and pays her broker a 1.5% broker fee. She sells her stock when it increases to $28,600 two years later, and uses a discount broker who charges $21 per trade. Compute Darlene's net proceeds after the broker fees are taken out. $8,279

10. Alex purchases x dollars worth of stock on his broker's advice and pays his broker a 1% broker fee. The value of the shares falls to y dollars years later, and Alex uses a broker who charges 1.25% commission to make the sale. Express his net proceeds algebraically. $(y - 0.0125y) - (x + 0.01x)$

11. Ron bought x dollars worth of stock and paid a y percent commission. Dave purchased p dollars worth of stock and paid a q percent commission, where $x > p$. Pick numbers for x, y, p, and q such that Ron's commission is less than Dave's. Answers vary. See margin.

12. Debbie buys 400 shares of stock for $23 per share, and pays a 1% commission. She sells them six years later for $23.25 per share, and pays a $30 flat fee. Are her net proceeds positive or negative? Explain. The net proceeds are negative. The cost of both broker fees exceeded the small gain in price.

13. Sal bought x shares of a stock that sold for $23.50 per share. He paid a 1% commission on the sale. The total cost of his investment, including the broker fee, was $3,560.25. How many shares did Sal purchase? 150

Perception is strong and sight is weak. In strategy, it is important to see distant things as if they were close and to take a distanced view of close things.

Miyamoto Musashi, Japanese Samaurai, Artist, and Strategist

Stock Splits 1-8

Key Terms

- stock split
- outstanding shares
- market capitalization or market cap
- traditional stock split
- reverse stock split
- penny stock
- fractional part of a share

Objectives

- Calculate the post-split outstanding shares and share price for a traditional split.
- Calculate the post-split outstanding shares and share price for a reverse split.
- Calculate the fractional value amount that a shareholder receives after a split.

Common Core

A-CED1, A-REI3

CCSS Warm-Up

Given: One half of x minus one half of y equals −4.

1. Write an equation.
2. Solve the equation for x.
3. Solve the equation for y.

1. $(1/2)x - (1/2)y = -4$
2. $x = 2(-4 + (1/2)y)$ or $x = -8 + y$
3. $y = -2(-4 - (1/2)x)$ or $y = 8 + x$

Why do corporations split stocks?

Suppose that someone approaches you to give you two ten-dollar bills in exchange for a twenty-dollar bill. That might appear to be a worthless transaction because the value of the exchanged monies is the same. Having two ten-dollar bills might better suit one party and having a single twenty dollar bill might better suit the other. This is exactly what happens when a corporation offers its shareholders a **stock split**. To understand what happens when stocks split, it is first necessary to understand two important and related terms, outstanding shares and market capitalization. **Outstanding shares** are the total number of all shares issued by a corporation that are in investors' hands. **Market capitalization**, or **market cap**, is the total value of all of a company's outstanding shares.

When a stock is split, a corporation changes the number of outstanding shares while at the same time adjusts the price per share so that the market cap remains unchanged. In the opening situation, the number of bills doubled, while the value of each bill was halved. The total value of twenty dollars remained unchanged.

Why would a corporation institute a split if it is a monetary non-event? Many say that the reason is *perception*. The psychology of a split depends on the type of split. In a **traditional stock split**, the value of a share and the number of shares are changed in such a proportional way that the value decreases as the number of shares increases while the market cap remains the same. These types of splits are announced in the form *a* for *b* where *a* is greater than *b*. For example, one of the most common traditional splits is the 2-for-1 split. The investor gets two shares for every one share held while the price per share is cut in half. Although nothing has changed in the market value of the shares, the perception is that the investor sees the stock as more affordable. Investors may be attracted to this stock because the market price per share has been lowered, and they can afford to buy more shares.

In a **reverse stock split**, the effect is just the opposite. The number of outstanding shares is reduced and the market price per share is increased. As the price per share increases, the investor perceives

EXAMINE THE QUESTION

Stock splits have been occurring for decades. IBM had its first split in 1926. Caterpillar had two splits in the same year, 1926. Disney has had seven splits in its history.

One reason for a split might be that the stock price has gotten too high and therefore out priced itself in the market. The other reason is that the stock price has gotten too low and appears to be a worthless investment.

CLASS DISCUSSION

How do you think the perception of change might lead to an increase in sales and market prices?

TEACH

Students use fractions, ratios, and proportions to interpret and calculate the effect that stock splits have on the market and an individual's investment.

EXAMPLE 1

The pre-split market capitalization is the value of all of the shares at the time right before the split is enacted.

CHECK YOUR UNDERSTANDING

Answer $96

Let C represent pre-split market cap, N represent number of shares outstanding, and P represent market price at the time of split. The pre-split market cap formula is $C = NP$. Students are given $C = \$24B$ and $N = 250M$. Solving for P; $P = \frac{C}{N}$.

EXAMPLE 2

Use a proportion. Students can set up ratios in the form of post-split/pre-split to determine the number of shares in either situation. Knowing that the split ratio is 2 to 1, the proportion is $\frac{2}{1} = \frac{x}{1.2}$ where 1.2 represents 1.2 billion shares. Impress upon students that the answer must make sense in the context of the problem. Because every shareholder gets 2 shares for every one share held, it makes sense that the post-split number of shares should be twice the pre-split number of shares for individual holdings and for the number of shares.

CHECK YOUR UNDERSTANDING

Answer 3,200

Let x represent the number of shares Elena owned prior to the split. The proportion is $\frac{4}{1} = \frac{12.800}{x}$

that the stock is worth more. This often happens to stocks known as **penny stocks**, whose value is less than $5 per share. To increase the perceived value, the corporation may increase the price per share while at the same time decreasing the number of shares outstanding. This type of split is also in the form *a* for *b* where *a* is less than *b*. For example, in a 1-for-2 split, the investor holding shares would now own one share for every two previously held. The price for that share would have doubled. The market capitalization remains the same.

The saying "perception is reality" holds true for the stock market. Although stock splits may not initially alter the value of shares held, the perception of change may lead to increases in sales and market prices.

Skills and Strategies

Here you will learn how to interpret and calculate stock splits.

EXAMPLE 1

On December 4, John Deere Corporation (DE) instituted a 2-for-1 stock split. Before the split, the market share price was $87.68 per share and the corporation had 1.2 billion shares outstanding. What was the pre-split market cap for John Deere?

SOLUTION The market cap before the split is determined by multiplying the number of outstanding shares by the market price at that time.

$$\begin{aligned}\text{Pre-split market cap} &= \text{Number of shares} \times \text{Market price}\\ &= 1{,}200{,}000{,}000 \times 87.68\\ &= 105{,}216{,}000{,}000\end{aligned}$$

The pre-split market cap is $105,216,000,000.

■ CHECK YOUR UNDERSTANDING

A corporation has a market capitalization of $24,000,000,000 with 250M outstanding shares. Calculate the price per share.

EXAMPLE 2

What was the post-split number of shares outstanding for John Deere?

SOLUTION Use a proportion to determine the number of outstanding shares available after the split. Let *x* be the post-split outstanding shares.

$\frac{\text{Post-split}}{\text{Pre-split}}$ $\qquad \frac{2}{1} = \frac{x}{1.2}$

Cross multiply. $\qquad x = 2 \times 1.2$

After the split, there will be 2.4B shares outstanding.

■ CHECK YOUR UNDERSTANDING

QualComm, Inc. instituted a 4-for-1 split in November. After the split, Elena owned 12,800 shares. How many shares had she owned before the split?

EXAMPLE 3

What was the post-split market price per share for John Deere in Example 1? How many shares are outstanding? Did the market cap change after the split?

SOLUTION This was a 2-for-1 stock split, so the new share price is $\frac{1}{2}$ the old share price.

$$\frac{1}{2} \times 87.68 = \$43.84$$

In a 2-for-1 split the number of shares are doubled, so there are now

$$2 \times 1.2 = 2.4\text{B shares}$$

The post-split market cap is $43.84 × 2.4B = $105,216,000,000, which is the same as it was before.

CHECK YOUR UNDERSTANDING

In October, Johnson Controls, Inc instituted a 3-for-1 split. After the split, the price of one share was $39.24. What was the pre-split price per share?

Post-Split Market Price and Number of Outstanding Shares

In general, in any *a*-for-*b* split, you can apply the following formulas.

$$\text{Post-split number of shares} = \frac{a}{b} \times \text{Pre-split number of shares}$$

$$\text{Post-split share price} = \frac{b}{a} \times \text{Pre-split share price}$$

EXAMPLE 4

On October 15, Palm, Inc. instituted a 1-for-20 reverse stock split. Before the split, the market share price was $0.64 and there were 580,000,000 shares. What was the post-split share price and number of shares?

SOLUTION Write the 1-for-20 reverse stock split as the ratio $\frac{1}{20}$.

$$\text{Post-split number of shares} = \frac{a}{b} \times \text{Pre-split number of shares}$$

$$= \frac{1}{20} \times 580{,}000{,}000 = 29{,}000{,}000$$

$$\text{Post-split share price} = \frac{b}{a} \times \text{Pre-split share price}$$

$$= \frac{20}{1} \times 0.64 = 12.80$$

After the split, there were 29M shares outstanding with each share having a value of $12.80. Notice that the pre-split market cap, 580M × $0.64, and the post-split market cap, 29M × $12.80, both equal $371,200,000.

EXAMPLE 3

The solution walks students through the process without using a proportion. In a 2-for-1 split, the number of shares is doubled and the price per share is cut in half. Find the product of twice the number of shares and half the pre-split price per share. This yields the post-split market cap. Notice the value of the shares outstanding remains exactly the same as before the split.

CHECK YOUR UNDERSTANDING

Answer $117.72

EXAMPLE 4

The formulas given before Example 4 are alternate forms of the following proportions.

$$\frac{\text{Post-split number of shares}}{\text{Pre-split number of shares}} = \frac{a}{b}$$

$$\frac{\text{Post-split number of shares}}{\text{Pre-split number of shares}} = \frac{b}{a}$$

Point out that in both proportions, multiplying both sides of the equation by the pre-split value in the denominator yields the formulas given.

CHECK YOUR UNDERSTANDING

Answer \$1.71B

Students might be tempted to use formulas here. They should be encouraged to read the question carefully. Understanding that a split is a monetary non-event means that the pre-split and the post-split market caps must be the same.

EXTEND YOUR UNDERSTANDING

Answer 1-for-3 split ratio

Students should be encouraged to use the proportion $\frac{\text{Post-split number of shares}}{\text{Pre-split number of shares}} = \frac{b}{a}$ where $\frac{7.05}{2.35} = \frac{b}{a}$. Simplifying the ratio on the left yields $\frac{3}{1} = \frac{b}{a}$. So, $a = 1$ and $b = 3$. Therefore, these prices represent *a*-for-*b* or a 1-for-3 split.

EXAMPLE 6

First determine the post-split number of shares and the post-split share price using either the proportions or the formulas. Students should understand that all share amounts are rounded down to the nearest whole number of shares. The fractional part that remains is multiplied by the post-split price and that amount is refunded to the shareholder.

CHECK YOUR UNDERSTANDING

Answer Gabriella will receive 1,567 shares and be refunded for the overage of 0.5 shares.

This is a multi-step problem. Students need to calculate the post-split price per share and the number of shares. Mathematically, the post-split number of shares is 1,567.5. In actuality, the refund is calculated by multiplying 0.5 by the post-split price per share ($0.5 \times 41.86 = \$20.93$).

■ CHECK YOUR UNDERSTANDING

A major drugstore chain whose stocks are traded on the New York Stock Exchange was considering a 2-for-5 reverse split. If the pre-split market cap was 1.71B, what would the post-split market cap be?

■ EXTEND YOUR UNDERSTANDING

Suppose that before a stock split, a share was selling for \$2.35. After the stock split, the price was \$7.05 per share. What was the stock-split ratio?

Fractional Part of a Share

The previous examples had shares that could be split into whole-number amounts. In reality, this may not be the case. Often the split would create a **fractional part of a share**. In other words, there is less than one share remaining. When this happens, the corporation buys the fractional share at the current market price.

EXAMPLE 5

Steve owned 942 shares of Graham Corporation. On January 3, a 5-for-4 split was announced. The stock was selling at \$56 per share before the split. How was Steve financially affected by the split?

SOLUTION Write the split as a ratio. Use the pre-split information to find the post-split values.

$$\text{Post-split number of shares} = \frac{a}{b} \times \text{Pre-split number of shares}$$

$$= \frac{5}{4} \times 942 = 1{,}177.5$$

$$\text{Post-split share price} = \frac{b}{a} \times \text{Pre-split share price}$$

$$= \frac{4}{5} \times 56 = 44.80$$

Fractional shares are not traded, so the corporation paid him the market value of 0.5 shares.

Fractional part × Market price $\qquad 0.5 \times 44.80 = 22.40$

Steve received \$22.40 in cash and 1,177 shares worth \$44.80 each.

■ CHECK YOUR UNDERSTANDING

Gabriella owned 1,045 shares of Hollow Corporation at a price of \$62.79. The stock split 3-for-2. How was Gabriella financially affected by the split?

Applications

Perception is strong and sight is weak. In strategy, it is important to see distant things as if they were close and to take a distanced view of close things.

Miyamoto Musashi, Japanese Samaurai, Artist, and Strategist

1. Why should investors be cautious when a split occurs? How might those words apply to what you have learned? See margin.
2. In February, Robbins and Myers, Inc. executed a 2-for-1 split. Janine had 470 shares before the split. Each share was worth $69.48.
   - **a.** How many shares did she hold after the split? 940
   - **b.** What was the post-split price per share? $34.74
   - **c.** Show that the split was a monetary non-event for Janine. Pre-split and post-split shares were both worth $32,655.60.
3. On June 5, CIGNA instituted a 3-for-1 stock split. Before the split, CIGNA had 200 million shares with a price of $168 per share.
   - **a.** How many shares were outstanding after the split? 600M
   - **b.** What was the post-split price per share? $56
   - **c.** Show that this split was a monetary non-event for the corporation. Pre-split and post-split market caps both were $33,600M.
4. Vilma owns 750 shares of Aeropostale. On August 22, the corporation instituted a 3-for-2 stock split. Before the split, each share was worth $34.89.
   - **a.** How many shares did Vilma hold after the split? 1,125
   - **b.** What was the post-price per share after the split? $23.26
   - **c.** Show that the split was a monetary non-event for Vilma. Pre-split and post-split shares both were worth $26,167.50.
5. Mike owns 2,400 shares of JDS Uniphase Corp. The company instituted a 1-for-8 reverse stock split on October 17. The pre-split market price per share was $2.13.
   - **a.** How many shares did Mike hold after the split? 300
   - **b.** What was the post-split price per share? $17.04
   - **c.** Show that the split was a monetary non-event for Mike. Pre-split and post-split shares both were worth $5,112.
6. Versant Corporation executed a 1-for-10 reverse split on August 22. At the time, the corporation had 35,608,800 shares outstanding and the pre-split price per share was $0.41.
   - **a.** How many shares were outstanding after the split? 3,560,880
   - **b.** What was the post-price per share after the split? $4.10
   - **c.** Show that this split was a monetary non-event for the corporation. Pre-split and post-split market caps both were $14,599,608.
7. Kristy owns 200 shares of Nortel stock. On November 30 the company instituted a 1-for-10 reverse split. The pre-split price per share was $2.15. The number of shares outstanding before the split was 4.34B.
   - **a.** How many shares did Kristy hold after the split? 20
   - **b.** What was the post-split price per share? $21.50
   - **c.** What was the post-split number of outstanding shares? 434M
   - **d.** What was the post-split market cap? $9.331B

TEACH

Exercises 2 and 3

Some students may need to solve these problems using a proportion while others may be able to calculate the solution through simple multiplication. Both methods are valid and should be addressed when reviewing the solutions.

Exercise 4

Stock splits that do not contain a 1 in the denominator are often difficult for students to understand. In this case, the stock holder gets 3 shares for every two shares owned. In reviewing the problem, you might show the equivalence of this situation and the split of 1.5 to 1.

Exercises 5–7

Before assigning these problems, make sure that students have an understanding of the reverse split. In particular, what such a split does to the number of shares held and what it does to the price per share.

ANSWERS

1. Musashi urges people to "see distant things as if they are close and take a close view of distant things." In other words, be cautious because things may not always appear to be what they really are. Perception changes reality.

TEACH

Exercises 11 and 12
Encourage students to try both methods when solving these problems. You should address both methods when reviewing the assignment.

ANSWERS

8. Post-split price per share = $\frac{\$203.8}{4}$ = \$50.95; post-split outstanding shares = 4 × 22,676,800 = 90,707,200

10a. Post-split share price = $\frac{5}{6}$ × 18 = \$15; post-split outstanding shares = $\frac{6}{5}$ × 4,800,000 = 5,760,000

Jon noticed that most traditional splits are in the form *x*-for-1. He says that in those cases, all you need do is multiply the number of shares held by *x* and divide the price per share by *x* to get the post-split numbers. Answer Exercises 8–9 based on Jon's method.

8. Verify that Jon's method works to determine the post-split price and shares outstanding for Hansen Natural Corporation which executed a 4-for-1 split on July 10 with 22,676,800 outstanding shares and a market price of \$203.80 per share before the split. See margin.

9. Jon also noticed that *every* traditional split ratio can be written in the form *x*-for-1. Examine how the 3-for-2 traditional split can be expressed as 1.5-for-1.

$$\frac{3}{2} = \frac{x}{1} \rightarrow 3 = 2x \rightarrow x = 1.5$$

Express each of the following traditional split ratios as *x*-for-1.

a. 5-for-4 1.25-for-1
b. 6-for-5 1.2-for-1
c. 5-for-2 2.5-for-1
d. 8-for-5 1.6-for-1

10. Monarch Financial Holdings, Inc. executed a 6-for-5 traditional split on October 5. Before the split there were approximately 4,800,000 shares outstanding, each at a share price of \$18.00.

a. Use the method outlined in Examples 2 and 3 on pages 46 and 47 to determine the post-split share price and number of shares outstanding. See margin.

b. Compare the results from part a. with that obtained by using Jon's method. Jon's method says that 6-for-5 is the same as 1.2-for-1. The post-split values are the same.

11. On June 19 California Pizza Kitchen, Inc. instituted a 3-for-2 split. At that time Krista owned 205 shares of that stock. The price per share was \$33.99. After the split, Krista received a check for a fractional part of a share. What was the amount of that check? \$11.33

12. On December 14, XTO Energy, Inc. executed a 5-for-4 split. At that time, Bill owned 325 shares of that stock. The price per share was \$65.80. After the split he received a check for a fractional part of a share. What was the amount of that check? \$13.16

Use the following spreadsheet to answer Exercises 13–15. The split-ratio is entered in cells B2 and C2. For example, the ratio of 2-for-1 would be entered as a 2 in B2 and a 1 in C2. The number of pre-split shares is entered in B3 and the pre-split price is entered in B4.

13. Write the spreadsheet formula that will calculate the post-split number of outstanding shares in C3. =B2/C2*B3

14. Write the spreadsheet formula that will calculate the post-split price per share in C4. =C2/B2*B4

15. Write the pre-split market cap formula in cell B5 and the post-split market cap formula in C5. =B4*B3; =C4*C3

	A	B	C
1		**Pre-split**	**Post-split**
2	Split ratio	2	1
3	Outstanding shares		
4	Price per share		
5	Market cap		

I believe non-dividend stocks aren't much more than baseball cards. They are worth what you can convince someone to pay for them.

Mark Cuban, Billionaire businessman

Dividend Income 1-9

Key Terms
- dividend
- dividend income
- income stock
- yield
- growth stock
- preferred stock
- common stock
- corporate bond
- face value
- matures

Objectives

- Understand the concept of shareowners splitting the profit of the corporation they own.
- Compute dividend income.
- Compute the yield for a given stock.
- Compute the interest earned on corporate bonds.

Common Core

A-SSE1

CCSS Warm-Up

***X* is the price of an item in dollars. *Y* is a percent.**
Interpret each expression.

1. $X(Y/100)$

2. $X + X(Y/100)$

1. The percent discount off an item in dollars or the percent tax on the item

2. The price with a percent increase or the price with Y percent tax added

If Shareholders Own a Corporation, Are They Entitled to Some of the Profits?

If you buy a stock and watch its price rise, it's exciting, but your profit is only realized when you actually sell it. Keep in mind that capital gains and net proceeds cannot be computed and are not assured until the stock is actually sold. However, your stock portfolio can earn income before you sell your shares. Remember, a shareholder is an owner of a corporation. As owners, shareholders are entitled to their portions of the corporation's profit. Profit split among shareholders is called a **dividend**. Money received from dividends is **dividend income**. Dividends are usually paid annually or quarterly. The board of directors of the corporation sets the dividend for one share of stock. For major public corporations this can be found under a column headed "Div" in newspaper or online stock tables. Your total dividend depends on the number of shares you own. Some corporations do not pay a dividend because the profit is being used to improve or grow the corporation. Some corporations do not pay a dividend because they have no profit. They are operating at a loss. Stocks that pay dividends are called **income stocks**, because they provide their owners with income.

Some people buy income stocks which pay dividends for the additional income. The **yield** of a stock is the percentage value of the dividend, compared to the current price per share. Investors use the yield to compare their dividend income to the interest they could have made if they put the money in the bank instead of buying the stock. Other investors are not concerned with dividend income. Instead, they want to buy low and sell high. Stocks that are bought for this reason are called **growth stocks**. A stock can be both an income and a growth stock.

Stocks are also classified as **preferred stock** or **common stock**. Preferred stockholders receive their dividends before common stockholders do, and they usually receive a set dividend which does not frequently change. Common stockholders receive dividends only when the board of directors elects to issue these dividends. Additionally, if a company goes out of business, preferred stockholders are entitled to assets and earnings of the company, ahead of common stockholders.

EXAMINE THE QUESTION

When you own shares of stock in a corporation you can receive a dividend check. That dividend check is your part of the profit, but depending on the corporation and the number of shares you own, the check may only be a few cents.

Have students research the history of dividend checks for major corporations. Some corporations issue quarterly dividends, some issue annual dividends, while some do not issue any dividends.

CLASS DISCUSSION

Corporations reinvest part of their profits into new products and services. Do you think this is a good business strategy?

Dividend payments are mailed to shareholders or electronically transferred to their accounts. Dividend payments can range in value from a few cents to thousands of dollars, because they depend on how much the dividend is and how many shares are owned. Remember that dividends are not guaranteed and can be cut or eliminated if the company decides they need the money. Although, most companies do not like to cut dividends and disappoint shareholders.

Skills and Strategies

If your stock pays a dividend, you want to make sure the amount you are receiving is correct. You also want to be aware of how dividend income compares to the bank interest you could have made if you decided to put the money in the bank instead of buying the stock.

EXAMPLE 1

Roberta is considering purchasing a common stock that pays an annual dividend of \$2.13 per share. If she purchases 700 shares for \$45.16 per share, what would her annual income be from dividends?

SOLUTION The price paid per share is not needed to compute the annual dividend. To find the annual income from dividends, multiply the number of shares by the annual dividend per share.

Income from dividends = Number of shares × Dividend per share

= 700 × 2.13 = 1,491

The annual income from dividends is \$1,491.

■ CHECK YOUR UNDERSTANDING

Jacques purchased x shares of a corporation that pays a y dollar annual dividend. What is his annual dividend income, expressed algebraically?

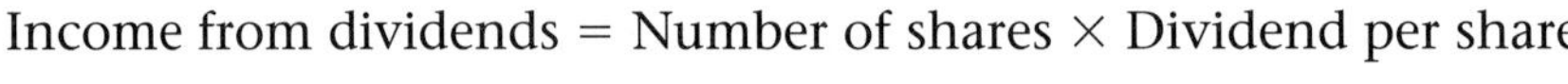

EXAMPLE 2

Elyse owns 2,000 shares of a corporation that pays a quarterly dividend of \$0.51 per share. How much should she expect to receive in a year?

SOLUTION First, compute her quarterly dividend by multiplying the total number of shares by the quarterly dividend per share.

Income from dividends = Number of shares × Dividend per share

= 2,000 × 0.51 = 1,020

To find the amount she should expect to receive in a year, multiply by 4.

1,020 × 4 = 4,080

Elyse should receive \$4,080 in a year.

TEACH

When calculating the profit and yield of stocks, students use basic operations and percents to interpret how much, if any amount, an investor will receive in dividends.

EXAMPLE 1

The Div column reports the annual dividend per share. Students should understand that an annual report gives data from a previous year and does not guarantee that owning that stock will yield the results every year.

CHECK YOUR UNDERSTANDING

Answer *xy*

Point out the importance of the word *annually*. Throughout the lesson, students will have to deal with variations on annual and quarterly dividends, so reading carefully is important.

■ CHECK YOUR UNDERSTANDING

Monique owns x shares of stock. The quarterly dividend per share is y dollars. Express Monique's annual dividend amount algebraically.

Yield

To find the yield of a stock, write the ratio of the annual dividend per share to the current price of the stock per share and convert to a percent. A yield can change even when a dividend amount does not because the price of the stock changes frequently.

EXAMPLE 3

Kristen owns common stock in Max's Toy Den. The annual dividend is \$1.40. The current price is \$57.40 per share. What is the yield of the stock to the nearest tenth of a percent?

SOLUTION Write the yield as a fraction. Then convert the fraction to a decimal. Finally write the decimal as a percent.

$$\text{Yield} = \frac{\text{Annual dividend per share}}{\text{Current price of one share}}$$

$$= \frac{1.40}{57.40} \approx 0.0243902, \text{ or } 2.4390\%$$

The yield is about 2.4%.

■ CHECK YOUR UNDERSTANDING

You bought x shares of a stock for \$$y$ per share. The annual dividend per share is \$$d$. Express the percent yield algebraically.

EXAMPLE 4

One share of BeepCo preferred stock pays an annual dividend of \$1.20. Today BeepCo closed at \$34.50 with a net change of –\$0.50. What was the stock's yield at yesterday's closing price?

SOLUTION Use today's close and the net change to find yesterday's close.

Today's close + Opposite of net change $\quad 34.50 - (-0.50) = 35$

Yesterday's close was \$35.00.

$$\text{Yield} = \frac{1.20}{35}$$

$$\approx 0.03429, \text{ or } 3.4\%$$

At yesterday's close, the yield was about 3.4%.

■ CHECK YOUR UNDERSTANDING

One share of Skroy Corporation stock pays an annual dividend of \$1.55. Today Skroy closed at x dollars with a net change of +0.40. Express the yield at yesterday's close algebraically.

CHECK YOUR UNDERSTANDING

Answer $4xy$

EXAMPLE 3

In stock data reports, yield is usually rounded to 1 or 2 decimal places. Instruct students to convert to a percent and then round to the nearest tenth or hundredth of a percent.

CHECK YOUR UNDERSTANDING

Answer $100\frac{d}{y}$

Remind students about multiplication by 100 to convert the decimal to an equivalent percent.

EXAMPLE 4

This reviews how the net change is used to compute a previous day's close.

CHECK YOUR UNDERSTANDING

Answer $100\frac{1.55}{x - 0.4C}$

Make sure students notice they are asked for yesterday's yield. If a student has an error, check the denominator used.

EXAMPLE 2

Guide students to understand that fractions of a penny cannot be on a dividend check. Amounts are rounded down to the nearest cent.

EXAMPLE 5

Point out that when a stock splits, the yield does not change, because the price of a share and the dividend are both divided by the same number.

CHECK YOUR UNDERSTANDING

Answer $1.40

This problem reviews skills learned about stock splits.

EXAMPLE 6

Point out to students that Adam will be paid interest each year that the bond is held. This means that the Labate Corporation pays Adam $57 to use his $1,000 for one year. You can remind students that multiplying by a power of 10 can be more easily done by moving the decimal point. In this case multiplying by 1,000 is the same as moving the decimal point in the rate (written as a decimal) to the right 3 places.

CHECK YOUR UNDERSTANDING

Answer $627

EXAMPLE 5

A stock paid an annual dividend of $2.14. The stock split 2-for-1. What is the annual dividend after the split?

SOLUTION After a 2-for-1 split, there are twice as many shares outstanding, so divide the dividend by 2: $2.14 \div 2 = 1.07$. The new annual dividend per share is $1.07.

■ CHECK YOUR UNDERSTANDING

A corporation was paying a $2.10 annual dividend. The stock underwent a 3-for-2 split. What is the new annual dividend per share?

Corporate Bonds

Buying stock has risk and rewards. If you do not want to take a significant risk, you can invest in corporate bonds. A **corporate bond** is a loan to a corporation. The corporation agrees to pay the bondholder back with interest, much like a bank does to customer with money on deposit. The interest is usually paid annually or semiannually. Usually, corporate bonds are for $1,000 or $5,000. This amount is the **face value** and is the amount paid when the bond **matures**. Bondholders do not share in any profits, and they do not own part of the corporation. Investors that buy bonds enjoy less risk and have less potential rewards.

The maturity date of a bond is a date in the future when the principal invested will be repaid to the investor The time to maturity can be a short period or as long as 30 years. Upon maturity, an investor will receive the amount originally invested back from the corporation. Bonds that take longer to mature generally pay a higher interest rate.

EXAMPLE 6

Adam bought a $1,000 corporate bond in the Labate Corporation. The bond pays 5.7% interest per year. How much does Adam receive in interest each year from this bond?

SOLUTION To find the annual interest, first convert the percent to an equivalent decimal.

$$5.7\% = 0.057$$

Then, multiply the interest expressed as a decimal by the face value.

Multiply interest by 1,000 $\quad 0.057 \times 1{,}000 = 57$

Adam receives $57 in annual interest.

■ CHECK YOUR UNDERSTANDING

If Adam holds the bond from Example 6 for 11 years, how much will he receive in total interest?

Applications

> *I believe non-dividend stocks aren't much more than baseball cards. They are worth what you can convince someone to pay for them.*
>
> **Mark Cuban,** Billionaire businessman

1. Based on what you learned about dividends, why are non-dividend stocks compared to baseball cards? See margin.
2. Years ago, Home Depot had an annual dividend of \$0.90. If you owned 4,000 shares of Home Depot, how much did you receive annually in dividends? \$3,600
3. Barnes and Noble had a \$1.00 annual dividend during 2008. If you owned 500 shares of Barnes and Noble, how much did you receive on a quarterly dividend check? \$125
4. If you own r shares of a stock with an annual dividend of p dollars, express the amount of your quarterly dividends algebraically. $\frac{rp}{4}$
5. The quarterly dividend for Tiffany, a jewelry company, was \$0.17 during the second quarter of 2008. What was the annual dividend for 2,000 shares? \$1,360
6. Mike owned 3,000 shares of Merck Corporation and received a quarterly dividend check for \$1,140. What was the annual dividend for one share of Merck? \$1.52
7. Jean owned x shares of a corporation and received a quarterly dividend check for y dollars. Express the annual dividend for one share algebraically. $\frac{4y}{x}$
8. The Walt Disney Company paid a \$0.35 annual dividend on a day it closed at a price of \$33.86 per share.
   a. What was the annual dividend for 500 shares? \$175
   b. What was the quarterly dividend for 500 shares? \$43.75
   c. Express the yield as a fraction. See margin.
   d. What was the yield to the nearest tenth of a percent? 1.0%
9. You own k shares of a stock that is selling for x dollars per share. The quarterly dividend is y dollars per share.
   a. Express the annual dividend for one share algebraically. $4y$
   b. Express the annual dividend for all k shares algebraically. $4yk$
   c. Express the yield as an algebraic fraction. $\frac{4y}{x}$
10. The spreadsheet on the right can be used to compute the yield. Write the formula that can be used to compute the yield in cell C2. =(B2/A2)*100
11. The Black Oyster Corporation is going out of business. All of the corporate assets are being sold. The money raised will be split by the stockholders. Which stockholders, the common or preferred, receive money first? preferred

	A	B	C
1	Price per Share	Annual Dividend	Yield
2	37.12	1.51	
3	44.55	1.77	
4	65.29	2.01	
5	14.35	0.48	

TEACH

Exercise 9
Remind students that they can "solve a simpler, related problem" using numbers in place of the variables if it helps them sort out what operations to use. Then they can substitute the variables back into their answer.

ANSWERS

1. If a stock does not pay a dividend, you can only make money on it by selling it to someone else for more than you paid. The buyer must be convinced that it is worth what you want for it. This is much like two kids trading baseball cards—you are relying on what another person thinks your item is worth.

8c. $\frac{0.35}{33.86}$

Name	Last Price	Dividend
3M Co	76.90	2.00
Alcoa, Inc	41.57	0.68
American Express Co	46.15	0.72
American International Group, Inc	34.91	0.80
AT&T, Inc	39.51	1.60
Bank of America Corp	33.87	2.56
Boeing Co	82.13	1.60
Caterpillar, Inc.	83.19	1.44
Chevron Corp	100.42	2.60
Citigroup, Inc.	21.60	1.28
Coca-Cola Co/The	57.44	1.52
El Du Pont de Nemours & Co	47.63	1.64
Exxon Mobil Corp	90.43	1.60

For Exercises 12–15, round answers to the nearest tenth of a percent.

12. The table gives the last price and the annual dividend for 15 corporations. Compute the yield for each corporation. See margin.

13. The Revreg Corporation pays an annual dividend of $1.60 per share. On Friday it closed at $44 per share with a net change of +0.35. The dividend did not change.

a. What was the yield on Friday? 3.6%

b. At what price did Revreg close on Thursday? $43.65

c. What was the yield at Thursday's close? 3.7%

d. Thursday's net change was +1.22. At what price did Reverg close on Wednesday? $42.43

e. If the dividend was $1.60 on Wednesday, what was the yield at Wednesday's close? 3.8%

f. Look at the yields for Wednesday, Thursday, and Friday. They are decreasing. Explain why this decrease is not "bad news" to the investor who owns stock in Revreg. See margin.

14. The Zeescore Corporation pays an annual dividend of $2 per share. On Wednesday it closed at $61 per share with a net change of –0.85. The dividend remained at $2 for a year.

a. What was the yield on Wednesday? 3.3%

b. At what price did Zeescore close on Tuesday? $61.85

c. What was the yield on Tuesday? 3.2%

d. Tuesday's net change was –1.96. At what price did Zeescore close on Monday? $63.81

e. What was Monday's yield? 3.1%

f. Look at the yields for Monday, Tuesday, and Wednesday. They are increasing. Explain why this increase is not "good news" to the investor who owns stock in Zeescore. See margin.

15. Sascha owns stock in Lewis Corp and she bought a $1,000 corporate bond. The bond pays 6.34% annual interest.

a. How much will Sascha receive in annual interest? $63.40

b. How much will Sascha receive in interest if she holds the bond for 14 years? $887.60

c. Sascha's stock is worth $46 per share, and it pays a $2 annual dividend. What is the yield? 4.3%

d. Which is higher, the yield on the stock or the interest rate on the bond? bond

e. How much does Lewis Corp. pay to Sascha when the bond matures? $1,000

16. Stock in Happy's Burger Chain was selling for $54.24 per share, and it was paying a $2.46 annual dividend. It underwent a 3-for-1 split.

a. What was the new price of one share after the split? $18.08

b. If you owned 200 shares before the split, how many shares did you own after the split? 600

c. Following the same pattern, what was the annual dividend per share after the split? $0.82

TEACH

Exercise 13b

Look out for students who compute Thursday's closing price incorrectly due to an incorrect interpretation of the sign of the net change.

Exercise 14b

Look out for students who compute Tuesday's closing price incorrectly due to an incorrect interpretation of the sign of the net change.

ANSWERS

12. 3M, 2.6%; Alcoa, 1.6%; Am Ex, 1.6%; AIG, 2.3%; AT&T, 4.0%; Bank of Am, 7.6%; Boeing, 1.9%; Cat, 1.7%; Chev, 2.6%; Citi, 5.9%; Coca-Cola, 2.6%; E!, 3.4%; Exxon, 1.8%

13f. The dividend has not changed. The price of the stock is going up, and that increases the denominator of the yield formula, decreasing the yield. The corporation's stock is rising, and that is good news to the investor.

14f. The dividend has not changed. The price of the stock is going down, and that decreases the denominator of the yield formula, increasing the yield. The corporation's stock is falling, and that is not good news to the investor.

Assessment

CHAPTER 1

Real Numbers

You Write the Story!!

Examine the graph below. Write a short newspaper-type article, using facts obtained online or at the library, centered around this graph. You can find an electronic copy of the graph at www.cengage.com/school/math/financialalgebra. Copy and paste it into your article.

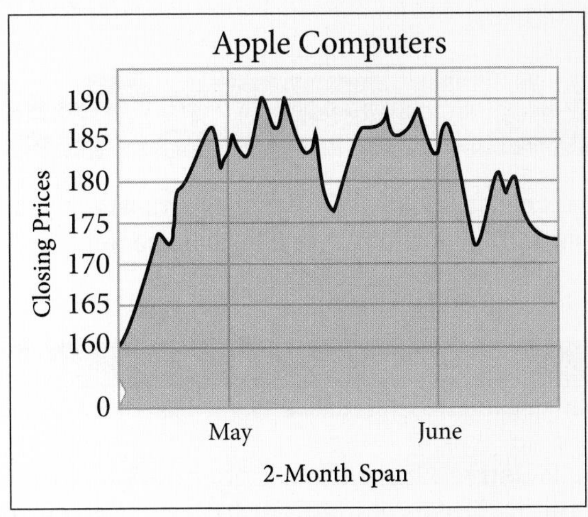

CHAPTER 1 ASSESSMENT

REAL NUMBERS

You Write the Story

Make sure students interpret the graph correctly, and do not use fictional or hypothetical anecdotes. If they want more information than the graph gives to write their articles, they can do an Internet search to acquire more facts.

REALITY CHECK

Reality Check projects are a terrific form of alternative assessment. They give students an additional avenue to show what they've learned, so their grades are not solely based on tests.

Projects can be presented to the class on any schedule that works for your program. These projects have students taking little field trips, so they don't conduct everything online.

Remind students who personally visit local businesses or community members that they are representing the school, and need to be cordial.

Reality Check

1. Choose a corporation that you are interested in following. Use the newspaper or Internet to find the daily low, high, close, and volume of your stock for the next three weeks. Set up a graph to record these prices and the volume. Discuss the trends for the three-week period. Check the corporation's website for major news about the corporation. Discuss the trend over the three-weeks and include any major corporate news that might have affected the trend.

2. Discuss stocks with your parents or guardians. Find out if they own any stocks currently, or ever did during their lives. If you earn money on your own, discuss with them the possibility of purchasing shares of stock for a corporation you are interested in following.

3. Survey your classmates and compile a list of questions your class has about stocks. Compile a list of the top five stocks they are interested in. Call a local stockbroker and request an appointment for a short meeting. Interview the broker. Ask the broker why these stocks may or may not be a good investment. Report your findings.

4. Visit a local bank and ask to speak to one of the representatives about United States Savings Bonds. Find out about the forms necessary to purchase a bond, the interest it pays, and how long the bonds take to reach their face value. Prepare a report and present your findings to the class.

REALLY? REALLY! REVISITED

The 6 by 5 grids that students draw should take up an entire page. In the corner of each box, have them put the date in June that the box refers to. Leave most of the room in the box for the dollar amounts.

Make sure students realize that they can just multiply the last calculator entry by 2 to get the next entry.

5. Contact a local stockbroker. Talk to your teacher about setting up a class session featuring the stockbroker as a guest speaker. During the broker's presentation, conduct a question-and-answer session.
6. Contact the New York Stock Exchange by mail or through its website. Request a list of publications that the Exchange offers.
7. Use the library or Internet to research a corporation. Prepare a poster board about the corporation. Include how and when the corporation was founded, where it got its name, major developments in its history, and why you may or may not want to invest in this company.
8. Work with a small group of classmates to select 5 to 10 stocks that will form a stock portfolio. Set up an online portfolio using any financial website such as yahoo.com or nyt.com with an initial investment of $10,000. Track the gains and losses of your entire portfolio for a month. Compare your total profit or loss with that of other groups.

Dollars and Sense — Your Financial News Update

Go to www.cengage.com/school/math/financialalgebra where you will find a link to a website containing current issues about the stock market.

Really? Really! REVISITED

The power of this activity is seeing the payment amounts increase slowly at first. Even after 2 weeks, the daily pay is relatively low. Students will see the power of exponents unfurl gradually as they complete this activity.

An extension of this activity is to have students fold a single sheet of paper in half several times. They can watch the thickness of the folded paper increase as they fold. After about 5 to 8 folds, they won't be able to physically fold the paper any longer. How many folds would it take to have the paper's thickness reach from the Earth to the Sun (about 93 million miles)? Although paper thicknesses vary, it is typically around 50 folds!

GOOGLE.COM® is derived from the number googol which is a 1 with 100 zeros following it. This is equivalent to 10^{100}. The change in spelling (but not pronunciation) still elicits the feel of something very large. How large is 10^{100}? There isn't a googol of anything on the planet!

Given that 1,000,000 pennies stacked one on top of another reaches about one mile high, how high will 1 googol pennies reach?

To get an idea of the "power" of exponents, investigate a famous problem in math. Imagine your teacher asks you to work at school for all of June. You can choose to be paid in one of two ways.

- One payment of $5,000, which you will receive on June 30.
- On the first day you get paid 1¢. On the second day you receive double that amount, which is 2¢. On the third day you receive 4¢, on the fourth day 8¢, and so on. Each day you get paid twice the amount you were paid the day before.

Draw a grid with six columns and five rows to represent the 30 days. Fill in the amount you are paid each day.

1. How much do you receive on June 14? June 27? June 30?
   $81.92; 671,088.64; 5,368,709.12
2. Another way to think of the payment on June 30 is 1 cent multiplied by 2 twenty-nine times. What is the product of 0.01 and 2^{29}? $5,368,709.12

Think about how much 29 multiplications by 2 inflated the original 1 cent! Imagine raising 10 to the 100th power! The stock market deals in billions and sometimes trillions of dollars, but remember that 1 billion = 10^9 and 1 trillion = 10^{12}. Nothing close to a googol. And that's reality!

Applications

1. Nick and Matt are the partners in a local health food store. They needed $73,000 to start the business. They invested in the ratio 3:7, Nick to Matt.
   a. How much money did each invest? Nick $21,900; Matt $51,100
   b. What percent of the business was owned by Matt? Round to the nearest tenth of a percent. 70%

2. Tom purchased shares of DuPont for $47.65 per share. He plans to sell the shares when the stock price rises 20%. At what price will he sell his shares? $57.18

3. The top three shareholders in a certain corporation each own s shares of a certain stock. The corporation's ownership is represented by a total of x shares of stock. Express the percent of the corporation owned by the top three shareholders algebraically. $\frac{3s}{x}100$

4. Marilyn purchased 2,000 shares of stock for $25.43 per share. She sold them for $44.10 per share. Express her capital gain to the nearest tenth of a percent. 73.4%

5. A local hairdresser bought 450 shares of a cosmetics corporation for $33.50 per share. He sold the shares for $39.01 per share.
   a. What was the percent increase in the price per share? Round to the nearest tenth of a percent. 16.4%
   b. What was the total purchase price for the 450 shares? $15,075
   c. What was the total selling price for the 450 shares? $17,554.50
   d. What was the percent capital gain for the 450 shares? Round to the nearest tenth of a percent. 16.4%

6. Deanna purchased $24,000 worth of stock and paid her broker a 1% broker fee. She sold the stock when it increased to $29,100 three years later and used a discount broker who charged $35 per trade. Compute her net proceeds after the broker fees were taken out. $4,825

7. The Bootle Corporation paid Leslie a quarterly dividend check for $828. Leslie owns 450 shares of Bootle. What was the quarterly dividend for one share of Bootle? $1.84

8. Aaron owned x shares of a corporation and received an annual dividend of y dollars. Express the quarterly dividend for one share algebraically. $\frac{y}{4}$

9. The Zyco Corporation pays an annual dividend of $2.10 per share. On Tuesday it closed at $72 per share with a net change of +0.95. The dividend remained at $2.10 for several months.
   a. What was the yield on Tuesday? Round to the nearest tenth of a percent. 2.9%
   b. At what price did Zyco close on Monday? $71.05
   c. What was the yield at Monday's close? Round to the nearest tenth of a percent. 3%

Market Data, Close on June 20								
52-week High	52-week Low	Symbol	Stock	Last	Change	Sales 100s	High	Low
143.25	73.25	PCU	Southern Copper Corp.	108.88	3.61	2643.7	110.68	105.68
42.97	32.95	T	AT&T, Inc.	34.43	−0.72	43386.8	35.59	34.41
131.82	42.24	ESI	ITT Ed Services	88.40	3.91	3429.5	90.71	82.06
50.48	36.01	JPM	JPMorgan Chase & Co.	37.86	−0.79	553772	39.19	36.95

10. Use the table above to answer the following questions.

a. What was the difference between the 52-week high and the 52-week low for one share of AT&T? $10.02

b. What was the difference between the day's high and low for one share of Southern Copper? $5.00

c. Which stock had a close that was furthest from the day's low? ITT Ed Services

d. Determine the close on June 19 for JPMorgan Chase. $38.65

e. How many shares of ITT were traded on June 20? 342,950

f. What was the percent net change from June 19 to June 20 for AT&T? Round to the nearest hundredth of a percent. −2.05%

g. Which stock had a day's high that was approximately 30% less than its 52-week high? ITT

h. On June 19, there were 59,945,400 shares of JPM traded. What was the difference in the number of shares traded from June 19 to June 20? 4,568,200

11. Use the stock bar chart to answer the questions below.

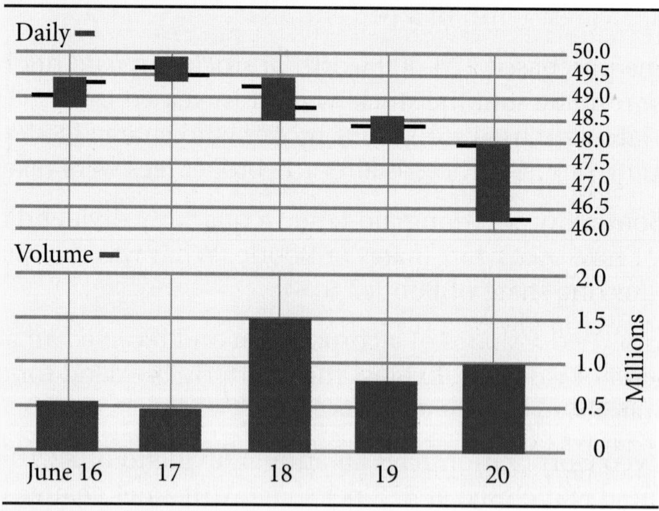

a. What was the day's open on June 17? about $49.60

b. What was the approximate difference between the day's high and low on June 18? approximately $49.45 – $48.50 = $0.95

c. On what day was the close also the day's low? June 20

d. Write the approximate volume for June 19. 750,000

12. Use the candlestick chart to answer the questions below.
   a. What was the approximate low on June 20? $24.13
   b. What was the approximate high on this date? $24.62
   c. What was the difference between the opening price and the close? $0.35
   d. What does the red candlestick color indicate? The opening price was greater than the closing price.

13. Lea owns 800 shares of ABC, Incorporated. On April 6 the corporation instituted a 5-for-2 stock split. Before the split, each share was worth $42.60.
   a. How many shares did Lea hold after the split? 2,000
   b. What was the post-split price per share? $17.04
   c. Show that the split was a monetary non-event for Lea. Pre-split value was $34,080; post-split value is $34,080.

14. Gene owns 1,200 shares of XYX Corporation. The company instituted a 1-for-10 reverse stock split on November 7. The pre-split market price per share was $1.20.
   a. How many shares did Gene hold after the split? 120
   b. What was the post-split price per share? $12.00
   c. Show that the split was a monetary non-event for Gene. Pre-split market value was $1,440; post-split market value is $1,440.

15. Use the table of closing prices for Microsoft. Round answers to the nearest cent. See margin.
   a. Determine the 3-day moving averages.
   b. Determine the 10-day moving averages.

Date	Close	3-day Averages	10-day Averages
23-May	28.05		
27-May	28.44		
28-May	28.18		
29-May	28.31		
30-May	28.32		
2-Jun	27.80		
3-Jun	27.31		
4-Jun	27.54		
5-Jun	28.30		
6-Jun	27.49		
9-Jun	27.71		
10-Jun	27.89		
11-Jun	27.12		
12-Jun	28.24		
13-Jun	29.07		
16-Jun	28.93		

Use the following stock market ticker to answer Exercises 16 and 17.

GE 12.5K@26.13▲1.13 F .67K@5.01▼0.38 C 3K@16.19▲ 1.47 T 1.6K@26.14▼1.08

16. Nick bought some shares of Ford Motor Company (F).
   a. How many shares did Nick buy? 670
   b. How much did each share cost? $5.01
   c. What was the value of Nick's trade? $3,356.70

17. Patrick sold his shares of AT&T (T).
   a. How many shares did he sell? 1,600
   b. For how much did each share sell? $26.14
   c. Based on Patrick's sale, what was the closing price of T on the previous trading day? $27.22

18. The stock in a real estate corporation was selling for $78 per share with an annual dividend of $1.86. It underwent a 3-for-2 split.
   a. What was the value of one share of the stock after the split? $52
   b. What was the annual dividend after the split? $1.24

19. A stock that was selling for $\$x$ per share underwent a y-for-p split. It was originally paying an annual dividend of $\$d$ per share. Express the annual dividend after the split algebraically. $\frac{pd}{y}$

20. Suki purchased $9,600 worth of stock and paid her broker a 1.75% broker fee. She had an immediate need for cash and was forced to sell the stock when it was worth $8,800. She used a discount broker who charged $32.50 per trade. Compute Suki's net loss after the broker fees were taken out. $1,000.50

ANSWERS

15a. 3-day averages: 28-May: 28.22; 29-May: 28.31; 30-May: 28.27; 2-Jun: 28.14; 3-Jun: 27.81; 4-Jun: 27.55; 5-Jun: 27.72; 6-Jun: 27.78; 9-Jun: 27.83; 10-Jun: 27.70; 11-Jun: 27.57; 12-Jun: 27.75; 13-Jun: 28.14; 16-Jun: 28.75

15b. 10-day averages: 6-Jun: 27.97; 9-Jun: 27.94; 10-Jun: 27.89; 11-Jun: 27.78; 12-Jun: 27.77; 13-Jun: 27.85; 16-Jun: 27.96

CHAPTER

2 Modeling a Business

Business, more than any other occupation, is a continual dealing with the future; it is a continual calculation, an instinctive exercise in foresight.

Henry R. Luce, Publisher and Philanthropist

What do you think Henry Luce meant in this quote?

What do you think?

Answers should contain a reference to the fact that in business, it is important to look ahead, to predict, and to calculate and weigh all options when making decisions.

TEACHING RESOURCES

Instructor's Resource CD

Exam *View*® CD, Ch. 2

eHomework, Ch. 2

www.cengage.com/school/math/financialalgebra

If you do an Internet search for the word *model*, you will find it used in a variety of contexts. There are computer models, medical models, working models, scientific models, business models, data models, and more. In each of these cases, a model is a representation. It is a well-formulated plan that can be used to represent a situation. Often, the model is a simplified version of the actual scenario. In this chapter, you will learn how to use mathematics to model a new business venture. You will use variables and examine relationships among those variables as you explore the business concepts of expense, revenue, and profit. Statistics play an important role in the creation and use of a business model. You will represent real-world situations with equations, analyze the data that has been derived from those equations, use data to make predictions, and generate and interpret graphs in order to maximize profit. As you work through this chapter, you will realize the importance of Henry Luce's words. The models you explore will examine the future success or failure of a product and will help you make decisions that will mold and shape its future.

Really?

Think of all the successful brand name products you use on a daily basis. Imagine all of the brain power and creative energy that went into inventing, perfecting, advertising, and selling these items. With all the resources major corporations have to make sure a product will sell, can you ever imagine a successful corporation producing a product that is a failure?

The business world is full of products that have failed. Some of the failures are from very well-known companies, such as The Coca-Cola Company, Ford Motor Company, and Sony Corporation of America. Below are three famous failures.

- **New Coke** In April 1985, The Coca-Cola Company changed the recipe of Coca-Cola, and the public was outraged. By July 1985, the company decided to bring back the original formula for Coca-Cola.
- **Edsel** The Ford Motor Company unveiled its new 1958 Edsel in the fall of 1957. The car had a radically different look and was often described as ugly. The buying public did not like the sound of the name, and the advertising campaign had flaws. By 1959, production ceased on the Edsel, and the term is still used as a synonym for a failed design.
- **Sony Betamax** In the late 1970s, Sony offered the first home video tape recorder, called the Betamax. Other manufacturers soon offered their own units. The units offered by other manufacturers all used the VHS tape format, and movies could be played on any brand's machine, except Sony's machine. Eventually, Sony had to abandon Betamax and issued its own VHS format tape recorders.

You can do online research to find more details on these and other famous product failures.

CHAPTER OVERVIEW

In this chapter, mathematical modeling is used to model a business. Point out that the word model can be used as a noun or a verb. You can create a mathematical *model*, or *model* a real-life situation mathematically. Students learn to graph and interpret scatterplots, linear functions, and parabolas.

REALLY? REALLY!

Encourage students to look on the Internet to find other product failures. Even Albert Einstein had failed inventions. Have students find the failed inventions of Einstein. Make sure students understand the difference between a failed invention and a product that just doesn't appeal to consumers.

Really!

To guess is cheap. To guess wrongly is expensive.
Ancient Chinese Proverb

2-1 Interpret Scatterplots

Objectives

- Graph bivariate data.
- Interpret trends based on scatterplots.
- Draw lines and curves of best fit.

Common Core

N-Q2, N-Q3, F-IF7a, F-IF8, S-ID6, S-ID9

Key Terms

- data
- univariate data
- bivariate data
- scatterplot
- trend
- correlation
- positive correlation
- negative correlation
- causal relationship
- explanatory variable
- response variable

CCSS Warm-Up

Use a table of values and graph paper to graph the line represented by the equation $y = 2x - 3$.

WARM-UP SOLUTION

The solution is a graph.

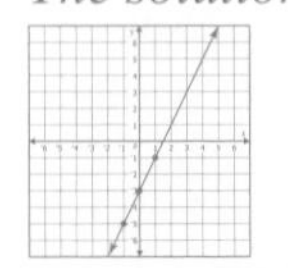

EXAMINE THE QUESTION

Show students how a scatterplot can depict a trend, and how trends affect business decisions.

Give students several examples of univariate and bivariate data.

How do scatterplots display trends?

Any set of numbers is called a set of **data**. A single set of numbers is called **univariate data**. When a business owner keeps a list of monthly sales amounts, the data in the list is univariate data. Data that lists pairs of numbers and shows a relationship between the paired numbers is called **bivariate data**. If a business owner keeps records of the number of units sold each month and the monthly sales amount, the set is bivariate data.

A **scatterplot** is a graph that shows bivariate data using points on a graph. Scatterplots may show a general pattern, or **trend**, within the data. A trend means a relationship exists between the two variables.

A trend may show a **correlation**, or *association*, between two variables. A **positive correlation** exists if the value of one variable increases when the value of the other increases. A **negative correlation** exists if the value of one variable decreases when the value of the other variable increases.

A trend may also show a **causal relationship**, which means one variable *caused* a change in the other variable. The variable which causes the change in the other variable is the **explanatory variable**. The affected variable is the **response variable**. While a trend may indicate a correlation or a causal relationship, it does not have to. If two variables are correlated, it does not mean that one caused the other.

Skills and Strategies

You can graph a scatterplot by hand. You can also graph a scatterplot on a graphing calculator.

EXAMPLE 1

Rachael runs a concession stand at the park, where she sells water bottles. She keeps a list of each day's high temperature and the number of water bottles she sells each day. Rachael is looking for trends that relate the daily high temperature to the number of water bottles she sells each day. She thinks these two variables might be related and wants to investigate possible trends using a scatterplot. Below is the list of her ordered pairs.

(65, 102), (71, 133), (79, 144), (80, 161), (86, 191),

(86, 207), (91, 235), (95, 237), (100, 243)

Construct a scatterplot by hand on graph paper. Then enter the data in a graphing calculator to create a scatterplot.

SOLUTION In each ordered pair, the first number is the high temperature for the day in degrees Fahrenheit. The second number is the number of water bottles sold. Think of these as the x- and y-coordinates. The scatterplot is drawn by plotting the points with the given coordinates.

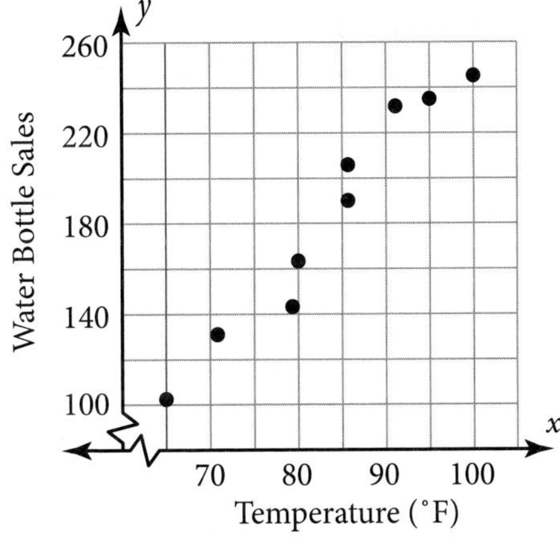

Choose a scale for each axis that allows the scatterplot to fit in the required space. To choose the scale, look at the greatest and least numbers that must be plotted for each variable. Label the axes accordingly. Then plot each point with a dot. Notice that you do not connect the dots in a scatterplot.

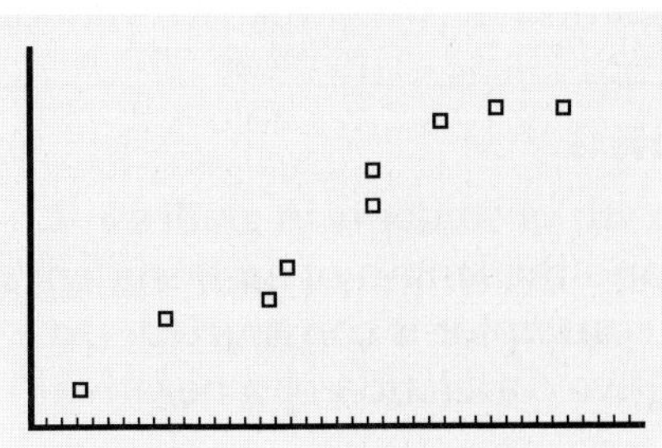

Use the statistics features on your graphing calculator to graph the scatterplot. Your display should look similar to the one shown.

TEACH

As students learn about scatterplots, be sure they realize that a scatterplot is a graph of a set of ordered pairs that may or may not show a relationship. They likely remember that to show an equation, ordered pairs are graphed on a coordinate plane and then connected. Point out that points graphed on a scatterplot are not connected. The position of the points are examined to determine the existence and strength of a correlation.

Spend time discussing the difference between correlation and causation. Students need to understand that just because two sets of data have a correlation, there may or may not be a causation between the sets.

EXAMPLE 1

Discuss with students the likelihood that this problem involves causation—the temperature is responsible for an increase in the water sales.

Compare this example to the following scenario:

As the sales of ice cream increase, the number of lifeguard rescues increases. Students should recognize that ice cream does not cause the need for rescues, but both increase as the temperature increases. When it gets hotter, more people swim (making for an increased need for lifeguard rescues), and more people eat ice cream.

CHECK YOUR UNDERSTANDING

Answer approximately 120 water bottles

■ **CHECK YOUR UNDERSTANDING**

If the temperature reaches 68 degrees Fahrenheit tomorrow, about how many water bottles do you predict will be sold? Explain.

EXAMPLE 2

Ask students what they think the scatterplot would look like if temperature was compared to sweater sales. They should realize that as temperatures increase, sales of sweaters decrease.

CHECK YOUR UNDERSTANDING

Answer Because sales decrease when the temperature increases, the correlation is negative. This correlation is probably causal, so temperature is the explanatory variable and hot chocolate sales is the response variable.

EXAMPLE 3

Compare the trends in the scatterplots to what students remember about slopes of lines. Explain that the sign of the "slope" of the scatterplot is the same as the sign of the correlation.

Ask students to think of two variables that are positively correlated, but one variable does not cause the other.

CHECK YOUR UNDERSTANDING

Answer Taller people generally have larger feet, so a positive correlation is expected. There is causation.

EXAMPLE 2

Rachael wants to interpret the trend shown in the scatterplot. What do you notice about the relationship between temperature and water bottle sales? Is there an explanatory variable and a response variable?

SOLUTION As the temperature rises, the water bottle sales generally increase. So, there is a correlation between the data. Because the y-values increase when the x-values increase, the correlation is *positive*. Additionally, the rise in temperature *caused* the increase in the number of bottles sold. Therefore, the temperature is the *explanatory variable* and the number of bottles sold is the *response variable*.

■ **CHECK YOUR UNDERSTANDING**

A local coffee shop sells hot chocolate. The manager keeps track of the temperature for the entire year and the hot chocolate sales. A scatterplot is graphed with temperature on the horizontal axis and hot chocolate sales on the vertical axis. Do you think the scatterplot shows a positive or negative correlation? Is there causation? Explain.

EXAMPLE 3

Determine if the following scatterplot depicts a positive correlation or a negative correlation.

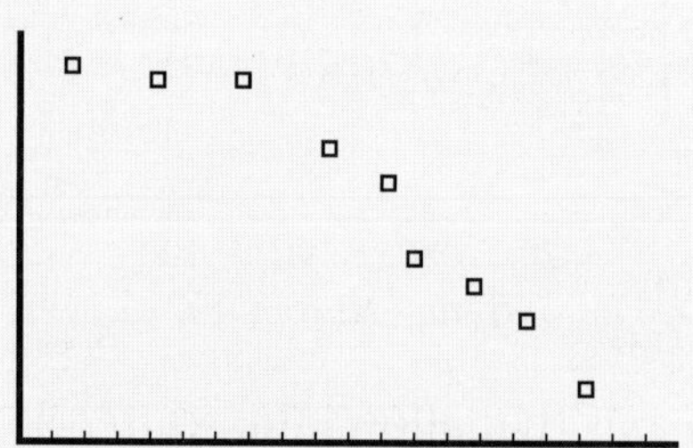

SOLUTION As the x-values increase, the y-values decrease. Therefore, this scatterplot shows a negative correlation between the two variables.

■ **CHECK YOUR UNDERSTANDING**

A local medical school is studying growth of students in grades 1–12. The height of each student in inches and the length of each student's foot in centimeters is recorded, and a scatterplot is constructed. Do you think the scatterplot shows a positive correlation or a negative correlation? Is there causation?

EXAMPLE 4

An elementary school principal compiled the following data about ten students at Compsett Elementary School. The first number represents a student's height in inches. The second number is the student's reading level. Create a scatterplot of the data. Do you think a person's height causes a higher reading level?

Height (inches)	Reading Level
48	5.8
63	9.2
49	5.5
43	4.1
46	6.1
55	7.6
59	8.1
60	10.0
47	4.9
50	7.7

SOLUTION The scatterplot shows a positive correlation.

A person's height does not cause a higher reading level. Most likely, both height and reading level for elementary school students increase with age. Keep in mind that if two variables are correlated, they are associated in some way. The student's height does not *cause* the reading levels to be a certain value.

■ CHECK YOUR UNDERSTANDING

Think of an example of data that might have a negative correlation but there is no causation.

EXAMPLE 5

The scatterplot at the right shows the relationship between the number of text messages made by each of ten juniors while studying for Mr. Galati's chemistry test last week and their scores on the test. Describe the trends you see in the data.

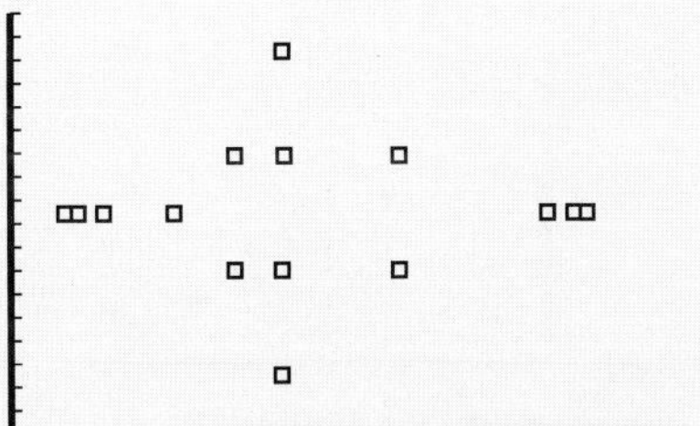

SOLUTION As the number of text messages increases, test grades do not increase, so there is no positive correlation. As the number of text messages increases, test grades do not decrease, so there is no negative correlation. There is no trend in the data, so there is no correlation.

■ CHECK YOUR UNDERSTANDING

Students in a biology class measure the circumference and diameter of every tree on the school property. The students create a table of ordered pairs and plan to draw a scatterplot. Should there be a positive correlation, a negative correlation, or no correlation?

EXAMPLE 4

Point out to students that reading level and height both increase due to their dependence on age. In this case, age is called a *lurking variable*.

CHECK YOUR UNDERSTANDING

Answer Answers will vary. Sample answer: miles a car is driven and balance of a loan on the car.

EXAMPLE 5

In the next lesson students will learn about describing a correlation numerically, using a correlation coefficient.

CHECK YOUR UNDERSTANDING

Answer Positive correlation based on the formula $C = \pi d$, as the diameter increases, the circumference increases.

Applications

To guess is cheap. To guess wrongly is expensive.
Ancient Chinese Proverb

TEACH

Vocabulary Review
Remind students that the terms *explanatory* and *response* are used when causation is implied. Have students offer original pairs of variables, tell how they are correlated, and determine if there seems to be causation.

ANSWERS

1. When making a business decision, it is wise to use available data and graphs to analyze trends, rather than guessing and subsequently investing money on a "hunch."

4c. hours-explanatory; paycheck-response

5a.

1. Use what you learned in this lesson to explain how the quote can be interpreted by a business person. See margin.

2. A scatterplot shows the number of days that have passed and the number of days left in a month. The explanatory variable is the number of days that have passed. The response variable is the number of days left. Is there a positive or negative correlation? Explain. Negative correlation; as the number of days that have passed increases, the number of days left decreases.

3. Examine each scatterplot. Identify each as showing a positive correlation, a negative correlation, or no correlation.

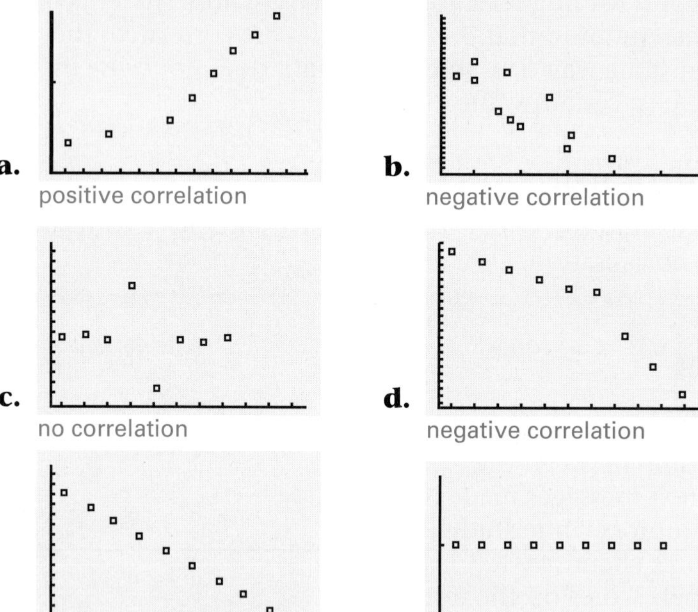

4. In a–d, each set of bivariate data has a causal relationship. Determine the explanatory and response variables for each set of data.

a. height and weight of a student height-explanatory; weight-response

b. grade on a math test and number of hours the student studied hours-explanatory; grade-response

c. number of hours worked and paycheck amount See margin.

d. number of gallons of gas consumed and weight of a car weight-explanatory; gallons-response

5. The table shows the personal income per capita (per person) in the United States for seven selected years.

a. Draw a scatterplot for the data. See margin.

b. Describe the correlation. positive correlation

Year	Per Capita Income in Dollars
2002	30,838
2003	31,530
2004	33,157
2005	34,690
2006	36,794
2007	38,615
2008	39,751

6. The following set of ordered pairs gives the results of a science experiment. Twelve people were given different daily doses of vitamin C, in milligrams, for a year. This is the x-value. They reported the number of colds they got during the year. This is the y-value.

(100, 4), (100, 4), (100, 3), (250, 3), (250, 2), (250, 2),

(500, 1), (500, 2), (500, 1), (1,000, 1), (1,000, 2), (1,000, 1)

a. Construct a scatterplot. See margin.
b. Describe the correlation. negative correlation
c. Should the scientists label the vitamin C intake the explanatory variable and the number of colds the response variable? Explain. Yes; it seems to be causal.

7. The enrollment at North Shore High School is given in the table. In each year, the number of students on the baseball team was 19.

Year	Enrollment
2006	801
2007	834
2008	844
2009	897
2010	922

a. If x represents the year and y represents the enrollment, draw a scatterplot to depict the data. See margin.
b. Describe the correlation from the scatterplot. positive correlation
c. If x represents the enrollment and y represents the number of students on the baseball team, draw a scatterplot to depict the data. See margin.
d. Describe the correlation from the scatterplot. no correlation

8. The MyTunes Song Service sells music downloads. Over the past few years, the service has lowered its prices. The table shows the price per song and the number of songs downloaded per day at that price.

Price per Song	Number of Downloads (in thousands)
\$0.89	1,212
\$0.79	1,704
\$0.69	1,760
\$0.59	1,877
\$0.49	1,944
\$0.39	2,011

a. Examine the data without drawing a scatterplot. Describe any trends you see. See margin.
b. Draw a scatterplot. Describe the correlation. See margin.
c. Approximate the number of downloads at a price of \$0.54 per song. Explain your reasoning. See margin.

9. Perform an online search to answer the questions below. Answers vary.
a. Find your state's population for each of the last ten years.
b. Create a table of bivariate data. Let x represent the year, and let y represent the population.
c. Create a scatterplot for the data.
d. Describe the correlation between the year and your state's population.

TEACH

Data Entry

Students need to double check calculator list entries before making calculations. The calculator will display incorrect answers just as quickly as it will correct answers if data are entered incorrectly. It is very easy to make a mistake entering data. Also remind them to check the number of pieces of data they entered, to make sure it agrees with the original list.

ANSWERS

6a.

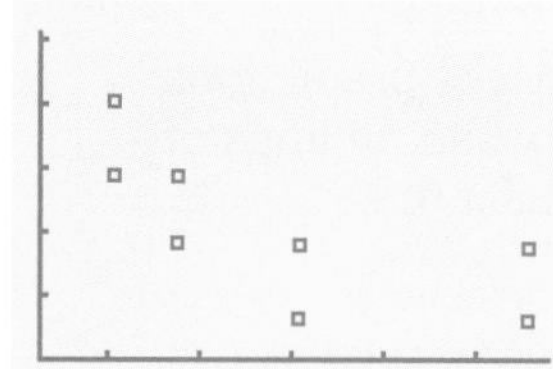

7a.

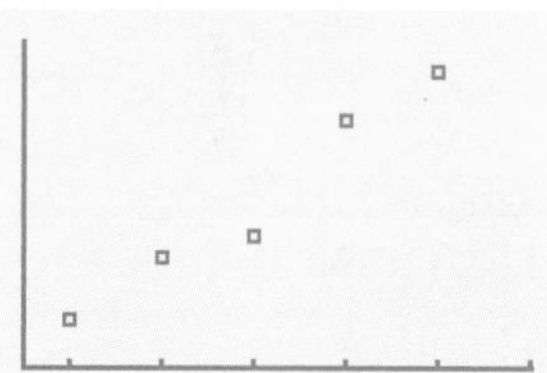

7c.

8a. As x decreases, y increases.
8b. There is a negative correlation.

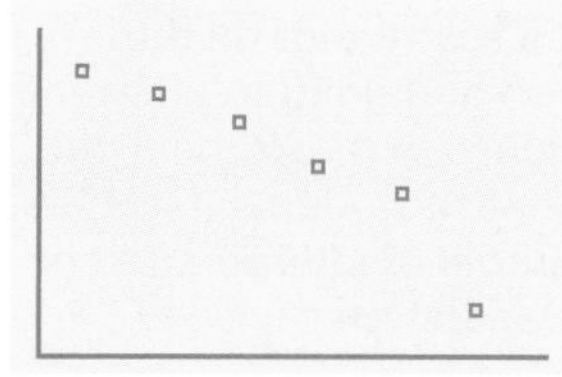

8c. Approximately 1,910,500 songs. The average of \$0.59 and \$0.49 is \$0.54 and the average of 1,877 and 1,944 is 1,910.5.

The only useful function of a statistician is to make predictions, and thus provide a basis for action.

William Edwards Deming, Professor and Statistician

2-2 Linear Regression

Objectives

- Be able to fit a regression line to a scatterplot.
- Find and interpret correlation coefficients.
- Make predictions based on lines of best fit.

Common Core

N-Q1, N-Q2, N-Q3, A-CED2, F-IF1, F-IF7a, F-IF8, S-ID6c, S-ID8

Key Terms

- line of best fit
- linear regression line
- least squares line
- domain
- range
- interpolation
- extrapolation
- correlation coefficient
- strong correlation
- weak correlation
- moderate correlation

CCSS Warm-Up

Find the slope and y-intercept of the graphs of each line.

1. $y = 8x - 70$ **2.** $2y = 8x - 70$ **3.** $2y + 8x = 70$

1. slope: 8; The y-intercept is -70.
2. slope: 4; The y-intercept is -35.
3. slope: -4; The y-intercept is 35.

EXAMINE THE QUESTION

The trends shown by scatterplots can be used to predict the future. But making a prediction without a line of best fit to guide you would be arbitrary. Point out that changes could make the prediction inaccurate. However, the predictions are based on current data and are better than haphazard guessing.

CLASS DISCUSSION

Put a scatterplot on the board and point to different x-values in the domain. For each, ask students if it is an example of interpolation or extrapolation.

What can you tell about the sign of the correlation coefficient and the slope of the regression line?

How can the past predict the future?

Many scatterplot points can be approximated by a single line that best fits the scattered points. This line may be called a: **line of best fit**, **linear regression line**, or **least squares line**. This line can be used to display a trend and predict corresponding variables for different situations. It is more efficient to rely on the single line rather than the scatterplot points because the line can be represented by an equation.

Recall that the **domain** is a set of first elements of the ordered pairs, and the **range** is the set of corresponding second elements. **Interpolation** means to predict corresponding y-values, given an x-value within the domain. **Extrapolation** means to predict corresponding y-values outside of the domain.

The scatterplot shown is from Example 1 in the previous lesson. The line shown is a line of best fit because it closely follows the trend of the data points. The blue labels are included to identify the axes, but will not be shown on a calculator display. Generally, the distance the points lie from the line of best fit determines how good a predictor the line is. If most of the points lie close to the line, the line is a better predictor of the trend of the data than if the points lie far from the line. If the points lie far from the line, the line is not good for predicting a trend.

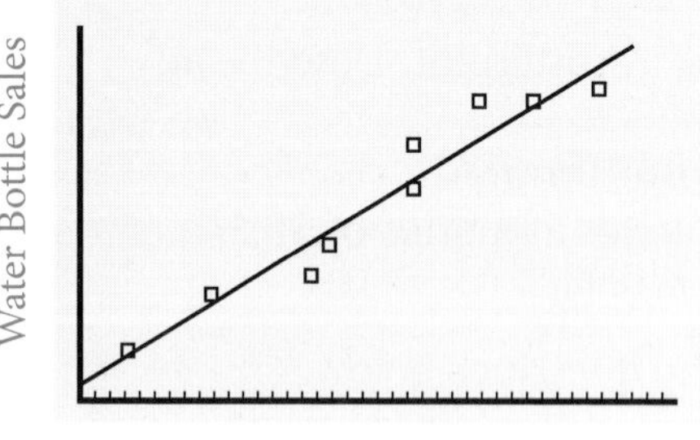

The **correlation coefficient**, r, is a number between -1 and 1 inclusive that is used to judge how closely the line fits the data. Negative correlation coefficients show negative correlations, and positive correlation coefficients show positive correlations. If the correlation coefficient is near 0, there is little or no correlation. Correlation coefficients with an absolute value greater than 0.75 are **strong correlations**. Correlation coefficients with an absolute value less than 0.3 are **weak correlations**. Any other correlation is a **moderate correlation**.

Skills and Strategies

The line of best fit and the correlation coefficient can be found using a graphing calculator.

EXAMPLE 1

Find the equation of the linear regression line for Rachael's scatterplot in Example 1 from Lesson 2-1. Round the slope and y-intercept to the nearest hundredth. The points are given below.

(65, 102), (71, 133), (79, 144), (80, 161), (86, 191),

(86, 207), (91, 235), (95, 237), (100, 243)

SOLUTION Although it is possible to find the linear regression equation using paper and pencil, it is a lengthy process. Using the linear regression feature on a graphing calculator produces more accurate results.

Enter the ordered pairs into your calculator. Then use the statistics menu to calculate the linear regression equation. The equation is of the form $y = mx + b$, where m is the slope and b is the y-intercept. Rounding the slope and y-intercept to the nearest hundredth, the equation of the regression line is $y = 4.44x - 187.67$.

Note that calculators may use different letters to represent the slope or the y-intercept. Remember that the coefficient of x is the slope.

CHECK YOUR UNDERSTANDING

Find the equation of the linear regression line of the scatterplot defined by these points: (1, 56), (2, 45), (4, 20), (3, 30), and (5, 9). Round the slope and y-intercept to the nearest hundredth.

EXAMPLE 2

Interpret the slope as a rate for Rachael's linear regression line. Use the equation from Example 1.

SOLUTION The formula for slope is $m = \frac{\Delta y}{\Delta x}$. The range values, y, represent bottles sold and the domain values, x, represent temperatures. The slope is a rate of bottles per degree. The slope is 4.44, which means that for each one-degree increase in temperature, 4.44 more water bottles will be sold. Rachael cannot sell a fraction of a water bottle, so she will sell approximately 4 more bottles for each degree the temperature rises.

CHECK YOUR UNDERSTANDING

Approximately how many more water bottles will Rachael sell if the temperature increases 2 degrees?

TEACH

To enter regression lines and have them graphed on the calculator's display along with the scatterplot, students need to be sure they have the scatterplot and the equation set to display on the same screen.

EXAMPLE 1

Different calculators have keys in different locations with different names, but the basic functions are similar. Remind students to input data carefully. An incorrect entry results in an incorrect answer.

CHECK YOUR UNDERSTANDING

Answer $y = -11.9x + 67.7$

EXAMPLE 2

Review the units of the slopes for the examples shown throughout Lesson 2-1, so students understand that the slope is a rate of change.

CHECK YOUR UNDERSTANDING

Answer 9 bottles

EXAMPLE 3

Ask students if this is an example of interpolation or extrapolation.

EXAMPLE 3

Rachael is stocking her concession stand for a day in which the temperature is expected to reach 106 degrees Fahrenheit. How many water bottles should she pack?

SOLUTION The linear regression equation tells Rachael the approximate number of bottles she should sell given a specific temperature. Substitute 106 for x in the equation, and compute y, the number of water bottles she should expect to sell.

Equation of the regression line	$y = 4.44x - 187.67$
Substitute 106 for x.	$y = 4.44(106) - 187.67$
Simplify.	$y = 282.97$

If the trend continues and the temperature reaches 106 degrees Fahrenheit, Rachael should expect to sell approximately 283 water bottles. She should stock 283 bottles. This is an example of extrapolation because 106 degrees Fahrenheit was not between the high and low x-values of the original domain.

CHECK YOUR UNDERSTANDING

Answer 181 water bottles; it is an example of interpolation.

CHECK YOUR UNDERSTANDING

How many water bottles should Rachael pack if the temperature forecasted were 83 degrees? Is this an example of interpolation or extrapolation? Round to the nearest integer.

EXAMPLE 4

Have students identify all correlations as strong, moderate, or weak.

It is a common error for students to ignore negative signs when reading correlation coefficients on calculator displays. Caution them to note the sign of the coefficient.

EXAMPLE 4

Find the correlation coefficient to the nearest hundredth for the linear regression for Rachael's data. Interpret the correlation coefficient.

SOLUTION Use a graphing calculator to find the correlation coefficient.

Round r to the nearest hundredth. $r = 0.97$

Because 0.97 is positive and greater than 0.75, there is a strong positive correlation between the high temperature and the number of water bottles sold.

CHECK YOUR UNDERSTANDING

Answer $r = -0.998$; this coefficient represents a strong negative correlation.

CHECK YOUR UNDERSTANDING

Find the correlation coefficient to the thousandth for the linear regression for the data in Check Your Understanding for Example 1. Interpret the correlation coefficient.

EXTEND YOUR UNDERSTANDING

Answer The correlation is weak and negative.

EXTEND YOUR UNDERSTANDING

Carlos entered data into his calculator and found a correlation coefficient of -0.28. Interpret this correlation coefficient.

Applications

The only useful function of a statistician is to make predictions, and thus provide a basis for action.
William Edwards Deming, Professor and Statistician

1. Apply what you have learned in this lesson to give an interpretation of the quote. See margin.

2. Over the past four years, Reggie noticed that as the price of a slice of pizza increased, her college tuition also increased. She found the correlation coefficient was $r = 0.49$. Which of the following scatterplots most accurately displays Reggie's data? Explain. See margin.

a. 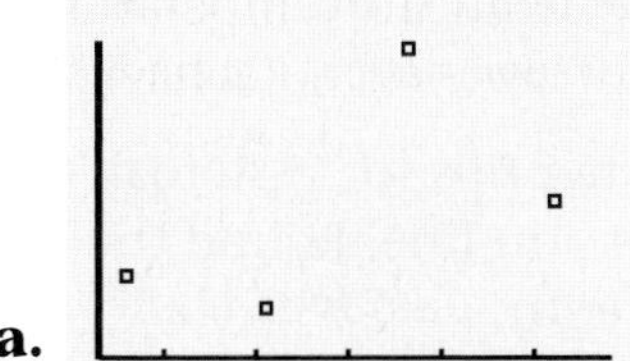

b. 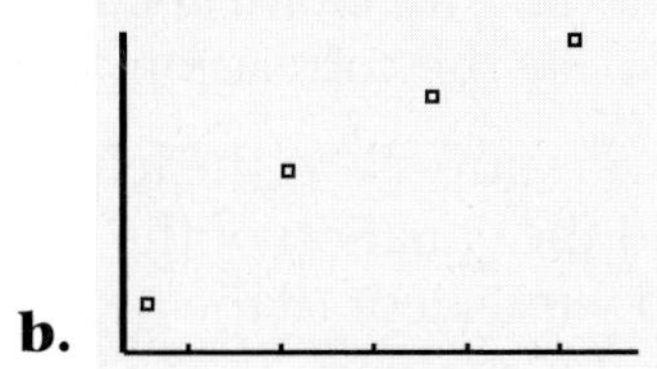

3. In Exercise 2, would the price of a slice of pizza be labeled as the explanatory variable and the tuition as the response variable? Explain. No, there is no apparent causation. Both prices may have increased due to inflation over time.

4. The table gives enrollments at North Shore High School.
   a. Find the equation of the regression line. Round the slope and y-intercept to the nearest hundredth. $y = 30.5x - 60{,}384.4$
   b. What is the slope of the linear regression line? 30.5
   c. What are the units of the slope expressed as a rate? students per year
   d. Based on the linear regression line, how many students will be enrolled in the year 2016? Round to the nearest integer. 1,104 students
   e. Is your answer to part d an example of interpolation or extrapolation? Explain. Extrapolation; 2016 is outside of the domain.
   f. Find the correlation coefficient to the nearest hundredth. $r = 0.98$
   g. Describe the correlation. strong positive correlation

Year	Enrollment
2006	801
2007	834
2008	844
2009	897
2010	922

5. Examine the data from Exercise 4.
   a. Find the mean (arithmetic average) of the five years. 2008
   b. Find the mean of the five enrollment figures. 859.6
   c. Create an ordered pair whose x-value is the mean of the years and whose y-value is the mean of the enrollments. (2008, 859.6)
   d. Show that the ordered pair satisfies the linear regression equation. What does this mean regarding the regression line? See margin.

6. Describe each of the following correlation coefficients using the terms strong, moderate, or weak and positive or negative.
   a. $r = 0.21$ weak positive
   b. $r = -0.87$ strong negative
   c. $r = 0.55$ moderate positive
   d. $r = -0.099$ weak negative
   e. $r = 0.99$ strong positive
   f. $r = -0.49$ moderate negative

TEACH

Investigate Correlation Coefficient
At some point, have students switch the x and y variables and find the correlation coefficient. They should see it remains the same. However, the slope of the regression line changes.

ANSWERS

1. The ability to make predictions is valuable in many fields. It allows you to be proactive in regards to the future, rather than just assuming you have no control over the future.
2. Graph a shows a moderate correlation that could be described by $r = 0.49$. Graph b is almost linear and shows a strong correlation.

5d. $y = 30.5x - 60{,}384.4$
$y = 30.5(2008) - 60{,}384.4 = 859.6$. The linear regression line always passes through the point formed by the averages of each set of data.

TEACH

Examine Scatterplots

For all examples, ask students about the shape of the scatterplots (linear or not), the sign of the association (positive or negative), and the strength (strong, moderate, weak) of the correlation. They should get comfortable using these terms to describe scatterplots.

7. The table gives the number of songs downloaded from MyTunes at different prices per song.

Price per Song	Number of Downloads (in thousands)
$0.89	1,212
$0.79	1,704
$0.69	1,760
$0.59	1,877
$0.49	1,944
$0.39	2,011

   a. Find the equation of the linear regression line. Round the slope and *y*-intercept to the nearest hundredth. $y = -1{,}380.57x + 2{,}634.90$

   b. What is the slope of the linear regression line? −1,380.57

   c. What are the units of the slope when it is expressed as a rate? thousands of downloads per dollar

   d. Based on the linear regression line, how many thousands of downloads would MyTunes expect if the price was changed to $0.45? Round to the nearest integer. 2,014

   e. Is your answer to part d an example of interpolation or extrapolation? interpolation

   f. Find the correlation coefficient to the nearest hundredth. $r = -0.90$

   g. Describe the correlation. strong negative correlation

Amount of Restaurant Bill ($)	Tip Amount ($)
45.55	7.00
52.00	15.00
66.00	6.00
24.44	6.00
57.90	15.00
89.75	23.00
33.00	8.00

8. Julie is a waitress. On the left is a log of her tips for yesterday's shift.

   a. Find the equation of the linear regression line. Round the slope and *y*-intercept to the nearest hundredth. $y = 0.22x - 0.27$

   b. What is the slope of the linear regression line? 0.22

   c. What are the units of the slope when it is expressed as a rate? See margin.

   d. Based on the linear regression line, what tip would Julie receive if the restaurant bill were $120? Round to the nearest dollar. $26

   e. Is your answer to part d an example of interpolation or extrapolation? Explain. Extrapolation; $120 is outside of the original domain.

   f. Find the correlation coefficient for this data. Round to the nearest hundredth. $r = 0.75$

   g. Describe the correlation. moderate positive correlation

   h. Based on the linear regression line, Julie creates a spreadsheet to compute predicted tips for any restaurant bill amount. Write the formula that can be used to compute the predicted tips in column B. =A2*0.22–0.27

	A	B
1	Restaurant Bill	Predicted Tip
2		
3		
4		
5		

9. Explain why the sign of the slope of a regression line must be the same as the sign of the correlation coefficient. See margin.

10. Which of the following scatterplots shows a correct line of best fit? c

a. 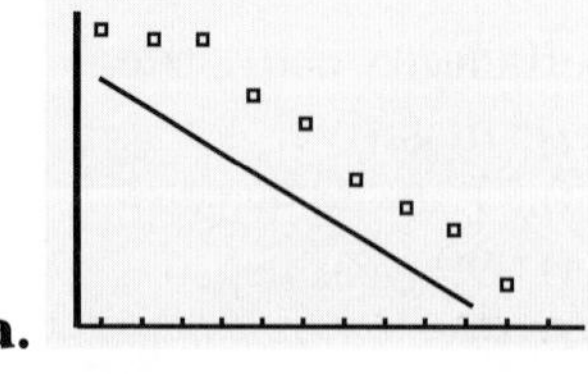

b. 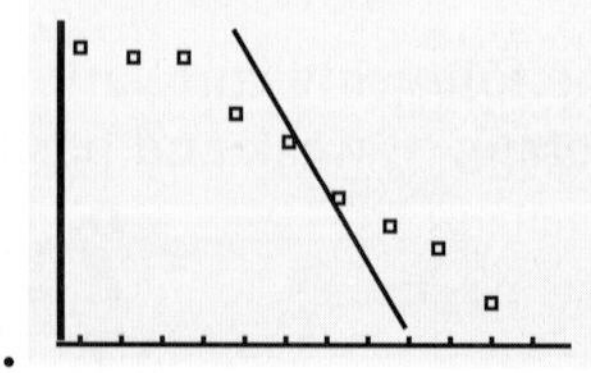

c. 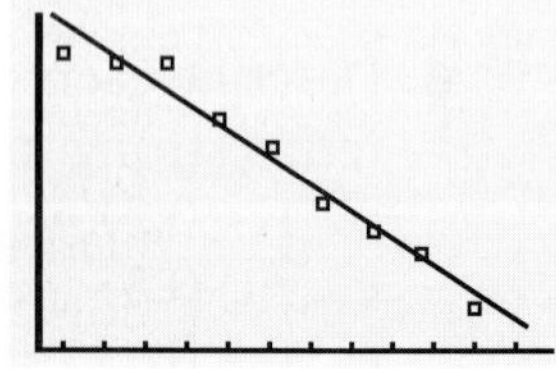

11. Is it possible for a linear regression line to go through every point on the scatterplot? Is it possible for a linear regression line to not go through any point on the scatterplot? See margin.

ANSWERS

8c. tip dollars per restaurant bill amount

9. A positive slope means the line is increasing, which means as *x* increases, *y* increases. If *y* increases as *x* increases, the correlation coefficient is positive. A negative slope means the line is decreasing, which means as *x* increases, *y* decreases. If *y* decreases as *x* increases, the correlation coefficient is negative.

11. Yes, if the points are linear, the regression line will go through every point. If the points are not linear, it may not go through any point on the scatterplot.

> *Teach a parrot the terms "supply and demand" and you've got an economist.*
>
> **Thomas Carlyle,** Philosopher

Supply and Demand 2-3

Key Terms
- widget
- function
- demand function
- demand
- supply
- wholesale price
- markup
- retail price
- equilibrium
- shift

Objectives
- Understand the slopes of the supply and demand curves.
- Find points of equilibrium.

Common Core
A-CED2, F-IF1, F-IF4, F-IF5, F-IF7a , F-IF8, S-ID6, S-ID8

CCSS Warm-Up

Determine the sign (+ or −) of the slope of each graph.

1. $3y = 9 - 4x$ **2.** $3y = 4x - 9$ **3.** $4x + 3y = 9$

1. negative 2. positive 3. negative

How do manufacturers decide the quantity of a product they will produce?

EXAMINE THE QUESTION
Have students imagine they are starting a new business. What are the dangers of overproducing? (excess inventory and wasted money) What are the dangers of underproducing? (lost income) Deciding how many items to produce is not guesswork.

Economists often call a new, unnamed product a **widget**. If a business develops a new product, the number of items they need to manufacture is a key question they need to address. Graphs may be used to help answer this question. Such graphs compare the price of an item, p, and the quantity sold, q. The horizontal axis is labeled p and the vertical axis is labeled q. The set of p values on the horizontal axis is the *domain*. The set of q values on the vertical axis is the *range*. A **function** is a rule that assigns a unique member of the range to each element of the domain.

Graphs using the p- and q- axes can be used to model a trend in consumers' interest in a product. A **demand function** relates the quantity of a product to its price. If a widget has a low price, many people may want it and will be able to afford it, so a large quantity may be sold. If it has a high price, fewer widgets will be sold. As the price increases, **demand** (the quantity consumers want) is likely to decrease, and as price decreases, demand increases. The graph of the demand function has a negative slope. However, its curvature varies.

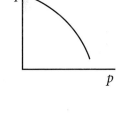

Graphs using p- and q- axes can also be used to model a trend in the manufacturing of a product. *Producers* provide **supply** (the quantity of items available to be sold). If a widget sells for a high price, the manufacturer may be willing to produce many items to maximize profit. If the widget sells for a lower price, the manufacturer may produce less. As price increases, supply increases. The graph of the supply function has a positive slope. Its curvature also varies.

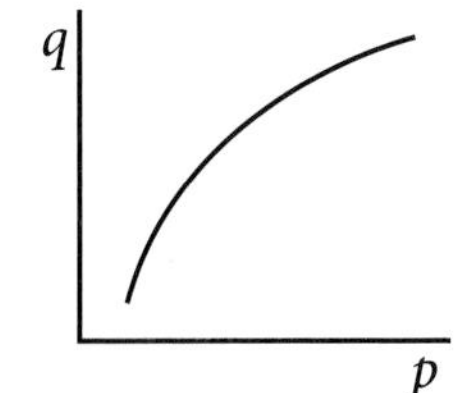

CLASS DISCUSSION

Give students other examples of functions, including non-numerical examples. For example, the initials function assigns first initials to people. The hair color function assigns a color to a person based on their hair color. Use examples such as these to show that two different elements of the domain could be mapped to the same element of the range.

Ask students about any products that are difficult to find because stores don't always have them in stock.

TEACH

Supply and demand are concepts that impact students' lives, yet they have probably never given much thought to them. Be sure they can give examples of the supply and demand for products they typically purchase or use.

EXAMPLE 1

Point out to students that the markup is not all profit. Markup costs are used to cover the store's expenses. Ask them to identify some of these expenses, which include rental costs, paying employees, advertising, utility costs, and purchasing store fixtures.

CHECK YOUR UNDERSTANDING

Answer $r - x$

Sometimes students have trouble expressing literal subtraction expressions, and they misplace the minuend and the subtrahend.

Economic decisions require research, and knowledge of the laws of supply and demand. To examine the law of supply and demand, graph both functions on the same axes. Examine what happens as the manufacturer sets different prices. Keep in mind that the manufacturer sells the items to retailers, such as stores, and not directly to the general public. The price the manufacturer charges the retailer is the **wholesale price**. Retailers increase the price a certain amount, called **markup**, so the retailer can make a profit. The price the retailer sells the item to the public for is the **retail price**.

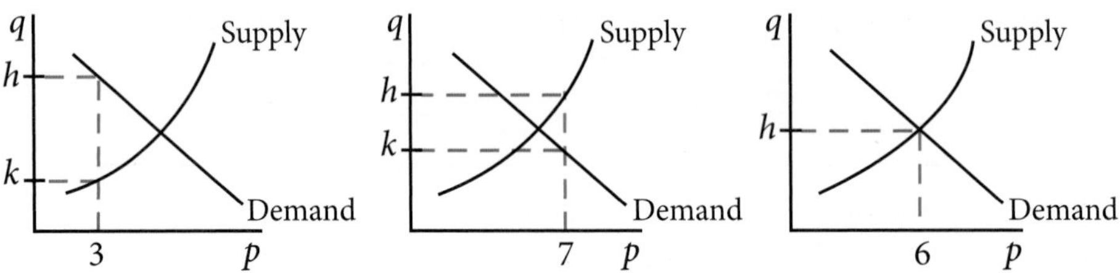

Look at the graph on the left. If the price is set at $3.00, consumers will demand h widgets, and manufacturers will be willing to supply k widgets. There will be a shortage of widgets. High demand and low supply often create a rise in price. The manufacturer knows that people want widgets, yet there are not enough of them. If the price rises, demand will fall.

Look at the center graph. If the price is set at $7.00, consumers will demand k widgets, and manufacturers will be willing to supply h widgets. There will be too much supply, and manufacturers will have to lower the price to try and sell the high inventory of widgets.

Look at the graph on the right. At a price of $6.00, the number of widgets demanded by consumers is equal to the number of widgets manufacturers will supply. Where the functions of supply and demand intersect, the market is in **equilibrium**.

Skills and Strategies

Supply depends on the expenses involved in producing a widget and the price for which it can be sold. The factors of supply will be outlined in Lesson 2-4. This lesson concentrates on demand.

EXAMPLE 1

The Wacky Widget Company sells widgets for $2.00 each wholesale. A local store has a markup of $1.59. What is the retail price?

SOLUTION Add the markup to the wholesale price.

Markup + Wholesale price = Retail price $2.00 + 1.59 = 3.59$

The retail price is $3.59.

CHECK YOUR UNDERSTANDING

The wholesale price of an item is x dollars. The retail price is r dollars. Express the markup algebraically.

EXAMPLE 2

The Robear Corporation sells teddy bears at a wholesale price of \$23.00. If a store marks this up 110%, what is the retail price?

SOLUTION Compute the markup amount. Then calculate the retail price.

Markup rate × Wholesale price = Markup $\quad 1.10 \times \$23 = \$25.30$

Wholesale price + Markup = Retail price $\quad \$23.00 + \$25.30 = \$48.30$

The retail price is \$48.30.

> **CHECK YOUR UNDERSTANDING**
>
> A banner company sells 5-foot banners to retailers for x dollars. The St. James Sign Shop marks them up 90%. Express the retail price at the St. James store algebraically.

EXAMPLE 3

The graph shows the supply and demand curves for a widget. Explain what happens if the price is set at \$9.00.

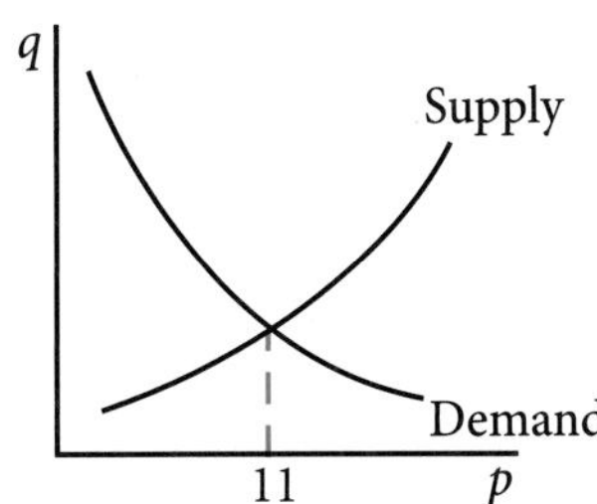

SOLUTION Because \$9.00 is less than the equilibrium price, demand will exceed supply. Suppliers will attempt to sell the widget at a higher price.

> **CHECK YOUR UNDERSTANDING**
>
> Use the graph to explain what happens if the price is set at \$15.00.

EXAMPLE 4

A company wants to base the price of its product on demand for the product, as well as on expenses. It takes a poll of several of its current retailers to find out how many widgets they would buy at different wholesale prices. The results are shown in the table. The company wants to use linear regression to create a demand function. What is the equation of the demand function? Round the slope and y-intercept to the nearest hundredth.

Wholesale Price (\$) (p)	Quantity Retailers Would Purchase (in thousands) (q)
15.25	3,456
15.50	3,005
15.75	2,546
16.00	2,188
16.25	1,678
16.50	1,290
16.75	889
17.00	310

SOLUTION Use the linear regression feature on your graphing calculator. The equation is $q = -1{,}756.19p + 30{,}238.82$. This represents the demand function.

> **CHECK YOUR UNDERSTANDING**
>
> Explain why it makes sense that the demand function has a negative slope.

EXAMPLE 2

Point out to students that a 100% markup is the same as doubling the wholesale price.

CHECK YOUR UNDERSTANDING

Answer $x + 0.9x$, or $1.9x$.

EXAMPLE 3

Point out the importance of labeling the axes and advise students to label all problems.

CHECK YOUR UNDERSTANDING

Answer Supply will exceed demand. Suppliers will attempt to sell the excess widgets by lowering the price.

EXAMPLE 4

Remind students that the linear regression line is an "average" line, and if they substitute the wholesale prices from the table into the regression equation, they will not get the quantity shown in the table, unless the regression line goes through the point with those coordinates. That is unlikely.

CHECK YOUR UNDERSTANDING

Answer As the price increases, less quantity is demanded, so the demand function slopes downward. This is indicated by a negative slope.

Applications

Teach a parrot the terms "supply and demand" and you've got an economist.

Thomas Carlyle, Philosopher

TEACH

Shifts of Demand Curves
Notice that when a demand curve is shifted to the right, some students may see this as shifted "up." Similarly, when a curve is shifted left, it may appear to be shifted "down." Try to have students use left and right to describe the shifts.

ANSWERS

1. Parrots repeat the things they hear over and over. Supply and demand is such an important concept in economics that it is constantly used by economists.

5b. Demand will exceed supply, and suppliers will attempt to sell the product at a higher price.

5e. Supply will exceed demand, and suppliers will attempt to sell the excess product at a lower price.

6b. Demand will exceed supply, and suppliers will attempt to sell the product at a higher price.

6c. Supply will exceed demand, and suppliers will attempt to sell the excess product at a lower price.

1. Interpret the quote in the context of what you learned in this lesson. See margin.

2. An automobile GPS system is sold to stores at a wholesale price of \$97. A popular store sells them for \$179.99. What is the store's markup? \$82.99

3. A CD storage rack is sold to stores at a wholesale price of \$18.
   a. If a store has a \$13 markup, what is the retail price of the CD rack? \$31
   b. Find the percent increase of the markup to the nearest percent. 72%

4. A bicycle sells for a retail price of b dollars from an online store. The wholesale price of the bicycle is w.
   a. Express the markup algebraically. $b - w$
   b. Express the percent increase of the markup algebraically. $\frac{b-w}{w} \cdot 100$

5. The graph shows supply and demand curves for the newest SuperWidget.

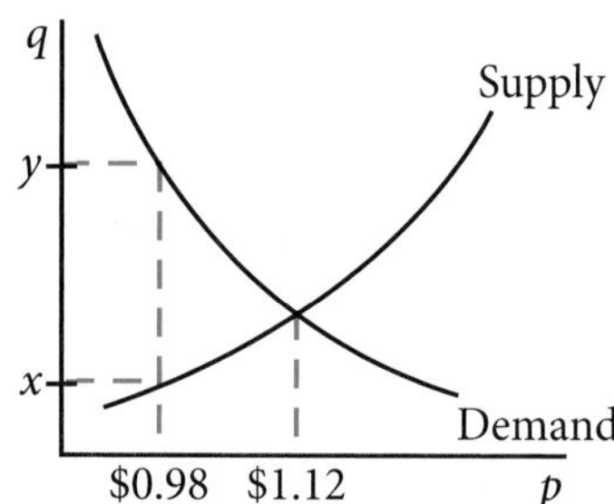

   a. What is the equilibrium price? \$1.12
   b. What will happen if the price is set at \$0.98? See margin.
   c. How many SuperWidgets are demanded at a price of \$0.98? y
   d. How many SuperWidgets are supplied at a price of \$0.98? x
   e. What will happen if the price is set at \$1.22? See margin.

6. The graph below shows supply and demand curves for a new mp3 player accessory.
   a. What is the equilibrium price? \$35
   b. Describe the relationship of supply and demand if the item were sold for \$20. See margin.
   c. Describe the relationship of supply and demand if the item were sold for \$40. See margin.
   d. Name the domain that will increase demand. $p < 35$
   e. Name the domain that will increase supply. $p > 35$

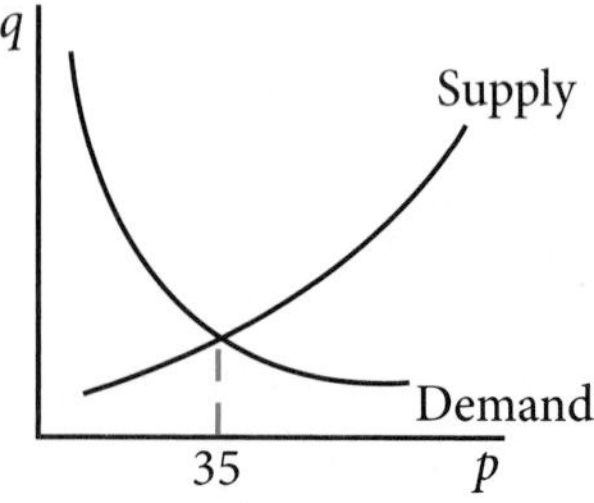

7. The supply and demand curves for a new widget are shown in the graph. Notice there are two demand curves. The original demand curve is d_1. Months after the product was introduced, there was a possible health concern over use of the product, and demand dropped to the new demand curve, d_2. The movement of the demand curve is called a **shift**.
   a. What was the equilibrium price before the demand shift? b
   b. What was the equilibrium quantity before the demand shift? e
   c. What was the equilibrium price after the demand shift? a
   d. What was the equilibrium quantity after the demand shift? c
   e. Express algebraically the difference in quantity demanded at price *b* before and after the shift. e – c
   f. Copy a rough sketch of the graph into your notebook. Label the curves. Where would the demand curve have shifted if a health benefit of the new widget was reported? It would shift to the right.

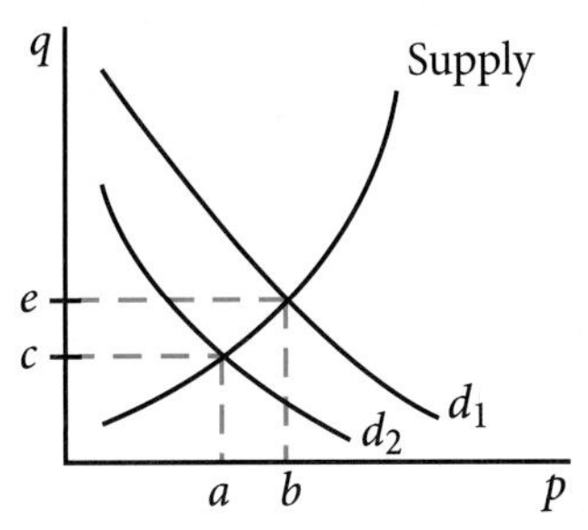

TEACH

Multi-part Exercises

These problems have many parts that depend on previous parts being answered correctly. Stress the fact that calculator list entries must be checked carefully.

ANSWERS

8b. The slope is –136.08. As a rate, the slope is expressed as garbage cans per dollar. For each dollar increase in price, about 136 less garbage cans are demanded.

8. Debbie is president of a company that produces garbage cans. The company has developed a new type of garbage can that is animal-proof, and Debbie wants to use the demand function to help set a price. She surveys ten retailers to get an approximation of how many garbage cans would be demanded at each price, and creates a table.
   a. Find the equation of the linear regression line. Round the slope and *y*-intercept to the nearest hundredth. $q = -136.08p + 2{,}535.79$
   b. Give the slope of the regression line and interpret the slope as a rate. See margin.
   c. Find the correlation coefficient and interpret it. Round to the nearest hundredth. $r = -0.99$; there is a strong negative correlation.
   d. Based on the linear regression line, how many garbage cans would be demanded at a wholesale price of $18.00? Round to the nearest hundred garbage cans. 86 hundred
   e. Was your answer to part d an example of extrapolation or interpolation? Explain. Extrapolation, $18.00 is not in the domain.
   f. Look at your answer to part d. If the company sold that many garbage cans at $18.00, how much money would the company receive from the garbage can sales? $154,800

Wholesale Price ($) (*p*)	Quantity Demanded By Retailers (in hundreds) (*q*)
13.00	744
13.50	690
14.00	630
14.50	554
15.00	511
15.50	456
16.00	400
16.50	300
17.00	207
17.50	113

9. A company that produces widgets has found its demand function to be $q = -1{,}500p + 90{,}000$.
   a. For each dollar increase in the wholesale price, how many fewer widgets are demanded? 1,500
   b. How many widgets would be demanded at a price of $20? 60,000
   c. How many widgets would be demanded at a price of $21? 58,500
   d. What is the difference in quantity demanded caused by the $1 increase in wholesale price? 1,500 less
   e. The company sets a price of $22.50. How many widgets will be demanded? 56,250
   f. How much will all of the widgets cost the store to purchase at a price of $22.50? $1,265,625
   g. If the store marks up the widgets that cost $22.50 at a rate of 50%, what is the retail price of each widget? $33.75

> *An economist is an expert who will know tomorrow why the things he predicted yesterday didn't happen today.*
>
> **Laurence J. Peter**, Professor

2-4 Fixed and Variable Expenses

Objectives

- Understand the difference between fixed and variable expenses.
- Create an expense equation based on fixed and variable expenses.

Common Core

A-CED2, A-CED3, A-REI2, A-REI6, A-REI12, F-IF8, S-ID8

Key Terms

- variable expenses
- fixed expenses
- expense equation
- revenue
- revenue equation
- profit
- loss
- breakeven point

CCSS Warm-Up

Graph each line on the same set of axes.

$y = 2x + 1$ $\qquad$ $y = -x + 4$

WARM-UP SOLUTION

The solution is a graph.

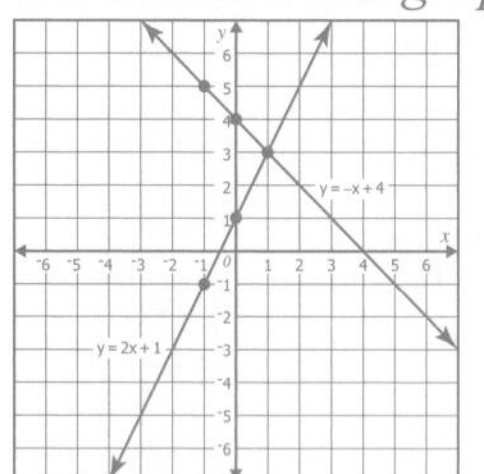

EXAMINE THE QUESTION

Students have possibly never brainstormed on all of the variables that affect the manufacturing process. Give them time to think and formulate answers before they read the text.

CLASS DISCUSSION

Can you think of any other expenses involved in the manufacturing process?

Point out that revenue depends on quantity sold, and the quantity sold depends on the price charged, so revenue ultimately depends on the price charged.

What expenses are involved in the manufacturing process?

A group of art school students have decided to start a business producing hand-painted jeans. They made a list of expenses for running the business. Some of these items must be purchased while others may be rented.

- factory space
- furniture
- delivery trucks
- electricity
- telephone
- computer
- office supplies
- jeans
- paint
- packaging
- postage
- labor

All of these expenses fall into one of two categories—variable expenses or fixed expenses. Expenses that depend on the number of items produced are **variable expenses**. Examples of variable expenses are costs for raw materials such as jeans, paint, office supplies, and labor expenses, because these costs change based on the quantity produced.

Some expenses do not change based on the quantity produced. These expenses are **fixed expenses**. Examples of fixed expenses are the cost of the furniture and the computer. The cost of having the lights on is the same regardless of how many items are produced, so this is also a fixed expense.

The *total expenses* is the sum of the fixed and variable expenses. The **expense equation** is

$E = V + F$ where E represents total expenses, V represents variable expenses, and F represents fixed expenses

The income a business receives from selling its product is **revenue**. Revenue is the price for which each product was sold times the number of products sold. The **revenue equation** is

$R = pq$ where R represents revenue, p represents the price of the product, and q represents the quantity of products sold

The difference obtained when expenses are subtracted from revenue is a **profit** when positive and a **loss** when negative. When the expenses and the revenue are equal, there is no profit or loss. This is the **breakeven point**.

Skills and Strategies

Business owners use mathematical models to analyze expenses and revenue to determine profitability of a product.

EXAMPLE 1

The art students have researched all of their potential expenses. The fixed expenses are \$17,600. The labor and materials required for each pair of painted jeans produced cost \$7.53. Represent the total expenses as a function of the quantity produced, q.

SOLUTION If q units are produced at a cost of \$7.53 per unit, the variable expenses can be represented by:

$$V = 7.53q$$

The fixed expenses, \$17,600, do not depend on the quantity produced. The total expenses, E, are the sum of the variable and the fixed expenses.

$$E = V + F$$
$$E = 7.53q + 17{,}600$$

The total expenses, E, are a function of the quantity produced, q.

■ CHECK YOUR UNDERSTANDING

A widget manufacturer's expense function is $E = 6.00q + 11{,}000$. What are the variable costs to produce one widget?

EXAMPLE 2

Kivetsky Ski Supply manufactures hand warmers for skiers. The expense function is $E = 1.18q + 12{,}000$. Find the average cost of producing one pair of hand warmers if 50,000 hand warmers are produced.

SOLUTION Find the total cost of producing 50,000 hand warmers by substituting 50,000 for q in the expense function.

	$E = 1.18q + 12{,}000$
Substitute.	$E = 1.18(50{,}000) + 12{,}000$
Multiply.	$E = 59{,}000 + 12{,}000$
Simplify.	$E = 71{,}000$

To find the average cost, divide the total cost by the number produced.

Divide by 50,000. $\dfrac{71{,}000}{50{,}000} = 1.42$

The average cost to produce one hand warmer is \$1.42 when 50,000 are produced.

■ CHECK YOUR UNDERSTANDING

The expense function for a certain product is $E = 3.40q + 189{,}000$. Express the average cost of producing q items algebraically.

TEACH

Relate what students know about variables and constants to the new vocabulary terms of variable expenses and fixed expenses.

EXAMPLE 1

Point out to students that the variable expenses part of the expense equation needs a variable. The fixed part of the equation is also called a constant.

CHECK YOUR UNDERSTANDING

Answer \$6.00

Ask students the costs of producing 500 widgets and 501 widgets. Find the difference and compare it to the slope of the expense function.

EXAMPLE 2

Point out to students that intuitively, the average cost decreases as the number of items produced increases, because the fixed costs are "spread out" over many items.

CHECK YOUR UNDERSTANDING

Answer $\dfrac{3.40q + 189{,}000}{q}$

EXAMPLE 3

Remind students that revenue depends on quantity sold, and the quantity sold depends on the price charged, so revenue depends on price. As a result, they can express revenue in terms of the variable p.

CHECK YOUR UNDERSTANDING

Answer

$E = -16.00p + 90{,}000$

You can give students similar problems to make sure they are substituting correctly.

EXAMPLE 4

Remind students to label the axes and to use these labels. Since the y-coordinates (the "heights") represent dollars, the revenue and expense heights can be compared to see which is greater.

You may put the graph on the board, and pick a specific value of q. Highlight the revenue and expenses at this q-value, and draw a vertical line connecting these two points. Explain that the length of this line represents the difference between revenue and expenses, and is a graphical representation of profit.

EXAMPLE 3

Willie's Widgets has created a demand function for its widgets, where q is the quantity demanded and p is the price of one widget.

$$q = -112p + 4{,}500$$

Its expense function is $E = 3.00q + 18{,}000$. Express the expense function as a function in terms of p.

SOLUTION Because E is a function of q, and q is a function of p, express E as a function of p using substitution.

	$E = 3.00q + 18{,}000$
Substitute for q.	$E = 3.00(-112p + 4{,}500) + 17{,}600$
Distribute.	$E = -336p + 13{,}500 + 17{,}600$
Simplify.	$E = -336p + 31{,}100$

The expense function in terms of the price, p, is $E = -336p + 31{,}100$.

CHECK YOUR UNDERSTANDING

A corporation's expense function is $E = 4.00q + 78{,}000$. The demand function was determined to be $q = -4p + 3{,}000$. Express E in terms of p.

EXAMPLE 4

Wally's Widget World created a monthly expense equation, $E = 1.10q + 4{,}200$. Wally's Widget World plans to sell its widgets to retailers at a wholesale price of \$2.50 each. How many widgets must be sold to reach the breakeven point?

SOLUTION Use a graphing calculator. Graph the revenue function, $R = 2.50q$, using R as revenue and q as the quantity sold. Notice that q is the independent variable, so the horizontal axis is labeled q. The labels on the graph below will not be shown on the calculator display.

Graph the revenue function on a coordinate grid.

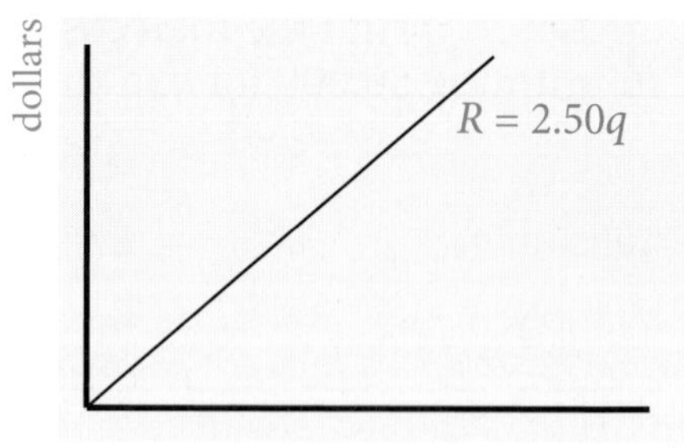

Graph the expense function on the same coordinate grid. Use your calculator's graph intersection feature to find the point of intersection.

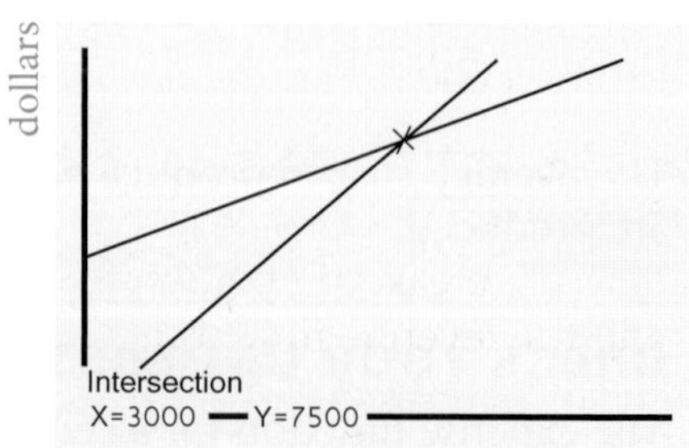

It will cost \$7,500 to manufacture 3,000 widgets. If 3,000 widgets are sold to stores for \$2.50 each, the company will receive \$7,500. Notice that no profit is made—the revenue equals the expense. The point (3,000, 7,500) is the breakeven point. Look at sections of the graph before and after the breakeven point to see if you understand what happens.

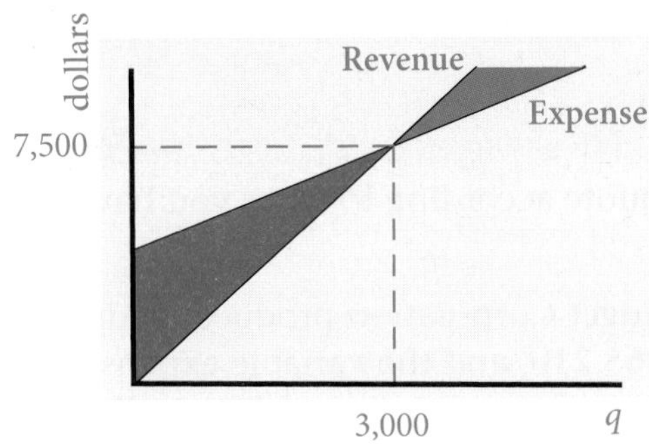

If more than 3,000 widgets are produced, the company will be operating in the green area of the graph, where $R > E$. A profit is made when revenue is greater than expenses.

If less than 3,000 widgets are produced, the company will be operating in the red area of the graph, where $E > R$. The company is not making enough revenue to pay its expenses.

CHECK YOUR UNDERSTANDING

If the company sells 2,900 widgets, is Wally's Widget World operating above or below the breakeven point? What is the difference between revenue and expense?

EXAMPLE 5

Find the solution to Example 4 algebraically.

SOLUTION To find the breakeven point, set the revenue and expense equations equal to each other.

$$R = E$$

Substitute. $\quad 2.50q = 1.10q + 4{,}200$

Subtract $1.10q$ from each side. $\quad 1.40q = 4{,}200$

Divide each side by 1.40. $\quad \dfrac{1.40q}{1.40} = \dfrac{4{,}200}{1.40}$

$$q = 3{,}000$$

The breakeven point occurs when the quantity produced, q, equals 3,000.

CHECK YOUR UNDERSTANDING

Find the breakeven point for the expense function, $E = 5.00q + 60{,}000$, and the revenue function, $R = 7.00q$.

CHECK YOUR UNDERSTANDING

Answer Wally's Widget World is operating below the breakeven point; expenses cost \$140 more than what is made in revenue.

For more practice, try other examples using other quantities.

EXAMPLE 5

You can give other examples of simultaneous linear equations and have the students solve them graphically and algebraically, as review.

CHECK YOUR UNDERSTANDING

Answer (30,000, 210,000) Remind students that the dollar sign should not be included in the ordered pair. They should properly label the axes on their graphs to understand the y-coordinate represents a dollar amount.

Applications

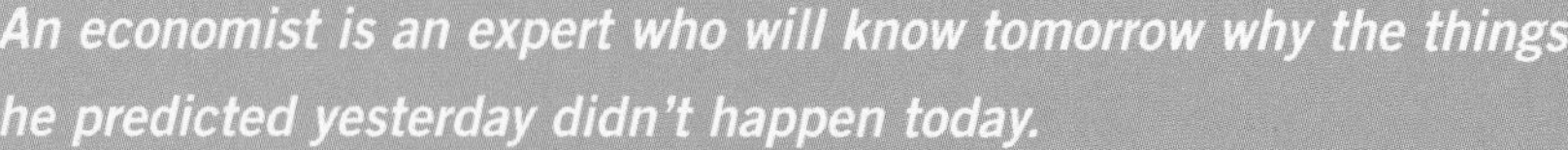

An economist is an expert who will know tomorrow why the things he predicted yesterday didn't happen today.

Laurence J. Peter, Professor

TEACH

Units in Answers

Point out to students that correlation coefficients have no units. Always require them to give answers, especially answers that are slopes, with the units. The more they hear it, read it, and say it, the more comfortable they will be with using the units. In science classes, they are encouraged/required to give units in answers.

ANSWERS

1. Many variables are considered when making business decisions. Although economists use math models to try to predict what will happen, a change in any variable can cause a change in the expected result.

1. Interpret the quote according to what you have learned in this chapter. See margin.

2. The Gidget Widget Corporation produces widgets. The fixed expenses are \$65,210, and the variable expenses are \$4.22 per widget. Express the expense function algebraically. $E = 4.22q + 65{,}210$

3. A corporation produces mini-widgets. The variable expenses are \$1.24 per mini-widget, and the fixed expenses are \$142,900.
- **a.** How much does it cost to produce 1 mini-widget? \$142,901.24
- **b.** How much does it cost to produce 20,000 mini-widgets? \$167,700
- **c.** Express the expense function algebraically. $E = 1.24q + 142{,}900$
- **d.** What is the slope of the expense function? 1.24
- **e.** If the slope is interpreted as a rate, give the units that would be used. dollars per mini-widget

4. The expense function for the Wonder Widget is $E = 4.14q + 55{,}789$.
- **a.** What is the fixed cost in the expense function? \$55,789
- **b.** What is the cost of producing 500 Wonder Widgets? \$57,859
- **c.** What is the average cost per widget of producing 500 Wonder Widgets? Round to the nearest cent. \$115.72
- **d.** What is the total cost of producing 600 Wonder Widgets? \$58,273
- **e.** What is the average cost per widget of producing 600 Wonder Widgets? Round to the nearest cent. \$97.12
- **f.** As the number of widgets increased from 500 to 600, did the average expense per widget increase or decrease? decrease
- **g.** What is the average cost per widget of producing 10,000 Wonder Widgets? Round to the nearest cent. \$9.72

5. The Royal Ranch Pool Supply Corporation manufactures chlorine test kits. The kits have an expense equation of $E = 5.15q + 23{,}500$. What is the average cost per kit of producing 3,000 test kits? Round to the nearest cent. \$12.98

6. The fixed costs of producing a Wild Widget are \$34,000. The variable costs are \$5.00 per widget. What is the average cost per widget of producing 7,000 Wild Widgets? Round to the nearest cent. \$9.86

7. Wanda's Widgets used market surveys and linear regression to develop a demand function based on the wholesale price. The demand function is $q = -140p + 9{,}000$. The expense function is $E = 2.00q + 16{,}000$.
- **a.** Express the expense function in terms of p. $E = -280p + 34{,}000$
- **b.** At a price of \$10.00, how many widgets are demanded? 7,600
- **c.** How much does it cost to produce the number of widgets from part b? \$31,200

8. Wind Up Corporation manufactures widgets. The monthly expense equation is $E = 3.20q + 56{,}000$. They plan to sell the widgets to retailers at a wholesale price of \$6.00 each. How many widgets must be sold to reach the breakeven point? 20,000

9. The Lerneg Corporation computed its monthly expense equation as $E = 11.00q + 76{,}000$. Its products will be sold to retailers at a wholesale price of \$20.00 each. How many items must be sold to reach the breakeven point? Round to the nearest integer. 8,444

10. Solve Exercise 9 using the graph intersection feature on your graphing calculator. Are the answers equivalent? Yes; see margin.

11. Variable costs of producing widgets account for the cost of gas required to deliver the widgets to retailers. A widget producer finds the average cost of gas per widget. The expense equation was recently adjusted from $E = 4.55q + 69{,}000$ to $E = 4.98q + 69{,}000$ in response to the increase in gas prices.
    a. Find the increase in the average cost per widget. \$0.43
    b. If the widgets are sold to retailers for \$8.00 each, find the breakeven point prior to the adjustment in the expense function. (20,000, 160,000)
    c. After the gas increase, the company raised its wholesale cost from \$8 to \$8.50. Find the breakeven point after the adjustment in the expense function. Round to the nearest integer. (19,602, 166,618)

12. Examine the graph of expense and revenue.
    a. What is the breakeven point? (*A*, *W*)
    b. If quantity *C* is sold and $C < A$, is there a profit or a loss? Explain. See margin.
    c. If quantity *D* is sold and $D > A$, is there a profit or a loss? Explain. See margin.
    d. The *y*-intercept of the expense function is *Z*. Interpret what the company is doing if it operates at the point (0, *Z*). See margin.

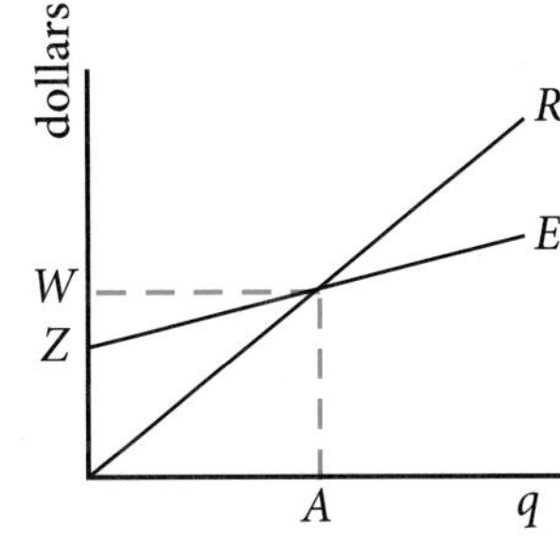

13. Billy invented an innovative baseball batting glove he named the Nokee and made his own TV infomercial to sell it. The expense function for the Nokee is $E = 6.21q + 125{,}000$. The Nokee sells for \$19.95.
    a. Represent the average expense *A* for one Nokee algebraically. See margin.
    b. Set your calculator viewing window to show *x*-values between 0 and 1,000, and *y*-values from 0 to 2,000. Let *x* represent *q* and let *y* represent *A*. Graph the average expense function. See margin.
    c. Is the average expense function linear? no
    d. Is the average expense function increasing or decreasing as *q* increases? decreasing
    e. If only one Nokee is produced, what is the average cost per Nokee to the nearest cent? \$125,006.21
    f. If 100,000 Nokees are produced, what is the average cost per Nokee to the nearest cent? \$7.46

14. Lorne has determined the fixed cost of producing his new invention is *N* dollars. The variable cost is \$10.75 per item. What is the average cost per item of producing *W* items? $10.75 + \frac{N}{W}$

TEACH

Domains and Breakeven Points

Constantly remind students what the domains before and after the breakeven points depict. For visual learners, this is crucial, and for non-visual learners, it may be difficult.

ANSWERS

10.

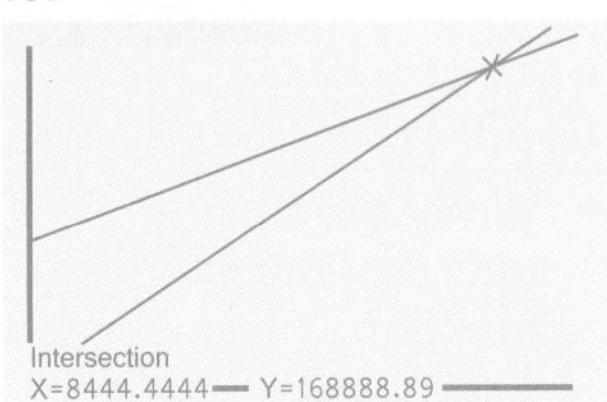

12b. There is a loss because expenses are greater than revenue at any quantity less than *A*.

12c. There is a profit because revenue is greater than expenses at any quantity greater than *A*.

12d. If no items are sold, the company still has to pay *Z* dollars for the fixed expenses.

13a. $\frac{6.21q + 125{,}000}{q}$

13b.

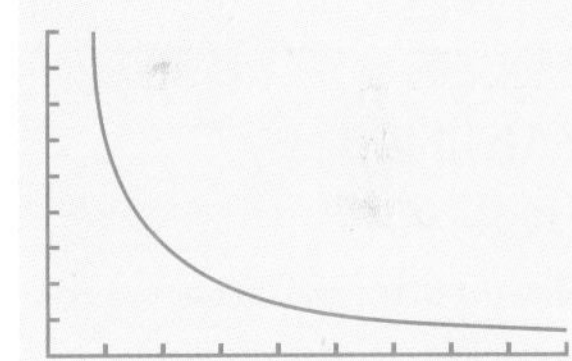

Money often costs too much.

Ralph Waldo Emerson, Poet

2-5 Graphs of Expense and Revenue Functions

Key Terms
- nonlinear function
- second-degree equation
- quadratic equation
- parabola
- leading coefficient
- maximum value
- vertex of a parabola
- axis of symmetry

Objectives

- Write, graph, and interpret the expense function.
- Write, graph, and interpret the revenue function.
- Identify the points of intersection of the expense and revenue functions.
- Identify breakeven points, and explain them in the context of the problem.

Common Core

N-Q1, N-Q2, N-Q3, A-SSE1a, A-CED2, A-CED3, A-REI4b, A-REI10, F-IF7a, F-IF8

CCSS Warm-Up

Find the vertex of the parabola with equation $y = x^2 + 8x + 15$.

$(-4, -1)$

EXAMINE THE QUESTION

A picture is worth 1,000 words. The graphs of expense and revenue equations yield pictorial insight into how expense and revenue interact.

CLASS DISCUSSION

How does price contribute to consumer demand? Name some other factors that might also play a role in the quantity of a product consumers purchase.

Why does a non-vertical line have slope but a nonlinear function does not?

Students often confuse $-ax^2$ with $(-ax)^2$. Highlight the difference and explain how the absence of parentheses changes the result.

How can expense and revenue be graphed?

The total expense for the production of a certain item is the amount of money it costs to manufacture and place it on the market. One contributor to consumer demand is the price at which an item is sold. Expense relies on the quantity produced and demand relies on price, so the expense function can be written in terms of price.

Recall that revenue is the total amount a company collects from the sale of a product or service. Revenue depends on the demand for a product, which is a function of the price of the product. The relationship between price, demand, expense, and revenue can be better understood when the functions are graphed on a coordinate plane.

Both the demand and expense functions are linear. However, as you will see, revenue is a **nonlinear function** when it is expressed in terms of price. That is, the graph of the revenue function is not a straight line. The revenue function has a variable raised to an exponent of 2, so it is a **second-degree equation** and is known as a **quadratic equation**. A quadratic equation can be written in the form

$$y = ax^2 + bx + c \text{ where } a, b, \text{ and } c \text{ are real numbers and } a \neq 0$$

The graph of a quadratic equation is called a **parabola**. In the revenue graph pictured, the horizontal axis represents the price of an item, and the vertical axis represents the revenue. If the **leading coefficient**, a, is *positive*, then the parabola opens upward.

Parabola with a Positive Leading Coefficient

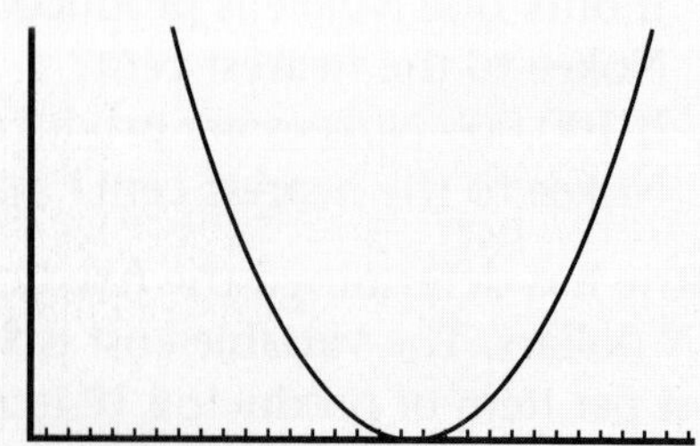

If the leading coefficient is *negative*, then the parabola opens downward. The downward parabola models the revenue function. In the graph, the parabola reaches a **maximum value** at its peak. This point is the **vertex of the parabola** and yields the price at which revenue can be maximized.

The **axis of symmetry** is a vertical line that can be drawn through the *vertex of the parabola* so that the dissected parts of the parabola are mirror images of each other. The point on the horizontal axis through which the *axis of symmetry* passes is determined by calculating $-\frac{b}{2a}$.

Parabola with a Negative Leading Coefficient

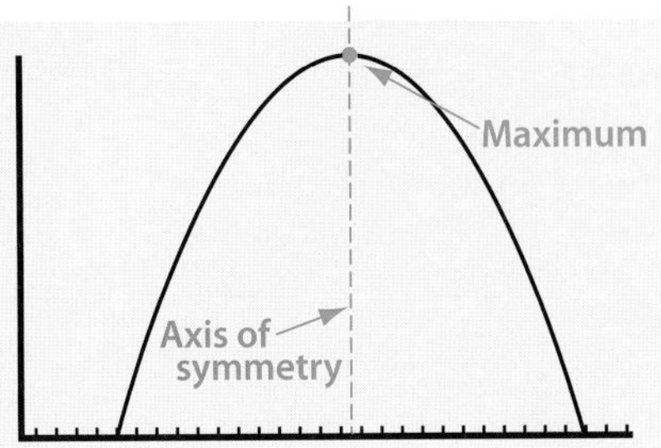

Skills and Strategies

The graphical relationship between revenue and expense reveals much information helpful to a business.

EXAMPLE 1

A particular item in the Picasso Paints product line costs \$7.00 each to manufacture. The fixed costs are \$28,000. The demand function is $q = -500p + 30{,}000$ where q is the quantity the public will buy given the price, p. Graph the expense function in terms of price on the coordinate plane.

SOLUTION The expense function is $E = 7.00q + 28{,}000$. Substitute for q to find the expense function in terms of price.

Expense function.	$E = 7.00q + 28{,}000$
Substitute.	$E = 7.00(-500p + 30{,}000) + 28{,}000$
Use the Distributive property.	$E = -3{,}500p + 210{,}000 + 28{,}000$
Simplify.	$E = -3{,}500p + 238{,}000$

The horizontal axis represents price, and the vertical axis represents expense. Both variables must be greater than 0, so the graph is in the first quadrant.

To determine a viewing window, find the points where the expense function intersects the vertical and horizontal axes. Neither p nor E can be 0 because both a price of 0 and an expense of 0 would be meaningless in this situation. But, you can use $p = 0$ and $E = 0$ to determine an appropriate viewing window.

To find the vertical axis intercept, let $p = 0$ and solve for E.

Let $p = 0$.

$$E = -3{,}500p + 238{,}000$$
$$E = -3{,}500(0) + 238{,}000$$
$$E = 238{,}000$$

To find the horizontal axis intercept, let $E = 0$ and solve for p.

Let $E = 0$.

$$0 = -3{,}500p + 238{,}000$$
$$3{,}500p = 238{,}000$$
$$p = 68$$

TEACH

Review a parabola and its related equation. Have students identify what is different in this equation from linear equations. Discuss how the leading coefficient, in this case the coefficient on the x^2 term, determines if the parabola opens upward or downward. Relate this concept to the leading coefficient of a linear equation, which is the coefficient on the x term and determines if the lines go up and to the right or down and to the right. In other words, the leading coefficient determines if the line has a positive slope or a negative slope.

EXAMPLE 1

It is very important that students understand the concept of writing a function *in terms of* a stated variable. In Example 1, they must first construct an expense function in terms of the variable q. Then, they must use the given demand function and substitute the expression for q so that the expense function is now in terms of the price p. This skill will be needed throughout the chapter.

CHECK YOUR UNDERSTANDING

Answer $E = -1{,}000p + 220{,}000$

Viewing window used:

Xmin = 0	Ymin = 200,000
Xmax = 15	Ymax = 250,000
Xscl = 1	Yscl = 1,000

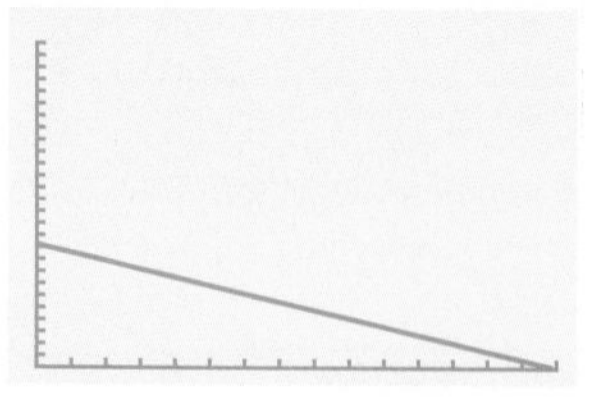

Students must first create the expense function in terms of q; $E = 5q + 20{,}000$. Then, substitute the expression for q given in the problem statement. This yields an expense function in terms of the price p. The horizontal intercept is 220. This can help you select viewing window values of 0 to 250 with a scale of 50. The vertical intercept is 220,000.

EXAMPLE 2

Students often confuse revenue and profit. Emphasize that revenue is merely the amount of money that the sale of an item brings in. It is therefore a function of the price of the item and the quantity sold. Profit is calculated taking into account the costs of making and selling the item.

CHECK YOUR UNDERSTANDING

Answer $437,500

This answer can also be found by determining the demand at that price and then multiplying that quantity by $25.

EXAMPLE 3

The revenue equation is a parabola, so students may need guidance in selecting an appropriate viewing window. Finding the axis of symmetry and the vertex will help set the vertical dimensions.

Use the intercepts to determine the size of the viewing window. In order to get a full picture, use window values that are slightly greater than the intercepts. Choose an appropriate scale for each axis. In this case, set the horizontal axis at 0 to 70 with a scale of 10 and the vertical axis at 0 to 240,000 with the scale at 50,000. Enter the function and graph.

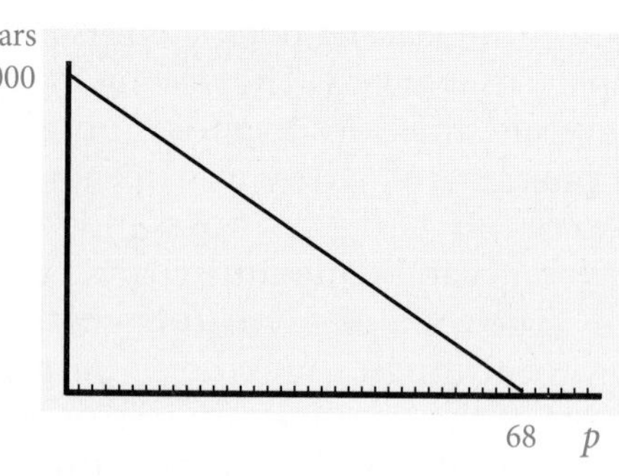

CHECK YOUR UNDERSTANDING

An electronics company manufactures earphones for portable music devices. Each earphone costs $5 to manufacture. Fixed costs are $20,000. The demand function is $q = -200p + 40{,}000$. Write the expense function in terms of q and determine a suitable viewing window for that function. Graph the expense function.

EXAMPLE 2

What is the revenue equation for the Picasso Paints product? Write the revenue equation in terms of the price.

SOLUTION Revenue is the product of the price and quantity, or $R = pq$. The quantity, q, is expressed in terms of the price, so the expression can be substituted into the revenue equation.

Revenue equation	$R = pq$
Substitute.	$R = p(-500p + 30{,}000)$
Distribute.	$R = p(-500p) + p(30{,}000)$
Simplify.	$R = -500p^2 + 30{,}000p$

The revenue function is a quadratic equation in the form $y = ax^2 + bx + c$ where $a = -500$, $b = 30{,}000$, and $c = 0$. Because the leading coefficient is negative, the graph is a parabola that opens downward.

CHECK YOUR UNDERSTANDING

Determine the revenue if the price per item is set at $25.00.

EXAMPLE 3

Graph the revenue equation on a coordinate plane.

SOLUTION The graph opens downward. It has a maximum height at the vertex. Here $b = 30{,}000$ and $a = -500$.

$$\frac{-b}{2a} = \frac{-30{,}000}{2(-500)} = \frac{-30{,}000}{-1{,}000} = 30$$

The axis of symmetry passes through 30 on the horizontal axis. To determine the height of the parabola at 30, evaluate the parabola when $p = 30$.

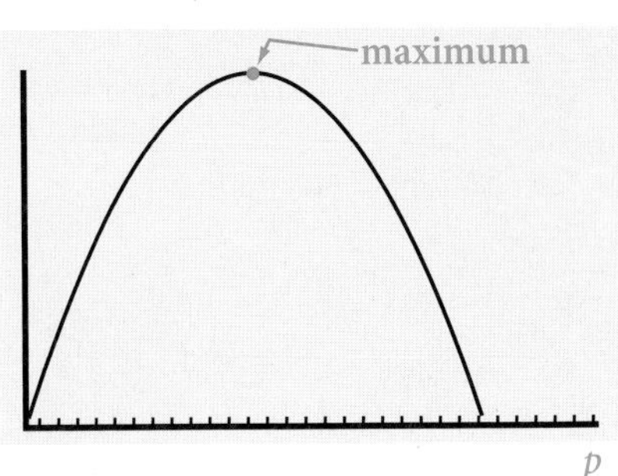

Revenue equation	$R = -500p^2 + 30{,}000p$
Substitute 30 for p.	$R = -500(30)^2 + 30{,}000(30)$
Simplify.	$R = 450{,}000$

When the price is set at $30, the maximum revenue is $450,000. The vertical axis must be as high as the maximum value. For the viewing window, use a number slightly greater than the maximum value, such as 500,000, so you can get the entire picture of the graph. Use the same horizontal values on the axis as used for the expense function.

■ **CHECK YOUR UNDERSTANDING**

Use the graph in Example 3. Which price would yield the higher revenue, $28 or $40?

EXAMPLE 4

The revenue and expense functions are graphed on the same set of axes. The points of intersection are labeled *A* and *B*. Explain what is happening at those two points.

SOLUTION Where the revenue and the expense functions intersect, revenue and expenses are equal. These are breakeven points. Notice there are two such points.

Before intersection point *A*, the expenses are greater than the revenue. The first breakeven price is approximately at $8.08. The second is approximately at $58.92. From point *A* to point *B*, the revenue is greater than the expenses. To the right of point *B*, the expenses again are greater than the revenue.

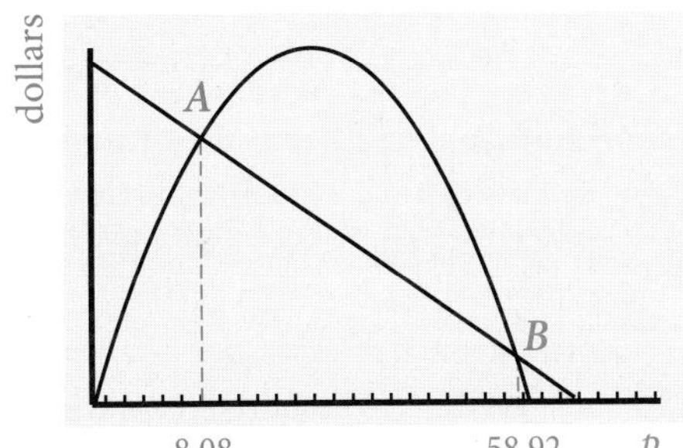

■ **CHECK YOUR UNDERSTANDING**

Why is using the prices of $7.50 and $61.00 not in the best interest of the company?

CHECK YOUR UNDERSTANDING

Answer Because $28 is closer to $30 than $40, it will yield a higher point on the parabola.

Students could test this statement by substitution but should be encouraged to think through the question before doing so. The very structure of a downward parabola yields a higher *y*-value as *x* approaches the axis of symmetry.

EXAMPLE 4

A and *B* are points of intersection. Ask students what is true about the *y*-value in each of the functions when evaluated at the *x*-values of points *A* and *B*. Once equality is establish, discuss what it means for the *y*-values to be the same for both functions at the points of intersection in the context of expense and revenue.

CHECK YOUR UNDERSTANDING

Answer At both prices, revenue is less than expenses. The price of $7.50 is too low for the incoming revenue to make up for the outgoing expenses. The price of $61 may be too high for consumers and would decrease the demand for the product. Therefore, with fewer items being sold, the revenue will be less.

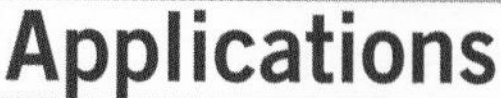

Applications

Money often costs too much.

Ralph Waldo Emerson, Poet

TEACH

Exercises 2 and 3
Students are introduced to a new product in each and given information necessary for creating an expense function. The independent variable for the expense function will be the quantity, q. Parts a–g of each question guide the students through the steps to graph the functions.

ANSWERS

1. Emerson cautions to be aware of the fact that the expenses involved in making revenue are often more than the revenue itself.

2c. The intercepts are (0, 10,000) and (10, 0), so the viewing window can be set from 0 to 12 with a scale of 1 for the horizontal axis and 0 to 12,000 for the vertical axis with a scale of 100.

2f. The maximum revenue of $18,062.50 is achieved when the price is $4.25; see additional answers for graph.

2g. (1.21, 8,794.36) and (8.29, 1,705.64); $1.21 and $8.29; see additional answers for graph.

3c. The intercepts are (0, 140,000) and (56, 0), so the viewing window can be set from 0 to 60 for the horizontal axis with a scale of 5 and 0 to 150,000 for the vertical axis with a scale of 10,000.

3f. The maximum revenue of $200,000 is achieved when the price is set at $20.00; see additional answers for graph.

1. How might the quote apply to what you have learned? See margin.

2. Rich and Betsy Cuik started a small business. They manufacture a microwavable coffee-to-go cup called Cuik Cuppa Coffee. It contains spring water and ground coffee beans in a tea-bag-like pouch. Each cup costs the company $1.00 to manufacture. The fixed costs for this product line are $1,500. Rich and Betsy have determined the demand function to be $q = -1{,}000p + 8{,}500$, where p is the price for each cup.

a. Write the expense equation in terms of the demand, q. $E = 1.00q + 1{,}500$

b. Express the expense equation found in part a in terms of the price, p. $E = -1{,}000p + 10{,}000$

c. Determine a viewing window on a graphing calculator for the expense function. Justify your answer. See margin.

d. Draw and label the graph of the expense function. See additional answers.

e. Write the revenue function in terms of the price. $R = -1{,}000p^2 + 8{,}500p$

f. Graph the revenue function in a suitable viewing window. What price will yield the maximum revenue? What is the revenue at that price? Round both answers to the nearest cent. See margin.

g. Graph the revenue and expense functions on the same coordinate plane. Identify the points of intersection using a graphing calculator. Round your answers to the nearest cent. Identify the price at the breakeven points. See margin.

3. Orange-U-Happy is an orange-scented cleaning product that is manufactured in disposable cloth pads. Each box of 100 pads costs $5 to manufacture. The fixed costs for Orange-U-Happy are $40,000. The research development group of the company has determined the demand function to be $q = -500p + 20{,}000$, where p is the price for each box.

a. Write the expense equation in terms of the demand, q. $E = 5q + 40{,}000$

b. Express the expense function in terms of the price, p. $E = -2{,}500p + 140{,}000$

c. Determine a viewing window on a graphing calculator for the expense function. Justify your answer. See margin.

d. Draw and label the graph of the expense function. See additional answers.

e. Write the revenue function in terms of the price. $R = -500p^2 + 20{,}000p$

f. Graph the revenue function in a suitable viewing window. What price will yield the maximum revenue? What is the revenue at that price? Round answers to the nearest cent. See margin.

g. Graph the revenue and expense functions on the same coordinate plane. Identify the points of intersection using a graphing calculator, and name the breakeven points. Round to the nearest cent. Identify the price at the breakeven points. (7.46, 121,354.02) and (37.54, 46,145.98)/$7.46 and $37.54; see additional answers for graph.

Risk comes from not knowing what you're doing.
Warren Buffet, Businessman

Breakeven Analysis 2-6

Key Terms
- zero net difference
- quadratic formula

Objectives
- Determine the breakeven prices and amounts using technology or algebra.

Common Core
A-CED2, A-CED3, A-REI4b, A-REI7, A-REI10, A-REI11, F-IF7a, F-IF8

CCSS Warm-Up

Graph each on the same set of axes.

$y = x^2$ $\qquad$ $y = -2x$

WARM-UP SOLUTION

The solution is a graph.

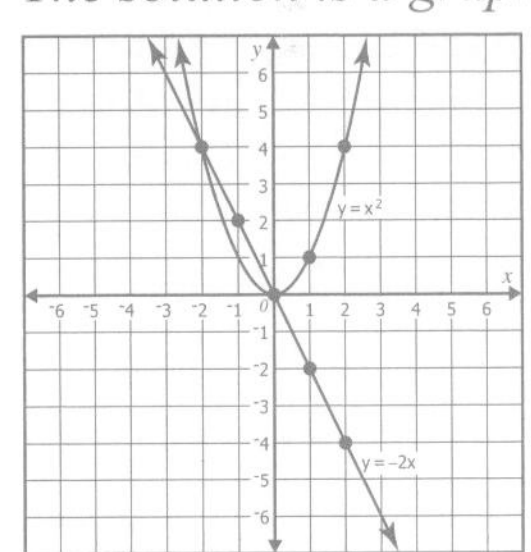

What happens when revenue equals expense?

When the revenue function is a quadratic equation, you can determine the values at which the expense and revenue functions are equal. Graph the revenue and expense functions on the same coordinate plane.

The functions intersect at the values at which the expense and revenue functions are equal (blue points), or the breakeven points. The difference between expense and revenue equals zero, which is a **zero net difference**.

Notice that the prices on the revenue function between the breakeven points result in revenue greater than expense. Prices beyond the breakeven points result in revenue less than expense. Decision makers must examine the breakeven points carefully to set appropriate prices to yield maximum revenue.

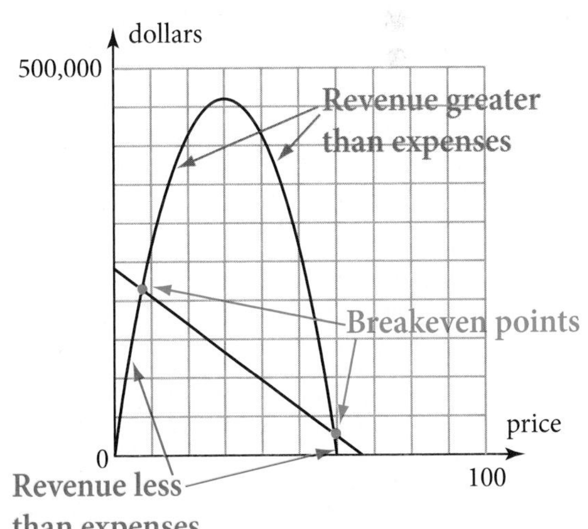

Breakeven points may be found algebraically or by using a graphing calculator. To find breakeven points algebraically, set the expense and revenue functions equal to each other. Rewrite the resulting equation with 0 on one side of the equal sign and all the remaining terms on the other side.

This gives a quadratic equation in the form $ax^2 + bx + c = 0$, where $a \neq 0$. The **quadratic formula** can then be used to solve this quadratic equation. The quadratic formula is

$$x = \frac{-b \pm \sqrt{b^2 - 4ac}}{2a}$$ where ± (read *plus or minus*) indicates the two solutions

$$x = \frac{-b + \sqrt{b^2 - 4ac}}{2a} \text{ and}$$

$$x = \frac{-b - \sqrt{b^2 - 4ac}}{2a}$$

EXAMINE THE QUESTION

This lesson examines what happens at the intersection of those functions. It might be helpful if you ask "What is true about the intersection of a street and an avenue?" Elicit responses that refer to the fact that the pavement at the intersection is shared by both the street and the avenue. Use this as a springboard for the discussion about intersection on graphs.

CLASS DISCUSSION

Why wouldn't a company set the price of an item at the breakeven point price? Are there always two breakeven points? Could there be a situation where there are more than two? Less than two?

Ask students to describe situations where a graph might also be a quadratic.

What are you finding when you solve a quadratic equation?

TEACH

Use the labeled graph from page 91 to be certain students can interpret these graphs when they create them in this lesson.

If your students do not remember the quadratic formula and want to know where it comes from, show the process of finding solutions by completing the square for the equation $y = ax^2 + bx + c$.

EXAMPLE 1

Make sure that students are comfortable with both methods of finding the breakeven points. Discuss the role that rounding plays in creating a possible discrepancy in the vertical axis values at the breakeven points. Some students might find the quadratic formula more accessible if it is stated as $x = -\frac{b}{2a} \pm \frac{\sqrt{b^2 - 4ac}}{2a}$. Here, students can see that the same amount is added to and subtracted from the axis of symmetry x-value, yielding roots that are symmetrical with respect to the axis of symmetry.

Skills and Strategies

Breakeven analysis can be used to make product price-setting decisions. Calculation and interpretation must be done during breakeven analysis.

EXAMPLE 1

Determine the prices at the breakeven points for the Picasso Paints product in Lesson 2-5. The expense function is $E = -3{,}500p + 238{,}000$, and the revenue function is $R = -500p^2 + 30{,}000p$.

SOLUTION The breakeven point occurs when the expense and revenue functions intersect. There are two ways to determine the breakeven point—using technology or algebra.

If a graphing calculator is used, let x represent the price, and express the equations in terms of x. Enter each function into the calculator, and graph them both using a suitable viewing window. Find the intersection points.

Because the calculator will display answers to many decimal places, round the intersection points to the nearest cent. The figures below show two graphing calculator screens after the Intersect feature has been used.

Shown below on the left is the leftmost breakeven point; the price is at $8.08.

On the right is the rightmost breakeven point; the price is $58.92.

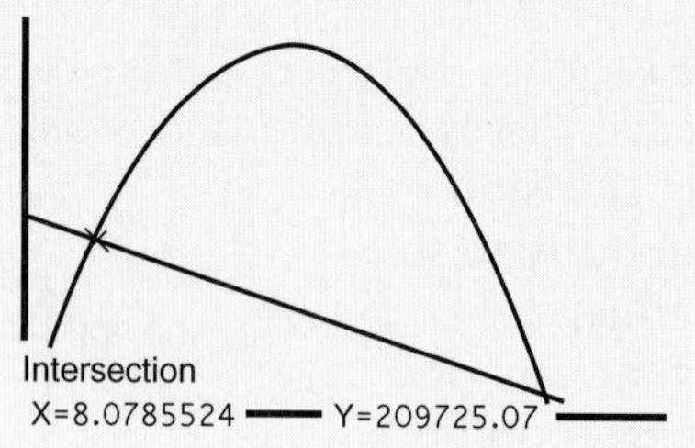

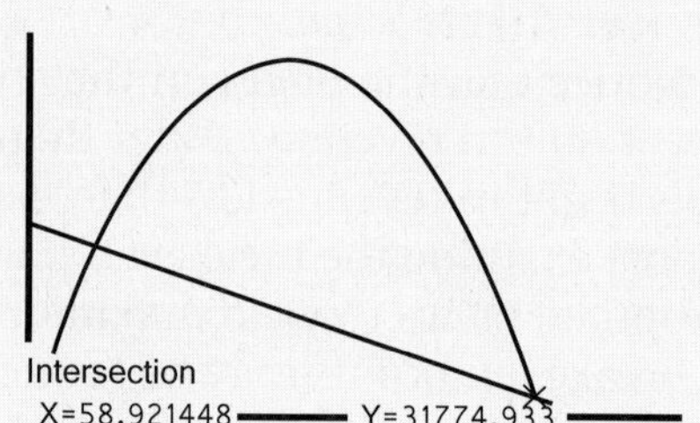

The breakeven point can also be found algebraically. Set the expense and revenue functions equal to each other. Rewrite the resulting equation with 0 on one side and all the remaining terms on the other side. The quadratic equation is usually written with the leading coefficient positive.

$$E = R$$

Set the expressions equal. $\quad -3{,}500p + 238{,}000 = -500p^2 + 30{,}000p$

Rewrite to set equal to 0. $\quad +500p^2 - 30{,}000p = +500p^2 - 30{,}000p$

$$500p^2 - 33{,}500p + 238{,}000 = 0$$

In the quadratic equation $500p^2 - 33{,}500p + 238{,}000 = 0$, $a = 500$, $b = -33{,}500$, and $c = 238{,}000$. Because the equation is written in terms of p, use p instead of x in the quadratic formula. Substitute values for a, b, and c, and calculate.

Quadratic formula $x = \dfrac{-b \pm \sqrt{b^2 - 4ac}}{2a}$

Use + in the formula.

$$p = \frac{-(-33{,}500) + \sqrt{(-33{,}500)^2 - 4(500)(238{,}000)}}{2(500)} \approx 58.92$$

Use – in the formula.

$$p = \frac{-(-33{,}500) - \sqrt{(-33{,}500)^2 - 4(500)(238{,}000)}}{2(500)} \approx 8.08$$

The prices at the breakeven points are \$8.08 and \$58.92.

■ CHECK YOUR UNDERSTANDING

The expense function for a particular product is $E = -2{,}000p + 125{,}000$. The revenue function for that product is $R = -600p^2 + 18{,}000p$. Determine the prices at the breakeven points for this product both algebraically and graphically.

■ EXTEND YOUR UNDERSTANDING

Knowing that the two breakeven prices have been rounded to the nearest cent, what would you expect when each is substituted into the expense and revenue equations?

EXAMPLE 2

Determine the revenue and expense for the Picasso Paints product at the breakeven points found in Example 1.

SOLUTION The y-value of the breakeven point will be both the revenue and expense values. These values can be determined by substituting the values of p into the expense and revenue equations.

Substitute 8.08 for p. $E = -3{,}500(8.08) + 238{,}000 = 209{,}720$

$R = -500(8.08)^2 + 30{,}000(8.08) = 209{,}756.80$

Substitute 58.92 for p. $E = -3{,}500(58.92) + 238{,}000 = 31{,}780$

$R = -500(58.92)^2 + 30{,}000(58.92) = 31{,}816.80$

When the breakeven price is approximately \$8.08, the expense and revenue values are each close to \$209,750.

When the breakeven price is approximately \$58.92, the expense and revenue values are each approximately \$31,800.

Because of rounding, the expense and revenue are not equivalent. They are, however, approximately equal.

■ CHECK YOUR UNDERSTANDING

How could you have improved on the error when calculating the expense and revenue values?

CHECK YOUR UNDERSTANDING

Answer The breakeven prices using both the quadratic formula method and the graphing calculator are \$8.33 and \$25. The former has been rounded to two decimal places.

EXTEND YOUR UNDERSTANDING

Answer The actual breakeven values have non-terminating decimal parts, so using the rounded values will not yield exact expense and revenue values. The expense and revenue values are approximately equal when $p = 8.08$ and $p = 58.92$.

EXAMPLE 2

Example 2 follows from the discussion in Extend Your Understanding. Notice that the expense and revenue values are approximately equal due to rounding.

CHECK YOUR UNDERSTANDING

Answer The error could have been improved by using more accurate prices with more decimal places in the calculation. But, for this purpose, it is acceptable to round to the nearest cent.

EXAMPLE 3

Carefully walk the students through the solution as stated here. Without a good understanding of the algebraic manipulations, students will not be able to create the spreadsheet formulas. Impress upon students that there are other acceptable correct solutions in spreadsheet form that will yield the same result.

CHECK YOUR UNDERSTANDING

Answer Because the value in B11 is the same as the value in B7, the formula in B11 is =B7. The value in B12 is the difference between *B* and *V*. Therefore, the formula in B12 is =(B8–B3). The value in B13 is the negative value in B4. The formula in B13 is =–B4.

If you want to stress to students that they are taking the opposite of the value in B4, you can have them write the formula for B13 as =–1*B4.

EXAMPLE 3

Use a spreadsheet to determine the breakeven price for the Picasso Paints product.

SOLUTION Develop general expense and revenue equations so the spreadsheet can calculate the breakeven prices regardless of the situations. The expense function is $E = Vp + F$, where p equals price, V equals variable costs, and F equals fixed costs. The revenue function is $R = Ap^2 + Bp$ where p equals price and A and B are values specific to the particular situation. Set the expense equation equal to the revenue equation.

$$E = R$$

Subtract $Vp + F$ from both sides.
$$Vp + F = Ap^2 + Bp$$
$$-Vp - F = -Vp - F$$
$$0 = Ap^2 + Bp - Vp - F$$

Combine like terms.
$$0 = Ap^2 + (B - V)p - F$$

This is a quadratic equation where $a = A$, $b = (B - V)$, and $c = -F$. Depending on the spreadsheet software, cell formulas may vary. The Picasso Paints functions are $E = -3{,}500p + 238{,}000$ and $R = -500p^2 + 30{,}000$.

The values of V and F from the expense function are entered into cells B3 and B4. The values of A and B from the revenue function are entered into cells B7 and B8. Cells B15 and B16 are the breakeven prices calculated using the quadratic formula.

For B15 the formula is =(–B12+SQRT(B12^2–4*B11*B13))/(2*B11).

For B16 the formula is =(–B12–SQRT(B12^2–4*B11*B13))/(2*B11).

	A	B
1	**Breakeven Calculator**	
2	The expense equation has the form $Vp + F$.	$-3{,}500p + 238{,}000$
3	Enter the value of V in cell B3.	–3,500
4	Enter the value of F in cell B4.	238,000
5		
6	The revenue equation has the form $Ap^2 + Bp$.	$-500p^2 + 30{,}000p$
7	Enter the value of A in cell B7.	–500
8	Enter the value of B in cell B8.	30,000
9		
10	Solve the quadratic equation.	$-500p^2 + 33{,}500p +$ $-238{,}000$
11	where $a =$	–500
12	$b =$	33,500
13	$c =$	–238,000
14		
15	The price at the first breakeven point is	$8.08
16	The price at the second breakeven point is	$58.92

CHECK YOUR UNDERSTANDING

What cell formulas were used to identify the a, b, and c values shown in B11, B12, and B13?

Applications

Risk comes from not knowing what you're doing.
Warren Buffet, Businessman

1. How might the quote apply to what you have learned? See margin.
2. A manufacturer has determined that the combined fixed and variable expenses for the production and sale of 500,000 items are $10,000,000. What is the price at the breakeven point for this item? $20
3. A supplier of school kits has determined that the combined fixed and variable expenses to market and sell G kits is W.
   a. What expression models the price of a school kit at the breakeven point? $\frac{W}{G}$
   b. Suppose a new marketing manager joined the company and determined that the combined fixed and variable expenses would only be 80% of the cost if the supplier sold twice as many kits. Write an expression for the price of a kit at the breakeven point using the new marketing manager's business model. $\frac{0.8W}{G}$
4. A jewelry manufacturer has determined the expense equation for necklaces to be $E = 1{,}250q + 800{,}000$, where q is the quantity demanded. At a particular price, the breakeven revenue is $2,600,000.
   a. What is the quantity demanded at the breakeven point? 1,440 necklaces
   b. If the breakeven revenue changes to 3.5 million, will the quantity demanded have increased or decreased? Explain. See margin.
5. A manufacturer determines that a product will reach the breakeven point if sold at either $80 or $150. At $80, the expense and revenue values are both $300,000. At $150, the expense and revenue values are both $100,000.

   On graph paper, graph possible revenue and expense functions that depict this situation. Circle the breakeven points. Answers vary.
6. iSports is considering producing a line of baseball caps with wireless cellphone earpieces attached. The breakeven point occurs when the price of a cap is $170 or $350. At $170, the expense and revenue values are both $2,600,000. At $350, the expense and revenue values are both $900,000.

   On graph paper, graph possible revenue and expense functions that depict this situation. Circle the breakeven points. Answers vary.
7. SeaShade produces beach umbrellas. The expense function is $E = -19{,}000p + 6{,}300{,}000$ and the revenue function is $R = -1{,}000p^2 + 155{,}000p$.
   a. Graph the expense and revenue functions. Label the maximum and minimum values for each axis. Circle the breakeven points. See additional answers.
   b. Determine the prices at the breakeven points. See margin.
   c. Determine the revenue and expense amounts for each of the breakeven points. See margin.

TEACH

Exercises 2 and 3
These questions are related and should be assigned together. Exercise 2 offers a purely numerical situation and Exercise 3 offers a related algebraic situation.

Exercises 5 and 6
These questions offer students numerical information about the relationship between revenue and expense. They are asked to use this data (rather than equations) to sketch graphs.

ANSWERS

1. Warren Buffet speaks to the need to be knowledgeable in order to minimize or eliminate risk. With the knowledge of the prices and subsequent revenue at breakeven points, the risk of putting a product on the market can be minimized.

4b. Increased; substitute 3,500,000 into the expense equation. When you solve for p, the solution is 2,160, which is greater than 1,440.

7b. $51.38 and $122.62

7c. When $p = \$51.38$, $E = \$5{,}323{,}780.00$ and $R = \$5{,}323{,}995.60$. When $p = \$122.62$, $E = \$3{,}970{,}220.00$ and $R = \$3{,}970{,}435.60$.

TEACH

Exercises 9 and 10

These questions are similar in structure and intent. Perhaps assign Exercise 9 to half the class and Exercise 10 to the other half. Have students from each group present the solutions to the other group.

ANSWERS

8c. When $p = \$210.27$, $E = \$7{,}248{,}650.00$ and $R = \$7{,}248{,}637.71$. When $p = \$394.73$, $E = \$6{,}326{,}350.00$ and $R = \$6{,}326{,}337.71$

9a. If the bookcase is set at $22.22 then the maximum revenue would be approximately $8,888.89.

10c. When $p = \$11.48$, $E = \$9{,}556.00$ and $R = \$9{,}558.71$. When $p = \$35.40$, $E = \$2{,}380.00$ and $R = \$2{,}378.88$. See additional answers for graph.

8. Where-R-U produces global positioning systems (GPS) that can be used in a car. The expense equation is $E = -5{,}000p + \$8{,}300{,}000$, and the revenue equation is $R = -100p^2 + 55{,}500p$.

a. Graph the expense and revenue functions. Circle the breakeven points. See additional answers.

b. Determine the prices at the breakeven points. Round to the nearest cent. $210.27 and $394.73

c. Determine the revenue and expense amounts for each of the breakeven points. Round to the nearest cent. See margin.

9. The student government at State College is selling inexpensive bookcases for dorm rooms to raise money for school activities. The expense function is $E = -200p + 10{,}000$ and the revenue function is $R = -18p^2 + 800p$.

a. At what price would the maximum revenue be reached? What would that maximum revenue be? Round to the nearest cent. See margin.

b. Graph the expense and revenue functions. Circle the breakeven points. See additional answers.

c. Determine the prices at the breakeven points. Round to the nearest cent. $13.08 and $42.48

d. Determine the revenue and expense amounts for each of the breakeven points. Round to the nearest cent. When $p = 13.08$, $E = 7{,}384.00$ and $R = 7{,}384.44$. When $p = 42.48$, $E = 1{,}504.00$ and $R = 1{,}502.09$.

10. An electronics store is selling car chargers for cell phones. The expense function is $E = -300p + 13{,}000$ and the revenue function is $R = -32p^2 + 1{,}200p$.

a. At what price would the maximum revenue be reached? $18.75

b. What would that maximum revenue be? Round to the nearest cent. $11,250

c. Graph the expense and revenue functions. Circle the breakeven points. See margin.

d. Determine the prices at the breakeven points. Round to the nearest cent. $11.48 and $35.40

e. Determine the revenue and expense amounts for each of the breakeven points. Round to the nearest cent. When $p = 11.48$, $E = 9{,}556.00$ and $R = 9{,}558.71$. When $p = 35.40$, $E = 2{,}380.00$ and $R = 2{,}378.88$.

Use the graph to answer Exercises 11–14.

11. At what price is the maximum profit reached? $60

12. What are the breakeven prices? $40 and $80

13. Name two prices where the revenue is greater than the expenses. Sample answers: $45 and $50

14. Name two prices where the revenue is less than the expenses. Sample answers: $35 and $150

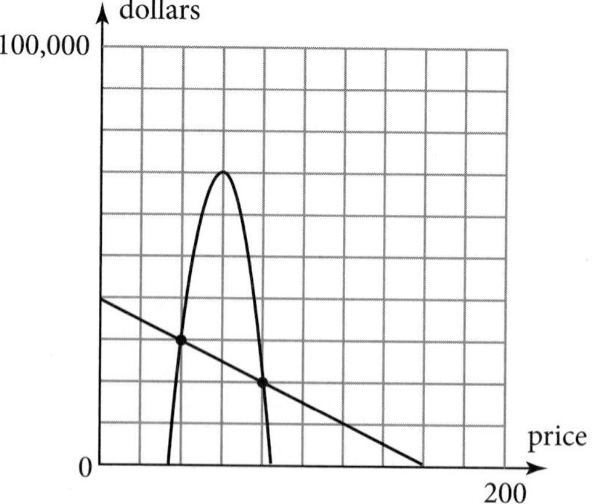

Nobody ever lost money taking a profit.

Bernard Baruch, Businessman

The Profit Equation 2-7

Key Terms
- profit
- maximum profit

Create an equation based on the following. **CCSS Warm-Up**

A company has fixed costs of \$30,000 and variable costs of \$2 per widget. Express the expenses E as a function of x.

$E = 2x + 30{,}000$

Objectives

- Determine a profit equation given the expense and revenue equations.
- Determine the maximum profit and the price at which that maximum is attained.

Common Core

N-Q1, N-Q2, N-Q3, A-CED2, A-CED3, A-REI7, A-REI10, A-REI11, F-IF7a, F-IF8

How do revenue and expenses contribute to profit calculation?

In the business world, two companies may produce and sell the same product. It is possible that both companies will have the same maximum revenue based on their individual revenue functions. However, other aspects of production may not be identical.

Revenue is the amount of money a company makes from the sale of goods or services. While the maximum revenue may be the same for each product, the revenue and expense equations may be different. Figure A displays the graph of the revenue function for the product. Figure B displays the graph of the revenue function of a similar product produced by a different company. The graphs of the revenue functions yield the same maximum values but model different situations.

EXAMINE THE QUESTION

Students have now explored the algebraic and graphical relationships between expense and revenue.

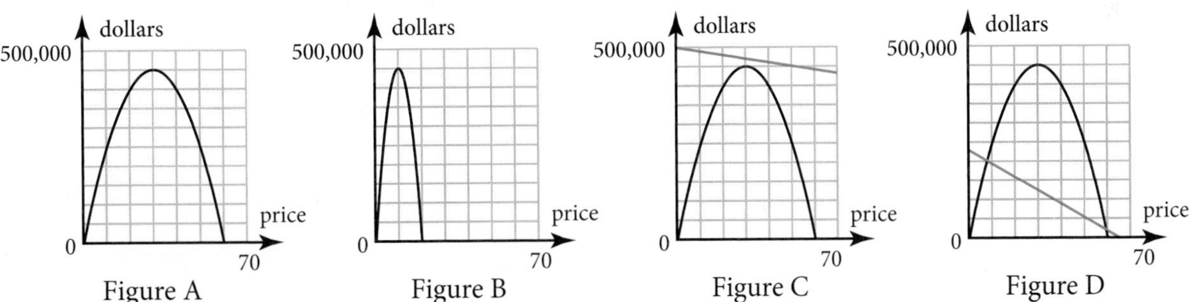

Figure A Figure B Figure C Figure D

Figures C and D depict the same revenue functions but different expense functions. Figure C shows an expense function that is always greater than the revenue graph. Therefore, the company makes no money on the manufacture and sale of the product. The company cannot even reach a breakeven point because there are no breakeven points. In Figure D, the expense function is greater than the revenue function at certain prices, but there are also prices at which the opposite is true. A company would prefer Figure D to model the sale of its product because there are prices at which money coming in is greater than money spent. The money a company makes after expenses have been deducted from revenue is **profit**.

This chapter is about profit and what factors contribute to profit. Ask students for their definition of profit. Then, ask them how revenue and expense contribute to profit. Their response will pave the way for the lesson and act as a first-step in answering the opening question.

CLASS DISCUSSION

Ask students for the names of different companies that produce the same product. Then, ask what aspects of the production might not be identical among the companies.

Describe a graph and a situation in which there is only one breakeven point. What does it mean for production and sales?

Have students examine the graph. Ask them to identify three different prices at which profit would be a small, medium, and large amount (not necessarily the maximum).

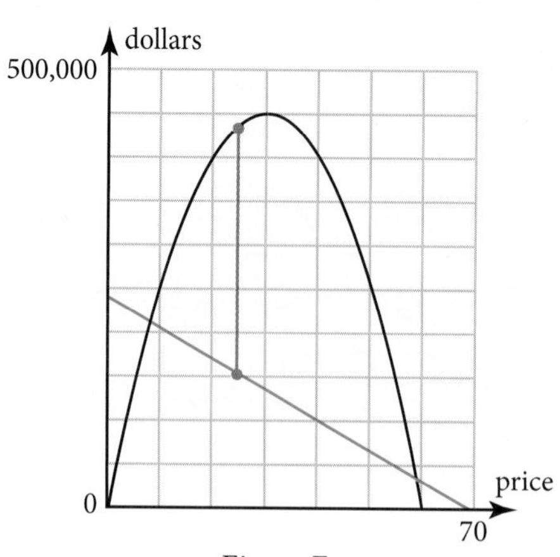

Figure E

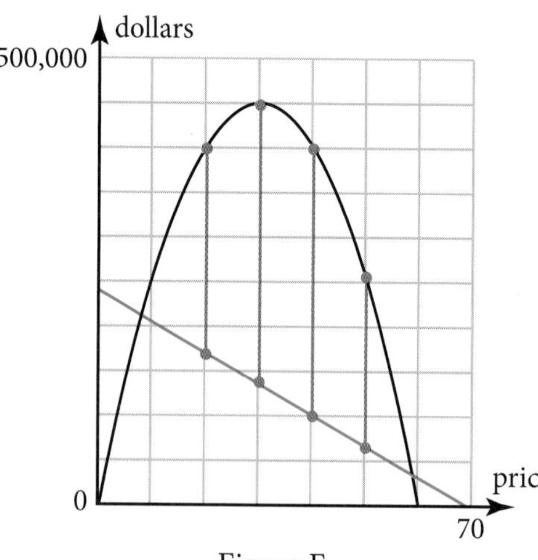

Figure F

In Figure D, there are prices at which the company will make a profit. In Figure C, no matter the price, the revenue is never enough to offset the expenses.

Graphically, *profit* is the vertical distance between the revenue and expense functions. In Figure E, the top of the vertical line segment (in purple) hits the revenue graph at \$437,500 when the price is about \$25.

The bottom of the vertical line segment hits the expense graph at \$150,500 at the same price. The vertical length of this segment is $437{,}500 - 150{,}500 = 287{,}000$ and is the *profit* the company makes when the price is about \$25.

$P = R - E$ where P is profit, R is revenue, and E is expenses

In Figure F, several profit line segments have been drawn for different prices. The longest segment would represent the greatest difference between revenue and expense at a given price. The greatest difference between revenue and expense denotes **maximum profit**.

It is difficult to make a visual determination as to where the maximum profit line might be drawn. Algebra and graphing must be used to make a more precise determination.

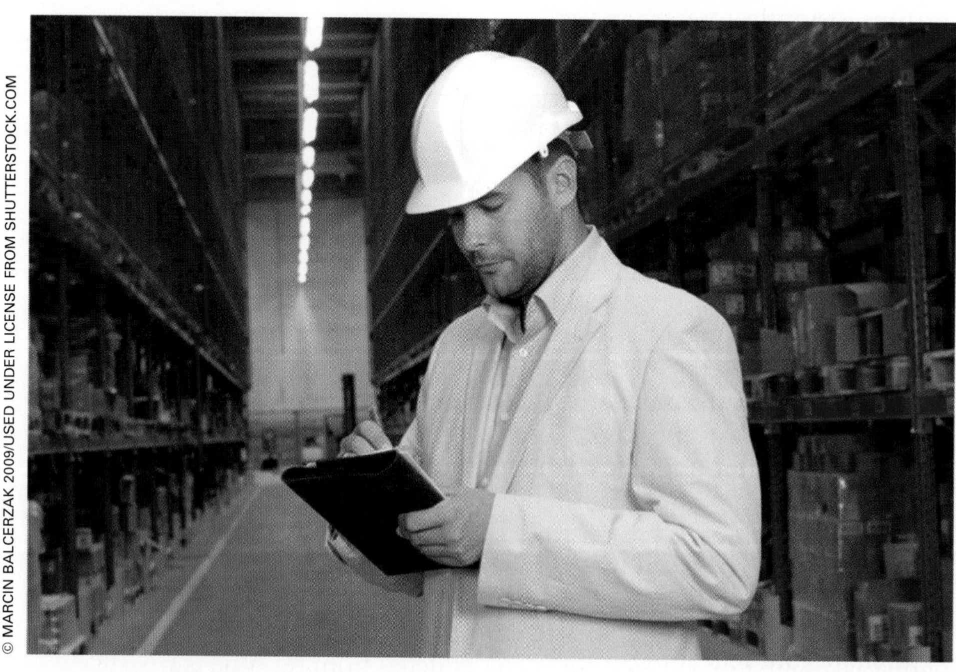

Skills and Strategies

The revenue and expense functions are both functions of price, p, so, you can create a profit function in terms of p.

EXAMPLE 1

Determine the profit equation for the Picasso Paints product in Lesson 2-5. The revenue and expense functions were

$$R = -500p^2 + 30{,}000p$$
$$E = -3{,}500p + 238{,}000$$

SOLUTION Profit is the difference between revenue and expense.

$$P = R - E$$

Substitute for R and E. $\quad P = -500p^2 + 30{,}000p - (-3{,}500p + 238{,}000)$

Distribute. $\quad P = -500p^2 + 30{,}000p + 3{,}500p - 238{,}000$

Combine like terms. $\quad P = -500p^2 + 33{,}500p - 238{,}000$

The profit equation is $P = -500p^2 + 33{,}500p - 238{,}000$. It is a downward parabola because the leading coefficient is negative.

CHECK YOUR UNDERSTANDING

Suppose that the revenue and expense functions are $R = -350p^2 + 18{,}000p$ and $E = -1{,}500p + 199{,}000$. Write the profit equation.

EXAMPLE 2

Use a graphing calculator to draw the graph of the profit equation from Example 1. What is the maximum profit?

SOLUTION Enter the profit equation $P = -500p^2 + 33{,}500p - 238{,}000$ into a graphing calculator. Use the same viewing window you used for the graphs of the revenue and expense functions in Lesson 2-5. The maximum profit is at the vertex of the parabola. Graphing calculators have a maximum feature that determines the value of the maximum point of a function. Let x represent the price, p. The maximum is 323,125 when $x = 33.50$.

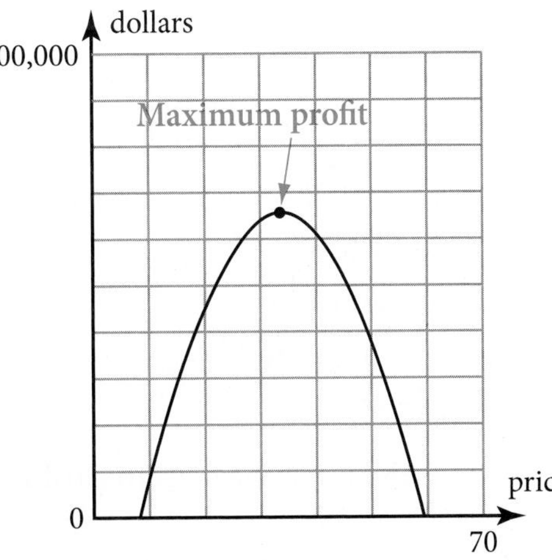

CHECK YOUR UNDERSTANDING

Sketch the graph. Identify the points where zero profit is made. Explain your reasoning.

TEACH

Before you begin Example 1, choose a product that students can relate to such as cell phones. Name two different companies that manufacture cell phones and have students describe the differences in Figures A–D on page 97 by relating them to the cell phones and their manufacturers.

EXAMPLE 1

Perhaps the most common error students make when generating the profit equation is the failure to distribute the subtraction over both terms in the expense expression. Make sure that you alert them to the importance of this part of the computation.

CHECK YOUR UNDERSTANDING

Answer $P = R - E$
$P = -350p^2 + 19{,}500p - 199{,}000$

EXAMPLE 2

Replace the variable p with x and P with Y.

CHECK YOUR UNDERSTANDING

Answer The two points where the profit function intersects the horizontal axis indicate item prices at which no profit is made. These prices are \$8.07 and \$58.93.

EXAMPLE 3

Students should maintain the same viewing window and all three graphs should be pictured in this window. Walk the students through each of the points mentioned in the problem statement and ask them to interpret the situation that is modeled at those points.

CHECK YOUR UNDERSTANDING

Answer No; the greatest difference between revenue and expense does not depend on the maximum revenue.

You might wish to use a ruler to show that the maximum revenue distance and the maximum profit are more than likely not the same.

EXAMPLE 4

To solve this problem algebraically, students need to first determine the profit quadratic and put it in standard form. Discuss where the maximum of a parabola always occurs (horizontal value is the axis of symmetry). Then, lead them through to the calculation of that maximum point. Although the question asks for the price at which the profit is a maximum, the solution shows students how to use that price to determine the maximum profit.

CHECK YOUR UNDERSTANDING

Answer Using $P = -350p^2 + 19{,}500p - 199{,}000$, a maximum profit of \$72,607.14 is attained at a price of \$27.86.

EXAMPLE 3

Graph the revenue, expense, and profit functions on the same coordinate plane. Interpret the zero-profit points, the maximum profit, and how the functions relate to each other.

SOLUTION The maximum profit is at the vertex of the profit graph. The price at this point yields the greatest difference between the revenue and expense functions. There are two zero-profit points on the graph of the profit function. No profit is made at the selling price where expense is equal to revenue. Visually, this is the price at which the revenue and expense functions intersect.

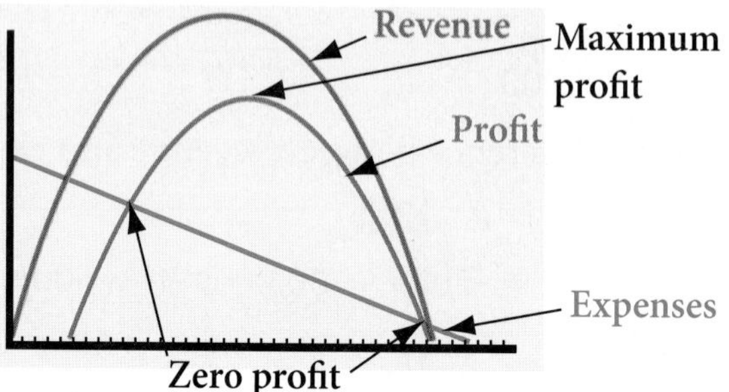

CHECK YOUR UNDERSTANDING

Must maximum profit occur at the same price as the maximum revenue?

EXAMPLE 4

Algebraically, determine the price of the Picasso Paints product that yields the maximum profit.

SOLUTION To determine the maximum profit algebraically, recall that the maximum value occurs on the axis of symmetry. For the profit function $P = -500x^2 + 33{,}500x - 238{,}000$, $a = -500$, $b = 33{,}500$, and $c = -238{,}000$. The x- intercept of the axis of symmetry is determined by calculating $\frac{-b}{2a}$.

$$\frac{-b}{2a} = \frac{-33{,}500}{2(-500)} = \frac{-33{,}500}{-1{,}000} = 33.5$$

The axis of symmetry intercepts the horizontal axis at 33.5. To determine the height of the parabola at 33.5, evaluate the function when $p = 33.5$.

Quadratic equation	$P = -500p^2 + 33{,}500p - 238{,}000$
Substitute 33.5 for *p*.	$P = -500(33.5)^2 + 33{,}500(33.5) - 238{,}000$
Simplify.	$P = 323{,}125$

At \$33.50, a maximum profit of \$323,125 is attained.

CHECK YOUR UNDERSTANDING

Use the profit function from Example 1 Check Your Understanding. Determine the price to the nearest cent that yields the maximum profit.

Applications

Nobody ever lost money taking a profit.
Bernard Baruch, Businessman

1. How might the quote apply to what has been outlined in this lesson? See margin.

Examine each of the graphs in Exercises 2–5. In each case, the blue graph represents the expense function and the black graph represents the revenue function. Describe the profit situation in terms of the expense and revenue functions. See margin.

2.

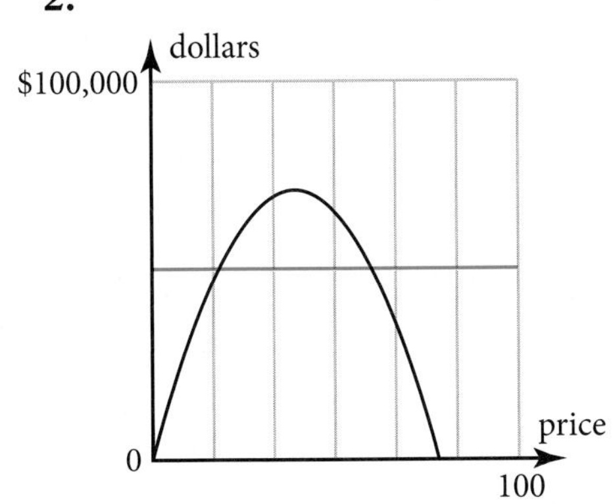

3.

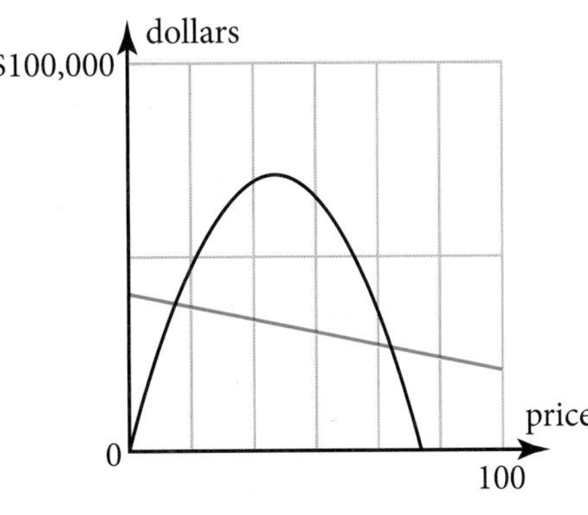

4.

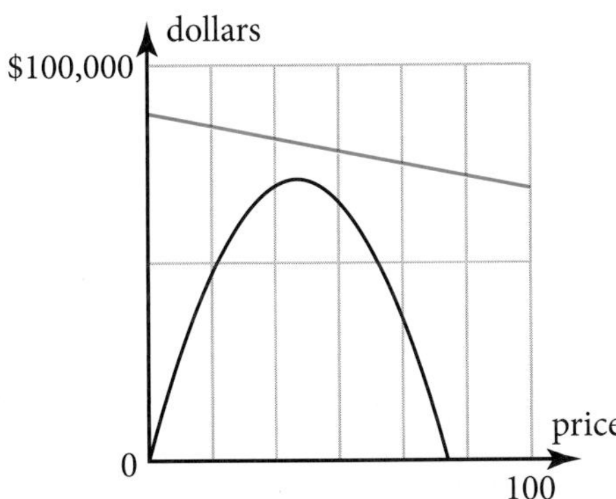

5.

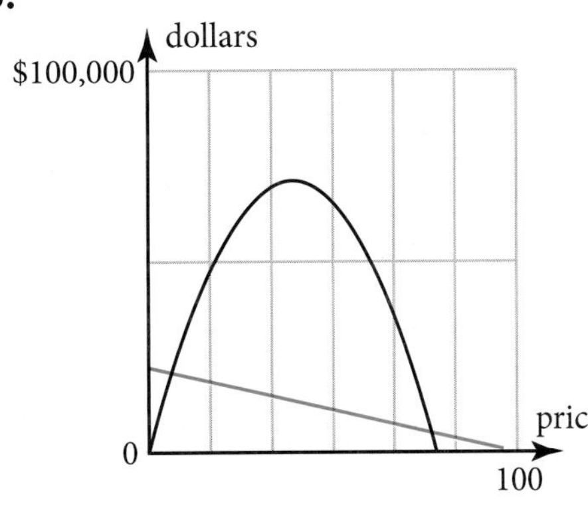

In Exercises 6–9, write the profit function for the given expense and revenue functions.

6. $E = -20{,}000p + 90{,}000$
$R = -2{,}170p^2 + 87{,}000p$ $P = -2{,}170p^2 + 107{,}000p - 90{,}000$

7. $E = -6{,}500p + 300{,}000$
$R = -720p^2 + 19{,}000p$ $P = -720p^2 + 25{,}500p - 300{,}000$

8. $E = -2{,}500p + 80{,}000$
$R = -330p^2 + 9{,}000p$ $P = -330p^2 + 11{,}500p - 80{,}000$

9. $E = -12{,}500p + 78{,}000$
$R = -1{,}450p^2 + 55{,}000p$ $P = -1{,}450p^2 + 67{,}500p - 78{,}000$

ANSWERS

1. A person would lose money when the expense is greater than the revenue. A true profit equation is found in the first quadrant and is the difference between the revenue and the expense. If the expense is greater than the revenue, then there is no profit. Therefore, no one would lose money if they take (make) a profit!
2. The expenses are fixed for this product. Regardless of price, the expenses are $500,000. A profit is made when the price is set approximately between $20 and $60.
3. This situation is similar to that examined in Skills and Strategies. Expenses decrease as the price of the item increases. Profit is made when the price is set approximately between $13 and $70.
4. The expenses are greater than the revenue at all possible prices. No profit can be made from the sale of this item.
5. This situation is similar to that examined in Skills and Strategies. Expenses decrease as the price of the item increases. Profit is made when the price is set approximately between $7 and $18.

TEACH

Exercise 12

Encourage students to attempt at least one of these problems in two different ways (graphically and algebraically).

Exercises 13–16

These questions are similar in intent. You might want to randomly assign two problems to each student so that when reviewing them the next day, students can listen to their peers explain the individual work that was done.

ANSWERS

10. Approximately \$26; it appears to have the greatest positive vertical distance from the revenue to the expense function.

11a. In Exercise 7 the expenses are always greater than the revenue.

12a. At \$15.50, the maximum profit would be \$46,100.

12b. At \$11.89, the maximum profit would be \$27,324.32.

12c. At \$261.18, the maximum profit would be \$11,541,235.29.

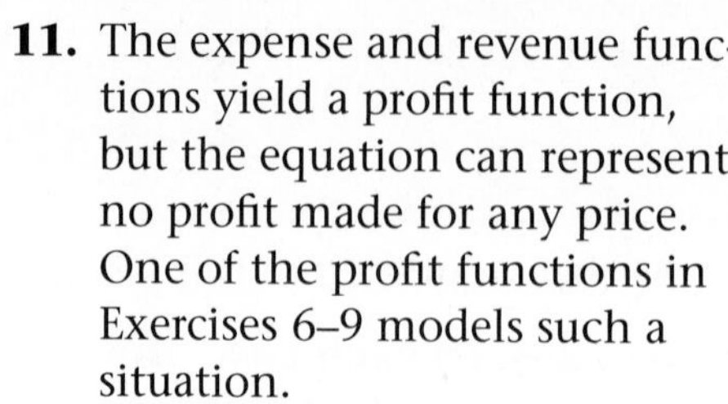

10. Examine the revenue (black) and expense (blue) functions. Estimate the price at the maximum profit. Explain your reasoning. See margin.

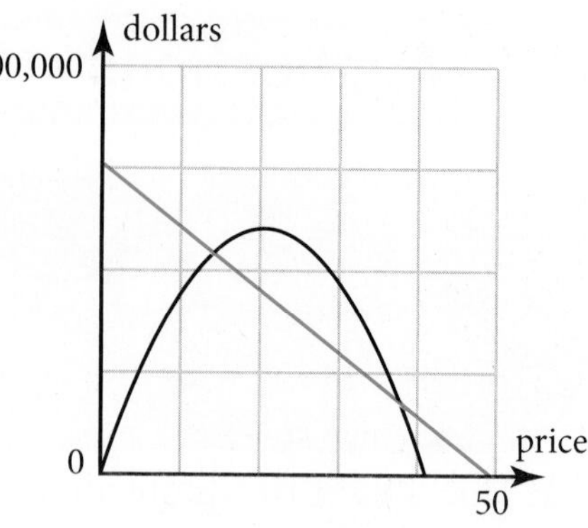

11. The expense and revenue functions yield a profit function, but the equation can represent no profit made for any price. One of the profit functions in Exercises 6–9 models such a situation.

a. Determine which profit function models a no profit situation. See margin.

b. What does a profit function look like when no profit can be made? If expenses are always greater than the revenue, the profit parabola will lie entirely below the horizontal axis.

12. Determine the maximum profit and the price that would yield the maximum profit for each. See margin.

a. $P = -400p^2 + 12{,}400p - 50{,}000$

b. $P = -370p^2 + 8{,}800p - 25{,}000$

c. $P = -170p^2 + 88{,}800p - 55{,}000$

13. Greenyard's manufactures and sells yard furniture made out of recycled materials. It is considering making a lawn chair from recycled aluminum and fabric products. The expense and revenue functions are $E = -1{,}850p + 800{,}000$ and $R = -100p^2 + 20{,}000p$.

a. Determine the profit function. $P = -100p^2 + 21{,}850p - 800{,}000$

b. Determine the price, to the nearest cent, that yields the maximum profit. \$109.25

c. Determine the maximum profit, to the nearest cent. \$393,556.25

14. Mountaineer Products Incorporated manufactures mountain-bike accessories. It is considering making a new type of reflector for night biking. The expense and revenue functions are $E = -450p + 90{,}000$ and $R = -185p^2 + 9{,}000p$.

a. Determine the profit function. $P = -185p^2 + 9{,}450p - 90{,}000$

b. Determine the price, to the nearest cent, that yields the maximum profit. \$25.54

c. Determine the maximum profit, to the nearest cent. \$30,679.05

15. Business Bargains manufactures office supplies. It is considering selling sticky-notes in the shape of the state in which they will be sold. The expense and revenue functions are $E = -250p + 50{,}000$ and $R = -225p^2 + 7{,}200p$.

a. Determine the profit function. $P = -225p^2 + 7{,}450p - 50{,}000$

b. Determine the price, to the nearest cent, that yields the maximum profit. \$16.56

c. Determine the maximum profit, to the nearest cent. \$11,669.44

16. FlipFlops manufactures beach sandals. Their expense and revenue functions are $E = -300p + 32{,}000$ and $R = -275p^2 + 6{,}500p$.

a. Determine the profit function. $P = -275p^2 + 6{,}800p - 32{,}000$

b. Determine the price, to the nearest cent, that yields the maximum profit. \$12.36

c. Determine the maximum profit, to the nearest cent. \$10,036.36

All models are wrong. Some models are useful.
George Box, Statistician and Quality Control Pioneer

Mathematically Modeling a Business

2-8

Key Terms
- dependence
- transitive property of dependence

CCSS Warm-Up

Use graph paper and a straightedge.
Find the points at which the graphs of the following equations intersect: $y = -x^2 + 4$ *and* $y = x + 2$.

(1, 3) and (−2, 0)

Objectives

- Recognize the transitive property of dependence as it is used in a business model.
- Use multiple pieces of information, equations, and methodologies to model a new business.

Common Core

N-Q1, N-Q2, A-CED2, A-CED3, A-REI7, A-REI10, A-REI11, F-IE4, F-IF7a, F-IF8

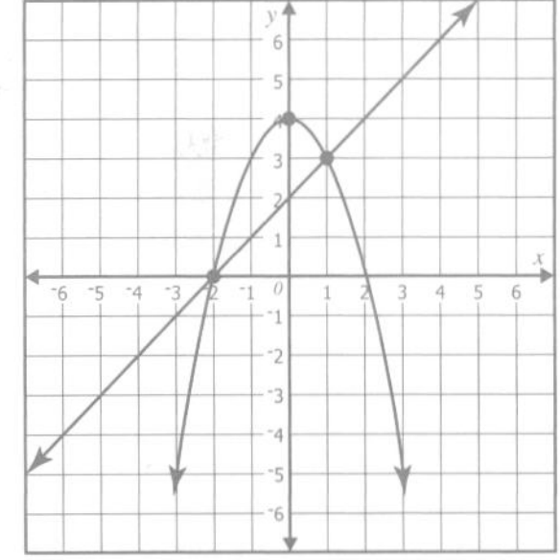

How can you mathematically model a start-up business?

Statistics are necessary in making business decisions. The relationship between supply and demand; expense, revenue, and profit; and breakeven points must be analyzed. All of the factors may be modeled together to assess business situations.

Dependence is used in many contexts.

- In sports, baseball fans *depend* on the manager of the team to lead the team to victory. In turn, the manager of the team *depends* on the players to work hard to succeed.
- In politics, voters *depend* on their local elected officials to represent them. Local elected officials *depend* on state government officials to give them the support they need to represent the voters.
- When starting a business venture, expenses *depend* on the demanded quantity of the product. Demand *depends* on the price of the product.

These are a few examples of dependence in daily life. In the first example, if the fans depend on the manager and the manager depends on the players, the fans depend on the players as well. In the second example, if the voters depend on the local elected officials and the local officials depend on the state officials, the voters depend upon the state officials, too. Finally, in the last example, if expenses depend on quantity and quantity depends on price, expenses also depend on price. These are examples of the **transitive property of dependence**.

If *x depends on y* and *y depends on z,* it follows that *x depends on z.*

The determination of the price that yields the maximum profit depends on a number of factors that precede it. Mathematical modeling using algebra is an illustration of the use of the transitive property in business.

EXAMINE THE QUESTION

In order for this question to make sense, students need a good understanding of what a mathematical model is and when those models are used. Discuss some situations where real life situations are modeled mathematically in order to gain information that would otherwise be difficult to attain.

CLASS DISCUSSION

Name other situations that illustrate dependence.

Have students use the situations identified in previous discussions and illustrate how they might be examples of the transitive property of dependence.

TEACH

Discuss with students how the models in this lesson differ from models used in math courses in earlier grades and how they are the same. Students will likely remember using models such as algebra tiles, fraction bars, and three-dimensional models of geometric solids. They will not, however, usually think of graphing on a coordinate plane or writing and solving an equation as a model. Guide students to see that the fundamental use of a model is the same, whether it is an equation or a cube.

EXAMPLE 1

It is important to work through both methods with students so that they can see the nature of mathematical dependency in this situation.

CHECK YOUR UNDERSTANDING

Answer Using either method, the expense is $5,248,000.

EXTEND YOUR UNDERSTANDING

Answer Once the value of *z* is known, then *y* can be calculated. With *y* calculated, then *x* can be determined. Once *x* is determined, it is substituted into the first equation, and *A* can be evaluated.

Skills and Strategies

Mathematically modeling a business situation helps you better understand the relationships between and among variables.

EXAMPLE 1

Determine the expense, E, for production of an item when the price, p, is \$60 given $E = 50q + 80{,}000$ and $q = 80p + 100{,}000$.

SOLUTION E depends on q, and q depends on p. To find the value of E at a particular price, p, use substitution or express the expense equation directly in terms of price. Both methods illustrate the transitive property of dependence.

The first method uses the price given to find a value for q that can be substituted into the equation for E.

Method 1

Use the equation for q.	$q = 80p + 100{,}000$
Substitute 60 for p.	$q = 80(60) + 100{,}000$
Simplify.	$q = 104{,}800$
Use the equation for E.	$E = 50q + 80{,}000$
Substitute 104,800 for q.	$E = 50(104{,}800) + 80{,}000$
Simplify.	$E = 5{,}320{,}000$

The second method substitutes the value of q in terms of p into the expense equation, and then uses the price given to find the value of E.

Method 2

Use the equation for E.	$E = 50q + 80{,}000$
Substitute $80p + 100{,}000$ for q.	$E = 50(80p + 100{,}000) + 80{,}000$
Distribute.	$E = 4{,}000p + 5{,}000{,}000 + 80{,}000$
Calculate.	$E = 4{,}000p + 5{,}080{,}000$
Substitute 60 for p.	$E = 4{,}000(60) + 5{,}080{,}000$
Simplify.	$E = 5{,}320{,}000$

The expenses total \$5,320,000.

CHECK YOUR UNDERSTANDING

Determine the expense, E, for production of an item when the price, p, is \$42 given $E = 50q + 80{,}000$ and $q = 80p + 100{,}000$.

EXTEND YOUR UNDERSTANDING

Suppose $A = 20x + 30$, $x = 30y + 40$, and $y = 40z + 50$. Describe how the value of A depends on the value of z.

EXAMPLE 2

A business model uses a summary analysis of the situation in terms of dependent variables. Examine the three graphs of a business situation for the production of widgets. The graphs depict numerical information that is needed to complete the summary analysis.

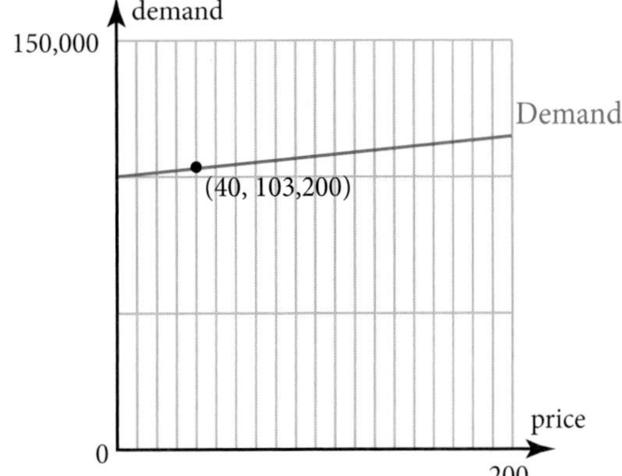

Write the summary analysis in terms of the data presented in the graphs. The summary analysis should have the following format.

In summary, to start this business, __?__ widgets should be manufactured. Each should be sold for \$__?__.

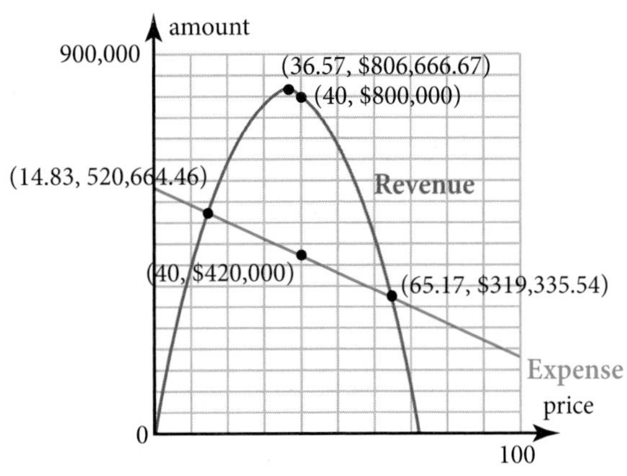

The breakeven point is reached at a price of \$__?__ or \$__?__, but a profit is made at any price between those prices.

At the selling price, there is revenue of \$__?__ and expenses of \$__?__, resulting in a profit of \$__?__.

SOLUTION In summary, to start this business, 103,200 widgets should be manufactured. Each should be sold for \$40.

This is asking the price that will yield the maximum profit and the quantity demanded at that price.

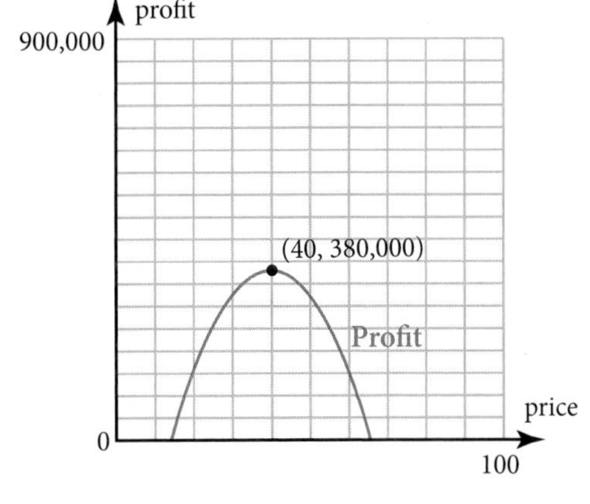

The breakeven point is reached at a price of \$14.83 or \$65.17, but a profit is made at any price between those prices.

These amounts can be found at the intersection points of the expense and revenue functions.

At the selling price, there is revenue of \$800,000 and expenses of \$420,000, resulting in a profit of \$380,000.

Use the price that yields the maximum profit, \$40, in both the expense and profit functions.

EXAMPLE 2

Students may need assistance with this activity in determining what type of information each graph yields. Before attempting a solution, ask students to examine each graph and determine what information can be gained from it.

CHECK YOUR UNDERSTANDING

Use the points labeled on the graphs to show that the maximum profit at the selling price is the difference between the revenue and expense values at that price.

CHECK YOUR UNDERSTANDING

Answer The maximum point on the profit function is (40, \$380,000). The expense at a price of \$40 is \$420,000, and the revenue at a price of \$40 is \$800,000.

800,000 – 420,000 = 380,000

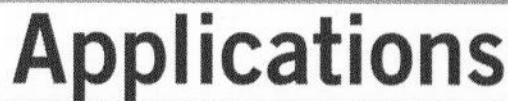

Applications

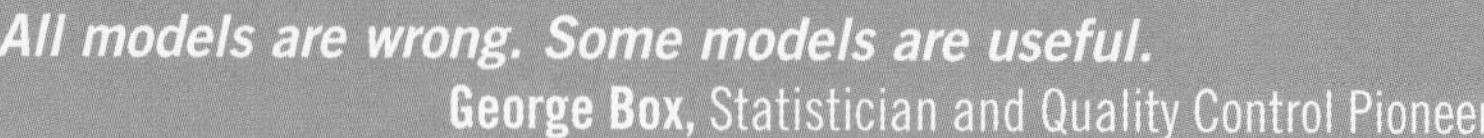

All models are wrong. Some models are useful.
George Box, Statistician and Quality Control Pioneer

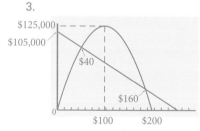

1. How might those words apply to what has been outlined in this lesson? See margin.

2. Use the following graph to answer the questions below.
Let Y_1 = expense function and Y_2 = revenue function.

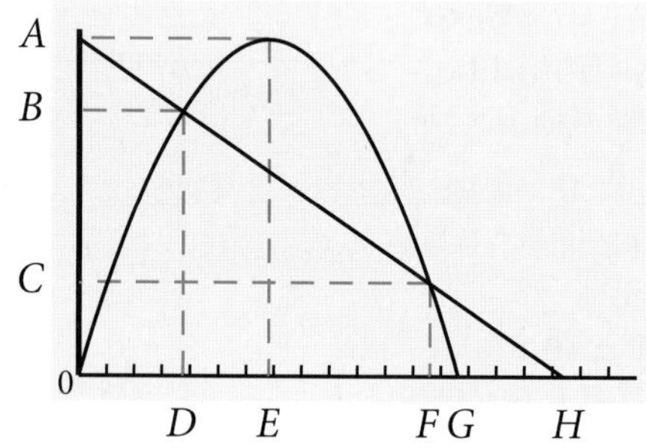

a. Explain the significance of point (D, B). It is the first breakeven point.
b. Explain the significance of point (E, A). It is the maximum revenue point.
c. Explain the significance of point (F, C). It is the second breakeven point.
d. Explain the significance of point (G, 0). It represents the price at which no revenue is made.
e. Explain the significance of point (H, 0). It represents the price at which there are no expenses.
f. Where do you think the maximum profit might occur? See margin.

3. Draw a graph of expense function Y_1 and revenue function Y_2 that meet the following criteria. See margin.

Maximum revenue: $125,000
Breakeven points: $40 and $160
Price at which no revenue is made: $200
Maximum expenses: $105,000

Use the following situation to answer Exercises 4–20.
A company produces a security device known as Toejack. Toejack is a computer chip that parents attach between the toes of a child, so parents can track the child's location at any time using an online system. The company has entered into an agreement with an Internet service provider, so the price of the chip will be low. Set up a demand function—a schedule of how many Toejacks would be demanded by the public at different prices.

4. As the price increases, what is expected to happen to the quantity demanded? decreases

5. The horizontal axis represents price, and the vertical axis represents quantity. Does the demand function have a positive or negative slope? Explain. The demand is decreasing; the slope is negative.

TEACH

Exercise 2

This question is a prerequisite for all of the exercises to follow. It is very important that students have an understanding of the points identified on the graphs and what those points represent in the context of a start-up business. You might want to do this problem in class as a closure piece for the lesson.

ANSWERS

1. Models simulate reality but they themselves are not reality. There are a fixed number of variables that are used in models. In reality, there are many more variables that contribute to the outcome of a situation. So, while models can be wrong, they can still be useful.

2f. The maximum profit occurs where there is the greatest vertical difference between the revenue and expense functions. It appears that this might happen at an x value slightly to the left of E.

3.

$125,000
$105,000
$40
$160
0
$100
$200

6. The company decides to conduct a market research survey to determine the best price for the device. The variable p represents price, and q represents quantity demanded. The points are listed as (p, q).

(14, 8,200), (11, 9,100), (16, 7,750), (16, 8,300), (14, 8,900), (17, 7,100), (13, 8,955), (11, 9,875), (11, 9,425), (18, 5,825)

Make a scatterplot of the data. Does the data look like it has a linear form? The scatterplot has a linear form. See margin.

7. Find the regression equation. Remember the quantity demanded, q, is the dependent variable. Round the slope and y-intercept to the nearest hundredth. $q = -423.61p + 14{,}315.94$

8. Is the linear regression line a good predictor? Explain. See margin.

9. Examine the data to see if there is any relationship between the price and the quantity demanded. Determine the correlation coefficient between price and demand, rounded to nearest hundredth. Explain the significance of the correlation coefficient. See margin.

10. Fixed costs are $24,500, and variable costs are $6.12 per Toejack. Express expenses, E, as a function of q, the quantity produced. $E = 6.12q + 24{,}500$

11. Express the revenue, R, in terms of p and q. $R = pq$

12. Express the revenue, R, in terms of p. $R = -423.61p^2 + 14{,}315.94p$

13. Use the transitive property of dependence to express expense, E, in terms of p. Round to the nearest hundredth. $E = -2{,}592.49p + 112{,}113.55$

14. Graph the expense and revenue functions.
   a. Determine an appropriate maximum horizontal-axis value. 50
   b. Determine an appropriate maximum vertical-axis value. 130,000
   c. Sketch the graphs of the expense and revenue functions. See additional answers.

15. Determine the coordinates of the maximum point on the revenue graph. Round the coordinates to the nearest hundredth. (16.90, 120,952.13)

16. Determine the breakeven points. Round to the nearest hundredth. (8.40, 90,343.87) and (31.52, 30,403.76)

17. Express the profit, P, in terms of p. $P = -423.61p^2 + 16{,}908.43p - 112{,}113.55$

18. Graph the profit function. Determine the coordinates of the maximum point of the profit graph. At what price, p, is profit maximized? Round to the nearest cent. This will be the price at which Toejack will sell! (19.96, 56,611.81); The profit is maximized at a price of $19.96. See additional answers for graph.

19. Write the business summary statement by filling in the blanks.

In summary, to start this business, _**a.**_ Toejacks should be manufactured. Each should be sold at $_**b.**_. The breakeven point is reached at a price of $_**c.**_ or $_**d.**_, but a profit is made at any price between those prices. At the selling price, there is a revenue of $_**e.**_ and expenses of $_**f.**_, resulting in a profit of $_**g.**_.

See margin.

20. If shares of stock are sold with an initial value of $5 each, how many shares must be sold to get enough money to start the business? 12,074

TEACH

Exercises 4–20

These problems guide students through the modeling process. They must be assigned in their entirety since they are cumulative and sequential.

ANSWERS

6.

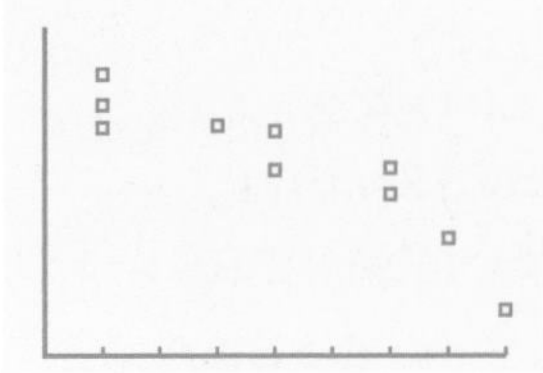

8. Based on the correlation coefficient of –0.92, the linear regression line is a good predictor.
9. $r = -0.92$; This is a significant correlation because the coefficient is close to –1.
19. a. 5,861; b. $19.96; c. $8.40; d. $31.52; e. $116,979.26; f. $60,367.45; g. $56,611.81.

CHAPTER 2

Assessment

Real Numbers

You Write the Story!!

CHAPTER 2 ASSESSMENT

REAL NUMBERS

You Write the Story
Students' answers will vary. Begin by having them focus on the shape of the curve. Why are the points at the beginning and at the end of the time cycle higher than those in the middle? Why are the mid-cycle points close to horizontal? Once they have established the nature of the graph, the article should be easy to write.

REALITY CHECK

The Reality Check projects are a terrific form of alternative assessment. They give students an additional avenue to show what they have learned, so their grades are not solely based on tests.

The Reality Check Projects in this lesson ask students to do research, interview business workers, read the business section of a newspaper, and more. Each project is designed so that students can use what they have learned in this chapter as a springboard for further work.

Examine the scatterplot below. It depicts the rate of failures reported for a single product. A product failure is when a product fails to do what it was manufactured to do. The diagram below is called a "bathtub curve." Write a short newspaper-type article centered on this graph, based on a hypothetical situation you create. An electronic copy of the graph can be found at school.cengage.com/math/financialalgebra. Copy and paste it into your article.

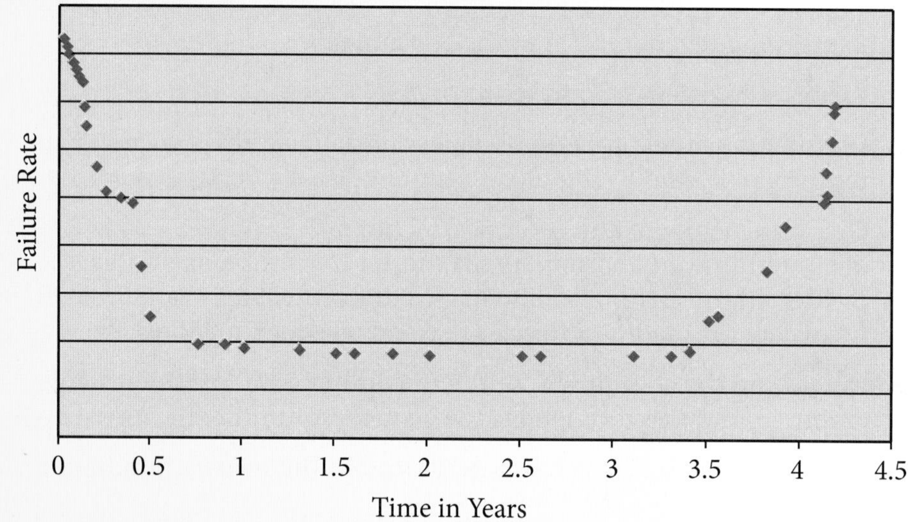

Reality Check

1. Corporations pride themselves on the recognition of their logos. This project involves creating a game. Use the library or the Internet to find logos of twelve popular brands. Look only for logos that do not include the corporate name. Paste the logos on a sheet of paper. With teacher approval, give the class the sheet of logos, and ask students to write the brand name next to each logo.
2. Use the Internet or library to find more details on the failures of the three products mentioned at the beginning of the chapter: New Coke, the Edsel, and the Sony Betamax. Write a report on the specific reasons for each failure.
3. Find an example of a product not mentioned in this chapter that failed. Prepare a report detailing the story behind the product's invention and its failure.

4. Interview a local businessperson. Ask for examples of fixed and variable expenses. Do not ask for amounts as that information is private. Make a comprehensive list. Also ask about the history of the business and how he or she became involved in it.

5. Trace the history of the portable, hand held calculator from inception to the present. Include brand names, sales figures, features, pictures, model names, etc. Prepare the findings in a report.

6. On January 1, 1962, the Beatles, looking for their first recording contract, had an audition with Decca records. They were turned down, and legend has it that Decca said " . . . guitar groups are on the way out." Use the library and/or the Internet to research the international sales of Beatles recordings over the past 5 decades and any other financially-related Beatles facts. Compare Decca's decision to the product failures discussed in this chapter. What are the similarities and differences? Prepare the findings in a report.

7. How prevalent are brand names in society? With teacher approval, get two copies of the same newspaper or magazine. Divide the class into two teams. First, give the number of pages in that publication. Next, have each team predict the number of times a brand name will be used. Have each team read through the entire publication (teams may split up the reading) and count every brand name that is written in the publication. If a name is written multiple times, count every time it is written. Write in the newspapers or magazines to easily keep track. Compare findings, and if they differ, find out where they differ. How did the findings compare to the predictions?

8. Search the Internet for three different websites that offer breakeven calculators. Compare and contrast them. What can one do that the other(s) can't? Write up a recommendation for the use of one of the three calculators and justify the recommendation.

9. Look either in the Business section of a newspaper or online to identify three companies that claim to have made a profit over a period of time. Research how they each define *profit,* and state the monetary amounts that each is quoting as their profit for the time period.

10. Many children set up lemonade stands in front of their homes when they were younger. What would the fixed costs of a lemonade stand be? What would be the variable costs? At what price would a glass of lemonade be sold? Explain how to decide the price. Estimate revenues and profit over a one-week period.

Dollars and Sense Your Financial News Update

Go to www.cengage.com/school/math/financialalgebra where you will find a link to a website containing current issues about modeling a business.

Really? Really! REVISITED

REALLY? REALLY! REVISITED

In the Really? Really! feature at the beginning of the chapter, students were introduced to products that were market failures. Certainly, the manufacturers of these products envisioned market success. But, for numbers of reasons, each individual to the product, consumers just didn't make the purchases. Here, students revisit one such product failure, the Edsel. The structure of this bar graph might be new to students and will need an explanation. The concepts of automobile depreciation and appreciation will be explored in detail in the Automobile chapter, but are worth mentioning here. Often some cars depreciate at the outset and then after numbers of years become a collector's item. Once that happens, the demand for them increases and the value of the car appreciates. This appears to be the case with the Edsel.

After completing the questions related to the graph, encourage students to follow up with the Internet research extension activity. Remind them of the role perception played in stock splits. Link that concept to how perception played a role in the sale of the Edsel.

Ford Motor Company predicted 1958 Edsel sales to exceed 200,000 cars. Only 63,107 of the 1958 models were sold. The 1960 model saw only 2,846 cars sold. During the three years of production, approximately 110,847 Edsels were manufactured.

Today, less than 6,000 of them remain. As a rare curiosity, they are prized by many car collectors and have grown in value.

The following bar graph gives the values of a 1958 Edsel Villager 9-Passenger Station Wagon during the years 1999–2008. Because the value depends on the condition of the car, car appraisers rate the condition of a classic car. On this graph, Condition 2 is the best condition and Condition 6 is the poorest condition.

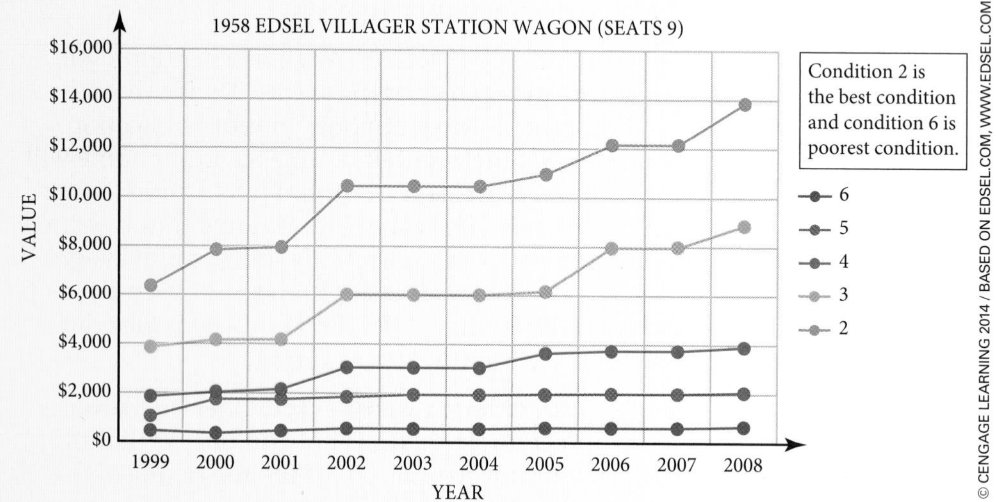

1. Give an approximate value for the 1958 Villager in a condition of 6 in 2008. $1,000
2. Give an approximate value for the 1958 Villager in a condition of 2 in 2008. $14,000
3. Approximate the difference between a 1958 Villager in a condition of 6 and in a condition of 2 in 2008. $13,000
4. Approximate the difference between a 1958 Villager in a condition of 2 in 1999 and in 2008. $7,000

Look at the general trend of the graph. If a failure is kept for long enough, it may prove to be a good decision! Go online and look for pictures of the original 1958 Edsel. Also find photos of the 1958 Chevrolet, the 1958 Chrysler, and the 1958 Buick. Does the Edsel look very different from the other cars? Consumers thought it did! And that's reality!

Applications

1. Examine each scatterplot. Identify each as showing a positive correlation, a negative correlation, or no correlation.

a. 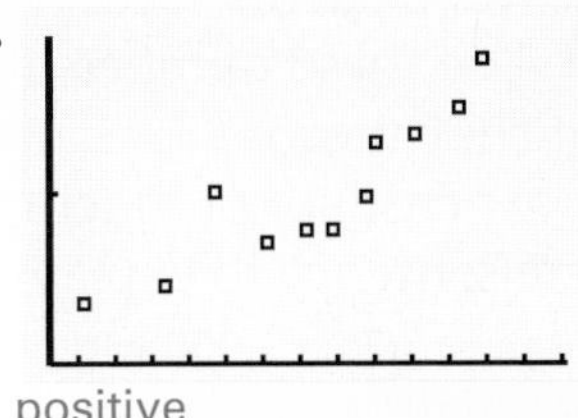
positive

b. 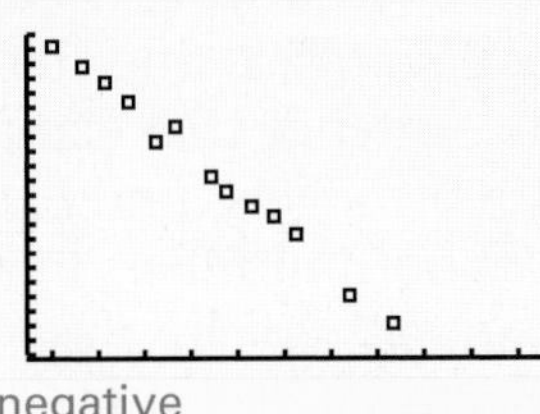
negative

c. 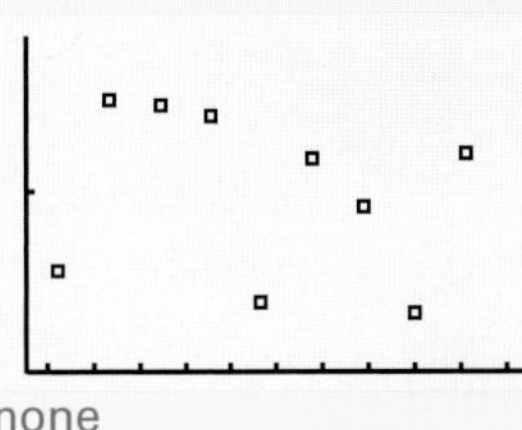
none

2. If each set of bivariate data has a causal relationship, determine the explanatory and response variables for each set of data.
   a. number of hours spent reading and page number on which you are reading hours-explanatory; page number-response
   b. calories burned and number of minutes of exercising minutes exercised-explanatory; calories-response
   c. amount paid as income tax and the amount of a paycheck paycheck-explanatory; taxes-response
   d. pounds of hamburger used to make a meatloaf and number of people that can be fed from the meatloaf pounds of hamburger-explanatory; people-response

3. Which of the following scatterplots does not show a line of best fit? b

a. 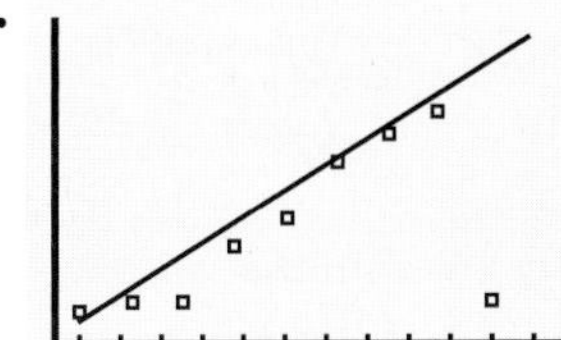

b. 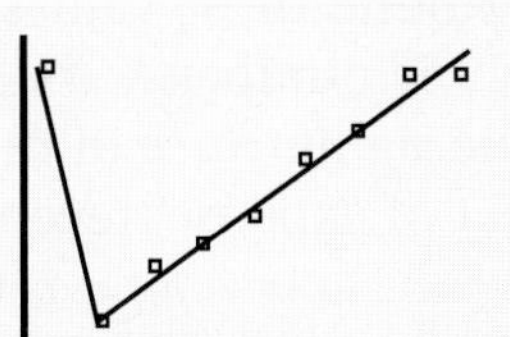

c. 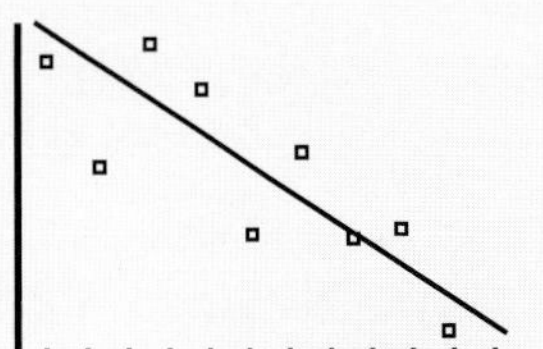

4. Describe each of the following correlation coefficients using the terms strong, moderate, or weak and positive or negative.
   a. $r = 0.17$ weak positive
   b. $r = -0.62$ moderate negative
   c. $r = -0.88$ strong negative
   d. $r = 0.33$ moderate positive
   e. $r = 0.49$ moderate positive
   f. $r = -0.25$ weak negative
   g. $r = 0.91$ strong positive

5. The graph shows supply and demand curves for the newest game controller for the VVV video game system.

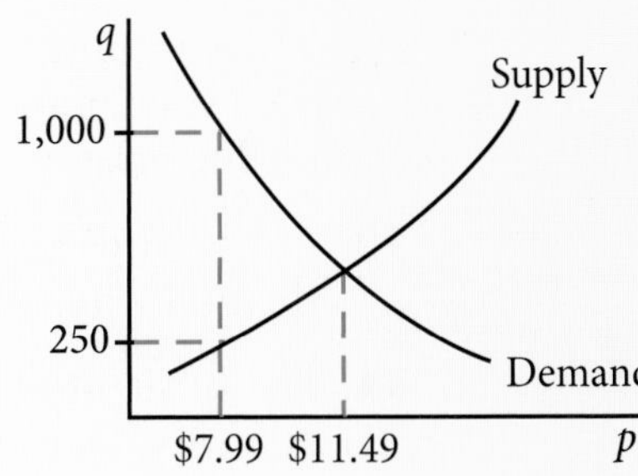

   a. What is the equilibrium price? $11.49
   b. What will happen if the price is set at $7.99? Demand will exceed supply.
   c. How many game controllers are demanded at a price of $7.99? 1,000
   d. How many game controllers are supplied at a price of $7.99? 250
   e. What will happen if the price is set at $12.99? Supply will exceed demand, and suppliers will attempt to sell the excess product at a lower price.

ANSWERS

6d. demand = 2,500; when price is set at \$25 per item, the demand for the item will be 2,500.

7a.

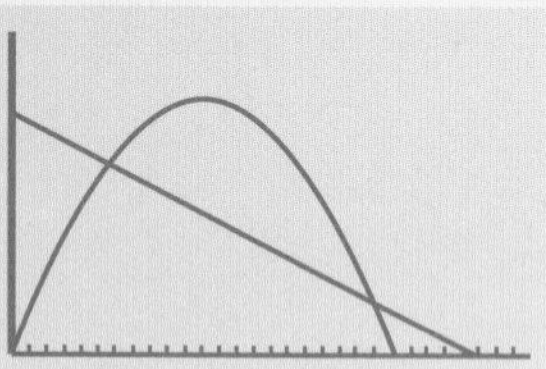

9b. The maximum profit price is approximately \$23.33. At that price, the maximum profit is approximately \$76,666.66.

6. The demand function for a certain product is $q = -300p + 10{,}000$. The fixed expenses are \$500,000 and the variable expenses are \$2 per item produced.
   a. Express the expense function in terms of q. $E = 2q + 500{,}000$
   b. Use substitution to express the expense function in terms of p. $E = -600p + 520{,}000$
   c. If the price is set at \$20, what quantity will be demanded? 4,000
   d. If price is set at \$25, find the demand. Use these numbers in a complete sentence that explains what they mean. See margin.
   e. If q = 1,000 widgets, find E, the cost (expense) of producing them. Use both numbers in a complete sentence to explain what they mean. E = 502,000; it costs \$502,000 to produce 1,000 widgets.
   f. If the price is set at p = \$15, how much will it cost to produce the correct number of widgets? Use these numbers in a complete sentence to explain what they mean. E = 511,000; it would cost \$511,000 to produce widgets that sell for \$15 each.
7. Let the expense function for a particular item be defined as $y = -1{,}950x + 53{,}000$. Let the revenue function be defined as $y = -450x^2 + 10{,}000x$, where x represents price in each equation. Use this window.
   a. Graph the two functions. See margin.
   b. Determine the x- and y-coordinates of the first point where the two graphs intersect. Round those values to the nearest whole number. x = 6 and y = 42,026
   c. Explain the significance of this point in the context of expense, revenue, and price. When the price is set at approximately \$6, both the revenue and the expense will be approximately \$42,026.

WINDOW
Xmin=0
Xmax=30
Xscl=1
Ymin=0
Ymax=70000
Yscl=1
Xres=1

8. Express the revenue equation in terms of price given the demand function.
   a. $q = -900p + 120{,}000$ $R = -900p^2 + 120{,}000p$
   b. $q = -88{,}000p + 234{,}000{,}000$ $R = -88{,}000p^2 + 234{,}000{,}000p$
9. The expense function for a widget is $E = -3{,}000p + 250{,}000$. The revenue function is $R = -600p^2 + 25{,}000p$.
   a. Write the profit equation in simplified form. $P = -600p^2 + 28{,}000p - 250{,}000$
   b. Use the axis of symmetry formula to determine the maximum profit price and the maximum profit. See margin.

Use this situation to answer Exercises 10–25.

A company is interested in producing and selling a new device called an eyePOD (eyewear personal optical device). The eyePOD is an MP3 and video player built into a pair of sunglasses. The user can listen to music from the small earphones and watch videos projected on the screen behind the glasses.

10. As the price of the eyePOD increases, what is expected to happen to the quantity demanded? decreases
11. The horizontal axis represents price, and the vertical axis represents quantity. Does the demand function have a positive or negative slope? Explain. The demand is decreasing; the slope is negative.

12. The market research department conducted consumer surveys at college campuses and reported its results. In these ordered pairs, the first number represents price, p, and the second number represents the quantity demanded, q. The points are listed as (p, q).

(300, 10,000), (325, 8,900), (350, 8,800), (375, 8,650), (400, 6,700), (425, 6,500), (450, 5,000), (475, 4,500), (500, 4,450), (525, 3,000)

Make a scatterplot of the data. See margin.

13. What is the correlation coefficient? Round it to the nearest hundredth. Is this line a good predictor? Explain. −0.98; because the absolute value of the correlation coefficient is greater than 0.75, this is a good predictor.

14. Write the regression equation. Remember that the demanded quantity, q, is the dependent variable. Round the slope and y-intercept to the nearest hundredth. $q = -30.74p + 19{,}330$

15. The accounting department has calculated that this could be the biggest product to hit the market in years. It anticipates the fixed costs to be $160,000 and the variable cost to be $150 per eyePOD. Express expenses, E, as a function of q, the quantity produced. $E = 150q + 160{,}000$

16. Express the revenue, R, in terms of p and q. $R = pq$

17. Express the revenue, R, in terms of p. $R = -30.74p^2 + 19{,}330p$

18. Recall the transitive property of dependence. Express expenses, E, in terms of p. Round to the nearest hundredth. $E = -4{,}611p + 3{,}059{,}500$

19. Graph the expense and revenue functions.

a. Determine an appropriate maximum horizontal-axis value. 700

b. Determine an appropriate maximum vertical-axis value. 3,100,000

c. Sketch the graphs of the expense and revenue functions. See additional answers.

20. Determine the coordinates of the maximum point on the revenue graph. Round to the nearest hundredth. 314.41, 3,038,784.16)

21. Determine the breakeven points. Round to the nearest hundredth. (161.13, 2,316,534.30) and (617.69, 211,315.67)

22. Express the profit, P, in terms of p. $P = -30.74p^2 + 23{,}941p - 3{,}059{,}500$

23. Graph the profit function. Determine the coordinates of the maximum point of the profit graph. At what price, p, is profit maximized? Round to the nearest cent. This will be the price at which one eyePOD will sell! (389.41, 1,601,946.66); the profit is maximized at a price of $389.41.

24. Write the business summary statement by filling in the blanks.

In summary, to start this business, __**a.**__ eyePODS should be manufactured. Each should be sold at $__**b.**__. The breakeven point is reached at a price of $__**c.**__ or $__**d.**__, but a profit is made at any price between those prices. At the selling price, there is a revenue of $__**e.**__ and expenses of $__**f.**__, resulting in a profit of $__**g.**__. See margin.

25. If shares of stock are sold with an initial value of $10 each, how many shares must be sold to get enough money to start the business? 126,394

12.

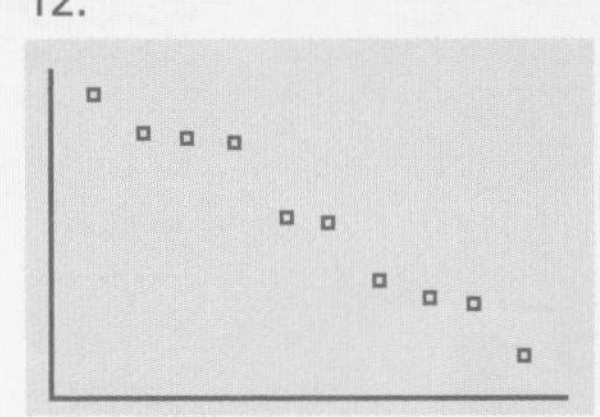

24. a. 7,360; b. $389.41; c. $161.13; d. $617.69; e. $2,865,877.15; f. $1,263,930.49; g. $1,601,946.66

CHAPTER

3 Banking Services

The entire essence of America is the hope to first make money—then make money with money—then make lots of money with lots of money.

Paul Erdman, Business and Financial Author

What does Paul Erdman mean in this quotation?

Chapters 1 and 2 introduced you to the business world. In that world, people take risks and make investments in businesses with the hope of making money. Where do people keep the money they earn? They keep it in checking accounts and savings accounts in banks. The money in their checking accounts is used to pay bills, and the money in their savings accounts is actually another form of investment. In Chapter 3, this less risky form of investment is examined. Although savings accounts may already be familiar, Chapter 3 answers questions about unknown factors of savings accounts. How safe is your money in a bank? Where do banks get the money they pay you in interest? Can you get rich from the interest? What requirements are involved in opening an account? Together, Chapters 1, 2, and 3 give an inside look at the different degrees of risk and reward inherent in investing money in different ways.

What do you think?

Most people feel that having money is a prerequisite to living the "American dream." Once you have money, you can save it and invest it to earn more money.

TEACHING RESOURCES

Instructor's Resource CD

Exam*View*® CD, Ch. 3

eHomework, Ch. 3

www.cengage.com/school/math/financialalgebra

Really?

Most people are familiar with the United States Secret Service as the group that guards the President. Its officers are frequently seen on television surrounding the President as he tends to the affairs of the country.

What most people do not realize is that the Secret Service, established in 1865, was created to help the United States government combat the widespread counterfeiting of U.S. currency at the time. Counterfeiting, one of the oldest crimes in history, had become a national problem. It is estimated that approximately $\frac{1}{3}$ to $\frac{1}{2}$ of the nation's currency in circulation at that time was counterfeit.

The problem, although not as severe, still exists today. Modern printing and scanning equipment makes counterfeiting easier, and the government has instituted changes in currency to make it harder to counterfeit. Although most citizens have no intentions of counterfeiting U.S. currency, Americans have a responsibility to learn about counterfeiting, because they may receive a counterfeit bill one day. If a counterfeit bill is received, try to recall where it was acquired. Contact the nearest Secret Service office. The bill will be taken and no compensation will be returned to you. If a counterfeit bill is deposited in a bank account, you will lose the bill and the credit for the value of the deposit. Go to the Federal Reserve Bank website and read tips for spotting counterfeit currency. The penalty for trying to pass a counterfeit bill is a fine or imprisonment.

CHAPTER OVERVIEW

The first three chapters focus on risk and reward. The degree of risk and the degree of reward depends upon the venture undertaken as well as the investor's comfort level with monetary risks. Use this discussion as a springboard for this chapter on banking services. Ask students about the perceived risks and rewards of savings accounts and checking accounts.

REALLY? REALLY!

Counterfeiting has always been troublesome for the government, for banks, and for the consumer. This feature introduces students to the federal agency that was instituted to combat counterfeiting in its early years. Students are encouraged to go to the Federal Reserve website to read more about how the counterfeiting problem can affect them and what they can do about it.

There have been three great inventions since the beginning of time: fire, the wheel, and central banking.

Will Rogers, Actor and Columnist

3-1 Checking Accounts

Objectives

- Understand how checking accounts work.
- Complete a check register.

Common Core

A-SSE1, A-SSE3, F-BF1a

Key Terms

- checking account
- check
- electronic funds transfer (EFT)
- payee
- drawer
- check clearing
- deposit slip
- direct deposit
- hold
- endorse
- canceled
- insufficient funds
- overdraft protection
- automated teller machine (ATM)
- personal identification number (PIN)
- maintenance fee
- interest
- single account
- joint account
- check register
- debit
- credit

CCSS Warm-Up

Examine the set of ordered pairs: (x, y): (1, 2), (2, 5), (3, 10), (4, 17), (5, 26), (6, 37).

1. Write a function $y = f(x)$ for the set of ordered pairs.
2. Use your function to determine y when $x = 11$.

1. $y = x^2 + 1$

2. 122

EXAMINE THE QUESTION

Access can be direct or indirect. Direct access to money in a bank account can be made by physically going to the bank or to the ATM. Indirect access can be attained through writing checks, using a debit card, or making any electronic transactions. In the latter case, the actual bills are not handled by the consumer.

CLASS DISCUSSION

Ask if anyone has a checking account. If there are some students who do, ask them how they use the account. What are the responsibilities of having a checking account? Why do they have one? What are the ways that they access the money in that account?

Why might a person need overdraft protection? Some people say that it is a form of a loan from the bank. Explain why they might think that.

Why is it important to use the check register?

How do people gain access to money they keep in the bank?

Consumers can have savings, checking, and loan accounts in a variety of different banks. A survey reported that most consumers consider their primary bank to be the one where they have their main checking account even when they use banking services at other banks. A **checking account** is an account at a bank that allows a customer to deposit money, make withdrawals, and make transfers from the funds on deposit.

A **check** is a written order used to tell a bank to pay money (transfer funds) from an account to the check holder. Payments can be made by writing a paper check or by making an electronic funds transfer. An **electronic funds transfer (EFT)** is the process of moving funds electronically from an account in one bank to an account in another bank. An EFT is often referred to as an *electronic check* or *e-check*. Because the transfer is electronic, the processing time is very short. Both the paper and electronic forms of a check are written to a **payee**, the receiver of the transferred funds. The account owner of the check is the **drawer**. Both the payee and the drawer can be a person, persons, or a company. The checking account needs to have enough money in it to cover the amount of a check in order for the check to *clear*, that is, to be paid by the bank. This process is known as **check clearing**.

You can make deposits using a **deposit slip**. Often **direct deposit** is used to deposit payroll or government checks directly into an account. The validity and financial worthiness of deposits must be verified before the bank will allow customers to draw on the funds. If you would like to receive cash back when you deposit a check, there must be sufficient funds already in the checking account. A **hold** is put on the checking account in the amount of the cash received. When the deposit is cleared, the hold is lifted and all of the money in the account is available.

When cashing a check, the payee must **endorse** the check either in writing, by stamp, or electronically. Once the money is paid to the payee, the check is **canceled**.

If a check is written for an amount that cannot be paid out of the account, the check is returned, or dishonored. This means that there are **insufficient funds** in the account and the payee will not receive the money. Banks charge a fee for processing returned checks. Some banks offer customers **overdraft protection** plans that pay a check even though there are not enough funds in the account. There is a fee for this service and the money must be repaid.

Most banks offer **automated teller machines (ATMs)** that give customers 24-hour access to banking services such as deposits and withdrawals. You need a bank card and a **personal identification number (PIN)** to use an ATM. Usually there is no charge if you use one of your bank's ATMs. If you use another ATM, there may be a fee by the bank that owns the ATM and your bank as well.

There are many types of checking accounts, the names of which vary from bank to bank. Each has a different name and different benefits and requirements. Some banks offer free checking while others have accounts that have a monthly **maintenance fee**. Some banks pay **interest** on their checking accounts, which is a percentage of the money that is in the account over a given period of time. Some popular checking accounts are listed and explained below.

- **Basic checking accounts** are the most widely used types of checking accounts. Customers can move money in and out of the account by making deposits and writing checks to pay bills or access money. Many of these accounts do not pay interest.
- **Interest-bearing checking accounts** pay customers interest, usually on a monthly basis, on the money that is in the account. A minimum balance is often required and a fee is charged if the account balance drops below that minimum.
- **Free checking accounts** require no minimum balance and charge no maintenance fees. The Federal Truth in Savings Act guarantees such accounts are available.
- **Joint checking accounts** are accounts owned by more than one person. All owners have equal access to the money in the account.
- **Express checking accounts** are accounts for people who want to avoid going to a traditional bank. Express accounts are often accessed electronically via telephone, computer, or ATM. Some banks charge a fee when an Express account owner uses the services of bank personnel.
- **NOW accounts** stand for *negotiable order of withdrawal*. These are free checking accounts that have interest payments attached to them.
- **Lifeline checking accounts** are available in many states for low-income consumers. Fees and minimum balances are low or nonexistent. Lifeline accounts are required by law in many states.

Bank accounts can be owned by an individual or a group of individuals or a business. In a **single account**, only one person can make withdrawals. These are also called *individual* or *sole owner* accounts. **Joint accounts** have more than one person listed as the owner. Any person listed on a joint account can make withdrawals.

TEACH

Students need to have an understanding of checking account terminology. The highlighted words in the text are critical and will be used throughout the lesson. Ask students to have a discussion about checking accounts with their parents. What kind of account do their parents have? Are there any fees? Are there any minimum balances? What is the bank's name for the type of account they own? Have a discussion with the students about what they have learned from their parents.

EXAMPLE 1

The purpose of this exercise is to make sure that students know the mathematical difference between a deposit and a withdrawal in a checking account and how each affects the balance. Have students make a list of situations in which a deposit might be made (a birthday check, a paycheck, and so on) and when a withdrawal might be made (a utility bill, tuition, and ATM fee).

CHECK YOUR UNDERSTANDING

Answer $x + b + 2c - d$

To obtain an expression for the new balance, begin with the old balance, add the deposits, $x + b + 2c$, and subtract the withdrawal, d.

Skills and Strategies

Here you will learn how to deposit money into a checking account and to track the transactions in the account on a monthly basis.

EXAMPLE 1

Allison currently has a balance of $2,300 in her checking account. She deposits a $425.33 paycheck, a $20 rebate check, and a personal check for $550 into her checking account. She wants to receive $200 in cash. How much will she have in her account after the transaction?

SOLUTION Allison must fill out a deposit slip and hand it to the bank teller along with her endorsed checks. Although deposit slips vary from bank to bank, there is usually a line for cash deposits and a few lines for individual check deposits and for cash received. Allison is not making a cash deposit, so the cash line is blank. She lists the three checks on the deposit slip separately. In order for Allison to get $200 back from this transaction, she must have at least that amount already in her account.

DEPOSIT TICKET

Allison Megham
7 Tome Way
Philadelphia, PA 19255

DATE *June 4*

DEPOSITS MAY NOT BE AVAILABLE FOR IMMEDIATE WITHDRAWAL

Allison Megham

SIGN HERE FOR CASH RECEIVED (IF REQUIRED)*

ROME
FINANCIAL BANK

⑆04 2000119131⑆ 5171151007⑈

	DOLLARS	CENTS
CASH		
LIST CHECKS SINGLY	425	33
	20	00
	550	00
SUB TOTAL	995	33
LESS CASH RECEIVED	200	00
TOTAL		

Add the check amounts.	$425.33
	20.00
	+550.00
	$995.33
Subtract the cash received.	−200.00
Total on deposit slip	$795.33

Allison's current balance is $2,300.

Add current balance and deposit amount. $2{,}300 + 795.33 = 3{,}095.33$

Allison's new balance is $3,095.33.

CHECK YOUR UNDERSTANDING

Lizzy has a total of x dollars in her checking account. She makes a deposit of b dollar in cash and two checks each worth c dollars. She would like d dollars in cash from this transaction. She has enough to cover the cash received in her account. Express her new checking account balance after the transaction as an algebraic expression.

Check Registers

You should keep a record of all transactions in your checking account, including checks written, deposits made, fees paid, ATM withdrawals, and so on. This record is a **check register**. The record can be handwritten or electronic. It tracks the **debits** (withdrawals) and **credits** (deposits) of a checking account.

EXAMPLE 2

Nick has a checking account with the Park Slope Savings Bank. He writes both paper and electronic checks. For each transaction, Nick enters the necessary information: check number, date, type of transaction, and amount. He uses E to indicate an electronic transaction. Determine the balance in his account after the Star Cable Co. check is written.

NUMBER OR CODE	DATE	TRANSACTION DESCRIPTION	PAYMENT AMOUNT		✓	FEE	DEPOSIT AMOUNT		$ BALANCE 3,672.27
3271	5/5	Dewitt Auto Body (Car Repair)	$ 1,721	00					
3272	5/7	Kate's Guitar Hut (Strings)	32	50					
	5/9	Deposit (Paycheck)					821	53	
E	5/10	Verizon Wireless	101	50					
E	5/10	Star Cable Co.	138	90					

SOLUTION Perform the calculations needed as shown below. The balance in Nick's register is $2,499.90.

NUMBER OR CODE	DATE	TRANSACTION DESCRIPTION	PAYMENT AMOUNT		✓	FEE	DEPOSIT AMOUNT		$ BALANCE 3,672.27
3271	5/5	Dewitt Auto Body (Car Repair)	$ 1,721	00					- 1,721.00 1,951.27
3272	5/7	Kate's Guitar Hut (Strings)	32	50					- 32.50 1,918.77
	5/9	Deposit (Paycheck)					821	53	+ 821.53 2,740.30
E	5/10	Verizon Wireless	101	50					- 101.50 2,638.80
E	5/10	Star Cable Co.	138	90					- 138.90 2,499.90

■ CHECK YOUR UNDERSTANDING

Nick writes a check to his friend James Sloan on May 11 for $150.32. What should he write in the check register and what should the new balance be?

■ EXTEND YOUR UNDERSTANDING

Would the final balance change if Nick had paid the cable bill before the wireless bill? Explain.

EXAMPLE 2

Many students may never have seen a check register and do not know how to use one. Make copies of a blank form. It can be downloaded at www.cengage.com/school/math/financialalgebra.

Work through the check register in the solution to Example 2 line by line, performing the calculations needed to attain the correct balance.

CHECK YOUR UNDERSTANDING

Answer 3273; 5/11; James Sloan; $150.32; $2,349.58

EXTEND YOUR UNDERSTANDING

Answer No

2,740.30 – 138.90 = 2,601.40; 2,601.40 – 101.50 also equals 2,499.90.

Applications

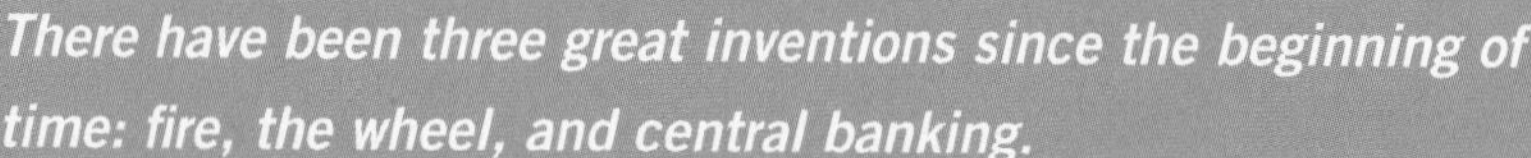

There have been three great inventions since the beginning of time: fire, the wheel, and central banking.

Will Rogers, Actor and Columnist

TEACH

Exercises 2 and 3

Notice that Exercises 2 and 3 are related. In Exercise 2, students are asked to find a numerical balance. In Exercise 3, students will mimic the process used in Exercise 2 but with variables. This balance will be represented as a variable expression. When reviewing these two exercises, make a connection between them.

Exercises 5 and 6

Get students into the habit of sorting checking account transactions by credits and debits. This will help organize the given information in both exercises.

ANSWERS

1. Will Rogers indicates that banking is as essential to your daily life as fire and the wheel.

1. How might the quote apply to what has been outlined in this lesson? See margin.

2. Jackie deposited a \$865.98 paycheck, a \$623 stock dividend check, a \$60 rebate check, and \$130 cash into her checking account. Her original account balance was \$278.91. Assuming the checks clear, how much was in her account after the deposit was made? \$1,957.89

3. Rich has t dollars in his checking account. On June 3, he deposited w, h, and v dollars, and cashed a check that he wrote to himself for k dollars. Write an algebraic expression that represents the amount of money in his account after the transactions. $t + w + h + v - k$

4. John cashed a check for \$630. The teller gave him three fifty-dollar bills, eighteen twenty-dollar bills, and t ten-dollar bills. Determine the value of t. $t = 12$

5. Gary and Ann have a joint checking account. Their balance at the beginning of October was \$9,145.87. During the month they made deposits totaling \$2,783.71, wrote checks totaling \$4,871.90, paid a maintenance fee of \$12, and earned \$11.15 in interest on the account. What was the balance at the end of the month? \$7,056.83

6. Anna has a checking account at Garden City Bank. Her balance at the beginning of February was \$5,195.65. During the month, she made deposits totaling \$6,873.22, wrote checks totaling c dollars, was charged a maintenance fee of \$15, and earned \$6.05 in interest. Her balance at the end of the month was \$4,200.00. What is the value of c? $c = \$7{,}859.92$

7. Queens Meadow Bank charges a monthly maintenance fee of \$13 and a check writing fee of \$0.07 per check. Last year, Mark wrote 289 checks from his account at Queens Meadow. What was the total of all fees he paid on that account last year? \$176.23

8. Joby had \$421.56 in her checking account when she deposited g twenty-dollar bills and k quarters. Write an expression that represents the amount of money in her account after the deposit. $421.56 + 20g + 0.25k$

9. Neka cashed a check for \$245. The teller gave him two fifty-dollar bills, six twenty-dollar bills and f five-dollar bills. Determine the value of f. $f = 5$

10. Olivia cashed a check for \$113. The teller gave her four twenty-dollar bills, x ten-dollar bills, and three one-dollar bills. Find the value of x. 3

11. Hector had y dollars in his savings account. He made a deposit of twenty-dollar bills and dollar coins. He had four times as many dollar coins as he had twenty-dollar bills and the total of his twenty-dollar bills was \$60. Write an expression for the balance in Hector's account after the deposit. $y + 72$

12. On September 1, Chris Eugene made the following band equipment purchases at Leslie's Music Store. Calculate her total bill. Complete a check for the correct amount. Print a copy of the check from www.cengage.com/school/math/financialalgebra. See additional answers.

DESCRIPTION	CATALOG NUMBER	LIST PRICE	QUANTITY	TOTAL
Speaker Cabinets	RS101	$400.00	2	
Speaker Cabinets	RG306	$611.00	2	
Horns	BG42	$190.00	2	
Audio Console	LS101	$1,079.00	1	
Power Amplifier	NG107	$416.00	5	
Microphones	RKG-1972	$141.92	8	
Microphone Stands	1957-210	$32.50	8	
			TOTAL	
			13% DISCOUNT	
			SALE PRICE	
			8% SALES TAX	
			TOTAL COST	

TEACH

Exercise 12
When reviewing this exercise, ask students if it would have made a difference if the 13% discount line and the 8% sales tax line had been switched on the equipment bill. Although it makes no difference in the total cost, this will be counterintuitive to many students. Show them that the switch will result in the same answer.

Exercise 13
Once again, it is important that students have a command of a credit (deposit) and a debit (a withdrawal). You might want to have students identify each before assigning this problem.

13. Create a check register for the transactions listed. There is a $2.25 fee for each ATM use. See additional answers.
   a. Your balance on 10/29 is $237.47
   b. You write check 115 on 10/29 for $18.00 to Fox High School.
   c. You deposit a paycheck for $162.75 on 10/30.
   d. You deposit a $25 check for your birthday on 11/4.
   e. On 11/5, you go to a sporting event and run out of money. You use the ATM in the lobby to get $15 for snacks.
   f. Your credit card bill is due on 11/10, so on 11/7 you write check 116 to Credit USA for $51.16.
   g. Your sister repays you $20 on 11/10. You deposit it.
   h. You withdraw $25 from the ATM to buy flowers on 11/12.
   i. You deposit your paycheck for $165.65 on 11/16.
   j. You deposit a late birthday check for $35 on 11/17.

14. Ridgewood Savings Bank charges a $27 per check overdraft protection fee. On July 8, Nancy had $1,400 in her account. Over the next four days, the following checks arrived for payment at her bank: July 9, $1,380.15; July 10, $670 and $95.67; July 11, $130; and July 12, $87.60. How much will she pay in overdraft protection fees? How much will she owe the bank after July 12? $108; $1,071.42

15. 123 Savings and Loan charges a monthly fee of $8 on checking accounts and an overdraft protection fee of $33. Neela's check register showed she had a balance of $456 when she wrote a check for $312. Three days later she realized her check register had an error and she actually only had $256. So she transferred $250 into her checking account. The next day, her monthly account statement was sent to her. What was the balance on her statement? $153

TEACH

Exercise 16

Review the ramifications of a voided check. Students need to realize that the destroyed check must be accounted for in the register so that when the user returns to balance the account he/she will have a record of that check. In part f of the problem, students will need to know that once the check is canceled, the very next check in the numerical sequence is recorded in the register and used.

ANSWERS

17. a. 623
    b. 629
    c. 630
    d. 71.10
    e. –500.00
    f. 1,292.80
    g. –51.12
    h. 1,241.68
    i. –25.00
    j. 1,216.68
    k. +650.00
    l. 1,866.68
    m. –200.00
    n. 1,666.68
    p. –90.00
    q. 1,576.68
    r. –49.00
    s. 1,527.68
    t. –65.00
    u. 1,462.68
    v. –300.00
    w. 1,162.68
    x. +400.00
    y. 1,562.68
    z. 1,191.02

16. Create a check register for the transactions listed. Download a blank check register from www.cengage.com/school/math/financialalgebra.

a. Your balance on 12/15 is $2,546.50. See additional answers.

b. On 12/16, you write check 2345 for $54 to Kings Park High School Student Activities.

c. On 12/17, you deposit your paycheck in the amount of $324.20.

d. Your grandparents send you a holiday check for $100 which you deposit into your account on 12/20.

e. On 12/22 you write three checks: 2346 to Best Buy in the amount of $326.89, 2347 to Macy's in the amount of $231.88, and 2348 to Target in the amount of $123.51.

f. On 12/24, you go to the Apple Store. As you are writing the check for $301.67, you make a mistake and must void that check. You pay with the next available check in your checkbook.

g. On 12/26, you return a holiday gift. The store gives you $98. You deposit that into your checking account.

h. On 12/28, you write an e-check to Allstate Insurance Company in the amount of $876.00 to pay your car insurance.

i. On 12/29, you withdraw $200 from an ATM. There is a $1.50 charge for using the ATM.

17. Download a copy of the check register shown below from www.cengage.com/school/math/financialalgebra. Complete items a through z. See margin.

PLEASE BE SURE TO DEDUCT CHANGES THAT AFFECT YOUR ACCOUNT

ITEM NO. FOR TRANSACTION CODE	DATE	DESCRIPTION OF TRANSACTION	SUBTRACTIONS: AMOUNT OF PAYMENT OR WITHDRAWAL	✓	OTHER	ADDITIONS: AMOUNT OF DEPOSIT OR INTEREST	BALANCE FORWARD
							1,863 90
621	10/3	TO Telephone Co. FOR Dec. Bill	d.				– 71 10 1,792 80
622	10/7	TO Banner Reality FOR Rent	500 00				e. f.
a.	10/8	TO Electric Co. FOR Dec. Bill	51 12				g. h.
624	10/10	TO Cathy Santoro FOR Piano Lesson	25 00				i. j.
	10/15	TO Deposit FOR				650 00	k. l.
625	10/16	TO Don's Day Camp FOR Kid's Summer Camp	200 00				m. n.
626	10/18	TO Ed's Sporting Goods FOR Winter Coat	90 00				p. q.
627	10/21	TO Maple Place Garage FOR antifreeze & hose	49 00				r. s.
628	10/22	TO Dr. Moe Goldstein FOR Check-up	65 00				t. u.
b.	11/4	TO Hicksville H.M.O. FOR yearly premium	300 00				v. w.
	11/5	TO Deposit FOR				400 00	x. y.
c.	11/9	TO State Insurance Co. FOR Auto Insurance	371 66				– 371 66 z.

My problem lies in reconciling my gross habits with my net income.

Errol Flynn, Actor

Reconcile a Bank Statement 3-2

Key Terms			
	• account number	• starting balance	• outstanding checks
	• bank statement	• ending balance	• balancing
	• statement period	• outstanding deposits	• reconciling

Objectives

- Reconcile a checking account with a bank statement by hand and by using a spreadsheet.

Common Core

A-CED4

CCSS Warm-Up

Solve the equation for the price, *P*.

The formula for finding the sale price, *S*, on an item costing *P* dollars after a *D*% discount is $S = P(1 - D/100)$.

$P = S/(1 - D/100)$

How do checking account users make sure that their records are correct?

EXAMINE THE QUESTION

There is a difference between keeping accurate records and checking that records are accurately kept. This question addresses both. Students will be introduced to the check register and the bank statement in this unit. Both should be accurate accountings of their transactions. But, both should be checked for accuracy.

A customer keeps a record of all transactions concerning a checking account in a paper or electronic check register. The bank also keeps a record of all transactions. Every month, the bank makes available a statement listing all of the transactions and balances for the account. The bank statement contains important information related to the account.

- The **account number** appears on all checks, deposit slips, and paper and electronic bank statements.
- The **bank statement** includes all transactions that have occurred for a period of approximately one month. The **statement period** indicates the dates in which the transactions occurred.
- The **starting balance** is the amount of money in a checking account at the beginning of a statement period.
- The **ending balance** is the amount of money in a checking account at the end of a statement period.
- The deposits section shows the money that was put into the account during the statement period. Deposits that do not appear on the statement are **outstanding deposits**.
- Checks that do not appear on the statement are **outstanding checks**.

Whether using paper or electronic statements, you should verify the bank's records to make sure no mistakes have been made. This process is called **balancing** a checkbook or **reconciling** a bank statement. Most bank statements include a checking account summary which guides the user through the reconciling process. Check registers contain a column to place a check mark for cleared items to assist in balancing.

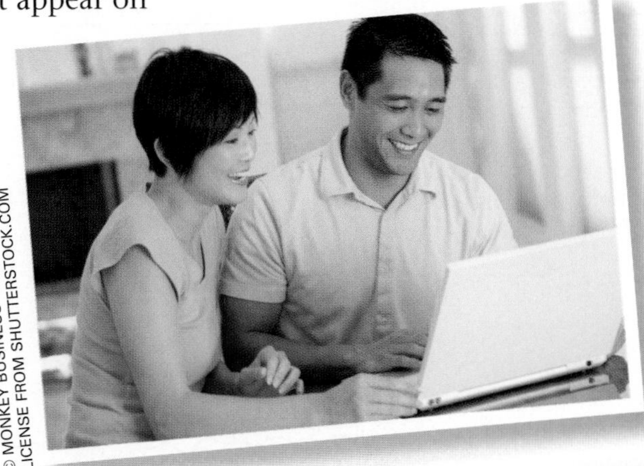

CLASS DISCUSSION

Discuss the importance of keeping accurate records and reconciling the check register on a monthly basis. In particular, focus on the problems that could arise if the balance you think you have in the account is more than the actual balance the bank knows you have.

TEACH

This lesson contains a great deal of terminology which must be introduced to students, many of whom may not have a checking account. Make sure that students have a firm understanding of these terms. You may want to make a word wall that lists these terms so that you can refer back to them as the lesson progresses.

EXAMPLE 1

Since reconciling a bank statement will be new to most students, it is important that you walk students through the steps necessary to complete this example. Students should know how the register and the bank statement interact with each other in order to determine if the account records balance. They also need to know what to do when the amounts do not balance.

One common error made in a check register is the transposition of numbers. For example, a check in the amount of $179 might be written as $197. Transposition errors always result in a difference that is divisible by 9. Have students make a transposition error then test this fact. Ask students how knowing that the difference is a multiple of 9 can be helpful.

Skills and Strategies

Here you will learn to reconcile a bank statement and a check register.

EXAMPLE 1

Below is a bank statement and check register for Michael Biak's checking account. What steps are needed to reconcile Michael's bank statement?

PLEASE BE SURE TO DEDUCT CHANGES THAT AFFECT YOUR ACCOUNT

ITEM NO. FOR TRANSACTION CODE	DATE	DESCRIPTION OF TRANSACTION	SUBTRACTIONS: AMOUNT OF PAYMENT OR WITHDRAWAL	✓	OTHER	ADDITIONS: AMOUNT OF DEPOSIT OR INTEREST	BALANCE FORWARD
							748 95
1763	10/13	TO Deepdale Country Club FOR Swimming lessons	50 00				− 50 00 / 698 95
1764	10/13	TO Joe's Sporting Goods FOR Tennis Racket	48 00	✓			− 48 00 / 650 95
1765	10/14	TO Ellio's Pizzeria FOR Pizza Party	19 50				− 19 50 / 631 45
1766	10/15	TO Bethpage Auto Parts FOR Air Filter	9 00	✓			− 9 00 / 622 45
	10/15	TO Deposit FOR		✓		100 00	+ 100 00 / 722 45
1767	10/16	TO Maple Place Garage FOR Inspection	18 00				− 18 00 / 704 45
1768	10/18	TO Ticket Man FOR Concert Tickets	46 50				− 46 50 / 657 95
1769	10/21	TO Caruso's Restaurant FOR Dinner	74 64				− 74 64 / 583 31
1770	10/22	TO Mickel's Home Center FOR Tool Chest	158 08				− 158 08 / 425 23
1771	11/4	TO Aunt Bella's Restaurant FOR Dinner	29 10				− 29 10 / 396 13
	11/5	TO Deposit FOR				35 00	+ 35 00 / 431 13
1772	11/9	TO Living Color Lab FOR Film Developing	15 00				− 15 00 / 416 13
	11/11	TO Deposit FOR				100 00	+ 100 00 / 516 13
	12/1	TO Deposit FOR				125 00	+ 125 00 / 641 13

Michael Biak
17 Breeze Way
Lake City, FL 32025

ACCOUNT NUMBER: 7843390
STATEMENT PERIOD: 11/01 - 11/30

STARTING BALANCE → **$ 791.95**

DATE	DESCRIPTION	CHECK NUMBER	TRANSACTION AMOUNT	BALANCE
11/05	DEPOSIT		35.00	$ 826.95
11/11	DEPOSIT		100.00	$ 926.95
11/13	W/D	1770	158.08	$ 768.87
11/17	W/D	1768	46.50	$ 722.37
11/19	W/D	1769	74.64	$ 647.73
11/27	W/D	1765	19.50	$ 628.23

ENDING BALANCE → $ 628.23

SOLUTION Compare the entries in Michael's check register with the bank statement. The entries marked with a ✓ appeared on a previous month's statement. Enter a check mark in the check register for each deposit and check listed on the monthly statement.

Some of the entries in his check register are not on his bank statement. List any outstanding checks or other withdrawals and find the total. Then list any outstanding deposits and find the total.

Outstanding Withdrawals	
ITEM	AMOUNT
1763	50.00
1767	18.00
1771	29.10
1772	15.00
TOTAL	112.10

Outstanding Deposits	
DATE	AMOUNT
12/1	125.00
TOTAL	125.00

Then complete the following steps.

Statement ending balance	\$628.24
Total deposits outstanding	+ \$125.00
Total withdrawals outstanding	– \$112.10
Revised statement balance	\$641.14
Check register balance	\$641.14

The revised statement balance equals the last balance in the check register, so the statement is reconciled.

If the balances are not equal, then there is an error. To find errors, check the arithmetic in the check register and on the statement. Be sure all fees, transaction charges, and interest have been included.

CHECK YOUR UNDERSTANDING

Name some reasons why a check may not have cleared during the monthly cycle and appear on the bank statement.

EXAMPLE 2

Use algebraic formulas and statements to model the check register balancing process.

SOLUTION Represent each line in the account summary with a variable.

Statement ending balance	a
Total deposits outstanding	b
Total withdrawals outstanding	c
Revised statement balance	d
Check register balance	r

The revised statement balance equals the statement balance plus the total outstanding deposits, b, minus the total withdrawals outstanding, c.

$$d = a + b - c$$

If the revised statement balance, d, equals the check register balance, r, the statement is reconciled.

CHECK YOUR UNDERSTANDING

Answer Sample answer: Many people and businesses hold on to checks and do not deposit or cash them immediately. If checks are written towards the end of a cycle, they will probably appear on the next monthly statement.

EXAMPLE 2

Some students may be able to jump right into the solution while others might have some difficulty writing the algebraic expression. For the latter, offer them an example using numbers, and then replace those numbers with the variables.

CHECK YOUR UNDERSTANDING

Answer Yes

Let $a = \$885.84$, $b = \$825$, $c = \$632.84$, $r = \$1{,}078$. Then $d = a + b - c = \$1{,}078$. Both d and r equal $1,078, so the check register is balanced.

EXAMPLE 3

Have students work through the computations first before assigning cell locations and writing the formulas. This will assist them in transferring from the arithmetic view to the algebraic view.

■ CHECK YOUR UNDERSTANDING

Nancy has a balance of $1,078 in her check register. The balance on her bank account statement is $885.84. Not reported on her bank statement are deposits of $575 and $250 and two checks for $195 and $437.84. Is her check register balanced? Explain.

EXAMPLE 3

Marina and Brian have a joint checking account. They have a balance of $3,839.25 in the check register. The balance on the bank statement is $3,450.10. Not reported on the statement are deposits of $2,000, $135.67, $254.77, and $188.76 and four checks for $567.89, $23.83, $598.33, and $1,000. Reconcile the bank statement using a spreadsheet.

SOLUTION Enter the outstanding deposits in cells A3 to A9.

Enter the outstanding checks in cells B3 to B9.

	A	B	C
1			
2	Outstanding Deposits	Outstanding Checks	
3	2,000.00	567.89	
4	135.67	23.83	
5	254.77	598.33	
6	188.76	1,000.00	
7			
8			
9			
10	2,579.20	2,190.05	Total
11			
12	Check register balance		3,839.25
13	Statement ending balance		3,450.10
14	Revised statement balance		3,839.25
15			
16	Statement is reconciled.		

Cell A10 calculates the total amount of the outstanding deposits and cell B10 calculates the total amount of the outstanding checks. The cell formula for the total of the outstanding deposits in A10 is =sum(A3:A9).

In the Check Your Understanding, you will be asked to write the cell formula for the total outstanding checks.

Enter the check register balance in cell C12.

Enter the statement ending balance in cell C13.

Cell C14 calculates the revised statement balance, which is the sum of the statement ending balance and total outstanding deposits minus the total outstanding checks. The formula is =C13+A10−B10.

You can make the spreadsheet check to see if the revised statement balance equals the check register balance. Use an IF statement in the form =IF(test, output if true, output if false).

The test portion of the statement must contain a mathematical equation or inequality. The spreadsheet uses the values in the cells to test the truth of the statement. If the statement is true, the first output will be printed. If the statement is false, the second output will be printed.

In the spreadsheet, cell A16 contains the IF statement, =IF(C12=C14, "Statement is reconciled.", "Statement is not reconciled."). Cell A16 states the statement is reconciled.

CHECK YOUR UNDERSTANDING

Answer Although formulas vary based on the spreadsheet being used, most spreadsheet programs would use the following formula to determine the sum: =sum(B3:B9)

■ CHECK YOUR UNDERSTANDING

Write a formula to calculate the sum of the outstanding checks.

Applications

My problem lies in reconciling my gross habits with my net income.

Errol Flynn, Actor

1. How might the quote apply to this lesson? See margin.

2. Rona filled out this information on her monthly statement. Find Rona's revised statement balance. Does her account reconcile? $864.52; yes

Checking Account Summary	
Ending Balance	$ 725.71
Deposits	+ $ 610.00
Checks Outstanding	– $ 471.19
Revised Statement Balance	
Check Register Balance	$ 864.52

3. Ken filled out this information on the back of his bank statement. Find Ken's revised statement balance. Does his account reconcile? $181.95; no

Checking Account Summary	
Ending Balance	$ 197.10
Deposits	+ $ 600.00
Checks Outstanding	– $615.15
Revised Statement Balance	
Check Register Balance	$ 210.10

4. Hannah wants to write a general formula and a comparison statement that she can use each month when she reconciles her checking account. Use the Checking Account Summary at the right to write a formula and a statement for Hannah. $B + D - C = S$; If $S = R$, the account is reconciled.

Checking Account Summary	
Ending Balance	B
Deposits	D
Checks Outstanding	C
Revised Statement Balance	S
Check Register Balance	R

5. Jill has not been able to maintain the $1,000 minimum balance required to avoid fees on her checking account. She wants to switch to a different account with a fee of $0.20 per check and a $12.50 monthly maintenance fee. Jill wants to estimate the fees for her new account. Below is a summary of the checks she has written from May to August.

Month	Number of Checks on Statement
May	14
June	19
July	23
August	24

a. What is the mean number of checks Jill wrote per month during the last four months? 20

b. Based on the mean, estimate how much Jill expects to pay in per-check fees each month after she switches to the new account. $4.00

c. Estimate the total monthly fees Jill will pay each month for the new checking account. $16.50

TEACH

Exercise 2 and 3
These similar exercises test the students' understanding of the components needed to be in place if a check register is to balance.
As an extension to these exercises, you might want to make up similar ones in which students have to find different amounts (ending balance, deposits, checks outstanding) when given all of the other values in a balanced check register.

Exercise 5
Ask students if using the median number of checks might change this problem.

ANSWERS

1. Errol Flynn used the word reconcile in the same way that it is used in a financial context. With a checking account, the problem lies in reconciling or balancing the check register amount with the revised statement amount. Errol Flynn's problem is in balancing his personal gross (monetary) habits such as making expensive purchases with the money he actually has coming in.

TEACH

Exercise 6
Students need to first locate or determine the amounts in question. They then should follow the reconciling process as outlined in Example 1.

ANSWERS

7. Let x = the number of checks Donna writes each month; let F = fee charged; $F = 9.75 + 0.15x$
8. no; adding $75 will correct that he subtracted $75 when he should not have. He will also need to add another $75 for the original deposit.

6. Use Tina Weaver's monthly statement and check register to reconcile her account.

a. What is the ending balance on the statement? $1,434.19
b. What is the total of the outstanding deposits? $700.00
c. What is the total of the outstanding withdrawals? $89.00
d. What is the revised statement balance? $2,045.19
e. What is the balance of the check register? $2,045.19
f. Does the account reconcile? yes

Tina Weaver
41 Slider Lane
Greenwich, CT 06830

ACCOUNT NUMBER: 766666600A
STATEMENT PERIOD: 3/01 - 3/31

STARTING BALANCE ⟶ $ 871.50

DATE	DESCRIPTION	CHECK NUMBER	TRANSACTION AMOUNT	BALANCE
3/3	W/D	395	$ 79.00	$ 792.50
3/4	DEPOSIT		$ 600.00	$ 1,392.50
3/10	W/D	396	$ 51.10	$ 1,341.40
3/14	W/D	393	$ 12.00	$ 1,329.40
3/19	W/D	394	$ 133.81	$ 1,195.59
3/24	DEPOSIT		$ 250.00	$ 1,445.59
3/30	W/D	398	$ 11.40	$ 1,434.19

ENDING BALANCE ⟶ $1,434.19

NUMBER OR CODE	DATE	TRANSACTION DESCRIPTION	PAYMENT AMOUNT		✓	FEE	DEPOSIT AMOUNT		$ BALANCE
									871.50
392	2/20	Conn Telephone Co.	$ 76	80	✓				
393	2/21	Rod's Bike Shop	12	00					859.50
394	3/1	Window's Restaurant	133	81					725.69
395	3/2	Centsible Bank	79	00					646.69
	3/4	Deposit					600	00	1,246.69
396	3/4	Spear's Department Store	51	10					1,195.59
397	3/15	Mary Lewis	50	00					1,145.59
398	3/21	Sea Cliff Records	11	40					1,134.19
	3/23	Deposit					250	00	1,384.19
399	4/2	Ciangiola Motors	39	00					1,345.19
	4/2	Deposit					700	00	2,045.19

7. Donna has a checking account that charges $0.15 for each check written and a monthly service charge of $9.75. Write a formula that Donna can use each month to find the fees she will be charged. Identify any variable you use in the formula. See margin.

8. Mason discovered that when he recorded a deposit of $75 two weeks ago, he mistakenly subtracted it from the running total in his check register. He decided that he would write a new entry after his most recent entry and add $75. Will this correct his mistake? Explain. See margin.

9. When Payne removed his bank statement from the envelope, it got caught on a staple and a corner was ripped from the page. Now he cannot read his ending balance. Explain the computations he can do to find his ending balance. See margin.

Payne Johnston
1234 Main Street
Miami, FL 33299

ACCOUNT NUMBER: 99887766D
STATEMENT PERIOD: 1/1 - 1/31

STARTING BALANCE → $754.33

DATE	DESCRIPTION	CHECK NUMBER	TRANSACTION AMOUNT	BALANCE
1/08	W/D	5502	121.28	$ 633.05
1/11	W/D	5501	140.00	$ 493.05
1/15	DEPOSIT		998.15	$ 1,491.20
1/24	W/D	5504	107.78	$ 1,383.42
1/27	W/D	5503	12.00	$ 1,371.42
1/30	W/D	5506	58.70	$ 1

ENDING BAL

10. Use Allison Shannon's bank statement and check register to reconcile her account. See margin.

Allison Shannon
3 Honey Drive
Dallas, TX 75372

ACCOUNT NUMBER: 76574709A
STATEMENT PERIOD: 12/01 - 12/31

STARTING BALANCE → $1,685.91

DATE	DESCRIPTION	CHECK NUMBER	TRANSACTION AMOUNT	BALANCE
12/08	W/D	1502	147.28	$ 1,538.63
12/10	W/D	1501	130.00	$ 1,408.63
12/15	DEPOSIT		749.00	$ 2,157.63
12/23	W/D	1504	250.00	$ 1,907.63
12/27	W/D	1503	72.00	$ 1,835.63
12/29	W/D	1506	26.00	$ 1,809.63

ENDING BALANCE → $1,809.63

PLEASE BE SURE TO DEDUCT CHANGES THAT AFFECT YOUR ACCOUNT

ITEM NO. FOR TRANSACTION CODE	DATE	DESCRIPTION OF TRANSACTION	SUBTRACTIONS: AMOUNT OF PAYMENT OR WITHDRAWAL	✓	OTHER	ADDITIONS: AMOUNT OF DEPOSIT OR INTEREST	BALANCE FORWARD
							1,685 91
1500	11/20	TO Girl Scouts FOR Cookies	32 00				− 32 00 1,653 91
1501	11/30	TO Bank of Seaford FOR Loan Payment	130 00	✓			− 130 00 1,523 91
1502	12/2	TO Lacy's Department Store FOR Radio	147 28	✓			− 147 28 1,376 63
1503	12/11	TO Charge Tix FOR Concert Tickets	72 00	✓			− 72 00 1304 63
	12/15	TO Deposit FOR		✓		749 00	+ 749 00 2,053 63
1504	12/16	TO FLASHCARD FOR Monthly payment	250 00	✓			− 250 00 1,803 63
1505	12/17	TO Red Cross FOR Donation	100 00				− 100 00 1,703 63
1506	12/18	TO Daily Newspaper FOR Subscription	26 00	✓			− 26 00 1,677 63
	1/5	TO Deposit FOR				150 00	+ 150 00 1,827 63

TEACH

Exercise 10

Although it is customary to mark off each transaction that is listed on the statement with a check mark, do not let students write in the text. Tell students to put a piece of blank paper over the Balance Forward column in the register and make their marks on that paper. This way, they will be able to easily account for the deposits and withdrawals that are outstanding.

ANSWERS

9. On the statement you can still see that the balance on 1/27 was $1,371.42 and the check written on 1/30 was for $58.70. Subtract to find the ending balance. 1,371.42 − $58.70 = 1,312.72
10. outstanding deposit: $150; outstanding checks: $132; 1,827.63 − 150 + 132 = 1,809.63; which reconciles with the statement balance.

TEACH

Exercise 11
Review the spreadsheet commands with students before assigning this problem.

11. Fill in the missing balances in Raymond Marshall's check register. Use the spreadsheet from www.cengage.com/school/math/financialalgebra to determine if Raymond's checking account reconciles with his statement. See additional answers.

Raymond Marshall
34 2630 Street
Oaks, NY 11004

ACCOUNT NUMBER: 6732281
STATEMENT PERIOD: 1/01 - 1/30

STARTING BALANCE → **$ 653.30**

DATE	DESCRIPTION	CHECK NUMBER	TRANSACTION AMOUNT	BALANCE
1/12	W/D	1776	28.00	$ 625.30
1/13	W/D	1778	56.73	$ 568.57
1/13	W/D	1777	120.00	$ 448.57
1/14	DEPOSIT		1,000.00	$1,448.57
1/17	W/D	1774	70.00	$1,378.57

ENDING BALANCE → **$1,378.57**

PLEASE BE SURE TO DEDUCT CHANGES THAT AFFECT YOUR ACCOUNT

ITEM NO. FOR TRANSACTION CODE	DATE	DESCRIPTION OF TRANSACTION	SUBTRACTIONS: AMOUNT OF PAYMENT OR WITHDRAWAL	✓	OTHER	ADDITIONS: AMOUNT OF DEPOSIT OR INTEREST	BALANCE FORWARD
							728 30
1773	12/28	TO Galaxy Theather FOR Tickets	75 00	✓			– 75 00
1774	12/30	TO American Electric Company FOR Electric Bill	70 00				– 70 00
1775	12/30	TO Hillsdake Water Co. FOR Water Bill	38 50				– 38 50
1776	1/2	TO Barbara's Restaurant FOR Dinner	28 00				– 28 00
1777	1/3	TO Platter Records FOR Compact Disc	120 00				– 120 00
1778	1/9	TO A1 Gas Co. FOR Gas Bill	56 73				– 56 73
1779	1/12	TO Al and Jean Adams FOR Wedding Gift	100 00				– 100 00
1780	1/12	TO Greene College FOR Fees	85 00				– 85 00
	1/14	TO Deposit FOR				1,000 00	+ 1,000 00
1780	1/25	TO Rob Gerver FOR Typing Fee	80 00				– 80 00
	2/1	TO Deposit FOR Salary				950 00	+ 950 00

12. When comparing his check register to his bank statement, Donté found that he had failed to record deposits of \$55.65, \$103.50, and \$25.00. What is the total of these amounts and how will he use this information to reconcile his account? \$184.15; these are the outstanding deposits.

13. Alisha has a February starting balance of \$678.98 in her checking account. During the month, she made deposits that totaled d dollars and wrote checks that totaled c dollars. Let E = her ending balance on February 28. Write an inequality using E and the starting balance to show the relationship of her starting and ending balances for each condition.

a. if $d > c$ $E > 678.98$

b. if $d < c$ $E < 678.98$

Anything that we can do to raise personal savings is very much in the interest of this country.

Alan Greenspan, Economist

Savings Accounts 3-3

Key Terms
- savings account
- interest
- interest rate
- principal
- simple interest
- simple interest formula
- statement savings
- minimum balance
- money market account
- certificate of deposit (CD)
- maturity

Objectives
- Learn the basic vocabulary of savings accounts.
- Compute simple interest using the simple interest formula.

Common Core

A-CED4

CCSS Warm-Up

Show that the two equations are the same.
Algebraically transform one equation into the other.

1. $A = (3B - C)D$ **2.** $C = 3B - DA$

1. $A = (3B - C)/D$
$DA = 3B - C \rightarrow C = 3B - DA$

2. $C = 3B - DA$
$DA = 3B - C \rightarrow A = (3B - C)/D$

What types of savings accounts do banks offer customers?

Most banks offer savings accounts, money market accounts, certificates of deposit (CDs), loans, life insurance policies, safe deposit boxes, and credit and debit cards, as well as checking accounts. Banks provide these services so they can attract customers and make a profit.

A **savings account** is an account in which the bank pays **interest** for the use of the money deposited in the account. The money on deposit with a bank is used by the bank to give loans. The people who borrow the money from a bank must pay it back with interest. The interest they pay is greater than the interest the bank pays for use of a customer's money. This way, the bank is able to pay depositors interest and still make a profit.

Interest is based on **interest rate** and **principal**, or balance. There are two classification for interest: *simple interest* and *compound interest.* Compound interest is discussed in the next lesson. **Simple interest**, explored in this lesson, is calculated on the principal only.

Simple Interest Formula

$I = prt$ where I = interest
p = principal
r = annual interest rate expressed as a decimal
t = number of years

Is there risk in putting money into a savings account? The Federal Deposit Insurance Corporation (FDIC) guarantees the safety of money in a bank by insuring each depositor for up to a specified amount. In 2008 the amount was $250,000 per depositor per bank depending on the type of account. It is important that all customers be aware if this amount is changed. If the bank fails, the money is replaced by the federal government.

EXAMINE THE QUESTION

Most students are familiar with savings accounts in general, yet they know little about the specifics. Most students can't even give a ballpark estimate of current savings account interest rates. Discuss with them what banking services their families have used. Ask them where the money that banks lend out for loans comes from.

CLASS DISCUSSION

Which banking services are you familiar with? What do you know about them?

Explain that compound interest will use the interest earned to increase the principal.

Explain direct deposit to students. Discuss advantages of direct deposit. (Money starts earning interest immediately, there is no check to get lost or stolen, and so on). Are there any disadvantages to direct deposit?

TEACH

Students have seen the simple interest formula before. Remind them that they need to change percents to equivalent decimals before substituting interest rates into the formula. You can review some of the more difficult percent conversions with fractions on the board. Remind them to write the formula in every problem in which they are using it.

EXAMPLE 1

Sometimes students enter division problems on the calculator in the incorrect order. Give students practice in entering division problems on the calculator, when they are given with the dividend/divisor notation or the divisor)dividend notation.

Filling in the extra zeroes on the right makes it easier to compare the numbers, because they will have the same number of decimal places and the decimal points can be lined up. All students may not need to do this, but it is a good method for students who need it.

CHECK YOUR UNDERSTANDING

Answer $5\frac{5}{8}$%, 5.6%, 5.51%, $5\frac{1}{2}$%, 5.099%

Students should write the final answers using the original forms of the percents.

Banks offer many forms of savings accounts. The most common type of savings account is a **statement savings** account where you receive a monthly statement showing all activity, including deposits, withdrawals, interest earned, and any fees. Some savings accounts require a **minimum balance**. With certain accounts, a fee is charged for each month the balance falls below the minimum amount. Some banks do not pay interest if a savings account falls below the minimum balance.

Another popular account is a **money market account**. It has a higher interest rate, but usually requires a greater initial deposit and a greater minimum balance requirement. You may be limited to a certain number of transactions per month in a money market account.

A **certificate of deposit (CD)** is a certificate that states you have a specific sum on deposit and guarantees the payment of a fixed interest rate until **maturity**, which is a specified date in the future. Maturity dates can be from seven days to ten years. Usually, the longer the term is, the higher the interest rate is. You cannot make deposits to or withdrawals from a CD without a penalty.

Skills and Strategies

All banks report interest rates as annual rates. When choosing a savings account at a bank, or which bank to use, compare the interest rates. Also, consider penalties, fees, minimum balances, and other banking services.

EXAMPLE 1

Grace wants to deposit $5,000 in a certificate of deposit for a period of two years. She is comparing interest rates quoted by three local banks and one online bank. Write the interest rates in ascending order. Which bank pays the highest interest for this two-year CD?

First State Bank: $4\frac{1}{4}$% E-Save Bank: $4\frac{3}{8}$%

Johnson City Trust: 4.22% Land Savings Bank: 4.3%

SOLUTION Numbers in ascending order are written from least to greatest. Convert the fractions to decimals and compare.

To convert a fraction to an equivalent decimal, divide the numerator by the denominator.	$4\frac{1}{4}\% = 4.25\%$ $4\frac{3}{8}\% = 4.375\%$
Add zeroes so they all have the same number of decimal places.	4.250% 4.375% 4.220% 4.300%
Then write the original numbers in order from least to greatest.	4.22%, $4\frac{1}{4}$%, 4.3%, $4\frac{3}{8}$%

E-Save Bank pays the highest interest on this two-year CD.

CHECK YOUR UNDERSTANDING

Write the following five interest rates in descending order (greatest to least):

5.51%, $5\frac{1}{2}$%, $5\frac{5}{8}$%, 5.099%, 5.6%

EXAMPLE 2

Raoul's savings account must have at least \$500, or he is charged a \$4 fee. His balance was \$716.23 when he withdrew \$225. What was his balance?

SOLUTION

Subtract the withdrawal. $716.23 - 225.00 = 491.23$

Compare to the minimum balance. $491.23 < 500$

Subtract the penalty. $491.23 - 4.00 = 487.23$

Raoul's balance after the withdrawal and penalty is \$487.23.

■ CHECK YOUR UNDERSTANDING

Mae has \$891 in her account. A \$7 fee is charged each month the balance is below \$750. She withdraws \$315. If she makes no deposits or withdrawals for the next x months, express her balance algebraically.

EXAMPLE 3

Mitchell deposits \$1,200 in an account that pays 4.5% simple interest. He keeps the money in the account for three years without any deposits or withdrawals. How much is in the account after three years?

SOLUTION Use the simple interest formula, $I = prt$. The interest rate is given as a percent, but you need to express it as a decimal.

Substitute to find the interest. $I = (1{,}200)(0.045)(3) = 162$

Add the interest and the principal. $162 + 1{,}200 = 1{,}362$

The balance after three years is \$1,362.

■ CHECK YOUR UNDERSTANDING

How much simple interest is earned on \$4,000 in $3\frac{1}{2}$ years at an interest rate of 5.2%?

EXAMPLE 4

How much simple interest does \$2,000 earn in 7 months at an interest rate of 5%?

SOLUTION Use the simple interest formula, $I = prt$. Convert 5% to a decimal and 7 months to years.

$r = 5\% = 0.05$ $t = 7 \text{ months} = \frac{7}{12} \text{ year}$

Substitute and simplify. Round. $I = (2{,}000)(0.05)\left(\frac{7}{12}\right) \approx 58.33$

The account earns \$58.33.

■ CHECK YOUR UNDERSTANDING

How much simple interest would \$800 earn in 300 days in a non-leap year at an interest rate of 5.71%? Round to the nearest cent.

EXAMPLE 2

Point out that some banks do not give interest on accounts that fall below a minimum balance, and that it is important for them to know their bank's policies.

CHECK YOUR UNDERSTANDING

Answer $576 - 7x$

EXAMPLE 3

Remind students that it is always a good idea to write the formula before starting these exercises. It makes the substitution easier, and allows a teacher to pinpoint an error that led to an incorrect answer.

CHECK YOUR UNDERSTANDING

Answer \$728

Give students additional practice on the board representing fractions of a year in months, and months as fractions of a year.

EXAMPLE 4

Students can ignore the fact that the months can have 28, 29, 30, or 31 days in them.

CHECK YOUR UNDERSTANDING

Answer \$37.55

This problem extends the fraction of a year notion to include days as the units. In a non-leap year, 300 days is 300/365 of a year.

EXAMPLE 5

Manipulating literal equations is important in algebra, and Examples 5, 6, and 7 give the students practice with it.

CHECK YOUR UNDERSTANDING

Answer \$4,615.38

Remind students that there are no additional withdrawals or deposits to this account over the two years.

EXAMPLE 6

Give students practice in manipulating literal equations that include addition and subtraction.

CHECK YOUR UNDERSTANDING

Answer approximately 9 years

EXAMPLE 7

Review the notation differences between equivalent quantities 0.04 and 4%. Point out that these expressions are not equivalent to 0.04%.

CHECK YOUR UNDERSTANDING

Answer 16%

Some students may assume that earning \$200 means "at least \$200", and can write any percent over 16%.

EXAMPLE 5

How much principal must be deposited to earn \$1,000 simple interest in 2 years at a rate of 5%?

SOLUTION Use the simple interest formula and solve for p.

Divide each side by rt and simplify. $\frac{I}{rt} = \frac{prt}{rt} \rightarrow \frac{I}{rt} = p$

Substitute and simplify. $p = \frac{1{,}000}{(0.05)(2)} = 10{,}000$

A principal of \$10,000 must be deposited.

■ CHECK YOUR UNDERSTANDING

How much principal must be deposited in a two-year simple interest account that pays $3\frac{1}{4}$% interest to earn \$300 in interest?

EXAMPLE 6

Derek has a bank account that pays 4.1% simple interest. The balance is \$910. When will the account grow to \$1,000?

SOLUTION Find the interest, $I = 1{,}000 - 910 = 90$.

Use the formula and solve for t. $t = \frac{I}{pr}$

Substitute and simplify. Round. $t = \frac{90}{(1{,}000)(0.041)} = 2.2$ years

Convert time to months. $t = (2.2)(12) = 26.4$

Derek's account will grow to \$1,000 in approximately 27 months.

■ CHECK YOUR UNDERSTANDING

How long will it take \$10,000 to double at 11% simple interest?

EXAMPLE 7

Kerry invests \$5,000 in a simple interest account for 5 years. What interest rate must the account pay so there is \$6,000 at the end of 5 years?

SOLUTION Subtract to find the interest, $I = 6{,}000 - 5{,}000 = 1{,}000$.

Use the formula and solve for r. $r = \frac{I}{pt}$

Substitute and simplify. $r = \frac{1{,}000}{(5{,}000)(5)} = 0.04 = 4\%$

The account must pay 4% annual simple interest.

■ CHECK YOUR UNDERSTANDING

Marcos deposited \$500 into a 2.5-year simple interest account. He wants to earn \$200 interest. What interest rate must the account pay?

Applications

Anything that we can do to raise personal savings is very much in the interest of this country.

Alan Greenspan, Economist

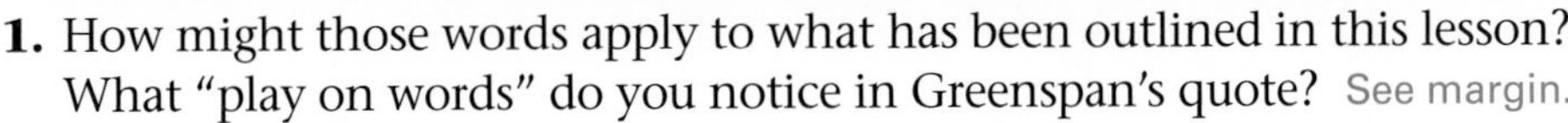

1. How might those words apply to what has been outlined in this lesson? What "play on words" do you notice in Greenspan's quote? See margin.

2. Arrange the following interest rates in ascending order: 3.4%, 3.039%, $3\frac{3}{16}\%$, 3.499%, $3\frac{1}{2}\%$. 3.039%, $3\frac{3}{16}\%$, 3.4%, 3.499%, $3\frac{1}{2}\%$

3. Josh has a savings account at a bank that charges a \$10 fee for every month his balance falls below \$1,000. His account has a balance of \$1,203.44 and he withdraws \$300. What will his balance be in six months if he makes no deposits or withdrawals? \$843.44

4. Linda's savings account has fallen below the \$1,000 minimum balance required to receive interest. It is currently \$871.43. The monthly fee charged by the bank for falling below the minimum is x dollars. Express algebraically how you compute the number of months it will take Linda's account to reach a zero balance if she makes no deposits. Explain. If $x = 9$, how many months will it take? See margin.

5. John, Paul, and George are having a disagreement over interest rates. John says that $6\frac{3}{4}\%$ can be expressed as 6.75%. George thinks that $6\frac{3}{4}\%$ can be expressed as 0.0675. Paul remembers converting percents to equivalent decimals and thinks it can be expressed as 0.0675%. Who is correct, and who is incorrect? Explain. See margin.

6. Beth and Mark would like to put some savings in the bank. They most likely will not need this money for 4 years, so Beth wants to put it in a four-year CD. Mark wants to put the money in a passbook savings account. What is the advantage of a CD? What is the disadvantage? See margin.

7. Find the simple interest on a \$2,350 principal deposited for six years at a rate of 4.77%. \$672.57

8. Ryan deposits \$775 in an account that pays 4.24% simple interest for four years. Brian deposits \$775 in an account that pays 4.24% simple interest for one year.
   a. What is Ryan's interest after the four years? \$131.44
   b. What is Ryan's balance after four years? \$906.44
   c. How much interest did Ryan's account earn the first year? \$32.86
   d. How much interest did Ryan's account earn the fourth year? \$32.86
   e. What is Brian's interest after the first year? \$32.86
   f. What is Brian's balance after the first year? \$807.86
   g. Suppose Brian withdraws all of the principal and interest after the first year and deposits it into another one-year account at the same rate, what is his interest for the second year? Round to the nearest cent. \$34.25
   h. Compare the interest Brian earns with the interest Ryan earns for the second year. Who earned more interest? Explain. Brian; Ryan earns the same amount of interest each year, \$32.86. Brian earned \$34.25 in interest the second year.

TEACH

Exercise 2
When students need to convert percents to fractions, have them convert the fractional part to a decimal first, and then move the decimal point.

Exercise 8
This exercise plants the seeds for the underlying concept of compound interest, which is in the next lesson. Notice that if Brian re-deposits his principal and interest each year, he is compounding his interest.

ANSWERS

1. In addition to the pun on 'interest', Greenspan thinks that savings help in several ways. First, they provide citizens with a financial cushion. They also give banks more money to lend for people to buy homes, cars, and so on.
4. $\frac{871.43}{x}$; 97 months; although the quotient is 96.825, it is not until the 97th month that the balance will reach zero.
5. John and George are correct. Paul is incorrect—when the percent is changed to an equivalent decimal, the percent sign is dropped.
6. The advantage is a higher rate of interest. The disadvantage is the CD has a penalty if the money is withdrawn before maturity.

TEACH

Exercise 9
Remind students that if the number of months is not a counting number, they need to round up.

Exercises 15 and 18
Remind students that if they have trouble with formulating literal algebraic expressions, they can solve the same problem with numbers first, to see how the variables should be manipulated.

Exercises 16 and 17
Point out that there are no deposits made to these accounts, and that might be unrealistic. Tell them they will learn how to handle long-term accounts with deposits being made in a later lesson.

ANSWERS

9. a. $268
   b. $179.38
   c. $1,211.51
   d. about 20 months
   e. about 21 months
   f. 5.56%
   g. $4,545.45
   h. $\frac{x}{0.03p}$

9. Use the simple interest formula to find the missing entries in the table. Round monetary amounts to the nearest cent. See margin.

Interest	Principal	Rate (to the nearest hundredth of a percent)	Time
a.	$2,000	3.35%	4 years
b.	$3,500	4.1%	15 months
c.	$20,100	5.5%	400 days
$100	$700	8.8%	**d.**
$250	$3,000	$4\frac{3}{4}\%$	**e.**
$500	$3,000	**f.**	3 years
$500	**g.**	4.4%	30 months
x	p	3%	**h.**

10. How much simple interest does $2,560 earn in 17 months at a rate of $5\frac{1}{8}\%$? Round to the nearest cent. $185.87

11. How long does it take $450 to double at a simple interest rate of 14%? approximately 86 months

12. How long does it take $450 to double at a simple interest rate of 100%? one year

13. What interest rate is needed for $9,500 to earn $900 in 19 months? Round to the nearest hundredth of a percent. 5.98%

14. Assume $20,000 is deposited into a savings account. Bedford Bank offers an annual rate of 4% simple interest for five years. Slick Bank offers a rate of 20% simple interest for one year. Which earns more interest? Neither; they are the same.

15. Assume $$x$ is deposited into a savings account. Blank Bank offers an annual rate of r% for y years. Thank Bank offers a rate of ry% for one year. Which earns more interest? Neither; they are the same.

16. A couple is planning a savings account for a newborn baby. They start with $3,450 received in newborn baby gifts. If no deposits or withdrawals are made, what is the balance of the account if it earns simple interest at 5% interest for 18 years? $6,555

17. Ron estimates that it will cost $400,000 to send his daughter to a private college in 18 years. He currently has $90,000 to deposit in an account. What simple interest rate must his account have to reach a balance of $400,000 in 18 years? Round to the nearest percent. 19%

18. Zoe creates a spreadsheet to make simple interest calculations. The user inputs values for the principal, rate, and time in years in row 2. Write each formula.

a. For A2 to compute the interest. =B2*C2*D2
b. For B2 to compute the principal. =A2/(C2*D2)
c. For C2 to compute the interest rate. =A2/(B2*D2)
d. For D2 to compute time in years, given the interest, rate, and the principal. =A2/(B2*C2)
e. For E2 to compute the time in months, given the time in years. =12*D2

	A	B	C	D	E
1	Interest	Principal	Rate	Time in Years	Time in Months
2					
3					
4					
5					

> *In the old days a man who saved money was a miser; nowadays he's a wonder.*
>
> **Author Unknown**

Explore Compound Interest 3-4

Key Terms
- compound interest
- annual compounding
- semiannual compounding
- quarterly compounding
- daily compounding
- crediting

Objectives
- Understand the concept of getting interest on your interest.
- Compute compound interest using a table.

Common Core
A-SSE1a, A-SSE1b

CCSS Warm-Up

Write an algebraic expression for each.

1. The product of R and the square of 1 more than X.
2. The quotient of one more than X and the square of R.

1. $R(X + 1)^2$
2. $\frac{x + 1}{R^2}$

What is compound interest?

EXAMINE THE QUESTION
When interest is added to principal, the principal increases, and the resulting interest for the next period increases.

When opening up any bank account, the annual interest rate is of major concern to most consumers. However, it is not enough to just know the interest rate. *How* the interest is computed should also be known.

Principal is used to compute interest. For simple interest, only the original principal is used to compute annual interest. Principal increases each time interest is added to the account. Sometimes, interest is computed using the new principal. That is, the account earns interest on the interest. **Compound interest** is money earned on the money deposited plus previous interest. This is not the case for simple interest. For simple interest, only the original principal is used to compute annual interest.

Interest can be compounded in different ways.

- **Annual compounding** is interest compounded once each year.
- **Semiannual compounding** is interest compounded twice per year, or every six months.
- **Quarterly compounding** is interest compounded four times per year, or every three months.
- **Daily compounding** is interest compounded every day. There are 365 days in a year and 366 days in a leap year.

The most common form of compounding is daily compounding. The bank pays interest every single day, based on that day's principal. The bank, however, does not add the interest every day. They keep a record of interest earned and add it into the account monthly or quarterly. This is called **crediting** an account. Compounding daily and crediting monthly is the most common procedure used by banks today.

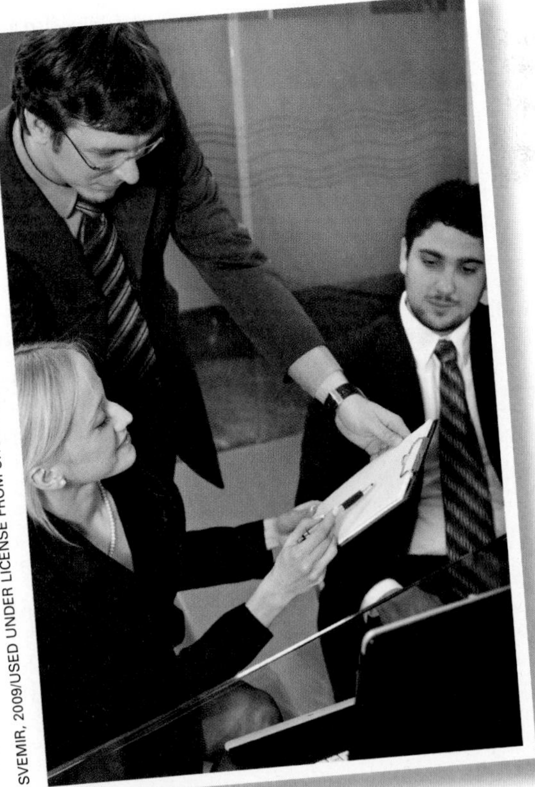

CLASS DISCUSSION

Point out that the interest for a subsequent interest period would be based on this adjusted principal—that the higher amount is used for the following interest period. It may sound obvious to some, but isn't necessarily to someone just being exposed to compound interest.

Could interest be compounded every hour? How many hours are in a year? Could interest be compounded every minute?

TEACH

Students will use the simple interest formula to make compound interest calculations. They will do a day-by-day analysis of a daily-compounded account so they can really see the interest being computed on a higher principal each day. After understanding these examples, students will be ready to learn the compound interest formula in the next lesson.

EXAMPLE 1

Since interest rates are reported for an annual interest period, yearly compounding is equivalent to simple interest for one year. However, point out that for the second year, under simple interest, the principal in this problem would still be $1,000, and under yearly compounding, it would be $1,060.

CHECK YOUR UNDERSTANDING

Answer 0.044*x* dollars

EXAMPLE 2

This problem uses the same numbers as Example 1 for comparison purposes. The only difference is the compounding period, so have students compare the answers to the two examples.

Skills and Strategies

Here you will get an understanding of how compound interest works. This will help you see how interest accumulates. As you read the examples, compare the results from each to the examples before it.

EXAMPLE 1

How much interest would $1,000 earn in one year at a rate of 6%, compounded annually? What would be the new balance?

SOLUTION The first year of interest compounded annually can be found using the simple interest formula.

Convert 6% to a decimal. $r = 6\% = 0.06$

Use the simple interest formula. $I = prt$

Substitute. $I = 1{,}000 \times 0.06 \times 1 = 60$

The account would earn $60 interest, and the balance after one year is $1,060.

CHECK YOUR UNDERSTANDING

How much would *x* dollars earn in one year at a rate of 4.4% compounded annually?

EXAMPLE 2

Maria deposits $1,000 in a savings account that pays 6% interest, compounded semiannually. What is her balance after one year?

SOLUTION Accounts that pay interest semiannually have the interest added on twice each year (every six months).

Convert 6% to a decimal. $r = 6\% = 0.06$

Convert 6 months to years. $t = 6 \text{ months} = 0.5 \text{ year}$

Use the simple interest formula. $I = prt$

Substitute and simplify. $I = 1{,}000 \times 0.06 \times 0.5 = 30$

Add the interest to the principal. $1{,}000 + 30 = 1{,}030$

This new principal, $1,030, is used to compute the next six months' interest.

Use the simple interest formula. $I = prt$

Substitute and simplify. $I = 1{,}030 \times 0.06 \times 0.5 = 30.90$

Add the interest to the principal. $1{,}030 + 30.90 = 1{,}060.90$

Maria's balance is $1,060.90 after one year. Compare this to the balance from Example 1.

CHECK YOUR UNDERSTANDING

Alex deposits $4,000 in a savings account that pays 5% interest, compounded semiannually. What is his balance after one year?

EXAMPLE 3

How much interest does $1,000 earn in three months at an interest rate of 6%, compounded quarterly? What is the balance after three months?

SOLUTION Accounts that pay interest quarterly earn interest every three months.

Convert 6% to a decimal.	$r = 6\% = 0.06$
Convert 1 quarter to years.	$t = 1$ quarter $= 3$ months $= 0.25$ year
Use the simple interest formula.	$I = prt$
Substitute and simplify.	$I = 1{,}000 \times 0.06 \times 0.25 = 15$
Add the interest to the principal.	$1{,}000 + 15 = 1{,}015$

The first quarter earns $15 interest, so the principal after one quarter is $1,015.

CHECK YOUR UNDERSTANDING

How much does $3,000 earn in six months at an interest rate of 4%, compounded quarterly?

EXAMPLE 4

How much interest does $1,000 earn in one day at an interest rate of 6%, compounded daily? What is the balance after a day?

SOLUTION Accounts that pay interest daily earn interest every day. There are 365 days in a year.

Convert 6% to a decimal.	$r = 6\% = 0.06$
Convert 1 day to years.	$t = 1 \text{ day} = \frac{1}{365} \text{ year}$
Use the simple interest formula.	$I = prt$
Substitute.	$I = 1{,}000 \times 0.06 \times \frac{1}{365} \approx 0.16$
Add the interest to the principal.	$1{,}000 + 0.16 = 1{,}000.16$

The first day's interest is approximately 16 cents, so the new balance is $1,000.16. This larger principal is used to compute the next day's interest.

CHECK YOUR UNDERSTANDING

How much interest does x dollars earn in one day at an interest rate of 5%, compounded daily? Express the answer algebraically.

CHECK YOUR UNDERSTANDING

Answer $4,202.50

EXAMPLE 3

Again the numbers from the previous two examples are used, with a change in the compounding method. You can have students compute the next three quarters' interest. Then they can compare the annual interest for the three examples.

CHECK YOUR UNDERSTANDING

Answer 3,060.30

EXAMPLE 4

Ask students how they would compute the interest for the entire year under daily compounding. Make sure they understand the drudgery of using this method repeatedly. Tell them that a better method will be introduced in the next lesson.

CHECK YOUR UNDERSTANDING

Answer $(x)(0.05)\left(\frac{1}{365}\right) = \frac{0.05x}{365}$

Encourage students to simplify the form of their answers.

EXAMPLE 5

The calendar tables allow students to see what is going on with daily compounding. The formula, which will be introduced in the next lesson, isn't as intuitive, so it is important that students understand the process. Also, the formula cannot be used if there are sporadic deposits and withdrawals.

EXAMPLE 5

Jennifer has a bank account that compounds interest daily at a rate of 3.2%. On July 11, the principal is $1,234.98. She withdraws $200 for a car repair. She receives a $34 check from her health insurance company and deposits it. On July 12, she deposits her $345.77 paycheck. What is her balance at the end of the day on July 12?

SOLUTION Organize the information in a table like the three-column table that is shown.

Date	July 11	July 12
Opening balance	$1,234.98	
Deposit (+)	$34.00	$345.77
Withdrawal (−)	$200.00	
Principal used to compute interest		
Day's interest rounded to the nearest cent		
Ending balance		

For July 11, the principal used to compute interest is computed by adding the $34 deposit and subtracting the $200 withdrawal.

The day's interest is the daily compounded interest.

To find the ending balance, add the July 11 interest to the principal used to compute interest to the nearest cent.

Date	July 11	July 12
Opening Balance	$1,234.98	
Deposit (+)	$34.00	$345.77
Withdrawal (−)	$200.00	
Principal used to compute interest	$1,068.98	
Day's interest rounded to the nearest cent	$0.09	
Ending balance	$1,069.07	

The opening balance for July 12 is the same as the ending balance from July 11.

The July 12 deposit must be added to the opening balance before the interest for July 12 is computed.

Compute interest to the nearest cent.

Add the interest to the principal used to compute interest, to compute the ending balance.

Date	July 11	July 12
Opening Balance	$1,234.98	$1,069.07
Deposit (+)	$34.00	$345.77
Withdrawal (−)	$200.00	—
Principal used to compute interest	$1,068.98	$1,414.84
Day's interest rounded to the nearest cent	$0.09	$0.12
Ending balance	$1,069.07	$1,414.96

Jennifer's balance is $1,414.96 at the end of the day on July 12.

CHECK YOUR UNDERSTANDING

Answer $976.37

A student could do this at the board so all table entries, and not just the final answer, can be scrutinized by students.

CHECK YOUR UNDERSTANDING

On January 7, Joelle opened a savings account with $900. It earned 3% interest, compounded daily. On January 8, she deposited her first paycheck of $76.22. What was her balance at the end of the day on January 8?

Applications

In the old days a man who saved money was a miser; nowadays he's a wonder.

Author Unknown

1. How might those words apply to what you learned in this lesson? See margin.
2. Jerome deposits \$3,700 in a certificate of deposit that pays $6\frac{1}{2}\%$ interest, compounded annually. How much interest does Jerome earn in one year? \$240.50
3. Sally deposits \$4,000 in a certificate of deposit that pays $6\frac{3}{4}\%$ simple interest. What is her balance after one year? \$4,270
4. Pierre deposits \$9,000 in a certificate of deposit that pays 8% interest, compounded semiannually. How much interest does the account earn in the first six months? What is the balance after six months? \$360; \$9,360
5. Kevin has x dollars in an account that pays 2.2% interest, compounded quarterly. Express his balance after one quarter algebraically. $x + 0.0055x$
6. Regina deposits \$3,500 in a savings account that pays $7\frac{1}{2}\%$ interest, compounded semiannually.
   a. How much interest does the account earn in the first six months? \$131.25
   b. What is the balance at the end of the first six months? \$3,631.25
   c. How much interest does the account earn in the second six months? \$136.17
   d. What is the balance at the end of the year? \$3,767.42
   e. How much interest does the account earn the first year? \$267.42
   f. How much interest would \$3,500 earn in one year at $7\frac{1}{2}\%$ interest, compounded annually? \$262.50
   g. How much more interest does Regina earn at an interest rate of $7\frac{1}{2}\%$ compounded semiannually than compounded annually? \$4.92
7. Liam deposits \$3,500 in a saving account that pays $7\frac{1}{2}\%$ interest, compounded quarterly.
   a. Find the first quarter's interest. \$65.63
   b. Find the first quarter's ending balance. \$3,565.63
   c. Find the second quarter's interest. \$66.86
   d. Find the second quarter's ending balance. \$3,632.49
   e. Find the third quarter's interest. \$68.11
   f. Find the third quarter's ending balance. \$3,700.60
   g. Find the fourth quarter's interest. \$69.39
   h. What is the balance at the end of one year? \$3,769.99
   i. How much interest does the account earn in the first year? \$269.99
8. Janine opens a savings account with a deposit of \$720. The account pays 3.4% interest, compounded daily. What is the first day's interest? Round to the nearest cent. \$0.07
9. Laura deposits \$2,000 in an account that has an annual interest rate of 3.96%, compounded monthly. How much interest will she earn at the end of 1 month? \$6.60

TEACH

Exercises 2 and 3
Note that exercise 2 asks for the interest and exercise 3 asks for the balance. Remind students not to skim math problems—every word is important.

Exercises 4–7
It is too much work to compute an entire year's interest using these methods of compounding.

Exercise 8
Ask students how much work it would be to compute an entire year's interest under daily compounding! This motivates the need for a formula, which is introduced in the next lesson.

ANSWERS

1. Compound interest is better than simple interest, but it won't make you rich. Time is very influential in making savings grow, so the earlier an account is started, the longer the money earns interest.

10. a. $0
b. $4,550.00
c. $4,550.00
d. $0.50
e. $4,550.50
f. $4,550.50
g. $300.00
h. $4,850.50
i. $0.53
j. $4,851.03
k. $4,851.03
l. $900.00
m. $3,951.03
n. $0.43
p. $3,951.46

11. a. $0
b. $6,000.00
c. $0
d. $6,000.00
e. $0.57
f. $6,000.57
g. $6,000.57
h. $500.00
i. $0
j. $6,500.57
k. $0.61
l. $6,501.18
m. $6,501.18
n. $0
p. $2,500.00
q. $4,001.18
r. $0.38
s. $4,001.56

14. a. $P + D$
b. $\frac{0.02(P+D)}{365}$
c. $P + D + \frac{0.02(P+D)}{365}$
d. $P + D + \frac{0.02(P+D)}{365}$
e. $P + D - W + \frac{0.02(P+D)}{365}$
f. $0.02\left(\frac{P + D - W + 0.02\left(\frac{P+D}{365}\right)}{365}\right)$
g. $(P + D - W) + \frac{0.02(P+D)}{365} + 0.02\left(\frac{P + D - W + 0.02\left(\frac{P+D}{365}\right)}{365}\right)$

10. Jacob opens a savings account in a non-leap year on August 10 with a $4,550 deposit. The account pays 4% interest, compounded daily. On August 11 he deposits $300, and on August 12 he withdraws $900. Find the missing amounts in the table. See margin.

Date	Aug. 10	Aug. 11	Aug. 12
Opening balance	a.	f.	k.
Deposit	b.	g.	-----
Withdrawal	-----	-----	l.
Principal used to compute interest	c.	h.	m.
Day's interest rounded to nearest cent	d.	i.	n.
Ending balance	e.	j.	p.

11. On December 18 of a leap year, Stacy opened a savings account by depositing $6,000. The account pays 3.45% interest, compounded daily. On December 19 she deposited $500, and on December 20 she withdrew $2,500. Find the missing amounts in the table. Round to the nearest cent. What is her opening balance on December 21? See margin; $4,001.56

Date	Dec. 18	Dec. 19	Dec. 20
Opening balance	a.	g.	m.
Deposit	b.	h.	n.
Withdrawal	c.	i.	p.
Principal used to compute interest	d.	j.	q.
Day's interest rounded to nearest cent	e.	k.	r.
Ending balance	f.	l.	s.

12. On May 29, Rocky had an opening balance of x dollars in an account that pays 3% interest, compounded daily. He deposits y dollars. Express his ending balance on May 30 algebraically. $x + y + \frac{0.03(x+y)}{365}$

13. Linda has d dollars in an account that pays 3.4% interest, compounded weekly. She withdraws w dollars. Express her first week's interest algebraically. $\frac{0.034(d-w)}{52}$

14. The table represents the compound interest calculations for an account that pays 2% interest compounded daily. Represent a–g algebraically. See margin.

Date	Feb. 2	Feb. 3
Opening balance	P	d.
Deposit	D	------
Withdrawal	-----	W
Principal used to compute interest	a.	e.
Interest	b.	f.
Ending balance	c.	g.

15. One day before the end of the month, George had an opening balance of m dollars in an account that pays 2.25% interest compounded monthly. On the last day of the month, he made a deposit equal to twice his opening balance. Express his ending balance on the last day of the month algebraically. $3m + \left[\frac{0.025(3m)}{12}\right]$

To make a million, start with $900,000.
Morton Shulman, Politician, Businessman, and Television Personality

Compound Interest Formula 3-5

Key Terms	• compound interest formula	• annual percentage rate (APR)	• annual percentage yield (APY)

Objectives

- Become familiar with the derivation of the compound interest formula.
- Make computations using the compound interest formula.

Common Core
A-SSE3c, F-IF8b

CCSS Warm-Up

Factor each expression.

1. $x^2 - x - 20$ **2.** $x^2 - 9x + 20$ **3.** $x^2 + x - 20$

1. $(x - 5)(x + 4)$ 2. $(x - 5)(x - 4)$ 3. $(x + 5)(x - 4)$

What are the advantages of using the compound interest formula?

Julio deposited $10,000 in a five-year CD, with the intention of using the money for his son's college education. The account pays 5.2% interest compounded daily. There will be no deposits or withdrawals during the five years. Julio wants to know how much the $10,000 will grow to by the end of the five years. Imagine if he set up a daily compound interest table as in the last lesson. There are over 1,800 days in five years, so the table would get quite tedious. It is not practical to solve this problem one day at a time.

EXAMINE THE QUESTION

Exercises 8–14 from the previous lesson illustrate how tedious weekly and

(continued on next page)

Calculating compound interest using the simple interest formula is tedious when there are numerous periods. The power of mathematics can turn this long procedure into a relatively small amount of work. Numerical examples and algebra can be combined to uncover a pattern that leads to a formula that finds compound interest. The **compound interest formula** relates principal, interest rate, the number of times interest is compounded per year, and the number of years the money will be on deposit, and the ending balance. The formula is used for any type of compounding: annually, semiannually, monthly, weekly, daily, and so on.

In Lesson 3-3, you used the annual interest rate to compute interest. Banks call this the **annual percentage rate (APR)**. Most banks advertise the **annual percentage yield (APY)** since it is higher than the APR for accounts compounded more than once per year. The bank takes the dollar amount of interest you earn under the compounding to create the APY. The APY is the simple interest rate that would be required to give the same dollar amount of interest that the compounding gave. Therefore, annual percentage yield (APY) is an annual rate of interest that takes into account the effect of compounding.

daily compound interest calculations can get. Ask students to imagine how difficult it would be for a bank to do this for thousands of customers, before there were computers! Explain that someone programmed a formula into the computers, and that they are about to learn that formula.

CLASS DISCUSSION

Remind students about the calendar computations from the last lesson. Have them approximate how long it would take them to do the computations for five years!

TEACH

Students will get to see how the compound interest formula can be derived. They will have a chance to look for patterns and generalize to discover the formula.

EXAMPLE 1

Elicit patterns the students see when the example is finished.

Skills and Strategies

Here you will solve some compound interest problems and then look for a pattern to derive the compound interest formula.

EXAMPLE 1

Jose opens a savings account with principal *P* dollars that pays 5% interest, compounded quarterly. What will his ending balance be after one year?

SOLUTION 1 Find the first quarter's interest, where $p = P$, $r = 0.05$, and $t = \frac{1}{4}$.

Use the simple interest formula. $I = prt$

Substitute. $I = (P)(0.05)\left(\frac{1}{4}\right)$

Simplify. $I = \frac{0.05}{4}P$

Let B_1 represent the first quarter's ending balance, the sum of *P* and the first quarter's interest.

Principal + Interest $B_1 = P + \frac{0.05}{4}P$

Factor out *P*. $B_1 = P\left(1 + \frac{0.05}{4}\right)$

To get the second quarter's ending balance, follow the same procedure with the new balance B_1.

Principal + Interest $B_2 = B_1 + \frac{0.05}{4}B_1$

Factor out B_1. $B_2 = B_1\left(1 + \frac{0.05}{4}\right)$

Substitute $P\left(1 + \frac{0.05}{4}\right)$ for B_1. $B_2 = p\left(1 + \frac{0.05}{4}\right)\left(1 + \frac{0.05}{4}\right)$

Write in exponential form. $B_2 = P\left(1 + \frac{0.05}{4}\right)^2$

To get the third quarter's ending balance, follow the same procedure with the new balance B_2.

Principal + Interest $B_3 = B_2 + \frac{0.05}{4}B_2$

Factor out B_2. $B_3 = B_2\left(1 + \frac{0.05}{4}\right)$

Substitute $P\left(1 + \frac{0.05}{4}\right)^2$ for B_2. $B_3 = P\left(1 + \frac{0.05}{4}\right)^2\left(1 + \frac{0.05}{4}\right)$

Write in exponential form. $B_3 = P\left(1 + \frac{0.05}{4}\right)^3$

To get the fourth quarter's ending balance, follow the same procedure with the new balance B_3.

Factor out B_4. $$B_4 = B_3 + \frac{0.05}{4}B_3 = B_3\left(1 + \frac{0.05}{4}\right)$$

Substitute $P\left(1 + \frac{0.05}{4}\right)^3$ for B_3. $$B_4 = P\left(1 + \frac{0.05}{4}\right)^3\left(1 + \frac{0.05}{4}\right)$$

Ending balance after one year $$B_4 = P\left(1 + \frac{0.05}{4}\right)^4$$

This is the balance after one year. Examine the formula for patterns.

CHECK YOUR UNDERSTANDING

Rico deposits $800 at 3.87% interest, compounded quarterly. What is his ending balance after one year? Round to the nearest cent.

EXAMPLE 2

If you deposit *P* dollars for one year at 5% compounded daily, express the ending balance algebraically.

SOLUTION Use the formula from Example 1 and make adjustments for daily compounding. When the interest was compounded quarterly, there was a denominator of 4 and an exponent of 4 in the formula.

$$B_4 = P\left(1 + \frac{0.05}{4}\right)^4$$

With daily compounding, these entries are replaced with 365. Rewrite the formula.

Ending balance after one year $$B = P\left(1 + \frac{0.05}{365}\right)^{365}$$

This is the ending balance expressed algebraically.

CHECK YOUR UNDERSTANDING

Nancy deposits $1,200 into an account that pays 3% interest, compounded monthly. What is her ending balance after one year? Round to the nearest cent.

EXTEND YOUR UNDERSTANDING

Nancy receives two offers in the mail from other banks. One is an account that pays 2.78% compounded daily. The other account pays 3.25% compounded quarterly. Would either of these accounts provide Nancy with a better return than her current account? If so, which account?

CHECK YOUR UNDERSTANDING

Answer $831.41

Show how parentheses must be placed when the expression is entered on a calculator. Make sure students enter the entire expression into the calculator, and do not compute separate parts of the expression, round them, and then make subsequent calculations.

EXAMPLE 2

Give other examples of weekly, hourly, monthly compounding using the formula, so students get used to adjusting the formula.

CHECK YOUR UNDERSTANDING

Answer $1,236.50

Have students compare this to the balance under simple interest, which is $1,236.

EXTEND YOUR UNDERSTANDING

Answer yes; the account that pays 3.25% compounded quarterly

Compound Interest Formula

Examples 1 and 2 involved accounts for one year. The exponent and the denominator in those formulas are the number of times the interest is compounded *in one year*. You can leave your money in for more than one year. The formula used to compute the ending balance includes the variable t, where t is the number of years.

Compound Interest Formula

$$B = p\left(1 + \frac{r}{n}\right)^{nt}$$

where B = ending balance
p = principal or original balance
r = interest rate expressed as a decimal
n = number of times interest is compounded annually
t = number of years

EXAMPLE 3

Marie deposits $1,650 for three years at 3% interest, compounded daily. What is her ending balance?

SOLUTION Use the compound interest formula. The values for the variables are $p = 1{,}650$, $r = 0.03$, $n = 365$, and $t = 3$.

Substitute the values for Marie's account.

$$B = 1{,}650\left(1 + \frac{0.03}{365}\right)^{365(3)}$$

Use your calculator to enter the expression. Enter the entire expression; try not to do it in separate terms. The keystrokes are:

1650(1+0.03/365)^(365×3) ENTER

```
1650(1+0.03/365)
^(365*3)
          1805.380891
```

Marie's ending balance, to the nearest cent, is $1,805.38.

■ CHECK YOUR UNDERSTANDING

Kate deposits $2,350 in an account that earns interest at a rate of 3.1%, compounded monthly. What is her ending balance after five years? Round to the nearest cent.

■ EXTEND YOUR UNDERSTANDING

Write an algebraic expression for the ending balance after k years of an account that starts with a balance of $2,000 and earns interest at a rate of 3.5%, compounded daily.

EXAMPLE 3

Point out that the product representing the exponent must be put in parentheses for the calculator to compute this correctly. Have students write calculator keystroke sequences given the formula for practice.

CHECK YOUR UNDERSTANDING

Answer $2,743.45

Look at the calculator entries of students who got incorrect answers. Look for parentheses placement errors.

EXTEND YOUR UNDERSTANDING

Answer

$2{,}000\left(1 + \frac{0.035}{365}\right)^{365k}$

EXAMPLE 4

Sharon deposits $8,000 in a one year CD at 3.2% interest, compounded daily. What is Sharon's annual percentage yield (APY) to the nearest hundredth of a percent?

SOLUTION Find the APY using the compound interest formula and the simple interest formula.

Use the compound interest formula. $B = p\left(1 + \frac{r}{n}\right)^{nt}$

Substitute. $B = 8{,}000\left(1 + \frac{0.032}{365}\right)^{365 \times 1}$

Simplify. $B = 8{,}260.13$

Subtract the principal from the new balance.

$$I = 8{,}260.13 - 8{,}000 = 260.13$$

Use the simple interest formula. $I = prt$

Solve for *r*. $r = \frac{I}{pt}$

Substitute. $r = \frac{260.13}{8{,}000 \times 1}$

Simplify. $r \approx 0.0325 = 3.25\%$

The annual percentage yield is 3.25%.

APY can also be found by using the formula $APY = \left(1 + \frac{r}{n}\right)^n - 1$, where *r* is the interest rate and *n* is the number of times interest is compounded per year.

Use the *APY* formula. $APY = \left(1 + \frac{r}{n}\right)^n - 1$

Substitute. $APY = \left(1 + \frac{0.032}{365}\right)^{365} - 1$

Simplify. $APY \approx 0.0325 = 3.25\%$

The annual percentage yield is 3.25%, which is the same as the previous answer.

CHECK YOUR UNDERSTANDING

Barbara deposits $3,000 in a one year CD at 4.1% interest, compounded daily. What is the APY to the nearest hundredth of a percent?

EXTEND YOUR UNDERSTANDING

Consider an amount *x* deposited into a CD at 2.4% interest compounded daily, and the same amount deposited into a CD at the same rate that compounds monthly. Explain why, after 1 year, the balance on a CD that compounds daily is greater than the CD that compounded monthly.

EXAMPLE 4

The annual percentage yield gives the simple interest rate that would have earned Sharon the same dollar amount of interest, if she began with the same $2,350. The APY is more than the APR since the APY doesn't give interest on the interest like compounding. Since the principals used to compute interest when compounding are not used in simple interest, the APY must be higher to compensate for the lower principal used throughout the process.

CHECK YOUR UNDERSTANDING

Answer 4.18%

EXTEND YOUR UNDERSTANDING

Answer Because there are more compounding periods for the interest to be earned on already accumulated interest, the balance grows quicker.

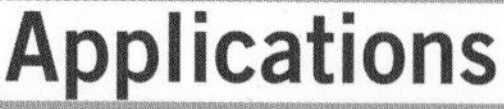

Applications

To make a million, start with $900,000.
Morton Shulman, Politician, Businessman, and Television Personality

TEACH

Exercises 1–11
Remind students to write the formula for each problem, and identify the value for each variable in the formula. This way, if they enter an incorrect keystroke sequence into the calculator, you can troubleshoot where their difficulties began. You can also use it to give partial credit on a graded assignment or exam.

ANSWERS

1. Bank interest on its own will not make you rich; the interest rates are much smaller than possible returns on business investments. However, there is much less risk.

1. How might these words apply to what is in this lesson? See margin.

2. Jimmy invests $4,000 in an account that pays 5% annual interest, compounded semiannually. What is his balance, to the nearest cent, at the end of 10 years? $6,554.47

3. On Olga's 16th birthday, her uncle invested $2,000 in an account that was locked into a 4.75% interest rate, compounded monthly. How much will Olga have in the account when she turns 18? Round to the nearest cent. $2,198.91

4. Samantha deposits $1,500 into the Park Street Bank. The account pays 4.12% annual interest, compounded daily. To the nearest cent, how much is in the account at the end of three non-leap years? $1,697.33

5. Joanne deposits $4,300 into a one-year CD at a rate of 4.3%, compounded daily.

a. What is her ending balance after the year? $4,488.92
b. How much interest does she earn? $188.92
c. What is her annual percentage yield to the nearest hundredth of a percent? 4.39%

6. Mike deposits $5,000 in a three-year CD account that yields 3.5% interest, compounded weekly. What is his ending balance at the end of three years? $5,553.36

7. Rob deposits $1,000 in a savings account at New York State Bank that pays 4.4% interest, compounded monthly.

a. How much is in his account at the end of one year? $1,044.90
b. What is the APY for this account to the nearest hundredth of a percent? 4.49%

8. How much more does $1,000 earn in eight years, compounded daily at 5%, than $1,000 over eight years at 5%, compounded semiannually? $7.27

9. If $3,000 is invested at an interest rate of 4.8%, compounded hourly for two years, what is the ending balance? $3,302.28

10. Mike and Julie receive $20,000 in gifts from friends and relatives for their wedding. They deposit the money into an account that pays 4.75% interest, compounded daily.

a. Will their money double in fourteen years? no
b. Will their money double in fifteen years? yes

11. Lindsay invests $80 in an account that pays 5% annual interest, compounded monthly. Michele invests $60 in an account that pays 8% annual interest, compounded weekly.

a. Whose balance is greater after one year? Lindsay's
b. Whose balance is greater after twelve years? Michele's

12. Investigate the difference between compounding annually and simple interest for parts a–j.

a. Find the simple interest for a one-year CD for $5,000 at a 6% interest rate. $300

b. Find the interest for a one-year CD for $5,000 at an interest rate of 6%, compounded annually. $300

c. Compare the results from parts a and b. The interest is the same.

d. Find the simple interest for a three-year CD for $5,000 at an interest rate of 6%. $900

e. Find the interest for a three-year CD for $5,000 at an interest rate of 6%, compounded annually. $955.08

f. Compare the results from parts d and e. See margin.

g. Find the simple interest for a six-year CD for $5,000 at an interest rate of 4%. $1,200

h. Find the interest for a six-year CD for $5,000 at an interest rate of 4%, compounded annually. $1,326.60

i. Compare the results from parts g and h. See margin.

j. Is interest compounded annually the same as simple interest? Explain. See margin.

13. Rodney invests a sum of money, *P*, into an account that earns interest at a rate of *r*, compounded yearly. Gerald invests half that amount into an account that pays twice Rodney's interest rate. Which of the accounts will have the higher ending balance after one year? Explain. See margin.

14. Island Bank is advertising a special 6.55% APR for CDs. Manny takes out a one-year CD for $40,000. The interest is compounded daily. Find the annual percentage yield for Manny's account to the nearest hundredth of a percent. 6.77%

15. Businesses deposit large sums of money into bank accounts. Imagine an account with 10 million dollars in it.

a. How much would the account earn in one year of simple interest at a rate of 5.12%? $512,000

b. How much would the account earn in one year at 5.12% if the interest was compounded daily? $525,296.00

c. How much more interest is earned by interest compounded daily compared to simple interest? $13,296

16. An elite private college receives large donations from successful alumni. The account that holds these donations has $955,000,000 currently.

a. How much would the account earn in one year of simple interest at a rate of 5.33%? $50,901,500

b. How much would the account earn in one year at 5.33% if the interest was compounded daily? Round to the nearest cent. $52,278,530.93

c. How much more interest is earned by compounded daily as compared to simple interest? $1,377,030.93

d. If the money is used to pay full scholarships, and the price of tuition is $61,000 per year to attend, how many more students can receive full four-year scholarships if the interest was compounded daily rather than using simple interest? 22

Exercises 15 and 16

Students get a glimpse into the world of high finance. Seldom do they get a chance to see the large amount of interest that can be earned on savings accounts with high principals.

ANSWERS

12f. The annual compounded interest earned $55.08 more than the simple interest.

12i. The annual compounded interest earned $126.60 more than the simple interest.

12j. No; they are the same for one year. For anything longer, compounded interest grows faster than simple interest.

13. Rodney's account balance will always be greater; $P\left(1+\frac{r}{1}\right)^{1.1} > 0.5P\left(1+\frac{2r}{1}\right)^{1.1}$, or $P(1+r) > P(0.5+r)$

The infinite! No other question has ever moved so profoundly the spirit of man.

David Hilbert, Mathematician

3-6 Continuous Compounding

Objectives

- Compute interest on an account that is continuously compounded.

Common Core

N-RN1, N-RN2, A-SSE1b, A-SSE3

Key Terms

- limit
- finite
- infinite
- continuous compounding
- exponential base (*e*)
- continuous compound interest formula

CCSS Warm-Up

Determine the exact value of each.

1. $\sqrt[3]{A}$ when $A = 8$

2. A^{bc} when $A = 9$, $b = 2$, $c = (1/4)$

1. 2

2. 3

EXAMINE THE QUESTION

Pose the idea of compounding daily, hourly, every minute, every second, and so on. Can you compound every half-second? Every millisecond? Microsecond?

At the end of the lesson introduction, students are asked about depositing $1,000 at 100% interest compounded continuously for one year. As they offer their estimates for the balance after one year, write their guesses on the board. Students may not realize that the frequent interest calculations counteract the smaller amounts of interest being added on each period.

CLASS DISCUSSION

You can have a student actually walk across the classroom, walking half of the remaining distances each time. They are really adding an infinite number of "half of the remaining distances." Yet they reach the other side of the room, proving that this infinite sum has a finite answer. You can point out that all infinite sums do not necessarily have a finite answer; for example, 1 + 2 + 3 + 4 + ... does not have a finite sum.

How can interest be compounded continuously?

Compounding interest daily makes money grow more quickly than simple interest. It is possible to compound interest every hour, every minute, even every second! There are over 31 million seconds in a year. The compound interest formula works with seconds just as it did for compounding daily. There are one million microseconds in one second! It works even if interest is compounded every microsecond!

How do millions of compounds affect the ending balance after a year? To understand this, you need to learn about **limits**. Imagine you want to walk all the way across a 64-foot wide room. The length 64 feet is a **finite** distance—it can be represented by a real number. To do this, you first must walk halfway across the room, or 32 feet. To continue the walk, you must cover half of the remaining 32 feet, which is 16 feet. Then you must cover half of the remaining 16 feet, which is 8 feet. Next, you must cover half of the remaining 8 feet, which is 4 feet. Then, you need to cover half of the remaining 4 feet, which is 2 feet. Next, you need to cover half of the remaining 2 feet, which is 1 foot. Then you need to cover $\frac{1}{2}$ foot, then $\frac{1}{4}$ foot, then $\frac{1}{8}$ foot, and so on. The distances walked so far are shown in the diagram below.

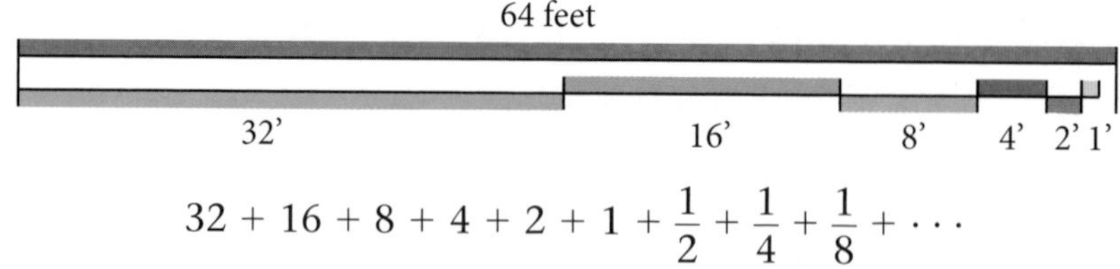

$$32 + 16 + 8 + 4 + 2 + 1 + \frac{1}{2} + \frac{1}{4} + \frac{1}{8} + \cdots$$

What do the three dots at the end of the expression mean? Because there will always be some distance between you and the wall, no matter how small, you will always have a positive number to take half of. You will be taking half of the remaining distance infinitely many times! The expression will never end. Yet, you know you can touch the wall you were walking towards. And you know it is 64 feet away. Conclusion? You can add an **infinite** amount of numbers and get a finite sum!

The infinite sum shown adds to 64. If you stopped adding at any time, you would not reach the sum of 64. The limit of the sum is 64 since every addition gets the sum closer to 64. The sum will never reach 64.

Now think about compound interest. Rather than compounding every minute, or every microsecond, imagine compounding infinitely many times each year. This is called **continuous compounding**. Will it make you rich? Consider: If you deposited $1,000 at 100% interest, compounded continuously, what would your ending balance be after one year?

Notice the extremely high interest rate. Before reading Skills and Strategies, write down your best guess for this balance. Compare your guess to the guesses of your classmates.

TEACH

The notion of limit is usually introduced in a precalculus class. Students may have some experience with asymptotes and infinity. A calculator is a helpful tool to illustrate patterns in sequences that depict properties of infinity.

Skills and Strategies

The question just posed will be answered through the following series of examples. Be sure to compare your guess to the correct answer.

EXAMPLE 1

Students should notice that due to the squaring, multiplication by 3, and addition, that the numbers will strictly increase, and there will be no limit.

EXAMPLE 1

Given the quadratic function $f(x) = x^2 + 3x + 5$, as the values of x increase to infinity, what happens to the values of $f(x)$?

SOLUTION Use your calculator. Find the value of $f(x)$ for each of the increasing values of x in the table.

x	$f(x)$
100	10,305
1,000	1,003,005
90,000	8,100,270,005
900,000	$> 8(10)^{11}$
8,000,000	$> 6(10)^{13}$
50,000,000	$> 2(10)^{15}$

As x approaches infinity, the value of $f(x)$ increases without bound. Therefore, $f(x)$ has no limit.

CHECK YOUR UNDERSTANDING

As the values of x increase towards infinity, what happens to the values of $g(x) = -5x + 1$?

CHECK YOUR UNDERSTANDING

Answer They decrease.

EXAMPLE 2

Given the function $f(x) = \dfrac{6x - 1}{3x + 2}$, as the values of x increase to infinity, what happens to the values of $f(x)$?

SOLUTION Set up a table with increasing values of x. The pattern in the table shows that as x approaches infinity, $f(x)$ approaches 2. It keeps getting closer to 2; it, never reaches 2. You can say, "The limit of $f(x)$, as x approaches infinity, is 2," written

$$\lim_{x \to \infty} f(x) = 2$$

x	$f(x)$
100	1.983443709
1,000	1.998334444
90,000	1.999981482
900,000	1.999998148
8,000,000	1.999999792
50,000,000	1.999999967
2,000,000,000	1.999999999

Lim is an abbreviation for limit. The arrow represents "approaching." The symbol for infinity is ∞.

CHECK YOUR UNDERSTANDING

If $f(x) = \dfrac{1}{x}$, use a table and your calculator to find $\lim_{x \to \infty} f(x)$.

CHECK YOUR UNDERSTANDING

Answer 0

EXAMPLE 3

Students should make a conjecture before using their calculators.

CHECK YOUR UNDERSTANDING

Answer 1

First ask students for the limits of 3^x, 4^x, 5^x, and so on before 1^x.

EXAMPLE 4

You can preface this example by asking the students for the limits as x increases for $\frac{1}{x}$, and then for $\left(1 + \frac{1}{x}\right)$.

Compare the designation of this limit as e to the designation of π for the ratio of a circle's circumference to its diameter. That's how important e is in mathematics!

CHECK YOUR UNDERSTANDING

Answer 1.05127

You can vary the numerator in the fraction of the expression and have students see what happens to the limits.

EXAMPLE 3

Given the function $f(x) = 2^x$, find $\lim_{x\to\infty} f(x)$.

SOLUTION You can use a table or your mathematical intuition. As the values of x increase, the values of $f(x)$ increase without bound, so the limit is undefined.

CHECK YOUR UNDERSTANDING

Given the function $f(x) = 1^x$, find $\lim_{x\to\infty} f(x)$.

EXAMPLE 4

If $f(x) = (1 + \frac{1}{x})^x$, find $\lim_{x\to\infty} f(x)$.

SOLUTION You can do this intuitively in gradual steps.

From Check Your Understanding for Example 3 $\lim_{x\to\infty} 1^x = 1$

From Check Your Understanding for Example 2 $\lim_{x\to\infty}\left(\frac{1}{x}\right) = 0$

As a result $\lim_{x\to\infty}\left(1 + \frac{1}{x}\right) = 1$

Keep in mind the expression in parentheses is always a little greater than 1. Because $\left(1 + \frac{1}{x}\right)$ is greater than 1, the expression $\left(1 + \frac{1}{x}\right)^x$ has a "battle" going on within it as x approaches infinity. As x approaches infinity, the expression in parentheses decreases. Simultaneously, the exponent increases. For this reason, it is difficult to tell what happens to the entire expression. You cannot use mathematical intuition to find the limit.

x	$f(x)$ to nine decimal places
100	2.704813829
1,000	2.716923932
90,000	2.718266724
900,000	2.718280046
8,000,000	2.718281659
50,000,000	2.718281801
2,000,000,000	2.718281828

Use a table. The pattern in the table shows that as x approaches infinity, $f(x)$ approaches a number around 2.718... This number is very special in mathematics. It is called the **exponential base**, and is abbreviated ***e***. Look for a key labeled e on your calculator. Press it.

$$e \approx 2.718281828$$

The exponential base e is an irrational number. It is a non-terminating, non-repeating decimal. Your calculator shows only the first few decimal places of e.

Therefore $\lim_{x\to\infty}\left(1 + \frac{1}{x}\right)^x = e$

CHECK YOUR UNDERSTANDING

Use a table and your calculator to find $\lim_{x\to\infty}\left(1 + \frac{0.05}{x}\right)^x$, rounded to five decimal places.

EXAMPLE 5

If you deposited \$1,000 at 100% interest, compounded continuously, what would your ending balance be after one year?

SOLUTION This is the original question posed in the beginning of the lesson. Compounding continuously requires taking a limit as the number of compounds approaches infinity.

$$\lim_{x \to \infty} 1{,}000\left(1 + \frac{1}{x}\right)^x = 1{,}000e \approx 1{,}000(2.7182818) = 2{,}718.28$$

Therefore, \$1,000 at 100% interest, compounded continuously would grow to \$2,718.28 in one year. You may have originally thought that, with 100% interest, and an infinite amount of compounds, that the \$1,000 would grow tremendously. Keep in mind that, as the exponent x increases, the fraction $\frac{1}{x}$ in the parentheses decreases, somewhat counteracting, or "battling" the exponent. Think of the result as a "compromise" of this battle.

CHECK YOUR UNDERSTANDING

The irrational, exponential base e is so important in mathematics that it has a single-letter abbreviation, e, and has its own key on the calculator. When you studied circles, you studied another important irrational number that has a single-letter designation and its own key on the calculator. The number was π. Recall that $\pi = 3.141592654$. Use the e and π keys on your calculator to find the difference between e^π and π^e. Round to the nearest thousandth.

EXAMPLE 6

If you deposit \$1,000 at 4.3% interest, compounded continuously, what would your ending balance be to the nearest cent after five years?

SOLUTION Using 4.3% instead of 100% changes the limit expression to $\lim_{x\to\infty} 1{,}000\left(1 + \frac{0.043}{x}\right)^x$. Use the following formula.

Continuous Compound Interest Formula

$B = pe^{rt}$ where
B = ending balance
p = principal
e = exponential base
r = interest rate expressed as a decimal
t = number of years

Substitute. $B = 1{,}000e^{0.043(5)}$

Calculate. $B = 1{,}239.86$

The ending balance would be \$1,239.86.

CHECK YOUR UNDERSTANDING

Craig deposits \$5,000 at 5.12% interest, compounded continuously for four years. What would his ending balance be to the nearest cent?

EXAMPLE 5

This answers the question posed at the beginning of the lesson. Look back at the student guesses and see who is closest. Ask students with high guesses what they didn't account for.

CHECK YOUR UNDERSTANDING

Answer 0.682

If any students have encountered the golden ratio, point out that it also has a letter designation, the Greek letter phi, φ.

EXAMPLE 6

The formula makes it easy to find the balance. Using the limit expression would require increasing substitutions into the calculator.

CHECK YOUR UNDERSTANDING

Answer \$6,136.40

Applications

The infinite! No other question has ever moved so profoundly the spirit of man.

David Hilbert, Mathematician

TEACH

So far in this chapter, students have used the simple interest formula and the compound interest formula. Now they also need to use the continuous compounding formula. Spiral the homework assignments so students have to do all three types for a few days.

Exercises 1–5

The use of parentheses in the continuous compounding formula is not as tricky as the compound interest formula, but students do need to make sure the entire exponent is in parentheses.

ANSWERS

1. People have a difficult time conceiving of infinity. The concept of infinite time, space, and number triggers the imagination and often boggles the mind.

3b. The exponent on e is only 0.0539 since the parentheses were closed before the 4 was included. Ed's expression raised e to the 0.0539 power, multiplied it by 20,000, and multiplied that result by 4.

5d. Sample answers: How close is the bank to her home? Will she still be living in the same place in two years? Does she have other banking business at that bank? What are the hours? How customer-friendly is the service?

1. How might these words apply to this lesson? See margin.

2. A bank representative studies compound interest, so she can better serve customers. She analyzes what happens when \$2,000 earns interest several different ways at a rate of 4% for 3 years.

a. Find the interest if it is computed using simple interest. \$240
b. Find the interest if it is compounded annually. \$249.73
c. Find the interest if it is compounded semiannually. \$252.32
d. Find the interest if it is compounded quarterly. \$253.65
e. Find the interest if it is compounded monthly. \$254.54
f. Find the interest if it is compounded daily. \$254.98
g. Find the interest if it is compounded hourly. \$254.99
h. Find the interest if it is compounded every minute. \$254.99
i. Find the interest if it is compounded continuously. \$254.99
j. What is the difference in interest between simple interest and interest compounded continuously? \$14.99

3. Ed computes the ending balance for an account he is considering. The principal is \$20,000, and the interest rate is 5.39%, compounded continuously for four years. He uses the formula $B = pe^{rt}$ and substitutes directly on his calculator. Look at the keystrokes he entered.

20,000*e*^(.0539)(4)

He presses ENTER and sees this display.

20000*e*^(.0539)(4) = 84430.32472

Ed's knowledge of compound interest leads him to believe that this answer is extremely unreasonable. To turn \$20,000 into over \$84,000 in just four years at 5.39% interest seems incorrect to him.

a. Find the correct ending balance. \$24,812.12
b. Explain what part of Ed's keystroke sequence is incorrect. See margin.

4. Find the interest earned on a \$50,000 deposited for six years at $4\frac{1}{8}$% interest, compounded continuously. \$14,040.97

5. Whitney deposits \$9,000 for two years. She compares two different banks. State Bank will pay her 4.1% interest, compounded monthly. Kings Savings will pay her 4.01% interest, compounded continuously.

a. How much interest does State Bank pay? \$767.74
b. How much interest does Kings Savings pay? \$751.53
c. Which bank pays higher interest? How much higher? State Bank; \$16.21
d. What other factors might affect Whitney's choice besides interest? See margin.

6. Interest rates fluctuate with the economy. In the 1980s, the highest CD interest rate was over 16%. By 2009, the highest CD interest rates were approximately 5%.
   a. If $1,000 is invested at 16% interest, compounded continuously, for five years, what is the ending balance? $2,225.54
   b. If $1,000 is invested at 5% interest, compounded continuously, for five years, what is the ending balance? $1,284.03
   c. What is the difference between the two ending balances? $941.51

7. Find the interest earned on a $30,000 deposit for six months at $4\frac{1}{2}$% interest, compounded continuously. $682.65

8. Caroline is opening a CD to save for college. She is considering a 3-year CD or a $3\frac{1}{2}$-year CD since she starts college around that time. She needs to be able to have the money to make tuition payments on time, and she does not want to have to withdraw money early from the CD and face a penalty. She has $19,400 to deposit.
   a. How much interest would she earn at 4.2% compounded monthly for three years? Round to the nearest cent. $2,600.23
   b. How much interest would she earn at 4.2% compounded monthly for $3\frac{1}{2}$ years? Round to the nearest cent. $3,066.30
   c. Caroline decides on a college after opening the $3\frac{1}{2}$-year CD, and the college needs the first tuition payment a month before the CD matures. Caroline must withdraw money from the CD early, after 3 years and 5 months. She faces two penalties. First, the interest rate for the last five months of the CD was lowered to 2%. Additionally, there was a $250 penalty. Find the interest on the last five months of the CD. Round to the nearest cent. $183.95
   d. Find the total interest on the $3\frac{1}{2}$ year CD after 3 years and 5 months. $2,784.18
   e. The interest is reduced by subtracting the $250 penalty. What does the account earn for the 3 years and 5 months? $2,534.18
   f. Find the balance on the CD after she withdraws $12,000 after 3 years and five months. $9,934.18
   g. The final month of the CD receives 2% interest. What is the final month's interest? Round to the nearest cent. $16.56
   h. What is the total interest for the $3\frac{1}{2}$ year CD? $2,550.74
   i. Would Caroline have been better off with the 3-year CD? Explain? Yes, with the penalty and reduced interest, the 3-year earned more.

9. Samuel wants to deposit $4,000 and keep that money in the bank without deposits or withdrawals for three years. He compares two different options. Option 1 will pay 3.8% interest, compounded quarterly. Option 2 will pay 3.5% interest, compounded continuously.
   a. How much interest does Option 1 pay? $480.60
   b. How much interest does Option 2 pay? $442.84

10. Write an algebraic expression for the interest earned on a $15,000 deposit for *t* months at 2.75% interest, compounded continuously.
$15{,}000e^{0.0275\left(\frac{t}{12}\right)}$

TEACH

Exercise 6
Have students compare the interest rates from the 1980s to today's rates. Point out that loan rates were also much higher in the 1980s than they are today.

Exercise 8
Committing money into a CD is something that needs to be undertaken with much thought about future financial expenses.

> *It is never too early to encourage long-term savings.*
> **Ron Lewis**, Politician

3-7 Future Value of Investments

Objectives

- Calculate the future value of a periodic deposit investment.
- Graph the future value function.
- Interpret the graph of the future value function.

Common Core

F-IF8b

Key Terms

- future value of a single deposit investment
- periodic investment
- biweekly
- future value of a periodic deposit investment

CCSS Warm-Up

Classify each exponential function as decreasing or increasing functions.

1. $f(x) = 5^x$ **2.** $f(x) = 0.5^x$ **3.** $f(x) = (1.5)^x$

1. increasing 2. decreasing 3. increasing

How can you effectively plan for the future balance in an account?

EXAMINE THE QUESTION

Many people deposit money in a savings account without much thought as to what the balance will be at some date in the future. Their only concern is that the balance grows over time. But some people want to know what needs to be deposited into an account now or at regular intervals so there is a certain amount of money after a fixed period of time.

CLASS DISCUSSION

In Lessons 3-7 and 3-8, students will learn about four different investment situations: future value of single deposit investments, future value of periodic deposit investments, present value of single deposit investments, and present value of periodic deposit investments. Students should know how to identify the correct situation.

Suppose you open an account that pays interest. You make no further contributions. You just leave your money alone and let compound interest work its magic. The balance your account grows to at some point in the future is called the **future value of a single deposit investment**. To calculate the future balance, use the compound interest formula $B = P\left(1 + \frac{r}{n}\right)^{nt}$, where B is the balance at the end of a time period in years t, P is the original principal, r is the interest rate expressed as a decimal, and n is the number of times the interest is compounded in one year.

Many people add money to their savings accounts on a regular basis. **Periodic investments** are the same deposits made at regular intervals, such as yearly, monthly, biweekly, weekly, or even daily. Suppose Enrique gets paid every other week and has \$200 directly deposited into his savings account. He wants to know how much he will have in the account after 5 years. In this case, Enrique makes an initial deposit of \$200 and continues to make deposits biweekly for five years. **Biweekly** means every two weeks and is a common schedule for paychecks. Because he will get 26 biweekly paychecks per year, he makes a total of 130 periodic direct deposits (26 × 5) each in the amount of \$200. Had the account offered no interest, he would have at least (130 × 200), or \$26,000 at the end of the five-year period. Banks offer compound interest, so Enrique needs a different formula to calculate his balance at the end of five years.

Future Value of a Periodic Deposit Investment

$$B = \frac{P\left(\left(1 + \frac{r}{n}\right)^{nt} - 1\right)}{\frac{r}{n}}$$

where
B = balance at end of investment period
P = periodic deposit amount
r = annual interest rate expressed as a decimal
n = number of times interest is compounded annually
t = length of investment in years

Skills and Strategies

Here you will learn how to calculate the balance in an account in which periodic investments have been made at a given compound interest rate.

EXAMPLE 1

Rich and Laura are both 45 years old. They open an account at the Rhinebeck Savings Bank with the hope that it will gain enough interest by their retirement at the age of 65. They deposit $5,000 each year into an account that pays 4.5% interest, compounded annually. What is the account balance when Rich and Laura retire?

SOLUTION You are looking to determine a balance at some point in the future, so this is a future value problem. Because $5,000 is deposited each year for 20 years, this is a periodic investment.

Use the formula for the future value of a periodic investment. $$B = \frac{P\left(\left(1 + \frac{r}{n}\right)^{nt} - 1\right)}{\frac{r}{n}}$$

Substitute. $$B = \frac{5{,}000\left(\left(1 + \frac{0.045}{1}\right)^{1(20)} - 1\right)}{\frac{0.045}{1}}$$

Calculate to the nearest cent. $B \approx 156{,}857.11$

The account balance will be $156,857.11 when Rich and Laura retire.

CHECK YOUR UNDERSTANDING

How much more would Rich and Laura have in their account if they decide to hold off retirement for an extra year?

EXTEND YOUR UNDERSTANDING

Carefully examine the solution to Example 1. During the computation of the numerator, is the 1 being subtracted from the 20? Explain your reasoning.

EXAMPLE 2

How much interest will Rich and Laura earn over the 20-year period?

SOLUTION The balance at the end of 20 years was $156,857.11. Rich and Laura deposited $5,000 into the account every year for 20 years.

Find the total amount deposited. $5{,}000 \times 20 = 100{,}000$

Subtract. $156{,}857.11 - 100{,}000 = 56{,}857.11$

Rich and Laura will earn $56,857.11 in interest.

TEACH

It is important that students have a working knowledge of the two formulas presented. Those formulas are algebraically manipulated in Lesson 3-8 in order to find a present rather than future balance. Ask students why someone might make a single deposit into an account and no further deposits (for example, a trust fund from the estate of a grandparent). Then, ask them to cite a situation where an account might be open and like amounts deposited at regular intervals (direct deposit accounts as employee deductions).

EXAMPLE 1

The formulas in Lessons 3-7 and 3-8 require the use of a calculator. Therefore, students need to know the correct keystroke sequences and where parentheses are necessary for calculator input.

CHECK YOUR UNDERSTANDING

Answer $12,058.57

Determine the amount that will be in the account after 21 years ($168,915.68) and subtract that from the answer to Example 1.

EXTEND YOUR UNDERSTANDING

Answer No

Using the order of operations, $(1 + 0.045)^{20}$ will be computed first. 1 is subtracted from that value, not from the exponent of 20.

EXAMPLE 2

Students must take into consideration what Rich and Laura deposited over the 20-year period. Subtracting that amount from the 20-year balance yields the interest made.

CHECK YOUR UNDERSTANDING

Answer Rich and Laura will earn $7,058.57 more by retiring one year later.

EXAMPLE 3

The formula remains the same but the value of n used twice in the formula is now 12 (to represent 12 monthly deposits/compounds per year).

CHECK YOUR UNDERSTANDING

Answer Not necessarily. It depends on the principal, rate, and length of time opened.

CHECK YOUR UNDERSTANDING

Answer

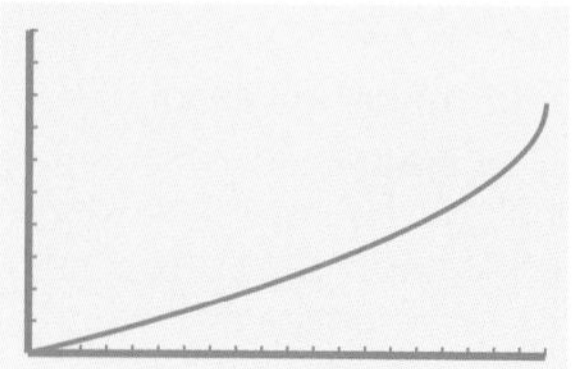

■ CHECK YOUR UNDERSTANDING

Use Example 1 Check Your Understanding. How much more interest would Rich and Laura earn by retiring after 21 years?

EXAMPLE 3

Linda and Rob open an online savings account that has a 3.6% annual interest rate, compounded monthly. If they deposit $1,200 every month, how much will be in the account after 10 years?

SOLUTION

Use the formula for the future value of a periodic investment.

$$B = \frac{P\left(\left(1 + \frac{r}{n}\right)^{nt} - 1\right)}{\frac{r}{n}}$$

Substitute.

$$B = \frac{1{,}200\left(\left(1 + \frac{0.036}{12}\right)^{12(10)} - 1\right)}{\frac{0.036}{12}}$$

Calculate to the nearest cent.

$$B \approx 173{,}022.87$$

Linda and Rob will have $173,022.87 in the account after 10 years.

■ CHECK YOUR UNDERSTANDING

Would opening an account at a higher interest rate for fewer years have assured Linda and Rob at least the same final balance?

EXAMPLE 4

Construct a graph of the future value function that represents Linda and Rob's account for each month. Use the graph to approximate the balance after 5 years.

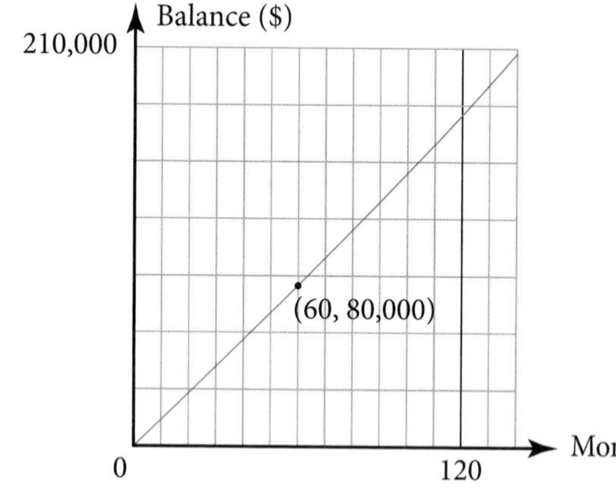

SOLUTION Let x represent each of the monthly interest periods. The minimum value of x is 0 and corresponds with the opening of the account. The maximum value of x is 120, because Linda and Rob make deposits for 120 months (10 years × 12 months). Use a graphing calculator to graph the future value function.

$$B = \frac{1{,}200\left(\left(1 + \frac{0.036}{12}\right)^{x} - 1\right)}{\frac{0.036}{12}}$$

In 5 years, the balance will be approximately $80,000.

■ CHECK YOUR UNDERSTANDING

Construct a graph for Rich and Laura's situation in Example 1.

Applications

It is never too early to encourage long-term savings.
Ron Lewis, Politician

1. How might those words apply to what has been outlined in this lesson? See margin.

2. Suppose that $1,000 is deposited into an account that yields 5% interest, compounded annually. How much money will be in that account at the end of 4 years? $1,215.51

3. Arianna deposits $500 in an account that pays 3% interest, compounded semiannually. How much is in the account at the end of two years? $530.68

4. When Derrick turned 15, his grandparents put $10,000 into an account that yielded 4% interest, compounded quarterly. When Derrick turns 18, his grandparents will give him the money to use toward his college education. How much does Derrick receive from his grandparents on his 18th birthday? $11,268.25

5. Barbara wants to restore her '66 Mustang in 4 years. She puts $200 into an account every month that pays 4.5% interest, compounded monthly. How much is in the account after 4 years? $10,496.77

6. Robbie opens an account at a local bank by depositing $100. The account pays 2.4% interest, compounded weekly. He deposits $100 every week for three years.
   a. How much is in the account after three years? $16,171.46
   b. Write the future value function if x represents the number of weeks. See margin.
   c. Use a graphing calculator to graph the future value function. See margin.
   d. Using the graph, what is the approximate balance after 2 years? $11,000

7. Suppose $600 is deposited into an account every quarter. The account earns 5% interest, compounded quarterly.
   a. What is the future value of the account after 5 years? $13,537.79
   b. Write the future value function if x represents the number of quarters. See margin.
   c. Use a graphing calculator to graph the future value function. See margin.
   d. Using the graph, what is the approximate balance after 3 years? $7,500

8. When Abram was born, his parents put $2,000 into an account that yielded 3.5% interest, compounded semiannually. When he turns 16, his parents will give him the money to buy a car. How much will Abram receive on his 16th birthday? $3,484.43

TEACH

Exercise 4
Alert students that the elapsed time of this account is not a number given in the problem statement but rather needs to be determined by using the time that elapsed from when Derrick turned 15 to his 18th birthday.

ANSWERS

1. Answers will vary but should include some mention of the fact that the longer an amount is in a savings account the more it will accrue in interest. Therefore, the earlier the start of the account, the better.

6b. $B = \dfrac{100\left(\left(1 + \frac{0.024}{52}\right)^x - 1\right)}{\frac{0.024}{52}}$

6c.

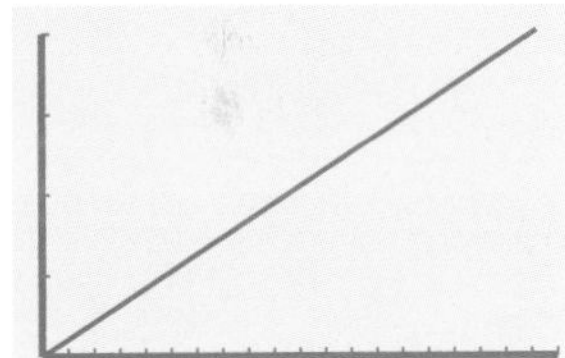

7b. $B = \dfrac{600\left(\left(1 + \frac{0.05}{4}\right)^x - 1\right)}{\frac{0.05}{4}}$

7c.

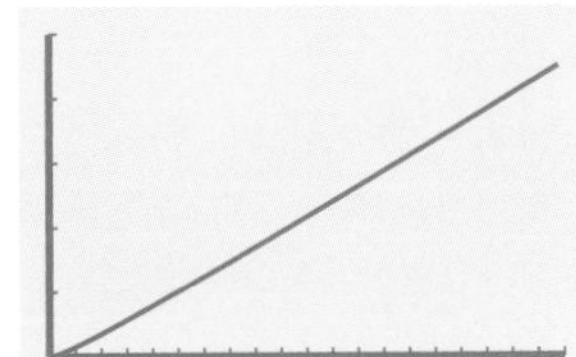

TEACH

Exercise 9

Ask students to predict who will have the most money in the account after 20 years and why. Then, after completing all the parts of the problem, ask if their predictions were backed by the math and the graph.

Exercise 11

This is an excellent guided discovery exercise. Here, students discover Einstein's Rule of 72. This problem is suitable as a stand-alone homework assignment or an in-class activity.

ANSWERS

9g. $B = \dfrac{100\left(\left(1+\dfrac{0.05}{12}\right)^x - 1\right)}{\dfrac{0.05}{12}}$

9h. $B = \dfrac{80\left(\left(1+\dfrac{0.08}{12}\right)^x - 1\right)}{\dfrac{0.08}{12}}$

9j. Sydney's balance starts out higher than Benny's but by about the 160th month (a little over 13 years), Benny's amount begins to overtake Sydney's.

9. Sydney invests $100 every month into an account that pays 5% annual interest, compounded monthly. Benny invests $80 every month into an account that pays 8% annual interest rate, compounded monthly.

a. Determine the amount in Sydney's account after 10 years. $15,528.23

b. Determine the amount in Benny's account after 10 years. $14,635.68

c. Who had more money in the account after 10 years? Sydney

d. Determine the amount in Sydney's account after 20 years. $41,103.37

e. Determine the amount in Benny's account after 20 years. $47,121.63

f. Who had more money in the account after 20 years? Benny

g. Write the future value function for Sydney's account where x represents the number of months. See margin.

h. Write the future value function for Benny's account where x represents the number of months. See margin.

i. Graph Benny and Sydney's future value function on the same axes. See additional answers.

j. Explain what the graph indicates. See margin.

10. You are constructing a future value spreadsheet. Users will be asked to enter the periodic investment in cell A3, the interest rate as an equivalent decimal in cell A4, the time in years in cell A5, and the number of times per year the interest is compounded in cell A6. Cell A8 will contain the future value of the periodic investment. Write the formula that will display this value in A8.
=(A3*((1+A4/A6)^(A6*A5)−1))/(A4/A6)

11. Albert Einstein said that compound interest was ". . .the most powerful thing I have ever witnessed." Work through the following exercises to discover a pattern Einstein discovered which is now known as the Rule of 72.

a. Suppose that you invest $2,000 at a 1% annual interest rate. Use your calculator to input different values for t in the compound interest formula. What whole number value of t will yield an amount closest to twice the initial deposit? 70 years

b. Suppose that you invest $4,000 at a 2% annual interest rate. Use your calculator to input different values for t in the compound interest formula. What whole number value of t will yield an amount closest to twice the initial deposit? 35 years

c. Suppose that you invest $20,000 at a 6% annual interest rate. Use your calculator to input different values for t in the compound interest formula. What whole number value of t will yield an amount closest to twice the initial deposit? 12 years

d. Albert Einstein noticed a very interesting pattern when an initial deposit doubles. In each of the three examples above, multiply the value of t that you determined times the percentage amount. For example, in a. multiply t by 1. What do you notice? You get a number close to 72.

e. Einstein called this the Rule of 72 because for any initial deposit and for any interest percentage, 72 ÷ (percentage) will give you the approximate number of years it will take for the initial deposit to double in value. Einstein also said that "If people really understood the Rule of 72 they would never put their money in banks." Suppose that a 10-year-old has $500 to invest. She puts it in her savings account that has a 1.75% annual interest rate. How old will she be when the money doubles? 51 years old

Before you can really start setting financial goals, you need to determine where you stand financially.

David Bach, Financial Consultant

Present Value of Investments 3-8

Key Terms
- present value
- present value of a single deposit investment
- present value of a periodic deposit investment

Objectives
- Calculate the present value of a single deposit investment.
- Calculate the present value of a periodic deposit investment.

Common Core

F-IF4, A-SSE3, A-CED4, F-IF8b

CCSS Warm-Up

Identify whether each graph intersects the x-axis only, the y-axis only, or both axes.

1. $y = 3^x$ **2.** $y = x^2 + 5x + 6$ **3.** $y = 3$

1. y-axis only 2. both axes 3. y-axis only

How can you determine what you need to invest now to reach a financial goal?

EXAMINE THE QUESTION

Many people make financial plans that include a fixed expenditure in the future. Perhaps they want to save for college, buy a home, or go on a vacation. This entails planning now by making decisions about money that should be deposited on a one-time or periodic basis. Ask students what large "purchases" they might foresee in their futures.

Everyone has future plans. Those plans may be more defined for some people than others. Look ahead to the future. What might you need to save for? An education? A car? A house? A family? While you don't know what the expense for these items will be in the future, you can probably be assured that they will cost more than they do now. Perhaps a college tuition that now costs $25,000 per year might be $30,000 per year five years from now.

You need to start now to plan for large expenses in the future. Planning for a large expense in the future requires financial planning for that expense in the present. It helps to know how much you need to save now or on a regular basis in order to meet your future financial goal.

Present value is the current value of a deposit that is made in the present time. You can determine the **present value of a single deposit investment**, meaning you can calculate how much a one-time deposit should earn at a specific interest rate in order to have a certain amount of money saved for a future savings goal.

You can also determine how much to save on a regular basis at a specific interest rate to meet that future goal by finding the **present value of a periodic deposit investment**. In both cases, you determine what you need to save now in order to have enough money in your account later on to meet a given expense.

CLASS DISCUSSION

Up to this point, students have been solving for a future balance. In this lesson, they have an amount in mind they will need at some point in the future and are asked to determine how much should be deposited once in the present time, or multiple times on a periodic basis. It is important that they understand the difference between what is asked in this lesson and what was asked in the previous lesson.

TEACH

You might want to set up the following diagram to assist students:

	Single	Periodic
Present		
Future		

Within each of the empty cells, enter the appropriate formulas. They have already studied future values, so those formulas can be entered now as a review of the last lesson. In this lesson, they will learn about the two formulas that are used for present value exercises. Those formulas can be entered during the review of Example 1 and Example 3. As students read a problem, they need to find the row and column that match the problem statement. This will get them into the habit of defining the situation in terms of the type of deposit and what balance is being determined.

EXAMPLE 1

This is a present value of a single deposit investment problem. Have students enter the formula into the chart that was created (see TEACH). Make sure they understand why the formula is entered in the designated location.

CHECK YOUR UNDERSTANDING

Answer Using the same formula, it would take approximately 14 years.

Skills and Strategies

Using algebra, the present value formulas are derived from the future value formulas that you studied in the previous lessons.

EXAMPLE 1

Mr. and Mrs. Johnson know that in 6 years, their daughter Ann will attend State College. She will need about $20,000 for the first year's tuition. How much should the Johnsons deposit into an account that yields 5% interest, compounded annually, in order to have that amount? Round your answer to the nearest thousand dollars.

SOLUTION Use the formula for the future value of a single deposit investment, where B = ending balance, P = principal or original balance, r = interest rate expressed as a decimal, n = number of times interest is compounded annually, and t = number of years.

Solve the formula for P.

$$B = P\left(1 + \frac{r}{n}\right)^{nt}$$

Divide each side by $\left(1 + \frac{r}{n}\right)^{nt}$.

$$\frac{B}{\left(1 + \frac{r}{n}\right)^{nt}} = \frac{P\left(1 + \frac{r}{n}\right)^{nt}}{\left(1 + \frac{r}{n}\right)^{nt}}$$

Simplify.

$$\frac{B}{\left(1 + \frac{r}{n}\right)^{nt}} = P$$

Rewrite the previous equation so that you have a new formula.

Present Value of a Single Deposit Investment

$$P = \frac{B}{\left(1 + \frac{r}{n}\right)^{nt}}$$

where B = ending balance
P = principal or original balance (present value)
r = interest rate expressed as a decimal
n = number of times interest is compounded annually
t = number of years

Substitute 20,000 for B, 0.05 for r, 1 for n, and 6 for t.

$$P = \frac{20{,}000}{\left(1 + \frac{0.05}{1}\right)^{1(6)}}$$

Simplify.

$$P = \frac{20{,}000}{(1 + 0.05)^6}$$

Calculate.

$$P \approx 14{,}924.31$$

The Johnsons should deposit approximately $15,000 into the account.

■ CHECK YOUR UNDERSTANDING

How many years would it take for $10,000 to grow to $20,000 in the same account?

EXAMPLE 2

Ritika just graduated from college. She wants \$100,000 in her savings account after 10 years. How much must she deposit in that account now at a 3.8% interest rate, compounded daily, in order to meet that goal? Round up to the nearest dollar.

SOLUTION Use the formula for the present value of a single deposit investment. Let $B = 100$, $r = 0.038$, $t = 10$, and $n = 365$.

$$P = \frac{B}{\left(1 + \frac{r}{n}\right)^{nt}}$$

Substitute. $$P = \frac{100{,}000}{\left(1 + \frac{0.038}{365}\right)^{365(10)}}$$

Calculate. $$P = 68{,}387.49$$

Ritika must deposit approximately \$68,388.

CHECK YOUR UNDERSTANDING

How does the equation from Example 2 change if the interest is compounded weekly?

EXAMPLE 3

Nick wants to install central air conditioning in his home in 3 years. He estimates the total cost to be \$15,000. How much must he deposit monthly into an account that pays 4% interest, compounded monthly, in order to have enough money? Round up to the nearest hundred dollars.

SOLUTION Use the formula for the future value of a periodic deposit investment, where B = ending balance, P = periodic deposit amount, r = interest rate expressed as a decimal, n = number of times interest compounded annually, and t = number of years.

Solve the formula for P. $$B = \frac{P\left(\left(1 + \frac{r}{n}\right)^{nt} - 1\right)}{\frac{r}{n}}$$

Multiply each side by $\frac{r}{n}$. $$B \times \frac{r}{n} = \frac{P\left(\left(1 + \frac{r}{n}\right)^{nt} - 1\right)}{\frac{r}{n}} \times \frac{r}{n}$$

Simplify. $$B \times \frac{r}{n} = P\left(\left(1 + \frac{r}{n}\right)^{nt} - 1\right)$$

Divide each side by $\left(1 + \frac{r}{n}\right)^{nt} - 1$. $$\frac{B \times \frac{r}{n}}{\left(1 + \frac{r}{n}\right)^{nt} - 1} = \frac{P\left(\left(1 + \frac{r}{n}\right)^{nt} - 1\right)}{\left(1 + \frac{r}{n}\right)^{nt} - 1}$$

Simplify. $$\frac{B \times \frac{r}{n}}{\left(1 + \frac{r}{n}\right)^{nt} - 1} = P$$

EXAMPLE 2

Example 2 represents a present value of a single deposit investment problem in which $n = 365$.

CHECK YOUR UNDERSTANDING

Answer Everything remains the same except $n = 52$.

EXAMPLE 3

This is a present value of a periodic investment problem since Nick will be making a deposit monthly. Have students enter the formula in the chart that was created (see TEACH). Make sure they understand why this formula is entered in the designated location.

CHECK YOUR UNDERSTANDING

Answer $P = \dfrac{x\left(\frac{r}{2}\right)}{\left(1 + \frac{r}{2}\right)^{2y} - 1}$

EXAMPLE 4

You may need to assist students in identifying the independent variable. Because the number of months is given in the example, the independent variable, x, replaces nt in the formula.

CHECK YOUR UNDERSTANDING

Answer Using the graph found in Example 3, the approximate values are: \$16,000; \$1,300; and \$500.

Rewrite the previous equation so that you have a new formula.

Present Value of a Periodic Deposit Investment

$$P = \frac{B \times \frac{r}{n}}{\left(1 + \frac{r}{n}\right)^{nt} - 1}$$

where B = ending balance
P = principal or original balance
r = interest rate expressed as a decimal
n = number of times interest is compounded annually
t = number of years

Substitute. $P = \dfrac{15{,}000 \times \frac{0.04}{12}}{\left(1 + \frac{0.04}{12}\right)^{12(3)} - 1}$

Calculate. $P \approx 392.86$

Nick must deposit about \$400 every month.

> **CHECK YOUR UNDERSTANDING**
>
> Write the formula to find the present value of an x-dollar balance that is reached by periodic investments made semiannually for y years at an interest rate of r.

EXAMPLE 4

Randy wants to have saved a total of \$200,000 by some point in the future. He is willing to set up a direct deposit account with a 4.5% APR, compounded monthly, but is unsure of how much to periodically deposit for varying lengths of time. Graph a present value function to show the present values for Randy's situation from 12 months to 240 months.

SOLUTION Let x represent the number of months. Begin with a one year investment. The minimum value of x is 12. The maximum value is 240.

Use the present value of a periodic investment formula. $P = \dfrac{B \times \frac{r}{n}}{\left(1 + \frac{r}{n}\right)^{nt} - 1}$

Substitute 200,000 for B, 0.045 for r, 12 for n, and x for nt. $P = \dfrac{200{,}000 \times \frac{0.045}{12}}{\left(1 + \frac{0.045}{12}\right)^{x} - 1}$

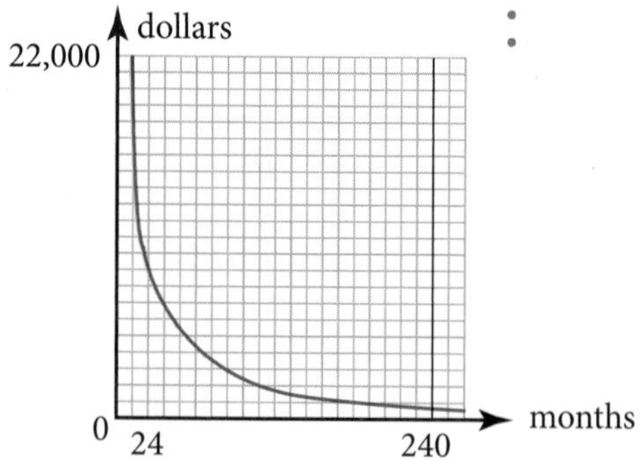

Graph the function.

The present value decreases as the number of months increases.

> **CHECK YOUR UNDERSTANDING**
>
> Use the graph to estimate how much to deposit each month for 1 year, 10 years, and 20 years.

Applications

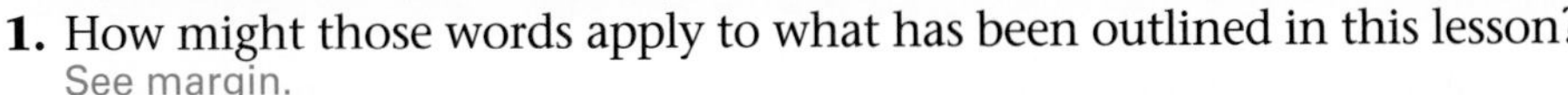

Before you can really start setting financial goals, you need to determine where you stand financially.

David Bach, Financial Consultant

1. How might those words apply to what has been outlined in this lesson? See margin.
2. Complete the table to find the single deposit investment amounts.

Future Value	Interest Rate	Interest Periods	Deposit
$1,000	4%, compounded annually	3 years	a.
$2,500	3%, compounded semiannually	5 years	b.
$10,000	5%, compounded quarterly	10 years	c.
$50,000	2.75%, compounded monthly	8 years	d.

See margin.

3. Complete the table to find the periodic deposit investment amounts.

Future Value	Interest Rate	Interest Periods	Deposit
$50,000	2%, compounded annually	8 years	a.
$25,000	1.5%, compounded semiannually	4 years	b.
$100,000	3.75%, compounded quarterly	10 years	c.
$1,000,000	4%, compounded monthly	20 years	d.

See margin.

4. Bob wants $50,000 at the end of 7 years in order to buy a car. If his bank pays 4.2% interest, compounded annually, how much must he deposit each year in order to reach his goal? $6,292.16
5. Grandpa Joe wants to open an account for his grandchildren that he hopes will have $80,000 in it after 20 years. How much must he deposit now into an account that yields 2.75% interest, compounded monthly, so he can be assured of reaching his goal? $46,185.04
6. Mary wants to go on a $10,000 vacation in 6 months. She has a bank account that pays 4.25% interest, compounded monthly. How much must she deposit each month to afford the vacation? $1,651.97
7. Janine is 21 years old. She opens an account that pays 4.4% interest, compounded monthly. She sets a goal of saving $10,000 by the time she is 24 years old. How much must she deposit each month? $260.36
8. Suni needs to repay her school loan in 4 years. How much must she semiannually deposit into an account that pays 3.9% interest, compounded semiannually, to have $100,000 to repay the loan? $11,671.58
9. Rich needs $50,000 for a down payment on a home in 5 years. How much must he deposit into an account that pays 6% interest, compounded quarterly, in order to meet his goal? $37,123.52
10. Marcy wants to have $75,000 saved sometime in the future. How much must she deposit into an account that pays 3.1% interest, compounded monthly? Use a graphing calculator to graph the present value function. See margin.

TEACH

Exercises 2–10
In each of these exercises a financial goal has been set. Students need to look for verbal clues that alert them to whether or not the problem is a single deposit or a periodic deposit.

Exercise 10
This exercise does not give students a fixed time by which the balance must be $75,000. Therefore finding a good viewing window might take a few trials. Encourage students to select maximum x-values systematically, increasing the max until the graph can be seen crossing $y = 75{,}000$.

ANSWERS

1. Answers will vary but should include the fact that to look ahead to a future value savings, it is necessary to carefully examine what you can afford to save in the present.
2. a. $889.00
   b. $2,154.17
   c. $6,084.13
   d. $40,136.04
3. a. $5,825.49/year
   b. $3,043.89/6 months
   c. $2,072.04/quarter
   d. $2,726.47/month

10.

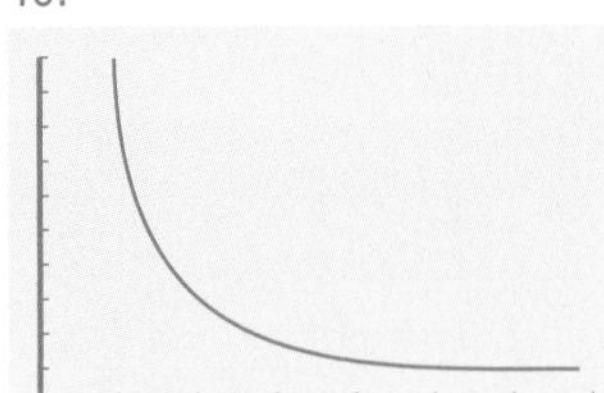

CHAPTER 3

Assessment

Real Numbers

You Write the Story!!

CHAPTER 3 ASSESSMENT

REAL NUMBERS

You Write the Story
Have the students list the points as ordered pairs. Then show them how to enter them and draw a time plot on their graphing calculators.

Have them go online and find out the interest rates for the years past 2008 to update the graph.

REALITY CHECK

Reality Check projects are a terrific form of alternative assessment. They give students an additional avenue to show what they've learned, so their grades are not solely based on tests.

Examine the line graph below. It depicts the average online savings account interest rates at the beginning of January for 8 years. Write a short newspaper-type article centered on the graph. Use the Internet if you need additional information and background to help you explain the graph. An electronic copy of the graph is at www.cengage.com/school/math/financialalgebra. Copy and paste it into the article.

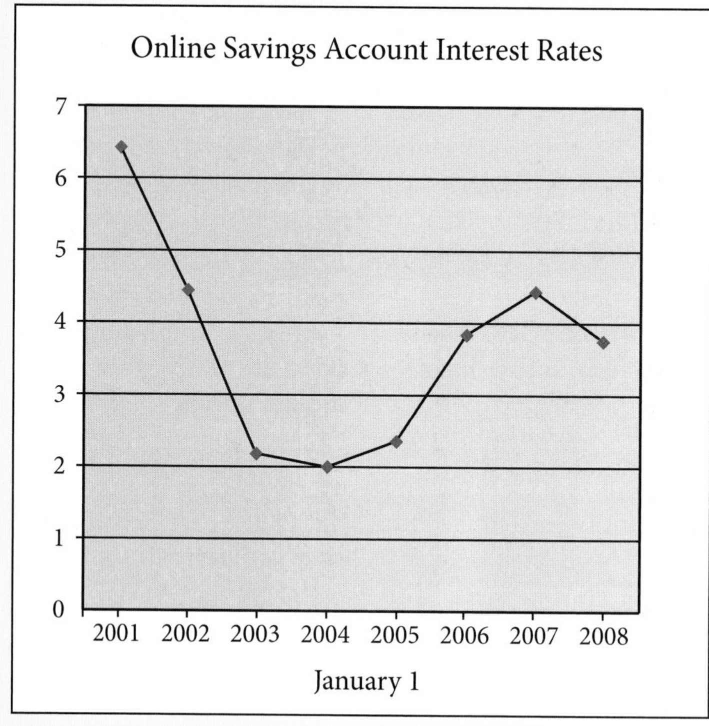

Reality Check

1. Go to the FDIC website. Find information on how a person can be insured at one bank for more than $250,000. Use the e-mail or phone contacts to ask questions. Speak to a representative at a bank to ask further questions. Create five different hypothetical families, the accounts they have, and how much of each account is insured. Prepare examples on a poster to present to the class.

2. Interview a bank representative about trust accounts. Find out what the abbreviations POD, ATF, and ITF mean. Prepare questions about FDIC insurance limits and beneficiaries. Ask for any brochures they offer about trust accounts. Prepare a report or a poster on trust accounts to present to the class.

3. Go to a bank or bank website to find three different types of checking accounts. Compare and contrast the accounts offered by the same bank. What are the benefits of each? What are the drawbacks of each? Who might be better served by each type of checking account? Explain which account might be best for your financial situation.

4. While the law states that free checking accounts cannot have minimum balances or per check fees, there are other fees and penalties that are allowable. Research the allowable fees and penalties on checking accounts. Make a list and explain the purpose and cost of each.

5. Visit two local banks. Speak to a bank representative at each bank. Prepare a list of services to compare. What are the CD rates at each bank? What are the penalties for withdrawing money from a CD before it is due? What are the minimum balances for different types of accounts? What are the fees for insufficient funds? What are the different types of checking accounts they offer? What are the fees and requirements for these accounts? What are the hours of service? Think of other questions to ask. Prepare the findings in a report.

6. Interest rates have historically fluctuated with the economy. Go online and/or use the library to find interest rates over the past 50 years. Make a graph to display the information.

7. Each year, there are contests in schools all over the nation to see how many decimal places of the number π students can memorize. The records are amazing! Go online and find out the decimal representation of e to as many decimal places as possible. Talk to the teacher about having a memorization contest in class. Research how experts memorize long sequences of digits. Visit a few local businesses to see if they would be willing to donate a prize for the contest. Ask the school newspaper to cover the contest. Emcee the contest in class.

8. Some employers allow employees to have money deducted from their accounts and automatically placed into a savings account. Interview three adults working in different professions. Ask them about employer-sponsored savings plans. Prepare a report on the findings.

9. Visit a local bank. Get brochures they offer about their services. If the brochures are two-sided, take two of each so you can cut them out and paste them onto a poster board. Pick several services to highlight. Cut out the portions of the brochures that explain each service. Give each service an original, short title, and print out your title. Organize the titles and descriptions of the banking services onto a poster board.

10. The Rule of 72 is a method for quickly estimating how many years it will take principal to double, assuming the interest was compounded. Go to the library and/or use the Internet to research the Rule of 72 beyond what was presented in Lesson 3-7. Prepare some examples to illustrate the rule. Discuss the history and the use of the rule. Display your research on a poster board.

Projects can be presented to the class on any schedule that works for your program. It may be too time-consuming for every student to present their project for every chapter.

Remind students who are personally visiting local businesses or community members that they are representing the school, and need to be cordial and patient. These projects deliberately have students taking little field trips, so they don't conduct everything online.

Point out that they need to thank any person who helps them in completing their Reality Check projects. A letter is the most personal way to do this.

You can offer students extra projects for extra credit.

Dollars and Sense — Your Financial News Update

Go to www.cengage.com/school/math/financialalgebra where you will find a link to a website containing current issues about banking. Try one of the activities.

Really? Really! REVISITED

REALLY? REALLY! REVISITED

The Publications Department of the Federal Reserve Bank offers materials on counterfeiting that can be accessed on-line. You can have students request some of the materials.

The Secret Service drastically reduced the occurrences of counterfeit money since the Civil War. Nevertheless, the problem still exists. Look at the following table.

U.S. Counterfeiting 1999–2005

Year	Dollar value of currency that was found after being in circulation, in millions	Dollar value of currency that was found before getting into circulation, in millions
1999	39.2	13.7
2000	39.7	20.9
2001	47.5	12.6
2002	42.9	9.7
2003	36.6	10.7
2004	43.6	10.3
2005	56.2	12.7

Source: U.S. Secret Service; Board of Governors of the Federal Reserve System; U.S. Department of the Treasury

1. Create a line graph for each column of data. Let the horizontal axis represent the year, and let the vertical axis represent dollars. Put both graphs on the same set of axes, in different colors. See additional answers.
2. Look at the graphs you created in Exercise 1. Do you think the pattern of catching counterfeit bills before and after circulation follows the same pattern of increases and decreases? The patterns are not identical. Changes in one category are not the same in direction or magnitude.

Applications

1. Go to www.cengage.com/school/math/financialalgebra and download a blank check register. Complete all of the necessary information in the check register. See additional answers.
   a. The balance on December 10 is $3,900.50.
   b. On December 11 check #1223 is written for $84 to North Shore High School Drama Club.
   c. On December 12 a paycheck in the amount of $240.80 is deposited.
   d. On December 13 a birthday check for $100 is received from grandparents. The check is deposited that afternoon.
   e. On December 17 three checks are written while holiday shopping. One is to Best Buy in the amount of $480.21, one is to Target in the amount of $140.58, and one is to Aeropostale in the amount of $215.60.
   f. Staples sells computers. On December 20 a laptop is purchased for $1,250. A mistake is made on the first check, and the check must be voided. A correct check for the right amount is then written with the next available check.
   g. On December 22 a gift is returned to Barnes and Noble. The $120 amount is deposited into the checking account.
   h. On December 24, $300 is withdrawn from an ATM for food at a holiday party. The company that owns the ATM charges $1.50 fee for the transaction, and the customer's bank charges a $2.50 fee for the transaction. The fees are taken directly out of the checking account.
   i. On December 28 a check for $521 is written to Len's Auto Body Shop to repair a dent in the fender of a car.
   j. On December 29 a check is written to AMTRAK for $150.80 to visit a cousin in Washington, D.C. for New Year's Eve.

2. Use the check register from Exercise 1. It is now one month later, and the checking account statement has arrived. Does the account balance? See margin.

Checking Account Statement				
Date	**Description**	**Check #**	**Amount**	**Balance**
12/12	Deposit		$240.80	$4,141.30
12/13	Deposit		$100.00	$4,241.30
12/19	W/D	1223	$ 84.00	$4,157.30
12/19	W/D	1226	$215.60	$3,941.70
12/20	W/D	1225	$140.58	$3,801.12
12/21	W/D	1224	$480.21	$2,320.91
12/24	ATM Withdrawal		$300.00	$3,020.91
12/24	ATM Fee		$ 1.50	$3,019.41
12/24	ATM Fee		$ 2.50	$3,016.91
01/15	W/D	1229	$521.00	$2,495.91
		Ending Balance: $2,495.91		

Ending balance from statement **a.** ______
Deposits outstanding **b.** ______
Checks outstanding **c.** ______
Revised statement balance **d.** ______
Balance from checkbook **e.** ______

ANSWERS

2a. $2,495.91
b. $120
c. $1,400.80
d. $1,215.11
e. $1,215.11

ANSWERS

7b. All of Matt's money is insured. The FDIC insures up to $250,000 at one bank, if the accounts are the same type.

9. a. $0
b. $5,200.00
c. $5,200.00
d. $0.57
e. $5,200.57
f. $5,200.57
g. $700.00
h. $5,900.57
i. $0.65
j. $5,901.22
k. $5,901.22
l. $500.00
m. $5,401.22
n. $0.59
p. $5,401.81

3. Find the simple interest on a $2,219 principal, deposited for six years at a rate of 5.11%. $680.35

4. Ruth has a savings account at a bank that charges a $3.50 fee for every month her balance falls below $1,500. Her account has $1,722 and then she withdraws $400. What is her balance in five months if her account balance never reaches $1,500? $1,304.50

5. Nine months ago Alexa deposited $7,000 in a three-year CD. She has received $224.16 in interest. She withdraws $1,000. This is before the CD matures, so she pays a $250 penalty. What is her balance after the withdrawal? $5,974.16

6. Ralph deposited $910 in an account that pays 5.2% simple interest, for $3\frac{1}{2}$ years.

a. How much interest did the account earn? $165.62
b. What is the ending balance? $1,075.62
c. How much interest did the account earn the first year? $47.32
d. How much interest did the account earn the third year? $47.32

7. Matt has two single accounts at Midtown Bank. One account has a balance of $74,112.09 and the other has a balance of $77,239.01.

a. What is the sum of Matt's balances? $151,351.10
b. Is all of Matt's money insured by the FDIC? Explain. See margin.

8. Rhonda deposits $5,600 in a savings account that pays $4\frac{1}{2}$% interest, compounded semiannually.

a. How much interest does the account earn in the first six months? $126
b. What is the ending balance after six months? $5,726
c. How much interest does the account earn in the second six months? $128.84
d. What is the balance after one year? $5,854.84
e. How much interest does the account earn the first year? $254.84

9. Rebecca opened a savings account on March 20, with a $5,200 deposit. The account pays 3.99% interest, compounded daily. On March 21 she made a $700 deposit, and on March 22 she made a $500 withdrawal. Use this information to find the missing amounts. See margin.

Date	March 20	March 21	March 22
Opening balance	a.	f.	k.
Deposit	b.	g.	-----
Withdrawal	-----	-----	l.
Principal used to compute interest	c.	h.	m.
Interest	d.	i.	n.
Ending balance	e.	j.	p.

10. Nick deposited $3,000 in a three-year CD account that pays 4.08% interest, compounded weekly. What is the ending balance? $3,390.46

11. How much more would $10,000 earn in three years compounded daily at 4.33%, than compounded semiannually at 4.33%? $15.69

ANSWERS

19.

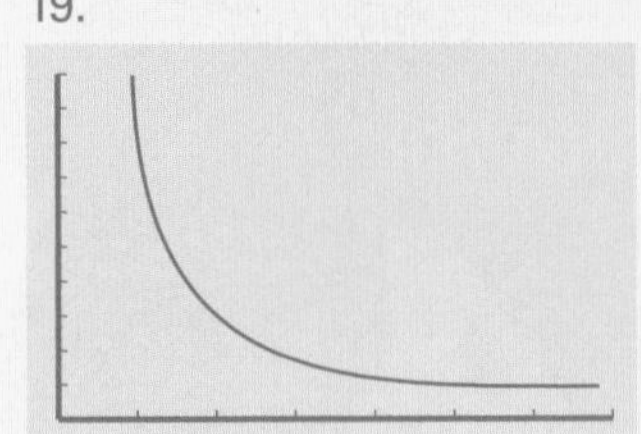

12. Austin deposits \$2,250 into a one-year CD at an interest rate of 5.3%, compounded daily.

a. What is the ending balance after the year? \$2,372.46

b. How much interest did the account earn during the year? \$122.46

c. What is the annual percentage yield? Round to the nearest hundredth of a percent. 5.44%

13. Find the interest earned on a \$25,000 deposit for $2\frac{1}{2}$ years at 4.7% interest, compounded continuously. \$3,117.04

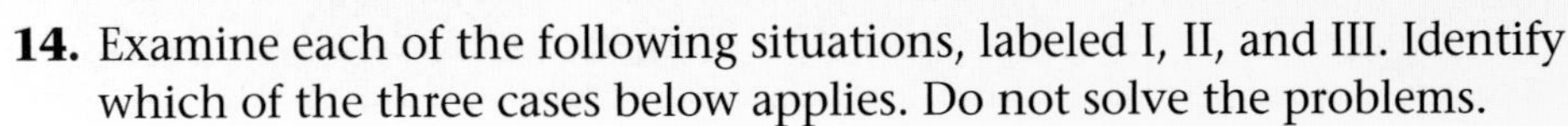

14. Examine each of the following situations, labeled I, II, and III. Identify which of the three cases below applies. Do not solve the problems.

I. future value of a single deposit investment
II. future value of a periodic deposit investment
III. present value of a periodic deposit investment

a. You want to save for a new car that you will buy when you graduate college in 4 years. How much will you be able to afford if you deposit \$1,000 per quarter in an account that compounds interest at a rate of 4.1% quarterly? future value of a periodic investment

b. You deposit \$3,000 into an account that yields 3.22% interest compounded semiannually. How much will you have in the account in 5 years? future value of a single deposit investment

c. You want to put a \$40,000 down payment on a store front for a new business that you plan on opening in 5 years. How much should you deposit monthly into an account with an APR of 3.75%, compounded monthly? present value of a periodic investment

15. Santos deposited \$1,800 in an account that yields 2.7% interest, compounded semiannually. How much is in the account after 54 months? \$2,030.89

16. Stephanie signed up for a direct deposit transfer into her savings account from her checking account. Every month \$150 is withdrawn from her checking account. The interest in this account is at 2.6% compounded monthly. How much will be in the account at the end of $6\frac{1}{2}$ years? \$12,731.79

17. Jazmine needs \$30,000 to pay off a loan at the end of 5 years. How much must she deposit monthly into a savings account that yields 3% interest, compounded monthly? \$464.06

18. Use a table of increasing values of x to find each of the following limits. If no limit exists, say the limit is undefined.

a. $\lim_{x\to\infty} f(x)$ if $f(x) = \dfrac{9x - 1}{3x - 5}$ 3

b. $\lim_{x\to\infty} g(x)$ if $g(x) = \dfrac{3x^2 + 9x}{4x + 1}$ undefined

c. $\lim_{x\to\infty} h(x)$ if $h(x) = \dfrac{7x}{x^2 - 41}$ 0

19. Tom wants to have \$50,000 saved sometime in the future. How much must he deposit every month into an account that pays 2.8% interest, compounded monthly. Use a graphing calculator to graph the present value function. See margin.

CHAPTER

4 Consumer Credit

Live within your income, even if you have to borrow money to do so.

Josh Billings, American Humorist

What do you think humorist Josh Billings meant in his quote?

Credit is a promise to pay in the future for goods and services you purchase today. When you think of consumer credit, you might think of loans and credit cards. Most people use credit. Using credit has advantages and disadvantages. Credit lets you enjoy purchases while you are paying for them. However, if you use credit irresponsibly, you may find yourself with debt that you cannot afford to pay. Being in debt is not a problem as long as you can make punctual payments to eliminate the debt. Imagine your life without credit. If you had to save several years to buy a car, what would you use for transportation during the years you were saving? If you had to save for many years to purchase a home, where would you live while you were saving? Credit provides you with a way to increase your standard of living, as long as your purchases are made with careful financial planning.

What do you think?

Traditionally, living within your income means that if you need to borrow money to buy something, you can't afford it. Living within your income does not mean not ever borrowing money. It means you should borrow what you can afford to repay. People who borrow are not automatically living beyond their means.

TEACHING RESOURCES

Instructor's Resource CD

Exam*View*® CD, Ch. 4

eHomework, Ch. 4

www.cengage.com/school/math/financialalgebra

Really?

The use of credit cards is incredibly prevalent in today's society. Those little plastic cards are everywhere!

- There are almost a billion MasterCard and Visa credit and debit cards in use in the United States.
- In 2006, Visa cardholders made more than $1,000,000,000,000 in purchases!
- Today's consumer owes money, on average, to 13 different lending institutions, including credit cards and loans!
- There are over 1 billion Visa cards used internationally!
- More than half of the United States population has at least two credit cards!

Clearly the small plastic card plays a major role in how you will conduct your financial life. A discussion about the credit card industry requires frequent use of numbers in the billions and trillions!

CHAPTER OVERVIEW

Discuss with students that credit is based on honesty, responsibility, and the ability to pay back.

Ask students if any of them have used their parents' credit cards.

REALLY? REALLY!

Have students read the bullet points aloud. In the second bullet, the number one trillion is written out with all of its place-holding zeroes. This may be the first time students have ever seen it written this way. This is an opportune time to review million, billion, quadrillion, and so on. You can even suggest that students do Internet research to find the quantity googol, which is the number 1 followed by 100 zeroes.

Really!

He that goes a borrowing goes a sorrowing.
Benjamin Franklin, American Statesman

4-1 Introduction to Consumer Credit

Objectives

- Become familiar with the basic vocabulary of credit terms.
- Become familiar with types of lending institutions.
- Compute finance charges for installment purchases.

Common Core

A-SSE1, A-SSE3, A-CED3, F-BF1a

Key Terms

- credit
- debtor
- creditor
- asset
- earning power
- credit rating
- credit reporting agency
- FICO score
- installment plan
- down payment
- interest
- finance charge

CCSS Warm-Up

If Sal saves \$55 per month, express his total savings for x years as an expression in terms of x.

$\$55(12)x = \$660x$

EXAMINE THE QUESTION

Credit is not extended to young children because it requires a degree of financial and legal responsibility. Ask students what they think credit worthiness should be based upon.

CLASS DISCUSSION

Why does credit tempt overspending?

Has anyone ever encountered advertisements about obtaining your credit score on television, radio, or in print? For now, explain to them that their credit score is like a credit "report card."

What do you need to know before using credit?

Goods and services can be purchased in one of two ways. The first is "buy now, pay now," and the second is "buy now, pay later." If you purchase something that you do not pay for immediately, you are using **credit**. People who use credit are called **debtors**. Every time you use electricity, you are using credit, because you use the electricity and do not pay for it until the monthly bill arrives. People who use credit cards or take out loans are also using credit. Organizations or people that extend credit to consumers are called **creditors**.

There are advantages to using credit. You can shop without carrying large amounts of cash. You do not have to wait until you can pay in full to purchase something. Credit allows you to get use out of something while still paying for it. There are also disadvantages to using credit. Creditors charge interest on all purchases. Some people also feel that there is a tendency to overspend when using credit.

Any type of credit is based on honesty. Creditors need to be sure that they will be paid back before they extend credit. They will have you fill out an application for credit and will check your financial history. This history includes three basic items.

- **Assets** Assets are everything you own—your home, car, bank accounts, and other personal possessions.
- **Earning Power** Earning power is your ability to earn money now and in the future. Creditors want to make sure you have enough income to repay the debt.
- **Credit Rating** A credit rating is your credit "report card." Every time you use credit, the creditor reports how well you met your financial obligations to a credit reporting agency.

A **credit reporting agency** compiles records on all users of credit. These records are used by creditors before they issue credit to a consumer. The best way to start a good credit history is to open savings and checking accounts, pay all your bills on time, and successfully handle all your credit transactions.

© DNY59/ISTOCKPHOTO.COM

Consumers are given credit scores based on these three criteria. The most popular score is the **FICO score**, named for its creator, Fair, Isaac and Company. The scores, which range from 300 to about 850, summarize the probability that debtors will repay their debts. A higher score indicates a better credit rating. A person with a score near 800 is less of a risk to a creditor than a person with a score near 500. The FICO score is widely accepted by creditors as a reliable way to judge credit worthiness. Gender, race, religion, nationality, and marital status do not affect credit scores.

Any transaction involving credit is a legal contract obligating you to make timely payments. To use credit responsibly, you need to know the language of credit, and the laws that protect creditors and debtors.

TEACH

Students may already be familiar with the terms down payment and interest. When they think of interest, they think of receiving interest from a bank. The term *finance charge* indicates that the consumer is being charged interest, not receiving any interest.

Skills and Strategies

Some stores offer creditworthy customers the convenience of paying for merchandise or services over a period of time. This is an **installment plan**. The customer pays *part* of the selling price at the time of purchase. This is the **down payment**. The scheduled payments, or installments, are usually made on a monthly basis. Installment buyers are charged a fee. This fee is the **interest**, or **finance charge**, and is added to the cost.

EXAMPLE 1

Heather wants to purchase an electric guitar. The price of the guitar with tax is \$2,240. If she can save \$90 per month, how long will it take her to save up for the guitar?

SOLUTION If Heather saves for the guitar, she is not using credit. But she will also not have use of the guitar while she is saving for it.

Divide 2,240 by 90. Round. $2{,}240 \div 90 \approx 24.9$

It will take Heather 25 months to save for the guitar.

EXAMPLE 1

Whenever problems involving how much to save are done, "normal" rounding rules are adjusted. If the answer is not an integer, always round up so that the amount saved is greater than the amount needed.

■ CHECK YOUR UNDERSTANDING

If Heather's guitar costs x dollars and she could save y dollars per month, express algebraically the number of months it would take Heather to save for the guitar.

CHECK YOUR UNDERSTANDING

Answer $\frac{x}{y}$

The answer must be rounded up if it is not an integer.

EXAMPLE 2

The finance charge is also called the interest. In Chapter 3 the consumer *earned* interest, and now the consumer is *paying* interest.

CHECK YOUR UNDERSTANDING

Answer $(0.2p + 12w) - p$, or $12w - 0.8p$

Students should get comfortable with the simplest form of the expression, but note that the expression that is not in simplest form is also valuable because it models the sequence of events more clearly.

EXAMPLE 3

Tell students that the finance charge, imposed if the entire balance is not paid in full, is usually a relatively high interest rate. The finance charge applies retroactively to the day the loan was initiated.

EXAMPLE 2

Heather, from Example 1, speaks to the salesperson at the music store who suggests that she buy the guitar on the installment plan. It requires a 15% down payment. The remainder, plus an additional finance charge, is paid back on a monthly basis for the next two years. The monthly payment is $88.75. What is the finance charge?

SOLUTION Find the down payment by taking 15% of $2,240.

Multiply $2,240 by 0.15. $0.15(2{,}240) = 336$

Heather pays the store $336 at the time of purchase.

She now has to make two years (24 months) of monthly payments of $88.75. The sum of the monthly payments is found by multiplying the number of payments by the monthly payment amount.

Multiply $88.75 by 24. $24(88.75) = 2{,}130$

The sum of the monthly payments is $2,130.

Add down payment plus sum of payments. $336 + 2{,}130 = 2{,}466$

The total cost is $2,466.

The finance charge is the extra money Heather paid for the use of credit. To find the finance charge, subtract the price of the guitar from the total cost.

Total cost – purchase price $2{,}466 - 2{,}240 = 226$

Heather paid a finance charge (interest) of $226. That is the "fee" she paid for not having to wait two years to start using the guitar.

CHECK YOUR UNDERSTANDING

Assume the original price of the guitar was p dollars, and Heather made a 20% down payment for a one-year installment purchase. The monthly payment was w dollars. Express the finance charge algebraically.

EXAMPLE 3

Carpet King is trying to increase sales, and it has instituted a new promotion. All purchases can be paid on the installment plan with no interest, as long as the total is paid in full within six months. There is a $20 minimum monthly payment required. If the Schuster family buys carpeting for $2,134 and makes only the minimum payment for five months, how much will they have to pay in the sixth month?

SOLUTION This is a common business practice today. It is almost like a discount, except instead of saving money off the purchase price, the customer saves the finance charge.

If the Schusters pay $20 for five months, they will have paid a total of $100. Subtract to find what they owe in the sixth month.

Purchase price – amount paid $2{,}134 - 100 = 2{,}034$

They will have to pay $2,034 in the sixth month. If this is not paid in full, there will be a finance charge imposed.

■ CHECK YOUR UNDERSTANDING

The Whittendale family purchases a new refrigerator on a no-interest-for-one-year plan. The cost is $1,385. There is no down payment. If they make a monthly payment of x dollars until the last month, express their last month's payment algebraically.

Credit Scores

Credit scores change as new data about a person's credit becomes available. FICO scores higher than 700 signify a good credit rating and those above 770 are considered excellent.

Any person with a credit score below 600 is considered a significant risk to the creditor. Individuals with scores at 700 or greater qualify for the best interest rates available.

EXAMPLE 4

Mike has a credit rating of 720. Tyler has a credit rating of 560. Mike and Tyler apply for identical loans from Park Bank. Mike is approved for a loan at 5.2% interest, and Tyler is approved for a loan that charged 3 percentage points higher because of his inferior credit rating. What interest rate is Tyler charged?

© MCFIELDS/ISTOCKPHOTO.COM

SOLUTION Add 3% to 5.2%.

$$3\% + 5.2\% = 8.2\%$$

Tyler will pay 8.2% interest for the same loan.

While the arithmetic in this problem may have been simplistic, the message is important: Credit scores will affect the interest you pay on loans. If you are a good credit risk, you will save money when you borrow money.

If you consider that Mike and Tyler took out loans for $3,000 to be paid back over 3 years, you can use the simple interest formula ($I = prt$) to get an idea of the impact a credit score can have on the cost of a loan.

Mike's loan $I = 3{,}000 \times 0.052 \times 3 = 468$

Tyler's loan $I = 3{,}000 \times 0.082 \times 3 = 738$

In the end Tyler's loan will have cost him almost $300 more than Mike's loan for the same amount over the same period of time.

■ CHECK YOUR UNDERSTANDING

Janet had a credit score of 660. She then missed three monthly payments on her credit cards, and her score was lowered x points. Express her new credit score algebraically.

CHECK YOUR UNDERSTANDING

Answer $1,385 − 11$x$

Point out that x could be a minimum monthly payment, and would not necessarily be equal to $\frac{1{,}385}{12}$, which would represent 12 equal payments.

EXAMPLE 4

Make students aware that their credit rating not only affects whether or not they get a loan, it affects the interest rate they pay.

CHECK YOUR UNDERSTANDING

Answer $660 - x$

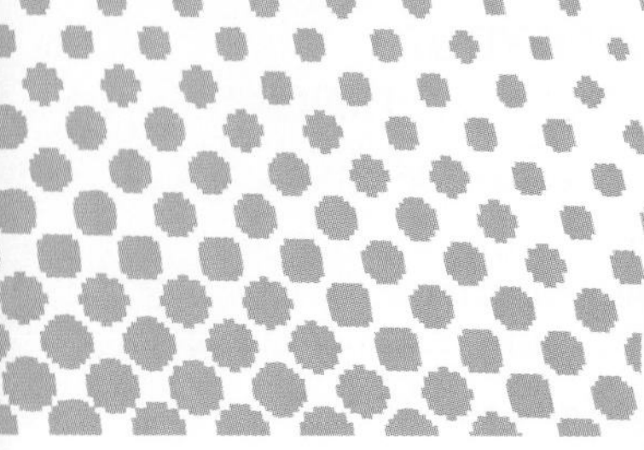

Applications

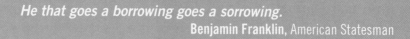

He that goes a borrowing goes a sorrowing.
Benjamin Franklin, American Statesman

TEACH

Algebraic Representations
Students having difficulty with algebraic representations should be reminded to mimic the previous numeric examples.

Options to Buy
Describe the difference between rent-to-own and layaway plans. In rent-to-own plans, the consumer has the use of the product before paying in full. In layaway, they do not get the product until payment is made in full.

Finance Charges
As each finance charge problem is completed, ask students if they feel that the interest is a worthwhile fee for having the use of the product sooner than if money were saved before making the purchase.

ANSWERS

1. Borrowing money is a tremendous responsibility; it ties up future income, and sometimes borrowers regret borrowing. Borrowers also pay a fee (interest) for borrowing.

1. Interpret the quote in the context of what you learned. See margin.

Solve each problem. Round monetary amounts to the nearest cent.

2. Monique buys a \$4,700 air conditioning system using an installment plan that requires 15% down. How much is the down payment? \$705

3. Craig wants to purchase a boat that costs \$1,420. He signs an installment agreement requiring a 20% down payment. He currently has \$250 saved. Does he have enough for the down payment? no

4. Jean bought a \$1,980 snow thrower on the installment plan. The installment agreement included a 10% down payment and 18 monthly payments of \$116 each.
- **a.** How much is the down payment? \$198
- **b.** What is the total amount of the monthly payments? \$2,088
- **c.** How much did Jean pay for the snow thrower on the installment plan? \$2,286
- **d.** What is the finance charge? \$306

5. Linda bought a washer and dryer from Millpage Laundry Supplies for y dollars. She signed an installment agreement requiring a 15% down payment and monthly payments of x dollars for one year.
- **a.** Express her down payment algebraically. $0.15y$
- **b.** How many monthly payments must Linda make? 12
- **c.** Express the total amount of the monthly payments algebraically. $12x$
- **d.** Express the total amount Linda pays for the washer and dryer on the installment plan algebraically. $12x + 0.15y$
- **e.** Express the finance charge algebraically. $12x + 0.15y - y$, or $12x - 0.85y$

6. Zeke bought a \$2,300 bobsled on the installment plan. He made a \$450 down payment, and he has to make monthly payments of \$93.50 for the next two years. How much interest will he pay? \$394

7. Gary is buying a \$1,250 computer on the installment plan. He makes a down payment of \$150. He has to make monthly payments of \$48.25 for $2\frac{1}{2}$ years. What is the finance charge? \$347.50

8. Mazzeo's Appliance Store requires a down payment of $\frac{1}{3}$ on all installment purchases. Norton's Depot requires a 30% down payment on installment purchases. Which store's down payment rate is lower? Norton's Depot

9. Ari purchased a microwave oven on the installment plan for m dollars. He made a 20% down payment and agreed to pay x dollars per month. Express the finance charge algebraically. $0.2m + 24x - m$, or $24x - 0.8m$

10. Adam bought a $1,670 custom video game/sound system on a special no-interest plan. He made a $100 down payment and agreed to pay the entire purchase off in $1\frac{1}{2}$ years. The minimum monthly payment is $10. If he makes the minimum monthly payment up until the last payment, what will be the amount of his last payment? $1,400

11. Max created a spreadsheet for installment purchase calculations.

	A	B	C	D	E	F	G	H
1	Purchase Price	Down Payment Percentage as a Decimal	Down Payment	Monthly Payment	Time in Years	Time in Months	Total of Monthly Payments	Finance Charge
2	$1,200	0.20	f.	$ 97.01	1	j.	n.	s.
3	$1,750	0.10	g.	$ 71.12	2	k.	p.	t.
4	$1,340	0.15	h.	$ 77.23	1.5	l.	q.	u.
5	$ 980	0.10	i.	$165.51	0.5	m.	r.	v.

a. Write a spreadsheet formula to compute the down payment in cell C2. =A2*B2
b. Write a spreadsheet formula to compute the time in months in cell F2. =12*E2
c. Write a spreadsheet formula to compute the total of monthly payments in cell G2. =D2*F2
d. Write the spreadsheet formula to compute the finance charge in cell H2. =C2+G2−A2
e. Use your answers to a–d to fill in the missing entries f–v. See margin.

12. A *layaway* plan is similar to an installment plan, but the customer does not receive the merchandise until it is paid for. It is held in the store for a fee. If you purchased a $1,700 set of golf clubs on a nine-month layaway plan and had to pay a monthly payment of $201, what is the sum of the monthly payments? What was the fee charged for the layaway plan? $1,809; $109

13. A *deferred payment plan* is also similar to an installment plan, except there are very low monthly payments until the end of the agreement. At that point, the entire purchase must be paid in full. If it is not paid, there will be high finance charges. Often, there is no interest—stores use no-interest deferred payment plans to attract customers. Many times there is also no down payment.
a. Chris purchases a living room furniture set for $4,345 from Halloran Gallery. She has a one-year, no interest, no money down, deferred payment plan. She does have to make a $15 monthly payment for the first 11 months. What is the sum of these monthly payments? $165
b. How much must Chris pay in the last month of this plan? $4,180
c. What is the difference between the layaway plan in Exercise 12 and the deferred payment plan? See margin.

14. Audrey purchases a riding lawnmower using the 2-year no-interest deferred payment plan at Lawn Depot for x dollars. There was a down payment of d dollars and a monthly payment of m dollars. Express the amount of the last payment algebraically. $x - d - 23m$

ANSWERS

11e. f. $240
g. $175
h. $201
i. $ 98
j. 12
k. 24
l. 18
m. 6
n. $1,164.12
p. $1,706.88
q. $1,390.14
r. $ 993.06
s. $204.12
t. $131.88
u. $251.14
v. $111.06

13c. With the layaway plan, you do not receive the merchandise until payment is made in full. With the deferred payment plan, you receive the merchandise immediately.

ANSWERS

18. No. Even if her low credit rating was 620, it would only increase to 660, which is not in the "good" range.
19. He had no credit history and had a low credit score as a result. He had no proof he could make timely payments over a period of time.

15. Some stores offer a *rent-to-own* plan. The customer makes a down payment, receives the merchandise at time of purchase, and makes monthly payments. The sum of the monthly payments is lower than the cost of the item. When the last payment is made, customers make a choice. They can purchase the item and apply their payments towards the cost. They can return the item, which means they rented it for a certain period of months.

a. Sharon bought a $2,100 high-definition television set (HDTV) on a six-month rent-to-own plan. The down payment was 10%. What was the dollar value of the down payment? $210

b. Her monthly payments were $75 per month. If she decides not to buy the HDTV after the six months, what was her cost to rent it? $660

16. Bernie bought a refrigerator at a special sale. The refrigerator regularly sold for $986. No down payment was required. Bernie has to pay $69 per month for $1\frac{1}{2}$ years. What is the average amount Bernie pays in interest each month? $14.22

17. Lillian purchased a guitar from Smash Music Stores. It regularly sold for $670, but was on sale at 10% off. She paid 8% tax. She bought it on the installment plan and paid 15% of the total cost with tax as a down payment. Her monthly payments were $58 per month for one year.

a. What is the discount? $67

b. What is the sale price? $603

c. What is the sales tax? $48.24

d. What is the total cost of the guitar? $651.24

e. What is the down payment? $97.69

f. What is the total of the monthly payments? $696

g. What is the total she paid for the guitar on the installment plan? $793.69

h. What is the finance charge? $142.45

18. The following inequalities give information on your credit scores. Let x represent your credit score.

- If $x > 700$, your credit score is excellent.
- If $680 < x < 700$, your credit score is good.
- If $620 < x < 680$, your credit score should be watched carefully.
- If $580 < x < 620$, your credit score is low
- If $x < 580$, your credit score is poor.

If Mary Ann's credit score is low, but she receives 40 points for paying off some delinquent debts, is it possible that her credit rating is now good? Explain. See margin.

19. Samantha's grandfather is debt-free—he bought his car and his house without taking out a loan. He saved and paid cash. He wanted to take out a loan to buy Samantha a car for college graduation. The bank turned him down. Explain why. See margin.

20. Bianka has a credit line of $8,000. She had a previous balance of $567.91 and made a payment of $1,200. Her total purchases are $986.79, and she has been charged a $10.00 finance charge. What is her available credit? $7,635.30

Lend money to an enemy, and thou will gain him, to a friend, and thou will lose him.

Benjamin Franklin, American Statesman, and Inventor

Loans 4-2

Key Terms
- promissory note
- principal
- annual percentage rate
- cosigner
- life insurance
- prepayment privilege
- prepayment penalty
- wage assignment
- wage garnishment
- balloon payment
- lending institution
- collateral

Objectives
- Read monthly payments from a table.
- Compute monthly payments using a formula.
- Compute finance charges on loans.

Common Core

A-SSE1b, A-SSE2, A-SSE3c, F-IF8b, F-LE5

CCSS Warm-Up

Evaluate each expression when $x = 3$.

1. $(1 + x)^x$ **2.** $\left(1 + \frac{1}{x}\right)^x$ **3.** x^x

1. 64 2. 64/27 3. 27

What information do you need to know before taking out a loan?

Whenever you borrow money, you must sign an agreement, called a **promissory note**, which states the conditions of the loan. Your signature is your promise to pay back the loan as outlined in the agreement. Always read an entire promissory note carefully before signing it.

The amount you borrow is the **principal**. The interest rate you pay is given per year and is the **annual percentage rate (APR)**. The promissory note contains information that the creditor is required to state, as stipulated in the *Truth in Lending Act*. This includes the principal, APR, monthly payment, number of payments that must be made, finance charge, due dates for each payment, and fees for late payments.

Not all loan agreements are the same, so each promissory note describes the features of that particular loan. Become familiar with the terms given below.

- **Cosigner** This person agrees to pay back the loan if the borrower is unable to do so. People without an established credit rating often need a cosigner.
- **Life Insurance** A creditor often requires a borrower to have life insurance that will cover the loan in the event the borrower dies before the loan is paid.
- **Prepayment Privilege** This feature allows the borrower to make payments before the due date to reduce the amount of interest.
- **Prepayment Penalty** This agreement requires borrowers to pay a fee if they wish to pay back an entire loan before the due date.
- **Wage Assignment** This is a voluntary deduction from an employee's paycheck, used to pay off debts. If a debtor's employer and the creditor agree, loans can be paid off using this form of electronic transfer.

EXAMINE THE QUESTION

Taking out a loan requires you to sign a legal document called a promissory note. There is a lot of fine print and it must all be read carefully.

Before taking out a loan, you would need to know the different types of lending institutions and understand legal terms presented in the promissory note.

CLASS DISCUSSION

Finance charge is another name for interest.

It is not a benefit to the bank for loans to be paid off early since it reduces the amount of interest collected.

Which types of lending institutions have you heard of? Are there any locally?

CLASS DISCUSSION

Highlight the differences between the types of lending institutions.

Which types of lending institutions have you heard of? Are there any locally? How would you decide which type of institution from which to borrow?

- **Wage Garnishment** This is an involuntary form of wage assignment, often enforced by court order. The employer deducts money from the employee's paycheck to pay the creditor.
- **Balloon Payment** The last monthly payment on some loans can be much higher than the previous payments. These high payments are called balloon payments.

Organizations that extend loans are called **lending institutions**. Lending institutions are businesses that make profit by charging interest. There are many types of lending institutions.

- **Banks** Most consumers apply for loans at banks. *Savings banks* offer good interest rates but require loan applicants to have good credit ratings. *Commercial banks* are banks used by businesses, so they have large amounts of money to lend. They also require a good credit rating.
- **Credit Unions** A credit union provides financial services for its members only. Members may work in the same office, be in the same profession, or live in the same apartment complex. Members deposit money in a credit union account. This money is made available to members who apply for loans from the credit union, usually at an interest rate that is lower than a bank can offer.
- **Consumer Finance Companies** These businesses primarily lend money to people with poor credit ratings, who cannot get a loan anywhere else. High interest are charged rates for this service.
- **Life Insurance Companies** Life insurance companies make loans to their policyholders. The amount that can be borrowed is based on the amount of life insurance purchased and the length of time the policy has been held. The interest rate is good because the life insurance company is not taking a tremendous risk because if the loan is not paid back, it can be deducted from the life insurance benefit when it is paid.
- **Pawnshops** Pawnshops are known for small, quick loans. A customer who needs money leaves a personal belonging, called **collateral**, with the pawn broker in exchange for the loan. Most loans are 30-, 60-, or 90-day loans. When the debtor returns with the principal plus interest, the collateral is returned.

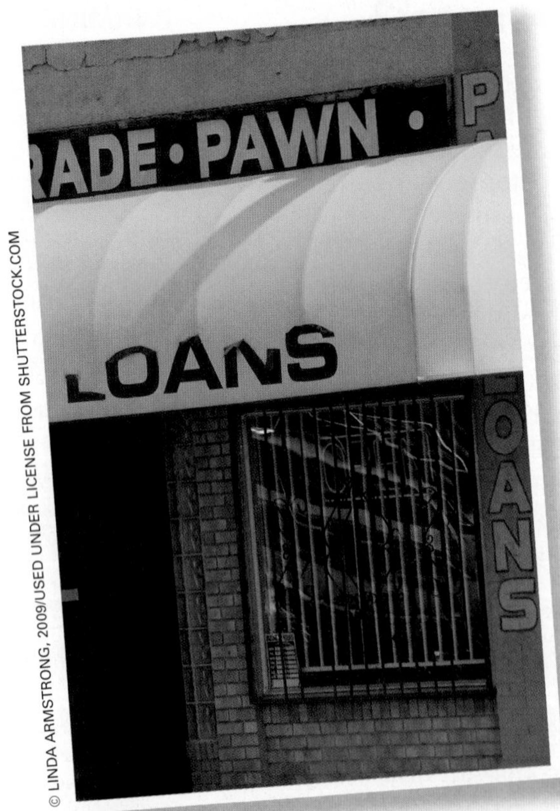

You may have seen *loan sharks* in the movies. Loan sharks charge extremely high interest rates and do not formally check your credit rating. Loan sharking is illegal.

Regardless of where you shop for a loan, the *Equal Credit Opportunity Act* requires a creditor to treat you fairly. If your application is turned down, you are protected by the *Fair Credit Reporting Act* which says that the lender must give you the reason in writing for the loan denial. Always compare the terms of the loan and the annual percentage rates when shopping for a loan.

Skills and Strategies

Monthly loan payments are computed using a formula. Payment information is often arranged in tables to make it easy for customers.

Table of Monthly Payments per $1,000 of Principal

Rate	1 yr	2 yr	3 yr	4 yr	5 yr	10 yr	Rate	1 yr	2 yr	3 yr	4 yr	5 yr	10 yr
6.50%	86.30	44.55	30.65	23.71	19.57	11.35	10.00%	87.92	46.14	32.27	25.36	21.25	13.22
6.75%	86.41	44.66	30.76	23.83	19.68	11.48	10.25%	88.03	46.26	32.38	25.48	21.37	13.35
7.00%	86.53	44.77	30.88	23.95	19.80	11.61	10.50%	88.15	46.38	32.50	25.60	21.49	13.49
7.25%	86.64	44.89	30.99	24.06	19.92	11.74	10.75%	88.27	46.49	32.62	25.72	21.62	13.63
7.50%	86.76	45.00	31.11	24.18	20.04	11.87	11.00%	88.38	46.61	32.74	25.85	21.74	13.78
7.75%	86.87	45.11	31.22	24.30	20.16	12.00	11.25%	88.50	46.72	32.86	25.97	21.87	13.92
8.00%	86.99	45.23	31.34	24.41	20.28	12.13	11.50%	88.62	46.84	32.98	26.09	21.99	14.06
8.25%	87.10	45.34	31.45	24.53	20.40	12.27	11.75%	88.73	46.96	33.10	26.21	22.12	14.20
8.50%	87.22	45.46	31.57	24.65	20.52	12.40	12.00%	88.85	47.07	33.21	26.33	22.24	14.35
8.75%	87.34	45.57	31.68	24.77	20.64	12.53	12.25%	88.97	47.19	33.33	26.46	22.37	14.49
9.00%	87.45	45.68	31.80	24.89	20.76	12.67	12.50%	89.08	47.31	33.45	26.58	22.50	14.64
9.25%	87.57	45.80	31.92	25.00	20.88	12.80	12.75%	89.20	47.42	33.57	26.70	22.63	14.78
9.50%	87.68	45.91	32.03	25.12	21.00	12.94	13.00%	89.32	47.54	33.69	26.83	22.75	14.93
9.75%	87.80	46.03	32.15	25.24	21.12	13.08	13.25%	89.43	47.66	33.81	26.95	22.88	15.08

EXAMPLE 1

What is the monthly payment for a $4,000 two-year loan with an APR of 8.50%?

SOLUTION The table lists monthly costs per $1,000 borrowed. Divide the amount you want to borrow by 1,000. Look across the row labeled 8.50% and down the column labeled 2 yr. The monthly cost per thousand dollars borrowed is $45.46. You are borrowing 4 sets of $1,000, so the table amount must be multiplied by 4.

$$45.46 \times 4 = 181.84$$

The monthly payment is $181.84.

CHECK YOUR UNDERSTANDING

Juan is borrowing $41,000 for 5 years at an APR of 6.5%. What is the monthly payment?

EXAMPLE 2

What is the total amount of the monthly payments for a $4,000, two-year loan with an APR of 8.50%?

SOLUTION There are 12 months in a year, so the borrower will make 24 monthly payments in two years. Use the monthly payment from Example 1, $181.84.

Multiply monthly payment by 24. $181.84 \times 24 = 4{,}364.16$

The total amount of monthly payments is $4,364.16.

TEACH

The formula to compute monthly payments requires careful placement of parentheses. Calculator entry must be done carefully. Students need to use their "financial number sense" to check each problem when they are finished.

EXAMPLE 1

The table is abbreviated; it only offers selected interest rates and numbers of years. Explain the need for an algebraic formula to handle any loan conditions.

CHECK YOUR UNDERSTANDING

Answer $802.37

Some students may forget that the table amounts are per each $1,000 of principal.

EXAMPLE 2

You can review the amount of months in 1, $1\frac{1}{4}$, $1\frac{1}{2}$, $1\frac{3}{4}$, years. Students should become familiar with yearly equivalents of 15 months, 18 months, 30 months, and so on.

CHECK YOUR UNDERSTANDING

Answer $6,000
Students can use trial and error after they get the monthly payment per $1,000 in the 5-year column.

EXAMPLE 3

Remind students that the finance charge is the same as the interest.

CHECK YOUR UNDERSTANDING

Answer $36y - x$

EXAMPLE 4

Ask students what purpose the fraction bar serves besides indicating division. Guide students to understand that the fraction bar also serves as a grouping symbol. When the formula is entered into the calculator they must think about the order of operations and if parentheses are needed for proper calculator entry.

After the discussion, you can have students insert the parentheses when they write the formula in their notes.

Also remind students that their answers must make sense, and often, if the numerical entries are put into the calculator incorrectly, an unreasonable answer is displayed.

CHECK YOUR UNDERSTANDING

Answer $86.76 (from the formula or the table)

Sometimes the table and the calculator will differ, due to rounding, and the bank will adjust the last payment to make sure the finance charge is correct.

■ **CHECK YOUR UNDERSTANDING**

The total of monthly payments for a 5-year loan is $7,171.20. The APR is 7.25%. How much money was originally borrowed?

EXAMPLE 3

Find the finance charge for a $4,000, two-year loan with an 8.5% APR?

SOLUTION Use the total amount of monthly payments from Example 2 and subtract the borrowed amount.

$$4{,}364.16 - 4{,}000 = 364.16$$

The finance charge for this loan is $364.16.

■ **CHECK YOUR UNDERSTANDING**

Karl is borrowing x dollars over a three-year period. The monthly payment is y dollars. Express his finance charge algebraically.

EXAMPLE 4

Mark bought a new car. The total amount he needs to borrow is $28,716. He plans on taking out a 4-year loan at an APR of 5.12%. What is the monthly payment?

SOLUTION Mark must use the monthly payment formula.

Monthly Payment Formula

$$M = \frac{p\left(\frac{r}{12}\right)\left(1 + \frac{r}{12}\right)^{12t}}{\left(1 + \frac{r}{12}\right)^{12t} - 1}$$

where M = monthly payment
p = principal
r = interest rate
t = number of years

Substitute $p = 28{,}716$, $r = 0.0512$, and $t = 4$.

$$M = \frac{28{,}716\left(\frac{0.0512}{12}\right)\left(1 + \frac{0.0512}{12}\right)^{12(4)}}{\left(1 + \frac{0.0512}{12}\right)^{12(4)} - 1}$$

Simplify the exponent to make calculator entry easier.

$$M = \frac{28{,}716\left(\frac{0.0512}{12}\right)\left(1 + \frac{0.0512}{12}\right)^{48}}{\left(1 + \frac{0.0512}{12}\right)^{48} - 1}$$

Use your calculator. Enter in one keystroke sequence, but work slowly and carefully. Round to the nearest cent.

```
(28716(.0512/12)
(1+.0512/12)^48)
/((1+.0512/12)^4
8-1)
```

The monthly payment is $662.87.

■ **CHECK YOUR UNDERSTANDING**

Find the monthly payment for a $1,000, one-year loan at an APR of 7.5%.

Applications

Lend money to an enemy, and thou will gain him, to a friend, and thou will lose him.

Benjamin Franklin, American Statesman, and Inventor

1. Interpret the quote in the context of what you learned, and on your general experiences. See margin.

2. Arrange the following lending institutions in descending order according to their APRs for a $10,000, two-year loan. Columbia, East Meadow, First Bank, Tivoli, Clinton Park

East Meadow Savings	$9\frac{1}{2}\%$
Clinton Park Credit Union	9%
Tivoli Trust	$9\frac{3}{8}\%$
First Bank of Rhinecliff	9.45%
Columbia Consumer Finance Corp.	$9\frac{9}{16}\%$

3. How many more monthly payments are made for a five-year loan than for a two-year loan? 36

4. How many monthly payments must be made for a $2\frac{1}{2}$-year loan? 30

5. Bart needs to borrow $7,000 from a local bank. He compares the monthly payments for a 9.75% loan for three different periods of time.
   a. What is the monthly payment for a one-year loan? $614.60
   b. What is the monthly payment for a three-year loan? $225.05
   c. What is the monthly payment for a five-year loan? $147.84

6. Rachel has a $10,000, three-year loan with an APR of 7.25%.
   a. What is the monthly payment? $309.90
   b. What is the total amount of the monthly payments? $11,156.40
   c. What is the finance charge? $1,156.40

7. Melissa wants to check the accuracy of the finance charge on her promissory note. She has a $6,000, four-year loan at an APR of 10%.
   a. What is the monthly payment? $152.16
   b. What is the total amount of the monthly payments? $7,303.68
   c. What is the finance charge? $1,303.68

8. The policy of the Broadway Pawnshop is to lend up to 35% of the value of a borrower's collateral. John wants to use a $3,000 ring and a $1,200 necklace as collateral for a loan. What is the maximum amount that he could borrow from Broadway? $1,470

9. Juliana is taking out an $8,700, $3\frac{1}{2}$-year loan with an APR of 9.31%. What will be the monthly payment for this loan? $243.52

10. Lavonda took out a $7,500 loan with an APR of 6.875% and agreed to pay it back monthly over six years. How many monthly payments did she make? 72

TEACH

Formulas
For exercises involving monthly payments, students should be provided with the formula for these exercises.

On tests, you can give them an option—to take a test with or without the formula sheet, and you can offer bonus points accordingly for students who elect to memorize the formula.

Exercise 4
This exercise requires students to use the number of months as a fraction of a year. Extra practice can be given at the board.

Exercise 5
This is a typical analysis most borrowers do so they can choose for how long to take out a loan. The advantage to a long period is a low monthly payment. The disadvantage is more total interest.

Exercise 7
Point out to the students that, equipped with their monthly payment formula, they can check to insure the bank is doing the calculations on their loans correctly.

ANSWERS

1. Borrowing money from a friend can create problems. Friends can take advantage of one another since repayment is not structured with a legal contract.

TEACH

Exercise 15

This exercise demonstrates the need to use parentheses carefully, and why students need to use number sense when reviewing their answers.

ANSWERS

15. The parentheses that group the entire numerator and the parentheses that group the entire denominator were omitted.

17b. =(A2*(B2/12)(1+B2/12)^D2)/((1+B2/12)^D2–1)

c. 36

d. 6

e. 12

f. 344.70

g. 152.98

h. 220.95

11. Solomon is taking out a $15,320, two-year loan with an APR of 10.29%. What will be the finance charge for this loan to the nearest dollar? $1,696

12. Reggie needs a quick *x*-dollar loan, just until his next payday in two weeks to take advantage of a sale on ski equipment. The bank would take too long in paperwork, so he goes to a pawnshop. The pawnshop will only lend him 25% of the value of his collateral. Express algebraically the amount of collateral Reggie must use for this loan. $4x$

13. Olivia is considering membership to the Regional Teachers Credit Union so that she can save money on a loan. The credit union will lend her $8,000 for three years at 8.25% APR. The same loan at her savings bank has an APR of 10.5%. How much would Olivia save in finance charges if she joined the credit union and took out her loan there? Round to the nearest ten dollars. $300

14. Rob wants to purchase a $5,000 drum set. The music store offers him a two-year installment agreement requiring $800 down and monthly payments of $202.50. Rob has a poor credit rating.

a. What is his interest on this installment agreement? $660

b. Instead of using the store's installment plan, Rob can borrow $5,000 at an APR of 13% from a local consumer finance company. What would be the monthly payment for this loan using the table? $237.70

c. How much interest would the finance company charge? $704.80

d. Should Rob use the installment plan or borrow the money from the finance company? The installment plan has a lower finance charge.

15. Lee wanted to compute the monthly payment on a 2-year, $8,400 loan at an APR of 7%. She entered the keystrokes on her calculator at the right. The display gives an answer of 48, which Lee knows is incorrect. Explain what was incorrectly entered. See margin.

```
8400(.07/12)(1+.
07/12)^24/(1+.07
/12)^24-1
```

16. A loan used for buying a home is called a *mortgage*. The Fortunato family is buying a $430,000 home. They are taking out a 30-year mortgage at a rate of 8%.

a. Compute the monthly payment. $3,155.19

b. Find the total of all of the monthly payments for the 30 years. $1,135,868.40

c. What is the finance charge? $705,868.40

d. Which is greater, the interest or the original cost of the home? interest

17. The following spreadsheet can be used to compute monthly payments given the APR, principal, and length of the loan.

	A	B	C	D	E
1	Principal	Interest Rate as a Decimal	Time in Years	Time in Months	Monthly Payment
2	11,000	0.08	3	**c.**	**f.**
3	900	0.0677	0.5	**d.**	**g.**
4	2,500	0.11	1	**e.**	**h.**

a. Write the spreadsheet formula to compute cell D2. =12*C2

b. Write the spreadsheet formula to compute cell E2. See margin.

c-h. Use your spreadsheet to fill in the missing entries. See margin.

> *Loans and debts make worries and frets.*
>
> Traditional Proverb

4-3 Loan Calculations and Regression

Key Terms
- monthly payment calculator
- natural logarithm
- cubic function
- cubic regression equation

Objectives
- Calculate the present value of a single deposit investment.
- Calculate the present value of a periodic deposit investment.

Common Core
S-ID6a

CCSS Warm-Up

Determine if the given point is on the graph of $2x - 3y = 12$.

1. (6, 4) **2.** (−6, −8) **3.** (0, 4)

1. no 2. yes 3. no

How can you calculate and model loan computations?

EXAMINE THE QUESTION
Students will model the monthly loan payment figures using the loan formula and regression analysis.

Before taking out a loan, you need a complete picture of what your payment responsibilities will be over the life of the loan. Part of the monthly payment decreases your principal and part is the finance charge or interest.

In a savings account, the interest is an amount of money that you get from the bank as a compensation for keeping your money there. For loans, interest is the amount of money that you have to give to the bank as a fee for using their money.

There are many **monthly payment calculators** available on the Internet that can give you a summary of the loan balance over the lifetime of the loan and on a monthly or yearly basis.

Examine the summary statement of a loan calculator for a \$100,000 loan with an APR of 7.5% for a period of 15 years, taken out in January 2010. Notice the interest you must pay is more than half the amount that was borrowed.

You can get a better idea of how your monthly payment is allocated by looking at a payment schedule for the first year of the loan. Notice, as the months pass, the principal that is paid off by your monthly payment of \$927.01 increases as the interest amount decreases. Pick any month. The sum of the *principal paid* and the *interest paid* will always be approximately equal to your monthly payment. But, in the beginning of the loan, more goes to paying the bank interest than paying off the principal.

Loan Amount	Interest Rate	Term	Start Date
\$ 100,000	7.5 %	15 years	Jan 2010

Payments & Interest	
Your Monthly Payment	\$ 927.01
Total Interest Paid (life of loan)	\$ 66,862.22

Payment Schedule for 2010			
Month	**Principal Paid**	**Interest Paid**	**Loan Balance**
Jan 2010	\$ 302.01	\$ 625.00	\$ 99,697.00
Feb 2010	\$ 303.90	\$ 623.11	\$ 99,394.09
Mar 2010	\$ 305.80	\$ 621.21	\$ 99,088.29
Apr 2010	\$ 307.71	\$ 619.30	\$ 98,780.58
May 2010	\$ 309.63	\$ 617.38	\$ 98,470.94
Jun 2010	\$ 311.57	\$ 615.44	\$ 98,159.38
Jul 2010	\$ 313.52	\$ 613.50	\$ 97,845.86
Aug 2010	\$ 315.48	\$ 611.54	\$ 97,530.38
Sep 2010	\$ 317.45	\$ 609.56	\$ 97,212.94
Oct 2010	\$ 319.43	\$ 607.58	\$ 96,893.50
Nov 2010	\$ 321.43	\$ 605.58	\$ 96,572.08
Dec 2010	\$ 323.44	\$ 603.58	\$ 96,248.64

Skills and Strategies

Here you will learn how to use formulas and regression analysis to make loan calculations in order to make wise credit decisions.

EXAMPLE 1

Determine the total interest owed on a 5-year \$10,000 loan at 6% APR.

SOLUTION

Use the monthly payment formula.

$$M = \frac{p\left(\frac{r}{12}\right)\left(1+\frac{r}{12}\right)^{12t}}{\left(1+\frac{r}{12}\right)^{12t}-1}$$

Substitute $p = 10{,}000$, $r = 0.06$, and $t = 5$.

$$M = \frac{10{,}000\left(\frac{0.06}{12}\right)\left(1+\frac{0.06}{12}\right)^{12(5)}}{\left(1+\frac{0.06}{12}\right)^{12(5)}-1}$$

Use your calculator. Enter in one keystroke sequence. Think about the order of operations to determine where parentheses are needed. $M = 193.3280$

The monthly payment is approximately \$193.33.

Multiply the amount of the monthly payments by the number of monthly payments to find the total of the monthly payments.

$$193.33 \times 60 = 11{,}599.80$$

The total of the monthly payments is \$11,599.80.

Keep in mind that this is not the exact amount. The amount of the monthly payment was rounded to the nearest cent, or two decimal places, but in reality, banks keep decimal amounts when performing calculations.

To find the interest you must pay, subtract the loan principal from the total payback.

$$11{,}599.80 - 10{,}000 = 1{,}599.80$$

The interest on a \$10,000 loan at 6% APR taken out for 5 years is approximately \$1,599.80.

■ CHECK YOUR UNDERSTANDING

Hannah is taking out a 4.3% loan to purchase an \$18,000 car. The length of the loan is 8 years. How much will she pay in interest?

CLASS DISCUSSION

Discuss how a loan balance works. Although the monthly payment remains the same, the contributions to principal and finance charge do not.

TEACH

Before focusing on the loan chart, ask students what the total interest charge might be on a \$100,000 15-year loan with an APR of 7.5%. How far off were their interest estimations from the actual amount?

EXAMPLE 1

Before students use their calculator, discuss the careful use of parentheses. Be sure they understand that the fraction bar makes parentheses unnecessary in the book, but the calculator is different.

CHECK YOUR UNDERSTANDING

Answer \$3,305.28
It is necessary to calculate the monthly payment using the formula (\$221.93) and then determine the total amount that will be paid back by multiplying the monthly payment by 96 (\$21,305.28). Subtracting the loan amount from the total yields \$3,305.28 extra that was paid toward interest.

EXAMPLE 2

Claude wants to borrow \$25,000 to purchase a car. After looking at his monthly budget, he realizes that all he can afford to pay per month is \$300. The bank is offering a 5.9% loan. What would the length of his loan need to be so that he can stay within his budget?

SOLUTION To solve this problem, it is necessary to perform some algebraic manipulations on the monthly loan payment formula.

To find the length of the loan given the amount of the monthly payment, you need to solve for the exponent t. To solve for an exponent, you need to understand the concept of a **natural logarithm**. In Lesson 3-6, you learned about the constant e. Examine the following equation.

$$y = e^x$$

To find the value of x when given a particular y, use the following algebraic transformation.

$$x = \ln y$$

This is read as "x equals the natural logarithm of y" or "when e is raised to the exponent x, the resulting value is y."

Before the use of calculators, people used a logarithm table to determine the exponent values. Now, graphing calculators have a natural logarithm key [LN]. For example, consider the following equation.

$$130 = e^x$$

To solve for x, that is, to find the exponent to which you need to raise e to get 130, you need to use the [LN] key and then enter 130 into the calculator. The result is approximately 4.9.

The development of the loan length formula is beyond the scope of this course. That formula requires the use of the natural logarithm in order to solve for the exponent t.

Loan Length Formula

$$t = \frac{\ln\left(\frac{M}{p}\right) - \left(\ln\left(\frac{M}{p} - \frac{r}{12}\right)\right)}{12\ln\left(1 + \frac{r}{12}\right)}$$

where M = monthly payment
p = principal
r = interest rate
t = number of years

Substitute $p = 25{,}000$, $M = 300$, and $r = 0.059$.

$$t = \frac{\ln\left(\frac{300}{25{,}000}\right) - \left(\ln\left(\frac{300}{25{,}000} - \frac{0.059}{12}\right)\right)}{12\ln\left(1 + \frac{0.059}{12}\right)}$$

Calculate to the nearest hundredth of a year. $t \approx 8.96$

Claude would need to take out a loan for about 9 years.

CHECK YOUR UNDERSTANDING

In Example 2, what impact would an increase in the monthly payment of \$50 have on the length of the loan?

EXAMPLE 2

Since the variable representing time in the monthly payment formula is an exponent, solving for that exponent requires the use of logarithms. Some students may already have been introduced to logs in a previous math course while for others, this may be their first introduction to the topic. This is not meant to be a comprehensive lesson on the use of logs. Rather, it is a lesson on how the natural log can be used in this particular case. The resulting formula is complex and again requires the proper placement of parentheses.

CHECK YOUR UNDERSTANDING

Answer The length of the loan would drop to about 7.35 years if the monthly payment is increased by \$50.

Students need to recalculate the time formula from Example 2 using \$350 as the monthly payment. Ask students what they expect will happen to the length of the loan before they actually do the calculations.

Year	Loan Balance
2010	$ 96,248.64
2011	$ 92,206.05
2012	$ 87,849.63
2013	$ 83,155.00
2014	$ 78,095.92
2015	$ 72,644.09
2016	$ 66,769.01
2017	$ 60,437.85
2018	$ 53,615.17
2019	$ 46,262.84
2020	$ 38,339.72
2021	$ 29,801.51
2022	$ 20,600.46
2023	$ 10,685.11
2024	$ 0.00

EXAMPLE 3

The purpose of this problem is to introduce students to other forms of regression equations. It walks them through linear, quadratic, and cubic regression. The information presented here is not to be interpreted as making the claim that the payment formula is a cubic regression. Rather, Example 3 shows that the cubic regression yields a better approximation of the values stated in the table.

CHECK YOUR UNDERSTANDING

Answer linear: $96,445.96; quadratic: $92,093.62; cubic: $92,190.73; chart: $92,206.05

EXAMPLE 3

This lesson opened with a discussion about a $100,000 loan with an APR of 7.5% taken out in January 2010 for a period of 15 years. Examine the table of decreasing loan balances over the 15-year period. Use regression to determine a curve of best fit for this data.

SOLUTION Use the statistics features on your graphing calculator to make a scatterplot of the ordered pairs (x, y) where x equals the year number and y equals the loan balance.

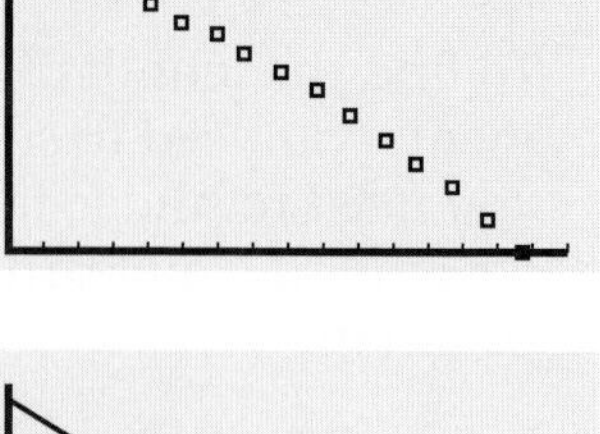

To simplify the data entry process, rather than using the actual years, let year 2010 be year 1, 2011 be year 2, and so on.

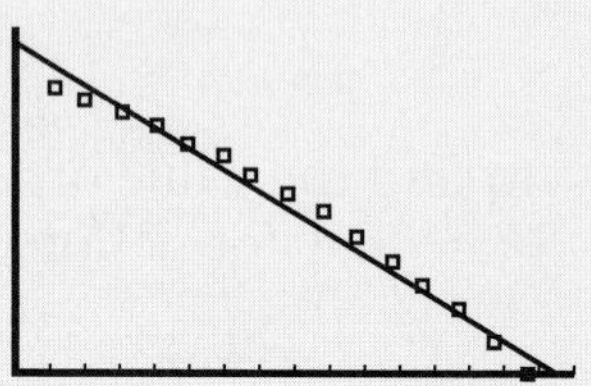

Use the Linear Regression feature to determine the linear regression equation, $y = -6{,}777.54x + 110{,}001.04$, with numbers rounded to the nearest hundredth. Notice that the line doesn't follow the shape of the points.

To get a more accurate regression equation, use the Quadratic Regression feature to find a second degree regression function in the form $y = ax^2 + bx + c$. It has the shape of a parabola. While the scatterplot may not look completely parabolic, the points might best fit on part of a parabola.

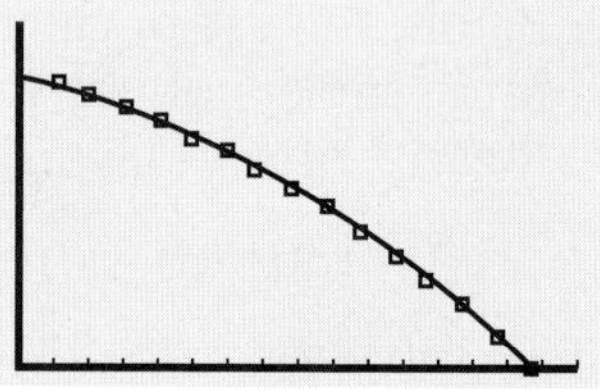

The quadratic regression equation is $y = -251.10x^2 - 2{,}760.02x + 98{,}618.06$, with numbers rounded to the nearest hundredth.

For even more accuracy, you can use the Cubic Regression feature to determine a third degree regression equation of the form $y = ax^3 + bx^2 + cx + d$. This function is known as a **cubic function**. The **cubic regression equation** is $y = -6.23x^3 - 101.67x^2 - 3{,}747.49x + 100{,}142.23$, with numbers rounded to the nearest hundredth.

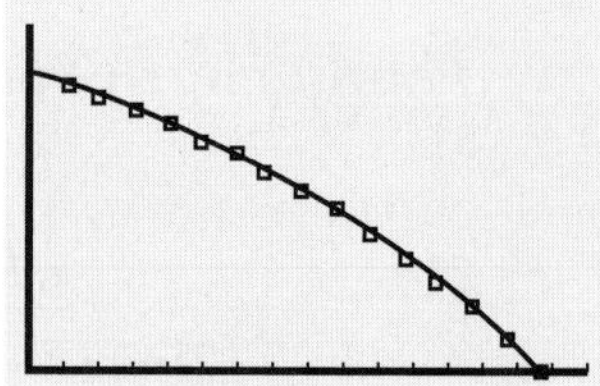

It appears that this regression equation approaches the shape of the points better than the quadratic or the linear equations. While the cubic above may not yield the exact equation to determine loan balances through the life of the loan, it does yield fairly accurate amounts.

CHECK YOUR UNDERSTANDING

Use the linear, quadratic, and cubic regression equations determined in Example 3 to compare the computed loan balances when $x = 2$ with the loan balance amount given in the chart for 2011.

Applications

Loans and debts make worries and frets.

Traditional Proverb

1. How might the quote apply to what you have learned? See margin.
2. What is the total interest on a ten-year 6.1% loan with a principal of $32,000? $10,824.40
3. Jamie wants to borrow $15,000 from South Western Bank. They offered her a 4-year loan with an APR of 5.5%. How much will she pay in interest over the life of the loan? $1,744.80
4. Charlie and Kathy want to borrow $20,000 to make some home improvements. Their bank will lend them the money for 10 years at an interest rate of $5\frac{3}{4}$%. How much will they pay in interest? $6,344.80
5. Devon is considering taking out a $7,000 loan. He went to two banks. Stevenson Trust Company offered him an 8-year loan with an interest rate of 8.6%. First National Bank offered him a 5-year loan with an interest rate of 10%. Which loan will have the lower interest over its lifetime? The First National loan will have the lower interest. (Stevenson: $2,705.60; First National: $1,923.80)
6. A bank offers a $25,000 loan at an interest rate of 7.7% that can be paid back over 2 to 10 years.
   - **a.** Write the monthly payment formula for this loan situation. Let t represent the number of years from 2 to 10 inclusive. See additional answers.
   - **b.** Write the total interest formula for this loan situation. Let t represent the number of years from 2 to 10 inclusive. See additional answers.
   - **c.** Construct a graph. Let the independent variable represent years and the dependent variable represent the interest paid. See additional answers.
   - **d.** Use your graph to estimate the interest for a $6\frac{1}{2}$-year loan. approx. $6,800
7. Jennifer wants to borrow $20,000. Her bank offers a 7.1% interest rate. She can afford $500 a month for loan payments. What should be the length of her loan to the nearest tenth of a year? 3.8 years
8. Louis wants to take out a $14,000 loan with a 6.8% APR. He can afford to pay no more than $400 per month for loan payments. What would be the length of his loan? Round to the nearest tenth of a year. 3.3 years
9. Use your answer and the loan information from Exercise 8 to determine what effect a $50 decrease in Louis' monthly payment would have on the length of his loan. The loan would increase to 3.8 years.
10. Dave wants to borrow $22,000 from First Finance Bank. The bank will give him a 15-year loan at an interest rate of 4.85%. How much will he pay the bank in interest over the life of the loan? Round to the nearest hundred dollars. $9,000

TEACH

Exercises 2–5
Here students are asked to determine the total interest over the life of the loan. They will need to first determine the monthly payment and then multiply that monthly payment by the loan length in months. Subtracting the principal from this amount will yield the desired result.

Exercise 6
Students may need some assistance in setting up an appropriate viewing window when graphing. Keep in mind that the formula calculates a monthly payment but the independent variable for the graph is stated in years.

ANSWERS

1. The proverb is a warning about loans and debts. Entering into any debt agreement should be made cautiously.

Year	Principal Paid	Interest Paid	Loan Balance
			$ 10,000.00
1	$ 680.52	$ 775.41	$ 9,319.48
2	$ 737.01	$ 718.92	$ 8,582.47
3	$ 798.18	$ 657.75	$ 7,784.29
4	$ 864.43	$ 591.50	$ 6,919.86
5	$ 936.17	$ 519.76	$ 5,983.69
6	$ 1,013.88	$ 442.05	$ 4,969.81
7	$ 1,098.03	$ 357.90	$ 3,871.78
8	$ 1,189.16	$ 266.77	$ 2,682.62
9	$ 1,287.86	$ 168.07	$ 1,394.76
10	$ 1,394.76	$ 61.18	$ 0.00

11. Use the given yearly payment schedule.

a. What is the loan amount? $10,000

b. What is the length of the loan? 10 years

c. What is the monthly payment? approx. $121.33

d. What is the total interest paid? $4,559.31

e. Construct a scatterplot using the data points (year, loan balance). See margin.

f. Write a linear regression equation that approximates the year/loan balance relationship. Round to the nearest hundredth. $y = -1{,}029.43x + 10{,}812.73$

g. Write a quadratic regression equation that approximates the year/loan balance relationship. Round to the nearest hundredth. $y = -40.85x^2 - 580.08x + 9{,}914.03$

h. Write a cubic regression equation that approximates the year/loan balance relationship. Round to the nearest hundredth. $y = -1.08x^3 - 22.98x^2 - 662.48x + 10{,}006.94$

TEACH

Exercises 11 and 12

Once the data has been entered into the calculator, the regression equations are easy to determine. Use the regression keystroke sequence that enters the equations into Y1, Y2, and Y3 respectively so that those equations are not overwritten and students can easily refer to them.

ANSWERS

11e.

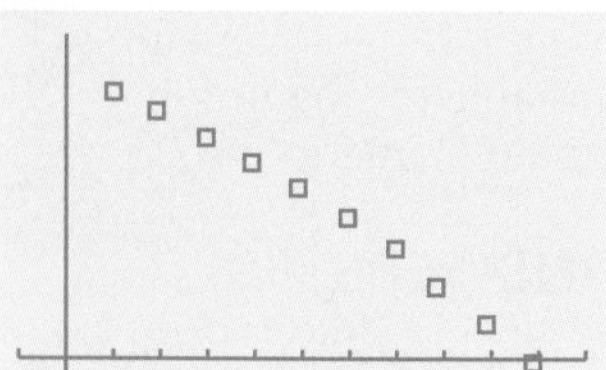

12e.

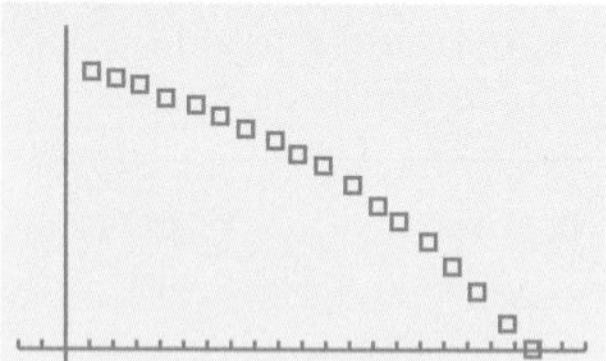

12f. $y = -1{,}945.42x + 39{,}737.05$

12g. $y = -90.18x^2 - 231.99x + 34{,}025.63$

12. Use the given payment schedule.

Yearly Payment Schedule			
Year	Principal Paid	Interest Paid	Loan Balance
			$ 35,000.00
2010	$ 773.32	$3,291.90	$ 34,226.68
2011	$ 850.08	$ 3,215.15	$ 33,376.60
2012	$ 934.44	$ 3,130.78	$ 32,442.16
2013	$ 1,027.18	$ 3,038.04	$ 31,414.97
2014	$ 1,129.13	$ 2,936.10	$ 30,285.84
2015	$ 1,241.19	$ 2,824.03	$ 29,044.65
2016	$ 1,364.38	$ 2,700.85	$ 27,680.27
2017	$ 1,499.79	$ 2,565.44	$ 26,180.48
2018	$ 1,648.64	$ 2,416.59	$ 24,531.84
2019	$ 1,812.26	$ 2,252.96	$ 22,719.57
2020	$ 1,992.13	$ 2,073.10	$ 20,727.45
2021	$2,189.84	$ 1,875.39	$ 18,537.61
2022	$ 2,407.18	$ 1,658.05	$ 16,130.43
2023	$ 2,646.08	$ 1,419.14	$ 13,484.34
2024	$ 2,908.70	$ 1,156.53	$ 10,575.64
2025	$ 3,197.38	$ 867.84	$ 7,378.26
2026	$ 3,514.72	$ 550.51	$ 3,863.54
2027	$ 3,863.54	$ 201.69	$ 0.00

a. What is the loan amount? $35,000

b. What is the length of the loan? 18 years

c. What is the approximate monthly payment rounded to the nearest cent? $338.77

d. What is the total interest paid over the life of the loan? $38,174.09

e. Construct a scatterplot using the data points (year, loan balance). See margin.

f. Write a linear regression equation that approximates the year/loan balance relationship. Round to the nearest hundredth. See margin.

g. Write a quadratic regression equation that approximates the year/loan balance relationship. Round to the nearest hundredth. See margin.

h. Write a cubic regression equation that approximates the year/loan balance relationship. Round to the nearest hundredth. $y = -2.81x^3 - 10.04x^2 - 857.63x + 35{,}147.55$

Life was a lot simpler when what we honored was father and mother rather than all major credit cards.

Robert Orben, American Comedy Writer

Credit Cards 4-4

Key Terms

- credit card
- impulse buying
- revolving charge account
- charge card
- Truth-in-Lending Act
- Fair Credit Billing Act
- Fair Debt Collection Practices Act
- debit card
- Electronic Funds Transfer Act
- average daily balance
- mean

Objectives

- Become familiar with the basic vocabulary of credit cards.
- Compute an average daily balance.

Common Core

N-Q1, N-Q2, A-SSE1

CCSS Warm-Up

A company has 50 employees. Forty earn $100 per day, and 10 earn $60 per day. What is the average daily salary of the 50 employees?

$92

What do I need to know to use credit cards?

Plastic credit cards were introduced in the 1950s. A **credit card** is a plastic card that entitles its holder to make purchases and pay for them later. The issuer of the card has given the person whose name is on the account a line of credit The account holder of a credit card has signed an agreement to pay for any purchase made using the card.

Credit cards are so prevalent today that they seem more popular than cash. Businesses that honor credit cards think that consumers spend more money when they just have to sign their names. It is mentally different than removing cash from your wallet when paying for something. The use of credit cards probably increases impulse buying. **Impulse buying** is when a consumer purchases something to which they suddenly were attracted to and had no intention of buying. The convenience of using credit cards also can attract new customers to stores that accept them. Consumers enjoy many advantages when using a credit card.

- There is no need to carry large sums of cash.
- Responsible use of a card helps a credit rating (FICO score).
- Customers receive or have access to a written record of all purchases.
- Some cards have rewards programs such as frequent flyer miles.

There are two types of credit card accounts. The most commonly used is the **revolving charge account**. This means that the entire bill does not have to be paid in full each month. There is a minimum monthly payment, and there is a finance charge the month following any month the bill is not paid in full. Customers have the convenience of stretching out payments over as many months as they choose. However, the interest costs for doing this are relatively high. Popular revolving charge accounts include Visa, MasterCard, American Express, and Discover Card.

EXAMINE THE QUESTION

Students have seen many people use credit cards in stores, but they know very little about the chain of events that using that card has started. They don't see people paying credit card bills, checking monthly statements, or dealing with problems. There is much more to using the cards than just saying, "Charge it!"

CLASS DISCUSSION

A charge card is a type of credit card. However, with a charge card, the credit is not extended over a long period of time.

Stores accept credit cards as a means to attract customers. Ask students how this would attract customers.

CLASS DISCUSSION

Students may inquire if it is possible to take a friend's card, use it extensively, and then have the friend report it lost, and only be responsible for $50. This is a crime, and with store video cameras always in use, it would be easy to get caught.

Ask students if any of them, or their older siblings, have debit cards.

A **charge card** is a special type of credit card. It allows the cardholder to make purchases in places that accept the card. The monthly bill for all purchases must be paid in full. There is no interest charged. Popular charge cards used today include Diner's Club and certain types of American Express cards. Most people informally use the words *charge card* and *credit card* interchangeably.

Using credit cards is both a convenience and a responsibility. There is a temptation to overspend, and the card also can be lost. The **Truth-in-Lending Act** protects you if your card is lost or stolen. If this happens, notify the creditor who issued the card immediately. You may be partially responsible for charges made by unauthorized users of cards you lose. The maximum liability is $50. You are not responsible for any charges that occur after you notify the creditor.

If the card number, and not the actual card, is stolen, you are not responsible for any purchases. It is the responsibility of the person selling the merchandise to make sure the purchaser is actually the card owner.

Cardholders receive a monthly statement of their purchases, and any payments they made to the creditor. The **Fair Credit Billing Act** protects you if there are any errors in your monthly statement.

It is your responsibility to notify the creditor about the error. You do not have to pay the amount that is disputed or any finance charge based on that amount, until the problem is cleared up.

If you find yourself unable to meet payments required by a creditor, notify that creditor immediately. The **Fair Debt Collection Practices Act** prohibits the creditor from harassing you or using unfair means to collect the amount owed. As you can see, you need to be knowledgeable to responsibly use credit and charge cards.

Another type of plastic card is known as a debit card. A **debit card** is not a credit or charge card, because there is no creditor extending credit. If you open a debit account, you deposit money into your account, and the debit card acts like an electronic check. You are deducting money directly from your account each time you make a purchase using the debit card.

You cannot make purchases that exceed the balance in your debit card account. Keeping a record of your debit card activity is exactly like keeping the check register you learned about in Lesson 3-1. The **Electronic Funds Transfer Act** protects debit card users against unauthorized use of their cards. They are not responsible for purchases made with a lost or stolen card after the card is reported missing.

Most debit cards carry the Visa or MasterCard logo and the holder can choose, at the time of a purchase, if the purchase acts as a debit card purchase or a credit card purchase. At some retailers, when you use a debit card you are charged a fee, similar to the fees charged at an ATM.

Skills and Strategies

Revolving credit cards can have high interest rates, so it is important to verify that the finance charge on your monthly statement is correct.

EXAMPLE 1

Frank lost his credit card in a local mall. He notified his creditor before the card was used. However, later in the day, someone found the card and charged $700 worth of hockey equipment on it. How much is Frank responsible for paying?

SOLUTION By the Truth in Lending Act, Frank is responsible for zero dollars, because he reported it lost before it was used.

■ CHECK YOUR UNDERSTANDING

Carrie's credit card was stolen. She didn't realize it for days, at which point she notified her creditor. During that time, someone charged $2,000. How much is Carrie responsible for paying?

EXAMPLE 2

Credit card companies issue a monthly statement, therefore APR (annual percentage rate) must be converted to a monthly percentage rate. If the APR is 21.6%, what is the monthly interest rate?

SOLUTION To change to a monthly interest rate, divide the APR by 12.

$$21.6 \div 12 = 1.8$$

The monthly APR is 1.8%. This is the percent that will be used to compute the monthly finance charge.

■ CHECK YOUR UNDERSTANDING

If a monthly statement shows a monthly interest rate of x percent, express the APR algebraically.

The **average daily balance** is the average of the amounts you owed each day of the billing period. It changes due to purchases made and payments made.

EXAMPLE 3

Rebecca did not pay last month's credit card bill in full. Below a list of Rebecca's daily balances for her last billing cycle.

For seven days she owed $456.11.
For three days she owed $1,177.60.
For six days she owed $990.08.
For nine days she owed $2,115.15.
For five days she owed $2,309.13.

Find Rebecca's average daily balance.

TEACH

Students will examine the average daily balance and its role in computing finance charges. Highlight the fact that interest rates are usually given as annual rates, and they need to compute a monthly rate to get the monthly finance charge.

In a month following a month in which the statement was paid in full, there is no finance charge. They can think of this as a no-interest loan—they got to pay for the items they bought a few weeks later, with no interest.

EXAMPLE 1

All computer cash registers record the time of the purchase, so it is easy for consumers to determine if they reported the call before or after the card was used.

CHECK YOUR UNDERSTANDING

Answer $50, the maximum liability under the Truth-in-Lending Act.

EXAMPLE 2

Credit card billing is usually done on a monthly basis.

CHECK YOUR UNDERSTANDING

Answer $12x$

EXAMPLE 3

If you purchased an item earlier in the billing cycle, you would have a higher average daily balance than if you purchased it later in the billing cycle. This fact actually drives when people make certain purchases.

CHECK YOUR UNDERSTANDING

Answer $\frac{6x + 12y + qw + 2d}{q + 20}$

EXAMPLE 4

Make sure students understand that if a bill is paid in full, there will be no finance charge the following month.

Also point out that the billing cycle months are not calendar months. Your bill is not a "January" bill; your billing cycle may go from January 11 through February 11.

CHECK YOUR UNDERSTANDING

Answer $\left(\frac{\frac{p}{100}}{12}\right)d$

Students often forget that they need to divide the percent by 100 because the percent sign is dropped in the algebraic expression.

SOLUTION The average daily balance is an arithmetic average. The arithmetic average is also called the **mean**. To find this average, you add the balances for the entire billing period, and divide by the number of days.

Add the number of days in the list to find the number of days in the cycle.

$$7 + 3 + 6 + 9 + 5 = 30$$

There were 30 days in Rebecca's billing cycle.

To find the sum of the daily balances, multiply the number of days by the amount owed. Then add these products.

7(456.11) =	3,192.77
3(1,177.60) =	3,532.80
6(990.08) =	5,940.48
9(2,115.15) =	19,036.35
5(2,309.13) =	11,545.65
Total	43,248.05

Divide the total by 30, and round to the nearest cent.

$$43{,}248.05 \div 30 \approx 1{,}441.60$$

The average daily balance is $1,441.60.

■ CHECK YOUR UNDERSTANDING

Last month, Paul had a daily balance of x dollars for 6 days, y dollars for 12 days, w dollars for q days, and d dollars for 2 days. Express the average daily balance algebraically.

Finance charges are not charged if, in the previous month, the revolving credit card bill was paid in full. If you pay your card in full every month, you will never pay a finance charge.

EXAMPLE 4

Rebecca (from Example 3) pays a finance charge on her average daily balance of $1,441.60. Her APR is 18%. What is her finance charge for this billing cycle?

SOLUTION Finance charges are computed monthly, so the 18% APR must be divided by 12 to get a monthly percentage rate of 1.5%. Take 1.5% of the average daily balance to get the finance charge.

Change 1.5% to an equivalent decimal, multiply, and round to the nearest cent.

$$0.015(1{,}441.60) \approx 21.62$$

The finance charge is $21.62.

■ CHECK YOUR UNDERSTANDING

Steve owes a finance charge this month because he didn't pay his bill in full last month. His average daily balance is d dollars and his APR is p percent. Express his finance charge algebraically.

Applications

Life was a lot simpler when what we honored was father and mother rather than all major credit cards.
Robert Orben, American Comedy Writer

1. Interpret the quote in the context of what you learned. See margin.
2. Janine's credit card was stolen, and the thief charged a $44 meal before she reported it stolen. How much of this is Janine responsible for paying? $44
3. Dan's credit card was lost on a vacation. He immediately reported it missing. The person who found it days later used it, and charged $$x$ worth of merchandise on the card, where $x > \$200$. How much of the $$x$ is Dan responsible for paying? $0
4. Felix and Oscar applied for the same credit card from the same bank. The bank checked both of their FICO scores. Felix had an excellent credit rating, and Oscar had a poor credit rating.
   a. Felix was given a card with an APR of 12%. What was his monthly percentage rate? 1%
   b. Oscar was given a card with an APR of 15%. What was his monthly percentage rate? 1.25%
   c. If each of them had an average daily balance of $800 and had to pay a finance charge, how much more would Oscar pay than Felix? $2
5. Vincent had these daily balances on his credit card for his last billing period. He did not pay the card in full the previous month, so he will have to pay a finance charge. The APR is 19.2%.

   nine days @ $778.12
   eight days @ $1,876.00
   four days @ $2,112.50
   ten days @ $1,544.31

   a. What is the average daily balance? $1,480.78
   b. What is the finance charge? $23.69
6. Express the average daily balance algebraically given this set of daily balances.

   x days @ y dollars w days @ d dollars
   r days @ q dollars m days @ p dollars $\frac{xy + wd + rq + mp}{x + w + r + m}$
7. Suzanne's average daily balance for last month was x dollars. The finance charge was y dollars.
   a. What was the monthly percentage rate? $\frac{y}{x}(100)$
   b. What was the APR? $\frac{12y}{x}(100)$
8. Jared's average daily balance for last month was $560. The finance charge was $8.12.
   a. What was the monthly percentage rate? 1.45%
   b. What was the APR? 17.4%

TEACH

Exercises 5 and 6
Exercise 5 will help students do the algebraic representation required for Exercise 6, if they are having trouble.

ANSWERS

1. The comedy writer is using the word "honor" as a pun. When a store honors a credit card, it just means they accept it as a means of payment. It is a different use of the word honor than the Ten Commandments used. Since using a credit card involves procedures and paperwork, he sees it as life getting less simple.

TEACH

Exercise 9

This exercise highlights the classic manipulation of the billing cycle. If they make a purchase right after the billing period ends, it will not appear on a statement for about a month.

Exercise 10

A debit card is not a loan, since you are taking money out of your own account. Although the plastic card and the purchase process seem similar, it is actually a very different process.

ANSWERS

10. a. $686.00
    b. $635.00
    c. $1,035.00
    d. $1,010.00
    e. $938.88
    f. $447.37

9. Helene's credit card has an APR of 16.8%. She never pays her balance in full, so she always pays a finance charge. Her next billing cycle starts today. The billing period is 30 days. Today's balance is $712.04. She is only going to use the credit card this month to make a $5,000 down payment on a new car.

a. If she puts the down payment on the credit card today, what will her daily balance be for each of the 30 days of the cycle? $5,712.04

b. Find her average daily balance for the 30-day period if she puts the down payment on the credit card today. $5,712.04

c. Find the finance charge for this billing period based on the average daily balance from part a. $79.97

d. Find her average daily balance for the 30-day period if she puts the down payment on the credit card on the last day of the billing cycle. $878.71

e. Find the finance charge on the average daily balance from part d. $12.30

f. How much can Helene save in finance charges if she makes the down payment on the last day, as compared to making it on the first day? $67.67

10. Gino has a debit card. The account pays no interest. He keeps track of his purchases and deposits in this debit card register. Find the missing entries a–f. See margin.

NUMBER OR CODE	DATE	TRANSACTION DESCRIPTION	PAYMENT AMOUNT	✓	FEE	DEPOSIT AMOUNT	$ BALANCE 778.19
	8/4	Baseball Bat	$ 92.19				92.19
							a.
	8/5	Gas	51.00				51.00
							b.
	8/7	Deposit				400.00	400.00
							c.
	8/7	Gas	25.00				25.00
							d.
	8/7	Dinner at Spooner's On the Beach	71.12				71.12
							e.
	8/11	Books for Fall Semester	491.51				491.51
							f.

11. Ron did not pay his credit card bill in full last month. He wants to pay it in full this month. On this month's bill, there is a mistake in the average daily balance. The credit card company lists the average daily balance on his bill as $510.50. Ron computed it himself and found that it is $410.50.

a. The APR is 18%. What finance charge did the credit card company compute on Ron's bill? $7.66

b. If Ron's average daily balance is correct, what should the finance charge be? $6.16

12. The terms of Medina's credit card state that the APR is 12.4%, and if a payment is not received by the due date, the APR will increase by w%. The credit card company received Medina's payment three days after the due date in February. Write the interest rate, in decimal form that she will be charged in March, assuming she carried a balance from February. $0.124 + 0.01w$

13. Express the missing entries in the debit card register algebraically. See margin.

NUMBER OR CODE	DATE	TRANSACTION DESCRIPTION	PAYMENT AMOUNT	✓	FEE	DEPOSIT AMOUNT	$ BALANCE
							m
	12/3	Arloff's Gifts	$ x				a.
	12/6	Bonnie's Boutique	z				b.
	12/7	Gas	y				c.
	12/11	Cable TV	v				d.
	12/12	Deposit				r	e.
	12/14	Gas	g				f.

14. Jill's credit card was stolen. The thief charged a $900 kayak on the card before she reported it stolen.

a. How much of the thief's purchase is Jill responsible for? $50

b. Jill's average daily balance would have been $1,240 without the thief's purchase. What was the sum of her daily balances for the 30-day billing period? Explain. See margin.

c. The thief's purchase was on her daily balances for 10 out of the 30 days during the billing cycle. What was the sum of Jill's daily balances with the thief's purchase included? $46,200

d. What was the average daily balance with the thief's purchase included? $1,540

15. Kristin's credit rating was lowered, and the credit card company raised her APR from 12% to 13.2%. If her average daily balance this month is x dollars, express algebraically the increase in this month's finance charge due to the higher APR. $0.001x$

16. It is important to check your credit card bill each month. In the next lesson, you will carefully examine a credit card statement and learn how to look for errors. Most people would notice a major, expensive purchase that they did not make. A smaller, incorrect charge of $6 for example, might go unnoticed unless the entire statement was checked with a calculator. If one million credit card holders were each over-charged $6 each month for five years, what would be the total amount that debtors were overcharged, not including the extra finance charges? $360 million

17. Naoko has these daily balances on his credit card for September's billing period. He paid his balance from the August billing in full.

two days @ $99.78
fifteen days @ $315.64
eleven days @ $515.64
two days @ $580.32

a. His APR is 15.4%. How much is the finance charge on his September bill? $0

b. Does the credit card company need to calculate his average daily balance? Explain. See margin.

c. Naoko calculated his average daily balance to be $377.85. Is he correct? If not, what was his average daily balance? no; $392.23

d. What mistake did Naoko make when calculating this average daily balance? See margin.

ANSWERS

13. a. $m - x$
b. $m - x - z$
c. $m - x - z - y$
d. $m - x - z - y - v$
e. $m - x - z - y - v + r$
f. $m - x - z - y - v + r - g$

14b. $37,200; multiply the average by the number of days.

17b. Because Naoko paid his balance in full, there will be no finance charges. The average daily balance is used to calculate finance charges, so the average daily balance will not be needed.

17d. He only added the given balances and divided by 5, instead of multiplying the balances by the number of days before adding.

Credit card companies pay college students generously to stand outside dining halls, dorms, and academic buildings and encourage their fellow students to apply for credit cards.

Louise Slaughter, American Congresswoman

4-5 Credit Card Statement

Objectives

- Identify and use the various entries in a credit card statement.

Common Core

N-Q1, A-SSE1

Key Terms

- billing cycle
- credit card statement
- account number
- credit line
- available credit
- billing date
- payment due date
- transactions
- debit/credit
- previous balance
- payments/credits
- new purchases
- late charge
- finance charge
- new balance
- minimum payment
- average daily balance
- number of days in billing cycle
- APR
- monthly periodic rate

CCSS Warm-Up

Solve each literal equation for *x*.

Express 15% of the difference between x and y algebraically.

$0.15|x - y|$

EXAMINE THE QUESTION

Most students have never seen a credit card statement so the answer to this question will evolve as the lesson progresses. Ask them what information they might find useful on a credit card statement at the end of a monthly cycle. Keep their responses at hand so that you can compare them with the actual information contained on the statement.

CLASS DISCUSSION

After reading the introductory material, ask students how the credit card company might benefit from a shorter billing cycle for a college student who has yet to establish a credit track record.

Discuss possible errors that a credit card user might find on the credit card statement. For example, double charging for a single purchase, failure to post a credit, transposition of digits in a purchase, or posting of an incorrect amount.

Have students research how they can establish credit responsibly.

What information does a credit card statement give you?

Credit cards can be used when making purchases in person, by mail, by phone, online, and more. In most situations you get a receipt for each transaction, but it can be difficult to keep track of the transactions over a billing cycle.

A **billing cycle** is a predetermined amount of time set by the credit card company that is used for calculating your credit card bill. This cycle can be adjusted by the company based upon your credit worthiness. For example, a college student with little or no track record of being able to keep up credit card payments may initially be given a 21-day billing cycle. A seasoned credit card holder who has proven to be financially responsible might get a longer billing cycle.

At the end of every cycle, the credit card company takes an accounting of your credits and debits and sends you that information in the form of a **credit card statement**. You should read the statement carefully and verify the charges. All credit card companies have a process through which the credit card holder can dispute errors on the statement.

Jane Sharp has a FlashCard revolving credit card. At the end of a 30-day cycle, Jane receives her FlashCard statement listing all of her purchases and the payments the company has received during that 30-day cycle. Jane's credit card statement is shown on the next page.

Locate each of the terms explained below on Jane's statement.

Jane Sharp							25 Main Street Sunrise, NY
ACCOUNT INFORMATION							
Account Number 2653 8987 6098				Billing Date 23 Jan		**Payment Due** 2 Feb	
TRANSACTIONS						DEBITS / CREDITS (−)	
2 Jan	Candida's Gift Shop					$75.00	
3 Jan	Skizza's Pizzas					$31.85	
5 Jan	Beekman Department Store					$139.10	
10 Jan	Festival Book Store					$38.50	
21 Jan	Payment					−$75.00	
SUMMARY	Previous Balance	Payments / Credits	New Purchases	Late Charge	Finance Charge	New Balance	**Minimum Payment**
	$150.50	$75.00	$284.45	$0.00	$3.53	$363.48	$20.00
Total Credit Line $ 8,000.00 Total Available Credit $ 7,636.52				Average Daily Balance	# Days in Billing Cycle	APR	Monthly Periodic Rate
				$235.10	30	18%	1.5%

- **Account Number** Each credit card account has a unique number.
- **Credit Line** The maximum amount you can owe at any time.
- **Available Credit** The difference between the maximum amount you can owe and the actual amount you owe.
- **Billing Date** The date the bill (statement) was written.
- **Payment Due Date** On this date the monthly payment must be received by the creditor.
- **Transactions** Lists where purchases were made and the date. Some companies use the date posted, which indicates when the creditor received its notification of the charge and processed it. Some companies list the date of transaction, which shows when purchases were made or payments were received. Some companies list both the posted and the transaction dates.
- **Debits/Credits** A debit is the amount charged to your account. A credit is a payment made to reduce your debt. Credits are identified by a negative (−) sign.
- **Previous Balance** Any money owed before current billing period.
- **Payments/Credits** Total amount received by the creditor.
- **New Purchases** The sum of purchases (debits) on the current bill.
- **Late Charge** The penalty for late payments from a previous month.
- **Finance Charge** The cost of using the credit card for the current billing period.
- **New Balance** The amount you currently owe.
- **Minimum Payment** This amount is the lowest payment the credit card company will accept for the current billing period.
- **Average Daily Balance** The average amount owed per day during the billing cycle.
- **Number of Days in Billing Cycle** The amount of time, in days, covered by the current bill.
- **APR** The yearly interest rate.
- **Monthly Periodic Rate** The APR divided by 12.

CLASS DISCUSSION

The list of terms included here may seem overwhelming to students. Take your time when explaining them. They are critical to the understanding of all component parts of the credit card process.

Emphasize that it is important to know what the date on your statement refers to.

TEACH

Display a list of the terms introduced in this lesson. Ask students to write as many definitions as they are able with the current knowledge that they already have about credit. Use their definitions as a springboard to giving more precise meanings to the terms.

EXAMPLE 1

This problem begins the unwrapping process that will help students understand how a credit card statement is built. The "New Purchases" is the sum of the purchases made during the cycle. A number of things contribute to the "New Balance." If there is a carryover balance from the previous month, begin with that amount. Note that the carryover balance necessitates a finance charge. If there is no carryover balance there will be no finance charge calculated on the new purchases for that cycle. A late charge is added if the payment from the last cycle arrives to the creditor late. You might want to discuss the benefits of online payments in avoiding late charges.

CHECK YOUR UNDERSTANDING

Answer =A2–B2+C2+D2+E2

If there is no entry in any cell, the spreadsheet will use a zero amount in the calculation.

Skills and Strategies

Here you will learn how to read and verify entries on a credit card statement.

EXAMPLE 1

The summary portion of Jane Sharp's credit card statement shown on the previous page looks as follows:

SUMMARY	Previous Balance	Payments / Credits	New Purchases	Late Charge	Finance Charge	New Balance	**Minimum Payment**
	$150.50	$75.00	$284.45	$0.00	$3.53	$363.48	$20.00

a. Explain how the new purchases amount was determined.
b. Explain how the new balance amount was determined.

SOLUTION

a. The new purchases amount is the sum of the purchases that appear as debits. This sum must equal the amount $284.45 listed in the New Purchases section of the statement summary.

ACCOUNT INFORMATION			
Account Number 2653 8987 6098		Billing Date 23 Jan	**Payment Due** 2 Feb
TRANSACTIONS			DEBITS / CREDITS (−)
2 Jan	Candida's Gift Shop		$75.00
3 Jan	Skizza's Pizzas		$31.85
5 Jan	Beekman Department Store		$139.10
10 Jan	Festival Book Store		$38.50
21 Jan	Payment		−$75.00

New purchases = 75 + 31.85 + 139.10 + 38.50 = 284.45

b. The new balance amount is determined by using the formula given below.

Previous Balance	−	Payments	+	New Purchases	+	Finance Charge	+	Late Charge	=	New Balance
150.50	−	75	+	284.45	+	3.53	+	0	=	363.48

CHECK YOUR UNDERSTANDING

Suppose you create the following spreadsheet that models the statement summary and input the values in row 2. Write the spreadsheet formula to compute the new balance in cell F2.

	A	B	C	D	E	F
1	**Previous Balance**	**Payments**	**New Purchases**	**Late Charge**	**Finance Charge**	**New Balance**
2						

EXAMPLE 2

Pascual has a credit line of $15,000 on his credit card. His summary looks as follows. How much available credit does Pascual have?

SUMMARY	Previous Balance	Payments / Credits	New Purchases	Late Charge	Finance Charge
	$4,598.12	$4,000.00	$1,368.55	$20.00	$5.78

SOLUTION Pascual needs to determine his new balance and then subtract that from his credit line in order to find his available credit.

$$4{,}598.12 - 4{,}000.00 + 1{,}368.55 + 20.00 + 5.78 = 1{,}992.45$$

He has a new balance of $1,992.45. Subtracting this from his credit line of $15,000 leaves him with an available credit of $13,007.55.

■ CHECK YOUR UNDERSTANDING

Rhonda had a previous balance of $567.91 and made an on-time credit card payment of $567.91. She has a credit line of x dollars and made purchases totaling y dollars. Write an algebraic expression that represents her current available credit.

EXAMPLE 3

Myrna is examining the summary section of her credit card statement. Myrna has checked all the entries on her bill and agrees with everything except the new balance. Determine where the error was made.

SUMMARY	Previous Balance	Payments / Credits	New Purchases	Late Charge	Finance Charge	New Balance
	$1,748.00	$100.00	$800.00	$9.15	$19.00	$2,576.15

SOLUTION Add the amounts that show money Myrna must pay to the credit card company.

$1,748.00	previous balance
800.00	purchases
9.15	finance charge
+ 19.00	late charge
$2,576.15	total to be paid

Subtract the $100 payment, and Myrna's new balance will be $2,476.15. It appears that Myrna was not credited for her payment. Under the Fair Credit Billing Act, Myrna must notify her creditor in writing within 60 days from the statement date on her bill.

■ CHECK YOUR UNDERSTANDING

Determine the error that was made using the following summary statement.

SUMMARY	Previous Balance	Payments / Credits	New Purchases
	$850.00	$560.00	$300.00
	Late Charge	**Finance Charge**	**New Balance**
	$3.00	$4.78	$507.78

EXAMPLE 2

Since a credit line is the maximum amount that a creditor is willing to lend, the available credit is the amount available to the creditor after the debits have been subtracted from the credit line.

CHECK YOUR UNDERSTANDING

Answer $x - y$

Students can use Example 2 as a guide to find the solution.

EXAMPLE 3

This problem offers students an excellent example of why every credit card statement must be checked for accuracy. Initially, it looks as if the statement is correct since the total to be paid and the new balance listed on the statement match. But, the $100 payment has not been credited to the account. Therefore, the actual new balance should be $100 less than stated. Discuss the Fair Credit Billing Act as a means of protecting consumers from these types of errors.

Explain to students that fax transmission and emails are not acceptable as written notification of an error on a bill.

CHECK YOUR UNDERSTANDING

Answer The new balance should be $597.78. It appears that the payment of $560 was recorded as $650.

Applications

Credit card companies pay college students generously to stand outside dining halls, dorms, and academic buildings and encourage their fellow students to apply for credits cards.
Louise Slaughter, American Congresswoman

TEACH

Have students work on Exercises 2–7 with a partner or in a small group. Walk around the room listening to the discussion that ensues. Misconceptions about terms and procedures may surface that you will need to address before assigning any further exercises.

Exercises 2–7

Exercises 2–7 led students through the completion of the statement through a guided approach. An incorrect answer in the early stages here could affect the subsequent answers.

ANSWERS

1. Students are targeted by credit card companies at colleges. The companies use their peers to get them to sign a contract. She wants everyone to be aware that this is advertising at its finest!

1. How might the quote apply to what you have learned? See margin.

Use the FlashCard statement to answer Exercises 2–7.

ACCOUNT INFORMATION							
Account Number		4-10700000		Billing Date	30 May	**Payment Due**	8 Jun
TRANSACTIONS						DEBITS / CREDITS (−)	
9 MAY	3291684271 Fanelli Furs						$975.00
12 MAY	594683219 Brooklyn Pets						$32.50
15 MAY	7677095385 Maple Garage						$178.21
18 MAY	8765713281 PAYMENT						−$150.00
21 MAY	321447162 Caruso's Restaurant						$41.53
SUMMARY	Previous Balance	Payments / Credits	New Purchases	Late Charge	Finance Charge	New Balance	**Minimum Payment**
	$420.50	$150.00	$1,227.24	$0.00	$19.80	$1,517.54	$30.00
Total Credit Line	$ 3,000.00			Average Daily Balance	# Days in Billing Cycle	APR	Monthly Periodic Rate
Total Available Credit	$ 1,661.51			$1,199.97	30	19.8%	1.65%

2. How many purchases were made during the billing cycle? 4

3. What is the sum of all purchases made during the billing cycle? $1,227.24

4. When is the payment for this statement due? June 8

5. What is the minimum amount that can be paid? $30

6. How many days are in the billing cycle? 30

7. What is the previous balance? $420.50

8. Rollie has a credit card with a line of credit at $4,000. He made the following purchases: $425.36, $358.33, $377.11, and $90.20. What is Rollie's available credit? $2,749

9. Rebecca has a credit line of $6,500 on her credit card. She had a previous balance of $398.54 and made a $250 payment. The total of her purchases is $1,257.89. What is Rebecca's available credit? $5,093.57

10. The APR on Leslie's credit card is currently 21.6%. What is the monthly periodic rate? 1.8%

11. Sheldon's monthly periodic rate is 1.95%. What is the APR? 23.4%

12. Zea has a credit limit of $2,000 on her credit card. Each month, she charges about $200 and makes a payment of $125.

a. Estimate the number of months that Zea can continue this pattern until she reaches her credit limit. 27

b. Consider that part of the $125 Zea pays each month will be for finance charges. How will the number of months from part a be affected by these charges? The number of months will be less than 27.

13. Examine this portion of the credit card summary.

Average Daily Balance	# Days in Billing Cycle	APR
W	*X*	*Y* %

a. Express the sum of the cycle's daily balances algebraically. *WX*

b. Express the monthly periodic rate as an equivalent decimal without the % symbol. $\frac{\frac{Y}{12}}{100}$

14. Fill in the missing amounts for a–d.

ACCOUNT INFORMATION							
Type Revolving		Account Number 234 98765 90		Billing Date 16 Aug		**Payment Due Date** 1 Sep	
TRANSACTIONS						DEBITS / CREDITS (−)	
6 AUG	Meghan's Shop					$85.63	
7 AUG	Payment					−$63.00	
8 AUG	Joe's Italian Restaurant					$47.60	
10 AUG	University of New York					$855.00	
15 AUG	SkyHigh Airlines					$370.50	
16 AUG	Payment					−$137.00	
SUMMARY	Previous Balance	Payments / Credits	New Purchases	Late Charge	Finance Charge	New Balance	**Minimum Payment**
	$215.88	**b.**	**c.**	$0.00	$6.70	**d.**	$25.00
Total Credit Line		$ 5,000.00		Average Daily Balance	# Days in Billing Cycle	APR	Monthly Periodic Rate
Total Available Credit		**a.**		$446.41	30	18%	1.5%

a. $3,618.69; b. $200.00; c. $1,358.73; d. $1,381.31

15. Examine the summary section of the monthly credit card statement below. Use the first five entries to determine whether the new balance is correct. If it is incorrect, write the correct amount.
It is incorrect; the correct new balance is 388.01.

SUMMARY	Previous Balance	Payments / Credits	New Purchases	Late Charge	Finance Charge	New Balance	**Minimum Payment**
	$359.02	$80.00	$103.65	$0.00	$5.34	$548.01	$18.00

16. Check the new balance entry on the monthly statement below by using the first five entries. If the new balance is incorrect, write the correct amount. It is correct.

SUMMARY	Previous Balance	Payments / Credits	New Purchases	Late Charge	Finance Charge	New Balance	**Minimum Payment**
	$424.41	$104.41	$103.38	$23.00	$7.77	$454.15	$54.00

17. A credit card statement is modeled using the following spreadsheet. Entries are made in columns A–F. Write the formula to calculate the available credit in cell G2. =F2−(A2−B2+C2+D2+E2)

	A	B	C	D	E	F	G
1	**Previous Balance**	**Payments**	**New Purchases**	**Late Charge**	**Finance Charge**	**Credit Line**	**Available Credit**
2							

18. Determine the amount of the payment made on this credit card. $250

SUMMARY	Previous Balance	Payments / Credits	New Purchases	Late Charge	Finance Charge	New Balance	**Minimum Payment**
	$939.81		$125.25	$3.00	$15.38	$833.44	$25.00

19. The previous balance after the last billing cycle is represented by *A*, recent purchases by *B*, payments by *C*, finance charge by *D*, late charge by *E*. Express the relationship among the variables that must be true in order for the new balance to be zero. $A + B + D + E = C$

TEACH

Exercises 14–18
This cluster of Exercises focuses on the summary section of the credit card statement. Consider completing Exercise 13 with the entire class before assigning the remaining problems.

14. Note that parts b–d must be completed before part a.

The best way to deal with credit card debt is to educate yourself.
Mark Rosen, Author

4-6 Average Daily Balance

Objectives

- Calculate the average daily balance using the credit calendar.
- Calculate the finance charge using the credit calendar.

Common Core

N-Q1, A-SSE1

Key Terms
- average daily balance
- credit calendar
- billing date

CCSS Warm-Up

The scores 4, 6, x, 8, 10 are written in ascending order. Find the value of x if the mean of the set equals the median.

$y = 7$

EXAMINE THE QUESTION

In this lesson, students will learn how the average daily balance is determined and then used in the calculation of a finance charge.

CLASS DISCUSSION

Make an overhead transparency of the "Terms and Conditions" section of a cardholder agreement. Students will be able to see why many card holders skip this information. Look for portions where "average daily balance" or "daily balance" are mentioned.

How are the entries on the monthly statement calculated?

Credit card users who do not pay their bills in full are charged a finance charge for the convenience of extra payment time. The finance charge is computed on any statement in which the consumer has a previous unpaid balance.

The charge is based on the average amount the consumer owed each day of the billing cycle. This average is the **average daily balance**. It is used with the monthly periodic rate to determine the finance charge. Billing cycles and interest rates differ from card to card and from user to user with the same credit card.

Skills and Strategies

Here you will learn how to calculate the average daily balance using a credit card billing calendar, often called a **credit calendar**.

Elena Kaye

44 Central Avenue
Onesburg, TX

ACCOUNT INFORMATION							
Account Number		07-3458-1299	Billing Date	13 Nov	**Payment Due**	5 Dec	
TRANSACTIONS					DEBITS / CREDITS (−)		
25 Oct	House Depot				$67.00		
29 Oct	Bubble Wrap Shipping Co.				$55.00		
5 Nov	Payment				−$160.00		
SUMMARY	Previous Balance	Payments / Credits	New Purchases	Late Charge	Finance Charge	New Balance	**Minimum Payment**
	$829.30	$160.00	$122.00	$0.00	$12.09	$803.39	$59.00
Total Credit Line Total Available Credit		$ 3,000.00 $ 2,196.61		Average Daily Balance	# Days in Billing Cycle	APR	Monthly Periodic Rate
				854.46	31	16.98%	1.415%

EXAMPLE 1

Use the information given in Elena Kaye's credit card statement to verify the accuracy of her average daily balance.

SOLUTION Carefully follow Steps 1–8.

Step 1 On a blank sheet of paper, draw a grid that has 7 boxes across and 5 boxes down. Draw an arc in each corner.

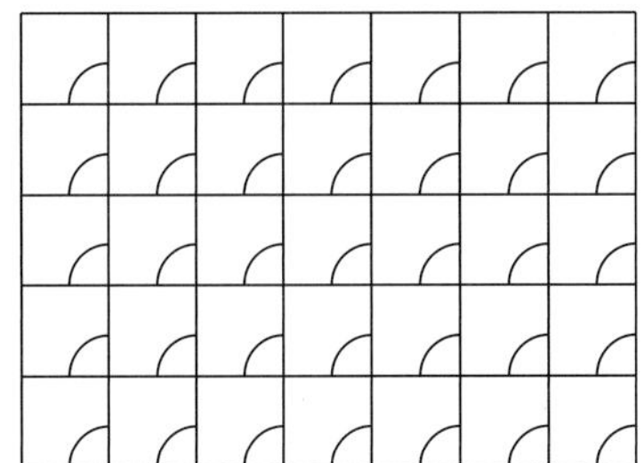

Step 2 On Elena's statement you can find that the number of days in the billing cycle is 31 days. Shade in the last 4 days that will not be used.

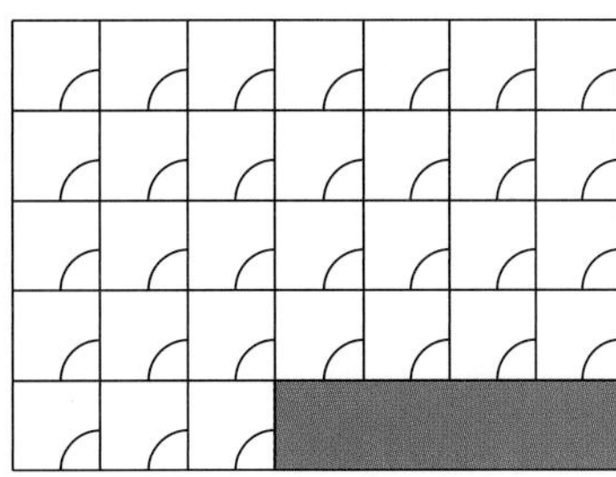

OCT. 14	15	16	17	18	19	20
21	22	23	24	25	26	27
28	29	30	31	NOV. 1	2	3
4	5	6	7	8	9	10
11	12	13				

Step 3 Enter the **billing date**, 11/13, in the corner section of the last day on the calendar. Number the days back from that date until the calendar is completely filled in. Notice that although the billing date is in November, the billing cycle includes some days from October. Enter the month of the first date in your calendar and the month of the first day of the next month.

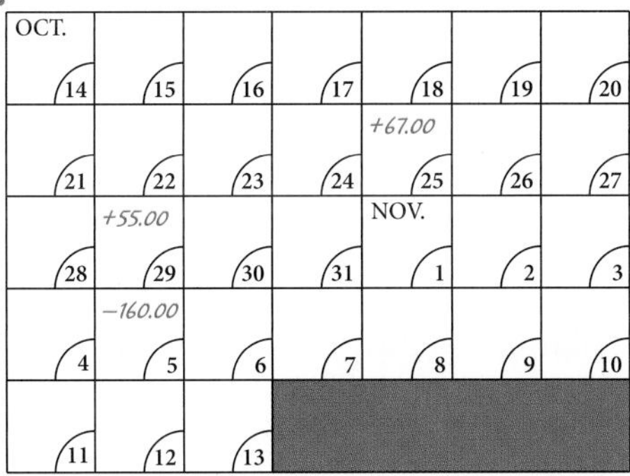

Step 4 Look at the posted dates of each of the charges (debits). Put a plus sign (+) and the charged amount on the calendar dates that have debits posted. Next look at the posted date of the payment made. Put a minus sign (−) and the payment made on that calendar date.

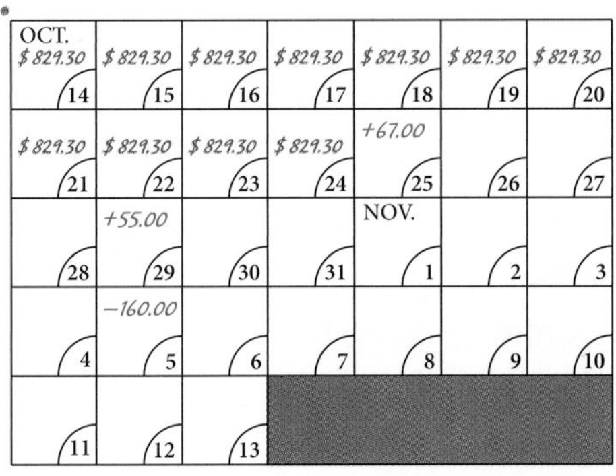

OCT.
$829.30
+67.00
+55.00
NOV.
−160.00

Step 5 The first day of the billing cycle is October 14. The previous balance of $829.30 is the amount Elena owed on October 14. Enter that balance on October 14. Notice that Elena made no purchases or payments until October 25, so on each day from October 14 to October 24, the daily balance is $829.30. Enter this number on each of these dates.

EXAMPLE 1

Work through this example using an overhead projector or some other form of projection device.

Distribute copies of the blank credit calendar which can be found at www.cengage.com/school/math/financialalgebra and project it for students to see. Carefully work through each of the steps with students. As you mark the template, they should be doing the same with their own copy.

CHECK YOUR UNDERSTANDING

Answer Students should understand that the closer the payment is made to the beginning of the cycle, the lower the average daily balance will be.

EXAMPLE 2

Some credit card statements include the monthly periodic rate while others do not. If the rate is missing, it is necessary for students to calculate the MPR by dividing the APR by 12. Then, express the MPR as an equivalent decimal and multiply that amount times the average daily balance.

CHECK YOUR UNDERSTANDING

Answer The later in the billing cycle purchases are made, the lower the average daily balance, which results in a lower finance charge.

Step 6 A $67.00 purchase was made on October 25. The amount Elena owes on October 25 is increased by $67.00. The amount owed from October 25 to October 28 is $896.30.

OCT. $829.30 14	$829.30 15	$829.30 16	$829.30 17	$829.30 18	$829.30 19	$829.30 20
$829.30 21	$829.30 22	$829.30 23	$829.30 24	+67.00 $896.30 25	$896.30 26	$896.30 27
$896.30 28	+55.00 29	30	31	NOV. 1	2	3
4	−160.00 5	6	7	8	9	10
11	12	13				

Step 7 A $55.00 purchase was made on October 29, and a payment of $160.00 was made on November 5. The purchase must be added to the daily balance of October 28, and the payment must be subtracted from the daily balance of November 4. There are no other transactions, so continue the daily balance amount through to the end of the billing cycle.

OCT. $829.30 14	$829.30 15	$829.30 16	$829.30 17	$829.30 18	$829.30 19	$829.30 20
$829.30 21	$829.30 22	$829.30 23	$829.30 24	+67.00 $896.30 25	$896.30 26	$896.30 27
$896.30 28	+55.00 $951.30 29	$951.30 30	$951.30 31	NOV. $951.30 1	$951.30 2	$951.30 3
$951.30 4	−160.00 $791.30 5	$791.30 6	$791.30 7	$791.30 8	$791.30 9	$791.30 10
$791.30 11	$791.30 12	$791.30 13				

Step 8 To find the average daily balance, add all the daily balances and divide by the number of days in the billing cycle, 31. The sum of the daily balances is $26,488.30. Divide that sum by 31.

$$26{,}488.30 \div 31 = 854.46$$

The average daily balance is $854.46.

■ CHECK YOUR UNDERSTANDING

Is there a better time during the billing cycle when Elena could have made her payment so that the average daily balance would have been less?

EXAMPLE 2

Determine the finance charge for Elena's billing cycle.

SOLUTION Once the average daily balance is computed using the calendar, find the finance charge using the average daily balance and the monthly periodic rate.

Balance × monthly periodic rate	854.46 × 1.415%
Express rate as a decimal.	854.46 × 0.01415
Simplify and round.	12.09

Her finance charge is $12.09.

■ CHECK YOUR UNDERSTANDING

When might Elena have made her purchases during the billing cycle in order to decrease her finance charge?

Applications

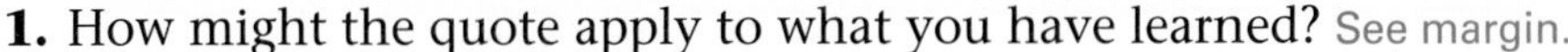

The best way to deal with credit card debt is to educate yourself.

Mark Rosen, Author

1. How might the quote apply to what you have learned? See margin.
2. Ralph just received his June FlashCard bill. He did not pay his May bill in full, so his June bill shows a previous balance and a finance charge. The average daily balance is $470, and the monthly periodic rate is 1.5%. What should Ralph's finance charge be? $7.05
3. Lauren did not pay her January FlashCard bill in full, so her February bill has a finance charge added on. The average daily balance is $510.44, and the monthly periodic rate is 2.5%. What should Lauren's finance charge be on her February statement? $12.76
4. Jennifer did not pay her FlashCard bill in full in September. Her October bill showed a finance charge, and she wants to see whether or not it is correct. The average daily balance is $970.50, and the APR is 28.2%. Find the finance charge for her October statement. $22.81
5. Daniyar paid his April FlashCard bill in full. His May bill shows an average daily balance of $270.31 and a monthly periodic rate of 1.95%. What is the finance charge on Daniyar's May statement? $0
6. Use Mark Gilley's FlashCard statement. There is an error in his bill. The average daily balance, finance charge, available credit, and new balance amounts are not filled in. You can find a copy of the blank calendar at www.cengage.com/school/math/financialalgebra.
   a. What is Mark's average daily balance? $999.81
   b. What is Mark's finance charge? $15.00
   c. What is Mark's new balance? $957.00
   d. What is Mark's available credit? $5,043.00
   e. If the $200 payment had been posted on 6/13, would Mark's finance charge for this billing cycle have been higher or lower? Lower; the average daily balance would be lower.
7. After Wade paid his May credit card bill, he still had a balance of z dollars. He made no additional payments or purchases before he received his next bill. The monthly periodic rate on this account is 2.015%. What expression represents the finance charge on his June statement? $0.02015z$

Mark Gilley — 700 West Street, Maintown, FL

ACCOUNT INFORMATION							
Account Number		7-6231-491	Billing Date	26 Jun		**Payment Due**	10 Jul
TRANSACTIONS						DEBITS / CREDITS (−)	
31 May	63214987261 Linda's Art Shop					$251.00	
12 Jun	62115497621 Artisign's Inc.					$72.50	
18 Jun	73216532116 Payment Thank you					−$200.00	
20 Jun	73162225142 Sylvart Corp.					$18.50	
SUMMARY	Previous Balance	Payments / Credits	New Purchases	Late Charge	Finance Charge	New Balance	**Minimum Payment**
	$800.00	$200.00	$342.00	$0.00			$25.00
Total Credit Line		$ 6,000.00		Average Daily Balance	# Days in Billing Cycle	APR	Monthly Periodic Rate
Total Available Credit					31	18%	1.5%

TEACH

Exercises 2–4
It is important that students understand the effect that a partial payment has on the following month's bill. Address this before assigning these exercises.

Exercise 5
Since a complete payment was made the prior month, it is not necessary to make any calculations. There will be no finance charge.

Exercise 6
Extend this exercise by having students develop a credit card statement that contains one or more errors. Once completed, they can switch with a partner and find the errors.

ANSWERS

1. The quote is a warning about loans and debts. Entering into any debt agreement should be made cautiously.

TEACH

Exercise 7

This exercise requires students to construct and use a credit calendar. Make sure that they understand the need to alter the calendar depending upon the number of days in the cycle. They also need to "date backwards" starting from the billing date listed in the statement. A reminder as to the number of days in a given month may be needed.

Exercise 8

This exercise extends the concepts learned in this lesson so that students can model the credit calendar process algebraically. Do not assign this problem until you are sure that students correctly answered Exercise 7. They should be encouraged to model the solution to this problem after the one in Exercise 7.

ANSWERS

9d. $7Y + 5(Y + X) + 7(Y + X - Z) + 2(Y + X - Z + W)$

9e. $\dfrac{(7Y + 5(Y + X) + 7(Y + X - Z) + 2(Y + X - Z + W))}{21}$

8. Ed Lubbock's FlashCard bill is below. There are entries missing.

Ed Lubbock — 1234 Algebra Street, Euclid, WA

ACCOUNT INFORMATION					
Account Number	7-6234712	Billing Date	10 Dec	**Payment Due**	21 Dec

TRANSACTIONS			DEBITS / CREDITS (−)
24 NOV	632174293	Rusty's Rib Palace	$48.00
1 DEC	321446253	Payment	−$100.00
6 DEC	333261114	Petrela Sailboats	$30.00

SUMMARY	Previous Balance	Payments / Credits	New Purchases	Late Charge	Finance Charge	New Balance	**Minimum Payment**
	$421.50	$100.00	$78.00				$30.00
Total Credit Line / Total Available Credit	$ 1,000.00			Average Daily Balance	# Days in Billing Cycle	APR	Monthly Periodic Rate
					30	19.8%	1.65%

a. What is Ed's average daily balance? $420.37

b. What is Ed's finance charge? $6.94

c. What is Ed's new balance? $406.44

d. What is Ed's available credit? $593.56

e. If the $30 charge to Petrela Sailboats had been posted on 12/9, would the finance charge be higher or lower for this billing cycle? Explain. lower; the average daily balance is lower.

9. Examine the following 21-day credit calendar. The opening balance is Y dollars. On March 23, a purchase of X dollars was made. On March 28, a payment of Z dollars was made. On April 4, a purchase of W dollars was made.

MARCH Y 16	Y 17	Y 18	Y 19	Y 20	Y 21	Y 22
Y + X 23	24	25	26	27	− Z 28	29
30	31	APRIL 1	2	3	+ W 4	5
6	7	8	9	10	11	12
13	14	15	16	17	18	19

a. What is the algebraic expression for the daily balance on March 23? Write it in on that date and on March 24–27. $Y + X$

b. What is the algebraic expression for the daily balance on March 28 after the payment is made? Write it in on that date and on March 29 to April 3. $Y + X - Z$

c. What is the algebraic expression that represents the daily balance on April 4 after the purchase is made? Write it in on that date and on April 5. $Y + X - Z + W$

d. Write the algebraic expression for the sum of the daily balances. See margin.

e. What is the algebraic expression for the average daily balance? See margin.

CHAPTER 4

Assessment

Real Numbers

You Write the Story!!

FICO scores are measures of your credit risk to a potential creditor. The graph gives the weighted contribution of several factors that affect your credit rating. The Fair Isaac Corporation, the creators of the FICO score, keeps their formulas for computing the scores a secret. Write a short newspaper-type article centered on the circle graph. You can find a copy of this graph at www.cengage.com/school/math/financialalgebra. Copy and paste it into your article.

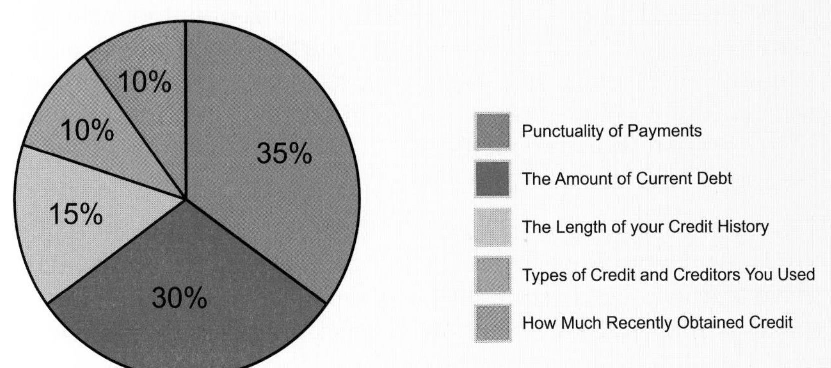

CHAPTER 4 ASSESSMENT

REAL NUMBERS

You Write the Story
Encourage students to do a web search on FICO scores before writing the story. They will notice that the actual formula used to calculate the scores is never stated. The only information given is the percent contributions as depicted in the graph.

ANSWER

Answers vary. The FICO score places a large emphasis on the debtor's ability to pay on time. This comprises 35% of the FICO score. The second most important factor is the amount of money the debtor currently owes. This obviously has an affect on their ability to continue to use credit. This represents 30% of the FICO score. The third most important factor is the length of the debtor's credit history. A long credit history gives the potential creditor lots of information on your payment behavior. This counts as 15%. The last two factors count 10% each. Types of credit include what types of credit the debtor has—installment loans, credit cards, bank loans, and so on. Recently obtained credit gives the creditor your recent financial activity.

Reality Check

1. There are six laws that regulate consumer credit in the United States. Find when each act was signed into law. What problem was the act trying to help solve? What are the major provisions of each act? Prepare a poster displaying your findings. The laws are listed below.
   - Equal Credit Opportunity Act
   - Electronic Funds Transfer Act
   - Fair Credit Reporting Act
   - Fair Credit Billing Act
   - Fair Debt Collection Practices Act
   - Truth-in-Lending Act
2. Visit two lending institutions in your area. Find the APR, monthly payment, and finance charge for a $15,000, three-year loan at the two lenders. Prepare a poster that includes a business card from each lender and the following mathematical information for the loan.
   - APR
   - monthly payment
   - total of all monthly payments
   - finance charge

REALITY CHECK

The Reality Check projects are excellent opportunities for alternative assessments. They give students an additional avenue to show what they have learned, so their grades are not solely based on tests.

The Reality Check projects in this lesson ask students to do research, go to a lending institution and gather current information, do online searches for credit protection agencies, invite guest speakers into the classroom to make presentations, interview parents/friends about their credit experiences, and more. Each project is designed so that students can use what they have learned in this chapter as a springboard for further investigation.

3. Go online and find information on the FICO score. What is the range of possible scores? How can each score be interpreted? What contributes to the FICO score? Summarize the information you find from the websites. Prepare your information in a report.

4. There are three major credit reporting agencies in the United States. They are named Equifax, Experian, and TransUnion. They keep records of your credit activity and provide your potential creditors with information on your financial habits. This helps a creditor decide how much of a credit risk each customer is. Go online or to a library and look up information about these three credit reporting agencies. Summarize the information you obtain in a report.

5. Find contact information for three credit unions in your area. Write to each credit union and explain that you are doing a report for school. Find the requirements to join each credit union. Find the APR, monthly payment, and finance charges for a $31,000 new-car loan over a five-year period. Prepare your information on a poster.

6. Talk to your teacher about having a local bank representative come to your class. Have the class prepare questions about loans and credit cards in advance. Plan a script of the questions that will be addressed. When the bank representative comes to speak, act as moderator for the discussion. Keep a log of the questions and which student asked them. Write a thank you letter to the bank representative after the session.

7. Interview your parents or relatives about their use of loans and credit cards. Find what they consider wise spending habits, and what they have learned about credit. If they agree to let you see their last credit card statement, show them how to check entries in the statement, including the average daily balance and the finance charge.

8. Find out if any local store has an installment plan. Go to the store and interview a customer service representative. Ask questions about how their installment plan works. Get the monthly payment and finance charge for a specific item in the store, purchased under the installment plan. Prepare a report for the class.

9. Find a website that lists the terms and conditions of major credit cards. Research two different cards by going to the provider's links. Compare and contrast the advantages and disadvantages of each.

10. Some credit card providers offer student credit cards. Research this type of card and discuss how it differs from a regular credit card.

Dollars and Sense — Your Financial News Update

Go to www.cengage.com/school/math/financialalgebra where you will find a link to a website containing current issues about credit cards. Try one of the activities.

REVISITED Really? Really!

How much is 1 billion credit cards? How far would they stretch end-to-end? The typical credit card measures 54 mm by 85 mm.

1. A credit card's length is 85 mm. Convert this to inches by using an online metric conversion table. Round to the nearest hundredth. 3.35 in.
2. There are 5,280 feet in a mile and 12 inches in each foot. How many inches are equivalent to a mile? 63,360 in.
3. How many credit cards, placed end to end, would it take to span a mile? Round to the nearest integer. 18,913
4. The circumference of the earth is approximately 24,901 miles at the equator. How many credit cards (end to end) would it take to circle the earth? 470,952,613
5. Write your answer to Exercise 4 in words. four hundred seventy million, nine hundred fifty-two thousand, six hundred thirteen
6. In Really? Really! you read facts involving 1 billion credit cards. How many times would 1 billion credit cards circle the earth at the equator? more than twice

REALLY? REALLY! REVISITED

In this feature, students get a sense of just what 1 billion credit cards are. They calculate the number of credit cards it would take to circle the earth at the equator. This expansive number and the fact that there are more than enough credit cards in use today worldwide that would accomplish that task, should underscore the fact that the use of credit and the credit industry is an integral part of our daily lives.

Applications

Round monetary amounts to the nearest cent.

1. Faith is taking an \$8,100, $2\frac{1}{2}$-year loan with an APR of 8.22%. What is the monthly payment for this loan? \$299.61
2. Shania bought a \$1,455 drum set on the installment plan. The installment agreement included a 15% down payment and 18 monthly payments of \$80.78 each.
   a. How much is the down payment? \$218.25
   b. What is the total amount of the monthly payments? \$1,454.04
   c. How much will Shania pay for the drum set on the installment plan? \$1,672.29
   d. What is the finance charge? \$217.29
3. Pauline's credit card was lost on a business trip. She immediately reported it missing to her creditor. The person who found it hours later used it, and charged *w* dollars worth of merchandise on the card, where $w < \$50$. How much of the *w* dollars is Pauline responsible for paying? \$0
4. Carly took a \$7,000, three-year loan with an APR of 8.15%.
   a. What is the monthly payment? \$219.84
   b. What is the total amount of the monthly payments? \$7,914.24
   c. What is the finance charge? \$914.24
5. Sarah is taking out a \$24,400, four-year new-car loan with an APR of 6.88%. What is the finance charge for this loan? Round to the nearest hundred dollars. \$3,600

ANSWERS

9b. $\frac{0.01p}{12}$

12. Incorrect; the APR should be divided by 12 before multiplying by the average daily balance. The correct finance charge is $7.47.

6. The policy of the Black Oyster Pawnshop is to lend up to 30% of the value of a borrower's collateral. Pete wants to use a $2,000 guitar and a $900 camera as collateral for a loan. What is the maximum amount that he could borrow from Black Oyster? $870

7. Juan purchased a tool set for $\$t$ on the installment plan. He made a 15% down payment and agreed to pay $\$m$ per month for the next y years. Express the finance charge algebraically. $0.15t + 12my - t$

8. Jake had these daily balances on his credit card for his last billing period. He did not pay the card in full the previous month, so he will have to pay a finance charge. The APR is 18.6%.

two days @ $331.98
eleven days @ $1,203.04
four days @ $996.71
thirteen days @ $1,002.76

a. What is the average daily balance? $1,030.67
b. What is the finance charge? $15.98

9. Kim's credit card was not paid in full last month so she will pay a finance charge this month. She had an average daily balance of $\$d$ during this billing period, which had 31 days. The APR was p%.
a. Express algebraically the APR as an equivalent decimal. $0.01p$
b. Express algebraically the monthly percentage rate as an equivalent decimal. See margin.
c. Express the finance charge algebraically. $\left(\frac{0.01p}{12}\right)d$

10. Michelle's credit card billing cycle is 30 days. She had a daily balance of b dollars for d days. Then she charged one item for $56, and that was all of the purchases she made for the rest of the month. There was no other activity on the credit card. Express her average daily balance algebraically. $\frac{bd + (30 - d)(b + 56)}{30}$

11. The finance charge on Lauren's credit card bill last month was $13.50. Her APR is 18%. What was her average daily balance? $900

12. Riel had an average daily balance of $415.22 on his May credit card statement. The bill showed that his APR was 21.6% and that his finance charge was $89.69. When he verified the finance charge, did he find that it was correct or incorrect? Explain. See margin.

13. What is the monthly periodic rate on a loan with an APR of 19.5%? 1.625%

14. Harold borrowed $8,000 for five years at an APR of 6.75%.
a. What is Harold's monthly payment? $157.47
b. What is the total amount that Harold paid in monthly payments for the loan? $9,448.20
c. What is the amount Harold will pay in finance charges? $1,448.20

15. Examine the summary section of the monthly credit card statement. Use the first five entries to determine the new balance. $0.00

SUMMARY	Previous Balance	Payments / Credits	New Purchases	Late Charge	Finance Charge	New Balance	**Minimum Payment**
	$421.36	$1,703.50	$1,273.11	$0.00	$9.03		$18.00

16. The table lists the balances at the end of each year for a 15-year, $50,000 loan with an 8% interest rate.

Year	Balance
0	$ 50,000.00
1	$ 48,201.08
2	$ 46,252.85
3	$ 44,142.91
4	$ 41,857.85
5	$ 39,383.13
6	$ 36,703.01
7	$ 33,800.44
8	$ 30,656.96
9	$ 27,252.57
10	$ 23,565.62
11	$ 19,572.66
12	$ 15,248.28
13	$ 10,564.98
14	$ 5,492.97
15	$ 0.00

a. Construct a scatterplot using the data points (year, loan balance). See margin.

b. Write a linear regression equation that approximates the year/loan balance relationship. Round to the nearest integer. $y = -3{,}271x + 54{,}077$

c. Write a quadratic regression equation that approximates the year/loan balance relationship. Round to the nearest integer. $y = -129x^2 - 1{,}338x + 49{,}566$

d. Write a cubic regression equation that approximates the year/loan balance relationship. Round to the nearest integer. $y = -3x^3 - 52x^2 - 1{,}782x + 50{,}030$

ANSWERS

16a.

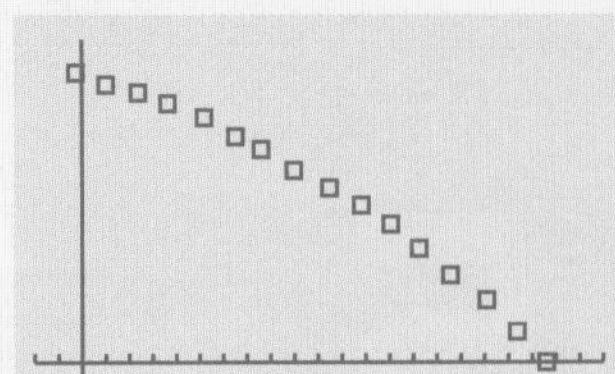

17. Bill can afford a monthly payment of $475. He wants to take out a $20,000 loan at 7% interest rate. What should the length of the loan be? Round your answer to the nearest year. 4 years

18. Ciana wants to take out a $7,500 loan with a 5.3% APR. She can afford to pay $128 per month for loan payments.

a. What should be the length of her loan? Round to the nearest tenth of a year. 5.7 years

b. What would an increase of $20 to the monthly payment do to the length of her loan? The loan would be for 4.8 years, nine-tenths of a year less.

19. Use the credit card statement and a blank credit card calendar.

ACCOUNT INFORMATION							
Account Number		3-22767195	Billing Date	5 May	Payment Due	18 May	
TRANSACTIONS					DEBITS / CREDITS (−)		
7 APR	124576893 Macy's				$676.00		
15 APR	762938471 Bedford Auto Body Shop				$721.80		
19 APR	309175832 Barnes and Noble Books				$93.15		
27 APR	100445638 Payment				−$1,340.00		
30 APR	876655411 FedEx				$115.75		
3 MAY	998430828 TicketMaster				$450.95		
SUMMARY	Previous Balance	Payments / Credits	New Purchases	Late Charge	Finance Charge	New Balance	**Minimum Payment**
	$978.00	$1,340.00	$2,057.65	$0.00			$115.00
Total Credit Line	$ 3,000.00			Average Daily Balance	# Days in Billing Cycle	APR	Monthly Periodic Rate
Total Available Credit					30	19.8%	1.65%

a. What is the total of all of the purchases made this billing cycle? $2,057.65

b. What is the amount of total payments? $1,340

c. What is sum of the daily balances? $55,672.70

d. What is the average daily balance? $1,855.76

e. What is the monthly periodic rate? 1.65%

f. What is the finance charge? $30.62

g. What is the new balance? $1,726.27

h. What is the available credit? $1,273.73

CHAPTER

5 Automobile Ownership

The car has become an article of dress without which we feel uncertain, unclad, and incomplete.

Marshall McLuhan, Canadian Educator and Philosopher

What do you think Marshall McLuhan meant in his quote?

The automobile is part of the American way of life. Many people commute to jobs that require them to own a car. Some students drive several miles to school. Stores and businesses are clustered in central locations often not near residential neighborhoods. When there is no mass transit system readily available to you, an automobile can provide convenient and necessary transportation.

Owning an automobile is a tremendous responsibility. The costs of gas, repairs, and insurance are high. Driving an automobile can also be dangerous. As a driver, you have a responsibility to yourself, your passengers, pedestrians, and other motorists. So, before embarking upon that first automobile purchase, you need to be aware of the physics and finances of operating a car. Being equipped with this knowledge will make your years on the road safer, less expensive, and more enjoyable.

What do you think?

Answers might include that the car is much more than a means of transportation. It has become a mode of self-expression as well as a mode of transportation. People pride themselves in automobile ownership; many even see it as a status symbol.

TEACHING RESOURCES

Instructor's Resource CD

Exam *View*® CD, Ch. 5

eHomework, Ch. 5

www.cengage.com/school/math/financialalgebra

Really?

How much does it cost to fill your car's gas tank today? Did your parents ever tell you stories about gas prices when they were young? Can you imagine people in gas lines in 1973, furious that gas prices had risen to over 50 cents per gallon?

The table shows the average price per gallon of gasoline from 1950–2005. Gas prices vary from region to region. They even differ from gas station to gas station, depending on the services the station provides and the neighborhood in which it is. Therefore, use the table as a general guide to gas prices.

Year	Price per Gallon ($)
1950	0.27
1955	0.30
1960	0.31
1965	0.31
1970	0.35
1975	0.53
1980	1.13
1985	1.19
1990	1.13
1995	1.14
2000	1.66
2005	2.33

Source: NBC

Imagine what it would cost to fill a tank in any of the years listed in the table. Imagine what new cars cost! The first Corvette, the 1953 model, had a base price of $3,498. There were only 300 of these cars manufactured. It cost about $5 to fill its 18-gallon gas tank! The 1953 Corvette buyer had an easy time picking a color. The car came in one color only—white.

CHAPTER OVERVIEW

This chapter offers 9 lessons pertaining to the automobile. Students explore formulas of varying degrees of mathematical sophistication as they work on pricing structures, insurance issues, automobile depreciation, and data that can assist them in making wise and safe driving decisions.

REALLY? REALLY!

The variability of gasoline prices has been of interest over the past few years. Looking at the table, students will notice a slow and small increase in prices in the early years. The seventies marked an era of increased automobile consumption and worldwide awareness of the power that oil ownership held in international relations. Prices have continued to rise. The inclusion of the data on the first Corvette, a highly desirable car, underscores how much things have changed in a relatively short period of time.

Really!

In auto sales, appearance is everything, or almost everything. It is certainly the most important single factor in a consumer's decision to buy this or that make.

Harley Earl, Designer/Inventor of the Corvette

5-1 Classified Ads

Objectives

- Compute the cost of classified ads for used cars.
- Compute the cost of sales tax on automobiles.

Common Core

A-CED2, F-IF1, F-IF2, F-IF7b

Key Terms
- sales tax
- domain
- piecewise function
- split function
- cusp

CCSS Warm-Up

$A(x)$ is the area function for an equilateral triangle given by $A(x) = (x^2\sqrt{3})/4$. Evaluate the function for each value of x.

1. $A(6)$ **2.** $A(\sqrt{2})$ **3.** $A(x + 1)$

1. $9\sqrt{3}$ 2. $\sqrt{3}/2$ 3. $((x^2 + 2x + 1)\sqrt{3})/4$

EXAMINE THE QUESTION

Classified ads provide a central place where buyers and sellers can be matched up according to what they want. They can then negotiate, agree on a price, and exchange their wares.

CLASS DISCUSSION

If you were looking for a 2009 Mustang, imagine trying to find someone who was selling one without using a classified ad.

What are some other options you might be looking for? Do you know their abbreviations?

How do buyers and sellers use classified ads for automobiles?

Most teenagers cannot wait to get their own set of "wheels." New cars are expensive, so many people buy used cars when they purchase their first car. They can buy used cars from a dealer or by looking at the classified ads in the newspaper or on the Internet.

Classified ads in newspapers use abbreviations to save space and lower the cost of the ad. Take a look at your local newspaper's classified ad section and see how many of the abbreviations you understand.

Words such as *mint* and *immaculate* are often used to describe cars in excellent condition. A car with many options is often listed as *loaded.* The number of thousands of miles the car has been driven is abbreviated as K. An ad that says "34K" tells you that the car has been driven a total of 34,000 miles. Take a look at some other abbreviations used in classified ads for used cars.

The asking price is usually given in the advertisement. *Negotiable* means that the seller is willing to bargain with you. *Firm* means that the owner is unwilling to change the price. *Sacrifice* means that the seller needs to sell the car quickly and believes that the price is lower than the car's worth.

By knowing what these expressions mean, you will be able to skim the classified ads and focus on the ones that describe the used car that would be best for you.

Abbreviation	Meaning
ac	air conditioning
auto	automatic transmission
cruise	cruise control
CD	compact disc player
cyl	number of cylinders
dr	number of doors
GPS	navigation system
lthr	leather interior
p/ant	power antenna
p/locks	power door locks
p/mirrors	power mirrors
p/seats	power seats
ps	power steering
pw	power windows

Skills and Strategies

Here you will learn some of the steps that may be involved when buying or selling a used car. You can contact your state's Department of Motor Vehicles to find specific information about cars in your state. In some states the buyer of a used car must pay a **sales tax** on the car.

EXAMPLE 1

Kerry purchased a used car for $7,400 and had to pay $8\frac{1}{2}\%$ sales tax. How much tax did she pay?

SOLUTION To find the sales tax, multiply the price of the item by the sales tax rate, expressed as a decimal.

$$\begin{aligned}\text{Sales tax} &= \text{Price of item} \times \text{Sales tax rate}\\ &= 7{,}400 \times 0.085 = 629.00\end{aligned}$$

Kerry must pay $629.00 in sales tax. This money goes to the state, not the seller of the car. Be sure you consider the sales tax expense on a car you are planning to purchase. It can be thousands of dollars on a new car.

■ **CHECK YOUR UNDERSTANDING**

The sales tax rate in Mary Ann's state is 4%. If she purchases a car for x dollars, express the total cost of the car with sales tax algebraically.

EXAMPLE 2

The cost of a classified ad is determined by its length. John plans to sell his car and places a 5-line ad. The newspaper charges $31 for the first two lines and $6 per extra line to run the ad for one week. What will John's ad cost to run for two weeks?

SOLUTION Subtract to find the number of lines over 2 lines.

$$5 - 2 = 3$$

Multiply 3 by $6 to find the cost of the extra 3 lines.

$$3(6) = 18$$

Add to find the cost of running the ad for one week.

$$31 + 18 = 49$$

Multiply by 2 to get the cost for the two-week ad.

$$49(2) = 98$$

The ad will cost John $98.

■ **CHECK YOUR UNDERSTANDING**

Ramon plans to sell his car and places an ad with x lines. The newspaper charges y dollars for the first g lines and p dollars per extra line to run the ad for a week. If $x > g$, express the cost of running the ad for a week.

TEACH

This lesson teaches students to compute sales tax, and shows them how large the sales tax on a car can be. It gives them practice on interpreting pricing schedules for classified ads. Once students understand these price schedules, they are introduced to a topic usually taught in precalculus: piecewise (split) functions. They will need to understand the role of the domain in these problems.

EXAMPLE 1

Underscore the fact that the sales tax on a used car is not paid to the seller in a private sale—it is paid to the state. For added practice, have them compute their state's sales tax on a $50,000 car.

CHECK YOUR UNDERSTANDING

Answer $x + 0.04x$, or $1.04x$

Show students both forms of the correct answer.

EXAMPLE 2

Point out that many newspaper and online ads are priced this way. Some cell phone plans are priced similarly.

CHECK YOUR UNDERSTANDING

Answer $y + p(x - g)$

Remind students they can mimic the algebraic steps with numbers if it makes it easier for them to form the algebraic expression.

EXAMPLE 3

Students are building their first piecewise function in this example. Point out that they can use the word "if" to replace the word "when" and the meaning is the same.

Recall that the **domain** is the set of values that can be input into a function.

EXAMPLE 3

Jason works for the *Glen Oaks News* and is writing a program to compute ad costs. He needs to enter an algebraic representation of the costs of an ad. His company charges \$42.50 for up to five lines for a classified ad. Each additional line costs \$7. Express the cost of an ad with x lines as a function of x algebraically.

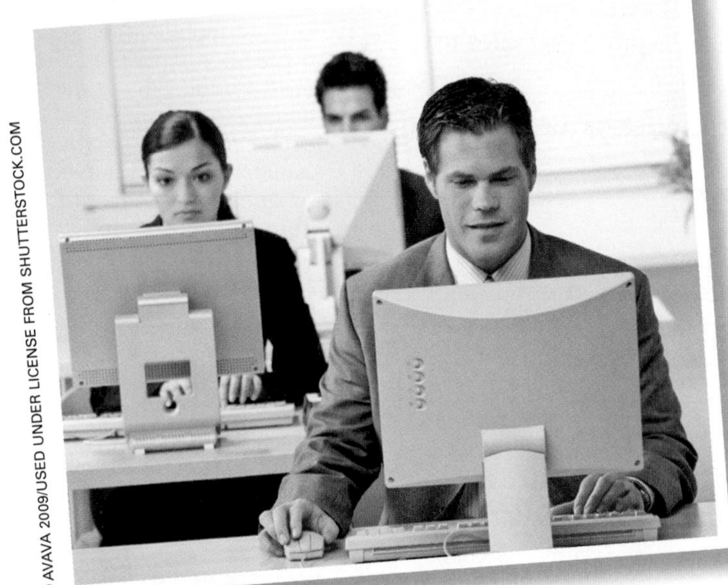

SOLUTION The algebraic representation of the classified ad cost function requires two rules. One rule is for ads with five or fewer lines and the other rule is for ads with more than five lines. You can view these two conditions as two different domains.

You will find the equation for the cost when $x \leq 5$, and then find the equation for the cost when $x > 5$. These are the two different domains.

Let $c(x)$ represent the cost of the classified ad. In this situation, x must be an integer.

If the ad has five or fewer lines, the cost is \$42.50.

$$c(x) = 42.50 \text{ when } x \leq 5$$

If the ad has more than five lines, the cost is \$42.50 plus the cost of the lines over 5 lines. Note that the domain is given by the inequality that follows *when* in the statement of the function.

If x is the number of lines, then the number of lines over five can be expressed as $x - 5$. These extra lines cost \$7 each.

$$c(x) = 42.50 + 7(x - 5) \text{ when } x > 5$$

These two equations can be written in mathematical shorthand using a **piecewise function**. Piecewise functions are sometimes called **split functions**.

A piecewise function gives a set of rules for each domain of the function. Notice that $c(x)$ is computed differently depending on the value of x. Here $c(x)$ is expressed as a piecewise function.

$$c(x) = \begin{cases} 42.50 & \text{when } x \leq 5 \\ 42.50 + 7(x - 5) & \text{when } x > 5 \end{cases}$$

The domain is defined by the inequalities that follow *when* in the above statement.

CHECK YOUR UNDERSTANDING

Answer

$$c(x) = \begin{cases} 38 & \text{when } x \leq 4 \\ 38 + 6.25(x - 4) & \text{when } x > 4 \end{cases}$$

Remind them to use two let statements:

Let x represent the number of lines.

Let $c(x)$ represent the cost of the ad.

■ CHECK YOUR UNDERSTANDING

The *Smithtown News* charges \$38 for a classified ad that is 4 or fewer lines long. Each line above four lines costs an additional \$6.25. Express the cost of an ad as a piecewise function.

EXAMPLE 4

Roxanne set up the following piecewise function which represents the cost of an auto classified from her hometown newspaper.

$$c(x) = \begin{cases} 41.55 & \text{when } x \le 6 \\ 41.55 + 5.50(x - 6) & \text{when } x > 6 \end{cases}$$

If x is the number of lines in the ad, use words to express the price $c(x)$ of a classified ad from this paper.

SOLUTION Look at the two domains. Look at the function rule in the first line. The inequality $x \le 6$ tells you that the cost is $41.55 if the number of lines is less than or equal to 6.

Next, look at the second line. The expression $x - 6$ gives the number of lines over six. That expression is multiplied by 5.50, so the cost of each extra line must be $5.50. The inequality $x > 6$ tells you that the cost is $41.55 for the first six lines, and $5.50 for each line over six lines.

CHECK YOUR UNDERSTANDING

The following piecewise function gives the price $p(w)$ of a classified ad in a classic car magazine. If w is the number of lines in the ad, use words to express the price $p(w)$ of a classified ad from this paper.

$$p(w) = \begin{cases} 60 & \text{when } w \le 5 \\ 60 + 8(w - 5) & \text{when } w > 5 \end{cases}$$

EXAMPLE 5

Graph the piecewise function Roxanne created in Example 4.

SOLUTION Use your graphing calculator to display functions with more than one domain.

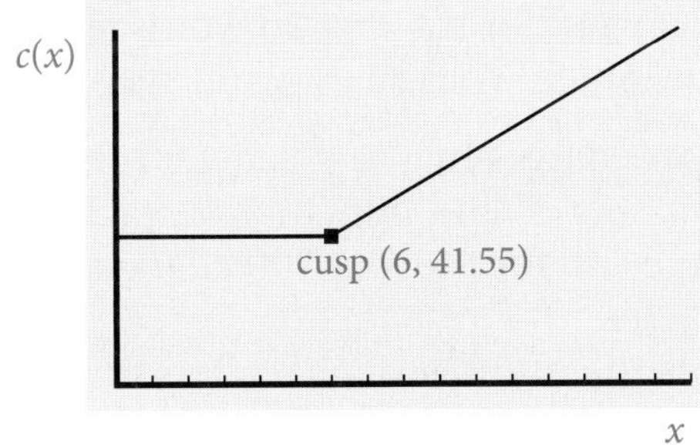

Notice that the graph is composed of two straight lines that meet at the point (6, 41.55). The point where the two lines meet is called a **cusp** because it resembles the sharp cusp on a tooth.

CHECK YOUR UNDERSTANDING

Find the cusp of the graph of the following piecewise function.

$$c(x) = \begin{cases} 42.50 & \text{when } x \le 5 \\ 42.50 + 7(x - 5) & \text{when } x > 5 \end{cases}$$

EXAMPLE 4

Interpreting a given piecewise function will help students understand them and create their own.

CHECK YOUR UNDERSTANDING

Answer The ad is $60 for the first five lines and $8 for each line over 5 lines.

EXAMPLE 5

This is probably the first time the students will see a cusp in a graph. Note to the students the dramatic increase in price after the cusp.

CHECK YOUR UNDERSTANDING

Answer (5, 42.50)

The graph in Example 5 has a discrete domain—x can only take on integer values. Therefore, the graph can be drawn as a scatterplot that is also a function.

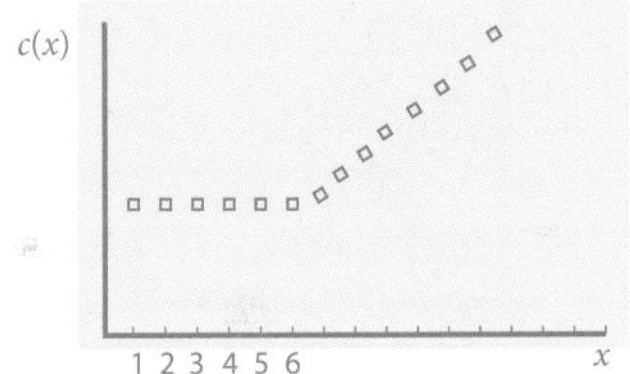

Often when line graphs depict discrete data, they are drawn as continuous curves. You can show this to students and explain that the domain is only integer values, and that the context of each problem will make it clear when a curve actually has a discrete domain.

Applications

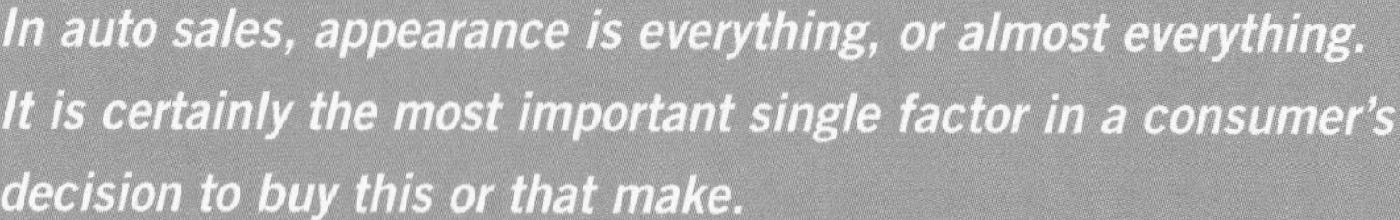

In auto sales, appearance is everything, or almost everything. It is certainly the most important single factor in a consumer's decision to buy this or that make.

Harley Earl, Designer/Inventor of the Corvette

TEACH

Exercise 5
Have the students also do the problem if $x < m$ just to point out the difference.

Exercises 8, 9, and 10 have discrete domains.

ANSWERS

1. Although consumers consider gas mileage, condition, options, status, and other things when purchasing a new or used car, the look of the car is a major determinant of what car people will buy.

9a.

$$c(x) = \begin{cases} 46 & \text{when } x \leq 200 \\ 46 + 0.15(x - 200) & \text{when } x > 200 \end{cases}$$

9b.

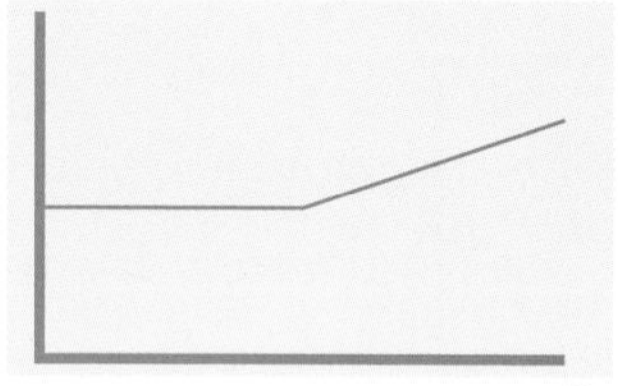

1. Interpret the quote in the context of what you learned. See margin.

2. The *North Shore News* charges $19.50 for a two-line classified ad. Each additional line costs $7. How much does a six-line ad cost? $47.50

3. The *Antique Auto News* charges $45 for a three-line classified ad. Each additional line costs $8.50. For an extra $40, a seller can include a photo in the ad. How much would a four-line ad with a photo cost? $93.50

4. A local newspaper charges g dollars for a four-line classified ad. Each additional line costs d dollars. Write an expression for the cost of a seven-line ad. $g + 3d$

5. The *Auto Times* charges g dollars for a classified ad with m or less lines. Each additional line is d dollars. If $x > m$, express the cost of an x-line ad algebraically. $g + d(x - m)$

6. Samantha purchased a used car for $4,200. Her state charges 4% tax for the car, $47 for license plates, and $35 for a state safety and emissions inspection. How much does Samantha need to pay for these extra charges, not including the price of the car? $250

7. Ralph placed a classified ad to sell his used Honda Odyssey minivan for $18,500. After two weeks, he didn't sell the minivan, and the newspaper suggested lowering the price 5%. What would the new price be if Ralph reduced it according to the suggestion? $17,575

8. The *Bayside Bugle* charges by the word to run classified ads. The newspaper charges $18 for the first 20 words and $0.35 for each additional word. How much would a 27-word classified ad cost? $20.45

9. A local newspaper charges by the character for its classified ads. Letters, numbers, spaces, and punctuation each count as one character. They charge $46 for the first 200 characters and $0.15 for each additional character.

  a. If x represents the number of characters in the ad, express the cost $c(x)$ of an ad as a piecewise function. See margin.

  b. Graph the function from part a. See margin.

  c. Find the coordinates of the cusp in the graph in part b. (200, 46)

10. The *Kings Park Register* gives senior citizens a 10% discount on classified ads. Mr. Quadrino, a senior citizen, is selling his car and wants to take out a four-line ad. The paper charges $6.50 per line. What is the price of the ad for Mr. Quadrino? $23.40

11. The *Good Ole Times* magazine charges for classified ads by the "column inch." A column inch is as wide as one column, and it is one inch high. The cost is $67 per column inch. How much would the magazine charge to print a $2\frac{1}{2}$-inch ad? $167.50

12. Leslie placed this ad in the *Collector Car Monthly*.

> 1957 Chevrolet Nomad station wagon. Tropical Turquoise, 6 cyl. auto, PS, PW, AM/FM, repainted, rebuilt transmission, restored two-tone interior. Mint! Moving, sacrifice, $52,900. 555-4231

a. If the newspaper charges $48 for the first three lines and $5 for each extra line, how much will this ad cost Leslie? $58

b. Ruth buys the car for 8% less than the advertised price. How much does she pay? $48,668

c. Ruth must pay her state 6% sales tax on the sale. How much must she pay in sales tax? $2,920.08

13. The *Online Car Auctioneer* charges a commission for classified ads. If the car sells, the seller is charged 4% of the *advertised* price, not of the price for which the car actually sells. If the car doesn't sell, the seller pays nothing. If Barbara advertises her Cadillac for $12,000 and sells it for $11,200, how much must she pay for the ad? $480

14. The cost of an ad in a local paper is given by the piecewise function

$$c(x) = \begin{cases} 38 & \text{when } x \leq 4 \\ 38 + 6.25(x - 4) & \text{when } x > 4 \end{cases}$$

a. Find the cost of a three-line ad. $38

b. Find the difference in cost between a one-line ad and a four-line ad. $0

c. Find the cost of a seven-line ad. $56.75

d. Graph this function on your graphing calculator. See margin.

e. Find the coordinates of the cusp from the graph in part d. (4, 38)

15. Express the following classified ad rate as a piecewise function. Use a let statement to identify what x and y represent.

$29 for the first five lines, and $6.75 for each additional line. See margin.

16. The piecewise function describes a newspaper's classified ad rates.

$$y = \begin{cases} 21.50 & \text{when } x \leq 3 \\ 21.50 + 5(x - 3) & \text{when } x > 3 \end{cases}$$

a. If x represents the number of lines, and y represents the cost, translate the function into words. See margin.

b. If the function is graphed, what are the coordinates of the cusp? (3, 21.50)

17. A local *Pennysaver* charges $11 for each of the first three lines of a classified ad, and $5 for each additional line.

a. What is the price of a two-line ad? $22

b. What is the price of a five-line ad? $43

c. If x is the number of lines in the ad, express the cost $c(x)$ of the ad as a piecewise function. See margin.

18. The *Position Posted* online job website charges $15 to place a classified ad plus $2.50 for each of the first five lines, and $8 for each additional line after the fifth line. If x is the number of lines in the ad, write a piecewise function for the cost of the ad, $c(x)$.

$$c(x) = \begin{cases} 15 + 2.5(5) & \text{when } x \leq 5 \\ 27.5 + 8(x - 5) & \text{when } x > 5 \end{cases}$$

TEACH

Exercises 12, and 14–18 have discrete domains.

Exercise 15

The more practice students get with this type of problem, the better. Make up similar problems for additional practice.

Exercise 16

See if students, based on patterns in the problems they have seen already, can find the coordinates of the cusp by just inspecting the piecewise function.

Exercise 17

Have students bring in a local *Pennysaver* and contact them to find the cost of their classified ads.

ANSWERS

14d.

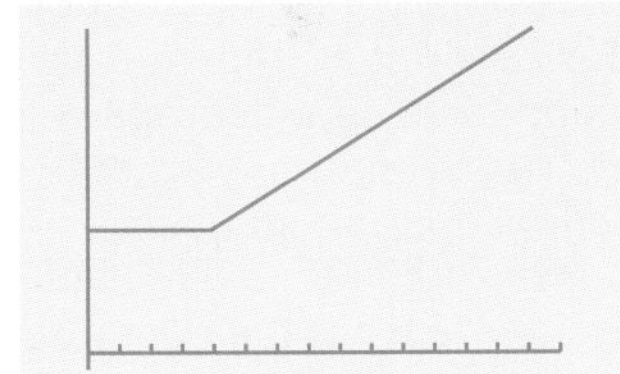

15. Let x = number of lines in the ad

Let $c(x)$ = cost of the ad

$$c(x) = \begin{cases} 29 & \text{when } x \leq 5 \\ 29 + 6.75(x - 5) & \text{when } x > 5 \end{cases}$$

16a. The cost is $21.50 for three lines or less, and $5 for each additional line.

17c.

$$c(x) = \begin{cases} 11x & \text{when } x \leq 3 \\ 33 + 5(x - 3) & \text{when } x > 3 \end{cases}$$

> *Statistical thinking will one day be as necessary for efficient citizenship as the ability to read and write.*
>
> **H.G. Wells,** English Science Fiction Author

5-2 Buy or Sell a Car

Objectives

- Compute mean, median, mode, range, quartiles, and interquartile range.

Common Core

S-ID2, S-ID3, S-ID4

Key Terms

- statistics
- data
- measures of central tendency
- mean
- arithmetic average
- outlier
- median
- ascending order
- descending order
- skew
- resistant
- range
- quartiles
- lower quartile
- upper quartile
- subscripts
- interquartile range (IQR)
- mode
- bimodal

CCSS Warm-Up

Write a simplified expression for the average of the three numbers described.

Let n represent the first number. The second number is four less than the first number. The third number is four more than twice the first.

$(n + (n - 4) + (2n + 4))/3 = 4n/3$

EXAMINE THE QUESTION

All buyers want to pay a lower price, and all sellers want the highest price possible. Negotiating out of *desire* is not as effective as using facts about comparable cars. Smart buyers and sellers do their statistical homework first so they can maximize what they get out of the transaction.

CLASS DISCUSSION

What is more important to you, the mechanical condition of the car or its appearance? Why?

Do you think the appearance is a reflection of the mechanical condition of the car?

There is a Reality Check project at the end of the chapter in which students can price a new car.

How can statistics help you negotiate the sale or purchase of a car?

You are planning to buy a used car. How can you tell what a reasonable price is for the car you want to buy? You can find a lot of information about used car prices on the Internet. You can also visit a used car dealer. The price of any car depends heavily on its condition and how desirable it is in the marketplace.

You will probably spend a few weeks shopping for your car. You can determine a reasonable price for a particular car by examining the prices of those and similar cars listed in classified ads.

The *Kelley Blue Book* (www.kbb.com) and Edmunds (edmunds.com) are two of many excellent sources on the Internet you can use to find the value of a used car. Ask questions as you do your research. You can contact sellers to find out about their cars. Be smart in your search, and if possible, bring a knowledgeable person with you when you go to test drive a used car.

NIKNIKON/ISTOCKPHOTO.COM

As you search, compile a list of advertised prices for the cars you want. Then, you can use **statistics** to help analyze the numbers, or **data**, that you compile. **Measures of central tendency** are single numbers designed to represent a "typical" value for the data.

You will find less variability in the prices of new cars, because all new cars are in the same condition. The price you will pay is based on the sticker price of the car. Different dealers can give different prices, and it is best to compare deals when buying a new car.

Skills and Strategies

Used car prices vary greatly, and a skilled negotiator will have an advantage when buying or selling a used car.

EXAMPLE 1

Jason wants to sell his Ford SUV. He compiles these prices from the Internet for cars similar to his: $11,000, $9,900, $12,100, $10,500, and $9,000. What is a reasonable price for Jason to consider for his SUV?

SOLUTION Jason should start by finding the **mean** or **arithmetic average** of the five prices. The mean is often called the average.

Add and then divide by 5.

$$\frac{11{,}000 + 9{,}900 + 12{,}000 + 10{,}500 + 9{,}000}{5} = 10{,}500$$

The mean is $10,500. Jason can adjust this mean price based on the condition of his car, the mileage it has on it, and the options it has.

■ CHECK YOUR UNDERSTANDING

Maxine compiled a list of these car prices: $7,500, $6,500, $5,750, $4,900, $6,250, and $4,200. Find the mean of the prices.

EXAMPLE 2

Dory is looking for a classic 1967 Firebird. She finds these prices on the Internet: $18,000, $77,000, $22,000, $21,200, $19,000, $17,500, and $22,500. She computes the mean as $28,171.43. This number doesn't seem to be a good representative of the data. How can she find a better representation?

SOLUTION There is an **outlier**—a piece of data that is extremely different than the rest of the data. When there are outliers, the mean is often not a good representation. In these cases you can use the **median**—the middle score—to best represent the data.

To find the median, arrange the values in **ascending order** (from least to greatest), or **descending order** (from greatest to least).

Pair the numbers starting from the ends of the list as shown, and circle the middle number that remains after the numbers are paired.

The median is the circled number. Notice there is the same number of scores below the median as there are above the median.

The median is $21,200. This price is a better representation of the data. When the mean of a data set is not equal to the median, the data is **skewed**.

The median is unaffected by the outlier. If the $77,000 price was $977,000, the median would remain the same. The median is **resistant** to extreme numbers.

17,500 18,000 12,000 (21,200) 22,000 22,500 77,000

TEACH

Students will revisit mean, median, and mode in this real-life context, and then be introduced to three measures that help describe spread: the range, quartiles, and interquartile range. They will also be introduced to outliers and formulas for finding outliers.

EXAMPLE 1

Students have already seen the mean. When students find the mean with a calculator they must group the addends in parentheses before dividing.

CHECK YOUR UNDERSTANDING

Answer $5,850

EXAMPLE 2

The advantage of the median, that it is less sensitive to extreme scores, is important for students to understand.

CHECK YOUR UNDERSTANDING

Answer $1,600; $1,600; no

EXAMPLE 3

Explain that in the case with an even number of numbers, the median may be a number that is not one of the numbers in the distribution. Remind students that the mean is often a number that is not one of the numbers in the data set.

CHECK YOUR UNDERSTANDING

Answer $9,900

EXAMPLE 4

A disadvantage of the range as a measure of spread is that it ignores all numbers in the distribution except the two end numbers. Have students create scenarios with the same minimum and maximum numbers but different other numbers to see how the range is unchanged.

CHECK YOUR UNDERSTANDING

Answer $3,300

CHECK YOUR UNDERSTANDING

Find the mean and median of the following prices for a used car extended warranty: $1,200, $1,650, $1,500, $2,000, $1,400, $1,850, and $1,600. Is the data skewed?

EXAMPLE 3

Find the median of the following used car prices: $6,700, $5,800, $9,100, $8,650, $7,700, and $7,800.

SOLUTION Put the numbers in ascending order. Then, pair the numbers. Since there is an even number of scores, there is no number left alone in the middle. Circle the last two numbers that were paired.

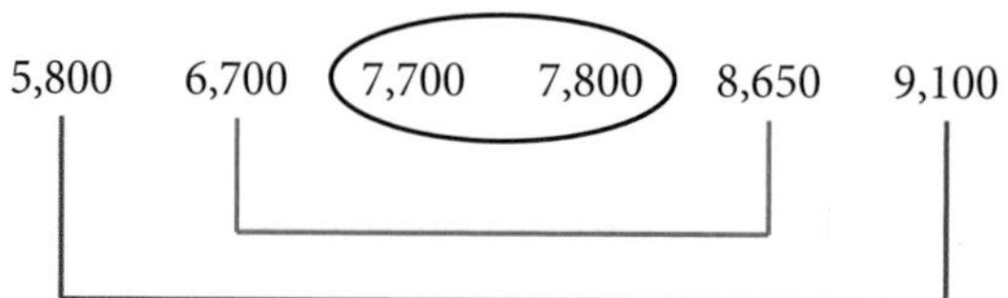

To find the median, find the mean of the two innermost circled numbers.

Add and then divide by 2. $\frac{7{,}700 + 7{,}800}{2} = 7{,}750$

The median is $7,750. Again, notice that there is the same number of scores below the median as there are above the median, and the median is resistant to extreme scores.

CHECK YOUR UNDERSTANDING

Find the median of these prices: $10,200, $9,300, $11,900, $2,999, $17,200, and $9,600.

EXAMPLE 4

Prices found online for the same GPS navigation system are $295, $345, $199, $225, and $200. Find the range of the GPS prices.

SOLUTION The **range** of a data set is a measure that shows dispersion (how spread out the data are). The range is the difference between the greatest and least numbers in the data.

The greatest price is $345 and the least is $199. The range is the difference between these two prices. Therefore, the range is $146, because 345 – 199 = 146.

CHECK YOUR UNDERSTANDING

Find the range of the used car prices in Example 3.

Quartiles

If you want to find out more about how the numbers are dispersed, you can use **quartiles**. Quartiles are three values represented by Q_1, Q_2, and Q_3 that divide the distribution into four subsets that each contain 25% of the data.

EXAMPLE 5

Find the quartiles for the tire pressures of cars at an auto clinic.

15, 17, 21, 25, 31, 32, 32, 32, 34

Tire pressure is measured in psi—pounds per square inch.

SOLUTION The numbers are in ascending order.

- Q_1 is the first quartile or **lower quartile**, and 25% of the numbers in the data set are at or below Q_1.
- Q_2 is the second quartile. Half the numbers are below Q_2, and half are above, so Q_2 is equal to the *median.*
- Q_3 is the third quartile, or **upper quartile**, and 75% of the numbers are at or below Q_3.
- Q_4 is the *maximum value* in the data set because 100% of the numbers are at or below that number.

The **subscripts** are used to name each quartile.

To find the quartiles, first find Q_2. Because Q_2 equals the median, $Q_2 = 31$.

For Q_1, find the median of the numbers below the median, which are 15, 17, 21, and 25. The median of these numbers is $Q_1 = 19$.

Add and then divide by 2. $\frac{17 + 21}{2} = 19$

For Q_3, find the median of the numbers in the data set that are above the median, which are 32, 32, 32, 34. The two middle numbers are 32, so $Q_3 = 32$.

The maximum value in the data set is 34. So, $Q_4 = 34$. The quartile values are $Q_1 = 19$, $Q_2 = 31$, $Q_3 = 32$, and $Q_4 = 34$.

You can use your graphing calculator to find quartiles.

CHECK YOUR UNDERSTANDING

What percent of the numbers in a data set are above Q_3?

EXAMPLE 6

What is the difference between Q_1 and Q_3 from the data set in Example 5?

SOLUTION The difference $Q_3 - Q_1$ is the **interquartile range (IQR)**. The interquartile range gives the range of the middle 50% of the numbers. A small interquartile range means that the middle 50% of the numbers are clustered together. A large interquartile range means that the middle 50% of the numbers are more spread out. To find the interquartile range, subtract. The interquartile range is $Q_3 - Q_1 = 32 - 19 = 13$.

EXAMPLE 5

The quartiles will help students create and understand box-and-whisker plots in the next lesson. Show the students how to use their calculator's statistical features to find quartiles.

CHECK YOUR UNDERSTANDING

Answer 25%

EXAMPLE 6

The interquartile range will be necessary to find the outliers, so students need to understand it before attempting Example 7.

CHECK YOUR UNDERSTANDING

Answer $1,950

EXAMPLE 7

Students should memorize the formulas for the outlier boundaries. Explain that the mean is very sensitive to outliers, but the median is not. The range is very sensitive to outliers, but the interquartile range is not.

CHECK YOUR UNDERSTANDING

Answer yes

EXAMPLE 8

This problem is relevant to students if their school does any voting in this manner. If three people were running for school president, the mode name wins even though it may not be the majority.

CHECK YOUR UNDERSTANDING

Answer 32

■ **CHECK YOUR UNDERSTANDING**

Find the interquartile range for the data in Example 3.

EXAMPLE 7

Find the outliers for these tire prices:

$45, $88, $109, $129, $146, $189, $202, $218, and $545

SOLUTION The interquartile range is used to identify outliers. Outliers may occur on the lower or upper end of the data set. The numbers are in ascending order. The median, Q_2, is $146.

$$Q_1 = \frac{88 + 109}{2} = 98.5 \qquad Q_3 = \frac{202 + 218}{2} = 210$$

$$IQR = 210 - 98.5 = 111.5$$

Use $Q_1 - 1.5(IQR)$ to compute the boundary for lower outliers.

$$98.5 - 1.5(111.5) = -68.75$$

Any number below −68.75 is an outlier. There are no lower outliers.

Use $Q_3 + 1.5(IQR)$ to compute the boundary for upper outliers.

$$210 + 1.5(111.5) = 377.25$$

Any number above 377.25 is an upper outlier, so $545 is an upper outlier.

■ **CHECK YOUR UNDERSTANDING**

The store that charged $545 for a tire in Example 7 had a sale and lowered its price to $399. Is the new price an upper outlier?

EXAMPLE 8

Each year, the 880 seniors in North Shore High School vote for one of the 110 teachers to receive the annual yearbook dedication. The teacher who receives the most votes wins. Can a teacher who receives 9 votes win, if every senior votes?

SOLUTION The **mode** is the most-occurring item and is often used with non-numerical variables, such as the winning teacher.

If each of the 880 votes were split among the 110 teachers, each teacher would get 8 votes. If one teacher received 7 votes, another received 9 votes, and everyone else received 8 votes, the teacher with 9 votes would win. A set can have no mode.

If there are two modes, the set is **bimodal**.

■ **CHECK YOUR UNDERSTANDING**

Find the mode of the tire pressures from Example 5.

Applications

Statistical thinking will one day be as necessary for efficient citizenship as the ability to read and write.

H.G. Wells, English Science Fiction Author

1. Interpret the quote in the context of what you learned. See margin.
2. Find the mean, median, mode, and range for each data set given.
   - **a.** 7, 12, 1, 7, 6, 5, 11 mean = 7; median = 7; mode = 7; range = 11
   - **b.** 85, 105, 95, 90, 115 mean = 98; median = 95; no mode; range = 30
   - **c.** 10, 14, 16, 16, 8, 9, 11, 12, 3 mean = 11; median = 11; mode = 16; range = 13
   - **d.** 10, 8, 7, 5, 9, 10, 7 mean = 8; median = 8; mode = 7 and 10; range = 5
   - **e.** 45, 50, 40, 35, 75 mean = 49; median = 45; no mode; range = 40
   - **f.** 15, 11, 11, 16, 16, 9 mean = 13; median = 13; mode = 11 and 16; range = 7
3. Which of the data sets from Exercise 2 are skewed? b and e
4. Courtney wants to sell her grandfather's antique 1932 Ford. She begins to set her price by looking at ads and finds these prices: \$24,600, \$19,000, \$33,000, \$15,000, and \$20,000. What is the mean price? \$22,320
5. Five Smithtown High School students are saving up to buy their first cars. They all have after-school jobs, and their weekly salaries are listed in the table.

Emily	\$110
Sam	\$145
Danielle	\$130
Katie	\$160
Stephanie	\$400

   - **a.** What is the mean weekly salary for these students? \$189
   - **b.** What is the median salary? \$145
   - **c.** Whose salary would you consider to be an outlier? Stephanie's
   - **d.** Which number do you think is a better representation of the data, the mean or the median? median
   - **e.** Explain your answer to part d. Because there is an outlier, the median is a better representation than the mean.

6. Rosanne is selling her Corvette. She wants to include a photo of her car in the ad. Three publications give her prices for her ad with the photograph:

Lake Success Shopsaver	\$59.00
Glen Head Buyer	\$71.00
Floral Park Moneysaver	\$50.00

   - **a.** What is the mean price of these ads? Round to the nearest cent. \$60.00
   - **b.** What would it cost her to run all three ads? \$180
   - **c.** If each of the three newspapers used the mean price as their ad price, what would it cost Rosanne to run ads in all three papers? \$180
   - **d.** Find the range of these ad prices. \$21.00

7. Dan's parents are going to pay for half of his car if he gets a 90 average in math for all four marking periods and the final exam. All grades are weighted equally. Here are his grades for the first four quarters: 91, 82, 90, and 89. What grade does he need on his final exam to have a 90 average? 98

TEACH

Exercise 5
When discussing their responses in class, try to get students to use the words *skew* and *resistant* so you can verify that they understand them.

Exercise 7
Students are frequently trying to figure out what they need on the next test to get a certain grade. Remind them that they have added another grade and should make sure they are dividing by the correct number.

ANSWERS

1. With the tremendous crunching and availability of data due to the prevalence of technology, we are bombarded by statistics on a daily basis. Understanding how to interpret this information is becoming increasingly important.

TEACH

Exercise 8

Remind students about the credit chapter they recently completed. If someone has to save years for a car, what would they drive while they are saving?

Exercises 14–18

Students can create their lists and trade with other students. Then have them perform the required computations to see if their numbers satisfy the problems posed.

8. Elliot is saving to buy a used car next year on his 18th birthday. He plans on spending $6,000. How much must he save each week, if he plans to work the entire year with only two weeks off? $120

9. The mean of five numbers is 16. If four of the numbers are 13, 20, 11 and 21, what is the fifth number? 15

10. The quartiles of a data set are $Q_1 = 50$, $Q_2 = 72$, $Q_3 = 110$, and $Q_4 = 140$. Find the interquartile range. 60

11. The following list of prices is for a used original radio for a 1955 Thunderbird. The prices vary depending on the condition of the radio.

$210, $210, $320, $200, $300, $10, $340,

$300, $245, $325, $700, $250, $240, $200

a. Find the mean of the radio prices. $275
b. Find the median of the radio prices. $247.50
c. Find the mode of the radio prices. $200, $210, and $300
d. Find the four quartiles. $Q_1 = 210$, $Q_2 = 247.50$, $Q_3 = 320$, $Q_4 = 700$
e. Find the interquartile range for this data set. 110
f. Find the boundary for the lower outliers. Are there any lower outliers? $45; yes, there is one lower outlier, $10.
g. Find the boundary for the upper outliers. Are there any upper outliers? $485; yes, there is one upper outlier, $700.

12. Bill is looking for original taillights for his 1932 Ford. The prices vary depending on the condition. He finds these prices: $450, $100, $180, $600, $300, $350, $300, and $400.
a. Find the four quartiles. $Q_1 = 240$; $Q_2 = 325$; $Q_3 = 425$; $Q_4 = 600$
b. Find the interquartile range. 185
c. Find the boundary for the lower outliers. Are there any lower outliers? –$37.50; there are no lower outliers.
d. Find the boundary for the upper outliers. Are there any upper outliers? $702.50; there are no upper outliers.

13. Eliza wants to sell a used car stereo online. From her research on the website she will post to, she found 8 similar stereos listed. She decides to list her stereo for 20% less than the mean price of the stereos already for sale on the site. Let *x* represent the sum of the prices of the stereos she found in her research. Write an expression to calculate the price she will list as the cost of her stereo. $\frac{x}{8} - 0.2\left(\frac{x}{8}\right)$ or $0.8\left(\frac{x}{8}\right)$

14. Create a list of five different numbers whose mean is 50. Answers vary.

15. Create a list of six different numbers whose median is 10. Answers vary.

16. Create a list of five numbers whose mean and median are both 12. Answers vary.

17. Create a list of numbers whose mean, median, and mode are all 10. Answers vary.

18. Create a list of numbers with two upper outliers and one lower outlier. Answers vary.

19. Explain why you cannot find the range of a data set if you are given the four quartiles. You need the least number, which is not one of the quartiles.

It is a capital mistake to theorize before one has data.
Sir Arthur Conan Doyle, Scottish Author (Sherlock Holmes novels)

Graph Frequency Distributions 5-3

Key Terms • frequency distribution • frequency • stem-and-leaf plot • box-and-whisker plot • boxplot • modified boxplot

Objectives

- Create a frequency distribution from a set of data.
- Use box-and-whisker plots and stem-and-leaf plots to display information.
- Use linear regression to negotiate the purchase or sale of a used car.

Common Core

S-ID1, S-ID2, S-ID3, S-ID4

CCSS Warm-Up

Laura has grades of 88, 92, 84, and 86 on the first four math tests. Find the fifth test grade for each situation.

1. She wants her average to be 90. **2.** She wants her average to be at least 85.

1. 100 2. at least 75

WHY ARE GRAPHS USED SO FREQUENTLY IN MATHEMATICS, AND IN DAILY LIFE?

Think of all the graphs you have seen in your mathematics textbooks over the years. Think of all of the graphs you have seen in newspapers, magazines, online, and on television. Why are graphs so prevalent? The answer is simple: "a picture is worth a thousand words." Graphs gather and present information in an easy-to-see format that can be interpreted quicker than information from a long list.

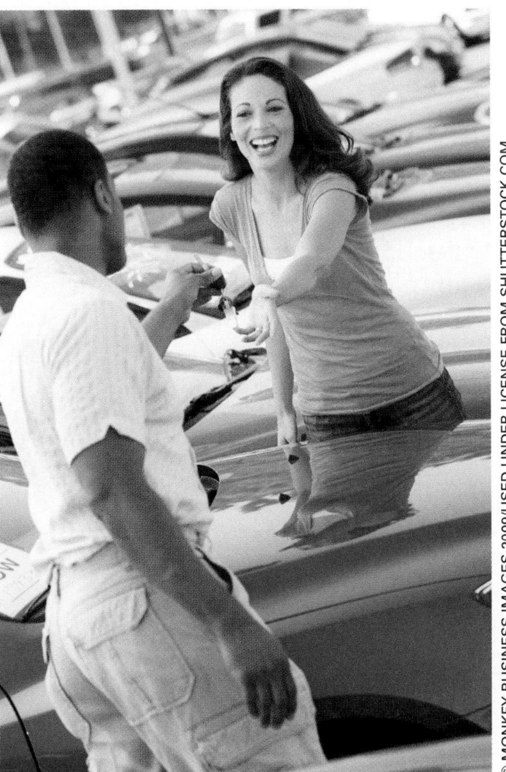

© MONKEY BUSINESS IMAGES 2009/USED UNDER LICENSE FROM SHUTTERSTOCK.COM

In your mathematical career, you have worked with bar graphs, histograms, circle graphs, and line graphs. Earlier in this book you learned about scatterplots. Trends in data that a long list can hide can be seen on a graph.

In the previous lesson you learned about measures of central tendency and measures of dispersion. In this lesson, you will learn about two graphs that present information about central tendency and dispersion pictorially. You can use these graphs to help negotiate car purchases and sales. If the graph supports your position, it can give the other party involved a quick look at the point you are trying to make.

EXAMINE THE QUESTION

Pictures tell a story. That is why they are used frequently. Find some graphs to show to students. Ask them basic questions about the graphs to reinforce this point.

Also discuss how graphs can display information that is too long for a list. Imagine a list of everyone in the U.S. and the prices paid for their cars. The list would be millions of numbers long. A graph of the numbers could be compact.

CLASS DISCUSSION

Show different graphs to students. Ask them to recall the names of the graphs.

Can graphs be used to mislead people?

EXAMPLE 1

Show students how to enter these numbers onto a list in their calculators. Show them how to use a second list as a frequency column.

Show students how to find the mean using a list. Explain to them that if the mean is reasonable given the data, they probably entered the numbers correctly.

Price, p ($)	Frequency, f
540	1
550	4
600	3
675	1
700	7
750	1
775	2
800	1
870	1
900	2
990	6
1,000	1
1,200	3
Total	33

CHECK YOUR UNDERSTANDING

Answer 19

EXAMPLE 2

To find the mean, Jerry could have added the 33 prices, instead of adding a column.

Make sure that when students add the numbers in the product column, they don't divide by the number of numbers they entered. They need to divide by 33, which is the number of pieces of data. This is a common error.

Skills and Strategies

Here you will learn how to organize data using a table and draw two types of graphs to display how the data is distributed.

EXAMPLE 1

Jerry wants to purchase a car stereo. He found 33 ads for the stereo he wants and arranged the prices in ascending order:

\$540 \$550 \$550 \$550 \$550 \$600 \$600 \$600 \$675 \$700 \$700 \$700
\$700 \$700 \$700 \$700 \$750 \$775 \$775 \$800 \$870 \$900 \$900 \$990
\$990 \$990 \$990 \$990 \$990 \$1,000 \$1,200 \$1,200 \$1,200

He is analyzing the prices, but having trouble because there are so many numbers. How can he organize his prices in a helpful format?

SOLUTION Jerry can set up a **frequency distribution**. A frequency distribution is a table that gives each price and the **frequency**—the number of stereos that are advertised at each price.

Jerry adds the numbers in the frequency column to find the total frequency—the total number of pieces of data in his data set. He wants to make sure he did not accidentally leave out a price.

Because there are 33 prices in the set, and the sum of the frequencies is 33, Jerry concludes his frequency distribution is correct.

CHECK YOUR UNDERSTANDING

Use the frequency distribution from Example 1 to find the number of car stereos selling for less than \$800.

EXAMPLE 2

Find the mean of the car stereos prices from Example 1.

SOLUTION Jerry creates another column in his table for the product of the first two column entries.

The sum of the entries in the third column, 26,425, is used to find the mean. This is the same sum you would find if you added the original 33 prices. Divide by 33 to find the mean, and round to the nearest cent.

$$26{,}425 \div 33 \approx 800.76$$

The mean of the prices is \$800.76.

You can use your graphing calculator to find the mean, median, and quartiles.

Price, p ($)	Frequency, f	Product, pf
540	1	540
550	4	2,200
600	3	1,800
675	1	675
700	7	4,900
750	1	750
775	2	1,550
800	1	800
870	1	870
900	2	1,800
990	6	5,940
1,000	1	1,000
1,200	3	3,600
Total	33	26,425

CHECK YOUR UNDERSTANDING

Jerry, from Example 1, decides he is not interested in any of the car stereos priced below $650 because they are in poor condition and need too much work. Find the mean of the data set that remains after those prices are removed.

EXAMPLE 3

Rod was doing Internet research on the number of gasoline price changes per year in gas stations in his county. He found the following graph, called a **stem-and-leaf plot**. What are the mean and the median of this distribution?

Stem	Leaves
1	1 1 2 3 7 9
2	0 3 6 6
3	8 8 9 9 9 9 9
4	0
5	2 2 4 5 5 5 6 7
6	3 4 4
7	2

5| 2 = 52

SOLUTION A stem-and-leaf plot displays data differently than a frequency table. To read the stem-and-leaf plot, look at the first row. In this plot, the numbers to the left of the vertical line represent the tens place digit, and are the stems. The numbers to the right of the vertical line represent the digits in the ones place, in ascending order, and are the leaves. The first row represents these numbers.

11, 11, 12, 13, 17, 19

The second row represents these numbers.

20, 23, 26, 26

The last row represents the number 72.

With one quick look at a stem-and-leaf plot, you can tell if there are many low numbers, many high numbers, or many numbers clustered in the center. Upon further investigation, you can find the total frequency and every piece of data in the data set. This allows you to find the mean, median, mode, range, and quartile values.

By counting the leaves, the entries on the right side of the vertical line, you find the frequency is 30. Add the data represented in the plot and divide to find the mean. The sum is 1,188.

Divide by 30 to find the mean. $1{,}188 \div 30 = 39.6$

The stem-and-leaf plot presents the numbers in ascending order. To find the median, locate the middle number. The frequency, 30, is even, so find the mean of the numbers in the 15th and 16th positions. The two middle numbers are both 39, so the median is 39.

Stem-and-leaf plots may have a slightly different look depending on what information is displayed. A stem-and-leaf plot should include a legend or key that describes how to read it.

CHECK YOUR UNDERSTANDING

Find the range and the upper and lower quartiles for the stem-and-leaf plot shown in Example 3.

CHECK YOUR UNDERSTANDING

Answer $875.40

EXAMPLE 3

Since there are different types of stem-and-leaf plots, they all need keys to identify how they should be read.

CHECK YOUR UNDERSTANDING

Answer range = 61; $Q_1 = 23$; $Q_3 = 55$

EXAMPLE 4

Box-and-whisker plots should be drawn to scale whenever possible. Explain that the mean cannot be computed using the information from a box-and-whisker plot. Also the median is not necessarily midway between the first and third quartiles. This is a common misconception.

You should provide several examples of boxplots where $Q_3 - Q_2$ does not equal $Q_2 - Q_1$ to show students all boxplots are not symmetrical.

CHECK YOUR UNDERSTANDING

Answer 75%

EXAMPLE 4

Rod, from Example 3, found another graph called a **box-and-whisker plot**, or **boxplot**. It is shown below.

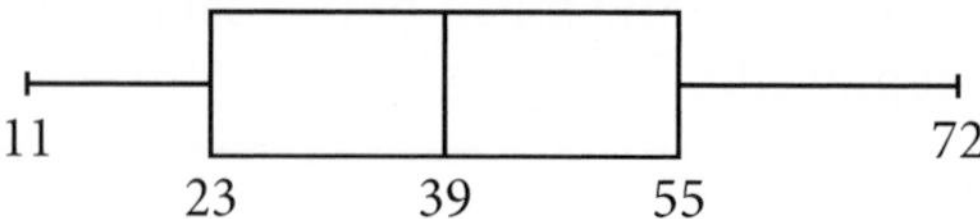

Find the interquartile range of the distribution.

SOLUTION Look at the information presented on the box-and-whisker plot.

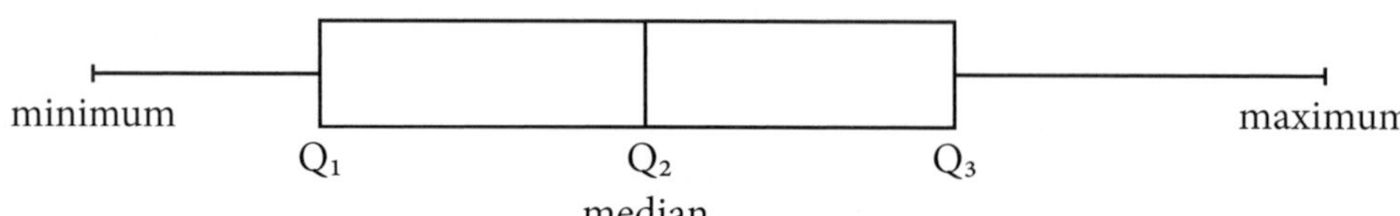

The box-and-whisker plot shows all four quartiles and the *least* number. It should be drawn to scale, so it changes shape depending on the distribution. Recall that the interquartile range can be computed by subtracting Q_1 from Q_3. The box part of the diagram helps you find the interquartile range, because it displays Q_1 and Q_3.

$$Q_3 - Q_1 = 55 - 23 = 32$$

The interquartile range is 32. That means 50% of all the gas prices are within this range. Notice that you can also find the range using a boxplot, but you cannot find the mean from a boxplot.

You can use the statistics menu on your graphing calculator to draw a box-and-whisker plot.

■ CHECK YOUR UNDERSTANDING

Based on the box-and-whisker plot from Example 4, what percent of the gas stations had 55 or fewer price changes?

EXAMPLE 5

The following box-and-whisker plot gives the purchase prices of the cars of 114 seniors at West High School. Are any of the car prices outliers?

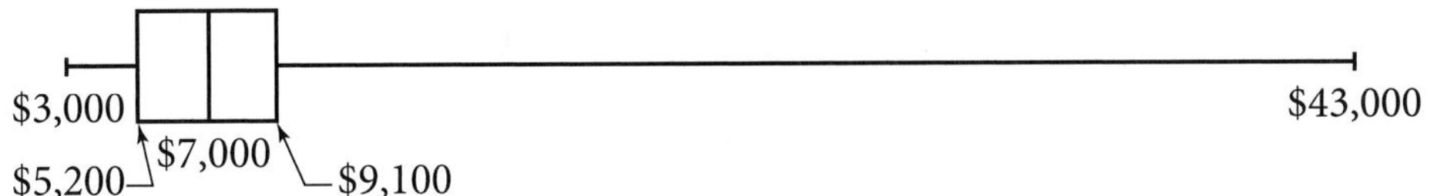

SOLUTION Quartiles are shown on the boxplot, so you can find the interquartile range. The interquartile range is

$$IQR = Q_3 - Q_1 = 9{,}100 - 5{,}200 = 3{,}900$$

The boundary for lower outliers is

$$Q_1 - 1.5(IQR) = 5{,}200 - 1.5(3{,}900) = -650$$

There are no lower outliers.

The boundary for upper outliers is

$$Q_3 + 1.5(IQR) = 9{,}100 + 1.5(3{,}900) = 14{,}950$$

There is at least one upper outlier, the high price of $43,000. From this boxplot, you cannot tell if there are any others, because the boxplot does not give all the original data. Boxplots are drawn to scale, so the long whisker on the right means that there could be more than one outlier.

If you want to show outliers on a boxplot, you can create a **modified boxplot**. A modified boxplot shows all the numbers that are outliers as single points past the whiskers. In the following modified boxplot, $43,000 is the only outlier. The greatest price less than $43,000 is $12,500.

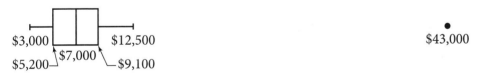

If there were three upper outliers, the modified boxplot would have three dots to the right of the whisker.

$3,000 $12,500 $21,000 $43,000

$5,200 $7,000 $9,100 $16,000

Modified boxplots give more information than standard box-and-whisker plots. Your calculator can draw modified boxplots.

CHECK YOUR UNDERSTANDING

Examine the modified boxplot. Is 400 an outlier?

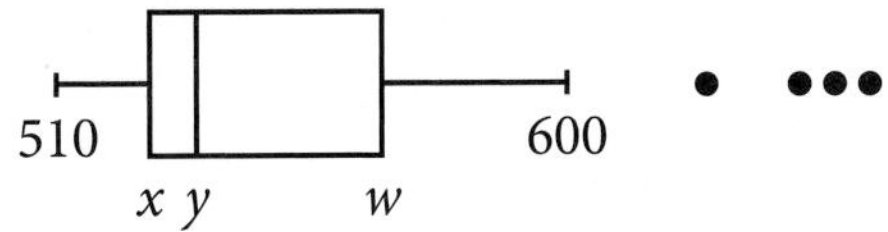

EXAMPLE 5

To help students visualize the scale of the boxplot, you may want to draw a number line above the box-plot from the example for demonstration purposes.

Reinforce that the right endpoint of the whisker in a modified box-plot with an upper outlier is not the boundary for the upper outlier; it is the greatest piece of data that is below the boundary for the upper outliers.

CHECK YOUR UNDERSTANDING

Answer yes

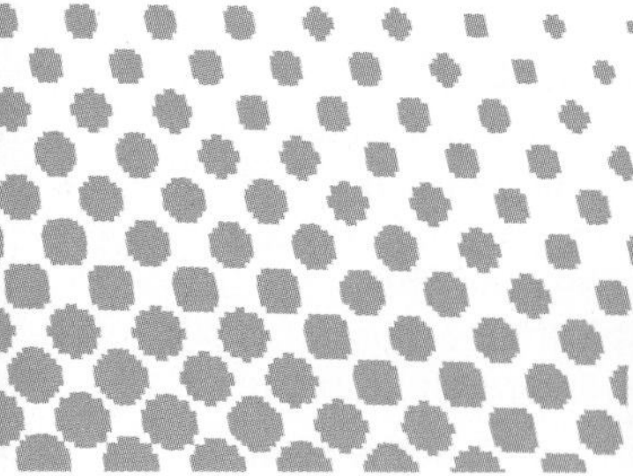

Applications

It is a capital mistake to theorize before one has data.
Sir Arthur Conan Doyle, Scottish Author (Sherlock Holmes novels)

TEACH

Exercise 6
If students are getting the wrong answers, analyze their work step by step to determine if they misunderstood a concept earlier in the process which is affecting their final answer.

ANSWERS

1. You need facts—data—to back up any theory you have. Using convenient anecdotal evidence to create a theory is not wise.

6a.

Price	Frequency
$ 8,500	3
$ 9.900	1
$10,800	2
$11,000	1
$12,500	2
$13,000	2
$14,500	1
$23,000	1

7b. If the data has an outlier, then a modified boxplot would more appropriately represent the data.

1. Interpret the quote in the context of what you learned. See margin.

2. Look at the frequency table in Example 2. Imagine the 33 prices listed in ascending order. If the prices were numbered using subscripts from p_1 to p_{33}, the middle price would be price number p_{17}. Use the frequency table to find the median. $750

3. Find the mode of the distribution from Example 1. $700

4. Find the range of the distribution from Example 1. $660

5. Martina found the mean of the data from Example 1 by adding the prices in the first column and dividing by the number of prices she added. Her answer was incorrect. Explain what error she made. Martina did not take into account the frequency of each price.

6. Brian looked up prices of thirteen used Chevrolet HHR "retro" trucks in the classified ads and found these prices: $8,500, $8,500, $8,500, $9,900, $10,800, $10,800, $11,000, $12,500, $12,500, $13,000, $13,000, $14,500, and $23,000.
- **a.** Make a frequency table for this data set. See margin.
- **b.** Find the mean. Round to the nearest dollar. $12,038
- **c.** Find the median. $11,000
- **d.** Find the mode. $8,500
- **e.** Find the range. $14,500
- **f.** Find the four quartiles. Q_1 = $9,200; Q_2 = $11,000; Q_3 = $13,000; Q_4 = $23,000
- **g.** Find the interquartile range. $3,800
- **h.** Find the boundary for the upper outliers. $18,700
- **i.** Find the boundary for the lower outliers. $3,500
- **j.** How many outliers are there? 1
- **k.** Draw a modified box-and-whisker plot. Label it. See additional answers.

7. Enter the data from Example 1 in your calculator.
- **a.** Create a box-and-whisker plot using the data from Example 1. See additional answers.
- **b.** How would you determine if it would be appropriate to create a modified boxplot for this data? See margin.
- **c.** How many outliers are there in this distribution? 0

8. Megan has a friend at work who is selling a used Honda. The car has 60,000 miles on it. Megan comparison shops and finds these prices for the same car.
- **a.** Find the mean price of the 5 prices listed. $18,320
- **b.** How many of these cars are priced below the mean? 3
- **c.** Find the median price. $18,000
- **d.** How many of these cars are priced below the median? 2

Price
$22,000
$19,000
$18,000
$16,700
$15,900

9. Megan, from Exercise 8, decides to get more information about the cars she researched. The table has prices and mileages for the same used car. In addition to the statistics she has learned in this chapter, Megan decides to use her linear regression skills from Chapter 2 to see if there is a relationship between the prices and the mileage. She hopes to use this knowledge to negotiate with sellers.

Mileage, x	Price, y
21,000	$22,000
30,000	$19,000
40,000	$18,000
51,000	$16,700
55,000	$15,900

a. Enter the data into your calculator. Find the regression equation. Round to the nearest hundredth. $y = -0.16x + 24{,}722.26$

b. Find the correlation coefficient r. Round to three decimal places. $r = -0.970$

c. Is the regression equation a good predictor of price, given the mileage? Explain. Yes; r is close to −1.

d. The car Megan is considering has 60,000 miles on it and the price is $19,000. Discuss her negotiating strategy. Explain on what grounds she should try to get a lower price. See margin.

10. The Cold Spring High School student government polled randomly selected seniors and asked them how much money they spent on gas in the last week. The following stem-and-leaf plot shows the data they collected.

1	7
4	1 1 2 9
5	3 3 3 3 3
6	1 3 4 6 7 8 9
7	1 3 5 5 7
8	2 2 3 4

8| 2 = 82

a. How many students were polled? 26

b. Find the mean to the nearest cent. $62.12

c. Find the median. $65

d. Find the mode. $53

e. Find the range. $67

f. Find the four quartiles. $Q_1 = \$53$; $Q_2 = \$65$; $Q_3 = \$75$; $Q_4 = \$84$

g. What percent of the students spent $53 or more on gas? 75%

h. Find the interquartile range. $22

i. What percent of the students spent from $53 to $75 on gas? 50%

j. Find the boundary for the lower outliers. $20

k. Find the boundary for the upper outliers. $108

l. How many outliers are there? 1

m. Draw a modified boxplot. See additional answers.

11. A group of randomly-selected recent college graduates were asked how much the monthly payment is on their student loan. The responses are shown in the stem-and-leaf plot.

16	2 3 5 5
17	5 7 8
18	7 7
19	2 4 6
20	1 1
21	
22	5 6 6 6

16| 2 = $162

a. What is the total frequency? 18

b. How many people had monthly payments between $210 and $219? 0

c. What is the mode monthly payment? $226

d. What is the median monthly payment? $189.50

12. Express the mean of the data set shown in the frequency table algebraically. $\frac{xy + 5w + 64 + 18v}{y + v + 9}$

Price	Frequency
x	y
w	5
16	4
18	v

TEACH

Exercise 10
Point out to students that if a distribution has no outliers, then the boxplot and modified boxplot are the same.

Exercise 11
This stem-and-leaf is different than the previous ones, but as long as the key is clear the format is acceptable.

Exercise 12
If a student has trouble with this problem, have them review Example 2 in Skills and Strategies. Then they can apply the operations shown to the algebraic representation required for this answer.

ANSWERS

9d. When 60,000 miles is substituted into the regression equation, the predicted price is approximately $15,122. That is almost $4,000 lower than the asking price for the car. That is sufficient reason to ask for the price to be lowered.

Never lend your car to anyone to whom you have given birth.
Erma Bombeck, Humor Writer

5-4 Automobile Insurance

Objectives

- Learn about different types of auto insurance coverage.
- Compute insurance costs.
- Compute payments on insurance claims.

Common Core

F-IF7a, S-ID7

Key Terms

- liable
- negligent
- automobile insurance
- premium
- claim
- liability insurance
- bodily injury liability (BI)
- property damage liability (PD)
- uninsured/underinsured motorist protection (UMP)
- personal injury protection (PIP)
- no-fault insurance
- comprehensive insurance
- collision insurance
- car-rental insurance
- emergency road service insurance
- actuary
- surcharge
- deductible

CCSS Warm-Up

Write a linear equation for each of the following.

1. slope: $-2/3$
y-intercept: -8

2. slope: 0
y-intercept: -8

3. no slope
x-intercept: -8

1. $y = (-2/3)x - 8$ 2. $y = -8$ 3. $x = -8$

EXAMINE THE QUESTION

What types of damages can you cause while driving? Initiate a discussion on "what could go wrong" when you are operating an automobile.

CLASS DISCUSSION

Do you know how much auto body work costs? How much a fire hydrant or lamp post costs?

What do you know about the cost of doctors and hospitals?

Discuss what specific items are covered by comprehensive insurance, and ask students if they personally know of any car damages caused by the listed disasters. You could refer to the intense damage caused to automobiles in New York City the day of the September 11 attacks, and how comprehensive insurance covered them.

WHY IS HAVING AUTO INSURANCE SO IMPORTANT?

Even responsible drivers run the risk of injuring themselves, hurting other people, and damaging property. By law, drivers are **liable** (responsible) to pay for the damages they cause with their automobiles. You could also be sued for being **negligent** (at fault) if you cause an accident.

Drivers purchase **automobile insurance** because most drivers cannot afford the costs that could result from an auto accident. An automobile insurance policy is a contract between a driver and an insurance company. The driver agrees to pay a fee (called the **premium**) and the company agrees to cover certain accident-related costs when the driver makes a **claim** (a request for money). **Liability insurance** is the most important coverage. States set minimum liability requirements. Insurance regulations vary by state. Liability insurance is required unless you can prove financial responsibility otherwise. Several types of coverages are available.

- **Bodily Injury Liability (BI)** BI liability covers bodily injury. If you are at fault in an automobile accident, you are responsible for paying the medical expenses of anyone injured in the accident. You can purchase as much BI liability as you want.
- **Property Damage Liability (PD)** This coverage pays for damage you cause to other people's property. You are financially responsible if you damage a telephone pole, fire hydrant, another car, or any other property. You can purchase as much PD liability insurance as you want.
- **Uninsured/Underinsured Motorist Protection (UMP)** This coverage pays for injuries to you or your passengers caused by a driver who has no insurance or does not have enough insurance to cover your medical losses.

- **Personal Injury Protection (PIP)** This is coverage, mandatory in some states, that pays for any physical injuries you or your passengers sustain while in the vehicle, even if you are not involved in a traffic accident. It compensates you regardless of who is at fault, so it is sometimes called **no-fault insurance**. Your PIP insurance will cover you and people injured in, on, around, or under your car for medical treatment.
- **Comprehensive Insurance** This covers the repair or replacement of parts of your car damaged by vandalism, fire, flood, wind, earthquakes, falling objects, riots, hail, damage from trees, and other disasters. It also covers your car if it is stolen. If your car is older, comprehensive coverage may not be cost-effective.
- **Collision Insurance** This pays you for the repair or replacement of your car if it's damaged in a collision with another vehicle or object, or if it overturns, no matter who is at fault. If you took out a loan to purchase your car, the lender will probably require you to have collision coverage. If your car is older, collision coverage may not be a worthwhile expense.
- **Car-Rental Insurance** This pays you for part of the cost of a rented car if your car is disabled because of a collision or comprehensive-covered repair.
- **Emergency Road Service Insurance** This coverage pays for towing or road service when your car is disabled. Only the road service fee is covered. Gas, oil, part, and labor are not covered.

Auto insurance companies are in business to make a profit. The company loses money if a high percentage of insured drivers get into accidents. Insurance companies classify drivers according to their age, sex, marital status, driving record, and locality. Statisticians called **actuaries** predict how often customers, based on these criteria, will submit claims.

CLASS DISCUSSION

If a driver has PIP insurance, causes an injury, and there are no lawsuits, then the PIP insurance, and not the BI insurance, takes care of covering the injuries. Students sometimes find this confusing, since it is easy to assume that "bodily injury" covers injuries.

TEACH

For students to be responsible drivers, they need to understand the language of auto insurance. They should share what they are learning with their parents, especially as they will soon be asking for car privileges.

The mathematics involves translating the vocabulary into appropriate math sentences.

EXAMPLE 1

Discuss the advantages of paying quarterly with students. Point out that the surcharge is paid with each quarterly payment.

Skills and Strategies

Once you learn more about auto insurance, you'll understand how you can save money and comparison shop for different insurance policies.

EXAMPLE 1

Kwan's annual premium is $1,284. If he pays quarterly, there is a $1 per payment **surcharge** (extra fee). What is the quarterly payment?

SOLUTION

Divide the annual premium by 4 $\quad 1{,}284 \div 4 = 321$

Add on the $1 surcharge. $\quad 321 + 1 = 322$

Each of the four quarterly payments is $322.

■ CHECK YOUR UNDERSTANDING

Leon's annual premium is x dollars. If he pays his premium semiannually, there is a y-dollar surcharge on each semiannual payment. Express the amount of his semiannual payment algebraically.

CHECK YOUR UNDERSTANDING

Answer $\frac{x}{2} + y$

EXAMPLE 2

Stress that property damage liability insurance does not cover damage you do to your own car in an accident.

CHECK YOUR UNDERSTANDING

Answer $x + y$

This amount will be paid in full if the coverage limit on the property damage is greater than $x + y$. The w-dollar damage is not covered under PD.

EXAMPLE 3

The deductible is per accident. Collision and comprehensive are sold on a deductible basis.

CHECK YOUR UNDERSTANDING

Answer $y - x$

EXAMPLE 2

Stan DeMille has $25,000 worth of property damage liability insurance. He caused an accident that damaged a $2,000 fire hydrant and did $5,600 worth of damage to another car. How much of the damage must Stan pay?

SOLUTION Find the sum of the damages.

$$2{,}000 + 5{,}600 = 7{,}600$$

$7,600 < $25,000, so the company will pay for all of the damage and Stan will pay nothing. Notice that this $25,000 coverage is *per accident.*

■ CHECK YOUR UNDERSTANDING

Keith ran his car into a telephone pole that had a bicycle leaning against it which was also damaged. The pole will cost x dollars to fix, the bicycle will cost y dollars to replace, and there was w dollars damage to the car. Express algebraically the amount that can be claimed under Keith's property damage liability insurance.

Deductibles

When you purchase an automobile insurance policy, you must choose a *deductible* amount that will be part of the policy. The **deductible** is the amount that the policy owner must pay before the insurance policy pays any money. Once an owner has paid the deductible amount, the insurance company pays the rest of the cost to get the repairs done. Collision insurance only covers damage to the policy owner's car, not property damaged, or another driver's vehicle. If a driver has $500 deductible and the repairs to this car cost $2,200, the driver pays the first $500 and the insurance company pays the balance, 2,200 – 500, or $1,700.

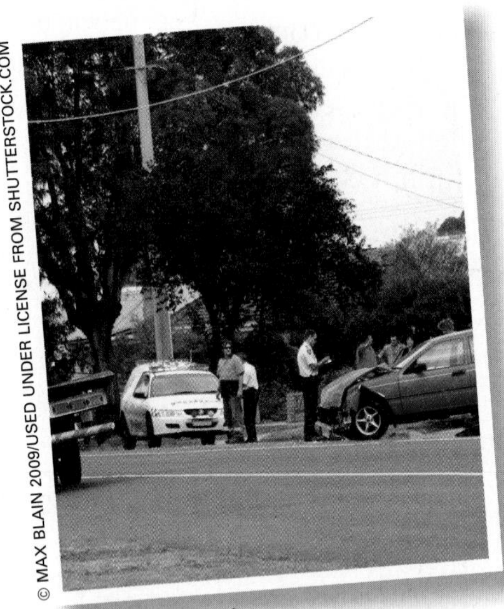

EXAMPLE 3

Peter has $1,000 deductible collision insurance. Peter backs his car into his garage and causes $4,300 worth of damage to the car. How much will his insurance company have to pay?

SOLUTION Subtract the deductible, which is $1,000, because Peter must pay that amount.

$$4{,}300 - 1{,}000 = 3{,}300$$

The company must pay $3,300.

■ CHECK YOUR UNDERSTANDING

Manuel has an x-dollar deductible on his comprehensive insurance. His car is stolen and never recovered. The value of his car is y dollars where $y > x$. How much must the insurance company pay him for his stolen car?

Bodily Injury and Property Damage

Bodily injury insurance coverage uses two numbers with a slash between them. The first number is the maximum amount per accident the insurance company will pay, in thousands of dollars, to any one person who is hurt and sues you due to your driving negligence. The second number represents the maximum amount per accident your insurance company will pay in total to all people who sue as a result of the accident. Sometimes, bodily injury and property damage are combined into a three number system with two slashes. The numbers 100/300/25 represent 100/300 BI insurance and $25,000 PD insurance.

EXAMPLE 4

Bob was in an auto accident caused by his negligence. He has 100/300 bodily injury insurance. The three people injured in the accident sued. One person was awarded $140,000, and each of the other two was awarded $75,000. How much does the insurance company pay?

SOLUTION Bob has 100/300 BI, so the company only pays $100,000 to the person who was awarded $140,000. The other two injured persons were awarded a total of $150,000. Each was under $100,000. The most Bob's company would pay out for any BI claim is $300,000.

Add the awarded amounts. $100{,}000 + 75{,}000 + 75{,}000 = 250{,}000$

$250,000 < $300,000, so the insurance company pays $250,000. The remaining $40,000 owed to one of the injured is Bob's responsibility.

CHECK YOUR UNDERSTANDING

Joan has 50/100 BI liability insurance. She hurts 28 children riding a school bus, and each child is awarded $10,000 as a result of a lawsuit. How much will the insurance company pay in total for this lawsuit?

EXAMPLE 5

Desmond has a policy with 50/150 BI, $50,000 PD, and $50,000 PIP. He causes an accident in which he hurts 7 people in a minivan and 4 people in his own car, including himself. The eleven people who are hurt have minor injuries and do not sue Desmond. The total medical bill for all involved is $53,233. How much does the insurance company pay?

SOLUTION Desmond is covered by his PIP, which has a limit of $50,000 per person, per accident. PIP takes care of medical payments without regard to who is at fault. The company pays the entire $53,233, as long as no individual person requests more than $50,000.

Notice that the bodily injury numbers were not relevant in this scenario.

CHECK YOUR UNDERSTANDING

Pat has 50/100 BI liability insurance and $100,000 PIP insurance. She hurts 28 children in a school bus and is not sued. However, if each child needs $10,000 for medical care, how much will the insurance company pay in total for these medical claims?

EXAMPLE 4

You can pose similar scenarios to students to make sure they understand the bodily injury numbering scheme. It will take several examples for all students to be clear on the different possibilities.

CHECK YOUR UNDERSTANDING

Answer $100,000

EXAMPLE 5

This example will help show the difference between PIP and BI insurance. There were no lawsuits, so BI did not take effect since the person had no-fault (PIP) insurance.

CHECK YOUR UNDERSTANDING

Answer $280,000

Remind students that the $100,000 PIP coverage limit is per person, per accident.

Applications

Never lend your car to anyone to whom you have given birth.
Erma Bombeck, Humor Writer

TEACH

Exercise 7
Under PIP, the fact that one person has a small claim has no effect on another person's claim that exceeds the coverage limit.

The person who exceeds the limit cannot receive funds from the unused money from the small claim.

ANSWERS

1. Driving a car is a tremendous responsibility, and often the source of parent-teenager conflicts. Teenage drivers have the highest frequency of accidents.

1. Interpret the quote in the context of what you learned. See margin.

2. Rachel has $25,000 worth of property damage insurance. She causes $32,000 worth of damage to a sports car in an accident.
  a. How much of the damages will the insurance company have to pay? $25,000
  b. How much will Rachel have to pay? $7,000

personal injury protection	$234
bodily injury liability	$266
property damage liability	$190
uninsured motorist protection	$11
comprehensive insurance	$344
collision insurance	$410
emergency road service	$12

3. Ronald Kivetsky bought a new car and received these price quotes from his insurance company.
  a. What is the annual premium? $1,467
  b. What is the semiannual premium? $733.50
  c. How much less would Ronald's semiannual payments be if he dropped the optional collision insurance? $205

4. Gloria pays her insurance three times each year. The first payment is 40% of the annual premium, and each of the next two payments is 30% of the annual premium. If the annual premium is $924, find the amounts of the three payments. $369.60; $277.20; $277.20

5. Ruth Fanelli has decided to drop her collision insurance because her car is getting old. Her total annual premium is $916, of which $170.60 covers collision insurance.
  a. What will her annual premium be after she drops the collision insurance? $745.40
  b. What will her quarterly payments be after she drops the collision coverage? $186.35

6. Gary Lieberman has $10,000 worth of property damage insurance. He collides with two parked cars and causes $12,000 worth of damage. How much money must Gary pay after the insurance company pays its share? $2,000

7. Craig Rosenberg has a personal injury protection policy that covers each person in, on, around, or under his car for medical expenses as a result of an accident. Each person can collect up to $50,000. Craig is involved in an accident and three people are hurt. One person has $23,000 of medical expenses, one person has $500 worth of medical expenses, and Craig himself has medical expenses totaling $70,000. How much money must the insurance company pay out for these three people? $73,500

8. Leslie has comprehensive insurance with a $500 deductible on her van. On Halloween her van is vandalized, and the damages total $1,766. Leslie submits a claim to her insurance company.
  a. How much must Leslie pay for the repair? $500
  b. How much must the insurance company pay? $1,266

9. Felix Madison has $10,000 worth of property damage insurance and a $1,000 deductible collision insurance policy. He had a tire blowout while driving and crashed into a $1,400 fire hydrant. The crash caused $1,600 in damages to his car.

a. Which insurance covers the damage to the fire hydrant? property damage

b. How much will the insurance company pay for the fire hydrant? $1,400

c. Which insurance covers the damage to the car? collision

d. How much will the insurance company pay for the damage to the car? $600

10. Jared's car slides into a stop sign during an ice storm. There is x dollars damage to his car, where $x > 1{,}000$, and the stop sign will cost y dollars to replace. Jared has $25,000 worth of PD insurance, a $1,000 deductible on his collision and comprehensive insurance, and $50,000 no-fault insurance.

a. Which insurance covers the damage to the sign? PD

b. How much will his company pay for the stop sign? See margin.

c. Which insurance covers the damage to his car? collision

d. How much will his company pay for the damage to the car? $x - 1{,}000$

11. Eric must pay his p dollar annual insurance premium by himself. He works at a job after school.

a. Express how much he must save each month to pay this premium algebraically. $\frac{p}{12}$

b. If he gets into a few accidents and his company raises his insurance 15%, express how much he must save each month to meet this new premium algebraically. $0.15\left(\frac{p}{12}\right)$

12. Mollie has 100/300/50 liability insurance and $50,000 PIP insurance. She drives through a stop sign and hits a telephone pole and bounces into a minivan with 8 people inside. Some are seriously hurt and sue her. Others have minor injuries. Three passengers in Mollie's car are also hurt.

a. The pole will cost $7,000 to replace. Mollie also did $6,700 worth of damage to the minivan. What insurance will cover this, and how much will the company pay? property damage; $13,700

b. The minivan's driver was a concert violinist. The injury to his hand means he can never work again. He sues for $4,000,000 and is awarded that money in court. What type of insurance covers this, and how much will the insurance company pay? BI; $100,000

c. The minivan's driver (from part b) had medical bills totaling $60,000 from his hospital trip and physical therapy after the accident. What type of insurance covers this, and how much will the insurance company pay? PIP; $50,000

d. The three passengers in Mollie's car are hurt and each requires $12,000 worth of medical attention. What insurance covers this, and how much will the company pay? PIP; $36,000

13. Julianne currently pays x dollars for her annual premium. She will be away at college for the upcoming year and will only use the car when she is home on vacations. Her insurance company offers her a 35% discount for her annual premium. Express algebraically the amount she must save each month to pay the new, lower premium. $\frac{x - 0.35x}{12}$ or $\frac{0.65x}{12}$

TEACH

Exercise 9

This is a good problem to ensure students understand PD and collision coverage.

Exercise 10

Remind students that no-fault is another name for PIP, and it never covers any physical damage to property.

ANSWERS

10b. y dollars, the cost of a stop sign is less than $25,000.

TEACH

Exercise 16

This stem-and-leaf plot differs from the ones previously discussed. Using the legend, students should be able to extend their knowledge of stem-and-leaf plots to decipher it.

14. The Schuster family just bought a third car. The annual premium would have been x dollars to insure the car, but they are entitled to a 10% discount since they have other cars with the company.

a. Express their annual premium after the discount algebraically. $x - 0.1x$, or $0.9x$

b. If they pay their premium quarterly and have to pay a y-dollar surcharge for this arrangement, express their quarterly payment algebraically. $\frac{0.9x}{4} + y$

15. Marc currently pays x dollars per year for auto insurance. Next year, his rates are going to increase 15%. If he completes a defensive driver course, the insurance company will lower his rate by d dollars.

a. Express his annual premium for next year algebraically if he completes the course. $x + 0.15x - d$ or $1.15x - d$

b. Express his semiannual premium for next year algebraically if he does not complete the course. $\frac{1.15x}{2}$

16. The stem-and-leaf plot gives the semiannual premiums for the girls and boys in Van Buren High School who currently drive. It is called a *back-to-back stem-and-leaf plot,* and combines two stem-and-leaf plots. The numbers between the two vertical lines represent the hundreds and tens digits. The numbers on the extreme left show the units digits for the girls. Notice they are written in ascending order as you move out from the middle. The numbers on the extreme right show the units digits for the boys.

Girls	Stem	Boys
9 8 1 1 1 1	87	1 2 2
3 2	88	2 4 6 7
7 5 4	89	1 3
7 6 6 6 6 5	90	2 7 7 7

1| 87 = $871

87| 1 = $871

a. How many girls at Van Buren HS drive? 17

b. How many boys at Van Buren HS drive? 13

c. Find the range of the annual premiums for all of the students. $36

17. The following stem-and-leaf plot gives the number of juniors who took a driver education course at Guy Patterson High School over the last two decades. Construct a box-and-whisker plot based on the data. See additional answers.

Stem	Leaf
4	1 2 3 5 5 6
5	1 1 8 8 8 9
6	0 0 0 1 2 5
7	1 1

1| 5 = 15

18. Express the boundary for the upper outliers algebraically, using the modified box-and-whisker plot given below. $d + 1.5(d - c)$

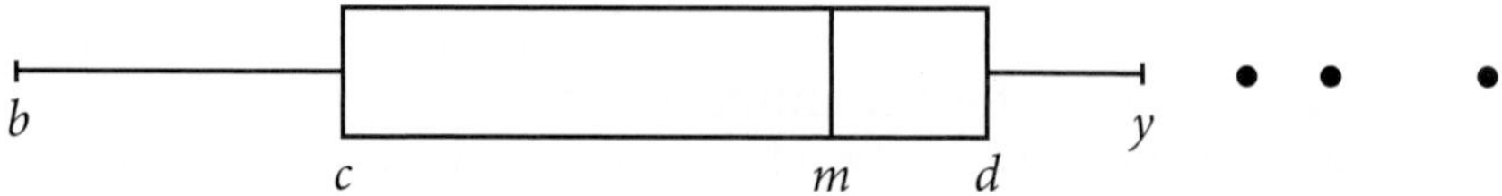

If the automobile had followed the same development cycle as the computer, a Rolls-Royce would today cost $100 [and] get a million miles per gallon.

Michael Moncur, Internet Consultant

Linear Automobile Depreciation

5-5

Key Terms
- depreciate
- appreciate
- straight line depreciation
- slope
- straight line depreciation equation

Objectives
- Write, interpret, and graph a straight line depreciation equation.

Common Core

A-CED2, A-CED3, F-IF6, F-IF7a, F-IF9, F-LE1b, F-LE5

CCSS Warm-Up

A parabola models a price function where x is the price and y is the number of items sold.
The vertex is (24, 3000) and the roots are (16, 0) and (32, 0). What do $x = 16$, $x = 24$, and $x = 32$ represent in this situation?
If the price is set at $16 or $32, no items will be sold. If the price is set at $24, the maximum number of items will be sold.

WHAT IS THE VALUE OF YOUR CAR?

Most cars will not be worth their purchase prices as they get older. Most cars **depreciate**; that is, they lose value over time. Some collectible cars increase in value over time, or **appreciate**. The simplest form of depreciation is **straight line depreciation**. When a car loses the same amount of value each year, the scatterplot that models this depreciation appears linear. By determining the equation of this linear model, you can find the value of the car at any time in its lifespan. There are many factors contributing to the depreciation of an automobile. The condition of the car, mileage, and make of the car are only a few of those factors. The straight line depreciation equation is a mathematical model that can be used as a starting point in examining auto depreciation.

In Chapter 2, you used the intercepts of linear equations when graphing expense and demand functions. Recall that the horizontal intercept always has the form $(a, 0)$ and the vertical intercept always has the form $(0, b)$. In addition to intercepts, straight lines also have slope. The **slope** of the line is the numerical value for the inclination or declination of that line. It is expressed as a ratio of the change in the vertical variable over the change in the horizontal variable from one point on the line to the next. Traditionally, the horizontal axis is called the x-axis and the vertical axis is called the y-axis. Using those variable names, the slope of a line would be represented by the following ratio.

$$\text{Slope} = \frac{\text{Change in } y\text{-value}}{\text{Change in } x\text{-value}}$$

If the coordinates of the two points are (x_1, y_1) and (x_2, y_2), then the slope can be modeled mathematically by the following ratio.

$$\textbf{Slope ratio} \quad \frac{y_2 - y_1}{x_2 - x_1}$$

The independent variable in a car's depreciation equation is *time in years* and the dependent variable is *car value*. By identifying the intercepts and slope of a straight line depreciation model, you will be able to determine the equation that represents the depreciation.

EXAMINE THE QUESTION

How do the automobile industry, car dealers, and individual owners define "car value"? The value of a car can be both personal and monetary. Ask the students what makes a car personally valuable? Ask students what factors might contribute to the monetary value of a car?

CLASS DISCUSSION

Ask students to list items that would appreciate/depreciate over time. Discuss the fact that straight line depreciation is merely a depreciation model and may not be the exact way that cars lose value over time. We introduce it here as a means for beginning the discussion on depreciation.

Use this opportunity to review the general equation for a straight line, $y = mx + b$. Discuss the slope, the intercepts, and the fact that all points on the line must satisfy the equation.

TEACH

This lesson serves as the introductory lesson to automobile depreciation. Students learn how to interpret, create, graph, and use the equation that models straight line depreciation by identifying the depreciation slope and the depreciation intercepts.

EXAMPLE 1

People say that a car depreciates the moment it is driven off the car lot. The original price of the car is established at year 0 (before it is driven off the lot). If points on the depreciation line are represented by (year, value), then the point (0, 27,000) must lie on the line. If the car has no value after 12 years, then the point (12, 0) must also lie on the line. Ask students where these points would be located on a coordinate grid. Do they determine a unique line?

CHECK YOUR UNDERSTANDING

Answer (0, *D*) and (*T*, 0)

EXAMPLE 2

Before starting this problem, ask students for their definition of slope. Some may say "rise over run" but press them further for a better explanation. The slope indicates vertical and horizontal distances from one point to another on the line. Before applying the slope formula, ask students to describe how they would vertically and horizontally jump from (0, 27,000) to (12, 0). Repeat the same question for (12, 0) to (0, 27,000).

CHECK YOUR UNDERSTANDING

Answer $\frac{-D}{T}$

Skills and Strategies

Here you will learn how to determine and use a **straight line depreciation equation**.

EXAMPLE 1

Suppose that you purchase a car for $27,000. According to your online research, this make and model of car loses all of its marketable value after 12 years. That is, it depreciates to a value of zero dollars 12 years after the purchase date. If this car depreciates in a straight line form, what are the intercepts of the depreciation equation?

SOLUTION Let x represent the time in years. The minimum x-value is 0 years, the purchase year of the car. Because the car totally depreciates after 12 years, the maximum x-value will be 12.

In a straight line depreciation equation, the intercepts are

(0, maximum car value) and (maximum lifespan, 0)

Let y represent the value of the car at any time during its lifetime. The minimum y-value is zero dollars and the maximum y-value is the purchase price of $27,000. Knowing this information, you can identify the intercepts as (0, 27,000) and (12, 0).

■ CHECK YOUR UNDERSTANDING

A car sells for D dollars and totally depreciates after T years. If this car straight line depreciates, what are the intercepts of the straight line depreciation equation?

EXAMPLE 2

Determine the slope of the straight line depreciation equation for the situation in Example 1.

SOLUTION Two points determine a line, so you only need two points to determine the slope of a line. Let the coordinates of the y-intercept be the first point. That is, $(x_1, y_1) = (0, 27{,}000)$. Let the coordinates of the x-intercept be the second point. That is, $(x_2, y_2) = (12, 0)$.

Use the slope ratio. $\frac{y_2 - y_1}{x_2 - x_1}$

Substitute and simplify. $\frac{0 - 27{,}000}{12 - 0} = \frac{-27{,}000}{12} = -2{,}250$

The slope of the depreciation line is $\frac{-2{,}250}{1}$.

■ CHECK YOUR UNDERSTANDING

Write the slope of the straight line depreciation equation that models the situation in which a car is purchased for D dollars and totally depreciates after T years.

EXAMPLE 3

Write the straight line depreciation equation for the situation discussed in Examples 1 and 2. Then draw the graph of the equation.

SOLUTION The general form for the equation of a straight line is

$$y = mx + b$$

where m represents the slope of the line and b represents the y-intercept.

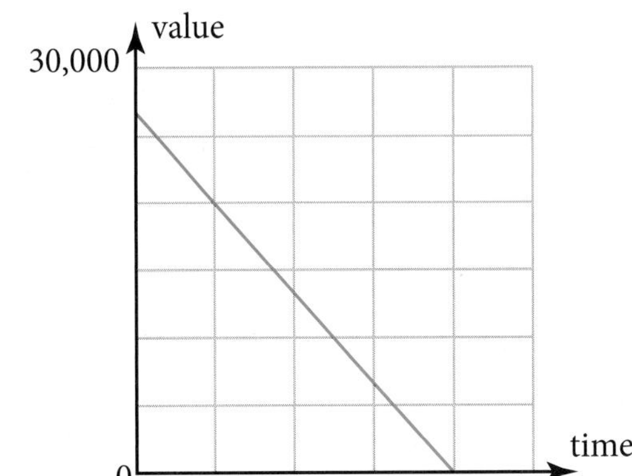

The slope is −2,250, and the y-intercept is 27,000. Therefore, the straight line depreciation equation is

$$y = -2{,}250x + 27{,}000$$

To graph the equation on a graphing calculator, first determine an appropriate graphing window. Use your maximum and minimum x- and y-values as a starting point. Choose x- and y-values that are larger than the maximum values you have determined so that you get a complete picture of the graph. One such pair could be a maximum of $30,000 on the y-axis and 15 on the x-axis as shown in the graph. Because time and car value are both positive numbers, the minimum x- and y-values will be zero.

EXAMPLE 3

Here students must determine the depreciation equation. Examples 1 and 2 had them work through all of the information they will need. Some students may want to express the slope as a fraction with 1 in the denominator. Indicate that it is not necessary to do so and eliminating the 1 makes the equation easier to interpret. Once the equation is established, ask students for the real-world significance of the numbers −2,250 and 27,000.

■ CHECK YOUR UNDERSTANDING

Write and graph the straight line depreciation equation for a car that was purchased for $22,000 and totally depreciates after 11 years.

CHECK YOUR UNDERSTANDING

Answer The equation is $y = -2{,}000x + 22{,}000$. The graph is

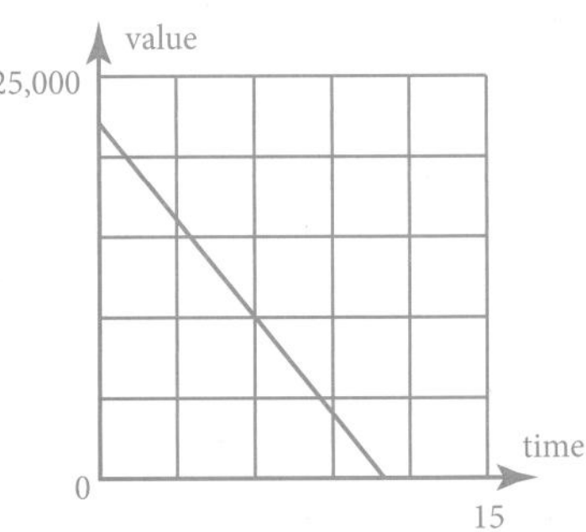

EXAMPLE 4

Suppose that Jack purchased a car five years ago at a price of $27,600. According to research on this make and model, similar cars have straight line depreciated to zero value after 12 years. How much will this car be worth after 66 months?

SOLUTION Determine the straight line depreciation equation. The intercepts are (0, 27,600) and (12, 0). Determine the slope.

$$\frac{y_2 - y_1}{x_2 - x_1} = \frac{0 - 27{,}600}{12 - 0} = \frac{-27{,}600}{12} = -2{,}300$$

Therefore, the straight line depreciation equation is $y = -2{,}300x + 27{,}600$. Because x represents years, it is necessary to convert 66 months into years by dividing by 12.

$$\frac{66}{12} = 5.5$$

Therefore, 66 months is equivalent to 5.5 years.

Use the depreciation equation.	$y = -2{,}300x + 27{,}600$
Substitute 5.5 for x.	$y = -2{,}300(5.5) + 27{,}600$
Simplify.	$y = 14{,}950$

The car will be worth $14,950 after 66 months.

EXAMPLE 4

Alert students that the time is in months but the variable, x, represents time in years. Elicit from them how to change 66 months into years.

CHECK YOUR UNDERSTANDING

Answer $y = -2{,}055x + 18{,}495$;

$-2{,}055\left(\frac{W}{12}\right) + 18{,}495$

EXAMPLE 5

Students must first calculate a specified car value, substitute that value for y, and then manipulate the equation in order to solve for x (the time in months).

CHECK YOUR UNDERSTANDING

Answer $\frac{(D - 32{,}000)}{-4{,}000}$

Students may have a tendency to write the answer as an equation. Explain that even though the solution contains variables, it is correctly written as an algebraic expression.

■ **CHECK YOUR UNDERSTANDING**

A car sells for $18,495 dollars and straight line depreciates to zero after 9 years. Write the straight line depreciation equation for this car and an expression for the value of the car after W months.

EXAMPLE 5

The straight line depreciation equation for a car is $y = -4{,}000x + 32{,}000$. In approximately how many years will the car's value decrease by 25%?

SOLUTION The original value of the car is the y-intercept, 32,000. You must determine the actual value of the car after it has dropped by 25%. This can be done in two ways.

You can find 25% of the original value of the car and then subtract that amount from the original value.	or	You can notice that once the car drops in value by 25%, it will be worth 75% of its original value.
$0.25 \times 32{,}000 = 8{,}000$		$0.75 \times 32{,}000 = 24{,}000$
$32{,}000 - 8{,}000 = 24{,}000$		
The value is $24,000.		The value is $24,000.

You are trying to determine a length of time. Solve the depreciation equation for x.

Use the depreciation equation.	$y = -4{,}000x + 32{,}000$
Substitute 24,000 for y.	$24{,}000 = -4{,}000x + 32{,}000$
Subtract 32,000 from each side.	$-8{,}000 = -4{,}000x$
Divide each side by –4,000.	$\frac{-8{,}000}{-4{,}000} = \frac{-4{,}000x}{-4{,}000}$
Simplify.	$2 = x$

The car will depreciate by 25% after 2 years.

■ **CHECK YOUR UNDERSTANDING**

Write an algebraic expression that represents the length of time it will take the car in Example 5 to have a value of D dollars.

Automobile Expense Function

In Chapter 2 you learned about expense functions. You can create an expense function for an automobile. While there are many expenses that contribute to the running and upkeep of a car, for the purposes here, the expense function is composed of the fixed expense down payment that you make when you purchase a car and the variable expense monthly payment that you make to the lending institution. Looking at the linear expense and depreciation functions simultaneously will give you insight into the value of your automotive investment.

EXAMPLE 6

Celine bought a new car for \$33,600. She made a \$4,000 down payment and pays \$560 each month for 5 years to pay off her loan. She knows from her research that the make and model of the car she purchased straight line depreciates to zero over 10 years.

a. Create an expense and depreciation function.

b. Graph these functions on the same axes.

c. Interpret the region before, at, and after the intersection point.

SOLUTION

a. Let x represent time in months and y represent dollars. Celine's expense function is the sum of her monthly payments over this time period and her initial down payment.

Expense function $y = 560x + 4{,}000$

The time, x, is in months rather than years. Express Celine's depreciation function in terms of months as well. Celine's car totally depreciates after 10 years, or 120 months. To determine her monthly depreciation amount, divide the original car value by 120.

$$\frac{33{,}600}{120} = 280$$

Celine's car depreciates \$280 per month. To calculate the slope of the depreciation equation, use the intercepts (0, 33,600) and (120, 0).

Slope $$\frac{0 - 33{,}600}{120 - 0} = \frac{-33{,}600}{120} = -280$$

Notice that the slope is the negative of the monthly depreciation amount. The straight line depreciation function for Celine's car is as follows.

Depreciation function $y = -280x + 33{,}600$

b. Determine an appropriate graphing window by using the largest coordinates of the intercepts for both functions to set up the horizontal and vertical axes. Graph both functions as shown.

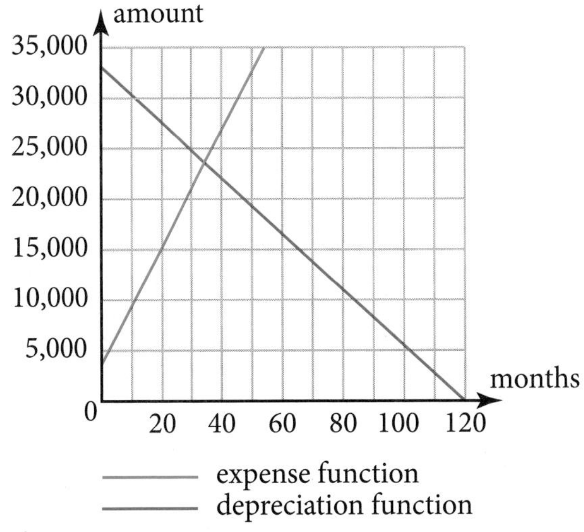

c. Using a graphing calculator, the coordinates of the intersection point, rounded to the nearest hundredth, are (35.24, 23,733.33). This means that after a little more than 35 months, both your expenses and the car's value are the same. In the region before the intersection point, the expenses are lower than the value of the car. The region after the intersection point indicates a period of time that the value of the car is less than what you have invested in it.

CHECK YOUR UNDERSTANDING

How might the expense function be altered so that it reflects a more accurate amount spent over time? What effect might that have on the graphs?

EXAMPLE 6

Students create both an expense and a depreciation function. They then plot them on the same coordinate grid and interpret the interactions of the graphs. You may want to review the component parts of an expense function (variable and fixed expenses) and how they contribute to the creation of an automobile expense function. Expense functions were introduced and used in Chapter 2.

CHECK YOUR UNDERSTANDING

Answer You can include your monthly maintenance and insurance costs with the monthly payment amount. This will yield a slope that is greater than the one depicted in the graph. Since the expense graph will be steeper, the intersection point will have an x-value that is less than 35.24. This will indicate that the value of the car will be less than the expenses-to-date earlier in the car's lifetime.

Applications

If the automobile had followed the same development cycle as the computer, a Rolls-Royce would today cost $100 [and] get a million miles per gallon.

Michael Moncur, Internet Consultant

TEACH

Exercise 2
Impress upon students that the slope represents depreciation and therefore must be negative.

Exercise 3
The intercepts that have been identified in 3a must satisfy the equation that the students create in 3c. Ask students to verify the accuracy of their work by testing the points in the equation.

1. How might those words apply to what you have learned? See margin.
2. Delia purchased a new car for $25,350. This make and model straight line depreciates to zero after 13 years.
   - **a.** Identify the coordinates of the x- and y-intercepts for the depreciation equation. (0, 25,350) and (13, 0)
   - **b.** Determine the slope of the depreciation equation. –1,950
   - **c.** Write the straight line depreciation equation that models this situation. $y = -1{,}950x + 25{,}350$
   - **d.** Draw the graph of the straight line depreciation equation. See additional answers.
3. Vince purchased a used car for $11,200. This make and model used car straight line depreciates to zero after 7 years.
   - **a.** Identify the coordinates of the x- and y-intercepts for the depreciation equation. (0, 11,200) and (7, 0)
   - **b.** Determine the slope of the depreciation equation. –1,600
   - **c.** Write the straight line depreciation equation that models this situation. $y = -1{,}600x + 11{,}200$
   - **d.** Draw the graph of the straight line depreciation equation. See additional answers.

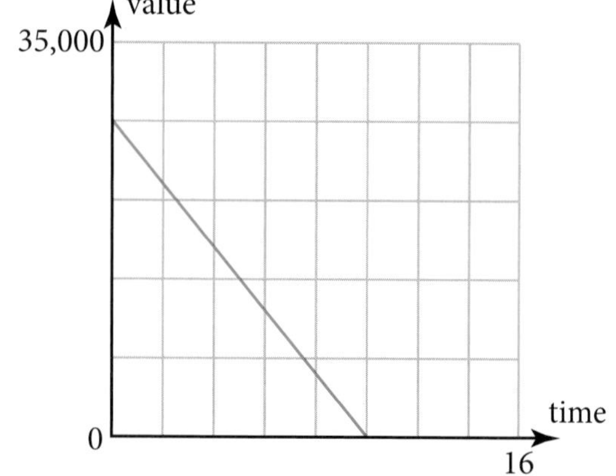

4. Examine the straight line depreciation graph for a car.
   - **a.** At what price was the car purchased? $28,000
   - **b.** After how many years does the car totally depreciate? 10 years
   - **c.** Write the equation of the straight line depreciation graph shown. $y = -2{,}800x + 28{,}000$
5. The straight line depreciation equation for a luxury car is $y = -3{,}400x + 85{,}000$.
   - **a.** What is the original price of the car? $85,000
   - **b.** How much value does the car lose per year? $3,400
   - **c.** How many years will it take for the car to totally depreciate? 25 years
6. The straight line depreciation equation for a motorcycle is $y = -2{,}150x + 17{,}200$.
   - **a.** What is the original price of the motorcycle? $17,200
   - **b.** How much value does the motorcycle lose per year? $2,150
   - **c.** How many years will it take for the motorcycle to totally depreciate? 8 years
7. The straight line depreciation equation for a car is $y = -2{,}750x + 22{,}000$.
   - **a.** What is the car worth after 5 years? $8,250
   - **b.** What is the car worth after 8 years? $0
   - **c.** Suppose that A represents a length of time in years when the car still has value. Write an algebraic expression to represent the value of the car after A years. $-2{,}750A + 22{,}000$

ANSWERS

1. This somewhat cynical quote compares the monetary value of computers to that of automobiles. As computer technology has become more sophisticated, the price of computers has drastically dropped. But, that is not the case for the automobile.

8. The straight line depreciation equation for a car is $y = -2{,}680x + 26{,}800$.

a. How much is the car worth after 48 months? $16,080

b. How much is the car worth after 75 months? $10,050

c. Suppose that M represents the length of time in months when the car still has value. Write an algebraic expression to represent the value of this car after M months. 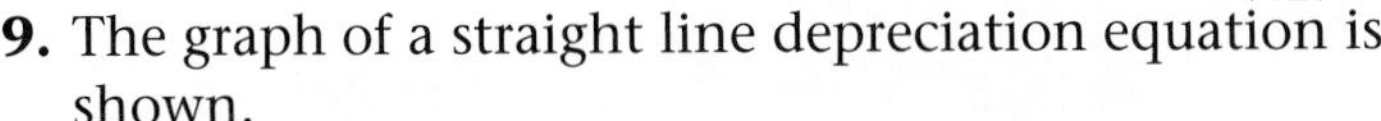 $-2{,}680\left(\frac{M}{12}\right) + 26{,}800$

9. The graph of a straight line depreciation equation is shown.

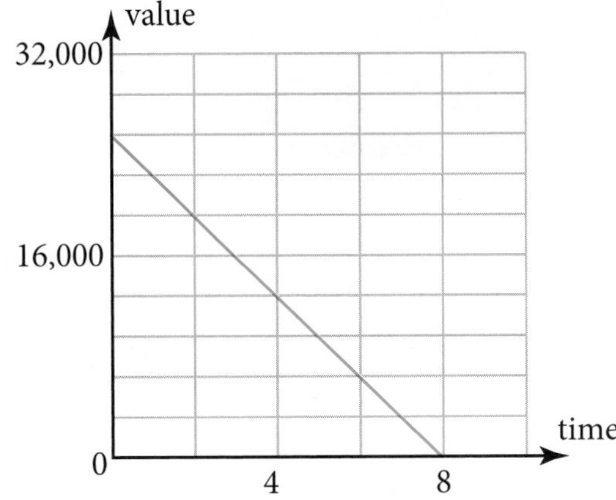

a. Use the graph to approximate the value of the car after 4 years. $12,800

b. Use the graph to approximate the value of the car after 5 years. $9,600

c. Use the graph to approximate when the car will be worth half its original value. 4 years

10. A car is originally worth $34,450. It takes 13 years for this car to totally depreciate.

a. Write the straight line depreciation equation for this situation. $y = -2{,}650x + 34{,}450$

b. How long will it take for the car to be worth half its value? 6.5 years

c. How long will it take for the car to be worth $10,000? Round your answer to the nearest tenth of a year. 9.2 years

11. The original price of a car is entered into spreadsheet cell A1 and the length of time it takes to totally depreciate is entered into cell B1.

a. Write the spreadsheet formula that calculates the amount that the car depreciates each year. =A1/B1

b. The spreadsheet user is instructed to enter a length of time in years that is within the car's lifetime in cell C1. Write the spreadsheet formula that will calculate the car's value after that period of time. =–(A1/B1)*C1+A1

12. The original price of a car is entered into spreadsheet cell A1 and the annual depreciation amount in cell B1.

a. Write the spreadsheet formula to determine the number of years it will take for the car to totally depreciate. =A1/B1

b. The spreadsheet user is instructed to enter a car value in cell D1. Write the spreadsheet formula to compute how long it will take for the car to depreciate to that value. =(D1–A1)/(–B1)

c. The spreadsheet user is instructed to enter a percent into cell E1. Write the spreadsheet formula to compute the length of time it will take for the car to decrease by that percent. =(((100–E1)/100)*A1–A1)/(–B1)

13. Winnie purchased a new car for $54,000. She has determined that it straight line depreciates to zero over 10 years. When she purchased the car, she made an $8,000 down payment and financed the rest with a 4-year loan at 4.875%. You can use the monthly payment formula from the last chapter to determine the monthly payment to the nearest cent. depreciation: $y = -450x + 54{,}000$; expense: $y = 1{,}056.74x + 8{,}000$

a. Create an expense and depreciation function.

b. Graph these functions on the same axes. See additional answers.

c. Interpret the region before, at, and after the intersection point in light of the context of this situation. See margin.

TEACH

Exercises 11 and 12

These problems require students to understand what the variables in the straight line depreciation equation represent. Remind them that the x-variable represents time in years and the y-variable represents car value after x years.

Exercise 13

Remind students that ordinarily x represents time in months in the expense equation and x represents time in years in the depreciation equation. To graph both equations on the same axes, change x in the depreciation equation to time in months.

ANSWERS

13c. Using a graphing tool the coordinates of the intersection point, rounded to the nearest hundredth, are (30.53, 40,261.73). This means that after a little more than 30.5 months, both the expenses-to-date and the car's value are the same. In the region before the intersection point, the expenses are lower than the value of the car. But, the region after the intersection point indicates a period of time that the value of the car is less than what was invested in it.

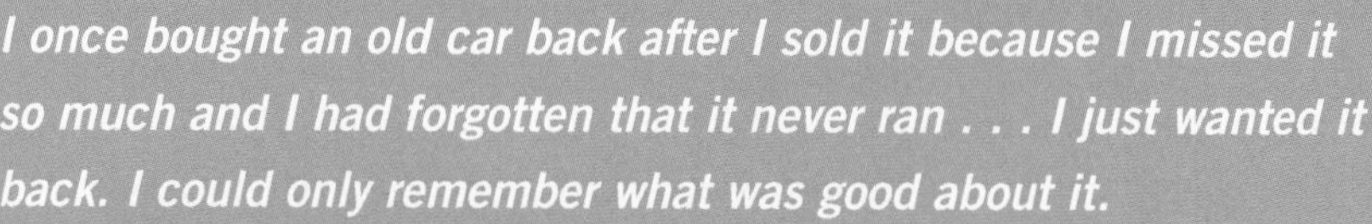

I once bought an old car back after I sold it because I missed it so much and I had forgotten that it never ran . . . I just wanted it back. I could only remember what was good about it.
Connie Chung, Television News Commentator

5-6 Historical and Exponential Depreciation

Objectives

- Write, interpret, and graph an exponential depreciation equation.
- Manipulate the exponential depreciation equation in order to determine time, original price, and depreciated value.

Common Core

A-CED2, A-CED3, F-IF7e, F-IF8b, F-IF9, F-LE1c, F-LE5, S-ID6

Key Terms
- dollar value
- historical data
- historical depreciation
- exponential decay
- exponential depreciation

CCSS Warm-Up

Answer true or false for each statement. Explain your reasoning.

1. $5 \cdot 2^x = 10^x$

2. $5^{2x} = 25^x$

3. $5^{2x} = (5^x)^2$

1. False, you cannot distribute the 5 times the base 2
2. True, $5^{2x} = (5^2)^x = 25x$
3. True, $5^{2x} = 5^{x \cdot 2} = (5^x)^2$

How does your car lose its value?

In the previous lesson, you examined the depreciation of cars where the car lost the same amount of **dollar value** each year. That may not always be the case. You can often get a good idea of how a car loses its value by looking at prices from the past. This information is known as **historical data**, and the devaluation of a car when using this type of data is called **historical depreciation**.

There are many websites that list the prices of used cars. One well-known site is *Kelley Blue Book*. Before the Internet, the *Kelley Blue Book* was an actual book of historical car prices that could be used to determine the current value of a used car. Today, the website gives the same information in a much easier to access format.

EXAMINE THE QUESTION

Ask students what the word *devaluation* means. Then, ask the same question in the context of automobile value. Elicit from the students some of the contributing factors to auto devaluation.

Examine the data of used car prices for a Chevrolet Corvette 2-door Coupe in good condition. The table shows the age of the car in years and the value of the car at that time. The prices quoted are for cars with similar usage for their age and offered for sale in the same geographic location.

Age	Value ($)	Age	Value ($)
1	24,230	6	15,245
2	22,355	7	14,075
3	20,645	8	13,100
4	18,070	9	12,325
5	16,265	10	11,525

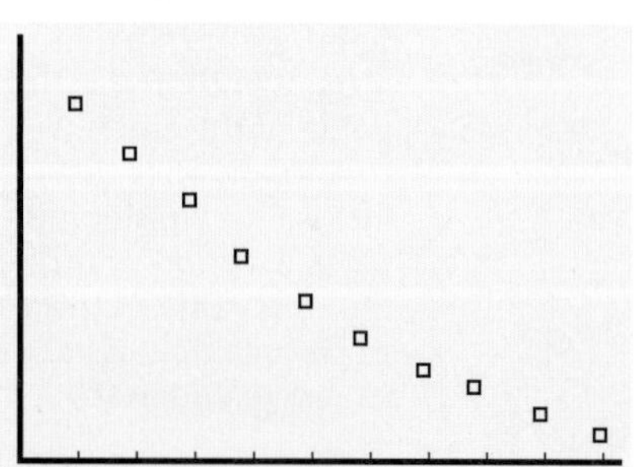

The scatterplot of this data is shown. Notice that it is not linear, but rather appears to be curved. The car values seem to have a greater drop at the beginning of the car's lifetime and less as each year passes. Notice that the depreciation is not constant from year to year. This scatterplot models an **exponential decay** function. Rather than the value decreasing by the same dollar amount each year, it decreases by the same percentage each year. In the context of auto devaluation, such a model is known as **exponential depreciation**. The general form of the exponential depreciation equation is

$$y = A(1 - r)^x$$

where A is the starting value of the car, r is the percent of depreciation expressed as a decimal, x is the elapsed time in years, and y is the car value after x years.

Skills and Strategies

The extent to which the exponential depreciation model fits the historical data varies from situation to situation. Here you will learn how to determine and use an exponential depreciation model.

CLASS DISCUSSION

If you have Internet access in the classroom, show students the *Kelley Blue Book* website (www.kbb.com).

EXAMPLE 1

Determine an exponential depreciation equation that models the data in the table from the previous page.

SOLUTION The exponential depreciation function can be determined using exponential regression calculated by hand, by computer software, or by a graphing calculator. When you use the statistics feature on a graphing calculator, the data is entered into two lists as shown. (Note that only 7 of the 10 data are shown on the calculator screen.) The independent variable is the age of the car and the dependent variable is the car value.

L1	L2	L3
1	24230	------
2	22355	
3	20645	
4	18070	
5	16265	
6	15245	
7	14075	

L2(1)=24230

The exponential regression equation is displayed in the graphing calculator screen at the right. Notice that the general form of the exponential regression equation used by the calculator is slightly different than the one introduced on the previous page. For ease of use, the numbers are rounded to the nearest hundredth. Using the format $y = a \times b^x$, where $a = 25{,}921.87$ and $b = 0.92$, the exponential depreciation function is $y = 25{,}921.87 \times (0.92)^x$. The graph of this function, superimposed over the scatterplot, appears to be a good fit.

ExpReg
y=a*b^x
a=25921.87218
b=.9189620427

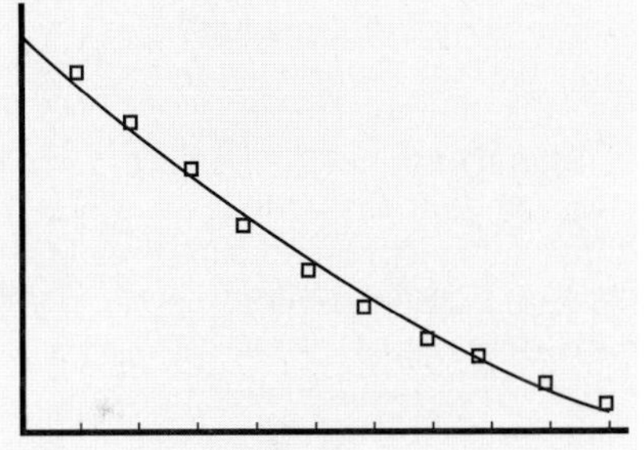

CHECK YOUR UNDERSTANDING

How might a better-fitting exponential depreciation equation look when superimposed over the same scatterplot?

EXAMPLE 1

Each number in List 2 is a percentage of the number that precedes it. The exponential regression formula calculates that percentage and assigns it to b.

CHECK YOUR UNDERSTANDING

Answer The graph would be closer to the data points.

EXAMPLE 2

What is the depreciation percentage for the 10 years of car prices as modeled by the exponential depreciation equation found in Example 1?

SOLUTION The exponential decay function was introduced as $y = A(1 - r)^x$. The graphing calculator uses the format $y = a*b^x$. Both formats are identical if you recognize that $b = 1 - r$.

Use the equation and solve for r. $\quad b = 1 - r$

Subtract 1 from each side. $\quad b - 1 = 1 - r - 1$

Simplify. $\quad b - 1 = -r$

Divide each side by −1. $\quad \dfrac{b-1}{-1} = \dfrac{-r}{-1}$

Simplify. $\quad 1 - b = r$

Since b is approximately 0.92, then $1 - 0.92 = 0.08$. The Corvette depreciated by about 8% per year.

EXAMPLE 2

Students have now been introduced to two exponential depreciation equations: $y = a(1 - r)^x$ and $y = ab^x$. This example shows how the two equations are related.

CLASS DISCUSSION

Note: This activity should accompany Example 1. Before examining the exponential depreciation example, have students explore the following exponential decay activity. Put students into groups and ask them to begin with the number 100. Record this step of the activity as the ordered pair (0, 100). Divide the second number in half and record the ordered pair as (1, 50). Divide the second number in half again and record as (2, 25). Have students repeat the process at least 10 more times. Ask them to graph the ordered pairs on a coordinate plane. Help students see that at the beginning, the original number "depreciated" faster than at the end. However, each depreciation was at 50%.

After the exponential depreciation formula is introduced remind students that the basic interest formula was an "appreciation formula" and was written using the exponential base $(1 + r)$. In that case, the initial value increased each time by a certain percentage. In the depreciation formula, subtracting r from 1 decreases the original value by a certain percentage.

CHECK YOUR UNDERSTANDING

Answer 12%

EXAMPLE 3

Students need to understand that the exponent $\frac{1}{a}$ represents $\sqrt[a]{\ }$. They have already learned that a square root is used to undo squaring. They may not be familiar with the undoing process for the *a*th root. In this example, students will raise both sides of the equation to the 4th root in order to remove the exponent that raises $(1 - r)$ to the 4th power.

■ CHECK YOUR UNDERSTANDING

After entering a set of automobile value data into a graphing calculator, the following exponential regression equation information is given: $y = a*b\text{^}x$, $a = 32{,}567.98722$, $b = 0.875378566$. Round the values to the nearest hundredth. Determine the depreciation percentage.

EXAMPLE 3

Eamon purchased a four-year-old car for $16,400. When the car was new, it sold for $23,000. Find the depreciation rate to the nearest tenth of a percent.

SOLUTION Let r equal the depreciation rate expressed as a decimal. The exponential depreciation formula for this situation is $16{,}400 = 23{,}000\,(1 - r)^4$. Notice that the variable r is in the base of an exponential expression. To solve for r, you must first isolate that expression.

Use the exponential depreciation formula. $\quad 16{,}400 = 23{,}000(1 - r)^4$

Divide each side by 23,000. $\quad \dfrac{16{,}400}{23{,}000} = \dfrac{23{,}000(1 - r)^4}{23{,}000}$

Simplify. $\quad \dfrac{16{,}400}{23{,}000} = (1 - r)^4$

To solve for r, you need to undo the exponent of 4 to which the expression $1 - r$ has been raised by raising each side of the equation to the reciprocal of 4, or $\frac{1}{4}$. $\quad \left(\dfrac{16{,}400}{23{,}000}\right)^{\frac{1}{4}} = \left((1 - r)^4\right)^{\frac{1}{4}}$

To simplify a power raised to an exponent, multiply the exponents. The exponent on the right side of the equation is 1. $\quad \left(\dfrac{16{,}400}{23{,}000}\right)^{\frac{1}{4}} = (1 - r)^1$

Simplify. $\quad \left(\dfrac{16{,}400}{23{,}000}\right)^{\frac{1}{4}} = 1 - r$

Subtract 1 from each side. $\quad \left(\dfrac{16{,}400}{23{,}000}\right)^{\frac{1}{4}} - 1 = -r$

Divide both sides by −1. $\quad \dfrac{\left(\dfrac{16{,}400}{23{,}000}\right)^{\frac{1}{4}} - 1}{-1} = \dfrac{-r}{-1}$

Simplify. $\quad 1 - \left(\dfrac{16{,}400}{23{,}000}\right)^{\frac{1}{4}} = r$

Calculate. $\quad 0.0810772512 = r$

Because r represents a percent expressed as a decimal, the depreciation rate rounded to the nearest tenth of a percent is 8.1%.

CHECK YOUR UNDERSTANDING

A car originally sells for D dollars. After A years, the value of the car has dropped exponentially to P dollars. Write an algebraic expression for the exponential depreciation rate expressed as a decimal.

CHECK YOUR UNDERSTANDING

Answer $1 - \left(\frac{P}{D}\right)^{\frac{1}{A}}$

EXAMPLE 4

This example lends itself to a graphical solution. The algebraic solution is beyond the scope of this course. The intersection of the exponential depreciation equation and the expense equation yields the point at which the values are the same.

Make sure that you emphasize that the depreciation equation uses time in years and the original statement of the expense equation uses time in months. Therefore, the monthly payment of $400 must be converted to a yearly payment of $4,800 in order that both equations can be graphed on the same axes.

EXAMPLE 4

A car originally sold for $26,600. It depreciates exponentially at a rate of 5.5% per year. When purchasing the car, Richard put $6,000 down and pays $400 per month to pay off the balance. After how many years will his car value equal the amount he paid to date for the car?

SOLUTION This problem is similar to Example 6 in Lesson 5-5. To find the solution, you need to set up both an expense equation and a depreciation equation.

The exponential depreciation equation is

$$y = 26{,}600(1 - 0.055)^x$$

where x represents time in years.

The expense equation is

$$y = 400x + 6{,}000$$

where x represents the number of months that have passed.

To graph these two equations on the same axes, the independent variable in each equation must represent the same unit of time.

If you let x represent time in years, then to make the expense equation work, you need to determine the yearly payment rather than the monthly payment.

Over the course of the year, Richard will have paid 400(12), or $4,800, in car payments.

The new yearly expense equation is

$$y = 4{,}800x + 6{,}000$$

where x is time in years.

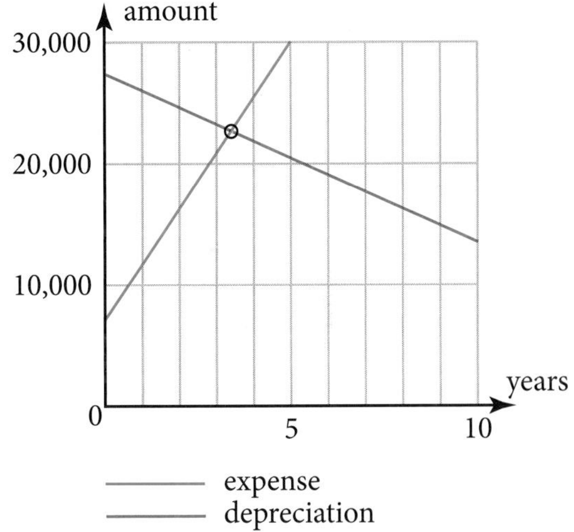

Use the graph shown to determine an appropriate viewing window to use on your graphing calculator. Use the calculation feature to find the coordinates of the point of intersection.

After approximately 3.3 years (about 40 months), Richard will have paid about $22,022.74 toward his loan payments and the car will have a value of that same amount.

CHECK YOUR UNDERSTANDING

Describe the situation pictured above after 4 years.

CHECK YOUR UNDERSTANDING

Answer The amount he has paid toward the loan of the car is more than what the car is worth.

EXAMPLE 5

Walk through the solution steps with students carefully since they may have difficulty deciding what operations need to be completed ahead of others. Remind students not to round values until the very end of the process.

CHECK YOUR UNDERSTANDING

Answer Approximately \$31,176.59

EXAMPLE 6

This example asks students to solve for an exponent. Remind them how the natural logarithm was used in Chapter 4 in a similar situation. Students should be given this formula and not required to memorize it.

CHECK YOUR UNDERSTANDING

Answer Students must first calculate half the original value of the car and use that amount in the formula involving the natural log. The car would be approximately 8.3 years old had it been purchased at half its original value.

ANSWERS (for page 257)

1. To some people, the value of a car is more than monetary. It is emotional as well. While a car may depreciate monetarily, some people find that it has increased in personal value.

EXAMPLE 5

A car exponentially depreciates at a rate of 6% per year. Beth purchased a 5-year-old car for \$18,000. What was the original price of the car when it was new?

SOLUTION

Use the exponential depreciation equation. $y = A(1 - r)^x$

Substitute 18,000 for y, 0.06 for r, and 5 for x. $18{,}000 = A(1 - 0.06)^5$

Simplify. $18{,}000 = A(0.94)^5$

Divide each side by $(0.94)^5$. $\dfrac{18{,}000}{0.94^5} = \dfrac{A(0.94)^5}{0.94^5}$

Simplify and calculate to the nearest cent. $24{,}526.37 = A$

The original price of this car was approximately \$24,526.37.

■ CHECK YOUR UNDERSTANDING

A car depreciates exponentially at a rate of 5% per year. If the car is worth \$30,000 after 9 months, what was the original price of the car?

EXAMPLE 6

Leah and Josh bought a used car valued at \$20,000. When this car was new, it sold for \$24,000. If the car depreciates exponentially at a rate of 8% per year, approximately how old is the car?

SOLUTION You need to solve for the variable x in the exponential depreciation equation

$$y = A(1 - r)^x$$

In the last chapter, you learned that solving for an exponent requires the use of natural logarithms. The length of time, x, can be determined using the following formula.

$$x = \frac{\ln\left(\frac{y}{A}\right)}{\ln(1 - r)}$$

Because y equals the value of the car after x years, $y = 20{,}000$. The new car price, A, is \$24,000. The variable r represents the depreciation rate expressed as a decimal. Therefore, $r = 0.08$.

Substitute and calculate. $x = \dfrac{\ln\left(\frac{20{,}000}{24{,}000}\right)}{\ln(1 - 0.08)} \approx 2.19$

At the time of the purchase, the car was about 2.19 years old.

■ CHECK YOUR UNDERSTANDING

How old would the car in Example 4 be had it been purchased at half its value?

Applications

I once bought an old car back after I sold it because I missed it so much and I had forgotten that it never ran . . . I just wanted it back. I could only remember what was good about it.

Connie Chung, Television News Commentator

1. How might the quote apply to what you have learned? See margin.

2. Seamus bought a car that originally sold for \$40,000. It exponentially depreciates at a rate of 7.75% per year. Write the exponential depreciation equation for this car. $y = 40{,}000(1 - 0.0775)^x$

3. Shannon's new car sold for \$28,000. Her online research indicates that the car will depreciate exponentially at a rate of $5\frac{1}{4}$% per year. Write the exponential depreciation formula for Shannon's car. $y = 28{,}000(1 - 0.0525)^x$

4. Chris purchased a used car for \$19,700. The car depreciates exponentially by 10% per year. How much will the car be worth after 6 years? Round your answer to the nearest penny. \$10,469.39

5. Laura's new car cost her \$21,000. She was told that this make and model depreciates exponentially at a rate of $8\frac{5}{8}$% per year. How much will her car be worth after 100 months? \$9,903.32

6. Lisa purchased a used car for D dollars. The car depreciates exponentially at a rate of E% per year. Write an expression for the value of the car in 5 years, in A years, and in M months. $D(1 - E/100)^5$; $D(1 - E/100)^A$; $D(1 - E/100)^{(M/12)}$

7. A graphing calculator has determined this exponential regression equation based upon car value data: $y = a*b^x$, $a = 20{,}952.11$, and $b = 0.785$. What is the rate of depreciation for this car? How much is this car worth after 6 years; 78 months; w years? 21.5%; \$4,902.82; \$4,343.91; $20{,}952.11 \times 0.785^w$

8. A graphing calculator has determined this exponential regression equation based upon car value data: $y = a*b^x$, $a = 18{,}547.23$, and $b = 0.8625$. What is the rate of depreciation for this car? How much is this car worth after 6 years, 78 months, and w months? 13.75%; \$7,635.43; \$7,091.09; $18{,}547.23 \times 0.8625^{(w/12)}$

9. The historical prices of a car are recorded for 11 years as shown.
   - **a.** Construct a scatterplot for the data. See margin.
   - **b.** Determine the exponential depreciation equation that models this data. Round to the nearest hundredth. See margin.
   - **c.** Determine the depreciation rate. approximately 11%
   - **d.** Predict the value of this car after $3\frac{1}{2}$ years. \$11,902.01

Age	Value (\$)	Age	Value (\$)
0	19,000	6	8,600
1	16,325	7	7,200
2	13,700	8	6,900
3	12,000	9	6,000
4	10,500	10	5,600
5	9,700		

10. The historical prices of a car are recorded for 17 years as shown.
    - **a.** Construct a scatterplot for the data. See margin.
    - **b.** Determine the exponential depreciation formula that models this data. Round to the nearest hundredth. See margin.
    - **c.** Determine the depreciation rate. approximately 11%
    - **d.** Predict the value of this car after 140 months. \$10,843.12

Age	Value	Age	Value
0	42,000	9	14,800
1	37,420	10	13,000
2	34,000	11	11,245
3	29,400	12	10,211
4	26,200	13	9,400
5	23,700	14	8,100
6	20,990	15	7,500
7	18,200	16	6,290
8	16,876		

ANSWERS

9a.

9b. $y = 17{,}895.97*(0.89)^x$

10a.

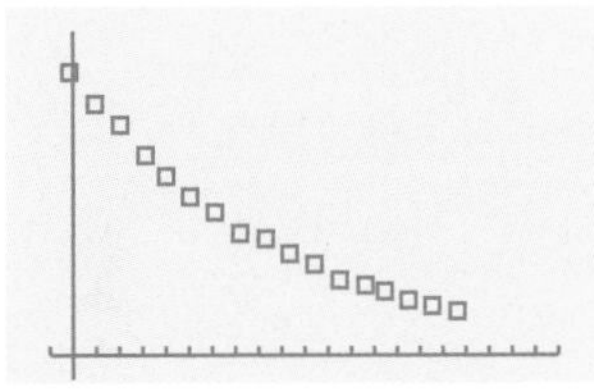

10b. $y = 42{,}228.36*0.89^x$

TEACH

Exercises 11–13
These problems require students to determine the original value of the car. Encourage them to use Example 5 as a model.

ANSWERS

20a. After 1967, the car appreciates exponentially in value.

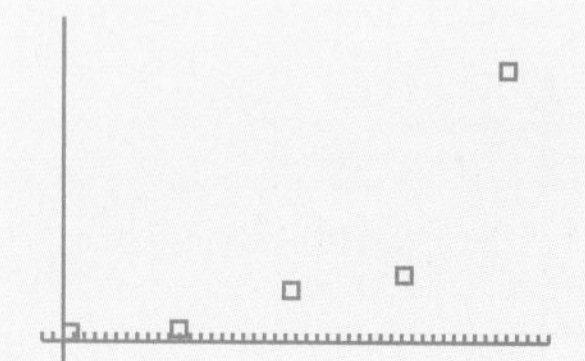

11. Raphael purchased a 3-year-old car for $16,000. He was told that this make and model depreciates exponentially at a rate of 5.45% per year. What was the original price of the car when it was new? $18,929.34

12. The car that Diana bought is 8 years old. She paid $6,700. This make and model depreciates exponentially at a rate of 14.15% per year. What was the original price of the car when it was new? $22,706.62

13. Chaz bought a two-year-old car. He paid *D* dollars. This make and model depreciates at a rate of *E* percent per year. Write an expression for the original selling price of the car when it was new. $D/(1 - E/100)^2$

14. What is the exponential depreciation rate, expressed as a percent to the nearest tenth of a percent, for a car that originally sells for $30,000 when new but exponentially depreciates after 5 years to $18,700? 9%

15. What is the exponential depreciation rate, expressed as a percent to the nearest tenth of a percent, for a car that originally sells for $52,000 when new but exponentially depreciates to $45,000 after 32 months? 5.3%

16. A new car sells for $27,300. It exponentially depreciates at a rate of 6.1% to $22,100. How long did it take for the car to depreciate to this amount? Round your answer to the nearest tenth of a year. 3.4 years

17. Amber bought a used car valued at $16,000. When this car was new, it was sold for $28,000. If the car depreciates exponentially at a rate of 9% per year, approximately how old is the car? 5.9 years

18. A car originally sold for $25,900. It depreciates exponentially at a rate of 8.2% per year. Nina put $10,000 down and pays $550 per month to pay off the balance. After how many years will her car value equal the amount she paid for the car to that point? What will that value be? 1.8 years; $22,131.10

19. Jazmine's car originally sold for $46,600. It depreciates exponentially at a rate of 10.3% per year. Jazmine put $12,000 down and pays $800 per month to pay off the balance. After how many years will her car value equal the amount she paid to date for the car? What will that value be? 2.5 years; $35,651.67

20. The July 2008 issue of *Hemmings Motor News* included a feature story on the 1957 Cadillac Eldorado Brougham. When sold as a new car in 1957, the price was $13,074. It depreciated in value over the next few years. Then, in 1967, something interesting began to happen as seen in this table of values.

Year	Value
1967	$2,500
1977	$5,500
1987	$18,500
1997	$25,000
2007	$95,000

a. Construct a scatterplot for the data. Let 1967 be year 1, 1977 be year 11, 1987 be year 21, and so on. What do you notice about the trend? See margin.

b. Find an exponential regression equation that models this situation. Round the numbers to the nearest hundredth. $y = 2{,}262.70 \times 1.09^x$

c. What kind of a rate has been used? What is the value of that rate to the nearest tenth of a percent? exponential appreciation rate; 9%

Is it sufficient that you have learned to drive the car, or shall we look and see what is under the hood? Most people go through life without ever knowing.

June Singer, Analyst and Writer

Driving Data 5-7

Key Terms

- odometer
- electronic odometer
- mechanical odometer
- trip odometer
- speedometer
- fuel economy measurement
- miles per gallon (mpg)
- kilometers per liter (km/L)
- English Standard System
- Metric System
- distance formula
- currency exchange rate

Objectives

- Write, interpret, and use the distance formula.
- Use the formula for the relationship between distance, fuel economy, and gas usage.

Common Core

A-CED4

CCSS Warm-Up

The volume of a cone is $V = (1/3)\pi r^2 h$, where r is the radius and h is the height.

1. Solve the formula for the radius, r.

2. Solve the formula for the height, h.

1. $r = \sqrt{\frac{3V}{\pi h}}$

2. $h = \frac{3V}{\pi r^2}$

What Data Is Important to a Driver?

The dashboard of an automobile is an information center. It supplies data on fuel, speed, time, and engine-operating conditions. It can also give information on the inside and outside temperature. Some cars even have a global positioning system mounted into the dashboard. This can help the driver find destinations or map out alternate routes. Your cellular phone can be wirelessly connected to your car so that you can send and receive hands-free calls. There have been many advances in the information that the driver has available to make trips safer, smarter, and more energy efficient.

The **odometer** indicates the distance a car has traveled since it left the factory. All automobiles have either an electronic or mechanical odometer. Some dashboard odometers can give readings in both miles and kilometers. An **electronic odometer** gives the readings digitally. A **mechanical odometer** consists of a set of cylinders that turn to indicate the distance traveled. Many cars also have a **trip odometer** which can be reset at the beginning of each trip. The trip odometer gives you the accumulated distance traveled on a particular trip. The **speedometer** tells you the rate at which the car is traveling. The rate, or speed, is reported in miles per hour (mi/h or mph) or kilometers per hour (km/h or kph).

Drivers are concerned not only with distance traveled and speed, but also with the amount of gasoline used. Gasoline is sold by the gallon or the liter. Over the past 20 years, the price of gasoline has changed dramatically. Economizing on fuel is a financial necessity. Car buyers are usually interested **fuel economy measurements**. These are calculated in **miles per gallon (mi/g** or **mpg)** or **kilometers per liter (km/L)**. In order to understand these fuel economy measurements, it is necessary to have a good sense of distances in both the **English Standard System** of measurement used in the United States, and the **Metric System** of measurement used in most countries throughout the world.

EXAMINE THE QUESTION

This is a very important question that will help you understand what students see as significant driving information. Newer cars give a variety of dashboard data that is helpful in knowing about average speed, time traveled, fuel efficiency, temperature, and so on. This question goes beyond the dashboard numbers and asks students to come up with other data that might at some time save their lives.

CLASS DISCUSSION

Based upon the equivalencies stated here, which is a greater distance—a mile or a kilometer? If a sign read "100 miles to the Canadian Border", would the numeral used to represent the number of kilometers be greater than 100 or less than 100?

TEACH

In this lesson, students learn about the relationship between distance, rate, and time; distance, mpg, and gallons of gas used. These basic formulas assist a driver in planning for a trip and analyzing the fuel efficiency of the car during that trip.

EXAMPLE 1

Students have likely used the distance formula for many years and are comfortable using it to find distances. Help students to understand that this formula can be rewritten so that it can be used to find the rate or the time.

CLASS DISCUSSION

Discuss the significance of understanding what 60 mi/h means. Be sure that students understand when a driver is going 60 mi/h that the driver will travel 60 miles in one hour. Guide students to use this rate as a benchmark when they are driving a long distance to estimate the length of time it will take to travel a specific distance.

Without using the formula, students should be able to do simple mental math and comparisons to know that the distance in Example 1 will be less than 360 miles.

CHECK YOUR UNDERSTANDING

Answer $R\left(\frac{M}{60}\right)$

EXAMPLE 2

Discuss with students how changes in Jack's speed affect how long the trip will take.

A mile equals 5,280 feet. A meter is a little more than 3 feet. Driving distances are not reported in feet or meters, but in miles and kilometers. A kilometer is equal to 1,000 meters. Miles and kilometers can be compared as follows.

1 kilometer ≈ 0.621371 mile
1 mile ≈ 1.60934 kilometers

The distance from Seattle, Washington, to Vancouver, British Columbia, is about 176 kilometers or 110 miles. When traveling, it is important to use the correct measurement system. Miles per gallon is a unit of measurement that gives the number of miles a car can be driven on one gallon of gas. A car that gets 28 mpg can travel about 28 miles on one gallon. A car that gets 11.9 km/L can travel about 11.9 kilometers on one liter. There are about 3.8 liters in a gallon and 0.26 gallons in a liter. When shopping for a new car, always ask for the fuel estimate.

Skills and Strategies

A smart automobile owner is aware that a working knowledge of driving data can help reduce the costs of automobile ownership. Here you will learn how to use and interpret driving data.

EXAMPLE 1

A car travels at an average rate of speed of 50 miles per hour for 6 hours. How far does this car travel?

SOLUTION The distance that a car travels is a function of its speed and the time traveled. This relationship is shown in the **distance formula**

$$D = R \times T$$

where D represents the distance traveled, R represents the rate at which the car is traveling, and T is the time in hours.

Substitute 50 for D and 6 for T. $D = 50 \times 6$

Calculate. $D = 300$

The car travels 300 miles.

CHECK YOUR UNDERSTANDING

A car is traveling at R miles per hour for M minutes. Write an algebraic expression for the distance traveled.

EXAMPLE 2

Jack lives in New York and will be attending college in Atlanta, Georgia. The driving distance between the two cities is 883 miles. Jack knows that the speed limit varies on the roads he will travel from 50 mi/h to 65 mi/h. He figures that he will average about 60 mi/h on his trip. At this average rate, for how long will he be driving? Express your answer rounded to the nearest tenth of an hour and to the nearest minute.

SOLUTION

Use the distance formula.	$D = R \times T$
Divide each side by *R*.	$\frac{D}{R} = \frac{R \times T}{R}$
Simplify.	$\frac{D}{R} = T$
Substitute 883 for *D* and 60 for *R*.	$\frac{883}{60} = T$
Calculate.	$14.71\overline{6} = T$

The answer is a non-terminating, repeating decimal as indicated by the bar over the digit 6. The time rounded to the nearest tenth of an hour is 14.7 hours.

If you are using a calculator and the display reads 14.71666667, the calculator has rounded the last digit, but it stores the repeating decimal in its memory. Because you know that the exact time is between 14 and 15 hours, use only the decimal portion of the answer. Once the answer is on the calculator screen, subtract the whole number portion.

$$14.7166666667 - 14 = 0.7166666667$$

The number of sixes displayed will depend upon the accuracy of your calculator. There are 60 minutes in an hour, so multiply by 60.

$$0.7166666667 \times 60 = 43$$

The decimal portion of the hour is 43 minutes. Jack will be driving for 14 hours and 43 minutes.

CHECK YOUR UNDERSTANDING

Danielle drove from Atlanta, Georgia, to Denver, Colorado, which is a distance of 1,401 miles. If she averaged 58 miles per hour on her trip, how long is her driving time to the nearest minute?

EXAMPLE 3

Kate left Albany, New York, and traveled to Montreal, Quebec. The distance from Albany to the Canadian border is approximately 176 miles. The distance from the Canadian border to Montreal, Quebec, is approximately 65 kilometers. If the entire trip took her about $3\frac{3}{4}$ hours, what was her average speed for the trip?

SOLUTION Kate's average speed can be reported in miles per hour or kilometers per hour. To report her speed in miles per hour, convert the entire distance to miles. To change 65 kilometers to miles, multiply by the conversion factor 0.621371.

$$65 \times 0.621371 = 40.389115$$

The distance from the Canadian border to Montreal is approximately 40.4 miles. Kate's total driving distance is the sum of the distances from Albany to the Canadian border and from the Canadian border to Montreal.

$$176 + 40.4 = 216.4 \text{ miles}$$

CHECK YOUR UNDERSTANDING

Answer 24 hours and 9 minutes

EXAMPLE 3

Students need notice that distance given in the problem are in different measuring systems. Explain to students that websites are available that will do conversions from the customary system to the metric and vice versa. Even though most students will not commit the equivalences to memory, it is good for them to have a general idea or benchmark to use. Tell students to think of one kilometer as being about the distance of one-half mile.

CHECK YOUR UNDERSTANDING

Answer yes

57.7 mph × 1.60934 = approximately 93 km/h

EXAMPLE 4

This example provides an opportunity to show how to utilize the distance formula in another way. Students need to understand that the rate they are using in this problem is fuel economy measurement per gallons of fuel used.

Now, solve for the rate. Let $D = 216.4$ and $T = 3.75$.

Use the distance formula.	$D = R \times T$
Divide each side by T.	$\frac{D}{T} = \frac{R \times T}{T}$
Simplify.	$\frac{D}{T} = R$
Substitute 216.4 for D and 3.75 for T.	$\frac{216.4}{3.75} = R$
Calculate.	$57.7 \approx R$

Kate traveled at approximately 58 miles per hour.

Follow the same reasoning to determine her speed in kilometers per hour. To change the portion of the trip reported in miles to kilometers, multiply 176 by the conversion factor 1.60934.

$$176 \times 1.60934 \approx 283.2$$

There are approximately 283.2 kilometers in 176 miles.

The distance from Albany to Montreal is 283.2 + 65, or 348.2 kilometers.

Let $D = 348.2$ and $T = 3.75$ in the distance formula.

$$\frac{348.2}{3.75} = R$$

$$92.85\overline{3} = R$$

Kate traveled approximately 93 kilometers per hour.

> **■ CHECK YOUR UNDERSTANDING**
>
> In Example 3 above, could Kate's km/h have been calculated by multiplying her miles per hour by the conversion factor? Explain your answer.

EXAMPLE 4

Juan has a hybrid car that averages 40 miles per gallon. His car has a 12-gallon tank. How far can he travel on one full tank of gas?

SOLUTION The distance traveled can also be expressed as a function of the fuel economy measurement and the number of gallons used.

$$\text{Distance} = \text{miles per gallon} \times \text{gallons}$$

$$\text{Distance} = \text{kilometers per liter} \times \text{liters}$$

Therefore, the distance that Juan can travel on one tank of gas is the product of his miles per gallon and the tank size in gallons.

$$\text{Distance} = 40 \times 12 = 480 \text{ miles}$$

When traveling at an average rate of 40 mpg, one full tank of gas in Juan's hybrid car can take him 480 miles.

CHECK YOUR UNDERSTANDING

Lily drove a total of 500 miles on g gallons of gas. Express her fuel economy measurement in miles per gallon as an algebraic expression.

EXAMPLE 5

When Barbara uses her car for business, she must keep accurate records so that she will be reimbursed for her car expenses. When she started her trip, the odometer read 23,787.8. When she ended the trip it read 24,108.6. Barbara's car gets 32 miles per gallon. Her tank was full at the beginning of the trip. When she filled the tank, it cost her $40.10. What price did she pay per gallon of gas on this fill-up?

SOLUTION Begin by computing the distance Barbara traveled. Find the difference between her ending and beginning odometer readings.

$$24{,}108.6 - 23{,}787.8 = 320.8$$

Barbara traveled 320.8 miles.

Since Barbara's car gets 32 mpg, you can determine the number of gallons of gas used on the trip with the formula

$$D = M \times G$$

where D is the distance traveled, M is the miles per gallon, and G is the number of gallons used.

Use the formula.	$D = M \times G$
Substitute 320.8 for D and 32 for M.	$320.8 = 32G$
Divide each side by 32.	$\frac{320.8}{32} = \frac{32G}{32}$
Simplify.	$\frac{320.8}{32} = G$
Calculate.	$10.025 = G$

Barbara used 10.025 gallons of gas on this trip.

If her total gas bill was $40.10, divide this total amount by the number of gallons used to get the price per gallon paid.

$$\frac{40.10}{10.025} = \text{Price per gallon}$$

Barbara paid $4 per gallon for this fill-up.

CHECK YOUR UNDERSTANDING

Suppose a person begins a trip with an odometer reading of A miles and ends the trip with an odometer reading of B miles. If the car gets C miles per gallon and the fill-up of gas for this trip cost D dollars, write an algebraic expression that represents the price per gallon.

CHECK YOUR UNDERSTANDING

Answer $\frac{500}{g}$

EXAMPLE 5

You can take this opportunity to discuss using your car for business. Students will likely think that the company will reimburse Barbara the money she spent on gasoline. You can explain that business reimburse on a set rate per mile driven. This discussion can lead to the how using your car for business means more than just the money you send for gasoline.

CHECK YOUR UNDERSTANDING

Answer $D \div \left(\frac{B-A}{C}\right)$

EXAMPLE 6

Students may have difficulty understanding when to multiply and when to divide to convert properly. Walking through this example using dimensional analysis will help them visualize the conversion process because they can see how the units cancel.

CHECK YOUR UNDERSTANDING

Answer $4.55 per gallon

EXAMPLE 7

Example 6 converts Mexican pesos per liter to U.S. dollars per gallon. Example 7 converts U.S. dollars per gallon to Mexican pesos per liter. Explaining to students that these are inverse operations may help them to more easily understand the conversions.

CHECK YOUR UNDERSTANDING

Answer approximately 0.70 per liter

EXAMPLE 6

David is driving in Mexico on his vacation. He notices that gas costs 8.50 Mexican pesos per liter. What is this equivalent to in U.S. dollars?

SOLUTION David must find the current currency exchange rate. The **currency exchange rate** is a number that expresses the price of one country's currency calculated in another country's currency. Up-to-date exchange rates are available on the Internet.

David needs to know what 1 U.S. dollar (USD) is worth in Mexican pesos. For the time of his travel, 1 USD = 13.3 Mexican pesos. Divide the foreign currency amount paid for gas by the exchange rate.

$$8.50 \div 13.3 \approx 0.64$$

Each liter would cost him about 64 cents of U.S. currency. He knows there are approximately 3.8 liters in a gallon, so he can multiply 0.64×3.8 to determine the equivalent gas price if it was purchased with U.S. dollars per gallon.

The price of 8.50 Mexican pesos per liter is approximately $2.43 per gallon.

■ CHECK YOUR UNDERSTANDING

On a trip through Canada, Angie noticed that the average price of gas per liter was 1.28 Canadian dollars. If 1 USD is equivalent to approximately 1.07 Canadian dollars, what is the equivalent gas price per gallon in U.S. currency?

EXAMPLE 7

David knows that the price of gas in his home town is about $2.90 per gallon. How can he compare this price to the price paid in Example 6 for a liter?

SOLUTION David needs to express the U.S. gas price as a price in USD per liter. There are approximately 3.8 liters in a gallon. Divide the price per gallon by 3.8 to determine the price per liter in USD.

$$2.90 \div 3.8 \approx 0.76$$

His home town gas price is equivalent to about 0.76 USD per liter. So gas is less expensive in Mexico, $\$0.64 < \$0.76$.

To compare the prices in pesos, multiply the USD amount by the exchange rate.

Exchange rate was 13.3. $0.76 \times 13.3 \approx 10.11$

The gas in his home town would sell for about 10.11 Mexican pesos. Just as the comparison in USD showed, the comparison in pesos shows that gas is less expensive in Mexico, $8.50 < 10.11$.

■ CHECK YOUR UNDERSTANDING

In the Example 6 Check Your Understanding, Angie knew that the price of gas in her home town was $2.50 per gallon. What is the equivalent price in Canadian dollars per liter?

Applications

Is it sufficient that you have learned to drive the car, or shall we look and see what is under the hood? Most people go through life without ever knowing.

June Singer, Analyst and Writer

1. How might the quote apply to what you have learned? See margin.
2. Arthur travels for 3 hours on the freeway. His average speed is 55 mi/h. How far does he travel? 165 miles
3. Yolanda is planning a 778-mile trip to visit her daughter in Maryland. She plans to average 50 miles per hour. At that speed, approximately how long will the trip take? Express your answer to the nearest tenth of an hour. Then express your answer to the nearest minute. 15.6 h and 15 h 34 min
4. Steve's SUV has a 17-gallon gas tank. The SUV gets an estimated 24 miles per gallon. Approximately how far can the SUV run on half a tank of gas? 204 mi
5. Becky is planning a 2,100-mile trip to St. Louis to visit a college. Her car averages 30 miles per gallon. About how many gallons will her car use on the trip? 70
6. Robbie's car gets *M* miles per gallon. Write an algebraic expression that represents the number of gallons he would use when traveling 270 miles. $\frac{270}{M}$
7. Michael used his car for business last weekend. When he reports the exact number of miles he traveled, the company will pay him 52 cents for each mile. At the beginning of the weekend, the odometer in Michael's car read 74,902.6 miles. At the end of the weekend, it read 75,421.1 miles.
   - **a.** How many miles did Michael drive during the weekend? 518.5 miles
   - **b.** How much money should his company pay him for the driving? $269.62
8. Lenny's car gets approximately 20 miles per gallon. He is planning a 750-mile trip.
   - **a.** About how many gallons of gas should Lenny plan to buy? 37.5 gallons
   - **b.** At an average price of $4.10 per gallon, how much should Lenny expect to spend for gas? $153.75
9. Francois' car gets about 11 kilometers per liter. She is planning a 1,200-kilometer trip.
   - **a.** About how many liters of gas should Francois plan to buy? Round your answer to the nearest liter. 109 liters
   - **b.** At an average price of $1.45 per liter, how much should Francois expect to spend for gas? $158.05
10. Nola's car gets approximately 42 miles per gallon. She is planning to drive *x* miles to visit her friends.
    - **a.** What expression represents the number of gallons of gas she should expect to buy? $\frac{x}{42}$
    - **b.** At an average price of $2.38 per gallon, write an expression for the amount that Nola will spend for gas. $\frac{2.38x}{42}$

TEACH

Exercise 7
Remind students that the distance traveled must be a positive number.

Exercises 8 and 9
These problems do not require students to convert between the two systems.

ANSWERS

1. Answers will vary. Although this analyst is probably using a car as a metaphor, she does infer that it isn't enough to just know how to drive a car but to know all of the important information about the car as well.

TEACH

Exercise 13
Students will need to use the problem-solving strategy of working backwards in order to solve this problem.

Exercise 15
Before assigning this problem, ask students how they would determine an appropriate graphing window.

ANSWERS

12. a. $39.90
    b. $48.96
    c. $70.55
    d. $111.80
    e. $15*D*
    f. $*GP*
    g. $9.98
    h. $9.79
    i. $23.52
    j. $18.63
    k. $\frac{\$15D}{4}$
    l. $\frac{\$GP}{C}$

11. Jason uses his car for business. He must keep accurate records so his company will reimburse him for his car expenses. When he started his trip, the odometer read 42,876.1. When he ended the trip it read 43,156.1. Jason's car gets 35 miles per gallon. His tank was full at the beginning of the trip. When he filled the tank, it cost $34.24. What price did he pay per gallon of gas on this fill-up? $4.28

12. Complete the chart for entries a–l. See margin.

Number of gallons purchased	Price per gallon	Total gas cost	Number of people in car pool	Gas cost per person
10	$3.99	a.	4	g.
12	$4.08	b.	5	h.
17	$4.15	c.	3	i.
26	$4.30	d.	6	j.
15	*D*	e.	4	k.
G	*P*	f.	*C*	l.

13. Alexandra uses her car for business. She knows that her tank was full when she started her business trip, but she forgot to write down the odometer reading at the beginning of the trip. When the trip was over, the odometer read 13,020.5. Alexandra's car gets 25 miles per gallon. When she filled up the tank with gas that cost $4.15 per gallon, her total bill for the trip was $59.76. Determine Alexandra's beginning odometer reading. 12,660.5

14. Bill left Burlington, Vermont, and traveled to Ottawa, Ontario, the capital of Canada. The distance from Burlington to the Canadian border is approximately 42 miles. The distance from the Canadian border to Ottawa is approximately 280 kilometers. If it took him 4.3 hours to complete the trip, what was his average speed in miles per hour? about 50 mi/h

15. A car averages 56 mi/h on a trip.

a. Write an equation that shows the relationship between distance, rate, and time for this situation. $D = 56T$

b. Let time be the independent variable and distance be the dependent variable. Draw and label the graph of this equation. See additional answers.

c. Use the graph to determine approximately how far this car would travel after 14 hours. about 800 miles

d. Use the graph to determine the approximate length of time a 500-mile trip would take. approximately 9 hours

16. A spreadsheet has been created so that the user enters information in the stated cells.

a. Write a formula to calculate the speed of the car for the trip in cell C1. =(A2–A1)/A4

b. Write a formula to calculate the number of gallons of gas used in cell C2. =(A2–A1)/A3

c. Write a formula to calculate the total cost of gas for the trip in cell C3. =C2*A5

	A	B	C
1		Starting odometer reading in A1	
2		Ending odometer reading in A2	
3		Fuel efficiency measure in mpg in A3	
4		Duration of trip in A4	
5		Gas price per gallon in A5	

Use the following information to complete Exercises 17–22. Round all answers to two decimal places.

1 USD ≈ 1.07 Canadian dollars (CAD)

1 USD ≈ 0.69 Euros (EUR)

1 USD ≈ 1.16 Australian dollars (AUD)

1 USD ≈ 89.85 Japanese yen (JPY)

1 USD ≈ 7.34 South African rand (ZAR)

1 USD ≈ 1.00 Swiss franc (CHF)

17. Complete the chart. See margin.

USD	CAD	EUR	AUD
3.80	a.	b.	c.
15.75	d.	e.	f.
20.00	g.	h.	i.
178.50	j.	k.	l.
250.00	m.	n.	p.
5500.00	q.	r.	s.

18. Complete the chart. See margin.

Foreign Currency	USD Equivalent	Foreign Currency	USD Equivalent
85 CAD	a.	130 CHF	d.
1000 EUR	b.	222 ZAR	e.
500 AUD	c.	36 JPY	f.

19. Reid will be driving through Spain this summer. He did some research and knows that the average price of gas in Spain is approximately 1.12 euros per liter.

a. What is this amount equivalent to in U.S. dollars? approx \$1.62 USD/L

b. What is this rate equivalent to in U.S. dollars per gallon? approx \$6.16/gal

20. Shyla will be driving through South Africa. She has found that the average price of gas in Johannesburg is about 19.24 ZAR per liter.

a. What is this amount equivalent to in U.S. dollars? approx \$2.62 USD/L

b. What is this rate equivalent to in U.S. dollars per gallon? approx \$9.96/gal

21. Brenda will be driving through Europe. She plans to pay an average price of *h* euros per liter for gasoline.

a. What is this amount equivalent to in U.S. dollars? $\frac{h}{0.69}$ USD/L

b. What is this rate equivalent to in U.S. dollars per gallon? $\frac{3.8h}{0.69}$ per gal

22. While Willie traveled in India, he paid an average of 87.42 Indian rupees for a liter of gas.

a. What expression represents the price of this gas in U.S. dollars if the exchange rate was *x*? $\frac{87.42}{x}$ USD/L

b. What is this rate equivalent to in U.S. dollars per gallon? $\frac{3.8(87.42)}{x}$ per gal

c. If Willie spent about \$115, how many gallons of gas did he buy? $115 \div \frac{3.8(87.42)}{x}$

d. If Willie spent about \$115, how many liters of gas did he buy? $115 \div \frac{87.42}{x}$

ANSWERS

17. a. 4.07
b. 2.62
c. 4.41
d. 16.85
e. 10.87
f. 18.27
g. 21.40
h. 13.80
i. 23.20
j. 191.00
k. 123.17
l. 207.06
m. 267.50
n. 172.50
p. 290.00
q. 5,885.00
r. 3,795.00
s. 6,380.00

18. a. 79.44
b. 1,449.28
c. 431.03
d. 130.00
e. 30.25
f. 0.40

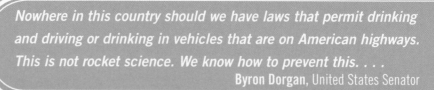

Nowhere in this country should we have laws that permit drinking and driving or drinking in vehicles that are on American highways. This is not rocket science. We know how to prevent this. . . .

Byron Dorgan, United States Senator

5-8 Driving Safety Data

Objectives

- Calculate reaction time and distance in the English Standard System.
- Calculate and use the braking distance in both the English Standard and Metric Systems.
- Calculate and use the total stopping distance in both the English Standard and Metric Systems.

Common Core

A-SSE1b, A-SSE3

Key Terms

- reaction time
- thinking time
- reaction distance
- braking distance
- total stopping distance

CCSS Warm-Up

Write each function in two equivalent ways.
You can partially or fully expand the function.

1. $f(x) = x^2 + 2x + 1$ **2.** $g(x) = (x - 1)^3$

1. $f(x) = (x + 1)(x + 1) = (x + 1)^2$
2. $g(x) = (x - 1)^2(x - 1) = (x^2 - 2x + 1)(x - 1) = x^3 - 3x^2 + 3x - 1$

EXAMINE THE QUESTION

In the last lesson, students used data to become a more informed driver. In this lesson, a working knowledge of mathematics is important for students to have their beliefs tested about the interaction between distance, rate, and time for safety purposes.

CLASS DISCUSSION

After reviewing the definitions of reaction time, reaction distance, and braking distance, elicit from students their best guess as to how long it takes to react, how far the car travels in that time, and how far the car travels when the brakes are applied before it stops.

How can you use mathematics to become a safer driver?

Although a dashboard can give you much information about the car's ability to *go*, it gives little or no information about the car's ability to *stop*. It takes time to stop a moving car safely. Even during the time your foot switches from the gas pedal to the brake pedal, the car continues to travel.

The average, alert driver takes from approximately three-quarters of a second to one and a half seconds to switch from the gas pedal to the brake pedal. This time is the **reaction time** or **thinking time**. During the reaction time, the car travels a greater distance than most people realize. That distance is the **reaction distance**. The distance a car travels while braking to a complete stop is the **braking distance**. Most people think they can stop on a dime. In reality, that is far from the truth. Take a look at these facts.

- There are 5,280 feet in a mile.
- A car traveling 55 mi/h covers 55 miles in one hour.
- A car traveling 55 mi/h covers 55 × 5,280 or 290,400 feet in one hour.
- A car traveling 55 mi/h covers 290,400 ÷ 60 or 4,840 feet in one minute.
- A car traveling 55 mi/h covers 4,840 ÷ 60 or 80.67 feet in one second.

Suppose that your reaction time is one second. That is, it takes you one second from the time you realize that you have to brake to the time you actually apply your foot to the brake pedal. When traveling at 55 mi/h, in that one second of time, you travel about 81 feet.

By thinking about these facts, you can understand how speeding, tailgating, texting while driving, and driving while intoxicated can cost you in damages or even your life!

Skills and Strategies

Here you will learn how to make driving decisions based upon reaction and braking distances.

EXAMPLE 1

What is the reaction distance for a car traveling approximately 48 miles per hour?

SOLUTION 1 The reaction distance is the approximate distance covered in the time it takes an average driver to switch from the gas pedal to the brake pedal.

Research has determined that the average driver takes from 0.75 to 1.5 seconds to react.

A car traveling at 55 mi/h travels about 81 feet per second.

Let x = the distance traveled when the reaction time is 0.75 seconds.

Write a proposition. $$\frac{81}{1} = \frac{x}{0.75}$$

Multiply each side by 0.75. $$\frac{81}{1} \times 0.75 = \frac{x}{0.75} \times 0.75$$

Simplify. $$81 \times 0.75 = x$$

Calculate. $$60.75 = x$$

Let x = the distance traveled when the reaction time is 1.5 seconds.

Write a proportion. $$\frac{81}{1} = \frac{x}{1.5}$$

Multiply each side by 1.5. $$\frac{81}{1} \times 1.5 = \frac{x}{1.5} \times 1.5$$

Simplify. $$81 \times 1.5 = x$$

Calculate. $$121.5 = x$$

If the average person's reaction time ranges from 0.75 to 1.5 seconds, the average person's reaction distance when traveling at 55 mi/h ranges from 60.75 to 121.5 feet. That's quite a span in the short time it takes for a person to apply the brakes.

The reaction distances and times are used to give you a sense of how far the car will go. *A conservative rule of thumb for the reaction distance is that a car travels about one foot for each mile per hour of speed.*

Therefore, a car traveling at 48 mi/h has a reaction distance of approximately 48 feet.

CHECK YOUR UNDERSTANDING

A car is traveling at 65 mi/h. Approximately how far will it travel during the average reaction time?

TEACH

Drivers must have an understanding of the basic mathematics of driving safety. This lesson offers students a variety of easy to use formulas in order to make them aware of things they can do as a driver to reduce the risk of an accident.

EXAMPLE 1

Students can use a proportion to solve this problem or they can realize that the distance traveled is three-fourths of the number of feet traveled in one second.

CHECK YOUR UNDERSTANDING

Answer 65 feet

EXAMPLE 2

Impress upon students the need for the correct placement of parentheses. Here, there is a big difference between $0.1s^2$ and $(0.1s)^2$.

CHECK YOUR UNDERSTANDING

Answer Road conditions such as rain, snow, and ice affect the efficiency of the car's brakes. The tire pressure, driver impairment and more could greatly affect the braking distance of a car.

EXAMPLE 3

Total stopping distance takes into account the reaction distance and the braking distance. It is the sum of both amounts and indicates how far a car will go (on average) from the moment that a driver realizes the need to stop to the moment that the car actually comes to a complete stop.

CHECK YOUR UNDERSTANDING

Answer Using the formula, the total stopping distance is 276.25 feet.

EXAMPLE 2

What is the approximate braking distance for a car traveling at 48 mi/h?

SOLUTION The general formula for the braking distance is

$$\frac{s^2}{20}$$

where *s* represents the speed of the car. Because this formula is not accessible without a calculator, an equivalent is often used.

$$(0.1 \times s)^2 \times 5$$

Notice the four expressions below are equivalent.

$$(0.1 \times s)^2 \times 5 \qquad \left(\frac{1}{10} \times s\right)^2 \times 5 \qquad \left(\frac{s}{10}\right)^2 \times 5 \qquad \frac{5s^2}{100} = \frac{s^2}{20}$$

Each of the expressions yields the braking distance when $s = 48$.

$$\frac{s^2}{20} = \frac{48^2}{20} = 115.2 \quad \text{or} \quad (0.1 \times s)^2 \times 5 = (0.1 \times 48)^2 \times 5 = 115.2$$

Once the brakes are applied, on average, a car traveling at 48 mi/h will come to a complete stop after the car has traveled approximately 115.2 feet.

CHECK YOUR UNDERSTANDING

What factors also need to be taken into account that might add to or subtract from the braking distance?

EXAMPLE 3

Rachel is driving at 48 mi/h on a one-lane highway. She sees an accident directly ahead of her about 200 feet away. Will she be able to stop in time?

SOLUTION The **total stopping distance** from the moment a driver realizes the need to stop to the time that the car is no longer moving is the sum of the reaction distance and the braking distance.

$$\text{Total stopping distance} = \text{Reaction distance} + \text{Braking distance}$$

Since the reaction distance of a car traveling at *s* miles per hour is approximated by using a distance of *s* feet, the formula can be represented by either of the following.

$$s + (0.1 \times s)^2 \times 5 \quad \text{or} \quad s + \frac{s^2}{20}$$

Rachel's total stopping distance is $48 + 115.2 = 163.2$ feet.

The accident is 200 feet away, so she should be able to stop in time.

CHECK YOUR UNDERSTANDING

What is the total stopping distance for a car traveling at 65 mi/h?

EXAMPLE 4

Desireé is traveling through Canada. The speedometer in her rented car indicates kilometers per hour and all of the road signs give distances in kilometers. She knows that one kilometer is equal to 1,000 meters and one meter is a little more than 3 feet. Determine Desireé's total stopping distance if she is traveling 88 kilometers per hour.

© JESSIE ELDORA ROBERTSON 2009/USED UNDER LICENSE FROM SHUTTERSTOCK.COM

SOLUTION Since 1 kilometer ≈ 0.6213712 miles, 88 kilometers per hour can be expressed in miles per hour by multiplying 88 by the conversion factor.

$$88 \times 0.621371 = 54.680648$$

$$88 \text{ km/h} \approx 54.68 \text{ mi/h}$$

Evaluate the total stopping distance formula $s + (0.1 \times s)^2 \times 5$ when $s = 54.68$.

$$s + (0.1 \times s)^2 \times 5 = 54.68 + (0.1 \times 54.68)^2 \times 5 \approx 204.17512 \text{ feet}$$

There are approximately 0.3048 meters in 1 foot.

Multiply the stopping distance in feet by this conversion factor.

$$204.17512 \times 0.3048 \approx 62.23 \text{ meters}$$

The approximate stopping distance of Desireé's car is 62.23 meters.

Notice that this gives an answer that has been determined through various stages of rounding since you used rounded versions of answers and conversion factors along the way.

There is a formula that can be used to determine the total stopping distance directly. Let s represent the speed in kilometers per hour.

$$\text{Total stopping distance in meters} = \frac{s^2}{170} + \frac{s}{5}$$

Substitute $s = 88$.

$$= \frac{88^2}{170} + \frac{88}{5} \approx 63.15 \text{ meters}$$

Notice that the two answers, 62.23 meters and 63.15 meters, are very close to each other.

CHECK YOUR UNDERSTANDING

A car is traveling at 78 km/h. What is the total stopping distance in meters? Round your answer to the nearest hundredth of a meter.

EXTEND YOUR UNDERSTANDING

Toni's car is traveling 75 km/h. Randy's car is behind Toni's car and is traveling 72 km/h. Toni notices a family of ducks crossing the road 50 meters ahead of her. Will she be able to stop before she reaches the ducks? What is the least distance that Randy's car can be from Toni's car to avoid hitting her car, if he reacts as soon as he sees her brakes?

EXAMPLE 4

The reaction and braking distance formulas used up to this point in this lesson require that the variables be measured in the customary system of measurement. Therefore, before using the formulas, it is necessary for the students to use the conversion factor to change metric measures into customary measures. The solution also shows students the formula that can be used when the units of measure are in the metric system. It compares the results when both methods are employed to solve the problem.

CHECK YOUR UNDERSTANDING

Answer approximately 51.39 meters

EXTEND YOUR UNDERSTANDING

Answer yes; 3.2 meters

Applications

> *Nowhere in this country should we have laws that permit drinking and driving or drinking in vehicles that are on American highways. This is not rocket science. We know how to prevent this. . . .*
>
> **Byron Dorgan,** United States Senator

TEACH

Exercises 2–4
Students should have completed Exercise 2 and/or Exercise 3 before working on Exercise 4.

Exercises 5–7
Students should have completed Exercise 5 and/or Exercise 6 before working on Exercise 7.

ANSWERS

1. The total braking distance is substantial for a normal, non-impaired driver. People driving under the influence of alcohol or drugs significantly increase their reaction time which increases the total stopping distance.

3g. $\frac{5{,}280x}{60}$

3h. $\frac{5{,}280x}{3{,}600}$

6c. $\frac{1{,}000x}{60}$

6d. $\frac{1{,}000x}{3{,}600}$

1. Explain how the quote can be interpreted from what you have learned. See margin.

2. There are 5,280 feet in a mile. Round answers to the nearest unit.
- **a.** How many miles does a car traveling at 65 mi/h go in one hour? 65
- **b.** How many feet does a car traveling at 65 mi/h go in one hour? 343,200
- **c.** How many feet does a car traveling at 65 mi/h go in one minute? 5,720
- **d.** How many feet does a car traveling at 65 mi/h go in one second? 95

3. There are 5,280 feet in a mile. Round answers to the nearest unit.
- **a.** How many miles does a car traveling at 42 mi/h go in one hour? 42
- **b.** How many feet does a car traveling at 42 mi/h go in one hour? 221,760
- **c.** How many feet does a car traveling at 42 mi/h go in one minute? 3,696
- **d.** How many feet does a car traveling at 42 mi/h go in one second? 62
- **e.** How many miles does a car traveling at x mi/h go in one hour? x
- **f.** How many feet does a car traveling at x mi/h go in one hour? $5{,}280x$
- **g.** How many feet does a car traveling at x mi/h go in one minute? See margin.
- **h.** How many feet does a car traveling at x mi/h go in one second? See margin.

4. Determine the distance covered by a car traveling 80 km/h for each unit and time given. Round answers to the nearest unit.
- **a.** kilometers in one hour 80
- **b.** meters in one hour 80,000
- **c.** meters in one minute 1,333
- **d.** meters in one second 22

5. Determine the distance covered by a car traveling 55 km/h for each unit and time given. Round answers to the nearest unit.
- **a.** kilometers in one hour 55
- **b.** meters in one hour 55,000
- **c.** meters in one minute 917
- **d.** meters in one second 15

6. Determine the distance covered by a car traveling x km/h for each unit and time given.
- **a.** kilometers in one hour x
- **b.** meters in one hour $1{,}000x$
- **c.** meters in one minute See margin.
- **d.** meters in one second See margin.

7. Mindy is driving 32 mi/h as she nears an elementary school. A first-grade student runs into the street after a soccer ball, and Mindy reacts in about three-quarters of a second. What is her approximate reaction distance? 32 feet

8. Determine the distance covered by a car traveling 68 mi/h for each unit and time given. Round answers to the nearest unit.
- **a.** miles in one hour 68
- **b.** feet in one hour 359,040
- **c.** feet in one minute 5,984
- **d.** feet in one second 99.73

9. Edward is driving 52 mi/h on a one-lane road. He must make a quick stop because there is a stalled car ahead.
   a. What is his approximate reaction distance? 52 feet
   b. What is his approximate braking distance? 135.2 feet
   c. About how many feet does the car travel from the time he switches pedals until the car has completely stopped? 187.2 feet

10. Complete the chart for entries a–j. See margin.

Speed	Reaction Distance	Braking Distance
40 mi/h	a.	f.
30 mi/h	b.	g.
20 mi/h	c.	h.
15 mi/h	d.	i.
5 mi/h	e.	j.

11. David is driving on the highway at the legal speed limit of 70 mi/h. He notices that there is an accident up ahead approximately 200 feet away. His reaction time is approximately $\frac{3}{4}$ of a second. Is he far enough away to bring the car safely to a complete stop? Explain your answer. See margin.

12. Martine is driving on an interstate at 70 km/h. She sees a traffic jam about 50 meters ahead and needs to bring her car to a complete stop before she reaches that point. Her reaction time is approximately $\frac{3}{4}$ of a second. Is she far enough away from the traffic jam to safely bring the car to a complete stop? Explain. See margin.

13. Model the total stopping distance by the equation $y = \frac{x^2}{20} + x$, where x represents the speed in miles per hour and y represents the total stopping distance in feet.
   a. Graph this equation for the values of x, where $x \leq 70$ mi/h. See additional answers.
   b. Use the graph to approximate the stopping distance for a car traveling at 53 mi/h. about 185 feet
   c. Use the graph to approximate the speed for a car that stops completely after 70 feet. about 28 mi/h

14. Model the total stopping distance by the equation $y = \frac{x^2}{170} + \frac{x}{5}$, where x represents the speed in km/h and y represents the total stopping distance in meters.
   a. Graph this equation for the values of x, where $x \leq 100$ km/h. See additional answers.
   b. Use the graph to approximate the stopping distance for a car traveling at 60 km/h. about 33 m
   c. Use the graph to approximate the speed for a car that stops completely after 60 meters. about 85 km/h

15. A spreadsheet user inputs a speed in miles per hour into cell A1.
   a. Write a formula that would enter the approximate equivalent of that speed in km/h in cell A2. =A1*1.60934
   b. Write a spreadsheet formula that would enter the approximate total stopping distance in feet in cell A3. =A1^2/20 + A1
   c. Write a spreadsheet formula that would enter the approximate total stopping distance in kilometers in cell A4. =A2^2/170 + A2/5

TEACH

Exercises 11–12

These exercises offer students an opportunity to assess a situation mathematically and come to a decision as to whether or not the driver can safely stop. In addition to these problems, you might want to have students make up and solve their own.

Exercises 13–14

Students are asked to graph the stopping distance equations offered in this lesson. You may want to assist them in determining a suitable viewing window.

ANSWERS

10. a. 40 ft
    b. 30 ft
    c. 20 ft
    d. 15 ft
    e. 5 ft
    f. 80 ft
    g. 45 ft
    h. 20 ft
    i. 11.25 ft
    j. 1.25 ft
11. David's total stopping distance is 315 feet. He does not have enough road ahead of him to bring the car to a safe stop before the accident.
12. Martine's total stopping distance is 42.8 meters which is less than the distance to the traffic jam.

It takes 8,460 bolts to assemble an automobile, and one nut to scatter it all over the road.

Author Unknown

5-9 Accident Investigation Data

Objectives

- Determine the minimum skid speed using the skid mark formula.
- Determine the minimum skid speed using the yaw mark formula.

Common Core

A-REI2, G-C5, F-IF4

Key Terms

- accident reconstructionist
- skid mark
- shadow skid mark
- anti-lock braking system (ABS)
- yaw mark
- skid speed formula
- drag factor
- braking efficiency
- skid distance
- chord
- middle ordinate

CCSS Warm-Up

Let $f(x) = (x - 2)/7$. Let $g(x) = 5/x$.
Solve the equation $f(x) = g(x)$.
$x = -5, x = 7$

EXAMINE THE QUESTION

The last two lessons have focused on driving data that assists drivers on the road. This lesson introduces students to data that can be collected at the scene of an accident in order to make decisions about fault. Before continuing with the lesson, have students answer the question in order to ascertain what they think is usable mathematical evidence at an accident scene.

CLASS DISCUSSION

Go on the internet and find images of car skid marks. Display them to the students and ask them what information those skid marks might give an accident reconstructionist.

What data might a car leave behind at the scene of an accident?

Auto accidents happen. Many times it is clear who is at fault, but that may not always be the case. When fault is uncertain, it is up to the authorities to get detailed and accurate information from witnesses and each of the parties involved. It may be necessary to examine the data that was left behind at the scene. That data is interpreted by **accident reconstructionists**, who have knowledge of both crime scene investigations and mathematics that can help them understand the circumstances surrounding the accident.

Reconstructionists pay very close attention to the marks left on the road by the tires of a car. A **skid mark** is a mark that a tire leaves on the road when it is in a locked mode, that is, when the tire is not turning, but the car is continuing to move. When the driver first applies the brakes, the skid mark is light and is a **shadow skid mark**. This mark darkens until the car comes to a complete stop either on its own or in a collision.

Some cars have an **anti-lock brake system (ABS)**, which does not allow the wheels to continuously lock. In cars equipped with this feature, the driver feels a pulsing vibration on the brake pedal and that pedal moves up and down. The skid marks left by a car with ABS look like uniform dashed lines on the pavement. A driver without ABS may try to simulate that effect by pumping the brakes. The skid marks left by these cars are also dashed, but they are not uniform in length.

When a car enters a skid and the brakes lock (or lock intermittently), the driver cannot control the steering. Therefore, the skid is usually a straight line. The vehicle is continuing to move straight ahead as the wheels lock making the tire marks straight. When the vehicle is slipping sideways while at the same time continuing in a forward motion, the tire marks appear curved. These are called **yaw marks**.

Taking skid and yaw measurements, as well as other information from the scene, can lead reconstructionists to the speed of the car when entering the skid. The formulas used are often presented in court and are recognized for their strength in modeling real world automobile accidents.

Skills and Strategies

Here you will learn how to use the skid and yaw formulas to examine the circumstances surrounding an automobile accident.

The **skid speed formula** is

$$S = \sqrt{30 \cdot D \cdot f \cdot n} = \sqrt{30Dfn}$$

where S is the speed of the car when entering the skid, D is the skid distance, f is the **drag factor**, and n is the **braking efficiency**.

Before using the equation, it is important that you understand its component parts. The number 30 is a constant; it is part of the equation and does not change from situation to situation. Simply put, the drag factor is the pull of the road on the tires. It is a number that represents the amount of friction that the road surface contributes when driving. Many accident reconstructionists perform drag factor tests with a piece of equipment known as a drag sled. The table lists acceptable ranges of drag factors for the road surfaces.

Road Surface	Drag Factor Range
Cement	0.55–1.20
Asphalt	0.50–0.90
Gravel	0.40–0.80
Snow	0.10–0.55
Ice	0.10–0.25

The **skid distance** is a function of the number and lengths of the skid marks left at the scene. If there are four marks of equal length, then that amount is used. But, if the lengths are different or there are fewer than four skid marks, then the average of the lengths is used in the formula. If there is only one skid mark, that length is used.

Finally, you need to know about the braking efficiency of the car. This number is determined by an examination of the rear and front wheel brakes. It can run from 0% efficiency (no brakes at all) to 100% efficiency (brakes are in excellent condition). The braking efficiency number is expressed as a decimal when used in the formula.

CLINTSPENCER/ISTOCKPHOTO.COM

TEACH

This lesson will introduce students to formulas involving square roots. It is important that they have a working understanding of the domain and the nature of the square root function. Here, they will see use the fact that the square root and the square functions are inverses.

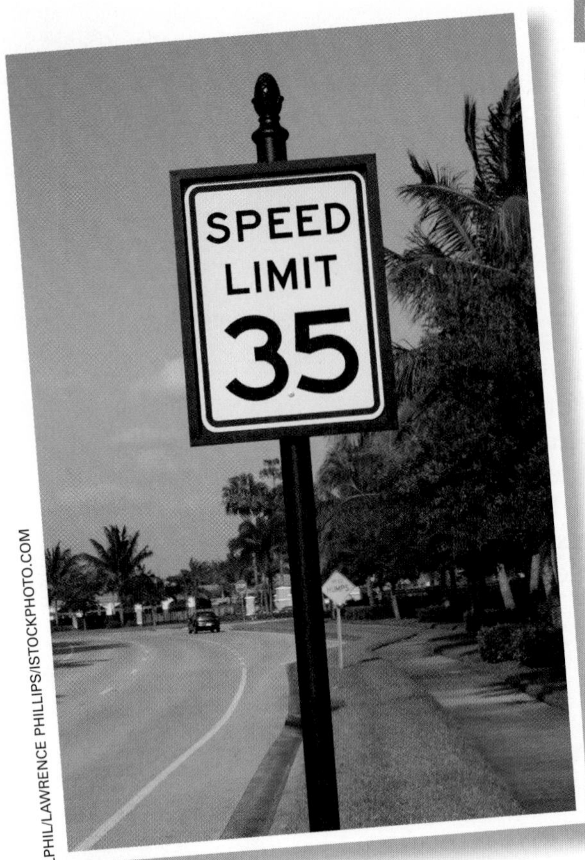

LPHIL/LAWRENCE PHILLIPS/ISTOCKPHOTO.COM

EXAMPLE 1

A car is traveling on an asphalt road with a drag factor of 0.78. The speed limit on this portion of the road is 35 mi/h. The driver just had his car in the shop and his mechanic informed him that the brakes were operating at 100% efficiency. The driver must make an emergency stop, when he sees an obstruction in the road ahead of him. His car leaves four distinct skid marks each 80 feet in length. What is the minimum speed the car was traveling when it entered the skid? Round your answer to the nearest tenth. Was the driver exceeding the speed limit when entering the skid?

SOLUTION Determine the car speed.

Use the skid speed formula.	$S = \sqrt{30Dfn}$
Substitute 80 for *D*, 0.78 for *f*, and 1.0 for *n*.	$S = \sqrt{30 \times 80 \times 0.78 \times 1.0}$
Simplify	$S = \sqrt{1{,}872}$
Take the square root.	$S \approx 43.3$

The car was traveling at approximately 43.3 miles per hour. The driver was exceeding the speed limit and could be fined.

EXAMPLE 1

Make sure students realize that there are many factors other than drag, brake efficiency, and road surface that can affect skid speed. But this formula is recognized by many law enforcement personnel as a good means of making an approximate determination.

■ CHECK YOUR UNDERSTANDING

A portion of road has a drag factor of *x*. A car with a *y* percent braking efficiency is approaching a traffic jam ahead, causing the driver to apply the brakes for an immediate stop. The car leaves four distinct skid marks of *z* feet each. Write an expression for determining the minimum speed of the car when entering into the skid.

CHECK YOUR UNDERSTANDING

Answer $\sqrt{30zx\left(\frac{y}{100}\right)}$

EXAMPLE 2

Melissa was traveling at 50 mi/h on a concrete road with a drag factor of 1.2. Her brakes were working at 90% efficiency. To the nearest tenth of a foot, what would you expect the average length of the skid marks to be if she applied her brakes in order to come to an immediate stop?

SOLUTION You are asked to find the skid distance given the speed, the drag factor, and the braking efficiency.

Use the skid speed formula.	$S = \sqrt{30Dfn}$
Substitute 50 for *S*, 1.2 for *f*, and 0.9 for *n*.	$50 = \sqrt{30 \times D \times 1.2 \times 0.9}$
Simplify the expression under the radical.	$50 = \sqrt{32.4D}$

EXAMPLE 2

In this example, students are asked to find the value of a variable under the square root sign. It is therefore necessary for them to have a working understanding of how to undo the effect of a square root by squaring both sides of the equation. Before attempting the problem solution, you may want to have students do some numerical examples of undoing a square root by squaring.

It is necessary to solve for a variable that is under a radical sign. To undo the square root, square both sides. $(50)^2 = (\sqrt{32.4D})^2$

Simplify. $2{,}500 = 32.4D$

Divide each side by 32.4. $\dfrac{2{,}500}{32.4} = \dfrac{32.4D}{32.4}$

Simplify. $\dfrac{2{,}500}{32.4} = D$

Round your answer to the nearest tenth. $77.2 \approx D$

Under the given conditions, you would expect the average of the skid marks to be approximately 77.2 feet.

CHECK YOUR UNDERSTANDING

Neil is traveling on a road at M miles per hour when he slams his foot on the brake pedal in order to avoid hitting a car up ahead. He is traveling on a gravel road with a drag factor of A and his brakes are operating at 100% efficiency. His car leaves three skid marks of length x, y, and z, respectively. Write an algebraic expression that represents the drag factor, A.

CHECK YOUR UNDERSTANDING

Answer $\dfrac{M^2}{\left(30A\dfrac{(x+y+z)}{3}\right)}$

Yaw Marks

Examine how the minimum speed can be determined from the data available by measuring the yaw marks. If S is the minimum speed, f is the drag factor, and r is the radius of the arc of the yaw mark, the most basic formula is

$$S = \sqrt{15fr}$$

To identify a radius, you must be able to pinpoint the center of the circle of which the arc is part. Here is how reconstructionists do just that. First, they select two points on the outer rim of the arc and connect them with a chord. A **chord** is the line segment that connects two points on an arc or circle as shown.

The center of the chord is located and a perpendicular line segment is drawn from that center to the arc. A line is perpendicular to another line if it meets at a right angle. This short line segment is the **middle ordinate**.

Reconstructionists use the following formula to determine the radius.

$$r = \frac{C^2}{8M} + \frac{M}{2}$$

M

r

C

where r is the radius of the yaw arc, C is the length of the chord, and M is the length of the middle ordinate.

EXAMPLE 3

In this problem, students are given the reconstructionist formula that is used when a yaw mark is left at the accident scene. In order to understand the formula, it is necessary that you explained the meaning of each variable used. Notice that there are two distinct and related parts to the solution of the problem. First, the radius must be determined by using the evidence left at the scene. Once the radius is established, it is entered into the skid speed formula.

CHECK YOUR UNDERSTANDING

Answer Using both the radius and the skid speed formulas, the minimum skid speed is approximately 42.4 mph.

EXAMPLE 3

An accident reconstructionist took measurements from yaw marks left at a scene. Using a 43-foot length chord, she determined that the middle ordinate measured approximately 4 feet. The drag factor for the road surface was determined to be 0.8. Determine the radius of the curved yaw mark to the nearest tenth of a foot. Determine the minimum speed that the car was going when the skid occurred to the nearest tenth.

SOLUTION Solve for r by substituting 43 for C and 4 for M in the equation.

$$r = \frac{C^2}{8M} + \frac{M}{2}$$

$$r = \frac{43^2}{8 \cdot 4} + \frac{4}{2}$$

$$r \approx 59.8$$

The radius of the curve is approximately 59.8 feet.

Solve for S by substituting $r = 59.8$ and $f = 0.8$ in the equation.

$$S = \sqrt{15fr}$$

$$S = \sqrt{15 \cdot 0.8 \cdot 59.8}$$

$$S \approx 26.8$$

The car entered the skid with an approximate minimum speed of 26.8 miles per hour.

■ CHECK YOUR UNDERSTANDING

Determine the minimum speed of a car at the point the brakes are immediately applied to avoid a collision based upon a yaw mark chord measuring 62.4 feet and a middle ordinate measuring 5 feet. The drag factor of the road surface is 1.2. Round your answer to the nearest tenth.

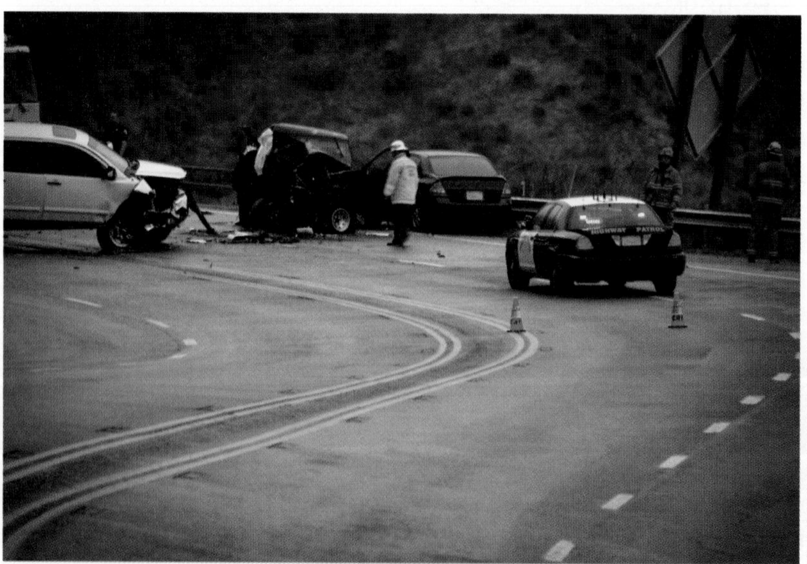

EYECRAVE/ISTOCKPHOTO.COM

Applications

It takes 8,460 bolts to assemble an automobile, and one nut to scatter it all over the road.

Author Unknown

1. Explain how the quote can be interpreted from what you have learned. See margin.

2. Ron's car left four skid marks on the road after he slammed his foot on the brake pedal to make an emergency stop. The police measured them to be 55 ft, 55 ft, 62 ft, and 62 ft. What skid distance will be used when calculating the skid speed formula? 58.5 ft

3. Jennie's car left three skid marks on the road surface in her highway accident. They measured 35 ft, 38 ft, and 47 ft. What skid distance will be used when calculating the skid speed formula? 40 ft

4. Kate's car left two skid marks each A feet long and two skid marks each B feet long after she had to immediately apply the brakes to avoid hitting a car. Write the algebraic expression that represents the skid distance that will be used in the skid speed formula. $\frac{A+B}{2}$

5. Rona was driving on an asphalt road that had a 35 mi/h speed limit posted. A deer jumped out from the side of the road causing Rona to slam on her brakes. Her tires left three skid marks of lengths 70 ft, 72 ft, and 71 ft. The road had a drag factor of 0.78. Her brakes were operating at 95% efficiency. The police gave Rona a ticket for speeding. Rona insisted that she was driving under the limit. Who is correct (the police or Rona)? Show your work. See margin.

6. In the spreadsheet, the prompts for entering data are in column A. The user enters the data in column B.
   a. Write the spreadsheet formula that will calculate the skid distance in cell B9. =sum(B5:B8)/B3
   b. Write the spreadsheet formula that will calculate the minimum skid speed in cell B9. The format for finding a square root in a spreadsheet is SQRT(number or expression). =sqrt(30*B1*B2*B9)
   c. Verify the accuracy of your formula for the following input values: drag factor, 0.6; braking efficiency, 0.8; and two skid marks, 45.3 ft and 48.2 ft. 25.9 mi/h

	A	B	C
1	Enter the road surface drag factor in B1.		
2	Enter the braking efficiency as a decimal in B2.		
3	Enter the number of skid marks on the road in B3.		
4	Enter lengths of skid marks. If fewer than 4 skid marks, enter measures and zero in the remaining cell(s).		
5	Skid mark #1 – cell B5		
6	Skid mark #2 – cell B6		
7	Skid mark #3 – cell B7		
8	Skid mark #4 – cell B8		
9	Calculated skid distance		
10	Minimum skid speed		

7. Ravi was driving on an asphalt road with a drag factor of 0.75. His brakes were working at 85% efficiency. He hit the brakes in order to avoid a dog that ran out in front of his car. Two of his tires made skid marks of 36 ft and 45 ft respectively. What was the minimum speed Ravi was going at the time he went into the skid? 27.8 mi/h

TEACH

Exercises 2–4

These problems should be completed in order together. Students work through the numerical then algebraic representation of tire skid mark distances.

ANSWERS

1. Clearly the quote is said in jest, but there is a great deal of truth in it. It highlights the fact that it is very easy to have an accident and drivers should always be alert and aware.
5. The police were correct since according to the formula, Rona's minimum skid speed was approximately 39.7 miles per hour.

TEACH

Exercise 8
Assist students in identify the variables, the function and an appropriate viewing window. Asks students where they will need to look on the graph in order to find the skid speeds for the given braking efficiencies.

Exercises 12–15
Remind students that rounding will change the accuracy of the solution.

8. A car leaves four skid marks each 50 feet in length. The drag factor for the road is 0.9. Let x represent the braking efficiency.

a. What is the range of values that can be substituted for x? 0 – 1 (0% – 100%)

b. Let the speed be represented by the variable y and x represent the braking efficiency. Write the skid speed equation in terms of x and y. $y = \sqrt{30 \cdot 50 \cdot 0.9 \cdot x} = \sqrt{1{,}350x}$

c. Graph the skid speed equation using the braking efficiency as the independent variable and the skid speed as the dependent variable. See additional answers.

d. Use your graph to estimate the skid speed for braking efficiencies of 20%, 40%, 60%, 80%, and 100%. 20%, 16 mi/h; 40%; 22 mi/h; 60%, 29 mi/h; 80%, 33 mi/h; 100%, 37 mi/h

9. A car is traveling at 57 mi/h before it enters into a skid. The drag factor of the road surface is 1.1, and the braking efficiency is 100%. How long might the average skid mark be to the nearest tenth of a foot? 98.5 ft

10. Steve is driving at 35 mi/h when he makes an emergency stop. His wheels lock and leave four skid marks of equal length. The drag factor for the road surface was 0.97 and his brakes were operating at 90% efficiency. How long might the skid marks be to the nearest foot? 47 ft

11. Marielle was in an accident. She was traveling down a road at 36 mi/h when she slammed on her brakes. Her car left two skid marks that averaged 50 ft in length with a difference of 4 ft between them. Her brakes were operating at 80% efficiency at the time of the accident.

a. What was the possible drag factor of this road surface? 1.08

b. What were the lengths of each skid mark? 52 ft and 48 ft

12. An accident reconstructionist takes measurements of the yaw marks at the scene of an accident. What is the radius of the curve if the middle ordinate measures 4.8 feet when using a chord with a length of 42 ft? Round your answer to the nearest tenth of a foot. 48.3 ft

13. The measure of the middle ordinate of a yaw mark is 6 ft. The radius of the arc is 70 ft. What was the length of the chord used in this situation? Round the answer to the nearest tenth of a foot. 56.7 ft

14. The following measurements from yaw marks left at the scene of an accident were taken by the authorities. Using a 31-ft length chord, the middle ordinate measured approximately 3 ft. The drag factor for the road surface is 1.02.

a. Determine the radius of the yaw mark to the nearest tenth of a foot. 41.5 ft

b. Determine the minimum speed that the car was going when the skid occurred to the nearest tenth. 25.2 mi/h

15. Juanita is an accident reconstruction expert. She measured a 70-ft chord from the outer rim of the yaw mark on the road surface. The middle ordinate measured 9 ft in length. The drag factor of the road surface was determined to be 1.13.

a. Determine the radius of the yaw mark to the nearest tenth of a foot. 72.6 ft

b. Determine the minimum speed that the car was going when the skid occurred to the nearest tenth. 35.1 mi/h

16. The formula used to determine the radius of the yaw mark arc is derived from a geometric relationship about two intersecting chords in a circle. In the figure, chords $\overline{AB}$ and $\overline{CD}$ intersect at point E in the circle. The product of the two segment lengths making up chord $\overline{AB}$, $AE \times EB$, is equal to the product of the two segment lengths making up chord $\overline{CD}$, $CE \times ED$.

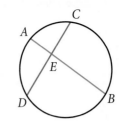

In the next figure, the yaw mark is darkened and it is continued to form a complete circle. A chord is drawn connecting two points on the yaw mark. The middle ordinate is also drawn. The length of the middle ordinate is M and the length of the chord is CD. The middle ordinate cuts the chord into two equal pieces with each half of the chord $\frac{CD}{2}$ units in length. The radius of the circle has length r as shown in the diagram. Applying the property to the two intersecting chords in this diagram, you get $AE \times EB = CE \times ED$.

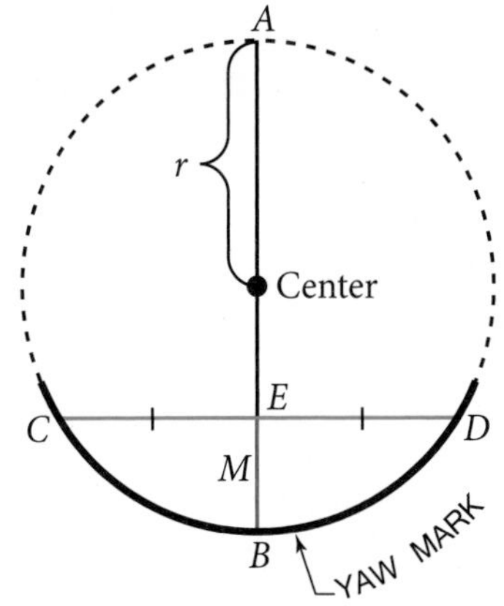

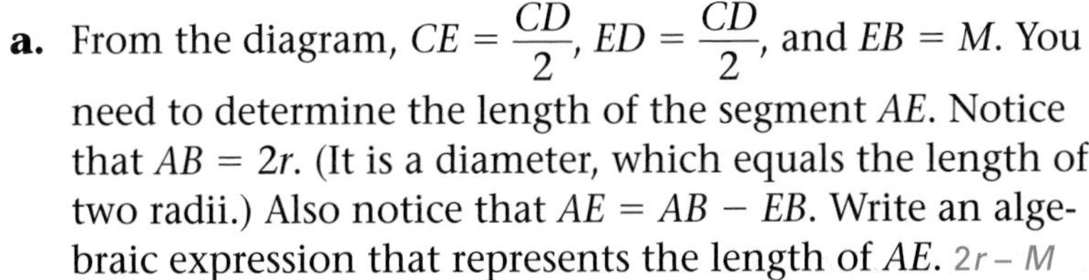

a. From the diagram, $CE = \frac{CD}{2}$, $ED = \frac{CD}{2}$, and $EB = M$. You need to determine the length of the segment AE. Notice that $AB = 2r$. (It is a diameter, which equals the length of two radii.) Also notice that $AE = AB - EB$. Write an algebraic expression that represents the length of AE. $2r - M$

b. Write the algebraic expression for the product of the segments of a chord that applies to this situation. Do not simplify. $(2r - M)M = \left(\frac{CD}{2}\right)\left(\frac{CD}{2}\right)$

c. Simplify the side of the equation that represents the product of the segments of chord $\overline{CD}$. Write the new equation. $(2r - M)M = \frac{(CD)^2}{4}$

d. Solve the equation for r by isolating the variable r on one side of the equation. Show your work. Compare your answer with the radius formula. $r = \frac{(CD)^2}{8M} + \frac{M}{2}$

TEACH

Exercise 16

This is a guided discovery that leads students to the development of certain algebraic relationships. It may not be appropriate for all students since it employs a higher degree of mathematical abstraction.

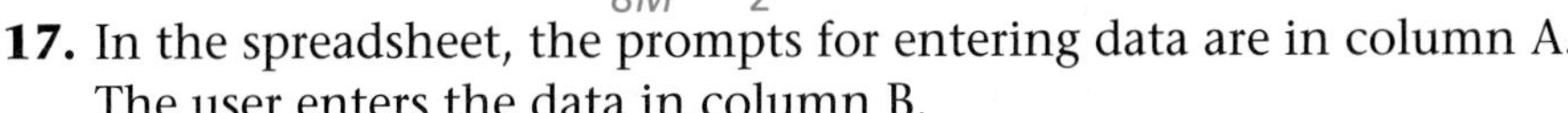

17. In the spreadsheet, the prompts for entering data are in column A. The user enters the data in column B.

a. Write the spreadsheet formula that will calculate the radius in cell B4. =(B2^2/(8*B3)+B3/2)

b. Write the spreadsheet formula that will calculate the minimum skid speed in cell B5. The formula for finding that speed is found by taking the $\sqrt{15}$ times the product of the drag factor and the radius. =sqrt(15*B1*B4)

c. Verify the accuracy of your formula for the following input values: drag factor, 0.97; chord length, 47 ft; and middle ordinate, 5 feet. approximately 29 mi/h

	A	B	C
1	Enter the road surface drag factor in B1.		
2	Enter the length of the chord connecting two points on the yaw mark in B2.		
3	Enter the length of the middle ordinate in B3.		
4	Calculated radius		
5	Minimum skid speed		

18. Ghada works for an insurance company as an accident reconstruction expert. She measured a 52-ft chord from the outer rim of the yaw mark on the road surface. The middle ordinate measured x ft in length. The drag factor of the road surface was determined to be 1.05.

a. What is the expression for the radius of the yaw mark? $\frac{x^2 + 676}{2x}$

b. Determine the expression for the minimum speed that the car was going when the skid occurred. $\sqrt{\frac{2x^2 + 31.5x + 676}{2x}}$

CHAPTER

5 Assessment

Real Numbers

You Write the Story!!

CHAPTER 5 ASSESSMENT

REAL NUMBERS

You Write the Story
Students have already seen linear and exponential regression. Make sure students interpret the graph correctly and do not use fictional or hypothetical anecdotes. If they want more information than the graph gives to write their articles, they can do an Internet search to acquire more facts. They should notice that the rate is increasing.

REALITY CHECK

Reality Check projects give students an additional avenue to show what they've learned, so their grades are not solely based on tests.

Projects can be presented to the class on any schedule that works for your program. It may be too time consuming for every student to present their project for every chapter.

Remind students who are personally visiting local businesses or community members that they are representing the school, and need to be cordial and patient. These projects deliberately have students taking little field trips, so they don't conduct everything online.

The graph below is a scatterplot and its regression curve. It gives actual hybrid electric vehicle (HEV) car sales in the United States for the years 2000–2012 and then predictions for HEV sales up to 2015. Write a short newspaper-type article centered on this graph. You can find an electronic copy at www.cengage.com/school/math/financialalgebra. Copy it and paste it into your article.

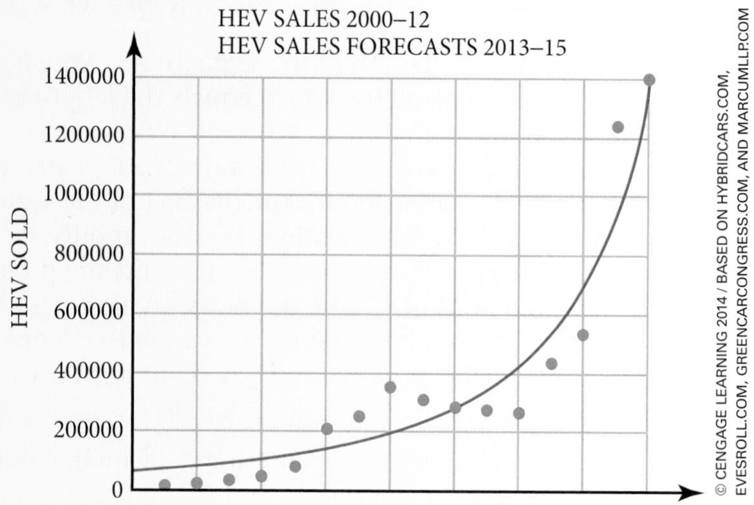

Write a short newspaper-type article centered on this graph. You can find an electronic copy at www.cengage.com/school/math/financialalgebra. Copy it and paste it into your article.

Reality Check

1. Go to a new car dealership. Pick out a car and make a list of the options you would order. Find the price of the car, the price of each option, and the total cost. Compute the sales tax and make a complete list of any extra charges for new car delivery. Report your findings to the class.
2. Pick any new or used car you would like to own. Make a list of the options you would like the car to have. Search for used car price on the Internet and find out what the car is worth. Print pages that summarize the car and its value. Visit a local insurance agent, and find out the cost of insurance for the car. Display your findings on a poster.
3. Visit your local motor vehicle department or their website. Make a list of the forms needed to register a car and get license plates. If possible, get sample copies of each form. Show and explain each form to the class.

4. Pick a road trip you would like to make. Estimate the gas cost. Get hotel prices for any overnight stays. Get the full cost of staying at your destination. Approximate food expenses. Interview a local travel agent. Before the interview, list questions you want to ask. Include the expenses, questions, and answers from the interview in a report.

5. Talk to your teacher about having an insurance agent speak to your class. Have the class submit questions about automobile insurance. Copy the questions neatly on a sheet of paper and give it to the agent before the talk.

6. Write an ad to sell a used car. Contact several newspapers online to find the price of both a print and online ad for one week. Report your findings to the class.

7. Pick out a new or used car that you would like to own. Choose one of the following repair jobs: complete brake job, complete tune-up, or complete exhaust system replacement. Go to a garage or repair shop and get a price estimate for the job. Be sure to include parts and labor. Then go to an auto supply store and find out what each of the parts would cost. Compare the garage or repair shop's estimate of parts and labor to the cost of repairing the car yourself.

8. Interview a local insurance agent. Find out when premiums must be paid, types of discounts offered, insurance that is mandatory in your state, optional insurance that is available, and any other questions you can think of. Summarize your interview in a report.

9. Go online and find the cost of renting a car of your choice for two weeks. Pay particular attention to the limited damage waiver they offer. If you rent a car, you will be asked if you want to pay a limited damage waiver. This will reduce your liability for physical damage to the car. This type of insurance is expensive. Certain credit cards provide this coverage as a service. Go online and get contact information for two credit card companies. Contact them and ask which of their cards includes coverage for the limited damage waiver for a rented car. Give a report.

10. Flamboyant cars have graced movie and television screens for decades. Go online and/or to the library and make a list of famous cars. Give the make, model, and year of each car. Include information on where these cars are now and the highest price paid for each car as it changed owners. Add photos and other interesting facts about each car. Present your information on a poster.

11. A nomograph or nomogram is a chart that graphs the relationships between three quantities. Nomographs have been used in many fields such as medicine, physics, information technology, geology, and more. One such nomograph charts the fuel economy relationship—distance is equal to the miles per gallon fuel consumption of the car times the number of gallons used. Research the creation and usages of nomographs and find one that relates to fuel economy. Write a short description of this nomograph, explaining how it works and how it can be helpful to drivers. Include an example of the nomograph.

REALITY CHECK

You can offer students extra projects for extra credit.

Students completing Project 1 can also visit a bank and price a loan for their car. They can also combine it with Project 10, and price insurance for that same car. The loan payment and monthly insurance cost can give them a glimpse at the monthly cost of owning the car.

If a student chooses Project 14, you can make copies of the nomograph they downloaded and the student can show the class how to use it.

Dollars and Sense — Your Financial News Update

Go to www.cengage.com/school/math/financialalgebra where you will find a link to a website containing current issues about automobile ownership. Try one of the activities.

Really? Really! REVISITED

Take another look at the gas price table. As you marvel at how inexpensive gas prices may have seemed, remember one word—*inflation*. If you research the price of gas on the Internet and look at prices adjusted for inflation, you will be surprised. In 1960, the median annual income of United States families was $5,600. Nevertheless, it is always fascinating to look at different prices over the course of history.

Year	Price per Gallon
1950	$0.27
1955	$0.30
1960	$0.31
1965	$0.31
1970	$0.35
1975	$0.53
1980	$1.13
1985	$1.19
1990	$1.13
1995	$1.14
2000	$1.66
2005	$2.33

1. Enter the data from the table of gas prices and draw a scatter plot on a sheet of graph paper. See margin.
2. Go online and find out the average cost of a gallon of gas today. Answers vary.
3. Add today's cost to your scatterplot. Answers vary.
4. Draw a smooth curve that, by eye, looks like the best fit to the points on your scatterplot. Answers vary.
5. Go online and look up the median U.S. income for last year. Also find out the base price of this year's Corvette. Answers vary.

REALLY? REALLY! REVISITED

As students plot gas prices, you can also have them chart other indicators for the same years:

- cost of a movie
- median US income
- cost of a Corvette
- median home price
- cost of a baseball game ticket

The graphs cannot be drawn on the same axes due to the very different price ranges for each item, but the shape of the graph tells the story of the rates of increase.

ANSWERS

1.

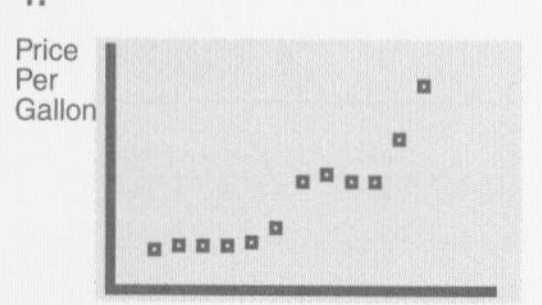

Applications

1. The college newspaper charges by the character for classified ads. Letters, numbers, spaces, and punctuation count as one character. They charge \$34 for the first 100 characters, and \$0.09 for each additional character. If x represents the number of characters, express the cost $c(x)$ of an ad as a piecewise function. Graph the function. See margin.

2. The *Classic Car Monthly* charges \$49 for a three-line classified ad. Each additional line costs \$9.50. For an extra \$30, a seller can include a photo. How much would a five-line ad with a photo cost? \$98

3. A local newspaper charges d dollars for a three-line classified ad. Each additional line costs a dollars. Express the cost of a six-line ad algebraically. $d + 3a$

4. The straight line depreciation equation for a car is $y = -2{,}400x + 36{,}000$.
   a. What is the original price of the car? \$36,000
   b. How much value does the car lose per year? \$2,400
   c. How many years will it take for the car to totally depreciate? 15 years

5. A car is originally worth \$43,500. It takes 12 years for this car to totally depreciate. $y = -3{,}625x + 43{,}500$
   a. Write the straight-line depreciation equation for this situation.
   b. How long will it take for the car to be worth one quarter of its original price? 9 years
   c. How long will it take for the car to be worth \$20,000? Round your answer to the nearest tenth of a year. 6.5 years

6. Prices for used stainless steel side trim for a 1957 Chevrolet convertible are \$350, \$350, \$390, \$400, \$500, \$500, \$500, \$600, \$650, \$725, \$800, \$850, \$900, and \$1,700. The prices vary depending on the condition.
   a. Find the mean of the trim prices to the nearest dollar. \$658
   b. Find the median of the trim prices. \$550
   c. Find the mode of the trim prices. \$500
   d. Find the four quartiles for this data. $Q_1 = \$400$; $Q_2 = \$550$; $Q_3 = \$800$; $Q_4 = \$1{,}700$
   e. Find the interquartile range for this data. \$400
   f. Find the boundary for the lower outliers. Are there any lower outliers? –\$200; there are no lower outliers.
   g. Find the boundary for the upper outliers. Are there any upper outliers? \$1,400; yes, there is one upper outlier: \$1,700.
   h. Draw a modified box-and-whisker plot. See additional answers.

7. Kathy purchased a new car for \$37,800. From her research she has determined that it straight-line depreciates over 14 years. She made a \$7,000 down payment and pays \$710 per month for her car loan.
   a. Create an expense and depreciation function where x represents the number of months. depreciation: $y = -225x + 37{,}800$; expense: $y = 710x + 7{,}000$
   b. Graph these functions on the same axes. See additional answers.
   c. Interpret the region before, at, and after the intersection point in the context of this situation. See margin.

ANSWERS

1. $c(x) = \begin{cases} 34 & \text{when } x \le 100 \\ 34 + 0.09(x - 100) & \text{when } x > 100 \end{cases}$

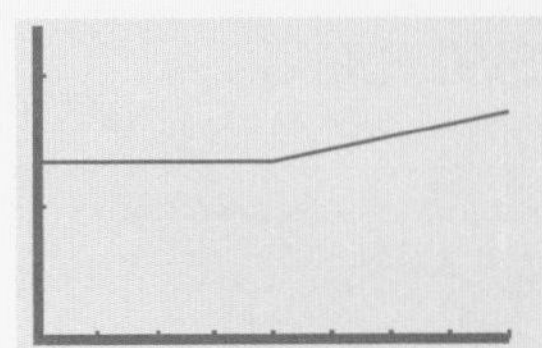

7c. Using a graphing tool, the coordinates of the intersection point, rounded to the nearest hundredth, are (31.87, 30628.88). This means that after a little less than 31 months, both the expenses-to-date and the car's value are the same. In the region before the intersection point, the expenses are lower than the value of the car. But, the region after the intersection point indicates a period of time that the value of the car is less than what was invested in it.

1	1 8 9 9
2	0 0 3
3	4 6 6 7 7 8
4	0 1 2
5	5 5 6 8 9 9
6	1 2 2

4| 1 = 41

ANSWERS

10a.

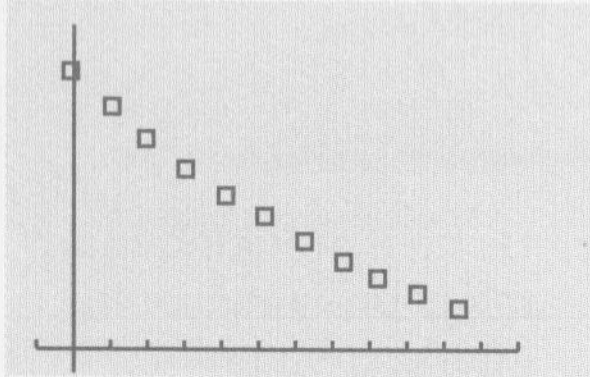

11c. $50,000 under PIP.

8. Grahamsville High School recently polled its teachers to see how many miles they drive to work each day. At the left is a stem-and-leaf plot of the results.

a. How many teachers were polled? 25

b. Find the mean to the nearest mile. 40

c. Find the median. 38

d. Find the mode(s). 19, 20, 36, 37, 55, 59, 62

e. Find the range. 51

f. Find the four quartiles. $Q_1 = 21.5$; $Q_2 = 38$; $Q_3 = 57$; $Q_4 = 62$

g. What percent of the teachers travel more than 38 miles to work? 48%

h. Find the interquartile range. 35.5

i. What percent of the teachers travel from 38 to 57 miles to work? 28%

9. Stewart has $25,000 worth of property damage insurance and a $1,000 deductible collision insurance policy. He crashed into a fence when his brakes failed and did $7,000 worth of damage to the fence. The crash caused $3,600 in damages to his car.

a. Which insurance covers the damage to the fence? property damage

b. How much will the insurance company pay for the fence? $7,000

c. Stewart's car still was drivable after the accident. On the way home from the accident, he hit an empty school bus and did $20,000 worth of damage to the bus and $2,100 worth of damage to his car. How much will the insurance company pay for this damage to the bus? $20,000

d. Which insurance covers the damage to Stewart's car? collision

e. How much will the insurance company pay for the damage to the car? $3,700

Historical Prices

Age	Value ($)
0	32,000
1	29,100
2	26,500
3	24,120
4	21,950
5	20,000
6	18,100
7	16,500
8	15,000
9	13,700
10	12,500

10. The historical prices of a car with the same make, model, and features are recorded for a period of 10 years as shown in the table.

a. Construct a scatterplot for the data. See margin.

b. Determine the exponential depreciation formula that models this data. Round all numbers to the nearest hundredth. $y = 31{,}985.36 \times 0.91^x$

c. Determine the depreciation rate to the nearest percent. approximately 9%

d. Use the model equation to predict the value of this car after 66 months. Round to the nearest thousand dollars. $19,000

11. Gina has 250/500/50 liability insurance and $50,000 PIP insurance. She changes lanes too quickly, hits the metal guard rail, and then hits a tour bus. Four people are seriously hurt and sue her. Twenty others have minor injuries. Gina's boyfriend, who was in her car, was also hurt.

a. The guard rail will cost $2,000 to replace. Gina also did $9,700 worth of damage to the bus. What insurance will cover this, and how much will the company pay? property damage under $11,700

b. The bus driver severed his hand and cannot drive a bus again. He sues for $2,500,000 and is awarded $1,750,000 in court. What type of insurance covers this? How much will the insurance company pay? $250,000 under BI

c. The bus driver (from part b) had medical bills totaling $90,000 from an operation after the accident. What type of insurance covers this, and how much will the insurance company pay? See margin.

d. Gina's boyfriend is hurt and requires $19,000 worth of medical attention. What insurance covers this, and how much will the company pay? $19,000 under PIP

12. Joshua just purchased a 4-year-old car for $12,000. He was told that this make and model depreciates exponentially at a rate of 5.8% per year. What was the original price to the nearest hundred dollars? $15,200

13. A graphing calculator has determined the following exponential regression equation: $y = a*b^x$, $a = 28{,}158.50$, $b = 0.815$.
    a. What is the rate of depreciation for this car? 18.5%
    b. How much is this car worth to the nearest dollar after 6 years? $8,252
    c. How much is this car worth to the nearest hundred dollars after 39 months? $14,500
    d. How much is this car worth after y years? $28{,}158.50(0.815^y)$

14. Jonathan's car gets approximately 25 miles per gallon. He is planning a 980-mile trip. About how many gallons of gas will his car use for the trip? At an average price of $4.00 per gallon, how much should Jonathan expect to spend for gas? Round to the nearest ten dollars. 39.2 gallons; $160

15. Ann's car gets about 12 kilometers per liter of gas. She is planning a 2,100 kilometer trip. To the nearest liter, how many liters of gas should Ann plan to buy? At an average price of $1.49 per liter, how much should Ann expect to spend for gas? 175 liters; $260.75

16. Max is driving 42 miles per hour. A dog runs into the street and Max reacts in about three-quarters of a second. What is his approximate reaction distance? 42 ft

17. Tricia is driving 64 miles per hour on an interstate highway. She must make a quick stop because there is an emergency vehicle ahead.
    a. What is her approximate reaction distance? 64 ft
    b. What is her approximate braking distance? 204.8 ft
    c. About how many feet does the car travel from the time she starts to switch pedals until the car has completely stopped? 268.8 ft

18. Marlena is driving on an interstate at 65 km/h. She sees a traffic jam about 30 meters ahead and needs to bring her car to a complete stop before she reaches that point. Her reaction time is approximately $\frac{3}{4}$ of a second. Is she far enough away from the traffic jam to safely bring the car to a complete stop? Explain. See margin.

19. Richie was driving on an asphalt road that had a 40 mi/h speed limit. A bicyclist darted out from the side of the road causing him to slam on his brakes. His tires left three skid marks of 69 ft, 70 ft, and 74 ft. The road had a drag factor of 0.95. His brakes were operating at 98% efficiency. The police gave Richie a ticket for speeding. Richie insisted that he was driving under the speed limit. Who is correct? Explain. See margin.

20. A car is traveling at 52 mi/h before it enters into a skid. It has been determined that the drag factor of the road surface is 1.05, and the braking efficiency is 80%. How long might the average skid mark be to the nearest tenth of a foot for this situation? 107.3 ft

21. A reconstructionist took measurements from yaw marks left at the scene of an accident. Using a 46-ft chord, the middle ordinate measured approximately 6 ft. The drag factor for the road surface was 0.95. Determine the radius of the yaw mark to the nearest tenth of a foot. Determine the minimum speed when the skid occurred to the nearest tenth mile. 47.1 ft; 25.9 mi/h

ANSWERS

18. She does not have enough room to stop. Marlena's total stopping distance is 37.85 meters which is more than the distance to the traffic jam.

19. The police were correct since according to the formula, Richie's minimum skid speed was approximately 44.53 miles per hour.

CHAPTER

6 Employment Basics

Choose a job you love, and you will never have to work a day in your life.

Confucius, Ancient Chinese Philosopher

What did Confucius mean by this statement?

About 70% of the time you are awake during your lifetime is spent at work. Knowing that this much of your waking time is spent at a job makes it extremely important to learn and understand as much as possible about the jobs you hold, the salaries you make, the benefits your job offers, and the taxes you pay. In this chapter, you will study employment basics so that you can become an educated employee. You won't have to wait years to use the information you will learn here. You will be able to apply this knowledge while you are searching, applying, accepting, and working at a job, whether it is in a part-time or full-time capacity. Many people start working in their early to mid-twenties, and continue working until they are in their 60s or 70s.

What do you think?

This quote tests personal definitions of job and work. Is a job still considered to be work if it is something that you love to do? Enjoyment in the job you perform can take the work out of work!

TEACHING RESOURCES

Instructor's Resource CD

Exam*View*® CD, Ch. 6

eHomework, Ch. 6

www.cengage.com/school/math/financialalgebra

Really?

The American workforce is vast, diverse, and strong. As of May 2008, there were approximately 155 million workers in the United States. The occupations of some of these workers are shown in the table, according to the *Statistical Abstract of the United States: 2009*.

Occupation	Number of Employees
Teachers	7.2 million
Hairdressers, hairstylists and cosmetologists	773,000
Chefs and head cooks	351,000
Taxi drivers and chauffeurs	373,000
Firefighters	293,000
Roofers	234,000
Pharmacists	243,000
Musicians, singers and related workers	186,000
Gaming industry (gambling)	111,000
Tax preparers	105,000
Service station attendants	87,000
Inspectors, testers, sorters, samplers, weighers	751,000

- 7.7 million workers are called *moonlighters*. They hold more than one job. Close to 300,000 of those moonlighters work two full-time jobs.
- 28% of workers work more than 40 hours per week.
- 17 million workers leave for work between midnight and 5:59 A.M.
- 3.1 million workers travel over 90 minutes to work.
- 10.4 million workers are self-employed.
- 5.7 million workers work from home.

CHAPTER OVERVIEW

Students will explore the world of work from the first time they begin to look for employment to years in the future when they will be concerned about retirement benefits. The focus of this chapter is to make them aware of the many aspects of the working world.

REALLY? REALLY!

The United States workforce is larger and more diverse than students might imagine. In this feature, students are given numerical data that offer insight into the who, what, where, and when of our working population.

Students can find more amazing work facts in the *Statistical Abstract of the United States* on the Census Bureau's website.

When the data for the 2010 U.S. Census is compiled and released, it may be interesting to see how the workforce has shifted. Ask students to find this information on the U.S. Census Bureau's website.

Really!

In today's competitive job market, it's important to realize that finding a job is in itself a full time job.

Lee Marc, American Businessman and Developer of Online Resume Site

6-1 Look for Employment

Objectives

- Compute periodic salary based on annual contract salary.
- Interpret abbreviations in classified ads.
- Express classified ad prices as piecewise functions.

Common Core

A-CED2, F-IF2

Key Terms

- employment agency
- fee paid
- resume
- Form W-4 Employee's Withholding Allowance Certificate
- benefits
- discount

CCSS Warm-Up

For each x, find the value of $f(x)$ if

$$f(x) = \begin{cases} 4x - 7 \text{ when } x < 3 \\ x^2 + 2x \text{ when } x \geq 3 \end{cases}$$

1. $x = 2$ **2.** $x = 3$ **3.** $x = 4$

1. 1 2. 15 3. 24

EXAMINE THE QUESTION

The material presented in the introduction may not reflect how your employed students got their part-time and/or summer jobs. However, all of your employed students should remember filling out Form W-4, although they may not remember its name. You may want to tell them how you found out about your current teaching job.

How do people in different stages of their careers find employment?

Many students take on after-school and summer jobs. Sometimes these are not related to their eventual career choice—they are jobs to meet the growing expenses of being a teenager. Many students find out about these jobs by signs in store windows, the school guidance department, bulletin board postings, and word-of-mouth.

When choosing a career, you usually choose a field of interest. You then need to develop skills in that area. Your career will be based on the training you receive in college, trade school, or as an on-the-job as an apprentice. All electricians, lawyers, teachers, plumbers, actors, dentists, and so on had to learn their trade and then practice it. How do you go about looking for employment? You can look in the classified ad section of the newspaper.

You can also look online. There are many Internet sites available to job seekers. These ads cover all types of employment, from summer jobs for teenagers to careers in all fields. You will find it helpful to learn the special shorthand that is used in help-wanted classified ads. There are many abbreviations that are special for individual fields. Some commonly used abbreviations are shown in the table.

agcy	employment agency
asst	assistant
bi/ling	you are bilingual
comp lit	you must be computer literate
email res	email your resume
eves	evenings
exp'd	experienced
fee paid	employer pays employment agency fee
F/T	full-time
gd	good
K	$1,000
P/T	part-time
pd vac	paid vacation
req	required
to $*m*	maximum pay is $*m* per hour
w/	with

You can also look for work through an employment agency. An **employment agency** is a business that has lists of job openings. Some employment agencies specialize in certain fields of work. If you are placed in a job by an employment agency, you may have to pay a fee to the agency. When the employer is willing to pay this fee, the job is listed as **fee paid**.

When you decide to apply for a specific job, you will have to send your resume to the employer. A **resume** is a short account of your education and qualifications for employment. Some employers want resumes submitted electronically online. Project 3 in the Chapter 6 Reality Check will help you familiarize yourself with resume writing. If the employer is impressed with your resume, you will be invited to an interview and you might be hired.

Once you are hired, you will need to fill out numerous forms, including a **Form W-4 Employee's Withholding Allowance Certificate**. This form is used by employers for income tax purposes. As you embark on your job search, salary isn't your only consideration. Among other factors, you need to consider **benefits**—additional compensation from your employer. Benefits can include health and dental insurance, child care, retirement, and travel expenses.

CLASS DISCUSSION

Ask the students if any of them are employed, or were in the summer.

Encourage students to view sample job resumes on the Internet.

Skills and Strategies

Here you will learn about interpreting classified ads, computing salaries, and employment agency fees.

EXAMPLE 1

Explain that many jobs have an annual salary rather than an hourly wage. Remind students that there are 52 weeks in a year.

CHECK YOUR UNDERSTANDING

Answer $5,608

EXAMPLE 1

Julianne found a job listed in the classified ads that pays a yearly salary of $41K. What is the weekly salary based on this annual salary?

SOLUTION Julianne must interpret $41K. The K stands for $1,000. Julianne multiplies to compute the annual salary.

$$41 \times 1{,}000 = 41{,}000$$

The annual salary is $41,000.

To compute the weekly salary, divide the annual salary by 52. There are 52 weeks in a year. Round to the nearest cent.

$$41{,}000 \div 52 \approx 788.46$$

The weekly salary is $788.46.

CHECK YOUR UNDERSTANDING

Karen found a job with an annual salary of $67.3K. What is her monthly pay, rounded to the nearest dollar?

EXAMPLE 2

Students might be surprised at the employment agency fees. Explain that the employment agency does much of the work it takes to look for a job, and they also have operating expenses. These expenses are paid by the fees they charge.

CHECK YOUR UNDERSTANDING

Answer $\frac{0.15x}{12}$

EXAMPLE 3

Students learned about piecewise functions when they learned about classified ads for used cars. This is a great refresher for that skill.

CHECK YOUR UNDERSTANDING

Answer

$$c(x) = \begin{cases} 13x & \text{when } x \leq 4 \\ 68 + 7.50(x - 4) & \text{when } x > 4 \end{cases}$$

EXTEND YOUR UNDERSTANDING

Answer
$13x$ would become kx and 68 would become $4k$.

EXAMPLE 2

Dylan took a job through an employment agency. The job pays \$395 per week. Dylan must pay a fee to the employment agency. The fee is 20% of his first four weeks' pay. How much money must Dylan pay the agency?

SOLUTION Dylan multiplies his weekly pay by four to compute his first four weeks' pay.

$$395 \times 4 = 1{,}580$$

He then finds 20% of \$1,580.

$$1{,}580 \times 0.20 = 316.00$$

The employment agency fee that Dylan must pay is \$316.00.

■ CHECK YOUR UNDERSTANDING

The Alpha Employment Agency is advertising a job in the construction industry. The fee is 15% of the first month's pay. If the job pays x dollars annually, express the agency fee algebraically.

EXAMPLE 3

Ken is a mechanic who owns Ace Auto Repair. He needs a foreign car expert and is placing a twelve-line classified ad. The cost of an ad x lines long is given by the following piecewise function.

$$c(x) = \begin{cases} 56 & \text{when } x \leq 4 \\ 56 + 6(x - 4) & \text{when } x > 4 \end{cases}$$

Find the cost of a twelve-line ad.

SOLUTION Because 12 is in the domain $x > 4$, Ken can substitute 12 into the second equation of the piecewise function.

Use the second equation.	$c(x) = 56 + 6(x - 4)$
Substitute.	$c(12) = 56 + 6(12 - 4)$
Calculate.	$c(12) = 104$

The total cost is \$104.

■ CHECK YOUR UNDERSTANDING

A local newspaper charges \$13 for each of the first four lines of a classified ad, and \$7.50 for each additional line. Express the cost of an x-line ad, $c(x)$, as a piecewise function.

■ EXTEND YOUR UNDERSTANDING

If the local newspaper from the Check Your Understanding above wanted the price of their per line charge for the first four lines to be k, what would change in the piecewise function?

EXAMPLE 4

An online job search site charges employers fees to post job listings. Their price list is shown in the table. The prices per posting decrease as the number of postings increase. What is the percent savings if an employer decides to post four jobs?

Number of Job Postings	Price per Job Posting
1	\$395.00 each
2	\$385.00 each
3	\$375.00 each
4	\$350.00 each
5–20	\$320.00 each
21–50	\$265.00 each
51–100	\$200.00 each
101–150	\$165.00 each
151–250	\$135.00 each

SOLUTION The price for posting one job is \$395. If four jobs are posted, the price per job is \$350. The amount the fee was lowered is the **discount**. There is a \$45 discount per job. Set up a fraction to find the percent of the discount.

$$\text{Percent discount} = \frac{\text{Original price} - \text{Discount price}}{\text{Original price}}$$

Substitute, solve, and round to the nearest percent.

$$\text{Percent discount} = \frac{395 - 350}{395} \approx 0.113 \approx 11\%$$

The employer saves 11% per posting.

CHECK YOUR UNDERSTANDING

JobFind charges employers x dollars to post a job on their website. They offer a 16% discount if 20 or more jobs are posted. If 31 jobs are posted by a specific employer, express the discount as a percent.

EXAMPLE 5

Jane's Printing Services charges \$29.95 to print 200 high quality copies of a one-page resume. Each additional set of 100 copies costs \$14. Express the cost, $r(x)$, of printing x sets of 100 resumes, as a piecewise function.

SOLUTION The printing service charges for multiples of 100 only. If you think in sets of 100 copies, 200 copies represent 2 sets. Split the function into rules for the two different domains.

$$r(x) = \begin{cases} 29.95 & \text{when } x \text{ is an integer and } x \leq 2 \\ 29.95 + 14(x - 2) & \text{when } x \text{ is an integer and } x > 2 \end{cases}$$

Notice the additional restriction on each domain. Notice that x must be a positive integer. These prices are for bulk orders only.

CHECK YOUR UNDERSTANDING

Pete needs 77 copies of his resume. Jane's charges 39 cents per resume-quality copy. Should he pay individually for the 77 copies or get 200 copies at the prices from Example 5? Explain.

EXTEND YOUR UNDERSTANDING

Write an inequality that compares the unit costs of a resume printed using each option Pete has in the Check Your Understanding above.

EXAMPLE 4

Students have seen percent discount problems for years. In science class, they have also calculated percent error, and percent increase and decrease. Example 4 reviews these skills.

CHECK YOUR UNDERSTANDING

Answer percent discount = $\frac{x - 0.84x}{x}(100)$

EXAMPLE 5

The piecewise function skills undergo an adjustment in this problem. The domain requires that x be an integer since the printing service sells copies in integral batches of 100.

CHECK YOUR UNDERSTANDING

Answer He should get 200 copies for \$29.95, since 77 copies at \$0.39 is \$30.03. He gets more copies for less money by ordering 200.

EXTEND YOUR UNDERSTANDING

Answer
$0.39 > 0.15$

Applications

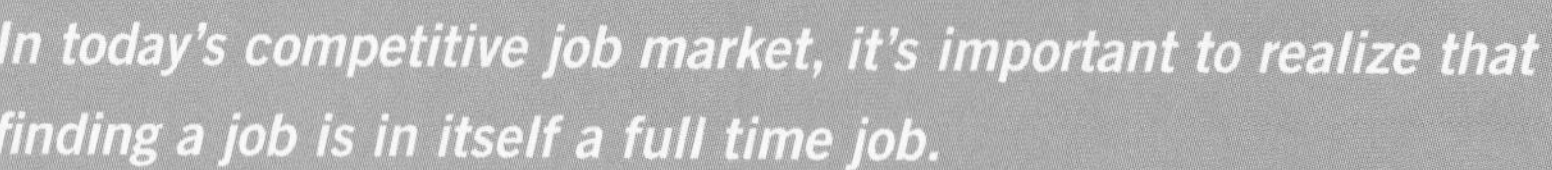

In today's competitive job market, it's important to realize that finding a job is in itself a full time job.
Lee Marc, American Businessman and Developer of Online Resume Site

TEACH

Exercises 1–7
These exercises require students to compute salaries and employment agency fees. Remind students not to skim problems and to read them carefully. They could be asked for annual, monthly, or weekly salaries, and agency fees are all slightly different from each other.

ANSWERS

1. In today's world, you need to know how to find job openings, and how to get your resume into the hands of prospective employers once you find them. With all of today's technology, your resume often exists in a sea of hundreds of resumes, and making it stand out is crucial.

8b.

$$r(x) = \begin{cases} 21.50 & \text{when } x \text{ is a positive integer and } x \le 2 \\ 21.50 + 10(x - 2) & \text{when } x \text{ is an integer and } x > 2 \end{cases}$$

1. Interpret the quote in the context of what you learned about job seeking. See margin.

2. Danny just answered a help-wanted ad. The ad states that the job pays $27K annually. What would Danny's monthly salary be if he gets this job? $2,250

3. Becky is looking for a new job as an account executive. She responds to a classified ad for a position that pays 34.5K. What would Becky's weekly salary be to the nearest cent, if she gets this job? $663.46

4. Enid got a job through an employment agency that charges a fee equal to 40% of the first five weeks' pay. The job pays $315 per week. How much does Enid have to pay the employment agency? $630

5. Melanie got a new job through the Jones Employment Agency. The job pays $32,400 per year, and the agency fee is equal to 45% of one month's pay. How much must Melanie pay the agency? $1,215

6. The Rockville Employment Agency just placed Howard Jacobson in a job as a junior pharmacist. The job pays $51.2K. The agency fee is equal to 40% of the first three weeks' pay.
  a. What is Howard's weekly salary to the nearest cent? $984.62
  b. What will Howard earn during the first three weeks? $2,953.86
  c. How much must Howard pay the employment agency to the nearest dollar? $1,182

7. Maple Place Garage is posting five job listings with the online service from Example 4.
  a. How much is each posting? $320
  b. How much less does Maple Place pay per posting compared to the price for one posting? $75
  c. What is the cost of the five postings? $1,600
  d. What is the total savings for the five postings? $375
  e. Express the total savings as a percent of the total cost for the five postings. Round to the nearest percent. 19%

8. Roger wants to have 400 copies of his resume printed. His local print shop charges $21.50 for the first 200 copies and $10 for every 100 additional copies.
  a. How much will the 400 copies cost, including a sales tax of 6%? $43.99
  b. If the number of sets of 100 resumes is represented by x, express the cost of the resumes, $r(x)$, as a piecewise function of x. See margin.

9. Pat earns $575 per week at her new job. Express her annual salary using the K abbreviation found in classified ads. $29.9K

10. Kareem earns y dollars per month at his accounting job. Express his annual salary using the K abbreviation found in classified ads. $\frac{12y}{1{,}000}K$

11. Mike is a veterinarian. He is placing a 9-line classified ad for an assistant. The following piecewise function gives the price of an x-line ad.

$$a(x) = \begin{cases} 45 & \text{when } x \leq 3 \\ 45 + 9(x - 3) & \text{when } x > 3 \end{cases}$$

a. Find the difference between the cost of a 2-line ad and the cost of a 3-line ad. $0

b. Find the cost of a 10-line ad. $108

c. Find the cost of an 11-line ad. $117

d. Can you find the difference between the cost of a 15-line ad and a 17-line ad, without finding out the cost of each ad first? Explain. See margin.

12. Joanne is looking for a job as a teacher. She plans to send resumes to 123 schools in her county. Her local printer charges $23 per 100 copies, and sells them only in sets of 100.

a. How many copies must Joanne purchase if she is to have enough resumes? 200

b. How much will the copies cost her, including 8% sales tax? $49.68

c. If the number of sets of 100 resumes is represented by x, express the cost, with 8% sales tax, of the resumes, $r(x)$, as a function of x. $r(x) = 1.08(23x)$

13. Cathy is looking for a job as a bookkeeper. One classified ad lists a job in a stereo store that pays 34.6K. Another job, in a clothing store, has a weekly salary of $620.

a. Which job is the higher-paying job? stereo store job

b. What is the difference in the weekly salaries of these two jobs? Round to the nearest dollar. $45

14. An online job seeking service allows job seekers to post their resumes for free. The service charges employers looking for applicants a fee to look through the resumes. The fee is based on how long the employer wants access to the resumes, and how many miles from the workplace address the employer wants to consider. The fees are $585 for a 100-mile radius for 3 weeks and $675 for a 150-mile radius for 3 weeks.

a. If there are 98 resumes within a 100-mile radius, what is the average cost to the nearest cent to the employer for looking at each resume? $5.97

b. If there are 208 resumes within a 150-mile radius, what is the average cost to the employer for looking at each resume? $3.25

c. Under the 150-mile radius option, an employer would see the same 98 resumes from part a that he would have seen under the 100-mile radius option. What is the average cost to the employer for looking at the extra resumes he would see if he opted for the more expensive plan? Explain. See margin.

d. Give an advantage and a disadvantage of opting for the more expensive plan. See margin.

TEACH

Exercise 10

This exercise asks for a literal expression. Whenever students have trouble with these, remind them to think of the variables as numbers. They might have an easier time understanding the letters after they perform computations on numbers.

Exercise 14

Point out that all applicants that live within a 100-mile radius also live within a 150-mile radius.

ANSWERS

11d. Yes; the additional two lines will cost $18, since each line over the first three lines costs $9.

14c. The employer sees 110 extra resumes for $90. The average cost per extra resume is approximately 82 cents.

14d. An advantage is that the price per extra resume is much less than the price of looking at the original 100 resumes ($5.97 vs. 82 cents). The disadvantage is that the extra resumes are from people far away, who would most likely have to relocate to take the job. Some may not be willing to, so time spent on interviewing those people might be wasted time.

Never confuse the size of your paycheck with the size of your talent.

Marlon Brando, Actor

6-2 Pay Periods and Hourly Rates

Objectives

- Compute weekly, semimonthly, and biweekly earnings given annual salary.
- Compute hourly pay and overtime pay given hourly rate.

Common Core

A-CED4

Key Terms

- weekly
- biweekly
- semimonthly
- monthly
- direct deposit
- hourly rate
- regular hours
- overtime hours
- overtime hourly rate
- time-and-a-half overtime
- double-time pay
- gross pay
- minimum wage

CCSS Warm-Up

Solve each literal equation for x.
Isolate x on one side of the equation.

1. $rx = t$ **2.** $1.5x = r + t$ **3.** $1.5(x + r) = 9$

1. $x = \frac{t}{r}$ 2. $x = \frac{r + t}{1.5}$ 3. $x = 6 - r$

EXAMINE THE QUESTION

Most paychecks today are computer-generated. Even so, encourage students to check their paychecks because computers can make mistakes. They also need to know about labor laws in their industry. Even part-time student jobs are protected by labor laws.

What do you need to know to make sure each paycheck is correct?

Everybody looks forward to payday. Most high school students are paid on a **weekly** basis, which means they receive 52 paychecks per year. Their paydays usually fall on the same day each week. However, not all jobs have a pay period of one week.

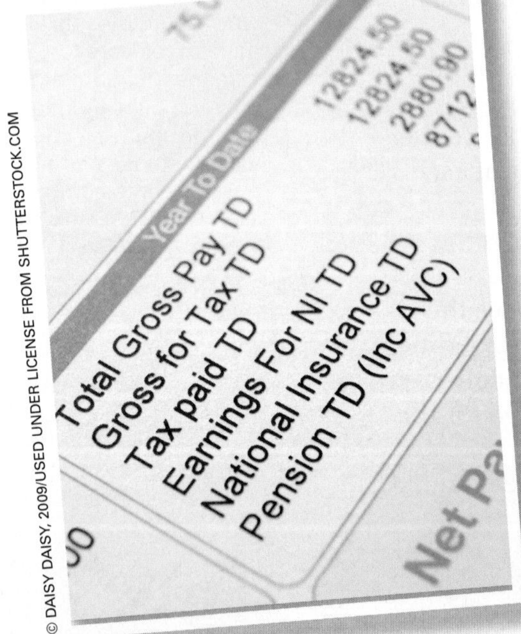

Some employees receive a paycheck every two weeks. They receive 26 paychecks per year. These people are paid **biweekly**. Their paydays fall on the same day of the week. Businesses that distribute paychecks biweekly save time, money, and paperwork, when compared with businesses that pay their employees weekly.

Some businesses pay their employees twice a month, or **semimonthly**. There are 12 months in a year, so these employees receive 24 paychecks per year. The paychecks are distributed on the same dates each month. For example, an employer may choose to pay employees on the 1st and 15th of each month. Note that biweekly and semimonthly payment schedules are slightly different.

Although it is not common, some businesses pay their employees **monthly**. These employees receive 12 paychecks per year. They are usually paid on the same date of each month, for example, the 15th.

Most employers offer their employees **direct deposit**. This means their paycheck amounts are automatically deposited electronically into their bank accounts on payday.

Most part-time jobs that students hold pay a set amount for each hour they work, called the **hourly rate**. Many people in full-time jobs also are paid at an hourly rate.

Certain jobs, whether full- or part-time, require the employee work a specific number of hours per week. These are the employee's **regular hours**. Employees may work more hours than their regular hours. These extra hours are called **overtime hours**. The **overtime hourly rate** is usually greater than the hourly rate for the regular hours. Often the overtime rate is $1\frac{1}{2}$ times the regular hourly rate, called **time-and-a-half overtime**. Sometimes the overtime rate is 2 times the hourly rate, called **double-time pay**. Your total pay, which is the sum of your hourly pay and your overtime pay, is your **gross pay**.

There are federal and state laws on the lowest hourly rate that can be paid to an employee in the United States. This rate is the **minimum wage**. Other laws involve the number of hours employees can work, and conditions in the workplace. It is important to have a clear understanding of your rights and responsibilities as an employee.

CLASS DISCUSSION

Highlight the difference between semimonthly and biweekly pay periods.

Discuss advantages of direct deposit. Ask students if any of their jobs offered direct deposit.

Tell students about Department of Labor postings that legally must be present in the workplace. The postings list labor laws specific to each industry. These laws have to do with pay rates, hours, overtime, breaks, and job safety.

Skills and Strategies

Here you will learn how to make computations involving different pay periods and hourly rates. When you take a job, be sure to ask about everything you need to know regarding your paycheck.

TEACH

After completing these examples, students should be able to start to check their own gross pay.

EXAMPLE 1

Christina is paid biweekly. Her annual salary is \$37,000. What is her biweekly salary, rounded to the nearest cent?

SOLUTION There are 26 biweekly paychecks per year. Christina divides her annual salary by the number of paychecks to compute her weekly salary.

$$37{,}000 \div 26 = 1{,}423.08$$

Christina earns \$1,423.08 per biweekly pay period.

CHECK YOUR UNDERSTANDING

Carlos earns x dollars biweekly. Express his annual salary algebraically.

EXAMPLE 1

It is common for students to mix up biweekly and semimonthly pay periods. If they know that there are 52 weeks in a year and 12 months in a year, they can figure out the correct number of paychecks. Some may choose to memorize the number of annual paychecks.

CHECK YOUR UNDERSTANDING

Answer $26x$

EXAMPLE 2

Manny is paid semimonthly. His semimonthly salary is \$1,239. What is his annual salary?

SOLUTION Manny receives 24 paychecks per year. He multiplies the monthly amount by the number of paychecks to calculate his annual salary.

$$1{,}239 \times 24 = 29{,}736$$

Manny's annual salary is \$29,736.

CHECK YOUR UNDERSTANDING

Alex is paid semimonthly. His annual salary is y dollars. Express his semimonthly salary algebraically.

EXAMPLE 2

Remind students to use their number sense as they get used to possible salaries. If they press an incorrect number into the calculator, or use an incorrect operation, they can get answers that don't make sense.

CHECK YOUR UNDERSTANDING

Answer $\frac{y}{24}$

EXAMPLE 3

Point out that regular hours are often 40 hours per week, but it can differ in certain industries. There are also child labor laws for students restricting the number of hours they can work. Students can look these up on the Internet.

CHECK YOUR UNDERSTANDING

Answer $52hd$

EXAMPLE 4

Students will have many chances to compute time-and-a-half rates for over-time work, so they should get used to multiplying the hourly rate by 1.5.

CHECK YOUR UNDERSTANDING

Answer $1.5y$

EXAMPLE 5

A solid understanding of Example 5 will insure that students can handle literal algebraic versions in similar problems, as in the Check Your Understanding problem.

CHECK YOUR UNDERSTANDING

Answer $40x + 1.5xy$

EXAMPLE 3

Maureen works at a local Chicken King restaurant. Her regular hourly wage is $9.70. If she regularly works 40 hours per week, what is her regular weekly pay?

SOLUTION Multiply the hours worked by the hourly wage.

$$9.70 \times 40 = 388$$

Maureen's regular weekly pay is $388.

■ CHECK YOUR UNDERSTANDING

Roger regularly works h hours per week at a rate of d dollars per hour. Express his annual salary algebraically.

EXAMPLE 4

If Maureen from Example 3 works overtime, she receives an hourly rate of $1\frac{1}{2}$ times her regular hourly rate. What is Maureen's hourly overtime rate?

SOLUTION Multiply her hourly rate by $1\frac{1}{2}$, which is 1.5 as a decimal.

$$9.70 \times 1.5 = 14.55$$

Maureen's hourly overtime rate is $14.55.

■ CHECK YOUR UNDERSTANDING

If Mary Ann earns y dollars per hour regularly, express her hourly overtime rate algebraically if she is paid time-and-a-half.

EXAMPLE 5

Janice earns $10 per hour. If her regular hours are 40 hours per week, and she receives time-and-a-half overtime, find her total pay for a week in which she works 45 hours.

SOLUTION

Find her regular pay for the 40 regular hours.	$40 \times 10 = 400$
Subtract to find the number of overtime hours.	$45 - 40 = 5$
Her overtime rate is 1.5 times the hourly rate.	$10 \times 1.5 = 15$
Multiply the overtime hourly rate by the number of overtime hours to find the overtime pay.	$15 \times 5 = 75$
Add her regular pay to her overtime pay.	$400 + 75 = 475$

Janice earned $475 for her 45 hours of work.

■ CHECK YOUR UNDERSTANDING

Ron regularly works 40 hours per week, at a rate of x dollars per hour. Last week he worked y overtime hours at time-and-a-half. Express his total weekly salary algebraically.

EXAMPLE 6

Samantha worked her 40 regular hours last week, plus 7 overtime hours at the time-and-a-half rate. Her gross pay was $611.05. What was her hourly rate?

SOLUTION Let x represent the hourly rate. Her regular pay is $40x$. Her overtime rate is $1.5x$. Her overtime pay is $7(1.5x)$.

$$\text{Regular pay} + \text{Overtime pay} = \text{Total pay}$$

Substitute.	$40x + 7(1.5x) = 611.05$
Simplify.	$40x + 10.5x = 611.05$
Combine like terms.	$50.5x = 611.05$
Divide each side by 50.5.	$x = 12.10$

Samantha's regular hourly rate is $12.10.

■ CHECK YOUR UNDERSTANDING

Jillian worked her 40 regular hours last week, plus 2 overtime hours at a double-time rate. Her gross pay was $484. What was her hourly rate?

EXAMPLE 7

Last week, Saul worked r regular hours and t overtime hours at a time-and-a-half rate. He earned $700. If x represents his hourly rate, express x in terms of r and h.

SOLUTION Regular gross pay is rx. Total overtime pay is $t(1.5x)$.

$$\text{Regular pay} + \text{Overtime pay} = \text{Total pay}$$

Substitute.	$rx + t(1.5x) = 700$
Remove the parentheses.	$rx + 1.5tx = 700$
Factor out x.	$x(r + 1.5t) = 700$
Divide each side by $(r + 1.5t)$.	$x = \dfrac{700}{r + 1.5t}$

Saul's hourly rate can be represented by $\dfrac{700}{r + 1.5t}$.

■ CHECK YOUR UNDERSTANDING

Jonathan worked h hours at an hourly rate of r dollars. He also worked w hours at an overtime rate of double time. Express his total pay for the week algebraically.

■ EXTEND YOUR UNDERSTANDING

Jovanna gets paid a regular-pay rate of r dollars for 40 hours worked. She is paid at a time-and-a-half rate for up to 16 overtime hours worked and a double-time rate for any overtime hours worked greater than 16 hours. Write a piecewise function, $p(z)$, for Jovanna's pay when she works z hours.

EXAMPLE 6

If students had trouble with Example 5, do not do Example 6 until their questions are cleared up.

CHECK YOUR UNDERSTANDING

Answer $11

Notice that the overtime rate in this problem differs from the Example because it involves double-time.

EXAMPLE 7

This is an algebraic model of what happened in Example 6. Refer to Example 6 as you work through this example.

CHECK YOUR UNDERSTANDING

Answer $hr + 2rw$

EXTEND YOUR UNDERSTANDING

Answer

$$p(z) = \begin{cases} 40r & \text{when } z \le 40 \\ 40r + \frac{3}{2}r(z - 40) & \text{when } 40 \le z \le 56 \\ 40r + \frac{3}{2}r(16) + 2r(z - 56) & \text{when } z > 56 \end{cases}$$

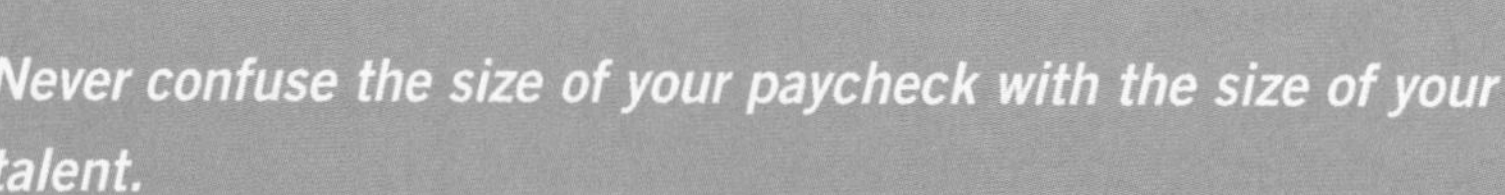

Applications

Never confuse the size of your paycheck with the size of your talent.

Marlon Brando, Actor

1. Interpret the quote in the context of what you learned about jobs and salaries. See margin.

2. Yoko is paid semimonthly. How many fewer paychecks does she receive in a year compared to someone who is paid weekly? 28

3. Sean is paid biweekly. His annual salary is $42,500. What is his biweekly salary to the nearest cent? $1,634.62

4. Cynthia's semimonthly salary is $1,371.50. What is her annual salary? $32,916

5. Baseball player Alex Rodriguez earned $27,708,525 in 2007. He played in 158 games. What was his salary per game to the nearest thousand dollars? $175,000

6. Ceil gets paid biweekly. Her biweekly salary is $1,763.28. What is her annual salary? $45,845.28

7. John's weekly salary is $478.25. His employer is changing the pay period to semimonthly.
   - **a.** What is John's annual salary? $24,869
   - **b.** What will John's semimonthly salary be to the nearest cent? $1,036.21

8. Ralph earns $72,000 annually as an architect and is paid semimonthly. Alice also earns $72,000 but she is paid biweekly.
   - **a.** How many more checks does Alice receive in a year when compared to Ralph? 2
   - **b.** What is the difference between Ralph's semimonthly salary and Alice's biweekly salary? Round to the nearest cent. $230.77

9. Last year Beth's annual salary was $38,350. This year she received a promotion and now earns $46,462 annually. She is paid biweekly.
   - **a.** What was her biweekly salary last year? $1,475
   - **b.** What is Beth's biweekly salary this year? $1,787
   - **c.** On a biweekly basis, how much more does Beth earn as a result of her promotion? $312

10. Justin is a golf pro. He works eight months per year, and is paid $76,000. During the winter months, he teaches golf privately and earns another $12,500. What is his average monthly salary based on his yearly earnings? $7,375

11. Last year Nancy's annual salary was x dollars. This year she received a raise of y dollars per year. She is paid semimonthly. See margin.
    - **a.** Express her semimonthly salary last year algebraically.
    - **b.** Express her semimonthly salary this year algebraically.
    - **c.** On a monthly basis, how much more does Nancy earn as a result of her raise?

TEACH

Exercise 5
Students can look up celebrity salaries on the Internet and make up their own problems for sports stars, television actors, and so on.

Exercise 11
This exercise treats the pay rate and pay period idea algebraically. Always remind students to recall what they did on the numerical problems while solving these.

ANSWERS

1. There are many talented people doing excellent work who are underpaid, and there are also many people being overpaid for mediocre or poor work. Brando, being an actor, may have been making a statement about overpaid mediocre actors, but it extends to the general workforce.

11. a. $\frac{x}{24}$
    b. $\frac{x+y}{24}$
    c. $\frac{y}{12}$

12. Hector works in a gas station and earns $8.60 per hour. Last week he worked 29 hours. What was his gross pay? $249.40

13. Eddie works at Beep-N-Kleen car wash. He earns $8.40 per hour. Last week he worked *x* hours at this rate. Express his gross pay algebraically. $8.40*x*

14. Lynn regularly works a 40-hour week and earns $9 per hour. She receives time-and-a-half pay for each hour of overtime she works. Last week she worked 43 hours.

a. What was her regular gross pay? $360.00
b. What was her hourly overtime rate? $13.50
c. What was her overtime pay? $40.50
d. What was her total pay for the week? $400.50

15. Amy regularly works 20 hours per week at Pook's Dry Cleaners from Monday through Friday. She earns $8.10 per hour and receives double-time pay for working Sundays. Next week she will work her regular 20 weekday hours, and an additional eight hours on Sunday. What will her total pay be for the week? $291.60

16. Tom earns $12.50 per hour at the Yankee Bowling Alley. He regularly works 40 hours per week. He is paid time-and-a-half for each hour of overtime work. Last week he worked 42 hours. What was his gross pay for the week? $537.50

17. Pedro works 35 regular hours per week at the Meadow Deli. His hours over 35 are considered overtime. He earns $9.20 per hour and receives time-and-a-half pay for each hour of overtime he works. Last week he worked 41 hours and received a gross pay of $305.80. This amount is incorrect. How much does Pedro's boss owe him? $99.00

18. Colby and Cheryl work in different local supermarkets. Colby regularly earns $8.90 per hour, and he is paid time-and-a-half for each hour of overtime he works. Cheryl regularly earns $7.10 per hour, and she is paid double time for an hour of overtime. Who earns more for one hour of overtime? How much more? Cheryl; $0.85 more

19. Ron earns *x* dollars per hour. He regularly works 40 hours per week. Express his annual salary algebraically. $52(40x)$

20. Michael earns $10 per hour and works 40 hours per week. How many overtime hours would he have to work in a week for his time-and-a-half overtime pay to be greater than his regular gross pay? 27

21. Jim worked 40 regular hours last week, plus 8 overtime hours at the time-and-a-half rate. His gross pay was $1,248.

a. What was his hourly rate? $24
b. What was his hourly overtime rate? $36

22. Julianne works as a waitress. She earns $5.90 per hour plus tips.

a. Today she worked *x* hours. Express her pay for these hours algebraically. $5.90x$
b. She served nine tables. The total bill for these nine tables was *y* dollars. Julianne received 18% in tips from these bills. Express the amount she received in tips algebraically. $0.18y$
c. Express Julianne's total earnings for the day algebraically. $5.90x + 0.18y$

TEACH

Exercise 23

Waiting on tables is a job where there is a monetary incentive to do good work. The next lesson deals exclusively with these types of jobs.

Exercise 27

Have students do this exercise on a grid or calendar, and let them see the answer unfold over a few minutes. This goes quickly with a calculator, but the gradual increases in daily salary amaze them and show the power of exponential functions.

Exercise 28

Explain that a lottery player, who buys a weekly ticket for 20 years and does not ever win, is not more likely to win next week than a first-time ticket buyer.

ANSWERS

25. Yes; Gary's weekly pay is $826.73, which exceeds the $562.42 total cost of his monthly car and insurance payments.

26. a. =B2*C2
    b. =A2–B2
    c. =1.5*C2
    d. =E2*F2
    e. =D2+G2

27e.

Salary

Date

28. The purchase of a $2 ticket each week for 20 years cost $2,080 and her winnings were $2,000. This was not a worthwhile investment.

23. Mike works at Cheesecake King. He earns $11 per hour as a busboy. The waiters he helps give him 25% of their tips.

a. If Mike worked 6 hours today, how much did he earn, without tips? $66

b. The waiters Mike assisted waited on 16 tables, and the total bill from all these tables was $1,188. The waiters earned 15% in tips, and gave 25% of these earning to Mike. How much did Mike make in tips? $44.55

c. What was Mike's total salary for the day? $110.55

d. What were Mike's average earnings per hour, including tips? Round to the nearest cent. $18.43

24. Max works x hours per week and has a 3-week vacation each year. Mindy works y hours per week and has a four-week vacation each year. Express their combined number of work hours per year. $49x + 48y$

25. Gary earns $42,990 per year. He is paid weekly. He currently has a $456-per-month car loan payment, and he pays $1,277 per year for auto insurance. Is one week's paycheck enough to pay for his monthly auto loan and his monthly cost of insurance? Explain. See margin.

26. The following spreadsheet can be used to compute total weekly pay, given the hours, hourly rate, and overtime rate. See margin.

	A	B	C	D	E	F	G	H
1	Hours Worked	Regular Hours	Hourly Rate	Regular Gross Pay	Overtime Hours	Time-and-a-Half Overtime Rate	Total Overtime Pay	Total Gross Pay
2	42	40	10.50					
3	44	40	9.00					
4	45	40	14.00					

a. Write the formula to compute the regular gross pay in cell D2.

b. Write the formula to compute the overtime hours in cell E2.

c. Write the formula to compute the time-and-a-half overtime hourly rate in cell F2.

d. Write the formula to find the total overtime pay in cell G2.

e. Write the formula to compute the total weekly pay in cell H2.

f. Use your spreadsheet to fill in the missing entries.

27. Marty is working with a math problem that defies intuition. He is going to pay his gardener for the entire month of July. He will pay the gardener every day. On the first day, he will pay the gardener $0.01. On the second day, he will pay double the first day, $0.02. On the third day, he will double the second day's pay and pay $0.04. See additional answers for a–c.

a. Make a grid that looks like a calendar with 7 columns and 5 rows.

b. Fill in the dates from July 1–July 31.

c. Enter the amount Marty pays his gardener on each day.

d. On what day will the gardener's pay exceed $1,000,000 for the first time? July 28

e. If x represents the day and y represents the salary for that day, draw a scatterplot for the first two weeks of July. See margin.

28. Melissa has bought a $2 lottery ticket every week for the past 20 years. This week she won for the first time—$2,000 in her state lottery. Compare these winnings to her total investment, and explain if the lottery was a worthwhile endeavor for her. See margin.

He that is of the opinion money will do everything may well be suspected of doing everything for money.
Benjamin Franklin, American Statesman

Commissions, Royalties, and Piecework Pay

6-3

Key Terms
- commission
- royalty
- pieceworker
- piecework rate

Objectives
- Compute pay based on percent commission.
- Compute piecework pay.
- Understand advantages and disadvantages of pay based on production.

Common Core
A-CED1, F-IF2

CCSS Warm-Up

Which of the following equations represents the statement,
"Three times the sum of x and 7 exceeds y by 23"?

a. $3x + 7 = y + 23$ **b.** $3(x + 7) = y + 23$ **c.** $3(x + 7) + 23 = y$

b

What jobs base their pay according to the amount produced?

Some employees are not paid by the number of hours they work. Their pay is based on the amount of sales they make. Stockbrokers, travel agents, authors, musicians, and salespersons may all be paid based upon money from sales. These people are paid a **commission**, or a **royalty**. The commission or royalty rate is usually expressed as a percent. People who get paid commissions or royalties earn more money as more sales are made. Even if they work many hours, they can earn very little money if they make very few sales. Some employees get a commission in addition to a regular salary. Can you think of any advantages or disadvantages of getting paid only by commission?

A real estate salesperson receives a commission on the sale of each home. Money is not made until there is a sale. When an author writes a book, the author's job is basically done. Royalties depend on sales, but the author does not have to do any more writing to make more money. However, an author can do promotional events and book signings to increase awareness of the book, which may increase sales of the book.

Compare commission workers to people who are paid according to the amount of items they produce. They are paid by production, rather than the length of time that it takes them to do the job. These employees are called **pieceworkers**. Pieceworkers are paid a certain amount of money, called a **piecework rate**, for each item they complete. Although piecework is not as common as in years past, there are still jobs in farming, manufacturing, and journalism where this method of payment is used.

Piecework pay is sometimes used in combination with an hourly wage. The employee gets paid by the hour and receives a certain amount of money for each piece of work completed. The greater the number of pieces of work completed, the more money the employee makes. What are the benefits to both the employer and the worker?

EXAMINE THE QUESTION

Workers paid based on what they sell or produce are often driven to work hard. Since they are not paid by the hour, they must get enough work done to earn their desired salary.

CLASS DISCUSSION

Ask students what they perceive are the advantages and disadvantages of commissions, royalties, and other forms of payments that are based on sales and/or production.

EXAMPLE 1

This example uses percents and piecework rates. Students compute earnings based on different payment structures.

CHECK YOUR UNDERSTANDING

Answer $0.08xy + 2,500$

EXAMPLE 2

Explain to students that this payment structure can be expressed as a piecewise function, such as:

$$p(x) = \begin{cases} 0.11x & \text{when } 0 \le x \le 900 \\ 99 + 0.17(x - 900) & \text{when } x > 900 \end{cases}$$

Skills and Strategies

In these examples you will examine how certain occupations pay their workers based on sales and production, not just on hours worked.

EXAMPLE 1

Adrianna wrote a textbook for high school students. She receives a 10% royalty based on the total sales of the book. The book sells for $47.95, and 17,000 copies were sold last year. How much did Adrianna receive in royalty payments for last year?

SOLUTION Determine the total amount of sales from the 17,000 books.

$$17,000 \times 47.95 = 815,150$$

The total amount of sales is $815,150.

Multiply the total sales by the commission rate expressed as a decimal.

$$815,150 \times 0.10 = 81,515$$

Adrianna received $81,515 in royalty payments for last year.

■ CHECK YOUR UNDERSTANDING

Xander writes math textbooks that sell for x dollars each. He received a bonus of $2,500 for signing a contract, and he receives 8% commission on each book sale. Express the total amount of income Xander earns from selling y books algebraically.

EXAMPLE 2

Allison sells cosmetics part-time from door-to-door. She is paid a monthly commission. She receives 11% of her first $900 in sales and 17% of the balance of her sales. Last month she sold $1,250 worth of cosmetics. How much commission did she earn last month?

SOLUTION Find the commission on the first $900 of sales by multiplying 900 by the commission rate expressed as a decimal.

$$900 \times 0.11 = 99.00$$

The commission based on the first $900 is $99.

Determine the amount over $900 by subtracting 900 from total sales.

$$1,250 - 900 = 350$$

The balance over $900 is $350.

Multiply 350 by the 17% commission rate expressed as a decimal.

$$350 \times 0.17 = 59.50$$

The commission on the balance of sales over $900 is $59.50.

Find the sum of the commission on the first $900 and the commission on the $350 balance.

$$99.00 + 59.50 = 158.50$$

The total commission for last month was $158.50.

■ CHECK YOUR UNDERSTANDING

Arthur sells electronics on commission. He receives 7% of his first x dollars in sales and 10% of the balance of his sales. Last week he sold y dollars worth of electronics. Express the commission he earned last month algebraically.

CHECK YOUR UNDERSTANDING

Answer

$$f(x) = \begin{cases} 0.07x + 0.10(y - x) & \text{when } y > x \\ 0.07x & \text{when } x \geq y \end{cases}$$

EXAMPLE 3

Of all the different payment schemes, piecework is the least familiar to students. Have them research it on the Internet to become more familiar with jobs that are paid this way.

EXAMPLE 3

Kate works in a dress factory that makes dresses for designer boutiques. She is paid a piecework rate of \$85 per unit (piece) produced. Yesterday she made 3 dresses. How much did she earn?

SOLUTION Multiply the number of pieces, 3, by the piecework rate, which is \$85.

$$3 \times 85 = 255$$

Kate earned \$255 yesterday.

■ CHECK YOUR UNDERSTANDING

Martin writes magazine articles. He is paid a rate of p dollars for each article he writes. Last year he wrote s articles. Express his total piecework earnings algebraically.

CHECK YOUR UNDERSTANDING

Answer ps

EXAMPLE 4

Point out that efficiency translates into earnings under a piecework pay system.

EXAMPLE 4

Tony picks strawberries and gets paid at a piecework rate of 45 cents per container for the first 200 containers picked. He receives 65 cents per container for every container over 200 that he picks. Last week, Tony picked 270 containers. How much did he earn?

SOLUTION Compute the piecework pay for 200 containers at a rate of 45 cents per container. Then compute the pay for the containers over 200. Add these amounts to find his total pay.

Multiply 200 by piecework pay.	$200 \times 0.45 = 90$
Subtract to find the amount picked over the initial 200 containers.	$270 - 200 = 70$
Multiply 70 by additional container pay.	$70 \times 0.65 = 45.50$
Total pay is the sum of the two amounts.	$90.00 + 45.50 = 135.50$

Tony earned \$135.50 in piecework pay last week.

■ CHECK YOUR UNDERSTANDING

Brianna picks tomatoes on a local farm. She receives 11 cents per crate. Last week, her total piecework earnings was x dollars. Express the number of crates she picked algebraically.

CHECK YOUR UNDERSTANDING

Answer $\frac{x}{0.11}$

EXAMPLE 5

Workers who sell high priced items such as cars and homes do not usually do a large volume of sales. They work hard, many hours, weeks, or even months, for a few sales which have a large payoff.

CHECK YOUR UNDERSTANDING

Answer $15.20

EXAMPLE 6

Advise students to check their work by taking their answer and computing the earnings on it to see if their answer is correct. This is better as a check than simply reviewing the algebraic steps they took.

CHECK YOUR UNDERSTANDING

Answer $2,300

EXAMPLE 5

Glassman Chevrolet pays commission to its car salespeople. They are paid a percent of the profit the dealership makes on the car, not on the selling price of the car. If the profit is under $750, the commission rate is 20%. If the profit is at least $750 and less than or equal to $1,000, the commission rate is 22% of the profit. If the profit is above $1,000, the rate is 25% of the profit. If x represents the profit, express the commission $c(x)$ as a piecewise function.

SOLUTION There is a different rule for each of the different domains.

The 20% commission rate is for profits less than $750.
The 22% commission rate is for profits from $750 to $1,000, inclusive.
The 25% commission rate is for profits greater than $1,000.

Translate the words into algebraic symbols.

$$c(x) = \begin{cases} 0.20x & \text{when } 0 \le x < 750 \\ 0.22x & \text{when } 750 \le x \le 1{,}000 \\ 0.25x & \text{when } x > 1{,}000 \end{cases}$$

■ CHECK YOUR UNDERSTANDING

Find the difference between the commission paid if a Glassman Chevrolet salesman, from Example 5, sells a car for a $750 profit compared to selling a car for a $749 profit.

EXAMPLE 6

Joyce works at Fortunato's Furniture. She is paid on commission. She receives 10% of her first $900 in sales and 15% of the balance of her sales. Last week she earned $750. What was the total value of the furniture she sold?

SOLUTION Let x represent the total value of the furniture.

Commission for the first $900. $0.10(900)$

Balance of sales after the first $900. $x - 900$

Commission for the balance. $0.15(x - 900)$

Add the two commissions. $0.10(900) + 0.15(x - 900) = 750$

Simplify. $90 + 0.15x - 135 = 750$

Combine like terms. $0.15x - 45 = 750$

Add 45 to each side. $0.15x = 795$

Divide each side by 0.15. $x = 5{,}300$

Joyce sold $5,300 worth of furniture last week.

■ CHECK YOUR UNDERSTANDING

Lauren is a salesperson at Koslow's Tires. She is paid a monthly commission. She receives 6% of her first $1,000 in sales and 11% of the balance of her sales. Today she earned $203. What was the total value of the tires she sold?

Applications

He that is of the opinion money will do everything may well be suspected of doing everything for money.
Benjamin Franklin, American Statesman

1. Interpret the quote in the context of your experiences with money. See margin.
2. Rock musician Donny West is paid 15% on his CD sales and tour video sales. Last year, he sold one million CDs and 550,000 videos. The CDs were sold to music stores for $5 each and the videos for $6 each.
   - **a.** What was the total amount of CD sales? $5,000,000
   - **b.** What was the total amount of video sales? $3,300,000
   - **c.** What was the combined total of CD and video sales? $8,300,000
   - **d.** How much did Donny West receive in royalties last year? $1,245,000
3. Joan sells new cars at a local dealership. She receives a 25% commission on the profit each car is sold for. Last month she sold 9 cars, for a total of $8,870 dealer profit. How much did she earn in commission? $2,217.50
4. Liz works at Heedle's Computer Outlet. She receives a weekly salary of $200 plus 3% commission on her sales. Last week, she sold $29,700 of computer equipment. How much did Liz earn last week? $1,091
5. Oscar sells Internet access subscriptions by telephone. He receives 12% of the first $1,000 and 15% on the balance over $1,000. Last month he sold $7,500 worth of Internet access subscriptions. What was his commission for last month? $1,095
6. Professional baseball player Rusty Raspberry earns $1,715,000 a year playing baseball. Last year, a biography that he had written sold 300,000 copies at a price of $24 each. Raspberry received 10% in royalties on the book sales. What was his total salary last year from the book and his baseball career? $2,435,000
7. Maram is a real estate agent. She earns 6.5% commission on each sale she makes. Last month she sold one house for $250,000 and another for $310,000. What did Maram earn in commissions for the month? $36,400
8. Glen has a job selling magazine subscriptions by phone. He makes a base salary of $9.60 per hour plus a 5% commission on all sales. Last week, Glen worked 35 hours and sold $230 worth of subscriptions. What was his gross pay for the week? $347.50
9. Hillside Travel pays its employees $10 per hour plus 8% commission on all trips booked. Tyrus worked 20 hours last week and booked trips amounting to $2,100. What was his gross pay for last week? $368
10. Silvan picks berries at Seymour's Berry Farm. He receives 28 cents for each small basket picked. Last weekend, he was able to pick 731 baskets. How much did he earn? $204.68

TEACH

Students should always use number sense to make sure their answers are reasonable. Most of the exercises in this lesson are numerical for that reason; students need to develop this financial number sense.

ANSWERS

1. To many people, money is a top priority. Many people feel that money buys happiness, and, as a result, they go to great lengths to acquire it.

TEACH

Exercise 20

Students should review the definitions of mean, median, and mode before they begin this exercise. Remind students that the mean and median can be values that are not actual elements in the set, but the mode must be a number that is in the set of data.

11. Alanna is a stockbroker. She receives a commission based on the value of the trades she makes.

a. If Alanna earns $50 for sales of $1,000, what is her percent of commission? 5%

b. If she earns *x* dollars for sales of *y* dollars, express her percent of commission algebraically. $\frac{x}{y}(100)$

12. Barb works in a local factory. She receives 92 cents for each of the first 100 units she produces and $1.01 for each unit over 100. Yesterday, she produced 120 units. How much did Barb earn? $112.20

13. Bill works for the Stuff-It Mailing Service. He receives 25 cents for each document he puts together and prepares for mailing. Last week, Bill prepared 2,000 documents for mailing for a local department store. He received a check with gross pay of $474 and is certain that the amount is incorrect.

a. What is Bill's correct total piecework pay? $500

b. How much does his boss owe him? $26

14. Audrey works in a factory. She receives a salary of $8 per hour and piecework pay of 12 cents per unit produced. Last week she worked 38 hours and produced 755 units.

a. What was her piecework pay? $90.60

b. What was her total hourly pay for the week? $304

c. What was her total pay for the week? $394.60

d. What would her total weekly salary have been if she produced 0 units? $304

15. Anton picks corn at a local farm. He is paid 80 cents per bushel for the first 50 bushels, 90 cents per bushel for the next 50 bushels, and $0.95 per bushel for all bushels picked over 100. Express algebraically the amount Anton earns if he picks *x* bushels, where $x > 100$. $85 + 0.95(x - 100)$

16. Danielle works in an exclusive dress factory. She is paid $156 for each dress she sews. Last month she sewed 30 dresses. What was her total pay for the month? $4,680

17. Jason types papers for local college students. He charges $6.50 per page. How much will he receive for a 22-page paper? $143

18. Neil sells subscriptions by phone. He makes $2.10 for each subscription sold. At the holiday time last year, he sold *n* subscriptions. Express his earnings algebraically. $2.10n$

19. Last week Eric received a total piecework paycheck of $252.48. He receives 12 cents per unit produced. How many units did he produce? 2,104

20. Arielle receives a piecework rate of 10 cents per unit from the Wiggy Factory. Her production record for last week was affected by a machinery breakdown on Tuesday. Her production results were: Monday, 375 units; Tuesday, 22 units; Wednesday, 410 units; Thursday, 390 units; and Friday, 390 units.

a. What is the mean number of units produced per day? 317.4

b. What is the median number of units produced? 390

c. What is the mode number of units produced? 390

21. Janice is a travel agent. She receives a 7% commission based on the value of the trips she books. Today she spent five hours arranging a $3,300 cruise for a newlywed couple.

a. How much commission did she earn? $231

b. What was her mean hourly pay for the work she did? $46.20

22. Linda is a salesperson for Spooner's Cleaning Service, which cleans office buildings. She receives a 14% commission for every office that signs a contract for the cleaning services. Last week she received $1,233.60 in commissions. What was the total value of the cleaning contracts she sold, rounded to the nearest dollar? $8,811

23. Appel's Music Store pays its sales staff a commission of 9.5% of the first $1,000 in sales and 15.5% of the balance of sales. Alex, the store's drum expert, received $1,234.25 in commission last week. What were his total sales for the week? $8,350

24. Salespersons at the Kings Park Auto Giant are paid a commission, $c(p)$, based on the profit, p. The following piecewise function gives the commission rules.

$$c(p) = \begin{cases} 0.20\,p \text{ when } 0 \le p < 900 \\ 0.23\,p \text{ when } 900 \le p < 1{,}500 \\ 0.25\,p \text{ when } p \ge 1{,}500 \end{cases}$$

a. If the profit is $1,500, what is the percent commission rate? 25%

b. If the profit is $900, what is the percent commission rate? 23%

c. What is the commission on a car sold for a $970 profit? $223.10

d. Kings Park Auto Giant purchases a car for $32,090 and sells it for $33,200. What commission is paid to the salesperson? $255.30

25. McCormack Chrysler pays their sales staff by commission. They are paid a percent of the profit the dealership makes on the car. If the profit is $500 or less, the commission rate is 17%. If the profit is greater than $500 and less than or equal to $1,100, the commission rate is 20%. If the profit is above $1,100, the rate is 22%.

a. If x represents the profit, express the commission $c(x)$ as a piecewise function. See margin.

b. If the dealer purchases the car for $21,696 and Kristin, a salesperson, sells it for $22,800, how much commission does Kristin earn for the sale? $242.88

c. Kristin is thinking of leaving McCormack Chrysler and working at Glassman Chevrolet, from Example 5. How much more commission would she have made for the same sale at Glassman? $33.12

26. A car dealer pays d dollars for a car, which is sold for c dollars. The commission paid to the salesperson is 24% of the profit. Express the commission algebraically. $0.24(c - d)$

27. Aileen is a salesperson at Lopez Sporting Goods. She is paid a monthly commission on all Little League uniforms she sells. She receives 10% of her first $2,000 in sales and 12% of the balance of her sales. Last week she earned $231.20. What was the total value of the uniforms she sold? $2,260

TEACH

Exercise 21

Explain that travel agents get paid based on the value of the trips they book.

Exercise 24

Students need to examine the domains carefully before picking the function rule to use.

ANSWERS

25a.

$$c(x) = \begin{cases} 0.17x \text{ when } 0 \le x \le 500 \\ 0.20x \text{ when } 500 < x \le 1{,}100 \\ 0.22x \text{ when } x > 1{,}100 \end{cases}$$

To find joy in work is to discover the fountain of youth.
Pearl S. Buck, American Novelist

6-4 Employee Benefits

Objectives

- Understand and calculate the value of certain employee benefits.

Common Core

A-CED1, A-REI3, F-BF1, F-LE1

Key Terms

- employee benefits
- insurance
- paid vacation time
- paid holiday time
- retirement plans
- stock ownership plans
- childcare leave
- family health care
- individual health care
- pension
- unemployment insurance
- base period
- worker's compensation

CCSS Warm-Up

An appliance salesman pays x dollars for a dishwasher, which he sells for y dollars. He receives a 12% commission on the profit. Express the commission algebraically.

$0.12(y - x)$

EXAMINE THE QUESTION

In order to have a discussion about the question posed here, it is necessary to first define job benefits. Ask students for their definition of the benefits of a job. Their responses could include a variety of benefits such as monetary, social, and emotional. Lay the groundwork for a discussion of employee benefits that are part of the salaried package that many workers receive.

CLASS DISCUSSION

The benefits listed may already be familiar to some students. Before describing any of the benefits, ask students what they know and how they learned about these benefits.

Be sure to emphasize that a criteria for unemployment insurance is that the laid off worker is actively looking for a job during the compensated period.

WHAT ARE THE BENEFITS OF A JOB?

The first time you get a full-time job, someone will probably ask you, "Does it come with benefits?" You might think this is a foolish question because the best benefit you know of is that the job is salaried. This is a monetary benefit. You might respond that you will find satisfaction in working in a career you trained for. This is an emotional benefit. But the questioner is probably asking you about employee benefits. **Employee benefits** are value-added options that an employer may choose to offer employees. Typically, benefits are in the forms of **insurance** (health, life, and disability), **paid vacation time**, **paid holiday time**, **retirement plans**, **stock ownership plans**, **childcare leave**, and more. **Family health care** covers all members of the immediate family for health care bills to the extent outlined in the health care coverage plan. **Individual health care** covers only the employee. A **pension** is compensation that an employee receives from an employer after retirement.

While the above benefits are not required, there are some benefits that are required. **Unemployment insurance** is a government program that offers benefits to eligible employees who, through no fault of their own, have become unemployed. These workers must meet certain eligibility requirements. The program is meant to offer temporary assistance to people who are out of a job, but looking for replacement employment. For example, suppose that you work for a telephone company. Over the last few years, land lines have increasingly been replaced by cellular phones. As a result, your employer found that she must reduce the workforce in order to stay in business. She informed you that you would no longer have a job in the company. Here, your impending loss of a job was not your fault. If you also meet other requirements as outlined by state law, you could be eligible for unemployment compensation. The amount you receive is based on a percentage of what you earned at your job over a qualifying period of employment. There is a state maximum for this benefit. The benefits are sometimes extended by federal and state agencies beyond the initial compensation period. The actual formula used to compute the weekly compensation varies from state to state, but most states make the determination on salaries that the employee earned during a fixed period of time known as a **base period**.

Another benefit that is required by the government is **worker's compensation**. The extent of compensation from this program is governed by state laws. But, the purpose of the program is to offer assistance to employees who are injured while working at their job.

The question that you may be asked about whether or not you have benefits when you get your job is the question you should be asking before you accept your job. Employee benefits add to the value of employment beyond the salary for that job.

CLASS DISCUSSION

Discuss why worker's compensation is a valuable benefit for all injured workers who qualify.

TEACH

The Skills and Strategies examples will expose students to a variety of employee benefits. Be sure to stress that the benefit plans that are addressed in the examples are just sample packages. The details of benefit plans vary from employer to employer.

Skills and Strategies

Here you will learn about a variety of employee benefits and the mathematics that is needed to get the most out of them.

EXAMPLE 1

Alan works for a printing company. It has been a little over four years since he was hired. He now makes $54,080 per year. When he was hired, he was told that he had five days of paid vacation time. For each year that he worked at the company, he would gain another two days of paid vacation time to a maximum of 20 days. How many paid vacation days does he now get at the end of four years of employment and how much will he make during the time he is on vacation?

SOLUTION Examine the table. Alan has completed four full years of work for his company. He is in his fifth year of employment and is entitled to 13 paid vacation days. Because he is making $54,080 per year, you can determine his weekly salary by dividing this amount by 52 weeks.

Number of Years Worked	Number of Paid Vacation Days
0	5
1	5 + 2 = 7
2	5 + 2 + 2 = 9
3	5 + 2 + 2 + 2 = 11
4	5 + 2 + 2 + 2 + 2 = 13

$$54{,}080 \div 52 = 1{,}040$$

Alan makes $1,040 per week. A typical workweek consists of five business days. Therefore, Alan has two work weeks plus three days of paid vacation coming to him this year. The remaining three vacation days can be expressed as a fractional part of a work week. The fraction $\frac{3}{5}$ can be written as 0.6. Alan gets 2.6 work weeks of paid vacation time.

Weekly salary × 2.6 $\qquad 1{,}040 \times 2.6 = 2{,}704$

Alan will make $2,704 while on vacation this year.

EXAMPLE 1

The problem solving skill of making a table is useful in finding the solution to this exercise. Once the table has been created, ask students if they see the pattern in the relationship between the number of years worked and the number of paid vacation days. This will lead into the algebraic modeling that is asked for in the Check Your Understanding that follows Example 1.

CHECK YOUR UNDERSTANDING

Let x represent the number of the working year and y represent the number of paid vacation days. Based on the table above, write an algebraic equation that models the relationship between these two variables.

CHECK YOUR UNDERSTANDING

Answer $y = 2x + 5$

EXAMPLE 2

Before addressing the solution, make sure that students understand the meaning of a biweekly pay period. In addition, discuss how most health care coverage consists of a shared contribution on the parts of both employee and employer.

CHECK YOUR UNDERSTANDING

Answer $\frac{26d}{p}$

EXAMPLE 3

The calculation of an individual's pension varies from work place to work place. In Example 3, a popular method is used which involves the average of the final salaries for a specified number of years.

EXAMPLE 2

Frieda's employer offers her family health care. Frieda must contribute 12% of the cost, and her employer will cover the rest. Frieda gets paid on a biweekly basis, and she notices that $88.50 is taken out of each paycheck for her portion of the contribution to the family health care coverage. How much does Frieda's employer contribute for her coverage?

SOLUTION Let x represent the cost of Frieda's family health care. Frieda's total contribution is 12% of that cost, or $0.12x$. Since Frieda has $88.50 taken out of her biweekly paychecks for the coverage, her total yearly contribution is determined by multiplying that biweekly amount times 26 which is the number of biweekly paychecks.

Frieda's health care contribution $88.50 \times 26 = 2{,}301$

Frieda's contribution of $2,301 is 12% of the total amount.

Write an equation and solve for x. $0.12x = 2{,}301$

Divide each side by 0.12. $\frac{0.12x}{0.12} = \frac{2{,}301}{0.12}$

$$x = 19{,}175$$

Frieda's family health care coverage costs $19,175. She contributes $2,301 to that amount, and her employer pays the rest.

Subtract to find her employer's contribution. $19{,}175 - 2{,}301 = 16{,}874$

The employer's contribution is $16,874.

CHECK YOUR UNDERSTANDING

Mark's employer offers individual health care. Mark pays d dollars out of his biweekly paycheck for his share of the total cost. If Mark's contribution is a percentage of the total cost, where p represents that percentage written as an equivalent decimal, represent the total cost of Mark's coverage in terms of d and p.

EXAMPLE 3

Marina works at Washington Performing Arts Center. Her employer offers her a pension. Marina's employer uses a formula to calculate the pension. A retiring employee will receive 1.5% of their average salary for the last five years of employment for every year worked. Marina is planning on retiring at the end of this year after 25 years of employment. Marina would receive this amount each year until her death. Her salaries for the last five years are $88,900, $92,200, $96,000, $98,000, and $102,000. Calculate Marina's pension.

SOLUTION Find Marina's 5-year average salary.

$$\frac{88{,}900 + 92{,}200 + 96{,}000 + 98{,}000 + 102{,}000}{5} = 95{,}420$$

Marina's average salary for her last five years of work is \$95,420. For each of the 25 years she worked at the Center, she will receive 1.5% of that average.

Find 1.5% of \$95,420. $0.015 \times 95{,}420 = 1{,}431.30$

Multiply this amount by 25 years. $1{,}431.30 \times 25 = 35{,}782.50$

Marina will receive a pension of \$35,782.50 per year until her death.

CHECK YOUR UNDERSTANDING

DeBrown Corporation offers employees a retirement plan based upon the following formula. The retiree will get 2% of the average of the final three year salaries times the number of years employed by the company. Suppose an employee's last three years of salaries are A, B, and C, and the employee worked at DeBrown for D years. Write the algebraic expression that represents the employee's yearly pension.

EXAMPLE 4

In Reese's state, the weekly unemployment compensation is 60% of the 26-week average for the two highest-salaried quarters. A quarter is three consecutive months. For July, August, and September, he earned a total of \$9,024. In October, November, and December, he earned a total of \$9,800. Determine Reese's unemployment compensation.

SOLUTION Find Reese's total earnings for the two quarters.

$$9{,}024 + 9{,}800 = 18{,}824$$

Divide the total of \$18,824 earned during these months by 26, since there are 26 weeks in this half-year period.

$$18{,}824 \div 26 = 724$$

His 26-week average is \$724 per week.

Find 60% of 724. $0.60 \times 724 = 434.40$

Some states have a maximum compensation amount. In Reese's state, \$434.40 falls below that maximum. He will receive that amount for the next 26 weeks or until he finds another job during that time.

CHECK YOUR UNDERSTANDING

Wanda lives in the same state as Reese. Her weekly unemployment compensation is \$360. What were the total 26-week earnings for her highest two consecutive quarters of employment?

EXTEND YOUR UNDERSTANDING

Lara lives in the same state as Reese. Lara made the same weekly salary for each of the 26 weeks in her two highest consecutive quarters. She will receive a weekly unemployment compensation check for \$570. What was Lara's weekly salary when she worked for her company?

CHECK YOUR UNDERSTANDING

Answer $0.02D\left(\frac{A+B+C}{3}\right)$

EXAMPLE 4

The exact formula used for unemployment compensation is a function of what has been approved in any given state. Example 4 serves as a model for the typical way that the compensation is calculated.

CHECK YOUR UNDERSTANDING

Answer \$15,600

EXTEND YOUR UNDERSTANDING

Answer \$950

Applications

To find joy in work is to discover the fountain of youth.
Pearl S. Buck, American Novelist

TEACH

Exercises 2 and 3
Encourage students to set up a table. This will assist them in determining the modeling equation.

Exercise 5
The equation that models this situation is an exponential equation. Alert students to the fact that the solutions may not always be linear.

ANSWERS

1. Perhaps one of the biggest employee benefits a person can attain from work is the joy of that work. Pearl Buck implies that if you find that joy, then you have discovered a treasure.

1. How can the quote be interpreted in light of what you have learned? See margin.

2. Roberto's employer offers a sliding paid vacation. When he started work, he was given three paid days of vacation. For each six-month period he stays at the job, his vacation is increased by two days.
   a. Let x represent the number of 6-month periods worked and y represent the total number of paid vacation days. Write an equation that models the relationship between these two variables. $y = 3 + 2x$
   b. How much vacation time will he have earned after working for 4.4 years? 19 days

3. When Lisa started at her current job, her employer gave her two days of paid vacation time with a promise of three additional paid vacation days for each year she remains with the company to a maximum of four work weeks of paid vacation time.
   a. Let x represent the number of years she has worked for this employer and y represent the number of paid vacation days she has earned. Write an equation that models the relationship between these two variables. $y = 2 + 3x$
   b. It has been five years since Lisa began working for this employer. How many paid vacation days has she earned? 17 days
   c. When will she reach the maximum number of paid vacation days allowed? After 6 years

4. When Lou started his current job, his employer told him that he would receive two vacation days for each full year he worked. Let x represent the number of years he has worked for the company and y represent the number of paid vacation days he earned.
   a. Write an equation that models the relationship between these two variables. $y = 2x$
   b. How long will it take him to earn 18 paid vacation days? 9 years

5. When George started his current job, his employer told him that at the end of the first year, he would receive two vacation days. After each year worked, his number of vacation days would double up to five work weeks of paid vacation.
   a. Let x represent the work year and y represent the number of paid vacation days. Write an equation that models the relationship between these two variables. $y = 2^x$
   b. How many vacation days will he have earned after four years? 16 days
   c. In what year will he have maxed out his vacation days? In the fifth year he will receive the maximum number.

6. Ruth contributes 18% of the total cost of her individual health care. This is a \$67.50 deduction from each of her biweekly paychecks. What is the total value of her individual coverage for the year? \$9,750

7. At Richardson Manufacturing Company, there are two factors that determine the cost of health care. If an employee makes less than $55,000 per year, he pays $40 per month for individual coverage and $85 per month for family coverage. If an employee makes at least $55,000 per year, individual coverage is $70 per month and family coverage is $165 per month.
   a. Arielle is an office assistant at Richardson. She makes $47,700 per year. She has individual health care. Her yearly contribution is 5% of the total cost. How much does her employer contribute? $9,120
   b. Catherine is a department manager at Richardson. Her annual salary is $68,300. She has family health care. Her employer contributes $935 per month towards her total coverage cost. What percent does Catherine contribute toward the total coverage? 15%

8. Eddie is a plant manager at North Salem Construction Company. He has been employed there for 20 years and will be retiring at the end of this year. His pension is calculated on the average of his last four years' salaries. In those years, he earned $82,000, $96,000, $105,000, and $109,000. His employer will give him 1.2% of that average for each year he worked. Calculate Eddie's pension. $23,520

9. As part of their employee benefits, all workers at Middletown Electronics receive a pension that is calculated by multiplying the number of years worked times 1.65% of the average of their three highest years' salary. Maureen has worked for Middletown for 27 years and is retiring. Her highest salaries are $97,000, $97,800, and $98,198. Calculate Maureen's pension. $43,510.20

10. The spreadsheet calculates a yearly pension. Users enter the pension percentage as a percent in cell B1, the number of years worked in cell B2, and the last four working years' salaries in cells B3–B6. That 4-year average salary is calculated and displayed in cell B7. The yearly pension amount is calculated and displayed in cell B8.
   a. Write the spreadsheet formula for cell B7. =average(B3:B6)
   b. Write the spreadsheet formula for cell B8. =B1/100*B7*B2

	A	B
1	Pension percentage	
2	Years worked	
3	Year 1 salary	
4	Year 2 salary	
5	Year 3 salary	
6	Year 4 salary	
7	Average salary	
8	Yearly pension	

11. Natalia worked in an automobile plant. She lost her job when the plant relocated to another state. She applied for unemployment compensation. In her state, the amount is calculated by taking 55% of the average of the last 26 weekly salary amounts. The gross incomes from her last 26 paychecks are listed in the table. Determine Natalia's unemployment compensation weekly amount to the nearest cent. $400.65

Week	1	2	3	4	5	6	7	8	9	10	11	12	13
Salary	$715	$700	$730	$730	$730	$720	$700	$720	$720	$720	$725	$720	$725
Week	14	15	16	17	18	19	20	21	22	23	24	25	26
Salary	$730	$730	$735	$735	$735	$740	$740	$740	$740	$740	$740	$740	$740

12. In Rodger's state, unemployment compensation is calculated by finding the total of the quarterly wages of two consecutive quarters and dividing by 26. The weekly unemployment is 65% of that amount. In the quarter of January, February, and March, Rodger made a total of $13,950.80. In the quarter of April, May, and June, he made a total of $14,250.10. Find Rodger's weekly unemployment amount. $705.02

TEACH

Exercise 7
There is a great deal of numerical information that needs to be sorted in this exercise. Students may find it easier if they organize the data in a chart.

Exercises 8 and 9
Once students have completed these exercises and you have reviewed the solutions with them, ask the class which pension plan might be more beneficial—using the average of the last four annual salaries or the average of the three highest year's salaries.

Exercise 11
Students may wish to write a spreadsheet in order to find the solution to this exercise. They can use the one listed next to Exercise 10 and alter it to fit 26 pay periods.

A nation's strength lies in the well-being of its people. The Social Security program plays an important part in providing for families, children, and older persons in the time of stress.

President John F. Kennedy

6-5 Social Security and Medicare

Objectives

- Compute paycheck deductions for Social Security.
- Compute paycheck deductions for Medicare.

Common Core

F-IF4, F-IF7b

Key Terms

- Social Security
- Federal Insurance Contributions Act (FICA)
- FICA tax
- Social Security tax
- Medicare tax
- maximum taxable income
- Social Security number

CCSS Warm-Up

For which of the following graphs is the range "all real numbers greater than or equal to 0"?

a. $y = x^2 - 11$ **b.** $y = |x - 15|$ **c.** $y = 12$

b

EXAMINE THE QUESTION

Most students have heard of Social Security and Medicare but probably know very little about them. They should be encouraged to learn more about them through the Reality Check projects at the end of the chapter.

CLASS DISCUSSION

Ask students if they have ever noticed a FICA box on their paycheck stubs.

Emphasize the importance of keeping their Social Security number secure to avoid identity theft.

Underscore the fact that their contributions to Social Security and Medicare are matched by their employers, but they are not being saved for them in a bank account. The amounts are being recorded, but the money is being spent on current benefits.

What Are Social Security and Medicare?

An insurance program is available jointly through your employer and the United States government. This insurance, **Social Security**, covers 90% of all American jobs. President Franklin D. Roosevelt started Social Security in 1935. It was established in the **Federal Insurance Contributions Act (FICA)**. Social Security provides income for people after they retire. Social Security also pays benefits to disabled workers. If an eligible worker dies, benefits are paid to surviving family members.

When you work at a job covered by Social Security, you must pay **FICA taxes**. Both **Social Security tax** and **Medicare tax** fall under this category. These taxes help cover the cost of these federal insurance programs. Medicare is the nation's largest health insurance program for people 65 years of age and older and some disabled people under 65.

The costs of Social Security and Medicare are split evenly between you and your employer. The amount of Social Security tax you pay depends on the Social Security percentage and the **maximum taxable income** for that year. A percentage of each worker's salary is taken out of each paycheck, up to a set maximum amount. Any annual income greater than that amount is not subject to Social Security tax. Medicare tax is paid on all of your income. The money that you and your employer contribute to Social Security and Medicare is used to pay the *current* benefits to someone else. When you become eligible for benefits, the people working at that time will be paying for your benefits.

The government keeps records of the amounts that you have paid to Social Security and Medicare under your own personal **Social Security number**. Your Social Security number is a unique nine-digit number that belongs only to you. It will be on all of your paycheck stubs, so be sure to check that it is correct every time you get paid. You will have the same Social Security number for your entire life. It is important to keep your Social Security number private to prevent identity theft.

Skills and Strategies

Here you will learn about Social Security and Medicare payments, and how they have changed over the years.

EXAMPLE 1

Ramiro got his first job in 2006. In that year, Social Security tax was 6.2% of income up to $94,200. Medicare tax was 1.45%. If Ramiro earned $73,210 in 2006, how much did he pay for Social Security and Medicare taxes?

SOLUTION Ramiro's income was below the 2006 maximum taxable income of $94,200, so he paid Social Security tax on all of his income.

Multiply his income by 6.2%. $73{,}210 \times 0.062 = 4{,}539.02$

His Social Security tax for 2006 was $4,539.02. Find the Medicare tax.

Multiply his income by 1.45%. $73{,}210 \times 0.0145 = 1{,}061.545$

His Medicare tax for 2006 was $1,061.55, rounded to the nearest cent.

To find his total Social Security and Medicare tax, add them together.

$$4{,}539.02 + 1{,}061.55 = 5{,}600.57$$

Ramiro paid $5,600.57 for Social Security and Medicare in 2006. He should verify that the government has these exact numbers in their files.

CHECK YOUR UNDERSTANDING

Lisa made a total of x dollars last year, which was less than the maximum taxable income for the year. Social Security tax was 6.2% and Medicare tax was 1.45%. Write an expression that represents what Lisa paid to Social Security and Medicare combined.

EXAMPLE 2

Express the Social Security tax for 2006 as a piecewise function.

SOLUTION Let x represent the income. Use the tax rate and maximum taxable income from Example 1. For incomes less than or equal to $94,200, Social Security tax is modeled by the equation

$$f(x) = 0.062x$$

All incomes over $94,200 pay the same Social Security tax, 6.2% of 94,200.

$$94{,}200(0.062) = 5{,}840.40$$

Social Security tax, $f(x)$, can be represented by a piecewise function, as

$$f(x) = \begin{cases} 0.062x & \text{when } 0 < x \leq 94{,}200 \\ 5{,}840.40 & \text{when } x > 94{,}200 \end{cases}$$

It is not necessary to use a piecewise function to represent the Medicare tax for 2006, because the Medicare tax for that year was 1.45% of total income. The Medicare tax function $m(x)$ is

$$m(x) = 0.0145x$$

TEACH

Even students who work know little about how Social Security is computed. They probably don't realize that there is a maximum taxable income. These exercises show them how these computations are made.

EXAMPLE 1

This exercise introduces students to the maximum taxable income, which none of them have earned in their part-time jobs. The very first dollar they earn is subject to Social Security tax.

CHECK YOUR UNDERSTANDING

Answer $0.062x + 0.0145x$ or $0.0765x$

Have students find the current maximum taxable income on the Internet.

EXAMPLE 2

Students revisit piecewise functions again here. They should start getting more skilled at this precalculus concept.

CHECK YOUR UNDERSTANDING

Answer $0.0765(x + y + z)$

EXAMPLE 3

The graph shows that all workers pay the same maximum amount for the year into Social Security.

CHECK YOUR UNDERSTANDING

Answer approximately $55,000

EXAMPLE 4

Show students how the maximum taxable income has changed since 1988.

CHECK YOUR UNDERSTANDING

Answer $38,000

ANSWERS

(Applications on page 319)

1. A nation is stronger when its people are cared for. The Social Security program does just that.
5. a. Social Security $3,571.20; Medicare $1,957.50

   b.
$$f(x) = \begin{cases} 0.062x & \text{when } 0 < x \leq 84{,}900 \\ 5{,}263.80 & \text{when } x > 84{,}900 \end{cases}$$

CHECK YOUR UNDERSTANDING

Ming worked three jobs in 2006. The total of her incomes was less than $94,200. At QuickMart, she made x dollars. At the College Book Store, she made y dollars. At the Mail Depot, she made z dollars. Express the combined total of her Social Security and Medicare taxes algebraically.

EXAMPLE 3

Graph the Social Security tax piecewise function from Example 2.

SOLUTION Determine appropriate values for the x- and y-axes. The maximum value you need to graph on the y-axis is $5,840.40. The x-axis should extend beyond $94,200. Social Security tax on 0 dollars is 0, so the point (0, 0) is on the graph. The maximum taxable income, $94,200, and the maximum you could pay to Social Security, $5,840.40, are coordinates of a second point. Draw a line segment connecting (94,200, 5,840.40) to (0, 0). This line segment has the equation $y = 0.062x$. The slope is the Social Security tax rate. For incomes greater than $94,200, the Social Security tax is $5,840.40, so a horizontal ray finishes the graph. The horizontal ray has a slope of 0. Notice that there is a sharp point where the ray and the line segment with different slopes meet. This point, located at (94,200, 5,840.40), is a *cusp*.

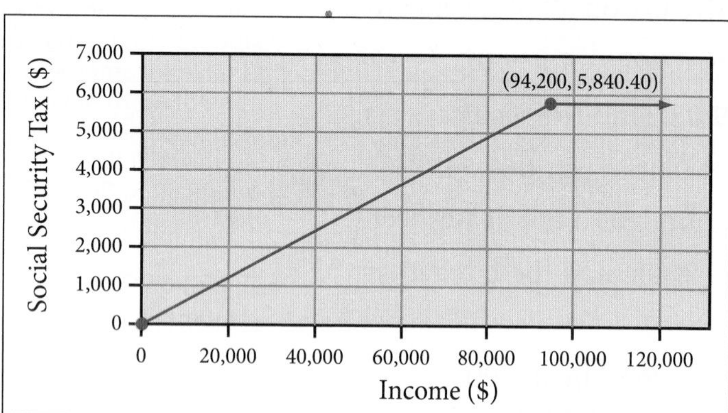

CHECK YOUR UNDERSTANDING

Mark's Social Security tax was $3,500 during the year in the graph in Example 3. Use the graph to approximate his taxable income.

EXAMPLE 4

In 1988, Social Security tax was 7.51%, to the maximum income of $45,000. If Grace earned $51,211 in 1988, how much Social Security did she pay?

SOLUTION Grace's income, $51,211, is over the maximum taxable income of $45,000 for that tax year.

Find 7.51% of income. $45{,}000 \times 0.0751 = 3{,}379.50$

Grace's Social Security tax for 1988 was $3,379.50.

This was the most anybody contributed to Social Security in 1988. Even if you earned millions of dollars, this is the amount you contributed to Social Security.

CHECK YOUR UNDERSTANDING

In 1988 Ramona paid $2,853.80 in Social Security tax. What was Ramona's taxable income in 1988?

Applications

A nation's strength lies in the well-being of its people. The Social Security program plays an important part in providing for families, children, and older persons in the time of stress.
President John F. Kennedy

1. How can the quote be interpreted in the context of what you have learned? See margin.

2. The table on the right gives a historical look at Social Security tax before there was a separate Medicare tax. Find the maximum you could pay into Social Security for each year. See below.

Year	Social Security (%)	Maximum Taxable Income ($)	Maximum You Could Pay Into Social Security
1978	6.05%	17,700	a.
1980	6.13%	25,900	b.
1982	6.7%	32,400	c.
1984	6.7%	37,800	d.
1986	7.15%	42,000	e.
1988	7.51%	45,000	f.
1990	7.65%	51,300	g.

a. \$1,070.85; b. \$1,587.67; c. \$2,170.80; d. \$2,532.60; e. \$3.003; f. \$3.379.50; g. \$3,924.45

3. In 1990, Jerry's gross pay was \$78,000.
   a. What was his monthly gross pay? \$6,500
   b. In what month did Jerry hit the maximum taxable Social Security income? August
   c. How much Social Security tax did Jerry pay in January? \$497.25
   d. How much Social Security tax did Jerry pay in December? \$0

4. In 1978, Dawn earned \$48,000.
   a. What was her monthly gross pay? \$4,000
   b. In what month did Dawn reach the maximum taxable Social Security income? May
   c. How much Social Security tax did Dawn pay in February? \$242
   d. How much Social Security tax did Dawn pay in May? \$102.85
   e. How much Social Security tax did Dawn pay in November? \$0

5. In 1991, Social Security and Medicare taxes were itemized separately on paycheck stubs and tax forms for the first time. The table on the right gives a historical look at Social Security and Medicare taxes. See additional answers.
   a. Find the maximum a person could contribute to Social Security and Medicare in 1993.
   b. If $f(x)$ represents the Social Security tax, and x represents income, express the 2002 Social Security tax as a piecewise function.

Year	Social Security (%)	Maximum Taxable Income for Social Security ($)	Medicare (%)	Maximum Taxable Income for Medicare ($)
1991	6.2%	53,400	1.45%	125,000
1992	6.2%	55,500	1.45%	130,200
1993	6.2%	57,600	1.45%	135,000
1994	6.2%	60,600	1.45%	All income
1995	6.2%	61,200	1.45%	All income
1996	6.2%	62,700	1.45%	All income
1997	6.2%	65,400	1.45%	All income
1998	6.2%	68,400	1.45%	All income
1999	6.2%	72,600	1.45%	All income
2000	6.2%	76,200	1.45%	All income
2001	6.2%	80,400	1.45%	All income
2002	6.2%	84,900	1.45%	All income
2003	6.2%	87,900	1.45%	All income
2004	6.2%	87,900	1.45%	All income
2005	6.2%	90,000	1.45%	All income
2006	6.2%	94,200	1.45%	All income
2007	6.2%	97,500	1.45%	All income
2008	6.2%	102,000	1.45%	All income
2009	6.2%	106,800	1.45%	All income

TEACH

Exercise 11
This exercise involves an interpretation of the slope. You may want to discuss it in depth.

Exercise 14
This exercise involves interpreting a discontinuity in a graph, another skill usually taught in precalculus.

Exercise 15
If you have two employers, you could have paid too much in Social Security taxes, since the employers do not know the earnings from the other job.

ANSWERS

11. If the slope was 1, then the Social Security contribution would be 100% of the income.
12. They will pay a very high Social Security tax and may pay more than they are able to get from the Social Security system.
14. If you make $99,999.99, you would pay very close to $6,000. But, if your income is just 2 cents more, $100,000.01, you would pay $2,000 more in taxes.
16. Yes; the player's per game salary is $154,320.99, which is greater than the taxable income of $106,800.

For Exercises 6–10, use the table on the previous page that provides a historical look at Social Security and Medicare.

6. Express the 1993 Social Security tax function as a piecewise function $t(x)$, where x is the annual income. Graph the function. What are the coordinates of the cusps on the graph? (57,600, 3,571.20); see additional answers for graph.
7. Graph the Social Security tax function for 1992. What are the coordinates of the cusp? On the same axes, graph the Medicare function. (55,500, 3,441); see additional answers for graph.
8. In 2007, Jessica earned p dollars, where $p > 100{,}000$. She was paid monthly. Express the amount her employer contributed to her Social Security tax in February algebraically. $0.062\left(\frac{p}{12}\right)$
9. In 1995, Eve earned d dollars, where $d < 50{,}000$. Express the amount she paid to Social Security and Medicare as a function of d. $0.062d + 0.0145d$, or $0.0765d$
10. Keesha earned x dollars per month in 2006, where $x <$ \$5,600.
    a. Did she earn more or less than the maximum taxable income for 2006? less
    b. Express her Social Security tax for the year algebraically. $0.062(12x)$, or $0.744x$
    c. Express her Medicare tax for the year algebraically. $0.0145(12x)$, or $0.174x$
11. Explain why the slope of the Social Security function, before it becomes horizontal, cannot equal 1. See margin.
12. A politician is considering removing the maximum taxable income and having all income subject to Social Security tax. Why might this be unfair to very affluent people? See margin.
13. Find the Social Security and Medicare tax rates for the current year. Also find the maximum taxable income for the Social Security tax. Use the information to graph this year's Social Security tax function. See students' work.
14. A politician is listening to a proposal for a new Social Security tax plan. The graph is shown. The two parts of the graph are disconnected where $x = 100{,}000$. Explain why this would be an unfair Social Security tax function. See margin.

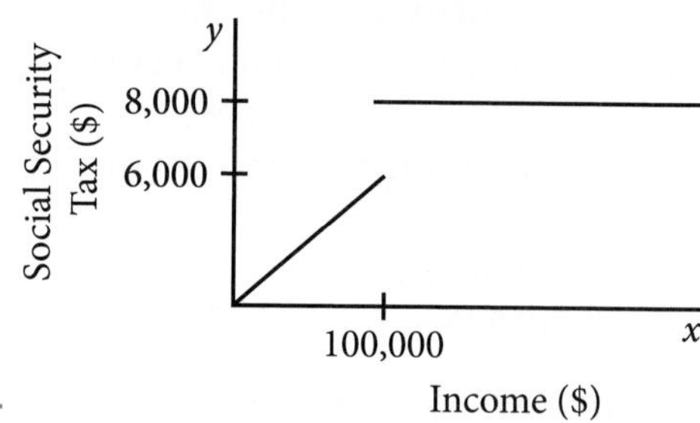

15. In a year when the maximum income for Social Security was $106,800, Bart worked at two jobs. In one job he earned $99,112. In his second job, he earned $56,222. Both of his employers took out Social Security tax. As a result, Bart had paid excess Social Security tax, and the government must return some of it to him. How much does the government owe him for excess Social Security paid? $3,009.11
16. An All-Star baseball player earning $25,000,000 per year plays 162 games per year. If you divide the salary by the number of games, does that baseball player reach this year's maximum taxable income in the first game of the year? See margin.

Assessment

CHAPTER 6

Real Numbers

You Write the Story!!

Write a short newspaper-type article based on the graph below. You can find an electronic copy at www.cengage.com/school/math/financialalgebra. Copy and paste it into your article.

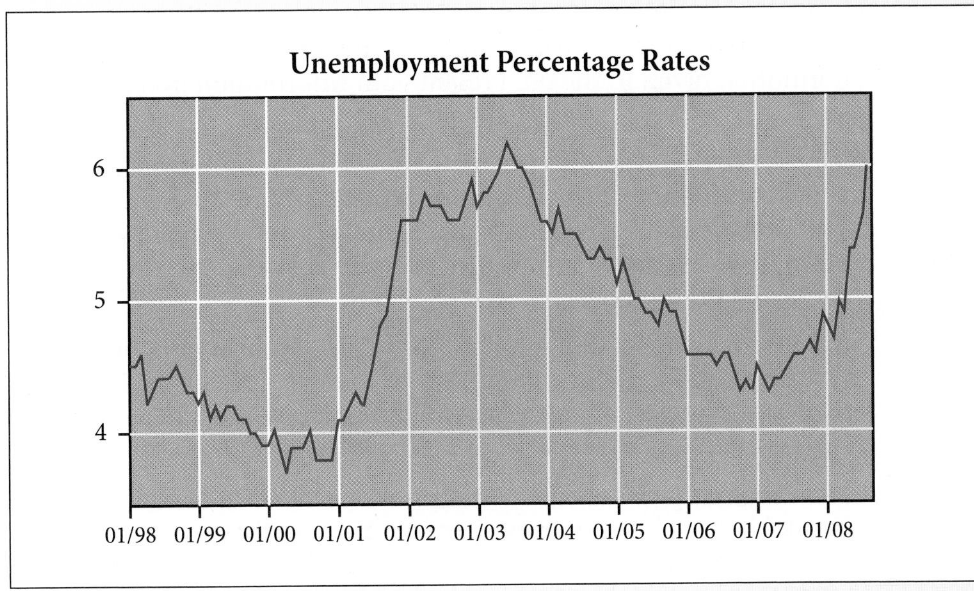

Source: Bureau of Labor Statistics

CHAPTER 6 ASSESSMENT

REAL NUMBERS

You Write the Story!
The unemployment rates for years beyond 2008 can be found by searching data available on the U.S. Bureau of Labor Statistics website.

REALITY CHECK

Reality Check projects are a terrific form of alternative assessment. They give students an additional avenue to show what they've learned, so their grades are not solely-based on tests. These Reality Checks have students doing research on topics involving Social Security, labor statistics, minimum wage, and more. In addition, students are encouraged to speak with parents and community members about employment related topics.

Reality Check

1. Every taxpayer should periodically ask the Social Security Administration for a copy of their Social Security records. This is a record of every dollar ever earned in a taxpayer's entire life, shown year-by-year. Visit the Social Security website for more information. Discuss this with your parents. Ask them if they might walk you through their record to illustrate their working history.

2. You are going to research benefits payable under Social Security. Go to the Social Security website. Do an Internet search for other sites about Social Security benefits. Read through each site and compile a list of benefits and a description of each benefit in a few sentences. Prepare a written report, oral report, or PowerPoint report on your findings.

REALITY CHECK

Projects can be presented to the class on any schedule that works for your program. It may be too time-consuming for every student to present their project for every chapter.

Remind students who are personally visiting local businesses or community members that they are representing the school, and need to be cordial and patient. These projects deliberately have students taking field trips, so they don't conduct everything online.

Explain that they need to thank any person who helps them in completing their Reality Check projects. A letter is the most personal way to do this.

You can offer students extra projects for extra credit.

3. Do an Internet search and speak to your librarian and English teacher about sources available to you so you can learn how to write a job resume. Pretend you are applying for a job of your choice. Prepare a cover letter and job resume about yourself that can include fictional colleges or trade schools, employment, community experience, and so on.
4. Contact the Department of Labor for your state by mail or email, or visit their Internet site. Gather information about unemployment insurance, state minimum wage for different industries, labor laws, child labor laws, and so on. Ask them to send you informative brochures, or download information from the website. Compile a list of facts you found in your readings. Create a presentation board to be displayed in your classroom.
5. Search a newspaper's help-wanted classified ads. Cut out 20 ads related to a specific profession. Interpret each ad in full sentences. Compute the annual, weekly, and monthly gross salary based on information given in the ad. Present your information in a report.
6. Do a library or Internet search on the federal minimum wage over the past two decades. Also research your state's minimum wage over the past two decades. The minimum wage could be different in different industries. Pick two of them. Create a graph that shows both federal and state minimum wages over the past 20 years. Present your graph on a poster.
7. Visit a local business that employs teenagers. Make an appointment to interview the manager. Prepare a list of questions for the manager about pay, pay periods, benefits, and other job-related facts. Prepare your information in a report.
8. Interview your parents about their opinions on what to consider when taking a job or choosing a career. How do they weigh benefits compared to salary? What other factors have their experiences taught them should be considered when planning a career?
9. Use the Internet to find the salaries of famous, highly paid athletes, movie stars, and other personalities. Set up rates that compare their salaries per day, per inning, per hour, per race, per pitch, per lap, per goal, per hour, per game, and so on. Present your information in graph form on a poster.
10. Call the help-wanted customer service line for several local newspapers. Find out the cost to an employer of placing a classified ad in the help-wanted section. Express the cost as a piecewise function. Present your findings on a poster.

Dollars and Sense — Your Financial News Update

Go to www.cengage.com/school/math/financialalgebra where you will find a link to a website containing current issues about employment. Try one of the activities.

Really? Really! REVISITED

In Really? Really! you were introduced to statistics about the American workforce. Now take a look at statistical predictions of how that workforce may look by the year 2016.

According to the U.S. Department of Labor's Bureau of Labor Statistics, the following is a list of the 10 fastest growing occupations from 2006 to 2016.

Job Title	Employment Number (in thousands)	
	2006	2016
Network systems and data communications analysts	262	402
Personal and home care aides	767	1,156
Home health aides	787	1,171
Computer software engineers, applications	507	733
Veterinary technologists and technicians	71	100
Personal financial advisors	176	248
Makeup artists, theatrical and performance	2	3
Medical assistants	417	565
Veterinarians	62	84
Substance abuse and behavioral disorder counselors	83	112

Based on the data in the list, explain how these ten jobs were sorted with network systems and data communications analyst as the fastest growing occupation and substance abuse and behavioral disorder counselors as the tenth fastest growing occupation. Justify your response. See margin.

REALLY? REALLY! REVISITED

In order to answer the question, it is important to have a discussion about the meaning of fastest growing jobs from 2006 to 2016. How does the data presented in the chart contribute to the sorting formula? You may need to suggest that the solution lies in setting up ratios.

ANSWERS

The sorting was done by determining the percent change in employment numbers from 2006 to 2016. For example, network analysts increased by 140,000 from 2006 to 2016. This represents a 53.4% increase over the ten year period. By calculating the percent increase over the ten year period for each occupation, you will see how the jobs have been ranked.

ANSWERS

9.

$$c(x) = \begin{cases} 0.18x \text{ when } x \le 900 \\ 0.20x \text{ when } 900 < x \le 1{,}500 \\ 0.25x \text{ when } x > 1{,}500 \end{cases}$$

Applications

1. Josephine is looking for a new part-time job as a plumber. She responds to a classified ad for a position that pays 44.5K. What would her weekly salary be to the nearest cent if she gets this job? $855.77

2. Frank got a new job through the Valley Employment Service. The job pays $51K per year, and the agency fee is equal to 35% of one month's pay. How much must Frank pay the agency? $1,487.50

3. Derek is placing a seven-line classified job for an assistant. The following piecewise function gives the price of an x-line ad.

$$a(x) = \begin{cases} 32 & \text{when } x \le 3 \\ 32 + 9(x - 3) & \text{when } x > 3 \end{cases}$$

Find the difference between the cost of a 6-line ad and the cost of a 7-line ad. $9

4. Carole worked her 40 regular hours last week plus 5 overtime hours at the time-and-a-half rate. Her gross pay was $451.25. What was her hourly rate? $9.50

5. Tania earns $13.50 per hour at the Glendale Florist. She regularly works 40 hours per week. She is paid time-and-a-half for each hour of overtime work. Last week she worked 43 hours. What was her gross pay for the week? $600.75

6. Patrick earns x dollars per hour for his regular 40 hours per week. He also works three hours overtime each week, at a time-and-a-half rate. Express his annual salary algebraically. $52(40x + 4.5x) = 52(44.5x)$

7. An author writes a computer self-help manual that sells for x dollars each. He received a bonus of $1,000 to sign with his publisher, and he receives 10% commission on each book sale. Express the total amount of income he earns from selling y books algebraically. $0.10xy + 1{,}000$

8. Jim received a total piecework paycheck of $291.81. He receives 71 cents per unit produced. How many units did he produce? 411

9. The Price King Auto Mall pays their sales staff by commission. They are paid a percent of the profit the dealership makes on each sold car. If the profit is $900 or less, the commission rate is 18%. If the profit is greater than $900 and less than or equal to $1,500, the commission rate is 20% of the profit. If the profit is above $1,500, the rate is 25% of the profit. If x represents the profit, express the commission $c(x)$ as a piecewise function. See margin.

10. Jean's Jeans pays its sales staff a commission of 4% of the first $1,000 in sales and 6% of the balance of sales, plus a weekly salary. If a salesperson sold x dollars worth of clothing and $x > \$1{,}000$, express the commission earned algebraically. $40 + 0.06(x - 1{,}000)$

11. Gabe contributes 15% of the total cost of his individual health care coverage. He pays $28.80 per week towards this contribution. What is the total value of Gabe's health care coverage for the year? $9,984

12. Anton works at First National Bank. His employer offers him a pension retirement plan which will be 1.45% of his average salary for the last five years of employment for every year worked. Anton is planning on retiring at the end of this year after 22 years of employment. His salaries for the last five years are \$92,000; \$92,800; \$99,000; \$100,500; and \$105,000. Calculate Anton's pension. \$31,217.34

13. In Don's state, the unemployment compensation is calculated by finding the total of the quarterly wages of two consecutive quarters and dividing that amount by 26. The weekly unemployment amount is 47% of that figure. In the quarter consisting of January, February, and March, Don made a total of \$19,574. In the quarter consisting of April, May, and June, he made a total of \$21,974. Find Don's weekly unemployment amount. \$751.06

14. In 2008, the Social Security percentage was 6.2% for the first \$102,000 earned. The Medicare percentage was 1.45% of your entire salary. Darby made \$143,000 in 2008.
   a. Write the combined taxes, y, as a piecewise function where x represents the income. See margin.
   b. How much did Darby pay in Social Security tax? \$6,324
   c. How much did Darby pay in Medicare tax? \$2,073.50

15. The percentages at the turn of the 21st century are shown in the table. Ray worked at the same job for those three years making \$80,400 without any increase in salary. See margin.

	Social Security	Maximum Taxable Income	Medicare	Maximum Taxable Income
2000	6.2%	\$76,200	1.45%	All income
2001	6.2%	\$80,400	1.45%	All income
2002	6.2%	\$84,900	1.45%	All income

   a. Calculate his Social Security and Medicare taxes for those years.
   b. Calculate the percent of his salary for the combined taxes in each year. What do you notice?

16. In many states, the weekly unemployment compensation is a certain percentage of the 26-week average for the two highest-salaried quarters. A quarter is three consecutive months. In the spreadsheet below, the user enters the two highest quarter salaries and the state unemployment compensation percentage in the indicated cells.

	A	B
1	Enter your state's unemployment compensation percentage.	
2	Enter the two highest quarter salaries for the year.	
3	Quarter 1	
4	Quarter 2	
5	Quarter 3	
6	Quarter 4	
8	Your weekly unemployment compensation will be:	

Write a spreadsheet formula that will calculate the weekly unemployment compensation. =(sum(B3:B6)/26*B1/100)

ANSWERS

14a.

$$y = \begin{cases} 0.062x + 0.0145x \text{ when } x < 102{,}000 \\ 6{,}324 + 0.0145x \text{ when } x \geq 102{,}000 \end{cases}$$

15a.

	Social Security	Medicare	Combined
2000	\$4,724.40	\$1,165.80	\$5,890.20
2001	\$4,984.80	\$1,165.80	\$6,150.60
2002	\$4,984.80	\$1,165.80	\$6,150.60

b. 7.3%, 7.65%; his percentage increased to the combined Social Security and Medicare rate of 7.65% when the salary was less than the maximum. The more you make, the smaller percentage of your salary is used.

CHAPTER

7 Income Taxes

Taxes are the price we pay for civilization.

Oliver Wendell Holmes, Jr.,
American Jurist

What did Oliver Wendell Holmes mean by his statement?

It takes a lot of money to run local, city, state, and federal governments. The money collected through taxes helps those agencies fund police forces, fire departments, political officers, teachers, research, military defense, public assistance programs, and much more. There are many different types of taxes, including sales taxes, property taxes, social security taxes, and income taxes. Although most people don't like to pay taxes, they do so because it is required by law. Plus, people realize that government services are an essential part of day-to-day life. In this chapter, you will be learning about how taxpayers compute and report their income taxes to the government.

What do you think?

What would our country be today without taxes? Would students sacrifice all the services government provides just to pay no tax? How would their lives be different? Exactly what services do taxes provide, and where would we be without them? Have students read the passage aloud and let them offer comments about the possibilities.

TEACHING RESOURCES

Instructor's Resource CD

Exam*View*® CD, Ch. 7

eHomework, Ch. 7

www.cengage.com/school/math/financialalgebra

Really?

The Tax Foundation is a nonpartisan educational organization whose mission is to ". . . educate taxpayers about sound tax policy and the size of the tax burden borne by Americans at all levels of government." Each year, the Foundation calculates the average number of days it would take Americans to earn enough money to pay off their entire year's income tax debt. Starting with January 1st, the Foundation determines the first date that average Americans would be working for themselves rather than working to pay off taxes. This date is called Tax Freedom Day. Tax Freedom Day changes from year to year based upon a variety of economic factors. Examine these Tax Freedom dates.

Year	Tax Freedom Day	Year	Tax Freedom Day
1993	April 21	2001	April 30
1994	April 23	2002	April 20
1995	April 25	2003	April 16
1996	April 26	2004	April 16
1997	April 28	2005	April 23
1998	April 30	2006	April 26
1999	May 1	2007	April 26
2000	May 3	2008	April 23

For example, if all of a person's income went to pay taxes from the beginning of 2008, the average American would have worked until April 23 before being free from his or her tax burden.

CHAPTER OVERVIEW

In this chapter students will use tax tables, as well as discover the equations and piecewise functions upon which the progressive tax system is based.

REALLY? REALLY!

Often, students who work part-time only pay Social Security. They don't pay federal or state withholding taxes. Consequently, they are not attuned to the idea that money is withheld from their paychecks which is used to provide government services.

Therefore, part of the money they earn goes to the government. Students can translate this into the fact that they spend some portion of their working time making money just to pay taxes. If this fraction of time spent is reallocated into one solid chunk of time starting January 1, the concept of Tax Freedom Day emerges.

Really!

The hardest thing in the world to understand is the income tax.
Albert Einstein

7-1 Tax Tables, Worksheets, and Schedules

Objectives

- Express tax schedules algebraically.
- Compute federal income taxes using a tax table and tax schedules.

Common Core

A-CED3

Key Terms

- property tax
- sales tax
- income tax
- taxable income
- tax
- Internal Revenue Service (IRS)
- single
- married filing jointly
- qualifying widow(er)
- married filing separately
- head of household

CCSS Warm-Up

Determine x and y given the constraints stated.

x and y are both integers; $-20 < x < 0$; $0 < y < 20$; $-10 < (2x + 3y) < 0$; $x - y = -15$.

$x = -10$ and $y = 5$

EXAMINE THE QUESTION

At first glance, this may appear to be a very basic question—everyone pays taxes! But who are the taxpayers? This lesson will inform students about the types of taxes that are levied and the categories of taxpayers who pay them.

CLASS DISCUSSION

After reviewing the three types of taxes listed, ask students which they pay now and which their parents pay now.

Ask students what the statement "Your annual tax changes as your annual income changes" means.

TEACH

In order to provide answers for exercises in this chapter, the tax schedules and forms used to complete the exercises are those that were available at www.irs.gov for 2008. You can enrich the exercise by having students obtain the most recent tax schedules and forms.

WHO PAYS TAXES?

Imagine how much money it takes to run your city, state, and federal governments. Where does the money come from for police forces, the space program, military defense and national security, health research, social programs, and other government programs? Taxpayers!

There are many different types of taxes. **Property taxes** are collected based on the value of the property you own. **Sales taxes** are collected based on the value of items you purchase. **Income taxes** are collected based on the amount of **taxable income** you earn. Your **tax** is the amount of money you must pay to the government. It is the price you pay to benefit from government services.

Federal taxes are collected by the **Internal Revenue Service (IRS)**. Although people don't like to pay taxes, they are required and people realize taxes are necessary. You report your taxable income on a form called a tax return.

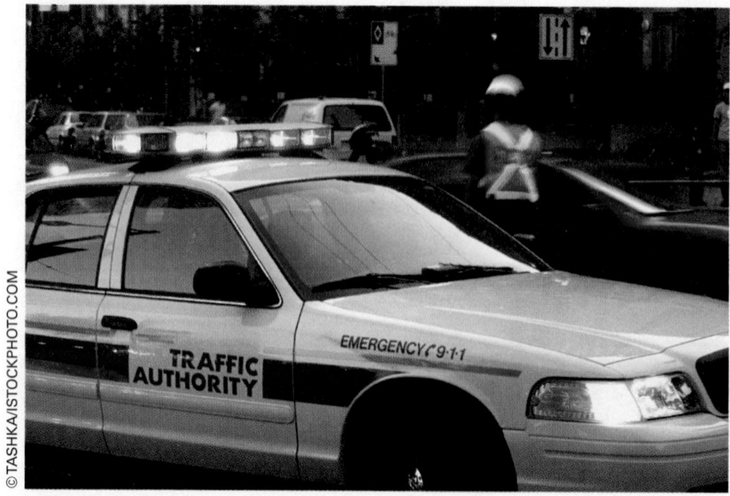

©TASHKA/ISTOCKPHOTO.COM

Your filing status is a description of your marital and family status on the last day of the year. You must indicate your filing status on your tax return. The choices for filing status are

- **Single** unmarried taxpayers.
- **Married Filing Jointly** or **Qualifying Widow(er)** married people who fill out one tax return together or a widow(er) who meets the qualifications outlined by the IRS.
- **Married Filing Separately** married people who file two separate returns.
- **Head of Household** a special filing status for certain unmarried taxpayers who support people in addition to supporting themselves.

Your annual tax changes as your annual income changes. To find the tax on your taxable income, you use a tax table or a tax schedule. Tax tables are easier to use than tax schedules, but with a little algebra, you can master the use of the tax schedule.

TEACH

Ask students to list services that communities, towns, villages, or cities supply to residents. Make sure they realize the services are paid for through a variety of local, state, and federal taxes.

EXAMPLE 1

In the tax table headings, relate the terms "at least" and "but less than" to mathematical symbols.

In *tax tables,* the first number in the range is included in the interval. In *tax schedules,* the second number in the range is included in the interval. This inconsistency may cause confusion when students are writing intervals.

Skills and Strategies

Here you will learn how to use tax tables, tax schedules, and tax worksheets to compute your taxes.

EXAMPLE 1

Ron is single. He is using an IRS tax form and calculates that his taxable income is $51,482. The instructions tell him to use the tax table to determine his taxes. How much does Ron owe in taxes?

SOLUTION Tax tables list the tax for an income interval. Examine the portion of a tax table shown at the right.

Notice that the headings in the two columns read *At least* and *But less than.* The first row is used by taxpayers whose taxable income is at least $51,000, but less than $51,050. Let t represent the taxable income. Using compound inequality notation, this can be expressed as

$$t \geq 51{,}000 \quad \text{and} \quad t < 51{,}050$$

This can also be symbolized using *interval notation* as

$$51{,}000 \leq t < 51{,}050$$

Ron's taxable income of $51,482 is at least $51,450 but less than $51,500. Look across this line until it intersects with the column titled Single. Ron owes $9,213 in taxes.

If line 43 (taxable income) is—		And you are —			
At least	But less than	Single	Married filing jointly *	Married filing separately	Head of a household
		Your tax is —			
51,000					
51,000	**51,050**	9,100	6,851	9,100	7,819
51,050	**51,100**	9,113	6,859	9,113	7,831
51,100	**51,150**	9,125	6,866	9,125	7,844
51,150	**51,200**	9,138	6,874	9,138	7,856
51,200	**51,250**	9,150	6,881	9,150	7,869
51,250	**51,300**	9,163	6,889	9,163	7,881
51,300	**51,350**	9,175	6,896	9,175	7,894
51,350	**51,400**	9,188	6,904	9,188	7,906
51,400	**51,450**	9,200	6,911	9,200	7,919
51,450	**51,500**	9,213	6,919	9,213	7,931
51,500	**51,550**	9,225	6,926	9,225	7,944
51,550	**51,600**	9,238	6,934	9,238	7,956
51,600	**51,650**	9,250	6,941	9,250	7,969
51,650	**51,700**	9,263	6,949	9,263	7,981
51,700	**51,750**	9,275	6,956	9,275	7,994
51,750	**51,800**	9,288	6,964	9,288	8,006
51,800	**51,850**	9,300	6,971	9,300	8,019
51,850	**51,900**	9,313	6,979	9,313	8,031
51,900	**51,950**	9,325	6,986	9,325	8,044
51,950	**52,000**	9,338	6,994	9,338	8,056

■ CHECK YOUR UNDERSTANDING

If r represents Ron's taxable income, express his tax interval as an inequality using interval notation.

CHECK YOUR UNDERSTANDING

Answer

$51{,}450 \leq r < 51{,}500$

EXAMPLE 2

Review the structure of the chart with the students. They will need to first subtract the amount in the last column from the taxable income before calculating the percent.

CHECK YOUR UNDERSTANDING

Answer $65,100

EXAMPLE 2

Maria and Don are married taxpayers filing a joint return. Their combined taxable income is $153,900. The IRS offers a tax schedule so that taxpayers can calculate their tax. Use the tax schedule below for married taxpayers filing jointly to calculate Maria and Don's tax.

Schedule Y-1— If your filing status is **Married filing jointly or Qualifying widow(er)**

If your taxable income is: Over—	But not over—	The tax is:	of the amount over—
$0	$16,050	**--------- 10%**	**$0**
16,050	65,100	**$1,605.00 + 15%**	**16,050**
65,100	131,450	**8,962.50 + 25%**	**65,100**
131,450	200,300	**25,550.00 + 28%**	**131,450**
200,300	357,700	**44,828.00 + 33%**	**200,300**
357,700	---------	**96,770.00 + 35%**	**357,700**

SOLUTION Maria and Don's taxable income is over $131,450, but not over $200,300. If *t* represents their taxable income, this can be expressed in interval notation as

$$131{,}450 < t \leq 200{,}300$$

They should use the information on line 4 to determine their tax.

Their tax is $25,550 + 28% of the amount over 131,450.

$$\text{Tax} = 25{,}550 + 0.28(153{,}900 - 131{,}450)$$

Their tax is $31,836.

CHECK YOUR UNDERSTANDING

Using the table above, what taxable income would yield a tax of exactly $8,962.50?

© HERJUA/ISTOCKPHOTO.COM

EXAMPLE 3

The IRS includes the tax schedule for information purposes only. For taxable incomes over \$100,000, taxpayers must use the tax worksheet. Here is a portion of the worksheet for married taxpayers filing jointly. Calculate Maria and Don's tax using this worksheet.

Section B — Use if your filing status is **Married filing jointly** or **Qualifying widow(er)**. Complete the row below that applies to you.

Taxable income If line 43 is—	**(a)** Enter the amount from line 43	**(b)** Multiplication amount	**(c)** Multiply (a) by (b)	**(d)** Subtraction amount	**Tax** Subtract (d) from (c). Enter the result here and on Form 1040, line 44
At least \$100,000 but not over \$131,450	\$	× 25% (.25)	\$	\$ 7,312.50	\$
Over \$131,450 but not over \$200,300	\$	× 28% (.28)	\$	\$ 11,256.00	\$
Over \$200,300 but not over \$357,700	\$	× 33% (.33)	\$	\$ 21,271.00	\$
Over \$357,700	\$	× 35% (.35)	\$	\$ 28,425.00	\$

SOLUTION Maria and Don's taxable income of \$153,900 is over \$131,450, but not over \$200,300, as indicated in the second line of the worksheet. To calculate their tax, they enter their taxable income in that line of column (a).

Over \$131,450 but not over \$200,300	\$ 153,900	× 28% (.28)	\$	\$ 11,256.00	\$

Column (b) asks them to take 28% of that income. That is, multiply the income by 0.28. That amount is entered in column (c).

$$153{,}900 \times 0.28 = 43{,}092$$

Over \$131,450 but not over \$200,300	\$ 153,900	× 28% (.28)	\$ 43,092	\$ 11,256.00	\$ 31,836

Column (d) says to subtract \$11,256.00 from the amount that was just calculated and to enter the difference in the last column.

$$43{,}092 - 11{,}256 = 31{,}836$$

Maria and Don owe \$31,836 in taxes. This agrees with the amount they computed using the tax schedule.

CHECK YOUR UNDERSTANDING

Davida and John have a taxable income of \$118,675. Use the Married Filling Jointly worksheet above to determine the amounts for columns (a) and (c). What is their calculated tax?

EXTEND YOUR UNDERSTANDING

Chase has a taxable income of x dollars. This amount is over \$100,000, but not over \$131,450. Express his tax algebraically.

EXAMPLE 3

Review the structure of the chart with the students. This worksheet is more user friendly than the schedule in the previous example. Here, students can perform the calculations from left to right.

CHECK YOUR UNDERSTANDING

Answer (a) 118,675; (c) 29,668.75; \$22,356.25

EXTEND YOUR UNDERSTANDING

Answer $0.25x - 7{,}312.50$

Applications

The hardest thing in the world to understand is the income tax.
Albert Einstein

1. How can the quote be interpreted in light of what you have learned? See margin.

Use these tax tables to answer Exercises 2–5.

If line 43 (taxable income) is—		And you are —			
At least	But less than	Single	Married filing jointly *	Married filing separately	Head of a household
		Your tax is —			
57,000					
57,000	**57,050**	10,600	7,751	10,600	9,319
57,050	**57,100**	10,613	7,759	10,613	9,331
57,100	**57,150**	10,625	7,766	10,625	9,344
57,150	**57,200**	10,638	7,774	10,638	9,356
57,200	**57,250**	10,650	7,781	10,650	9,369
57,250	**57,300**	10,663	7,789	10,663	9,381
57,300	**57,350**	10,675	7,796	10,675	9,394
57,350	**57,400**	10,688	7,804	10,688	9,406
57,400	**57,450**	10,700	7,811	10,700	9,419
57,450	**57,500**	10,713	7,819	10,713	9,431
57,500	**57,550**	10,725	7,826	10,725	9,444
57,550	**57,600**	10,738	7,834	10,738	9,456
57,600	**57,650**	10,750	7,841	10,750	9,469
57,650	**57,700**	10,763	7,849	10,763	9,481
57,700	**57,750**	10,775	7,856	10,775	9,494
57,750	**57,800**	10,788	7,864	10,788	9,506
57,800	**57,850**	10,800	7,871	10,800	9,519
57,850	**57,900**	10,813	7,879	10,813	9,531
57,900	**57,950**	10,825	7,886	10,825	9,544
57,950	**58,000**	10,838	7,894	10,838	9,556

If line 43 (taxable income) is—		And you are —			
At least	But less than	Single	Married filing jointly *	Married filing separately	Head of a household
		Your tax is —			
60,000					
60,000	**60,050**	11,350	8,201	11,350	10,069
60,050	**60,100**	11,363	8,209	11,363	10,081
60,100	**60,150**	11,375	8,216	11,375	10,094
60,150	**60,200**	11,388	8,224	11,388	10,106
60,200	**60,250**	11,400	8,231	11,400	10,119
60,250	**60,300**	11,413	8,239	11,413	10,131
60,300	**60,350**	11,425	8,246	11,425	10,144
60,350	**60,400**	11,438	8,254	11,438	10,156
60,400	**60,450**	11,450	8,261	11,450	10,169
60,450	**60,500**	11,463	8,269	11,463	10,181
60,500	**60,550**	11,475	8,276	11,475	10,194
60,550	**60,600**	11,488	8,284	11,488	10,206
60,600	**60,650**	11,500	8,291	11,500	10,219
60,650	**60,700**	11,513	8,299	11,513	10,231
60,700	**60,750**	11,525	8,306	11,525	10,244
60,750	**60,800**	11,538	8,314	11,538	10,256
60,800	**60,850**	11,550	8,321	11,550	10,269
60,850	**60,900**	11,563	8,329	11,563	10,281
60,900	**60,950**	11,575	8,336	11,575	10,294
60,950	**61,000**	11,588	8,344	11,588	10,306

If line 43 (taxable income) is—		And you are —			
At least	But less than	Single	Married filing jointly *	Married filing separately	Head of a household
		Your tax is —			
63,000					
63,000	**63,050**	12,100	8,651	12,100	10,819
63,050	**63,100**	12,113	8,659	12,113	10,831
63,100	**63,150**	12,125	8,666	12,125	10,844
63,150	**63,200**	12,138	8,674	12,138	10,856
63,200	**63,250**	12,150	8,681	12,150	10,869
63,250	**63,300**	12,163	8,689	12,163	10,881
63,300	**63,350**	12,175	8,696	12,175	10,894
63,350	**63,400**	12,188	8,704	12,188	10,906
63,400	**63,450**	12,200	8,711	12,200	10,919
63,450	**63,500**	12,213	8,719	12,213	10,931
63,500	**63,550**	12,225	8,726	12,225	10,944
63,550	**63,600**	12,238	8,734	12,238	10,956
63,600	**63,650**	12,250	8,741	12,250	10,969
63,650	**63,700**	12,263	8,749	12,263	10,981
63,700	**63,750**	12,275	8,756	12,275	10,994
63,750	**63,800**	12,288	8,764	12,288	11,006
63,800	**63,850**	12,300	8,771	12,300	11,019
63,850	**63,900**	12,313	8,779	12,313	11,031
63,900	**63,950**	12,325	8,786	12,325	11,044
63,950	**64,000**	12,338	8,794	12,338	11,056

2. Determine the tax for each filing status and taxable income amount.

a. single \$57,723 \$10,775 **b.** head of household \$60,950 \$10,306

c. married filing jointly \$63,999 \$8,794 **d.** married filing separately \$57,521 \$10,725

3. Given a taxable income amount, express the tax table line that would be used in compound inequality notation.

a. i = \$60,124 $i \geq 60{,}100$ and $i < 60{,}150$ **b.** i = \$57,333 $i \geq 57{,}300$ and $i < 57{,}350$

4. Given the taxable income amount, express the tax table line that would be used in interval notation. See margin.

a. i = \$57,555 **b.** i = \$63,411 **c.** i = \$60,002 **d.** i = \$63,301

5. Given the filing status and the tax, identify the taxable income interval that was used to determine the tax.

a. head of household \$9,406 at least \$57,350 but less than \$57,400

b. single \$12,275 at least \$63,700 but less than \$63,750

c. single \$11,538 at least \$60,750 but less than \$60,800

d. married filing jointly \$8,291 at least \$60,600 but less than \$60,650

e. married filing separately \$10,788 at least \$57,750 but less than \$57,800

TEACH

Exercise 5

Students must work backwards. Impress upon them that only the interval can be determined, not the exact taxable income.

ANSWERS

1. When you think of smart people, you may think of Einstein. Yet, he found the tax system confusing. Therefore, the average citizen needs to take time to understand the system.
4. a. $57{,}550 \leq i < 57{,}600$
   b. $63{,}400 \leq i < 63{,}450$
   c. $60{,}000 \leq i < 60{,}050$
   d. $63{,}300 \leq i < 63{,}350$

Use these tax schedules to answer Exercises 6–10.

Schedule Z— If your filing status is **Head of household**

If your taxable income is: Over—	But not over—	The tax is:	of the amount over—
$0	$11,450	--------- 10%	$0
11,450	43,650	$1,145.00 + 15%	11,450
43,650	112,650	5,975.00 + 25%	43,650
112,650	182,400	23,225.00 + 28%	112,650
182,400	357,700	42,755.00 + 33%	182,400
357,700	---------	100,604.00 + 35%	357,700

6. Calculate the tax for each taxable income of a head of household.

a. $400,000 $115,409 **b.** $10,954 $1,095.40

c. $108,962 $22,303 **d.** $201,102 $48,926.66

7. For what taxable income would a taxpayer have to pay $5,975.00 in taxes? Explain your reasoning. $43,650; it is the minimum amount in that interval.

8. According to the tax schedule, Rich has to pay $25,000 in taxes. What is Rich's taxable income? $118,989.29

9. Kelly's taxable income is $110,000. Approximately what percent of her taxable income is her tax? 21%

10. Maureen's taxable income, t, is between $182,400 and $357,700. Write an algebraic expression that represents her tax. $42{,}755 + 0.33(t - 182{,}400)$

Use this tax computation worksheet to answer Exercises 11–14.

Section D — Use if your filing status is **Head of household**. Complete the row below that applies to you.

Taxable income. If line 43 is—	(a) Enter the amount from line 43	(b) Multiplication amount	(c) Multiply (a) by (b)	(d) Subtraction amount	**Tax** Subtract (d) from (c). Enter the result here and on Form 1040, line 44
At least $100,000 but not over $112,650	$	× 25% (.25)	$	$ 4,937.50	$
Over $112,650 but not over $182,400	$	× 28% (.28)	$	$ 8,317.00	$
Over $182,400 but not over $357,700	$	× 33% (.33)	$	$ 17,437.00	$
Over $357,700	$	× 35% (.35)	$	$ 24,591.00	$

11. Calculate the tax for each of the taxable incomes of a head of household taxpayer.

a. $400,000 $115,409 **b.** $108,962 $22,303

c. $201,102 $48,926.66 **d.** $106,000 $21,562.50

12. Let x represent a head of household taxpayer's taxable income that is over $357,700. Write an expression for this taxpayer's tax in terms of x.
$0.35x - 24{,}591$

13. Let w represent the tax for any taxable income t on the interval $182{,}400 < t \leq 357{,}700$.

a. Calculate the lowest tax on this interval. $42,755

b. Calculate the highest tax on this interval. $100,604

c. Given the interval, $182{,}400 < t \leq 357{,}700$, express the tax in terms of w. $0.33w - 17{,}437$

TEACH

Exercises 6–10
These exercises offer students practice with a tax schedule. Before assigning the problems, make sure that they have a grasp of the structure of the schedule.

TEACH

Exercise 20

This exercise is included to give students a historical perspective on tax rates then (1990) and now. Once students have completed this problem using the 1990 tax schedule, it is suggested that you get the most recent tax schedule and have them use those figures in answering the same exercises. Ask students to compare the results. What changes have been made to the schedule and to the amount of tax owed?

ANSWERS

20a. 1990 tax: $32,853.50; Exercise 6 tax: $25,283

20b. 1990: ≈27%; Exercise 6: ≈21%

20c. Answers vary depending on the current tax schedules.

14. Calculate the tax using the computation worksheet for a head of household taxpayer with a taxable income of $115,700. $24,079

15. Using the tax schedule from Exercise 6, calculate the tax for the person in Exercise 14. $24,079

16. Is there a difference in the tax in Exercises 14 and 15? If so, how much and which method favors the taxpayer? They are the same.

17. Use the tax table at the right to calculate the tax of a head of household taxpayer with a taxable income of $27,811. $3,601

18. Use Schedule Z from Exercise 6 to calculate the tax for the taxpayer in Exercise 17. $3,599.15

If line 43 (taxable income) is—		And you are —			
At least	But less than	Single	Married filing jointly *	Married filing sepa-rately	Head of a house-hold
		Your tax is —			
27,000					
27,000	27,050	3,653	3,251	3,653	3,481
27,050	27,100	3,660	3,259	3,660	3,489
27,100	27,150	3,668	3,266	3,668	3,496
27,150	27,200	3,675	3,274	3,675	3,504
27,200	27,250	3,683	3,281	3,683	3,511
27,250	27,300	3,690	3,289	3,690	3,519
27,300	27,350	3,698	3,296	3,698	3,526
27,350	27,400	3,705	3,304	3,705	3,534
27,400	27,450	3,713	3,311	3,713	3,541
27,450	27,500	3,720	3,319	3,720	3,549
27,500	27,550	3,728	3,326	3,728	3,556
27,550	27,600	3,735	3,334	3,735	3,564
27,600	27,650	3,743	3,341	3,743	3,571
27,650	27,700	3,750	3,349	3,750	3,579
27,700	27,750	3,758	3,356	3,758	3,586
27,750	27,800	3,765	3,364	3,765	3,594
27,800	27,850	3,773	3,371	3,773	3,601
27,850	27,900	3,780	3,379	3,780	3,609
27,900	27,950	3,788	3,386	3,788	3,616
27,950	28,000	3,795	3,394	3,795	3,624

19. Is there a difference in the tax in Exercises 17 and 18? If so, how much and which method favors the taxpayer? yes; by $1.85; Schedule Z

20. In 1990, taxpayers used the following tax schedule. See margin.

1990 Tax Rate Schedules

Caution: *Use ONLY if your taxable income (Form 1040, line 37) is $50,000 or more. If less, use the **TAX Table**. (Even thught you cannot use the tax rate schedules below if your taxable income is less than $50,000, we show all levels of taxable income so that taxpayers can see the tax rate that applies to each level.)*

Schedule X— If your filing status is **Single**

If the amount on Form 1040 line 37, is: Over—	*But not Over—*	Enter on Form 1040 line 38	*of the amount Over—*
$0	$19,450	--------- 15%	**$0**
19,450	47,050	**$2,917.50 + 28%**	**18,450**
47,050	97,620	**10,645.50 + 33%**	**47,050**
97,620	--------	Use Worksheet below to figure your tax.	

Schedule Z— If your filing status is **Head of household**

If the amount on Form 1040 line 37, is: Over—	*But not Over—*	Enter on Form 1040 line 38	*of the amount Over—*
$0	$26,050	--------- 15%	**$0**
26,050	67,200	**$3,907.50 + 28%**	**26,050**
67,200	134,930	**15,429.50 + 33%**	**67,200**
134,930	--------	Use Worksheet below to figure your tax.	

a. Compare the tax of a head of household taxpayer whose taxable income in 1990 was $120,000 with a head of household taxpayer's tax, using the tax schedule from Exercise 6, who earns the same amount.

b. What percent of the taxable income was the tax in each year?

c. Go to the IRS website (www.irs.gov) and find the most recent tax rate schedule. Compare the tax of the same head of household taxpayer from part a with a head of household taxpayer making the same salary today. What percent increase has there been in the tax from then to now?

Taxes are paid in the sweat of every man who labors.
Franklin D. Roosevelt

Modeling Tax Schedules 7-2

Key Terms
- flat tax
- proportional tax
- progressive tax system
- tax bracket
- regressive tax schedule

Objective
- Construct income tax graphs using compound equations.

Common Core
F-IF1, F-IF2, F-IF7b, F-IF8, F-BF1a

CCSS Warm-Up

Match the functions $f(x) = \sqrt{x}$; $g(x) = |x|$; $h(x) = x^2$ with the true statements.

1. always greater than or equal to zero
2. has vertical symmetry

1. $f(x)$, $g(x)$, $h(x)$
2. $g(x)$, $h(x)$

How can you graph tax schedules?

When you pay a sales tax, the tax percentage remains the same whether you purchase a $13 item or a $13,000 item. Sales tax is a **flat tax**, or a **proportional tax**. The tax rate does not depend on the cost of the item you purchase.

How does the tax schedule work? Does the person with taxable income of $13,000 pay the same percent as the person who earns $13,000,000? There are different percentages on tax schedules. This is a distinct feature of a **progressive tax system**. In a progressive income tax system, the tax rate increases as the income increases. People with greater incomes are subject to higher tax rates on part of their income. Look at the first line of the tax schedule shown.

Schedule Y-1— If your filing status is **Married filing jointly or Qualifying widow(er)**

If your taxable income is: Over—	But not over—	The tax is:	of the amount over—
$0	$16,050	--------- 10%	$0
16,050	65,100	$1,605.00 + 15%	16,050
65,100	131,450	8,962.50 + 25%	65,100
131,450	200,300	25,550.00 + 28%	131,450
200,300	357,700	44,828.00 + 33%	200,300
357,700	---------	96,770.00 + 35%	357,700

Notice that all married couples filing jointly pay a 10% tax on the first $16,050 they earn. If the couple earns $16,051 or 15 million dollars for the year, the tax on the first $16,050 of taxable income you earn is taxed at the same rate, 10%.

The next bracket of income is taxed at the 15% rate. Each line of the tax schedule has a different percent. This percent is called a **tax bracket**. You may have heard the expression "I'm in the 35% tax bracket." That means the couple earns an income that is partly taxed at a 35% rate. Keep in mind that the first $16,050 of this couple's income is still taxed at the 10% rate.

EXAMINE THE QUESTION

Our tax system is a series of tables, schedules, and worksheets. By creating tax equations and graphs, we can get a better picture of how the tax burden is levied among the different income levels.

CLASS DISCUSSION

Before examining the schedule presented on this page, ask students how sales tax might work if it was a progressive rather than a proportional tax. Present them with a schedule in which the shopper would have to pay 6% on the first $50 and 8% on the amount over $50. Ask them to calculate this tax and discuss the difference between this system and what is currently in place.

TEACH

Students have likely heard their parents, adult friends, and co-workers complain about the tax system in the U.S. The examples in this lesson look at the nature of the progressive tax system and how it is related to intervals, equations, slopes, and piecewise functions.

EXAMPLE 1

This example sets the stage for creating the piecewise function. The compound interval notation leads to the compound inequality notation. It is the latter that is used when graphing the piecewise function on the graphing calculator.

CHECK YOUR UNDERSTANDING

Answer Over $131,450 but not over $200,300; $131{,}450 < x \leq 200{,}300$; $x > 131{,}450$ and $x \leq 200{,}300$

There are people who support changing the current progressive tax schedule to a flat tax system, to simplify income taxes. In a **regressive tax schedule**, the tax rate decreases as income increases. The debate between flat, progressive, and regressive taxes can be a lively one. Which system would you recommend? Why?

Skills and Strategies

Previously, you used the tax worksheet and the tax schedule to calculate the tax of married taxpayers filing a joint return. Now you will examine how percentages depend on income in the tax schedules.

EXAMPLE 1

Model the schedule shown in tax schedule notation, interval notation, and compound inequality notation.

Schedule Y-1— If your filing status is **Married filing jointly or Qualifying widow(er)**

If your taxable income is: Over—	But not over—	The tax is:	of the amount over—
$0	$16,050	--------- **10%**	**$0**
16,050	65,100	**$1,605.00 + 15%**	**16,050**
65,100	131,450	**8,962.50 + 25%**	**65,100**
131,450	200,300	**25,550.00 + 28%**	**131,450**
200,300	357,700	**44,828.00 + 33%**	**200,300**
357,700	---------	**96,770.00 + 35%**	**357,700**

SOLUTION There are six taxable income intervals. If x represents any taxable income, then those intervals can be expressed in tax schedule notation, interval notation, and compound inequality notation as follows:

Tax Schedule Notation	Interval Notation	Compound Inequality Notation
Over $0 but not over $16,050	$0 < x \leq 16{,}050$	$x > 0$ and $x \leq 16{,}050$
Over $16,050 but not over $65,100	$16{,}050 < x \leq 65{,}100$	$x > 16{,}050$ and $x \leq 65{,}100$
Over $65,100 but not over $131,450	$65{,}100 < x \leq 131{,}450$	$x > 65{,}100$ and $x \leq 131{,}450$
Over $131,450 but not over $200,300	$131{,}450 < x \leq 200{,}300$	$x > 131{,}450$ and $x \leq 200{,}300$
Over $200,300 but not over $357,700	$200{,}300 < x \leq 357{,}700$	$x > 200{,}300$ and $x \leq 357{,}700$
Over $357,700	$x > 357{,}700$	$x > 357{,}700$

■ CHECK YOUR UNDERSTANDING

Write the tax schedule notation, interval notation, and compound inequality notation that would apply to an income of $172,876.99.

Tax Equation

For each interval in the tax schedule beyond the first, the tax is calculated by adding a fixed tax to a percentage of the difference between the taxable income and some number that is stated in the schedule. Let y represent the tax and x represent the taxable income. The tax for each of these intervals can be expressed algebraically as shown in this chart.

Tax Schedule Notation	Tax Equation
Over \$0 but not over \$16,050	$y = 0.10x$
Over \$16,050 but not over \$65,100	$y = 1{,}605 + 0.15(x - 16{,}050)$
Over \$65,100 but not over \$131,450	$y = 8{,}962.50 + 0.25(x - 65{,}100)$
Over \$131,450 but not over \$200,300	$y = 25{,}550 + 0.28(x - 131{,}450)$
Over \$200,300 but not over \$357,700	$y = 44{,}828 + 0.33(x - 200{,}300)$
Over \$357,700	$y = 96{,}770 + 0.35(x - 357{,}700)$

If $f(x)$ represents the entire tax function for married taxpayers filing jointly, then this function can be written in piecewise function notation.

$$f(x) = \begin{cases} 0.10x & 0 < x \le 16{,}050 \\ 1{,}605 + 0.15(x - 16{,}050) & 16{,}050 < x \le 65{,}100 \\ 8{,}962.50 + 0.25(x - 65{,}100) & 65{,}100 < x \le 131{,}450 \\ 25{,}550 + 0.28(x - 131{,}450) & 131{,}450 < x \le 200{,}300 \\ 44{,}828 + 0.33(x - 200{,}300) & 200{,}300 < x \le 357{,}700 \\ 96{,}770 + 0.35(x - 357{,}700) & x > 357{,}700 \end{cases}$$

CLASS DISCUSSION

Ask students who have a job or have had a job about their experiences with paying income taxes.

Discuss with students why they think the tax system is difficult for the average American to understand.

EXAMPLE 2

With the piecewise function created, you can now examine how the same mathematical results can be achieved using the tax computation worksheet. This is an important example and you should work through it meticulously with the class. They will have opportunities to do the same with worksheets for different filing statuses.

EXAMPLE 2

How does the piecewise function relate to the tax computation worksheet?

SOLUTION Examine the tax computation worksheet for married taxpayers filing jointly.

Section B — Use if your filing status is **Married filing jointly** or **Qualifying widow(er)**. Complete the row below that applies to you.

Taxable income If line 43 is—	(a) Enter the amount from line 43	(b) Multiplication amount	(c) Multiply (a) by (b)	(d) Subtraction amount	Tax Subtract (d) from (c). Enter the result here and on Form 1040, line 44
At least \$100,000 but not over \$131,450	\$	× 25% (.25)	\$	\$ 7,312.50	\$
Over \$131,450 but not over \$200,300	\$	× 28% (.28)	\$	\$ 11,256.00	\$
Over \$200,300 but not over \$357,700	\$	× 33% (.33)	\$	\$ 21,271.00	\$
Over \$357,700	\$	× 35% (.35)	\$	\$ 28,425.00	\$

Although the numbers in column (d) appear to have no mathematical significance, they can be found by using the distributive property for each of the equations in the piecewise function.

CHECK YOUR UNDERSTANDING

Answer $y = 0.28x - 11{,}256$; the slope is the multiplication amount in that row of the tax computation worksheet and the y-intercept, 11,256, is the subtraction amount

EXAMPLE 3

This example picks up where Example 2 left off. It asks students to follow the structure outlined in the previous example to express the equations in $y = mx + b$ form.

CHECK YOUR UNDERSTANDING

Answer $6,097.50

Looking at the incomes that are at least $65,100 but not over $131,450, the equation is

$$y = 8{,}962.5 + 0.25(x - 65{,}100)$$

where y represents the tax and x represents the taxable income. Use the distributive property and combine like terms as follows:

Start with the equation.	$y = 8{,}962.5 + 0.25(x - 65{,}100)$
Use the distributive property.	$y = 8{,}962.5 + 0.25x - 0.25(65{,}100)$
Multiply.	$y = 8{,}962.5 + 0.25x - 16{,}275$
Add like terms.	$y = 0.25x - 7{,}312.50$

The final equation is in the slope-intercept form of a linear equation. Recall the slope-intercept form of a linear equation is $y = mx + b$ where m represents the slope and b represents the y-intercept. The slope of this tax equation is 0.25 and the y-intercept is $-7{,}312.5$.

Return to the first line of the worksheet. For incomes that are at least $100,000 but not over $131,450, you are instructed to compute 25% of your taxable income and then subtract $7,312.50 from it to compute the tax.

Expressing the tax schedule equation in $y = mx + b$ form illustrates where the numbers in the tax computation worksheet came from.

CHECK YOUR UNDERSTANDING

The tax equation for incomes over $131,450 but not over $200,300 is $y = 25{,}550 + 0.28(x - 131{,}450)$. Simplify the equation and explain the numerical significance of the slope and the y-intercept.

EXAMPLE 3

Express the equations in the married taxpayers filing jointly schedule in $y = mx + b$ form.

SOLUTION Using the distributive property and combining like terms, each of the equations can be expressed as follows:

Tax Equation	$y = mx + b$ Form
$y = 0.10x$	$y = 0.10x$
$y = 1{,}605 + 0.15(x - 16{,}050)$	$y = 0.15x - 802.5$
$y = 8{,}962.50 + 0.25(x - 65{,}100)$	$y = 0.25x - 7{,}312.50$
$y = 25{,}550 + 0.28(x - 131{,}450)$	$y = 0.28x - 11{,}256$
$y = 44{,}828 + 0.33(x - 200{,}300)$	$y = 0.33x - 21{,}271$
$y = 96{,}770 + 0.35(x - 357{,}700)$	$y = 0.35x - 28{,}425$

CHECK YOUR UNDERSTANDING

Use the appropriate equation from Example 3 to determine the tax for an income of $46,000.

EXAMPLE 4

Examine the piecewise function $f(x)$ composed of the first three equations in Example 3.

$$f(x) = \begin{cases} 0.10x & 0 < x \le 16{,}050 \\ 0.15x - 802.5 & 16{,}050 < x \le 65{,}100 \\ 0.25x - 7{,}312.5 & 65{,}100 < x \le 131{,}450 \end{cases}$$

Graph the function on the appropriate interval.

SOLUTION Most graphing calculators have a feature that allows you to graph the parts of a piecewise function only on the given domains.

First, enter each of the three component equations of the piecewise function into the calculator as Y1, Y2, and Y3. Define them only on the appropriate domains using compound inequalities.

```
Plot1  Plot2  Plot3
\Y1■(.10X)(X>0 a
nd X≤16050)
\Y2■(.15X-802.5)
(X>16050 and X≤6
5100)
\Y3■(.25X-7312.5)
(X>65100 and X≤
131450)
```

Using a window of Xmin = 0, Xmax = 150000, Xscl = 15000, Ymin = 0, Ymax = 25000, and Yscl = 2500, the graph is shown.

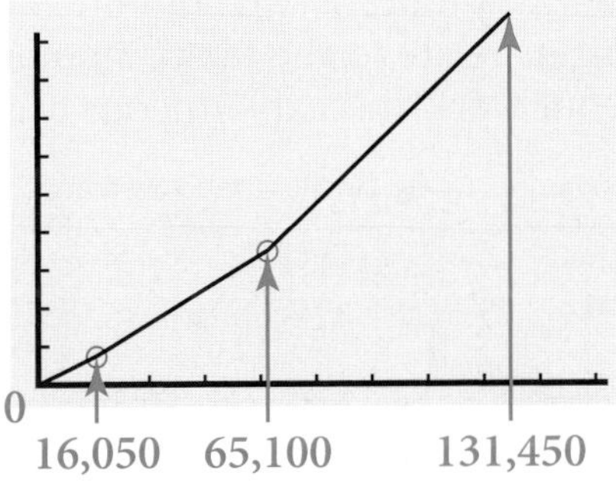

Notice that the three line segments do not have the same slope. The circled points on the graph are the cusps. The graph helps you understand the progressive tax rate system.

■ CHECK YOUR UNDERSTANDING

If you were to graph the fourth equation in the piecewise function, $y = 0.28x - 11{,}256$, where would you expect the last point in that equation to be? Explain your reasoning.

■ EXTEND YOUR UNDERSTANDING

What are the monetary implications of the fact that the slope of the last segment of the piecewise function is greater than the slope of the segment preceding it?

EXAMPLE 4

Students now learn how to use the graphing calculator to enter and graph the piecewise function. Be aware of the fact that each brand of calculator may use a different set of keystroke sequences for piecewise functions. Included is the most widely used type of graphing calculator. For this brand, it is important that the equation and the domain are both encased in separate sets of parentheses. Check your calculator owner's manual to make sure that you are familiar with the piecewise function process.

CHECK YOUR UNDERSTANDING

Answer (200,300, 44,828); it is the highest tax for that tax bracket.

EXTEND YOUR UNDERSTANDING

Answer The percent of income paid in federal taxes is greater; therefore, the amount of taxes paid is greater.

Applications

Taxes are paid in the sweat of every man who labors.
Franklin D. Roosevelt

1. How can the quote be interpreted in light of what you have learned? See margin.

Use the tax schedule for a single taxpayer for Exercises 2 and 3.

Schedule X— If your filing status is **Single**

If your taxable income is: Over—	But not over—	The tax is:	of the amount over—
$0	$8,025	.... 10%	$0
8,025	32,550	$802.50 + 15%	8,025
32,550	78,850	4,481.25 + 25%	32,550
78,850	164,550	16,056.25 + 28%	78,850
164,550	357,700	40,052.25 + 33%	164,550
357,700	....	103,791.75 + 35%	357,700

2. There are six taxable income intervals in this chart. Let x represent any taxable income. Express those intervals in tax schedule notation, interval notation, and compound inequality. See additional answers.

3. Let y represent the tax and x represent the taxable income of a single taxpayer. See margin.

a. Use the tax schedule to write three equations in $y = mx + b$ form for values of x that are greater than or equal to $100,000.

b. Use the distributive property and combine like terms to show how the equations relate to the tax computation worksheet below. Show your work and explain your reasoning.

TEACH

Exercise 4

Make sure that students have identified the correct domain for each portion of the piecewise function. It is important that the endpoints are included (or excluded) correctly.

ANSWERS

1. Income taxes are workers' taxes. Therefore, the taxes that are collected are a direct function of the work that the taxpayers do.
3. a. $y = 0.28x - 6{,}021.75$; $y = 0.33x - 14{,}249.25$; $y = 0.35x - 21{,}403.25$
   b. The equations demonstrate the transformation from the tax schedule to the tax worksheet.

Section A — Use if your filing status is **Single**. Complete the row below that applies to you.

Taxable income If line 43 is—	(a) Enter the amount from line 43	(b) Multiplication amount	(c) Multiply (a) by (b)	(d) Subtraction amount	**Tax** Subtract (d) from (c). Enter the result here and on Form 1040, line 44
At least $100,000 but not over $164,550	$	× 28% (.28)	$	$ 6,021.75	$
Over $164,550 but not over $357,700	$	× 33% (.33)	$	$ 14,249.25	$
Over $357,700	$	× 35% (.35)	$	$ 21,403.25	$

4. Write a piecewise function to represent the tax $f(x)$ for the first three taxable income intervals in the schedule for a married taxpayer who is filing separately. See additional answers.

Schedule Y-2— If your filing status is **Married filing separately**

If your taxable income is: Over—	But not over—	The tax is:	of the amount over—
$0	$8,025	.... 10%	$0
8,025	32,550	$802.50 + 15%	8,025
32,550	65,725	4,481.25 + 25%	32,550
65,725	100,150	12,775.00 + 28%	65,725
100,150	178,850	22,414.00 + 33%	100,150
178,850	....	48,385.00 + 35%	178,850

5. Use the 2000 tax schedule for a married taxpayer filing jointly. Write an equation in $y = mx + b$ form for a taxable income in the interval over $105,950 but not over $161,450. $y = 0.31x - 8{,}879$

6. Use the 2006 tax schedule for a married taxpayer filing jointly. Write the piecewise function for the tax intervals. See additional answers.

7. Use the tax schedule from Example 1 and Exercises 5 and 6. Select any income. Write an equation for that income for the three different years. Answers vary.

8. In 1998, a single taxpayer used this tax schedule. Let x represent the single taxpayer's taxable income and y represent that taxpayer's tax. Express the tax schedule as a piecewise function. See additional answers.

9. Use the tax computation worksheet for a head of household taxpayer. Let x represent the taxpayer's taxable income and y represent the tax. Express each line of the worksheet as a linear equation in $y = mx + b$ form. Use interval notation to define the income range on which each of your equations is defined. See margin.

2000 Tax Rate Schedule

Schedule Y-1— If your filing status is **Married filing jointly** or **Qualifying widow(er)**

If the amount on Form 1040 line 39, is: *Over—*	*But not over—*	Enter on Form 1040 line 40	*of the amount over—*
$0	$43,850	--------- 15%	$0
43,850	105,950	$6,577.50 + 28%	43,850
105,950	161,450	23,965.50 + 31%	105,950
161,450	288,350	41,170.50 + 36%	161,450
288,350	---------	86,854.50 + 39.6%	288,350

2006 Tax Rate Schedule

Schedule Y-1— If your filing status is **Married filing jointly** or **Qualifying widow(er)**

If your taxable income is: Over—	But not over—	The tax is:	of the amount over—
$0	$15,100	--------- 10%	$0
15,100	61,300	$1,510.00 + 15%	15,100
61,300	123,700	8,440.00 + 25%	61,300
123,700	188,450	24,040.00 + 28%	123,700
188,450	336,550	42,170.00 + 33%	188,450
336,550	---------	91,043.00 + 35%	336,550

1998 Tax Rate Schedule

Schedule X— If your filing status is **Single**

If the amount on Form 1040 line 39, is: *Over—*	*But not over—*	Enter on Form 1040 line 40	*of the amount over—*
$0	$25,350	--------- 15%	$0
25,350	61,400	$3,802.50 + 28%	25,350
61,400	128,100	13,896.50 + 31%	61,400
128,100	278,450	34,573.50 + 36%	128,100
278,450	---------	88,699.50 + 39.6%	278,450

Exercises 6–8
Offer students practice with a variety of different schedules from the turn of the century to the current date.

Section D — Use if your filing status is **Head of household**. Complete the row below that applies to you.

Taxable income. If line 43 is—	(a) Enter the amount from line 43	(b) Multiplication amount	(c) Multiply (a) by (b)	(d) Subtraction amount	Tax Subtract (d) from (c). Enter the result here and on Form 1040, line 44
At least $100,000 but not over $112,650	$	× 25% (.25)	$	$ 4,937.50	$
Over $112,650 but not over $182,400	$	× 28% (.28)	$	$ 8,317.00	$
Over $182,400 but not over $357,700	$	× 33% (.33)	$	$ 17,437.00	$
Over $357,700	$	× 35% (.35)	$	$ 24,591.00	$

ANSWERS

9. $y = 0.25x - 4{,}937.50$
$x \geq 100{,}000$ and $x \leq 112{,}650$
$y = 0.28x - 8{,}317.00$
$x > 112{,}650$ and $x \leq 182{,}400$
$y = 0.33x - 17{,}437.00$
$x > 182{,}400$ and $x \leq 357{,}700$
$y = 0.35x - 24{,}591.00$
$x > 357{,}700$

Exercises 9 and 10
Make sure that the keystroke sequences are written correctly. A misplaced or missing parenthesis can cause an error message or an incorrect graph.

ANSWERS

10a. $y = 0.28x - 6{,}083.50$;
$y = 0.33x - 12{,}951$;
$y = 0.35x - 19{,}530$

10. You are given this portion of a tax schedule from a previous year for single taxpayers with incomes over $71,950.

If your taxable income is: Over—	But not over—	The tax is:	of the amount over—
71,950	150,150	**14,062.50 + 28%**	**71,950**
150,150	326,450	**36,598.50 + 33%**	**150,150**
326,450	--------	**94,727.75 + 35%**	**326,450**

a. Model each of the three rows as a simplified equation in $y = mx + b$ form. See margin.

b. Create an associated tax computation spreadsheet for the tax schedule using the linear equations you have identified. A template for the worksheet is shown below. See additional answers.

	A	B	C	D	E	F
1	**Taxable Income**	**(a) Enter taxable income**	**(b) Multiplication amount**	**(c) Multiply (a) by (b)**	**(d) Subtraction amount**	**Tax Subtract (d) from (c)**
2	At least $71,950 but not over $150,150					
3	Over $150,150 but not over $326,450					
4	Over $326,450					

11. Examine the following tax computation worksheet. Let x represent the taxable income and y represent the tax.

Section C — Use if your filing status is **Married filing separately**. Complete the row below that applies to you.

Taxable income If line 43 is—	(a) Enter the amount from line 43	(b) Multiplication amount	(c) Multiply (a) by (b)	(d) Subtraction amount	**Tax** Subtract (d) from (c). Enter the result here and on Form 1040, line 44
At least $100,000 but not over $100,150	$	× 28% (.28)	$	$ 5,628.00	$
Over $100,150 but not over $178,850	$	× 33% (.33)	$	$ 10,635.50	$
Over $178,850	$	× 35% (.35)	$	$ 14,212.50	$

a. Let Y1 represent the graphing calculator function for taxable incomes on the interval over $100,150 but not over $178,850. Write the calculator keystroke sequence for the equation that models the tax on this interval. Be sure to include the interval definition. $(0.33x-10635.5)(x\geq100150 \text{ and } x<178850)$

b. Let Y2 represent the graphing calculator function for taxable incomes on the interval "Over 178,850." Write the calculator keystroke sequence for the equation that models the tax on this interval. Be sure to include the interval definition. $(0.35x-14212.5)(x\geq178850)$

12. Examine this tax schedule. Let x represent the taxable income and y represent the tax.

a. What is the calculator keystroke sequence for an equation that models the tax on the interval over 32,550 but not over 65,725? See margin.

b. What is the calculator keystroke sequence for an equation that models the tax on the interval over 100,150 but not over 178,850? $22414 + 0.33(x - 100150)(x > 100150 \text{ and } x \leq 178850)$

Schedule Y-2— If your filing status is **Married filing separately**

If your taxable income is: Over—	But not over—	The tax is:	of the amount over—
$0	$8,025	--------- 10%	$0
8,025	32,550	$802.50 + 15%	8,025
32,550	65,725	4,481.25 + 25%	32,550
65,725	100,150	12,775.00 + 28%	65,725
100,150	178,850	22,414.00 + 33%	100,150
178,850	---------	48,385.00 + 35%	178,850

13. Use the graph of a piecewise function with three equations.

a. A taxpayer has a taxable income of $39,800. What is her tax? $5,448

b. A taxpayer will owe $21,197. What is his taxable income? $102,800

c. What is the approximate tax for an income of $30,000? $4,500

d. What is the approximate tax for an income of $99,000? $20,500

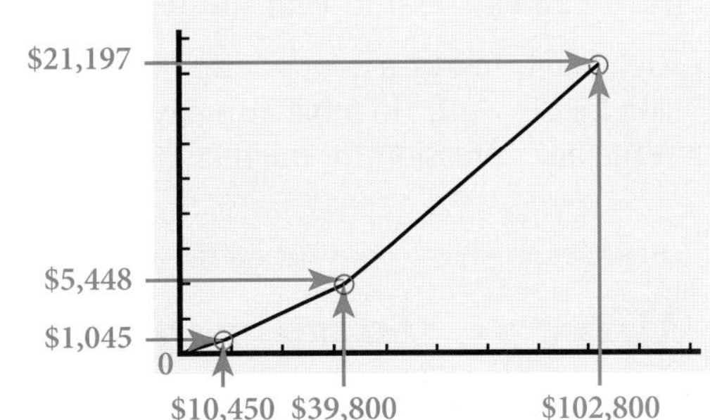

e. Nick is paid every other week. He has $390 taken out of each paycheck for federal taxes. What is his approximate taxable income? $68,000

14. Many people claim that once they are married, they pay more taxes than they did before they were married. Many call this a marriage penalty. Could this be true?

Suppose that Alli and DeWitt are lawyers and each has a taxable income of $140,000. They can't decide if they should be married in December or in January. If they marry in December, then they are considered married for the entire tax year and could file a joint return. If they get married in January of the next year, they would file a separate return each as a single taxpayer. Which filing status would yield the lower tax and by how much? single taxpayer; $4,772.50

Schedule X— If your filing status is **Single**

If your taxable income is: Over—	But not over—	The tax is:	of the amount over—
$0	$8,025	--------- 10%	$0
8,025	32,550	$802.50 + 15%	8,025
32,550	78,850	4,481.25 + 25%	32,550
78,850	164,550	16,056.25 + 28%	78,850
164,550	357,700	40,052.25 + 33%	164,550
357,700	--------	103,791.75 + 35%	357,700

Schedule Y-1— If your filing status is **Married filing jointly** or **Qualifying widow(er)**

If your taxable income is: Over—	But not over—	The tax is:	of the amount over—
$0	$16,050	--------- 10%	$0
16,050	65,100	$1,605.00 + 15%	16,050
65,100	131,450	8,962.50 + 25%	65,100
131,450	200,300	25,550.00 + 28%	131,450
200,300	357,700	44,828.00 + 33%	200,300
357,700	---------	96,770.00 + 35%	357,700

Exercise 14

Before assigning this problem, either have a discussion about the "Marriage Tax penalty" or ask students to do an Internet search on the subject.

ANSWERS

12a. $(4481.25+0.25(x-32550))(x>32550 \text{ and } x\leq 65725$

They take the money out of your paycheck before you can go out and spend it.

Robert Hopkins, Financial Advisor

7-3 Income Statements

Objectives

- Interpret and use the information on a pay stub, W-2 form, and 1099 form.

Common Core

A-SSE1, F-BF1

Key Terms

- gross pay
- net pay
- take-home pay
- paycheck
- pay stub
- Form W-4
- withholding tax
- Form W-2
- Form 1099
- tax-deferred contribution
- cafeteria plan
- flexible spending account (FSA)

CCSS Warm-Up

Write an expression that models this situation.

Rich wants to buy a coat priced at x dollars. It is on sale for 20% off. He must also pay 7.25% sales tax. Write an expression for the final price of the coat.

$(x - 0.20x) + 0.0725(x - 0.20x) = 0.80x + 0.0725x - 0.0145x = 0.858x$

EXAMINE THE QUESTION

Salary is a monetary agreement between an employee and employer for work performed. Unfortunately, the actual amount that an employee takes home is often far less than the agreed upon amount due to deductions from the salary. Before beginning the lesson, pre-assess students' knowledge of the types of deductions employees can have taken from their salaries.

CLASS DISCUSSION

Ask students to recall the definition of net proceeds from Chapter 1. How might the terms net proceeds and net pay be related?

Go to the IRS website (www.irs.gov) to find a copy of the W-4 form.

Why is your take-home pay lower than your salary?

Employees have many expenses. These include federal income tax, state income tax, city income tax, Social Security tax, Medicare tax, disability insurance fees, pension plan contributions, dental insurance fees, and medical insurance fees. These expenses can add to thousands of dollars each year. Rather than having employees pay these costs in a single yearly payment, they are distributed throughout the year. Amounts are deducted, or subtracted, from the employee's **gross pay**, or total pay. The amount of money that the employee takes home is the **net pay**, or **take-home pay**. With each **paycheck** on a **pay stub**, or pay slip, employees receive a listing of their wages and what amounts were deducted. These deductions are based on information that employees submit to their employers. The deductions for tax withholdings are based on information that employees submit on **Form W-4**, *Employees Withholding Allowance Certificate*. The employer withholds the deductions and sends the amount to the appropriate government or private agency. Federal, state, and local income taxes are **withholding taxes** since employers withhold these taxes and send them to the government. Social Security and Medicare payments are also withheld and sent to the government.

At the end of the year, an employer compiles a list of each employee's deductions. This information is usually on the last pay stub of the year. The withholding data is put on **Form W-2**, *Wage and Tax Statement*, which must be given to employees by the end of January. This information is used to compute federal, state, and local income taxes. When filing your income tax forms, you must submit a copy of your W-2.

Not all income comes from wages, salaries, and tips. People make money from interest on bank accounts, interest from stocks, royalties, and more. These types of income are not wages. It is up to taxpayers to report this income on their yearly tax forms. Rather than getting a W-2 form from these sources, taxpayers are sent a **Form 1099**. These amounts are reported to the government as well as the taxpayer.

Skills and Strategies

Here you will learn how to make calculations based on reading pay stubs, W-2, and 1099 forms.

EXAMPLE 1

Barbara started a new job and wants to verify that her net pay has been computed correctly. Her gross pay per pay period is $269.75. She has the following deductions: FICA tax 6.2%, Medicare tax 1.45%, federal withholding tax $47.51, state withholding tax $16.62, retirement insurance contribution $9.00, disability insurance fee $2.56, medical insurance fee $12.00, and dental insurance fee $6.00. What should her net pay be for this pay period?

SOLUTION First, calculate the Social Security and Medicare taxes to the nearest cent by multiplying the gross pay times the tax rate.

Social Security tax $269.75 \times 0.062 = 16.7245 \approx 16.72$

Medicare tax $269.75 \times 0.0145 = 3.911375 \approx 3.91$

Add all of the deductions to determine the total deductions.

$16.72 + 3.91 + 47.51 + 16.62 + 9.00 + 2.56 + 12.00 + 6.00 = 114.32$

Subtract deductions from gross pay. $269.75 - 114.32 = 155.43$

The net pay is $155.43.

CHECK YOUR UNDERSTANDING

What percentage of Barbara's gross pay for this pay period accounts for all of her deductions? Round to the nearest tenth of a percent.

EXAMPLE 2

Examine Lorna's biweekly pay stub. Assuming that Lorna's salary and deductions remain the same throughout the calendar year, how much will be taken out of her total annual gross salary for federal and state taxes?

EARNINGS		
PERIOD	AMOUNT	YTD AMOUNT
3/15 - 3/28	$4,596.39	$32,174.73
DEDUCTIONS		
TAX TYPE	AMOUNT	YTD AMOUNT
Social Security	$280.79	$1,999.63
Medicare	$65.67	$467.67
Federal Tax	$1,001.47	$7,067.89
State Tax	$280.89	$1,977.50
ADJUSTMENTS		
ITEM	AMOUNT	YTD AMOUNT
Union Dues	$61.00	$427.00
Family Health Ins.	$67.55	$472.85
Retirement	$50.00	$350.00

SOLUTION Lorna receives 26 paychecks a year. The federal and state deductions are constant. To find the total amount contributed to taxes, multiply the biweekly amounts by 26 and find the sum of those deductions.

Federal deduction $\times$ 26 = Federal deduction for year

$1{,}001.47 \times 26 = 26{,}038.22$

State deduction $\times$ 26 = State deduction for year

$280.89 \times 26 = 7{,}303.14$

Add the federal and state deductions. $26{,}038.22 + 7{,}303.14 = 33{,}341.36$

The total deduction for state and federal taxes for the year is $33,341.36.

TEACH

Discuss deductions that are taken from your paycheck (federal, state, and local taxes, medical insurance, union dues). Explain that taxes are withheld from salary and sent by the employer to the tax agency.

EXAMPLE 1

It is a good practice to periodically check the accuracy of the pay stub. The order that the deductions are made is irrelevant. Remind students that Medicare tax is paid on all income while there is a ceiling on the taxable income for Social Security tax.

CHECK YOUR UNDERSTANDING

Answer 42.4%

EXAMPLE 2

The assumption is made in this problem that Lorna will not reach the Social Security income limit.

CHECK YOUR UNDERSTANDING

Answer Yes; 35.4% of her annual salary will be deducted for taxes.

EXAMPLE 3

This may be the first time that students have seen a W-2 form. Before beginning this example, take a few moments to review the information that is included in this W-2 and discuss other data that could be included as well.

It is a taxpayer's responsibility to either complete tax forms on their own or use a tax preparation agency to do it. It is the employer's responsibility to give each employee a W-2 form no later than a specified date which can change from year to year. The due date is usually the end of January following the tax year.

CHECK YOUR UNDERSTANDING

Answer approximately 70.8%

Make sure that students read this problem correctly. The exercise is asking for the percent of the income she actually takes home and not the percent that she is taxed.

CHECK YOUR UNDERSTANDING

Employees can choose to increase their tax withholding if they feel that the amount calculated for the tax deductions may not be enough to meet the total tax at the end of the year. From her past records, Lorna knows that her total tax is usually 30% of her annual salary. At the rate of deduction shown on this pay stub, will Lorna's employer have taken enough out of each paycheck to meet her tax obligation for the year? Explain your answer.

The W-2 Form

Your personal W-2 form is a yearly accounting of your tax withholdings. It includes personal information about you as an employee, such as your name, address, and place of employment, Social Security number, taxable earnings, taxes paid, and more. If you work more than one job during a tax year, you will receive a W-2 form from each employer.

EXAMPLE 3

On January 30th, Joanne Toscano received this W-2 form from her employer. How much did Joanne pay in taxes during the year?

a Employee's social security number **000-00-0000** OMB No. 1545-0008 Safe, accurate, FAST! Use IRS e-file Visit the IRS website at www.irs.gov/efile.

b Employer identification number (EIN) **00-0000000**	1 Wages, tips, other compensation **$76,350.00**	2 Federal income tax withheld **$15,851.00**
c Employer's name, address, and ZIP code **Crawfish Castle 500 Pecan Parkway Colfax, Louisiana 71417**	3 Social security wages **$76,350.00**	4 Social security tax withheld **$4,733.70**
	5 Medicare wages and tips	6 Medicare tax withheld
	7 Social security tips	8 Allocated tips
d Control number	9 Advance EIC payment	10 Dependent care benefits
e Employee's first name and initial **Joanne S.** Last name **Toscano** Suff.	11 Nonqualified plans	12a See instructions for box 12
3 Delta Queen Drive Colfax, Louisiana 71417	13 Statutory employee / Retirement plan / Third-party sick pay	12b
	14 Other	12c
f Employee's address and ZIP code		12d

15 State Employer's state ID number	16 State wages, tips, etc.	17 State income tax	18 Local wages, tips, etc.	19 Local income tax	20 Locality name
00-0000000	$76,350.00	$5,344.50	$76,350.00	$1,092.00	

SOLUTION In this W-2 form, the Federal income tax withheld is listed in Box 2. The state tax is listed in Box 17, and the local income tax is listed in Box 19. The total amount that Joanne paid that year in taxes is the sum of the amounts in these three boxes.

$$15{,}851 + 5{,}344.50 + 1{,}092 = 22{,}287.50$$

Joanne's total amount paid in taxes for the year is $22,287.50.

CHECK YOUR UNDERSTANDING

What percent of Joanne's gross income did she actually take home?

EXAMPLE 4

Amy Springfield works for Pound Ridge Financial Planners. Her employer uses an electronic W-2 form as shown at the right. What accounts for the difference between her wages listed in Box 1 and her Social Security and Medicare wages listed in Boxes 3 and 5?

a Employee's social security number: 000-00-0000	OMB No. 1545-0008	Safe, accurate, FAST! Use IRS e-file	Visit the IRS website at www.irs.gov/efile.
b Employer identification number (EIN): 00-0000000		1 Wages, tips, other compensation: $78,900.00	2 Federal income tax withheld: $15,780.00
c Employer's name, address, and ZIP code: Pound Ridge Financial Planners, 2000 Hazelwood Lane, Riverdale, New York 10463		3 Social security wages: $92,100.00	4 Social security tax withheld: $5,710.20
		5 Medicare wages and tips: $92,100.00	6 Medicare tax withheld: $1,335.45
		7 Social security tips	8 Allocated tips
d Control number: 246-8977		9 Advance EIC payment	10 Dependent care benefits
e Employee's first name and initial: Amy	Last name: Springfield	11 Nonqualified plans	12a See instructions for box 12: E $12,200.00
8 Coughlin Drive, Ridgewood, NY 11385	Suff.	13 Statutory employee ☐ Retirement plan ☒ Third-party sick pay ☐	12b
		14 Other: caf125 $1,000.00	12c
f Employee's address and ZIP code			12d

15 State	Employer's state ID number	16 State wages, tips, etc.	17 State income tax	18 Local wages, tips, etc.	19 Local income tax	20 Locality name
	00-0000000	$78,900.00	$5,523.00			

SOLUTION There is a $13,200 difference between the amount in Box 1, $78,900, and the amount listed in both Boxes 3 and 5, $92,100. Both are earned wages, but they reflect different income amounts used for the calculation of Amy's taxes. The 6.2% Social Security tax and the 1.45% Medicare tax were calculated on $92,100, her total income.

Amy made **tax-deferred contributions** to her retirement plan. The $12,200, shown in Box 12a, was deducted from her gross earnings before any federal or state taxes were calculated. The money is being placed in a qualified retirement account; therefore, taxes on this money are deferred until Amy makes a withdrawal from the account after she retires.

The tax-deferred contribution to Amy's retirement fund only accounts for part of the difference. There is still $1,000 that must be identified. Box 14 lists Caf125 $1,000.

Section 125 of the U.S. Tax Code outlines a **cafeteria plan** in which employees can hold back a portion of their pre-tax wages for the payment of certain medical, childcare, parental care, and nonreimbursed medical insurance expenses. The cafeteria plan is a type of **flexible spending account (FSA)**. This is an employer-sponsored plan in which employees choose to deposit funds that will be used for the sole purposes outlined above and only in the specified 12-month period of time.

This is a "use it or lose it" plan. If all of the money in the plan is not spent by the end of the 12-month period, the money cannot return to the employee. Box 14 indicates that Amy deposited $1,000 into this account.

The sum of the tax-deferred contribution and the FSA deposit accounts for the difference in wage totals.

CHECK YOUR UNDERSTANDING

Amy pays 20% federal tax and 7% state tax. How much did she save in taxes by putting money in her tax deferred and flexible spending accounts?

EXAMPLE 4

The fact that this is an electronic W-2 form has no bearing on the information or the calculations. It is just an alternative way that an employer can provide the information to the employee. This example discusses tax-deferred contributions. Make sure that students understand the meaning of the word deferred. The contributions made to any tax-deferred plan will be taxed at some point in the future (usually after retirement) but at a different rate.

CHECK YOUR UNDERSTANDING

Answer $3,564

This problem can be solved in more than one way. Once students have a solution, encourage them to find an alternative method.

1099 Form

Another type of income statement is the Internal Revenue Service's Form 1099. This form is used to report different types of income other than wages, salaries, and tips such as bank interest, royalties, contracted work, and so on. Different 1099 forms are used depending upon the income type. An example of a 1099 form is shown here for a taxpayer who makes royalties from the sale of a book that he wrote.

Unlike the wages reported on the W-2 form, 1099 income has yet to be taxed. It will be added to the employee's total income and used in the calculation of taxes when filling out the income tax return.

☐ CORRECTED (if checked)

PAYER'S name, street address, city, state, ZIP code, and telephone no.		1 Rents	OMB No. 1545-0115	
North-Eastern Publishing Co. **2112 South Street** **Cincinnati, Ohio 45231**		$ 2 Royalties $ **5,678.90**	Form **1099-MISC**	**Miscellaneous Income**
		3 Other income $	**4 Federal income tax withheld** $	Copy B For Recipient
PAYER'S federal identification number **00-0000000**	RECIPIENT'S identification number **000-00-0000**	5 Fishing boat proceeds $	6 Medical and health care payments $	
RECIPIENT'S name **Avdi Eamon**		7 Nonemployee compensation $	8 Substitute payments in lieu of dividends or interest $	This is important tax information and is being furnished to the Internal Revenue Service. If you are required to file a return, a negligence penalty or other sanction may be imposed on you if this income is taxable and the IRS determines that it has not been reported.
Street address (including apt. no.) **PO Box 1234** City, state, and ZIP code **Delphia, KY 41735**		9 Payer made direct sales of $5,000 or more of consumer products to a buyer (recipient) for resale ► ☐ 11	10 Crop insurance proceeds $ 12	
Account number (see instructions) **0008733**		13 Excess golden parachute payments $	14 Gross proceeds paid to an attorney $	
15a Section 409A deferrals $	15b Section 409A income $	16 State tax withheld $ $	17 State/Payer's state no.	18 State income $ $

Form **1099-MISC**

Avdi must report this royalty amount as income when filling out her income tax forms.

All of the IRS forms and instruction booklets can be accessed on the Internal Revenue website at www.irs.gov.

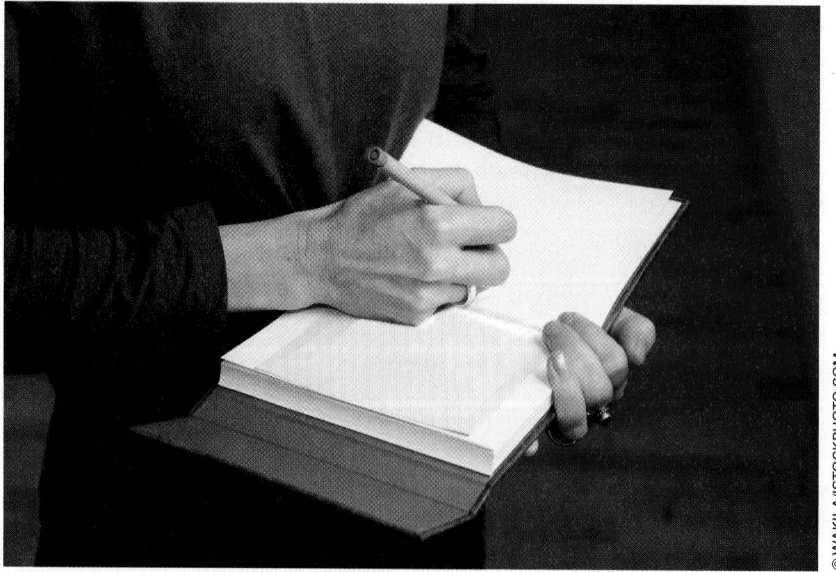

© WAKILA/ISTOCKPHOTO.COM

Applications

They take the money out of your paycheck before you can go out and spend it.

Robert Hopkins, Financial Advisor

1. How can the quote be interpreted in light of what you have learned? See margin.

2. Joe makes an hourly wage of $8.10. For hours worked over 40, he is paid at a rate of $12.15 per hour. Last week, Joe worked 45 hours.
   a. What is Joe's gross pay for this pay period? $384.75
   b. What is Joe's Social Security deduction? $23.85
   c. What is Joe's Medicare tax deduction? $5.58
   d. Joe's other deductions are: federal tax $61.12, state tax $21.03, city tax $6.01, retirement insurance $4.12, disability insurance $1.31, medical insurance $13.05, and dental insurance $5.46. What are Joe's total deductions for this pay period? $141.53
   e. What is Joe's net pay for this pay period? $243.22
   f. If Joe pays the same amount for medical insurance each weekly pay period, what is his annual premium? $678.60
   g. Does Joe receive time-and-a-half, double-time, or triple-time for each hour of overtime? time-and-a-half

3. Leslie works for Blanck Corporation. His annual salary is $57,285.50.
   a. What is Leslie's annual Social Security deduction? $3,551.70
   b. What is Leslie's annual Medicare deduction? $830.64
   c. Leslie is paid every other week. What is his biweekly gross pay? $2,203.29
   d. Each pay period, Leslie's employer deducts $418.63 for federal withholding tax. What percentage of Leslie's yearly salary is deducted for federal withholdings? approximately 19%
   e. If Leslie is taxed at an annual rate of 3.65% for city tax, how much is deducted from his salary per paycheck for city tax? $80.42
   f. Leslie's net pay for each pay period is $1,347.34. What percent of his biweekly gross pay is deducted from his salary to yield this net pay amount? approximately 39%
   g. As of January 1, Leslie will receive a 12.5% raise. What will Leslie's new annual salary be? $64,446.19
   h. If the percentage of his biweekly deductions remains the same, what should Leslie's new net pay be for each pay period? $1,512.01

4. Use the partial information given in this electronic W-2 form to calculate the amount in Box 1. $66,694

45-0008 Safe, accurate, FAST! Use IRS e-file. Visit the IRS website at www.irs.gov/efile.

1 Wages, tips, other compensation	2 Federal income tax withheld
3 Social security wages	4 Social security tax withheld
5 Medicare wages and tips $73,094.00	6 Medicare tax withheld
7 Social security tips	8 Allocated tips
9 Advance EIC payment	10 Dependent care benefits
11 Nonqualified plans	12a See instructions for box 12 Code E $1,900.00
13 Statutory employee / Retirement plan / Third-party sick pay	12b Code
14 Other caf125 $4,500.00	12c Code
	12d Code

me tax	18 Local wages, tips, etc.	19 Local income tax	20 Locality name

TEACH

Exercises 2, 3, and 5
These exercises assess students' knowledge of pay periods and the pay stub data. It is important that students complete either (or both) of the first two exercises before attempting the algebraic representations in Exercise 5.

ANSWERS

1. The intent of Hopkins's quote was to make a point about direct withdrawals into savings and retirement accounts. But, it applies to the multitude of deductions discussed in this lesson. Money is taken out of your paycheck and sent to the appropriate governmental agencies and/or banks before you have a chance to spend it.

Exercise 6
An incorrect answer at the beginning of this exercise can cause subsequent responses to also be incorrect. Make sure that students double check their work for accuracy before moving on to the next part of this problem.

Exercises 7, 12, and 13
These exercises offer students different scenarios in which taxable income is reduced by tax-deferred withholdings. Although similar, they each ask students to solve for a different variable. Make sure that students fully understand what is being asked before attempting each problem.

5. Let A represent the number of the paycheck for the year. For example, if the paycheck was the fifth of the year, A is 5. Let B represent the biweekly gross pay. Let C represent the biweekly union dues contribution. Let D represent the biweekly health insurance deduction. Let E represent the biweekly retirement plan contribution.

a. Write an expression for the calendar year-to-date gross pay. AB
b. Write an expression for the pay period Social Security tax. $0.062B$
c. Write an expression for the calendar year-to-date Social Security tax (assume that the maximum will not be met). $0.062AB$
d. Write an expression for the pay period Medicare tax. $0.0145B$
e. Write an expression for the calendar year-to-date Medicare tax. $0.0145AB$
f. Write an expression for the calendar year-to-date union dues. AC
g. Write an expression for the calendar year-to-date health insurance deduction. AD
h. Write an expression for the calendar year-to-date retirement plan deduction. AE
i. Assume that the taxpayer pays 21% federal taxes. Write an expression for the pay period federal tax deduction. $0.21B$
j. Assume that the taxpayer pays 11% state taxes. Write an expression for the state tax deduction for a pay period. $0.11B$
k. Write an algebraic expression that represents the net pay for this pay period. $B - 0.062B - 0.0145B - C - D - E - 0.21B - 0.11B$

6. Complete the missing entries in the following pay stub.

EARNINGS		
PERIOD	AMOUNT	YTD AMOUNT
WEEKLY - #18	**a.**	$21,510
DEDUCTIONS		
TAX TYPE	AMOUNT	YTD AMOUNT
Social Security	**b.**	**c.**
Medicare	**d.**	**e.**
Federal Tax	$322.65	$5,807.70
State Tax	$191.20	$3,441.60
ADJUSTMENTS		
ITEM	AMOUNT	YTD AMOUNT
Union Dues	**f.**	$216.00
Family Health Ins.	$23.95	**g.**

a. As indicated in the paycheck number box, this is the 18th paycheck of the year. Determine the current gross pay. $1,195
b. What is the Social Security tax for this pay period? $74.09
c. What is the year-to-date Social Security tax? $1,333.62
d. What is the Medicare tax for this pay period? $17.33
e. What is the year-to-date Medicare tax? $311.94
f. What are the union dues for this pay period if it is paid weekly? $12
g. What is the year-to-date health insurance contribution if it is paid weekly? $431.10
h. What is the state tax rate? 16%
i. What is the federal tax rate? 27%

7. Andres is taxed at a 17% tax rate for his federal taxes. Last year, he reduced his taxable income by contributing $350 per biweekly paycheck to his tax deferred retirement account and $50 per biweekly paycheck to his FSA. How much did he reduce his annual federal taxes by if his gross biweekly pay is $1,870? $1,768

8. Examine this portion of a taxpayer's W-2 form. Assume that the taxpayer's wages for the year are under the Social Security limit. What entry should be in Box 1? $77,255

Safe, accurate, FAST! Use IRS e-file. Visit the IRS website at www.irs.gov/efile. 545-0008

1 Wages, tips, other compensation	2 Federal income tax withheld
3 Social security wages	4 Social security tax withheld $4,789.81
5 Medicare wages and tips	6 Medicare tax withheld
7 Social security tips	8 Allocated tips
9 Advance EIC payment	10 Dependent care benefits

9. Let the Medicare tax withheld in Box 6 be represented by *x* as shown. Write an algebraic expression that represents the federal income tax withheld assuming that the taxpayer pays 28% of his income in federal taxes and that there are no tax deferred entries for the year. $0.28\left(\frac{x}{0.0145}\right)$

Safe, accurate, FAST! Use IRS e-file. Visit the IRS website at www.irs.gov/efile. 45-0008

1 Wages, tips, other compensation	2 Federal income tax withheld
3 Social security wages	4 Social security tax withheld
5 Medicare wages and tips	6 Medicare tax withheld *x*
7 Social security tips	8 Allocated tips
9 Advance EIC payment	10 Dependent care benefits

10. Determine the correct entry for Box 4. $5,758.56

Safe, accurate, FAST! Use IRS e-file. Visit the IRS website at www.irs.gov/efile. 45-0008

1 Wages, tips, other compensation	2 Federal income tax withheld
3 Social security wages	4 Social security tax withheld
5 Medicare wages and tips	6 Medicare tax withheld $1,346.76
7 Social security tips	8 Allocated tips
9 Advance EIC payment	10 Dependent care benefits

11. Determine the correct entry for Box 1 assuming that the taxpayer pays 33% of his total income in federal taxes. $121,900

Safe, accurate, FAST! Use IRS e-file. Visit the IRS website at www.irs.gov/efile. 45-0008

1 Wages, tips, other compensation	2 Federal income tax withheld $40,227.00
3 Social security wages	4 Social security tax withheld
5 Medicare wages and tips	6 Medicare tax withheld
7 Social security tips	8 Allocated tips
9 Advance EIC payment	10 Dependent care benefits

12. Martina is taxed at a rate of 25% for her federal taxes. Last year, she reduced her taxable income by contributing to a flexible savings plan in the amount of $2,700. If her wages before the deduction were $68,000, how much did she save in federal taxes by using the FSA? $675

13. Laurel's W-2 form reported total Medicare wages as $100,750. She contributed $30 per weekly paycheck to her FSA and $75 per weekly paycheck to her retirement plan. She received a 1099 form from her bank for her savings account interest in the amount of $690 and a 1099 form from an employer that she did some consulting work for in the amount of $2,600. What is Laurel's taxable income? $98,580

Exercises 8–11
Point out to students that the W-2 forms shown in these exercises are just a portion of a complete form. Although W-2 forms do not all look alike, they must all contain the same information of the employee. These partial W-2 forms are shown this way to save space in the textbook.

> *It is my belief that one's salary is between an individual and the IRS.*
>
> **Jessica Savitch,** American Journalist

7-4 Forms 1040EZ and 1040A

Objectives

- Complete Form 1040EZ.
- Complete Form 1040A.

Common Core

A-SSE1, A-CED3

Key Terms

- Form 1040EZ
- Form 1040A
- Form 1040
- dependent
- exemption
- itemize
- standard deduction

CCSS Warm-Up

Determine whether the point (5, 36) is in the solution set for each inequality.

1. $y - 2x \geq -3$ **2.** $y > 2^x$ **3.** $y \leq x^2 - 4x + 4$

1. yes 2. yes 3. no

EXAMINE THE QUESTION

Taxpayers report income, deductions, and exemptions to the government in the yearly forms they submit to the Internal Revenue Service. The forms presented in the next two lessons are the three basic tax forms. But, there are hundreds of other forms that can be completed by the taxpayer. You can show students a list of the names of forms so that they have an understanding of the enormity of the tax reporting system.

How do taxpayers report their income to the government?

It is common for a person's tax to be several thousand dollars, and most people pay their tax regularly through payroll deductions. The employer withholds federal, state, and local taxes from each paycheck. At the end of the year, each employee's annual income and the amounts withheld are reported on Form W-2. Once you get your W-2 form from your employer, you need to determine your actual tax for the past year, based on your earnings and your deductions. You then compare the tax you must pay to the amount your employer withheld during that year. If your tax is exactly equal to the amount withheld, your taxes are paid for the year. However, this is an unlikely event. It is very difficult to estimate exactly what your tax will be in advance.

If your employer withholds more than the tax you owe, you are entitled to a refund. If your employer withholds less than the tax you owe, you must pay the government the difference. You must furnish all of this information to the government on a tax return. If you owe the government money, you must pay that amount when you file your return. If the government owes you money, you will receive it after your return has been processed.

There are three basic Internal Revenue Service tax returns. **Form 1040EZ** and **Form 1040A** are short forms, and **Form 1040** is a long form. The two short forms will be addressed in this lesson and the long form will be covered in the next lesson. On all of these forms, the IRS allows the taxpayer to round monetary entries to the nearest dollar.

CLASS DISCUSSION

The text introduces students to the three possible tax situations: underpayment of taxes, overpayment of taxes, and exact payment of taxes.

Skills and Strategies

Here you will learn the skills that are essential for accurately filling out Forms 1040EZ and 1040A. On any tax form, you must fill out your name, address, Social Security number, and filing status. Depending upon the form, you must also supply information about family members that you support financially. Each person you support is a **dependent**. You receive an **exemption** for each of your dependents, which lowers the amount of your taxable income. You can also claim yourself as an exemption.

While exact payment is a statistical improbability, there are many people who prefer overpaying their taxes so that they have a "forced savings plan". Ask students why a bank savings account would be a better option.

Why do you think that the IRS allows a taxpayer to claim him/herself as an exemption?

FORM 1040EZ

It is important to select the correct short form based upon the requirements outlined by the IRS. There is a list of the requirements at the front of the instruction booklets for each of these tax forms. Some of the major requirements to file form 1040EZ are

- Your filing status must be single or married filing jointly only.
- You have no dependents, other than yourself and your spouse, to claim.
- Your taxable income is less than $100,000.
- Your income is only from wages, salaries, tips, taxable scholarships, fellowship grants, unemployment compensation, or Alaska Permanent Fund dividends.
- Your taxable interest is not over $1,500.

TEACH

Before teaching this lesson, you could contact the IRS for a class set of forms and instruction booklets.

Give students an assignment to go on the IRS website and research the three basic tax forms (1040EZ, 1040A, and 1040). Let them know that there are requirements that must be in place to use each type of form.

EXAMPLE 1

Elizabeth Allison is a food editor for a magazine. She has received a W-2 form from her employer and a 1099 form from her savings bank. What is Elizabeth's taxable income for the year if she files as a single taxpayer?

a Employee's social security number: 000-00-0000	OMB No. 1545-0008; Safe, accurate, FAST! Use IRS e-file; Visit the IRS website at www.irs.gov/efile.
b Employer identification number (EIN): 00-0000000	1 Wages, tips, other compensation: $83,600.00 — 2 Federal income tax withheld: $15,884.00
c Employer's name, address, and ZIP code: Food For Thought, 15 Chestnut Street, Philadelphia, Pennsylvania 19144	3 Social security wages: $83,600.00 — 4 Social security tax withheld: $5,183.20
	5 Medicare wages and tips: $83,600.00 — 6 Medicare tax withheld: $1,212.20
	7 Social security tips — 8 Allocated tips
d Control number	9 Advance EIC payment — 10 Dependent care benefits
e Employee's first name and initial: Elizabeth; Last name: Allison; Suff.	11 Nonqualified plans — 12a See instructions for box 12
	13 Statutory employee / Retirement plan / Third-party sick pay — 12b
6204 Lincoln Street, Philadelphia, Pennsylvania 19144	14 Other — 12c — 12d
f Employee's address and ZIP code	

15 State	Employer's state ID number	16 State wages, tips, etc.	17 State income tax	18 Local wages, tips, etc.	19 Local income tax	20 Locality name
	00-0000000	$83,600.00	$10,032.00			

EXAMPLE 1

Here, students are given a taxpayer's W-2 and 1099 form. The information on these forms will be used in Examples 1, 2, and 3 as students complete a 1040EZ for the taxpayer in 3 stages. Example 1 is the first stage of the form. Students use the W-2 and 1099 information to determine the taxable income for the taxpayer.

CHECK YOUR UNDERSTANDING

Answer Line 5 would be $17,900, which would make line 6 $66,656. Lines 1–4 would remain the same.

☐ CORRECTED (if checked)

PAYER'S name, street address, city, state, ZIP code, and telephone no.	Payer's RTN (optional)	OMB No. 1545-0112	
First National Bank 1517 Pine Street Philadelphia, PA 14145	1 Interest income $ 956.00 2 Early withdrawal penalty $	Form 1099-INT	Interest Income
PAYER'S federal identification number 00-0000000 / RECIPIENT'S identification number 000-00-0000	3 Interest on U.S. Savings Bonds and Treas. obligations $		Copy B For Recipient This is important tax information and is being furnished to the Internal Revenue Service. If you are required to file a return, a negligence penalty or other sanction may be imposed on you if this income is taxable and the IRS determines that it has not been reported.
RECIPIENT'S name Elizabeth Allison	4 Federal income tax withheld $	5 Investment expenses $	
Street address (including apt. no.) 6201 Linclon Street	6 Foreign tax paid $	7 Foreign country or U.S. possession	
City, state, and ZIP code Philadelphia, PA 14144	8 Tax-exempt interest	9 Specified private activity bond interest	
Account number (see instructions)	$	$	

Form **1099-INT**

SOLUTION Elizabeth's gross income as reported on her W-2 was $83,600.

She also made $956 in interest as reported on her 1099 form.

After she completes the label portion of the 1040EZ form, she must list her income and interest amounts. The sum of these amounts is her adjusted gross income.

$$83{,}600 + 956 = 84{,}556$$

Since Elizabeth is filing as a single taxpayer and no one can claim her as a dependent, she can take an $8,950 deduction from her adjusted gross income. That deduction is entered and her taxable income is the difference between her adjusted gross income and the deduction, or $75,606.

This amount is entered as shown in Elizabeth's 1040EZ form below.

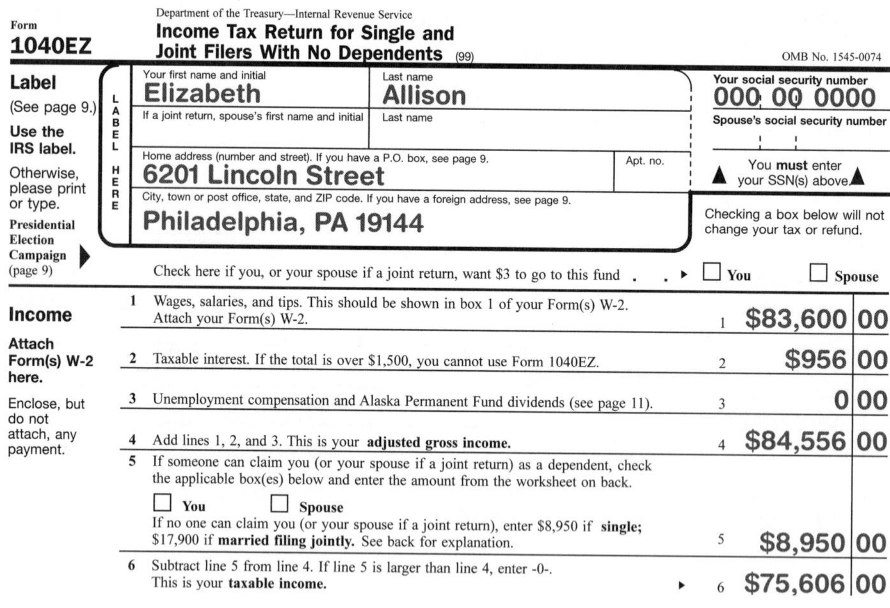

Form **1040EZ** Department of the Treasury—Internal Revenue Service
Income Tax Return for Single and Joint Filers With No Dependents (99) OMB No. 1545-0074

Label (See page 9.) **Use the IRS label.** Otherwise, please print or type. LABEL HERE

Your first name and initial: Elizabeth | Last name: Allison | Your social security number: 000 00 0000

If a joint return, spouse's first name and initial | Last name | Spouse's social security number

Home address (number and street). If you have a P.O. box, see page 9.: 6201 Lincoln Street | Apt. no. | ▲ You **must** enter your SSN(s) above.▲

City, town or post office, state, and ZIP code. If you have a foreign address, see page 9.: Philadelphia, PA 19144

Presidential Election Campaign (page 9) ▶ Check here if you, or your spouse if a joint return, want $3 to go to this fund . ▶ ☐ You ☐ Spouse — Checking a box below will not change your tax or refund.

Income			
Attach Form(s) W-2 here. Enclose, but do not attach, any payment.	1 Wages, salaries, and tips. This should be shown in box 1 of your Form(s) W-2. Attach your Form(s) W-2.	1	$83,600 00
	2 Taxable interest. If the total is over $1,500, you cannot use Form 1040EZ.	2	$956 00
	3 Unemployment compensation and Alaska Permanent Fund dividends (see page 11).	3	0 00
	4 Add lines 1, 2, and 3. This is your **adjusted gross income.**	4	$84,556 00
	5 If someone can claim you (or your spouse if a joint return) as a dependent, check the applicable box(es) below and enter the amount from the worksheet on back. ☐ You ☐ Spouse If no one can claim you (or your spouse if a joint return), enter $8,950 if **single;** $17,900 if **married filing jointly.** See back for explanation.	5	$8,950 00
	6 Subtract line 5 from line 4. If line 5 is larger than line 4, enter -0-. This is your **taxable income.** ▶	6	$75,606 00

■ **CHECK YOUR UNDERSTANDING**

How would Elizabeth's tax form above differ if she were married, filing a joint return, assuming that her spouse had no income to report?

EXTEND YOUR UNDERSTANDING

Suppose that a single taxpayer's wages are *w* dollars and taxable interest is *d* dollars. Write an algebraic expression for the taxpayer's taxable income.

EXAMPLE 2

What is Elizabeth's tax?

SOLUTION Through employer withholding, Elizabeth has already paid $15,884 in federal taxes. She must use the tax tables to determine the tax she owes. From the tax table, Elizabeth owes $15,250. She enters her income tax withheld from her W-2 and the tax table amount in the payments and tax section of the tax form as shown.

Payments and tax				
7	Federal income tax withheld from box 2 of your Form(s) W-2.	7	$15,884	00
8a	**Earned income credit (EIC)** (see page 12).	8a	0	00
b	Nontaxable combat pay election. 8b			
9	Recovery rebate credit (see worksheet on pages 17 and 18).	9		
10	Add lines 7, 8a, and 9. These are your **total payments.** ▶	10	$15,884	00
11	**Tax.** Use the amount on **line 6 above** to find your tax in the tax table on pages 28–36 of the booklet. Then, enter the tax from the table on this line.	11	$15,250	00

CHECK YOUR UNDERSTANDING

Suppose that Elizabeth had been filing as married filing jointly with her husband, and their combined taxable income was the same as reported on line 6. Why is that tax lower?

EXAMPLE 3

Does Elizabeth get a refund or owe the government money? In either case, determine that amount.

SOLUTION Elizabeth compares the amount her employer withheld with the amount she actually owes. Form 1040EZ leads taxpayers through the steps necessary to make the determination as to whether they owe or are owed money. Elizabeth is asked whether the total withheld payments are greater than the calculated tax from the tax table. If yes, then Elizabeth overpaid her taxes and she would get a refund. This is the case for Elizabeth. As instructed, Elizabeth subtracts the calculated tax from the total payments to determine her refund.

$$15{,}884 - 15{,}250 = 634$$

Elizabeth will get $634 as her federal tax refund.

Notice that Elizabeth has included her bank information so that her refund can be directly deposited into her bank account. To complete her return, Elizabeth must sign it, attach the federal copy of her W-2 form to the return, and mail it to the appropriate IRS office for processing.

Refund Have it directly deposited! See page 18 and fill in 12b, 12c, and 12d or Form 8888.	12a	If line 10 is larger than line 11, subtract line 11 from line 10. This is your **refund.** If Form 8888 is attached, check here ▶ ☐	12a	$634	00
	▶ b	Routing number 123456789 ▶ c Type: ☒ Checking ☐ Savings			
	▶ d	Account number 00011122233344455			
Amount you owe	13	If line 11 is larger than line 10, subtract line 10 from line 11. This is the **amount you owe.** For details on how to pay, see page 19. ▶	13		

EXTEND YOUR UNDERSTANDING

Answer $w + d - 8{,}950$

EXAMPLE 2

In this example, students are asked to use the partially completed form from Example 1 to calculate the taxpayer's tax. Elizabeth's taxable income is $75,606. Students are given a partial tax table to determine the tax.

If Form 1040EZ, line 6, is– At least	But less than	And you are– Single	Married filing jointly
		Your tax is–	
75,000			
75,000	75,050	15,100	11,444
75,050	75,100	15,113	11,456
75,100	75,150	15,125	11,469
75,150	75,200	15,138	11,481
75,200	75,250	15,150	11,494
75,250	75,300	15,163	11,506
75,300	75,350	15,175	11,519
75,350	75,400	15,188	11,531
75,400	75,450	15,200	11,544
75,450	75,500	15,213	11,556
75,500	75,550	15,225	11,569
75,550	75,600	15,238	11,581
75,600	75,650	15,250	11,594
75,650	75,700	15,263	11,606
75,700	75,750	15,275	11,619
75,750	75,800	15,288	11,631
75,800	75,850	15,300	11,644
75,850	75,900	15,313	11,656
75,900	75,950	15,325	11,669
75,950	76,000	15,338	11,681

CHECK YOUR UNDERSTANDING

Answer Because the income is from two taxpayers, which means that individually, each had a lower taxable income.

EXAMPLE 3

Students need to refer back to the W-2 form presented on page 347. After computing Elizabeth's tax liability, they need to compare that amount with the amount withheld by her employer. Since the tax due is less than the withheld amount, Elizabeth gets a refund.

CHECK YOUR UNDERSTANDING

Answer He owes money; $1,045

EXTEND YOUR UNDERSTANDING

Answer If $w > t$, then the taxpayer receives a refund of $w - t$ dollars.

■ CHECK YOUR UNDERSTANDING

Leo is filling out his 1040EZ form. His employer withheld $12,907 in federal taxes. He has calculated that he owes $13,952. Does he get a refund or owe money? In either case, what is the amount?

■ EXTEND YOUR UNDERSTANDING

Suppose a taxpayer's withheld tax from line 7 is represented by w and the calculated federal tax from line 10 is represented by t. Write an inequality that represents the conditions when the taxpayer would get a refund. Then write an algebraic expression that represents the amount of the refund.

FORM 1040A

Kenya and Robin Omar are married with one child, Kenya is a pharmacist and Robin is a store manager. Their W-2 forms are shown below. They received $987 interest on bank deposits and $1,200 in stock dividends.

a Employee's social security number 000-00-0000	OMB No. 1545-0008	Safe, accurate, FAST! Use IRS e-file	Visit the IRS website at www.irs.gov/efile.
b Employer identification number (EIN) 00-0000000		1 Wages, tips, other compensation $65,120.97	2 Federal income tax withheld $8,765.99
c Employer's name, address, and ZIP code SuperBuy Department Store 7 Highway B Novelty, Ohio 44072		3 Social security wages $65,120.97	4 Social security tax withheld $4,037.50
		5 Medicare wages and tips $65,120.97	6 Medicare tax withheld $944.25
		7 Social security tips	8 Allocated tips
d Control number 09564		9 Advance EIC payment	10 Dependent care benefits
e Employee's first name and initial Robin · Last name Omar · Suff.		11 Nonqualified plans	12a See instructions for box 12
14 Rachel Drive Walnut Creek, Ohio 44684		13 Statutory employee · Retirement plan · Third-party sick pay	12b
		14 Other	12c
f Employee's address and ZIP code			12d

15 State	Employer's state ID number	16 State wages, tips, etc.	17 State income tax	18 Local wages, tips, etc.	19 Local income tax	20 Locality name
	00-0000000	$65,120.97	$7,654.91			

a Employee's social security number 000-00-0000	OMB No. 1545-0008	Safe, accurate, FAST! Use IRS e-file	Visit the IRS website at www.irs.gov/efile.
b Employer identification number (EIN) 00-0000000		1 Wages, tips, other compensation $52,126.76	2 Federal income tax withheld $6,198.65
c Employer's name, address, and ZIP code Ruby Ridge Hospital 76 Ridge Road Walnut Creek, Ohio 44684		3 Social security wages $52,126.76	4 Social security tax withheld $3,231.86
		5 Medicare wages and tips $52,126.76	6 Medicare tax withheld $755.84
		7 Social security tips	8 Allocated tips
d Control number 09564		9 Advance EIC payment	10 Dependent care benefits
e Employee's first name and initial Kenya · Last name Omar · Suff.		11 Nonqualified plans	12a See instructions for box 12
14 Rachel Drive Walnut Creek, Ohio 44684		13 Statutory employee · Retirement plan · Third-party sick pay	12b
		14 Other	12c
f Employee's address and ZIP code			12d

15 State	Employer's state ID number	16 State wages, tips, etc.	17 State income tax	18 Local wages, tips, etc.	19 Local income tax	20 Locality name
	00-0000000	$52,126.76	$3,198.10			

The Omars have a dependent child, so they cannot use form 1040EZ. They have looked over their records for the year and determined that they do not have enough deductions to **itemize** (list), so they will not use the long 1040 form. In order to use Form 1040A, they must have a combined taxable income of less than \$100,000. Although their combined gross income is slightly greater than this amount, they know that amount will be reduced because of exemptions and deductions they will claim. An exemption is an allowable amount that reduces the taxable income based upon certain requirements as outlined in the IRS instruction booklet.

EXAMPLE 4

How many exemptions can Mr. and Mrs. Omar claim?

SOLUTION After the label portion of the 1040A tax form is completed, Mr. and Mrs. Omar identify their filing status as married filing jointly by checking the appropriate box. They then list their exemptions. The Omars can take themselves as an exemption and therefore enter 2 on the line to the right in the exemptions section. The form asks for the name and Social Security number of any dependents. They enter the information about their son and since he does live with them, 1 is placed on the line indicating the number of dependents living at home. There are no other dependents. The total exemptions, 3, is entered at the bottom.

Form **1040A** Department of the Treasury—Internal Revenue Service
U.S. Individual Income Tax Return (99) IRS Use Only—Do not write or staple in this space.
OMB No. 1545-0074

Label (See page 17.)
LABEL HERE

Use the IRS label. Otherwise, please print or type.

Your first name and initial: **Kenya**	Last name: **Omar**	**Your social security number**: 000 : 00 : 0000
If a joint return, spouse's first name and initial: **Robin**	Last name: **Omar**	**Spouse's social security number**: 000 : 00 : 0000
Home address (number and street). If you have a P.O. box, see page 17.: **14 Rachel Drive**	Apt. no.	▲ You **must** enter your SSN(s) above ▲
City, town or post office, state, and ZIP code. If you have a foreign address, see page 17.: **Walnut Creek, Ohio 44684**		Checking a box below will not change your tax or refund.

Presidential Election Campaign ▶ Check here if you, or your spouse if filing jointly, want \$3 to go to this fund (see page 17) ▶ ☐ You ☐ Spouse

Filing status Check only one box.
1 ☐ Single
2 ☒ Married filing jointly (even if only one had income)
3 ☐ Married filing separately. Enter spouse's SSN above and full name here. ▶
4 ☐ Head of household (with qualifying person). (See page 18.) If the qualifying person is a child but not your dependent, enter this child's name here. ▶
5 ☐ Qualifying widow(er) with dependent child (see page 19)

Exemptions
6a ☒ **Yourself.** If someone can claim you as a dependent, do not check box 6a.
b ☒ **Spouse**
} Boxes checked on 6a and 6b: **2**

c **Dependents:**

(1) First name Last name	(2) Dependent's social security number	(3) Dependent's relationship to you	(4) ✓ if qualifying child for child tax credit (see page 20)
Robert Omar	000 : 00 : 0000		☐
			☐
			☐
			☐
			☐
			☐

If more than six dependents, see page 20.

No. of children on 6c who:
• lived with you: **1**
• did not live with you due to divorce or separation (see page 21): ____
Dependents on 6c not entered above: ____

d Total number of exemptions claimed. Add numbers on lines above ▶ **3**

The number of exemptions that the Omars claim on this return is 3.

■ CHECK YOUR UNDERSTANDING

Jack and Janine Jones are married and will be filing a joint 1040A tax return. They have x dependent children living at home and they are the sole supporters for y dependent adults. Write an algebraic expression for the number of exemptions they will claim.

EXAMPLE 4

This is the first of 4 examples that lead the students through the completion of a 1040A tax form for the Omar family. In this example, the number of exemptions is calculated by identifying the number of dependents.

CHECK YOUR UNDERSTANDING

Answer $2 + x + y$

EXAMPLE 5

Additions to and deductions from wages are introduced in this example, and the adjusted gross income is calculated.

CHECK YOUR UNDERSTANDING

Answer $86,380

EXAMPLE 5

Determine the Omars' adjusted gross income. They received $987 interest on bank deposits and $1,200 in stock dividends.

SOLUTION From Kenya Omar's W-2, his gross income is $52,126.76. From Robin Omar's W-2, her gross income is $65,120.97. Their total income rounded to the nearest dollar is

$$52{,}127 + 65{,}121 = 117{,}248$$

The Omars have interest income that is below $1,500 and dividends that are below $1,500.

It is not necessary for them to complete and attach Schedule 1, which gives a detailed accounting when one or both are in excess of the limit.

The income, interest, and dividends are listed in the income section. Since they had no other income that year, their total income is the sum of these amounts.

$$\text{Total income} = 117{,}248 + 987 + 1{,}200 = 119{,}435$$

The next section allows taxpayers to adjust that total by reducing the amount for a number of qualifying expenses.

The Omars had no adjustments to make, so their adjusted gross income remains at $119,435.

Income Attach Form(s) W-2 here. Also attach Form(s) 1099-R if tax was withheld.	7	Wages, salaries, tips, etc. Attach Form(s) W-2.		7	$117,248 00
	8a	**Taxable** interest. Attach Schedule 1 if required.		8a	$987 00
	b	**Tax-exempt** interest. **Do not** include on line 8a.	8b		
	9a	Ordinary dividends. Attach Schedule 1 if required.		9a	$1,200 00
	b	Qualified dividends (see page 24).	9b		
If you did not get a W-2, see page 23.	10	Capital gain distributions (see page 24).		10	
	11a	IRA distributions. 11a	**11b** Taxable amount (see page 24).	11b	
Enclose, but do not attach, any payment.	12a	Pensions and annuities. 12a	**12b** Taxable amount (see page 25).	12b	
	13	Unemployment compensation and Alaska Permanent Fund dividends.		13	
	14a	Social security benefits. 14a	**14b** Taxable amount (see page 27).	14b	
	15	Add lines 7 through 14b (far right column). This is your **total income.** ▶		15	$119,435 00
Adjusted gross income	16	Educator expenses (see page 29).	16		
	17	IRA deduction (see page 29).	17		
	18	Student loan interest deduction (see page 31).	18		
	19	Tuition and fees deduction. Attach Form 8917.	19		
	20	Add lines 16 through 19. These are your **total adjustments.**		20	
	21	Subtract line 20 from line 15. This is your **adjusted gross income.** ▶		21	$119,435 00

For Disclosure, Privacy Act, and Paperwork Reduction Act Notice, see page 78. Cat. No. 11327A Form **1040A** (2008)

■ CHECK YOUR UNDERSTANDING

Lisa and Bob Zee have a combined income from salaries of $87,980. They received 1099 forms for $1,100 in interest from their bank and $1,300 in stock dividends. They have a total of $4,000 in adjustments to their gross income. Determine their adjusted gross income.

EXAMPLE 6

Determine the Omars tax for the year.

SOLUTION The **standard deduction** is an allowable reduction that is based on the filing status. These amounts are set by the government and may change from year to year.

The Omars are married and filing a joint return, so they can take the standard deduction of $10,900.

Since they are claiming 3 exemptions, they can reduce their adjusted gross income by 3 times the exemption deduction amount. In this case, $3 \times 3{,}500$, or $10,500.

Their taxable income is calculated as shown.

Adjusted gross income − Standard deduction − Exemption deduction

$$119{,}435 - 10{,}900 - (3 \times 3{,}500) = 98{,}035$$

Their taxable income has been reduced to $98,035. They use the tax tables to determine their tax as shown.

98,000	98,050	21,425	17,194	21,819	19,569
98,050	98,100	21,439	17,206	21,833	19,581
98,100	98,150	21,453	17,219	21,847	19,594
98,150	98,200	21,467	17,231	21,861	19,606
98,200	98,250	21,481	17,244	21,875	19,619
98,250	98,300	21,495	17,256	21,889	19,631
98,300	98,350	21,509	17,269	21,903	19,644
98,350	98,400	21,523	17,281	21,917	19,656

Their tax is $17,194. They have no further reductions. This is the total tax that they owe as shown on the completed form below.

Form 1040A (2008) Page **2**

Tax, credits, and payments

22	Enter the amount from line 21 (adjusted gross income).	22	$119,435 00
23a	Check if: ☐ **You** were born before January 2, 1944, ☐ Blind; ☐ **Spouse** was born before January 2, 1944, ☐ Blind } **Total boxes checked** ▶ 23a ☐		
b	If you are married filing separately and your spouse itemizes deductions, see page 32 and check here ▶ 23b ☐		
c	Check if standard deduction includes real estate taxes (see page 32) ▶ 23c ☐		
24	Enter your **standard deduction** (see left margin).	24	$10,900 00
25	Subtract line 24 from line 22. If line 24 is more than line 22, enter -0-.	25	$108,535 00
26	If line 22 is over $119,975, or you provided housing to a Midwestern displaced individual, see page 32. Otherwise, multiply $3,500 by the total number of exemptions claimed on line 6d.	26	$10,500 00
27	Subtract line 26 from line 25. If line 26 is more than line 25, enter -0-. This is your **taxable income.** ▶	27	$98,035 00
28	**Tax,** including any alternative minimum tax (see page 33).	28	$17,194 00
29	Credit for child and dependent care expenses. Attach Schedule 2. 29		
30	Credit for the elderly or the disabled. Attach Schedule 3. 30		
31	Education credits. Attach Form 8863. 31		
32	Retirement savings contributions credit. Attach Form 8880. 32		
33	Child tax credit (see page 37). Attach Form 8901 if required. 33		
34	Add lines 29 through 33. These are your **total credits.**	34	0 00
35	Subtract line 34 from line 28. If line 34 is more than line 28, enter -0-.	35	$17,194 00
36	Advance earned income credit payments from Form(s) W-2, box 9.	36	
37	Add lines 35 and 36. This is your **total tax.** ▶	37	$17,194 00

Standard Deduction for—
- People who checked any box on line 23a, 23b, or 23c **or** who can be claimed as a dependent, see page 32.
- All others:

Single or Married filing separately, $5,450

Married filing jointly or Qualifying widow(er), $10,900

Head of household, $8,000

■ CHECK YOUR UNDERSTANDING

Raul and Hannah have an adjusted gross income of A dollars. They are married and filing a joint return. They reported a total of E exemptions on their form and have no further deductions. Write an algebraic expression for their taxable income.

EXAMPLE 6

This example introduces students to the standard deduction. This deduction can vary from year to year and is determined by the filing status. In addition, the number of exemptions times the exemption amount is now factored into the adjusted gross income as a deduction. Taxes are calculated in this example. Although there are other categories of deductions (credits), they are beyond the scope of this course. You should mention to the students that they exist. The total tax is calculated at the end of this example.

CHECK YOUR UNDERSTANDING

Answer $A - 10{,}900 - 3{,}500E$

This answer is correct based upon the tax information at the time of this printing. The deduction and exemption amounts are subject to change.

EXAMPLE 7

The final portion of the 1040A is now completed so it can be determined whether or not the Omar's get a refund or owe money. Their tax paid is less than the tax owed, so they need to send money in along with their 1040A form in the amount due the government.

CHECK YOUR UNDERSTANDING

Answer $7,498.65; they would still owe $929.

EXAMPLE 7

Do the Omars get a refund or owe the government money? In either case, determine that amount.

SOLUTION The Omars now complete the final portion of the form. They need to find the total of the federal taxes that were withheld by their employers during the year. These amounts are on their W-2 forms. Robin paid $8,765.99 and Kenya paid $6,198.65 in taxes. The sum of those amounts is $14,964.64, and they can use $14,965 as the rounded dollar amount. Find the difference between these two amounts.

$$17{,}194 - 14{,}965 = 2{,}229$$

The tax paid is less than the tax owed, so they owe the government $2,229.

They must each sign the completed form, attach their W-2 forms, and enclose a check for $2,229.

	37	Add lines 35 and 36. This is your **total tax.**			▶ 37	$17,194 00
	38	Federal income tax withheld from Forms W-2 and 1099.	38	$14,965 00		
	39	2008 estimated tax payments and amount applied from 2007 return.	39			
If you have a qualifying child, attach Schedule EIC.	40a	**Earned income credit (EIC).**	40a			
	b	Nontaxable combat pay election. 40b				
	41	Additional child tax credit. Attach Form 8812.	41			
	42	Recovery rebate credit (see worksheet on pages 53 and 54).	42			
	43	Add lines 38, 39, 40a, 41, and 42. These are your **total payments.**			▶ 43	$14,965 00
Refund	44	If line 43 is more than line 37, subtract line 37 from line 43. This is the amount you **overpaid.**			44	
Direct deposit? See page 55 and fill in 45b, 45c, and 45d or Form 8888.	45a	Amount of line 44 you want **refunded to you.** If Form 8888 is attached, check here ▶ ☐			45a	
	▶ b	Routing number ▶ c Type: ☐ Checking ☐ Savings				
	▶ d	Account number				
	46	Amount of line 44 you want applied to your **2009 estimated tax.**	46			
Amount you owe	47	**Amount you owe.** Subtract line 43 from line 37. For details on how to pay, see page 56.			▶ 47	$2,229 00
	48	Estimated tax penalty (see page 57).	48			

CHECK YOUR UNDERSTANDING

Suppose that Kenya had an additional $50 withheld from each of his biweekly paychecks. How would that change the amount reported on his W-2 form? With the additional money withheld, would they have gotten a refund or owed the government money?

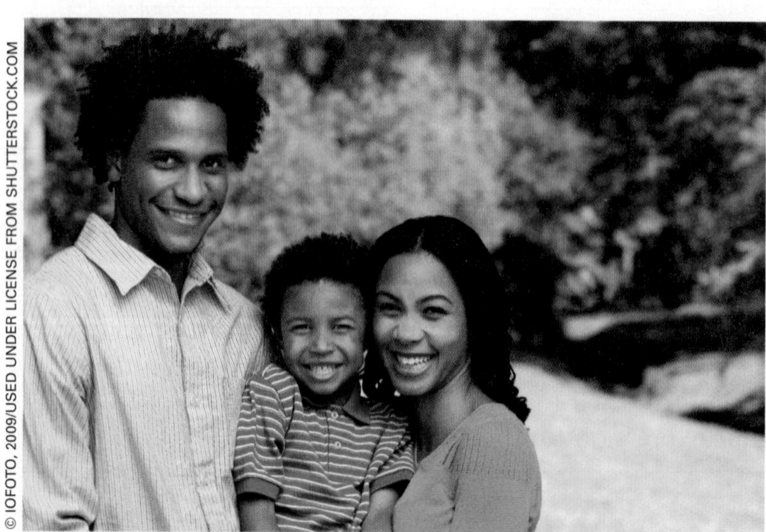

Applications

It is my belief that one's salary is between an individual and the IRS.

Jessica Savitch, American Journalist

1. How can the quote be interpreted in light of what you have learned? See margin.

Round all monetary answers to the nearest dollar.

2. William Base's employer withheld $13,956.95 in federal income tax. After completing his return, William determined that his tax is $11,874.82. Will William get a refund or does he owe the government money? William will receive an income tax refund of $2,082.
3. Ralph is a teacher who works as a musician on weekends. Here is part of his tax worksheet: wages from teaching $43,871.82, wages from music jobs $15,873.00, interest $863.90, dividends $350.70, and royalties $1,200.60. What is Ralph's total income? $62,160
4. Kate is filling out her income tax return. Her tax for last year is $973. Her employer withheld $712 in federal taxes.
   - **a.** Does Kate get a refund or does she owe the government money? owe
   - **b.** What is the difference between Kate's tax and the amount withheld by her employer? $261
5. Dale's employer withheld $9,873.33 in federal taxes last year. His tax is $8,792.75.
   - **a.** Does Dale get a refund or does he owe the government money? refund
   - **b.** What is the difference between Dale's tax and the amount withheld by his employer? $1,081
6. Katrina is single with a taxable income for last year of $75,431. Her employer withheld $14,870 in federal taxes.
   - **a.** Use the tax table from Example 2 in Lesson 7-4 to determine Katrina's tax. $15,200
   - **b.** Does Katrina get a refund? no
   - **c.** Find the difference between Katrina's tax and the amount withheld by her employer. $330
7. Oscar is single with a taxable income for last year of $75,555. His employer withheld $16,381 in federal taxes.
   - **a.** Use the tax table from Example 2 in Lesson 7-4 to determine Oscar's tax. $15,238
   - **b.** Does Oscar get a refund? yes
   - **c.** Find the difference between Oscar's tax and the amount withheld by his employer. $1,143
8. Tony is paying off a car loan. The monthly payment is $211.28. He is hoping to receive an income tax refund that is large enough to make one monthly payment. His tax is $1,722 and his employer withheld $2,071 in federal taxes.
   - **a.** How much of a refund will Tony receive? $349
   - **b.** Will Tony be able to make one car loan payment with the refund? Explain your answer. Yes; $349 > $211.28

TEACH

Exercises 2–5

These exercises do not require the use of any forms or tables. All of the information needed is included in the problem statements.

ANSWERS

1. Most people believe that their salary is personal and they do not bring it up in conversation. Ms. Savitch's comment indicates an awareness of the fact that no matter how personal you believe your salary amount to be, it is still known to the IRS.

Exercises 9–14
These exercises were completed using 2008 tax schedules and forms. The 2008 tax forms are available at www.cengage.com/school/math/financialalgebra. You can have students do these exercises using the current tax tables, found at www.irs.gov.

ANSWERS

9. adjusted gross income: \$21,559; taxable income: \$12,609; tax due: \$1,493; owe: \$362
10. adjusted gross income: \$118,726; taxable income: \$93,826; tax due: \$16,144; refund: \$7,991
11. adjusted gross income: \$110,187; taxable income: \$92,287; tax due: \$15,756; refund: \$2,687

For each of the following questions, complete the form indicated to find the adjusted gross income, taxable income, tax due, and amount of refund or amount owed. Round all answers to the nearest whole number. A complete tax table is in the Appendix.

9. Laurie Tenser is single and works in a clothing store. The following information was reported on her W-2 form: federal income tax withheld, \$1,131.00; wages, \$21,265.50; and state income tax withheld, \$900. Laurie received \$293 in interest from her bank account. Fill out a Form 1040EZ for Laurie. See margin.

10. Betsy and Rich Crosmour are married with two children. Rich is a chef and Betsy is a designer. This information was reported on their W-2 forms. Betsy and Rich received \$1,287.43 in interest on bank deposits and \$976 in stock dividends. Fill out a Form 1040A for Betsy and Rich. See margin.

	Betsy Crosmour	Rich Crosmour
Federal income tax withheld	\$11,900	\$12,235
Wages	\$57,742	\$58,721
State income tax withheld	\$ 8,873	\$ 5,872

a Employee's social security number	000-00-0000
OMB No. 1545-0008	Safe, accurate, FAST! Use IRS e-file. Visit the IRS website at www.irs.gov/efile.
b Employer identification number (EIN)	00-0000000
c Employer's name, address, and ZIP code	Rockland School, 76 Rickety Road, Rockford, Illinois 61126
1 Wages, tips, other compensation	\$42,126.76
2 Federal income tax withheld	\$8,198.00
3 Social security wages	\$42,126.76
4 Social security tax withheld	\$2,611.81
5 Medicare wages and tips	\$42,126.76
6 Medicare tax withheld	\$610.83
7 Social security tips	
8 Allocated tips	
d Control number	09945
9 Advance EIC payment	
10 Dependent care benefits	
e Employee's first name and initial / Last name / Suff.	Mukul / Racket
11 Nonqualified plans	
12a See instructions for box 12	
13 Statutory employee / Retirement plan / Third-party sick pay	
12b	
14 Other	
12c	
12d	
f Employee's address and ZIP code	5 Rockefeller Drive, Rockford, Illinois 61126
15 State / Employer's state ID number	00-0000000
16 State wages, tips, etc.	\$42,126.76
17 State income tax	\$3,198.10
18 Local wages, tips, etc.	
19 Local income tax	
20 Locality name	

a Employee's social security number	000-00-0000
OMB No. 1545-0008	Safe, accurate, FAST! Use IRS e-file. Visit the IRS website at www.irs.gov/efile.
b Employer identification number (EIN)	00-0000000
c Employer's name, address, and ZIP code	Racket's Rackets, 3 Net Highway, Rockford, Illinois 61126
1 Wages, tips, other compensation	\$66,199.00
2 Federal income tax withheld	\$10,245.00
3 Social security wages	\$66,199.00
4 Social security tax withheld	\$4,104.34
5 Medicare wages and tips	\$66,199.00
6 Medicare tax withheld	\$959.89
7 Social security tips	
8 Allocated tips	
d Control number	88345
9 Advance EIC payment	
10 Dependent care benefits	
e Employee's first name and initial / Last name / Suff.	Mukul / Racket
11 Nonqualified plans	
12a See instructions for box 12	
13 Statutory employee / Retirement plan / Third-party sick pay	
12b	
14 Other	
12c	
12d	
f Employee's address and ZIP code	5 Rockefeller Drive, Rockford, Illinois 61126
15 State / Employer's state ID number	00-0000000
16 State wages, tips, etc.	\$66,199.00
17 State income tax	\$3,267.00
18 Local wages, tips, etc.	
19 Local income tax	
20 Locality name	

11. Mukul is a teacher at Rockland School and he runs a tennis shop called Racket's Rackets. He and his wife Nikki have combined bank interest of \$1,011. Nikki made \$850 in tips last year. If they get a refund, they would like their money deposited into their checking account (number 88535244, with routing number 100078456). Complete their 1040EZ form. See margin.

12. Darcelle teaches skiing at the Snow School. Jack runs a ski shop called Up Hill, Down Hill. Their combined bank interest is $1,000. If they get a refund, they would like the money deposited into their checking account (number 89764251, with routing number 114466872). Complete a 1040EZ form for Darcelle and Jack. See margin.

a Employee's social security number	000-00-0000
OMB No. 1545-0008	Safe, accurate, FAST! Use IRS e-file. Visit the IRS website at www.irs.gov/efile.
b Employer identification number (EIN)	00-0000000
c Employer's name, address, and ZIP code	Snow School 76 Winter Road White Bird, Idaho 83554
d Control number	02435
e Employee's first name and initial / Last name / Suff.	Darcelle Hill
f Employee's address and ZIP code	5 Falldown Drive Woodruff, Idaho 83252
1 Wages, tips, other compensation	$40,126.00
2 Federal income tax withheld	$7,198.00
3 Social security wages	$40,126.00
4 Social security tax withheld	$2,487.81
5 Medicare wages and tips	$40,126.00
6 Medicare tax withheld	$581.83
7 Social security tips	
8 Allocated tips	
9 Advance EIC payment	
10 Dependent care benefits	
11 Nonqualified plans	
12a See instructions for box 12	
12b	
12c	
12d	
13 Statutory employee / Retirement plan / Third-party sick pay	☐ ☐ ☐
14 Other	
15 State / Employer's state ID number	00-0000000
16 State wages, tips, etc.	$40,126.00
17 State income tax	$3,611.00
18 Local wages, tips, etc.	
19 Local income tax	
20 Locality name	

a Employee's social security number	000-00-0000
OMB No. 1545-0008	Safe, accurate, FAST! Use IRS e-file. Visit the IRS website at www.irs.gov/efile.
b Employer identification number (EIN)	00-0000000
c Employer's name, address, and ZIP code	Up Hill, Down Hill 3 Net Highway Woodruff, Idaho 83252
d Control number	09435
e Employee's first name and initial / Last name / Suff.	Jack Hill
f Employee's address and ZIP code	5 Falldown Drive Woodruff, Idaho 83252
1 Wages, tips, other compensation	$68,199.00
2 Federal income tax withheld	$11,245.00
3 Social security wages	$68,199.00
4 Social security tax withheld	$4,228.34
5 Medicare wages and tips	$68,199.00
6 Medicare tax withheld	$988.89
7 Social security tips	
8 Allocated tips	
9 Advance EIC payment	
10 Dependent care benefits	
11 Nonqualified plans	
12a See instructions for box 12	
12b	
12c	
12d	
13 Statutory employee / Retirement plan / Third-party sick pay	☐ ☐ ☐
14 Other	
15 State / Employer's state ID number	00-0000000
16 State wages, tips, etc.	$68,199.00
17 State income tax	$6,137.00
18 Local wages, tips, etc.	
19 Local income tax	
20 Locality name	

13. Complete a 1040A form for Kevin Hooper. Kevin is a butcher. He is single with two children, which he can claim as dependents. He also takes care of his dad, who lives with his family. Use the following amounts and his W-2 form that is shown: bank interest: $1,300; dividends: $672; and unemployment insurance: $900. See margin.

a Employee's social security number	000-00-0000
OMB No. 1545-0008	Safe, accurate, FAST! Use IRS e-file. Visit the IRS website at www.irs.gov/efile.
b Employer identification number (EIN)	00-0000000
c Employer's name, address, and ZIP code	Butchers Block 130 Burger Blvd. Sea Cliff, New York 11579
d Control number	03764
e Employee's first name and initial / Last name / Suff.	Kevin Hooper
f Employee's address and ZIP code	15 Yonder Road Glen Head, New York 11545
1 Wages, tips, other compensation	$32,619.00
2 Federal income tax withheld	$3,908.00
3 Social security wages	$32,619.00
4 Social security tax withheld	$2,022.38
5 Medicare wages and tips	$32,619.00
6 Medicare tax withheld	$472.98
7 Social security tips	
8 Allocated tips	
9 Advance EIC payment	
10 Dependent care benefits	
11 Nonqualified plans	
12a See instructions for box 12	
12b	
12c	
12d	
13 Statutory employee / Retirement plan / Third-party sick pay	☐ ☐ ☐
14 Other	
15 State / Employer's state ID number	00-0000000
16 State wages, tips, etc.	$32,619.00
17 State income tax	$1,007.00
18 Local wages, tips, etc.	
19 Local income tax	
20 Locality name	

ANSWERS

12. adjusted gross income: $109,325; taxable income: $91,425; tax due: $15,544; refund: $2,899

13. adjusted gross income: $35,491; taxable income: $16,041; tax due: $2,003; refund: $1,905

a Employee's social security number **000-00-0000**

OMB No. 1545-0008 | Safe, accurate, FAST! Use IRS e-file | Visit the IRS website at www.irs.gov/efile.

b Employer identification number (EIN): **00-0000000**

c Employer's name, address, and ZIP code:
North Shore Schools
112 Franklin Avenue.
Jamaica, New York 11433

1 Wages, tips, other compensation **$47,900.00**	2 Federal income tax withheld **$7,955.00**
3 Social security wages **$47,900.00**	4 Social security tax withheld **$2,969.80**
5 Medicare wages and tips **$47,900.00**	6 Medicare tax withheld **$694.55**
7 Social security tips	8 Allocated tips
9 Advance EIC payment	10 Dependent care benefits
11 Nonqualified plans	12a See instructions for box 12
13 Statutory employee / Retirement plan / Third-party sick pay	12b
14 Other	12c
	12d

d Control number: **13764**

e Employee's first name and initial: **Winnie** Last name: **Johnston** Suff.

199 Wild Boulevard
Jamaica, New York 11433

f Employee's address and ZIP code

15 State	Employer's state ID number	16 State wages, tips, etc.	17 State income tax	18 Local wages, tips, etc.	19 Local income tax	20 Locality name
	00-0000000	$47,900.00	$1,971.00			

14. Winnie Johnston is a teacher who files her taxes as a Head of Household and takes care of her mother and her grandmother, both of whom live with her. Her W-2 form is shown and she also has $65 in bank interest and has $250 in educator expenses that she can claim. Complete a 1040A form. See margin.

a Employee's social security number **000-00-0000**

OMB No. 1545-0008 | Safe, accurate, FAST! Use IRS e-file | Visit the IRS website at www.irs.gov/efile.

b Employer identification number (EIN): **00-0000000**

c Employer's name, address, and ZIP code:
Financial Planning
1040 A Street
Benson, AZ 85602

1 Wages, tips, other compensation **$56,940.00**	2 Federal income tax withheld **$11,289.00**
3 Social security wages **$56,940.00**	4 Social security tax withheld **$3,530.28**
5 Medicare wages and tips **$56,940.00**	6 Medicare tax withheld **$825.63**
7 Social security tips	8 Allocated tips
9 Advance EIC payment	10 Dependent care benefits
11 Nonqualified plans	12a See instructions for box 12
13 Statutory employee / Retirement plan / Third-party sick pay	12b
14 Other	12c
	12d

d Control number: **822356**

e Employee's first name and initial: **Charles** Last name: **Friend** Suff.

234 Locust Lane
Benson, AZ 85602

f Employee's address and ZIP code

15 State	Employer's state ID number	16 State wages, tips, etc.	17 State income tax	18 Local wages, tips, etc.	19 Local income tax	20 Locality name
	00-0000000	$56,940.00	$5,007.00			

15. Charlie Friend is an accountant and his wife, Monica, is a cook. They have four children. They also take care of Monica's mother, who lives with them. Use the following amounts and their W-2 forms that are given: bank interest of $500 from Chase Bank and dividends of $304 from GM. Complete a 1040A tax form for them. See margin.

a Employee's social security number **000-00-0000**

OMB No. 1545-0008 | Safe, accurate, FAST! Use IRS e-file | Visit the IRS website at www.irs.gov/efile.

b Employer identification number (EIN): **00-0000000**

c Employer's name, address, and ZIP code:
The Eatery
4 Dinner Drive
Bisbee, AZ 85603

1 Wages, tips, other compensation **$52,190.00**	2 Federal income tax withheld **$8,345.00**
3 Social security wages **$52,190.00**	4 Social security tax withheld **$3,235.78**
5 Medicare wages and tips **$52,190.00**	6 Medicare tax withheld **$756.76**
7 Social security tips	8 Allocated tips
9 Advance EIC payment	10 Dependent care benefits
11 Nonqualified plans	12a See instructions for box 12
13 Statutory employee / Retirement plan / Third-party sick pay	12b
14 Other	12c
	12d

d Control number: **77543**

e Employee's first name and initial: **Monica** Last name: **Friend** Suff.

234 Locust Lane
Benson, AZ 85602

f Employee's address and ZIP code

15 State	Employer's state ID number	16 State wages, tips, etc.	17 State income tax	18 Local wages, tips, etc.	19 Local income tax	20 Locality name
	00-0000000	$52,190.00	$4,764.00			

ANSWERS

14. adjusted gross income: $47,715; taxable income: $29,215; tax due: $3,811; refund: $4,144

15. adjusted gross income: $109,934; taxable income: $74,534; tax due: $11,319; refund: $8,315

Our forefathers made one mistake. What they should have fought for was representation without taxation.

Fletcher Knebel, American Author

Form 1040 and Schedules A and B

7-5

Key Terms

- voluntary compliance
- Form 1040
- Schedule B—Interest and Dividend Income
- Schedule A—Itemized Deductions
- tax credit
- tax avoidance
- tax evasion

Objectives

- File Form 1040 with itemized deductions.
- Understand the difference between a tax credit and a tax deduction.

Common Core

A-SSE1, A-CED3

CCSS Warm-Up

Determine if the given point is in the solution set for the system $2x - 4y > 8$ and $y + x < -2$.

1. $(-2, -4)$ **2.** $(0, -2)$ **3.** $(2, -3)$

1. yes 2. no 3. no

What is the Difference Between Tax Evasion and Tax Avoidance?

People don't like paying taxes, but they realize it is a necessity to raise money for government services, and they cooperate with the procedure. This is known as **voluntary compliance**. You can lower your tax burden if you learn about taxes—the more you know, the more you can save.

On Form 1040A, you can report income from wages, interest, stock dividends, pensions, unemployment insurance, and Social Security benefits. There are many other sources of income a citizen can have, including alimony and prizes. A taxpayer cannot report these other types of income on Form 1040A. They need to use **Form 1040**, often called the long form. **Schedule B—Interest and Dividend Income** is used to list sources of interest and dividend income. It tells the IRS who paid you interest and dividends and how much you received from each.

Deductions lower your taxable income, which means you pay a lower income tax. Form 1040A allows some deductions from income, including some educational expenses. There are many deductions that the government allows taxpayers to use to lower the amount they pay in taxes, including

medical expenses	alimony paid
property taxes paid	mortgage interest paid
state and local income taxes paid	charitable contributions
casualty and theft losses	gambling losses
moving expenses	job-seeking expenses
business expenses	tax preparation fees

These deductions are filed using Form 1040, on an additional form, **Schedule A—Itemized Deductions**. You can file Schedule A only if you are filing Form 1040. The information needed for calculating and claiming deductions is found in the Form 1040 instruction booklet.

EXAMINE THE QUESTION

Tax evasion cases are often in the news, especially when they involve celebrities. Tax evasion is illegal; however, tax avoidance is within the law, and advantageous to taxpayers. Tax avoidance is the result of maximizing one's deductions and tax credit to lower the amount of tax due.

This motivation often leads to a true life-long learning experience. As tax laws and forms change, and as students grow into working adults, the knowledge gained in this lesson will need to be updated. Most likely, the financial benefits will ensure that students keep abreast of tax changes for their entire lives.

CLASS DISCUSSION

Discuss if students can name any high-profile cases of tax evasion. Have students research to see the lengths of prison sentences that such criminals have done.

TEACH

The examples in this lesson will indoctrinate students to the major lines of Form 1040 and Schedules A and B. Download a copy of the current tax year's form to point out any changes.

There are 11 examples in this lesson. The long form is divided up into digestible snippets so students do not get overwhelmed. This is sophisticated subject matter. Do not expect to finish the entire lesson in one day, since each example could spark some questions and comments.

EXAMPLE 1

After completing the biographical section of Form 1040, taxpayers must compute their income from all sources.

Schedule B is used for filers who have bank interest and stock dividends exceeding a given amount, which changes every few years.

Tax credits are another way to reduce your taxes. A tax credit is an amount you subtract from your tax *after* you looked it up on the tax table. Deductions are subtracted from your income *before* you look up your tax on the tax table. Two popular credits are the Child Care Tax Credit and the Earned Income Credit. The amount of any credit is dependent on many different factors. The IRS offers credit worksheets on which taxpayers can determine if they qualify to claim a credit. If they do, the amount is then transferred to their tax return and used to reduce the taxes owed.

All tax deductions and tax credits are subject to certain limitations and restrictions, and it is important that you know the rules that apply. If you use a rule to your advantage to lower your tax burden, you are not breaking any laws. This is called **tax avoidance**. If you lie about items on your tax return, you are committing **tax evasion**, which is a crime. You can learn about all tax laws by reading literature available online or by mail from the Internal Revenue Service (IRS). Even if you choose to have an accountant do your taxes, you need to know what aspects of your financial life affect your taxes, so that you can tell your accountant everything needed to file your form.

Skills and Strategies

Here you will learn how to file Form 1040 with Schedules A and B. Schedule A is used to list your deductions. Schedule B is used to list dividend and interest incomes.

EXAMPLE 1

Margaret and Brian O'Sullivan are married. They have one child, Carole. Margaret works for a sports cable station and Brian is a cameraman. The O'Sullivans had combined wages of $76,521. They also had interest of $812 from Seaford Bank and $877 from Buffalo Bank. They received stock dividends of $444 from GM stock and $1,200 from Kodak stock. During the year, Margaret won $300 in the lottery. Find the total income from wages, bank interest, stock dividends, and the prize.

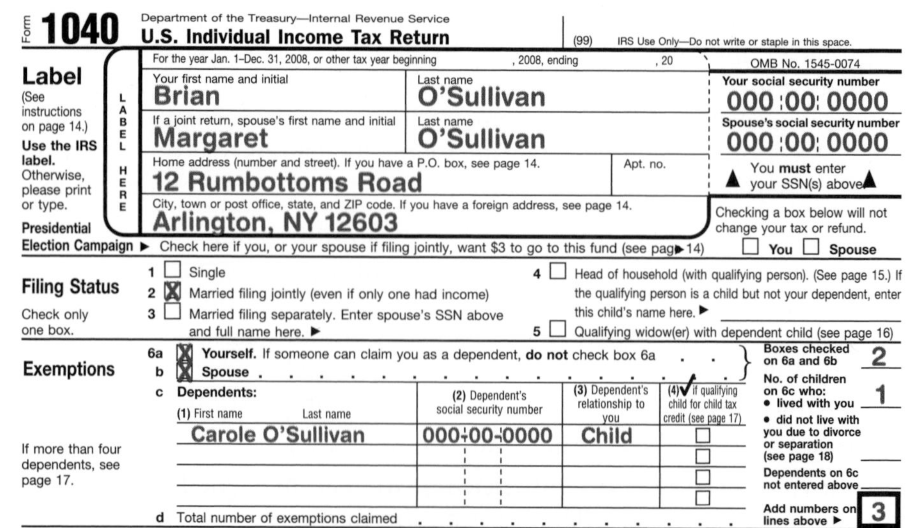

Form **1040** Department of the Treasury—Internal Revenue Service
U.S. Individual Income Tax Return (99) IRS Use Only—Do not write or staple in this space.

For the year Jan. 1–Dec. 31, 2008, or other tax year beginning , 2008, ending , 20 OMB No. 1545-0074

Label (See instructions on page 14.) **Use the IRS label.** Otherwise, please print or type. LABEL HERE

Your first name and initial: **Brian** | Last name: **O'Sullivan** | Your social security number: **000 00 0000**

If a joint return, spouse's first name and initial: **Margaret** | Last name: **O'Sullivan** | Spouse's social security number: **000 00 0000**

Home address (number and street). If you have a P.O. box, see page 14. **12 Rumbottoms Road** | Apt. no. | ▲ You **must** enter your SSN(s) above ▲

City, town or post office, state, and ZIP code. If you have a foreign address, see page 14. **Arlington, NY 12603** | Checking a box below will not change your tax or refund.

Presidential Election Campaign ▶ Check here if you, or your spouse if filing jointly, want $3 to go to this fund (see page 14) ☐ You ☐ Spouse

Filing Status
Check only one box.
1 ☐ Single
2 ☒ Married filing jointly (even if only one had income)
3 ☐ Married filing separately. Enter spouse's SSN above and full name here. ▶
4 ☐ Head of household (with qualifying person). (See page 15.) If the qualifying person is a child but not your dependent, enter this child's name here. ▶
5 ☐ Qualifying widow(er) with dependent child (see page 16)

Exemptions
6a ☒ **Yourself.** If someone can claim you as a dependent, **do not** check box 6a
b ☒ **Spouse**
Boxes checked on 6a and 6b: **2**

c Dependents:

(1) First name Last name	(2) Dependent's social security number	(3) Dependent's relationship to you	(4) ✓ if qualifying child for child tax credit (see page 17)
Carole O'Sullivan	000-00-0000	Child	☐
			☐
			☐
			☐

If more than four dependents, see page 17.

No. of children on 6c who: • lived with you **1**
• did not live with you due to divorce or separation (see page 18)
Dependents on 6c not entered above

d Total number of exemptions claimed . . . Add numbers on lines above ▶ **3**

SOLUTION

Add to find the total interest. $812 + 877 = 1{,}689$

They received $1,689 in bank interest. Since this amount is greater than $1,500, they must list this on Schedule B.

Add to find the total stock dividends. $444 + 1{,}200 = 1{,}644$

They received $1,644 in stock dividends. Since this amount is greater than $1,500, they must list this on Schedule B.

Here is their Schedule B filled out. Notice their name is not filled in because Schedule B is on the reverse side of Schedule A.

Schedules A&B (Form 1040) 2008 — OMB No. 1545-0074 — Page **2**

Name(s) shown on Form 1040. Do not enter name and social security number if shown on other side. | **Your social security number**

Schedule B—Interest and Ordinary Dividends — Attachment Sequence No. **08**

			Amount
Part I Interest (See page B-1 and the instructions for Form 1040, line 8a.)	1 List name of payer. If any interest is from a seller-financed mortgage and the buyer used the property as a personal residence, see page B-1 and list this interest first. Also, show that buyer's social security number and address ▶		
	Seaford Bank	1	$812 00
	Buffalo Bank		$877 00
	2 Add the amounts on line 1	2	$1,689 00
	3 Excludable interest on series EE and I U.S. savings bonds issued after 1989. Attach Form 8815	3	
	4 Subtract line 3 from line 2. Enter the result here and on Form 1040, line 8a ▶	4	
	Note. If line 4 is over $1,500, you must complete Part III.		Amount
Part II Ordinary Dividends	5 List name of payer ▶ **GM**	5	$444 00
	Kodak		$1,200 00
	6 Add the amounts on line 5. Enter the total here and on Form 1040, line 9a ▶	6	$1,644 00
	Note. If line 6 is over $1,500, you must complete Part III.		

There are lines on Form 1040 for each type of income. The sum of wages, bank interest, stock dividends, and the prize gives their total income.

$$76{,}521 + 1{,}689 + 1{,}644 + 300 = 80{,}154$$

Their total income is $80,154.

Look at the Income section of their Form 1040. Notice the lines for other types of income that the O'Sullivans did not have, but some people do.

Income	7 Wages, salaries, tips, etc. Attach Form(s) W-2	7	$76,521 00
	8a **Taxable** interest. Attach Schedule B if required	8a	$1,689 00
Attach Form(s) W-2 here. Also attach Forms W-2G and 1099-R if tax was withheld.	b **Tax-exempt** interest. **Do not** include on line 8a — 8b		
	9a Ordinary dividends. Attach Schedule B if required	9a	$1,644 00
	b Qualified dividends (see page 21) — 9b		
	10 Taxable refunds, credits, or offsets of state and local income taxes (see page 22)	10	
	11 Alimony received	11	
	12 Business income or (loss). Attach Schedule C or C-EZ	12	
	13 Capital gain or (loss). Attach Schedule D if required. If not required, check here ▶ ☐	13	
If you did not get a W-2, see page 21.	14 Other gains or (losses). Attach Form 4797	14	
	15a IRA distributions — 15a — b Taxable amount (see page 23)	15b	
	16a Pensions and annuities — 16a — b Taxable amount (see page 24)	16b	
Enclose, but do not attach, any payment. Also, please use **Form 1040-V.**	17 Rental real estate, royalties, partnerships, S corporations, trusts, etc. Attach Schedule E	17	
	18 Farm income or (loss). Attach Schedule F	18	
	19 Unemployment compensation	19	
	20a Social security benefits — 20a — b Taxable amount (see page 26)	20b	
	21 Other income. List type and amount (see page 28) **Prize -- Lottery**	21	$300 00
	22 Add the amounts in the far right column for lines 7 through 21. This is your total income ▶	22	$80,154 00

■ CHECK YOUR UNDERSTANDING

A family had $1,123 in bank interest. Must they report this on Schedule B? Explain.

CHECK YOUR UNDERSTANDING

Answer No; it is below the threshold amount.

EXAMPLE 2

The Adjusted Gross Income section allows taxpayers to enter certain tax deductions. Deductions lower the income before the tax is computed; providing the taxpayer with a lower tax burden. Other deductions will be on Schedule A.

CHECK YOUR UNDERSTANDING

Answer $x - d$

EXAMPLE 3

This example starts the Schedule A deductions. The first section is Medical Expenses, which do not count in full. Only the excess over 7.5% of adjusted gross income can be taken as a deduction.

Point out to students that decades ago, all medical expenses were deductible; there was not a threshold a taxpayer had to exceed.

EXAMPLE 2

Margaret O'Sullivan teaches a night course at the local college and had \$133 in educator expenses. The O'Sullivans also had \$3,009 worth of moving expenses. These two expenses are deductions from income. Find their adjusted gross income.

SOLUTION Add to find the total adjustments (deductions).

$$133 + 3{,}009 = 3{,}142$$

The total to be deducted is \$3,142.

Subtract from total income. $80{,}154 - 3{,}142 = 77{,}012$

Their adjusted gross income is \$77,012 as shown in the Adjusted Gross Income section of their Form 1040.

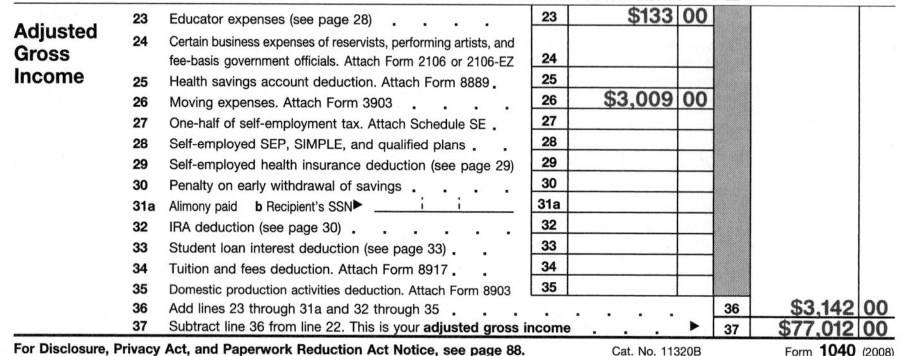

Adjusted Gross Income					
23	Educator expenses (see page 28)	23	\$133 00		
24	Certain business expenses of reservists, performing artists, and fee-basis government officials. Attach Form 2106 or 2106-EZ	24			
25	Health savings account deduction. Attach Form 8889	25			
26	Moving expenses. Attach Form 3903	26	\$3,009 00		
27	One-half of self-employment tax. Attach Schedule SE	27			
28	Self-employed SEP, SIMPLE, and qualified plans	28			
29	Self-employed health insurance deduction (see page 29)	29			
30	Penalty on early withdrawal of savings	30			
31a	Alimony paid b Recipient's SSN ▶	31a			
32	IRA deduction (see page 30)	32			
33	Student loan interest deduction (see page 33)	33			
34	Tuition and fees deduction. Attach Form 8917	34			
35	Domestic production activities deduction. Attach Form 8903	35			
36	Add lines 23 through 31a and 32 through 35			36	\$3,142 00
37	Subtract line 36 from line 22. This is your **adjusted gross income** ▶			37	\$77,012 00

For Disclosure, Privacy Act, and Paperwork Reduction Act Notice, see page 88. Cat. No. 11320B Form **1040** (2008)

CHECK YOUR UNDERSTANDING

The Lamberti family had a total income of x dollars. They also had d dollars in adjustments to income. Express their adjusted gross income algebraically.

EXAMPLE 3

The O'Sullivans had \$18,800 in medical expenses last year. Medical insurance covered 80% of these expenses, so they only had to pay 20% of the medical bills. The IRS allows medical and dental expenses deductions for the amount that exceeds 7.5% of a taxpayer's adjusted gross income. How much can they claim as a medical deduction?

SOLUTION Determine the amount that the O'Sullivans paid out-of-pocket for medical bills. Since the insurance company covered 80% of the costs, the family paid 20%.

$$18{,}800 \times 0.20 = 3{,}760$$

To determine if they can claim any medical expenses, calculate 7.5% of their adjusted gross income and compare it to out-of-pocket cost.

$$77{,}012 \times 0.075 = 5{,}775.90$$

Subtract to find the amount of medical expenses over 5,775.90.

$$3{,}760 - 5{,}775.90 = -2{,}015.90$$

Since their medical expenses do not exceed 7.5% of their adjusted gross income, the O'Sullivans medical expense deduction was 0. If medical expenses are less than 7.5% of adjusted gross income, the medical deduction is 0. Look at the Medical and Dental Expenses section of Schedule A. Notice how the instructions guide the taxpayer.

SCHEDULES A&B (Form 1040) Department of the Treasury Internal Revenue Service (99)	Schedule A—Itemized Deductions (Schedule B is on back) ▶ Attach to Form 1040. ▶ See Instructions for Schedules A&B (Form 1040).				OMB No. 1545-0074 Attachment Sequence No. 07
Name(s) shown on Form 1040	Brian and Margaret O'Sullivan				Your social security number 000: 00 : 0000
Medical and Dental Expenses	**Caution.** Do not include expenses reimbursed or paid by others.				
	1 Medical and dental expenses (see page A-1)	1	$3,760 00		
	2 Enter amount from Form 1040, line 38 [2] $77,012 00				
	3 Multiply line 2 by 7.5% (.075)	3	$5,782 65		
	4 Subtract line 3 from line 1. If line 3 is more than line 1, enter -0-.			4	0 00

■ CHECK YOUR UNDERSTANDING

Mary's adjusted gross income was x dollars last year. If she had m dollars of medical expenses not covered by insurance, express her medical expense deduction algebraically.

EXAMPLE 4

The O'Sullivans paid $3,298 in state income taxes and $3,567 in real estate taxes. They paid $3,096 in mortgage interest. What is the total amount they paid in state income and real estate taxes?

SOLUTION Find the sum of the state income and real estate taxes.

$$3{,}298 + 3{,}567 = 6{,}865$$

The total taxes were $6,865 as shown in the Taxes and Interest sections.

The amount of mortgage interest is entered into line 10 and line 15.

Taxes You Paid (See page A-2.)	5 State and local **(check only one box):** a ☒ Income taxes, or b ☐ General sales taxes }	5	$3,298 00		
	6 Real estate taxes (see page A-5)	6	$3,567 00		
	7 Personal property taxes	7			
	8 Other taxes. List type and amount ▶ ----------------	8			
	9 Add lines 5 through 8			9	$6,865 00
Interest You Paid (See page A-5.)	10 Home mortgage interest and points reported to you on Form 1098	10	$3,096 00		
	11 Home mortgage interest not reported to you on Form 1098. If paid to the person from whom you bought the home, see page A-6 and show that person's name, identifying no., and address▶ ----------------	11			
Note. Personal interest is not deductible.	12 Points not reported to you on Form 1098. See page A-6 for special rules.	12			
	13 Qualified mortgage insurance premiums (see page A-6)	13			
	14 Investment interest. Attach Form 4952 if required. (See page A-6.)	14			
	15 Add lines 10 through 14			15	$3,096 00

■ CHECK YOUR UNDERSTANDING

The Keenan family paid t dollars in state income taxes and r dollars in real estate taxes. Represent their Schedule A taxes paid algebraically.

CHECK YOUR UNDERSTANDING

Answer $m - 0.075x$ if $m > 0.075x$

EXAMPLE 4

Taxes and interest are also tax-deductible. The mortgage interest deduction is one reason people buy homes instead of just paying rent. Rent is not deductible.

CHECK YOUR UNDERSTANDING

Answer $t + r$

EXAMPLE 5

Charitable contributions are fully deductible, but careful records need to be kept. Advise students to always get receipts when making charitable contributions.

Explain that even Girl Scout cookie purchases are deductible. However, the deduction is the difference between what the cookies would have cost in a store, and what was donated to the Girl Scouts.

Also, cash contributions and deductions of items (such as clothes, toys, and furniture) are viewed as two separate categories.

CHECK YOUR UNDERSTANDING

Answer $x + bc$

EXAMPLE 6

Casualty and theft losses are not fully deductible, so make sure students understand the multi-step procedure required to compute the deduction.

If money was received for the damages from an insurance company, then there is no loss to deduct.

CHECK YOUR UNDERSTANDING

Answer $(c + s + v - 300) - 0.10x$, only if the answer is positive.

EXAMPLE 5

The O'Sullivans gave $987 to different charities. The highest amount they gave to any single charity was $100. They also donated $450 worth of old clothes to different charities. The most they gave to any single charity was $120. Find the total of their charitable contributions.

SOLUTION Add the two different types of donations.

$$987 + 450 = 1{,}437$$

The total of their charitable contributions is $1,437. This is entered in the Gifts to Charity section of Schedule A on two different lines, as shown below. Some of the donations are monetary, and others were donated items.

Gifts to Charity						
	16	Gifts by cash or check. If you made any gift of $250 or more, see page A-7	16	$987 00		
If you made a gift and got a benefit for it, see page A-7.	17	Other than by cash or check. If any gift of $250 or more, see page A-8. You **must** attach Form 8283 if over $500	17	$450 00		
	18	Carryover from prior year	18			
	19	Add lines 16 through 18			19	$1,437 00

■ CHECK YOUR UNDERSTANDING

Pete donated *x* dollars to charity over the last tax year. He also donated *b* bags of used clothing valued at *c* dollars each. Express his total charitable contributions algebraically.

EXAMPLE 6

The O'Sullivans had $9,230 worth of flood damage that was not covered by insurance. Find their casualty deduction.

SOLUTION The IRS requires that $100 be deducted for each casualty.

$$9{,}230 - 100 = 9{,}130$$

Only part of the remaining casualty loss is deductible. To find out how much, subtract 10% of the adjusted gross income from $9,130.

$$9{,}130 - 0.10(77{,}012) = 9{,}130 - 7{,}701.20 = 1{,}428.80$$

Rounded to the nearest dollar, the casualty deduction is $1,429. This is entered in the Casualty and Theft Losses section of Schedule A. They also must fill out an additional form to explain the casualty loss.

Casualty and Theft Losses	20	Casualty or theft loss(es). Attach Form 4684. (See page A-8.)	20	$1,429 00

■ CHECK YOUR UNDERSTANDING

Scott's adjusted gross income was *x* dollars. He had three different casualties last year that were not covered by insurance. A car was stolen, and he did not have comprehensive insurance, so he lost *c* dollars. A storm caused *s* dollars damage, and his vintage violin, worth *v* dollars, was destroyed in a fire. Express his casualty loss algebraically.

EXAMPLE 7

Brian O'Sullivan had $541 in expenses for job travel. This is not from driving to work because that is not tax deductible. This is traveling as part of work. It is based on the miles covered. Margaret and Brian belong to unions and pay a total of $1,439 in union dues. Brian took two college classes related to his employment, for a total tuition of $2,315. Find their miscellaneous expenses deduction.

SOLUTION Add the miscellaneous expenses.

$$541 + 1{,}439 + 2{,}315 = 4{,}295$$

They can only deduct miscellaneous expenses that exceed 2% of their adjusted gross income. Find 2% of their adjusted gross income.

$$0.02(77{,}012) = 1{,}540.24$$

Rounded to the nearest dollar, this amount is $1,540. Subtract this from their total miscellaneous expenses.

$$4{,}295 - 1{,}540 = 2{,}755$$

The Schedule A miscellaneous deductions are $2,755 as shown.

Job Expenses and Certain Miscellaneous Deductions	21	Unreimbursed employee expenses—job travel, union dues, job education, etc. Attach Form 2106 or 2106-EZ if required. (See page A-9.) ▶	21	$4,295 00		
	22	Tax preparation fees	22			
(See page A-9.)	23	Other expenses—investment, safe deposit box, etc. List type and amount ▶	23			
	24	Add lines 21 through 23 . . .	24	$4,295 00		
	25	Enter amount from Form 1040, line 38 25 | $77,012 | 00				
	26	Multiply line 25 by 2% (.02)	26	$1,540 00		
	27	Subtract line 26 from line 24. If line 26 is more than line 24, enter -0- . .			27	$2,755 00

CHECK YOUR UNDERSTANDING

Edgardo's miscellaneous expenses were m dollars, and his adjusted gross income was a dollars. Express his Schedule A miscellaneous deduction algebraically.

EXAMPLE 8

Find the O'Sullivans' total itemized deductions from Schedule A.

SOLUTION Add the numbers in the right column of Schedule A that you found in Examples 3–7.

$$6{,}865 + 3{,}096 + 1{,}437 + 1{,}429 + 2{,}755 = 15{,}582$$

Their total itemized deductions are $15,582. For some high incomes, the Schedule A total is reduced, but the O'Sullivan's income is below that number. Look at the bottom of the Schedule A form. It is now completed.

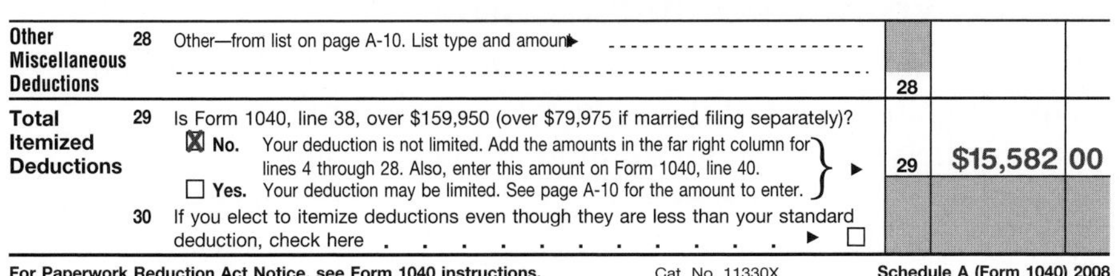

Other Miscellaneous Deductions	28	Other—from list on page A-10. List type and amount ▶	28	
Total Itemized Deductions	29	Is Form 1040, line 38, over $159,950 (over $79,975 if married filing separately)? ☒ **No.** Your deduction is not limited. Add the amounts in the far right column for lines 4 through 28. Also, enter this amount on Form 1040, line 40. ☐ **Yes.** Your deduction may be limited. See page A-10 for the amount to enter. } ▶	29	$15,582 00
	30	If you elect to itemize deductions even though they are less than your standard deduction, check here . . . . ▶ ☐		

For Paperwork Reduction Act Notice, see Form 1040 instructions. Cat. No. 11330X **Schedule A (Form 1040) 2008**

EXAMPLE 7

Job-seeking expenses, travel to a second job, business travel, and job related education expenses are some of many miscellaneous deductions. If you pay a tax preparer to do your taxes, that is also a miscellaneous deduction.

Explain to students that even if they have an accountant do their taxes, they need to be knowledgeable to tell the accountant all their financial activities that affect their taxes.

Note that miscellaneous deductions, at one time fully deductible, are now subject to meeting a threshold and deducting the excess.

CHECK YOUR UNDERSTANDING

Answer $m - 0.02a$, as long as $m > 0.02a$

EXAMPLE 8

The deductions in the right hand column of Schedule A are added to find the total Schedule A deduction. Even this total is subject to a threshold—it may not be fully deductible for people with higher incomes.

CHECK YOUR UNDERSTANDING

Answer $412 per hour

EXTEND YOUR UNDERSTANDING

Answer $470

EXAMPLE 9

After Schedule A is completed, the Schedule A deduction is entered on the back of Form 1040 and then subtracted. This is where the taxable income is lowered.

After exemptions for dependents are deducted, taxable income is obtained, and the tax can be computed using a table or a tax schedule/worksheet, as discussed in previous sections.

CHECK YOUR UNDERSTANDING

Answer 6*d*

Remind students that the amount per exemption often changes each year.

CHECK YOUR UNDERSTANDING

The Volp family took three hours to gather information and fill out their Schedule A. The itemized deductions saved them $1,236 in taxes. What was the mean savings per hour to fill out Schedule A?

EXTEND YOUR UNDERSTANDING

Orli spent $700 on job travel, but this deduction saved her $230 in taxes. What was the net cost to Orli of the job travel?

EXAMPLE 9

Once Schedule A is completed, the O'Sullivans return to Form 1040 to finish computing their taxes. Each exemption from the total number of exemptions line allows them a deduction on Form 1040. The amount can change from year to year, and usually increases. If the deduction for an exemption is $3,500, find the total amount the O'Sullivans can deduct. For higher income families, this deduction may be reduced. How much can the O'Sullivans deduct for their exemptions?

SOLUTION They have three exemptions, so multiply to find the total deduction for exemptions.

$$3 \times 3{,}500 = 10{,}500$$

They can deduct $10,500. Look at the lines on their Form 1040 that include the subtraction of the itemized deductions, $15,582, and the subtraction of the deductions for the three exemptions, $10,500.

Form 1040 (2008) Page **2**

Tax and Credits	38	Amount from line 37 (adjusted gross income)	38	$77,012 00
	39a	Check if: ☐ You were born before January 2, 1944, ☐ Blind. ☐ Spouse was born before January 2, 1944, ☐ Blind. **Total boxes checked** ▶ **39a** ☐		
	b	If your spouse itemizes on a separate return or you were a dual-status alien, see page 34 and check here ▶ **39b** ☐		
Standard Deduction for—	c	Check if standard deduction includes real estate taxes or disaster loss (see page 34) ▶ **39c** ☐		
• People who checked any box on line 39a, 39b, or 39c **or** who can be claimed as a dependent, see page 34.	40	**Itemized deductions** (from Schedule A) **or** your **standard deduction** (see left margin)	40	$15,582 00
	41	Subtract line 40 from line 38	41	$61,430 00
	42	If line 38 is over $119,975, or you provided housing to a Midwestern displaced individual, see page 36. Otherwise, multiply $3,500 by the total number of exemptions claimed on line 6d	42	$10,500 00
	43	**Taxable income.** Subtract line 42 from line 41. If line 42 is more than line 41, enter -0-	43	$50,930 00
	44	**Tax** (see page 36). Check if any tax is from: a ☐ Form(s) 8814 b ☐ Form 4972	44	$6,836 00
	45	**Alternative minimum tax** (see page 39). Attach Form 6251	45	
	46	Add lines 44 and 45 ▶	46	$6,836 00

These deductions lowered their income *before* they looked on the tax table. They looked up $50,930 instead of $80,154, for their total income, by using tax deductions allowed by the IRS.

Their tax, found on the tax table, is $6,836. It is shown on their Form 1040 above.

CHECK YOUR UNDERSTANDING

The Trobiano family consists of two parents, three children, and a live-in grandparent. If the deduction per exemption is d dollars, express their deduction for exemptions algebraically.

EXAMPLE 10

The O'Sullivans both work, and they pay for child care while they are at work. They can get a tax credit of $780. They installed some energy-saving items in their home, and can receive a $133 tax credit for that. What is their tax after the credits are subtracted?

SOLUTION Tax credits are subtracted from the tax found in the tax table. From Example 9, the tax was $6,836.

Subtract the sum of the two tax credits from this amount.

Tax − Credits	6,836 − (780 + 133)
Simplify.	6,836 − 913
Subtract.	5,923

The tax has been reduced to $5,923. Look at the tax credits entered on Form 1040.

The O'Sullvans' employers withheld $7,622 in federal income tax. Since the O'Sullivans' tax is $5,923, they subtract and find that they will receive a $1,699 refund.

Single or Married filing separately, $5,450	47	Foreign tax credit. Attach Form 1116 if required	47			
	48	Credit for child and dependent care expenses. Attach Form 2441	48	$780 00		
	49	Credit for the elderly or the disabled. Attach Schedule R	49			
Married filing jointly or Qualifying widow(er), $10,900	50	Education credits. Attach Form 8863	50			
	51	Retirement savings contributions credit. Attach Form 8880	51			
	52	Child tax credit (see page 42). Attach Form 8901 if required	52			
	53	Credits from Form: a ☐ 8396 b ☐ 8839 c ☒ 5695	53	$133 00		
Head of household, $8,000	54	Other credits from Form: a ☐ 3800 b ☐ 8801 c ☐ ____	54			
	55	Add lines 47 through 54. These are your **total credits**			55	$913 00
	56	Subtract line 55 from line 46. If line 55 is more than line 46, enter -0- ▶			56	$5,923 00
Other Taxes	57	Self-employment tax. Attach Schedule SE			57	
	58	Unreported social security and Medicare tax from Form: a ☐ 4137 b ☐ 8919			58	
	59	Additional tax on IRAs, other qualified retirement plans, etc. Attach Form 5329 if required			59	
	60	Additional taxes: a ☐ AEIC payments b ☐ Household employment taxes. Attach Schedule H			60	
	61	Add lines 56 through 60. This is your total tax ▶			61	$5,923 00
Payments	62	Federal income tax withheld from Forms W-2 and 1099	62	$7,622 00		
	63	2008 estimated tax payments and amount applied from 2007 return	63			
If you have a qualifying child, attach Schedule EIC.	64a	**Earned income credit (EIC)**	64a			
	b	Nontaxable combat pay election 64b				
	65	Excess social security and tier 1 RRTA tax withheld (see page 61)	65			
	66	Additional child tax credit. Attach Form 8812	66			
	67	Amount paid with request for extension to file (see page 61)	67			
	68	Credits from Form: a ☐ 2439 b ☐ 4136 c ☐ 8801 d ☐ 8885	68			
	69	First-time homebuyer credit. Attach Form 5405	69			
	70	Recovery rebate credit (see worksheet on pages 62 and 63)	70			
	71	Add lines 62 through 70. These are your total payments ▶			71	$7,622 00
Refund	72	If line 71 is more than line 61, subtract line 61 from line 71. This is the amount you overpaid			72	$1,699 00
Direct deposit? See page 63 and fill in 73b, 73c, and 73d, or Form 8888.	73a	Amount of line 72 you want **refunded to you.** If Form 8888 is attached, check here ▶ ☐			73a	$1,699 00
	▶ b	Routing number ▶ c Type: ☐ Checking ☐ Savings				
	▶ d	Account number				
	74	Amount of line 72 you want **applied to your 2009 estimated tax** ▶	74			
Amount You Owe	75	**Amount you owe.** Subtract line 71 from line 61. For details on how to pay, see page 65 ▶			75	
	76	Estimated tax penalty (see page 65)	76			

Third Party Designee Do you want to allow another person to discuss this return with the IRS (see page 66)? ☐ **Yes.** Complete the following. ☐ **No**

Designee's name ▶ Phone no. ▶ ( ) Personal identification number (PIN) ▶

Sign Here Under penalties of perjury, I declare that I have examined this return and accompanying schedules and statements, and to the best of my knowledge and belief, they are true, correct, and complete. Declaration of preparer (other than taxpayer) is based on all information of which preparer has any knowledge.

Joint return? See page 15. Keep a copy for your records.

Your signature	Date	Your occupation	Daytime phone number ( )
Spouse's signature. If a joint return, **both** must sign.	Date	Spouse's occupation	

Paid Preparer's Use Only

Preparer's signature ▶	Date	Check if self-employed ☐	Preparer's SSN or PTIN
Firm's name (or yours if self-employed), address, and ZIP code ▶		EIN	
		Phone no.	( )

Form **1040** (2008)

The O'Sullivans will receive a check from the U.S. government in the amount of $1,699.

EXAMPLE 10

At this point, students are ready for the difference between a tax credit and a tax deduction. Both are legal forms of tax avoidance. Deductions are taken before the income is looked up on a tax table or schedule, and tax credits are taken after. Tax credits are deductions directly from the tax amount. This difference can be difficult for students who are new to this whole topic.

CHECK YOUR UNDERSTANDING

Answer $x - d$; the tax credits have no affect on the taxable income. The taxable income is the income that is used to compute the tax, and the tax credit is taken after the tax is computed.

EXAMPLE 11

This example illustrates the benefits of knowing about your taxes in one succinct problem. Students also gain practice in computing taxes. Students could use the tax table in the Appendix instead of calculating the taxes due using Schedule X.

CHECK YOUR UNDERSTANDING

Answer \$2,297; be sure students use the Head of Household category when looking at the table.

■ CHECK YOUR UNDERSTANDING

The Safran family's income was x dollars. Their total deductions for the year were d dollars. They had c dollars of tax credits. Represent their taxable income algebraically.

EXAMPLE 11

Gloria is single. Her taxable income without deductions was \$25,760. She was able to reduce her total income by \$5,381 when she listed her allowable deductions on Schedule A. How much did she save in tax by using Schedule A?

SOLUTION Use Schedule X for Single Taxpayers, from Lesson 7-1 Applications, to determine her tax before deductions.

$(25{,}760 - 8{,}025)0.15 + 802.50$

The tax for a single person with taxable income \$25,760 is \$3,463.

Subtract the deductions from the income.

$25{,}760 - 5{,}381 = 20{,}379$

Determine the tax on the lower income.

$(20{,}379 - 8{,}025)0.15 + 802.50$

The tax on \$20,379 for a single person is \$2,656.

Subtract the tax after deductions from the tax before deductions.

$$3{,}463 - 2{,}656 = 807$$

Gloria saved \$807 by filing Schedule A with her Form 1040. Since she saved all of her bills, checks, and receipts that applied to Schedule A deductions in an envelope throughout the year, it only took her two hours to organize the receipts and fill out Schedule A.

■ CHECK YOUR UNDERSTANDING

Denise is divorced with one child, so she files her taxes as Head of Household. Her taxable income was \$76,312 before she filled out Schedule A. She had \$9,200 in Schedule A deductions. How much did using Schedule A save Denise in taxes?

Applications

Our forefathers made one mistake. What they should have fought for was representation without taxation.
Fletcher Knebel, American Author

1. How can the quote be interpreted in light of what you have learned? See margin.

Round all monetary answers to the nearest dollar. Use the tax tables in the Appendix or the appropriate schedule based on filing status.

2. Chiara had $5,700 in medical expenses last year. Her medical insurance covered 80% of these expenses. The IRS allows medical and dental expenses deductions for the amount that exceeds 7.5% of a taxpayer's adjusted gross income. If Chiara's adjusted gross income is $35,432, how much can she claim as a medical deduction? Explain See margin.
3. Maria and Don had $20,800 in medical expenses. Their family medical insurance covered 60% of these expenses. The IRS allows medical and dental expense deductions for the amount that exceeds 7.5% of a taxpayer's adjusted gross income. If their adjusted gross income is $101,598, how much can they claim as a medical deduction? $700
4. Jonathan is a single taxpayer. His total income before deductions was $63,110. He was able to reduce his total income by $10,312 when he filled out Schedule A. How much did he save in tax by using Schedule A? $2,587
5. Vito is single. His total income before deductions was $147,760. He was able to reduce his total income by $14,198 when he filled out Schedule A. How much did he save in tax by using Schedule A? Use the schedule on page 333. $3,976
6. Mr. and Mrs. Delta are filing a joint tax return. Together they had an income of $100,830 last year. Their total deductions were $16,848.
   a. What was Mr. and Mrs. Delta's taxable income? $83,982
   b. What is the tax on the amount in part a? $13,681
   c. The Delta's received a combined education and child tax credit of $2,500. How much tax must they pay after applying the tax credits? $11,181
   d. If their employers withheld $10,201 in federal income tax, how much money will they owe to the federal government? $980
7. Complete this chart. See margin.

Total Income Before Deductions	Filing Status	Total Deductions from Form 1040, Schedule A, and Exemptions	Taxable Income	Tax
$69,940	single	$3,500	a.	b.
$69,940	married filing separately	$3,500	c.	d.
$69,940	head of household	$6,900	e.	f.
$69,940	married filing separately	$6,900	g.	h.
$69,940	single	$6,900	i.	j.

TEACH

Exercises 1–7
These exercises do not deal with the tax forms; they examine how much can be saved by using deductions and credits. They give the students practice using tax tables and schedules. They summarize the taxpayer experience, without getting into the line-by-line specifics of the forms. This "big picture" is important—it is easy to lose sight of the net effect when getting so entrenched in the forms.

ANSWERS

1. "Taxation without representation" was a battle cry for American colonists before the Revolutionary War. Colonists felt it was unfair to pay taxes to a government in which you had no say. Knebel's quote underscores how people don't love paying taxes.
2. 0; 20% of $5,700 does not exceed 7.5% of $35,432.
7. a. 66,440
   b. 12,950
   c. 66,440
   d. 12,971
   e. 63,040
   f. 10,819
   g. 63,040
   h. 12,100
   i. 63,040
   j. 12,100

Exercises 8 and 9
Have students check their answers with you every few lines. Walk around the room with your key and place a check next to the last item. Filling in these forms are not ideal homework assignments; students need frequent feedback to learn the forms better.

For each family, complete a form 1040, Schedule A, and Schedule B to find total itemized deductions, interest and ordinary dividends, adjusted gross income, taxable income, tax due, and amount of refund or amount owed. Round all answers to the nearest dollar.

8. Donald and Barbara Mims are married with one child, Ashley. Donald is a piano tuner and Barbara is a car detailer. Donald's W-2 is shown and Barbara's W-2 provided her wages as $49,800 and the amount withheld for federal income tax as $8,123.

a Employee's social security number	000-00-0000
OMB No. 1545-0008	Safe, accurate, FAST! Use IRS e-file. Visit the IRS website at www.irs.gov/efile.
b Employer identification number (EIN)	00-0000000
c Employer's name, address, and ZIP code	Frank's Pianos, 231 Royal Guardsman Road, Plano, TX 75074
d Control number	
e Employee's first name and initial / Last name / Suff.	Donald / Mims
f Employee's address and ZIP code	175 Rickenbacker Road, Plano, TX 75074
1 Wages, tips, other compensation	$57,890.00
2 Federal income tax withheld	$9,765.00
3 Social security wages	$57,890.00
4 Social security tax withheld	
5 Medicare wages and tips	$57,890.00
6 Medicare tax withheld	
7 Social security tips	
8 Allocated tips	
9 Advance EIC payment	
10 Dependent care benefits	
11 Nonqualified plans	
12a See instructions for box 12	
12b	
12c	
12d	
13 Statutory employee / Retirement plan / Third-party sick pay	☐ ☐ ☐
14 Other	
15 State / Employer's state ID number	00-0000000
16 State wages, tips, etc.	$57,890.00
17 State income tax	$1,340.00
18 Local wages, tips, etc.	
19 Local income tax	
20 Locality name	

They received $556 in bank interest and $412 in stock dividends.

Their itemized deductions are:
Medical expenses: doctors $1,770, dentists $2,300
Taxes: $7,600
Interest Paid: $5,290
Contributions: cash $270, used clothing $200
Casualty and Theft Loss: $12,000
Job Expenses: union dues $400, tax preparation fees $175 See margin.

9. Mike and Julianne Heedles both work.

Julianne is a part-time environmental lawyer whose W-2 provided the following information.

Wages, tips, other compensation: $51,122.00
Social Security wages: $51,122.00
Medicare wages: $51,122.00
Federal income tax withheld: $5,004.00
State income tax withheld: $1,096.00

Mike is a gym teacher whose W-2 provided the following information.

Wages, tips, other compensation: $77,851.00
Social security wages: $77,851.00
Medicare wages: $77,851.00
Federal income tax withheld: $10,121.00
State income tax withheld: $3,215.00

They have two children. They received $1,897 in bank interest and $876 in stock dividends. Mike had $400 in educational expense deductions he can report on Form 1040.

Their itemized deductions are as follows.

Medical Expenses: prescriptions $600, doctors $5,240, dentists $2,300, eyeglasses $510
Taxes: State income from W-2, real estate $9,213
Interest Paid: home mortgage loan $7,110
Contributions: cash $980, used clothing $450, old furniture $250
Casualty and Theft Loss: storm damage to home not covered by insurance $3,450; camera stolen while on vacation $600
Job Expenses: union dues $1,200, tax preparation fees $395 See margin.

ANSWERS

8. total itemized deductions: $14,391; interest: $556; dividends: $412; adjusted gross income: $94,267; taxable income: $83,767; tax due: $13,631; refund: $4,257
9. total itemized deductions: $22,314; interest: $1,897; dividends: $876; adjusted gross income: $131,346; taxable income: $95,032; tax due: $16,444; owe: $1,319

Assessment

CHAPTER 7

Real Numbers

You Write the Story!!

Examine the graph. Write a short newspaper-type article based on this circle graph. You can find an electronic copy of this graph at www.cengage.com/school/math/financialalgebra. Copy and paste it into your article.

Revenue Sources for the Federal Government

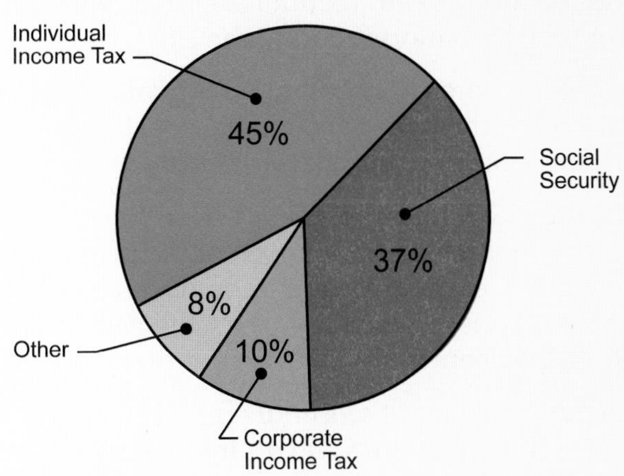

CHAPTER 7 ASSESSMENT

REAL NUMBERS

You Write the Story

The graph shown is often included on the IRS website and sometimes appears in the paper instruction booklets that go with the different forms.

REALITY CHECK

Reality Check projects are a terrific form of alternative assessment. They give students an additional avenue to show what they've learned, so their grades are not solely-based on tests.

Reality Check

1. Interview an accountant or tax preparer in your community. Before the interview, make a list of tax questions that you might ask. Prepare a written report including the questions and the accountant's answers. Ask for their fees and what determines the filing costs. Make a presentation to the class on the answers to your questions and about what accountants do besides help people with their income taxes.
2. Most people can find answers to basic tax form questions in the IRS publication *Your Federal Income Tax*. It is also called *Publication 17*. Download (www.irs.gov) or send for a free copy of *Publication 17*, by filling out a form in the current year's Instructions for Preparing Tax Forms. Go to the section on Schedule A: Itemized Deductions. Skim through the section. Make a list of 25 events, and whether or not they are tax deductible. Prepare a "quiz" for your classmates, listing the events, and asking other students what they think.
3. Download Tax Form 1040, Schedule A, Schedule B, and Form W-2 (www.irs.gov) or get copies at your local post office. Create an original story similar to those in Lesson 7-5. Complete the tax forms needed for your story as an answer key. Ask your teacher about assigning the story as homework, class work, or for extra practice.

Reality Check 2 can be done using online publications, or students can send away for their own paper copies of *Publication 17: Your Federal Income Tax*. It explains common procedures, forms, deductions, and credits.

Reality Check 4 brings a guest speaker into the classroom. Students always have lots of questions. You can stockpile these questions as they come up during the unit.

Realty Check 12 allows students to examine taxes on very high incomes.

The projects can be presented to the class on any schedule that works for your program. It may be too time-consuming for every student to present their project for every chapter.

Remind students who are personally visiting local businesses or community members that they are representing the school, and need to be cordial and patient. These projects deliberately have students taking little field trips, so they don't conduct everything online.

They need to thank any person who helps them in completing their Reality Check projects. A letter is the most personal way to do this.

You can offer students extra projects for extra credit.

4. Speak with your teacher about the possibility of having a guest speaker come to your classroom. Compile a list of local accountants, their email addresses, and their phone numbers. If there is an IRS office or Social Security office near your school, inquire there, too. Present the list to your teacher and discuss the logistics involved in having the speaker come to one of your classes and make a presentation, followed by a question-and-answer session.

5. Have a discussion with your parents about how they organize their tax information for the current tax year. Is there a special system they have for saving receipts and important tax documents so they are ordered and accessible at the end of the year? How do they remember all of their tax-related events at the end of the year?

6. Do an Internet search on IRS tax audit procedures, rules, rights, and regulations. Visit the IRS website and other websites you find in your search. Check out your local library, or arrange to interview an accountant. Prepare a written report on some of the major facts people should know about tax audits. Discuss with your teacher how you can present this information to the class.

7. Research tax software packages that are available in stores and on the Internet. Give the price of each package. Use the advertising or product description to give a specific feature of each.

8. Every year the IRS publishes a list of "What's New" for the tax year. Research what has been new for each of the last 5 years. Find out what new initiatives are still in place and which were abandoned over the 5-year period. Describe each of the new initiatives, and explain how they benefit the taxpayer or the government.

9. One of the nation's largest seasonal employers is H & R Block, an organization of tax preparers. Do an Internet search and/or visit a local H & R Block office, and find out the requirements for becoming a tax preparer for them. Include a job description of the tasks their employees perform, and for what months they are employed.

10. Over the years, the percent of federal tax for the highest tax bracket has changed. Do library or Internet research on these top bracket percents and prepare a graph showing the changes year by year.

Dollars and Sense — Your Financial News Update

Go to www.cengage.com/school/math/financialalgebra where you will find a link to a website containing current issues about income tax. Try one of the activities.

REVISITED Really? Really!

1. Use the Tax Freedom Day data to create a line graph. Let the x-axis represent that calendar year and the y-axis represent the numerical day of the year on which Tax Freedom Day falls. Hint: April 1st is the 91st day of a non-leap year.
2. Use the statistical features of your graphing calculator to determine the 4th degree quartic regression curve for the Tax Freedom Day data. Since we are beginning our list with the 1993 Tax Freedom Day, that year will be represented as year 1. The ordered pairs in the list should have the form (year number, day number). For example, the April 21st, 1993 Tax Freedom Day would be represented as the ordered pair (1, 111). That is, 1993 is the first year in our chart and April 21st is the 111th day of that year. Write the equation as displayed on the calculator. See margin.
3. Use your regression equation to predict the Tax Freedom Day for this year. Then, search the Internet to find the day that has been named as this year's Tax Freedom Day. How good of a predictor was your regression equation? Answers will vary depending on year.

REALLY? REALLY! REVISITED

Before students do these regression calculations, make sure that the class is comfortable with coordinates.

ANSWERS

2. $0.20x - 0.075y$ if 20% of medical expenses exceeds 7.5% of adjusted gross income, otherwise the amount is 0.

Applications

1. Jake and Gloria are married, filing jointly. Their taxable income without deductions was \$120,440. They were able to reduce their total income by \$25,381 using Form 1040 and Schedule A. How much did they save in tax by claiming these deductions? Use the tax tables in the Appendix and the schedule on page 333. \$8,950
2. The Lerners had x dollars in medical expenses. Medical insurance covered 80% of these expenses, so they had to pay 20% of the medical bills. The IRS allows medical and dental expenses deductions for the amount that exceeds 7.5% of a taxpayer's adjusted gross income. Their adjusted gross income was y dollars. Express the amount they can claim as a medical deduction algebraically. See margin.
3. Determine the tax for each filing status and taxable income amount listed using the tax tables in the Appendix.
   - **a.** single \$97,642 \$21,313
   - **b.** head of household \$95,100 \$18,844
   - **c.** married filing jointly \$99,999 \$17,681
   - **d.** married filing separately \$99,002 \$22,099
   - **e.** Given a taxable income amount t = \$97,226, express the tax table line that would be used in compound inequality notation. $t \geq 97{,}200$ and $t < 97{,}250$
   - **f.** Given the taxable income amount t = \$95,656, express the tax table line that would be used in interval notation. $95{,}650 \leq t < 95{,}700$

TEACH

Exercise 7

For Exercise 7, students need the maximum taxable income and correct Social Security and Medicare percents.

ANSWERS

6.

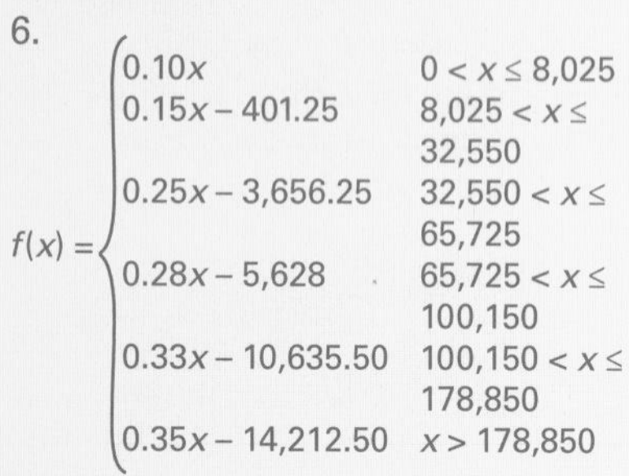

$$f(x) = \begin{cases} 0.10x & 0 < x \le 8{,}025 \\ 0.15x - 401.25 & 8{,}025 < x \le 32{,}550 \\ 0.25x - 3{,}656.25 & 32{,}550 < x \le 65{,}725 \\ 0.28x - 5{,}628 & 65{,}725 < x \le 100{,}150 \\ 0.33x - 10{,}635.50 & 100{,}150 < x \le 178{,}850 \\ 0.35x - 14{,}212.50 & x > 178{,}850 \end{cases}$$

4. Use the table to answer the questions below.

Schedule Y-1— If your filing status is **Married filing jointly or Qualifying widow(er)**

If your taxable income is: Over—	But not over—	The tax is:	of the amount over—
$0	$16,050	--------- 10%	$0
16,050	65,100	$1,605.00 + 15%	16,050
65,100	131,450	8,962.50 + 25%	65,100
131,450	200,300	25,550.00 + 28%	131,450
200,300	357,700	44,828.00 + 33%	200,300
357,700	---------	96,770.00 + 35%	357,700

a. What is the tax for taxpayers filing jointly with a combined taxable income of $134,786? $26,484.08

b. A married couple's tax is approximately $30,000. What is their approximate taxable income? $147,343

5. Let x represent the taxpayer's taxable income and y represent the tax. Express the line of the worksheet below as a linear equation in $y = mx + b$ form. Use interval notation to define the income range on which each of your equations is defined. $y = 0.25x - 4{,}937.50$ when $100{,}000 \le x < 112{,}650$

Section D — Use if your filing status is **Head of household**. Complete the row below that applies to you.

Taxable income. If line 43 is—	**(a)** Enter the amount from line 43	**(b)** Multiplication amount	**(c)** Multiply (a) by (b)	**(d)** Subtraction amount	**Tax** Subtract (d) from (c). Enter the result here and on Form 1040, line 44
At least $100,000 but not over $112,650	$	× 25% (.25)	$	$ 4,937.50	$

6. Write a piecewise function to represent the tax y for the taxable income interval in the schedule below for a taxpayer whose filing status is married filing separately. See margin.

Schedule Y-2— If your filing status is **Married filing separately**

If your taxable income is: Over—	But not over—	The tax is:	of the amount over—
$0	$8,025	--------- 10%	$0
8,025	32,550	$802.50 + 15%	8,025
32,550	65,725	4,481.25 + 25%	32,550
65,725	100,150	12,775.00 + 28%	65,725
100,150	178,850	22,414.00 + 33%	100,150
178,850	---------	48,385.00 + 35%	178,850

7. Ann's W-2 form reported total Medicare Wages as $88,340. She contributed $50 per weekly paycheck to her FSA and $90 per weekly paycheck to her retirement plan. She received a 1099 form from her bank for her savings account interest in the amount of $800 and a 1099 form from a book publisher for royalties in the amount of $3,700. What is Ann's adjusted gross income? $85,560

8. Mike pays $8,000 in property taxes, but receives a 28% tax deduction for it. What is Mike's net expense for property taxes? $5,760

9. Identify the error(s) on Rorie's W-2 form below.
Box 1 and Box 16 should be $86,100.

a Employee's social security number: 000-00-0000	OMB No. 1545-0008	Safe, accurate, FAST! Use IRS e-file	Visit the IRS website at www.irs.gov/efile.
b Employer identification number (EIN): 00-0000000		1 Wages, tips, other compensation: $96,900.00	2 Federal income tax withheld: $23,256.00
c Employer's name, address, and ZIP code: Saturn Publishing Company, 251 Broadway, Taftsville, VT 05073		3 Social security wages: $96,900.00	4 Social security tax withheld: $6,007.80
		5 Medicare wages and tips: $96,900.00	6 Medicare tax withheld: $1,405.05
		7 Social security tips	8 Allocated tips
d Control number: 2187690		9 Advance EIC payment	10 Dependent care benefits
e Employee's first name and initial: Rorie	Last name: Welles	11 Nonqualified plans	12a See instructions for box 12: E | $7,600.00
		13 Statutory employee ☐ Retirement plan ☒ Third-party sick pay ☐	12b
615 Memorial Dr., Sudbury, VT 05233		14 Other: caf125 $3,200.00	12c
f Employee's address and ZIP code			12d

15 State Employer's state ID number	16 State wages, tips, etc.	17 State income tax	18 Local wages, tips, etc.	19 Local income tax	20 Locality name
	$96,900.00	$9,978.00			

For each exercise, complete the indicated forms to find adjusted gross income, taxable income, tax due, and amount of refund or amount owed. If appropriate, find the total itemized deductions, and the interest and ordinary dividends. Round all answers to the nearest dollar. Use the tax tables in the Appendix.

10. Katie and Ken are married with three children. The following information was reported on their W-2 forms.

They received $924.78 in interest on bank deposits and $1,011 in stock dividends. Fill out a Form 1040A for Katie and Ken.

	Katie	Ken
Federal income tax withheld	$ 9,800	$11,500
Wages	$49,000	$52,000

11. Von is a single taxpayer. His wages for the year are $66,200. The amount withheld for federal taxes was $9,930. His bank interest is $1,200. Fill in his 1040EZ form.

12. Connor and Samantha Lamberti are married with three children. Their total wages for the year were $90,114. The total amount withheld from their paychecks for federal taxes was $7,209.12. They received $1,328 in bank interest and $776 in dividends. Samantha had $400 in educational expense deductions.

Their itemized deductions are: Medical Expenses: prescriptions $550, doctors $1,340, dentists $1,761, eyeglasses $430; Taxes: State income tax withheld $7,108, real estate tax $8,219; Interest Paid: home mortgage loan $6,629; Contributions: cash, $1,000; used clothing, $550; old toys $150; Casualty and Theft Loss: Luggage stolen while on vacation $4,600; and Job Expenses: union dues, $1,350; resume costs, $75.

Complete a current Form 1040 for them, including Schedules A and B. Round all entries to the nearest dollar.

TEACH

Exercises 10–12

In Exercises 10–12, students complete tax forms. Have students check their answers with you every few lines. Walk around the room with your key and place a check next to the last item you corrected. Then, when you see that student again during the period or the next day, you will know what you have already checked. For this reason, filling in these forms are not ideal homework assignments; students need frequent feedback to learn the forms better.

ANSWERS

10. adjusted gross income: $102,936; taxable income: $74,536; tax due: $11,319; refund: $9,981
11. adjusted gross income: $67,400; taxable income: $58,450; tax due: $10,963; owe: $1,033
12. total itemized deductions: $23,656; interest: $1,328; dividends: $776; adjusted gross income: $91,818; taxable income: $50,662; tax due: $6,799; refund: $410

CHAPTER

8 Independent Living

I long, as does every human being, to be at home wherever I find myself.

Maya Angelou, American Poet

What do you think Maya Angelou meant in her quote?

You may have heard the expressions "Be it ever so humble, there's no place like home" and "Home is where the heart is." A home can be many things. It can be a tent, an igloo, a hotel room, a tree house, an apartment, a condominium, a co-op, a house, a penthouse, or a mansion. A home is a place where a person establishes him or herself. The end of your schooling will mark a time in your life when you begin to become independent. When this happens, you may find that you will be spending a large part of your income on housing and household expenses. For most people, a home represents the largest financial undertaking of their lives. There are many factors that influence how and where you will live. With so much money involved, you will want to make wise, well-thought-out decisions. In this chapter, you will learn how to embark on the road to independent living.

What do you think?

Physical structure and amenities describe a house. A home is more of an emotional place, as the two quotes at the beginning of the paragraph stress. Students embarking on young adulthood will not have the financial resources to afford lavish homes. Nevertheless, they will be able to create a place that will afford them lifelong memories and fond recollections.

TEACHING RESOURCES

Instructor's Resource CD

Exam*View*® CD, Ch. 8

eHomework, Ch. 8

www.cengage.com/school/math/financialalgebra

Really?

Moving yourself to a new location is a big undertaking. But what about moving an entire building to a new location! This happens more often than you think.

Sometimes, prospective buyers fall in love with a home but not the location. Or, a developer is willing to sell an old structure for a cheap price so that he can build new structures on that location. Homes are not the only structures that take to the road. Here are the five heaviest buildings whose owners moved the buildings to different locations.

- The Shubert Theater, Minneapolis, Minnesota—2,908 tons
- The Hotel Montgomery, San Jose, California—4,816 tons
- Cape Hatteras Lighthouse, Outer Banks, North Carolina—4,830 tons
- Newark International Airport Building 51, Newark, New Jersey—7,400 tons
- Fu Gang Building, Guangxi Provence, China—15,140 metric tons

Moving a building to a new location takes a great deal of mathematics. Math plays a central role in the planning, engineering, approvals, finances, and more.

CHAPTER OVERVIEW

Students use algebra and geometry skills to investigate the processes of looking for a place to live, understanding the layout of the living space, and calculating the costs of renting or buying a home.

REALLY? REALLY!

The photo shows moving the Cape Hatteras Lighthouse. Moving a house or large building is something that most people have never seen in person. Many airplanes are much heavier than most houses, and they fly! The thought of moving an immense structure through narrow streets, under power lines, and around corners is fascinating. There are television programs on house-moving, and students can also learn more searching the Internet.

Really!

What is more agreeable than one's home?
Marcus Tullius Cicero, Ancient Roman Writer, Scholar, and Statesman

8-1 Find a Place to Live

Objectives

- Calculate the affordability of a monthly rent.
- Determine the relationship between square footage and monthly rent.
- Determine lease signing costs.
- Calculate moving expenses.

Common Core

A-CED2, A-CED3, A-REI6, S-ID6a, S-ID6c, S-ID8

Key Terms

- apartment
- tenant
- landlord
- furnished
- unfurnished
- lease
- expire
- evict
- single-family home
- square footage
- application deposit
- security deposit

CCSS Warm-Up

Find the linear regression equation for the scatterplot with the points below.
(1, 14); (2, 16.4); (3, 19); (4, 27); (5, 26)
$y = 9.46x - 1.9$

EXAMINE THE QUESTION

This is a question about life transitions. You might ask yourself, where will I be living in a few years? You may remain at home with your parents or rent an apartment. You might be living on a base as a member of the military or in a dorm room during your college years. When it comes time to decide where to live, knowing your options makes it a less stressful decision.

WHERE WILL YOU LIVE?

Have you ever imagined what it would be like to have a place of your own? For many teenagers, the usual progression of living arrangements is from family home to dorm room to apartment to homeownership. Finding a place to live isn't easy. There are many decisions to make.

Your first experience in independent living will probably be in a rented **apartment**. When you rent an apartment, you are the **tenant**, and the owner of the apartment is the **landlord**. As you look for an apartment to rent, you will see that they come **furnished** or **unfurnished**. The cost of renting a furnished apartment includes the use of the landlord's furniture in that apartment. You must provide your own furniture when you rent an unfurnished apartment. Before you move into any apartment, you must sign a **lease**. A lease is a written agreement between the landlord and the tenant that details the amount of rent and the length of time that you will rent the apartment. The lease states the rules and regulations that must be followed by the tenant and the landlord. After a lease **expires** or ends, the tenant may sign a new lease for a new period of time and this lease may have an increase in the rent. If, for any reason, a tenant stops paying rent, they have defaulted on the lease, and may be **evicted** from the apartment.

While renting is a suitable option for many, others find owning a home is their goal. There are many options for ownership. You can purchase a **single-family home**, a multiple-family home, a condominium, or a cooperative.

Rather than renting an apartment, there is a possibility that you can purchase and own that apartment if it is part of a cooperative or condominium. A condominium is a form of home ownership where each unit is individually owned. Each individual unit is called a condominium or condo. Condominium owners own everything from the walls inward and are responsible for the maintenance of the inside of their own units. The owners are charged a maintenance fee that is used to maintain common areas such as a lobby, lawn, roof, sidewalks, and roads.

A co-op apartment or residence is another form of home ownership. A cooperative is a corporation. Cooperative owners own shares in the corporation and the right to live in a unit. They are also responsible for the maintenance of the inside of their units.

Skills and Strategies

Here you will learn how to make sound decisions when considering rentals or purchases based on data available.

Affording the Rent

Every 10 years, the U.S. Census Bureau collects data. The following chart illustrates the average amount that people paid for rent as a percentage of their incomes.

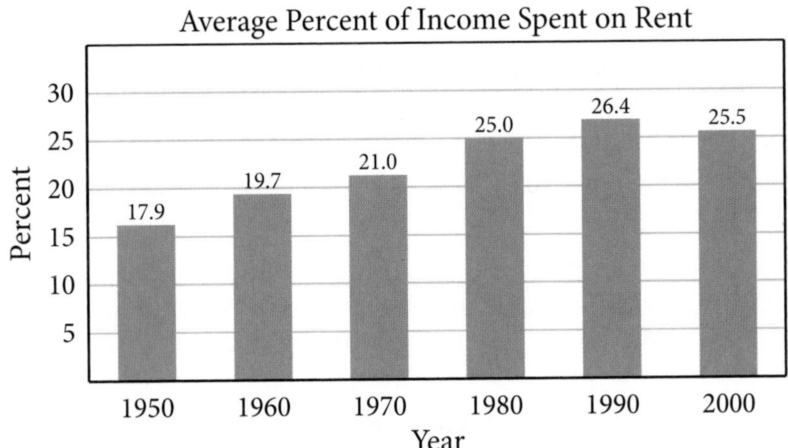

Notice how the percentage appears to be hovering around 25% since 1980. Experts agree that as a rule, a prospective renter should budget 25% to 30% of their gross income for rent.

TEACH

The topic of housing options may be new to students. Students should know the options, opportunities, and financial responsibilities that are involved. As you begin this chapter, create a large poster (or reserve a portion of board space that can remain untouched over the life of this chapter). Create a graphic organizer and add to it as new information surfaces. Start with the heading "Independent Living" then branch off with two paths: "Renting" and "Owning". Tailor the organizer to meet the needs of your students. The paths can include options, benefits, concerns, or a combination. As the organizer builds, students will be able to see the decisions they will have to make in planning for their futures.

EXAMPLE 1

Alex makes $61,992 per year and pays about 25% of his gross monthly income in federal and state taxes. He wants to find an apartment to rent. Estimate how much he can afford to pay for rent each month. Then determine how much money he will have after taxes and rent are paid.

SOLUTION The recommended rule is to budget 25% to 30% of the gross income for rent. A good estimate to use is 28%. Rent is paid on a monthly basis, so find Alex's gross monthly income.

Divide annual income by 12. $61{,}992 \div 12 = 5{,}166$

Alex's gross monthly income is $5,166. Find 28% of his monthly income to estimate an affordable amount.

Multiply by 0.28. $5{,}166 \times 0.28 = 1{,}446.48$

Alex can afford an apartment with a monthly rent of about $1,446.

Alex pays 25% of his gross monthly income in federal and state taxes.

Multiply by 0.25. $5{,}166 \times 0.25 = 1{,}291.50$

Alex pays about $1,291 in taxes each month. To find the amount remaining each month, subtract the amounts for rent and taxes from Alex's monthly income.

$$5{,}166 - 1{,}446 - 1{,}292 = 2{,}430$$

Alex will have approximately $2,430 remaining.

EXAMPLE 1

Although the computation involved in this example is fairly basic, the importance of the question is not. Before any individual begins the process of looking to rent or buy, they need to assess what they can afford. Using the 25–30% ceiling as a rule of thumb helps people put options in perspective.

CHECK YOUR UNDERSTANDING

Answer No; after paying her taxes, loan, and credit card company, she is left with less than $1,800. She should find a less expensive apartment.

You could also find the remaining amount by determining the percent of Alex's income that is not spent on taxes and rent. Subtracting these percents from 100% yields 47% since 100 − 25 − 28 = 47. You can verify that 47% of $5,166 equals $2,428.02, which is close to the estimate found previously.

■ CHECK YOUR UNDERSTANDING

Bethany's monthly gross income is $3,840. She pays 24% of her monthly gross earnings in federal and state taxes and 15% for her student loan. Bethany uses 15% of her monthly gross income to pay toward her credit card balance. She wants to rent an apartment that will cost $1,800 per month. Will she be able to make the payments without changing the amounts she pays toward her student loans and credit card balances?

Shopping for a Rental

Once you have determined what you can afford to pay in rent, it is time to start looking at the classified ads for rental property. As with automobile classifieds, you should become familiar with the abbreviations that are used. Here are a few of the common ones.

ba or bth, bathroom
br, bedroom
DW or D/W or dshwr, dishwasher
DR, dining room
Drmn, doorman
EIK, eat-in-kitchen
elev, elevator in building
gar, garage
h/w, hardwood floors
htd, heat is included in rent
incl ht/hw, includes heat and hot water
mint, excellent condition
renov, renovated
rm, room
stu, studio
spac, spacious
WIC, walk-in closet
W/D, washer and dryer
w/d hkup, washer and dryer hookup
w/w, wall-to-wall carpeting
yd, yard

In addition to explaining what the apartment has to offer, classified ads often include the **square footage** of each apartment. This number is the amount of floor space available in the apartment.

EXAMPLE 2

Students are familiar with regression analysis. This example asks them to see if a relationship exists between the size of an apartment and the rent. Impress upon them that the apartments listed have similar layouts and amenities and are in comparable neighborhoods. Square footage alone may not be the single factor that determines price. But, when similar dwellings are examined, it can be a powerful indicator.

EXAMPLE 2

Rufus and Maria have both been offered new jobs in a different city. A real estate broker sent them a listing of apartments in their desired location showing the square footage in each apartment. Use linear regression analysis to determine if there is a correlation between the square footage of rental property and the amount charged for the monthly rent. What is the linear regression equation? Interpret the correlation coefficient.

Square Feet	Monthly Rent ($)
664	995
735	1,045
787	1,095
872	1,205
903	1,245
993	1,325
976	1,295
1,133	1,295
1,150	1,595
1,244	1,595
1,474	1,595
1,697	1,995

SOLUTION Use the statistics features on your graphing calculator to create a scatterplot. Graph the linear regression line.

```
LinReg
 y=ax+b
 a=.9061573426
 b=403.0870898
 r²=.9229477794
 r=.960701712
```

The linear regression equation is $y = 0.91x + 403.09$ to the nearest hundredth.

The correlation coefficient of 0.96 indicates that square footage is a good predictor of the amount charged as rent for these apartments.

CHECK YOUR UNDERSTANDING

Based on Example 2, what is a good estimate for the amount of monthly rent charged for an 880-square foot apartment?

CHECK YOUR UNDERSTANDING

Answer approximately $1,200

Lease Signing Costs

It isn't enough just to have the first month's rent available. There are a number of fees that are associated with the rental of any property. Usually, there is an **application deposit**. This amount, which is sometimes refundable, may vary between $100 and $400. It covers the cost of processing the application for the rental. Often a credit report is required. The fee for this report is usually under $25.

A **security deposit** is money given to the landlord from the tenant as protection in the event that the tenant causes damage to the rented property. This deposit is refunded when the tenant moves out if there is no damage. The security deposit can range from 1 to 4 month's rent.

EXAMPLE 3

Students might be surprised by the upfront costs of renting. Remind them that some of the costs are refundable at a later date.

CHECK YOUR UNDERSTANDING

Answer $125 + 4.6r$

In addition to the first month's rent paid in advance, many landlords also require the last month's rent to be paid at the time of move in. This protects the landlord in the event that the tenant decides to break the lease and vacate the apartment earlier than agreed in the contract.

If you use a broker to find an apartment, there will be an additional fee for the broker's services; usually a percentage of a year's rent.

EXAMPLE 3

Rufus and Maria paid a $200 application deposit for the 1,150-square foot apartment in Example 2. They are required to provide a credit report that costs $25 and pay a security deposit equal to one month's rent. The landlord also requires the last month's rent at the time of signing the lease. The broker charged 10% of the yearly rent. How much should they expect to pay to be able to move into the apartment?

SOLUTION Rufus and Maria should plan on paying the following:

Application deposit	$ 200
Credit report fee	$ 25
Security deposit: 1 month's rent	$1,595
Last month's rent	$1,595
Broker's fee: 0.1(1,595 × 12)	$1,914
First month's rent	$1,595
Add these amounts to find the total.	$6,924

Rufus and Maria should expect to pay $6,924 before moving into their apartment.

CHECK YOUR UNDERSTANDING

Larry is renting an apartment that will cost *r* dollars per month. He must pay a $100 application fee and a $25 credit report fee. His security deposit is two month's rent, and he must also pay the last month's rent upon signing the lease. His broker charges 5% of the total year's rent as the fee for finding the apartment. Express in terms of *r* the total cost of signing the lease.

Moving Costs

Whether you are renting or purchasing a home, you need to budget for moving expenses. When planning a move, you should consider all of the options available to you.

You can elect to have someone do all of the packing, loading, transporting, unloading, and unpacking for you. Or, you can do all or part of it yourself, with or without help from professionals.

The cost of making a move depends upon a variety of factors: how much of the work you choose to do, the distance you are moving, the weight and size of your belongings, how accessible the items are to street level (Are you on the first floor? Are there many flights of stairs? Is there an elevator?), and the location of the pick up and drop off of your items. These are only a few of the factors that come into play when you are given a moving estimate. Many companies offer online services to help you.

EXAMPLE 4

Jay is moving from an apartment in Miami to one in Orlando. If Jay moves on a weekday, he will need more movers' time to pack, load, unload, and unpack because his friends will not be able to help him. If he moves on a weekend, he can get his friends to help, cutting down on the number of hours he will need to hire movers. MoveOut is a moving company that supplies movers, trucks, and moving equipment. They have given him the following moving estimates.

Weekday Move	**Weekend Move**
6 hours of loading/unloading	4 hours of loading/unloading
5 hours of packing/unpacking	2 hours of packing/unpacking
\$720 total cost	\$400 total cost

MoveOut charges a set hourly moving team rate for loading and unloading, and a different set hourly moving team rate for packing and unpacking. Determine the MoveOut hourly rates.

SOLUTION Solve this problem by setting up a system of two equations. First, identify the variables to use. Let x represent the hourly cost for loading/unloading. Let y represent the hourly cost for packing/unpacking.

Two equations can be written that model the moving costs.

Weekday Move $6x + 5y = 720$ Weekend Move $4x + 2y = 400$

To graph these linear equations, first solve for y.

$$6x + 5y = 720 \qquad\qquad 4x + 2y = 400$$

$$5y = -6x + 720 \qquad\qquad 2y = -4x + 400$$

$$\frac{5y}{5} = \frac{-6x + 720}{5} \qquad\qquad \frac{2y}{2} = \frac{-4x + 400}{2}$$

$$y = -\frac{6}{5}x + 144 \qquad\qquad y = -2x + 200$$

WINDOW
Xmin=1
Xmax=130
Xscl=10
Ymin=0
Ymax=210
Yscl=10
Xres=1

Use values slightly greater than the x- and y-intercepts to determine an appropriate viewing window. In the weekday equation, the x-intercept is 120, and the y-intercept is 144. In the weekend equation, the x-intercept is 100, and the y-intercept is 200.

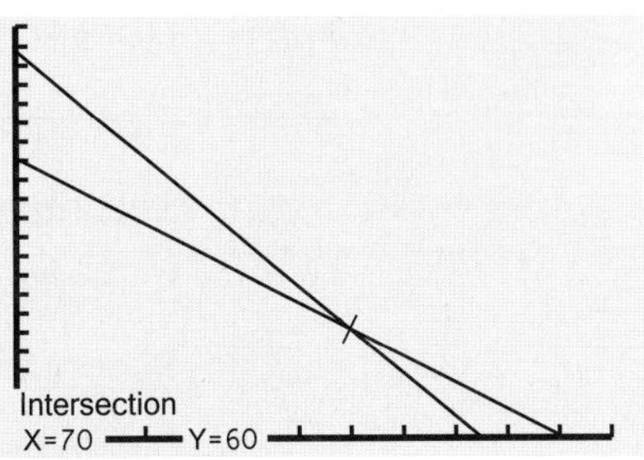

The setting for the viewing window and the graphs of the two equations are shown.

Using the intersection feature on your calculator, you can determine that the two lines intersect at the point (70, 60). This indicates that MoveOut charges \$70 per hour for loading/unloading and \$60 per hour for packing/unpacking.

CHECK YOUR UNDERSTANDING

Using the information above, suppose that Jay hired the movers for P hours to pack and unpack and for L hours to load and unload. Write an expression that represents his moving cost for these services.

EXAMPLE 4

In Chapter 2, students determined the solution to a system of two equations with two unknowns graphically. In this example, they will solve the system in a similar way. Make sure that they identify the variables at the outset and are careful with the equation statement. The initial equation will be written in the standard form of $ax + by = c$. In order to graph the linear equations, it is necessary to rewrite them in $y = mx + b$ form. Using the graphing calculator, students will be able to find the point of intersection and determine the rates for loading/unloading and packing/unpacking.

CHECK YOUR UNDERSTANDING

Answer $60P + 70L$

EXAMPLE 5

Students will now use the method of elimination to solve a system of two equations with two unknowns. They should be familiar with this method from a previous algebra course.

CHECK YOUR UNDERSTANDING

Answer (75, 5)

Systems of equations can also be solved algebraically. The *elimination method* is the process of algebraically manipulating one or both equations so that the coefficients of one set of variable terms are opposite and will drop out when the equations are combined as shown in Example 5.

EXAMPLE 5

Samantha is moving from Madison, WI to La Crosse, WI. She will do all of the packing and unpacking by herself with her brother. The moving company quoted a price of $1,250 for 8 hours of loading and unloading and driving 130 miles. The company quoted the same price if the truck drives an extra 30 miles to pick up Samantha's brother. Samantha figures that with her brother's help she only needs to hire the movers for 6 hours. How much does the company charge per hour for the loading/unloading? How much do they charge per mile for driving?

SOLUTION Let x represent the hourly cost for loading and unloading. Let y represent the per-mile cost for renting the truck.

	Load/Unload Hours	Mileage
Situation without brother	8	130
Situation with brother	6	160
Cost	$1,250	$1,250

Write the equations that model each situation.

Labor cost + Truck rental cost = Total cost

$$8x + 130y = 1{,}250$$

$$6x + 160y = 1{,}250$$

Use the elimination method to solve the system of equations. Multiply the first equation by –3, and multiply the second equation by 4 so the coefficients of the x-terms are opposites.

$$-3(8x + 130y) = -3(1{,}250) \quad \rightarrow \quad -24x - 390y = -3{,}750$$

$$4(6x + 160y) = 4(1{,}250) \quad \rightarrow \quad 24x + 640y = 5{,}000$$

Add the equations. $\quad 250y = 1{,}250$

Solve for y. Divide each side by 250. $\quad y = 5$

Use $y = 5$ to substitute into either of the original equations to solve for x.

First equation $\quad 8x + 130y = 1{,}250$

Substitute 5 for y. $\quad 8x + 130(5) = 1{,}250$

Simplify. $\quad 8x + 650 = 1{,}250$

Subtract 650 from each side. $\quad 8x = 600$

Divide by 8. $\quad x = 75$

Samantha will pay $75 per hour for loading/unloading and $5 per mile for the truck rental.

CHECK YOUR UNDERSTANDING

If you graph the two equations in Example 5, what is the point of intersection?

Applications

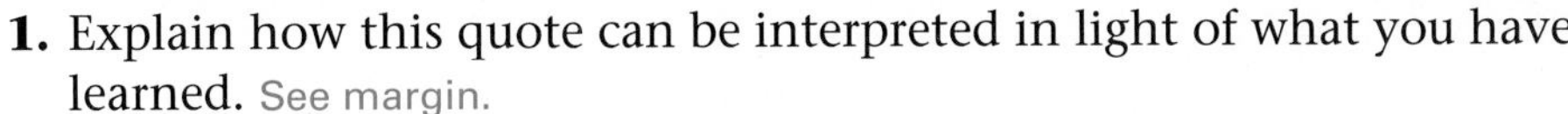

What is more agreeable than one's home?
Marcus Tullius Cicero, Ancient Roman Writer, Scholar, and Statesman

1. Explain how this quote can be interpreted in light of what you have learned. See margin.
2. Use the interval 25%–30% to find the monetary range that is recommended for the monthly housing budget in each situation. Round to the nearest dollar.
   a. Mark makes $86,000 per year. $1,792–$2,150
   b. Linda makes $7,000 per month. $1,750–$2,100
   c. Meghan makes $1,500 per week. $1,625–$1,950
3. Jessica's financial advisor believes that she should spend no more than 28% of her gross monthly income for housing. She has determined that amount is $1,400 per month. Based on this amount and her advisor's recommendation, what is Jessica's annual salary? $60,000
4. Abe makes $18.50 per hour. He works 37 hours a week. He pays 23% of his gross earnings in federal and state taxes and saves 5% of his monthly gross income. He is considering renting an apartment that will cost $1,500 per month.
   a. Is this monthly rental fee within the recommended 25%–30% housing expense range? no
   b. Based upon his expenses, can he make the monthly payments? Yes, but it is not recommended because he will have only about $600 for all other expenses.
5. Rachel is considering moving into a one-bedroom apartment in Glen Gardens. The apartment has a monthly rent of $1,300. Here are the fees that she has been quoted. How much is she expected to pay up front in order to rent this apartment? $5,808

   Application fee: 2% of one month's rent
   Credit application fee: $10
   Security deposit: 1 month's rent
   Last month's rent
   Broker's fee: 12% of one year's rent

6. Milena has a gross biweekly income of $2,200. She pays 18% in federal and state taxes, puts aside 10% of her income to pay off her school loan, and puts 5% of her income aside for savings. She is considering an apartment that rents for $1,200 per month.
   a. Is this monthly rental fee within the recommended 25%–30% housing expense range? yes
   b. Based on her expenses, can she make the monthly payments? yes
7. A moving helper company gave Mike these two quotes. Use a system of equations to determine the hourly rates for loading/unloading and packing/unpacking. See margin.

3 hours of loading/unloading	5 hours of loading/unloading
2 hours of packing/unpacking	2 hours of packing/unpacking
Total cost: $480	Total cost: $680

8. Jaden received these two estimates from a moving company. Write and solve a system of equations to determine the hourly loading/unloading fee and the mileage charge for the truck rental. See margin.

   Situation A: He hires 5 helpers to load and unload the truck and travels 80 miles on back roads for a total cost of $780.

   Situation B: He hires 6 helpers to load and unload the truck and takes a highway route which adds 20 miles to the trip but gets the truck to the destination faster for a total cost of $960.

ANSWERS

1. Perhaps this is the earliest version of the phrase "There is no place like home." Cicero implies that sentiment in his quote, and Americans still believe it to be true to this day.
7. $100 per hour for loading/unloading and $90 per hour for packing/unpacking
8. $5x + 80y = 780$; $6x + 100y = 960$; $x = \$60$ (per helper), $y = \$6$ per mile

Square Feet	Monthly Rent	Square Feet	Monthly Rent
400	$ 980	500	$1,200
1,000	$2,000	700	$1,600
650	$1,500	900	$1,900
800	$1,700	750	$1,550
850	$1,725	480	$1,050

9. Ann obtained this list of apartments.
   a. Use linear regression analysis to determine if there is a correlation between the square footage and the monthly rent. See margin.
   b. Determine the regression equation. Round the numbers in the equation to the nearest hundredth. $y = 1.74x + 299.46$
   c. Use your regression equation to determine the price you might expect to pay for an 810-square foot apartment. $1,708.86

Exercises 12 and 13
In Exercise 12, students can algebraically determine the square footage (y-value) using the equation or they can enter the regression equation into the calculator and use the table feature.

10. Use the information from Exercise 9.
    a. Determine the correlation coefficient and linear regression equation that expresses the square footage as a function of the monthly rent. Round the numbers in the equation to the nearest hundredth. correlation coefficient = 0.987; $y = 0.56x - 149.07$
    b. Use your regression equation to determine the square footage you might expect if renting a $1,710 apartment. approximately 809 square feet

Application Fee: 1.5% of one month's rent
Credit Application Fee: $10
Security Deposit: 1 month's rent
Last month's rent
Broker's Fee: 9% of one year's rent

11. Dave wants to rent a two-bedroom apartment in City Fields. The apartment has a monthly rent of D dollars. Here are the fees that he has been quoted. Write an algebraic expression that represents the amount he is expected to pay before renting the apartment. $D + 0.015D + 10 + D + D + 0.09(12D) = 4.095D + 10$

Exercise 13 asks students to again use a regression equation, but now determine the monthly rent.

Exercises 14 and 15
These exercises should be assigned together. The first has students doing calculations to find an exact moving cost. The second uses the same procedure but has an algebraic expression as the answer.

12. The square footage and monthly rental of 10 similar one-bedroom apartments yield the linear regression $y = 0.775x + 950.25$, where x represents the square footage of the apartment and y represents the monthly rental price. Grace can afford $1,500 per month rent. Using the equation, what size apartment should she expect to be able to rent for that price? about 709 square feet
13. The square footage and monthly rental of 10 similar two-bedroom apartments yield the linear regression formula $y = 1.165x + 615.23$ where x represents the square footage of the apartment and y represents the monthly rental price.
    a. Use the formula to determine the monthly rent for an apartment that has 1,500 square feet. $2,362.73
    b. Based upon the recommendation that you should spend no more than 28% of your monthly gross income on housing, can Jacob afford this rental if he makes $8,000 each month. Explain. No, the recommendation is to spend no more than $2,240.

ANSWERS

9a. correlation coefficient = 0.987

$85 per hour for loading/unloading service
$70 per hour for packing/unpacking service
$5 per mile for truck rental

14. WeMoveU charges for moving according to the rate schedule shown. Nicky is moving a distance of 150 miles and needs 7 hours of loading/unloading and 5 hours of packing/unpacking. What will her moving cost be if the service also charges 8% tax on the total? $1,830.60

L dollars per hour for loading and loading service
P dollars per hour for packing and unpacking service
M dollars per mile for truck rental

15. Van4Hire charges for moving according to this rate schedule. Nicky is moving a distance of D miles and needs A hours of loading/unloading and B hours of packing/unpacking. Write an algebraic expression that represents her total moving cost. $AL + BP + MD$

A good home must be made, not bought.
Joyce Maynard, American Author

Read a Floor Plan 8-2

Key Terms			
	• floor plan • area • congruent	• apothem • perimeter • Monte Carlo method	• volume • British Thermal Units (BTUs)

Objectives

- Compute the perimeter and the area of a polygon.
- Compute areas of irregular regions.
- Compute volumes of rectangular solids.

Common Core

G-C5, G-MG3

CCSS Warm-Up

A circle has diameter 10 feet. It is cut into two semicircles. Find the area of the semicircle to the nearest hundredth.

39.27 ft^2

How much space do I want? How much space do I need?

When you begin to look for a place to live, price and location are not the only factors you should consider. One important consideration is the number of rooms, room sizes, and the layout of the living space. This information is shown on a floor plan. A **floor plan** is a drawing of the layout and dimensions of rooms. The floor plan shown is for a one-bedroom apartment. Here is some of the information that the floor plan shows you:

- This apartment has a kitchen, a dining room, a living room, a bedroom, and a bathroom.
- The bathroom has a sink, a toilet, a bathtub, and one window.
- The bedroom is 15 feet by 12 feet; it has two windows and one doorway.
- The living room is 20 feet by 12 feet; it has one large window and three entrances, one being the outside entrance.
- The dining area is 8 feet by 7 feet and has three entrances and no windows.
- The kitchen has cabinets, counter space, a sink, a stove, a refrigerator, one window, and one entrance.

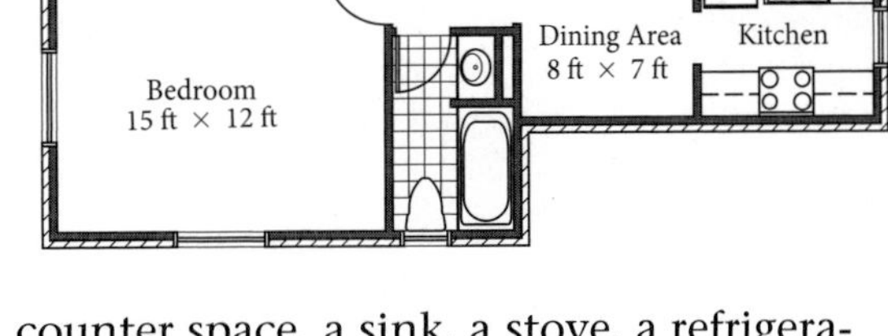

Examining a floor plan allows you to make intelligent decisions before you move in. It helps you determine what furniture will fit in each room. Everybody likes to have ample space that suits their living style, family size, and hobbies. Larger spaces usually are more expensive, so deciding what you want and what you need is a balancing act with what you can afford.

EXAMINE THE QUESTION

Different people have different needs when it comes to living space. How many people are in the family? How many bedrooms do you need? Do you need office space at home? Do you need a dining room or is the kitchen big enough to eat in? Will your furniture fit in the rooms? These are just a few of the many questions you will have to ask yourself before you select a home.

CLASS DISCUSSION

Discuss the type of apartment students would like as their first places to live when they move out on their own.

Ask students how houses that have the same floor plan can look different from the street.

TEACH

These examples are all geometric in nature. They involve areas and perimeters of regular and irregular plane figures. Volumes of rooms are also scrutinized, since volume relates to air-conditioning and heating costs.

EXAMPLE 1

Some students may have seen pictures of floor plans drawn by an architect. These drawings must be to scale so the contractors can purchase the correct amount of materials. The most-used scale for homes is $\frac{1}{4}$-inch represents 1 foot.

You can create floor plans by hand or by using computer software specifically designed to draw floor plans. Floor plans are drawn to scale—they are drawn in the same proportion as the actual home. Even if you never need to draw your own floor plan, you need to know how to read them.

Skills and Strategies

Here you will learn to read floor plans and use information in the floor plans to make buying decisions.

EXAMPLE 1

Jerry is using the floor plans for his new home to help him purchase base molding for the place where the walls meet the floor. The plans are drawn using a scale of $\frac{1}{4}$ inch represents 1 foot. He measures the walls on the floor plan with a ruler and finds that they total $23\frac{1}{2}$ inches. If molding costs \$2.10 per foot, how much will Jerry spend on molding?

SOLUTION Jerry needs to use a proportion to convert the scale measurements to the actual measurements in feet. Recall that a proportion is created when two ratios are set equal to each other.

When setting up a proportion, keep like units in the numerators and like units in the denominators.

$$\frac{0.25 \text{ inch}}{1 \text{ foot}} = \frac{\text{Number of inches on the floor plan}}{\text{Actual number of feet in the room}}$$

Substitute. $\frac{0.25 \text{ inch}}{1 \text{ foot}} = \frac{23.5 \text{ inches}}{x}$

Cross multiply. $0.25x = 23.5(1)$

Divide each side by 0.25. $x = 94$

Jerry needs 94 feet of molding.

To find the total cost, multiply the number of feet of molding by the cost per foot.

$$94(2.10) = 197.40$$

The molding will cost Jerry \$197.40.

CHECK YOUR UNDERSTANDING

Answer $4\frac{1}{4}$ inches

■ **CHECK YOUR UNDERSTANDING**

The length of a room is 17 feet. When using $\frac{1}{4}$ inch = 1 foot scale, what is the length of the room on a floor plan?

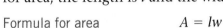

EXAMPLE 2

Gabriela plans to carpet her living room, except for the quarter-circle shown in the corner. That area will be a wood floor where she will put her piano. The radius of the quarter circle is 8 feet. If carpeting costs \$9.55 per square foot, what is the cost of the carpeting she will use in her living room?

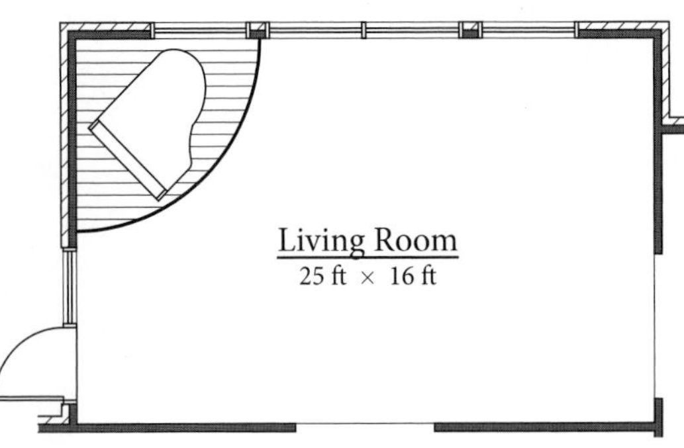

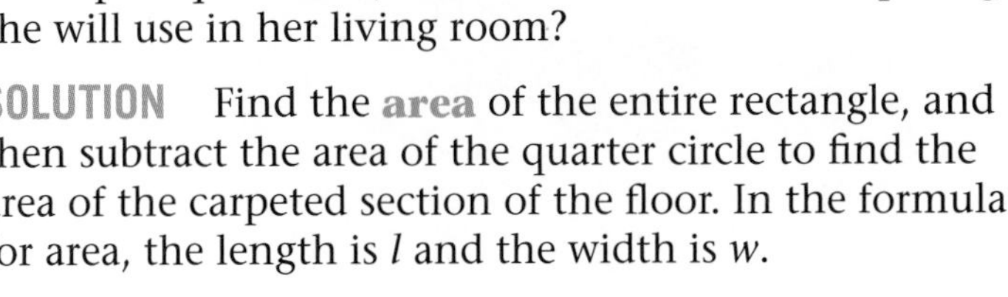

SOLUTION Find the **area** of the entire rectangle, and then subtract the area of the quarter circle to find the area of the carpeted section of the floor. In the formula for area, the length is l and the width is w.

Formula for area $\quad A = lw$

Substitute and multiply. $\quad A = 25(16) = 400$

The area of the room is 400 square feet.

The area of a circle with radius r is given by the formula

$$A = \pi r^2$$

Therefore, the area of the quarter-circle is given by the formula

$$A = \frac{1}{4}\pi r^2$$

Substitute 8 for r and 3.14 for π. $\quad A = \frac{1}{4}(3.14)(8)^2$

Simplify. $\quad A = 0.25(3.14)(64) = 50.24$

The area of the quarter-circle is approximately 50.24 square feet.

Subtract to find the area of the carpeted region. $\quad 400 - 50.24 = 349.76$

Gabriela needs approximately 350 square feet of carpeting.

Multiply the number of square feet needed by \$9.55 to find the total cost of the carpeting that will be used.

$$350(9.55) = 3{,}342.50$$

The carpeting will cost approximately \$3,342.50.

Due to the shape of the carpeted area, Gabriela may have to purchase a few extra square feet of carpet to make sure the installers have enough. This is determined at the time of purchase.

■ CHECK YOUR UNDERSTANDING

Express the area of the shaded region in the room shown algebraically.

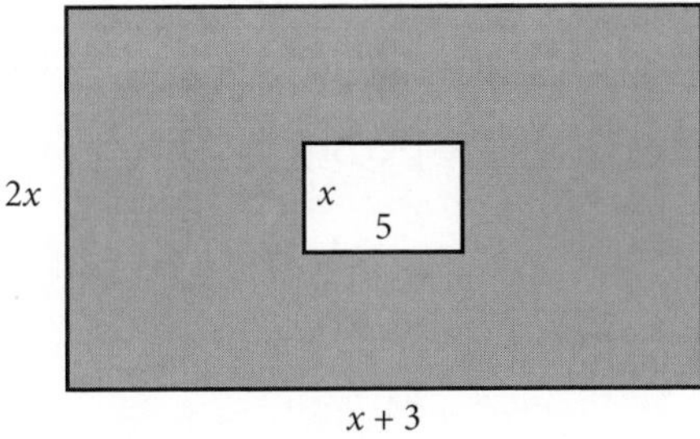

EXAMPLE 2

In this problem, a carpet seller would not sell the exact amount of carpet used because they would sell the rectangle for the size of the room and then the installers would cut out the quarter circle for the space where the piano sits. If a student raises this issue, you can point out that the question asks for the cost of the carpet used, not the cost of the carpet that Gabriela would likely have to purchase.

You can also stress that the answer for the area of the quarter circle is an approximated answer because 3.14 for is an approximation for π.

For a more precise and accurate square footage, have students use the π key on their calculators and then round to the nearest hundredth. The square footage is 50.27.

You can give extra problems demonstrating subtraction of areas since they give students practice with the concept and the area formulas.

CHECK YOUR UNDERSTANDING

Answer $2x^2 + x$

EXAMPLE 3

Relate the apothem to the altitude of a triangle by dividing the regular polygon into congruent triangles. You can derive the $A = \frac{1}{2}ap$ formula by adding the areas of the triangles and then factoring out the apothem (height of each triangle).

EXAMPLE 3

Delgado's Landscape Design is building a large gazebo for a backyard. It is in the shape of a regular octagon as shown in the diagram. Each side of the gazebo is 10 feet. They need to purchase wood for the floor. It costs $14 per square foot for a special type of wood. Find the cost of the gazebo's floor.

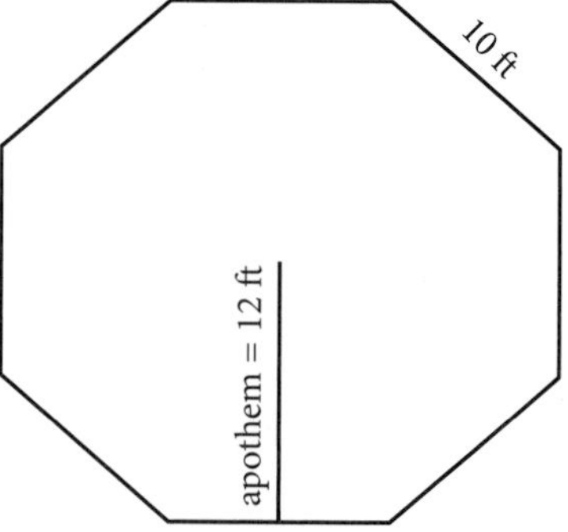

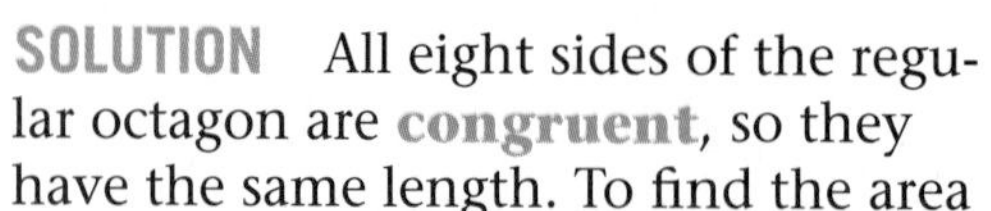

SOLUTION All eight sides of the regular octagon are **congruent**, so they have the same length. To find the area of a regular octagon, you need its apothem and its **perimeter**. The **apothem**, as shown in the diagram, is a line segment through the center of a regular polygon that is perpendicular to a side.

$A = \frac{1}{2}ap$ where A is the area of the regular polygon, a is the apothem, and p is the perimeter

The perimeter is the product of the number of sides and the length of each side.

An octagon has 8 sides. $p = 8(10) = 80$

The apothem is 12 feet long.

Substitute and simplify. $A = \frac{1}{2}ap$

$A = \frac{1}{2}(12)(80) = 480$

The area is 480 square feet.

Multiply the area by the price per square foot to obtain the total cost.

Square feet × cost per foot $480(14) = 6{,}720$

The flooring will cost $6,720.

CHECK YOUR UNDERSTANDING

A regular pentagon (5 sides) has an area of 440 square units, and each side measures x units. Express the apothem of the pentagon algebraically in terms of x.

EXAMPLE 4

Don sculpts out a region for a flower garden, as shown. He takes a digital picture of the garden. The irregular region would fit inside a rectangle that is 15 yards by 20 yards. He superimposes a 15 by 20 grid over the photo on his computer. The area of the garden impacts the cost of mulch, plants, fertilizer, and so on. What is the area of the garden?

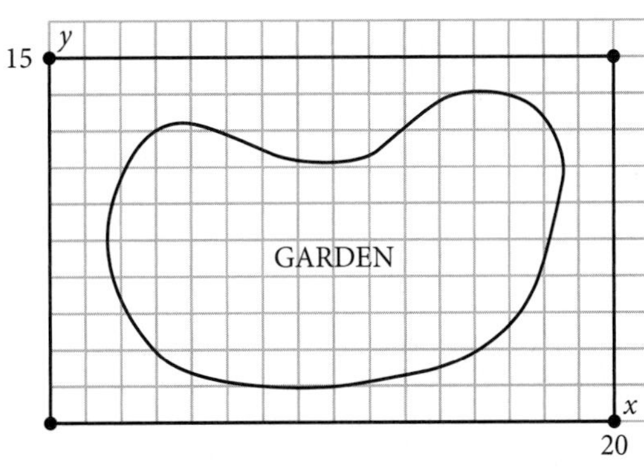

SOLUTION The garden is not a polygon. It is a free-form plane figure. Don can use probability to find the area. First, he frames the irregular region with a 15 by 20 rectangle, whose area is 300 square units. Then, he generates 1,000 random points (x, y) with a domain $0 \le x \le 20$ and a range $0 \le y \le 15$. Most graphing calculators have a random number feature that can generate x- and y-values for this problem.

Don plots the points and determines the number of points that landed inside the garden region. He finds that 631 points landed inside the garden region. He uses the following proportion.

$$\frac{\text{Number of points inside the region}}{\text{Total number of random points}} = \frac{\text{Area of irregular region}}{\text{Area of rectangle used to frame irregular region}}$$

Substitute. $\quad \dfrac{631}{1{,}000} = \dfrac{x}{300}$

Cross multiply. $\quad 1{,}000x = 631(300)$

Multiply. $\quad 1{,}000x = 189{,}300$

Solve for x. $\quad x = 189.3$

The area of the free-form garden is approximately 189 square feet.

The method used in this example is the **Monte Carlo method**. It is based on probability. The theory is that the ratio of points that land inside the region to the total points should equal the ratio of the area of the irregular region to the area of the rectangle. The more points you use, the more accurate your approximation.

CHECK YOUR UNDERSTANDING

An irregular plane figure is framed inside of a 20 by 20 square that represents a 20-foot by 20-foot square. To find its area, 2,000 random points are generated, and 910 of them land inside the irregular region. What is the area of the irregular region, to the nearest integer?

CHECK YOUR UNDERSTANDING

Answer $\frac{176}{x}$

EXAMPLE 4

You can have students practice the Monte Carlo method using graph paper. Have students draw a polygon on graph paper, and then find the area by square-counting or using formulas. They can check the accuracy of the Monte Carlo method by generating points and comparing the result to the actual areas. Many (thousands) points must be generated to get a good approximation. If each student contributes 100 points, the aggregate as a class would yield many points.

CHECK YOUR UNDERSTANDING

Answer 182 square feet

EXAMPLE 5

Explain to students how the volume of a room affects heating and air-conditioning costs. These costs include the purchase of the equipment as well as the costs of running the equipment.

CHECK YOUR UNDERSTANDING

Answer $\frac{1,900}{x^2}$

EXAMPLE 6

Make sure students understand how the insulation and orientation of the house can affect the cost of air-conditioning. This is because rooms that face the sun cost more to keep cool.

CHECK YOUR UNDERSTANDING

Answer 12,096 BTUs

Volume is the amount of space inside a three-dimensional region, such as a room. Volume is measured in cubic units. Most rooms are in the shape of rectangular solids and have length, width, and height.

EXAMPLE 5

Find the volume of a room 14 feet by 16 feet with an 8-foot ceiling.

SOLUTION The formula for the volume of a rectangular solid with length l, width w, and height h, is

$$V = lwh$$

Substitute and simplify. $V = (16)(14)(8) = 1,792$

The volume of the room is 1,792 cubic feet.

■ CHECK YOUR UNDERSTANDING

A square room with sides x units long has volume 1,900 cubic units. Express the height of the ceiling algebraically in terms of x.

EXAMPLE 6

Mike's bedroom measures 16 feet by 14 feet and has a 9-foot ceiling. It is well insulated and on the west side of his house. How large of an air conditioner should he purchase?

SOLUTION Air conditioners are sold according to their **BTU (British Thermal Units)** rating. The air conditioner with the right BTU rating will cool and dehumidify a room. If the rating is too low, the room may not cool sufficiently. If the rating is too high, it may shut off before removing the humidity. Many appliance salespeople use the formula known as "while divided by 60" to compute the correct BTU rating.

In this formula, w represents the width of the room, h represents the height, and l represents the length. The level of insulation is represented by i. If the room is well insulated, $i = 10$, and if the room is poorly insulated, $i = 18$. The variable e represents the exposure—the direction the outside wall of the room faces. If it faces north, $e = 16$. If it faces east, $e = 17$. If it faces south, $e = 18$, and if it faces west, $e = 20$.

$$\text{BTU rating} \approx \frac{while}{60}$$

Substitute. $\text{BTU rating} \approx \frac{(14)(9)(10)(16)(20)}{60}$

Simplify. $\text{BTU rating} \approx 6,720$

Mike should purchase an air conditioner rated at 7,000 BTUs.

■ CHECK YOUR UNDERSTANDING

In Example 6, find the recommended BTUs if Mike's room was poorly insulated, and the other variables remained the same.

Applications

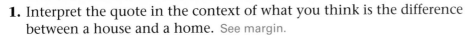

A good home must be made, not bought.
Joyce Maynard, American Author

1. Interpret the quote in the context of what you think is the difference between a house and a home. See margin.
2. A rectangular room measures 13 feet by 15 feet. It is going to be carpeted with carpeting that sells for $68 per square yard.
   - **a.** What is the area of the room in square feet? 195 sq ft
   - **b.** If the room is drawn so $\frac{1}{4}$ inch represents 1 foot scale, give the dimensions of the room in inches on the scale drawing. See margin.
   - **c.** A yard equals 3 feet. How many square feet are in a square yard? 9
   - **d.** How many square yards will it take to carpet the room? Round up to the next greater integer. 22 sq yd
   - **e.** What is the total price for the carpeting? $1,496
   - **f.** In the early mid-2000s, there was a dramatic increase in the price of carpeting, since it was a petroleum-based product. As a result, selling by the yard made it look expensive. Some stores started selling carpet by the square foot. How much would a square yard of carpet selling for $8.95 per square foot cost? $80.55
   - **g.** This room is well-insulated and is on the south side of the house. It has an 8-foot-high ceiling. How large an air conditioner would this room require? Round to the nearest thousand BTUs. 5,000 BTUs
3. A rectangular room has length L and width W, where L and W are measured in feet.
   - **a.** Express the area in square feet algebraically. LW
   - **b.** If carpeting costs x dollars per square yard, express the cost of carpeting this room algebraically. See margin.
4. A rectangular room is 14 feet by 20 feet. The ceiling is 8 feet high.
   - **a.** Find the length and width of the smaller wall. 14 ft by 8 ft
   - **b.** Find the area of the smaller wall. 112 sq ft
   - **c.** Find the area of the larger wall. 160 sq ft
   - **d.** Find the total area of the four walls in the room. 544 sq ft
   - **e.** If a gallon of paint costs $36.50 and it covers 350 square feet on average, what is the cost of painting the room with two coats of paint? Explain your answer. See margin.
   - **f.** This room is well-insulated and is on the north side of the house. How large an air conditioner would this room require? Round to the nearest thousand BTUs. 6,000 BTUs
5. A gazebo in the shape of a regular octagon has equal sides of 9 feet and an apothem of 10.9 feet.
   - **a.** If one side of a gazebo is open, and the other sides have a railing, find the cost of the railing if it sells for $7.90 per foot. $497.70
   - **b.** Find the area of the gazebo. 392.4 sq ft
   - **c.** Find the cost of the gazebo's floor if the flooring costs $3 per square foot. Round to the nearest hundred dollars. $1,200

TEACH

Exercises 2 and 3
Knowing the area of the floor is needed when covering the floor with carpeting or tiles. You may want to point out that carpet installers have other restrictions that dictate how they will cut the carpet to fit in certain floor plans. Since it is usually sold in 12-foot widths, consumers sometimes have to purchase more carpet than they need so there are fewer seams in the installation process.

Exercises 4 and 6
These exercises deal with painting the walls of a room. Make sure students understand how the length and width of each wall can be determined from the dimensions of the room. They might want to draw a rectangular solid on paper and label the sides to understand which dimensions are used for each surface.

ANSWERS

1. A house is a physical structure. A home is not—it is the spiritual and emotional component of all that goes on inside a house.

2b. $3\frac{1}{4}$ by $3\frac{3}{4}$

3b. $\frac{LW}{9}x$

4e. To paint the room twice, you will need to cover 1,088 square feet. This will require more than 3 gallons of paint, so you will need a fourth gallon. At a cost of $36.50, the four gallons will cost $146.

TEACH

Exercise 8

Point out that consumers need to take doors and windows into account when purchasing wall coverings, such as brick, paint, or wallpaper.

Exercises 9 and 10

These exercises use the Monte Carlo method to find area. Remind students that this method can be used to find the area of any plane figure; it does not need to be a polygon.

Imagine an environmentalist trying to find the area of an oil spill, which could take on any possible shape. A photograph could be taken and superimposed with a grid, and the area could be found using the Monte Carlo method.

Keep in mind that the Monte Carlo method cannot be used to find the perimeter.

ANSWERS

6d. $\frac{2xc + 2yc + xy}{400}$ gallons

10. $\frac{p}{10{,}000}xy$

6. A rectangular room measures x feet by y feet, where $x < y$. The ceiling is c feet high. The walls and the ceiling will be painted the same color.

a. Express the area of the smaller wall and the larger wall algebraically. small, xc; large, yc

b. Express the total area of the room algebraically. $2xc + 2yc$

c. Express the area of the ceiling algebraically. xy

d. If a gallon of paint covers 400 square feet, express the amount of paint you will need algebraically. See margin.

7. A gazebo in the shape of a regular hexagon has side length s and apothem a. If the cost per square unit of flooring is c, express the total cost T of the floor algebraically. $T = 0.5a(6s)c$, or $T = 3asc$

8. Giuliana is having one wall of her den covered in brick. She needs to find the area of the wall, excluding the doors and the windows. A diagram of the room is shown.

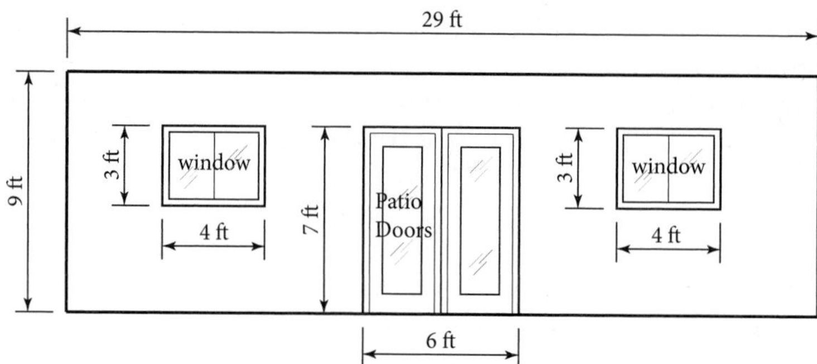

a. Giuliana creates a scale drawing to bring to the contractor. She uses the scale $\frac{1}{4}$ inch represents 1 foot. Copy the diagram and label the scale drawing dimensions in inches. See additional answers.

b. Find the area of the wall that will be covered in brick. 195 sq ft

c. If the brick, with installation, costs $18 per square foot, find the total cost of the job. $3,510

9. Elizabeth is a landscape designer. She created a small pond with a fountain that her company plans to manufacture and market. It is a free-form shape and the company wants to include the area of the pond on the packaging.

a. She takes a diagram of the pond and places it inside a 25-ft by 25-ft square. What is the area of the square? 625 sq ft

b. She then uses a graphing calculator to generate 5,000 random points inside the square. She finds that 3,200 of these points landed inside the pond outline. What percent of the points landed in the pond? 64%

c. What is the area of the pond, to the nearest square foot? 400 sq ft

10. Elizabeth (from Exercise 9) is designing another backyard pond design for her company. She follows the same procedure to find the area. She first creates an x by y rectangle to frame her pond diagram. She generates 10,000 random points inside the rectangle and p points land inside the pond. Express the area of the pond algebraically. See margin.

There's no place like home.
Judy Garland, American Actress, as Dorothy in *The Wizard of Oz*

Mortgage Application Process 8-3

Key Terms
- market value
- property tax
- real estate tax
- assessed value
- down payment
- mortgage
- fixed rate mortgage
- adjustable rate mortgage
- foreclose
- homeowner's insurance
- escrow
- front-end ratio
- back-end ratio
- debt-to-income ratio
- balloon mortgage
- interest-only mortgage

Objectives
- Compute the monthly cost of paying for a house.
- Understand the research that is necessary before you purchase a home.

Common Core
A-SSE1, A-CED3, A-APR6, F-BF1

CCSS Warm-Up

Find, to the nearest hundredth, the value of M for each value of r if using the expression for M on the right.

1. $r = 0.05$ **2.** $r = 0.06$

$$M = \frac{1000\left(\frac{r}{12}\right)\left(1 + \frac{r}{12}\right)^{12}}{\left(1 + \frac{r}{12}\right)^{12} - 1}$$

1. 85.61 2. 86.07

What do you need to know about mortgages?

Buying a house is probably the most expensive investment you will ever make. **Market value** is the amount for which a house could be sold. Homeowners pay **property taxes**, also called **real estate taxes**. The **assessed value** of a home is an amount used to determine the property taxes. The assessed value may not be the same as the market value. Property taxes help pay for government services, such as schools, libraries, and police.

After making the required **down payment**, most people take out a loan to pay the balance owed on their new home. These loans are **mortgages**. Because interest rates differ, shopping for a mortgage can be important. You should become familiar with the following mortgage vocabulary.

- **Fixed rate mortgage** A fixed rate mortgage is a mortgage in which the monthly payment and annual percentage rate (APR) remain the same throughout the entire loan period.
- **Adjustable rate mortgage** An adjustable rate mortgage is a mortgage in which the monthly payment and the APR may change, as specified in the signed agreement.
- **Foreclosure** The bank forecloses on (takes possession of) the home and sells it if the homeowner cannot pay the mortgage.
- **Homeowner's insurance** Insurance that covers damage to the home due to fire, and other natural disasters. It also covers the contents of the home in case of theft or vandalism.

Most mortgage loans are repaid over 15 to 30 years, which means a home buyer is taking on a long-term financial responsibility.

EXAMINE THE QUESTION

Students need to see the financial implications buying a home will have on their lives. In this lesson, students will get an idea what it costs to purchase a home.

Combined with their knowledge of income taxes, students will get a better picture of what salary it will take to purchase the kind of home they want.

Additionally, combining this lesson's skills with the credit chapter will show students how much interest they pay over the life of a mortgage.

CLASS DISCUSSION

Discuss situations when the students' families have made insurance claims and the circumstances that caused the damage. Did having insurance save the family a lot of money?

TEACH
This lesson examines the costs of a mortgage, property taxes, homeowner's insurance, and other periodic payments related to housing.

EXAMPLE 1
Students will see that the interest on a home purchase can be hundreds of thousands of dollars. Point out that the interest on the loan in Example 1 is actually more than the principal.

Have students consider the order of operations and the formula use in the solution to determine if additional parentheses need to be included when entering the equation into a calculator. Some students will benefit by rewriting the formula, placing parentheses around the numerator and denominator when they make the substitutions.

CHECK YOUR UNDERSTANDING
Answer $I = (360M - p)$

Skills and Strategies

Here you will examine what costs must be researched by a prospective home buyer before committing to the responsibility of a monthly mortgage payment for many years.

EXAMPLE 1

Heather is planning to buy a home. She has some money for a down payment already. She sees a home she would like and computes that she would need to borrow \$190,000 from a bank over a 30-year period. The APR is 6.4%. What will be her total interest for the 30 years?

© ALTERFALTER, 2009/USED UNDER LICENSE FROM SHUTTERSTOCK.COM

SOLUTION Recall the monthly payment formula from Chapter 4.

$$M = \frac{p\left(\frac{r}{12}\right)\left(1 + \frac{r}{12}\right)^{12t}}{\left(1 + \frac{r}{12}\right)^{12t} - 1}$$

where M = monthly payment
p = principal
r = interest rate expressed as a decimal
t = number of years

Substitute and simplify. Round to the nearest cent.

$$M = \frac{190{,}000\left(\frac{0.064}{12}\right)\left(1 + \frac{0.064}{12}\right)^{12(30)}}{\left(1 + \frac{0.064}{12}\right)^{12(30)} - 1} \approx 1{,}188.46$$

The monthly payment is \$1,188.46.

There are 12 payments per year, so there are 360 payments over the 30 years. Multiply to find the sum of all 360 payments.

$$360(1{,}188.46) = 427{,}845.60$$

The sum of the monthly payments is \$427,845.60. To find the interest, subtract the principal from this amount.

$$427{,}845.60 - 190{,}000 = 237{,}845.60$$

Heather will pay \$237,845.60 in interest. This is almost a quarter of a million dollars, and it is just interest! Buying a home is an expensive proposition.

■ **CHECK YOUR UNDERSTANDING**

Don and Barbara Weinstein are looking for a home for which they would have to borrow p dollars. If they take out a 30-year loan with a monthly payment equal to M, express their interest I algebraically.

EXAMPLE 2

Jessica and Darryl Delaware are looking at a house, and they contacted the tax assessor to find out what the property taxes would be. In their town, the tax is based on the square footage and other features of the house. The classified ad describing their house is shown below. What is the annual property tax on their house if the town has a tax rate of 0.89%?

> 2-story Colonial with 2.5 bath, frpl, full basement, CAC, 30 × 30 ft deck, 3/4 acre, 600 sq ft first flr, 1500 sq ft second flr, 20 × 20 ft dormer, 12 × 21 ft garage, 16 × 32 ft vinyl pool, gas ht, excellent cond. $289K

EXAMPLE 2

Students may have heard adults complaining about property taxes being high in certain locations. Remind them what services are paid for by property taxes.

Explain to students that property taxes are not usually collected annually—they are collected monthly or semiannually.

SOLUTION Property tax is based on the assessed value of the house. The Delaware's received a copy of how the assessed values are computed, shown at the right. Some of the assessed values are based on square footage, and some are flat rates. Compute the assessed value for each part.

Add all the assessed values to find the total assessed value of the home.

Structural Rates per Square Foot	Flat Rates
1st floor over basement $3.00	land $1,000 per acre
1st floor over slab $2.25	1st bathroom $0
2nd floor $2.25	extra full bathroom $100
garage $1.00	half bathroom $50
dormer $1.00	fireplace $125
barn $0.75	tennis court $375
deck $0.50	spa $125
shed $0.70	central air conditioning $200
vinyl-lined pool $0.75	gas heat $700

	Square Footage	Assessed Value
first floor	600	$600 \times 3 = 1{,}800$
second floor	1,500	$1{,}500 \times 2.25 = 3{,}375$
dormer	$20 \times 20 = 400$	$400 \times 1 = 400$
garage	$12 \times 21 = 252$	$252 \times 1 = 252$
deck	$30 \times 30 = 900$	$900 \times 0.5 = 450$
pool	$16 \times 32 = 512$	$512 \times 0.75 = 384$
land		$\frac{3}{4} \times 1{,}000 = 750$
extra bathrooms		$1\frac{1}{2} = 100 + 50 = 150$
fireplace		125
central air conditioning		200
gas heat		700

$$1{,}800 + 3{,}375 + 400 + 252 + 450 + 384 + 750 + 150 + 125 + 200 + 700 = 8{,}586$$

The assessed value is $8,586.

Multiply the assessed value by the tax rate to compute the annual property tax. The town has a tax rate of 89%. Find 89% of $8,586 to find the annual property tax.

$$0.89(8{,}586) = 7{,}641.54$$

The property tax on the house is $7,641.54 per year.

CHECK YOUR UNDERSTANDING

Answer $P = ar$

EXAMPLE 3

Explain to students that a common practice is to have the bank collect property tax and homeowner's insurance payments with the mortgage.

■ CHECK YOUR UNDERSTANDING

The assessed value of a home is *a* dollars and the tax rate, expressed as a decimal, is *r*. Express the property tax *P* algebraically.

EXAMPLE 3

Kevin and Cathy Mackin have a mortgage with National Trust Bank. The bank requires that the Mackins pay their homeowner's insurance, property taxes, and mortgage in one monthly payment to the bank. Their monthly mortgage payment is $1,233.56, their semi-annual property tax bill is $5,206, and their annual homeowner's insurance bill is $1,080. How much is the monthly payment they make to National Trust?

SOLUTION The bank wants the insurance and taxes paid monthly so the Mackins do not have large bills to pay at the end of the year. The bank holds the insurance and property tax money and pays those bills for the Mackins when they are due. This is holding money in **escrow**.

Divide the annual insurance by 12 to get a monthly amount.

$$1{,}080 \div 12 = 90$$

The Mackins must pay $90 per month into escrow for their homeowner's insurance.

Divide the semi-annual property tax by 6, and round to the nearest cent to get a monthly amount for the property tax.

$$5{,}206 \div 6 = 867.67$$

The Mackins must pay $867.67 per month into escrow for their property taxes.

The monthly payment to National Trust is the sum of the monthly mortgage, insurance, and taxes.

$$1{,}233.56 + 90 + 867.67 = 2{,}191.23$$

The Mackins pay the bank $2,191.23 each month.

CHECK YOUR UNDERSTANDING

Answer $m + \frac{h}{3} + \frac{p}{12}$

■ CHECK YOUR UNDERSTANDING

Michelle and Dan Zlotnick pay their mortgage, insurance, and property taxes in one monthly payment to the bank. If their monthly mortgage payment is *m* dollars, their annual property tax payment is *p* dollars, and their quarterly homeowner's insurance payment is *h* dollars, express the amount they pay the bank monthly algebraically.

EXAMPLE 4

Tom and Lori Courtney are considering buying a house and are researching the potential costs. Their adjusted gross income is $135,511. The monthly mortgage payment for the house they want would be $1,233. The annual property taxes would be $9,400, and the homeowner's insurance premium would cost them $876 per year. Will the bank lend them $190,000 to purchase the house?

SOLUTION Banks use several factors, including credit rating, to decide if they will lend money. The bank wants to be paid back. They want assurance that the borrowers can afford the monthly payments.

One indicator is the **front-end ratio**, which is a ratio of monthly housing expenses to monthly gross income.

$$\text{Front-end ratio} = \frac{\text{Monthly housing expenses}}{\text{Monthly gross income}}$$

Banks often want the front-end ratio to be 28% or less before they lend the money.

Find the monthly amount for property tax.

Annual property tax ÷ 12 $\quad \dfrac{9{,}400}{12} \approx 783.33$

Rounded to the nearest cent, the monthly property tax is $783.33.

Find the monthly amount for homeowner's insurance.

Annual insurance ÷ 12 $\quad \dfrac{876}{12} = 73$

Find the monthly gross income.

Annual gross income ÷ 12 $\quad \dfrac{135{,}511}{12} \approx 11{,}292.58$

The monthly gross income is $11,292.58, rounded to the nearest cent.

Substitute these values into the front-end ratio. Convert the decimal equivalent to a percent.

$$\text{Front-end ratio} = \frac{1{,}233 + 783.33 + 73}{11{,}292.58} = \frac{2{,}089.33}{11{,}292.58} \approx 0.185 = 18.5\%$$

The front-end ratio is 18.5%.

The Courtneys' front-end ratio is less than 28%, so the bank would say they can afford the mortgage on this house based on the front-end ratio.

CHECK YOUR UNDERSTANDING

Ken and Julie Frederick have an adjusted gross income of x dollars. They are looking at a new house. Their monthly mortgage payment would be m dollars. Their annual property taxes would be p dollars, and their annual homeowner's premium would be h dollars. Express their front-end ratio algebraically.

EXAMPLE 4

Explain to students that the bank does not want to have to repossess the house—they want to make sure the borrowers can afford the mortgage, so they set up the front-end ratio to create a benchmark for mortgage approvals.

CHECK YOUR UNDERSTANDING

Answer $\dfrac{m + \frac{p}{12} + \frac{h}{12}}{\frac{x}{12}}$

EXAMPLE 5

The back-end ratio takes into account the aggregate of a borrower's monthly debts. Together with the front-end ratio, it paints a picture of how credit-worthy the borrower is for the mortgage in question.

CHECK YOUR UNDERSTANDING

Answer 51%

EXAMPLE 5

Bill and Terry Noke are considering buying a house and need to figure out what they can afford and what a bank will lend them. Their adjusted gross income is $166,988. Their monthly mortgage payment for the house they want would be $1,544. Their annual property taxes would be $9,888, and the homeowner's insurance premium would cost them $1,007 per year. They have a $510 per month car loan, and their average monthly credit card bill is $5,100. Would the bank lend them $210,000 to purchase their house?

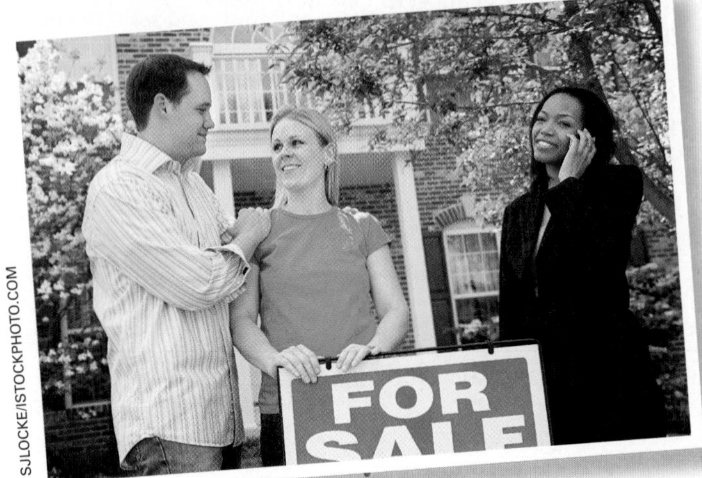

© SJLOCKE/ISTOCKPHOTO.COM

SOLUTION In Example 4 you learned about the front-end ratio that banks use to assess potential borrowers. Banks also use the **back-end ratio**, or **debt-to-income ratio**, which takes into account a borrower's regular monthly debts, such as car loans, alimony, child support, and credit card bills.

$$\text{Back-end ratio} = \frac{\text{Total monthly expenses}}{\text{Monthly gross income}}$$

Banks generally want a back-end ratio less than 36% to approve a mortgage application.

Find the monthly amounts for the homeowner's insurance and the property taxes to the nearest dollar.

Monthly homeowner's insurance $1{,}007 \div 12 \approx 84$

Monthly property tax $9{,}888 \div 12 = 824$

The total monthly expenses are the sum of the mortgage payment, property tax, homeowners insurance, car payment, and credit card payments.

Add. $1{,}544 + 824 + 84 + 510 + 5{,}100 = 8{,}062$

Find the Noke's monthly gross income by dividing by 12 and rounding to the nearest dollar.

$$166{,}988 \div 12 \approx 13{,}916$$

Substitute these values into the back-end ratio.

$$\text{Back-end ratio} = \frac{8{,}062}{13{,}916} \approx 0.579$$

The back-end ratio for the Noke's is 58%.

The back-end ratio for the Nokes is greater than 36%. The bank will not give them a loan for $210,000.

CHECK YOUR UNDERSTANDING

Find the back-end ratio to the nearest percent for the Nokes in Example 5, if they pay off their car, and Terry gets a $12,000 raise.

EXAMPLE 6

Chris and Scott Halloran are opening a new restaurant. They take out a 6.1%, 15-year, \$300,000 mortgage on the building, but they do not have a lot of money because they are spending what they have to get the business started. Years in the future they intend to have much more money from the success of the restaurant. Can they get a loan that will fit well with their current and future incomes? How much will they pay in interest for the loan? What are the monthly payments?

SOLUTION The Hallorans can take out a balloon mortgage. A **balloon mortgage** features a very high last payment, with all other payments being relatively low.

One type of balloon loan is an **interest-only** balloon mortgage where only the interest is paid until the final month.

Use the monthly payment formula. Substitute, simplify, and round to the nearest cent.

$$M = \frac{300{,}000\left(\frac{0.061}{12}\right)\left(1 + \frac{0.061}{12}\right)^{12(15)}}{\left(1 + \frac{0.061}{12}\right)^{12(15)} - 1} \approx 2{,}547.81$$

To find the interest due on the Halloran's loan, first find the total amount due for the loan. Then subtract the \$300,000 principal from the total paid.

The loan is for 15 years, so there will be $12 \times 15 = 180$ payments.

Payment amount × 180 $\quad 2{,}547.81 \times 180 = 458{,}605.80$

Total paid – principal $\quad 458{,}605.80 - 300{,}000 = 158{,}605.80$

The interest on the Halloran's loan, rounded to the nearest dollar, is \$158,606.

If the last payment is the \$300,000 balloon, the first 179 payments equal the interest only.

Divide. $\quad 158{,}606 \div 179 \approx 886.07$

The first 179 monthly payments are \$886.07, and the 180th (last) payment, at the end of the 15 years, is the balloon payment of \$300,000. Notice that the initial monthly payments were low, allowing the Hallorans to put money into their business.

Keep in mind that they had to start saving for the balloon payment years in advance since it is so high.

There are other ways to set up balloon payments, but all of them feature the large final payment.

CHECK YOUR UNDERSTANDING

The total interest on a 20-year balloon mortgage with principal p dollars is x dollars. If just the interest is paid before the final balloon payment, express the monthly payment before the balloon payment amount algebraically.

EXAMPLE 6

Discuss the advantages and disadvantages of the large balloon payment at the end of the loan. It makes the monthly payments lower when the business starts, which is helpful to a new business. However, the final payment must be saved for in advance since it is so large.

CHECK YOUR UNDERSTANDING

Answer $\frac{x}{239}$

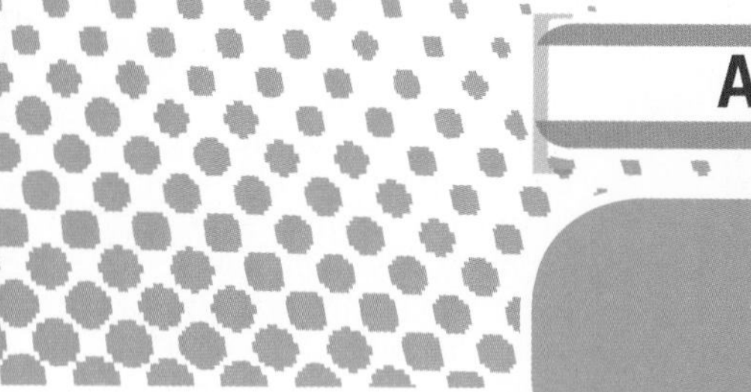

Applications

There's no place like home.
Judy Garland, American Actress, as Dorothy in *The Wizard of Oz*

TEACH

Exercise 3
This exercise allows students to see the savings from paying a loan off in 25 years instead of 30 years. Although this increases the monthly payment, it lowers the total interest and gives the borrower the extra 5 years of no monthly payments. Discuss with students that if they can afford the higher monthly payment, it pays to go with the shorter loan.

Exercises 5–7, and 9
These exercises all deal with property taxes.

ANSWERS

1. In the movie, Dorothy runs away from home, and eventually realizes that nothing matches the comfort of your own home. It is easy to take this feeling for granted, or not even realize it.

4e. United, by approximately $58,460

1. Interpret the quote in the context of your own home. See margin.

2. The Smiths took out a $130,000, 30-year mortgage at an APR of 6.5%. The monthly payment was $821.69. What will be their total interest charges after 30 years? $165,808.40

3. If you borrow $120,000 at an APR of 7% for 25 years, you will pay $848.13 per month. If you borrow the same amount at the same APR for 30 years, you will pay $798.36 per month.

a. What is the total interest paid on the 25-year mortgage? $134,439
b. What is the total interest paid on the 30-year mortgage? $167,409.60
c. How much more interest is paid on the 30-year loan? Round to the nearest dollar. $32,971
d. If you can afford the difference in monthly payments, you can take out the 25-year loan and save all the interest from part c. What is the difference between the monthly payments of the two different loans? Round to the nearest dollar. $50

4. United Bank offers a 15-year mortgage at an APR of 6.2%. Capitol Bank offers a 25-year mortgage at an APR of 6.5%. Marcy wants to borrow $120,000.

a. What would the monthly payment be from United Bank? $1,025.64
b. What would the total interest be from United Bank? Round to the nearest ten dollars. $64,620
c. What would the monthly payment be from Capitol Bank? $810.25
d. What would the total interest be from Capitol Bank? Round to the nearest ten dollars. $123,080
e. Which bank has the lower total interest, and by how much? See margin.
f. What is the difference in the monthly payments? $215.39
g. How many years of payments do you avoid if you decide to take out the shorter mortgage? 10

5. The assessed value of the Weber family's house is $186,000. The annual property tax rate is 2.15% of assessed value. What is the property tax on the Weber's home? $3,999

6. The monthly payment on a mortgage with a principal of p dollars is m dollars. The mortgage is taken out for y years. Express the interest I as a function of p, m, and y. $I = 12my - p$

7. The market value of Christine and Gene's home is $275,000. The assessed value is $230,000. The annual property tax rate is $17.50 per $1,000 of assessed value.

a. What is the property tax on their home? $4,025
b. How much do they pay monthly toward property taxes? Round your answer to the nearest cent. $335.42

8. Jim is taking out a \$135,000 mortgage. His bank offers him an APR of 6.25%. He wants to compare monthly payments on a 20- and a 30-year loan. Find, to the nearest dollar, the difference in the monthly payments for these two loans. \$156

9. The Joseph family took out a \$175,000, 25-year mortgage at an APR of 6%. The assessed value of their house is \$9,000. The annual property tax rate is 97.22% of assessed value. What is the annual property tax? \$8,749.80

10. The Jordans are considering buying a house with a market value of \$250,000. The assessed value of the house is *a* dollars. The annual property tax is \$2.45 per \$100 of assessed value. What is the property tax on this house? See margin.

11. Allison has a mortgage with North End Bank. The bank requires that she pay her homeowner's insurance, property taxes, and mortgage in one monthly payment. Her monthly mortgage payment is \$1,390, her semi-annual property tax bill is \$3,222, and her quarterly homeowner's bill is \$282. How much does Allison pay North End Bank each month? \$2,021

12. Mike and Cheryl had an adjusted gross income of *a* dollars. Mike just got a \$3K raise and Cheryl got a \$1.5K raise. They are considering moving to a new house with monthly mortgage payments of *m* dollars, annual property taxes of *p* dollars, and annual homeowner's premium of *h* dollars. Express their front-end ratio algebraically. See margin.

13. The Ungers have an adjusted gross income of \$117,445. They are looking at a new house that would carry a monthly mortgage payment of \$1,877. Their annual property taxes would be \$6,780, and their semi-annual homeowner's premium would be \$710.
    a. Find their front-end ratio to the nearest percent. 26%
    b. Assume that their credit rating is good. Based on the front-end ratio, would the bank offer them a loan? Explain. See margin.
    c. The Ungers have a monthly car loan of \$430, and their average monthly credit card bill is \$5,100. Mr. Unger is also paying \$1,000 per month in child support from a previous marriage. Compute the back-end ratio to the nearest percent. 93%
    d. If the bank used both the front-end and back-end ratios to decide on mortgage approval, would the Ungers get their mortgage? Explain. See margin.

14. Andy is a single father who wants to purchase a home. His adjusted gross income for the year is *a* dollars. His monthly mortgage is *m* dollars, and his annual property tax bill is *p* dollars. His monthly credit card bill is *c* dollars, and he has a monthly car loan for *d* dollars. His quarterly homeowner's bill is *h* dollars. Express Andy's back-end ratio algebraically. See margin.

15. Ron has a homeowner's insurance policy, which covers theft, with a deductible of *d* dollars. Two bicycles, worth *b* dollars each, and some tools, worth *t* dollars, were stolen from his garage. If the value of the stolen items was greater than the deductible, represent the amount of money the insurance company will pay algebraically. $2b + t - d$

16. Find the monthly payment (before the balloon payment) for a 20-year, interest-only balloon mortgage for \$275,000 at an APR of 8%. Round to the nearest ten dollars. \$1,160

TEACH

Exercises 12 and 13
Front-end and back-end ratios are examined.

ANSWERS

10. $\$2.45\left(\frac{a}{100}\right)$

12. $\dfrac{m + \frac{p}{12} + \frac{h}{12}}{\frac{(a + 4{,}500)}{12}}$

13b. Yes; because the front-end ratio is less than 28%.

13d. No; because 93% > 36%. Based on the total of their monthly expenses, they cannot afford this loan.

14. $\dfrac{m + \frac{p}{12} + \frac{h}{3} + c + d}{\frac{a}{12}}$

ANSWERS

20. c. 594.50
 d. 3,574.44
 e. 861.08
 f. 5,177.28
 g. 873.67
 h. 5,252.93
 i. 772.92
 j. 4,647.17

17. Siegell's Locksmith Shop is taking out a mortgage on a new building. It is going to be an interest-only, 12-year balloon mortgage for \$350,000. The APR is 7.1%. The last payment will be the balloon payment of the full principal.

a. Find the total interest for the 12-year mortgage. \$170,994.88

b. Find the total number of monthly payments, not including the final balloon payment. 143

c. Find the amount of each monthly payment if the payments are interest-only. Round to the nearest cent. \$1,195.77

d. Find the difference between the regular monthly payment and the balloon payment, to the nearest hundred dollars. \$348,800.

e. If the mortgage was not a balloon mortgage, what would be the amount of the monthly payment, rounded to the nearest cent? \$3,618.02

18. An interest-only balloon mortgage for a principal of p dollars for 18 years has total interest of t dollars. Express the amount of each monthly payment before the balloon payment algebraically. $\frac{t}{215}$

New Listing: Cape-Cod style home w/ 2 baths, 700 sq. ft first flr., upstairs 15 × 26 dormer, 12 × 20 garage, gas heat, frpl, basement. Property 1/2 acre plot w/ 5 ×12 shed and tennis court.
\$301K

19. Using the table from Example 2, find the assessed value of the house in this classified ad. \$4,572

20. Mark and Beth are looking at four different homes. They created this spreadsheet to estimate escrow calculations more easily. They will pay the property tax and homeowner's insurance each month with their mortgage payment. The bank will hold these two amounts in escrow until those bills need to be paid, which is every six months. Each line represents data for a different home they are looking at. Mark and Beth input values for the mortgage, property tax, and homeowner's insurance in rows 2–5, columns A, B, and C.

	A	B	C	D	E
1	Monthly Mortgage	Annual Property Tax	Annual Homeowner's Insurance	Monthly Escrow Payment	Escrow Balance with Interest after Six Months
2	1,435	5,900	1,234	c.	d.
3	1,987	8,766	1,567	e.	f.
4	2,081	8,944	1,540	g.	h.
5	1,873	7,711	1,564	i.	j.

Future Value of a Periodic Deposit

$$B = \frac{P\left(\left(1+\frac{r}{n}\right)^{nt}-1\right)}{\frac{r}{n}}$$

where B = balance at the end of the six months
P = periodic deposit amount, which is the monthly escrow
r = annual interest rate expressed as a decimal
n = number of times the interest is compounded annually
t = length of the investment in years

a. Write the spreadsheet formula for cell D2 that will compute the escrow balance after one month. =B2/12+C2/12

If the monthly escrow payments get 1% interest compounded monthly, Mark and Beth can compute the value of the escrow account in six months. Look at this as finding the future value of a periodic deposit. Recall the formula from Lesson 3-8 shown at the left.

b. Write the spreadsheet formula for cell E2 that will compute the escrow balance after six months, with the given interest rate and monthly compounding. =D2*((1+0.01/12)^(12*0.5)–1)/(0.01/12)

c–j. Fill in the missing entries. See margin.

Owning a home is a keystone of wealth . . . both financial affluence and emotional security.

Suze Orman, Author, TV Personality, and Personal Finance Expert

Purchase a Home 8-4

Key Terms

- recurring costs
- non-recurring costs
- closing
- closing costs
- earnest money deposit
- attorney fee
- origination fee
- title
- title search
- points
- origination points
- discount points
- prepaid interest
- arrears
- transfer tax
- amortization table
- initial rate
- adjustment period
- hybrid ARM

Objectives

- Estimate closing costs.
- Create an amortization table for a fixed rate mortgage.
- Create an amortization table for a fixed rate mortgage with extra payments.
- Investigate the amortization table for an adjustable rate mortgage.

Common Core

A-SSE1, F-BF1

CCSS Warm-Up

Jordan saves $x per month for 30 years. Express his savings after 30 years algebraically.

$360x$

What will the American dream cost you?

Once you have your mortgage approval, you are a big step closer to home ownership. Below are a few questions that you must investigate thoroughly before buying a home

- What is the cost of the home?
- Will you need to make a down payment?
- Where is the home located?
- How many rooms does the home have?
- What is the size of the property you will own?
- What condition is the house and property in?
- What type of heating/cooling system does the house have?
- What is the approximate cost of running the house (electricity, gas, water, and so on)?

One of the biggest concerns for a prospective homeowner is the costs in both the immediate and the distant future. These costs are in two categories: recurring costs and non-recurring costs. **Recurring costs** are costs that occur on a regular basis. Some examples of recurring costs are mortgage payments, insurance payments, and property taxes.

Non-recurring costs are one-time costs. Moving costs and many of the costs at the closing are non-recurring. The **closing** is a meeting attended by the buyer, seller, their attorneys, and a representative of the lending institution. The official sale takes place at this meeting. The buyer is responsible for paying **closing costs**. Although they can differ from state to state, some of the most common non-recurring closing costs are listed and explained on the next page.

EXAMINE THE QUESTION

The American dream is usually thought of as home ownership. Attaining that dream is often very costly. This lesson walks students through some of the costs incurred in purchasing a home.

CLASS DISCUSSION

Before addressing the opening questions in the text, ask students to come up with some questions of their own that they believe need to be answered before buying a home.

Ask students to identify some recurring and non-recurring costs that they are responsible for now.

Why is it important for a prospective buyer to have a title search?

Ask students for other financial responsibilities that are paid in arrears (for example, credit card balances).

- **Earnest Money Deposit** The earnest money, or good-faith deposit, is the money paid to the seller by an interested buyer to show that the buyer is serious about buying the house.
- **Attorney Fees** These are fees paid to the attorney in return for representation at the closing.
- **Origination Fee** This fee is money paid to the lending institution for the paperwork involved in the loan application process.
- **Title** The title is the legal claim of property ownership. It is common practice that before property can change hands, a **title search** is conducted. A title search is a procedure used to make sure that the seller does actually hold title to the property being sold.
- **Points** Points are extra fees charged by the lending institution for the use of their money. Each point is equivalent to 1% of the loan amount. There are two types of points. **Origination points** are similar to origination fees. They are collected from the buyer as a means of paying for the loan application process. **Discount points** are points that reduce the interest rate of the loan. They generally lower the interest rate about 0.25% on a fixed rate mortgage and 0.375% on an adjustable rate mortgage. These percentages vary depending upon the lending institution.
- **Prepaid Interest** Mortgage interest is not paid like rent. Rent is paid ahead of the time you live in the home. Mortgage interest is paid in **arrears**. Interest starts accruing (building) at the beginning of each month and continues throughout the month. When you make your mortgage payment, you are paying the interest that has built up on money borrowed during the month that just passed. Prepaid interest at the closing is the amount of mortgage interest due to cover the time from the closing date to when the first mortgage payment is due. For example, if you close on the 10th day of a 30-day month, you will need to prepay 20 days of interest at the closing.
- **Transfer Tax** This is a fee that is charged for the transfer of title from the seller to the buyer.

Skills and Strategies

Here you will learn about the financial aspects of the closing and the years that follow the purchase of a home.

EXAMPLE 1

Leah and Josh are buying a \$600,000 home. They have been approved for a 7.25% APR mortgage. They made a 15% down payment and will be closing on September 6th. How much should they expect to pay in prepaid interest at the closing?

SOLUTION First determine the amount that Josh and Leah borrowed. Since they made a 15% down payment, multiply \$600,000 by 0.15. Then subtract the down payment from the original amount.

Down payment $600{,}000 \times 0.15 = 90{,}000$

Loan amount $600{,}000 - 90{,}000 = 510{,}000$

You can also calculate the loan amount by recognizing that 15% of the purchase price was the down payment. Therefore, subtract 15% from 100% to find the percent of the purchase price that is the loan amount.

$$100\% - 15\% = 85\%$$

Then multiply the purchase price by the percent that remains to be financed by the mortgage to find the loan amount.

$$600{,}000 \times 0.85 = 510{,}000$$

Josh and Leah's first mortgage payment will be due on October 1. At that time they will prepay interest from September 7 to September 30 for a total of 24 days. The amount of prepaid interest is calculated as follows.

Determine the annual interest by multiplying the APR times the amount borrowed.

$$510{,}000 \times 0.0725 = 36{,}975$$

There is \$36,975 in annual interest for this loan.

Determine the daily amount of interest due by dividing the annual interest by 365 calendar days.

$$36{,}975 \div 365 \approx \$101.30$$

It will cost \$101.30 in interest per day.

Multiply the daily interest rate by the number of days to be paid in arrears.

$$101.30 \times 24 = 2{,}431.20$$

Leah and Josh will owe \$2,431.20 in prepaid interest for the remainder of September.

■ CHECK YOUR UNDERSTANDING

How much will be charged in prepaid interest on a \$400,000 loan with an APR of 6% that was closed on December 17?

TEACH

Purchasing a home is a financial, emotional, and time-consuming endeavor. Students need to understand the complexity of the process. There are many online sites that offer advice about home purchases. Encourage students to do some research. You might also want to ask a local realtor to make a presentation in your class about the steps involved in purchasing a home.

EXAMPLE 1

The steps involved in determining the prepaid interest at the closing need to be thoroughly developed and explained to the students. Because the closing is on September 6th, interest is due from September 7th to the end of that month for a total of 24 days. The daily interest owed on the loan is computed by finding the annual interest on the \$510,000 borrowed and dividing that amount by 365. The buyers will have to pay 24 times that amount since there are 24 days remaining until September 30th.

CHECK YOUR UNDERSTANDING

Answer \$920.50

This amount is computed as follows:

$$\left(\frac{400{,}000 \times 0.06}{365}\right) \times 14$$

EXAMPLE 2

There is no fixed amount that lending institutions charge at closing. These amounts vary depending upon location and the financial circumstances surrounding the sale. The usual expectation for closing fees is somewhere between 2–7% of the purchase price. Lending institutions will send the purchaser an accounting of the exact fees that will be incurred so there are no surprises.

CHECK YOUR UNDERSTANDING

Answer \$8,000–\$28,000

Since the mortgage is \$340,000, Shannon has already made a 15% down payment. Calculate the purchase price by dividing the mortgage amount by 0.85. Then apply the percentage interval to that amount.

EXAMPLE 3

Make sure that you thoroughly review the change in the loan formula. The new monthly payment formula is adjusted so that the rate is entered as a percent rather than as an equivalent decimal.

EXAMPLE 2

Leah and Josh know that they will have to bring their checkbook to the closing. What might they expect to pay in total at the closing?

SOLUTION Although there are no guarantees about what they will pay, the rule of thumb is that they can expect the closing costs to run from 2% to 7% of the purchase price. These numbers vary depending upon the location of the house and on any special circumstances.

$$600{,}000 \times 0.02 = 12{,}000$$

$$600{,}000 \times 0.07 = 42{,}000$$

Leah and Josh should be prepared to write checks that will total from \$12,000 to \$42,000 at the closing.

■ CHECK YOUR UNDERSTANDING

Shannon had to make a down payment of 15% of the selling price of her house. She was approved for a \$340,000 mortgage. What range of costs might she expect to pay at the closing?

EXAMPLE 3

Trudy and Tom have been approved for a \$300,000, 15-year mortgage with an APR of 5.75%. How much of their first monthly payment will go to interest and principal?

SOLUTION The amount allocated to principal and interest changes from month to month. At the beginning of the loan, the interest payment is high and the principal payment is lower. Towards the end of the loan the amount the principal payment becomes larger than the interest payment. To calculate each amount, you need to determine the monthly payment. You will use a slightly altered loan formula that allows you to enter the rate as a percent rather than as an equivalent decimal. Since the decimal is needed in the calculation, the monthly rate of $\frac{r}{12}$ is divided by 100.

$$\frac{r}{12} \div 100 = \frac{r}{12} \times \frac{1}{100} = \frac{r}{1{,}200}$$

The new monthly payment formula is

$$M = \frac{p\left(\frac{r}{1{,}200}\right)\left(1 + \frac{r}{1{,}200}\right)^{12t}}{\left(1 + \frac{r}{1{,}200}\right)^{12t} - 1}$$

where M = monthly payment
p = principal
r = interest rate expressed as a percent
t = length of loan in years

Substitute and simplify.

$$M = \frac{300{,}000\left(\frac{5.75}{1{,}200}\right)\left(1 + \frac{5.75}{1{,}200}\right)^{12(15)}}{\left(1 + \frac{5.75}{1{,}200}\right)^{12(15)} - 1} = 2491.23$$

The monthly payment on this loan is \$2,491.23.

The monthly interest can be determined using the monthly interest formula.

$$I = p \times \frac{r}{1{,}200} \quad \text{where} \quad \begin{aligned} I &= \text{interest} \\ p &= \text{principal} \\ r &= \text{interest rate expressed as a percent} \end{aligned}$$

Substitute. $I = 300{,}000 \times \dfrac{5.75}{1{,}200} = 1{,}437.50$

The first monthly interest amount is \$1,437.50.

Subtract that amount from the monthly payment to get the amount paid towards the principal.

$$2{,}491.23 - 1{,}437.50 = 1{,}053.73$$

The amount paid towards the principal is \$1,053.73.

CHECK YOUR UNDERSTANDING

What percent of the monthly payment went to principal and what percent went to interest?

EXAMPLE 4

How can Trudy and Tom get an accounting of where their monthly payments will go for the first year of their mortgage?

SOLUTION In Example 3, you calculated the principal and interest for a single month. Here, Trudy and Tom need data over the course of 12 months. To determine the principal and interest amounts for an extended period of time, they should review an amortization table for their loan. An **amortization table** is a listing of the unpaid principal, the monthly payment, the amount allocated to paying down the principal, and the amount allocated to interest. There are many websites that offer mortgage amortization calculators. Some of them generate the amortization table.

Trudy and Tom can set up their own spreadsheet to generate the amortization table. They first set up rows 1–4 of the spreadsheet where the user will input the necessary data. Here the information is entered into the cells in column B in rows 1–4.

	A	B	C	D	E	F
1	Principal	300,000				
2	Interest rate as a percent	5.75				
3	Length of loan	15				
4	Number of yearly payments	12				
5	Payment Number	Beginning Balance	Monthly Payment	Towards Interest	Towards Principal	Ending Balance

Next, determine the information that they will need in the amortization table. It should contain the payment number, the beginning balance, the monthly payment, the amounts allocated towards principal and interest, and the ending balance as shown in row 5.

CHECK YOUR UNDERSTANDING

Answer approximately 58% to interest and 42% to principal

EXAMPLE 4

This example mimics the mathematics that is used in online mortgage calculators. Students learn how to use the mortgage formula in a spreadsheet so that the monthly interest and principal can be calculated and displayed.

Row 6 contains the formulas needed to generate the table.

A6	1	Begin with number 1.
B6	=B1	The beginning balance is the principal.
C6	=(B1*(B2/1200)*(1+B2/1200)^(B4*B3))/((1+B2/1200)^(B4*B3)–1)	Monthly payment formula from Example 3.
D6	=B6*B2/1200	This is the interest formula.
E6	=C6–D6	The monthly payment less the interest.
F6	=B6–E6	The ending balance is the beginning balance minus the amount towards principal.

	A	B	C	D	E	F
1	**Principal**	300,000				
2	**Interest rate as a percent**	5.75				
3	**Length of loan**	15				
4	**Number of yearly payments**	12				
5	**Payment Number**	**Beginning Balance**	**Monthly Payment**	**Towards Interest**	**Towards Principal**	**Ending Balance**
6	1	300,000.00	2,491.23	1,437.50	1,053.73	298,946.27
7	2	298,946.27	2,491.23	1,432.45	1,058.78	297,887.49
8	3	297,887.49	2,491.23	1,427.38	1,063.85	296,823.64
9	4	296,823.64	2,491.23	1,422.28	1,068.95	295,754.69
10	5	295,754.69	2,491.23	1,417.16	1,074.07	294,680.61
11	6	294,680.61	2,491.23	1,412.01	1,079.22	293,601.40
12	7	293,601.40	2,491.23	1,406.84	1,084.39	292,517.01
13	8	292,517.01	2,491.23	1,401.64	1,089.59	291,427.42
14	9	291,427.42	2,491.23	1,396.42	1,094.81	290,332.61
15	10	290,332.61	2,491.23	1,391.18	1,100.05	289,232.56
16	11	289,232.56	2,491.23	1,385.91	1,105.32	288,127.23
17	12	288,127.23	2,491.23	1,380.61	1,110.62	287,016.61

Set up row 7 so it can be copied into subsequent rows (filled down). When copying formulas, the spreadsheet advances the cell address in the formula down by one row. If you add $ to the cell address, it won't change when copying. The entries in row 9 should be as follows.

A7	=A6+1	This will add 1 to each payment number.
B7	=F6	The beginning balance is last month's ending balance.
C7	=$C$6	Put $ in the cell address to keep it from changing.
D7	=B7*$B$2/1200	Again add $ to keep cell address fixed.
E7	=C7–D7	
F7	=B7–E7	

The completed table for the first 12 payments is shown above.

■ **CHECK YOUR UNDERSTANDING**

Adding a sum cell to the bottom of the *monthly payment, towards interest,* and *towards principal* columns yields the following totals at the end of the first year of payments.

Payments for 12 Months: $29,894.76
Interest for 12 Months: $16,911.38
Principal for 12 Months: $12,983.39

At the end of the 12-month period, what percent of the principal has been paid off?

CHECK YOUR UNDERSTANDING

Answer approximately 4.3%

EXAMPLE 5

Students may need to see how this spreadsheet is built following the directions in the text. If possible, use a projection device connected to a computer in your classroom or take students to a computer lab and have them walk through the steps outlined in the text.

EXAMPLE 5

Trudy and Tom decide to make an extra payment of $100 each month to reduce their principal. They adjust their spreadsheet as shown. What formula change(s) did they make in row 6 so that the extra payment could be accounted for?

	A	B	C	D	E	F	G
1	**Principal**	300,000					
2	**Interest rate as a percent**	5.75					
3	**Length of loan**	15					
4	**Number of yearly payments**	12					
5	**Payment Number**	**Beginning Balance**	**Monthly Payment**	**Extra Payment**	**Towards Interest**	**Towards Principal**	**Ending Balance**
6	1	300,000.00	2,491.23	100.00	1,437.50	1153.73	298,846.27
7	2	298,846.27	2,491.23	100.00	1,431.97	1159.26	297,687.01
8	3	297,687.01	2,491.23	100.00	1,426.42	1164.81	296,522.20
9	4	296,522.20	2,491.23	100.00	1,420.84	1170.39	295,351.80
10	5	295,351.80	2,491.23	100.00	1,415.23	1176.00	294,175.80
11	6	294,175.80	2,491.23	100.00	1,409.59	1181.64	292,994.16
12	7	292,994.16	2,491.23	100.00	1,403.93	1187.30	291,806.86
13	8	291,806.86	2,491.23	100.00	1,398.24	1192.99	290,613.87
14	9	290,613.87	2,491.23	100.00	1,392.52	1198.71	289,415.17
15	10	289,415.17	2,491.23	100.00	1,386.78	1204.45	288,210.72
16	11	288,210.72	2,491.23	100.00	1,381.01	1210.22	287,000.50
17	12	287,000.50	2,491.23	100.00	1,375.21	1216.02	285,784.48

SOLUTION There is a new column D, so the formulas need to be adjusted in the following columns.

E6 =B6*B2/1200

F6 =C6+D6–E6 The monthly payment plus the extra payment less the monthly interest is the amount that goes towards the principal.

G6 =B6–F6

CHECK YOUR UNDERSTANDING

Answer $9,811.37 in interest and 10 monthly payments were saved.

■ **CHECK YOUR UNDERSTANDING**

Examine the loan summaries below for each of the two situations outlined on the previous page. How much interest and loan time was saved by making the extra $100 in payments toward principal each month?

	Without Extra Payment	With Extra Payment
Monthly Payment	2,491.23	2,591.23
Scheduled Payments	180	180
Actual Payments	180	170
Total Extra Payments	0	16,900.00
Total Interest	148,421.45	138,610.08

Adjustable Rate Mortgages (ARMs)

In the previous examples, each of the homebuyers had a fixed rate mortgage. In a fixed rate mortgage, the interest rate remains the same throughout the term of the loan. In an *adjustable rate mortgage or ARM,* the interest rate can change periodically. Therefore, the monthly payments change as well, based upon those rates.

Here is how an adjustable mortgage works. Lenders quote you an **initial rate** that stays in effect for an agreed upon period of time. This can be as short as 1 month to several years. The monthly payment is based upon that initial rate. Often, the initial interest rate quoted is tied into a customer's credit worthiness. In an ARM, the interest rate and monthly payment will change periodically. The period between rate changes is known as the **adjustment period**. A loan with a 1-year adjustment period is known as a 1-year ARM. Here, the interest rate and the monthly payment may change at the end of one year's adjustment period.

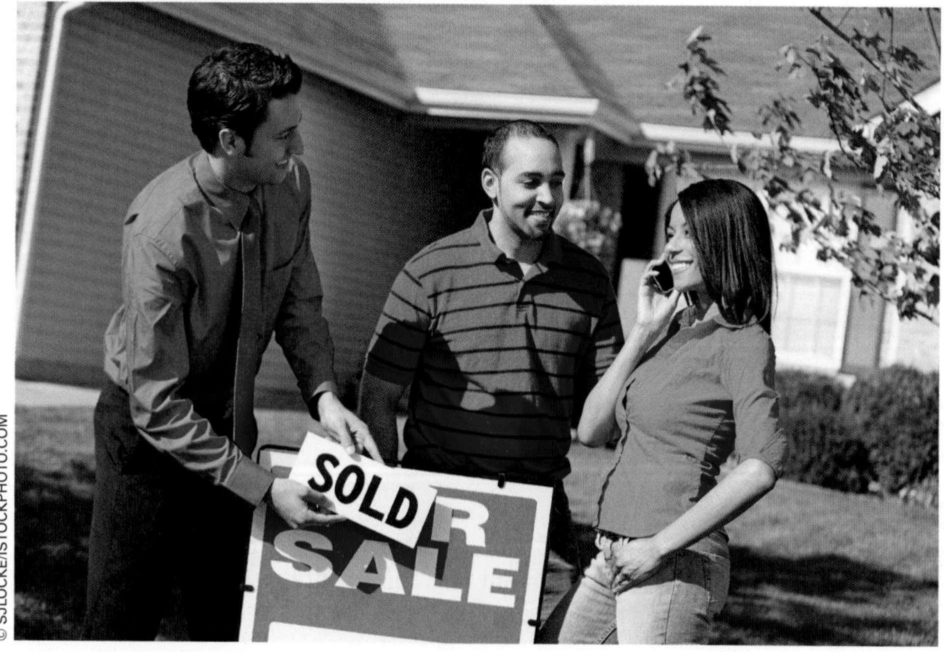

© SJLOCKE/ISTOCKPHOTO.COM

Some ARMS, known as **hybrid ARMs**, are a combination of a fixed rate period of time with an adjustable rate period of time. A 3/1 hybrid ARM indicates that the initial interest rate is fixed for the first 3 years and then there is an adjustment period every year thereafter for the life of the loan. There are many types of adjustable mortgages and many different rules and regulations attached to those mortgages. This is just another example of "Buyer Beware!" You must always be sure to read the fine print.

EXAMPLE 6

This example begins similar to Example 4. The interest rates and lengths of the loans differ. Students can build formulas for row 6 by referencing to Example 4. The formulas are:
C6 =(B1*(B2/1200)*(1+B2/1200)^(B4*B3))/((1+B2/1200)^(B4*B3)–1)
D6 = B6*B2/1200
E6 = C6–D6
F6 = B6–E6

The formulas change for row 7. The adjusted formulas are:

C12 =(B12*(C2/1200)*(1+C2/1200)^(B4*C3))/((1+C2/1200)^(B4*C3)–1)
D12 = B12*C2/1200
E12 = C12–D12
F12 = B12–E12

EXAMPLE 6

Chris and Gene have a 6-month adjustable 15-year mortgage. They borrowed $300,000 and were quoted an initial rate of 5%. After 6 months, their rate increased by 1%. Examine the following spreadsheet for the first year of payments. How were the amounts for payment 7 calculated?

	A	B	C	D	E	F	G
1	**Principal**	300,000					
2	**Interest rate as a percent**	5	6				
3	**Length of loan**	15	14.5				
4	**Number of yearly payments**	12					
5	**Payment Number**	**Beginning Balance**	**Monthly Payment**	**Towards Interest**	**Towards Principal**	**Ending Balance**	**Interest Rate**
6	1	300,000.00	2,372.38	1,250.00	1,122.38	298,877.62	5%
7	2	298,877.62	2,372.38	1,245.32	1,127.06	297,750.56	5%
8	3	297,750.56	2,372.38	1,240.63	1,131.75	296,618.81	5%
9	4	296,618.81	2,372.38	1,235.91	1,136.47	295,482.34	5%
10	5	295,482.34	2,372.38	1,231.18	1,141.20	294,341.13	5%
11	6	294,341.13	2,372.38	1,226.42	1,145.96	293,195.17	5%
12	7	293,195.17	2,526.94	1,465.98	1,060.96	292,134.21	6%
13	8	292,134.21	2,526.94	1,460.67	1,066.27	291,067.94	6%
14	9	291,067.94	2,526.94	1,455.34	1,071.60	289,996.34	6%
15	10	289,996.35	2,526.94	1,449.98	1,076.96	288,919.39	6%
16	11	288,919.39	2,526.94	1,444.60	1,082.34	287,837.05	6%
17	12	287,837.05	2,526.94	1,439.19	1,087.75	286,749.30	6%

SOLUTION In the spreadsheet you need to adjust the formulas for payments 7–12. Enter an interest rate of 6% in cell C2 and a length of loan of 14.5 years in cell C3. Adjust the formulas in row 12 so they use the adjusted interest rate, length of loan, and current principal balance. Then copy those formulas into rows 13 to 17.

The new ending balance is $286,749.30.

■ CHECK YOUR UNDERSTANDING

What effect did the 1% adjustment in interest rate have on the monthly payment and the amounts towards interest and principal?

CHECK YOUR UNDERSTANDING

Answer The monthly payment increased by $154.56. The amount toward interest increased and the amount toward principal decreased.

Applications

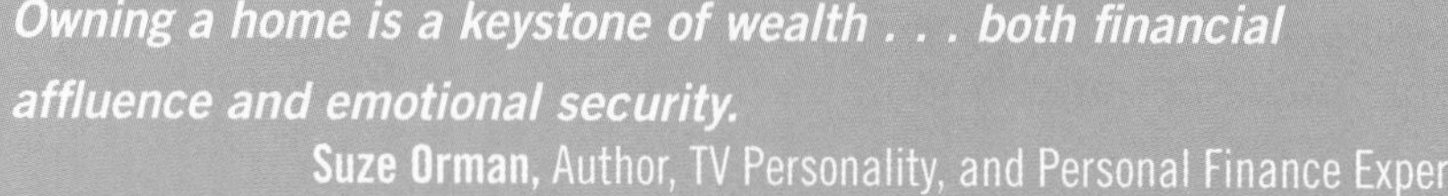

Owning a home is a keystone of wealth . . . both financial affluence and emotional security.
Suze Orman, Author, TV Personality, and Personal Finance Expert

TEACH

Exercises 2, 3, and 4
These exercises should be assigned together. In the first two, students find the prepaid interest. Using these two exercises as a guide, students can then convert the steps into formulas for the spreadsheet in Exercise 4.

Exercise 7
Make sure that students understand what each column heading represents. The sum of the interest and principal amounts must equal the monthly payment amount.

ANSWERS

1. For many, home ownership is a sign of financial stability, security, and an indication that "we've made it". Suze Orman goes even further and indicates that it is a key component of what it means to be wealthy.

1. Explain how the quote can be interpreted. See margin.

2. Del is buying a $250,000 home. He has been approved for a 5.75% mortgage. He was required to make a 15% down payment and will be closing on the house on July 15. How much should he expect to pay in prepaid interest at the closing? approximately $535.68

3. Bonnie is purchasing an apartment for $180,000. She has been approved for a 6% mortgage. She put 10% down and will be closing on April 22. How much should she expect to pay in prepaid interest? approximately $213.04

	A	B
1	Enter the loan amount.	
3	Enter the day of the month for closing.	
5	Enter number of days in month.	
7	Enter the APR for the loan.	
9	Interest due for one year.	
10	Daily interest due.	
11	Interest due from closing date until the end of the month.	

4. This spreadsheet can be used to calculate the amount of prepaid interest a buyer will need to pay at the closing. Write formulas for cells B9, B10, and B11. B9: =B1*B7/100; B10: =B9/365; B11: =(B5–B3)*B10

5. Jason is closing on a $430,000 home. He made a 13% down payment and is borrowing the rest. What is the approximate range of costs that he might expect to pay at the closing? $8,600 – $30,100

6. Becky was told that based on the price of her home, her approximate closing costs would range from $4,000 to $14,000. How much was the price of her home? $200,000

7. Celine and Don have been approved for a $400,000, 20-year mortgage with an APR of 6.55%. Using the mortgage and interest formulas, set up a two-month amortization table with the headings shown and complete the table for the first two months. See additional answers.

Payment Number	Beginning Balance	Monthly Payments	Towards Interest	Towards Principal	Ending Balance

8. Rob has been approved for a $275,000, 15-year mortgage with an APR of 5.9%. Using the mortgage and interest formulas, set up a table with the above headings and complete the table for the first two months. See additional answers.

9. Use a spreadsheet to generate the first year of payments in a loan amortization table for a $200,000, 10-year mortgage with an APR of 7%. See additional answers.

10. Use a spreadsheet to generate the last year of payments in a loan amortization table for a $600,000, 15-year mortgage with an APR of 5.5% See additional answers.

11. Shannon took out a $300,000, 15-year mortgage with an APR of 7%. The first month she made an extra payment of $400. What was her ending balance at the end of that first month? $298,653.52

12. Examine the loan amortization table for the last 5 months of a $500,000, 15-year mortgage with an APR of 5.75%. Determine the missing table amounts. See margin.

Payment Number	Beginning Balance	Monthly Payment	Towards Interest	Towards Principal	Ending Balance
176	20,465.13	a.	98.06	4,053.99	16,411.14
177	b.	a.	78.64	4,073.41	12,337.73
178	12,337.73	a.	c.	4,092.93	8,244.79
179	8,244.79	a.	39.51	d.	4,132.25
180	4,132.25	a.	19.80	4,132.25	e.

13. Examine the loan amortization table for a $210,000, 15-year mortgage with an APR of 6%. The borrower paid an extra $100 each month towards the principal. Determine the missing amounts. See margin.

Payment Number	Beginning Balance	Monthly Payment	Extra Payment	Towards Interest	Towards Principal	Ending Balance
1	210,000.00	a.	100.00	1,050.00	822.10	209,177.90
2	b.	a.	100.00	1,045.89	826.21	c.
3	208,351.69	a.	100.00	d.	830.34	207,521.35
4	207,521.35	a.	100.00	1,037.61	e.	206,686.86
5	206,686.86	a.	100.00	1,033.43	838.67	205,848.19

14. Examine this portion of an amortization table for an adjustable rate mortgage that had a 1-year initial rate period of 4.25% and increased to 5.25% after that period ended. Determine the missing amounts.
a. $1,300.39 b. $203,767.35 c. $1,410.14 d. $886.67 e. $525.76

Interest Rate	Payment Number	Beginning Balance	Monthly Payment	Towards Interest	Towards Principal	Ending Balance
4.25%	11	204,344.02	a.	723.72	576.67	b.
4.25%	12	b.	a.	721.68	578.71	203,188.63
5.25%	13	203,188.63	c.	888.95	521.19	202,667.44
5.25%	14	202,667.44	c.	d.	523.47	202,143.96
5.25%	15	202,143.96	c.	884.38	e.	201,618.20

15. Tom took out a $440,000 15-year adjustable rate mortgage with a 4% initial 6-month rate. The amortization table for the initial rate period is shown. After the first 6 months, the rate went up to 5%. Calculate the next line of the table. See margin.

Payment Number	Beginning Balance	Monthly Payment	Toward Interest	Toward Principal	Ending Balance
1	440,000.00	3,254.63	1,466.67	1,787.96	438,212.04
2	438,212.04	3,254.63	1,460.71	1,793.92	436,418.12
3	436,418.12	3,254.63	1,454.73	1,799.90	434,618.22
4	434,618.22	3,254.63	1,448.73	1,805.90	432,812.32
5	432,812.32	3,254.63	1,442.71	1,811.92	431,000.40
6	431,000.40	3,254.63	1,436.67	1,817.96	429,182.44

TEACH

Exercise 15

Make sure that students understand that there will be a change in the monthly payment for the new row they are calculating. This monthly payment must reflect an increase of 1% in the APR.

ANSWERS

12. a. $4,152.05
b. $16,411.14
c. $59.12
d. $4,112.54
e. 0

13. a. $1,772.10
b. $209,177.90
c. $208,351.69
d. $1,041.76
e. $834.49

15. Payment 7; Beginning Balance: $429,182.44; Monthly Payment: $3,472.72; Towards Interest: $1,788.26; Towards Principal: $1,684.46; Ending Balance: $427,497.98

> *Home is a place you grow up wanting to leave, and grow old wanting to get back to.*
>
> **John Ed Pearce,** Journalist

8-5 Rentals, Condominiums, and Cooperatives

Objectives

- Compute costs of purchasing a cooperative or a condominium.
- Understand the advantages and disadvantages of different forms of homes.

Common Core

A-SSE1b, F-BF1, F-LE1

Key Terms

- condominium
- maintenance fee
- co-op apartment
- cooperative
- landominium
- board of directors
- equity

CCSS Warm-Up

Find, to the nearest thousandth, the value of B given $B = \left(1 + \frac{1}{x}\right)^x$ for each value of x.

1. $x = 5$ **2.** $x = 50$ **3.** $x = 500$

1. 2.488 2. 2.692 3. 2.716

What alternatives are there to purchasing a single-family home?

Maintaining your own house requires time as well as money. Mowing lawns, shoveling snow, and making repairs keep the average homeowner very busy. Some people prefer not to be responsible for these chores.

As discussed in Lesson 8-1, you can rent an apartment. Apartments have rules regarding pets, noise, sanitation, and physical appearance that all tenants must follow. Since tenants are not buying the home, they do not have to make a large down payment. They make monthly rental payments. Since tenants do not own the apartment that they occupy, they cannot deduct property taxes or mortgage interest on their income tax forms, and they can't make a profit from the sale of their homes.

A **condominium** is a form of home ownership where each unit is individually owned. The common parts of the property, such as the grounds, are jointly owned. Condominium owners are responsible for

EXAMINE THE QUESTION

There are a variety of options available that fall under the category of home ownership. A home need not be a single family dwelling. Assess your students' familiarity with these options. Before beginning the lesson, ask them to list some of the home ownership alternatives.

CLASS DISCUSSION

What responsibilities does a homeowner have for the upkeep of a home? Which of these responsibilities do renters also have?

Ask students if they know of any condominiums in the school district. Discuss the structures. Are they single family dwellings? Are they townhouses? Are they apartments?

What might the benefits be of owning a landominium?

the maintenance of the inside of their own units. Condominium owners are charged a **maintenance fee**, which is used to hire workers to maintain common areas, such as lawns, outside walls, decks, roofs, sidewalks, and roads. Like single-family houses, condominiums can be purchased and sold. There are deeds, closing costs, property taxes, points, mortgage payments, and so on.

A **co-op apartment** or **cooperative** is another form of homeownership. A cooperative is a corporation that owns a group of apartments. The corporation takes out a mortgage to buy the entire apartment complex. Investors purchase shares in the co-op, and these shares allow them to occupy the apartments. Co-op owners do not own their individual apartment. They own a portion of the entire cooperative development. They can sell their shares of ownership and keep any profit from the sale. Co-op owners pay a monthly maintenance fee that covers their share of the maintenance of the apartment complex. Part of this fee covers the payment that the cooperative corporation must make toward the mortgage loan each month.

Condominiums and cooperatives usually have a **board of directors** elected by the homeowners to manage business matters. Condo and co-op owners may vote on major issues.

There are also **landominiums** where the owner owns both the home and the land on which the home is built. As with a condominium, a homeowner's association provides landscaping, maintenance, and other services and amenities such as swimming pools and tennis courts.

There are advantages and disadvantages that characterize all types of independent living. You must decide what type best suits your lifestyle and financial situation.

TEACH

Either bring in the real estate section of your local newspaper or access a real estate website. Show students a variety of housing alternatives that are available for purchase in your area. Be sure to include apartments, multiple- and single-family stand-alone residences, condominiums, co-ops, and landominiums.

EXAMPLE 1

Make sure that students understand that only part of the condominium maintenance fee is deductible as property taxes. Homeowners usually get a statement from the condominium association indicating the formula for the deduction. In Example 1, the owner knows that 15% of the fees are for the taxes and can easily calculate that amount for inclusion on his IRS return.

Skills and Strategies

EXAMPLE 1

Last year, Burt paid a monthly condominium maintenance fee of $912. Fifteen percent of this fee covered his monthly property taxes. How much did Burt pay last year in property taxes on his condo?

SOLUTION Burt finds 15% of his monthly maintenance fee by multiplying.

$$0.15 \times 912 = 136.80$$

The monthly property tax is $136.80.

Multiply that by 12 to get the annual property tax.

$$12 \times 136.80 = 1{,}641.60$$

The annual property tax is $1,641.60.

CHECK YOUR UNDERSTANDING

Maggie's monthly maintenance fee is m dollars, of which 27% is tax deductible for property tax purposes. Express the annual property tax deduction algebraically.

CHECK YOUR UNDERSTANDING

Answer $12(0.27m)$

EXAMPLE 2

The concept of ownership of a cooperative is not dissimilar to that of ownership of a corporation. Both involve shareholding. Janet's 550 shares represent a partial ownership of the Seaford Cove Cooperative in the amount of 1.1%.

CHECK YOUR UNDERSTANDING

Answer $100\left(\frac{r}{s}\right)$

EXAMPLE 3

To rent or to buy is a question that faces most people at some point in their lives. The purpose of Example 3 is to outline how to mathematically examine the question and make an informed decision based upon the financials. The assumption in this problem is that there will be an increase in rent each year when Gary renegotiates his rental agreement.

Make sure that you discuss the concept of equity and how that may be a factor in making this decision.

EXAMPLE 2

The Seaford Cove Cooperative is owned by the shareholders. The co-op has a total of 50,000 shares. Janet has an apartment at Seaford Cove and owns 550 shares of the cooperative. What percentage of Seaford Cove does Janet own?

SOLUTION Express Janet's shares as a fraction of the total number of shares. Janet owns $\frac{550}{50{,}000}$ of the corporation.

Divide. $\frac{550}{50{,}000} = 0.011$

Janet owns 1.1% of the Seaford Cove Cooperative.

CHECK YOUR UNDERSTANDING

The Glen Oaks Village Co-op is represented by *s* shares. Sage owns *r* shares. Express the percent of shares he owns algebraically.

EXAMPLE 3

Gary Larson's job is relocating to a new city. He knows he will be there for at least 10 years. Gary is uncertain as to whether he should rent an apartment or buy a home for the time he will be working there. He knows that he eventually wants to return to his home city. Gary wants to compare the accumulated mortgage costs versus the accumulated rental costs before making a decision. Gary knows that he can afford a monthly rent of $2,500. If he buys, he can put $100,000 down and take out a $350,000 mortgage for 20 years with an APR of 6%. Create a spreadsheet similar to the one created in Lesson 8-4 to assist Gary in making the comparison.

SOLUTION There are many factors that could enter into a comparison between renting and buying. In this case, you will only examine mortgage costs versus rental costs.

Gary's yearly rent increase can be modeled using an exponential function. Let *R* represent the yearly rent, *A* represent his initial annual rent, *B* represent the rate of increase expressed as a percent, and *D* represent the year number.

$$R = A\left(1 + \frac{B}{100}\right)^{D-1}$$

For example, suppose that Gary signs a contract for a monthly rent of $800 and the annual rate of increase is 2%.

In the formula, *A* equals the amount paid annually for rent. When you substitute a value for *A*, multiply the monthly rent by 12. The total rent paid is

First year $R = 12{*}800{*}(1{+}0.02)^{1-1} = 9{,}600{*}(1.02)^0 = \$9{,}600$

Second year $R = 12{*}800{*}(1 + 0.02)^{2-1} = 9{,}600{*}(1.02)^1 = \$9{,}792$

Create a rental spreadsheet that has cells where the user can enter the initial monthly rent and the average yearly rent increase as shown in rows 2 and 3 in the spreadsheet on the next page.

The first row, B5, after the table headings, should have the following entries.

B5	1	Begin with number 1.
C5	=12*$B$2*(1+$B$3/100)^(B5−1)	Yearly rent
D5	=C5	Running rent paid

The second row should have the following entries.

B6	=B5+1	Adds 1 to each payment number.
C6	=12*$B$2*(1+$B$3/100)^(B6−1)	Yearly rent
D6	=D5+C6	Running rent paid

Copy cells B6, C6, and D6 to create the spreadsheet values for 10 years.

If Gary takes out a 20-year mortgage for $350,000 at 6%, he would have a monthly payment of $2,507.51. Using the spreadsheet from Lesson 8-4, and entering the information for this mortgage, you obtain the spreadsheet below.

From the first spreadsheet, Gary would pay a total of $328,491.63 in rent after 10 years. From the second spreadsheet, Gary would still owe the lending institution $225,859.97. Out of his 120 payments, $124,140.03 would have gone to pay down the principal and $176,761.01 to interest on the loan. Gary's **equity** in the home would be $224,140.03 (the amount paid toward the principal plus his $100,000 down payment). While there are many other factors involved in the decision, based solely on the mortgage and rent costs, Gary might be better off making a purchase because of the equity he will build over the 10-year period.

	A	B	C	D
1	**RENTING**			
2	**Initial Rent**	2,500		
3	**Yearly Inflation Rate**	2		
4		**End of Year**	**Total Rent Paid for Year**	**Running Rent Paid**
5		1	30,000	30,000.00
6		2	30,600.00	60,600.00
7		3	31,212.00	91,812.00
8		4	31,836.24	123,648.24
9		5	32,472.96	156,121.20
10		6	33,122.42	189,243.63
11		7	33,784.87	223,028.50
12		8	34,460.57	257,489.07
13		9	35,149.78	292,638.85
14		10	35,852.78	328,491.63

	A	B	C	D	E	F
1	**Principal**	350,000				
2	**Interest rate as a percent**	6				
3	**Length of loan**	20				
4	**Number of yearly payments**	12				
5	**Payment Number**	**Beginning Balance**	**Monthly Payment**	**Towards Interest**	**Towards Principal**	**Ending Balance**
6	1	350,000.00	2,507.51	1,750.00	757.51	349,242.49
7	2	349,242.49	2,507.51	1,746.21	761.30	348,481.20
124	119	228,595.85	2,507.51	1,142.98	1,364.53	227,231.32
125	120	227,231.32	2,507.51	1,136.16	1,371.35	225,859.97
126					124,140.03	

CHECK YOUR UNDERSTANDING

Answer Answers will vary but should include: renting: utilities, renter's insurance; buying: closing costs, insurance, utilities, home upkeep, and so on.

EXAMPLE 4

Review the component parts of the exponential growth function $y = A(1 + r)^n$ where A is the initial amount, r is the percent increase, and n is the growth period. Remind students that the amount in the parentheses represents the decimal equivalent of 100% plus the percent increase.

CHECK YOUR UNDERSTANDING

Answer $y = 60x + 1{,}900$

CHECK YOUR UNDERSTANDING

Make a list. What other yearly costs might Gary have to consider for making this decision?

EXAMPLE 4

Jake and Gloria moved into an apartment and pay \$1,900 rent per month. The landlord told them that the rent has increased 4.1% per year on average. Express the rent y as an exponential function of the number of years they rent the apartment and determine the amount rent will be when they renew their lease for year 14.

SOLUTION Set up the exponential function you will enter where y is the monthly rent amount and x is the number of years Jake and Gloria have been renting.

$$y = 1{,}900(1 + 0.041)^{x-1}$$

Jake and Gloria's rent will not increase during the first year, so when $x = 1$, $(1 + 0.041)^{x-1}$ is equal to 1, so the rent is the initial rent of \$1,900.

X	Y1	
9	2620.4	
10	2727.8	
11	2839.6	
12	2956	
13	3077.2	
14	3203.4	
15	3334.8	

X=13

Use the table feature on your graphing calculator to list the amount of rent each year. Because rent only increases one time a year (at the time of contract renewal), set the x-values of the tables to begin with 1 and only display whole number values for x.

To find the amount of rent charged in the 13th year, find the row in the table where $x = 13$. Jake and Gloria will pay \$3,077.20 each month of their 14th year in the apartment.

CHECK YOUR UNDERSTANDING

In Example 4, suppose that the rent goes up \$60 per year. If y represents the rent and x represents the number of years, express Jake and Gloria's rent as a function of x.

EXAMPLE 5

Year	Monthly Rent ($)
2002	2,425
2003	2,500
2004	2,675
2005	2,800
2006	2,950
2007	3,100
2008	3,250
2009	3,400
2010	3,575

The monthly rents for two-bedroom apartments at the luxury Cambridge Hall Apartments, for a 9-year period, are given in the table. Find and use an exponential regression equation to predict the rent in 2015.

SOLUTION Enter the data into your calculator. To make the calculations easier, use 2, 3, 4, 5, 6, 7, 8, 9, and 10 for the respective years.

The exponential regression equation with coefficients rounded to the nearest thousandth is

$$y = 2{,}185.288(1.051)^{x-1}$$

Substitute $x = 15$ to represent the year 2015.

$$y = 2{,}185.288(1.051)^{14}$$

The rent in 2015, rounded to the nearest cent, is predicted to be $4,384.77.

■ CHECK YOUR UNDERSTANDING

Examine the regression equation from Example 5. To the nearest tenth of a percent, what was the approximate annual rent increase at Cambridge Hall Apartments?

EXAMPLE 6

In the 2000s the price of cooperative apartments soared, until the economic recession of 2009. In 1995, Ruth and Gino bought a co-op for $98,000. They borrowed $75,000 from the bank to buy their co-op. Years passed and they wanted to sell their co-op, but the price dipped to $61,000. Their equity was $6,744. If they sold the co-op, they would have to pay off the mortgage. How much money did they need to pay the bank back?

SOLUTION Ruth and Gino borrowed $75,000 and paid the bank $6,744 in principal. Subtract to find what they owed the bank.

$$75{,}000 - 6{,}744 = 68{,}256$$

They owed the bank $68,256.

They could sell the co-op for $61,000, but would have to pay the bank $68,256. Subtract to find how much they would need to sell their co-op.

$$68{,}256 - 61{,}000 = 7{,}256$$

Ruth and Gino would have to add $7,256 to pay the bank, since the price decreased.

■ CHECK YOUR UNDERSTANDING

Paul borrowed b dollars from a bank years ago when he bought his co-op for c dollars. He has built up equity and paid back d dollars towards his principal. The price dropped $23,000 since he bought it. Write an inequality that expresses the fact that the new, decreased price of the co-op is less than what Paul owes the bank.

EXAMPLE 5

In this example, students are using an exponential regression equation to predict rent at a future date. Once you have completed the solution, ask students to adjust the year data from the data in the table to the current year and determine the regression equation. Does that equation change? Does the prediction change? Why or why not?

CHECK YOUR UNDERSTANDING

Answer 5.1%

EXAMPLE 6

The phenomenon cited in Example 6 also occurred in the 1990s. At that time, the phrase "prisoners of their co-op" was coined to refer to people who had to raise extra money just to sell their apartments. The phrase also refers to the housing difficulties of 2009.

CHECK YOUR UNDERSTANDING

Answer $c - 23{,}000 < b - d$

Applications

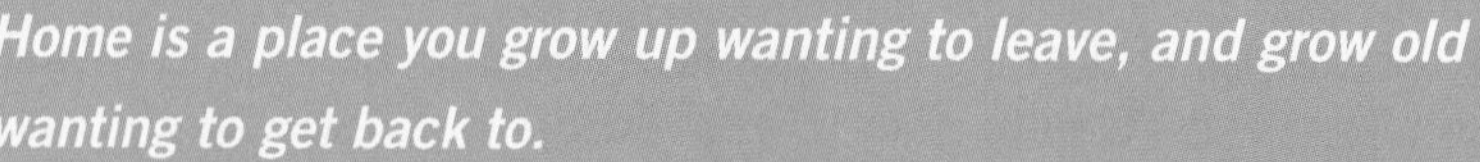

Home is a place you grow up wanting to leave, and grow old wanting to get back to.

John Ed Pearce, Journalist

TEACH

Exercises 2 and 3
These exercises should be assigned together. Exercise 2 uses numerical values while Exercise 3 uses variables to determine the expression for the property taxes.

Exercise 8
Discuss both the positives and negatives of subletting before assigning this problem. Students should know that although many owners sublet apartments, some may not do so with the approval of the landlord or co-op/condo board. In those cases, the people who are subletting could be legally asked to vacate the premises.

ANSWERS

1. Many young people can't wait to leave their parents' home and gain independence in a home of their own. Once they get older, they often long for "the good old days" and want to recapture the parts of their youth at their "growing up" home, which they recall with fond memories.

1. What does this quote mean to you? See margin.

2. Three years ago, Jerry purchased a condo. This year his monthly maintenance fee is $1,397. Twenty percent of this fee is for Jerry's property taxes. How much will Jerry pay this year in property taxes? $3,352.80

3. Last year, Anna paid x dollars for a co-op maintenance fee and one-third paid property taxes. How much property tax did Anna pay last year? $x \div 3$

4. Ron has a co-op in Astor Cooperative. The total shares in the cooperative are 40,000 shares. If Ron owns 500 shares, what percentage of the cooperative corporation does he own? 1.25%

5. The Jacobs Family owned a condo in Bethpage Acres. They bought it for $130,000 six years ago and sold it last week for $195,000. Who keeps the profit from the sale? the Jacobs family

6. Ethel rented an apartment from a landlord in Sullivan County. Her rent was $1,200 per month until she moved out last week. The new tenants pay $1,350 per month. Represent the rent increase as a percent, to the nearest tenth of a percent. 12.5%

7. Linda wants to purchase a Leisure Heights condominium apartment. She will borrow $100,000 from the Duchess Savings Bank. The bank is presently offering a 30-year fixed rate mortgage with an APR of 7.1%. Her monthly maintenance fee will be $310.
   a. What is the monthly mortgage payment to the nearest cent? $672.03
   b. What will be her combined monthly payment? $982.03

8. The Basil family has a summer co-op apartment on a beach and pays a monthly mortgage payment of $1,120 and a monthly maintenance fee of $800. The Basils get approval from the co-op board of directors to *sublet* their apartment, since they do not plan to use it this summer. This means they will continue to make all the payments, but they will rent the apartment to a tenant for the three months they are away. The Basils will charge $2,300 per month to the tenants.
   a. What is the total of the three months' mortgage payments and maintenance fees? $5,760
   b. How much rent will the Basils receive? $6,900
   c. Will the rent cover the monthly fees that the Basils must pay? Yes
   d. What is the difference between the rent the Basils will collect and their monthly payments for the three months? $1,140

9. Helene and Vick moved into an apartment and pay $1,875 rent per month. The landlord told them that the rent has increased 3.28% per year on average. Express the rent y as an exponential function of the number of years they rent the apartment. $y = 1{,}875(1.0328)^{x-1}$

10. Andrew and Meghan moved into an apartment in the city and pay \$2,700 rent per month. The landlord told them the rent has increased 11.1% per year on average.
   a. Express the rent y as an exponential function of x, the number of years they rent the apartment. $y = 2{,}700(1 + 0.111)^{x-1}$
   b. Suppose the rent has increased \$200 each year. Express the rent y as a function of the number of years x. $y = 200x + 2{,}700$
   c. Graph the functions from parts a and b on the same axes. See margin.
   d. Describe the difference between how the two graphs show the increase in rent. See margin.

11. Maria borrowed \$120,000 from a bank when she bought her co-op for \$156,000. The price dropped x dollars since she bought it. She now owes the bank \$114,000, which is more than she could sell the co-op for. Write an inequality that expresses the fact that the new, decreased price of the co-op is less than what Maria owes the bank. $156{,}000 - x < 114{,}000$

12. Monthly rent at Countryside Co-ops has increased annually, modeled by the exponential equation $y = 12(2{,}155)(1.062)^{x-1}$. What was the percent increase per year? 6.2%

13. The monthly rent for a one-bedroom apartment at North Shore Towers for six consecutive years is shown in the table.
   a. Represent the years using the numbers 5, 6, 7, 8, 9, and 10 respectively. Draw a scatterplot for the data. See margin.
   b. Find the exponential regression equation that models the rent increases. Round to the nearest thousandth. $y = 2{,}141.940(1.032)^{x-1}$
   c. Predict the rent in the year 2021. Round to the nearest dollar. \$4,022

14. The Tensers bought a mobile home for \$89,500. They rent space in a trailer park for \$900 per month. The rent increases 2% per year.
   a. If they put a down payment of \$10,000 on the trailer, how much must they borrow? \$79,500
   b. If they borrow the amount from part a for 15 years at an APR of 6%, what will the monthly payment be to the nearest cent? \$670.87
   c. What will be the first monthly payment? final monthly payment? \$670.87
   d. How much will they pay each month for their trailer and the space for the first year? \$1,570.87
   e. What will the space rental be to the nearest cent when they are making their final payment on the trailer? \$1,187.53

15. Joe wants to rent an apartment with an initial monthly rent of \$1,400. He has been told that the landlord raises the rent 1.25% each year. Set up an exponential function that models this situation. Calculate the rent after 12 years. Round to the nearest dollar. $y = 1{,}400(1.0125)^{x-1}$; \$1,605

16. Use spreadsheets to compare these situations after 5 years. See additional answers.

total paid and total paid to the principal for a \$250,000, 20-year mortgage with a 5.75% APR	total amount paid for a \$2,100 monthly rent that has an annual increase of 1.5%

17. Use spreadsheets to compare these situations after 10 years. See additional answers.

total paid and total paid to the principal for a \$300,000, 15-year mortgage with a 6.5% APR	total amount paid for a \$2,600 monthly rent that has an annual increase of 2% after 10 years

TEACH

Exercise 10
Make sure that students understand that 10b is asking for a linear rather than exponential equation.

Exercise 12
The base in this exponential equation is 1.062. This can be written as 1 + 0.062 which is the decimal equivalent of 100% + 6.2%. The percent increase is what is added to 100% in the equation.

Exercises 16 and 17
Inform students that the spreadsheets given in Lessons 8-4 and 8-5 can be used to answer these exercises.

Year	Monthly Rent
2005	\$2,500
2006	2,590
2007	2,675
2008	2,750
2009	2,850
2010	2,925

ANSWERS

10c.

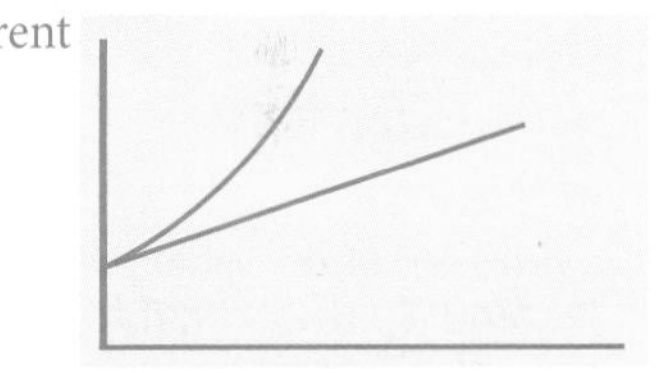

10d. The steepness of the exponential graph shows how each increase is greater than the constant increase, which is represented by a linear function.

13a.

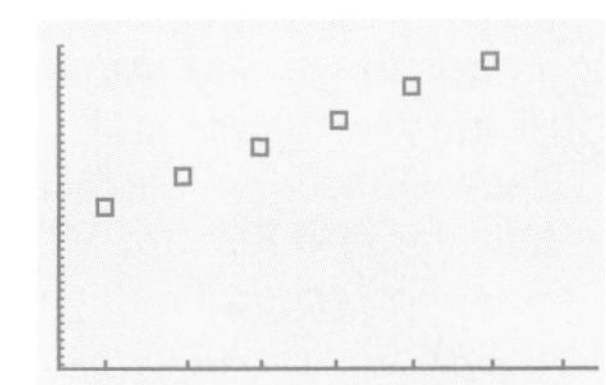

CHAPTER

8 Assessment

Real Numbers

You Write the Story!!

CHAPTER 8 ASSESSMENT

REAL NUMBERS

You Write the Story
Owning a home is often called "The American Dream." The bar graph shows census data for home ownership. Students may decide to add data from the 2010 Census, which they can look up online.

REALITY CHECK

These Reality Check projects have students doing online research and visiting real estate agents, lawyers, and banks.

The Reality Check projects are a terrific form of alternative assessment. They give students an additional avenue to show what they've learned, so their grades are not solely based on tests.

Projects can be presented to the class on any schedule that works for your program. It is too time-consuming for every student to present their project for every chapter.

The December 2009/January 2010 issue of the *Mathematics Teacher* features an article entitled "Algebra, Home Mortgages and Recessions" by Jean Miller-Mariner and Richard Millar. You can access a copy of it through www.nctm.org and use it as an optional topic or student extra credit assignment.

Examine the bar graph below. Write a short newspaper-type article centered on this graph. You can find an electronic copy of this graph at www.cengage.com/school/math/financialalgebra. Copy it, and paste it into your article. The graph depicts the historical census of housing from 1900 to 2000 in the United States.

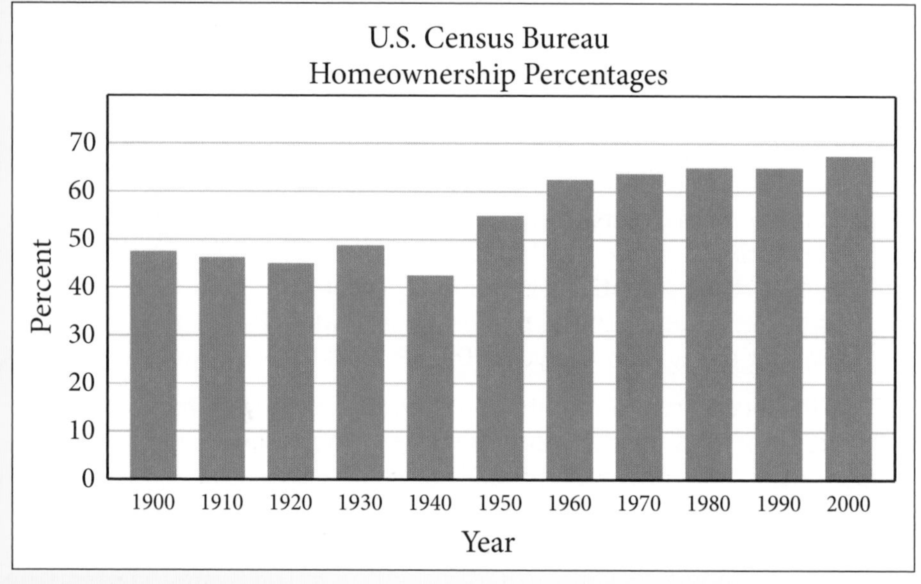

Reality Check

1. Make a poster with columns labeled Less than \$100,000; \$100,000–\$200,000; \$200,000–\$300,000; and so on. Then, look in the real estate section of a local newspaper or a local online source. Cut out a picture or description of a house for each column of your poster. Give as much information about the dwelling as possible.
2. Search real estate websites for cities outside of your state. Print an image of a house that is priced in each of the categories on the poster from Exercise 1 above. Give as much information as possible. Compare the houses with those in your area.
3. Search for an online calculator that will determine payments required for mortgages. Enter a value for a house, an interest rate, and a payment term, and calculate the monthly payment. Figure the total amount you would pay, including interest, for the house.
4. Search for an online calculator that will determine mortgage payments. Experiment with different loan amounts and different mortgage terms. Can you determine a pattern for the increase in your monthly payment for each additional \$1,000 that you borrow?

5. Design the first floor of a house. Make a scale drawing using a scale of $\frac{1}{4}$ inch = 1 foot. Include bedrooms, bathrooms, a kitchen, a living room, and anything else you choose.

6. Visit a real estate broker. Find information on homes for sale in your area including price range of homes, average price of a home, average price of a rental, average price of a co-op or condo, and range of property taxes. Prepare a report that includes your findings.

7. Visit your local bank. Find out information about mortgage loans they offer. Determine the rates for a fixed-rate mortgage and an adjustable-rate mortgage. Ask about the required down payment.

8. Interview a lawyer who represents clients at closings. Ask the lawyer to describe a typical closing and what prospective buyers need so that the closing goes smoothly. Prepare a report of your findings.

9. Search for an online calculator that will generate an amortization table when you make extra payments each month. Use the calculator to determine the difference in total interest on a $500,000, 20-year mortgage with an APR of 7% when the homeowner makes monthly extra payments of $50, $100, and $200.

10. Search online for examples and prices of modular housing. Make a list of advantages and disadvantages of modular housing as compared to houses built on-site. Prepare a report that includes any other facts and figures you find out about modular housing.

11. Search online for prices, fees, rules, and regulations related to trailer parks and mobile homes. List advantages and disadvantages of each. Find facts and figures about trailer park locations, prices, and popularity. Restrict your investigation to year-round trailer-park housing, not RV campgrounds and vacation parks. Prepare a report.

12. Talk to your teacher about planning a class debate on the issue of renting versus buying a home. Split the class into two teams and have each team do research. Have your teacher moderate the debate and formulate questions to be addressed by each side.

13. Determine a comparable monthly rent and mortgage payment. Find an apartment and a home you could rent and buy for that amount. Determine the current rate for a 15-year mortgage and the yearly rent increase percentage for your area (look online or ask a real estate broker). Run the numbers for a 5-, 10-, and 15-year stay in each. Make a display board about your findings.

14. Go online and find how property tax is determined where you live. Search for property tax in your city or county. Prepare a poster that describes the assessment and property tax computation procedures.

REALITY CHECK

Remind students who are personally visiting local businesses or community members, they are representing the school, and need to be cordial and patient. These projects deliberately have students taking little field trips, so they don't conduct everything online.

Emphasize that they need to thank any person who helps them in completing their Reality Check projects. A letter is the most personal way to do this.

You can offer students extra projects for extra credit. Adjust the requirements of any of the projects as appropriate.

DOLLARS AND SENSE

This activity requires students to look up a current financial news item on the Internet. These change periodically to keep the information updated, so the specific activities are not included in this teacher's edition. Use the link www.cengage.com/school/math/financialalgebra to get started.

Dollars and Sense — Your Financial News Update

Go to www.cengage.com/school/math/financialalgebra where you will find a link to a website containing current issues about home purchases, rentals, condos, and co-ops. Try one of the activities.

Really?
Really! REVISITED

REALLY? REALLY! REVISITED

Have the students look up weights online of other heavy objects, including an airplane, the space shuttle, a whale, and so on. Comparisons can be made to the Fu Gang Building.

At the beginning of the chapter, you were given the weights of the heaviest buildings ever moved. The Fu Gang Building in China was quoted in metric tones. A metric ton is about 10% heavier than an English Standard ton. Let's try to get a feeling for how much that building really did weigh.

1. How many pounds are in an English Standard ton? 2,000 lb
2. What do you get when you increase that amount by 10%? 2,200 lb
3. The answer to Exercise 2 is the approximate number of pounds in a metric ton. If the Fu Gang Building weighed approximately 15,140 metric tons, what is its equivalent weight in pounds? 33,308,000 lb
4. Assuming that the average weight of an elephant is 9,000 pounds, what was the equivalent weight of the Fu Gang Building in average elephants? approximately 3,701 average elephants

Applications

1. A rectangular room measures 18 feet by 25 feet. It is going to be carpeted with carpeting that sells for $8.45 per square foot.
   a. What is the area of the room in square feet? 450 sq ft
   b. If the room is drawn to a scale of $\frac{1}{4}$ inch represents 1 foot, give the dimensions of the room in inches on the scale drawing. $4\frac{1}{2}$ by $6\frac{1}{4}$
   c. This room is well-insulated and on the south side of the house. It has an 8-foot-high ceiling. How large an air conditioner would this room require? Round to the nearest thousand BTUs. 11,000 BTUs
2. Ricky took out a $268,000, 30-year mortgage at an APR of 6.34%.
   a. What is the monthly payment to the nearest cent? $1,665.84
   b. What will be his total interest charges after 30 years, to the nearest thousand dollars? $332,000
3. Adam is taking out a $197,000 mortgage. His bank offers him an APR of 7.45%. He wants to compare monthly payments on a 20- and a 30-year loan. Find, to the nearest ten dollars, the difference in the monthly payments for these two loans. $210
4. Eduardo owns a condominium. This year his monthly maintenance fee is m dollars. Twenty-seven percent of this fee pays for Eduardo's property taxes, and 11% pays for the mortgage on the entire development. Both of theses expenses are tax-deductible. Express the amount that is tax-deductible algebraically. $0.38m$
5. A gazebo in the shape of a regular decagon (10 sides) has side length s and apothem a. Express the area of the floor A, algebraically. $A = 5as$

6. Brianna just signed a lease on a rental apartment. The current rent is $1,330 per month, and she estimates a 6% increase each year. Use her estimate to predict the sum of the next five years' worth of monthly rental expenses. Round to the nearest thousand dollars. $90,000

7. The Bricely family borrowed $176,000 from Glen Bank several years ago when they bought their co-op for $246,000. The price dropped d dollars since they bought it. After making years of payments and paying some of the principal, they now owe the bank b dollars, which is more than the price for which they could sell the co-op.
   a. Write an inequality that expresses the fact that the new, decreased price of the co-op is less than what the Bricelys owe the bank. $246{,}000 - d < b$
   b. Express the amount of extra money the Bricelys need to raise to pay the bank if they wanted to sell their co-op for d dollars less than the price for which they could sell the co-op. $b - (246{,}000 - d)$

8. The Maxwell family took out a $275,000, 20-year mortgage at an APR of 6.1%. The assessed value of their house is $9,400. The annual property tax rate is 90.82% of assessed value. What is the annual property tax? $8,537.08

9. The market value of a home is $311,000. The assessed value is x dollars. The annual property tax rate is a dollars per $1,000 of assessed value. Express the semi-annual property tax bill algebraically. See margin.

10. Katherine and Alex had an adjusted gross income of g dollars. Katherine just got a $2,000 raise. They are considering moving to a new house with monthly mortgage payment m dollars, semiannual property taxes s dollars, and quarterly homeowner's premium q dollars. Express their front-end ratio algebraically. See margin.

11. The Xiomaras have an adjusted gross income of $137,865. They are looking at a new house that would have a monthly mortgage payment of $1,687. Their annual property taxes would be $7,550 and their semi-annual homeowner's premium would be $835.
   a. Find their front-end ratio to the nearest percent. 21%
   b. Assume that their credit rating is good. Based on the front-end ratio, would the bank offer them a loan? Explain. See margin.
   c. The Xiomaras have a $344 per month car loan, and their average monthly credit card bill is $420. Compute the back-end ratio to the nearest percent. 28%
   d. Based on the back-end ratio, would the bank offer them a loan? Explain. Yes, the back-end ratio is less than 36%.

12. Lexi moved into an apartment in the suburbs and pays $1,975 rent per month. The landlord told her that the rent has increased 3.6% per year on average. Express the rent y as an exponential function of x, the number of years she rents the apartment. $y = 1{,}975(1.036)^{x-1}$

13. Harley built a concrete patio in her backyard. It is a free-form shape and she needs to find the area of it for property tax purposes.
   a. She takes a diagram of the patio and places it inside a 30-ft by 25-ft rectangle. What is the area of the rectangle? 750 sq ft
   b. She then has a graphing calculator generate 20,000 random points inside the rectangle. She finds that 12,451 of these points landed in the patio outline. What percent of the points landed in the patio? Round to the nearest percent. 62%
   c. What is the area of the patio, to the nearest square foot? 465 sq ft

ANSWERS

9. $\dfrac{ax}{1{,}000}$

10. $\dfrac{m + \dfrac{s}{6} + \dfrac{q}{3}}{\dfrac{(g + 2{,}000)}{12}}$

11b. Yes; because the front-end ratio is less than 28%.

14. Ivana Chase has a gross bimonthly income of \$2,900. She pays 16% in federal and state taxes, puts aside 12% of her income to pay off her school loan, and puts 5% of her income aside for savings. She is considering an apartment that will rent for \$1,700 per month.
   a. Does this monthly rental fee fall within the recommended 25–30% housing expense range? yes
   b. Based upon her expenses, can she make the monthly payments? How much will remain after she pays for the rent and other expenses? yes, \$2,186
15. The square footage and monthly rental of 15 similar two-bedroom apartments in Martha's Cove yield the following linear regression formula: $y = 1.137x + 598.98$ where x represents the square footage of the apartment and y represents the monthly rental price.
   a. Use the formula to determine the monthly rent for an apartment that has 1800 square feet. \$2,645.58
   b. Using the recommendation that you should spend no more than 28% of your monthly gross income on housing, can Stephanie afford this rental if she makes \$9,800 per month? Explain. Yes; she can spend up to \$2,744 to be within the recommendation.
16. Johnny took out a \$500,000 30-year mortgage with an APR of 6.95%. The first month he made an extra payment of \$1,000. What was his balance at the end of that first month? \$498,586.09
17. James rents an apartment with an initial monthly rent of \$1,600. He was told that the rent goes up 1.75% each year. Write an exponential function that models this situation to calculate the rent after 15 years. Round the monthly rent to the nearest dollar. $y = 1{,}600(1.0175)^{x-1}$; \$2,040
18. Elizabeth is moving from a one bedroom apartment in one city to a similar apartment in another city. She has been quoted a flat fee for the truck rental and has two estimates for wages of the movers she will hire depending on her needs and when she moves.

Weekday Move	**Weekend Move**
5 hours of loading and unloading services	4 hours of loading and unloading services
4 hours of packing and unpacking services	5 hours of packing and unpacking services
\$730 total cost	\$710 total cost

   Luke's Moving Company charges a set hourly moving team rate for loading and unloading, and a different set hourly moving team rate for packing and unpacking. Determine the hourly rates. \$70 for loading/unloading, \$95 for packing/unpacking
19. Fill in the missing entries in this loan amortization table for a \$220,000 20-year mortgage with an APR of 5.95%. a. 1,569.81 b. 219,521.02 c. 1,086.07 d. 486.14 e. 217,581.25

Payment Number	Beginning Balance	Monthly Payment	Towards Interest	Towards Principal	Ending Balance
1	220,000.00	a.	1,090.83	478.98	b.
2	b.	a.	1,088.46	481.35	219,039.67
3	219,039.67	a.	c.	483.74	218,555.94
4	218,555.94	a.	1,083.67	d.	218,069.80
5	218,069.80	a.	1,081.26	488.55	e.

20. Joanne and Matt have been approved for a $350,000, 15-year mortgage with an APR of 6.25%. Using the mortgage and interest formulas, set up a two-month amortization table with the following headings and complete the table for the first two months. See additional answers.

Payment Number	Beginning Balance	Monthly Payments	Towards Interest	Towards Principal	Ending Balance

21. Use the spreadsheets from Lessons 8-4 and 8-5 to compare the following two situations after an 8-year period. See margin.

total amount paid and total amount paid to principal for a $250,000, 18-year mortgage with an APR of 6.35%	total amount paid for a $1,700 monthly rent that has an annual increase of 1.8%

22. Use the spreadsheets from Lessons 8-4 and 8-5 to compare the following two situations after a 7-year period. See margin.

total amount paid and total amount paid to principal for a $370,000, 20-year mortgage with an APR of 7.1%	total amount paid for a $2,600 monthly rent that has an annual increase of 2%

23. Michelle took out a $370,000 30-year adjustable rate mortgage with a 3.8% initial 6-month rate. The amortization table for the initial rate period is shown. After the first 6 months, the rate went up to 4.8%. Calculate the next line of the amortization table. See margin.

Payment Number	Beginning Balance	Monthly Payment	Towards Interest	Towards Principal	Ending Balance
1	370,000.00	1,724.04	1,171.67	552.38	369,447.62
2	369,447.62	1,724.04	1,169.92	554.12	368,893.50
3	368,893.50	1,724.04	1,168.16	555.88	368,337.62
4	368,337.62	1,724.04	1,166.40	557.64	367,779.98
5	367,779.98	1,724.04	1,164.64	559.41	367,220.57
6	367,220.57	1,724.04	1,162.87	561.18	366,659.40

24. Calculate the missing amounts in the amortization table which shows extra payments toward the principal made each month.

Payment Number	Beginning Balance	Monthly Payment	Towards Interest	Towards Principal	Ending Balance	Extra Payment
1	210,000.00	1,628.13	1,225.00	403.13	**a.**	100
2	**a.**	1,628.13	1,222.07	**b.**	208,890.81	200
3	208,890.81	1,628.13	**c.**	409.60	208,381.21	100
4	208,381.21	1,628.13	1,215.56	412.57	207,918.64	**d.**
5	207,918.64	1,628.13	1,212.86	415.27	**e.**	100

a. $209,496.87 b. $406.06 c. $1,218.53 d. $50 e. $207,403.37

ANSWERS

21. 1st situation: total amount paid = $186,706.20 total to principal = $86,937.88; 2nd situation: $173,860.19
22. 1st situation: total amount paid: $242,832.02 total to principal: $97,590.61; 2nd situation: total paid = $231,949.64
23. 7th month, Beginning Balance: $366,659.40; Monthly Payment: $1,938.38; Towards Interest: $1,466.64; Towards Principal: $471.74; Ending Balance: $366,187.66

CHAPTER

9 Planning for Retirement

If we ... accept our generation's responsibility, that's going to mean that we give our children no less retirement security than we inherited.

Carol Moseley Braun, American Politician

What do you think the author meant in her quote?

What do you think?

Carol Moseley Braun talks about the obligation of the current generation to secure the retirement future of upcoming generations. It should be responsible and not offer less.

TEACHING RESOURCES

Instructor's Resource CD

Exam*View*® CD, Ch. 9

eHomework, Ch. 9

www.cengage.com/school/math/financialalgebra

Most people eventually stop working—they retire—yet they still have all of the expenses you have encountered in this course. Everybody needs to make arrangements to have steady income for their retirement years. Imagine someone who retires at age 65 and lives to age 85. For 20 years after they stopped working, they need income. You need to start planning for retirement early in your working life. If you don't, you may not have enough money to fund your retirement. Retirement planning can actually affect what job you choose to do when you start working in your 20s!

There are many avenues you can take. There are special savings accounts that you can open for retirement income. Some jobs offer pension plans. Social Security provides benefits for retirees. You can't ignore the issue even when retirement seems a "lifetime" away. It is important to become knowledgeable about the pros and cons of each type of retirement income, so you are ready when you retire!

Really?

"**A** tsunami is building and ready to hit future generations, but this won't be set off by earthquakes or other natural disasters. Instead, it will be a fiscal calamity created by the failure of government and business leaders to deal with the financial drain of millions of retiring baby boomers," said former U.S. Comptroller General, David Walker. Who are these baby boomers that Walker is so worried about? Baby boomers are defined as those people born from 1946 to 1964. This was a time right after World War II when the United States experienced a huge increase in births. Examine these birth statistics.

1940 2,559,000 births per year
1946 3,311,000 births per year
1955 4,097,000 births per year
1957 4,300,000 births per year
1964 4,027,000 births per year
1974 3,160,000 births per year

Look at the rise in birthrates during the "boomer" years. In 2008, the first baby boomers reached the age when they could begin collecting full retirement benefits from the federal government. It is very likely that your grandparents were part of the baby boom generation. It is reported that as these baby boomers age, close to 9,000 Americans will reach the age of 65 each day. With that many baby boomers nearing the time when they leave the workforce, using Social Security benefits, and tapping into retirement savings accounts, it is reasonable to expect that there will be an effect on business, banking, and the economy.

CHAPTER OVERVIEW

This chapter focuses on retirement vocabulary and formulas. The purpose of the chapter is to assist students in realizing that although retirement may be in their very distant future, planning for it should not be. There are things they can do as soon as they get their first job that will help them to be financially secure in their retirement.

REALLY? REALLY!

The Baby Boomer generation has entered retirement age and there is a big fear that there will be more retirees asking for federal assistance from Social Security than the system can handle. This feature offers students the data that supports these claims. Have students research data on the number of births that were reported in the United States 65 years ago from this date. What impact might those numbers have today?

A whole generation of Americans will retire in poverty instead of prosperity, because they simply are not preparing for retirement now.

Scott Cook, American Businessman

9-1 Retirement Income from Savings

Objectives

- Calculate future values of retirement investments that are both single deposit and periodic.
- Compare the tax savings by making contributions to pre-tax retirement savings accounts.
- Calculate an employer's matching contribution to a retirement account.

Common Core

F-IF8b

Key Terms

- retirement
- semi-retired
- pre-tax dollars
- after-tax investments
- individual retirement account (IRA)
- traditional IRA
- tax-deferred
- Roth IRA
- tax-exempt
- 401k
- Keogh plan
- 403b

CCSS Warm-Up

Evaluate each of the following expressions when $a = 4$, $b = 1/2$, $c = \sqrt{2}$, and $d = -2$.

1. $\left(\frac{ac}{bd}\right)^2$ **2.** $d\sqrt{c^a}$ **3.** $(ab)^d$

1. 32 2. −4 3. 1/4

EXAMINE THE QUESTION

If asked this question, many students would offer the answer of a savings account. Plans for retirement are so far in their future that they are unaware of options that are available to them as young employees that will help them provide for themselves in their retirement years. This lesson examines the options at their disposal when they are ready to begin retirement savings. As with all financial decisions, some of the plans are secure and others come with risks.

How can you save for your retirement?

Retirement is a specific point in a person's life when he or she stops working. People can be partially, or **semi-retired**. That is, they continue to work at a full- or part-time job out of choice or financial necessity. Many people begin planning for their retirement at an early age in order to be financially secure when they are no longer employed. There are many options available that can provide you with some form of income in your retirement. Some retirement accounts are made with **pre-tax dollars**. A pre-tax investment is a deposit made to a retirement account that is taken out of your wages before taxes have been calculated and deducted. Pre-tax investments lower your current taxable income. Other types of accounts are made with **after-tax investments**. This is money that is deducted from your income after taxes have been deducted.

Some retirement plans are sponsored by employers and others are opened by individuals. Here are a few of the most common retirement savings plans.

- An **individual retirement account**, or **IRA**, is an account that is opened by an individual. There are two types of IRAs. A **traditional IRA** is a savings plan in which the income generated by the account is **tax-deferred** until it is withdrawn from that account. If you withdraw money from the account before the age of $59\frac{1}{2}$, then you may have to pay an early withdrawal penalty of 10% on that amount, as well as income tax. The penalty can be waived for certain exceptions such as qualified higher education expenses. The second type of IRA is a **Roth IRA**. All deposits into a Roth IRA are taxable. But, when the money is withdrawn from the account after having been there for at least 5 years and the saver is at least $59\frac{1}{2}$ years old, the money and the income earned is **tax-exempt**, or free from taxes. There is an income limit for being able to open a Roth IRA or a traditional IRA.

- A **401k** plan is a retirement savings plan that is sponsored by an employer for its employees. Like other retirement plans, there are strict rules as to when the money can be withdrawn without a penalty. There are also contribution limits that change from year to year.
- A **Keogh plan** is a retirement savings plan for a self-employed professional or the owner of a small business. The pre-tax money invested in this type of an account is tax-deferred until it is withdrawn.
- A **403b** plan is a tax-deferred retirement savings program for employees of educational institutions and some non-profit organizations.

CLASS DISCUSSION

Ask if students have family members or friends who are currently retired. How are they spending their retirement days?

Discuss the difference between tax deferred and tax exempt. In which case does the taxpayer have to pay some taxes and when might that happen?

After reviewing the retirement plans mentioned at the beginning of this lesson, ask students which plan they think is better and why.

Skills and Strategies

In Chapter 3, you learned about present and future values of single and periodic investment accounts. Often, these are retirement accounts.

EXAMPLE 1

Blythe is 40 years old. She is planning on retiring in 25 years. She has opened an IRA with an APR of 3.8% compounded monthly. If she makes monthly deposits of $500 to the account, how much will she have in the account when she is ready to retire?

SOLUTION Recall the formula in Lesson 3-7 for determining the future value of a periodic deposit investment.

$$B = \frac{P\left(\left(1 + \frac{r}{n}\right)^{nt} - 1\right)}{\frac{r}{n}}$$

where
B = balance at end of investment period
P = periodic deposit amount
r = annual interest rate expressed as a decimal
n = number of times interest is compounded annually
t = length of investment in years

Use the formula to determine the amount in Blythe's account after 25 years.

$$B = \frac{500\left(\left(1 + \frac{0.038}{12}\right)^{12(25)} - 1\right)}{\frac{0.038}{12}} \approx 249{,}762.8564$$

Blythe will have approximately $249,763 in her account after 25 years.

CHECK YOUR UNDERSTANDING

Which would have a greater effect on the final balance in Blythe's account—half the monthly deposit or half the interest rate?

TEACH

Retirement is a point that is so far in the future for many of your students that they are apt to ask the question "Why am I learning about this now?" The purpose of the lesson is to show them how early planning can benefit them when they are ready to retire.

EXAMPLE 1

Ask students where they have seen a problem similar to this. Hopefully, they will mention that this example falls into the category of finding the future value of a periodic investment. Have them look back to Lesson 3-7 and reread the information given there. Then, ask students to make the connection between the Examples of 3-7 and this example.

CHECK YOUR UNDERSTANDING

Answer Half the deposit; half the monthly deposit yields a final balance of $124,881.43, and half the interest rate (1.9%) yields a final balance of $191,813.77.

EXAMPLE 2

The taxable income in this example reflects that Blythe made monthly contributions in the amount of $500. Therefore, she contributed a total of $6,000 to her retirement account. Her taxable income has been reduced by that $6,000 and she is paying taxes on that revised income amount. To determine the difference requested, raise the taxable income by the $6,000 that had been subtracted and use that income amount and the tax table to calculate what would have been her tax liability.

© SANDY JONES/ISTOCKPHOTO.COM

CHECK YOUR UNDERSTANDING

Answer $A - D$

EXAMPLE 2

Suppose that Blythe's annual contribution was pre-tax. How much did she save in taxes in one year if her taxable income for that year was $72,500?

SOLUTION Blythe's taxable income was $72,500 for the tax year. Using the tax table on the left below, Blythe owes $14,475 in taxes.

Blythe contributed $500 for each of 12 months during the year.

$$12 \times 500 = 6{,}000$$

By using pre-tax dollars for her retirement investments, her income was reduced by $6,000.

Had her retirement deductions not been in pre-tax dollars, her taxable income would be $6,000 higher.

Taxable income plus pre-tax dollars $72{,}500 + 6{,}000 = 78{,}500$

Suppose Blythe's income was $78,500. Using the tax table on the right below, her tax would have been $15,975.

If line 43 (taxable income) is— At least	But less than	Single
72,000		
72,000	72,050	14,350
72,050	72,100	14,363
72,100	72,150	14,375
72,150	72,200	14,388
72,200	72,250	14,400
72,250	72,300	14,413
72,300	72,350	14,425
72,350	72,400	14,438
72,400	72,450	14,450
72,450	72,500	14,463
72,500	72,550	14,475
72,550	72,600	14,488
72,600	72,650	14,500
72,650	72,700	14,513
72,700	72,750	14,525
72,750	72,800	14,538
72,800	72,850	14,550
72,850	72,900	14,563
72,900	72,950	14,575
72,950	73,000	14,588

If line 43 (taxable income) is— At least	But less than	Single
78,000		
78,000	78,050	15,850
78,050	78,100	15,863
78,100	78,150	15,875
78,150	78,200	15,888
78,200	78,250	15,900
78,250	78,300	15,913
78,300	78,350	15,925
78,350	78,400	15,938
78,400	78,450	15,950
78,450	78,500	15,963
78,500	78,550	15,975
78,550	78,600	15,988
78,600	78,650	16,000
78,650	78,700	16,013
78,700	78,750	16,025
78,750	78,800	16,038
78,800	78,850	16,050
78,850	78,900	16,063
78,900	78,950	16,077
78,950	79,000	16,091

To find how much Blythe saved, subtract the tax without the reduction from the tax with the reduction.

$$15{,}975 - 14{,}475 = 1{,}500$$

By opening up an account in which her retirement savings were tax deferred, Blythe saved $1,500 in taxes.

CHECK YOUR UNDERSTANDING

Suppose Jacob invested D dollars in an after-tax retirement account. His taxable income for the year was A dollars. Represent his taxable income had he invested that same amount in a pre-tax account.

EXAMPLE 3

Chelsea is 45 years old. She plans to open a retirement account. She wants to have $300,000 in the account when she retires at age 62. How much must she deposit each month into an account with an APR of 2.25% to reach her goal?

SOLUTION Recall the formula in Lesson 3-8 for determining present value of a periodic deposit investment.

$$P = \frac{B\left(\frac{r}{n}\right)}{\left(1 + \frac{r}{n}\right)^{nt} - 1}$$

where B = ending balance
P = periodic deposit amount
r = annual interest rate expressed as a decimal
n = number of times interest is compounded annually
t = length of investment in years

Chelsea can compute the amount she will need to deposit each month for the next 17 years as follows.

$$P = \frac{30{,}000\left(\frac{0.0225}{12}\right)}{\left(1 + \frac{0.0225}{12}\right)^{12(17)} - 1} \approx 1{,}208.59$$

Chelsea should deposit $1,209 each month to reach her goal.

■ CHECK YOUR UNDERSTANDING

Which would result in a need for a larger monthly deposit: half the interest rate or half the number of years before the money is withdrawn from the account?

EXAMPLE 4

Zander is a 50-year-old married man who files taxes separately from his wife. He has been making monthly contributions into his traditional IRA for many years. Last year, he entered into a new business partnership and decided to withdraw $50,000 from his IRA to make the initial investment in the partnership. Zander's taxable income for the year, excluding the $50,000 from his IRA, was $97,000. How much extra did he pay in both penalty and taxes because of this withdrawal?

SOLUTION Using the tax table shown, Zander's taxable income of $97,000 would have made his tax $21,539.

If line 43 (taxable income) is—		And you are —			
At least	But less than	Single	Married filing jointly *	Married filing sepa-rately	Head of a house-hold
		Your tax is —			
97,000					
97,000	**97,050**	21,145	16,944	21,539	19,319
~~**97,050**~~	~~**97,100**~~	~~21,159~~	~~16,956~~	~~21,553~~	19,331
97,100	**97,150**	21,173	16,969	21,567	19,344
97,150	**97,200**	21,187	16,981	21,581	19,356
97,200	**97,250**	21,201	16,994	21,595	19,369
97,250	**97,300**	21,215	17,006	21,609	19,381
97,300	**97,350**	21,229	17,019	21,623	19,394
97,350	**97,400**	21,243	17,031	21,637	19,406
97,400	**97,450**	21,257	17,044	21,651	19,419
97,450	**97,500**	21,271	17,056	21,665	19,431
97,500	**97,550**	21,285	17,069	21,679	19,444
97,550	**97,600**	21,299	17,081	21,693	19,456
97,600	**97,650**	21,313	17,094	21,707	19,469
97,650	**97,700**	21,327	17,106	21,721	19,481
97,700	**97,750**	21,341	17,119	21,735	19,494
97,750	**97,800**	21,355	17,131	21,749	19,506
97,800	**97,850**	21,369	17,144	21,763	19,519
97,850	**97,900**	21,383	17,156	21,777	19,531
97,900	**97,950**	21,397	17,169	21,791	19,544
97,950	**98,000**	21,411	17,181	21,805	19,556

Zander's withdrawal will increase his taxable income to $147,000.

$$97{,}000 + 50{,}000 = 147{,}000$$

EXAMPLE 3

Have students read the problem statement and then go back to Lesson 3-8. Ask them to identify the similarities between what was introduced there and this example. They should recognize that this is a present value of a periodic deposit investment problem.

CHECK YOUR UNDERSTANDING

Answer Half the number of years; half the interest rate would yield a need for a monthly deposit of approximately $1,335, and half the length of the savings plan would yield a need for a monthly deposit of approximately $2,671.

EXAMPLE 4

It is important that students realize there is a two-tier penalty for an early withdrawal. Not only is Zander required to pay the back taxes he owes, but he will also incur a 10% penalty because of his decision to take the money out before he is of retirement age. Impress upon students that before such a decision to withdraw is made, Zander should explore other financial options such as a short term loan and compare the financial impact of both situations.

Because his taxable income is more than $100,000, he must use the tax computation worksheet to calculate his tax. The portion of the worksheet that pertains to Zander is shown here.

Section C — Use if your filing status is **Married filing separately**. Complete the row below that applies to you.

Taxable income. If line 43 is—	(a) Enter the amount from line 43	(b) Multiplication amount	(c) Multiply (a) by (b)	(d) Subtraction amount	Tax. Subtract (d) from (c) Enter the result here and on Form 1040, line 44
At least $100,000 but not over $100,150	$	× 28% (.28)	$	$ 5,628.00	$
Over $100,150 but not over $178,850	$ 147,000	× 33% (.33)	$ 48,510	$ 10,635.50	$ 37,874.50
Over $178,850	$	× 35% (.35)	$	$ 14,212.00	$

CHECK YOUR UNDERSTANDING

Answer $0.33(D + A) - 10,635.50$

EXAMPLE 5

Assist students in making sense of the problem statement by laying out all of the pertinent pieces. Consider a graphic organizer that will lead the students through the process. What does the company offer? What are the restrictions that the company has put on this employee contribution plan?

Zander's tax is now $37,874.50, which is $16,335.50 more than if he had not made the early withdrawal from his IRA.

$$37{,}874.50 - 21{,}539 = 16{,}335.50$$

Because Zander made a withdrawal before age $59\frac{1}{2}$ he must pay a penalty of 10% of the withdrawal amount.

$$0.10 \times 50{,}000 = 5{,}000$$

Add the penalty and the amount of additional taxes.

$$16{,}335.50 + 5{,}000 = 21{,}335.50$$

Zander had to pay $21,335.50 in combined taxes and penalty.

CHECK YOUR UNDERSTANDING

Suppose that Rachel's taxable income is D dollars. She withdraws A dollars from her IRA, which brings her taxable income between $100,150 and $178,850. Using the tax computation worksheet above, write an algebraic expression for her tax.

Employer Matching Plans

Some employers offer 401k retirement plans in which they match the employee's contribution up to a fixed amount of the salary made. This is extremely beneficial to the employee and is an excellent employee benefit. The money contributed by both the employer and the employee earns interest and is tax-deferred. Most companies only allow employee contributions to the 401k plan up to a certain percentage of the salary earned, based on government rules. There is also a maximum allowable contribution, which may change each year. The employer matching contribution is not calculated into the 401k yearly contribution limit.

EXAMPLE 5

Leo makes $75,000 per year. His company offers a 401k retirement plan in which they match 50% of his contributions to the 401k up to 6% of his salary. The company allows employees to make contributions to the 401k to a maximum of 15% of their salary. The maximum allowable contribution to any 401k is $16,500. How much should Leo contribute per month in order to maximize his employer's matching contribution?

SOLUTION Determine the maximum that Leo's employer will allow him to contribute this year to the 401k.

$$75{,}000 \times 0.15 = 11{,}250$$

Leo can contribute \$11,250, which is below the 401k limit of \$16,500 for the year.

To find the monthly contribution Leo can make, divide by 12.

$$11{,}250 \div 12 = 937.50$$

Leo can contribute \$937.50 per month and will reach his employer's maximum contribution limit by the end of the year.

Suppose Leo only wants to contribute an amount up to his employer's matching contribution level. He finds 6% of his salary and divides that amount by 12.

$$75{,}000 \times 0.06 = 4{,}500$$

$$4{,}500 \div 12 = 375$$

Leo will make a monthly contribution of \$375 to his 401k account.

His employer will make a matching contribution of 3%.

$$75{,}000 \times 0.03 = 2{,}250$$

$$2{,}250 \div 12 = 187.50$$

Leo's employer will contribute \$187.50 each month, or \$2,250 annually, to match Leo's contribution.

Add the two contributions. $375.00 + 187.50 = 562.50$

Each month \$562.50 will be put into Leo's 401k account. The total annual deposit to his 401k account will be 12×562.50, bringing his total annual deposit to \$6,750.

CHECK YOUR UNDERSTANDING

Robin makes D dollars. Her employer will match her IRA contributions up to P percent of her salary. Write an algebraic expression for Robin's monthly contribution if she only wants the total to match the maximum amount that will be matched by her employer.

CHECK YOUR UNDERSTANDING

Answer $\dfrac{D \times \frac{P}{100}}{12}$

Applications

A whole generation of Americans will retire in poverty instead of prosperity, because they simply are not preparing for retirement now.

Scott Cook, American Businessman

TEACH

Exercises 2, 3, 7, and 9
These exercises are related. Have students first identify which are future values of periodic investment and which are present values of periodic investment problems.

Exercise 4
Here, students first have to calculate the future value of a single deposit investment in order to determine the amount from which the withdrawal will be made.

Exercise 5
This is a good guided discovery activity to use during class. Students can work in small groups through each step.

ANSWERS

1. Retirement requires advanced planning and preparation. A retirement savings plan requires years to grow. Mr. Cook warns all of us (young and old) that without advanced planning for retirement, we could face years of poverty rather than a comfortable old age.

1. Explain how the quote can be interpreted. See margin.

2. Ricky is 35 years old. He plans to retire when he is 63. He has opened a retirement account that pays 3.2% interest compounded monthly. If he makes monthly deposits of $400, how much will he have in the account by the time he retires? $217,029.69

3. Jay just graduated from college and he has decided to open a retirement account that pays 1.75% interest compounded monthly. If he has direct deposits of $100 per month taken out of his paycheck, how much will he have in the account after 42 years? $74,356.50

4. At the age of 30, Jasmine started a retirement account with $50,000 which compounded interest semi-annually with an APR of 4%. She made no further deposits. After 25 years, she decided to withdraw 50% of what had accumulated in the account so that she could contribute towards her grandchild's college education. She had to pay a 10% penalty on the early withdrawal. What was her penalty? $6,728.97

5. A taxpayer who pays 22% in taxes each year has these two accounts.

Account 1: $10,000 is placed in a tax-deferred account that pays 5% interest compounded annually for 25 years.

Account 2: $10,000 is placed in a taxable account that pays 5% interest compounded annually for 25 years.

a. How much is in Account 1 after the 25-year period? $33,863.55

b. Since the taxpayer pays 22% of all income in taxes, 22% of the interest he makes each year will go towards taxes. Therefore, his annual interest rate in actuality is 22% less than the 5% quoted rate. What is his real annual interest rate? 3.9%

c. How much will he actually have made after the 25-year period in Account 2 if taxes are taken into consideration? $26,024.88

6. Laura has been contributing to a retirement account that pays 4% interest with pre-tax dollars. This account compounds interest monthly. She has put $500 per month into the account. At the end of 10 years, she needed to pay some medical bills and had to withdraw 15% of the money that was in the account.

a. Rounded to the nearest dollar, how much did she withdraw? $11,044

b. Laura pays 23% of her income in taxes. What was her tax on the amount of the withdrawal (rounded to the nearest dollar)? $2,540

c. She had to pay a 10% early withdrawal penalty. How much was she required to pay, rounded to the nearest dollar? $1,104

7. Fiona opened a retirement account that has an annual yield of 6%. She is planning on retiring in 20 years. How much must she deposit into that account each year so that she can have a total of $600,000 by the time she retires? $16,310.73

8. John is 60 years old. He plans to retire in two years. He now has $400,000 in a savings account that yields 2.9% interest compounded continuously (see Lesson 3-6). He has calculated that his final working year's salary will be $88,000. He has been told by his financial advisor that he should have 60–70% of his final year's annual income available for use each year when he retires.

a. What is the range of income that his financial advisor thinks he must have per year once he retires? $52,800–$61,600

b. Use the continuous compounding formula to determine how much he will have in his account at the ages of 61 and 62. $411,769.84 and $423,886, respectively

c. Assume that John is planning on using 65% of his current salary in each of his first 5 years of retirement. What should that annual amount be? $57,200

d. John has decided that he will need $20,000 each year from his savings account to help him reach his desired annual income during retirement. Will John be able to make withdrawals of $20,000 from his savings account for 20 years? Explain your reasoning. Yes; 20,000 × 20 = 400,000 and 400,000 < 423,886.

9. Bob can afford to deposit $400 a month into a retirement account that compounds interest monthly with an APR of 3.9%. His plan is to have $200,000 saved so that he can then retire. Approximately how long will it take him to reach this goal? 25 years

10. Jack contributed $400 per month into his retirement account in pre-tax dollars during the last tax year. His taxable income for the year was $62,350. He files taxes as a single taxpayer.

a. What would his taxable income have been had he contributed to the account in after-tax dollars? $67,150

b. Use the tax table below to calculate his tax in both the pre-tax and after-tax contribution situations. See margin.

c. How much did Jack save in taxes during that year? $1,200

If line 43 (taxable income) is—		And you are —			
At least	But less than	Single	Married filing jointly *	Married filing separately	Head of a household
		Your tax is —			
62,000					
62,000	**62,050**	11,850	8,501	11,850	10,569
62,050	**62,100**	11,863	8,509	11,863	10,581
62,100	**62,150**	11,875	8,516	11,875	10,594
62,150	**62,200**	11,888	8,524	11,888	10,606
62,200	**62,250**	11,900	8,531	11,900	10,619
62,250	**62,300**	11,913	8,539	11,913	10,631
62,300	**62,350**	11,925	8,546	11,925	10,644
62,350	**62,400**	11,938	8,554	11,938	10,656
62,400	**62,450**	11,950	8,561	11,950	10,669
62,450	**62,500**	11,963	8,569	11,963	10,681
62,500	**62,550**	11,975	8,576	11,975	10,694
62,550	**62,600**	11,988	8,584	11,988	10,706
62,600	**62,650**	12,000	8,591	12,000	10,719
62,650	**62,700**	12,013	8,599	12,013	10,731
62,700	**62,750**	12,025	8,606	12,025	10,744
62,750	**62,800**	12,038	8,614	12,038	10,756
62,800	**62,850**	12,050	8,621	12,050	10,769
62,850	**62,900**	12,063	8,629	12,063	10,781
62,900	**62,950**	12,075	8,636	12,075	10,794
62,950	**63,000**	12,088	8,644	12,088	10,806

If line 43 (taxable income) is—		And you are —			
At least	But less than	Single	Married filing jointly *	Married filing separately	Head of a household
		Your tax is —			
67,000					
67,000	**67,050**	13,100	9,444	13,139	11,819
67,050	**67,100**	13,113	9,456	13,153	11,831
67,100	**67,150**	13,125	9,469	13,167	11,844
67,150	**67,200**	13,138	9,481	13,181	11,856
67,200	**67,250**	13,150	9,494	13,195	11,869
67,250	**67,300**	13,163	9,506	13,209	11,881
67,300	**67,350**	13,175	9,519	13,223	11,894
67,350	**67,400**	13,188	9,531	13,237	11,906
67,400	**67,450**	13,200	9,544	13,251	11,919
67,450	**67,500**	13,213	9,556	13,265	11,931
67,500	**67,550**	13,225	9,569	13,279	11,944
67,550	**67,600**	13,238	9,581	13,293	11,956
67,600	**67,650**	13,250	9,594	13,307	11,969
67,650	**67,700**	13,263	9,606	13,321	11,981
67,700	**67,750**	13,275	9,619	13,335	11,994
67,750	**67,800**	13,288	9,631	13,349	12,006
67,800	**67,850**	13,300	9,644	13,363	12,019
67,850	**67,900**	13,313	9,656	13,377	12,031
67,900	**67,950**	13,325	9,669	13,391	12,044
67,950	**68,000**	13,338	9,681	13,405	12,056

TEACH

Exercise 8

Before assigning this exercise, encourage students to go back to Chapter 3 and review the lesson on continuous compounding.

ANSWERS

10b. Pre-tax: tax is $11,938;
After-tax: tax is $13,138

TEACH

Exercise 11

If you anticipate some students experiencing difficulty with the algebraic expressions in this exercise, give them a similar problem with numbers first. Once completed, ask them to do Exercise 11 using the simpler problem as a guide.

Exercises 13 and 14

Be sure to assign (and possibly review) Exercise 13 before having students work on Exercise 14. They are related.

11. Mark is an accountant who has been contributing to his retirement account for the last 15 years with pre-tax dollars. The account compounds interest semi-annually at a rate of 5%. He contributes x dollars after each 6-month period, and this has not changed over the life of the account.

a. How much will he have in the account after 20 years of saving? Round numbers to the nearest hundredth. $67.40x$

b. After 20 years of contributions, he needed to withdraw 20% of the money in his account to pay for his children's education. Write an expression for the withdrawal amount. $13.48x$

c. Mark pays t percent of his income in taxes. Write an algebraic expression for the combined total of his tax and the 10% early withdrawal penalty. $\frac{(13.48x)\,t}{100} + 1.348x$

12. Jhanvi is a 40-year-old executive for a department store. She files taxes as head of household. She needed to withdraw $45,000 from her tax-deferred retirement account to put a down payment on a new condominium. Jhanvi's taxable income for that year was $110,550, excluding the $45,000 early withdrawal from her retirement account.

a. Use the tax computation worksheet shown below to calculate Jhanvi's tax had she not made the early withdrawal. $22,700

Section D – Use if your filing status is **Head of household**. Complete the row below that applies to you.

Taxable income. If line 43 is–	**(a)** Enter the amount from line 43	**(b)** Multiplication amount	**(c)** Multiply (a) by (b)	**(d)** Subtraction amount	**Tax** Subtract (d) from (c). Enter the result here and on Form 1040, line 44
At least $100,000 but not over $112,650	$	× 25% (.25)	$	$ 4,937.50	$
Over $112,650 but not over $182,400	$	× 28% (.28)	$	$ 8,317.00	$
Over $182,400 but not over $357,700	$	× 33% (.33)	$	$ 17,437.00	$
Over $357,700	$	× 35% (.35)	$	$ 24,591.00	$

b. Use the same worksheet to calculate her tax with an increase in her taxable income of $45,000. $35,237

c. How much more in taxes did she pay because of the early withdrawal? $12,537

d. If Jhanvi paid a 10% early withdrawal fee, what was her early withdrawal penalty? $4,500

13. Nelson makes $120,000 per year. His employer offers a 401k plan in which they will match 40% of his contributions up to a maximum of 7% of his annual salary. His employer allows contributions up to a maximum of 15% of Nelson's salary per year. If Nelson contributes $200 out of each biweekly paycheck, how much will his employer contribute to his 401k? $2,080

14. Mike makes Y dollars per year. His company offers a matching retirement plan in which they agree to match M percent of his contributions up to P percent of his salary. Write an algebraic expression for the maximum value of the employer's matching contribution. $\frac{YMP}{10{,}000}$

We can never insure one hundred percent of the population against one hundred percent of the hazards and vicissitudes of life, but we have tried to frame a law which will give some measure of protection to the average citizen and to his family against the loss of a job and against poverty-ridden old age.

President Franklin Delano Roosevelt upon signing Social Security Act, 1935

Social Security Benefits 9-2

Key Terms
- Old-Age, Survivors, and Disability Insurance (OASDI)
- Social Security benefit
- full retirement age
- Social Security statement
- Social Security credit

Objectives
- Understand the benefits paid by Social Security.
- Understand how benefits are computed.
- Compute federal income tax on benefits that are paid under Social Security.

Common Core
A-SSE1, A-CED3

CCSS Warm-Up

Let A = number of airplane first-class seats sold at \$$B$.
Let C = number of airplane coach seats sold at \$$D$.
Interpret the expression $(AB + CD)/(A + C)$ in the context of airplane seat revenue.
The average price per sold seat on the airplane

How does the government help me finance my retirement?

There are many expenses involved in maintaining a comfortable, healthy lifestyle when you are not working. Being prepared to meet these challenges requires careful and early planning. In addition to your own savings plans, the government has an insurance program that helps workers in their retirement by providing financial assistance.

After the stock market crash of 1929, the United States entered a period of very harsh economic times. Millions of people were unemployed; banks and businesses failed, and the elderly had trouble paying expenses just to survive. These circumstances led to the Social Security Act of 1935. This act created an insurance program that paid workers benefits after they retired.

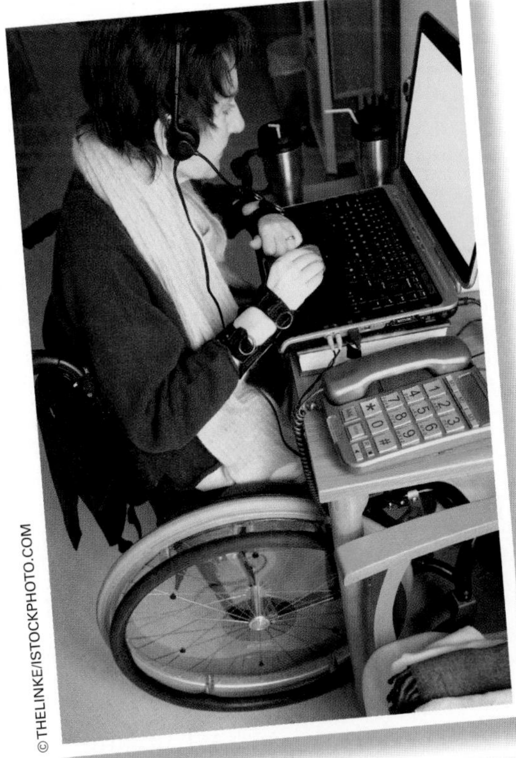
©THELINKE/ISTOCKPHOTO.COM

In Chapters 6 and 7 you learned about paying Social Security and Medicare taxes. Social Security taxes fund **Old-Age, Survivors, and Disability Insurance (OASDI)**. This insurance pays benefits to retired workers that help them meet their financial obligations. It also provides benefits to families of retired workers and disabled workers under certain conditions. Medicare taxes fund a health insurance program that provides benefits to people over age 65 and to some disabled persons under 65. It helps pay for doctor's costs, hospital costs, and prescription drugs.

Younger employees are usually more concerned with these programs because they are funded through taxes taken out of employee paychecks. There is a maximum amount of earnings subject to Social Security taxes. This maximum holds no matter how many jobs you have—it is a per-person maximum for the year.

EXAMINE THE QUESTION

In Chapter 6, students learned about the Social Security deductions taken from their paychecks. In Chapter 7, they saw how Social Security benefits are taxed as income on federal tax forms. What was the purpose of the deduction? What benefits does Social Security provide? As a retiree, Social Security will play an important financial role.

CLASS DISCUSSION

Remind students what happens to prices over 10, 20, or 30 years. Prices are apt to rise over retirement years. Therefore, all sources of income are significant.

Ask students where the money sent to recipients comes from. (It is the money withheld from the paychecks of current employees.)

TEACH

These problems show how a lifetime of earnings translates into Social Security payments. Remind students that laws and monetary amounts can change over the years.

EXAMPLE 1

There is a maximum taxable amount and a maximum Social Security tax for each year. People with two employers must determine if they have overpaid, since the two different employers do not know each other's Social Security deductions for that employee.

CHECK YOUR UNDERSTANDING

Answer $0.062(x + y - 97{,}500)$

When you get close to retirement age, you will be concerned with the benefits these services provide—benefits that you contributed to over your entire working career. The money that is taken out of your paycheck for Social Security is paying for the benefits of the people who are currently receiving them. Your benefits will be paid by the people who are working when you are receiving the benefits.

Social Security benefits are based on your earnings over your working lifetime. Benefits can start as early as age 62, but are reduced. People born after 1960 must wait to start collecting their full retirement benefit until age 67, their **full retirement age**.

You can keep track of every year's earnings by requesting a Social Security statement each year from the IRS. Compare the entries on the form to your W-2 each year. Be sure keep the copies on file.

Skills and Strategies

Here you will be introduced to some of the details on how Social Security works. When you get close to retirement, you will want to read lots of material on the rules and procedures involved.

EXAMPLE 1

In 2009, Jose had two jobs. He earned $73,440 working at a nursing home the first 8 months. He switched jobs in September and began to work in a hospital, where he earned $42,566. How much Social Security tax did he overpay?

SOLUTION In 2009, the maximum taxable income for Social Security taxes was $106,800. Each of Jose's employers took out the required 6.2% for Social Security. The nursing home took out 6.2% of $73,440.

$$0.062 \times 73{,}440 = 4{,}553.28$$

The hospital took out 6.2% of $42,565.

$$0.062 \times 42{,}565 = 2{,}639.03$$

Jose adds to find the total he paid into Social Security in 2009.

$$4{,}553.28 + 2{,}639.03 = 7{,}192.31$$

The two employers withheld $7,192.31 in Social Security taxes in 2009. This is too much tax. The maximum an individual should have paid in 2009 was 6.2% of $106,800, which equals $6,621.60. Subtract to find out how much Jose overpaid.

$$7{,}192.31 - 6{,}621.60 = 570.71$$

Jose overpaid $570.71 and needs to fill out a line on his Form 1040 to claim a refund of this amount. Notice that this is not a refund of federal income tax. It is a refund of overpaid FICA tax.

■ CHECK YOUR UNDERSTANDING

Monique had two employers in 2007. Both employers took out 6.2% Social Security tax. The maximum taxable income was $97,500. Monique earned x dollars at one job and y dollars at her second job, and $x + y > 97{,}500$. Express her refund algebraically.

Social Security Credits

Your **Social Security statement** is a record of the money you earned every year. You get a certain number of credits each working year. It includes the number of **Social Security credits** you have earned. You can earn a maximum of four credits for each year. Before 1978, employers reported earnings every three months or quarter. You earned one credit for each quarter in which you earned a specific amount of money. Since 1978, employers report earnings once a year and credits are based on your total wages and self-employment income during the year, no matter when you did the actual work. You might work all year to earn four credits, or you might earn enough for all four in a shorter length of time. The amount of earnings it takes to earn a credit changes each year. In 2009, you must earn $1,090 in covered earnings to get one credit. People born after 1929 need 40 credits in their lifetime to qualify for Social Security benefits.

EXAMPLE 2

Fran requests her annual Social Security statement from the Social Security Administration each year. She wants to check how many Social Security credits she received for 2009. She worked all year and earned $8,102 per month. How many credits did she earn in 2009?

SOLUTION Fran goes to the Social Security website. To earn a credit in 2009, she needed to earn at least $1,090. To earn the maximum 4 credits, Fran needed to earn 4 times the amount for one credit anytime during the year.

$$4 \times 1{,}090 = 4{,}360$$

Fran earned over $8,102 in one month, which is greater than $4,360, so her statement should show that she earned 4 credits for the year. Keep track of your credits carefully.

CHECK YOUR UNDERSTANDING

Beth earned $5,600 working part-time during the first half of the year in 2009. She then left for college and didn't work. How many Social Security credits did she receive?

Social Security Benefit

Your Social Security benefit is based on the 35 highest years of earnings throughout your lifetime. The earnings are adjusted for inflation—earning $5,000 in 1955 is not like earning $5,000 today. The adjusted earnings are used to find the average adjusted monthly earnings. Keep in mind that benefit computations can change, and you must be sure to keep up to date on how your particular benefit will be computed.

EXAMPLE 3

Marissa reached age 62 in 2007. She did not retire until years later. Over her life, she earned an average of $2,300 per month after her earnings were adjusted for inflation. What is her Social Security full retirement benefit?

EXAMPLE 2

The amount of money you earn each year translates to between 0 and 4 credits for Social Security. Remind students that Social Security is a federal assistance program. If you live long, you may receive more than you paid into Social Security. If you do not live as long, you may pay more into Social Security than you actually receive in benefits.

CHECK YOUR UNDERSTANDING

Answer 4

EXAMPLE 3

The rules for computing the benefit are much like the lines on the income tax forms.

CHECK YOUR UNDERSTANDING

Answer $0.90(680) + 0.32(4{,}100 - 680) + 0.15(x - 4{,}100) = 0.15x + 1{,}091.40$

EXAMPLE 4

Explain to students that reductions for early retirement cause employees near retirement age to think through whether it is worth working another few years to increase their benefit.

CHECK YOUR UNDERSTANDING

Answer \$791.28

At age 62, benefits are reduced by 30%. So, 0.3 × 1,130.40 = 339.12 and 1,130.40 – 339.12 = 791.28.

SOLUTION Marissa was born in 1945 and turned 62 in 2007. For people turning 62 in 2007, the formula for computing Social Security benefits is

- 90% of the first \$680 of monthly earnings
- 32% of the monthly earnings between \$680 and \$4,100
- 15% of the earnings over \$4,100

Marissa's monthly earnings were \$2,300.

Find 90% of the first \$680.	$0.90 \times 680 = 612$
Subtract to find the earnings over \$680.	$2{,}300 - 680 = 1{,}620$
Find 32% of \$1,620 by multiplying.	$0.32 \times 1{,}620 = 518.40$
Find the sum of \$612 and \$518.40.	$612 + 518.40 = 1{,}130.40$

Marissa's monthly full retirement benefit at age 67 is \$1,130.40.

■ CHECK YOUR UNDERSTANDING

Ron reached age 62 in 2007. His monthly adjusted earnings were x dollars, where $x > \$4{,}100$. Express his monthly benefit algebraically.

EXAMPLE 4

Marissa from Example 3 retired at age 65. What will her monthly benefit be, since she did not wait until age 67 to receive full retirement benefits?

SOLUTION Age 67 is considered to be full retirement age if you were born in 1945. If you start collecting Social Security before age 67, your full retirement benefit is reduced, according to the following schedule.

- If you start at collecting benefits at 62, the reduction is about 30%.
- If you start at collecting benefits at 63, the reduction is about 25%.
- If you start at collecting benefits at 64, the reduction is about 20%.
- If you start at collecting benefits at 65, the reduction is about 13.3%.
- If you start at collecting benefits at 66, the reduction is about 6.7%.

Marissa's full retirement benefit was \$1,130.40. Since she retired at age 65, the benefit will be reduced about 13.3%.

Find 13.3% of \$1,130.40, and round to the nearest cent.

$$0.133 \times 1{,}130.40 \approx 150.34$$

Subtract to find the benefit Marissa would receive.

$$1{,}130.40 - 150.34 = 980.06$$

Marissa's benefit would be about \$980.06.

■ CHECK YOUR UNDERSTANDING

Find the difference between Marissa's monthly benefit if she retires at age 62 instead of age 67.

Reporting Social Security Benefits on Form 1040

If your total taxable income (wages, pensions, interest, dividends, and so on) plus any tax-exempt income, plus half of your Social Security benefits exceed $25,000 for singles, $32,000 for married couples filing jointly, or $0 for married couples filing separately, you will pay federal income tax on your benefits.

The taxable portion can range from 50% to 85% of your benefits. The numbers can change from year to year, and the government prints worksheets to help taxpayers compute the part of their Social Security benefit that is taxed.

EXAMPLE 5

The Social Security worksheet is not a tax form; it is part of the instructions, and the result from it is entered on a tax return. It is a somewhat lengthy exercise in reading instructions involving mathematical operations and following them carefully.

EXAMPLE 5

Rob is 64 years old, and collected $19,612 in Social Security last year. He is married filing a joint return. On his Form 1040, the total of lines 7, 8a, 9a, 10 through 14, 15b, 16b, 17 through 19, and 21 is $80,433. Line 8b on his Form 1040 shows $519 and lines 23 to 32 on his Form 1040 total $1,239. Line 36 on his Form 1040 does not have an amount. What are Rob's taxable Social Security benefits for the year?

SOLUTION The Social Security Benefits Worksheet is used to determine the taxable benefit amount. It is not a form filed with your taxes. The worksheet is used to help you compute the part of the Social Security benefit that is taxed.

Rob starts filling out Form 1040 and gets to the line for Social Security benefits. He must now fill out the 18-line worksheet.

His Social Security benefit is entered on line 1.

Notice the information on lines 3 and 4 of the worksheet comes directly from the information given about Rob's Form 1040.

Line 6 also requires information from Rob's Form 1040.

Social Security Benefits Worksheet—Lines 20a and 20b

1. Enter the total amount from **box 5** of **all** your **Forms SSA-1099** and **Forms RRB-1099.** Also, enter this amount on Form 1040, line 20a 1. $19,612.00
2. Enter one-half of line 1 . . . . . . 2. $9,806.00
3. Enter the total of the amounts from Form 1040, lines 7, 8a, 9a, 10 through 14, 15b, 16b, 17 through 19, and 21 . . . . . . 3. $80,433.00
4. Enter the amount, if any, from Form 1040, line 8b 4. $519.00
5. Add lines 2, 3, and 4 . . . . . . 5. $90,758.00
6. Enter the total of the amounts from Form 1040, lines 23 through 32, plus any write-in adjustments you entered on the dotted line next to line 36 . . . . . . 6. $1,239.00
7. Is the amount on line 6 less than the amount on line 5?
   - ☐ **No.** STOP None of your social security benefits are taxable. Enter -0- on Form 1040, line 20b.
   - ☒ **Yes.** Subtract line 6 from line 5 . . . . . . 7. $89,519.00
8. If you are:
   - Married filing jointly, enter $32,000
   - Single, head of household, qualifying widow(er), or married filing separately and you **lived apart** from your spouse for all of 2008, enter $25,000
   - Married filing separately and you lived with your spouse at any time in 2008, skip lines 8 through 15; multiply line 7 by 85% (.85) and enter the result on line 16. Then go to line 17

   . . . . . . 8. $32,000.00
9. Is the amount on line 8 less than the amount on line 7?
   - ☐ **No.** STOP None of your social security benefits are taxable. Enter -0- on Form 1040, line 20b. If you are married filing separately and you **lived apart** from your spouse for all of 2008, be sure you entered "D" to the right of the word "benefits" on line 20a.
   - ☒ **Yes.** Subtract line 8 from line 7 . . . . . . 9. $57,519.00

CHECK YOUR UNDERSTANDING

Answer $100\left(\frac{t}{x}\right)$

EXAMPLE 6

Certain Medicare programs are not free to beneficiaries who contributed to it over their lifetimes. They reduce the cost of health-related issues.

CHECK YOUR UNDERSTANDING

Answer $12p$

The instructions for lines 10–18 use only lines from the worksheet. The instructions for each line guide Rob as he progresses.

10.	Enter: $12,000 if married filing jointly; $9,000 if single, head of household, qualifying widow(er), or married filing separately and you **lived apart** from your spouse for all of 2008 . .	**10.**	$12,000.00
11.	Subtract line 10 from line 9. If zero or less, enter -0-	**11.**	$45,519.00
12.	Enter the **smaller** of line 9 or line 10	**12.**	$12,000.00
13.	Enter one-half of line 12	**13.**	$6,000.00
14.	Enter the **smaller** of line 2 or line 13	**14.**	$6,000.00
15.	Multiply line 11 by 85% (.85). If line 11 is zero, enter -0-	**15.**	$38,691.15
16.	Add lines 14 and 15	**16.**	$44,691.15
17.	Multiply line 1 by 85% (.85)	**17.**	$16,670.20
18.	**Taxable social security benefits.** Enter the **smaller** of line 16 or line 17. Also enter this amount on Form 1040, line 20b	**18.**	$16,670.20

Rob's taxable Social Security benefits are $16,670.20 as shown on line 18. Rob must enter this amount on his Form 1040 and pay taxes on that amount. He received $19,612 in Social Security benefits, but only had to pay income tax on $16,670.20 of that money.

■ CHECK YOUR UNDERSTANDING

Maria filled out a Social Security benefits worksheet. She received x dollars in Social Security benefits, but had to pay taxes on t dollars of it. Express the fraction of her Social Security income that she had to pay tax on as a percent.

Medicare Benefit

When you apply for Social Security, you may also apply to receive Medicare. Medicare has four parts. Part A is hospital insurance that helps pay for inpatient care in a hospital. Part B is medical insurance and helps pay for doctor's visits. Part C is Medicare advantage and is available in some areas. Part D is prescription drug coverage.

You must pay a monthly premium for Part B. In 2008 the standard premium was $96.40. The premium may be higher if your adjusted gross income is greater than $85,000.

EXAMPLE 6

Ryan has retired and is qualified to receive Medicare. In 2008, he paid the standard monthly premium. How much did he pay for the year?

SOLUTION Ryan paid 12 monthly premiums.

Multiply. $12 \times 96.40 = 1{,}156.80$

Ryan paid $1,156.80 in Medicare premiums for the year.

■ CHECK YOUR UNDERSTANDING

Claire has retired. She pays a Medicare Part B premium of p dollars per month. Express the total amount she spent on Medicare last year algebraically.

Applications

We can never insure one hundred percent of the population against one hundred percent of the hazards and vicissitudes of life, but we have tried to frame a law which will give some measure of protection to the average citizen and to his family against the loss of a job and against poverty-ridden old age.

President Franklin Delano Roosevelt upon signing Social Security Act, 1935

1. Interpret the quote in the context of what you know about American history and/or challenges facing senior citizens. See margin.

2. In 2008, the maximum taxable income for Social Security was \$102,000 and the tax rate was 6.2%.

a. What is the maximum Social Security tax anyone could have paid in the year 2008? \$6,324

b. Randy had two jobs in 2008. One employer paid him \$67,010 and the other paid him \$51,200. Each employer took out 6.2% for Social Security taxes. How much did Randy overpay for Social Security taxes in 2008? \$1,005.02

3. In a certain year, the maximum taxable income for Social Security was x dollars and the tax rate was 6.2%.

a. What is the maximum Social Security tax anyone could have paid in that year? $0.062x$

b. Paul had two jobs that year. One employer paid him y dollars and the other paid him p dollars. His total income was greater than x. Each employer took out 6.2% for Social Security. Express the amount that Paul overpaid for Social Security taxes in that year algebraically. $0.062(y + p) - 0.062x$

4. In 1978, the amount of earnings required to earn one Social Security credit was \$250. Thirty years later, in 2008, this amount was \$1,050. What was the percent increase in the amount required to earn a credit, over this 30-year span? 320%

5. Go to the Social Security website. What is the amount of earnings needed to earn one Social Security credit for the current year? Answers vary.

6. In 1980, the amount of earnings required to earn one Social Security credit was \$290. Back then, Mike earned \$55 per week. How many credits did he earn in 1980? 4

7. Stacy was a stay-at-home mom for most of her adult life. At age 46, she started working outside the home. Each year she earns the maximum number of Social Security credits. Until what age must she work to qualify to receive Social Security benefits when she retires? 56

8. Rachael turned 62 in 2007.

a. Compute her Social Security full retirement benefit if her average monthly salary over her 35 highest-paying years was \$3,100. \$1,386.40

b. If she starts collecting her benefit at age 66, what will her benefit be? Round to the nearest dollar. \$1,294

TEACH

Exercise 2

This exercise allows students to take a historical look at the Social Security maximum taxable income and maximum Social Security tax from 2008. They should compare it to rates from previous years that were given in Chapter 6.

Exercise 5

In Exercise 5, students need to look at the amount of income required to earn a credit. Have them also find this tax year's maximum taxable income and maximum Social Security tax. Have them find out if the numbers for the next tax year have been released.

Exercises 7–12

These exercises deal with Social Security benefits. Remind students that benefit amounts and rules can change from year to year.

Invite students to do some research on the Social Security Trust Fund and report whether they think Social Security is in danger.

ANSWERS

1. When people retire, their income falls and their medical expenses increase. Living expenses also increase with inflation. President Roosevelt created Social Security to provide assistance to people who put in a lifetime of qualified work, to help them in their old age.

ANSWERS

11. a. $14,461
b. $67,649
c. $64,438
d. $25,000
e. $39,438
f. $9,000
g. $30,438
h. $9,000
i. $4,500
j. $4,500
k. $25,872.30
l. $30,372.30
m. $24,583.70
n. $24,583.70

9. Michelle turned 62 in 2007. She earned an average of x dollars per month (adjusted for inflation) over her highest-paying 35 years, where $x > 4{,}100$. Express her Social Security full retirement benefit algebraically. $1,706.40 + 0.15(x – 4,100)

10. Sascha's Social Security full retirement benefit is x dollars. She started collecting Social Security at age 65, so her benefit is reduced. Express her approximate Social Security benefit algebraically. $x - 0.133x$, or $0.867x$

11. Dominique is single. She is filling out the Social Security worksheet so she can determine the amount of her Social Security benefits that she will pay federal income tax on. Fill in the following lines which were taken from Dominique's tax information.

- Line 1—she received $28,922 in Social Security benefits.
- Line 3—the total of her other sources of income is $52,888.
- Line 4—the amount from line 8b is $300.
- Line 6—the total to enter is $3,211.

a–n. Fill in the correct entries for the rest of the lines on her Social Security worksheet. See margin.

p. How much of Dominique's Social Security benefit must she pay Federal income tax on? $24,583.70

Social Security Benefits Worksheet—Lines 20a and 20b

1. Enter the total amount from **box 5** of **all** your **Forms SSA-1099** and **Forms RRB-1099.** Also, enter this amount on Form 1040, line 20a 1. $28,922.00

2. Enter one-half of line 1 . . . . . . 2. a.

3. Enter the total of the amounts from Form 1040, lines 7, 8a, 9a, 10 through 14, 15b, 16b, 17 through 19, and 21 . . . . . . 3. $52,888.00

4. Enter the amount, if any, from Form 1040, line 8b 4. $300.00

5. Add lines 2, 3, and 4 . . . . . . 5. b.

6. Enter the total of the amounts from Form 1040, lines 23 through 32, plus any write-in adjustments you entered on the dotted line next to line 36 . . . . . . 6. $3,211.00

7. Is the amount on line 6 less than the amount on line 5?

☐ **No.** STOP None of your social security benefits are taxable. Enter -0- on Form 1040, line 20b.

☐ **Yes.** Subtract line 6 from line 5 . . . . . . 7. c.

8. If you are:

- Married filing jointly, enter $32,000
- Single, head of household, qualifying widow(er), or married filing separately and you **lived apart** from your spouse for all of 2008, enter $25,000
- Married filing separately and you lived with your spouse at any time in 2008, skip lines 8 through 15; multiply line 7 by 85% (.85) and enter the result on line 16. Then go to line 17

} . . . . . . 8. d.

9. Is the amount on line 8 less than the amount on line 7?

☐ **No.** STOP None of your social security benefits are taxable. Enter -0- on Form 1040, line 20b. If you are married filing separately and you **lived apart** from your spouse for all of 2008, be sure you entered "D" to the right of the word "benefits" on line 20a.

☐ **Yes.** Subtract line 8 from line 7 . . . . . . 9. e.

10. Enter: $12,000 if married filing jointly; $9,000 if single, head of household, qualifying widow(er), or married filing separately and you **lived apart** from your spouse for all of 2008 . . 10. f.

11. Subtract line 10 from line 9. If zero or less, enter -0- . . . . . . 11. g.

12. Enter the **smaller** of line 9 or line 10 . . . . . . 12. h.

13. Enter one-half of line 12 . . . . . . 13. i.

14. Enter the **smaller** of line 2 or line 13 . . . . . . 14. j.

15. Multiply line 11 by 85% (.85). If line 11 is zero, enter -0- . . . . . . 15. k.

16. Add lines 14 and 15 . . . . . . 16. l.

17. Multiply line 1 by 85% (.85) . . . . . . 17. m.

18. **Taxable social security benefits.** Enter the **smaller** of line 16 or line 17. Also enter this amount on Form 1040, line 20b . . . . . . 18. n.

12. Roberta's Social Security full retirement benefit is $2,101. She started collecting Social Security at age 64, and her benefit is reduced since she started collecting before age 67. Find her approximate Social Security benefit. $1,680.80

13. Linda and Rob are married filing a joint Form 1040. Rob is collecting Social Security, but Linda is not. They are filling out the Social Security worksheet (shown in Exercise 11) so they can determine the amount of Rob's Social Security benefits that they will pay federal income tax on. Fill in the following lines which were taken from their tax information:

- Line 1—Rob received $33,191 in Social Security benefits.
- Line 3—the total of their other sources of income is $112,543.
- Line 4—the amount from line 8b is $650.
- Line 6—the total to enter is $5,899.

a–n. Fill in the correct entries for the rest of the lines on their Social Security worksheet. See margin.

p. How much of Rob's Social Security benefit must they pay Federal income tax on? $28,212.35

14. If George pays x dollars monthly for Medicare Part B coverage, express his annual cost for Part B coverage algebraically. $12x$

15. This year Frank pays m dollars for Medicare Part B coverage. He reads that this cost will go up 12.3% next year. Express next year's cost algebraically. $1.123m$

16. You can receive Social Security payments for being disabled even if you have not retired or reached age 62. You need a certain number of Social Security credits to qualify for this.

- If you become disabled before age 24, you generally need six credits in the three years before you became disabled.
- If you are 24 through 30, you generally need credits for half of the time between age 21 and the time you became disabled, and at least six credits.
- If you are disabled at age 31 or older, you generally need at least 20 credits in the 10 years immediately before you became disabled. The table shows examples of how many credits you would need if you became disabled at various selected ages.

Age at Which You Become Disabled	Credits Needed
31 through 42	20
44	22
46	24
48	26
50	28
52	30
54	32
56	34
58	36
60	38
62 or older	40

a. How many credits would you need to qualify for disability if you became disabled at age 28? 14

b. How many credits would you need to qualify if you became disabled at age 22? 6

c. Express algebraically the number of credits you would need to qualify if you became disabled at age a, where $a > 21$ and $a < 30$. $\frac{4(a-21)}{2} = 2a - 42$

ANSWERS

13. a. $16,595.50
b. $129,788.50
c. $123,889.50
d. $32,000
e. $91,889.50
f. $12,000
g. $79,889.50
h. $12,000
i. $6,000
j. $6,000
k. $67,906.08
l. $73,906.08
m. $28,212.35
n. $28,212.35

Goodbye tension, hello pension!

Author Unknown

9-3 Pensions

Objectives

- Calculate pension benefits using various formulas.
- Calculate pension benefits during and after vesting periods.

Common Core

F-BF1

Key Terms

- deferred compensation
- pension
- defined benefit plan
- vested
- single life annuity
- qualified joint and survivor annuity
- lump-sum payment
- Pension Benefit Guaranty Corporation (PBGC)
- Employee Retirement Income Security Act (ERISA)
- Pension Protection Act
- cost of living adjustment (COLA)
- Consumer Price Index (CPI)

CCSS Warm-Up

Write a linear function, $f(x)$, that describes the relationship in each set of ordered pairs (x, y).

1. $(-2,4), (0,8), (2,12), (4,16)$

2. $(-1,-7), (1,-1), (3,5), (5,11)$

1. $f(x) = 8 + 2x$

2. $f(x) = 3x - 4$

EXAMINE THE QUESTION

Students should be familiar with the word *deferred*. Ask them for a definition. *Compensation* is another word that should be in their vocabulary although they may not use it in terms of monetary benefits. Once the separate definitions have been established, ask for their definition of the term *deferred compensation*. Ask why anyone might want to put off getting monetarily compensated for something.

CLASS DISCUSSION

Examine the sentence "The compensation from the plan is usually tax-deferred..." How does the employee benefit when the compensation is tax-deferred and how does the employer benefit when the compensation is tax-deductible?

Ask students if they think it is fair that the employer makes all of the decisions on the defined benefit plan investments. Ask what other options they would rather see in place and why.

Review the paragraph on vesting. Although it appears to be a strange term, ask students why they think it is appropriate here.

What is deferred compensation?

Deferred compensation is money that is given or received at a later date usually in return for services that have been given or received at the present time. A **pension** is a deferred compensation plan. A pension is income given to an employee after retirement that is given at the discretion of an employer. There is no mandate for an employer to fund a pension plan for employees. The compensation from the plan is usually tax-deferred and the contributions that the employer makes for the employees are tax-deductible for the employer.

There are two types of traditional occupational pension plans—the defined benefit plan and the defined contribution plan, such as 401k plans. In a **defined benefit plan**, the employee pension benefits are calculated based upon a formula that may involve the average salary before retirement, the age of the employee at retirement, the length of employment, and some predetermined percentage multiplier. The employer makes all decisions on the investment options for the money in the plan. There is no individual account for any one specific employee but a pooled fund upon which benefits are drawn upon retirement.

In almost every defined benefit plan, the employee must participate in the plan for a certain number of years before being **vested**, or having the right to it. There are two types of vesting. In *cliff vesting* the employee is entitled to a pension after having participated in the plan for a fixed number of years. Suppose you are in a plan with a 5-year cliff vesting formula. If you work for the employer for at least 5 years, you will be entitled to receive a pension even if you leave the company. If you leave before 5 years, you will not be entitled to a pension.

Graded vesting does not set an all or nothing time period. The employee gets a certain percentage of the pension after each set number of years has passed. For example, you might own only 20% of your pension after the first three years of employment and then for every year you work afterwards, your ownership increases by 20% to a maximum of 100%.

When it is time to have your pension benefits paid out to you (usually upon retirement), there are some common options that are available. A **single life annuity** offers the retired employee a fixed monthly amount until death, when all benefits stop. A **qualified joint and survivor annuity** offers the retiree a smaller monthly payment but, upon death, the spouse will continue to receive reduced payments until his or her death. A retiree can sometimes choose to take a **lump-sum payment** in which all of the money owed to you is given in a single payment and no further payments are made to either you or your beneficiaries.

There are different formulas that are used to calculate a pension.

- **Flat-Benefit Formula** Pays a fixed (flat) monthly pension based solely on the years that the retiree has worked for the employer.
- **Career-Average Formula** Pays a pension that is based on a fixed percentage of the average earnings of all of the years the retiree has worked for the employer.
- **Final-Average Formula** Pays a pension that is based on a fixed percentage of the average earnings of the last several years (often 3 to 5) of work with the employer.

Most defined benefit plans are insured under a federal pension insurance program known as the **Pension Benefit Guaranty Corporation (PBGC)**. The PBGC is a federal government agency that insures most defined benefit pension plans. It was created under the **Employee Retirement Income Security Act of 1974 (ERISA)** to protect the pension benefits of retirees. In 2006, the **Pension Protection Act** was passed which amended ERISA and offered legislation to strengthen and protect many types of pensions.

Some benefit plans are fixed throughout the life of the retiree while others can reflect an annual **cost of living adjustment (COLA)**. A cost of living adjustment is a small increase in the retiree's benefits that is based on the **Consumer Price Index (CPI)** or cost-of-living index. The CPI is an indicator of inflation that measures the change in the total cost of a specific list of services and products.

CLASS DISCUSSION

Discuss the three possible pension payouts (single life annuity, qualified joint and survivor annuity, and lump-sum payment). Ask students to define situations in which each would be beneficial to the retiree.

Review the three pension formulas. Although the examples in this lesson will examine them in detail, ask students for their reaction to the ways that pensions are calculated. Do they think each is fair to the retiree?

TEACH

There are a lot of new vocabulary terms that will be unfamiliar to students. A graphic organizer may assist them.

EXAMPLE 1

Remind students that whether or not pensions are offered is at the sole discretion of the employer. They may think that the employer in this example is offering a meager plan but it is a voluntary plan, not a mandate.

CHECK YOUR UNDERSTANDING

Answer $(x + y)z$ or $xz + yz$

EXAMPLE 2

Students should not be led to believe that a cost of living adjustment is a given. There are years when the economy warrants the adjustment and there are years when no adjustment is needed. In this example, there were two consecutive year adjustments made. After completing the example, ask students if the same answer could have been achieved if the two year adjustment percentages were added together and applied to the $800. (No, the combined percentage results in a lower cumulative adjustment.)

CHECK YOUR UNDERSTANDING

Answer $D(1.01)^5$

Skills and Strategies

Here you will learn how to calculate a variety of pension benefits.

EXAMPLE 1

Roberto worked for the Surgical Tools Corporation for 20 years. His employer offers a pension benefit package with a flat benefit formula using the flat amount of $40 for each year of service to calculate his monthly pension. How much will Roberto's monthly pension benefit be?

SOLUTION Roberto's monthly pension benefit is his number of years of service for the company times the flat amount of $40.

$$20 \times 40 = 800$$

Roberto will receive a monthly pension of $800 from Surgical Tools Corporation upon retirement.

CHECK YOUR UNDERSTANDING

Maddy has worked for the same company as Roberto for the last x years. She is considering working for y more years, at which time the flat benefit that Surgical Tools offers will be z dollars for each year of service. Write an algebraic expression that represents Maddy's monthly pension benefit.

EXAMPLE 2

After one year of retirement, Roberto's employer (from Example 1), offered a 2.21% cost of living adjustment to his monthly pension benefit. This year, the employer is offering a 2.35% COLA. Determine Roberto's current monthly pension benefit.

SOLUTION In Example 1, Roberto's monthly pension benefit was $800. Multiply the monthly pension benefit by the first cost of living adjustment, 2.21%.

$$800 \times 0.0221 = 17.68$$

Roberto's cost of living adjustment is $17.68. His new monthly pension benefit after one year is $817.68 ($800 + $17.68).

You can also calculate this by recognizing that Roberto's new monthly pension is 102.21% of his old benefit (100% + 2.21%). The new benefit is

$$800 \times 1.0221 = 817.68$$

To calculate his latest monthly benefit with the 2.35% COLA, multiply

$$817.68 \times 1.0235 = 836.89548$$

Roberto's new monthly pension benefit is $836.90.

CHECK YOUR UNDERSTANDING

Jackie's monthly pension benefit was originally D dollars. Each year for the last 5 years, she has received a 1% COLA. Write an exponential expression that represents Jackie's current monthly pension benefit.

EXAMPLE 3

Alex's employer offers an annual pension benefit calculated by multiplying 1.5% of his career average salary times the number of years employed. Alex has kept a list of his annual salaries in a spreadsheet as shown at the right. Add cells to the spreadsheet to calculate Alex's annual pension benefit.

	A	B
1	**Year**	**Salary**
2	1984	63,000
3	1985	63,000
4	1986	64,300
5	1987	65,000
6	1988	66,000
7	1989	66,300
8	1990	67,000
9	1991	67,000
10	1992	68,500
11	1993	68,500
12	1994	69,190
13	1995	70,300
14	1996	70,300
15	1997	70,799
16	1998	71,250
17	1999	73,000
18	2000	73,000
19	2001	74,190
20	2002	74,190
21	2003	75,000
22	2004	77,230
23	2005	77,230
24	2006	77,230
25	2007	81,002
26	2008	82,156

SOLUTION Alex added labels for the career average salary, percentage multiplier, years of service, and annual pension benefit in column C.

	A	B	C	D
1	**Year**	**Salary**	Career average salary	70,986.68
2	1984	63,000	Percentage multiplier	1.5
3	1985	63,000	Years of service	25
4	1986	64,300	Annual pension benefit	26,620.01

Alex put the formula =average(B2:B26) that calculates the career average salary in cell D1. The calculated amount, 70,986.68, is in cell D1.

Alex entered the percentage multiplier, 1.5 in cell D2.

He entered his years of service, 25, in cell D3.

The annual pension benefit is the product of the career average salary, the percentage multiplier expressed as an equivalent decimal, and the years of service. Alex entered the following formula in cell D4 =(D1*D2/100*D3).

His annual pension benefit, rounded to the nearest penny, is $26,620.01.

CHECK YOUR UNDERSTANDING

Suppose Alex wants to determine his annual pension benefit after any cost of living adjustments. He labels cell C5 as COLA and cell C6 as Adjusted pension. He then enters the COLA percentage in cell D5. Write the formula for cell D6 that will yield the pension with the cost of living adjustment.

EXAMPLE 4

Brian and Marina are married and each is planning on retiring after 30 years of employment. Marina worked the entire 30 years for Santa Fe Corporation. For the last three years she has been making $110,000 per year. Brian has been making the same salary for the last three years at Santa Fe, but has only been working there for 15 years. Prior to his current job, he worked for 15 years at a competitor and had a final average salary of $60,000. Both employers offered a defined benefit plan that calculated the annual pension as the product of the final three-year average salary, the number of years of service, and a 2% multiplier. Calculate and compare Marina and Brian's annual pension upon retirement from Santa Fe.

EXAMPLE 3

You might want to have students complete this problem by hand first. This will help them in the creation of the correct spreadsheet formulas.

CHECK YOUR UNDERSTANDING

Answer = D4 + (D1*D2/100*D3*D5/100)

EXAMPLE 4

Make sure that students understand the summary paragraph given in the solution. Working the same number of years does not necessitate the same pension in this case.

CHECK YOUR UNDERSTANDING

Answer $110,000; this is unlikely since over a 15-year period, a person's salary usually increases.

EXAMPLE 5

Before working on the solution with the students, ask them why the vesting percentage increases with the years of employment. How does this protect the employer?

CHECK YOUR UNDERSTANDING

Answer $1,848

SOLUTION Marina's annual pension can be calculated as follows.

Three-year average salary × Years of service × Percentage multiplier

$$110{,}000 \times 30 \times 0.02 = 66{,}000$$

Marina will receive an annual pension of $66,000.

Although Brian worked a total of 30 years, he received two pensions—one for his first 15 years of service and one for his last 15 years. His annual pension benefit is the sum of these two pension amounts.

Annual benefit from Job 1 = 60,000 × 15 × 0.02 = $18,000

Annual benefit from Job 2 = 110,000 × 15 × 0.02 = $33,000

Total annual pension benefit = 18,000 + 33,000 = $51,000

Although Brian and Marina worked the same number of years and ended their career at the same salary, because Brian's average salary for the first 15 years was lower, his annual pension benefit is $15,000 less than Marina's.

CHECK YOUR UNDERSTANDING

What would Brian's average salary have to have been for his first job so the total of his pensions matches Marina's pension amount?

EXAMPLE 5

Ann's employer offers a pension plan that calculates the annual pension as the product of the final three-year average salary, the number of years of service, and a 2% multiplier. Her employer uses a graded 6-year vesting formula as shown. After 5 years, Ann decides to leave her job. Her average salary was $50,000. How much pension will she receive?

Years Employed	Vesting Percentage
0	0%
1	0%
2	20%
3	40%
4	60%
5	80%
6	100%

SOLUTION Ann's annual pension can be calculated as follows.

Average salary × Years of service × Percentage multiplier

$$50{,}000 \times 5 \times 0.02 = 5{,}000$$

Find 80% of the pension amount.

$$0.80 \times 5{,}000 = 4{,}000$$

Ann will receive an annual pension of $4,000.

CHECK YOUR UNDERSTANDING

Use the vesting schedule from Example 5. Ralph is leaving his company after 4 years. Ralph's salary was $38,500 per year. How much pension will Ralph receive?

Applications

Goodbye tension, hello pension!

Author Unknown

1. Explain how that quote can be interpreted in light of what you have learned in this lesson. See margin.

2. Pete is retiring after working for 27 years at a major bank. The company offers him a flat monthly retirement benefit of $55 for each year of service. What will his monthly pension be? $1,485

3. Janet is retiring after working for a major department store for 20 years. The company offered her a flat retirement benefit of $50 per year for each year of service.
   - **a.** What was her monthly income in the first year after retirement? $1,000
   - **b.** What was her annual income for the first year of retirement? $12,000
   - **c.** After one year of retirement, she received a 1.54% cost of living adjustment to her monthly pension benefit. What was her new monthly benefit? $1,015.40

4. Integrated Technologies offers employees a flat pension plan in which a predetermined dollar amount (multiplier) is multiplied by the number of years of service to determine the monthly pension benefit using the schedule shown. After working at Integrated Technologies for 22 years, Al has decided to retire. He has been told there will be a 2.2% cost of living adjustment soon after he retires. Which will yield a higher retirement benefit, calculating the COLA on the multiplier or calculating the COLA on the monthly benefit using the chart? Both are exactly the same.

Years Employed	Multiplier
15–19	$40
20–25	$45
30+	$55

5. Martina's employer offers an annual pension benefit calculated by multiplying 2.35% of the career average salary times the number of years employed. Here are Martina's annual salaries over the last 24 years of employment.

28,800	29,300	30,250	31,000	35,500	42,000	45,000	50,000
28,800	29,900	30,350	35,000	35,700	43,000	48,000	52,000
29,210	29,900	30,450	35,000	38,000	43,900	48,800	52,000

   - **a.** What is Martina's career average salary? $37,577.50
   - **b.** What is Martina's annual pension under this plan? $21,193.71
   - **c.** What percentage of her final annual salary will her annual retirement salary be to the nearest percent? 41%
   - **d.** What is Martina's monthly pension benefit to the nearest penny? $1,766.14

6. The Morning Sun offers employees 1.65% of the average of their last three years of annual compensation for each year of service. Ramon began working for the Morning Sun in 1988. He retired in 2010. In 2008, he made $76,000 per year. Thereafter, he received a 3% salary increase each year until he retired. How much was his annual retirement benefit? $28,423.92

TEACH

Exercise 4

As an extension to this exercise, ask students for the yearly increase based upon this COLA. Does the yearly increase reflect the same 1.54% monthly increase?

Exercise 5

Remind students to be meticulous in entering the data into their calculators. Suggest that they check over all of the entries before continuing with the problem.

ANSWERS

1. Although this quote is more likely to be seen on a T-shirt given to a newly retired person, it expresses the sentiment that the tension of a 9 to 5 job is relieved once the pension begins. But, this "less-stress" situation is due to the fact that someone planned for their pension in the years prior to retirement.

TEACH

Exercises 7 and 8

Have students complete Exercise 7 first and then apply the structure to the spreadsheet in Exercise 8.

Exercises 9 and 10

As an extension to these exercises, ask students what multiplier Emily's employer (Exercise 9) would have to have offered so that her pension would match Grant's (Exercise 10).

7. Office Industries uses a final average formula to calculate employees' pension benefits. The calculations use the salary average of the final four years of employment. The retiree will receive an annual benefit that is equivalent to 1.4% of the final average for each year of employment. Charlotte and Krista are both retiring at the end of this year. Calculate their annual retirement pensions.

a. Krista's years of employment: 18 $18,746.28
Final four annual salaries: $72,000, $74,780, $74,780, $76,000

b. Charlotte's years of employment: 23 $26,186.65
Final four annual salaries: $81,000, $81,000, $81,400, $81,900

8. A certain company offers a 5-year average retirement formula for their employees. The accountant uses a spreadsheet to keep track of employee benefits. The salaries from the last five years of employment are listed in cells B5, B6, B7, B8, and B9. The percentage multiplier is listed in cell B10. The number of years of employment is listed in cell B11. Write the spreadsheet formula that will calculate the annual pension benefit for the employee. =(average(B5:B9)*(B10/100)*B11)

9. Emily's employer offers a pension plan that calculates the annual pension as the product of the final average salary, the number of years of service, and a 2% multiplier. Her employer uses a graded 5-year vesting formula as shown. After 4 years, Emily leaves her job. Her average salary was $65,000. How much pension will she receive? $3,900

Years Employed	Vesting Percentage
0	0%
1	0%
2	25%
3	50%
4	75%
5	100%

10. Grant's employer offers a pension plan that calculates the annual pension as the product of the final average salary, the number of years of service, and a 2% multiplier. His employer uses a graded 5-year vesting formula as shown. Grant's starting salary with his company 4 years ago was $80,000. Each year, he received a 2.5% raise. After 4 years, Grant leaves his job. How much pension will he receive? $4,650.82

Years Employed	Vesting Percentage
0	0%
1	10%
2	25%
3	45%
4	70%
5	100%

11. Peterson Products calculates its pension benefits as follows:

Years of service × 1.98% multiplier × Average of last two annual salaries

What is Mary's monthly pension benefit if she worked for Peterson for 28 years and her last two annual salaries were $78,000 and $80,000? $3,649.80

12. Jamal is retiring after working 45 years for the same company. The company pays a monthly retirement benefit of $35 for each year of service less than 20 years. The benefit increases by $\frac{1}{10}$% for each year of service beyond 20 years.

a. What is Jamal's multiplier? $35.89

b. What is his monthly income in his retirement? $1,615.05

c. What is his annual income in his retirement? $19,380.60

13. Sunshine Living calculates its pension benefits as follows: Years of service × 2.25% multiplier × Average of last five annual salaries. What is Killian's annual pension benefit if he worked for Sunshine Living for 16 years and his last annual salaries were $38,600, $39,990, $41,000, $41,500, and $55,200? $15,572.88

14. Sara works for the City of Northbeck. The city calculates an employee's pension according to the following formula.

- Determine the average of the highest 3 years of annual earnings.
- Determine the monthly average using the above amount.
- Subtract $600 from that amount.
- Multiply the result by 30%.
- Add $400 to that result.
- For each year of employment over 15 years, add 1% of the average monthly salary, not to exceed $100 for each year.
- The final result is the monthly pension benefit.

Sara's three highest annual salaries are $90,000, $92,598, and $93,000. Calculate Sara's monthly pension benefit to the nearest penny if she retires after 18 years of employment. $2,746.33

Use the following information to answer Exercises 15–18. The Merrick Oaks School District offers their employees the following annual pension benefit.

First 15 Years of Service	Service in Excess of 15 Years
2.12% multiplier	2.25% multiplier
Years of service up to 15	Years of service in excess of 15
Average of final 3 annual salaries	Average of final 3 annual salaries

15. Phil is a custodian who has been working for the Merrick Oaks School District for the last 12 years and has decided to retire. His last three years of annual salaries are $50,000, $50,000, and $52,100. Determine Phil's annual pension. $12,898.08

16. Carmen is a teacher in the district who began working there in 1995 and will retire in 2010 after 15 years of service. In the 2007–08 school year, she made $60,000. She received a 2% cost of living pay increase to her salary for each of the last two years before she retired. Determine her monthly pension. $1,622.01

17. Martha has been a principal in the district for the last 18 years. The average of her last 3 annual salaries is $100,000. Determine Martha's monthly pension if she retires after 18 years. $3,212.50

18. Ralph is a district employee. His final three years of annual salaries were D, E, and F dollars. If he worked for A years (where $A > 15$), write an algebraic expression that represents his annual pension benefit. $0.0212 \times 15 \times \frac{(D+E+F)}{3} + 0.0225 \times (A-15) \times \frac{(D+E+F)}{3}$

TEACH

Exercise 13
As an extension, ask students to create a spreadsheet to answer this exercise.

Exercises 14–17
These exercises should be assigned together.

Life is what happens to you while you're busy making other plans.

John Lennon, English Songwriter

9-4 Life Insurance

Objectives

- Compute the cost of different types of life insurance.
- Understand advantages and disadvantages of different types of life insurance.

Common Core

S-MD1, S-MD2, S-MD4, S-MD5

Key Terms

- beneficiary
- premium
- mortality table
- face value
- term life insurance
- group term life insurance
- level term insurance
- decreasing term insurance
- increasing term insurance
- permanent life insurance
- whole life insurance
- cash value
- universal life insurance
- variable life insurance

CCSS Warm-Up

Three red cards and two white cards are in a bag. A card is randomly selected, the color recorded, and the card returned to the bag. What is the probability when three cards are picked from the bag that all the cards are red? Write the answer as a fraction.

27/125

EXAMINE THE QUESTION

Life insurance is not a typical topic of conversation for teenagers. The feeling of immortality is natural for many high school students. However, many of them may have dealt with deceased parents, grandparents, friends, or neighbors.

CLASS DISCUSSION

Give students an example of why people might buy term life insurance. Imagine parents who want to make sure their child's college tuition is paid even if they pass away. They could take out inexpensive term life insurance for the duration of the college education. Around the time their child graduates and goes to work, the term policy will expire.

Point out that purchasing insurance policies is often less expensive for younger people.

What are the advantages of purchasing financial protection for your loved ones?

Many people want to provide their families with some financial protection after they die, so they buy life insurance. Life insurance provides cash benefits to **beneficiaries**, people chosen by the policyholder whose names are on the life insurance policy. Life insurance can help pay funeral costs, lawyer's fees, loans, mortgages, and other living expenses that dependents might not be able to afford after the death of the primary income provider.

Life insurance **premiums** are the amount you pay for the policy. Premiums are based on many factors. One is the age of the policyholder. For each age group, the insurance company estimates the number of people expected to die and the number of years that the remainder of the people will live. These facts are used to calculate a death rate for males and females in each age group. The computations are done by an actuary. The death rates are listed in a **mortality table**. The death rate for a person's age group is a key element in determining the premium. People with a higher probability of death pay higher insurance premiums. Insurance premiums are also based on the amount of coverage you purchase and the type of policy you buy. The amount of coverage that a policy provides is called the **face value** of the policy. There are four main types of life insurance policies.

Term life insurance provides protection for the policyholder. Term insurance covers the policyholder for a specified period of time, usually 5, 10, or 20 years. After that time, the policy is no longer in effect, unless it is renewed for another term. If the policyholder dies during the term of the policy, the beneficiaries receive a settlement from the insurance company. Many people get

group term life insurance through their employers. They are covered as long as they work for that employer.

Level term insurance pays the same death benefit over the term of the policy. The premiums you pay usually remain level throughout the term. **Decreasing term insurance** pays a decreasing death benefit over time, and as a result, has a lower premium than other types of term insurance. This is often purchased by parents who feel their children will need less as they get older or by couples looking to cover a declining balance on a mortgage. **Increasing term insurance** pays an increasing death benefit and has increasing premium as the policyholder ages.

Permanent life insurance covers you for your lifetime or to a specified age. Whole life, universal life, and variable life are types of permanent insurance. These polices are very complicated. Be sure to read carefully before investing in this type of policy.

Whole life insurance combines a life insurance policy with an investment feature. Policyholders pay a premium that is divided between the insurance portion and the investment portion. The investment portion has a **cash value**. As the policyholder gets older, more money goes into the insurance component and less into the investment component. If the policyholder wishes to change the death benefit, they must apply for a new policy, which will be based on their current age and health. Policyholders pay premiums to guarantee the death benefit. If the policyholder cancels the insurance before their death, they receive the cash value, and the insurance is no longer in effect.

Universal life insurance is similar to whole life insurance. The cash value can be used to pay the insurance premium if the policyholder doesn't pay it. But if the cash value is not enough to pay the insurance, the policy can lapse. The death benefit can be changed without having to get a new policy.

Variable life insurance combines an insurance part with a variety of investment components. These may include stocks, bonds, and money market funds. Financial advisors often caution clients that this is one of the riskiest insurance policies.

TEACH

These problems deal with the cost and the expected value of different life insurance policies. Expected value will be a new concept for students.

EXAMPLE 1

Explain that once the policy is in effect, a benefit can be collected in the event of a death, even if only a relatively small amount was paid in premiums.

Skills and Strategies

Here you will learn how to solve problems involving life insurance. Life insurance policies must be read carefully—be sure to know exactly what you are paying for.

EXAMPLE 1

Jack is 40 years old. In ten years, his house will be paid off and his daughter will have completed college. He wants to take out a 10-year level term insurance policy with a face value of $750,000. The monthly premium is $76. What will be Jack's total cost over the 10-year period?

SOLUTION There are 120 payments over the 10 years. Multiply to find the total cost.

$$120 \times 76 = 9{,}120$$

The term policy will cost Jack $9,120.

CHECK YOUR UNDERSTANDING

Answer \$0; term life insurance expires after the term is up.

EXAMPLE 2

Elderly people or people in poor health may pay higher premiums. The life insurance company is in business to make a profit, and these people present a risk.

It is a good idea to "lock in" a low premium at a young age. Unfortunately, most young people have many other pressing financial needs, and do not consider life insurance as early as they should, to get a better price.

CHECK YOUR UNDERSTANDING

Answer 35%

EXAMPLE 3

One provision of universal life insurance is that the cash value can be used to pay the premium and keep the policy in effect.

■ **CHECK YOUR UNDERSTANDING**

Joanne took out a 15-year term policy with a face value of x dollars. Over the lifetime of the policy, she pays monthly payments of m dollars. She dies after 16 years. How much will her beneficiaries receive from the insurance company?

EXAMPLE 2

Logan purchased a whole life policy with a face value of \$100,000 when he was 28 years old. The annual premium was c dollars. He wanted to increase the face value to \$250,000, so he had to apply for a new policy. Since his current age was higher, and he had some health issues, the premium increased to x dollars. Express the percent increase algebraically.

SOLUTION The increase is partially due to the increase in face value, but it is substantially affected by the fact that Logan is older and has some health issues. He is a greater risk to the insurance company, so they must charge him more. Subtract to find the monthly premium increase.

$$x - c$$

Divide the increase by the original premium c, and multiply by 100 to change the decimal to an equivalent percent.

$$\frac{x - c}{c}(100)$$

The percent increase can be represented by $\frac{x - c}{c}(100)\%$.

■ **CHECK YOUR UNDERSTANDING**

Gabriella's whole life premium increased from \$123 to \$166 per month when she increased the policy's face value. Find the percent increase to the nearest percent.

EXAMPLE 3

Mario has a universal life insurance policy with a face value of \$250,000. The current cash value of the policy is \$8,260. If the premium is \$97 per month, for how many months can the cash value be used to pay the premium?

SOLUTION With universal life insurance, the premium can be paid by having money taken out of the cash value. Divide to find how many months the current cash value could pay for.

$$8{,}260 \div 97 \approx 85.15464$$

The greatest number of payments the cash value can cover is 85.

In Chapter 8 you were introduced to the greatest integer function, which has its own notation, $[x]$.

The greatest integer less than or equal to 85.15464 is written

$$[85.15464]$$

If a number is not an integer, the greatest integer of that number is the integer to its left on the number line.

$$[85.15464] = 85$$

The current cash value could pay 85 months of premiums.

CHECK YOUR UNDERSTANDING

Zoe pays a monthly premium of m dollars for her universal life policy. Express algebraically the number of years of premiums that could be covered by a cash value of c dollars.

EXAMPLE 4

Joe is an insurance agent. Zach, a 45-year-old man, inquires about a life insurance policy. How can Joe assess the risk his company is taking on when they offer a life insurance policy to Zach?

SOLUTION Joe uses the mortality table for males, which was created by insurance company actuaries. The death probability is the probability that a man of a given age will die before his next birthday. Recall that a probability is a number from 0 to 100%. It can be expressed as a percent, a fraction, or a decimal.

Joe finds a probability of 0.003732 for a 45-year-old male. This means that there is, on average, a 0.37% chance—less than 1%—of a 45-year-old man dying before he reaches age 46.

Zach's rate will be based on this probability, the type of policy he wants, his overall health, where he lives, and how much coverage he wants.

	Mortality Table for Males	
Exact Age	Death Probability	Life Expectancy
41	0.002629	36.36
42	0.002863	35.46
43	0.003127	34.56
44	0.003418	33.67
45	0.003732	32.78
46	0.004967	31.90
47	0.004424	31.03
48	0.004805	30.17
49	0.005208	29.31
50	0.005657	28.46

CHECK YOUR UNDERSTANDING

The mortality rate for a certain female elderly age category is 0.043. A company insures 7,000 people in this category. About how many of them will die before their next birthday?

EXAMPLE 5

The Umbrella State Insurance Company sells a five-year term insurance policy with face value of $150,000 to a 41-year-old man for an annual premium of $648. What is the profit the company receives from selling this policy for each age of death?

SOLUTION The company collects $648 per year for this term policy. If the person dies within the policy period, the company loses a lot of money on the policy. They will have collected much less in premiums than the $150,000 in benefits they would have to pay out.

If the person dies after a year of payments, the company's revenue for this policy is $648, and they have to pay out $150,000. Subtract to find the profit.

$$648 - 150,000 = -149,352$$

CHECK YOUR UNDERSTANDING

Answer $\left[\frac{c}{12m}\right]$

EXAMPLE 4

Actuaries are statisticians who compute mortality tables for insurance companies. It is a very lucrative career for students interested in mathematics.

CHECK YOUR UNDERSTANDING

Answer 301

EXAMPLE 5

It is interesting to look at life insurance from the vantage point of the company, which is trying to earn a profit. Explain to students that each policyholder is a risk for the company, so they must rely on probability theory extensively.

CHECK YOUR UNDERSTANDING

Answer $17m - 100{,}000$

EXAMPLE 6

Example 6 again takes a look at life insurance through the eyes of the corporation. Remind students what they learned in Chapter 2 about starting a business. You can discuss revenue, profit, and fixed and variable expenses with respect to the life insurance companies.

CHECK YOUR UNDERSTANDING

Answer $0.7x + 0.1y + 0.2p$

The profit is negative, showing that there was a loss of $149,352.

Profit after 2 years of payments	$2 \times 648 - 150{,}000 = -148{,}704$
Profit after 3 years of payments	$3 \times 648 - 150{,}000 = -148{,}056$
Profit after 4 years of payments	$4 \times 648 - 150{,}000 = -147{,}408$
Profit after 5 years of payments	$5 \times 648 - 150{,}000 = -146{,}760$

At an age of death of 46 or greater, the term policy is ended, and the profit is found by multiplying the annual premium by 5 years.

$$5 \times 648 = 3{,}240$$

The company makes a profit of $3,240 if the person does not die during the five-year term.

CHECK YOUR UNDERSTANDING

An insurance company sells a $100,000 five-year term policy to a female. The monthly policy is *m* dollars. If the person dies 17 months after taking out the policy, express the insurance company's profit algebraically.

EXAMPLE 6

In Example 5, you witnessed how the company takes on a great risk when they sell a policy. The mortality rates and amount of profit are shown in the table. If the company sold 10,000 of the same policies, what would their expected profit be for the 10,000 policies?

Age at death	41	42	43	44	45	Age ≥ 46
Profit at end of each year	–149,352	–148,704	–148,056	–147,408	–146,760	$3,240
Mortality rate	0.0026	0.0029	0.0031	0.0034	0.0037	0.9843

SOLUTION Notice the sum of the probabilities in the table is 1. The *expected value* is the expected profit based on the probabilities. Add the products of each profit and its probability.

$$(-149{,}352)(0.0026) + (-148{,}704)(0.0029) + (-148{,}056)(0.0031) + (-147{,}408)(0.0034) + (-146{,}760)(0.0037) + (3{,}240)(0.9843) = 866.4024$$

The expected profit per policy is about $866.40. This is an average—it cannot occur for one policy. If the company sells 10,000 policies, on average it will earn $866.40 per policy. Multiply to find the profit on 10,000 policies.

$$10{,}000(866.40) = 8{,}664{,}000$$

The expected profit is $8,664,000. The company has made over 8 million dollars on these 10,000 term policies.

CHECK YOUR UNDERSTANDING

Express the expected profit algebraically for the mortality table.

Profit	x	y	p
Probability	0.7	0.1	0.2

Applications

Life is what happens to you while you're busy making other plans.

John Lennon, English Songwriter

1. Interpret the quote in the context of what you have learned throughout your financial algebra course. See margin.

2. Premiums for the Sun-Belt Insurance Company are given in the table. Find the annual premiums for $250,000 of the following Sun-Belt life insurance policies.
   a. A 10-year life insurance policy purchased by a 30-year-old male. $432
   b. A 20-year term policy for a 40-year-old female. $720
   c. A 10-year term life insurance policy for a 40-year-old male. $612
   d. A 20-year term life insurance policy for a 50-year-old female. $12*x*

Sun-Belt Life Insurance Company Term Life Premiums

Monthly Premiums for $250,000 Coverage

Age	Male		Female	
	10 year	20 year	10 year	20 year
20	$26	$ 35	$22	$32
30	$36	$ 46	$33	$45
40	$51	$ 67	$48	$60
50	$98	$111	$95	$*x*

3. New City Insurance Company offers a term life insurance policy with a renewable annual premium. The first year premium is $140. Premiums increase 6% each year.
   a. What will the premium be in the second year? $148.40
   b. What will the premium be in the third year? $157.30
   c. What will the premium be in the fifth year? $176.75
   d. What will the premium be in the *x*th year? $140(1.06)^{x-1}$

4. Candida purchased an insurance policy with an annual premium of $780. In the first year, 60% of the annual premium is allocated to the insurance component and 40% to the cash value. The investment earns 2.2% interest, compounded annually. How much will Candida have in the investment portion of her policy after the first year? $318.86

5. Explain why a ten-year, $200,000 term life insurance policy for a 20-year-old male would have a lower premium than a ten-year, $200,000 insurance policy for a 50-year-old male. The probability of death is less for the 20-year-old over the ten-year period of the policy.

6. Jonathan has a universal life insurance policy with a face value of $500,000. The current cash value of the policy is $11,260. Jonathan wants to stop paying premiums for a few months while he changes jobs. The premium is $134 per month.
   a. What will the cash value of the policy be, without adding any interest, if he doesn't pay the premiums for a year? $9,652
   b. For how many months could Jonathan use the cash value (without interest) to pay for the $134 premiums? 84

TEACH

Exercises 2–4
These exercises deal with premiums paid for life insurance coverage.

Exercise 6
A feature of universal life insurance and a scenario in which it could be used is highlighted.

ANSWERS

1. We get preoccupied with day-to-day experiences in life. We also get consumed by major events such as births, graduations, marriages, and so on. This causes time to go by very fast.

TEACH

Exercise 7

Remind students that life expectancy in this table is the number of years left to live. Traditionally, life expectancy is the total number of years a person is expected to live.

Exercise 8

In this exercise, students interpret the greatest integer function, which is usually taught in precalculus. Have them graph it on their graphing calculators using the greatest integer function command. It is a series of "steps" and it is discontinuous.

7. Use the mortality table below to answer parts a–f.

	Mortality Table for Males		Mortality Table for Females	
Exact Age	Death Probability	Life Expectancy	Death Probability	Life Expectancy
56	0.008467	23.52	0.005148	26.94
57	0.009121	22.71	0.005627	26.07
58	0.009912	21.92	0.006166	25.22
59	0.010827	21.13	0.006765	24.37
60	0.011858	20.36	0.007445	23.53
61	0.012966	19.60	0.08187	22.71
62	0.014123	18.85	0.08959	21.89
63	0.015312	18.11	0.09747	21.08
64	0.016567	17.38	0.010582	20.29
65	0.017976	16.67	0.011511	19.50
66	0.019564	15.96	0.012572	18.72
67	0.021291	15.27	0.013772	17.95
68	0.023162	14.59	0.015130	17.19
69	0.025217	13.93	0.016651	16.45

a. The life expectancy column gives the number of years a person of that age is expected to live. What is the life expectancy for a 67-year-old female, rounded to the nearest year? 18 years

b. To what age is a 56-year-old male expected to live, rounded to the nearest year? 80

c. If the company insures 20,000 69-year-old females, how many are expected to die before their 70th birthday? Round to the nearest integer. 333

d. If the company insures 14,000 59-year-old males, how many are expected to die before their 60th birthday? Round to the nearest integer. 152

e. If the company insures x number of 61-year-old females, how many are expected to die before their 62nd birthday? Express your answer algebraically. $0.008187x$

f. Based on the table, what is the probability that a 60-year-old male will live to his 61st birthday? $1 - 0.011858 = 0.988142$

8. Use the definition of the greatest integer function to evaluate each of the following.

a. $[55.9]$ 55 **b.** $[55.001]$ 55

c. $[0.65]$ 0 **d.** $[-34.11]$ −35

e. $\left[16\frac{3}{14}\right]$ 16 **f.** $[-8.21]$ −9

g. $[19]$ 19 **h.** $[-0.45]$ −1

i. $\left[-8\frac{1}{2}\right]$ −9 **j.** $\left[\frac{2}{3}\right]$ 0

9. Zeke has a universal life insurance policy with a face value of $200,000. The current cash value of the policy is x dollars. The premium is m dollars per month. He is going to use the cash value to pay for premiums for as long as it can. In those months, the cash value will earn y dollars in interest. Express algebraically the number of months the cash value can be used to pay the premium. $\frac{x+y}{m}$

10. Johan took out a 10-year term policy with a face value of x dollars. Over the lifetime of the policy, he pays monthly payments of m dollars. He dies after making payments for $3\frac{1}{4}$ years.

a. How many payments did he make? 39

b. Express the total he paid for the policy algebraically. \$39m

c. How much will his beneficiary receive from the insurance company? x dollars

11. The Durham Insurance Company sells a five-year term insurance policy with a face value of \$100,000 to a 47-year-old man for a monthly premium of \$63. The mortality table is given below.

Age at Death	47	48	49	50	51	Age ≥ 51
Mortality Rate	0.0032	0.0034	0.0038	0.0043	0.0049	x

a. Find the value of x from the table. 0.9804

b. A man buys a policy on his 47th birthday. He dies after making 15 payments. What is the sum total of the payments he made? \$945

c. How much do this man's beneficiaries receive upon his death? \$100,000

d. What is the insurance company's profit on this policy? –\$99,055

e. If 8,000 men aged 47 bought one of these policies, about how many would die at age 50? Round to the nearest integer. 34

f. What is the annual premium for this policy? \$756

g. Assume a policyholder pays the premium annually. What is the profit of this policy for each year of death? See margin.

h. What is the expected profit from selling one of these policies? Round to the nearest cent. \$1,793.62

i. What is the expected profit from selling 8,000 of these policies? \$14,348,960

12. Life insurance companies take risks much like arcade game owners take risks. Mollie has a booth on a popular beach boardwalk. She charges \$2 per game. Winners receive a \$5 prize. The probability of winning the game is 0.1.

a. What is the probability of losing the game? 0.9

b. What profit does Mollie earn if a person wins the game? –\$3

c. What profit does Mollie earn if the person loses the game? \$2

d. Set up a table indicating the profit and the probability of winning and losing. See margin.

e. What is Mollie's expected profit per game? \$1.50

f. If 500 people play this game on a summer weekend, what is Mollie's profit for the weekend? \$750

TEACH

Exercises 11 and 12

These exercises deal with expected value, a concept taught in probability and statistics courses. It can be extended to involve expected profit for carnival games and casinos. The Internet and many statistics books have examples that could be shared.

11g. Death at 47: –\$99,244
Death at 48: –\$98,488
Death at 49: –\$97,732
Death at 50: –\$96,976
Death at 51: –\$96,220
Death after 51: \$3,780

12d.

Profit	–\$3	\$2
Probability	0.1	0.9

CHAPTER 9

Assessment

Real Numbers

You Write the Story!!

CHAPTER 9 ASSESSMENT

REAL NUMBERS

You Write the Story

This graph resembles a back-to-back stem plot introduced in Chapter 5. It is really four histograms on a graph. It represents predicted data on the labor force and the population, for men and women.

Write a short newspaper-type article centered on this chart below. You can find an electronic copy at www.cengage.com/school/math/financialalgebra. Copy it, and paste it into your article.

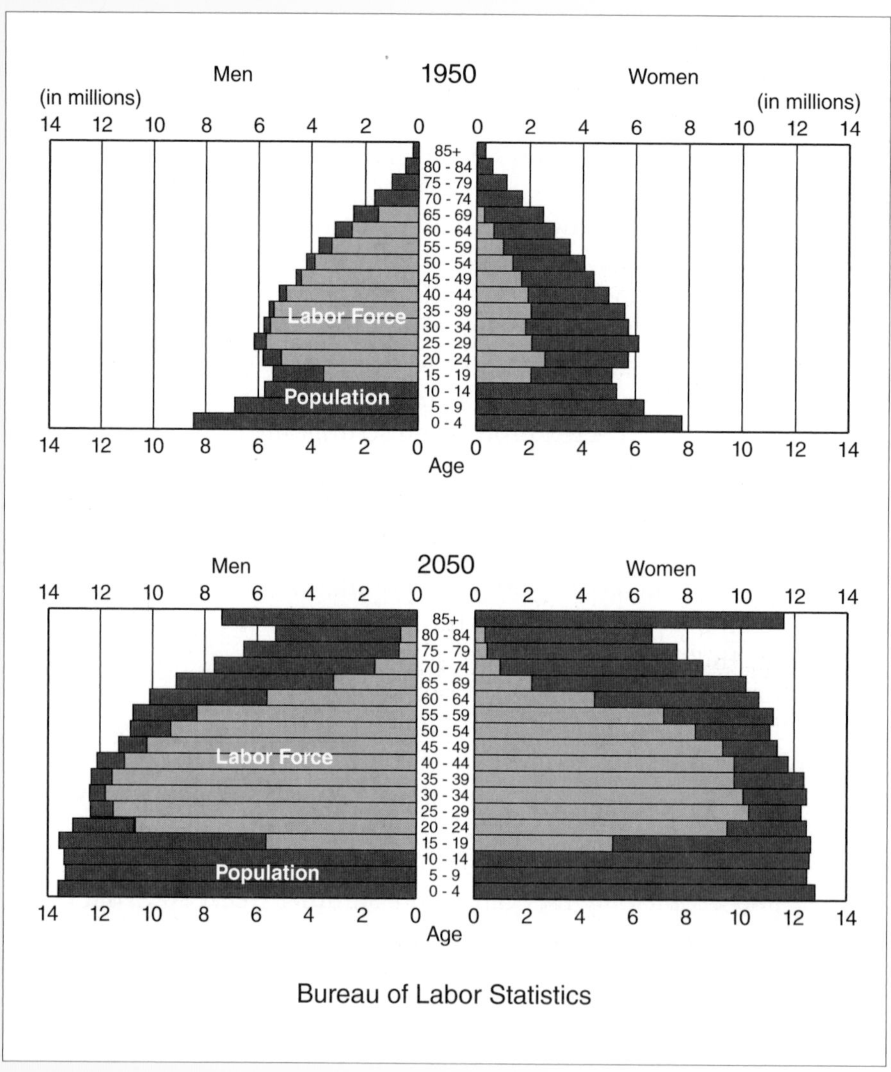

Bureau of Labor Statistics

1. Talk to your teacher about inviting a life insurance agent to your classroom. Contact a local life insurance agent and set up a session at your school. Gather questions about life insurance on index cards from your classmates. Ask these questions during the session.
2. Talk to your parents about their retirement plans. See if they have pensions or retirement savings plans. Find out if there are any savings accounts for your college or post–high school plans. Discuss with them their plans for financing their retirement years.
3. Too often, it is not practical to compare funeral costs. Usually, the person planning the funeral is too sad to take time to compare prices. This is an extremely disadvantageous position for a consumer. Funerals can be very expensive, so you should become familiar with funeral costs. Visit a local funeral parlor and discuss the price of a funeral with a representative. Ask questions about prices and different options. Prepare a report on your findings.
4. Go to the Social Security website and download a form to request a copy of your Social Security statement. Have your parent or guardian fill one out and send it in. If you have ever worked, you should fill one out too. When the statement arrives, check to see that it is correct. Be sure to keep it in a safe place.
5. Find a local law office and contact them. See if they would be willing to set up an appointment for you to talk to a lawyer about the costs and other aspects of setting up a will. Do some research online so you are prepared with some knowledge about a will. Make a list of key vocabulary words that a consumer needs to know when making out a will. Define each word. Prepare some questions for your interview. Summarize your findings in a report.
6. Interview your parent/guardian about the health insurance your family has. Find out if it is a benefit from employment or purchased by your family independently. Find out if there are benefits for dentistry, orthodontic care, vision care, and prescription drugs. Find out how much you pay for a visit to the doctor. Do not compile a report since this is private, personal information. Instead, have your parent/guardian write a note to the teacher stating that this interview has taken place.
7. Talk to your teacher about inviting a financial advisor to your classroom. You can find a local financial advisor through your bank. Gather questions about retirement savings plans on index cards from your classmates. Ask these questions during the visit.
8. Log on to the Social Security website. Using what you learned in this chapter, search for frequently asked questions on different aspects of Social Security, including credits and benefits. Select the frequently asked questions and answers that you understand. Paste them into a new document you create for a poster you will present to the class.

REALITY CHECK

Some of the Reality Check projects for Chapter 9 cover sensitive topics—age, health-related issues, and mortality. Remind students that whatever project they choose, to always be aware of this when they are asking questions.

9. Visit a local bank and set up an appointment with a bank representative and their in-house financial advisor. Make a list of the savings plans they offer for retirement. Get all information they can give you on these types of savings plans. Find out interest rates, fees, tax advantages, and get sample examples on how much your money can grow. Prepare a poster on your findings to present to the class.

10. Interview your grandparents about their Social Security benefits. Find out how many years each one of them worked in their lifetime and when they started collecting benefits. Ask them about anything they remember about applying for the benefits and when they started collecting Social Security. Do not include this information in a report for your class since it is private. Instead, have a parent or guardian write a note to the teacher stating that the interview did take place.

11. There has been much debate over recent years about the very large number of people in the United States who do not have health insurance because they cannot afford it. Do some Internet research on the current state of this problem. Find out how different politicians plan to address this issue. Look in the newspaper. Research how medical insurance is handled in other countries. Prepare a report on your findings.

12. Go to your local drug store and inquire about interviewing your local pharmacist. Talk to the pharmacist about the difference between generic and brand-name prescription drugs. Get some examples of the different prices of each. Prepare your information on a poster you can present to your class.

13. Log on to the Medicare website. Using what you learned in this chapter, search for frequently asked questions on different aspects of Medicare, including costs and coverage. Select the frequently asked questions and answers that you understand. Paste them into a new document you create for a poster you will present to the class.

Dollars and Sense — Your Financial News Update

Go to www.cengage.com/school/math/financialalgebra where you will find a link to a website containing current issues about retirement. Try one of the activities.

REVISITED Really? Really!

During the baby boomer years, approximately 76 million Americans were born. In 1957, 4.3 million babies were born in the United States. This is more than any year before or since. One of the baby boomers reaches 50 every seven seconds. That is around 12,340 people a day and 4 million a year.

In 2006, the oldest of the baby boomers, the generation born around 1946, turned 60 years old. Among the Americans celebrating their 60th birthday in 2006 were two recent presidents, George W. Bush and Bill Clinton. A host of world famous rock stars and entertainers reached their 60s by 2010.

Nearly 6,000 Americans turn 65 every day. That figure will jump to 9,000 as the baby boomers age. By 2030, there will be over a million centenarians in this country.

1. How many baby boomers reach the age of 50 each day? about 12,343
2. When 9,000 baby boomers per day reach the age of 65, how many will reach the age of 65 per year? 3,285,000
3. In 1957, how often was a baby born, on average? one every 7.3 seconds
4. There is constant concern that the Social Security Trust Fund will run out of money, since so many people are living longer. If, around 2030, there are 1 million people over the age of 100, estimate the total number of years they would have collected Social Security. Explain your answer. See margin.

REALLY? REALLY! REVISITED

If students research baby boomers on the Internet, they will find an abundance of information. Talk to their history teachers and find out if there is a window of opportunity to do a meaningful inter-disciplinary project on the baby boomers. This could involve their birth after World War II, and lead up to their future retirement-related financial issues. It includes fascinating information on the rise of the suburbs in American history.

ANSWERS

4. If 1 million people collect Social Security for the ages 65–100, the total number of years is approximately 35 million. This does not include the millions of others who did not reach age 100, but who are collecting Social Security.

Applications

1. In 2009, the maximum taxable income for Social Security was $106,800. The FICA tax rate was 6.2%.
   a. What is the maximum anyone could have paid into FICA tax in the year 2009? $6,621.60
   b. Bill had two jobs in 2009. One employer paid him $77,090 and the other paid him $31,280. Each employer took out 6.2% for Social Security. How much did Bill overpay in Social Security for 2009? $97.34
2. In 1990, the amount of earnings required to earn one Social Security credit was $520. In the tax year 1990, Maggie earned $187 biweekly. How many Social Security credits did she earn in 1990? 4
3. Anna turned 62 in 2007, and she is computing Social Security benefits. Using the formula from Example 3 in Lesson 9-2, compute her Social Security full retirement benefit if her average monthly salary over her 35 highest-paying years was $3,766. $1,599.52
4. Nick's annual salary is $90,000. His employer matches his 401k contributions at $0.75 for each dollar up to 8% of his annual salary. Nick contributes $350 from each biweekly paycheck to his 401k account. What is the combined total of his annual contribution and his employer's contribution? $14,500

5. Juanita's Social Security full monthly retirement benefit is $2,128. She started collecting Social Security at age 65. Her benefit is reduced since she started collecting before age 67. Using the reduction percents from Example 4 in Lesson 9-2, find her approximate monthly Social Security benefit to the nearest dollar. $1,845

6. Charleen is single. She is filling out the Social Security worksheet shown on page 451 so she can determine the amount of her Social Security benefits that she will pay federal income tax on. The following lines were taken from her tax information.
   - Line 1 She received $38,121 in Social Security benefits.
   - Line 3 The total of her other sources of income is $23,907.
   - Line 4 The amount from line 8b is $450.
   - Line 6 The total to enter is $3,211.

   How much of Charleen's Social Security benefit must she pay federal income tax on? $9,775.53

7. Reliable Insurance Company offers a term life insurance policy with a renewable annual premium. The first year premium is $795. Premiums increase by 4.1% each year. What will premiums be in the *n*th year? $795(1.041)^{n-1}$

8. Alex took out a 15-year term policy with a face value of *f* dollars. Over the lifetime of the policy, he pays monthly payments of *m* dollars. He dies after making payments for $1\frac{1}{2}$ years. Express algebraically the difference between the amount Alex paid in premiums and the amount his beneficiaries received when he died. $f - 18m$

9. Paul has a universal life insurance policy with a face value of *f* dollars. The current cash value of the policy is *c* dollars. The premium is *m* dollars per month. He is going to use the cash value to pay for premiums for as long as it can. In those months the cash value will earn *i* dollars in interest. Express algebraically the number of months the cash value can be used to pay the premium. $\left\lfloor \frac{c+i}{m} \right\rfloor$

10. Use the mortality table to answer parts a and b.

Exact Age	Death Probability	
	Males	Females
62	0.014123	0.08959
63	0.015312	0.09747
64	0.016567	0.010582
65	0.017976	0.011511
66	0.019564	0.012572
67	0.021291	0.013772

   a. If the company insures 10,000 63-year-old males, how many are expected to die before their 64th birthday? Round to the nearest integer. 153

   b. Based on the table, what is the probability that a 63-year-old male will live to his 64th birthday? $1 - 0.015312 = 0.984688$

11. The Lieberman Insurance Company sells a 5-year term insurance policy with face value of $250,000 to a 39-year-old man for an annual premium of $973. The mortality table is given below.

Age at Death	40	41	42	43	44	Age > 44
Mortality Rate	0.0008	0.0009	0.0011	0.0012	0.0013	p

a. Assume the policyholder pays the premium annually. What is the insurance company profit on this policy for each year of death? See margin.

b. What is the expected profit from selling one of these policies? Round to the nearest cent. $3,530.95

c. What is the expected profit from selling 5,000 of these policies? $17,654,750

12. Deanna is 62 years old. She plans to retire in 3 years. She has $300,000 in a savings account that yields 2.25% interest compounded daily. She has calculated that her final working year's salary will be $94,000. She has been told by her financial advisor that she should have 65% of her final year annual income available for use each year when she retires.

a. What is the income that her financial advisor feels she must have per year once she retires? $61,100

b. Use the compounding formula to determine how much she will have in her account at the ages of 63, 64, and 65. See margin.

c. Assume that Deanna is planning on using 60% of her current salary in each of her first 5 years of retirement. What should that annual amount be? $56,400

d. Deanna has decided that she will need $20,000 each year from her savings account to help her reach her desired annual income during retirement. Will Deanna be able to make withdrawals of $20,000 from her savings account for 20 years? Explain your reasoning. No; 20,000 × 20 = 400,000 and 400,000 > 320,948.

13. Mitch opened a retirement account that has an annual yield of 4.2%. He is planning on retiring in 13 years. How much must he deposit into that account each year so that he can have a total of $1,000,000 by the time he retires? Round to the nearest $10,000 dollars. approximately $60,000

14. Hillary's employer offers an annual pension benefit, for employees that have worked for the company for more than 10 years. The benefit is calculated by multiplying 5.08% of the career average salary by the number of years that exceeds 10 that the employee has worked for the company. Hillary's salary for the first five years was $26,745. After that she earned the following salaries:

29,000 29,400 30,100 32,500 32,500 33,200 33,400 34,700
35,000 35,000 35,000 35,000 36,700 38,000 39,000 39,500

a. What is Hillary's career average salary? $32,463.10

b. What is Hillary's annual pension under this plan? $18,140.38

c. What percentage of her final annual salary will her annual retirement salary be? Round your answer to the nearest percent. 46%

ANSWERS

11a. –$249,027, –$248,054, –$247,081, –$246,108, –$245,135, $4,8657

12b. $306,820.04, 313,795.14, and 320,928.79, respectively

15. Hannah contributed $300 per month into her retirement account in pre-tax dollars during the last tax year. Her taxable income for the year was $72,000. She files taxes as a single taxpayer.

a. What would her taxable income have been had she contributed to the account in after-tax dollars? $75,600

b. Use the tax tables below to calculate her tax in both the pre-tax and after-tax contribution situations. pre-tax $14,350; after-tax $15,250

If line 43 (taxable income) is—		And you are —			
At least	But less than	Single	Married filing jointly *	Married filing sepa-rately	Head of a house-hold
		Your tax is —			
72,000					
72,000	**72,050**	14,350	10,694	14,539	13,069
72,050	**72,100**	14,363	10,706	14,553	13,081
72,100	**72,150**	14,375	10,719	14,567	13,094
72,150	**72,200**	14,388	10,731	14,581	13,106
72,200	**72,250**	14,400	10,744	14,595	13,119
72,250	**72,300**	14,413	10,756	14,609	13,131
72,300	**72,350**	14,425	10,769	14,623	13,144
72,350	**72,400**	14,438	10,781	14,637	13,156
72,400	**72,450**	14,450	10,794	14,651	13,169
72,450	**72,500**	14,463	10,806	14,665	13,181
72,500	**72,550**	14,475	10,819	14,679	13,194
72,550	**72,600**	14,488	10,831	14,693	13,206
72,600	**72,650**	14,500	10,844	14,707	13,219
72,650	**72,700**	14,513	10,856	14,721	13,231
72,700	**72,750**	14,525	10,869	14,735	13,244
72,750	**72,800**	14,538	10,881	14,749	13,256
72,800	**72,850**	14,550	10,894	14,763	13,269
72,850	**72,900**	14,563	10,906	14,777	13,281
72,900	**72,950**	14,575	10,919	14,791	13,294
72,950	**73,000**	14,588	10,931	14,805	13,306

If line 43 (taxable income) is—		And you are —			
At least	But less than	Single	Married filing jointly *	Married filing sepa-rately	Head of a house-hold
		Your tax is —			
75,000					
75,000	**75,050**	15,100	11,444	15,379	13,819
75,050	**75,100**	15,113	11,456	15,393	13,831
75,100	**75,150**	15,125	11,469	15,407	13,844
75,150	**75,200**	15,138	11,481	15,421	13,856
75,200	**75,250**	15,150	11,494	15,435	13,869
75,250	**75,300**	15,163	11,506	15,449	13,881
75,300	**75,350**	15,175	11,519	15,463	13,894
75,350	**75,400**	15,188	11,531	15,477	13,906
75,400	**75,450**	15,200	11,544	15,491	13,919
75,450	**75,500**	15,213	11,556	15,505	13,931
75,500	**75,550**	15,225	11,569	15,519	13,944
75,550	**75,600**	15,238	11,581	15,533	13,956
75,600	**75,650**	15,250	11,594	15,547	13,969
75,650	**75,700**	15,263	11,606	15,561	13,981
75,700	**75,750**	15,275	11,619	15,575	13,994
75,750	**75,800**	15,288	11,631	15,589	14,006
75,800	**75,850**	15,300	11,644	15,603	14,019
75,850	**75,900**	15,313	11,656	15,617	14,031
75,900	**75,950**	15,325	11,669	15,631	14,044
75,950	**76,000**	15,338	11,681	15,645	14,056

c. How much did Hannah save in taxes during that year? $900

16. Regina is a 45-year-old supervisor for a communications company. She files taxes as married filing separately. She withdrew $50,000 from her tax-deferred retirement account to pay off her loans. Regina's taxable income for that year was $100,040, excluding the $50,000 early withdrawal from her retirement account.

a. Use the tax computation worksheet shown to calculate Regina's tax had she not made the early withdrawal. $22,383.20

Section C – Use if your filing status is **Married filing separately**. Complete the row below that applies to you.

Taxable income If line 43 is–	**(a)** Enter the amount from line 43	**(b)** Multiplication amount	**(c)** Multiply (a) by (b)	**(d)** Subtraction amount	**Tax** Subtract (d) from (c). Enter the result here and on Form 1040, line 44
At least $100,000 but not over $100,150	$	× 28% (.28)	$	$ 5,628.00	$
Over $100,150 but not over $178,850	$	× 33% (.33)	$	$ 10,635.50	$
Over $178,850	$	× 35% (.35)	$	$ 14,212.50	$

b. Use the same worksheet to calculate her tax with an increase in her taxable income of $50,000. $38,877.70

c. How much more in taxes did she pay because of the early withdrawal? $16,494.50

d. What was her early withdrawal penalty? $5,000

17. Circuit Technologies offers their employees a flat pension plan in which a predetermined dollar amount (multiplier) is multiplied by the number of years of service to determine the monthly pension benefit using the schedule shown.

Years Employed	Multiplier
15–19	$52
20–25	$57
30+	$60

After working at Circuit for 23 years, Jane has decided to change careers and leave her current job. She has been told that there will be a 2.05% cost of living adjustment soon after she retires. Calculate Jane's pension after the COLA. $1,337.88

18. Petra's employer offers an annual pension benefit calculated by multiplying 2.46% of the career average salary times the number of years employed. Here are Petra's annual salaries over the last 16 years of employment:

54,000 54,000 55,100 55,800 55,800 56,200 56,400 57,000
60,000 61,000 61,000 61,000 61,700 62,000 63,000 63,500

a. What is Petra's career average salary? $58,593.75
b. What is Petra's annual pension under this plan? $23,062.50
c. What percentage of her final annual salary will her annual retirement salary be? Round your answer to the nearest percent. 36%
d. What is Petra's monthly pension benefit? Round your answer to the nearest penny. $1,921.88

19. NuEditions Book Company uses a final average salary formula to calculate an employee's pension benefits. The amount used in the calculations is the salary average of the final 3 years of employment. The retiree will receive an annual benefit that is equivalent to 1.75% of the final average for each year of employment. Mike and Rob are both retiring at the end of this year. Calculate their annual retirement pension given the following information:

Mike: Years of employment: 25; $37,140.83

Final three annual salaries: $84,780, $84,900, $85,000

Kristy: Years of employment: 27; $35,122.50

Final three annual salaries: $71,600, $73,400, $78,000

20. Esteban's employer offers a pension plan that calculates the annual pension as the product of the final average salary, the number of years of service, and a 2% multiplier. His employer uses a graded vesting formula according to the schedule shown. Esteban has decided to change jobs after 3 years of service. What percent of his pension will he receive when he retires? 45%

Years Employed	Vesting Percentage
0	0%
1	0%
2	28%
3	45%
4	78%
5	100%

CHAPTER

10 Prepare a Budget

A budget tells us what we can't afford, but it doesn't keep us from buying it.

William Feather, American Author

What do you think William Feather meant in his quote?

What do you think?
Have students list some of the expenses they have learned about so far in this course. Did they realize before this course how much money it takes to run a household?

TEACHING RESOURCES

Instructor's Resource CD

Exam *View*® CD, Ch. 10

eHomework, Ch. 10

www.cengage.com/school/math/financialalgebra

Car insurance, mortgages, credit cards, investments, loans, life insurance, pensions, savings accounts, sales taxes, income taxes, and property taxes are just some of the expenses you will have to account for as you manage your finances. How do you organize all of these expenses so you can plan responsibly? You need to create a budget. *Budget* is a multi-purpose word. As a noun, it can mean a spending and saving plan as in, "I need to keep within my household budget." As a verb, it can mean to allocate money to certain spending categories, as in "My wife and I budget \$100 per month for entertainment." As an adjective, it means something that is reasonably priced, as in "He bought himself a budget suit." The word budget is said to derive from a Gallic word meaning "sack." It has a Latin root (bulga) and is also found in the French language as bougette. It wasn't until the 1700s that budget took on a financial meaning. Since that time, it has become a pivotal aspect of financial planning at home, in education, in government, and in industry. Whether you are planning for just yourself or for an entire family, a sound budget makes both sense and cents!

Really?

It has often been said that budgeting can help you save big bucks! But what do big bucks look like? U.S. currency is printed in $1, $2, $5, $10, $20, $50, and $100 denominations. Bills of higher amounts—$500, $1,000, $5,000, and $10,000—were printed through 1945. These denominations were discontinued by the Federal Reserve System in 1969.

Although the $500, $1,000, $5,000, and $10,000 bills were in circulation at one period of time, the $100,000 bill was never used by the general public. It was only used for monetary transactions between Federal Reserve Banks.

CHAPTER OVERVIEW

In this chapter, students are introduced to the typical utility bills homeowners must pay. These include electricity, gas, water, and so on. Lesson 10-2 on electronic utilities covers cell phones, Internet providers, and cable television. Budgeting includes annual, semi-annual, quarterly, monthly, and weekly expenses, and shows students how to organize and track these expenses. Finally, Lesson 10-4 examines how a homeowner can manage the balance of income with debt.

REALLY? REALLY!

The concept of large bills fascinates students. Imagine if you lost one! Students can view pictures of large denomination bills that are out of print on the Internet. Some Federal Reserve Banks have them on display in their visitor centers. If you live near a Federal Reserve Bank, find out if they offer tours and/or publications.

Really!

I'd put my money on the sun and solar energy. What a source of power! I hope we don't have to wait 'til oil and coal run out before we tackle that.

Thomas Edison, Scientist and Inventor

10-1 Utility Expenses

Objectives

- Compute the cost of electric, gas, oil, and water for the home.
- Compute the cost of using specific appliances for specific lengths of time.
- Compute the time it takes an energy-saving appliance to pay for itself.

Common Core

N-Q1, N-Q2, A-SSE1a, A-SSE1b

Key Terms

- utility
- meter
- watt
- watt-hour
- kilowatt-hour (kWh)
- cubic foot
- ccf
- volume
- previous reading
- present reading

CCSS Warm-Up

Tammy draws a scatterplot and regression line plotting her hours worked (x) and tips (y). Which represents the units of the slope?

a. dollars **b.** hours/dollar **c.** dollars/hour

c

EXAMINE THE QUESTION

Students may not have realized that they were spending money every time they turned on a light or brushed their teeth. Explain that they are using credit, since the bill wasn't paid until the end of the current billing cycle.

How much will it cost to run the utilities in your home?

If you own a home or rent an apartment, you are charged for using electricity, natural gas, heating oil, and water. These services are **utilities**. You pay for utilities after you use them, so you are actually using credit when you purchase utilities. Many people don't think about the costs of these services as they are using them.

How much electricity do you use? You probably don't know the exact amount, but it is recorded by a **meter**. An employee of the electric company comes to your home to read this meter to determine how much electricity you used. Every electrical appliance uses electricity. Electricity is measured in **watts**. The amount of electricity used is measured in **watt-hours**. For example, a 60-watt light bulb burning for two hours uses 120 watt-hours. A **kilowatt-hour (kWh)** is equivalent to 1,000 watt-hours of electrical use. Electricity is sold by the kilowatt-hour.

Natural gas and water are sold by the **cubic foot**, which represents the amount of space the gas or water occupies, not the weight. The unit **ccf** represents 100 cubic feet. The amount of space is the **volume**. You can think of one cubic foot as the space occupied by a box that measures one foot on each edge. Natural gas usage is also checked by someone reading a meter in your home. Most communities use water meters to monitor your water consumption.

Skills and Strategies

Here you will learn how your use of natural gas, water, and electricity is measured and how to read meters and utility bills. Electric and gas meters have dials that display usage. The units for natural gas are 100 cubic feet (ccf) and the units for electric usage are in kilowatt-hours (kWh). A **previous reading** is the last time the meter was read. A **present reading** is the current meter reading.

EXAMPLE 1

Tom's October water bill listed two meter readings. The previous reading was 3,128 ccf and the present reading is 3,141 ccf. How much water did Tom's household use during the billing period?

SOLUTION Subtract to find the number of ccf of water used.

$$3,141 - 3,128 = 13$$

Tom's household used 13 ccf of water during the billing period.

■ CHECK YOUR UNDERSTANDING

Ron used x ccf of water during a summer month. Express the number of cubic feet of water he used algebraically.

EXAMPLE 2

Janet works for a utility company and is reading the Saevitz household's electric meter. What is the reading?

SOLUTION Notice where the arrow points on each dial. The correct reading is the lower of the two numbers closest to the arrow, with one exception. If the arrow points between 0 and 9, this is read as 9.

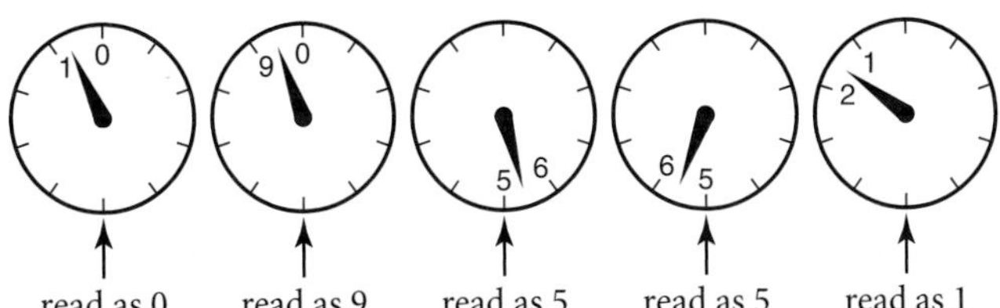

This meter shows a reading of 9,551 kWh of electricity. Some utility companies are installing digital meters which can be read more easily.

■ CHECK YOUR UNDERSTANDING

What is the ccf reading indicated by the dials?

TEACH

These problems investigate reading utility meters and utility bills. Students need to become acquainted with some vocabulary specific to utilities.

EXAMPLE 1

Many utility bills feature previous and present readings. The usage can be computed by subtracting. Sometimes utility companies give estimates one month, and actual readings the next month.

CHECK YOUR UNDERSTANDING

Answer $100x$

EXAMPLE 2

Many meters still use dials to display usage. Digital displays will eventually replace these meters.

CHECK YOUR UNDERSTANDING

Answer 3,359

EXAMPLE 3

Students may get the impression that a household's electric bill is small based on the small usage cost of this one example. Ask them to discuss the electric bill with their parents, so they can see how little usages can add up to hundreds of dollars.

CHECK YOUR UNDERSTANDING

Answer $c\left(\frac{w(m \div 60)}{1{,}000}\right)$

EXAMPLE 3

A certain electric mixer requires 125 watts. How much would it cost to run the mixer for a total of 90 minutes at a cost of \$0.10 per kilowatt-hour?

SOLUTION Calculate the operating cost of an electrical appliance by checking its wattage and the time it is being used.

Convert minutes to hours. $90 \text{ minutes} = \frac{90}{60} \text{ hour} = 1.5 \text{ hours}$

The number of watt-hours is the product of the watts and the number of hours the appliance is in use.

Find watt-hours. $125 \times 1.5 = 187.5$ watt-hours

Electric usage is billed by the kilowatt-hour, which is 1,000 watt-hours. To express the 187.5 watt-hours as kilowatt-hours, divide by 1,000.

Find kilowatt-hours. $187.5 \text{ watt-hours} = \frac{187.5}{1{,}000} = 0.1875 \text{ kilowatt-hours}$

If a kilowatt-hour costs \$0.10, multiply the kilowatt-hours by \$0.10 to find the cost of using the mixer for 90 minutes.

Find cost per kilowatt-hour. $0.1875 \times 0.10 = 0.01875$

The mixer costs \$0.01875 to run for 90 minutes, or 1.9¢. This is between 1 and 2 cents.

CHECK YOUR UNDERSTANDING

An appliance uses w watts. If you run it for m minutes, and the cost per kilowatt-hour is c, express the cost of running the appliance for m minutes algebraically.

EXAMPLE 4

Depending on the climate, utility usage can vary according to the seasons. Electric bills can be higher in the summer due to air conditioning use, and gas and oil usage can be higher in winter due to heating needs. For this reason, some utility companies offer balanced billing. This evens out the monthly cost of utilities to make the homeowner's payments predictable. Last year, the Ross family spent $3,336 for electricity. They are opting to use balanced billing for next year. What will their monthly payment be?

SOLUTION Balanced billing uses the previous year to determine monthly payments for the upcoming year. Divide the annual cost by 12 to get the monthly cost.

$$\frac{\text{annual utility cost}}{\text{12 months per year}} = \frac{3{,}336}{12} = 278$$

The Ross' monthly electric bill will be $278 under the balanced billing program.

CHECK YOUR UNDERSTANDING

Two years ago, the Halloran family used y dollars of electricity. Last year, they used balanced billing. During last year, they used x dollars of electricity, and their balanced billing payments were not enough to pay for their electric usage. They had to pay the difference at the end of the year. Express algebraically the amount they owed the utility company.

EXAMPLE 5

Energy savings often pay for themselves. This means that the savings in energy usage can equal, or offset, the cost of the item after a certain number of years. The Thomson's old water heater costs them $455 per year to run. The new one they purchased for $1,240 will save them 31% annually in energy costs to run it. In how many years will it pay for itself?

SOLUTION Compute the savings per year by finding 31% of $455.

$$455 \times 0.31 = 141.05$$

Divide the cost of the new appliance by the annual savings in energy.

$$\frac{1{,}240}{141.05} \approx 8.791$$

The water heater will pay for itself in about 9 years, since it will take more than 8 years to save more than $1,240.

CHECK YOUR UNDERSTANDING

An old dishwasher costs r dollars to run for a year. It is replaced by a new energy-efficient dishwasher that costs c dollars, but saves p percent per year in energy usage. Express algebraically the number of years it will take for the dishwasher to pay for itself.

EXAMPLE 4

Discuss with students when they think electric and gas bills are higher during the year, and for what reasons. Air conditioners, heat, stoves, appliances, lighting, and so on, all affect usage.

CHECK YOUR UNDERSTANDING

Answer $x - y$

EXAMPLE 5

This example examines an energy-saving appliance. Most new appliances are efficient enough to pay for themselves in a few years, but not always. It usually pays to calculate the savings to see if it is a worthwhile investment at that time.

CHECK YOUR UNDERSTANDING

Answer $\left[\frac{c}{\frac{p}{100}(r)}\right] + 1$

Applications

I'd put my money on the sun and solar energy. What a source of power! I hope we don't have to wait 'til oil and coal run out before we tackle that.

Thomas Edison, Scientist and Inventor

TEACH

Exercises 2–4 and 12
These exercises require students to read meters or utility bills. Ask them to check their meter readings at home and see which type of meters they have.

ANSWERS

1. Edison was foreshadowing our current attempt to switch to an energy policy based increasingly on solar and even wind power, as opposed to oil.

1. Interpret the quote in the context of what you know about the major issues in energy consumption today. See margin.

2. Emily's last water bill listed a previous reading of 7,123 ccf and a present reading of 7,171 ccf. Her water company charges $0.73 per ccf of water. What should Emily have been charged on her last water bill? $35.04

3. What is the meter reading, in ccf, indicated by each of the gas meters shown? a. 657 b. 9,416 c. 8,443 d. 8,513

a. 

b. 

c. 

d. 

4. Bill Heckle's last electric bill is shown below.

WATTCO LIGHTING CORPORATION

FOR SERVICES TO: Bill Heckle, 12 Cavern St., Linwood, KS 66052			ACCOUNT NUMBER		8761-21	
			BILL DATE		AUG 11	
	SERVICE PERIOD		METER READING			
SERVICE	FROM	TO	PREVIOUS	PRESENT	USAGE	AMOUNT
ELECTRIC	JUL 3	AUG 4	21,780	24,100	2,320	$255.20

a. What was the previous reading? 21,780 kWh
b. What is the present reading? 24,100 kWh
c. How many kilowatt-hours of electricity did Bill use during the service period shown? 2,320
d. What did Wattco charge per kilowatt-hour of electricity? $0.11
e. The bill covers 31 days of electric use. What was Bill's average daily expense for electricity for this service period? Round to the nearest cent. $8.23

5. Home heating oil is sold by the gallon. Last winter, the Romano family used 370 gallons of oil at a price of $3.91 per gallon. If the price increases 9% next year, what will their approximate heating expense be? Round to the nearest ten dollars. $1,580

6. The PA system at North High School requires 400 watts when it is switched on. How much would it cost to run for 3 hours, at a cost of $0.10 per kilowatt-hour? $0.12

7. The Zwerling family installed central air conditioning in their house this summer. They are comparing the electric bills of this summer and last summer. The data is shown.

Month	This Summer	Last Summer
June	$311.20	$179.90
July	300.65	$203.40
August	302.50	$201.11

a. What was the total electric bill this summer? $914.35
b. What was the total electric bill last summer? $584.41
c. Did the bill increase more or less than 50%? more than 50%

8. Last winter, Anne was charged $838.35 for 9,315 kWh of electricity. What did her company charge per kilowatt-hour of electricity? $0.09

9. A certain appliance requires 225 watts when it is switched on. How much would it cost to run for *m* minutes, at a cost of *d* dollars per kilowatt-hour? Express your answer algebraically. See margin.

10. Jessica's parents are always telling her to turn off the lights when she leaves a room. A light bulb requires 75 watts to run when it is turned on. The fixture in Jessica's room requires four of these bulbs.
a. Jessica's parents estimate that she leaves the lights on unnecessarily for 2.5 hours per day. How many watt-hours of electricity are used by these bulbs during 2.5 hours? 750
b. Approximately how many kilowatt-hours of electricity are used in a year to keep these bulbs lit for 2.5 hours per day? 273.75
c. At a cost of $0.09 per kilowatt-hour, how much money is wasted per year by keeping these lights on unnecessarily? Round to the nearest dollar. $25
d. If five million teenagers keep lights on as Jessica does, how much is wasted in unnecessary electric expenses? $125,000,000

11. The Smithtown Water Company uses water meters that measure water usage in gallons. They charge $0.12 per gallon of water. If Jack's previous meter reading was 45,621 gallons and his present water reading is 46,555 gallons, what is the amount of his water bill? $112.08

12. Ron Sargeant's electric bill from the Longwood Power Authority is shown. If his meter reading for December 17 is 52,344, find the total charges for the December bill. Include all rates and charges as shown on the November bill. $199.60

LONGWOOD POWER AUTHORITY

ELECTRIC USAGE		DELIVERY AND SYSTEM CHARGES	
METER READING		Basic Services	
NOVEMBER 17	50,361	31 days @ .18	$ 5.58
OCTOBER 17	49,356	1,005 kWh @ .095 ..	95.48
kWh USED IN 31 DAYS	1,005	Subtotal	101.06
		Sales Tax (3%)	3.04
		Total charges	$104.10

13. Last year, the Forrester family spent $1,882.56 for electricity. They are opting to use balanced billing for next year.
a. What will their monthly payment be under balanced billing? $156.88
b. Last year, they had their highest bill in the summer, for $405.67. Their lowest bill was in the winter. Explain why their lowest bill could not be $178. See margin.

TEACH

Exercises 13 and 14
These exercises deal with balanced billing. Discuss the advantages and disadvantages of balanced billing. Have students research balanced billing and see if the local utility company offers this feature.

ANSWERS

9. $225d\left(\frac{m \div 60}{1{,}000}\right)$

13b. The balanced billing amount is the average monthly expense, and their average monthly expense was $156.88. If the lowest month was $178, the average could not be $156.88.

TEACH

Exercise 18
This exercise can be extended to involve many political issues that center around our country's consumption of imported oil.

Exercise 19
In this exercise students revisit the concept of BTUs, which was covered in Lesson 8-2.

14. The Zlotnick family pays $223 per month for electricity under balanced billing. At the end of the year, they had used more electricity than the balanced billing covered, and they owed the utility company x dollars. Express their total electricity expenses for the year algebraically. $x + 12(223)$, or $x + 2{,}676$

15. The Waldner family paid their electric bill using balanced billing all last year. The monthly payment was m dollars. At the end of the year, the electric company told them they had a credit of c dollars due to overpayment. This meant they paid for more electricity than they used. Express the value of the electricity used by the Waldners last year algebraically. $12m - c$

16. A certain appliance uses w watts to run. If you run it for m minutes, and the cost per kilowatt-hour is c, the cost of running the appliance for m minutes is given by the formula

$$\frac{w\left(\frac{m}{60}\right)}{1{,}000}(c)$$

Find the cost of running an appliance that requires 500 watts for 25 minutes at a cost of $0.125 per kWh. Round to the nearest cent. $0.03

17. A large appliance such as a water heater is only running when it has clicked on and is actually heating water. The time your water heater is on varies according to how much you do laundry, take showers, or run the dishwasher. The national average is 3 hours per day.

a. If a water heater uses 4,200 watts, find the daily cost of running it at a cost of $0.11 per kilowatt-hour. Round to the nearest ten cents. $1.40

b. Find the annual cost of running the water heater to the nearest ten dollars. $510

c. A certain energy-saving water heater sells for $1,100. It will save 36% in energy costs per year compared to the water heater from parts a and b. What will be the approximate annual cost of running this water heater? Round to the nearest ten dollars. $330

d. In how many years will the new water heater "pay for itself"? 6

18. In September 1997, the average cost for 1 gallon of home heating oil in New York City was $1.192 per gallon. By September 2008, it had risen to $4.173 per gallon. What was the percent increase in those 11 years? Round to the nearest percent. 250%

19. Air conditioners are rated by BTUs. You learned about BTUs in Lesson 8-2, Example 6. One watt-hour is equivalent to 3.413 BTUs per hour.

a. How many BTUs per hour are equivalent to a kilowatt-hour? 3,413

b. If an air conditioner is rated at 16,000 BTUs, how many watts does it require per hour? Round to the nearest 100 watts. 4,700

c. Express your answer to part b in kilowatt-hours. 4.7

d. If you run an air conditioner for 18 hours per day for 31 days in July, how many kilowatt-hours will it require for the month? Round to the nearest 100 kilowatt-hours. 2,600

e. Based on your answer to part d, and a rate of $0.13 per kilowatt-hour, estimate the cost of running the air conditioner for July to the nearest 10 dollars. $340

Globalization, as defined by rich people like us, is a very nice thing . . . you are talking about the Internet; you are talking about cell phones; you are talking about computers. This doesn't affect two-thirds of the people of the world.

Jimmy Carter, 39th President of the United States, in 2002

Electronic Utilities 10-2

Key Terms
- electronic utilities

Objectives
- Compute the cost of cell phone calls, text messaging, Internet service, and cable television.
- Compare different plans for these services.

Common Core
A-SSE1a, F-IF7a, F-IF7b

CCSS Warm-Up

Find the two closest integers to each real number.

1. $\sqrt{17}$ **2.** $\sqrt{80}$ **3.** $\sqrt{65}$

1. 4 and 5 2. 8 and 9 3. 8 and 9

How much do electronic utilities cost to use?

When people first landed on the moon in the summer of 1969, cell phones, graphing calculators, personal home computers, and the Internet were more likely to appear in a science fiction movie than anywhere else! Cable television, computers, and digital electronics were in their infancy. Hand-held calculators were bulky, expensive, and rare and had very simple features. The digital wristwatch was new. The explosion of technological advancements has affected our lives tremendously. Imagine life without **electronic utilities** such as Internet access, cell phones, and television. Including these items as a part of daily life has a big affect on a household budget. Whether or not you pay your own bills, as a user of these services you need to know about the costs involved.

- Do you spend much time on the Internet?
- How many text messages do you send and receive each month?
- Do you know the provisions of your cell phone contract?
- Do you watch cable or satellite television?
- What do you know about the different plans available to users of these services?
- Are you sure you have the optimal plan for your specific usage?
- Are you checking your bills each month to see that they are correct?
- Could you change or adjust your usage to lower your costs?

In a year, a household could spend thousands of dollars on electronic utilities. The same household could save hundreds of dollars by using cell phone family plans, combining Internet, cable TV, and phone providers, or switching companies or plans.

EXAMINE THE QUESTION

It's amazing how cell phones and the Internet, both recent innovations, have consumed the American public. Every time a cell phone comes out with a new feature, everyone has to have it. Ask students when they use cell phones, the Internet, or watch cable TV if they consider the cost. Many students will not have considered the costs because they are not responsible for the bill.

TEACH

These problems will expose students to different types of plans typically available for cell phones, Internet providers, and cable television.

EXAMPLE 1

Ask students if they can name a local place that still has a pay phone. Many small local businesses do not have them; however, they are common in airports.

CHECK YOUR UNDERSTANDING

Answer \$2.25

EXAMPLE 2

The use of the greatest integer function in Example 2 is tricky, so go over it carefully. Offer students similar practice examples.

Skills and Strategies

The next examples will help you understand billing procedures and costs of different electronic utilities. Policies vary from company to company and from state to state. Remember that plan offerings change frequently.

EXAMPLE 1

Even with cell phones, there are still hundreds of thousands of pay phones across the United States. A pay phone at a local airport charges \$0.35 for the first three minutes (or part of) and \$0.19 for each extra minute (or part of). You get charged for an entire minute regardless of the portion of that minute you used. Find the cost of a $7\frac{1}{2}$-minute phone call.

SOLUTION The first three minutes cost \$0.35. Subtract to find the number of minutes over the 3 minutes.

$$7\frac{1}{2} - 3 = 4\frac{1}{2}$$

The call went $4\frac{1}{2}$ minutes over the initial 3 minutes. Therefore, you must pay for an additional 5 minutes.

Multiply to find the cost of the extra 5 minutes.

$$5 \times 0.19 = 0.95$$

The extra 5 minutes cost \$0.95.

Add to find the total cost of the call.

$$0.35 + 0.95 = 1.30$$

The total cost of the call is \$1.30.

■ CHECK YOUR UNDERSTANDING

Find the cost of a $12\frac{1}{4}$-minute phone call using the prices above.

EXAMPLE 2

Use the greatest integer function to express the payment from Example 1 as a piecewise (split) function.

SOLUTION Let m represent the length of the call in minutes. Let $c(x)$ represent the cost of the call.

First, represent the cost of a call that is 3 minutes or less, which is 35 cents.

$$c(m) = \{0.35 \quad \text{when } m \leq 3$$

Next, represent the cost of a call longer than 3 minutes, when m is an integer. The first 3 minutes cost \$0.35, but you must add on a charge of \$0.19 for each minute over the three minutes.

Therefore, use $m - 3$ to represent the number of minutes over 3.

$$c(m) = \begin{cases} 0.35 & \text{when } m \le 3 \\ 0.35 + 0.19(m - 3) & \text{when } m > 3 \text{ and } m \text{ is an integer} \end{cases}$$

If m is greater than 3 but is not an integer, use the *greatest integer function*. If you use a portion of a minute, you must pay for the entire minute.

If m is greater than 3, and m is not an integer, you must pay for

$$[m - 3] + 1 \text{ minutes}$$

You need to add 1 minute because the greatest integer function removes the portion of your last minute.

Add this line to the piecewise function.

$$c(m) = \begin{cases} 0.35 & \text{when } m \le 3 \\ 0.35 + 0.19(m - 3) & \text{when } m > 3 \text{ and } m \text{ is an integer} \\ 0.35 + 0.19([m - 3] + 1) & \text{when } m > 3 \text{ and } m \text{ is not an integer} \end{cases}$$

This is the completed piecewise function.

If you substitute $7\frac{1}{2}$ for m in the piecewise function, you need to use the third line of the function.

$$0.35 + 0.19\left(\left[7\frac{1}{2} - 3\right] + 1\right) = 0.35 + 0.19(4 + 1) = 1.30$$

Notice your answer is the same: $1.30.

The key step to remember is adding the extra +1 because the greatest integer function removes the portion of your last minute.

CHECK YOUR UNDERSTANDING

A pay phone at a baseball stadium charges $0.65 for the first five minutes (or part of) and $0.22 for each extra minute (or part of). Express the cost $c(m)$ of an m-minute phone call as a piecewise function using the greatest integer function.

EXAMPLE 3

The Call-Tech cellular phone company has many different calling plans. The Tell-Cell plan has a basic charge per month, which includes a certain number of free minutes. There is a charge for each additional minute. The piecewise function below gives the price, $f(x)$, of an x-minute phone call. Fractions of a minute are charged as if they were a full minute.

$$f(x) = \begin{cases} 40 & \text{when } x \le 750 \\ 40 + 0.35(x - 750) & \text{when } x > 750 \text{ and } x \text{ is an integer} \\ 40 + 0.35([x - 750] + 1) & \text{when } x > 750 \text{ and } x \text{ is not an integer} \end{cases}$$

Describe the cost of Call-Tech's Tell-Cell plan by interpreting the piecewise function.

TEACH

Remind students that when writing piecewise functions, the expression following the "when" defines the domain for each piece of the function. Students can use "if" in place of when and not change the function.

CHECK YOUR UNDERSTANDING

Answer

$$c(m) = \begin{cases} 0.65 & \text{when } m \le 5 \\ 0.65 + 0.22(m - 5) & \text{when } m > 5 \text{ and } m \text{ is an integer} \\ 0.65 + 0.22([m - 5] + 1) & \text{when } m > 5 \text{ and } m \text{ is not an integer} \end{cases}$$

EXAMPLE 3

Interpreting piecewise functions that include the greatest integer function will help students write them.

CHECK YOUR UNDERSTANDING

Answer \$209.40

EXAMPLE 4

All students need to be able to do the mathematics that allows them to compare cell phone plans. They need to read the fine print, and compare different companies as well as different plans.

CHECK YOUR UNDERSTANDING

Answer 375

SOLUTION Notice that, regardless of the number of minutes, there is a basic charge of \$40 per month. This is highlighted in yellow below.

$$f(x) = \begin{cases} 40 & \text{when } x \leq 750 \\ 40 + 0.35(x - 750) & \text{when } x > 750 \text{ and } x \text{ is an integer} \\ 40 + 0.35([x - 750] + 1) & \text{when } x > 750 \text{ and } x \text{ is not an integer} \end{cases}$$

Notice that x, the number of minutes, is always being compared to the number 750 as shown highlighted in blue below. The 750 is the number of free minutes.

$$f(x) = \begin{cases} 40 & \text{when } x \leq 750 \\ 40 + 0.35(x - 750) & \text{when } x > 750 \text{ and } x \text{ is an integer} \\ 40 + 0.35([x - 750] + 1) & \text{when } x > 750 \text{ and } x \text{ is not an integer} \end{cases}$$

The expression $x - 750$ gives the number of additional minutes. Notice that each additional minute costs \$0.35, which is highlighted in green below.

$$f(x) = \begin{cases} 40 & \text{when } x \leq 750 \\ 40 + 0.35(x - 750) & \text{when } x > 750 \text{ and } x \text{ is an integer} \\ 40 + 0.35([x - 750] + 1) & \text{when } x > 750 \text{ and } x \text{ is not an integer} \end{cases}$$

The basic charge is \$40 per month with 750 free minutes, with a charge of \$0.35 per minute for minutes over the 750.

CHECK YOUR UNDERSTANDING

Find the monthly cost for someone who had the plan in Example 3 who used 1,234 minutes last month.

EXAMPLE 4

Julianne has a cell phone and gets charged for text messages each month. She is thinking of paying a flat fee of \$40 for unlimited text messaging. If the cost is \$0.15 per text message, how much would she save by using the unlimited plan instead of the pay-per-message plan if she sends about 800 messages each month?

SOLUTION Julianne must first compute the cost of 800 texts at the cost of \$0.15 per text by multiplying.

$$0.15 \times 800 = 120$$

The 800 texts would cost her \$120.

Subtract the cost of unlimited texting to find out how much she saves.

$$120 - 40 = 80$$

Julianne would save \$80 by using the unlimited plan.

CHECK YOUR UNDERSTANDING

Kristin's phone company charges \$45 for unlimited texting per month, or \$0.12 per text message sent or received. For what amount of text messages would the unlimited plan cost the same as the per-text plan?

EXAMPLE 5

The Optizone cable TV/Internet/phone provider advertises a flat \$95 per month for all three services for a new customer's first year. The company estimates that this will increase 10% for the second year. Pauline normally pays \$49 for her monthly home phone service, \$35 for Internet service, and \$50 for cable television. If Pauline's usage remains the same, how much will she save per month in the second year?

SOLUTION Compute the monthly sum of Pauline's three services.

$$49 + 35 + 50 = 134$$

Pauline regularly pays \$134 per month for these three services.

Increase the \$95 fee by 10%. $95(0.10) + 95 = 9.50 + 95 = 104.50$

After the first year promotion, Pauline will pay \$104.50.

Subtract to find how much she would save. $134 - 104.50 = 29.50$

Pauline would save \$29.50 per month.

CHECK YOUR UNDERSTANDING

How much would Pauline save if the second-year increase was 25% instead of 10%?

EXAMPLE 6

The piecewise function below gives the cost $c(x)$ of x text messages from Horizon Cellular. Graph the function.

$$c(x) = \begin{cases} 32 & \text{when } x \leq 400 \\ 32 + 0.11(x - 400) & \text{when } x > 400 \end{cases}$$

SOLUTION Notice there is a flat fee of \$32 if the number of text messages is 400 or less. Because the domain is the number of text messages sent, the values of x must be integers. For integral values of x from 0 to 400, this can be graphed as ordered pairs that lie on a horizontal line

$$c(x) = 32$$

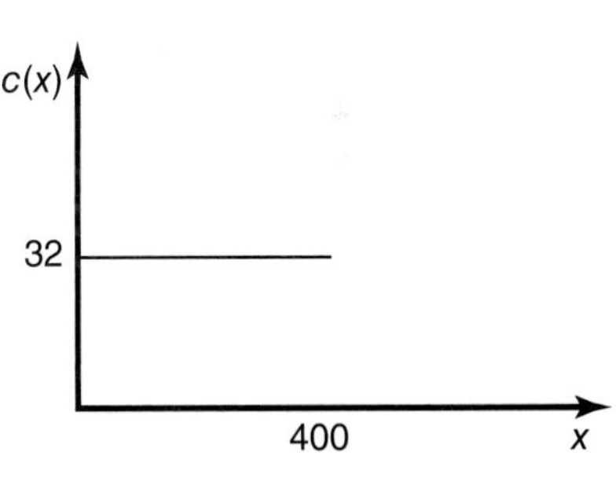

If the number of texts exceeds 400, there is a charge of \$0.11 per text for the texts over 400. There are $x - 400$ texts over 400. Multiply to find the cost of these texts.

$$0.11(x - 400)$$

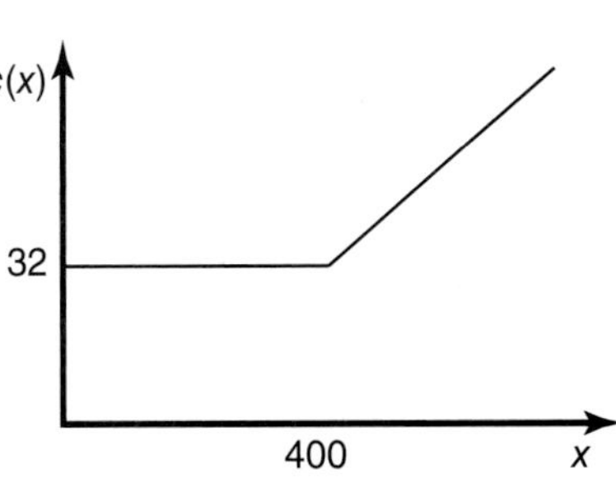

Add the \$32 fee. $32 + 0.11(x - 400)$

For the integral values of x greater than 400, the ordered pairs lie on the line

$$c(x) = 32 + 0.11(x - 400)$$

CHECK YOUR UNDERSTANDING

For the graph in Example 6, what are the coordinates of the cusp?

EXAMPLE 5

Promotions for the three popular electronic utilities are common in radio, television, and print ads. Students can research the plans given by the major providers, and you can discuss them in class. Make them aware of the fine print and other requirements in each plan.

CHECK YOUR UNDERSTANDING

Answer \$15.25

EXAMPLE 6

Point out that only integer values of x make sense for these functions; they are technically a discontinuous series of points.

CHECK YOUR UNDERSTANDING

Answer (400, 32)

Applications

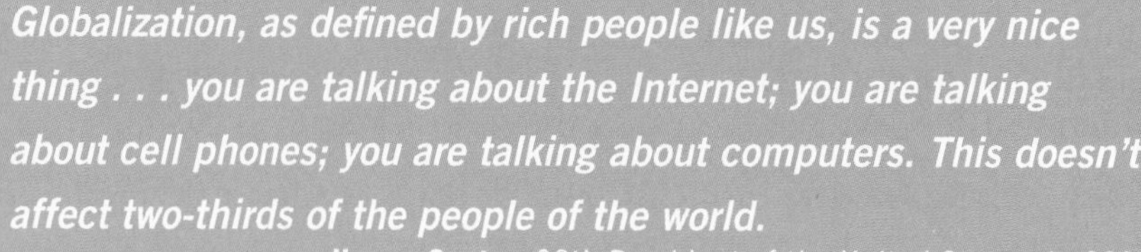

Globalization, as defined by rich people like us, is a very nice thing . . . you are talking about the Internet; you are talking about cell phones; you are talking about computers. This doesn't affect two-thirds of the people of the world.

Jimmy Carter, 39th President of the United States, in 2002

TEACH

Exercises 2–5 and 12
Remind students that the domain is positive integers, since fractional parts of minutes are not used.

Exercise 5
Suggest that students take a look at an actual utility bill with their parents when completing this exercise.

ANSWERS

1. While in the U.S. many middle- and upper-class neighborhoods are obsessed with the technological age, much of the world is still more preoccupied with securing food, a decent living, and adequate health care.

4.
$$c(m) = \begin{cases} 0.58 & \text{if } m \leq 1 \\ 0.58 + 0.21(m - 2) & \text{if } m > 2 \text{ and } m \text{ is an integer} \\ 0.58 + 0.21([m - 2] + 1) & \text{if } m > 2 \text{ and } m \text{ is not an integer} \end{cases}$$

5d. $\frac{e}{b}(100)$

1. Interpret the quote in the context of what you know about the standard of living throughout the world. See margin.

2. A pay phone at a shopping mall charges $0.68 for the first four minutes and $0.21 for each extra minute (or part of a minute).

a. Find the cost of a 10-minute call on this phone. $1.94

b. Find the cost of a 13.44-minute call on this phone. $2.78

3. A phone company set the following rate schedule for an m-minute call from any of its pay phones.

$$c(m) = \begin{cases} 0.70 & \text{when } m \leq 6 \\ 0.70 + 0.24(m - 6) & \text{when } m > 6 \text{ and } m \text{ is an integer} \\ 0.70 + 0.24([m - 6] + 1) & \text{when } m > 6 \text{ and } m \text{ is not an integer} \end{cases}$$

a. What is the cost of a call that is under six minutes? $0.70

b. What is the cost of a 14-minute call? $2.62

c. What is the cost of a $9\frac{1}{2}$-minute call? $1.66

4. The Tell-All Phone Company charges $0.58 for the first two minutes and $0.21 for each extra minute (or part of a minute). Express their rate schedule as a piecewise function. Let m represent the number of minutes and let $c(m)$ represent the cost of the call. See margin.

5. Phone companies itemize charges on monthly bills. There are several fees, call surcharges, and taxes. There could be charges for maintenance of the phone wiring within the home. These charges inflate the bill because they are not included in the advertised basic service rate. Be sure to inquire about all extra fees when choosing a phone company. A bill from the Tell-All Phone Company is shown.

a. Find the total amount, a, that must be paid for just the extra charges shown on the bill. $12.86

b. Find the total, b, that must be paid for this billing period. $52.85

c. What was the percent increase of the total bill when compared to the basic service cost? Round to the nearest percent. 32%

d. If the basic service cost is b dollars, and the extra charges are e dollars, represent the extra charges as a percent of the basic cost algebraically. See margin.

TELL-ALL PHONE COMPANY	
Basic Services	$39.99
Additional charges	
FCC Line charge	$6.42
Federal surcharge	0.73
9-11 Surcharge	0.35
Federal tax.............	0.17
State and Local tax	0.64
Wire Maintenance Option	4.55
Total (Additional charges)	$ a
Billing Period (May 30 - Jun 30)	
Total charges	$ b

6. Vicki's phone company charges x dollars for unlimited texting per month, or t dollars per text message sent or received. If she has m text messages for the month, express the difference in cost between the per-text plan and the unlimited plan algebraically. $mt - x$

7. A local cable TV/Internet/phone provider charges new customers $99 for all three services, per month, for the first year under their "3 for 99" promotion. Joanne normally pays $54 for her monthly home phone service, $39 for Internet service, and $49 for cable television.
   a. What are her percent savings if she switches to the "3 for 99" plan? Round to the nearest percent. 30%
   b. If, after the first year, the flat fee for all three services is $129, what are her percent savings? 9%
   c. Craig usually pays p dollars for phone service, i dollars for Internet service, and c dollars for cable TV service monthly. Represent his savings under the "3 for 99" plan algebraically, as a percent. See margin.

8. A cable TV/Internet/phone provider charges Janet $90 per month for all three services. In addition, Janet's monthly bill for cell phone calls and text messages averages $77 per month.
   a. What does Janet pay annually for these services? $2,004
   b. What is her average cost per day for these services? Round to the nearest cent. $5.49

9. Text-Time charges $25 for a texting plan with 300 text messages included. If the customer goes over the 300 messages, the cost is $0.10 per message. They have an unlimited plan for $48 per month.
   a. If x represents the number of text messages, and $c(x)$ represents the cost of the messages, express $c(x)$ as a piecewise function. See margin.
   b. Graph the function from part a. See margin.
   c. What are the coordinates of the cusp in your graph from part b? (300, 25)
   d. On the same axes as your graph from part b, graph the function $c(x) = 48$, which represents the cost under the unlimited plan. See margin.
   e. For what number of text messages are the costs of the two different plans the same? 530

10. The Fi-Zone cable TV/Internet/phone provider charges $100 per month for all three services for a new customer's first year. Tobi normally pays p dollars for her monthly home phone service, i dollars for Internet service, and c dollars for cable television. If Fi-Zone estimates a 10% increase in the monthly rate after the first-year special rate, and Tobi's usage remains the same, how much will she save per month in the second year? Express your answer algebraically. $p + i + c - 1.1(100)$

11. Throughout this lesson you have used the greatest integer function $y = [x]$. Use your graphing calculator to view the graph of this function and find the y-coordinate for each of the following x-values.
   a. 2.3 2 **b.** 2.99 2 **c.** 3 3 **d.** 3.01 3 **e.** 3.99 3

12. The piecewise function below gives the cost $f(x)$ of x text messages per month. Which would be the least expensive plan for a person who had d text messages: a plan in which $c = 31$ or a plan in which $c = 40$? Explain. The $c = 31$ plan is less expensive. The cost of d text messages is c.

$$f(x) = \begin{cases} c & \text{when } x \le d \\ c + p(x - d) & \text{when } x > d \end{cases}$$

TEACH

Exercise 9
Remind students that the number of text messages must be a positive integer.

Exercise 11
Explain that the calculator can graph the greatest integer function, but the screen may not show the open end-points on each segment.

ANSWERS

7c. $100\left(\dfrac{p + i + c - 99}{p + i + c}\right)$

9a.
$$c(x) = \begin{cases} 25 & \text{when } x \le 300 \\ 25 + 0.10(x - 300) & \text{when } x > 300 \end{cases}$$

9b.

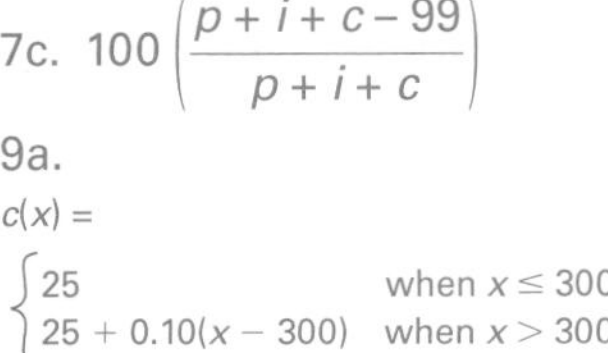

9d.

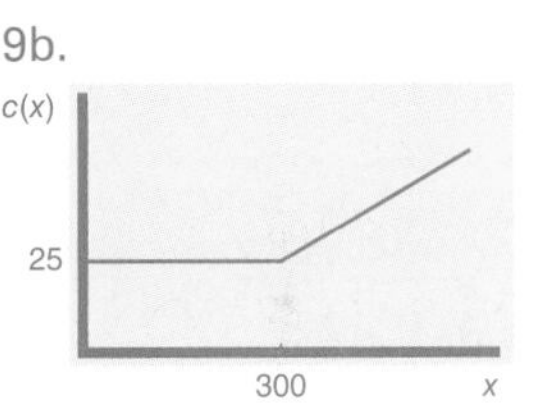

> *Any sensible family has a budget that lays out how much will be spent for household and other purposes. Without such planning, things would quickly go awry.*
>
> **Walter Ulbricht**, Politician

10-3 Charting A Budget

Objectives

- Create and use a budget check-off matrix.
- Visualize and interpret a budget using a pie chart, a bar graph, a line graph, and a budget line graph.

Common Core

N-VM6, A-REI10, F-IF4, F-IF5, F-IF7a

Key Terms

- budget matrix
- matrix
- row
- column
- electronic matrix
- budget check-off matrix
- order of a matrix
- pie chart
- line graph
- bar graph
- budget line graph
- sector
- central angle

CCSS Warm-Up

Which of the following points is on the line $y = 3x - 1$ and the curve $y = 2x^2 - x - 17$?

a. (4, 60) **b.** (4, 11) **c.** (4, 10)

b

How can you visualize your budget?

EXAMINE THE QUESTION

A budget is a personal accounting of income and expenses over a fixed period of time. Budgets can take on many different forms. They can be charts, spreadsheets, checklists, or even graphs. A budget helps you step back and get the big picture of your finances.

In Chapter 1 you learned to chart stock market data to get a picture of trends, make predictions, examine market strengths and weaknesses, and make decisions on where to invest your money. Those charts served as graphic organizers for understanding the stock market at any given time. Charts that relate to your personal budget can help you understand how and when money is coming in and going out. Perhaps the most common budget chart is the **budget matrix**. A **matrix** is a rectangular array of information. It consists of **rows** and **columns**. A spreadsheet is an **electronic matrix**. A budget matrix can contain numeric entries or information on when certain account deposits and withdrawals are made over a period of time. Examine these samples of two such budget matrices.

CLASS DISCUSSION

Why is it so important to know "how and when money is coming in and going out"?

Identify any differences and similarities between the two budget matrices presented here.

Ask students to give an example of these charts that they have seen through this book. (Hint: Look at the Real Numbers feature at the end of each chapter.)

Sample A	Jan	Feb	Mar	Apr	May	Jun	Jul	Aug	Sep	Oct	Nov	Dec
Health												
Insurance			✓			✓			✓			✓
Prescriptions (copayments)		✓		✓		✓		✓		✓		✓
Over-the-Counter Meds	✓	✓	✓	✓	✓	✓	✓	✓	✓	✓	✓	✓
Doctor Visits	✓						✓					
Life Insurance				✓				✓				✓
Health Club Dues									✓			

Sample B	Jan	Feb	Mar	Apr	May	Jun	Jul	Aug	Sep	Oct	Nov	Dec
Health												
Insurance			450			450			450			450
Prescriptions (copayments)		90		90		90		90		90		90
Over-the-Counter Meds	30	30	30	50	50	50	50	50	50	30	30	30
Doctor Visits	200						200					
Life Insurance				300				300				300
Health Club Dues									600			

Sample A shows a portion of a yearly budget matrix that relates to health expenses as a monthly **budget check-off matrix**. Notice there are no amounts in this budget. Rather, the check marks indicate at what time of the year the expenses for the categories will occur. Notice December has the most check marks, indicating that the highest health-related expenses *may* be incurred during that month. The user of this budget will have to plan accordingly.

Sample B can be used in addition to the budget shown in Sample A or in place of it. It too shows when expenses will be incurred over the course of a year, but it also gives the amounts of those expenses. Although December had the most number of check marks, notice that September is the month with the highest expenses.

The rectangular format of both budget matrices is exactly the same. Excluding the column and row labels, they each have 6 rows and 12 columns. The number of rows and columns in a matrix is the **order of the matrix**. The order is reported using the form "row × column" (pronounced "row by column"). Each budget matrix above is a 6 by 12 order matrix.

Budget matrices are not the only ways to visualize financial obligations over time. Other forms of graphical displays are as follows:

- **Pie Chart** A pie chart is a graphic display in the form of a circle divided into pie-shaped segments. A pie chart (or circle graph) is used to present data in percentages.
- **Line Graph** A line graph is used to depict changes over time on a coordinate grid.
- **Bar Graph** A bar graph uses rectangular bars to compare categories of data.
- **Budget Line Graph** This type of graph is used when a consumer is comparing two categories of expenses. It indicates the amount that can be allotted to each expense so that both categories can be afforded within a certain income.

TEACH

Most students at this point in their lives may have little need for an extensive budget. Their expenses may be minimal, so they can easily manage their money. Impress upon students that once they are employed and out on their own, it will be extremely important for them to have a working knowledge of their personal finances. This will minimize the financial surprises from paycheck to paycheck. Ask students to have a discussion with their parents about household budgets. Perhaps parents may want to share the method they are currently using.

EXAMPLE 1

Before working on the solution, review the periodic names and definitions with the students. They have seen these terms before in the banking and credit chapters. If possible, use a blank 12 x 12 grid and work with the students to complete each of the row entries.

CHECK YOUR UNDERSTANDING

Answer semimonthly; bimonthly means every two months, while semimonthly means twice per month.

Skills and Strategies

Here you will learn to use matrices, pie charts, bar graphs, line graphs, and budget line graphs.

EXAMPLE 1

Create a year-long budget check-off matrix that keeps track of the following household expenses and when they are due.

Mortgage: monthly
Utilities: monthly
Sanitation: quarterly
Insurance: semiannually
Internet: semiannually
Land Line Telephone: monthly
Cellular Telephone: monthly
Lawn and Garden: monthly, April–September only
Snow Removal: November, January, March only
Food: monthly
Childcare: every other month beginning with February
Vet Expenses: semiannually

SOLUTION Based upon the information listed above, construct a 12×12 budget check-off matrix. In addition to these 144 cells (12×12), the top row should include the labels for the months and the first column should include the budget categories as shown.

	Jan	Feb	Mar	Apr	May	Jun	Jul	Aug	Sep	Oct	Nov	Dec
Mortgage	✓	✓	✓	✓	✓	✓	✓	✓	✓	✓	✓	✓
Utilities	✓	✓	✓	✓	✓	✓	✓	✓	✓	✓	✓	✓
Sanitation			✓			✓			✓			✓
Insurance						✓						✓
Internet	✓	✓	✓	✓	✓	✓	✓	✓	✓	✓	✓	✓
Land Line	✓	✓	✓	✓	✓	✓	✓	✓	✓	✓	✓	✓
Cell	✓	✓	✓	✓	✓	✓	✓	✓	✓	✓	✓	✓
Lawn/Garden				✓	✓	✓	✓	✓	✓			
Snow	✓		✓								✓	
Food	✓	✓	✓	✓	✓	✓	✓	✓	✓	✓	✓	✓
Childcare		✓		✓		✓		✓		✓		✓
Vet						✓						✓

CHECK YOUR UNDERSTANDING

When setting up a budget, it is important to understand the meaning of the terms used in Example 1 (monthly, quarterly, and semiannually). Suppose that you decide to put two checks in a box when the expense occurred twice in that month. Use a dictionary to determine if that is a *bimonthly expense* or a *semimonthly expense*. Explain the difference between the two terms.

Pie Chart

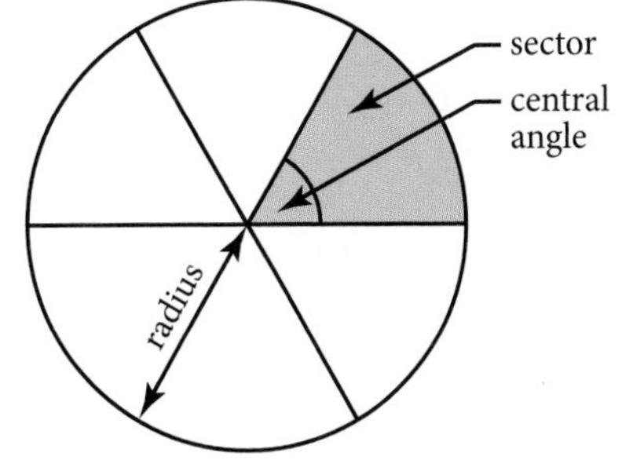

In order to construct a pie chart, you need to understand a few important characteristics of a circle. The six radii (plural of radius) divide 100% of the area of the circle into six regions called **sectors**. The sectors of the circle are constructed around the center of the circle. The angles formed at the center of the circle are **central angles**. Recall that the sum of the measures of the central angles in a circle is 360 degrees.

EXAMPLE 2

Jeff budgets his monthly expenses as follows.

Household: 40%
Education: 25%
Transportation: 15%
Health: 5%
Savings: 10%
Miscellaneous: 5%

Jeff's Monthly Budget

Savings 10%
Miscellaneous 5%
Health 5%
Household 40%
Transportation 15%
Education 25%

He used a software program to construct this pie chart to show his expense percentages. How did his category percentages affect the construction of the chart?

SOLUTION The percentage of the total area of each sector corresponds to the percentage of Jeff's money budgeted for each category. Household expenses make up 40% of Jeff's monthly budget, so the central angle forming the household sector is 40% of 360 degrees, or 144 degrees. Once the percentage is determined, the measure of the central angle is calculated by multiplying the decimal equivalent of that percentage by 360 degrees.

Category	%	Measure of Central Angle
Household	40	$0.40 \times 360 = 144$
Education	25	$0.25 \times 360 = 90$
Transportation	15	$0.15 \times 360 = 54$
Health	5	$0.05 \times 360 = 18$
Savings	10	$0.10 \times 360 = 36$
Miscellaneous	5	$0.05 \times 360 = 18$
	100%	360°

The sum of the percentages for this budget equals 100%. The sum of the measures of the central angles of the pie chart equals 360 degrees as shown in the table.

CHECK YOUR UNDERSTANDING

Martha budgets x percent of her monthly income for rent. Express the measure of the central angle for a pie chart sector that represents Martha's rent budget.

EXAMPLE 2

Although spreadsheet and other chart building programs will create the pie chart based upon the data, it is important that students have a working understanding of how the sector size relates to the category percentage. You might want to construct the sectors with the students as you work through the determination of the measures of the central angles. You can use a board protractor or available geometric construction software.

CHECK YOUR UNDERSTANDING

Answer $360\left(\frac{x}{100}\right)$

EXAMPLE 3

This is an excellent extrapolation exercise for students. Offer them a copy of the pie chart and ask them to extract as much information as they can, knowing solely that the chart represents an $800 transportation budget. Once they have exhausted their findings, compare them with what is listed in the text. As a follow-up to this activity, you might wish to have students construct another pie chart representing a different budget category. They then can switch pie charts with a partner and interpret the situations using the chart.

CHECK YOUR UNDERSTANDING

Answer The fuel budget is $200 and the parking and repairs budgets are each $100.

EXAMPLE 4

A bar chart is used to depict categorical data. In this case, the categories are the months of the year. The students need to first determine the monthly expenses, and then find a suitable scale for the vertical axis. Remind students that the bars in this type of chart do not touch.

EXAMPLE 3

Kate and Paul budget $800 per month for transportation as shown in the pie chart. What information can you conclude from the pie chart?

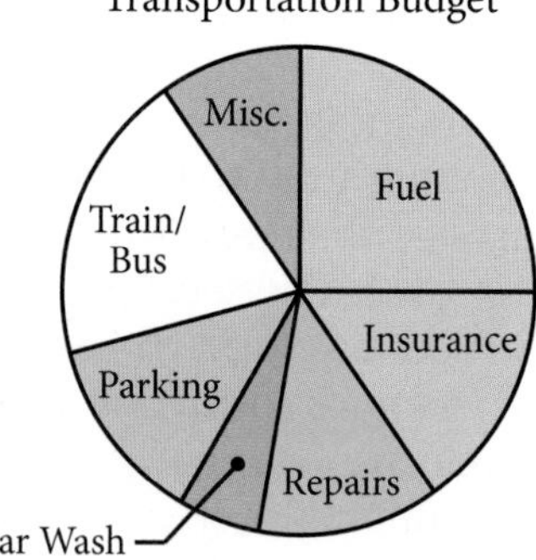

SOLUTION Without a protractor to measure the central angles, it is impossible to determine the exact amounts budgeted for each category. However, the following useful information can be seen in the chart.

- Kate and Paul spend the majority of their transportation budget on fuel.
- Repairs and parking appear to have the same amount budgeted.
- Public transportation costs account for the second highest budgeted amount.
- They spend the least amount per month on car washes.
- The amount budgeted for repairs appears to be half the amount budgeted for fuel costs.
- Miscellaneous expenses appear to be half of that budgeted for public transportation.

CHECK YOUR UNDERSTANDING

Based upon the information above and knowing that the central angle for the fuel sector is 90 degrees, what information can be determined?

EXAMPLE 4

Construct a bar graph using the information about health-related costs from Sample B on page 496.

Sample B	Jan	Feb	Mar	Apr	May	Jun	Jul	Aug	Sep	Oct	Nov	Dec
Health												
Insurance			450			450			450			450
Prescriptions (copayments)		90		90		90		90		90		90
Over-the-Counter Meds	30	30	30	50	50	50	50	50	50	30	30	30
Doctor Visits	200						200					
Life Insurance				300				300				300
Health Club Dues									600			

SOLUTION Find the total health-related expenses for each month. The health-related expenses are prescriptions (copayments), over-the-counter medications, and doctor visits.

Jan	Feb	Mar	Apr	May	June	July	Aug	Sept	Oct	Nov	Dec
230	120	480	440	50	590	250	440	1,100	120	30	870

Let the horizontal axis represent months and the vertical axis represent the health-related costs.

Determine the range of the values for the vertical axis. The minimum amount budgeted was $30 in November. The maximum amount budgeted was $1,100 in September. Therefore, use a minimum of $0 and a maximum of $1,200, with increments of $200.

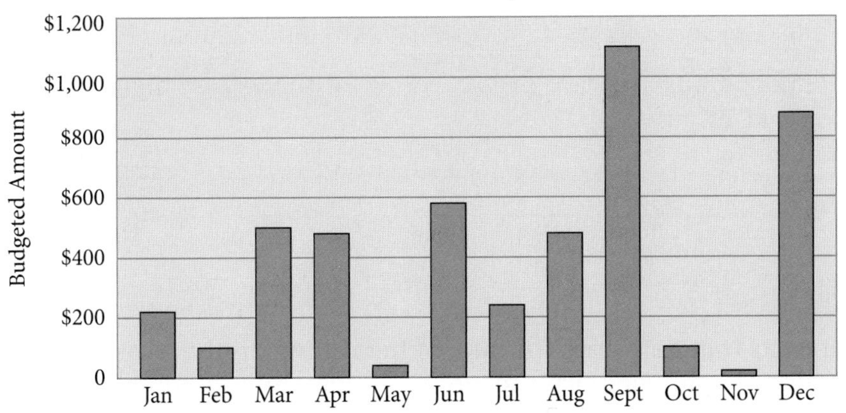

CHECK YOUR UNDERSTANDING

At what amount would a horizontal line be drawn to represent the average monthly budget to the nearest dollar for health-related expenses? In which months was the budgeted amount above average?

EXAMPLE 5

Over the last few months Kate has spent more than her budgeted amount for her cell phone bill. She decided to track her daily usage to see if she should change plans. She went online to her cell phone account and got the usage data below for the last three weeks. Construct a multiple line graph to identify any of Kate's usage trends.

	Week 1	Week 2	Week 3
Mon	18	10	13
Tues	17	19	12
Wed	12	15	18
Thurs	19	20	23
Fri	24	29	40
Sat	35	24	30
Sun	30	22	27

CHECK YOUR UNDERSTANDING

Answer $393; March, April, June, August, September, December

EXAMPLE 5

It is very important that students determine a suitable scale for the axes before beginning this problem. The scale must capture all of the data in the chart. Have students look for the maximum and minimum amounts listed and then adjust those amounts up and down so that a full graphing window can be established.

CHECK YOUR UNDERSTANDING

Answer $110

SOLUTION Kate is trying to determine if she needs to adjust her billing plan based upon her cell phone usage. She creates a multiple line graph chart comparing three weeks of phone use. The horizontal axis represents the days of the week and the vertical axis represents the minutes used. Since the maximum number of minutes used was 40 (Friday, Week 3), her vertical scale should be large enough to graph at least that amount. She decided to let the maximum minutes on the vertical scale be 45 with increments of 5.

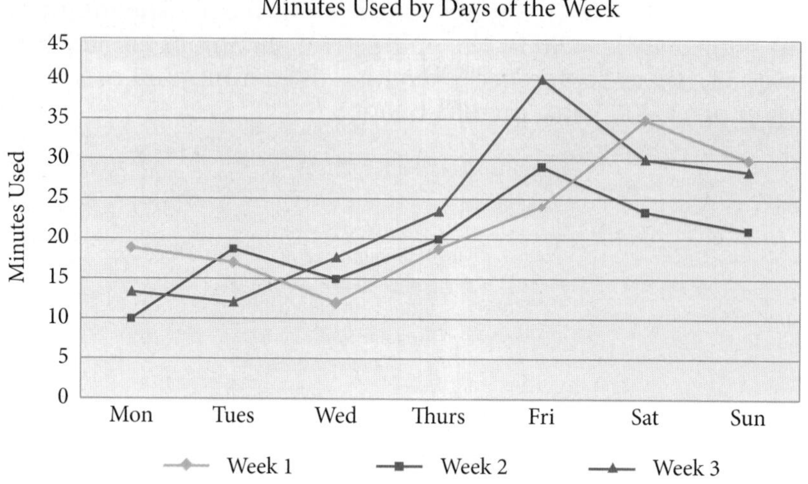

It appears that Kate does the bulk of her calling on the weekends with the highest number of calls made on a Friday. She should contact her cell phone provider to see if there is a weekend plan available that might reduce her costs and allow her to stay within her budget.

CHECK YOUR UNDERSTANDING

Examine the following line graph depicting Claire's electric usage for the first six months of last year.

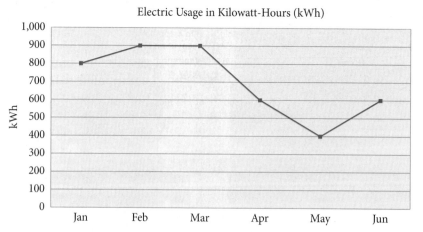

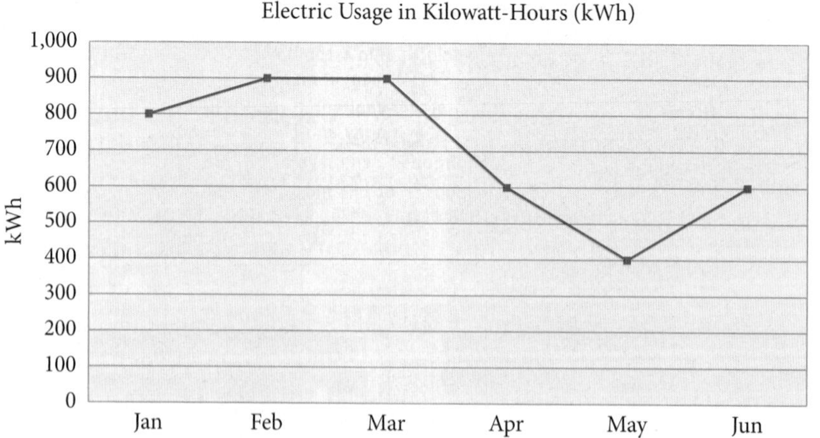

Her electric company uses this data to calculate her monthly budget for electricity, which is the average of the monthly usage costs. If electricity costs $0.15714 per kilowatt-hour, how much will her monthly electric budget be? Round your answer to the nearest dollar amount.

EXAMPLE 6

Beth is a coffee lover. In her budget, Beth has a section for coffee. She has budgeted \$90 per month to spend on the coffee she buys in two different locations. At *GasMart*, a cup of coffee costs \$1. At *The Perfect Coffee Company*, a cup of coffee costs \$3. She tries to balance both through a month. Construct a budget line that shows the different combinations of the two types of coffee purchase options which allow her to stay within her budget. Then, suppose she has to decrease her coffee budget by 20%. Identify and graph the new budget line.

SOLUTION If two items, x and y, are budgeted under a single category, their costs C_x and C_y generate the following budget line equation.

$C_x x + C_y y = B$ where B is the budgeted amount

Let x represent the number of cups of coffee purchased at *GasMart* and y represent the number of cups purchased at *The Perfect Coffee Company*.

Budget line equation $\quad C_x x + C_y y = B$

Substitute $C_x = 1$, $C_y = 3$, and $B = 90$. $\quad x + 3y = 90$

Solve for y. Subtract x from each side. $\quad 3y = -x + 90$

Divide each side by 3. $\quad y = -\frac{1}{3}x + 30$

The budget line graph is shown at the right. Three points are shown on the budget line graph.

Point A is in the set of all points below the budget line. Any of these points are within the \$90 coffee budget. Therefore, 20 cups of *GasMart* coffee and 6 cups of *The Perfect Coffee Company* coffee cost 20(1) + 6(3), or \$38, which is less than the \$90 budgeted.

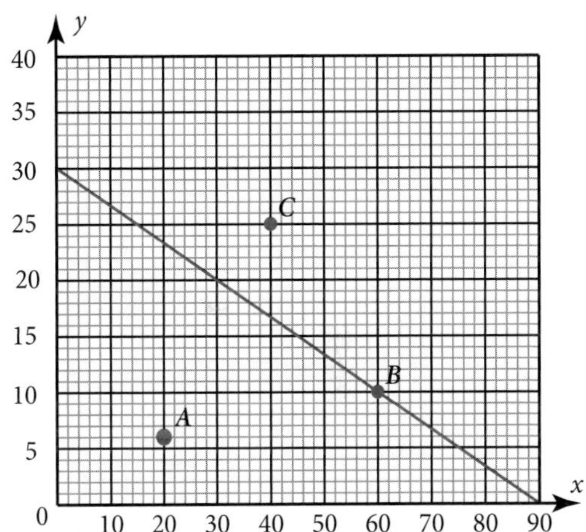

Point B is in the set of all points that lie on the budget line. If the combination B is chosen (60 *GasMart* cups and 10 *The Perfect Coffee Company* cups), the total cost is exactly the amount budgeted.

Point C is in the set of all points that lie above the budget line. If the combination C is chosen, Beth will be over her budget since $40(1) + 25(3) > 90$.

If Beth has to decrease her coffee budget by 20%, the new budget amount is 0.80(90), or \$72. The new budget line equation is $x + 3y = 72$ or $y = -\frac{1}{3}x + 24$. The new budget line (in blue) and the original line are shown in the graph at the right.

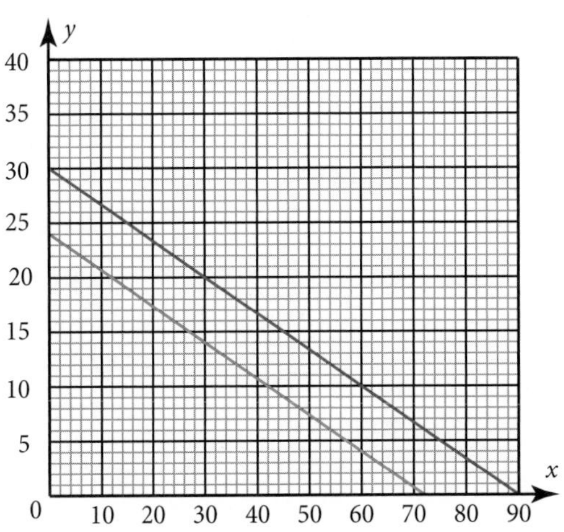

Notice that a decrease in the amount budgeted shifts the budget line to the left and decreases the number of combinations that will stay within the budget.

■ CHECK YOUR UNDERSTANDING

Using the coffee budget of \$72, suppose that the price of coffee doubles at *GasMart*. Identify and graph the new budget line equation.

EXAMPLE 6

Make sure students understand subscripted variables are for notation purposes so that C can represent the cost of each coffee situation. You may also want to show students how the equation of the line would change if the x and y variables are interchanged. Although the line changes, the solutions do not change.

CHECK YOUR UNDERSTANDING

Answer $y = -\frac{2}{3}x + 24$

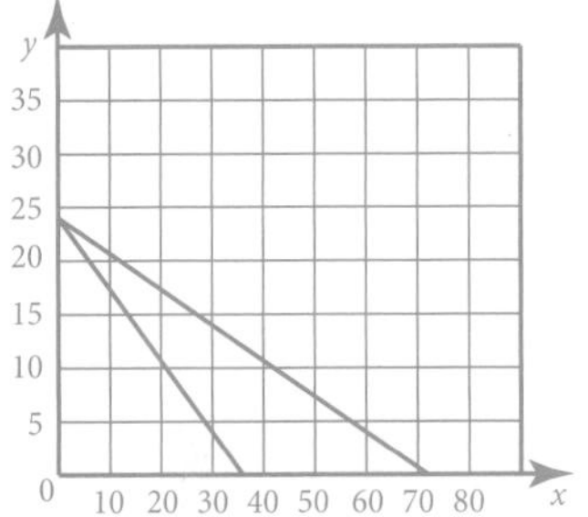

Applications

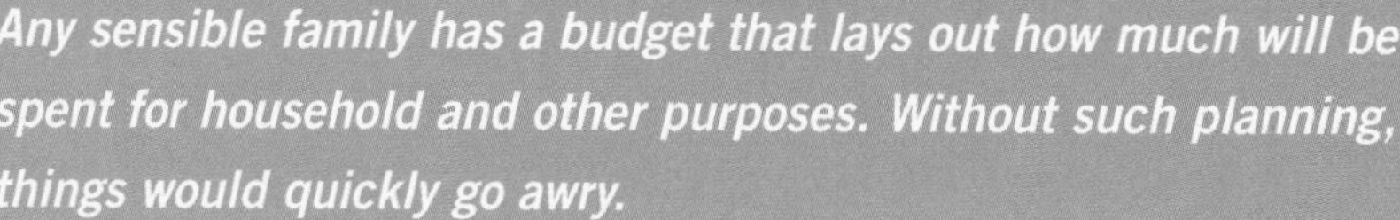

Any sensible family has a budget that lays out how much will be spent for household and other purposes. Without such planning, things would quickly go awry.

Walter Ulbricht, Politician

1. Explain how that quote can be interpreted in light of what you have learned in this lesson. See margin.

2. Create a year-long budget check-off matrix to chart the following transportation related expenses: Fuel: monthly; Insurance: quarterly; Servicing: every three months; Car wash: bimonthly; Parking: semi-annually; Public transportation: monthly. See additional answers.

3. Create a year-long budget matrix to chart these expenses: Savings: $600 bimonthly (starting in January); Retirement account: $2,000 quarterly; Checking account: $1,000 semi-monthly; Credit card: $500 monthly; Life insurance: $400 semi-annually; Real estate taxes: $1,300 every four months beginning in April. See additional answers.

4. Use the pie chart of a monthly entertainment budget.
   a. Suppose $600 was budgeted. Determine the exact amount for each category. See margin.
   b. Suppose $72 was budgeted for day trips. What would be the total amount budgeted for entertainment? $720
   c. Suppose $310 was budgeted for the summer vacation fund. What would be the total amount budgeted for entertainment? $775

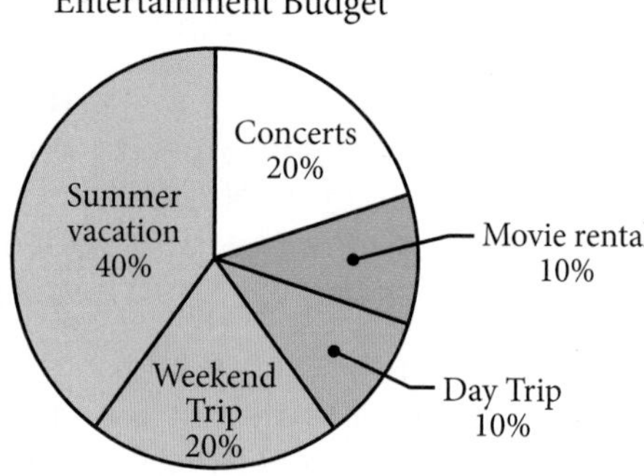

5. Use the pie chart of a person's monthly income.
   a. Suppose the total monthly income is $5,800. Determine the amounts in each income category. See margin.
   b. Suppose the income from the secondary job was $1,225. What would be the total monthly income? $4,900
   c. Suppose the income from interest was $315. What would be the income from the primary job? $3,780

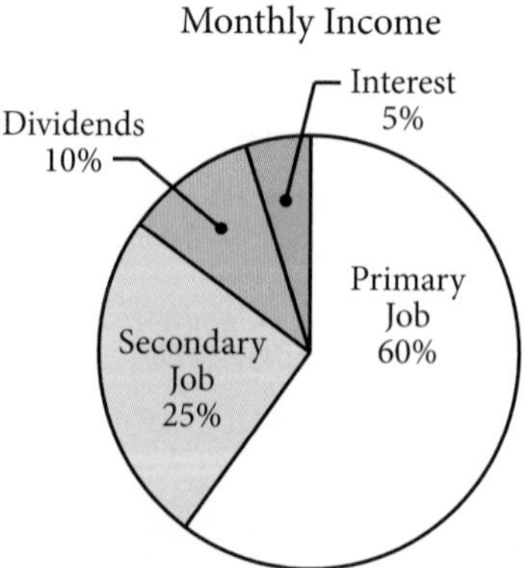

TEACH

Exercises 2 and 3
Have students use the sample matrices offered in the examples of this lesson as a guide for structuring the solutions to these two exercises.

Exercises 4
Remind students that the percentage not only gives the size of the central angle for the sector representing the category, it also is used to determine the actual portion of the total that is allocated to that category.

ANSWERS

1. It appears that the author of the quote is cautioning us all that it would be very difficult for a family to function financially if budget planning did not take place. He is trying to impress upon us the importance of such planning.

4a. Summer vacation: $240; Concerts: $120; Movies: $60; Day Trip: $60; Weekend Trip: $120

5a. Primary Job: $3,480; Secondary Job: $1,450; Dividends: $580; Interest: $290

6. Rachel's health-related budget is as follows: The percentage budgeted for health insurance is four times the percentage for health club dues. The percentage budgeted for prescriptions is equal to one-fourth the percentage budgeted for health insurance. The percentage budgeted for doctor visits is twice the percentage budgeted for prescriptions.

a. What is the percentage for health insurance? 50%

b. What are the percentages budgeted for all categories? See margin.

c. If $900 is budgeted for health-related expenses, how much is budgeted for health insurance? $450

7. Construct a pie chart that shows the following transportation-related expenses: Fuel: $240; Insurance: $80; Public transportation: $200; Parking garage: $120; Repairs: $160. See additional answers.

8. Examine the following bar graph that shows budgeted monthly utility expenses for a one-year period.

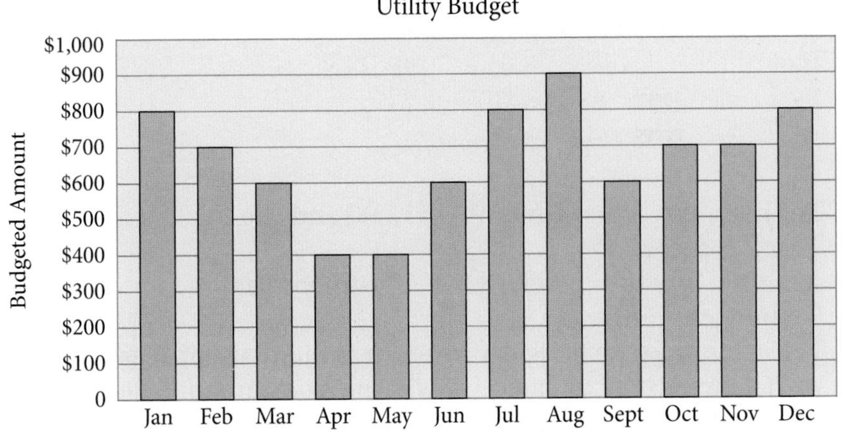

a. In which months was the same amount budgeted? See margin.

b. What is the total annual amount budgeted for utilities? $8,000

c. What percent of the total yearly amount was budgeted for the warm-weather months of June–September? 36.25%

d. Between which months was there a 100% increase in the amounts budgeted for utilities? April/May and Jan/July/Dec

e. At the end of December in the year shown, the homeowners replaced their furnace with a more energy-efficient one. They were told that they could decrease their utility budget for the upcoming month of January by 20% from the previous January amount. How much will they budget for utilities in January? $640

9. Construct a bar graph for Jason's transportation budget expenses.

400	550	400	650	400	350	200	300	450	500	650	500
Jan	Feb	Mar	Apr	May	June	July	Aug	Sept	Oct	Nov	Dec

See additional answers.

10. Construct a bar graph for the September budget category "Personal Items" using the following amounts: Haircut: $20, Clothing purchases: $60, Books: $20, Newspapers/Magazines: $65, Online subscriptions: $30, Gifts: $80, Donations $40, Other: $50.
See additional answers.

TEACH

Exercise 7
Students can either use a software program or construct the pie chart by hand (depending upon your preference). If you choose the latter, they will need protractors.

Exercise 9
Remind students that if they choose to begin the first vertical interval at 400, they must show a break in the vertical axis.

ANSWERS

6b. Health Insurance: 50%, Health Club Dues: 12.5%, Prescriptions: 12.5%, Doctor's Visits: 25%,

8a. Jan/July/Dec; Feb/Oct/Nov; Mar/June/Sept; April/May

TEACH

Exercise 11
Before assigning this exercise, ask students why a double bar graph is a better choice for this problem than using two separate bar graphs.

11. Aida created the following double bar graph. It illustrates the actual amount spent this year for household expenses per month and the budgeted amounts for the following year. The following year's amounts reflect a 5% increase over the cost of living adjustment (COLA).

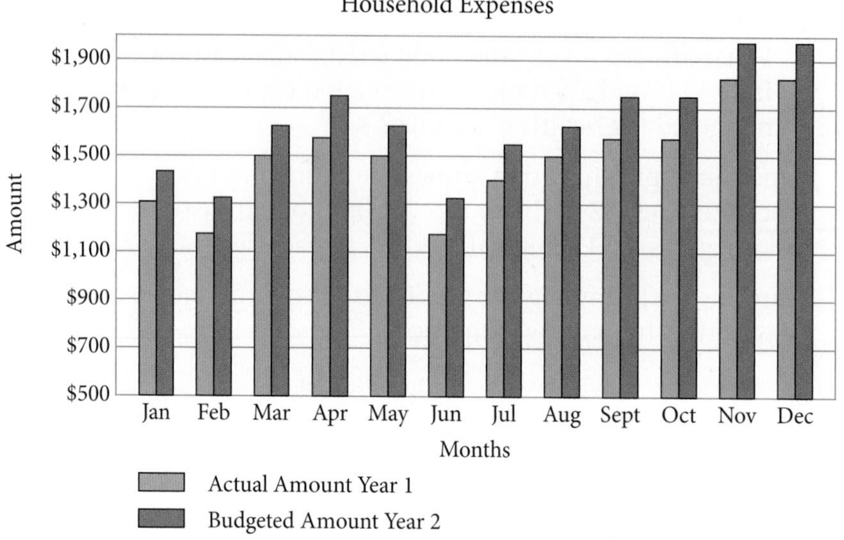

For June, the actual amount is $1,200 and the budgeted amount for Year 2 is $1,320.

a. What was the cost of living adjustment that Aida used to get the budgeted amount? 5%

b. Determine the budgeted amount for January of Year 2. $1,430

c. The August actual amount was the exact amount Aida had budgeted for. This actual amount reflected an 8% increase over the previous year's actual amount for August. What was the previous year's actual amount for August rounded to the nearest dollar? $1,389

12. Mark works at two jobs. His primary job is a commission-paid job. Therefore, his monthly income from this job varies. His secondary job has a fixed monthly income. His quarterly dividend checks and interest income have varied but not by a large amount. He used actual amounts from the previous year to set up this budget for the upcoming year.

	Jan	Feb	Mar	Apr	May	June	July	Aug	Sept	Oct	Nov	Dec
Primary Job	7,000	8,500	9,000	8,000	8,000	8,500	9,000	8,000	7,000	6,500	7,000	7,000
Secondary Job	2,000	2,000	2,000	2,000	2,000	2,000	2,000	2,000	2,000	2,000	2,000	2,000
Interest			380			390			400			410
Dividends			150			150			150			150
Other						3,000						3,000

a. What is his budgeted income for each month? See additional answers.

b. Construct a line graph to depict this budget. See additional answers.

c. Determine the average monthly income. Round your answer to the nearest dollar. $10,473

d. Draw a horizontal line on your graph representing that amount. What months fell below the average? See additional answers.

13. Rich budgets $2,500 in expenses for the month of January. He constructed the two graphs below.

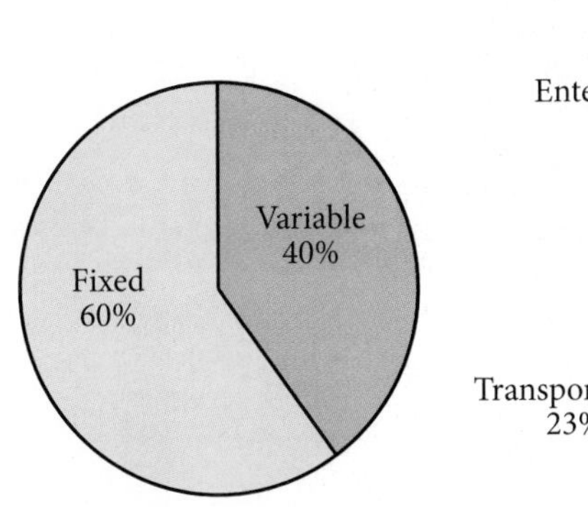

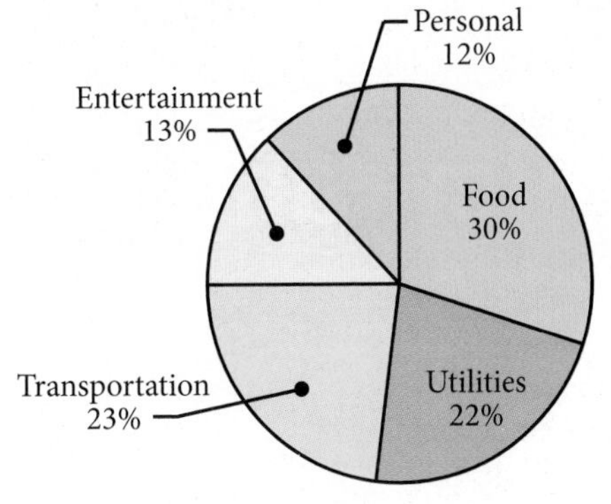

Using prior year's data and the budget he has created, he has budgeted the transportation category for the year as follows.

Jan	Feb	Mar	Apr	May	June	July	Aug	Sept	Oct	Nov	Dec
Use charts	+10%	+5%	+3%	+5%	+8%	+2%	−5%	−3%	+5%	+8%	+10%

Each of the monthly percentages is an increase or decrease from the January amount.

a. How much did Rich budget for fixed and variable expenses in January? fixed: $1,500; variable: $1,000

b. How much did he budget for transportation? $230

c. Determine the monthly budgeted amounts for transportation based upon your answer to part b. See additional answers.

d. Construct a line graph to chart the changes in Rich's transportation budget over time. See additional answers.

14. Under his household expense budget category, Mark has allocated $60 per month for pet food. He can purchase wet food in a can for $1.50 per can or dry food in a bag for $3 per bag.

a. Determine a budget line equation for this situation. $1.50x + 3y = 60$ or $3x + 1.50y = 60$

b. Graph the budget line that will depict the different combinations of cans and bags that Mark can purchase while still remaining within his budget. See additional answers.

c. Name a combination of bags and cans that will allow him to meet his budget exactly. any point on the line

d. Name a combination of bags and cans that will keep him under budget. any point below the line

e. Name a combination of bags and cans that will cause him to be over budget. any point above the line

15. A consumer budgets $480 per month for transportation. She has determined that the cost of a round-trip train ride is $4 and the cost of each round-trip car ride (factoring in gas, oil, etc.) is $3.

a. Write a budget line equation for this situation. $3x + 4y = 480$ or $4x + 3y = 480$

b. Construct the budget line graph that models this situation. See additional answers.

c. What do the points on the budget line represent? See margin.

d. What do points below the budget line represent? See margin.

e. Suppose that the budgeted amount increases to $516. Construct the new budget line and the old budget line on the same axes. See additional answers.

f. What does the region in between the two lines represent?
the gain in combinations of train/car rides that will stay within the budget

TEACH

Exercises 14 and 15
Be sure that students identify the variables before setting up the budget line equations.

ANSWERS

15c. combinations of car and train rides that stay exactly at the budgeted amount

15d. combinations of car and train rides that stay within the budgeted amount

> *Budget: a mathematical confirmation of your suspicions.*
>
> A. A. Latimer

10-4 Cash Flow and Budgeting

Objectives

- Develop and interpret a cash flow chart.
- Develop and interpret a frequency budget plan.
- Develop and interpret a year-long expense budget plan.

Common Core

A-SSE1, F-BF1

Key Terms

- cash flow analysis
- cash flow
- pro-rate
- envelope accounting system
- frequency budget plan
- year-long expense budget plan
- net worth
- assets
- liabilities
- debt reduction plan
- debt-to-income ratio

CCSS Warm-Up

Express algebraically:

"The average of x, y, and 2w is k more than 15."

$$\frac{x + y + 2w}{3} = k + 15$$

EXAMINE THE QUESTION

Before addressing the "how", ask students, "Why should you plan for expenses, reduce debt, and grow savings?" This will lead them to an acknowledgement of the need for a budget. With recognition of the need, the material offered in this lesson will have purpose.

What types of modifications might a person make to his/her lifestyle based upon a budget?

CLASS DISCUSSION

Ask students if they have any monthly expenses. Then have them explain how they plan to pay for those expenses each month.

Discuss saving money and ask students for what purposes they might be saving money. Stress the importance of looking to the future and foreseeing when and for what reasons they might need to have money in reserve.

How do you plan for expenses, reduce debt, and grow savings?

A budget is more than just a matrix of numbers that charts your income and expenditures. It is a well-thought-out plan that is the result of careful examination of your financial goals and obligations. Budgets allow you to plan for future spending and saving. They give you control over your financial situation and allow you to make financially sound modifications to your lifestyle based upon comparing what was planned and what actually occurred.

Budgets can also be motivators. You can celebrate when you accomplish your goals, and you can reflect and adjust when you find that you were not able to attain what you had planned for. A budget can be the product of both financial and nonfinancial goals. For example, you might have a goal of taking a vacation in the upcoming year, or eating healthier, or improving your public speaking. Each of these goals could contribute to the formation of your budget. Perhaps the most common financial goals that people make have to do with growing their savings and reducing their debt. Once you have selected your goals, it is then important to take a close look at your current income and spending habits. This is a **cash flow analysis**. A cash flow analysis is not a budget. It has nothing to do with a financial plan nor does it incorporate goals. Rather, it is a detailing of how money comes in and how money goes out over a fixed period of time. By carefully monitoring your **cash flow**, you can get a better sense of the possibility of meeting your goals.

There are many cash flow analyzers and budget planners on the Internet. You can find many sites with a variety of templates that you can adjust to meet your own specific needs. Cash flow analysis will help you determine whether or not you are "living within your means." If your monthly cash flow is a positive number, this implies that your income is more than what you spend. You can decide whether to carry the extra over to the following month, to increase your savings, or to increase the amount to pay off debt. If your monthly cash flow is negative, it means you are spending more money than you are making. You will have to readjust your plan so that you do not end up borrowing money at the end of each month.

Skills and Strategies

Here you will learn how to use cash flow analysis to set up a budget.

EXAMPLE 1

Dave and Joan want to chart their monthly cash flow. Create a spreadsheet that will help them keep track of their income and expenses for the month.

SOLUTION Dave and Joan should begin by collecting monthly amounts for the following categories.

- **Income** Make a list of all after-tax income. This includes primary and secondary jobs, unemployment benefits, Social Security, interest, dividends, child support, alimony, annuity income, gifts, etc.
- **Fixed Expenses** These expenses are the same from month to month. For example, mortgage/rent, loan payments, insurance premiums, and so on.
- **Variable Expenses** These expenses change each month. Your food and utility expenses are variable.
- **Savings** Financial advisors suggest that savings be considered a fixed expense.

The cash flow analysis spreadsheet shown on the next page asks the user to input after-tax income in cells B2–B4. Dave and Joan's combined after-tax income is $5,600 from their primary jobs. They both make extra money helping out at a family-owned business on Saturdays. That income is entered in cell B3. The total income is in cell B5.

© STEVECOLEIMAGES/VETTA COLLECTION/ISTOCKPHOTO.COM

TEACH

As a homework assignment, ask students to find a cash flow analysis website. Have them review what the site has to offer. On the following day, conduct a discussion of what they found on the various sites. Compare and contrast their findings.

EXAMPLE 1

The text offers a few examples of fixed and variable expenses. Ask students what those expenses might be for a college student.

Carefully review all of the component pieces in the spreadsheet (on the next page). Make sure students understand how the formulas are constructed and how each of the cells interacts.

	A	B	C	D	E
1	**Income**				
2	Primary Employment	5,600			
3	Secondary Employment	500			
4	Other Income				
5	**Total Income**	**6,100**			
6	**Fixed Expenses**			**Non-Monthly Expenses (per year)**	
7	Rent/Mortgage	2,400		Medical/Dental	600
8	Car Loan Payment	200		Auto Related	700
9	Education Loan Payment	150		Home Related	500
10	Personal Loan Payment	80		Life Insurance	600
11	Health Insurance Premium	50		Tuition	3,000
12	Life Insurance Premium			Vacation	1,200
13	Car Insurance Premium	60		Gifts	400
14	Homeowner's/Renter's Insurance	50		Contributions	400
15	Cable TV			Repairs	600
16	**Total Fixed Expenses**	**2,990**		Taxes	4,000
17				Other	
18	**Variable Expenses**			**Total Non-Monthly Expenses (per year)**	**12,000**
19	Groceries (Food)	800			
20	Dining Out	150		**Total Non-Monthly Expenses (per month)**	**1,000**
21	Fuel (Car)	160			
22	Cell Phone	120		**Total Expenses**	**5,990**
23	Land Line Phone			**Monthly Cash Flow**	**110**
24	Electricity	80			
25	Water	30			
26	Sewer				
27	Sanitation				
28	Medical				
29	Entertainment	200			
30	Savings	300			
31	Debt Reduction	160			
32	Other				
33	**Total Variable Expenses**	**2,000**			

The fixed and variable expenses categories are monthly bills. Notice that Dave and Joan left some of those cells empty. They only have cellular phones, and they do not pay any fees for sewer usage. Their life insurance, sanitation, and medical expenses are not billed monthly so those expenses are accounted for in another category.

Not all bills are monthly. Some, like insurance, tuition, vacation, medical/dental may be bimonthly, quarterly, semi-annually, or at varying intervals. It is still possible to prepare for those bills by examining their impact if spread evenly over the 12 months of the year.

The cash flow spreadsheet category Non-Monthly Expenses (per year) asks the user to input the accumulated yearly amount for any expense that does not occur on a monthly basis. For example, Dave and Joan pay their life insurance bill of $150 every three months. That is four times a year for a year-long total of $600. Six hundred dollars has been entered in cell E10.

The total year-long amount appears in cell E18. The cash flow spreadsheet divides that amount by 12, and enters the monthly amount in cell E20.

In order to be prepared for these non-monthly expenses, it is important to **pro-rate** them, that is, to divide them proportionately as if they were monthly expenses. Notice that Dave and Joan have a total of $12,000 in non-monthly expenses for the year. They need to account for $1,000 each month in order to be able to meet those expenses when the bills arrive. This monthly amount can be deposited into a special savings account and drawn upon when needed at various intervals in the year.

Cell D23 indicates that Dave and Joan have a positive cash flow of $110. They can carry that money over to the following month for emergency situations or they can choose to increase their savings or decrease their debt by that amount.

CHECK YOUR UNDERSTANDING

Suppose that the cash flow had been −$160. What advice might you give to Dave and Joan?

EXAMPLE 2

The Consumer Credit Counseling Service suggests that transportation expenses be between 6–20% of your budget and savings be between 5–9%. Using Dave and Joan's cash flow analysis, determine whether they remain within the guidelines for these categories.

SOLUTION Dave and Joan allocated $200 monthly for their car loan payment, $50 for their car insurance premium, and $160 for gasoline. They had $700 worth of auto-related expenses spread over the course of the year. Rounding up, this is approximately $59 per month. The total transportation expenses budgeted is $469. Since their total monthly income is $6,100, transportation accounts for approximately 7.7% (469 ÷ 6,100) of their budget. This is slightly over the suggested amount.

Their budgeted amount of $300 per month for savings is about 4.9% (300 ÷ 6,100) of their income, which is slightly lower than the suggested percentage.

CHECK YOUR UNDERSTANDING

Dave and Joan want to include a section in their cash flow spreadsheet that will calculate the monthly percentage allocated to certain categories suggested by the Consumer Credit Counseling Service. Write the spreadsheet formula that will calculate the transportation percentage for the month.

CHECK YOUR UNDERSTANDING

Answer Unless they borrow the $160, they will not be able to meet their financial responsibilities as outlined in the cash flow analysis. Dave and Joan should reconsider expendable expenses such as dining out and entertainment. If they can reduce that amount by $160, the money coming in and the money going out will break even.

EXAMPLE 2

This problem can also be solved by determining the suggested monetary interval first and then seeing if the allocated amount falls within that interval.

CHECK YOUR UNDERSTANDING

Answer =(((B8+B13+B21+E8)/12)/B5)*100

EXAMPLE 3

Students will need some guidance on the structure of this frequency budget plan. Ask them the following questions: What do the frequencies represent? What are the periodic names of these frequencies? How is the annual amount column calculated? What are "after tax" income categories? Why might someone wish to separate weekly from monthly expenses? Can you think of any other expenses that could be added to the list? How would you know if there was a surplus or a deficit?

CHECK YOUR UNDERSTANDING

Answer The cash flow of $110 per month approximately translates to an annual surplus of $1,284 (110 x 12 = 1,320).

Create, Use, and Modify a Budget

Once the cash flow analysis has been completed, it is time to convert what you have learned into a working budget. A budget is a personalized plan. A budget that works for one person may not work for another. A budget can be a simple system. The **envelope accounting system** is a way to manage your income with real dollars rather than with formulas and numbers in a matrix. Envelopes are set up to hold the allocated amount for weekly or monthly budget categories. Suppose you decide to budget $50 per week for dining out. This could include breakfast, lunch, dinner, or even snacks and coffee. Any time you pay for any item in this category, you take the money from the dining-out envelope. Once the money runs out, you have to wait until the next envelope allocation period comes around (usually on payday). If there is money remaining in the envelope at the end of a cycle, that money can be transferred to another envelope where funds are needed more. This system can work for people who have very few budgeting categories. College students might find this advantageous.

As financial responsibilities and expenses grow, so too does the sophistication of the budget. Examples 3 and 4 show two spreadsheet budgets using Dave and Joan's cash flow worksheet from Example 1. Example 3 shows a household budget in terms of the frequency that payments or credits are made over the course of a year, called a **frequency budget plan**. Example 4 shows a **year-long expense budget plan** in which entries are made under each of the months of the year.

Whichever budget structure you decide to use, it is important to review your budget periodically. Make alterations where necessary. Shift allocations to increase savings and reduce debt. Always pay your bills on time to avoid late charges. Keep accurate records. Set achievable goals and review them regularly.

EXAMPLE 3

Create a frequency budget plan for Dave and Joan using their cash flow analysis from Example 1.

SOLUTION On the next page is a frequency budget plan using the data from Dave and Joan's cash flow analysis. A budget need not be electronic. Everything a spreadsheet can be programmed to do can also be done by hand (with or without a calculator). The frequency budget shown is a template that can be filled in by hand. In the applications, you will be asked to convert it into a spreadsheet.

The frequency budget plan is built on the premise that most expenses and income deposits occur at predetermined intervals over the course of the year. Income and the frequency of that income are recorded at the top of the budget worksheet. The annual income is calculated by finding the product of the interval income and the frequency. The expenses are categorized by the frequency.

CHECK YOUR UNDERSTANDING

The frequency budget, shown on the facing page, states that Dave and Joan have an annual surplus of $1,284. How does this relate to the monthly positive cash flow that was computed in Example 1?

Frequency Budget Plan			
After-Tax Income Categories	**Income Amounts**	**Frequency**	**Annual Amount**
Primary Employment	2,800	24	67,200
Secondary Employment	500	12	6,000
Interest			
Dividends			
Other Income			
Total Income			73,200
Weekly Expenses	**Expense Amounts**		
Food	185	52	9,620
Personal Transportation	37	52	1,924
Public Transportation		52	0
Household		52	0
Childcare		52	0
Dining Out	35	52	1,820
Entertainment	46	52	2,392
Other		52	0
Total Weekly Expenses			15,756
Monthly Expenses			
Mortgage	2,400	12	28,800
Utilities	110	12	1,320
Land Line/Cellular Telephone	120	12	1,440
Car Loan	200	12	2,400
Education Loan	150	12	1,800
Personal Loan	80	12	960
Car Insurance	60	12	720
Homeowner's Insurance	50	12	600
Savings	300	12	3,600
Debt Reduction	160	12	1,920
Other	50	12	600
Total Monthly Expenses			44,160
Other Frequency Expenses			
Medical/Dental	600	1	600
Auto-Related	700	1	700
Home-Related	250	2	500
Life Insurance	150	4	600
Tuition	1,500	2	3,000
Vacation	1,200	1	1,200
Gifts	200	2	400
Contributions	400	1	400
Repairs	600	1	600
Taxes	2,000	2	4,000
Other			
Total Other Frequency Expenses			12,000
Total Expenses			71,916
Annual Surplus or Deficit			1,284

EXAMPLE 4

Again, the best way to explain this chart is through direct questioning, such as "Why do some months have more entries than others? How do those months influence Dave and Joan's plans for the year? If Dave and Joan find themselves with extra money at the end of the month, what suggestions might you have for them? Which entries are merely estimates and which are predetermined? How can the estimated categories be used to adjust the monthly amounts?"

CHECK YOUR UNDERSTANDING

Answer =sum(B8:B42); totals are: Jan 6,490; Feb 7,190; Mar 5,140; Apr 5,240; May 5,390; June 5,140; July 6,190; Aug 6,740; Sept 7,140; Oct 6,290; Nov 5,190; Dec 5,740

EXAMPLE 4

Construct a year-long expense budget spreadsheet using the cash flow data from Dave and Joan.

SOLUTION A year-long expense budget spreadsheet lays out the year's income and expenses by month. It gives the user a snapshot of financial expectations throughout the year. It can be modified as the year progresses.

The sample year-long budget shown on the next page is a month-by-month accounting of money coming in and money going out. It should be used in conjunction with a cash flow analysis. Every few months, the budget should be reevaluated and adjusted based upon any changes in the financial situation. Dave and Joan's year-long budget indicates that there are some months in which the expenses will be higher than others and they will have to plan accordingly.

CHECK YOUR UNDERSTANDING

Use the spreadsheet to create row 43 in which the totals for each month will be calculated. What formula would be used for January? What entries will appear for each of the months in this row if the same formula is applied to the remaining months?

	A	B	C	D	E	F	G	H	I	J	K	L	M
1	**Income**	Jan	Feb	Mar	Apr	May	Jun	Jul	Aug	Sep	Oct	Nov	Dec
2	Primary Employment	5,600	5,600	5,600	5,600	5,600	5,600	5,600	5,600	5,600	5,600	5,600	5,600
3	Secondary Employment	500	500	500	500	500	500	500	500	500	500	500	500
4	Other Income												
5	**Total Income**	6,100	6,100	6,100	6,100	6,100	6,100	6,100	6,100	6,100	6,100	6,100	6,100
6													
7	**Fixed Expenses**												
8	Rent/Mortgage	2,400	2,400	2,400	2,400	2,400	2,400	2,400	2,400	2,400	2,400	2,400	2,400
9	Car Loan Payment	200	200	200	200	200	200	200	200	200	200	200	200
10	Education Loan Payment	150	150	150	150	150	150	150	150	150	150	150	150
11	Personal Loan Payment	80	80	80	80	80	80	80	80	80	80	80	80
12	Health Insurance Premium	50	50	50	50	50	50	50	50	50	50	50	50
13	Life Insurance Premium												
14	Car Insurance Premium	60	60	60	60	60	60	60	60	60	60	60	60
15	Homeowner's Insurance	50	50	50	50	50	50	50	50	50	50	50	50
16	Cable TV												
17	Life Insurance			150			150			150			150
18	Tuition	1,500							1,500				
19	Taxes		2,000							2,000			
20													
21	**Variable Expenses**												
22	Groceries (Food)	800	800	800	800	800	800	800	800	800	800	800	800
23	Dining Out	150	150	150	150	150	150	150	150	150	150	150	150
24	Fuel (Car)	160	160	160	160	160	160	160	160	160	160	160	160
25	Cell Phone	120	120	120	120	120	120	120	120	120	120	120	120
26	Land Line Phone												
27	Electricity	80	80	80	80	80	80	80	80	80	80	80	80
28	Water	30	30	30	30	30	30	30	30	30	30	30	30
29	Sewer												
30	Sanitation												
31	Medical												
32	Medical/Dental												600
33	Auto-related										700		
34	Home-related				250				250				
35	Vacation							1,200					
36	Gifts		200									200	
37	Contributions					400							
38	Repairs										600		
39	Entertainment	200	200	200	200	200	200	200	200	200	200	200	200
40	Savings	300	300	300	300	300	300	300	300	300	300	300	300
41	Debt Reduction	160	160	160	160	160	160	160	160	160	160	160	160
42	Other												

EXAMPLE 5

Ask students to review Liam's assets. Can they think of any other assets that a person might add to this list? Why are the values of the computer and the guitar considered assets? Are there any other liabilities that a person might have that would add to this list? Students have already seen the term *net* (net proceeds, net pay). Ask them how the word net used in those contexts is similar to that used in the phrase net worth.

CHECK YOUR UNDERSTANDING

Answer Save more and pay down his debt.

Net Worth

Budgeting and cash flow help you understand how to manage your money so that there is a financially responsible balance between the money coming in and the money going out.

In addition to this type of planning, it is also a good idea to ask yourself the question "Where do I stand financially today?" To do so, you need to calculate your net worth. **Net worth** is the difference between your **assets** (what you own) and your **liabilities** (what you owe). The result can be a positive or a negative number.

You should calculate your net worth at regular intervals of perhaps once or twice a year, to determine if there have been changes in your financial status.

EXAMPLE 5

Liam Brown is single, in his mid-twenties, and owns a condo in a big city. He has calculated the following assets and liabilities.

Assets
Current value of condo: $580,000
Current value of car (as listed in Kelley Blue Book): $17,000
Balance in checking account: $980
Combined balance in all savings accounts: $22,500
Current balance in retirement account: $24,800
Current value of computer: $2,900
Current value of collector bass guitar: $6,700
Current value of stocks/bonds: $18,300

Liabilities
Remaining balance owed on home mortgage: $380,000
Remaining balance owed on student loans: $51,000
Combined credit card debt: $1,600

Calculate Liam's net worth. Last year at this time, he calculated his net worth as $205,780. Compare both values. What do the changes mean?

SOLUTION Net worth is the difference between assets and liabilities.

Find the sum of the assets.

580,000 + 17,000 + 980 + 22,500 + 24,800 + 2,900 + 6,700 + 18,300 = 673,180

Find the sum of the liabilities. 380,000 + 51,000 + 1,600 = 432,600

Find the difference. 673,180 − 432,600 = 240,580

Liam's current net worth is $240,580.

This is a $34,800 increase in net worth from the previous year. This increase represents an improving trend in Liam's financial well-being.

■ **CHECK YOUR UNDERSTANDING**

What can Liam do to continue his improving net worth trend?

Debt Reduction Planning

One of the most important things that Liam can do is to create a **debt reduction plan**. A thoughtful debt reduction plan requires an honest accounting of an individual's net worth as well as a calculation of a personal **debt-to-income ratio**. This ratio, expressed as a percent, offers some stark reality as to where you stand financially with the amount of debt presently being carried.

A ratio of 15% and under is recommended. A ratio of 20% and higher should alert you to the fact that you need to put a debt reduction and spending plan in place.

Debt reduction advice can be found in book, video, and online formats. It is often suggested that you can improve your debt-to-income ratio by setting up a debt reduction plan that contains some or all of the following.

- Lower debts that have the highest interest rates.
- Pay more than the minimum amount whenever possible.
- Look for ways to cut costs daily.
- Use an online debt management calculator.
- Face your debt. Make a list of what you owe and keep that handy to discourage you from incurring more debt.
- Slow down or eliminate your credit card spending.

After doing some research, you should develop a plan that is best for you and above all, do everything you can to stick with that plan.

EXAMPLE 6

Facing debt means taking personal stock in all that you owe in light of all of the income you have. In this example, Tome lists all of his current monthly debts and all of the monthly income that could be used to pay off that debt. Since a ratio is merely a comparison, the sum of his debts and the sum of his income amounts are compared in fraction form with debt in the numerator. That decimal is then converted to a percent. An amount over 15% signals that debt is over an acceptable limit in comparison to income.

CHECK YOUR UNDERSTANDING

Answer approximately 27.5%

EXAMPLE 6

Tome's monthly liabilities and assets are as shown in the table.

Monthly Liabilities (Debt)		Monthly Pre-Tax Assets (Income)	
Mortgage Payment	$2,300	Gross Salary	$7,800
Student Loan Payment	$ 750	Stock Dividends	$ 380
Minimum Credit Card Payment	$ 200	Interest	$ 120
Car Loan Payment	$ 150		

Find Tome's debt-to-income ratio. Express that ratio as a percent.

SOLUTION

Find the sum of Tome's assets. $7{,}800 + 380 + 120 = 8{,}300$

Find the sum of Tome's liabilities. $2{,}300 + 750 + 200 + 150 = 3{,}400$

$$\text{Debt-to-income ratio} = \frac{\text{Debt}}{\text{Pre-tax income}} = \frac{3{,}400}{8{,}300} \approx 0.405$$

Tome's debt-to-income ratio is approximately 40.5%, which is very high.

■ CHECK YOUR UNDERSTANDING

Tome anticipates that next year, his car and student loans will have been paid off and he will have received a 10% salary increase. If everything else remains the same, calculate that debt-to-income ratio.

Applications

Budget: a mathematical confirmation of your suspicions.
A. A. Latimer

ANSWERS

1. Many people avoid making a budget. They think that they know where their money is going but for a variety of reasons, never confront the realities of their finances. A budget is a mathematical financial reality. It puts numbers to paper and forces the user to make decisions based on facts, not on suspicions.
2. a. $785
   b. $150
   c. $260
   d. $117
   e. $83
   f. $135
   g. $55

3e. Removing the highest and lowest amounts from each data set made little change in the averages.

4d. Bob's net worth has shown an increase over this period of time. These numbers imply that he is managing his debt and/or increasing his savings with respect to his assets.

1. Explain how the quote can be interpreted in light of what you learned. See margin.

Use the table below for Exercises 2 and 3.

	July	Aug	Sept	Oct	Nov	Dec	Average
Groceries (Food)	740	800	650	820	820	880	a.
Dining Out	120	150	300	80	100	150	b.
Fuel (car)	200	240	320	300	280	220	c.
Cell Phone	104	108	126	140	120	104	d.
Land Line Phone	80	90	60	80	100	88	e.
Electricity	140	160	120	90	140	160	f.
Water	52	58	62	48	48	62	g.

2. The Larsons use the average of six months as their budget starting point in each category. Find each average. See margin.

3. The Larsons (from Exercise 2) decided they would not use the September amounts, when they were on vacation, nor the December amounts, when cousins stayed with them. Assume the chart is a spreadsheet with row 1 as the month labels and column A as the expense categories.

a. Write a spreadsheet formula to calculate the adjusted average for food. =(B2+C2+E2+F2)/4

b. What is the adjusted average for food? $795

c. Write a spreadsheet formula to calculate the adjusted average for electricity. =(B7+C7+E7+F7)/4

d. What is adjusted average for electricity? $132.50

e. Why do you think that the adjusted average is not that far off from the six-month average in each category? See margin.

Assets	
Current value of home	$422,000
Current value of car (*Kelley Blue Book*)	$22,000
Balance in checking account	$2,380
Balance of savings accounts	$140,500
Balance of retirement account	$250,000
Value of computer	$1,800
Value of stocks/bonds	$67,000
Liabilities	
Balance owed on home mortgage	$120,000
Balance owed on home equity loan	$21,000
Combined credit card debt	$940

4. Bob Forrester is retired and owns a home. He has these assets and liabilities.

a. Calculate Bob's net worth. $763,740

b. Two years ago, Bob's net worth was $650,000. Last year, his net worth as $740,500. What is the approximate percent of increase or decrease between two years ago and last year? an increase of approximately 14%

c. What is the approximate percent of increase or decrease between last year and this year? an increase of approximately 3.1%

d. Compare the values. What do the changes imply? See margin.

Use the budget information for Laura Shannon for Exercises 5–11.

Laura's Financial Report			
Income			
Teacher, monthly after-tax income: $5,000			
Tutor, monthly after-tax income: $1,200			
Monthly Expenses			
Rent	$2,200	Groceries	$600
Car loan	$180	Personal loan	$100
Electricity	$80	Land line phone	$60
Sanitation	$50	Auto insurance	$70
Cable/Internet	$40	Savings	$400
Dining out	$200	College loan	$250
Gasoline	$200	Cell phone	$80
Water	$40	Medical insurance	$60
Renter's insurance	$30	Entertainment	$250
Debt reduction	$200		
Non-Monthly Expenses			
Medical: $250 in April, $250 in September			
Auto-related: $400 in October			
Home-related: $250 in February, $250 in November			
Life insurance: $110 in April, August, December			
Tuition: $2,000 in May (summer) and August (fall)			
Vacation: $800 in July			
Gifts: $250 in March and December			
Contributions: $10 each week of the year			
Repairs: $280 in October			
Taxes: $1,500 in January and September			

5. The Consumer Credit Counseling Service suggests that the monthly food budget be between 15–30% of income.

  a. What is Laura's total monthly food bill including dining out? $800

  b. What percent of her income is spent on food? approximately 13%

  c. Is Laura below, in, or above the recommended interval? See margin.

6. Examine Laura's non-monthly expenses.

  a. Which month has the greatest expenses? August

  b. How might Laura prepare for those expenses? See margin.

7. Use a cash flow template to construct a cash flow plan for Laura. What is her monthly cash flow? See additional answers.

8. Create a frequency budget for Laura as on page 513. Although her food, fuel, dining out, and entertainment expenses were listed monthly for the cash flow, they should be considered weekly expenses here. Round the weekly amount up to the nearest dollar. Combine electricity, water, and sanitation under the utilities category. Any categories not mentioned belong in the other section. According to this frequency budget plan, what is Laura's surplus or deficit for the year? See additional answers.

9. Create a spreadsheet for the frequency budget in Exercise 8. See additional answers.

10. Create a year-long budget for Laura as on page 515. See additional answers.

11. Add row 43 to your matrix from Exercise 10. Calculate each month's total expenses.

  a. Draw a line graph to chart Laura's monthly budgeted expenses. Include horizontal lines to indicate the average monthly expense and the monthly income. See additional answers.

  b. What advice would you give to Laura based upon the graph you have constructed? See margin.

12. Marina's monthly liabilities and assets are as shown in the table.

  a. Find Marina's debt-to-income ratio. Express that ratio as a percent. approx. 28%

  b. How would you categorize her debt-to-income ratio? See margin.

Monthly Liabilities (Debt)		Monthly Pre-Tax Assets (Income)	
Rent	$1,400	Gross Salary	$8,900
Student Loan Payment	$ 350	Stock Dividends	$ 350
Minimum Credit Card Payment	$ 140	Interest	$ 190
Car Loan Payment	$ 130		
Graduate School Loan	$ 600		

ANSWERS

5c. She falls just below the interval.

6b. She could divide those expenses into equal portions to be put away during the months prior to when they are due.

11b. There will be months when she will have a surplus. She must save that money in order to pay the expenses during the months where those expenses are more than her monthly income.

12b. Marina should develop a debt reduction plan.

CHAPTER

10 Assessment

Real Numbers

You Write the Story!!

CHAPTER 10 ASSESSMENT

REAL NUMBERS

You Write the Story

Before assigning this activity, review the structure of this type of bar graph with students. They may not be familiar with the interpretation of downward bars.

REALITY CHECK

Reality Check projects are a terrific form of alternative assessment. They give students an additional avenue to show what they've learned, so their grades are not solely-based on tests.

Projects can be presented to the class on any schedule that works for your program. It may be too time-consuming for every student to present their project for every chapter.

Write a short newspaper-type article centered on this graph. You can find an electronic copy at www.cengage.com/school/math/financialalgebra. Copy it, and paste it into your article. The graph shows a comparison of consumer disposable income and consumer spending over a four-month period. Disposable income is the amount of money left that a consumer has to spend and save after taxes have been paid on the original amount. Consumer spending is the amount of money a consumer spends on goods and services.

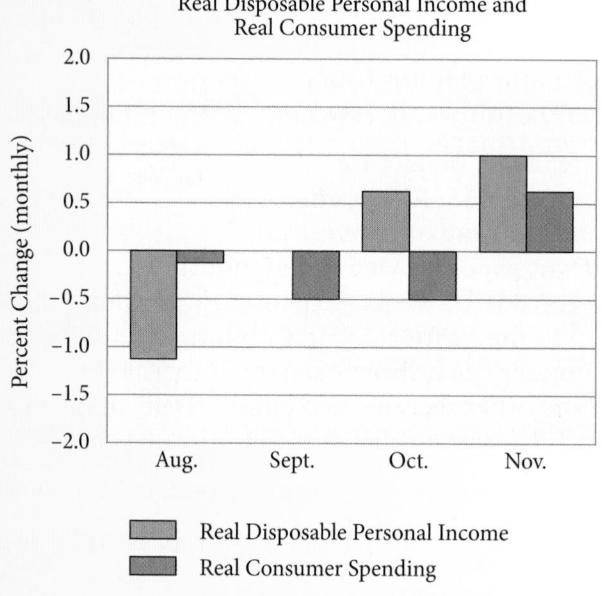

Reality Check

1. Contact your local natural gas, water, and electric companies. Find out information on their rates and how they are computed. Get pictures of their meters. Get information on how their bills are organized. Prepare your information on a poster for presentation to your class.
2. Take a look at your cell phone bill. It's probably several pages long. Make a detailed analysis of it. List each type of charge that appears on the bill. If there is a charge you do not understand, contact the company to have it explained. List the mode number—the number you called or texted the most—and its frequency. Find the mean length of a phone call. Prepare your information in a report.
3. Look over your cell phone bill carefully. List the charges that appear on your bill. Research other cell phone service providers. Choose one of

these providers. Compare your cell phone plan features and charges to the other plan you picked. Prepare your information in a report.

4. Talk to your parents about looking at your family's cable TV, Internet provider, and home phone bills. Find the average total monthly cost for these three items for as many months as you can locate the bills for. Research other available plans on the Internet and compare them to your monthly costs. Discuss with your parents if money can be saved by switching to another plan. Prepare your information in a report.

5. Select a group of students you would like to study. Have each person find out the number of cell phone calls they sent and received last month. Have them report the number of text messages sent and received. Record this data carefully. Find the mean and the median of each type of data. Draw a box and whisker plot for each type of data. Prepare the information you found on a poster.

6. Visit a supermarket and compare nationally advertised items to store-brand items. First, create a list of goods your family usually buys each week. Use only pre-packaged items, such as items in boxes and cans. Choose 30 items and enter them in a spreadsheet. Include the name, brand, and size. Take your list to a local supermarket. Copy the price of each item on your list. As you find the price of each item, look for the store-brand equivalent of the same item in the same size, and copy its price down. Find the total weekly cost of buying your 30 items as national brands and as store brands. Compute the annual savings if the 30 items are bought as store brands instead of national brands.

7. People protect themselves against loss, fire, and theft with insurance policies. Some buy homeowner's insurance, some buy renter's insurance, and some purchase floater policies for items that leave their homes, such as jewelry, cameras, laptops, and musical instruments. You need to talk to your parents. You are going to take a picture of valuable items in your home. You can attach a receipt if you have one for the item, or just list an appraised value. List each item, when it was purchased, its model number, serial number, and value. Print out the pages and staple them together into a book. The completed book should be placed in a safe-deposit box in a bank. If you are ever the victim of loss, fire, or theft, the book will be very helpful to the insurance company. Have your parents write a note to your teacher when the project is completed.

8. For this project you are going to visit two supermarkets and compare nationally advertised items from both stores. First, create a list of 30 items and enter them in a spreadsheet. Include the name, brand, and size. Take your list to two local supermarkets. Copy the price of each item on your list. Find the total weekly cost of buying your 30 items in each store. Compute the annual savings if the 30 items are bought at the store with the lowest prices.

9. Certain expenses are not periodic; they only happen occasionally. One of these expenses is a wedding. A wedding must be carefully planned and budgeted for. Visit several places to find out the cost of a wedding and a honeymoon trip. Include a catering hall, photographer, music agency, florist, and travel agent. Prepare your information in a scrapbook. Include estimates, photos, sample items, brochures, business cards, and anything else you acquire. Summarize the total cost in an itemized list.

REALITY CHECK

Remind students who are personally visiting local businesses or community members that they are representing the school, and need to be cordial and patient. These projects deliberately have students taking little field trips, so they don't conduct everything online.

Point out that they need to thank any person who helps them in completing their Reality Check projects. A letter is the most personal way to do this.

You can offer students extra projects for extra credit.

In this Reality Check, students will be extending their knowledge about utility rates, performing action research using real cell phone usage data, taking a trip to a supermarket, planning for a wedding, and using cash flow analysis to track their own spending habits.

REALLY? REALLY! REVISITED

Have students read this feature in its entirety before attempting the solutions. Ask them to take a guess at the answer to Exercise 5 and write that guess down. Then, have them work through the exercises and finally compare their guess with the answer that was arrived at by using the exponential equation. How close or far off were their guesses?

10. You might have never thought how much it costs to raise a child. Think of the clothing, food, and many other costs involved! For this project, you are going to concentrate on just the cost of having a baby. Go to a local hospital, explain the project, make an appointment to talk to someone in their billing department. Before the interview, list some questions you and your classmates have. Prepare the information you find in a report.

11. Use the cash flow and budget spreadsheets from Lesson 10-4 to track your spending and saving for a one-month period. Adjust the budget categories so that they pertain to your lifestyle. Analyze the data. How can you increase your savings each month?

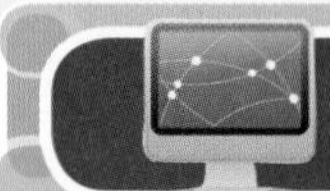

Dollars and Sense — Your Financial News Update

Go to www.cengage.com/school/math/financialalgebra where you will find a link to a website containing current issues about preparing a budget. Try one of the activities.

Really? Really! REVISITED

The facts about United States money represent a colorful part of our country's history. You can see paper currency manufactured at the Bureau of Engraving and Printing in Washington, DC. You can learn about the artwork on our currency from library books and Internet searches.

As an adult keeping a budget, you will always be asking yourself, "How far will my money go?" In this activity, you will take a literal look at how far those dollar bills can take you!

1. The sun is approximately 93 million miles from the Earth. Use your calculator to figure out how many inches away the sun is from the Earth. Your answer will be shown in scientific notation. Keep all the digits from your calculator display and convert from scientific notation to standard notation. 5,892,480,000,000

2. The thickness of a dollar bill is approximately 0.0043 in. If you folded the bill once, how thick would the folded bill be? 0.0086 in.

3. If you folded it a second time, how thick would the folded bill be? 0.0172 in.

4. If you folded it a third time, how thick would the folded bill be? 0.0344 in.

5. Notice that you are doubling the thickness each time you fold. You are building an exponential function for the thickness $t(x)$ after x folds, which is $t(x) = 0.0043(2^x)$.

Experiment with different values for x, and your answer to Exercise 1. How many folds will it take for the thickness of the folded bill to reach from the Earth to the sun? approximately 50

Applications

1. Jessica pays health, car, home, and life insurance over the course of a year. The chart below indicates her monthly insurance budget expenses. Create a bar graph to chart these expenses. See additional answers.

Jan	Feb	Mar	Apr	May	Jun	Jul	Aug	Sep	Oct	Nov	Dec
0	250	200	300	200	600	200	300	300	0	200	600

2. The Kings Park Water Works uses water meters that measure water usage in ccf. They charge $0.18 per ccf of water. If Jack's previous meter reading was 34,765 ccf and his present water reading is 36,900 ccf, what was his water bill for the service period? $384.30

3. Marissa's Beauty Salon has six hairdryers that each require 500 watts when switched on. How much would it cost to run all six dryers for seven hours, at a cost of $0.15 per kWh? $3.15

4. Leonard works as a waiter in an upscale city restaurant. He makes a very good salary plus tips. His monthly income varies based upon the nights he works. His quarterly dividend checks and interest income have varied but not by a large amount. He used actual amounts from the previous year to set up this budget for the upcoming year.

	Jan	Feb	Mar	Apr	May	Jun	Jul	Aug	Sep	Oct	Nov	Dec
Primary Job	4,500	5,000	3,500	4,500	4,000	6,000	7,000	6,000	5,000	4,500	5,000	5,500
Interest			450			500			510			540
Dividends			200			200			200			200

a. What is his budgeted income for each month? See additional answers.
b. Construct a line graph to depict this budget. See additional answers.
c. Determine the average monthly income. Round your answer to the nearest dollar. $5,275
d. Draw a horizontal line on your graph representing that amount. What percentage of the months fall above the average? approximately 42%

5. Last year, the Montvilo family spent $1,988.40 for electricity. They are opting to use balanced billing for next year. What will their monthly payment be under balanced billing? $165.70

6. The pie chart shows a monthly utility budget.
a. Suppose that $800 was budgeted for the month. Determine the exact amount for each category. See margin.
b. Suppose that $117 was budgeted for water. What would be the amount budgeted for cell phones? $180
c. Suppose that $204 was budgeted for gas. What would be the total amount budgeted for utilities? $1,200

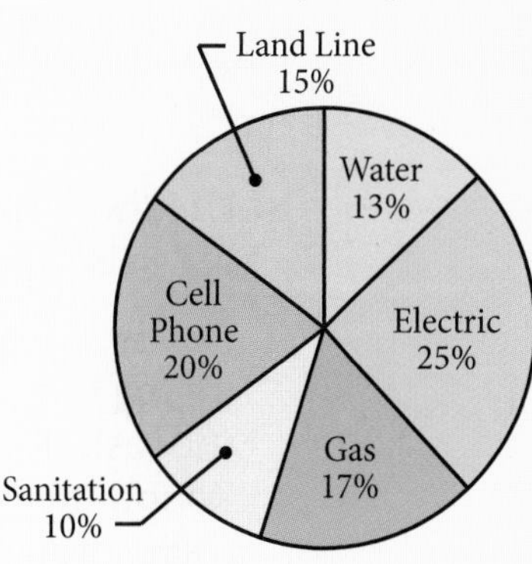

ANSWERS

6a. Land Line: $120, Cell: $160, Sanitation: $80, Gas: $136, Electric: $200, Water: $104

ANSWERS

7d. Any point that is both below the budget line and below the days line.

7. Under her Dinner budget category, Diane allocated $600 per month for eating in and dining out. She figures that eating in will cost her approximately $8 and dining out will cost her approximately $24. Let x represent the number of dinners eaten in, and y represent the number of dinners eaten out.
   - **a.** Determine a budget line equation for this situation. $8x + 24y = 600$
   - **b.** In a typical 30-day month, the sum of the dinners eaten in and out must be less than or equal to 30. Write the budget equation for the exact number of dinners for the month. $x + y = 30$
   - **c.** Graph the budget line and the equation from part b on the same axes. See additional answers.
   - **d.** Based on the graph, name a combination of dinners eaten in and out that will allow her to be within her Dinner budget. See margin.
   - **e.** Name a combination of dinners that will cause her to be over budget. any point above the budget line and/or above the days line

Use the budget information for Nelson Shapiro for Exercises 8 and 9.

Nelson's Financial Report

Income

Musician, monthly after-tax income: $7,000
Music lessons, monthly after-tax income: $1,000

Monthly Expenses

Mortgage	$2,800	Groceries	$500
Car loan	$200	Personal loan	$100
Electricity	$90	Land line phone	$50
Sanitation	$60	Auto insurance	$90
Cable/Internet	$50	Savings	$500
Dining out	$200	College loan	$200
Gasoline	$300	Cell phone	$100
Water	$50	Medical insurance	$80
Home insurance	$120	Entertainment	$350
Debt reduction	$200		

Non-Monthly Expenses

Medical: $350 in March, $350 in August
Auto-related: $600 in November
Home-related: $250 in February, $250 in November
Life insurance: $120 in April, August, December
Vacation: $1,800 in July
Gifts: $300 in May and December
Contributions: $40 each week of the year
Repairs: $600 in July
Taxes: $2,500 in January and September

8. Use the cash flow template on page 504 to construct a cash flow plan for Nelson. What is his monthly cash flow? $940

9. Create a frequency budget plan for Nelson. Although his food, fuel, dining out, and entertainment expenses were listed as monthly for the cash flow, they should be considered as weekly expenses here. Round the weekly amount up to the nearest dollar. Combine electricity, water, and sanitation under the utilities category. Any categories not mentioned in the template belong in the appropriate other section. According to this frequency budget plan, what is Nelson's surplus or deficit for the year? See additional answers.

10. The Seinfeld family pays m dollars per month for electricity under balanced billing. At the end of the year, they had used less electricity than the balanced billing covered, and the utility company owed them a credit of c dollars. Express their total electricity expenses for the year algebraically. $12m - c$

11. A pay phone at a railroad station charges \$0.55 for the first five minutes (or part of) and \$0.25 for each extra minute (or part of). Express the cost $c(m)$ of an m-minute phone call as a piecewise function using the greatest integer function. See margin.

12. Phone-Phriends charges \$37 for a text-message plan with 400 text messages included. If the customer goes over the 400 messages, the cost is \$0.12 per text message. They have an unlimited plan which costs \$49 per month.
   - **a.** If x represents the number of text messages, and $c(x)$ represents the cost of the messages, express $c(x)$ as a piecewise function in terms of x. See margin.
   - **b.** Graph the function from part a. See margin.

13. A local cable TV/Internet/phone provider charges new customers \$90 for all three services, per month, for the first year under their 90 NOW promotion. Alice normally pays \$59 for her monthly home phone service, \$29 for Internet service, and \$69 for cable television.
   - **a.** What are her percent savings if she switches to the 90 NOW plan? Round to the nearest percent. 43%
   - **b.** Craig usually pays x dollars for phone service, half of that for Internet service, and twice that for cable TV service monthly. Represent his annual cost for these services algebraically. $42x$

14. The information below is entered in a spreadsheet. Write a spreadsheet formula that will calculate the net worth. =(sum(B2:B8)–sum(D2:D4))

Assets	
Current value of home	B2
Current value of car (*Kelley Blue Book*)	B3
Balance in checking account	B4
Balance of savings accounts	B5
Balance of retirement account	B6
Value of computer	B7
Value of stocks/bonds	B8
Liabilities	
Balance owed on home mortgage	D2
Balance owed on home equity loan	D3
Combined credit card debt	D4

15. Abram's monthly liabilities equal \$2,400 and his monthly assets are \$6,800. What is his debt-to-income ratio, expressed as a percent? 35%

16. Kalani has these monthly liabilities: rent \$879, car payment \$315, credit card payment \$102. She has an annual income of \$96,448. What is her debt-to-income ratio, expressed as a percent? 16%

17. What is the debt-to-income ratio for a person who has monthly liabilities equal to x dollars and an annual income equal to y dollars? $\frac{x}{\frac{y}{12}}$

ANSWERS

11.

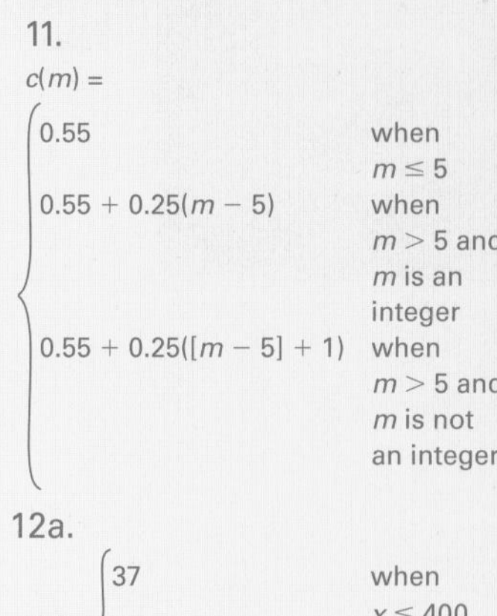

c(m) =
0.55 when m ≤ 5
0.55 + 0.25(m − 5) when m > 5 and m is an integer
0.55 + 0.25([m − 5] + 1) when m > 5 and m is not an integer

12a.

$$c(x) = \begin{cases} 37 & \text{when } x \le 400 \\ 37 + 0.12(x - 400) & \text{when } x > 400 \end{cases}$$

12b.

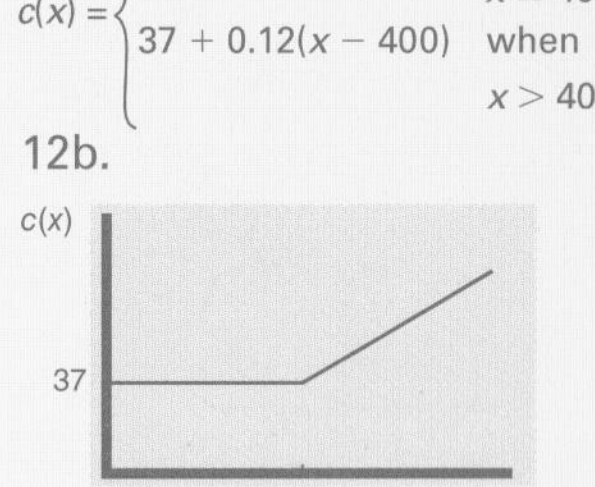

SAMPLE TAX TABLE

Sample Tax Table

See the instructions for line 44 that begin on page 36 to see if you must use the Tax Table below to figure your tax.

Example. Mr. and Mrs. Brown are filing a joint return. Their taxable income on Form 1040, line 43, is $25,300. First, they find the $25,300–25,350 taxable income line. Next, they find the column for married filing jointly and read down the column. The amount shown where the taxable income line and filing status column meet is $2,996. This is the tax amount they should enter on Form 1040, line 44.

Sample Table

At least	But less than	Single	Married filing jointly *	Married filing sepa-rately	Head of a house-hold
		Your tax is—			
25,200	**25,250**	3,383	2,981	3,383	3,211
25,250	**25,300**	3,390	2,989	3,390	3,219
25,300	**25,350**	3,398	(2,996)	3,398	3,226
25,350	**25,400**	3,405	3,004	3,405	3,234

If line 43 (taxable income) is—		And you are—			
At least	But less than	Single	Married filing jointly *	Married filing sepa-rately	Head of a house-hold
		Your tax is—			
0	**5**	0	0	0	0
5	**15**	1	1	1	1
15	**25**	2	2	2	2
25	**50**	4	4	4	4
50	**75**	6	6	6	6
75	**100**	9	9	9	9
100	**125**	11	11	11	11
125	**150**	14	14	14	14
150	**175**	16	16	16	16
175	**200**	19	19	19	19
200	**225**	21	21	21	21
225	**250**	24	24	24	24
250	**275**	26	26	26	26
275	**300**	29	29	29	29
300	**325**	31	31	31	31
325	**350**	34	34	34	34
350	**375**	36	36	36	36
375	**400**	39	39	39	39
400	**425**	41	41	41	41
425	**450**	44	44	44	44
450	**475**	46	46	46	46
475	**500**	49	49	49	49
500	**525**	51	51	51	51
525	**550**	54	54	54	54
550	**575**	56	56	56	56
575	**600**	59	59	59	59
600	**625**	61	61	61	61
625	**650**	64	64	64	64
650	**675**	66	66	66	66
675	**700**	69	69	69	69
700	**725**	71	71	71	71
725	**750**	74	74	74	74
750	**775**	76	76	76	76
775	**800**	79	79	79	79
800	**825**	81	81	81	81
825	**850**	84	84	84	84
850	**875**	86	86	86	86
875	**900**	89	89	89	89
900	**925**	91	91	91	91
925	**950**	94	94	94	94
950	**975**	96	96	96	96
975	**1,000**	99	99	99	99
1,000					
1,000	**1,025**	101	101	101	101
1,025	**1,050**	104	104	104	104
1,050	**1,075**	106	106	106	106
1,075	**1,100**	109	109	109	109
1,100	**1,125**	111	111	111	111
1,125	**1,150**	114	114	114	114
1,150	**1,175**	116	116	116	116
1,175	**1,200**	119	119	119	119
1,200	**1,225**	121	121	121	121
1,225	**1,250**	124	124	124	124
1,250	**1,275**	126	126	126	126
1,275	**1,300**	129	129	129	129

If line 43 (taxable income) is—		And you are—			
At least	But less than	Single	Married filing jointly *	Married filing sepa-rately	Head of a house-hold
		Your tax is—			
1,300	**1,325**	131	131	131	131
1,325	**1,350**	134	134	134	134
1,350	**1,375**	136	136	136	136
1,375	**1,400**	139	139	139	139
1,400	**1,425**	141	141	141	141
1,425	**1,450**	144	144	144	144
1,450	**1,475**	146	146	146	146
1,475	**1,500**	149	149	149	149
1,500	**1,525**	151	151	151	151
1,525	**1,550**	154	154	154	154
1,550	**1,575**	156	156	156	156
1,575	**1,600**	159	159	159	159
1,600	**1,625**	161	161	161	161
1,625	**1,650**	164	164	164	164
1,650	**1,675**	166	166	166	166
1,675	**1,700**	169	169	169	169
1,700	**1,725**	171	171	171	171
1,725	**1,750**	174	174	174	174
1,750	**1,775**	176	176	176	176
1,775	**1,800**	179	179	179	179
1,800	**1,825**	181	181	181	181
1,825	**1,850**	184	184	184	184
1,850	**1,875**	186	186	186	186
1,875	**1,900**	189	189	189	189
1,900	**1,925**	191	191	191	191
1,925	**1,950**	194	194	194	194
1,950	**1,975**	196	196	196	196
1,975	**2,000**	199	199	199	199
2,000					
2,000	**2,025**	201	201	201	201
2,025	**2,050**	204	204	204	204
2,050	**2,075**	206	206	206	206
2,075	**2,100**	209	209	209	209
2,100	**2,125**	211	211	211	211
2,125	**2,150**	214	214	214	214
2,150	**2,175**	216	216	216	216
2,175	**2,200**	219	219	219	219
2,200	**2,225**	221	221	221	221
2,225	**2,250**	224	224	224	224
2,250	**2,275**	226	226	226	226
2,275	**2,300**	229	229	229	229
2,300	**2,325**	231	231	231	231
2,325	**2,350**	234	234	234	234
2,350	**2,375**	236	236	236	236
2,375	**2,400**	239	239	239	239
2,400	**2,425**	241	241	241	241
2,425	**2,450**	244	244	244	244
2,450	**2,475**	246	246	246	246
2,475	**2,500**	249	249	249	249
2,500	**2,525**	251	251	251	251
2,525	**2,550**	254	254	254	254
2,550	**2,575**	256	256	256	256
2,575	**2,600**	259	259	259	259
2,600	**2,625**	261	261	261	261
2,625	**2,650**	264	264	264	264
2,650	**2,675**	266	266	266	266
2,675	**2,700**	269	269	269	269

If line 43 (taxable income) is—		And you are—			
At least	But less than	Single	Married filing jointly *	Married filing sepa-rately	Head of a house-hold
		Your tax is—			
2,700	**2,725**	271	271	271	271
2,725	**2,750**	274	274	274	274
2,750	**2,775**	276	276	276	276
2,775	**2,800**	279	279	279	279
2,800	**2,825**	281	281	281	281
2,825	**2,850**	284	284	284	284
2,850	**2,875**	286	286	286	286
2,875	**2,900**	289	289	289	289
2,900	**2,925**	291	291	291	291
2,925	**2,950**	294	294	294	294
2,950	**2,975**	296	296	296	296
2,975	**3,000**	299	299	299	299
3,000					
3,000	**3,050**	303	303	303	303
3,050	**3,100**	308	308	308	308
3,100	**3,150**	313	313	313	313
3,150	**3,200**	318	318	318	318
3,200	**3,250**	323	323	323	323
3,250	**3,300**	328	328	328	328
3,300	**3,350**	333	333	333	333
3,350	**3,400**	338	338	338	338
3,400	**3,450**	343	343	343	343
3,450	**3,500**	348	348	348	348
3,500	**3,550**	353	353	353	353
3,550	**3,600**	358	358	358	358
3,600	**3,650**	363	363	363	363
3,650	**3,700**	368	368	368	368
3,700	**3,750**	373	373	373	373
3,750	**3,800**	378	378	378	378
3,800	**3,850**	383	383	383	383
3,850	**3,900**	388	388	388	388
3,900	**3,950**	393	393	393	393
3,950	**4,000**	398	398	398	398
4,000					
4,000	**4,050**	403	403	403	403
4,050	**4,100**	408	408	408	408
4,100	**4,150**	413	413	413	413
4,150	**4,200**	418	418	418	418
4,200	**4,250**	423	423	423	423
4,250	**4,300**	428	428	428	428
4,300	**4,350**	433	433	433	433
4,350	**4,400**	438	438	438	438
4,400	**4,450**	443	443	443	443
4,450	**4,500**	448	448	448	448
4,500	**4,550**	453	453	453	453
4,550	**4,600**	458	458	458	458
4,600	**4,650**	463	463	463	463
4,650	**4,700**	468	468	468	468
4,700	**4,750**	473	473	473	473
4,750	**4,800**	478	478	478	478
4,800	**4,850**	483	483	483	483
4,850	**4,900**	488	488	488	488
4,900	**4,950**	493	493	493	493
4,950	**5,000**	498	498	498	498

* This column must also be used by a qualifying widow(er).

If line 43 (taxable income) is—		And you are—			
At least	But less than	Single	Married filing jointly *	Married filing separately	Head of a household
		Your tax is—			
5,000					
5,000	**5,050**	503	503	503	503
5,050	**5,100**	508	508	508	508
5,100	**5,150**	513	513	513	513
5,150	**5,200**	518	518	518	518
5,200	**5,250**	523	523	523	523
5,250	**5,300**	528	528	528	528
5,300	**5,350**	533	533	533	533
5,350	**5,400**	538	538	538	538
5,400	**5,450**	543	543	543	543
5,450	**5,500**	548	548	548	548
5,500	**5,550**	553	553	553	553
5,550	**5,600**	558	558	558	558
5,600	**5,650**	563	563	563	563
5,650	**5,700**	568	568	568	568
5,700	**5,750**	573	573	573	573
5,750	**5,800**	578	578	578	578
5,800	**5,850**	583	583	583	583
5,850	**5,900**	588	588	588	588
5,900	**5,950**	593	593	593	593
5,950	**6,000**	598	598	598	598
6,000					
6,000	**6,050**	603	603	603	603
6,050	**6,100**	608	608	608	608
6,100	**6,150**	613	613	613	613
6,150	**6,200**	618	618	618	618
6,200	**6,250**	623	623	623	623
6,250	**6,300**	628	628	628	628
6,300	**6,350**	633	633	633	633
6,350	**6,400**	638	638	638	638
6,400	**6,450**	643	643	643	643
6,450	**6,500**	648	648	648	648
6,500	**6,550**	653	653	653	653
6,550	**6,600**	658	658	658	658
6,600	**6,650**	663	663	663	663
6,650	**6,700**	668	668	668	668
6,700	**6,750**	673	673	673	673
6,750	**6,800**	678	678	678	678
6,800	**6,850**	683	683	683	683
6,850	**6,900**	688	688	688	688
6,900	**6,950**	693	693	693	693
6,950	**7,000**	698	698	698	698
7,000					
7,000	**7,050**	703	703	703	703
7,050	**7,100**	708	708	708	708
7,100	**7,150**	713	713	713	713
7,150	**7,200**	718	718	718	718
7,200	**7,250**	723	723	723	723
7,250	**7,300**	728	728	728	728
7,300	**7,350**	733	733	733	733
7,350	**7,400**	738	738	738	738
7,400	**7,450**	743	743	743	743
7,450	**7,500**	748	748	748	748
7,500	**7,550**	753	753	753	753
7,550	**7,600**	758	758	758	758
7,600	**7,650**	763	763	763	763
7,650	**7,700**	768	768	768	768
7,700	**7,750**	773	773	773	773
7,750	**7,800**	778	778	778	778
7,800	**7,850**	783	783	783	783
7,850	**7,900**	788	788	788	788
7,900	**7,950**	793	793	793	793
7,950	**8,000**	798	798	798	798

If line 43 (taxable income) is—		And you are—			
At least	But less than	Single	Married filing jointly *	Married filing separately	Head of a household
		Your tax is—			
8,000					
8,000	**8,050**	803	803	803	803
8,050	**8,100**	810	808	810	808
8,100	**8,150**	818	813	818	813
8,150	**8,200**	825	818	825	818
8,200	**8,250**	833	823	833	823
8,250	**8,300**	840	828	840	828
8,300	**8,350**	848	833	848	833
8,350	**8,400**	855	838	855	838
8,400	**8,450**	863	843	863	843
8,450	**8,500**	870	848	870	848
8,500	**8,550**	878	853	878	853
8,550	**8,600**	885	858	885	858
8,600	**8,650**	893	863	893	863
8,650	**8,700**	900	868	900	868
8,700	**8,750**	908	873	908	873
8,750	**8,800**	915	878	915	878
8,800	**8,850**	923	883	923	883
8,850	**8,900**	930	888	930	888
8,900	**8,950**	938	893	938	893
8,950	**9,000**	945	898	945	898
9,000					
9,000	**9,050**	953	903	953	903
9,050	**9,100**	960	908	960	908
9,100	**9,150**	968	913	968	913
9,150	**9,200**	975	918	975	918
9,200	**9,250**	983	923	983	923
9,250	**9,300**	990	928	990	928
9,300	**9,350**	998	933	998	933
9,350	**9,400**	1,005	938	1,005	938
9,400	**9,450**	1,013	943	1,013	943
9,450	**9,500**	1,020	948	1,020	948
9,500	**9,550**	1,028	953	1,028	953
9,550	**9,600**	1,035	958	1,035	958
9,600	**9,650**	1,043	963	1,043	963
9,650	**9,700**	1,050	968	1,050	968
9,700	**9,750**	1,058	973	1,058	973
9,750	**9,800**	1,065	978	1,065	978
9,800	**9,850**	1,073	983	1,073	983
9,850	**9,900**	1,080	988	1,080	988
9,900	**9,950**	1,088	993	1,088	993
9,950	**10,000**	1,095	998	1,095	998
10,000					
10,000	**10,050**	1,103	1,003	1,103	1,003
10,050	**10,100**	1,110	1,008	1,110	1,008
10,100	**10,150**	1,118	1,013	1,118	1,013
10,150	**10,200**	1,125	1,018	1,125	1,018
10,200	**10,250**	1,133	1,023	1,133	1,023
10,250	**10,300**	1,140	1,028	1,140	1,028
10,300	**10,350**	1,148	1,033	1,148	1,033
10,350	**10,400**	1,155	1,038	1,155	1,038
10,400	**10,450**	1,163	1,043	1,163	1,043
10,450	**10,500**	1,170	1,048	1,170	1,048
10,500	**10,550**	1,178	1,053	1,178	1,053
10,550	**10,600**	1,185	1,058	1,185	1,058
10,600	**10,650**	1,193	1,063	1,193	1,063
10,650	**10,700**	1,200	1,068	1,200	1,068
10,700	**10,750**	1,208	1,073	1,208	1,073
10,750	**10,800**	1,215	1,078	1,215	1,078
10,800	**10,850**	1,223	1,083	1,223	1,083
10,850	**10,900**	1,230	1,088	1,230	1,088
10,900	**10,950**	1,238	1,093	1,238	1,093
10,950	**11,000**	1,245	1,098	1,245	1,098

If line 43 (taxable income) is—		And you are—			
At least	But less than	Single	Married filing jointly *	Married filing separately	Head of a household
		Your tax is—			
11,000					
11,000	**11,050**	1,253	1,103	1,253	1,103
11,050	**11,100**	1,260	1,108	1,260	1,108
11,100	**11,150**	1,268	1,113	1,268	1,113
11,150	**11,200**	1,275	1,118	1,275	1,118
11,200	**11,250**	1,283	1,123	1,283	1,123
11,250	**11,300**	1,290	1,128	1,290	1,128
11,300	**11,350**	1,298	1,133	1,298	1,133
11,350	**11,400**	1,305	1,138	1,305	1,138
11,400	**11,450**	1,313	1,143	1,313	1,143
11,450	**11,500**	1,320	1,148	1,320	1,149
11,500	**11,550**	1,328	1,153	1,328	1,156
11,550	**11,600**	1,335	1,158	1,335	1,164
11,600	**11,650**	1,343	1,163	1,343	1,171
11,650	**11,700**	1,350	1,168	1,350	1,179
11,700	**11,750**	1,358	1,173	1,358	1,186
11,750	**11,800**	1,365	1,178	1,365	1,194
11,800	**11,850**	1,373	1,183	1,373	1,201
11,850	**11,900**	1,380	1,188	1,380	1,209
11,900	**11,950**	1,388	1,193	1,388	1,216
11,950	**12,000**	1,395	1,198	1,395	1,224
12,000					
12,000	**12,050**	1,403	1,203	1,403	1,231
12,050	**12,100**	1,410	1,208	1,410	1,239
12,100	**12,150**	1,418	1,213	1,418	1,246
12,150	**12,200**	1,425	1,218	1,425	1,254
12,200	**12,250**	1,433	1,223	1,433	1,261
12,250	**12,300**	1,440	1,228	1,440	1,269
12,300	**12,350**	1,448	1,233	1,448	1,276
12,350	**12,400**	1,455	1,238	1,455	1,284
12,400	**12,450**	1,463	1,243	1,463	1,291
12,450	**12,500**	1,470	1,248	1,470	1,299
12,500	**12,550**	1,478	1,253	1,478	1,306
12,550	**12,600**	1,485	1,258	1,485	1,314
12,600	**12,650**	1,493	1,263	1,493	1,321
12,650	**12,700**	1,500	1,268	1,500	1,329
12,700	**12,750**	1,508	1,273	1,508	1,336
12,750	**12,800**	1,515	1,278	1,515	1,344
12,800	**12,850**	1,523	1,283	1,523	1,351
12,850	**12,900**	1,530	1,288	1,530	1,359
12,900	**12,950**	1,538	1,293	1,538	1,366
12,950	**13,000**	1,545	1,298	1,545	1,374
13,000					
13,000	**13,050**	1,553	1,303	1,553	1,381
13,050	**13,100**	1,560	1,308	1,560	1,389
13,100	**13,150**	1,568	1,313	1,568	1,396
13,150	**13,200**	1,575	1,318	1,575	1,404
13,200	**13,250**	1,583	1,323	1,583	1,411
13,250	**13,300**	1,590	1,328	1,590	1,419
13,300	**13,350**	1,598	1,333	1,598	1,426
13,350	**13,400**	1,605	1,338	1,605	1,434
13,400	**13,450**	1,613	1,343	1,613	1,441
13,450	**13,500**	1,620	1,348	1,620	1,449
13,500	**13,550**	1,628	1,353	1,628	1,456
13,550	**13,600**	1,635	1,358	1,635	1,464
13,600	**13,650**	1,643	1,363	1,643	1,471
13,650	**13,700**	1,650	1,368	1,650	1,479
13,700	**13,750**	1,658	1,373	1,658	1,486
13,750	**13,800**	1,665	1,378	1,665	1,494
13,800	**13,850**	1,673	1,383	1,673	1,501
13,850	**13,900**	1,680	1,388	1,680	1,509
13,900	**13,950**	1,688	1,393	1,688	1,516
13,950	**14,000**	1,695	1,398	1,695	1,524

* This column must also be used by a qualifying widow(er).

Sample Tax Table–*Continued*

If line 43 (taxable income) is—		And you are—			
At least	But less than	Single	Married filing jointly *	Married filing separately	Head of a household
		Your tax is—			
14,000					
14,000	**14,050**	1,703	1,403	1,703	1,531
14,050	**14,100**	1,710	1,408	1,710	1,539
14,100	**14,150**	1,718	1,413	1,718	1,546
14,150	**14,200**	1,725	1,418	1,725	1,554
14,200	**14,250**	1,733	1,423	1,733	1,561
14,250	**14,300**	1,740	1,428	1,740	1,569
14,300	**14,350**	1,748	1,433	1,748	1,576
14,350	**14,400**	1,755	1,438	1,755	1,584
14,400	**14,450**	1,763	1,443	1,763	1,591
14,450	**14,500**	1,770	1,448	1,770	1,599
14,500	**14,550**	1,778	1,453	1,778	1,606
14,550	**14,600**	1,785	1,458	1,785	1,614
14,600	**14,650**	1,793	1,463	1,793	1,621
14,650	**14,700**	1,800	1,468	1,800	1,629
14,700	**14,750**	1,808	1,473	1,808	1,636
14,750	**14,800**	1,815	1,478	1,815	1,644
14,800	**14,850**	1,823	1,483	1,823	1,651
14,850	**14,900**	1,830	1,488	1,830	1,659
14,900	**14,950**	1,838	1,493	1,838	1,666
14,950	**15,000**	1,845	1,498	1,845	1,674
15,000					
15,000	**15,050**	1,853	1,503	1,853	1,681
15,050	**15,100**	1,860	1,508	1,860	1,689
15,100	**15,150**	1,868	1,513	1,868	1,696
15,150	**15,200**	1,875	1,518	1,875	1,704
15,200	**15,250**	1,883	1,523	1,883	1,711
15,250	**15,300**	1,890	1,528	1,890	1,719
15,300	**15,350**	1,898	1,533	1,898	1,726
15,350	**15,400**	1,905	1,538	1,905	1,734
15,400	**15,450**	1,913	1,543	1,913	1,741
15,450	**15,500**	1,920	1,548	1,920	1,749
15,500	**15,550**	1,928	1,553	1,928	1,756
15,550	**15,600**	1,935	1,558	1,935	1,764
15,600	**15,650**	1,943	1,563	1,943	1,771
15,650	**15,700**	1,950	1,568	1,950	1,779
15,700	**15,750**	1,958	1,573	1,958	1,786
15,750	**15,800**	1,965	1,578	1,965	1,794
15,800	**15,850**	1,973	1,583	1,973	1,801
15,850	**15,900**	1,980	1,588	1,980	1,809
15,900	**15,950**	1,988	1,593	1,988	1,816
15,950	**16,000**	1,995	1,598	1,995	1,824
16,000					
16,000	**16,050**	2,003	1,603	2,003	1,831
16,050	**16,100**	2,010	1,609	2,010	1,839
16,100	**16,150**	2,018	1,616	2,018	1,846
16,150	**16,200**	2,025	1,624	2,025	1,854
16,200	**16,250**	2,033	1,631	2,033	1,861
16,250	**16,300**	2,040	1,639	2,040	1,869
16,300	**16,350**	2,048	1,646	2,048	1,876
16,350	**16,400**	2,055	1,654	2,055	1,884
16,400	**16,450**	2,063	1,661	2,063	1,891
16,450	**16,500**	2,070	1,669	2,070	1,899
16,500	**16,550**	2,078	1,676	2,078	1,906
16,550	**16,600**	2,085	1,684	2,085	1,914
16,600	**16,650**	2,093	1,691	2,093	1,921
16,650	**16,700**	2,100	1,699	2,100	1,929
16,700	**16,750**	2,108	1,706	2,108	1,936
16,750	**16,800**	2,115	1,714	2,115	1,944
16,800	**16,850**	2,123	1,721	2,123	1,951
16,850	**16,900**	2,130	1,729	2,130	1,959
16,900	**16,950**	2,138	1,736	2,138	1,966
16,950	**17,000**	2,145	1,744	2,145	1,974
17,000					
17,000	**17,050**	2,153	1,751	2,153	1,981
17,050	**17,100**	2,160	1,759	2,160	1,989
17,100	**17,150**	2,168	1,766	2,168	1,996
17,150	**17,200**	2,175	1,774	2,175	2,004
17,200	**17,250**	2,183	1,781	2,183	2,011
17,250	**17,300**	2,190	1,789	2,190	2,019
17,300	**17,350**	2,198	1,796	2,198	2,026
17,350	**17,400**	2,205	1,804	2,205	2,034
17,400	**17,450**	2,213	1,811	2,213	2,041
17,450	**17,500**	2,220	1,819	2,220	2,049
17,500	**17,550**	2,228	1,826	2,228	2,056
17,550	**17,600**	2,235	1,834	2,235	2,064
17,600	**17,650**	2,243	1,841	2,243	2,071
17,650	**17,700**	2,250	1,849	2,250	2,079
17,700	**17,750**	2,258	1,856	2,258	2,086
17,750	**17,800**	2,265	1,864	2,265	2,094
17,800	**17,850**	2,273	1,871	2,273	2,101
17,850	**17,900**	2,280	1,879	2,280	2,109
17,900	**17,950**	2,288	1,886	2,288	2,116
17,950	**18,000**	2,295	1,894	2,295	2,124
18,000					
18,000	**18,050**	2,303	1,901	2,303	2,131
18,050	**18,100**	2,310	1,909	2,310	2,139
18,100	**18,150**	2,318	1,916	2,318	2,146
18,150	**18,200**	2,325	1,924	2,325	2,154
18,200	**18,250**	2,333	1,931	2,333	2,161
18,250	**18,300**	2,340	1,939	2,340	2,169
18,300	**18,350**	2,348	1,946	2,348	2,176
18,350	**18,400**	2,355	1,954	2,355	2,184
18,400	**18,450**	2,363	1,961	2,363	2,191
18,450	**18,500**	2,370	1,969	2,370	2,199
18,500	**18,550**	2,378	1,976	2,378	2,206
18,550	**18,600**	2,385	1,984	2,385	2,214
18,600	**18,650**	2,393	1,991	2,393	2,221
18,650	**18,700**	2,400	1,999	2,400	2,229
18,700	**18,750**	2,408	2,006	2,408	2,236
18,750	**18,800**	2,415	2,014	2,415	2,244
18,800	**18,850**	2,423	2,021	2,423	2,251
18,850	**18,900**	2,430	2,029	2,430	2,259
18,900	**18,950**	2,438	2,036	2,438	2,266
18,950	**19,000**	2,445	2,044	2,445	2,274
19,000					
19,000	**19,050**	2,453	2,051	2,453	2,281
19,050	**19,100**	2,460	2,059	2,460	2,289
19,100	**19,150**	2,468	2,066	2,468	2,296
19,150	**19,200**	2,475	2,074	2,475	2,304
19,200	**19,250**	2,483	2,081	2,483	2,311
19,250	**19,300**	2,490	2,089	2,490	2,319
19,300	**19,350**	2,498	2,096	2,498	2,326
19,350	**19,400**	2,505	2,104	2,505	2,334
19,400	**19,450**	2,513	2,111	2,513	2,341
19,450	**19,500**	2,520	2,119	2,520	2,349
19,500	**19,550**	2,528	2,126	2,528	2,356
19,550	**19,600**	2,535	2,134	2,535	2,364
19,600	**19,650**	2,543	2,141	2,543	2,371
19,650	**19,700**	2,550	2,149	2,550	2,379
19,700	**19,750**	2,558	2,156	2,558	2,386
19,750	**19,800**	2,565	2,164	2,565	2,394
19,800	**19,850**	2,573	2,171	2,573	2,401
19,850	**19,900**	2,580	2,179	2,580	2,409
19,900	**19,950**	2,588	2,186	2,588	2,416
19,950	**20,000**	2,595	2,194	2,595	2,424
20,000					
20,000	**20,050**	2,603	2,201	2,603	2,431
20,050	**20,100**	2,610	2,209	2,610	2,439
20,100	**20,150**	2,618	2,216	2,618	2,446
20,150	**20,200**	2,625	2,224	2,625	2,454
20,200	**20,250**	2,633	2,231	2,633	2,461
20,250	**20,300**	2,640	2,239	2,640	2,469
20,300	**20,350**	2,648	2,246	2,648	2,476
20,350	**20,400**	2,655	2,254	2,655	2,484
20,400	**20,450**	2,663	2,261	2,663	2,491
20,450	**20,500**	2,670	2,269	2,670	2,499
20,500	**20,550**	2,678	2,276	2,678	2,506
20,550	**20,600**	2,685	2,284	2,685	2,514
20,600	**20,650**	2,693	2,291	2,693	2,521
20,650	**20,700**	2,700	2,299	2,700	2,529
20,700	**20,750**	2,708	2,306	2,708	2,536
20,750	**20,800**	2,715	2,314	2,715	2,544
20,800	**20,850**	2,723	2,321	2,723	2,551
20,850	**20,900**	2,730	2,329	2,730	2,559
20,900	**20,950**	2,738	2,336	2,738	2,566
20,950	**21,000**	2,745	2,344	2,745	2,574
21,000					
21,000	**21,050**	2,753	2,351	2,753	2,581
21,050	**21,100**	2,760	2,359	2,760	2,589
21,100	**21,150**	2,768	2,366	2,768	2,596
21,150	**21,200**	2,775	2,374	2,775	2,604
21,200	**21,250**	2,783	2,381	2,783	2,611
21,250	**21,300**	2,790	2,389	2,790	2,619
21,300	**21,350**	2,798	2,396	2,798	2,626
21,350	**21,400**	2,805	2,404	2,805	2,634
21,400	**21,450**	2,813	2,411	2,813	2,641
21,450	**21,500**	2,820	2,419	2,820	2,649
21,500	**21,550**	2,828	2,426	2,828	2,656
21,550	**21,600**	2,835	2,434	2,835	2,664
21,600	**21,650**	2,843	2,441	2,843	2,671
21,650	**21,700**	2,850	2,449	2,850	2,679
21,700	**21,750**	2,858	2,456	2,858	2,686
21,750	**21,800**	2,865	2,464	2,865	2,694
21,800	**21,850**	2,873	2,471	2,873	2,701
21,850	**21,900**	2,880	2,479	2,880	2,709
21,900	**21,950**	2,888	2,486	2,888	2,716
21,950	**22,000**	2,895	2,494	2,895	2,724
22,000					
22,000	**22,050**	2,903	2,501	2,903	2,731
22,050	**22,100**	2,910	2,509	2,910	2,739
22,100	**22,150**	2,918	2,516	2,918	2,746
22,150	**22,200**	2,925	2,524	2,925	2,754
22,200	**22,250**	2,933	2,531	2,933	2,761
22,250	**22,300**	2,940	2,539	2,940	2,769
22,300	**22,350**	2,948	2,546	2,948	2,776
22,350	**22,400**	2,955	2,554	2,955	2,784
22,400	**22,450**	2,963	2,561	2,963	2,791
22,450	**22,500**	2,970	2,569	2,970	2,799
22,500	**22,550**	2,978	2,576	2,978	2,806
22,550	**22,600**	2,985	2,584	2,985	2,814
22,600	**22,650**	2,993	2,591	2,993	2,821
22,650	**22,700**	3,000	2,599	3,000	2,829
22,700	**22,750**	3,008	2,606	3,008	2,836
22,750	**22,800**	3,015	2,614	3,015	2,844
22,800	**22,850**	3,023	2,621	3,023	2,851
22,850	**22,900**	3,030	2,629	3,030	2,859
22,900	**22,950**	3,038	2,636	3,038	2,866
22,950	**23,000**	3,045	2,644	3,045	2,874

* This column must also be used by a qualifying widow(er).

If line 43 (taxable income) is—		And you are—			
At least	But less than	Single	Married filing jointly *	Married filing sepa-rately	Head of a house-hold
		Your tax is—			
23,000					
23,000	**23,050**	3,053	2,651	3,053	2,881
23,050	**23,100**	3,060	2,659	3,060	2,889
23,100	**23,150**	3,068	2,666	3,068	2,896
23,150	**23,200**	3,075	2,674	3,075	2,904
23,200	**23,250**	3,083	2,681	3,083	2,911
23,250	**23,300**	3,090	2,689	3,090	2,919
23,300	**23,350**	3,098	2,696	3,098	2,926
23,350	**23,400**	3,105	2,704	3,105	2,934
23,400	**23,450**	3,113	2,711	3,113	2,941
23,450	**23,500**	3,120	2,719	3,120	2,949
23,500	**23,550**	3,128	2,726	3,128	2,956
23,550	**23,600**	3,135	2,734	3,135	2,964
23,600	**23,650**	3,143	2,741	3,143	2,971
23,650	**23,700**	3,150	2,749	3,150	2,979
23,700	**23,750**	3,158	2,756	3,158	2,986
23,750	**23,800**	3,165	2,764	3,165	2,994
23,800	**23,850**	3,173	2,771	3,173	3,001
23,850	**23,900**	3,180	2,779	3,180	3,009
23,900	**23,950**	3,188	2,786	3,188	3,016
23,950	**24,000**	3,195	2,794	3,195	3,024
24,000					
24,000	**24,050**	3,203	2,801	3,203	3,031
24,050	**24,100**	3,210	2,809	3,210	3,039
24,100	**24,150**	3,218	2,816	3,218	3,046
24,150	**24,200**	3,225	2,824	3,225	3,054
24,200	**24,250**	3,233	2,831	3,233	3,061
24,250	**24,300**	3,240	2,839	3,240	3,069
24,300	**24,350**	3,248	2,846	3,248	3,076
24,350	**24,400**	3,255	2,854	3,255	3,084
24,400	**24,450**	3,263	2,861	3,263	3,091
24,450	**24,500**	3,270	2,869	3,270	3,099
24,500	**24,550**	3,278	2,876	3,278	3,106
24,550	**24,600**	3,285	2,884	3,285	3,114
24,600	**24,650**	3,293	2,891	3,293	3,121
24,650	**24,700**	3,300	2,899	3,300	3,129
24,700	**24,750**	3,308	2,906	3,308	3,136
24,750	**24,800**	3,315	2,914	3,315	3,144
24,800	**24,850**	3,323	2,921	3,323	3,151
24,850	**24,900**	3,330	2,929	3,330	3,159
24,900	**24,950**	3,338	2,936	3,338	3,166
24,950	**25,000**	3,345	2,944	3,345	3,174
25,000					
25,000	**25,050**	3,353	2,951	3,353	3,181
25,050	**25,100**	3,360	2,959	3,360	3,189
25,100	**25,150**	3,368	2,966	3,368	3,196
25,150	**25,200**	3,375	2,974	3,375	3,204
25,200	**25,250**	3,383	2,981	3,383	3,211
25,250	**25,300**	3,390	2,989	3,390	3,219
25,300	**25,350**	3,398	2,996	3,398	3,226
25,350	**25,400**	3,405	3,004	3,405	3,234
25,400	**25,450**	3,413	3,011	3,413	3,241
25,450	**25,500**	3,420	3,019	3,420	3,249
25,500	**25,550**	3,428	3,026	3,428	3,256
25,550	**25,600**	3,435	3,034	3,435	3,264
25,600	**25,650**	3,443	3,041	3,443	3,271
25,650	**25,700**	3,450	3,049	3,450	3,279
25,700	**25,750**	3,458	3,056	3,458	3,286
25,750	**25,800**	3,465	3,064	3,465	3,294
25,800	**25,850**	3,473	3,071	3,473	3,301
25,850	**25,900**	3,480	3,079	3,480	3,309
25,900	**25,950**	3,488	3,086	3,488	3,316
25,950	**26,000**	3,495	3,094	3,495	3,324
26,000					
26,000	**26,050**	3,503	3,101	3,503	3,331
26,050	**26,100**	3,510	3,109	3,510	3,339
26,100	**26,150**	3,518	3,116	3,518	3,346
26,150	**26,200**	3,525	3,124	3,525	3,354
26,200	**26,250**	3,533	3,131	3,533	3,361
26,250	**26,300**	3,540	3,139	3,540	3,369
26,300	**26,350**	3,548	3,146	3,548	3,376
26,350	**26,400**	3,555	3,154	3,555	3,384
26,400	**26,450**	3,563	3,161	3,563	3,391
26,450	**26,500**	3,570	3,169	3,570	3,399
26,500	**26,550**	3,578	3,176	3,578	3,406
26,550	**26,600**	3,585	3,184	3,585	3,414
26,600	**26,650**	3,593	3,191	3,593	3,421
26,650	**26,700**	3,600	3,199	3,600	3,429
26,700	**26,750**	3,608	3,206	3,608	3,436
26,750	**26,800**	3,615	3,214	3,615	3,444
26,800	**26,850**	3,623	3,221	3,623	3,451
26,850	**26,900**	3,630	3,229	3,630	3,459
26,900	**26,950**	3,638	3,236	3,638	3,466
26,950	**27,000**	3,645	3,244	3,645	3,474
27,000					
27,000	**27,050**	3,653	3,251	3,653	3,481
27,050	**27,100**	3,660	3,259	3,660	3,489
27,100	**27,150**	3,668	3,266	3,668	3,496
27,150	**27,200**	3,675	3,274	3,675	3,504
27,200	**27,250**	3,683	3,281	3,683	3,511
27,250	**27,300**	3,690	3,289	3,690	3,519
27,300	**27,350**	3,698	3,296	3,698	3,526
27,350	**27,400**	3,705	3,304	3,705	3,534
27,400	**27,450**	3,713	3,311	3,713	3,541
27,450	**27,500**	3,720	3,319	3,720	3,549
27,500	**27,550**	3,728	3,326	3,728	3,556
27,550	**27,600**	3,735	3,334	3,735	3,564
27,600	**27,650**	3,743	3,341	3,743	3,571
27,650	**27,700**	3,750	3,349	3,750	3,579
27,700	**27,750**	3,758	3,356	3,758	3,586
27,750	**27,800**	3,765	3,364	3,765	3,594
27,800	**27,850**	3,773	3,371	3,773	3,601
27,850	**27,900**	3,780	3,379	3,780	3,609
27,900	**27,950**	3,788	3,386	3,788	3,616
27,950	**28,000**	3,795	3,394	3,795	3,624
28,000					
28,000	**28,050**	3,803	3,401	3,803	3,631
28,050	**28,100**	3,810	3,409	3,810	3,639
28,100	**28,150**	3,818	3,416	3,818	3,646
28,150	**28,200**	3,825	3,424	3,825	3,654
28,200	**28,250**	3,833	3,431	3,833	3,661
28,250	**28,300**	3,840	3,439	3,840	3,669
28,300	**28,350**	3,848	3,446	3,848	3,676
28,350	**28,400**	3,855	3,454	3,855	3,684
28,400	**28,450**	3,863	3,461	3,863	3,691
28,450	**28,500**	3,870	3,469	3,870	3,699
28,500	**28,550**	3,878	3,476	3,878	3,706
28,550	**28,600**	3,885	3,484	3,885	3,714
28,600	**28,650**	3,893	3,491	3,893	3,721
28,650	**28,700**	3,900	3,499	3,900	3,729
28,700	**28,750**	3,908	3,506	3,908	3,736
28,750	**28,800**	3,915	3,514	3,915	3,744
28,800	**28,850**	3,923	3,521	3,923	3,751
28,850	**28,900**	3,930	3,529	3,930	3,759
28,900	**28,950**	3,938	3,536	3,938	3,766
28,950	**29,000**	3,945	3,544	3,945	3,774
29,000					
29,000	**29,050**	3,953	3,551	3,953	3,781
29,050	**29,100**	3,960	3,559	3,960	3,789
29,100	**29,150**	3,968	3,566	3,968	3,796
29,150	**29,200**	3,975	3,574	3,975	3,804
29,200	**29,250**	3,983	3,581	3,983	3,811
29,250	**29,300**	3,990	3,589	3,990	3,819
29,300	**29,350**	3,998	3,596	3,998	3,826
29,350	**29,400**	4,005	3,604	4,005	3,834
29,400	**29,450**	4,013	3,611	4,013	3,841
29,450	**29,500**	4,020	3,619	4,020	3,849
29,500	**29,550**	4,028	3,626	4,028	3,856
29,550	**29,600**	4,035	3,634	4,035	3,864
29,600	**29,650**	4,043	3,641	4,043	3,871
29,650	**29,700**	4,050	3,649	4,050	3,879
29,700	**29,750**	4,058	3,656	4,058	3,886
29,750	**29,800**	4,065	3,664	4,065	3,894
29,800	**29,850**	4,073	3,671	4,073	3,901
29,850	**29,900**	4,080	3,679	4,080	3,909
29,900	**29,950**	4,088	3,686	4,088	3,916
29,950	**30,000**	4,095	3,694	4,095	3,924
30,000					
30,000	**30,050**	4,103	3,701	4,103	3,931
30,050	**30,100**	4,110	3,709	4,110	3,939
30,100	**30,150**	4,118	3,716	4,118	3,946
30,150	**30,200**	4,125	3,724	4,125	3,954
30,200	**30,250**	4,133	3,731	4,133	3,961
30,250	**30,300**	4,140	3,739	4,140	3,969
30,300	**30,350**	4,148	3,746	4,148	3,976
30,350	**30,400**	4,155	3,754	4,155	3,984
30,400	**30,450**	4,163	3,761	4,163	3,991
30,450	**30,500**	4,170	3,769	4,170	3,999
30,500	**30,550**	4,178	3,776	4,178	4,006
30,550	**30,600**	4,185	3,784	4,185	4,014
30,600	**30,650**	4,193	3,791	4,193	4,021
30,650	**30,700**	4,200	3,799	4,200	4,029
30,700	**30,750**	4,208	3,806	4,208	4,036
30,750	**30,800**	4,215	3,814	4,215	4,044
30,800	**30,850**	4,223	3,821	4,223	4,051
30,850	**30,900**	4,230	3,829	4,230	4,059
30,900	**30,950**	4,238	3,836	4,238	4,066
30,950	**31,000**	4,245	3,844	4,245	4,074
31,000					
31,000	**31,050**	4,253	3,851	4,253	4,081
31,050	**31,100**	4,260	3,859	4,260	4,089
31,100	**31,150**	4,268	3,866	4,268	4,096
31,150	**31,200**	4,275	3,874	4,275	4,104
31,200	**31,250**	4,283	3,881	4,283	4,111
31,250	**31,300**	4,290	3,889	4,290	4,119
31,300	**31,350**	4,298	3,896	4,298	4,126
31,350	**31,400**	4,305	3,904	4,305	4,134
31,400	**31,450**	4,313	3,911	4,313	4,141
31,450	**31,500**	4,320	3,919	4,320	4,149
31,500	**31,550**	4,328	3,926	4,328	4,156
31,550	**31,600**	4,335	3,934	4,335	4,164
31,600	**31,650**	4,343	3,941	4,343	4,171
31,650	**31,700**	4,350	3,949	4,350	4,179
31,700	**31,750**	4,358	3,956	4,358	4,186
31,750	**31,800**	4,365	3,964	4,365	4,194
31,800	**31,850**	4,373	3,971	4,373	4,201
31,850	**31,900**	4,380	3,979	4,380	4,209
31,900	**31,950**	4,388	3,986	4,388	4,216
31,950	**32,000**	4,395	3,994	4,395	4,224

* This column must also be used by a qualifying widow(er).

Sample Tax Table–*Continued*

If line 43 (taxable income) is—		And you are—			
At least	But less than	Single	Married filing jointly *	Married filing sepa-rately	Head of a house-hold
		Your tax is—			
32,000					
32,000	**32,050**	4,403	4,001	4,403	4,231
32,050	**32,100**	4,410	4,009	4,410	4,239
32,100	**32,150**	4,418	4,016	4,418	4,246
32,150	**32,200**	4,425	4,024	4,425	4,254
32,200	**32,250**	4,433	4,031	4,433	4,261
32,250	**32,300**	4,440	4,039	4,440	4,269
32,300	**32,350**	4,448	4,046	4,448	4,276
32,350	**32,400**	4,455	4,054	4,455	4,284
32,400	**32,450**	4,463	4,061	4,463	4,291
32,450	**32,500**	4,470	4,069	4,470	4,299
32,500	**32,550**	4,478	4,076	4,478	4,306
32,550	**32,600**	4,488	4,084	4,488	4,314
32,600	**32,650**	4,500	4,091	4,500	4,321
32,650	**32,700**	4,513	4,099	4,513	4,329
32,700	**32,750**	4,525	4,106	4,525	4,336
32,750	**32,800**	4,538	4,114	4,538	4,344
32,800	**32,850**	4,550	4,121	4,550	4,351
32,850	**32,900**	4,563	4,129	4,563	4,359
32,900	**32,950**	4,575	4,136	4,575	4,366
32,950	**33,000**	4,588	4,144	4,588	4,374
33,000					
33,000	**33,050**	4,600	4,151	4,600	4,381
33,050	**33,100**	4,613	4,159	4,613	4,389
33,100	**33,150**	4,625	4,166	4,625	4,396
33,150	**33,200**	4,638	4,174	4,638	4,404
33,200	**33,250**	4,650	4,181	4,650	4,411
33,250	**33,300**	4,663	4,189	4,663	4,419
33,300	**33,350**	4,675	4,196	4,675	4,426
33,350	**33,400**	4,688	4,204	4,688	4,434
33,400	**33,450**	4,700	4,211	4,700	4,441
33,450	**33,500**	4,713	4,219	4,713	4,449
33,500	**33,550**	4,725	4,226	4,725	4,456
33,550	**33,600**	4,738	4,234	4,738	4,464
33,600	**33,650**	4,750	4,241	4,750	4,471
33,650	**33,700**	4,763	4,249	4,763	4,479
33,700	**33,750**	4,775	4,256	4,775	4,486
33,750	**33,800**	4,788	4,264	4,788	4,494
33,800	**33,850**	4,800	4,271	4,800	4,501
33,850	**33,900**	4,813	4,279	4,813	4,509
33,900	**33,950**	4,825	4,286	4,825	4,516
33,950	**34,000**	4,838	4,294	4,838	4,524
34,000					
34,000	**34,050**	4,850	4,301	4,850	4,531
34,050	**34,100**	4,863	4,309	4,863	4,539
34,100	**34,150**	4,875	4,316	4,875	4,546
34,150	**34,200**	4,888	4,324	4,888	4,554
34,200	**34,250**	4,900	4,331	4,900	4,561
34,250	**34,300**	4,913	4,339	4,913	4,569
34,300	**34,350**	4,925	4,346	4,925	4,576
34,350	**34,400**	4,938	4,354	4,938	4,584
34,400	**34,450**	4,950	4,361	4,950	4,591
34,450	**34,500**	4,963	4,369	4,963	4,599
34,500	**34,550**	4,975	4,376	4,975	4,606
34,550	**34,600**	4,988	4,384	4,988	4,614
34,600	**34,650**	5,000	4,391	5,000	4,621
34,650	**34,700**	5,013	4,399	5,013	4,629
34,700	**34,750**	5,025	4,406	5,025	4,636
34,750	**34,800**	5,038	4,414	5,038	4,644
34,800	**34,850**	5,050	4,421	5,050	4,651
34,850	**34,900**	5,063	4,429	5,063	4,659
34,900	**34,950**	5,075	4,436	5,075	4,666
34,950	**35,000**	5,088	4,444	5,088	4,674

If line 43 (taxable income) is—		And you are—			
At least	But less than	Single	Married filing jointly *	Married filing sepa-rately	Head of a house-hold
		Your tax is—			
35,000					
35,000	**35,050**	5,100	4,451	5,100	4,681
35,050	**35,100**	5,113	4,459	5,113	4,689
35,100	**35,150**	5,125	4,466	5,125	4,696
35,150	**35,200**	5,138	4,474	5,138	4,704
35,200	**35,250**	5,150	4,481	5,150	4,711
35,250	**35,300**	5,163	4,489	5,163	4,719
35,300	**35,350**	5,175	4,496	5,175	4,726
35,350	**35,400**	5,188	4,504	5,188	4,734
35,400	**35,450**	5,200	4,511	5,200	4,741
35,450	**35,500**	5,213	4,519	5,213	4,749
35,500	**35,550**	5,225	4,526	5,225	4,756
35,550	**35,600**	5,238	4,534	5,238	4,764
35,600	**35,650**	5,250	4,541	5,250	4,771
35,650	**35,700**	5,263	4,549	5,263	4,779
35,700	**35,750**	5,275	4,556	5,275	4,786
35,750	**35,800**	5,288	4,564	5,288	4,794
35,800	**35,850**	5,300	4,571	5,300	4,801
35,850	**35,900**	5,313	4,579	5,313	4,809
35,900	**35,950**	5,325	4,586	5,325	4,816
35,950	**36,000**	5,338	4,594	5,338	4,824
36,000					
36,000	**36,050**	5,350	4,601	5,350	4,831
36,050	**36,100**	5,363	4,609	5,363	4,839
36,100	**36,150**	5,375	4,616	5,375	4,846
36,150	**36,200**	5,388	4,624	5,388	4,854
36,200	**36,250**	5,400	4,631	5,400	4,861
36,250	**36,300**	5,413	4,639	5,413	4,869
36,300	**36,350**	5,425	4,646	5,425	4,876
36,350	**36,400**	5,438	4,654	5,438	4,884
36,400	**36,450**	5,450	4,661	5,450	4,891
36,450	**36,500**	5,463	4,669	5,463	4,899
36,500	**36,550**	5,475	4,676	5,475	4,906
36,550	**36,600**	5,488	4,684	5,488	4,914
36,600	**36,650**	5,500	4,691	5,500	4,921
36,650	**36,700**	5,513	4,699	5,513	4,929
36,700	**36,750**	5,525	4,706	5,525	4,936
36,750	**36,800**	5,538	4,714	5,538	4,944
36,800	**36,850**	5,550	4,721	5,550	4,951
36,850	**36,900**	5,563	4,729	5,563	4,959
36,900	**36,950**	5,575	4,736	5,575	4,966
36,950	**37,000**	5,588	4,744	5,588	4,974
37,000					
37,000	**37,050**	5,600	4,751	5,600	4,981
37,050	**37,100**	5,613	4,759	5,613	4,989
37,100	**37,150**	5,625	4,766	5,625	4,996
37,150	**37,200**	5,638	4,774	5,638	5,004
37,200	**37,250**	5,650	4,781	5,650	5,011
37,250	**37,300**	5,663	4,789	5,663	5,019
37,300	**37,350**	5,675	4,796	5,675	5,026
37,350	**37,400**	5,688	4,804	5,688	5,034
37,400	**37,450**	5,700	4,811	5,700	5,041
37,450	**37,500**	5,713	4,819	5,713	5,049
37,500	**37,550**	5,725	4,826	5,725	5,056
37,550	**37,600**	5,738	4,834	5,738	5,064
37,600	**37,650**	5,750	4,841	5,750	5,071
37,650	**37,700**	5,763	4,849	5,763	5,079
37,700	**37,750**	5,775	4,856	5,775	5,086
37,750	**37,800**	5,788	4,864	5,788	5,094
37,800	**37,850**	5,800	4,871	5,800	5,101
37,850	**37,900**	5,813	4,879	5,813	5,109
37,900	**37,950**	5,825	4,886	5,825	5,116
37,950	**38,000**	5,838	4,894	5,838	5,124

If line 43 (taxable income) is—		And you are—			
At least	But less than	Single	Married filing jointly *	Married filing sepa-rately	Head of a house-hold
		Your tax is—			
38,000					
38,000	**38,050**	5,850	4,901	5,850	5,131
38,050	**38,100**	5,863	4,909	5,863	5,139
38,100	**38,150**	5,875	4,916	5,875	5,146
38,150	**38,200**	5,888	4,924	5,888	5,154
38,200	**38,250**	5,900	4,931	5,900	5,161
38,250	**38,300**	5,913	4,939	5,913	5,169
38,300	**38,350**	5,925	4,946	5,925	5,176
38,350	**38,400**	5,938	4,954	5,938	5,184
38,400	**38,450**	5,950	4,961	5,950	5,191
38,450	**38,500**	5,963	4,969	5,963	5,199
38,500	**38,550**	5,975	4,976	5,975	5,206
38,550	**38,600**	5,988	4,984	5,988	5,214
38,600	**38,650**	6,000	4,991	6,000	5,221
38,650	**38,700**	6,013	4,999	6,013	5,229
38,700	**38,750**	6,025	5,006	6,025	5,236
38,750	**38,800**	6,038	5,014	6,038	5,244
38,800	**38,850**	6,050	5,021	6,050	5,251
38,850	**38,900**	6,063	5,029	6,063	5,259
38,900	**38,950**	6,075	5,036	6,075	5,266
38,950	**39,000**	6,088	5,044	6,088	5,274
39,000					
39,000	**39,050**	6,100	5,051	6,100	5,281
39,050	**39,100**	6,113	5,059	6,113	5,289
39,100	**39,150**	6,125	5,066	6,125	5,296
39,150	**39,200**	6,138	5,074	6,138	5,304
39,200	**39,250**	6,150	5,081	6,150	5,311
39,250	**39,300**	6,163	5,089	6,163	5,319
39,300	**39,350**	6,175	5,096	6,175	5,326
39,350	**39,400**	6,188	5,104	6,188	5,334
39,400	**39,450**	6,200	5,111	6,200	5,341
39,450	**39,500**	6,213	5,119	6,213	5,349
39,500	**39,550**	6,225	5,126	6,225	5,356
39,550	**39,600**	6,238	5,134	6,238	5,364
39,600	**39,650**	6,250	5,141	6,250	5,371
39,650	**39,700**	6,263	5,149	6,263	5,379
39,700	**39,750**	6,275	5,156	6,275	5,386
39,750	**39,800**	6,288	5,164	6,288	5,394
39,800	**39,850**	6,300	5,171	6,300	5,401
39,850	**39,900**	6,313	5,179	6,313	5,409
39,900	**39,950**	6,325	5,186	6,325	5,416
39,950	**40,000**	6,338	5,194	6,338	5,424
40,000					
40,000	**40,050**	6,350	5,201	6,350	5,431
40,050	**40,100**	6,363	5,209	6,363	5,439
40,100	**40,150**	6,375	5,216	6,375	5,446
40,150	**40,200**	6,388	5,224	6,388	5,454
40,200	**40,250**	6,400	5,231	6,400	5,461
40,250	**40,300**	6,413	5,239	6,413	5,469
40,300	**40,350**	6,425	5,246	6,425	5,476
40,350	**40,400**	6,438	5,254	6,438	5,484
40,400	**40,450**	6,450	5,261	6,450	5,491
40,450	**40,500**	6,463	5,269	6,463	5,499
40,500	**40,550**	6,475	5,276	6,475	5,506
40,550	**40,600**	6,488	5,284	6,488	5,514
40,600	**40,650**	6,500	5,291	6,500	5,521
40,650	**40,700**	6,513	5,299	6,513	5,529
40,700	**40,750**	6,525	5,306	6,525	5,536
40,750	**40,800**	6,538	5,314	6,538	5,544
40,800	**40,850**	6,550	5,321	6,550	5,551
40,850	**40,900**	6,563	5,329	6,563	5,559
40,900	**40,950**	6,575	5,336	6,575	5,566
40,950	**41,000**	6,588	5,344	6,588	5,574

* This column must also be used by a qualifying widow(er).

If line 43 (taxable income) is— At least	But less than	And you are— Single	Married filing jointly *	Married filing separately	Head of a household
		Your tax is—			
41,000					
41,000	**41,050**	6,600	5,351	6,600	5,581
41,050	**41,100**	6,613	5,359	6,613	5,589
41,100	**41,150**	6,625	5,366	6,625	5,596
41,150	**41,200**	6,638	5,374	6,638	5,604
41,200	**41,250**	6,650	5,381	6,650	5,611
41,250	**41,300**	6,663	5,389	6,663	5,619
41,300	**41,350**	6,675	5,396	6,675	5,626
41,350	**41,400**	6,688	5,404	6,688	5,634
41,400	**41,450**	6,700	5,411	6,700	5,641
41,450	**41,500**	6,713	5,419	6,713	5,649
41,500	**41,550**	6,725	5,426	6,725	5,656
41,550	**41,600**	6,738	5,434	6,738	5,664
41,600	**41,650**	6,750	5,441	6,750	5,671
41,650	**41,700**	6,763	5,449	6,763	5,679
41,700	**41,750**	6,775	5,456	6,775	5,686
41,750	**41,800**	6,788	5,464	6,788	5,694
41,800	**41,850**	6,800	5,471	6,800	5,701
41,850	**41,900**	6,813	5,479	6,813	5,709
41,900	**41,950**	6,825	5,486	6,825	5,716
41,950	**42,000**	6,838	5,494	6,838	5,724
42,000					
42,000	**42,050**	6,850	5,501	6,850	5,731
42,050	**42,100**	6,863	5,509	6,863	5,739
42,100	**42,150**	6,875	5,516	6,875	5,746
42,150	**42,200**	6,888	5,524	6,888	5,754
42,200	**42,250**	6,900	5,531	6,900	5,761
42,250	**42,300**	6,913	5,539	6,913	5,769
42,300	**42,350**	6,925	5,546	6,925	5,776
42,350	**42,400**	6,938	5,554	6,938	5,784
42,400	**42,450**	6,950	5,561	6,950	5,791
42,450	**42,500**	6,963	5,569	6,963	5,799
42,500	**42,550**	6,975	5,576	6,975	5,806
42,550	**42,600**	6,988	5,584	6,988	5,814
42,600	**42,650**	7,000	5,591	7,000	5,821
42,650	**42,700**	7,013	5,599	7,013	5,829
42,700	**42,750**	7,025	5,606	7,025	5,836
42,750	**42,800**	7,038	5,614	7,038	5,844
42,800	**42,850**	7,050	5,621	7,050	5,851
42,850	**42,900**	7,063	5,629	7,063	5,859
42,900	**42,950**	7,075	5,636	7,075	5,866
42,950	**43,000**	7,088	5,644	7,088	5,874
43,000					
43,000	**43,050**	7,100	5,651	7,100	5,881
43,050	**43,100**	7,113	5,659	7,113	5,889
43,100	**43,150**	7,125	5,666	7,125	5,896
43,150	**43,200**	7,138	5,674	7,138	5,904
43,200	**43,250**	7,150	5,681	7,150	5,911
43,250	**43,300**	7,163	5,689	7,163	5,919
43,300	**43,350**	7,175	5,696	7,175	5,926
43,350	**43,400**	7,188	5,704	7,188	5,934
43,400	**43,450**	7,200	5,711	7,200	5,941
43,450	**43,500**	7,213	5,719	7,213	5,949
43,500	**43,550**	7,225	5,726	7,225	5,956
43,550	**43,600**	7,238	5,734	7,238	5,964
43,600	**43,650**	7,250	5,741	7,250	5,971
43,650	**43,700**	7,263	5,749	7,263	5,981
43,700	**43,750**	7,275	5,756	7,275	5,994
43,750	**43,800**	7,288	5,764	7,288	6,006
43,800	**43,850**	7,300	5,771	7,300	6,019
43,850	**43,900**	7,313	5,779	7,313	6,031
43,900	**43,950**	7,325	5,786	7,325	6,044
43,950	**44,000**	7,338	5,794	7,338	6,056

If line 43 (taxable income) is— At least	But less than	And you are— Single	Married filing jointly *	Married filing separately	Head of a household
		Your tax is—			
44,000					
44,000	**44,050**	7,350	5,801	7,350	6,069
44,050	**44,100**	7,363	5,809	7,363	6,081
44,100	**44,150**	7,375	5,816	7,375	6,094
44,150	**44,200**	7,388	5,824	7,388	6,106
44,200	**44,250**	7,400	5,831	7,400	6,119
44,250	**44,300**	7,413	5,839	7,413	6,131
44,300	**44,350**	7,425	5,846	7,425	6,144
44,350	**44,400**	7,438	5,854	7,438	6,156
44,400	**44,450**	7,450	5,861	7,450	6,169
44,450	**44,500**	7,463	5,869	7,463	6,181
44,500	**44,550**	7,475	5,876	7,475	6,194
44,550	**44,600**	7,488	5,884	7,488	6,206
44,600	**44,650**	7,500	5,891	7,500	6,219
44,650	**44,700**	7,513	5,899	7,513	6,231
44,700	**44,750**	7,525	5,906	7,525	6,244
44,750	**44,800**	7,538	5,914	7,538	6,256
44,800	**44,850**	7,550	5,921	7,550	6,269
44,850	**44,900**	7,563	5,929	7,563	6,281
44,900	**44,950**	7,575	5,936	7,575	6,294
44,950	**45,000**	7,588	5,944	7,588	6,306
45,000					
45,000	**45,050**	7,600	5,951	7,600	6,319
45,050	**45,100**	7,613	5,959	7,613	6,331
45,100	**45,150**	7,625	5,966	7,625	6,344
45,150	**45,200**	7,638	5,974	7,638	6,356
45,200	**45,250**	7,650	5,981	7,650	6,369
45,250	**45,300**	7,663	5,989	7,663	6,381
45,300	**45,350**	7,675	5,996	7,675	6,394
45,350	**45,400**	7,688	6,004	7,688	6,406
45,400	**45,450**	7,700	6,011	7,700	6,419
45,450	**45,500**	7,713	6,019	7,713	6,431
45,500	**45,550**	7,725	6,026	7,725	6,444
45,550	**45,600**	7,738	6,034	7,738	6,456
45,600	**45,650**	7,750	6,041	7,750	6,469
45,650	**45,700**	7,763	6,049	7,763	6,481
45,700	**45,750**	7,775	6,056	7,775	6,494
45,750	**45,800**	7,788	6,064	7,788	6,506
45,800	**45,850**	7,800	6,071	7,800	6,519
45,850	**45,900**	7,813	6,079	7,813	6,531
45,900	**45,950**	7,825	6,086	7,825	6,544
45,950	**46,000**	7,838	6,094	7,838	6,556
46,000					
46,000	**46,050**	7,850	6,101	7,850	6,569
46,050	**46,100**	7,863	6,109	7,863	6,581
46,100	**46,150**	7,875	6,116	7,875	6,594
46,150	**46,200**	7,888	6,124	7,888	6,606
46,200	**46,250**	7,900	6,131	7,900	6,619
46,250	**46,300**	7,913	6,139	7,913	6,631
46,300	**46,350**	7,925	6,146	7,925	6,644
46,350	**46,400**	7,938	6,154	7,938	6,656
46,400	**46,450**	7,950	6,161	7,950	6,669
46,450	**46,500**	7,963	6,169	7,963	6,681
46,500	**46,550**	7,975	6,176	7,975	6,694
46,550	**46,600**	7,988	6,184	7,988	6,706
46,600	**46,650**	8,000	6,191	8,000	6,719
46,650	**46,700**	8,013	6,199	8,013	6,731
46,700	**46,750**	8,025	6,206	8,025	6,744
46,750	**46,800**	8,038	6,214	8,038	6,756
46,800	**46,850**	8,050	6,221	8,050	6,769
46,850	**46,900**	8,063	6,229	8,063	6,781
46,900	**46,950**	8,075	6,236	8,075	6,794
46,950	**47,000**	8,088	6,244	8,088	6,806

If line 43 (taxable income) is— At least	But less than	And you are— Single	Married filing jointly *	Married filing separately	Head of a household
		Your tax is—			
47,000					
47,000	**47,050**	8,100	6,251	8,100	6,819
47,050	**47,100**	8,113	6,259	8,113	6,831
47,100	**47,150**	8,125	6,266	8,125	6,844
47,150	**47,200**	8,138	6,274	8,138	6,856
47,200	**47,250**	8,150	6,281	8,150	6,869
47,250	**47,300**	8,163	6,289	8,163	6,881
47,300	**47,350**	8,175	6,296	8,175	6,894
47,350	**47,400**	8,188	6,304	8,188	6,906
47,400	**47,450**	8,200	6,311	8,200	6,919
47,450	**47,500**	8,213	6,319	8,213	6,931
47,500	**47,550**	8,225	6,326	8,225	6,944
47,550	**47,600**	8,238	6,334	8,238	6,956
47,600	**47,650**	8,250	6,341	8,250	6,969
47,650	**47,700**	8,263	6,349	8,263	6,981
47,700	**47,750**	8,275	6,356	8,275	6,994
47,750	**47,800**	8,288	6,364	8,288	7,006
47,800	**47,850**	8,300	6,371	8,300	7,019
47,850	**47,900**	8,313	6,379	8,313	7,031
47,900	**47,950**	8,325	6,386	8,325	7,044
47,950	**48,000**	8,338	6,394	8,338	7,056
48,000					
48,000	**48,050**	8,350	6,401	8,350	7,069
48,050	**48,100**	8,363	6,409	8,363	7,081
48,100	**48,150**	8,375	6,416	8,375	7,094
48,150	**48,200**	8,388	6,424	8,388	7,106
48,200	**48,250**	8,400	6,431	8,400	7,119
48,250	**48,300**	8,413	6,439	8,413	7,131
48,300	**48,350**	8,425	6,446	8,425	7,144
48,350	**48,400**	8,438	6,454	8,438	7,156
48,400	**48,450**	8,450	6,461	8,450	7,169
48,450	**48,500**	8,463	6,469	8,463	7,181
48,500	**48,550**	8,475	6,476	8,475	7,194
48,550	**48,600**	8,488	6,484	8,488	7,206
48,600	**48,650**	8,500	6,491	8,500	7,219
48,650	**48,700**	8,513	6,499	8,513	7,231
48,700	**48,750**	8,525	6,506	8,525	7,244
48,750	**48,800**	8,538	6,514	8,538	7,256
48,800	**48,850**	8,550	6,521	8,550	7,269
48,850	**48,900**	8,563	6,529	8,563	7,281
48,900	**48,950**	8,575	6,536	8,575	7,294
48,950	**49,000**	8,588	6,544	8,588	7,306
49,000					
49,000	**49,050**	8,600	6,551	8,600	7,319
49,050	**49,100**	8,613	6,559	8,613	7,331
49,100	**49,150**	8,625	6,566	8,625	7,344
49,150	**49,200**	8,638	6,574	8,638	7,356
49,200	**49,250**	8,650	6,581	8,650	7,369
49,250	**49,300**	8,663	6,589	8,663	7,381
49,300	**49,350**	8,675	6,596	8,675	7,394
49,350	**49,400**	8,688	6,604	8,688	7,406
49,400	**49,450**	8,700	6,611	8,700	7,419
49,450	**49,500**	8,713	6,619	8,713	7,431
49,500	**49,550**	8,725	6,626	8,725	7,444
49,550	**49,600**	8,738	6,634	8,738	7,456
49,600	**49,650**	8,750	6,641	8,750	7,469
49,650	**49,700**	8,763	6,649	8,763	7,481
49,700	**49,750**	8,775	6,656	8,775	7,494
49,750	**49,800**	8,788	6,664	8,788	7,506
49,800	**49,850**	8,800	6,671	8,800	7,519
49,850	**49,900**	8,813	6,679	8,813	7,531
49,900	**49,950**	8,825	6,686	8,825	7,544
49,950	**50,000**	8,838	6,694	8,838	7,556

* This column must also be used by a qualifying widow(er).

Sample Tax Table–*Continued*

If line 43 (taxable income) is— At least	But less than	Single	Married filing jointly *	Married filing sepa-rately	Head of a house-hold
		Your tax is—			
50,000					
50,000	**50,050**	8,850	6,701	8,850	7,569
50,050	**50,100**	8,863	6,709	8,863	7,581
50,100	**50,150**	8,875	6,716	8,875	7,594
50,150	**50,200**	8,888	6,724	8,888	7,606
50,200	**50,250**	8,900	6,731	8,900	7,619
50,250	**50,300**	8,913	6,739	8,913	7,631
50,300	**50,350**	8,925	6,746	8,925	7,644
50,350	**50,400**	8,938	6,754	8,938	7,656
50,400	**50,450**	8,950	6,761	8,950	7,669
50,450	**50,500**	8,963	6,769	8,963	7,681
50,500	**50,550**	8,975	6,776	8,975	7,694
50,550	**50,600**	8,988	6,784	8,988	7,706
50,600	**50,650**	9,000	6,791	9,000	7,719
50,650	**50,700**	9,013	6,799	9,013	7,731
50,700	**50,750**	9,025	6,806	9,025	7,744
50,750	**50,800**	9,038	6,814	9,038	7,756
50,800	**50,850**	9,050	6,821	9,050	7,769
50,850	**50,900**	9,063	6,829	9,063	7,781
50,900	**50,950**	9,075	6,836	9,075	7,794
50,950	**51,000**	9,088	6,844	9,088	7,806
51,000					
51,000	**51,050**	9,100	6,851	9,100	7,819
51,050	**51,100**	9,113	6,859	9,113	7,831
51,100	**51,150**	9,125	6,866	9,125	7,844
51,150	**51,200**	9,138	6,874	9,138	7,856
51,200	**51,250**	9,150	6,881	9,150	7,869
51,250	**51,300**	9,163	6,889	9,163	7,881
51,300	**51,350**	9,175	6,896	9,175	7,894
51,350	**51,400**	9,188	6,904	9,188	7,906
51,400	**51,450**	9,200	6,911	9,200	7,919
51,450	**51,500**	9,213	6,919	9,213	7,931
51,500	**51,550**	9,225	6,926	9,225	7,944
51,550	**51,600**	9,238	6,934	9,238	7,956
51,600	**51,650**	9,250	6,941	9,250	7,969
51,650	**51,700**	9,263	6,949	9,263	7,981
51,700	**51,750**	9,275	6,956	9,275	7,994
51,750	**51,800**	9,288	6,964	9,288	8,006
51,800	**51,850**	9,300	6,971	9,300	8,019
51,850	**51,900**	9,313	6,979	9,313	8,031
51,900	**51,950**	9,325	6,986	9,325	8,044
51,950	**52,000**	9,338	6,994	9,338	8,056
52,000					
52,000	**52,050**	9,350	7,001	9,350	8,069
52,050	**52,100**	9,363	7,009	9,363	8,081
52,100	**52,150**	9,375	7,016	9,375	8,094
52,150	**52,200**	9,388	7,024	9,388	8,106
52,200	**52,250**	9,400	7,031	9,400	8,119
52,250	**52,300**	9,413	7,039	9,413	8,131
52,300	**52,350**	9,425	7,046	9,425	8,144
52,350	**52,400**	9,438	7,054	9,438	8,156
52,400	**52,450**	9,450	7,061	9,450	8,169
52,450	**52,500**	9,463	7,069	9,463	8,181
52,500	**52,550**	9,475	7,076	9,475	8,194
52,550	**52,600**	9,488	7,084	9,488	8,206
52,600	**52,650**	9,500	7,091	9,500	8,219
52,650	**52,700**	9,513	7,099	9,513	8,231
52,700	**52,750**	9,525	7,106	9,525	8,244
52,750	**52,800**	9,538	7,114	9,538	8,256
52,800	**52,850**	9,550	7,121	9,550	8,269
52,850	**52,900**	9,563	7,129	9,563	8,281
52,900	**52,950**	9,575	7,136	9,575	8,294
52,950	**53,000**	9,588	7,144	9,588	8,306

If line 43 (taxable income) is— At least	But less than	Single	Married filing jointly *	Married filing sepa-rately	Head of a house-hold
		Your tax is—			
53,000					
53,000	**53,050**	9,600	7,151	9,600	8,319
53,050	**53,100**	9,613	7,159	9,613	8,331
53,100	**53,150**	9,625	7,166	9,625	8,344
53,150	**53,200**	9,638	7,174	9,638	8,356
53,200	**53,250**	9,650	7,181	9,650	8,369
53,250	**53,300**	9,663	7,189	9,663	8,381
53,300	**53,350**	9,675	7,196	9,675	8,394
53,350	**53,400**	9,688	7,204	9,688	8,406
53,400	**53,450**	9,700	7,211	9,700	8,419
53,450	**53,500**	9,713	7,219	9,713	8,431
53,500	**53,550**	9,725	7,226	9,725	8,444
53,550	**53,600**	9,738	7,234	9,738	8,456
53,600	**53,650**	9,750	7,241	9,750	8,469
53,650	**53,700**	9,763	7,249	9,763	8,481
53,700	**53,750**	9,775	7,256	9,775	8,494
53,750	**53,800**	9,788	7,264	9,788	8,506
53,800	**53,850**	9,800	7,271	9,800	8,519
53,850	**53,900**	9,813	7,279	9,813	8,531
53,900	**53,950**	9,825	7,286	9,825	8,544
53,950	**54,000**	9,838	7,294	9,838	8,556
54,000					
54,000	**54,050**	9,850	7,301	9,850	8,569
54,050	**54,100**	9,863	7,309	9,863	8,581
54,100	**54,150**	9,875	7,316	9,875	8,594
54,150	**54,200**	9,888	7,324	9,888	8,606
54,200	**54,250**	9,900	7,331	9,900	8,619
54,250	**54,300**	9,913	7,339	9,913	8,631
54,300	**54,350**	9,925	7,346	9,925	8,644
54,350	**54,400**	9,938	7,354	9,938	8,656
54,400	**54,450**	9,950	7,361	9,950	8,669
54,450	**54,500**	9,963	7,369	9,963	8,681
54,500	**54,550**	9,975	7,376	9,975	8,694
54,550	**54,600**	9,988	7,384	9,988	8,706
54,600	**54,650**	10,000	7,391	10,000	8,719
54,650	**54,700**	10,013	7,399	10,013	8,731
54,700	**54,750**	10,025	7,406	10,025	8,744
54,750	**54,800**	10,038	7,414	10,038	8,756
54,800	**54,850**	10,050	7,421	10,050	8,769
54,850	**54,900**	10,063	7,429	10,063	8,781
54,900	**54,950**	10,075	7,436	10,075	8,794
54,950	**55,000**	10,088	7,444	10,088	8,806
55,000					
55,000	**55,050**	10,100	7,451	10,100	8,819
55,050	**55,100**	10,113	7,459	10,113	8,831
55,100	**55,150**	10,125	7,466	10,125	8,844
55,150	**55,200**	10,138	7,474	10,138	8,856
55,200	**55,250**	10,150	7,481	10,150	8,869
55,250	**55,300**	10,163	7,489	10,163	8,881
55,300	**55,350**	10,175	7,496	10,175	8,894
55,350	**55,400**	10,188	7,504	10,188	8,906
55,400	**55,450**	10,200	7,511	10,200	8,919
55,450	**55,500**	10,213	7,519	10,213	8,931
55,500	**55,550**	10,225	7,526	10,225	8,944
55,550	**55,600**	10,238	7,534	10,238	8,956
55,600	**55,650**	10,250	7,541	10,250	8,969
55,650	**55,700**	10,263	7,549	10,263	8,981
55,700	**55,750**	10,275	7,556	10,275	8,994
55,750	**55,800**	10,288	7,564	10,288	9,006
55,800	**55,850**	10,300	7,571	10,300	9,019
55,850	**55,900**	10,313	7,579	10,313	9,031
55,900	**55,950**	10,325	7,586	10,325	9,044
55,950	**56,000**	10,338	7,594	10,338	9,056

If line 43 (taxable income) is— At least	But less than	Single	Married filing jointly *	Married filing sepa-rately	Head of a house-hold
		Your tax is—			
56,000					
56,000	**56,050**	10,350	7,601	10,350	9,069
56,050	**56,100**	10,363	7,609	10,363	9,081
56,100	**56,150**	10,375	7,616	10,375	9,094
56,150	**56,200**	10,388	7,624	10,388	9,106
56,200	**56,250**	10,400	7,631	10,400	9,119
56,250	**56,300**	10,413	7,639	10,413	9,131
56,300	**56,350**	10,425	7,646	10,425	9,144
56,350	**56,400**	10,438	7,654	10,438	9,156
56,400	**56,450**	10,450	7,661	10,450	9,169
56,450	**56,500**	10,463	7,669	10,463	9,181
56,500	**56,550**	10,475	7,676	10,475	9,194
56,550	**56,600**	10,488	7,684	10,488	9,206
56,600	**56,650**	10,500	7,691	10,500	9,219
56,650	**56,700**	10,513	7,699	10,513	9,231
56,700	**56,750**	10,525	7,706	10,525	9,244
56,750	**56,800**	10,538	7,714	10,538	9,256
56,800	**56,850**	10,550	7,721	10,550	9,269
56,850	**56,900**	10,563	7,729	10,563	9,281
56,900	**56,950**	10,575	7,736	10,575	9,294
56,950	**57,000**	10,588	7,744	10,588	9,306
57,000					
57,000	**57,050**	10,600	7,751	10,600	9,319
57,050	**57,100**	10,613	7,759	10,613	9,331
57,100	**57,150**	10,625	7,766	10,625	9,344
57,150	**57,200**	10,638	7,774	10,638	9,356
57,200	**57,250**	10,650	7,781	10,650	9,369
57,250	**57,300**	10,663	7,789	10,663	9,381
57,300	**57,350**	10,675	7,796	10,675	9,394
57,350	**57,400**	10,688	7,804	10,688	9,406
57,400	**57,450**	10,700	7,811	10,700	9,419
57,450	**57,500**	10,713	7,819	10,713	9,431
57,500	**57,550**	10,725	7,826	10,725	9,444
57,550	**57,600**	10,738	7,834	10,738	9,456
57,600	**57,650**	10,750	7,841	10,750	9,469
57,650	**57,700**	10,763	7,849	10,763	9,481
57,700	**57,750**	10,775	7,856	10,775	9,494
57,750	**57,800**	10,788	7,864	10,788	9,506
57,800	**57,850**	10,800	7,871	10,800	9,519
57,850	**57,900**	10,813	7,879	10,813	9,531
57,900	**57,950**	10,825	7,886	10,825	9,544
57,950	**58,000**	10,838	7,894	10,838	9,556
58,000					
58,000	**58,050**	10,850	7,901	10,850	9,569
58,050	**58,100**	10,863	7,909	10,863	9,581
58,100	**58,150**	10,875	7,916	10,875	9,594
58,150	**58,200**	10,888	7,924	10,888	9,606
58,200	**58,250**	10,900	7,931	10,900	9,619
58,250	**58,300**	10,913	7,939	10,913	9,631
58,300	**58,350**	10,925	7,946	10,925	9,644
58,350	**58,400**	10,938	7,954	10,938	9,656
58,400	**58,450**	10,950	7,961	10,950	9,669
58,450	**58,500**	10,963	7,969	10,963	9,681
58,500	**58,550**	10,975	7,976	10,975	9,694
58,550	**58,600**	10,988	7,984	10,988	9,706
58,600	**58,650**	11,000	7,991	11,000	9,719
58,650	**58,700**	11,013	7,999	11,013	9,731
58,700	**58,750**	11,025	8,006	11,025	9,744
58,750	**58,800**	11,038	8,014	11,038	9,756
58,800	**58,850**	11,050	8,021	11,050	9,769
58,850	**58,900**	11,063	8,029	11,063	9,781
58,900	**58,950**	11,075	8,036	11,075	9,794
58,950	**59,000**	11,088	8,044	11,088	9,806

* This column must also be used by a qualifying widow(er).

If line 43 (taxable income) is—		And you are—			
At least	But less than	Single	Married filing jointly *	Married filing separately	Head of a household
		Your tax is—			
59,000					
59,000	**59,050**	11,100	8,051	11,100	9,819
59,050	**59,100**	11,113	8,059	11,113	9,831
59,100	**59,150**	11,125	8,066	11,125	9,844
59,150	**59,200**	11,138	8,074	11,138	9,856
59,200	**59,250**	11,150	8,081	11,150	9,869
59,250	**59,300**	11,163	8,089	11,163	9,881
59,300	**59,350**	11,175	8,096	11,175	9,894
59,350	**59,400**	11,188	8,104	11,188	9,906
59,400	**59,450**	11,200	8,111	11,200	9,919
59,450	**59,500**	11,213	8,119	11,213	9,931
59,500	**59,550**	11,225	8,126	11,225	9,944
59,550	**59,600**	11,238	8,134	11,238	9,956
59,600	**59,650**	11,250	8,141	11,250	9,969
59,650	**59,700**	11,263	8,149	11,263	9,981
59,700	**59,750**	11,275	8,156	11,275	9,994
59,750	**59,800**	11,288	8,164	11,288	10,006
59,800	**59,850**	11,300	8,171	11,300	10,019
59,850	**59,900**	11,313	8,179	11,313	10,031
59,900	**59,950**	11,325	8,186	11,325	10,044
59,950	**60,000**	11,338	8,194	11,338	10,056
60,000					
60,000	**60,050**	11,350	8,201	11,350	10,069
60,050	**60,100**	11,363	8,209	11,363	10,081
60,100	**60,150**	11,375	8,216	11,375	10,094
60,150	**60,200**	11,388	8,224	11,388	10,106
60,200	**60,250**	11,400	8,231	11,400	10,119
60,250	**60,300**	11,413	8,239	11,413	10,131
60,300	**60,350**	11,425	8,246	11,425	10,144
60,350	**60,400**	11,438	8,254	11,438	10,156
60,400	**60,450**	11,450	8,261	11,450	10,169
60,450	**60,500**	11,463	8,269	11,463	10,181
60,500	**60,550**	11,475	8,276	11,475	10,194
60,550	**60,600**	11,488	8,284	11,488	10,206
60,600	**60,650**	11,500	8,291	11,500	10,219
60,650	**60,700**	11,513	8,299	11,513	10,231
60,700	**60,750**	11,525	8,306	11,525	10,244
60,750	**60,800**	11,538	8,314	11,538	10,256
60,800	**60,850**	11,550	8,321	11,550	10,269
60,850	**60,900**	11,563	8,329	11,563	10,281
60,900	**60,950**	11,575	8,336	11,575	10,294
60,950	**61,000**	11,588	8,344	11,588	10,306
61,000					
61,000	**61,050**	11,600	8,351	11,600	10,319
61,050	**61,100**	11,613	8,359	11,613	10,331
61,100	**61,150**	11,625	8,366	11,625	10,344
61,150	**61,200**	11,638	8,374	11,638	10,356
61,200	**61,250**	11,650	8,381	11,650	10,369
61,250	**61,300**	11,663	8,389	11,663	10,381
61,300	**61,350**	11,675	8,396	11,675	10,394
61,350	**61,400**	11,688	8,404	11,688	10,406
61,400	**61,450**	11,700	8,411	11,700	10,419
61,450	**61,500**	11,713	8,419	11,713	10,431
61,500	**61,550**	11,725	8,426	11,725	10,444
61,550	**61,600**	11,738	8,434	11,738	10,456
61,600	**61,650**	11,750	8,441	11,750	10,469
61,650	**61,700**	11,763	8,449	11,763	10,481
61,700	**61,750**	11,775	8,456	11,775	10,494
61,750	**61,800**	11,788	8,464	11,788	10,506
61,800	**61,850**	11,800	8,471	11,800	10,519
61,850	**61,900**	11,813	8,479	11,813	10,531
61,900	**61,950**	11,825	8,486	11,825	10,544
61,950	**62,000**	11,838	8,494	11,838	10,556
62,000					
62,000	**62,050**	11,850	8,501	11,850	10,569
62,050	**62,100**	11,863	8,509	11,863	10,581
62,100	**62,150**	11,875	8,516	11,875	10,594
62,150	**62,200**	11,888	8,524	11,888	10,606
62,200	**62,250**	11,900	8,531	11,900	10,619
62,250	**62,300**	11,913	8,539	11,913	10,631
62,300	**62,350**	11,925	8,546	11,925	10,644
62,350	**62,400**	11,938	8,554	11,938	10,656
62,400	**62,450**	11,950	8,561	11,950	10,669
62,450	**62,500**	11,963	8,569	11,963	10,681
62,500	**62,550**	11,975	8,576	11,975	10,694
62,550	**62,600**	11,988	8,584	11,988	10,706
62,600	**62,650**	12,000	8,591	12,000	10,719
62,650	**62,700**	12,013	8,599	12,013	10,731
62,700	**62,750**	12,025	8,606	12,025	10,744
62,750	**62,800**	12,038	8,614	12,038	10,756
62,800	**62,850**	12,050	8,621	12,050	10,769
62,850	**62,900**	12,063	8,629	12,063	10,781
62,900	**62,950**	12,075	8,636	12,075	10,794
62,950	**63,000**	12,088	8,644	12,088	10,806
63,000					
63,000	**63,050**	12,100	8,651	12,100	10,819
63,050	**63,100**	12,113	8,659	12,113	10,831
63,100	**63,150**	12,125	8,666	12,125	10,844
63,150	**63,200**	12,138	8,674	12,138	10,856
63,200	**63,250**	12,150	8,681	12,150	10,869
63,250	**63,300**	12,163	8,689	12,163	10,881
63,300	**63,350**	12,175	8,696	12,175	10,894
63,350	**63,400**	12,188	8,704	12,188	10,906
63,400	**63,450**	12,200	8,711	12,200	10,919
63,450	**63,500**	12,213	8,719	12,213	10,931
63,500	**63,550**	12,225	8,726	12,225	10,944
63,550	**63,600**	12,238	8,734	12,238	10,956
63,600	**63,650**	12,250	8,741	12,250	10,969
63,650	**63,700**	12,263	8,749	12,263	10,981
63,700	**63,750**	12,275	8,756	12,275	10,994
63,750	**63,800**	12,288	8,764	12,288	11,006
63,800	**63,850**	12,300	8,771	12,300	11,019
63,850	**63,900**	12,313	8,779	12,313	11,031
63,900	**63,950**	12,325	8,786	12,325	11,044
63,950	**64,000**	12,338	8,794	12,338	11,056
64,000					
64,000	**64,050**	12,350	8,801	12,350	11,069
64,050	**64,100**	12,363	8,809	12,363	11,081
64,100	**64,150**	12,375	8,816	12,375	11,094
64,150	**64,200**	12,388	8,824	12,388	11,106
64,200	**64,250**	12,400	8,831	12,400	11,119
64,250	**64,300**	12,413	8,839	12,413	11,131
64,300	**64,350**	12,425	8,846	12,425	11,144
64,350	**64,400**	12,438	8,854	12,438	11,156
64,400	**64,450**	12,450	8,861	12,450	11,169
64,450	**64,500**	12,463	8,869	12,463	11,181
64,500	**64,550**	12,475	8,876	12,475	11,194
64,550	**64,600**	12,488	8,884	12,488	11,206
64,600	**64,650**	12,500	8,891	12,500	11,219
64,650	**64,700**	12,513	8,899	12,513	11,231
64,700	**64,750**	12,525	8,906	12,525	11,244
64,750	**64,800**	12,538	8,914	12,538	11,256
64,800	**64,850**	12,550	8,921	12,550	11,269
64,850	**64,900**	12,563	8,929	12,563	11,281
64,900	**64,950**	12,575	8,936	12,575	11,294
64,950	**65,000**	12,588	8,944	12,588	11,306
65,000					
65,000	**65,050**	12,600	8,951	12,600	11,319
65,050	**65,100**	12,613	8,959	12,613	11,331
65,100	**65,150**	12,625	8,969	12,625	11,344
65,150	**65,200**	12,638	8,981	12,638	11,356
65,200	**65,250**	12,650	8,994	12,650	11,369
65,250	**65,300**	12,663	9,006	12,663	11,381
65,300	**65,350**	12,675	9,019	12,675	11,394
65,350	**65,400**	12,688	9,031	12,688	11,406
65,400	**65,450**	12,700	9,044	12,700	11,419
65,450	**65,500**	12,713	9,056	12,713	11,431
65,500	**65,550**	12,725	9,069	12,725	11,444
65,550	**65,600**	12,738	9,081	12,738	11,456
65,600	**65,650**	12,750	9,094	12,750	11,469
65,650	**65,700**	12,763	9,106	12,763	11,481
65,700	**65,750**	12,775	9,119	12,775	11,494
65,750	**65,800**	12,788	9,131	12,789	11,506
65,800	**65,850**	12,800	9,144	12,803	11,519
65,850	**65,900**	12,813	9,156	12,817	11,531
65,900	**65,950**	12,825	9,169	12,831	11,544
65,950	**66,000**	12,838	9,181	12,845	11,556
66,000					
66,000	**66,050**	12,850	9,194	12,859	11,569
66,050	**66,100**	12,863	9,206	12,873	11,581
66,100	**66,150**	12,875	9,219	12,887	11,594
66,150	**66,200**	12,888	9,231	12,901	11,606
66,200	**66,250**	12,900	9,244	12,915	11,619
66,250	**66,300**	12,913	9,256	12,929	11,631
66,300	**66,350**	12,925	9,269	12,943	11,644
66,350	**66,400**	12,938	9,281	12,957	11,656
66,400	**66,450**	12,950	9,294	12,971	11,669
66,450	**66,500**	12,963	9,306	12,985	11,681
66,500	**66,550**	12,975	9,319	12,999	11,694
66,550	**66,600**	12,988	9,331	13,013	11,706
66,600	**66,650**	13,000	9,344	13,027	11,719
66,650	**66,700**	13,013	9,356	13,041	11,731
66,700	**66,750**	13,025	9,369	13,055	11,744
66,750	**66,800**	13,038	9,381	13,069	11,756
66,800	**66,850**	13,050	9,394	13,083	11,769
66,850	**66,900**	13,063	9,406	13,097	11,781
66,900	**66,950**	13,075	9,419	13,111	11,794
66,950	**67,000**	13,088	9,431	13,125	11,806
67,000					
67,000	**67,050**	13,100	9,444	13,139	11,819
67,050	**67,100**	13,113	9,456	13,153	11,831
67,100	**67,150**	13,125	9,469	13,167	11,844
67,150	**67,200**	13,138	9,481	13,181	11,856
67,200	**67,250**	13,150	9,494	13,195	11,869
67,250	**67,300**	13,163	9,506	13,209	11,881
67,300	**67,350**	13,175	9,519	13,223	11,894
67,350	**67,400**	13,188	9,531	13,237	11,906
67,400	**67,450**	13,200	9,544	13,251	11,919
67,450	**67,500**	13,213	9,556	13,265	11,931
67,500	**67,550**	13,225	9,569	13,279	11,944
67,550	**67,600**	13,238	9,581	13,293	11,956
67,600	**67,650**	13,250	9,594	13,307	11,969
67,650	**67,700**	13,263	9,606	13,321	11,981
67,700	**67,750**	13,275	9,619	13,335	11,994
67,750	**67,800**	13,288	9,631	13,349	12,006
67,800	**67,850**	13,300	9,644	13,363	12,019
67,850	**67,900**	13,313	9,656	13,377	12,031
67,900	**67,950**	13,325	9,669	13,391	12,044
67,950	**68,000**	13,338	9,681	13,405	12,056

* This column must also be used by a qualifying widow(er).

Sample Tax Table–*Continued*

If line 43 (taxable income) is—		And you are—			
At least	But less than	Single	Married filing jointly *	Married filing sepa-rately	Head of a house-hold
		Your tax is—			
68,000					
68,000	**68,050**	13,350	9,694	13,419	12,069
68,050	**68,100**	13,363	9,706	13,433	12,081
68,100	**68,150**	13,375	9,719	13,447	12,094
68,150	**68,200**	13,388	9,731	13,461	12,106
68,200	**68,250**	13,400	9,744	13,475	12,119
68,250	**68,300**	13,413	9,756	13,489	12,131
68,300	**68,350**	13,425	9,769	13,503	12,144
68,350	**68,400**	13,438	9,781	13,517	12,156
68,400	**68,450**	13,450	9,794	13,531	12,169
68,450	**68,500**	13,463	9,806	13,545	12,181
68,500	**68,550**	13,475	9,819	13,559	12,194
68,550	**68,600**	13,488	9,831	13,573	12,206
68,600	**68,650**	13,500	9,844	13,587	12,219
68,650	**68,700**	13,513	9,856	13,601	12,231
68,700	**68,750**	13,525	9,869	13,615	12,244
68,750	**68,800**	13,538	9,881	13,629	12,256
68,800	**68,850**	13,550	9,894	13,643	12,269
68,850	**68,900**	13,563	9,906	13,657	12,281
68,900	**68,950**	13,575	9,919	13,671	12,294
68,950	**69,000**	13,588	9,931	13,685	12,306
69,000					
69,000	**69,050**	13,600	9,944	13,699	12,319
69,050	**69,100**	13,613	9,956	13,713	12,331
69,100	**69,150**	13,625	9,969	13,727	12,344
69,150	**69,200**	13,638	9,981	13,741	12,356
69,200	**69,250**	13,650	9,994	13,755	12,369
69,250	**69,300**	13,663	10,006	13,769	12,381
69,300	**69,350**	13,675	10,019	13,783	12,394
69,350	**69,400**	13,688	10,031	13,797	12,406
69,400	**69,450**	13,700	10,044	13,811	12,419
69,450	**69,500**	13,713	10,056	13,825	12,431
69,500	**69,550**	13,725	10,069	13,839	12,444
69,550	**69,600**	13,738	10,081	13,853	12,456
69,600	**69,650**	13,750	10,094	13,867	12,469
69,650	**69,700**	13,763	10,106	13,881	12,481
69,700	**69,750**	13,775	10,119	13,895	12,494
69,750	**69,800**	13,788	10,131	13,909	12,506
69,800	**69,850**	13,800	10,144	13,923	12,519
69,850	**69,900**	13,813	10,156	13,937	12,531
69,900	**69,950**	13,825	10,169	13,951	12,544
69,950	**70,000**	13,838	10,181	13,965	12,556
70,000					
70,000	**70,050**	13,850	10,194	13,979	12,569
70,050	**70,100**	13,863	10,206	13,993	12,581
70,100	**70,150**	13,875	10,219	14,007	12,594
70,150	**70,200**	13,888	10,231	14,021	12,606
70,200	**70,250**	13,900	10,244	14,035	12,619
70,250	**70,300**	13,913	10,256	14,049	12,631
70,300	**70,350**	13,925	10,269	14,063	12,644
70,350	**70,400**	13,938	10,281	14,077	12,656
70,400	**70,450**	13,950	10,294	14,091	12,669
70,450	**70,500**	13,963	10,306	14,105	12,681
70,500	**70,550**	13,975	10,319	14,119	12,694
70,550	**70,600**	13,988	10,331	14,133	12,706
70,600	**70,650**	14,000	10,344	14,147	12,719
70,650	**70,700**	14,013	10,356	14,161	12,731
70,700	**70,750**	14,025	10,369	14,175	12,744
70,750	**70,800**	14,038	10,381	14,189	12,756
70,800	**70,850**	14,050	10,394	14,203	12,769
70,850	**70,900**	14,063	10,406	14,217	12,781
70,900	**70,950**	14,075	10,419	14,231	12,794
70,950	**71,000**	14,088	10,431	14,245	12,806
71,000					
71,000	**71,050**	14,100	10,444	14,259	12,819
71,050	**71,100**	14,113	10,456	14,273	12,831
71,100	**71,150**	14,125	10,469	14,287	12,844
71,150	**71,200**	14,138	10,481	14,301	12,856
71,200	**71,250**	14,150	10,494	14,315	12,869
71,250	**71,300**	14,163	10,506	14,329	12,881
71,300	**71,350**	14,175	10,519	14,343	12,894
71,350	**71,400**	14,188	10,531	14,357	12,906
71,400	**71,450**	14,200	10,544	14,371	12,919
71,450	**71,500**	14,213	10,556	14,385	12,931
71,500	**71,550**	14,225	10,569	14,399	12,944
71,550	**71,600**	14,238	10,581	14,413	12,956
71,600	**71,650**	14,250	10,594	14,427	12,969
71,650	**71,700**	14,263	10,606	14,441	12,981
71,700	**71,750**	14,275	10,619	14,455	12,994
71,750	**71,800**	14,288	10,631	14,469	13,006
71,800	**71,850**	14,300	10,644	14,483	13,019
71,850	**71,900**	14,313	10,656	14,497	13,031
71,900	**71,950**	14,325	10,669	14,511	13,044
71,950	**72,000**	14,338	10,681	14,525	13,056
72,000					
72,000	**72,050**	14,350	10,694	14,539	13,069
72,050	**72,100**	14,363	10,706	14,553	13,081
72,100	**72,150**	14,375	10,719	14,567	13,094
72,150	**72,200**	14,388	10,731	14,581	13,106
72,200	**72,250**	14,400	10,744	14,595	13,119
72,250	**72,300**	14,413	10,756	14,609	13,131
72,300	**72,350**	14,425	10,769	14,623	13,144
72,350	**72,400**	14,438	10,781	14,637	13,156
72,400	**72,450**	14,450	10,794	14,651	13,169
72,450	**72,500**	14,463	10,806	14,665	13,181
72,500	**72,550**	14,475	10,819	14,679	13,194
72,550	**72,600**	14,488	10,831	14,693	13,206
72,600	**72,650**	14,500	10,844	14,707	13,219
72,650	**72,700**	14,513	10,856	14,721	13,231
72,700	**72,750**	14,525	10,869	14,735	13,244
72,750	**72,800**	14,538	10,881	14,749	13,256
72,800	**72,850**	14,550	10,894	14,763	13,269
72,850	**72,900**	14,563	10,906	14,777	13,281
72,900	**72,950**	14,575	10,919	14,791	13,294
72,950	**73,000**	14,588	10,931	14,805	13,306
73,000					
73,000	**73,050**	14,600	10,944	14,819	13,319
73,050	**73,100**	14,613	10,956	14,833	13,331
73,100	**73,150**	14,625	10,969	14,847	13,344
73,150	**73,200**	14,638	10,981	14,861	13,356
73,200	**73,250**	14,650	10,994	14,875	13,369
73,250	**73,300**	14,663	11,006	14,889	13,381
73,300	**73,350**	14,675	11,019	14,903	13,394
73,350	**73,400**	14,688	11,031	14,917	13,406
73,400	**73,450**	14,700	11,044	14,931	13,419
73,450	**73,500**	14,713	11,056	14,945	13,431
73,500	**73,550**	14,725	11,069	14,959	13,444
73,550	**73,600**	14,738	11,081	14,973	13,456
73,600	**73,650**	14,750	11,094	14,987	13,469
73,650	**73,700**	14,763	11,106	15,001	13,481
73,700	**73,750**	14,775	11,119	15,015	13,494
73,750	**73,800**	14,788	11,131	15,029	13,506
73,800	**73,850**	14,800	11,144	15,043	13,519
73,850	**73,900**	14,813	11,156	15,057	13,531
73,900	**73,950**	14,825	11,169	15,071	13,544
73,950	**74,000**	14,838	11,181	15,085	13,556
74,000					
74,000	**74,050**	14,850	11,194	15,099	13,569
74,050	**74,100**	14,863	11,206	15,113	13,581
74,100	**74,150**	14,875	11,219	15,127	13,594
74,150	**74,200**	14,888	11,231	15,141	13,606
74,200	**74,250**	14,900	11,244	15,155	13,619
74,250	**74,300**	14,913	11,256	15,169	13,631
74,300	**74,350**	14,925	11,269	15,183	13,644
74,350	**74,400**	14,938	11,281	15,197	13,656
74,400	**74,450**	14,950	11,294	15,211	13,669
74,450	**74,500**	14,963	11,306	15,225	13,681
74,500	**74,550**	14,975	11,319	15,239	13,694
74,550	**74,600**	14,988	11,331	15,253	13,706
74,600	**74,650**	15,000	11,344	15,267	13,719
74,650	**74,700**	15,013	11,356	15,281	13,731
74,700	**74,750**	15,025	11,369	15,295	13,744
74,750	**74,800**	15,038	11,381	15,309	13,756
74,800	**74,850**	15,050	11,394	15,323	13,769
74,850	**74,900**	15,063	11,406	15,337	13,781
74,900	**74,950**	15,075	11,419	15,351	13,794
74,950	**75,000**	15,088	11,431	15,365	13,806
75,000					
75,000	**75,050**	15,100	11,444	15,379	13,819
75,050	**75,100**	15,113	11,456	15,393	13,831
75,100	**75,150**	15,125	11,469	15,407	13,844
75,150	**75,200**	15,138	11,481	15,421	13,856
75,200	**75,250**	15,150	11,494	15,435	13,869
75,250	**75,300**	15,163	11,506	15,449	13,881
75,300	**75,350**	15,175	11,519	15,463	13,894
75,350	**75,400**	15,188	11,531	15,477	13,906
75,400	**75,450**	15,200	11,544	15,491	13,919
75,450	**75,500**	15,213	11,556	15,505	13,931
75,500	**75,550**	15,225	11,569	15,519	13,944
75,550	**75,600**	15,238	11,581	15,533	13,956
75,600	**75,650**	15,250	11,594	15,547	13,969
75,650	**75,700**	15,263	11,606	15,561	13,981
75,700	**75,750**	15,275	11,619	15,575	13,994
75,750	**75,800**	15,288	11,631	15,589	14,006
75,800	**75,850**	15,300	11,644	15,603	14,019
75,850	**75,900**	15,313	11,656	15,617	14,031
75,900	**75,950**	15,325	11,669	15,631	14,044
75,950	**76,000**	15,338	11,681	15,645	14,056
76,000					
76,000	**76,050**	15,350	11,694	15,659	14,069
76,050	**76,100**	15,363	11,706	15,673	14,081
76,100	**76,150**	15,375	11,719	15,687	14,094
76,150	**76,200**	15,388	11,731	15,701	14,106
76,200	**76,250**	15,400	11,744	15,715	14,119
76,250	**76,300**	15,413	11,756	15,729	14,131
76,300	**76,350**	15,425	11,769	15,743	14,144
76,350	**76,400**	15,438	11,781	15,757	14,156
76,400	**76,450**	15,450	11,794	15,771	14,169
76,450	**76,500**	15,463	11,806	15,785	14,181
76,500	**76,550**	15,475	11,819	15,799	14,194
76,550	**76,600**	15,488	11,831	15,813	14,206
76,600	**76,650**	15,500	11,844	15,827	14,219
76,650	**76,700**	15,513	11,856	15,841	14,231
76,700	**76,750**	15,525	11,869	15,855	14,244
76,750	**76,800**	15,538	11,881	15,869	14,256
76,800	**76,850**	15,550	11,894	15,883	14,269
76,850	**76,900**	15,563	11,906	15,897	14,281
76,900	**76,950**	15,575	11,919	15,911	14,294
76,950	**77,000**	15,588	11,931	15,925	14,306

* This column must also be used by a qualifying widow(er).

If line 43 (taxable income) is—		And you are—			
At least	But less than	Single	Married filing jointly *	Married filing separately	Head of a household
		Your tax is—			
77,000					
77,000	**77,050**	15,600	11,944	15,939	14,319
77,050	**77,100**	15,613	11,956	15,953	14,331
77,100	**77,150**	15,625	11,969	15,967	14,344
77,150	**77,200**	15,638	11,981	15,981	14,356
77,200	**77,250**	15,650	11,994	15,995	14,369
77,250	**77,300**	15,663	12,006	16,009	14,381
77,300	**77,350**	15,675	12,019	16,023	14,394
77,350	**77,400**	15,688	12,031	16,037	14,406
77,400	**77,450**	15,700	12,044	16,051	14,419
77,450	**77,500**	15,713	12,056	16,065	14,431
77,500	**77,550**	15,725	12,069	16,079	14,444
77,550	**77,600**	15,738	12,081	16,093	14,456
77,600	**77,650**	15,750	12,094	16,107	14,469
77,650	**77,700**	15,763	12,106	16,121	14,481
77,700	**77,750**	15,775	12,119	16,135	14,494
77,750	**77,800**	15,788	12,131	16,149	14,506
77,800	**77,850**	15,800	12,144	16,163	14,519
77,850	**77,900**	15,813	12,156	16,177	14,531
77,900	**77,950**	15,825	12,169	16,191	14,544
77,950	**78,000**	15,838	12,181	16,205	14,556
78,000					
78,000	**78,050**	15,850	12,194	16,219	14,569
78,050	**78,100**	15,863	12,206	16,233	14,581
78,100	**78,150**	15,875	12,219	16,247	14,594
78,150	**78,200**	15,888	12,231	16,261	14,606
78,200	**78,250**	15,900	12,244	16,275	14,619
78,250	**78,300**	15,913	12,256	16,289	14,631
78,300	**78,350**	15,925	12,269	16,303	14,644
78,350	**78,400**	15,938	12,281	16,317	14,656
78,400	**78,450**	15,950	12,294	16,331	14,669
78,450	**78,500**	15,963	12,306	16,345	14,681
78,500	**78,550**	15,975	12,319	16,359	14,694
78,550	**78,600**	15,988	12,331	16,373	14,706
78,600	**78,650**	16,000	12,344	16,387	14,719
78,650	**78,700**	16,013	12,356	16,401	14,731
78,700	**78,750**	16,025	12,369	16,415	14,744
78,750	**78,800**	16,038	12,381	16,429	14,756
78,800	**78,850**	16,050	12,394	16,443	14,769
78,850	**78,900**	16,063	12,406	16,457	14,781
78,900	**78,950**	16,077	12,419	16,471	14,794
78,950	**79,000**	16,091	12,431	16,485	14,806
79,000					
79,000	**79,050**	16,105	12,444	16,499	14,819
79,050	**79,100**	16,119	12,456	16,513	14,831
79,100	**79,150**	16,133	12,469	16,527	14,844
79,150	**79,200**	16,147	12,481	16,541	14,856
79,200	**79,250**	16,161	12,494	16,555	14,869
79,250	**79,300**	16,175	12,506	16,569	14,881
79,300	**79,350**	16,189	12,519	16,583	14,894
79,350	**79,400**	16,203	12,531	16,597	14,906
79,400	**79,450**	16,217	12,544	16,611	14,919
79,450	**79,500**	16,231	12,556	16,625	14,931
79,500	**79,550**	16,245	12,569	16,639	14,944
79,550	**79,600**	16,259	12,581	16,653	14,956
79,600	**79,650**	16,273	12,594	16,667	14,969
79,650	**79,700**	16,287	12,606	16,681	14,981
79,700	**79,750**	16,301	12,619	16,695	14,994
79,750	**79,800**	16,315	12,631	16,709	15,006
79,800	**79,850**	16,329	12,644	16,723	15,019
79,850	**79,900**	16,343	12,656	16,737	15,031
79,900	**79,950**	16,357	12,669	16,751	15,044
79,950	**80,000**	16,371	12,681	16,765	15,056

If line 43 (taxable income) is—		And you are—			
At least	But less than	Single	Married filing jointly *	Married filing separately	Head of a household
		Your tax is—			
80,000					
80,000	**80,050**	16,385	12,694	16,779	15,069
80,050	**80,100**	16,399	12,706	16,793	15,081
80,100	**80,150**	16,413	12,719	16,807	15,094
80,150	**80,200**	16,427	12,731	16,821	15,106
80,200	**80,250**	16,441	12,744	16,835	15,119
80,250	**80,300**	16,455	12,756	16,849	15,131
80,300	**80,350**	16,469	12,769	16,863	15,144
80,350	**80,400**	16,483	12,781	16,877	15,156
80,400	**80,450**	16,497	12,794	16,891	15,169
80,450	**80,500**	16,511	12,806	16,905	15,181
80,500	**80,550**	16,525	12,819	16,919	15,194
80,550	**80,600**	16,539	12,831	16,933	15,206
80,600	**80,650**	16,553	12,844	16,947	15,219
80,650	**80,700**	16,567	12,856	16,961	15,231
80,700	**80,750**	16,581	12,869	16,975	15,244
80,750	**80,800**	16,595	12,881	16,989	15,256
80,800	**80,850**	16,609	12,894	17,003	15,269
80,850	**80,900**	16,623	12,906	17,017	15,281
80,900	**80,950**	16,637	12,919	17,031	15,294
80,950	**81,000**	16,651	12,931	17,045	15,306
81,000					
81,000	**81,050**	16,665	12,944	17,059	15,319
81,050	**81,100**	16,679	12,956	17,073	15,331
81,100	**81,150**	16,693	12,969	17,087	15,344
81,150	**81,200**	16,707	12,981	17,101	15,356
81,200	**81,250**	16,721	12,994	17,115	15,369
81,250	**81,300**	16,735	13,006	17,129	15,381
81,300	**81,350**	16,749	13,019	17,143	15,394
81,350	**81,400**	16,763	13,031	17,157	15,406
81,400	**81,450**	16,777	13,044	17,171	15,419
81,450	**81,500**	16,791	13,056	17,185	15,431
81,500	**81,550**	16,805	13,069	17,199	15,444
81,550	**81,600**	16,819	13,081	17,213	15,456
81,600	**81,650**	16,833	13,094	17,227	15,469
81,650	**81,700**	16,847	13,106	17,241	15,481
81,700	**81,750**	16,861	13,119	17,255	15,494
81,750	**81,800**	16,875	13,131	17,269	15,506
81,800	**81,850**	16,889	13,144	17,283	15,519
81,850	**81,900**	16,903	13,156	17,297	15,531
81,900	**81,950**	16,917	13,169	17,311	15,544
81,950	**82,000**	16,931	13,181	17,325	15,556
82,000					
82,000	**82,050**	16,945	13,194	17,339	15,569
82,050	**82,100**	16,959	13,206	17,353	15,581
82,100	**82,150**	16,973	13,219	17,367	15,594
82,150	**82,200**	16,987	13,231	17,381	15,606
82,200	**82,250**	17,001	13,244	17,395	15,619
82,250	**82,300**	17,015	13,256	17,409	15,631
82,300	**82,350**	17,029	13,269	17,423	15,644
82,350	**82,400**	17,043	13,281	17,437	15,656
82,400	**82,450**	17,057	13,294	17,451	15,669
82,450	**82,500**	17,071	13,306	17,465	15,681
82,500	**82,550**	17,085	13,319	17,479	15,694
82,550	**82,600**	17,099	13,331	17,493	15,706
82,600	**82,650**	17,113	13,344	17,507	15,719
82,650	**82,700**	17,127	13,356	17,521	15,731
82,700	**82,750**	17,141	13,369	17,535	15,744
82,750	**82,800**	17,155	13,381	17,549	15,756
82,800	**82,850**	17,169	13,394	17,563	15,769
82,850	**82,900**	17,183	13,406	17,577	15,781
82,900	**82,950**	17,197	13,419	17,591	15,794
82,950	**83,000**	17,211	13,431	17,605	15,806

If line 43 (taxable income) is—		And you are—			
At least	But less than	Single	Married filing jointly *	Married filing separately	Head of a household
		Your tax is—			
83,000					
83,000	**83,050**	17,225	13,444	17,619	15,819
83,050	**83,100**	17,239	13,456	17,633	15,831
83,100	**83,150**	17,253	13,469	17,647	15,844
83,150	**83,200**	17,267	13,481	17,661	15,856
83,200	**83,250**	17,281	13,494	17,675	15,869
83,250	**83,300**	17,295	13,506	17,689	15,881
83,300	**83,350**	17,309	13,519	17,703	15,894
83,350	**83,400**	17,323	13,531	17,717	15,906
83,400	**83,450**	17,337	13,544	17,731	15,919
83,450	**83,500**	17,351	13,556	17,745	15,931
83,500	**83,550**	17,365	13,569	17,759	15,944
83,550	**83,600**	17,379	13,581	17,773	15,956
83,600	**83,650**	17,393	13,594	17,787	15,969
83,650	**83,700**	17,407	13,606	17,801	15,981
83,700	**83,750**	17,421	13,619	17,815	15,994
83,750	**83,800**	17,435	13,631	17,829	16,006
83,800	**83,850**	17,449	13,644	17,843	16,019
83,850	**83,900**	17,463	13,656	17,857	16,031
83,900	**83,950**	17,477	13,669	17,871	16,044
83,950	**84,000**	17,491	13,681	17,885	16,056
84,000					
84,000	**84,050**	17,505	13,694	17,899	16,069
84,050	**84,100**	17,519	13,706	17,913	16,081
84,100	**84,150**	17,533	13,719	17,927	16,094
84,150	**84,200**	17,547	13,731	17,941	16,106
84,200	**84,250**	17,561	13,744	17,955	16,119
84,250	**84,300**	17,575	13,756	17,969	16,131
84,300	**84,350**	17,589	13,769	17,983	16,144
84,350	**84,400**	17,603	13,781	17,997	16,156
84,400	**84,450**	17,617	13,794	18,011	16,169
84,450	**84,500**	17,631	13,806	18,025	16,181
84,500	**84,550**	17,645	13,819	18,039	16,194
84,550	**84,600**	17,659	13,831	18,053	16,206
84,600	**84,650**	17,673	13,844	18,067	16,219
84,650	**84,700**	17,687	13,856	18,081	16,231
84,700	**84,750**	17,701	13,869	18,095	16,244
84,750	**84,800**	17,715	13,881	18,109	16,256
84,800	**84,850**	17,729	13,894	18,123	16,269
84,850	**84,900**	17,743	13,906	18,137	16,281
84,900	**84,950**	17,757	13,919	18,151	16,294
84,950	**85,000**	17,771	13,931	18,165	16,306
85,000					
85,000	**85,050**	17,785	13,944	18,179	16,319
85,050	**85,100**	17,799	13,956	18,193	16,331
85,100	**85,150**	17,813	13,969	18,207	16,344
85,150	**85,200**	17,827	13,981	18,221	16,356
85,200	**85,250**	17,841	13,994	18,235	16,369
85,250	**85,300**	17,855	14,006	18,249	16,381
85,300	**85,350**	17,869	14,019	18,263	16,394
85,350	**85,400**	17,883	14,031	18,277	16,406
85,400	**85,450**	17,897	14,044	18,291	16,419
85,450	**85,500**	17,911	14,056	18,305	16,431
85,500	**85,550**	17,925	14,069	18,319	16,444
85,550	**85,600**	17,939	14,081	18,333	16,456
85,600	**85,650**	17,953	14,094	18,347	16,469
85,650	**85,700**	17,967	14,106	18,361	16,481
85,700	**85,750**	17,981	14,119	18,375	16,494
85,750	**85,800**	17,995	14,131	18,389	16,506
85,800	**85,850**	18,009	14,144	18,403	16,519
85,850	**85,900**	18,023	14,156	18,417	16,531
85,900	**85,950**	18,037	14,169	18,431	16,544
85,950	**86,000**	18,051	14,181	18,445	16,556

* This column must also be used by a qualifying widow(er).

Sample Tax Table–*Continued*

If line 43 (taxable income) is—		And you are—			
At least	But less than	Single	Married filing jointly *	Married filing separately	Head of a household
		Your tax is—			
86,000					
86,000	**86,050**	18,065	14,194	18,459	16,569
86,050	**86,100**	18,079	14,206	18,473	16,581
86,100	**86,150**	18,093	14,219	18,487	16,594
86,150	**86,200**	18,107	14,231	18,501	16,606
86,200	**86,250**	18,121	14,244	18,515	16,619
86,250	**86,300**	18,135	14,256	18,529	16,631
86,300	**86,350**	18,149	14,269	18,543	16,644
86,350	**86,400**	18,163	14,281	18,557	16,656
86,400	**86,450**	18,177	14,294	18,571	16,669
86,450	**86,500**	18,191	14,306	18,585	16,681
86,500	**86,550**	18,205	14,319	18,599	16,694
86,550	**86,600**	18,219	14,331	18,613	16,706
86,600	**86,650**	18,233	14,344	18,627	16,719
86,650	**86,700**	18,247	14,356	18,641	16,731
86,700	**86,750**	18,261	14,369	18,655	16,744
86,750	**86,800**	18,275	14,381	18,669	16,756
86,800	**86,850**	18,289	14,394	18,683	16,769
86,850	**86,900**	18,303	14,406	18,697	16,781
86,900	**86,950**	18,317	14,419	18,711	16,794
86,950	**87,000**	18,331	14,431	18,725	16,806
87,000					
87,000	**87,050**	18,345	14,444	18,739	16,819
87,050	**87,100**	18,359	14,456	18,753	16,831
87,100	**87,150**	18,373	14,469	18,767	16,844
87,150	**87,200**	18,387	14,481	18,781	16,856
87,200	**87,250**	18,401	14,494	18,795	16,869
87,250	**87,300**	18,415	14,506	18,809	16,881
87,300	**87,350**	18,429	14,519	18,823	16,894
87,350	**87,400**	18,443	14,531	18,837	16,906
87,400	**87,450**	18,457	14,544	18,851	16,919
87,450	**87,500**	18,471	14,556	18,865	16,931
87,500	**87,550**	18,485	14,569	18,879	16,944
87,550	**87,600**	18,499	14,581	18,893	16,956
87,600	**87,650**	18,513	14,594	18,907	16,969
87,650	**87,700**	18,527	14,606	18,921	16,981
87,700	**87,750**	18,541	14,619	18,935	16,994
87,750	**87,800**	18,555	14,631	18,949	17,006
87,800	**87,850**	18,569	14,644	18,963	17,019
87,850	**87,900**	18,583	14,656	18,977	17,031
87,900	**87,950**	18,597	14,669	18,991	17,044
87,950	**88,000**	18,611	14,681	19,005	17,056
88,000					
88,000	**88,050**	18,625	14,694	19,019	17,069
88,050	**88,100**	18,639	14,706	19,033	17,081
88,100	**88,150**	18,653	14,719	19,047	17,094
88,150	**88,200**	18,667	14,731	19,061	17,106
88,200	**88,250**	18,681	14,744	19,075	17,119
88,250	**88,300**	18,695	14,756	19,089	17,131
88,300	**88,350**	18,709	14,769	19,103	17,144
88,350	**88,400**	18,723	14,781	19,117	17,156
88,400	**88,450**	18,737	14,794	19,131	17,169
88,450	**88,500**	18,751	14,806	19,145	17,181
88,500	**88,550**	18,765	14,819	19,159	17,194
88,550	**88,600**	18,779	14,831	19,173	17,206
88,600	**88,650**	18,793	14,844	19,187	17,219
88,650	**88,700**	18,807	14,856	19,201	17,231
88,700	**88,750**	18,821	14,869	19,215	17,244
88,750	**88,800**	18,835	14,881	19,229	17,256
88,800	**88,850**	18,849	14,894	19,243	17,269
88,850	**88,900**	18,863	14,906	19,257	17,281
88,900	**88,950**	18,877	14,919	19,271	17,294
88,950	**89,000**	18,891	14,931	19,285	17,306

If line 43 (taxable income) is—		And you are—			
At least	But less than	Single	Married filing jointly *	Married filing separately	Head of a household
		Your tax is—			
89,000					
89,000	**89,050**	18,905	14,944	19,299	17,319
89,050	**89,100**	18,919	14,956	19,313	17,331
89,100	**89,150**	18,933	14,969	19,327	17,344
89,150	**89,200**	18,947	14,981	19,341	17,356
89,200	**89,250**	18,961	14,994	19,355	17,369
89,250	**89,300**	18,975	15,006	19,369	17,381
89,300	**89,350**	18,989	15,019	19,383	17,394
89,350	**89,400**	19,003	15,031	19,397	17,406
89,400	**89,450**	19,017	15,044	19,411	17,419
89,450	**89,500**	19,031	15,056	19,425	17,431
89,500	**89,550**	19,045	15,069	19,439	17,444
89,550	**89,600**	19,059	15,081	19,453	17,456
89,600	**89,650**	19,073	15,094	19,467	17,469
89,650	**89,700**	19,087	15,106	19,481	17,481
89,700	**89,750**	19,101	15,119	19,495	17,494
89,750	**89,800**	19,115	15,131	19,509	17,506
89,800	**89,850**	19,129	15,144	19,523	17,519
89,850	**89,900**	19,143	15,156	19,537	17,531
89,900	**89,950**	19,157	15,169	19,551	17,544
89,950	**90,000**	19,171	15,181	19,565	17,556
90,000					
90,000	**90,050**	19,185	15,194	19,579	17,569
90,050	**90,100**	19,199	15,206	19,593	17,581
90,100	**90,150**	19,213	15,219	19,607	17,594
90,150	**90,200**	19,227	15,231	19,621	17,606
90,200	**90,250**	19,241	15,244	19,635	17,619
90,250	**90,300**	19,255	15,256	19,649	17,631
90,300	**90,350**	19,269	15,269	19,663	17,644
90,350	**90,400**	19,283	15,281	19,677	17,656
90,400	**90,450**	19,297	15,294	19,691	17,669
90,450	**90,500**	19,311	15,306	19,705	17,681
90,500	**90,550**	19,325	15,319	19,719	17,694
90,550	**90,600**	19,339	15,331	19,733	17,706
90,600	**90,650**	19,353	15,344	19,747	17,719
90,650	**90,700**	19,367	15,356	19,761	17,731
90,700	**90,750**	19,381	15,369	19,775	17,744
90,750	**90,800**	19,395	15,381	19,789	17,756
90,800	**90,850**	19,409	15,394	19,803	17,769
90,850	**90,900**	19,423	15,406	19,817	17,781
90,900	**90,950**	19,437	15,419	19,831	17,794
90,950	**91,000**	19,451	15,431	19,845	17,806
91,000					
91,000	**91,050**	19,465	15,444	19,859	17,819
91,050	**91,100**	19,479	15,456	19,873	17,831
91,100	**91,150**	19,493	15,469	19,887	17,844
91,150	**91,200**	19,507	15,481	19,901	17,856
91,200	**91,250**	19,521	15,494	19,915	17,869
91,250	**91,300**	19,535	15,506	19,929	17,881
91,300	**91,350**	19,549	15,519	19,943	17,894
91,350	**91,400**	19,563	15,531	19,957	17,906
91,400	**91,450**	19,577	15,544	19,971	17,919
91,450	**91,500**	19,591	15,556	19,985	17,931
91,500	**91,550**	19,605	15,569	19,999	17,944
91,550	**91,600**	19,619	15,581	20,013	17,956
91,600	**91,650**	19,633	15,594	20,027	17,969
91,650	**91,700**	19,647	15,606	20,041	17,981
91,700	**91,750**	19,661	15,619	20,055	17,994
91,750	**91,800**	19,675	15,631	20,069	18,006
91,800	**91,850**	19,689	15,644	20,083	18,019
91,850	**91,900**	19,703	15,656	20,097	18,031
91,900	**91,950**	19,717	15,669	20,111	18,044
91,950	**92,000**	19,731	15,681	20,125	18,056

If line 43 (taxable income) is—		And you are—			
At least	But less than	Single	Married filing jointly *	Married filing separately	Head of a household
		Your tax is—			
92,000					
92,000	**92,050**	19,745	15,694	20,139	18,069
92,050	**92,100**	19,759	15,706	20,153	18,081
92,100	**92,150**	19,773	15,719	20,167	18,094
92,150	**92,200**	19,787	15,731	20,181	18,106
92,200	**92,250**	19,801	15,744	20,195	18,119
92,250	**92,300**	19,815	15,756	20,209	18,131
92,300	**92,350**	19,829	15,769	20,223	18,144
92,350	**92,400**	19,843	15,781	20,237	18,156
92,400	**92,450**	19,857	15,794	20,251	18,169
92,450	**92,500**	19,871	15,806	20,265	18,181
92,500	**92,550**	19,885	15,819	20,279	18,194
92,550	**92,600**	19,899	15,831	20,293	18,206
92,600	**92,650**	19,913	15,844	20,307	18,219
92,650	**92,700**	19,927	15,856	20,321	18,231
92,700	**92,750**	19,941	15,869	20,335	18,244
92,750	**92,800**	19,955	15,881	20,349	18,256
92,800	**92,850**	19,969	15,894	20,363	18,269
92,850	**92,900**	19,983	15,906	20,377	18,281
92,900	**92,950**	19,997	15,919	20,391	18,294
92,950	**93,000**	20,011	15,931	20,405	18,306
93,000					
93,000	**93,050**	20,025	15,944	20,419	18,319
93,050	**93,100**	20,039	15,956	20,433	18,331
93,100	**93,150**	20,053	15,969	20,447	18,344
93,150	**93,200**	20,067	15,981	20,461	18,356
93,200	**93,250**	20,081	15,994	20,475	18,369
93,250	**93,300**	20,095	16,006	20,489	18,381
93,300	**93,350**	20,109	16,019	20,503	18,394
93,350	**93,400**	20,123	16,031	20,517	18,406
93,400	**93,450**	20,137	16,044	20,531	18,419
93,450	**93,500**	20,151	16,056	20,545	18,431
93,500	**93,550**	20,165	16,069	20,559	18,444
93,550	**93,600**	20,179	16,081	20,573	18,456
93,600	**93,650**	20,193	16,094	20,587	18,469
93,650	**93,700**	20,207	16,106	20,601	18,481
93,700	**93,750**	20,221	16,119	20,615	18,494
93,750	**93,800**	20,235	16,131	20,629	18,506
93,800	**93,850**	20,249	16,144	20,643	18,519
93,850	**93,900**	20,263	16,156	20,657	18,531
93,900	**93,950**	20,277	16,169	20,671	18,544
93,950	**94,000**	20,291	16,181	20,685	18,556
94,000					
94,000	**94,050**	20,305	16,194	20,699	18,569
94,050	**94,100**	20,319	16,206	20,713	18,581
94,100	**94,150**	20,333	16,219	20,727	18,594
94,150	**94,200**	20,347	16,231	20,741	18,606
94,200	**94,250**	20,361	16,244	20,755	18,619
94,250	**94,300**	20,375	16,256	20,769	18,631
94,300	**94,350**	20,389	16,269	20,783	18,644
94,350	**94,400**	20,403	16,281	20,797	18,656
94,400	**94,450**	20,417	16,294	20,811	18,669
94,450	**94,500**	20,431	16,306	20,825	18,681
94,500	**94,550**	20,445	16,319	20,839	18,694
94,550	**94,600**	20,459	16,331	20,853	18,706
94,600	**94,650**	20,473	16,344	20,867	18,719
94,650	**94,700**	20,487	16,356	20,881	18,731
94,700	**94,750**	20,501	16,369	20,895	18,744
94,750	**94,800**	20,515	16,381	20,909	18,756
94,800	**94,850**	20,529	16,394	20,923	18,769
94,850	**94,900**	20,543	16,406	20,937	18,781
94,900	**94,950**	20,557	16,419	20,951	18,794
94,950	**95,000**	20,571	16,431	20,965	18,806

* This column must also be used by a qualifying widow(er).

If line 43 (taxable income) is—		And you are—			
At least	But less than	Single	Married filing jointly *	Married filing sepa-rately	Head of a house-hold
		Your tax is—			
95,000					
95,000	**95,050**	20,585	16,444	20,979	18,819
95,050	**95,100**	20,599	16,456	20,993	18,831
95,100	**95,150**	20,613	16,469	21,007	18,844
95,150	**95,200**	20,627	16,481	21,021	18,856
95,200	**95,250**	20,641	16,494	21,035	18,869
95,250	**95,300**	20,655	16,506	21,049	18,881
95,300	**95,350**	20,669	16,519	21,063	18,894
95,350	**95,400**	20,683	16,531	21,077	18,906
95,400	**95,450**	20,697	16,544	21,091	18,919
95,450	**95,500**	20,711	16,556	21,105	18,931
95,500	**95,550**	20,725	16,569	21,119	18,944
95,550	**95,600**	20,739	16,581	21,133	18,956
95,600	**95,650**	20,753	16,594	21,147	18,969
95,650	**95,700**	20,767	16,606	21,161	18,981
95,700	**95,750**	20,781	16,619	21,175	18,994
95,750	**95,800**	20,795	16,631	21,189	19,006
95,800	**95,850**	20,809	16,644	21,203	19,019
95,850	**95,900**	20,823	16,656	21,217	19,031
95,900	**95,950**	20,837	16,669	21,231	19,044
95,950	**96,000**	20,851	16,681	21,245	19,056
96,000					
96,000	**96,050**	20,865	16,694	21,259	19,069
96,050	**96,100**	20,879	16,706	21,273	19,081
96,100	**96,150**	20,893	16,719	21,287	19,094
96,150	**96,200**	20,907	16,731	21,301	19,106
96,200	**96,250**	20,921	16,744	21,315	19,119
96,250	**96,300**	20,935	16,756	21,329	19,131
96,300	**96,350**	20,949	16,769	21,343	19,144
96,350	**96,400**	20,963	16,781	21,357	19,156
96,400	**96,450**	20,977	16,794	21,371	19,169
96,450	**96,500**	20,991	16,806	21,385	19,181
96,500	**96,550**	21,005	16,819	21,399	19,194
96,550	**96,600**	21,019	16,831	21,413	19,206
96,600	**96,650**	21,033	16,844	21,427	19,219
96,650	**96,700**	21,047	16,856	21,441	19,231
96,700	**96,750**	21,061	16,869	21,455	19,244
96,750	**96,800**	21,075	16,881	21,469	19,256
96,800	**96,850**	21,089	16,894	21,483	19,269
96,850	**96,900**	21,103	16,906	21,497	19,281
96,900	**96,950**	21,117	16,919	21,511	19,294
96,950	**97,000**	21,131	16,931	21,525	19,306
97,000					
97,000	**97,050**	21,145	16,944	21,539	19,319
97,050	**97,100**	21,159	16,956	21,553	19,331
97,100	**97,150**	21,173	16,969	21,567	19,344
97,150	**97,200**	21,187	16,981	21,581	19,356
97,200	**97,250**	21,201	16,994	21,595	19,369
97,250	**97,300**	21,215	17,006	21,609	19,381
97,300	**97,350**	21,229	17,019	21,623	19,394
97,350	**97,400**	21,243	17,031	21,637	19,406
97,400	**97,450**	21,257	17,044	21,651	19,419
97,450	**97,500**	21,271	17,056	21,665	19,431
97,500	**97,550**	21,285	17,069	21,679	19,444
97,550	**97,600**	21,299	17,081	21,693	19,456
97,600	**97,650**	21,313	17,094	21,707	19,469
97,650	**97,700**	21,327	17,106	21,721	19,481
97,700	**97,750**	21,341	17,119	21,735	19,494
97,750	**97,800**	21,355	17,131	21,749	19,506
97,800	**97,850**	21,369	17,144	21,763	19,519
97,850	**97,900**	21,383	17,156	21,777	19,531
97,900	**97,950**	21,397	17,169	21,791	19,544
97,950	**98,000**	21,411	17,181	21,805	19,556
98,000					
98,000	**98,050**	21,425	17,194	21,819	19,569
98,050	**98,100**	21,439	17,206	21,833	19,581
98,100	**98,150**	21,453	17,219	21,847	19,594
98,150	**98,200**	21,467	17,231	21,861	19,606
98,200	**98,250**	21,481	17,244	21,875	19,619
98,250	**98,300**	21,495	17,256	21,889	19,631
98,300	**98,350**	21,509	17,269	21,903	19,644
98,350	**98,400**	21,523	17,281	21,917	19,656
98,400	**98,450**	21,537	17,294	21,931	19,669
98,450	**98,500**	21,551	17,306	21,945	19,681
98,500	**98,550**	21,565	17,319	21,959	19,694
98,550	**98,600**	21,579	17,331	21,973	19,706
98,600	**98,650**	21,593	17,344	21,987	19,719
98,650	**98,700**	21,607	17,356	22,001	19,731
98,700	**98,750**	21,621	17,369	22,015	19,744
98,750	**98,800**	21,635	17,381	22,029	19,756
98,800	**98,850**	21,649	17,394	22,043	19,769
98,850	**98,900**	21,663	17,406	22,057	19,781
98,900	**98,950**	21,677	17,419	22,071	19,794
98,950	**99,000**	21,691	17,431	22,085	19,806
99,000					
99,000	**99,050**	21,705	17,444	22,099	19,819
99,050	**99,100**	21,719	17,456	22,113	19,831
99,100	**99,150**	21,733	17,469	22,127	19,844
99,150	**99,200**	21,747	17,481	22,141	19,856
99,200	**99,250**	21,761	17,494	22,155	19,869
99,250	**99,300**	21,775	17,506	22,169	19,881
99,300	**99,350**	21,789	17,519	22,183	19,894
99,350	**99,400**	21,803	17,531	22,197	19,906
99,400	**99,450**	21,817	17,544	22,211	19,919
99,450	**99,500**	21,831	17,556	22,225	19,931
99,500	**99,550**	21,845	17,569	22,239	19,944
99,550	**99,600**	21,859	17,581	22,253	19,956
99,600	**99,650**	21,873	17,594	22,267	19,969
99,650	**99,700**	21,887	17,606	22,281	19,981
99,700	**99,750**	21,901	17,619	22,295	19,994
99,750	**99,800**	21,915	17,631	22,309	20,006
99,800	**99,850**	21,929	17,644	22,323	20,019
99,850	**99,900**	21,943	17,656	22,337	20,031
99,900	**99,950**	21,957	17,669	22,351	20,044
99,950	**100,000**	21,971	17,681	22,365	20,056

$100,000 or over — use the Tax Computation Worksheet on page 80

* This column must also be used by a qualifying widow(er)

401k, p. 439 A retirement savings plan that is sponsored and set up by an employer for its employees; like other retirement plans, there are strict rules as to when the money can be withdrawn without a penalty and strict contribution limits which change from year to year.

403b, p. 439 A tax-deferred retirement savings program for employees of educational institutions and some non profit organizations.

52-week high, p. 10 The highest price at which one share was traded over the last year.

52-week low, p. 10 The lowest price at which one share was traded over the last year.

A

accident reconstructionist, p. 274 Person with knowledge of both crime scene investigations and the mathematics that can help to explain the circumstances surrounding the accident.

account number (banking), p. 123 This number appears on all checks, deposit slips, and bank statements.

account number (credit card), p. 201 A unique number that identifies a credit card holder.

actuary, p. 239 A statistician who predicts how many customers will submit claims based on criteria such as age, sex, marital status, driving record, and residence.

adjustable rate mortgage, p. 401 A mortgage in which the monthly payment and the APR may change, as specified in the signed agreement.

adjustment period, p. 418 The period between rate changes in an ARM; a loan with a 1-year adjustment period is known as a 1-year ARM, which means that the interest rate and the monthly payment may change at the end of one year.

after-hours trading, p. 10 Trades that are made after the stock market closes.

after-tax investments, p. 438 Money that is deducted from your income after taxes have been deducted for the purpose of investing.

amortization table, p. 415 A listing of the unpaid principal, the monthly payment, the amount allocated to paying down the principal, and the amount allocated to interest.

annual compounding, p. 137 A method for calculating interest so that it is paid once a year.

annual percentage rate (APR), pp. 143, 181, 201 The interest rate paid per year or charged per year.

anti-lock braking system (ABS), p. 274 A system which most cars have that does not allow the wheels to continuously lock; in cars equipped with this feature, the driver feels a pulsing vibration on the brake pedal and that pedal moves up and down; the skid marks left by a car with ABS look like uniform dashed lines on the pavement.

apartment, p. 384 A home that is rented or leased by the people who live in it; also called a rental property.

apothem, p. 396 A line segment that goes through the center of a polygon that is perpendicular to a side.

application deposit, p. 387 Money that Covers the cost of processing the application for the rental.

appreciate, p. 245 Increase in value over time.

area, p. 395 The amount of space inside a two-dimensional region, such as a floor; area is measured in square units; the living space in a property.

arithmetic average (mean), p. 22 A measure of central tendency found by calculating the sum of numbers in a data set and then dividing by the number of elements in the data set.

arithmetic average, p. 225 The same as the mean; the sum of all the numbers in a data set divided by the number of elements in the data set.

arrears, p. 411 The manner that interest occurs throughout the month before it is paid with the mortgage payment.

ascending order, p. 225 Numbers that are in order from the least value to the greatest value.

assessed value, p. 401 An assigned value made by the local government on the value of a house for taxation purposes.

assets, pp. 174, 516 A person's property or what is owned.

at the market, p. 40 Instructions to the broker to get the best possible price.

attorney fee, p. 411 Fees paid to an attorney in return for representation at a closing.

automated teller machine (ATM), p. 117 Provides 24-hour bank access to make deposits, transfers, and withdrawals.

automobile insurance, p. 238 A contract between a driver and an insurance company, where the driver agrees to pay a fee (called the premium) and the company agrees to cover certain accident-related costs when the driver makes a claim (request).

available credit, p. 201 The difference between the maximum amount allowed and the actual amount owed on a credit card.

average daily balance, pp. 195, 206 The average amount owed per day during a billing cycle.

axis of symmetry, p. 87 A vertical line that can be drawn through the vertex of a parabola so that the dissected parts of the parabola are mirror images of each other; the point on the horizontal axis through which the axis of symmetry passes is determined by calculating $-\frac{b}{2a}$.

B

back-end ratio, p. 406 A factor that banks use when deciding whether to lend money for a mortgage that takes into account a borrower's regular monthly debts, such as car loans, alimony, child support, and credit card bills, to gross monthly income.

balancing, p. 123 The process of verifying the bank's records to make sure no errors have been made.

balloon mortgage, p. 407 A mortgage with a very large last payment, with all other payments being relatively low.

balloon payment, p. 182 The last monthly payment on some loans that is much greater than the previous payments.

bank statement, p. 123 A statement that includes all transactions that have occurred for a period of approximately one month.

bar graph, p. 497 A type of graph or data display that uses rectangular bars to compare categories of data.

base period, p. 311 A fixed period of time that most states use in an unemployment insurance formula to determine weekly benefits.

beneficiary, p. 457 A person chosen by the policyholder whose name is on the life insurance policy and who receives the benefits of the policy after the policyholder's death.

benefits, p. 291 Additional compensation from an employer; benefits can include health and dental insurance, child care, retirement, and travel expenses.

billing cycle, p. 200 A predetermined amount of time set by the credit card company that is used for calculating a credit card bill.

billing date, pp. 201, 207 The date that a credit card statement was written.

bimodal, p. 228 A set of data that has two modes.

bivariate data, p. 64 Data given as pairs of numbers and show a relationship between the pairs.

biweekly, pp. 156, 296 Every two weeks.

board of directors, p. 423 A group of people who are elected by the condominium or landominium homeowners to manage business matters.

bodily injury (BI) liability, p. 238 Covers bodily injury if a driver is at fault in an accident.

box-and-whisker plot, p. 234 Also called a boxplot; a type of graph that shows all four quartiles and the least number; it is drawn to scale.

boxplot, p. 234 Also called a box-and-whisker plot; a type of graph that shows all four quartiles and the least number; it should be drawn to scale.

braking distance, p. 268 The distance a car travels while braking to a complete stop.

braking efficiency, p. 275 A number determined by an examination of the rear and front wheel brakes; it can run from 0% efficiency (no brakes at all) to 100% efficiency (brakes are in excellent condition); the braking efficiency number is expressed as a decimal when used in the skid speed formula.

breakeven point, p. 80 When the expenses and the revenue are equal, so that there is no profit or loss.

British Thermal Units (BTUs), p. 398 A unit of measure by which air conditioners are sold.

broker fee, p. 40 A flat fee or commission that a stockbroker charges for trade stocks.

budget check-off matrix, p. 497 Where there are no amounts in the budget, but rather check marks that indicate at what time of the year the expenses for the indicated categories will occur.

budget line graph, p. 497 A type of graph used when a consumer is comparing two categories of expenses; it indicates the amount that can be allotted to each expense so that both categories can be afforded within a certain income.

budget matrix, p. 396 An organizer that contains numerical entries or information on when certain account deposits and withdrawals are made over a period of time.

C

cafeteria plan, p. 347 A portion of pre-tax wages set aside for the payment of certain medical, childcare, parental care, and nonreimbursed medical insurance expenses.

canceled, p. 117 A check that has been processed so that the money is paid to the payee of a check.

candlestick chart, p. 19 A chart, like a stock chart, but with a top line that indicates the high price, and a low line that indicates the low price for a given period; the rectangular region, known as the real body, is displayed in two different colors; the green candlestick indicates that the closing price is greater than the opening price and the red candlestick indicates the closing price is less than the opening price.

capital, p. 4 Money that is used to start or expand a business.

car-rental insurance, p. 239 A type of insurance that pays for part of the cost of a rented car if a car is disabled because of a collision or comprehensive-covered repair.

cash flow, p. 508 The money that goes in and out of a budget within a fixed period of time.

cash flow analysis, p. 499 A detailing of how money comes in and how money goes out over a fixed period of time.

cash value, p. 465 The value of the investment portion of a whole life insurance policy.

causal relationship, p. 64 When one variable causes a change in another variable.

ccf, p. 482 A unit of measure that represents 100 cubic feet.

cell, p. 12 The intersection of a column and row in a spreadsheet where data is entered.

central angle, p. 499 The angle formed around the center of a pie chart by the radii that make the sectors.

certificate of deposit (CD), p. 132 A certificate that states there is a specific sum of money on deposit and guarantees the payment of a fixed interest rate after a certain period of time, usually seven days to ten years; deposits and withdrawals cannot be made with a CD.

charge card, p. 194 A special type of credit card where the monthly bills for all purchases must be paid in full and there is no interest charged.

check, p. 116 A written order used to tell a bank to pay money (transfer funds) from an account to the check holder.

check clearing, p. 116 The process that happens when a bank pays for a check out of a checking account; a check is cleared when the bank has transferred the funds from the checking account.

check register, p. 119 A record of all transactions in a checking account, including checks written, deposits made, fees paid, ATM withdrawals, and so on.

checking account, p. 116 An account at a bank that allows a customer to deposit money and make withdrawals from the funds on deposit using a paper check or electronic transfer.

childcare leave, p. 310 An employee benefit that allows employees paid time off to care for sick children or newborns.

chord, p. 277 A line segment that connects two points on a circle.

claim, p. 238 A request for payment by a driver involved in an accident to an insurance company that provides automobile insurance for the driver.

close, p. 9 Also called closing price; The last price at which a stock was traded on a regular trading day.

closing, p. 411 A meeting attended by a buyer, seller, attorneys, and a representative of a lending institution for the official sale of a property.

closing costs, p. 411 Costs that are paid at closing that include origination fees, attorney fees, points, prepaid interest, transfer tax, and title insurance.

collateral, p. 182 Security, such as a personal belonging, car or boat title, CD, or stock certificates, that insures a loan will be repaid.

collision insurance, p. 239 A type of insurance that pays for the repair or replacement of an insured car if it is damaged in a collision with another vehicle or object, or if it overturns, no matter who is at fault. This type of insurance is usually required if there is a loan on the car.

column, p. 496 A vertical line of values in a matrix or spreadsheet.

commission (as compensation), p. 303 A method of payment where an employee receives a percentage of the amount of sales produced by that employee.

commission (of stock trades), p. 40 A percentage of the value of a stock trade.

compound interest, p. 137 Interest that is earned on the money deposited into an account plus previous interest.

common stock, p. 51 A type of stock where the stockholders receive dividends only when the board of directors elects to issue dividends.

compound interest formula, p. 143 Formula that can be used to calculate compound interest; $B = p(1 + \frac{r}{n})^{nt}$ where B is the ending balance, p is the principal or original balance, r is the interest rate, n is the number of times that interest is compounded annually, and t is the number of years.

comprehensive insurance, p. 239 A type of insurance that covers the repair or replacement of parts of an insured car damaged by vandalism, fire, flood, wind, earthquakes, missiles, falling objects, riots, tree sprays, and other disasters; it also covers if the car is stolen.

condominium, p. 422 A form of home ownership where each unit is individually owned.

congruent, p. 396 Figures that have the same shape and size.

Consumer Price Index (CPI), p. 457 An indicator of inflation that measures the change in the total cost of a specific list of services and products.

continuous compound interest formula, p. 150 A formula for calculating continuous compound interest; $B = pe^{rt}$, where B is the ending balance, p is the principal, e is the exponential base, r is the interest rate, and t is the number of years the principal earns interest.

continuous compounding, p. 150 A method of calculating interest so that it is compounded an infinite number of times each year rather than being compounded every minute, or every microsecond.

co-op apartment, p. 423 A form of home ownership where an investor purchases shares of a cooperative and then is able to live in the apartment.

cooperative, p. 423 A form of home ownership where a corporation owns a group of apartments and takes out a mortgage to buy the entire apartment complex; investors purchase shares which allow them to occupy the apartments; co-op owners do not own their individual apartment; instead they own a portion of the entire cooperative development.

corporate bond, p. 54 A loan to a corporation; the corporation agrees to pay the bondholder back with interest, much like a bank pays a customer with money on deposit.

corporation, p. 4 A business organization that is owned by one person or group of people, in which the owner has limited liability in the business, and therefore, is not personally liable.

correlation, p. 64 An association between two variables.

correlation coefficient, p. 70 Represented by r, it is a number between –1 and 1, inclusive, that is used to judge how closely a line fits the data.

cosigner, p. 181 A person that signs a promissory note along with the borrower and agrees to pay back the loan if the borrower does not.

cost of living adjustment (COLA), p. 457 A small increase in a retiree's benefits based on the Consumer Price Index (CPI) or cost of living index.

credit (banking), p. 119 Deposits into a bank account.

credit (purchases), p. 174 When something is bought that is not paid for at the time of purchase.

credit calendar, p. 206 A calendar method of finding the average daily balance of a credit card.

credit card, p. 193 A plastic card that entitles its holder to make purchases and pay for them later.

credit card statement, p. 200 An accounting of the credits and debits in the form of a monthly report sent to a credit card holder.

credit line, p. 201 The maximum amount that a person can owe on a credit card at one time.

credit rating, p. 174 A credit report card that shows how well a user of credit meets financial obligations; these records are used by creditors when they decide to issue credit.

credit reporting agency, p. 175 Organizations that compile records on users of credit as to how well they repay their debts.

crediting, p. 137 Interest that is compounded daily, but is paid either quarterly or semiannually.

creditor, p. 174 Organization or person who extends credit to debtors.

crossover, p. 26 Occurs when one time interval moving average graph crosses over another moving average; this is a possible signal that a stock trend reversal might be near.

cubic foot, p. 482 A unit of measure by which natural gas and water are sold; it represents the amount of space occupied, not the weight.

cubic function, p. 190 A function or equation raised to an exponent of three.

cubic regression equation, p. 190 A third-degree regression equation of the form $y = ax^3 + bx^2 + cx + d$ that can be used to determine the loan balance throughout the life of a loan.

currency exchange rate, p. 264 A rate used to convert one country's currency to another country's currency.

cusp, p. 221 On a graph, where two lines of a piecewise function meet.

D

daily compounding, p. 137 A method for calculating interest so that it is paid daily.

daily money flow, p. 32 A calculated indicator that is the average of a day's high, low, and close, multiplied by the volume for the day.

data, pp. 64, 224 A set of numbers.

debit, p. 119 Withdrawals from a bank account.

debit card, p. 194 A card that acts like an electronic check and is not a credit or charge card; with each purchase, the amount is deducted from a checking account; purchases may not exceed the balance in the account.

debit/credit, p. 201 A debit is the amount charged to an account; a credit is payment made to reduce your debt; credits are identified by a negative (–) sign.

debt reduction plan, p. 517 A plan to improve a debt-to-income ratio by doing some or all of the following: lower debts with the highest interest rates, pay more than the minimum amount, look for ways to cut costs daily, use an online debt management calculator, make a list of what you owe and keep it handy as a reminder not to incur more debt, and slow down or eliminate your credit card spending.

debtor, p. 174 Organization or person who uses credit.

debt-to-income ratio, pp. 406, 517 A ratio of monthly expenses to monthly gross income; offers a realistic view as to where a person stands financially with the amount of debt presently being carried.

decreasing term insurance, p. 465 A type of life insurance policy that pays a decreasing death benefits over time, and as a result, has a lower premium than other types of term insurance.

deductible, p. 240 Part of the repair or damages that a driver has to pay before the insurance company pays.

deferred compensation, p. 456 Money that is given or received at a later date usually in return for services that have been given or received at the present time.

defined benefit plan, p. 456 An employee pension benefit that is calculated based upon a formula that may involve the average salary before retirement, the age of the employee at retirement, the length of employment, and some predetermined percentage multiplier; the employer makes all decisions on the investment options for the money in the plan.

demand, p. 75 The quantity that consumers (as a whole) want.

demand function, p. 75 A function that relates the quantity of a product to its price.

dependence, p. 103 When x depends on y and y depends on z, it follows that x depends on z.

dependent, p. 353 A person reported on a taxpayer's income tax form that a taxpayer supports financially.

deposit slip, p. 116 A form to fill out when adding money to a bank account.

depreciate, p. 245 Decrease in value over time.

descending order, p. 225 Numbers that are in order from the greatest to the least.

direct deposit, pp. 116, 296 Payroll or other types of checks that are directly and electronically deposited into a bank account.

directional arrow, p. 30 Arrows that indicate whether the traded price of a single share is greater than the previous day's closing price (▲) or less than the previous day's closing price (▼).

discount, p. 293 The amount that a charge, cost, or fee is lowered.

discount broker, p. 40 A broker who trades stocks, but does not give investment advice.

discount points, p. 411 Points that reduce the interest rate of the loan; they generally lower the interest rate about 0.25% on a fixed rate mortgage and 0.375% on an adjustable rate mortgage; these percentages vary depending upon the lending institution.

distance formula, p. 260 A formula for the distance a car travels that is a function of the rate and time that it travels, or $d = rt$.

dividend, p. 51 A corporation's profit that is split among shareholders.

dividend income, p. 51 Money received because a person owns stock in a company and the company paid part of its profit to shareholders.

dollar value, p. 252 Value of money that something is worth, depreciates, or appreciates.

domain, pp. 70, 220 The set of all first elements,(x-values) of ordered pairs.

double-time pay, p. 297 An overtime rate that is two times the hourly rate.

Dow Jones Industrial Average (DJIA), p. 29 A published information system, the Dow follows the daily trading action of 30 large public companies; it is a well-respected average that offers a broad picture of how the market is performing from day to day.

down payment, pp. 175, 401 The upfront money applied to a purchase that is made using a loan (credit).

downtick, p. 32 A tick that indicates the price is lower than the previous trade.

drag factor, p. 275 The pull of the road on the tires; it is a number that represents the amount of friction that the road surface contributes when driving.

drawer, p. 116 The account owner of a check; the person who writes the check.

E

earnest money deposit, p. 411 The earnest money, or good-faith deposit paid to the seller by an interested buyer to show that the buyer is serious about buying the house.

earning power, p. 174 A person's ability to earn money now and in the future.

electronic funds transfer, (EFT), p. 116 The process of moving funds electronically from an account in one bank to an account in another bank; also referred to as an electronic check or e-check.

Electronic Funds Transfer Act, p. 194 The law that protects debit card users against unauthorized use of their cards; users are not responsible for purchases made with a lost or stolen card after the card is report missing.

electronic matrix, p. 496 A spreadsheet.

electronic odometer, p. 259 An odometer which gives the distance readings digitally.

electronic utilities, p. 489 Technologically advanced utilities such as Internet access, cell phones, and television.

emergency road service insurance, p. 239 A type of insurance coverage that pays for towing or road service when a car is disabled.

employee benefits, p. 310 Value-added options that an employer may choose to offer employees; typically, benefits are in the forms of insurance (health, life, and disability), paid vacation time, paid holiday time, retirement plans, stock ownership plans, and childcare leave.

Employee Retirement Income Security Act (ERISA), p. 457 The federal act that established protection of pension plans and the PBGC.

employment agency, p. 291 A business that has lists of job openings and charges a fee to find jobs for people.

ending balance, p. 123 The amount of money in a checking account at the end of a statement period.

endorse, p. 117 The act of signing the back of a check when cashing it.

English Standard System, p. 259 System of measurement used in the United States.

envelope accounting system, p. 512 A system of using envelopes that are set up to hold the allocated amounts for weekly or monthly budget categories.

equilibrium, p. 76 Where the functions of supply (what is available to be sold) and demand (the quantity that consumers want to buy) intersect.

equity The amount of a home that an owner actually owns.

escrow, p. 404 The money the bank collects from borrowers, for insurance and property taxes; the bank pays those bills for the homeowner when they are due.

evict, p. 384 The act of legally forcing a tenant to leave a rental property for failure to pay rent or follow the rules and regulations of the lease.

exemption, p. 353 Information included on tax forms that lowers taxes; exemptions include dependents as well as the taxpayer.

expense equation, p. 80 The sum of the fixed and variable expenses.

expire, p. 384 The time when a lease ends.

explanatory variable, p. 64 In a causal relationship, the variable which causes the change in another variable.

exponential base (*e*), p. 150 The exponential base *e* is an irrational number which is a non-terminating, non-repeating decimal with an approximate value of $e \approx 2.718281828 \ldots$.

exponential decay, p. 252 Rather than the value decreasing by the same dollar amount each year, it decreases by the same percentage each year.

exponential depreciation, p. 252 The model of exponential decay in the context of auto devaluation.

extrapolation, p. 70 To predict corresponding variables outside of the domain.

F

face value (bond), p. 54 The amount paid when a bond matures.

face value (life insurance), p. 464 The amount of coverage that a life insurance policy provides.

Fair Credit Reporting Act, p. 194 The law that gives protection to a consumer in the case of errors on a monthly credit card statement; consumers are not responsible for a disputed amount or the finance charges that amount accrues, until the error is resolved.

Fair Debt Collection Practices Act, p. 194 The law that prohibits the creditor from harassing or using unfair means to collect the amount owed.

family health care, p. 310 A type of health insurance that covers all members of the immediate family for health care bills to the extent outlined in the health care coverage plan.

fast moving average, p. 26 When a stock chart depicts moving averages for two different intervals, the graph with the shorter time interval is known as the fast moving average; as changes in closing prices occur on a day-to-day basis, the fast moving average will reflect those changes quicker than the slow moving average.

Federal Insurance Contributions Act (FICA), p. 316 The federal act that established Social Security insurance.

fee paid, p. 291 When the employer, instead of the employee, pays the fee to an employment agency.

FICA tax, p. 316 Social Security and Medicare taxes both fall in this category; the money that an employee and employer contribute to Social Security and Medicare is used to pay current benefits to others.

FICO score, p. 175 A score that summarizes the probability that a debtor will pay a debt and is a reliable way that creditors judge credit worthiness.

finance charge, pp. 175, 201 The interest that is charged to a buyer when paying for a purchase or service over time.

finite, p. 150 Something that has an end and can be represented by a real number.

fixed expenses, p. 80 Expenses that do not change based on the quantity produced, such as furniture or machinery.

fixed rate mortgage, p. 401 A mortgage in which the monthly payment and average percentage rate (APR) remain the same throughout the entire loan period.

flat tax, p. 335 A tax that is the same percentage or rate for everyone, such as sales tax.

flexible spending account (FSA), p. 347 An employee-sponsored cafeteria plan in which employees choose to deposit funds that will be used in a specified 12-month period of time. This is a "use it or lose it" plan; if all of the money in the plan is not spent by the end of the 12-month period, the money cannot be returned to the employee.

floor plan, p. 393 A drawing of the layout and the dimensions of rooms.

foreclose, p. 401 The act by a bank of taking possession of a home when the homeowner cannot pay the mortgage.

Form 1040, pp. 353, 365 A tax form used by people that have other types of income such as royalties, alimony, or prizes; also called the long form.

Form 1040A, p. 353 A short form that taxpayers can use to report their earnings and pay their taxes.

Form 1040EZ, p. 353 A short form that taxpayers can use to report their earnings and pay their taxes. This form has certain requirements.

Form 1099, p. 344 A form used to report other income made from interest on bank accounts, interest from stocks, and royalties.

Form W-2, p. 344 A form used to report The withholding data; a Wage and Tax Statement given to employees to compute federal, state, and local income taxes; a copy of the W-2 is submitted along with tax forms.

Form W-4 Employee's Withholding Allowance Certificate, p. 291 A form that is filled out by a new employee that gives directions to the government on how much money in taxes to deduct from an employee's pay.

fractional part of a share, p. 48 When a split creates a situation where less than one share remains.

frequency, p. 232 The number of times a particular piece of data appears in a set.

frequency budget plan, p. 512 A household budget in terms of the frequency that payments or credits are made over the course of a year.

frequency distribution, p. 232 A table or chart that gives each piece of data in the set and the frequency, or the number of times that it appears in the data set.

front-end ratio, p. 405 A factor that banks use when deciding whether to lend money for a mortgage; a ratio of monthly housing expenses to monthly gross income.

fuel economy measurement, p. 259 How much gasoline a car uses to travel a certain distance.

full retirement age, p. 448 Age at which a person receives full retirement Social Security benefits.

function, p. 75 A rule that assigns a unique member of the range to each element of the domain.

furnished, p. 384 A rental property that has furniture included.

future value of a periodic deposit investment, p. 56 The balance of an account will grow based on periodic investments; this can be calculated with the future value of a single deposit investment formula, $B = \dfrac{P\left(\left(1 + \frac{r}{n}\right)^{nt} - 1\right)}{\frac{r}{n}}$, where B is the balance at end of investment period, p is the periodic deposit amount, r is the annual interest rate, n is the number of times interest is compounded annually, and t is the time of investment in years.

future value of a single deposit investment, p. 156 The balance of an account grows to at some point in the future.

G

gross capital gain, p. 35 The difference between the selling price and the purchase price of a stock when the shares are sold at a greater price than they were purchased.

gross capital loss, p. 35 The difference between the selling price and the purchase price of a stock when the shares are sold at a lesser price than they were purchased.

gross pay, pp. 297, 344 The total pay, which is the sum of an employee's hourly pay and overtime pay.

group term life insurance, p. 465 Life insurance that employees get through their employers.

growth stock, p. 51 Stocks bought by investors who want to buy low and sell high.

H

head of household, p. 329 Special status for unmarried taxpayers who support other people besides themselves and their children.

high, p. 9 The highest price one share of a particular stock was traded on a particular day.

historical data, p. 252 The prices from the past that a car was worth.

historical depreciation, p. 252 The devaluation of a car using historical data.

hold, p. 116 The money in a bank account that is held until the issuing bank of a check pays for a check.

homeowner's insurance, p. 401 Required by mortgage holders, a type of insurance that covers damage to the home due to fire and other natural disasters; also covers the contents of the home in case of theft or vandalism.

hourly rate, p. 296 A set amount that an employee is paid for each hour of work.

hybrid ARM, p. 419 A combination of a fixed rate period of time with an adjustable rate period of time. A $\frac{3}{1}$ hybrid ARM indicates that the initial interest rate is fixed for the first 3 years and then there is an adjustment period every year thereafter for the life of the loan.

I

impulse buying, p. 93 When a consumer purchases something to which they suddenly were attracted and had no intention of buying.

income stock, p. 51 Stocks that pay dividends.

income tax, p. 328 Taxes that are based on the amount of taxable income that you earn.

increasing term insurance, p. 465 A type of life insurance policy that pays increasing death benefit over time and, as a result, has a lower premium than other types of term insurance.

individual health care, p. 310 A type of health insurance that covers only the individual to the extent outlined in the health care coverage plan.

individual retirement account (IRA), p. 438 An account that is opened by an individual, rather than sponsored by an employer.

infinite, p. 150 Something without end, that cannot be represented by a real number.

initial rate, p. 418 The beginning rate of an adjustable loan.

installment plan, p. 175 A method of payment of a purchase or services over a period of time.

insufficient funds, p. 117 When an account does not have enough money to cover a check that has been issued against it.

interest (banking), pp. 117, 131 A percentage of the money that is in an account that a bank pays on some accounts.

interest (credit), p. 175 The finance charge or fee that is charged to an installment buyer when paying for a purchase or service over time.

interest rate, p. 131 The percentage rate that is paid by a bank on money that is in some accounts.

interest-only mortgage, p. 407 A type of balloon mortgage where only the interest is paid in full every month.

Internal Revenue Service (IRS), p. 328 Government agency that collects federal taxes.

interpolation, p. 70 To predict corresponding variables within the domain.

interquartile range (IQR), p. 227 The difference between the upper and lower quartiles; found by subtracting $Q_3 - Q_1$.

itemize, p. 357 When deductions are listed on an income tax form.

J

joint account, p. 117 An account with more than one owner where all the owners have equal access.

K

Keogh plan, p. 439 A retirement savings plan for a self-employed professional or the owner of a small business; pre-tax money invested in this type of account is tax-deferred until it is withdrawn.

kilometers per liter (km/L), p. 259 A type of fuel economy measurement, which uses the metric system.

kilowatt-hour (kWh), p. 482 A unit of measure by which electricity is sold; equivalent to 1,000 watt-hours of electrical use.

L

lagging indicators, p. 22 Indicators that use past data. An example is simple moving averages which investors use when they want to identify and follow a trend in prices.

landlord, p. 384 The person or people that own a rented house or apartment.

landominium, p. 423 Similar to a condominium, except the owner owns both the home and the land on which the home is built.

last, p. 9 The price per share of the last trade that was made for a particular stock; in the newspaper, this is usually the closing price; online, it is the price of the last trade made for one share of stock.

late charge, p. 201 The penalty charged for late payments from a previous month.

leading coefficient, p. 86 The first coefficient in a quadratic equation when written in standard form, usually denoted by *a*.

lease, p. 384 A written agreement between the landlord and a tenant that details the amount of rent, the length of time the apartment is to be rented, and the rules and regulations that must be followed by the tenant and the landlord.

least squares line, p. 70 A line that approximates the points on a scatterplot which can be used to show a trend and make predictions; also called a line of best fit or linear regression line.

lending institutions, p. 182 Organizations that extend loans; they make their profit by charging interest; lending institutions include banks, savings and loans, credit unions, consumer finance companies, life insurance companies, and pawnshops.

level term insurance, p. 465 A type of life insurance policy that pays the same death benefit over the term of the policy. The premiums paid usually remain level throughout the term.

liabilities, p. 516 A person's debts or amount that is owed.

liability insurance, p. 238 A type of insurance that covers a person from damages; most states set minimum liability requirements.

liable, p. 238 Responsible for damages caused.

life insurance, p. 181 A type of insurance that pays a specified amount upon the policy holder's death.; a creditor often requires a borrower to take out life insurance to cover the loan in the event the borrower dies before the loan is paid.

limit, p. 150 A concept in calculus which means an unreachable value.

limited liability, p. 4 Not being able to lose any more than the value of owned shares if a corporation fails or does not make a profit.

limit order, p. 40 Instructions to the broker that name a specific price for a share of stock.

line graph, p. 497 A type of graph or data display that is used to depict changes over time (on a coordinate grid).

line of best fit, p. 70 A line that approximates the points on a scatterplot which can be used to show a trend and make predictions; also called a linear regression or least squares line.

linear regression line, p. 70 A line that approximates the points on a scatterplot which can be used to show a trend and make predictions; also called a line of best fit or least squares line.

loss, p. 80 The negative difference obtained when expenses are subtracted from revenue.

low, p. 9 The lowest price one share of a particular stock was traded on a particular day.

lower quartile, p. 227 Q_1 is the first quartile or lower quartile, and 25% of the numbers in the data set are at or below Q_1.

lump-sum payment, p. 457 Where all of the money owed to a retiree is given in a single payment and no further payments are made to either the retiree or the beneficiary.

M

maintenance fee (banking), p. 117 A fee that some banks charge on accounts to provide access to checking or savings accounts.

maintenance fee (condo), p. 422 A fee paid monthly by condo owners and used to hire workers to maintain common areas, such as lawns, outside walls, decks, roofs, sidewalks, and roads.

market capitalization or **market cap**, p. 45 The total value of all of a company's outstanding shares.

market value, p. 401 The amount that a house can be sold for.

markup, p. 76 The amount that retailers add on to the wholesale price of an item.

married filing jointly, p. 329 Filing status for married taxpayers who chose to fill out separate income tax returns.

married filing separately, p. 329 Filing status for married taxpayers who chose to fill out one income tax return together.

matrix, p. 496 A rectangular array of information consisting of rows and columns.

mature, p. 54 When a bond is due for repayment to the bondholder.

maturity, p. 132 A specified date at which interest is paid on a CD.

maximum profit, p. 97 The greatest difference between revenue and expense.

maximum taxable income, p. 316 The maximum income on which a person must pay Social Security tax in a given year.

maximum value, p. 87 The peak or vertex of a parabola; the point where revenue can be maximized.

mean, pp. 196, 225 Often referred to as average; the sum of all the numbers in a data set divided by the number of elements in the data set.

measures of central tendency, p. 224 Single numbers, such as the mean, median, and mode, designed to represent a "typical" value for the data.

mechanical odometer, p. 259 An odometer that consists of a set of cylinders that turn to indicate the distance traveled.

median, p. 225 The middle number when numbers are in ascending or descending order.

Medicare tax, p. 316 The amount of Medicare tax an employee pays is a set percentage of the entire income with no maximum amounts; the amount paid is split between the employee and employer.

meter, p. 482 A device that records how much of a particular utility is used.

metric system, p. 259 System of measurement used in other countries outside of the United States.

middle ordinate, p. 277 A segment drawn from the center of a chord to the arc of a yaw mark; this perpendicular segment is used to find the radius of a circle.

miles per gallon (mpg), p. 259 A type of fuel economy measurement, which uses the English Standard system.

minimum balance, p. 132 A certain amount of money that must be kept in an account as required by that particular bank.

minimum payment, p. 201 An amount that is the lowest payment the credit card company will accept for the current billing period.

minimum wage, p. 297 The hourly rate that federal law allow as the least hourly rate be paid to an employee in the United States.

mode, p. 228 The most often occurring value in a data set; there can be more than one mode or no modes at all.

moderate correlation, p. 70 Correlations that are not strong or weak.

modified boxplot, p. 235 A special type of boxplot that shows all the numbers that are outliers as single points past the whiskers.

money flow, p. 32 A type of market analysis known as money flow.

money market account, p. 132 An account that pays a higher interest rate than other types of accounts, but usually requires a higher initial deposit and a higher minimum balance often with a limit on the number of transactions per month.

Monte Carlo method, p. 397 A way to find area; the theory is that the ratio of points that land inside the region to the total points should equal the ratio of the area of the irregular region to the area of the rectangle; the more points used, the more accurate the approximation

monthly, p. 296 Twelve times a year.

monthly payment calculator, p. 187 A way to calculate information about the balance over the lifetime of the loan and on a monthly or yearly basis.

monthly periodic rate, p. 201 The APR divided by 12; the rate of interest charged each month.

mortality table, p. 464 A table that lists death rates according to age groups.

mortgage, p. 401 A loan taken out by people to purchase a house.

N

NASDAQ, p. 9 A stock market called the National Association of Securities Dealers Automated Quotation System.

natural logarithm, p. 189 An exponent of the power to which a base number must be raised to equal a given number; a natural logarithm is a logarithm where *e*, which is represented by a non-terminating, non-repeating decimal 2.71828182 . . . , is the base.

negative correlation, p. 64 When the value of one variable decreases as the value of the other variable increases.

negative money flow, p. 32 When stock is purchased on a downtick.

negligent, p. 238 At fault for damages caused.

net change, p. 10 Abbreviated Chg; shows the change between the previous day's closing price and the current day's closing price; it can be expressed as a dollar amount or a percentage; a positive change indicates the current day closed at a greater price than the previous day; a negative change indicates the current day closed at a lesser price than the previous day.

net money flow, p. 32 The difference between the price paid for a stock and its market value.

net pay, p. 344 The amount of money a worker takes home after deductions.

net proceeds, p. 40 The amount of money made on a stock trade after the brokerage fees are paid.

net worth, p. 512 The difference between a person's assets (what is owned) and that person's liabilities (what is owed).

new balance, p. 201 The amount currently owed on a credit card.

new purchases, p. 201 The sum of purchases or debits on an account.

no-fault insurance, p. 239 Same as PIP, or personal injury protection.

nonlinear function, p. 86 A function that has a graph that is not a straight line.

non-recurring costs, p. 411 Costs that occur only once.

number of days in billing cycle, p. 201 The amount of time, in days, covered by the current bill.

NYSE, p. 9 A stock market called the New York Stock Exchange.

O

odd lot, p. 35 A group of stocks that is less than 100 shares.

odometer, p. 259 A gauge on the dashboard of a car that indicates the distance the car has traveled since it left the factory.

Old-Age, Survivors, and Disability Insurance (OASDI), p. 449 An insurance that pays benefits to retired workers that help them meet their financial obligations and provides benefits to families of retired workers and disabled workers under certain conditions.

order of a matrix, p. 497 The number of rows and columns in a matrix; the order is reported using the form "row × column" (read "row by column").

origination fee, p. 411 This fee is money paid to the lending institution for the paperwork involved in the loan application process.

origination points, p. 411 Similar to origination fees that are collected from the buyer as a means of paying for the loan application process.

outlier, p. 225 Numbers in a data set that are extreme values; calculate outliers in a data set by multiplying 1.5 times the IQR; subtract this product from Q_1 to compute the boundary for lower outliers and add this value to Q_3 to compute the boundary for upper outliers.

outstanding checks, p. 123 Checks that do not appear on the bank statement.

outstanding deposits, p. 123 Deposits that do not appear on the bank statement.

outstanding shares, p. 45 The total number of all shares issued to investors by a corporation.

overdraft protection, p. 117 Protection pays a check even though there are not enough funds in the account; there is a fee for this service and the money must be repaid.

overtime hourly rate, p. 297 The hourly wage an employee receives for any overtime hours.

overtime hours, p. 297 The extra hours an employee works beyond their regular hours.

P

paid holiday time, p. 310 Paid time off for holidays that an employer may offer to employees as an employee benefit.

paid vacation time, p. 310 Paid time off that an employer may offer to employees as an employee benefit.

parabola, p. 86 The shape of the graph of a quadratic function.

partnership, p. 4 A business that is owned by more than one person; partners are each personally liable for the business.

pay stub, p. 344 A list of wages and the amounts deducted from a paycheck that can be detached from the actual paycheck.

paycheck, p. 344 A form of payment to employees for their work.

payee, p. 116 The receiver of the transferred funds or the person to whom the check is written.

payment due date, p. 201 The due date, or the date the monthly payment must be received by the creditor.

payments, p. 201 The total amount received by the creditor that is applied to the account.

penny stock, p. 46 A stock whose value is less than $5 per share.

Pension Benefit Guaranty Corporation (PBGC), p. 457 A federal government agency that insures most defined benefit pension plans.

Pension Protection Act, p. 457 The act which amended ERISA and offered legislation to strengthen and protect many types of pensions.

pension, pp. 310, 456 A type of retirement plan where an employee receives compensation from an employer after retirement.

perimeter, p. 396 The sum of all the side lengths of a figure.

periodic investment, p. 156 The same deposits made at regular intervals, such as yearly, monthly, bi-weekly, weekly, or even daily.

personal injury protection (PIP), p. 239 An added type of insurance coverage mandatory in some states, that pays for any physical injuries that the driver or the passengers sustain while in the vehicle, even if there is no traffic accident; sometimes called no-fault insurance.

personal identification number (PIN), p. 117 A password that allows access to an ATM.

personally liable, p. 4 A business owner who is personally responsible for the debts of the business whether or not there is a profit.

pie chart, p. 497 A pie chart is a graphic display in the form of a circle divided into pie-shaped sectors that are used to present data in percentages.

piecewise function, p. 220 Also called a split function; it gives a set of rules for each domain of the function; $c(x)$ is computed differently depending on the value of x.

piecework rate, p. 303 The set amount of money that a worker receives for each item the individual produces.

pieceworker, p. 303 A type of worker who is paid for each item the employee produces.

points, p. 411 Extra fees charged by the lending institution for the use of their money; each point is equivalent to 1% of the loan amount.

portfolio, p. 35 A grouping of all the stocks that an investor owns.

positive correlation, p. 64 A relationship where the value of one variable increases as the value of the other variable increases.

positive money flow, p. 32 When stock is purchased on an uptick.

preferred stock, p. 51 Preferred stockholders received dividends before common stockholders.

premium, pp. 464, 238 The amount paid for an insurance policy.

prepaid interest, p. 411 Interest starts accruing (building) at the beginning of each month and continues throughout the month; prepaid interest at the closing is the amount of mortgage interest due to cover the time from the closing date to when the first mortgage payment is due.

prepayment penalty, p. 181 An amount borrowers pay as a fee if they wish to pay back an entire loan before the due date.

prepayment privilege, p. 181 An agreement that allows the borrower to make payments before the due date to reduce the amount of interest.

present reading, p. 483 The current meter reading.

present value of a single investment, p. 161 The value, which can be calculated, for how much a one-time deposit should be at a specific interest rate in order to have a certain amount of money saved for a future savings goal; this can be calculated using the present value of a single investment formula; $P = \dfrac{B}{\left(1+\frac{r}{n}\right)^{nt}}$, where B is the balance at the end of investment period, p is the periodic deposit amount, r is the annual interest rate, n is the number of times interest is compounded annually, and t is the time of investment in years.

present value of a periodic deposit investment, p. 161 A determination to find how much to save on a regular basis at a specific interest rate to meet a future goal; this can be calculated with the present value of a periodic deposit investment formula; $P = \dfrac{B \times \frac{r}{n}}{\left(1+\frac{r}{n}\right)^{nt} - 1}$, where B is the balance at the end of the investment period, p is the periodic deposit amount, r is the annual interest rate, n is the number of times interest is compounded annually, and t is the time of investment in years.

present value, p. 161 The current value of a deposit that is made in the present time.

pre-tax dollars, p. 438 A deposit made to a retirement account that is deducted from wages before taxes, and therefore not taxed; pre-tax investments lower a person's current taxable income.

previous balance, p. 201 Any money owed prior to the current billing period.

previous reading, p. 483 The reading as of the last time the meter was read.

principal, pp. 131, 181 The balance, or amount of money, in an account, or amount borrowed.

profit, pp. 4, 80, 97 The positive difference obtained when expenses are subtracted from revenue.

progressive tax system, p. 336 A tax that increases as income increases; the percentage or rate increases.

promissory note, p. 181 An agreement which states the conditions of a loan; a borrower's signature confirms a promise to pay back the loan as outlined in the agreement.

property damage (PD) liability, p. 238 Insurance coverage that pays for damage a driver causes to another person's property.

property tax, pp. 328, 401 Taxes that are based on the assessed value of property owned.

proportional tax, p. 335 The same as a flat tax; a tax that is the same percentage or rate, such as sales tax.

pro-rate, p. 511 The process of dividing expenses proportionately as if they were monthly expenses.

public corporation, p. 4 A corporation where any person can purchase a share of stock in the corporation.

Q

quadratic equation, p. 86 An equation written in the form $y = ax^2 + bx + c$ where a, b, and c are real numbers and $a \neq 0$.

quadratic formula, p. 91 A formula used to solve for x given a quadratic equation;

$$x = \frac{-b \pm \sqrt{b^2 - 4ac}}{2a}.$$

qualified joint and survivor annuity, p. 457 A type of retirement account that offers the retiree a smaller monthly payment but, upon death, the spouse will continue to receive reduced payments until his or her death.

qualifying widow(er), p. 329 Filing status for a taxpayer who is a widow or widower and meets specific guidelines.

quarterly compounding, p. 137 A method for calculating interest so that it is paid four times a year, or every three months.

quartiles, p. 227 Three values represented by Q_1, Q_2, and Q_3 that divide the distribution into four subsets that each contains 25% of the data.

R

range (measure of dispersion), p. 226 A value that tells how dispersed or spread out a data set is.

range, p. 70 The set of second elements (y-values) that correspond with a set of x-values (domain).

reaction distance, p. 268 The distance a car travels during a reaction or thinking time.

reaction time, p. 268 The time that the average, alert driver takes to switch from the gas pedal to the brake pedal; usually from approximately 0.75 second to 1.5 seconds.

real estate tax, p. 401 Property tax that is based on the assessed value of the home; money collected in property taxes from homeowners helps pay for government services, such as schools, libraries, and a police force.

reconciling, p. 123 Same as balancing; the process of verifying the bank's records to make sure no errors have been made.

recurring costs, p. 411 Costs that occur on a regular basis.

regressive tax schedule, p. 337 A tax rate schedule that decreases as income increases.

regular hours, p. 297 The set number of hours that an employee is expected to work.

resistant, p. 225 When a value or measure of central tendency does not change easily or significantly due to an extreme value.

response variable, p. 64 In a causal relationship, the variable which is affected by the explanatory variable.

resume, p. 291 A short accounting of a job-seeker's education and qualifications for employment.

retail price, p. 76 The price for which retailers sell an item.

retirement, p. 438 The time when a person stops working for an employer.

retirement plans, p. 310 A means that employers may offer as to save for retirement; these types of plans may include pensions or 410(K).

revenue, p. 80 The income a business receives from selling a product.

revenue equation, p. 80 $R = pq$, where R represents revenue, p represents the price, and q represents the quantity of products sold.

reverse stock split, p. 45 When the number of outstanding shares is reduced and the market price per share is increased; as the price per share increases, the investor perceives that the stock is worth more.

revolving charge account, p. 193 A type of credit card where the entire bill does not have to be paid in full each month; there is a minimum monthly payment and finance charge the month following any month in which the bill is not paid in full.

Roth IRA, p. 438 Deposits are taxable, but when the money is withdrawn after having been there for at least 5 years and the saver is at least $59\frac{1}{2}$ years old, the money and the income earned is tax-exempt, or free from all taxes.

round lot, p. 35 A multiple of 100 shares; stocks are usually bought and sold in round lots.

row, p. 496 A horizontal line of values in a matrix or spreadsheet.

royalty, p. 303 Money that employees or others receive based on sales, for example an author or musician.

S

sales in 100s, p. 10 Groups of 100 shares that were traded within a given day.

sales tax, p. 219 A percentage paid to the government of sales on products or services.

savings account, p. 131 An account in which the bank pays interest for the use of the money deposited in the account.

scatterplot, p. 64 A graph that shows the relationship of bivariate data using points on the coordinate grid.

Schedule A—Itemized Deductions, p. 365 A form used to list or itemize deductions; deductions are subtracted from a taxpayer's income before the amount of tax owed is looked up on the tax table.

Schedule B—Interest and Dividend Income, p. 365 A form used to report interest income and income from dividends.

second-degree equation, p. 86 A function with a variable raised to an exponent of 2.

sector, p. 499 The radii (plural of radius) in a pie chart or circle graph divide the 100% of the area of the circle into these regions; sectors of the circle are constructed around the center of the circle.

security deposit, p. 387 The money given to the landlord from the tenant as protection in the event that the tenant causes damage to the rented property; refunded when the tenant moves out if there is no damage, and can range from 1 to 4 month's rent.

semiannual compounding, p. 137 A method for calculating interest so that it is paid twice a year, or every six months.

semimonthly, p. 296 Two times a month.

semi-retired, p. 438 A person of retirement age who works only partially or part-time.

shadow skid mark, p. 274 When a driver first applies the brakes and the skid mark is light.

shareholders, p. 4 People who own shares of stocks in a corporation.

shares of stock, p. 4 Represent a share of ownership in the corporation.

shift, p. 679 A movement, or change, of a demand curve.

simple interest formula, p. 131 The formula $I = prt$, where p is principal, r is the interest rate, and t is the time in years.

simple interest, p. 131 Interest that is calculated on the principal in an account, using the formula $I = prt$.

simple moving average (SMA), p. 22 A smoothing technique calculated by determining the arithmetic average or mean closing price over a given period of time.

single account, p. 117 An account that has just one owner who is able to make account transactions.

single life annuity, p. 457 Offers the retired employee a fixed monthly amount until death, when all benefits stop.

single, p. 329 Filing status for unmarried taxpayers that is indicated on tax forms which determine the tax rate paid.

single-family home, p. 384 A home where one family lives.

skew, p. 225 When the mean of a data set is not equal to the median.

skid distance, p. 275 A function of the number and lengths of the skid marks left at the scene of an accident.

skid mark, p. 274 A mark that a tire leaves on the road when it is in a locked mode, that is, when the tire is not turning, but the car is continuing to move.

skid speed formula, p. 275 The formula is $S = \sqrt{30 \cdot D \cdot f \cdot n} = \sqrt{30Dfn}$, where S is the speed of the car when entering the skid, D is the skid distance, f is the drag factor, and n is the braking efficiency.

slope, p. 245 The slope of a line is the numerical value for the inclination or declination of that line and is expressed as a ratio of the change in the vertical variable over the change in the horizontal variable from one point on the line to the next.

slow moving average, p. 26 When a stock chart depicts moving averages for two different intervals, the graph with the longer time interval is known as the slow moving average; as changes in closing prices occur on a day-to-day basis, the fast moving average will reflect those changes quicker than the slow moving average will.

smoothing techniques, p. 22 A statistical tool that allows an investor to reduce the impact of price fluctuations and to focus on patterns and trends; an example is the simple moving average (SMA).

Social Security, p. 316 An insurance program available through the United States government that provides income to people who retire, become disabled, or who receive survivor's benefits.

Social Security benefit, p. 449 Benefit based on earnings over a person's working lifetime; reduced benefits can start as early as age 62; people born after 1960 must wait to start collecting full retirement benefits until age 67, their full retirement age.

Social Security credit, p. 449 Based on total wages and self-employment income during the year; the amount of earnings it takes to earn a credit changes each year; in 2009, a person had to earn $1,090 in covered earnings to get one credit; people born after 1929 need 40 credits in their lifetime to qualify for Social Security benefits.

Social Security number, p. 316 A unique, nine-digit number that identifies a resident of the United States; this number is used to keep track of social security taxes that are paid.

Social Security statement, p. 449 A record of the money a individual earned every year; it includes the number of credits you have earned.

Social Security tax, p. 316 The amount of Social Security a worker pays depends on the Social Security percentage and the maximum taxable income for that year; the amount is split between the employee and the employer.

sole proprietorship, p. 4 A business that is owned by one person.

speedometer, p. 259 A device that tells the rate at which the car is traveling.

split function, p. 220 Also called a piecewise function; it gives a set of rules for each domain of the function; $c(x)$ is computed differently depending on the value of x.

spreadsheet, p. 12 An electronic worksheet where data is entered into cells that can contain numbers, words, or formulas.

square footage, p. 387 Indicates how much floor space is available in a living space.

standard deduction, p. 359 An allowable reduction on income tax forms that is based on the filing status; these amounts are set by the government and may change from year to year.

starting balance, p. 123 The amount of money in a checking account at the beginning of a statement period.

statement period, p. 123 Dates on a bank statement that indicate the range of dates in which the transactions occurred.

statement savings, p. 132 An account where a consumer receives a monthly statement showing all activity, including deposits, interest earned, and any fees.

statistics, p. 224 Mathematics that deals with the collection, analysis, and interpretation of numerical facts or data.

stem-and-leaf plot, p. 233 A type of graph or data display that shows frequency; the numbers to the left of the vertical line (stem) represent the tens place digit; the numbers to the right of the vertical line (leaf) represent the digits in the ones place, in ascending order.

stock bar chart, p. 16 A chart made up of two graphs; the top part shows daily information about the day's high, low, open, and close prices of that particular stock; the bottom part shows the daily volume.

stock chart, p. 16 Pictorial information on stocks from a day's worth of data to multi-year data trends; most stock charts present historical information about the trading prices and volumes of a particular stock.

stock market, p. 9 An institution where stocks are bought and sold.

stock ownership plans, p. 310 A plan that allows employees to buy or receive company stock; offered as an employee benefit.

stock split, p. 45 A corporation changes the number of outstanding shares while at the same time adjusts the price per share so that the market cap remains unchanged.

stock symbol, p. 30 Same as a ticker symbol; the letter or letters used to identify a corporation on a ticker.

stockbroker, p. 40 A person who sells shares of stocks to investors and gives investment advice.

straight line depreciation, p. 245 A line that show a constant decline in the value of something, something, such as a car that loses the same value each year.

straight line depreciation equation, p. 246 The general form for the equation of a straight line is $y = mx + b$, where m represents the slope of the line and b represents the y-intercept.

strong correlation, p. 70 Correlation coefficients with an absolute value greater than 0.75.

subscripts, p. 227 Small numbers, similar to exponents, except in the descending position that are used to name quartiles.

supply, p. 75 The quantity of an item available to be sold.

surcharge, p. 239 An extra fee paid to an automobile insurance company for dividing an annual premium into monthly, quarterly, or semiannual payments.

T

take-home pay, p. 344 The amount of money a worker takes home after deductions.

tax, p. 328 The amount of money a person must pay to the government to benefit from government services.

tax avoidance, p. 366 When a taxpayer uses a tax rule to lower the amount of tax due.

tax bracket, p. 336 Where each line of the tax schedule has an increasing percent based on increasing income.

tax credit, p. 366 An amount subtracted from the income tax owed; the most popular credits are the Child Care Tax Credit and the Earned Income Credit.

tax-deferred contribution, p. 347 When money is placed in a qualified retirement account, the taxes are deferred until the taxpayer makes a withdrawal from the account after retirement.

tax evasion, p. 366 When a taxpayer lies about information on a tax return form in an attempt to avoid paying taxes.

taxable income, p. 328 Earnings that are taxable.

tax-deferred, p. 438 Taxes are paid at the time the money is withdrawn from the account, not when the money is actually earned.

tax-exempt, p. 439 Money that is not taxed.

tenant, p. 384 A person who rents a house or apartment.

term life insurance, p. 464 A type of insurance that provides protection for the policyholder; term insurance covers the policyholder for a specified period of time, usually 5, 10, or 20 years; after that time, the policy is no longer in effect, unless it is renewed for another term.

thinking time, p. 268 Same as reaction time.

ticker symbol, p. 30 Same as a stock symbol; the letter or letters used to identify a corporation on a ticker.

ticker, p. 29 An information transmission machine that has been replaced by electronic scrolling, which uses symbols to provide up-to-date information during the trading day.

time-and-a-half overtime, p. 297 The hourly rate an employee usually gets paid for overtime hours.

title, p. 411 The legal claim of property ownership.

title search, p. 411 A procedure used to make sure that the seller does actually hold the title to the property being sold.

total stopping distance, p. 270 The sum of the reaction distance and the braking distance.

total value of a trade, p. 31 A value determined by multiplying the number of shares traded by the trading price, without including any fees.

trade, p. 35 When a stock is bought or sold.

trades, p. 9 Transactions on the stock market.

trading price, p. 30 A price displayed on the ticker, sometimes followed by a @ symbol.

trading volume, p. 30 The number of shares traded in a single transaction; trading volumes are listed on the ticker; 10K indicates that 10,000 shares traded, 10M indicates that 10,000,000 shares traded, and 10B means that 10,000,000,000 shares traded.

traditional IRA, p. 438 A savings plan in which the income generated by the account is tax-deferred until it is withdrawn from that account.

traditional stock split, p. 45 A split where the value of a share and the number of shares are changed in such a proportional way that the value decreases as the number of shares increases, while the market cap remains the same.

transaction, p. 201 A purchase, cash advance, or payment made using a credit card.

transfer tax, p. 412 A fee that is charged for the transfer of the title from the seller to the buyer.

transitive property of dependence, p. 103 An example is if expenses depend on quantity and quantity depends on price, then expenses also depend on price.

trend, p. 64 A relationship that exists between the two variables in a bivariate data set.

trip odometer, p. 259 Another odometer that gives the accumulated distance traveled on a particular trip.

Truth in Lending Act, p. 194 A law that offers protection if a credit card is lost or stolen; if a consumer contacts the credit card company immediately after losing a credit card or the card is stolen, the maximum liability is $50.

U

unemployment insurance, p. 310 A government program that offers benefits to eligible employees who, through no fault of their own, have become unemployed.

unfurnished, p. 384 A rental property that does not include furniture.

uninsured/underinsured motorist protection (UMP), p. 238 Coverage that pays for injuries to a driver or passengers caused by a driver who has no insurance or does not have enough insurance to cover the medical losses.

univariate data, p. 64 A single set of numbers.

universal life insurance, p. 465 Similar to whole life insurance; the cash value can be used to pay the insurance premium if the policyholder doesn't pay it, but if the cash value is not enough to pay the insurance, the policy can lapse.

upper quartile, p. 227 Q_3 is the third quartile or upper quartile, and 75% of the numbers in the data set are at or below Q_3.

uptick, p. 32 A tick that indicates the price is greater than the previous trade.

utility, p. 482 Expenses for electricity, natural gas, heating oil, and water that are incurred while living in a home.

V

variable expenses, p. 80 Expenses that depend on the number of items produced, such as raw materials.

variable life insurance, p. 465 Combines an insurance part with a variety of investment components; these may include stocks, bonds, and money market funds; one of the riskiest types of insurance policies.

vertex of a parabola, p. 87 The peak of the parabola and the point where revenue is maximized; the point of maximum value in a quadratic equation.

vested, p. 456 The number of years an employee must participate in the plan before having the right to the investment or part of the investment.

volume, pp. 398, 482 The amount of space inside a three-dimensional region, such as a room; volume is measured in cubic units.

volume (stock market), p. 10 The number of shares traded within a given amount of time, usually a day.

voluntary compliance, p. 354 When taxpayers cooperate with the taxpaying process.

W

wage assignment, p. 181 A voluntary deduction from an employee's paycheck, used to pay off debts.

wage garnishment, p. 182 An involuntary form of wage assignment, often done by court order.

watt, p. 482 A unit measure used for electricity.

watt-hour, p. 482 A unit for the usage of electricity; for example, a 60-watt light bulb burning for two hours uses 120 watt-hours.

weak correlation, p. 70 Correlation coefficients with an absolute value less than 0.3.

weekly, p. 296 Once per week.

whole life insurance, p. 465 A type of insurance that combines a life insurance policy with an investment feature; policyholders pay a premium that is divided between the insurance portion and the investment portion.

wholesale price, p. 76 The price that manufacturers charge the retailer.

widget, p. 75 A new, unnamed product.

withholding tax, p. 344 Federal, state, and local income taxes that are withheld by employers, who then send the money to the government.

worker's compensation, p. 311 Assistance to employees who are injured while working at their job; a program that is governed by state laws.

Y

yaw mark, p. 274 Curved tire marks that indicate the vehicle was slipping sideways while at the same time continuing in a forward motion.

year-long expense budget plan, p. 512 A plan where entries are made under each of the months of the year.

yield, p. 51 The percentage value of the dividend, compared to the current price per share.

Z

zero net difference, p. 91 When the difference between expense and revenue equals zero; meaning that the values of both are equal; also called breakeven points when revenue and expenses are graphed on the same coordinate plane.

INDEX

D

M

N

O

P

Q

R

T

U

V

W

X

Y

Z

CHAPTER 1

1-3, pp. 20–21

12.

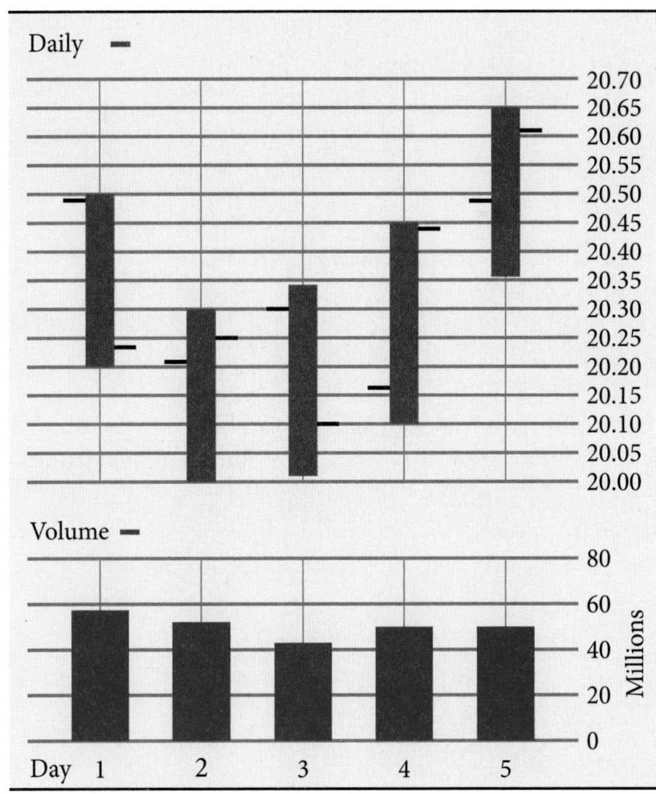

13.

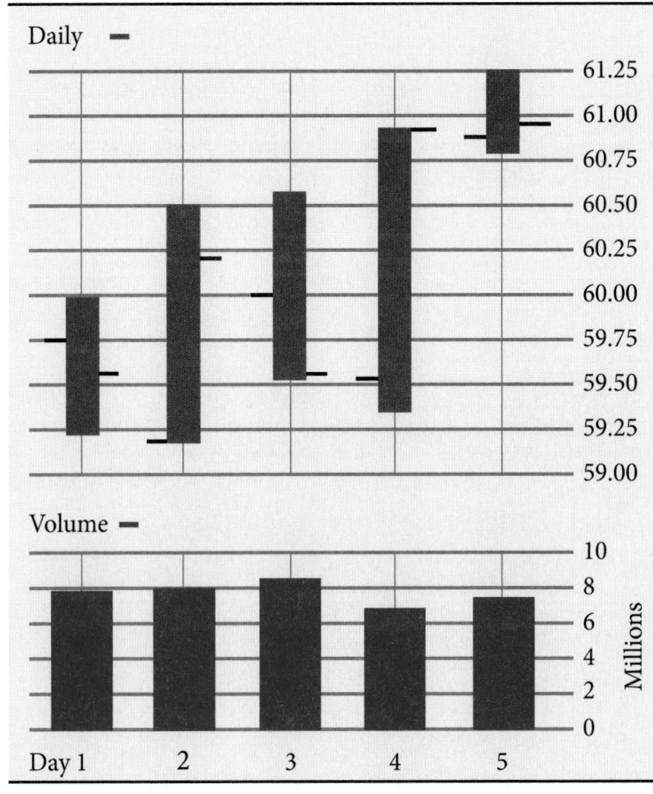

15.

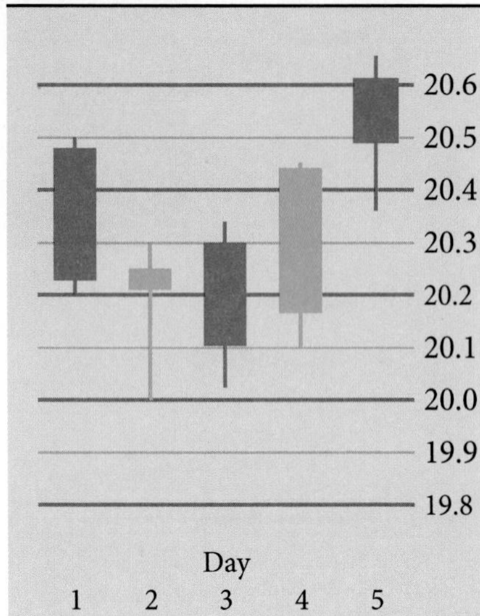

16.

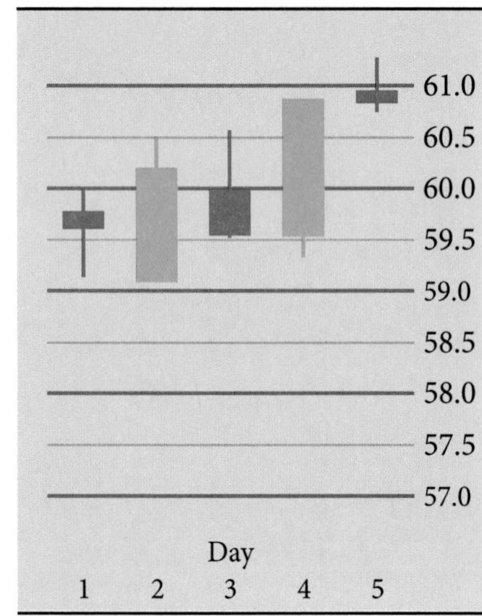

1-4, pp. 27–28

10.

Date	Closing Price	7-Day SMA
7-Apr	24.60	
8-Apr	23.76	
9-Apr	23.58	
10-Apr	23.71	
11-Apr	23.36	
14-Apr	22.51	
15-Apr	22.80	23.47
16-Apr	23.44	23.31
17-Apr	24.03	23.35
18-Apr	25.11	23.57
21-Apr	25.03	23.75

(Continued)

10. (*Continued*)

22-Apr	25.12	24.01
23-Apr	24.63	24.31
24-Apr	25.76	24.73
25-Apr	26.60	25.18
28-Apr	26.81	25.58
29-Apr	26.32	25.75
30-Apr	25.27	25.79
1-May	25.99	25.91
2-May	26.39	26.16
5-May	25.75	26.16
6-May	25.87	26.06
7-May	24.48	25.72
8-May	24.30	25.44
9-May	23.63	25.20

11.

Date	Closing Price	10-Day SMA
31-Mar	19.92	
1-Apr	20.33	
2-Apr	19.95	
3-Apr	20.12	
4-Apr	19.53	
7-Apr	19.23	
8-Apr	19.00	
9-Apr	18.69	
10-Apr	18.77	
11-Apr	18.50	19.40
14-Apr	18.24	19.24
15-Apr	18.28	19.03
16-Apr	18.72	18.91
17-Apr	19.05	18.80
18-Apr	19.47	18.80
21-Apr	19.56	18.83
22-Apr	19.05	18.83
23-Apr	19.05	18.87
24-Apr	19.14	18.91
25-Apr	19.11	18.97
28-Apr	18.87	19.03
29-Apr	18.97	19.10
30-Apr	18.63	19.09
1-May	19.08	19.09
2-May	19.32	19.08
5-May	19.10	19.03
6-May	19.19	19.05
7-May	18.90	19.03

(*Continued*)

11. (*Continued*)

Date	Closing Price	10-Day SMA
8-May	18.84	19.00
9-May	19.03	18.99

12.

Date	Closing Price	2-Day SMA	3-Day SMA	5-Day-SMA
31-Mar	440.47			
1-Apr	465.71	453.09		
2-Apr	465.70	465.71	457.29	
3-Apr	455.12	460.41	462.18	
4-Apr	471.09	463.11	463.97	459.62
7-Apr	476.82	473.96	467.68	466.89
8-Apr	467.81	472.32	471.91	467.31
9-Apr	464.19	466.00	469.61	467.01
10-Apr	469.08	466.64	467.03	469.80
11-Apr	457.45	463.27	463.57	467.07
14-Apr	451.66	454.56	459.40	462.04
15-Apr	446.84	449.25	451.98	457.84
16-Apr	455.03	450.94	451.18	456.01
17-Apr	449.54	452.29	450.47	452.10
18-Apr	539.41	494.48	481.33	468.50
21-Apr	537.79	538.60	508.91	485.72
22-Apr	555.00	546.40	544.07	507.35
23-Apr	546.49	550.75	546.43	525.65
24-Apr	543.04	544.77	548.18	544.35
25-Apr	544.06	543.55	544.53	545.28
28-Apr	552.12	548.09	546.41	548.14
29-Apr	558.47	555.30	551.55	548.84
30-Apr	574.29	566.38	561.63	554.40
1-May	593.08	583.69	575.28	564.40
2-May	581.29	587.19	582.89	571.85
5-May	594.90	588.10	589.76	580.41
6-May	586.36	590.63	587.52	585.98
7-May	579.00	582.68	586.75	586.93
8-May	583.01	581.01	582.79	584.91
9-May	573.20	578.11	578.40	583.29

13. Crossovers occur at Days 4 and 19. On Day 4, the fast moving average rises above the slow moving average indicating a possible signal to buy. On Day 19, the fast moving average dips below the slow moving average indicating a possible signal to sell.

14. Crossover occurs on Day 9 where the 3-Day SMA dips below the 5-Day SMA indicating a possible sell signal. On Day 11, that trend reverses. On Day 14, the 5-Day SMA rises above the 3-Day SMA and the 10-Day SMA rises above the 3-day, signaling a possible sell trend. Finally, on Day 15, the 10-day SMA crosses above the 5-Day SMA graph again, indicating a continuing sell trend.

15.

Date	Closing Price	2-Day SMA	5-Day SMA
21-Apr	28.55		
22-Apr	28.54	28.55	
23-Apr	28.08	28.31	
24-Apr	27.30	27.69	
25-Apr	26.8	27.05	27.85
28-Apr	26.43	26.62	27.43
29-Apr	27.36	26.90	27.19
30-Apr	27.41	27.39	27.06
1-May	26.81	27.11	26.96
2-May	28.67	27.74	27.34
5-May	24.37	26.52	26.92
6-May	25.72	25.05	26.60
7-May	25.64	25.68	26.24
8-May	26.22	25.93	26.12
9-May	25.93	26.08	25.58

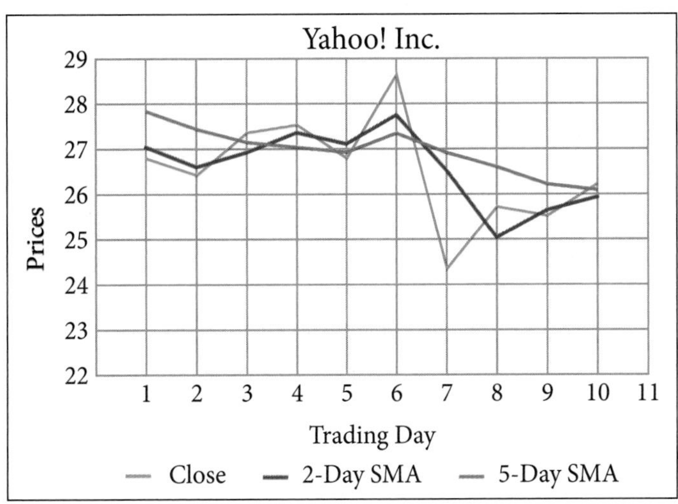

CHAPTER 2

2-5, p. 90

2d.

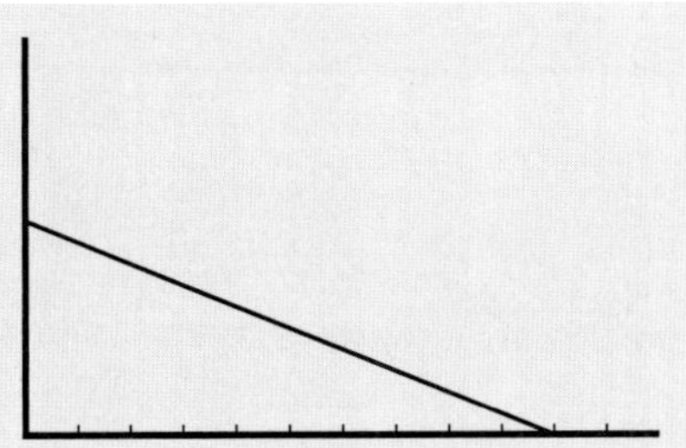

2f.

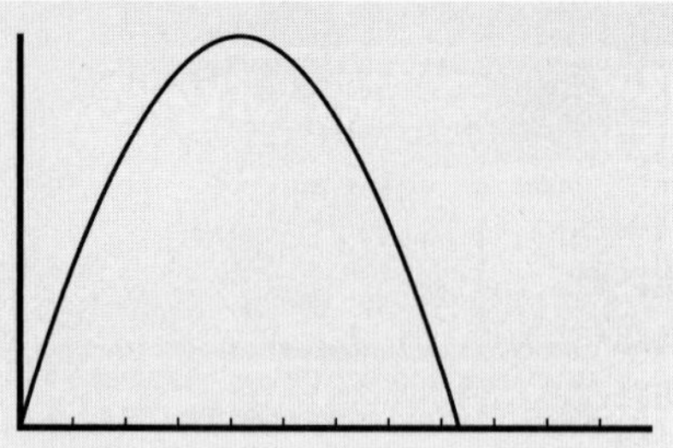

2g.

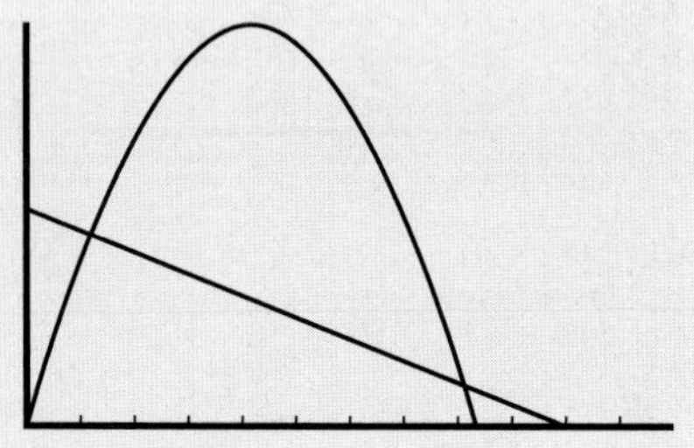

3d.

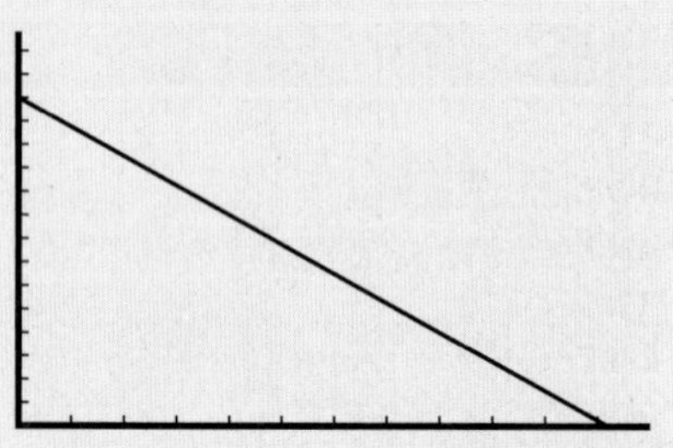

3f.

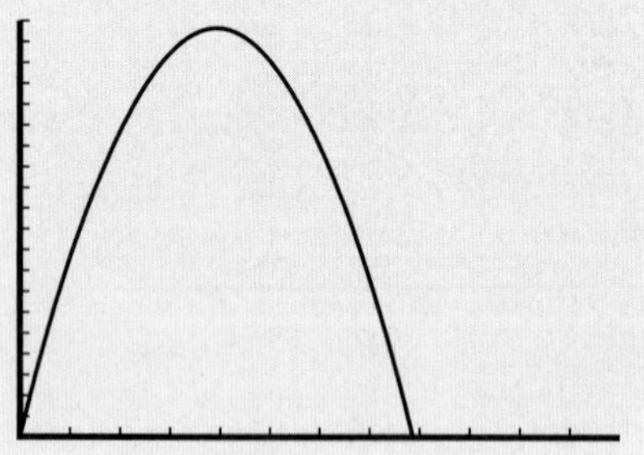

3g.

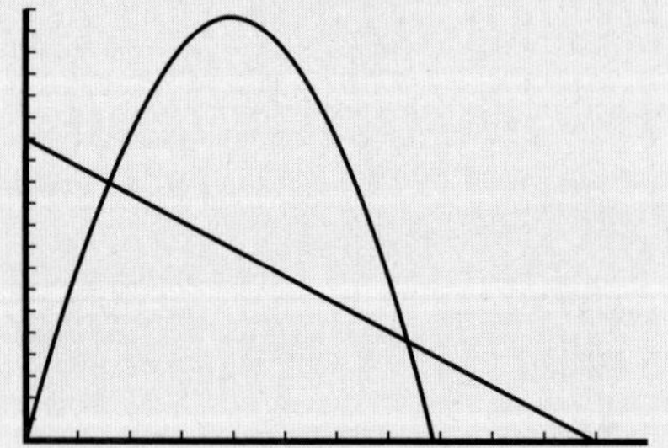

2-6, pp. 95–96

7a.

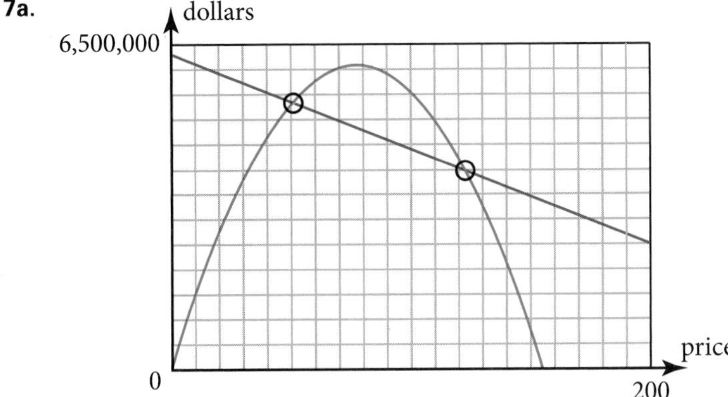

8a.

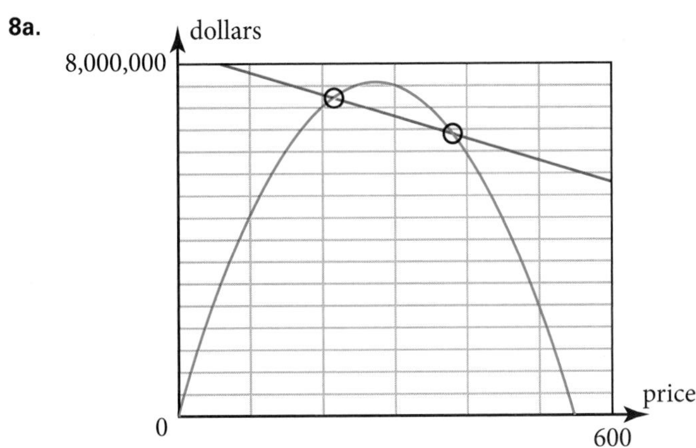

9b.

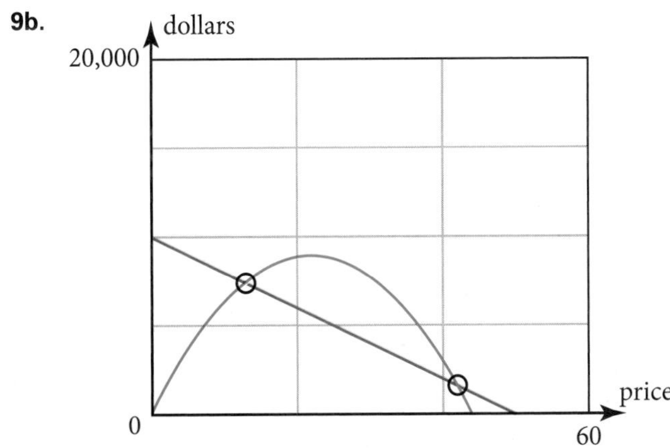

10c.

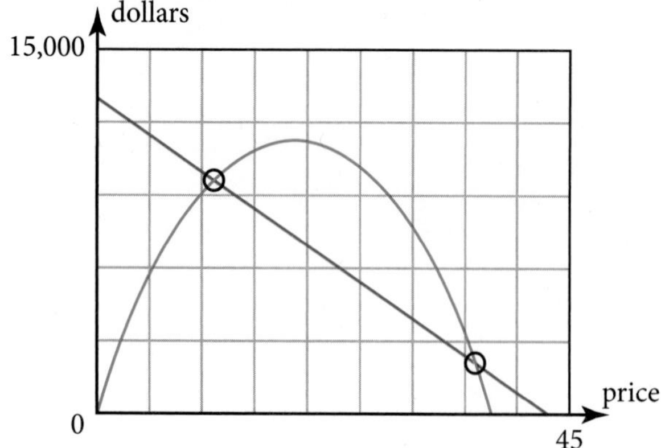

2-8, pp. 106–107

14c.

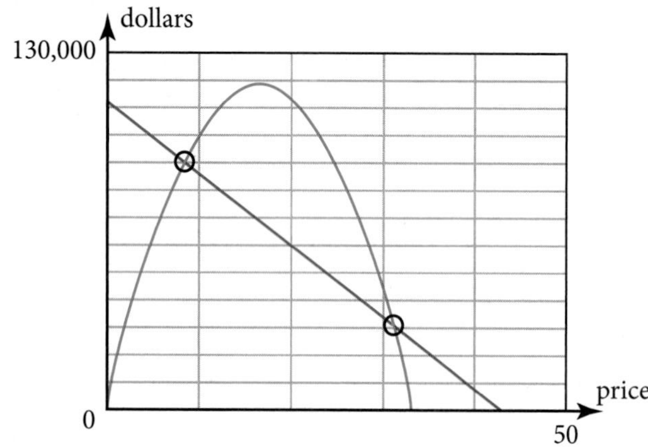

18.

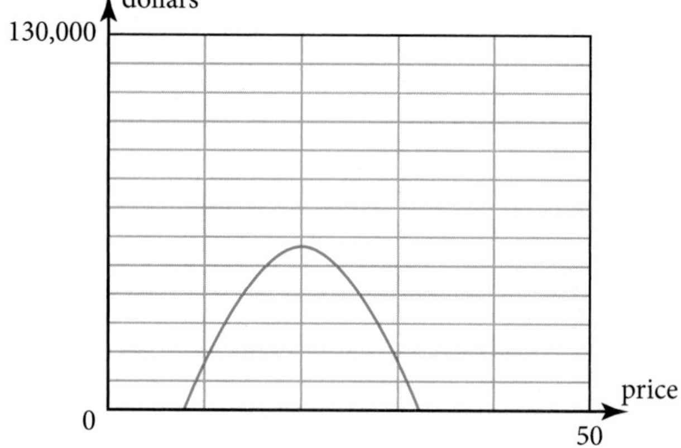

Assessment Applications, pp. 111–113

19c.

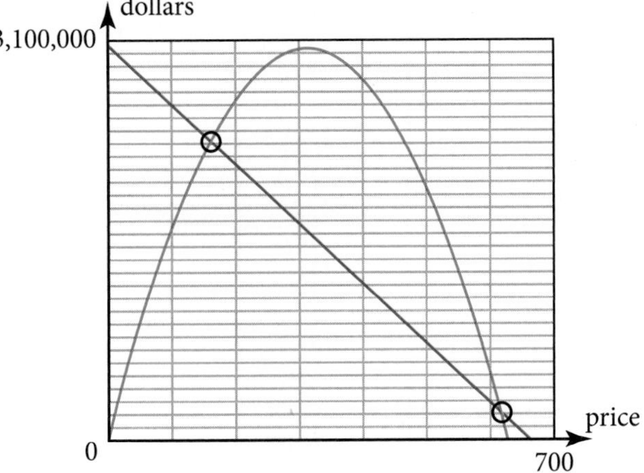

CHAPTER 3

3-1, pp. 120–122

12.

DESCRIPTION	CATALOG NUMBER	LIST PRICE	QUANTITY	TOTAL
Speaker Cabinets	RS101	$400.00	2	$800.00
Speaker Cabinets	RG306	$611.00	2	$1,222.00
Horns	BG42	$190.00	2	$380.00
Audio Console	LS101	$1,079.00	1	$1,079.00
Power Amplifier	NG107	$416.00	5	$2,080.00
Microphones	RKG-1972	$141.92	8	$1,135.36
Microphone Stands	1957-210	$32.50	8	$260.00
			TOTAL	$6,956.36
			13% DISCOUNT	$904.33
			SALE PRICE	$6,052.03
			8% SALES TAX	$484.16
			TOTAL COST	$6,536.19

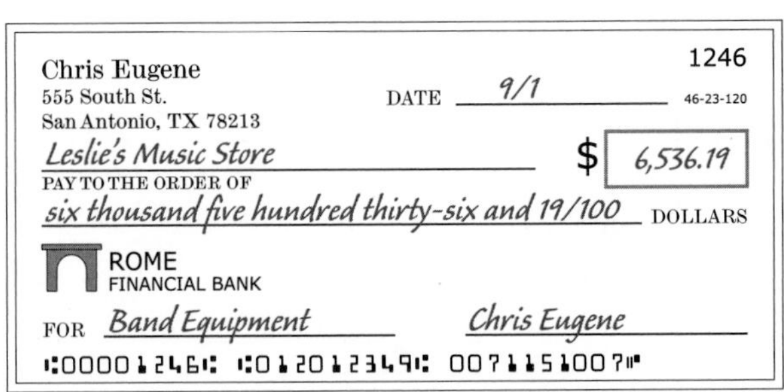
Chris Eugene
555 South St.
San Antonio, TX 78213

1246

DATE 9/1

46-23-120

PAY TO THE ORDER OF Leslie's Music Store $ 6,536.19

six thousand five hundred thirty-six and 19/100 DOLLARS

ROME
FINANCIAL BANK

FOR Band Equipment

Chris Eugene

⑆0000124б⑆ ⑆01201234 9⑆ 007115100 7⑈

13.

NUMBER OR CODE	DATE	TRANSACTION DESCRIPTION	PAYMENT AMOUNT		✓	FEE	DEPOSIT AMOUNT		$ BALANCE
	10/29		$						237.47
115	10/29	Fox High School	18	00					− 18.00 219.47
	10/30	Deposit					162	75	+ 162.75 382.22
	11/4	Deposit					25	00	+ 25.00 407.22
	11/5	ATM	15	00					− 15.00 392.22
	11/5	ATM fee	2	25					− 2.25 389.97
116	11/7	Credit USA	51	16					− 51.16 338.81
	11/10	Deposit					20	00	+ 20.00 358.81
	11/12	ATM	25	00					− 25.00 333.81
	11/12	ATM fee	2	25					− 2.25 331.56
	11/16	Deposit					165	65	+ 165.65 497.21
	11/17	Deposit					35	00	+ 35.00 532.21

16.

NUMBER OR CODE	DATE	TRANSACTION DESCRIPTION	PAYMENT AMOUNT		✓	FEE	DEPOSIT AMOUNT		$ BALANCE
	12/15		$						2,546.50
2345	12/16	Kings Park HSSA	54	00					− 54.00 2,492.50
	12/17	Deposit					324	20	+ 324.20 2,816.70
	12/20	Deposit					100	00	+ 100.00 2916.70
2346	12/22	Best Buy	326	89					− 326.89 2,589.81
2347	12/22	Macy's	231	88					− 231.88 2,357.93
2348	12/22	Target	123	51					− 123.51 2,234.42
2349	12/24	VOID							
2350	12/24	Apple	301	67					− 301.67 1,932.75
	12/26	Deposit					98	00	+ 98.00 2,030.75
EFT	12/28	Allstate	876	00					− 876.00 1,154.75
	12/29	ATM	200	00					− 200.00 954.75
	12/29	ATM fee	1	50					− 1.50 953.25

3-2, pp. 127–130

11.

Checking Account Summary	
Ending Balance	$1,378.57
Deposits	+ $950.00
Checks Outstanding	– $303.50
Revised Statement Balance	
Check Register Balance	$2,025.07

PLEASE BE SURE TO DEDUCT CHANGES THAT AFFECT YOUR ACCOUNT

ITEM NO. FOR TRANSACTION CODE	DATE	DESCRIPTION OF TRANSACTION	SUBTRACTION: AMOUNT OF PAYMENT OR WITHDRAWAL		✓	OTHER	ADDITIONS: AMOUNT OF DEPOSIT OR INTEREST		BALANCE FORWARD	
									728	30
1773	12/28	TO Galaxy Theather	75	00	✓				– 75	00
		FOR Tickets							653	30
1774	12/30	TO American Electric Company	70	00	✓				– 70	00
		FOR Electric Bill							583	30
1775	12/30	TO Hillsdake Water Co.	38	50					– 38	50
		FOR Water Bill							544	80
1776	1/2	TO Barbara's Restaurant	28	00	✓				– 28	00
		FOR Dinner							516	80
1777	1/3	TO Platter Records	120	00	✓				– 120	00
		FOR Compact Disc							396	80
1778	1/9	TO A1 Gas Co.	56	73	✓				– 56	73
		FOR Gas Bill							340	07
1779	1/12	TO Al and Jean Adams	100	00					– 100	00
		FOR Wedding Gift							240	07
1780	1/12	TO Greene College	85	00					– 85	00
		FOR Fees							155	07
	1/14	TO Deposit			✓		1,000	00	+ 1,000	00
		FOR							1,155	07
1780	1/25	TO Rob Gerver	80	00					– 80	00
		FOR Typing Fee							1,075	07
	2/1	TO Deposit					950	00	+ 950	00
		FOR Salary							2,025	07

Yes, Raymond's checking account balances.

3-7, pp. 159–160

9i.

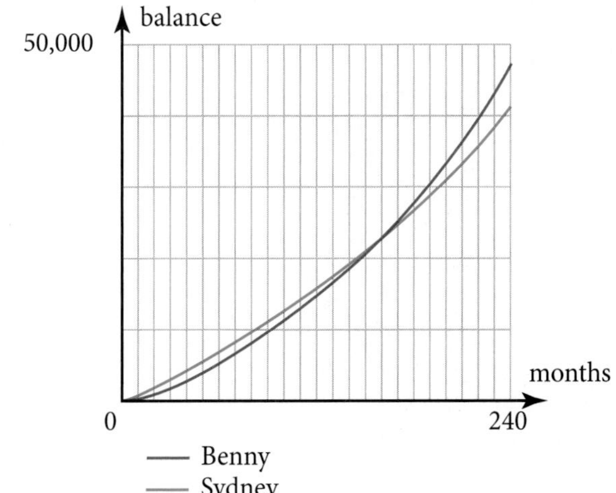

Really? Really! Revisited, p. 168

1.

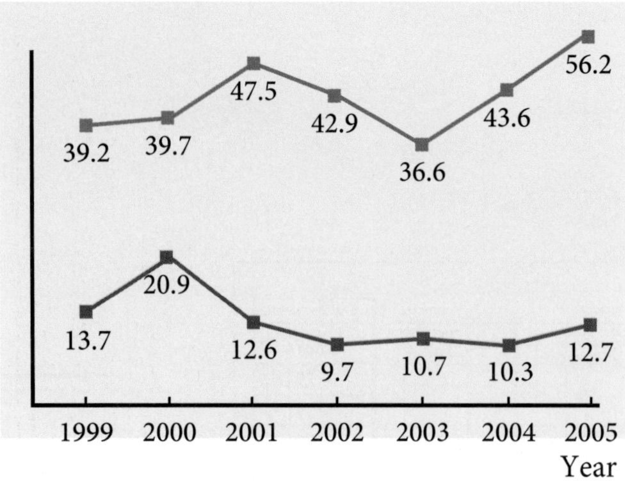

Assessment Applications, pp. 169–171

1.

NUMBER OR CODE	DATE	TRANSACTION DESCRIPTION	PAYMENT AMOUNT $		✓	FEE	DEPOSIT AMOUNT		$ BALANCE
	12/10								3,900.50
1223	12/11	North Shore HS Drama Club	84	00	✓				– 84.00 3,816.50
	12/12	Deposit (paycheck)			✓		240	80	+ 240.80 4,057.30
	12/13	Deposit (birthday check)			✓		100	00	+ 100.00 4,157.30
1224	12/17	Best Buy	480	21	✓				– 480.21 3,677.09
1225	12/17	Target	140	58	✓				– 140.58 3,536.51
1226	12/17	Aeropostale	215	60	✓				– 215.60 3,320.91
1227	12/20	VOID							
1228	12/20	Staples	1250	00					– 1,250.00 2,070.91
	12/22	Barnes & Nobles Return					120	00	+ 120.00 2,190.91
	12/24	ATM Withdraw	300	00	✓				– 300.00 1,890.91
	12/24	ATM Fee	1	50		✓			– 1.50 1,889.41
	12/24	Bank Fee	2	50		✓			– 2.50 1,886.91
1229	12/28	Len's Auto Body Shop	521	00	✓				– 521.00 1,365.91
1230	12/29	Amtrak	150	80					– 150.80 1,215.11

CHAPTER 4

4-3, pp. 191–192

6a. $$M = \frac{25{,}000 \cdot \frac{0.077}{12} \cdot \left(1 + \frac{0.077}{12}\right)^{12t}}{\left(1 + \frac{0.077}{12}\right)^{12t} - 1}$$

6b. $$\text{Interest} = 12t\left(\frac{25{,}000 \cdot \frac{0.077}{12} \cdot \left(1 + \frac{0.077}{12}\right)^{12t}}{\left(1 + \frac{0.077}{12}\right)^{12t} - 1}\right) - 25{,}000$$

6c.

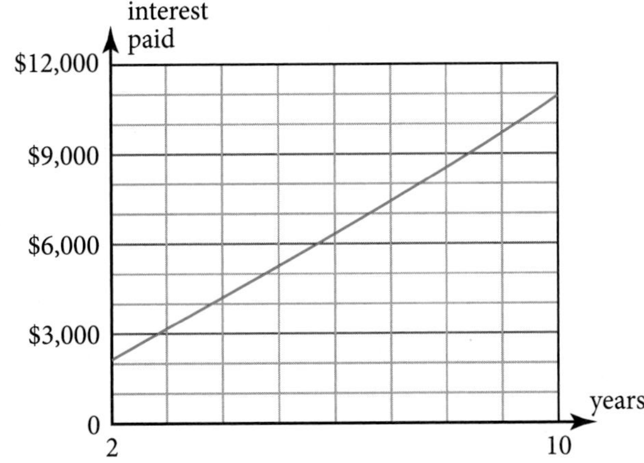

CHAPTER 5

5-3, pp. 236–237

6k.

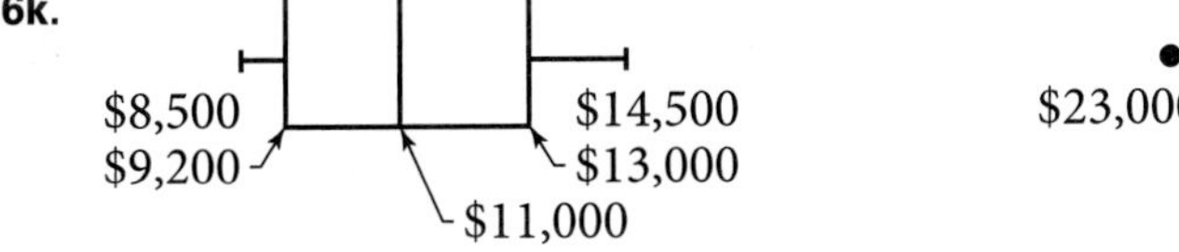

7a.

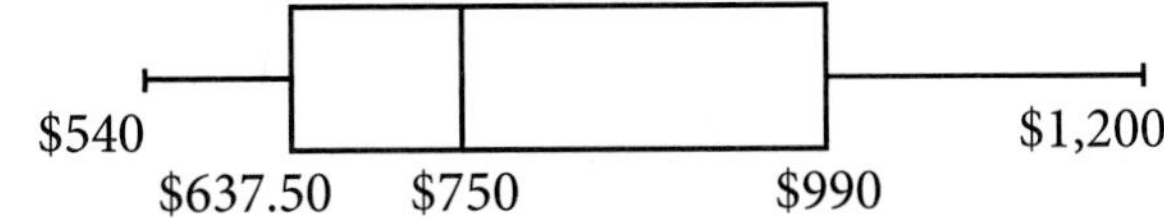

10m.

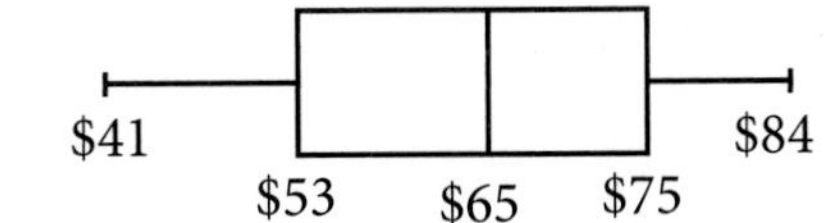

5-4, pp. 242–244

17.

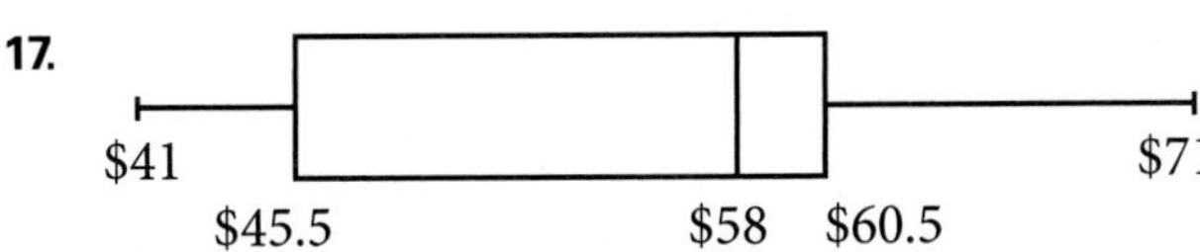

5-5, pp. 250–251

3d.

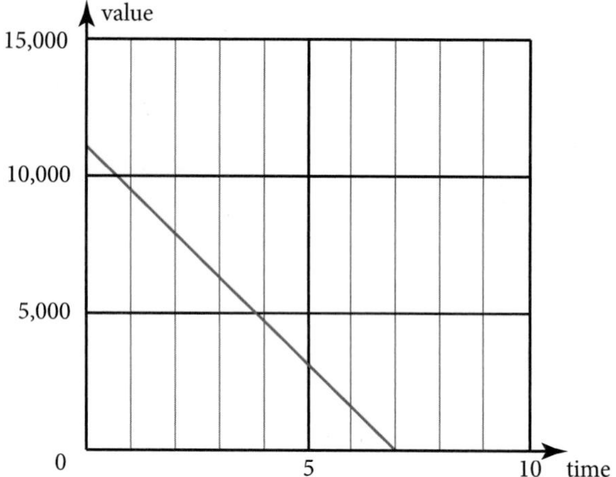

13b.

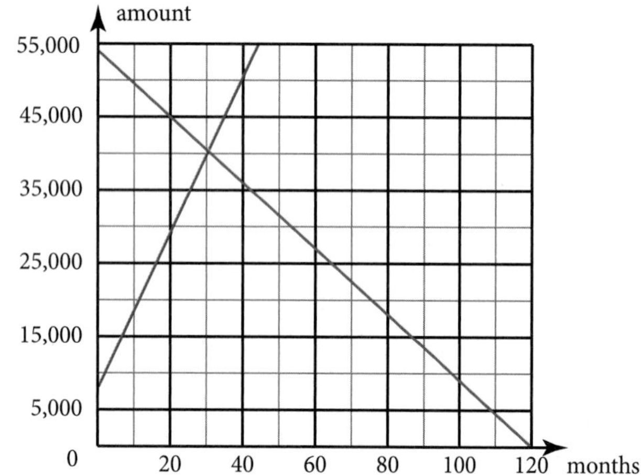

5-7, pp. 265–267

15b.

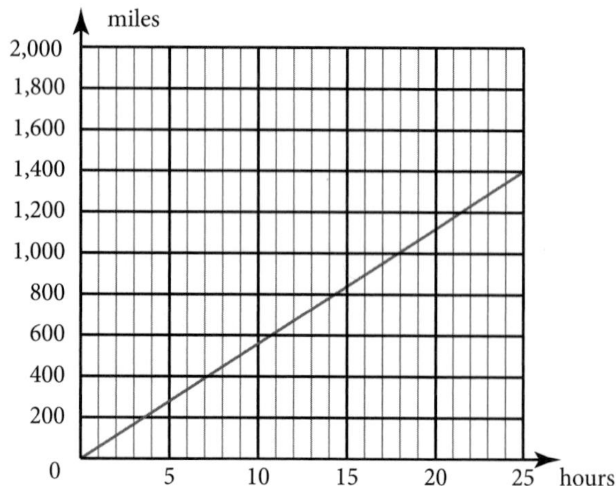

5-8, pp. 272–273

13a.

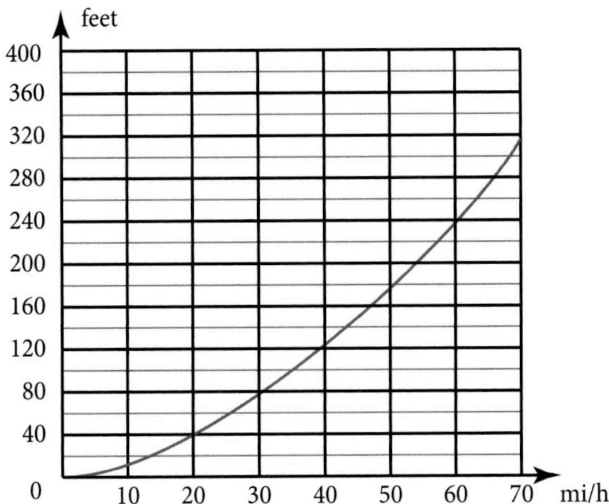

14a.

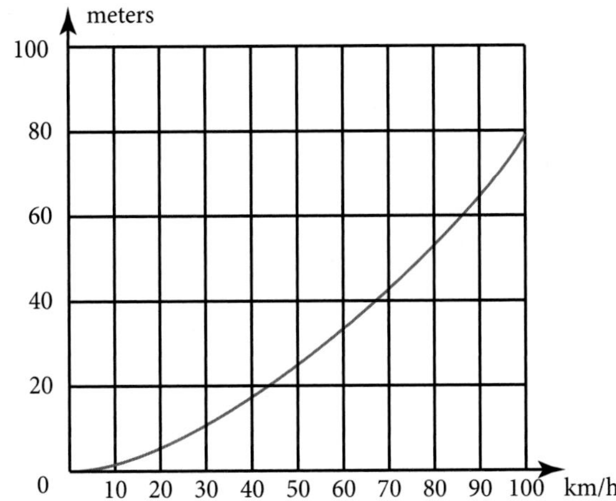

5-9, pp. 279–281

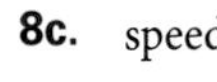

8c.

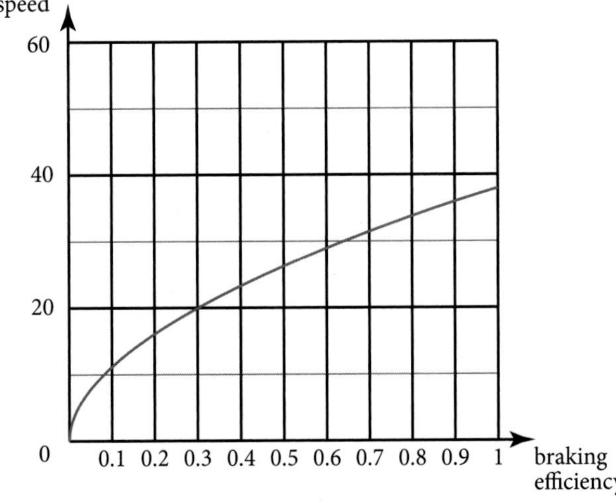

Assessment Applications, pp. 285–287

6h.

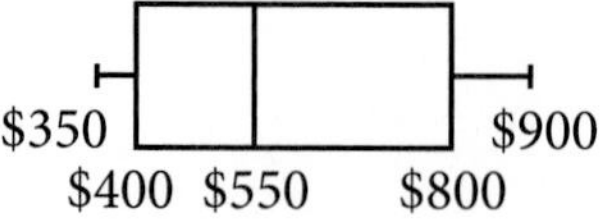

7b.

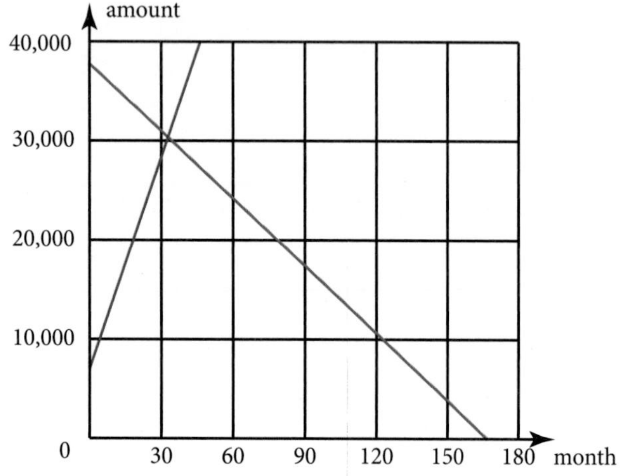

CHAPTER 6

6-2, pp. 300–302

27a–c.

1 0.01	2 0.02	3 0.04	4 0.08
5 0.16	6 0.32	7 0.64	8 1.28
9 2.56	10 5.12	11 10.24	12 20.48
13 40.96	14 81.92	15 163.84	16 327.68
17 655.36	18 1,310.72	19 2,621.44	20 5,242.88
21 10,485.76	22 20,971.52	23 41,943.04	24 83,886.08
25 167,772.16	26 335,544.32	27 671,088.64	28 1,342,177.28
29 2,684,354.56	30 5,368,709.12	31 10,737,418.24	

6-5, pp. 319–320

5a. Social Security, $3,571.20; Medicare, $1,957.50

5b. $f(x) = \begin{cases} 0.062x & \text{when } 0 < x \leq 84{,}900 \\ 5{,}263.80 & \text{when } x > 84{,}900 \end{cases}$

6. $t(x) = \begin{cases} 0.062x & \text{when } 0 < x \leq 57{,}600 \\ 3{,}571.20 & \text{when } x > 57{,}600 \end{cases}$

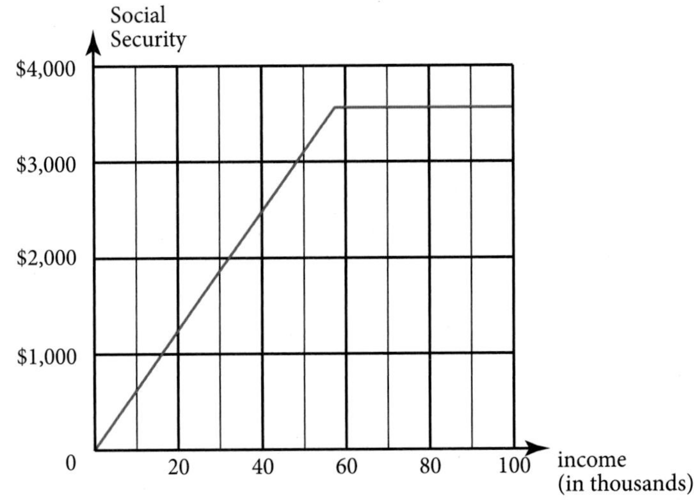

7.

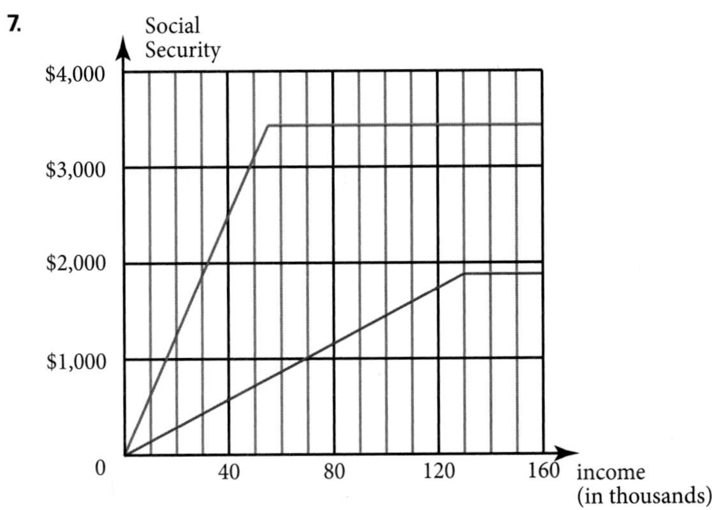

CHAPTER 7

7-2, pp. 340–343

2.

Tax Schedule Notation	Interval Notation	Compound Inequality Notation
Over $0 but not over $8,025	$0 < x \leq 8{,}025$	$(x > 0$ and $x \leq 8{,}025)$
Over $8,025 but not over $32,550	$8{,}025 < x \leq 32{,}550$	$(x > 8{,}025$ and $x \leq 32{,}550$
Over $32,550 but not over $78,850	$32{,}550 < x \leq 78{,}550$	$(x > 32{,}550$ and $x \leq 78{,}550)$
Over $78,550 but not over $164,550	$748{,}550 < x \leq 164{,}550$	$(x > 78{,}550$ and $x \leq 164{,}550)$
Over $164,550 but not over $357,700	$164{,}550 < x \leq 357{,}700$	$(x > 164{,}550$ and $x \leq 357{,}700)$
Over $357,700	$x > 357{,}700$	$(x > 357{,}700)$

4.

$$f(x) = \begin{cases} 0.10x & 0 < x \leq 8{,}025 \\ 0.15x - 401.25 & 8{,}025 < x \leq 32{,}550 \\ 0.25x - 3{,}656.25 & 32{,}550 < x \leq 65{,}725 \end{cases}$$

6.

$$f(x) = \begin{cases} 0.10 & 0 < x \leq 15{,}100 \\ 1{,}510 + 0.15(x - 15{,}100) & 15{,}100 < x \leq 61{,}300 \\ 8{,}440 + 0.25(x - 61{,}300) & 61{,}300 < x \leq 123{,}700 \\ 24{,}040 + 0.28(x - 123{,}700) & 123{,}700 < x \leq 188{,}450 \\ 42{,}170 + 0.33(x - 18.450) & 188{,}450 < x \leq 336{,}550 \\ 91{,}043 + 0.35(x - 336{,}550) & x > 336{,}550 \end{cases}$$

8.

$$f(x) = \begin{cases} y = 0.15x & 0 < x \leq 25{,}350 \\ y = 3{,}802.50 + 0.28(x - 25{,}350) & 25{,}350 < x \leq 61{,}400 \\ y = 13{,}896.50 + 0.31(x - 61{,}400) & 61{,}400 < x \leq 128{,}100 \\ y = 34{,}573.50 + 0.36(x - 128{,}100) & 128{,}100 < x \leq 278{,}450 \\ y = 88{,}699.50 + 0.396(x - 278{,}450) & x > 278{,}450 \end{cases}$$

10b.

Taxable Income	(a) Enter taxable income	(b) Multiplication amount	(c) Multiply (a) by (b)	(d) Subtraction amount	Tax Subtract (d) from (c)
At least $71,950 but not over $150,150	x	28% (0.28)	$0.28x$	6,083.50	$0.28x - 6{,}083.50$
Over $150,150 but not over $326, 450	x	33% (0.33)	$0.33x$	12,951	$0.33x - 12{,}951$
Over $326,450	x	35% (0.35)	$0.35x$	19,530	0.25 – 19,530

Really? Really! Revisited, p. 373

1.

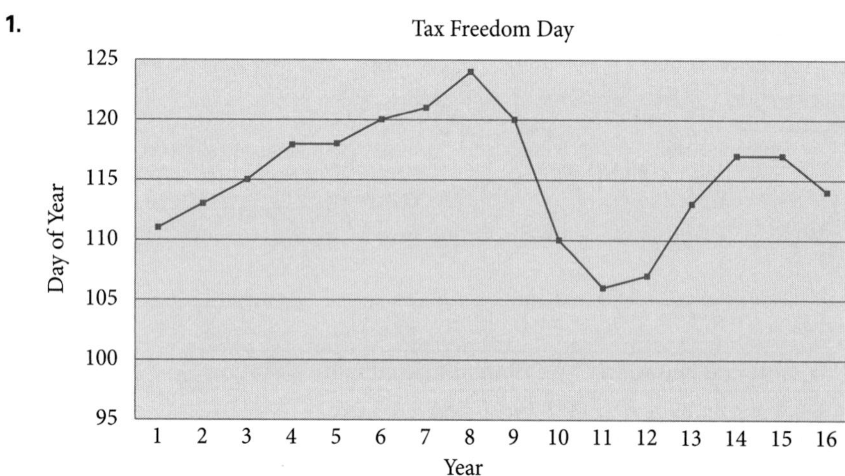

CHAPTER 8

8-2, pp. 399–400

8a.

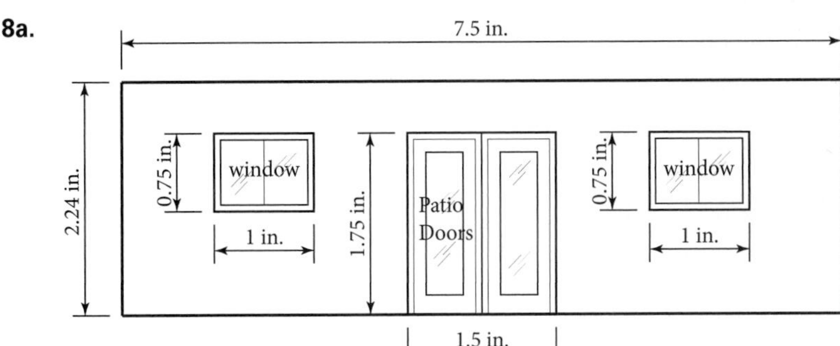

8-4, pp. 420–421

7.

Payment	Beginning Balance	Monthly Payment	Towards Interest	Towards Principal	Ending Balance
1	400,000.00	2,994.08	2,183.33	810.75	399,189.25
2	399,189.25	2,994.08	2,178.91	815.17	398,374.08

8.

Payment	Beginning Balance	Monthly Payment	Towards Interest	Towards Principal	Ending Balance
1	275,000.00	2,305.78	1,352.08	953.70	274,046.30
2	274,046.30	2,305.78	1,347.39	958.39	273,087.91

9.

Payment	Beginning Balance	Monthly Payment	Towards Interest	Towards Principal	Ending Balance
1	200,000.00	2,322.17	1,166.67	1,155.50	198,844.50
2	198,844.50	2,322.17	1,159.93	1,162.24	197,682.25
3	197,682.25	2,322.17	1,153.15	1,169.02	196,513.23
4	196,513.23	2,322.17	1,146.33	1,175.84	195,337.39
5	195,337.39	2,322.17	1,139.47	1,182.70	194,154.69
6	194,154.69	2,322.17	1,132.57	1,189.60	192,965.09
7	192,965.09	2,322.17	1,125.63	1,196.54	191,768.55
8	191,768.55	2,322.17	1,118.65	1,203.52	190,565.03
9	190,565.03	2,322.17	1,111.63	1,210.54	189,354.49
10	189,354.49	2,322.17	1,104.57	1,217.60	188,136.88
11	188,136.88	2,322.17	1,097.47	1,224.70	186,912.18
12	186,912.18	2,322.17	1,090.32	1,231.85	185,680.33

10.

Payment	Beginning Balance	Monthly Payment	Towards Interest	Towards Principal	Ending Balance
169	57,114.22	4,902.50	261.77	4,640.73	52,473.49
170	52,473.49	4,902.50	240.50	4,662.00	47,811.49
171	47,811.49	4,902.50	219.14	4,683.36	43,128.13
172	43,128.13	4,902.50	197.67	4,704.83	38,423.30
173	38,423.30	4,902.50	176.11	4,726.39	33,696.90
174	33,696.90	4,902.50	154.44	4,748.06	28,948.85
175	28,948.85	4,902.50	132.68	4,769.82	24,179.03
176	24,179.03	4,902.50	110.82	4,791.68	19,387.35
177	19,387.35	4,902.50	88.86	4,813.64	14,573.71
178	14,573.71	4,902.50	66.80	4,835.70	9,738.00
179	9,738.00	4,902.50	44.63	4,857.87	4,880.13
180	4,880.13	4,902.50	22.37	4,880.13	0.00

8-5, pp. 428–429

16. Rent: total paid $129,837.13; Purchase: total paid: $105,312.53, Paid toward principal: $42,717.12

17. Rent: $341,631.30; Purchase: total paid $313,598.65; Total paid toward principal: $169,935.92

Assessment Applications, pp. 432–435

20.

Payment	Beginning Balance	Monthly Payment	Towards Interest	Towards Principal	Ending Balance
1	350,000	3,000.98	1,822.92	348,821.94	274,046.30
2	348,821.94	3,000.98	1,816.78	1,184,20	347,637.74

CHAPTER 10

Lesson 10-3, pp. 504–505

2.

	Jan	Feb	Mar	Apr	May	June	July	Aug	Sept	Oct	Nov	Dec
Fuel	✓	✓	✓	✓	✓	✓	✓	✓	✓	✓	✓	✓
Insurance			✓	✓		✓			✓			✓
Servicing			✓			✓			✓			✓
Car Wash	✓		✓		✓		✓		✓		✓	
Parking						✓						✓
Public Transportation	✓	✓	✓	✓	✓	✓	✓	✓	✓	✓	✓	✓

3.

	Jan	Feb	Mar	Apr	May	June	July	Aug	Sept	Oct	Nov	Dec
Savings	600		600		600		600		600		600	
Retirement			2,000			2,000			2,000			2,000
Checking	2,000	2,000	2,000	2,000	2,000	2,000	2,000	2,000	2,000	2,000	2,000	2,000
Credit Card	500	500	500	500	500	500	500	500	500	500	500	500
Life Insurance						400						400
Real Estate taxes				1,300				1,300				1,300

7.

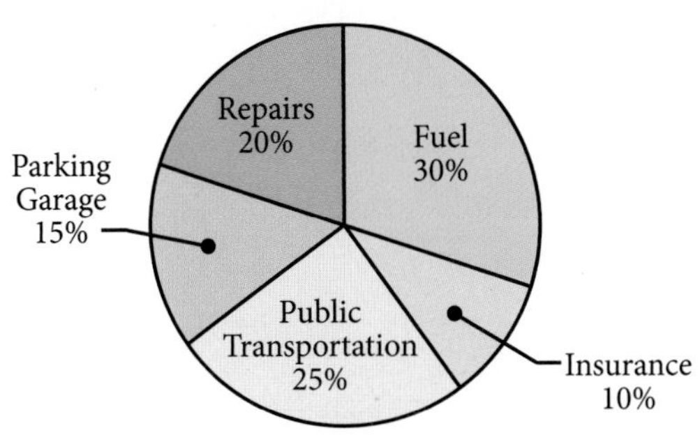

9.

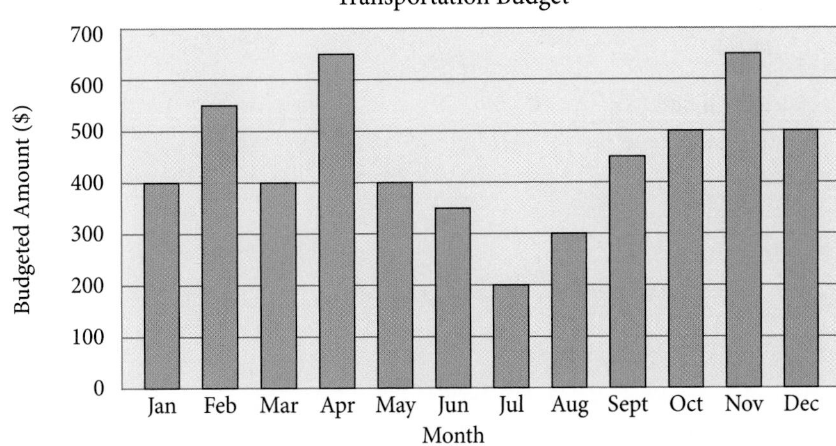

10.

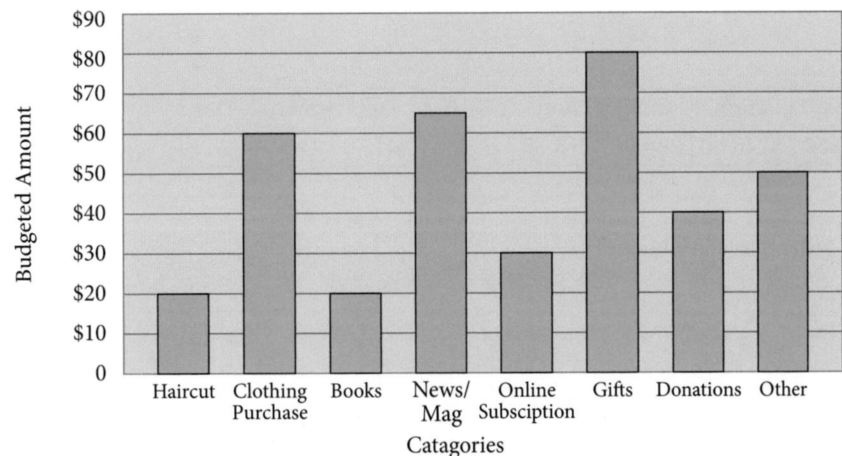

12a.

Jan	Feb	Mar	Apr	May	June	July	Aug	Sept	Oct	Nov	Dec
9,000	10,500	11,530	10,000	10,000	14,040	11,000	10,000	9,550	8,500	9,000	12,560

12b.

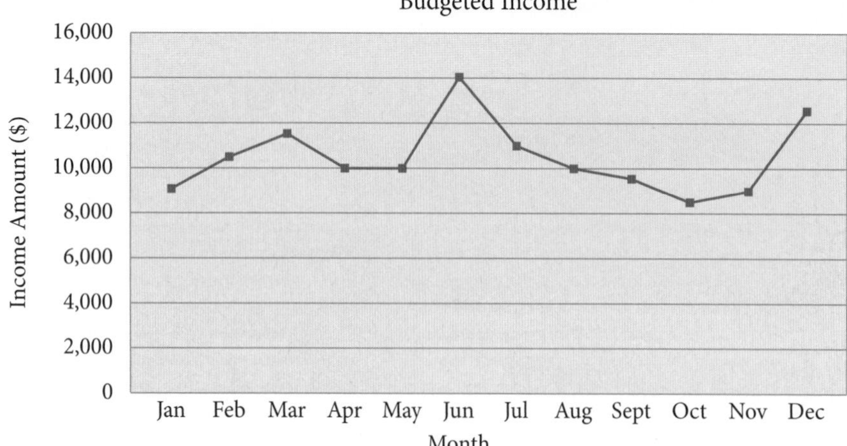

12d.

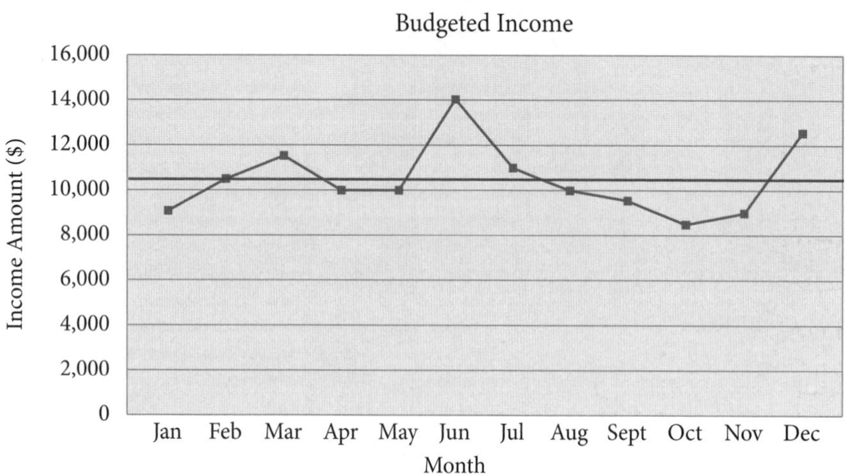

13c.

Jan	Feb	Mar	Apr	May	June	July	Aug	Sept	Oct	Nov	Dec
230	253	241.50	236.90	$241.50	$248.40	234.60	218.50	223.10	241.50	248.40	253

13d.

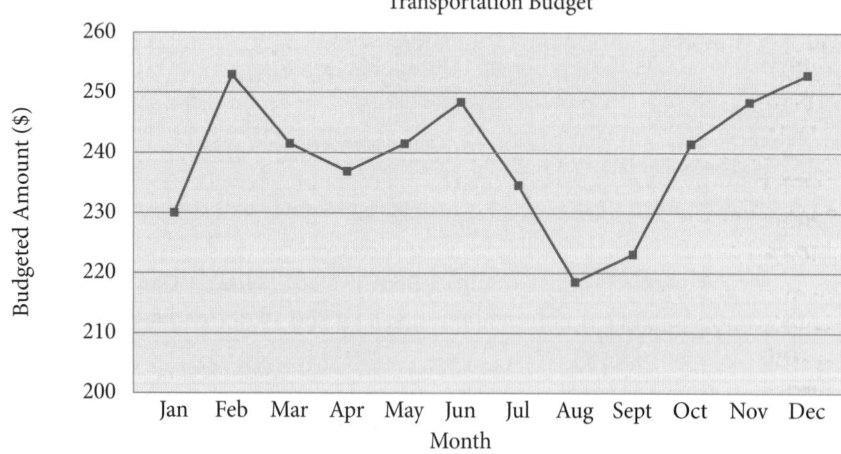

14b.

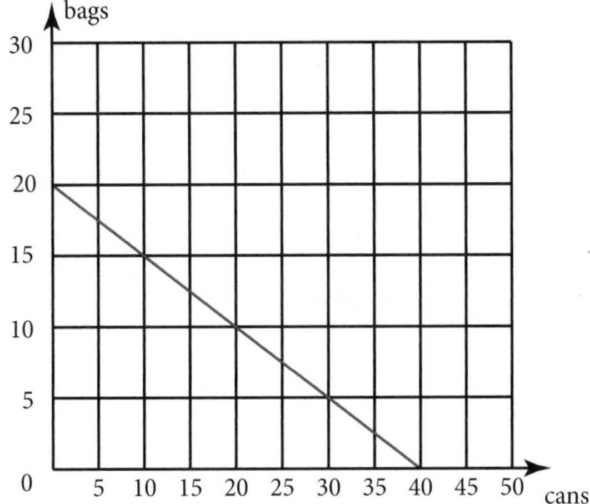
bags
30
25
20
15
10
5
0
5 10 15 20 25 30 35 40 45 50
cans

15b.

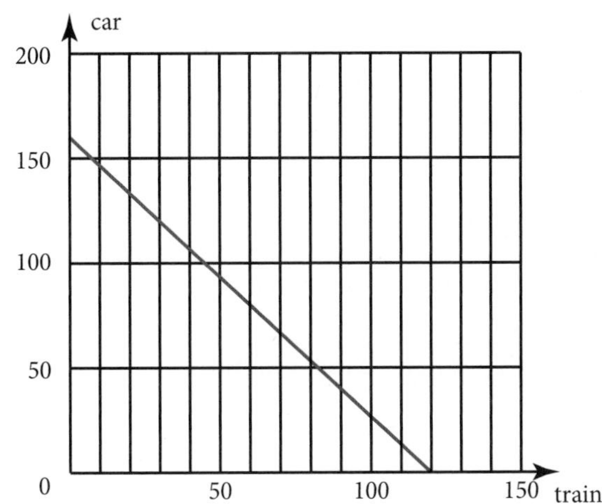
car
200
150
100
50
0
50 100 150
train

15e.

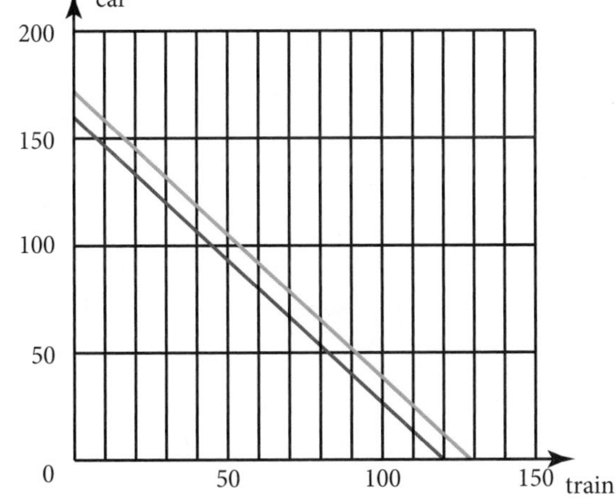
car
200
150
100
50
0
50 100 150
train

7.

Income				
Primary Employment	5,000			
Secondary Employment	1,200			
Other Income				
Total Income	**6,200**			
Fixed Expenses			**Non-Monthly Expenses (per year)**	
Rent/Mortgage	2,200		Medical/Dental	500
Car Loan Payment	180		Auto Related	400
Education Loan Payment	250		Home Related	500
Personal Loan Payment	100		Life Insurance	330
Health Insurance Premium	60		Tuition	4,000
Life Insurance Premium			Vacation	800
Car Insurance Premium	70		Gifts	500
Homeowner's/Renter's Insurance	30		Contributions	520
Cable TV	40		Repairs	280
Total Fixed Expenses	**2,930**		Taxes	3,000
			Other	
Variable Expenses			**Total Non-Monthly Expenses (per year)**	**10,830**
Groceries (Food)	600			
Dining Out	200		**Total Non-Monthly Expenses (per month)**	**902.50**
Fuel (car)	200			
Cell Phone	80		**Total Expenses**	**5,992.50**
Land Line Phone	60		**Monthly Cash Flow**	**207.50**
Electricity	80			
Water	40			
Sewer				
Sanitation	50			
Medical				
Entertainment	250			
Savings	400			
Debt Reduction	200			
Other				
Total Variable Expenses	**2,160**			

8.

Frequency Budget Plan			
After Tax Income Categories	**Income Amounts**	**Frequency**	**Annual Amount**
Primary Employment	2,500	24	60,000
Secondary Employment	1,200	12	14,400
Interest			
Dividends			
Other Income			
Total Income			**74,400**

(*Continued*)

8. (*Continued*)

Weekly Expenses	**Expense Amounts**		
Food	139	52	7,228
Personal Transportation (fuel)	47	52	2,444
Public Transportation		52	
Household		52	
Childcare		52	
Dining Out	47	52	2,444
Entertainment	58	52	3,016
Other (contributions)	10	52	520
Total Weekly Expenses			**15,652**
Monthly Expenses			
Rent	2,200	12	26,400
Utilities	170	12	2,040
Land Line/Cellular Telephone	140	12	1,680
Car Loan	180	12	2,160
Education Loan	250	12	3,000
Personal Loan	100	12	1,200
Car Insurance	70	12	840
Renter's Insurance	30	12	360
Savings	400	12	4,800
Debt Reduction	200	12	2,400
Other (health ins. prem.; cable)	100	12	1,200
Total Monthly Expenses			**46,080**
Other Frequency Expenses			
Medical/Dental	250	2	500
Auto Related	400	1	400
Home Related	250	2	500
Life Insurance	110	3	330
Tuition	2,000	2	4,000
Vacation	800	1	800
Gifts	250	2	500
Repairs	280	1	280
Taxes	1,500	2	3,000
Other			
Total Other Frequency Expenses			**10,310**
Total Expenses			**72,042**
Annual Surplus Or Deficit			**2,358**

9.

	A	B	C	D
1	**After Tax Income Categories**	**Income Amounts**	**Frequency**	**Annual Amount**
2	Primary Employment	2,500	24	=B2*C2
3	Secondary Employment	1,200	12	=B3*C3
4	Interest			
5	Dividends			
6	Other Income			
7	**Total Income**			=sum(D2:D6)
8				
9	**Weekly Expenses**	**Expense Amounts**		
10	Food	139	52	=B10*C10
11	Personal Transportation(fuel)	47	52	=B11*C11
12	Public Transportation		52	=B12*C12
13	Household		52	=B13*C13
14	Childcare		52	=B14*C14
15	Dining Out	47	52	=B15*C15
16	Entertainment	58	52	=B16*C16
17	Other (contributions)	10	52	=B17*C17
18				
19	**Total Weekly Expenses**			=sum(D10:D17)
20				
21	**Monthly Expenses**			
22	Rent	2,200	12	=B22*C22
23	Utilities	170	12	=B23*C23
24	Land Line/Cellular Telephone	140	12	=B24*C24
25	Car Loan	180	12	=B25*C25
26	Education Loan	250	12	=B26*C26
27	Personal Loan	100	12	=B27*C27
28	Car Insurance	70	12	=B28*C28
29	Renter's Insurance	30	12	=B29*C29
30	Savings	400	12	=B30*C30
31	Debt Reduction	200	12	=B31*C31
32	Other	100	12	=B32*C32
33				
34	**Total Monthly Expenses**			=sum(D22:D32)
35				
36	Other Frequency Expenses			
37	Medical/Dental	250	2	=B37*C37
38	Auto Related	400	1	=B38*C38
39	Home Related	250	2	=B39*C39
40	Life Insurance	110	3	=B40*C40
41	Tuition	2,000	2	=B41*C41
42	Vacation	800	1	=B42*C42
43	Gifts	250	2	=B43*C43
44	Repairs	280	1	=B44*C44

(*Continued*)

9. (*Continued*)

45	Taxes	1,500	2	=B45*C45
46	Other			=B46*C46
47				
48	**Total Other Frequency Expenses**			=sum(D37:D46)
49				
50	**Total Expenses**			=(D19+D34+D48)
51	**Annual Surplus or Deficit**			=(D7–D50)

10.

	A	B	C	D	E	F	G	H	I	J	K	L	M
1	**Income**	**Jan**	**Feb**	**Mar**	**Apr**	**May**	**June**	**July**	**Aug**	**Sept**	**Oct**	**Nov**	**Dec**
2	Primary Employment	5,000	5,000	5,000	5,000	5,000	5,000	5,000	5,000	5,000	5,000	5,000	5,000
3	Secondary Employment	1,200	1,200	1,200	1,200	1,200	1,200	1,200	1,200	1,200	1,200	1,200	1,200
4	Other Income												
5	**Total Income**	6,200	6,200	6,200	6,200	6,200	6,200	6,200	6,200	6,200	6,200	6,200	6,200
6													
7	**Fixed Expenses**												
8	Rent/Mortgage	2,200	2,200	2,200	2,200	2,200	2,200	2,200	2,200	2,200	2,200	2,200	2,200
9	Car Loan Payment	180	180	180	180	180	180	180	180	180	180	180	180
10	Education Loan Payment	250	250	250	250	250	250	250	250	250	250	250	250
11	Personal Loan Payment	100	100	100	100	100	100	100	100	100	100	100	100
12	Health Insurance Premium	60	60	60	60	60	60	60	60	60	60	60	60
13	Life Insurance Premium												
14	Car Insurance Premium	70	70	70	70	70	70	70	70	70	70	70	70
15	Homeowner's/ Renter's Insurance	30	30	30	30	30	30	30	30	30	30	30	30
16	Cable TV	40	40	40	40	40	40	40	40	40	40	40	40
17	Life Insurance				110				110				110
18	Tuition					2,000			2,000				
19	Taxes	1,500								1,500			
20													
21	**Variable Expenses**												
22	Groceries (Food)	600	600	600	600	600	600	600	600	600	600	600	600
23	Dining Out	200	200	200	200	200	200	200	200	200	200	200	200

(*Continued*)

10. (*Continued*)

24	Fuel (car)	200	200	200	200	200	200	200	200	200	200	200	200
25	Cell Phone	80	80	80	80	80	80	80	80	80	80	80	80
26	Land Line Phone	60	60	60	60	60	60	60	60	60	60	60	60
27	Electricity	80	80	80	80	80	80	80	80	80	80	80	80
28	Water	40	40	40	40	40	40	40	40	40	40	40	40
29	Sewer												
30	Sanitation	50	50	50	50	50	50	50	50	50	50	50	50
31	Medical												
32	Medical/Dental				250					250			
33	Auto Related										400		
34	Home Related		250									250	
35	Vacation							800					
36	Gifts			250									250
37	Contributions	44	44	44	44	44	44	44	44	44	44	44	44
38	Repairs										280		
39	Entertainment	250	250	250	250	250	250	250	250	250	250	250	250
40	Savings	400	400	400	400	400	400	400	400	400	400	400	400
41	Debt Reduction	200	200	200	200	200	200	200	200	200	200	200	200
42	Other												

11a.

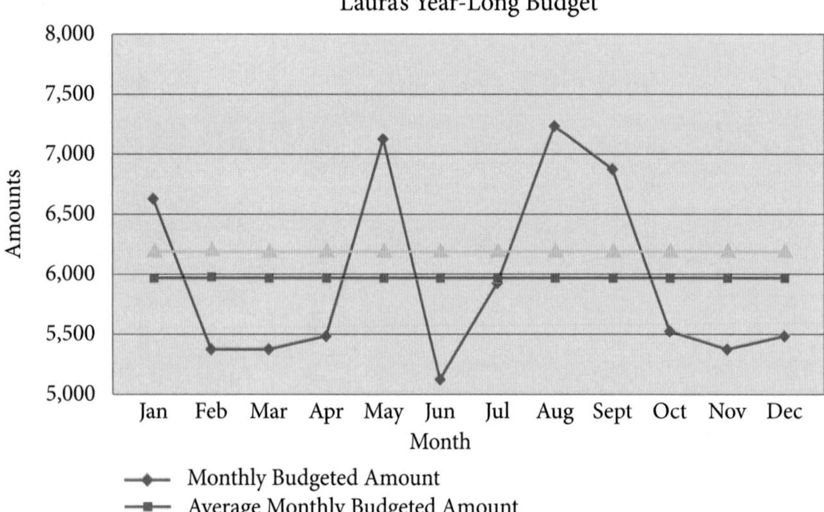

Assessment Applications, pp. 523–525

1.

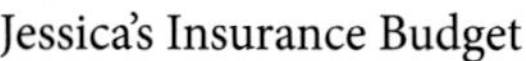

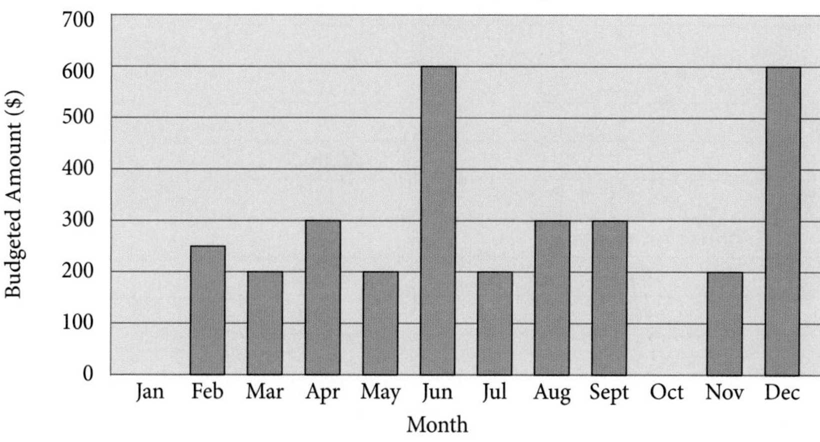

4a.

	Jan	Feb	Mar	Apr	May	June	July	Aug	Sept	Oct	Nov	Dec
Budgeted Income	4,500	5,000	4,150	4,500	4,000	6,700	7,000	6,000	5,710	4,500	5,000	6,240

4b.

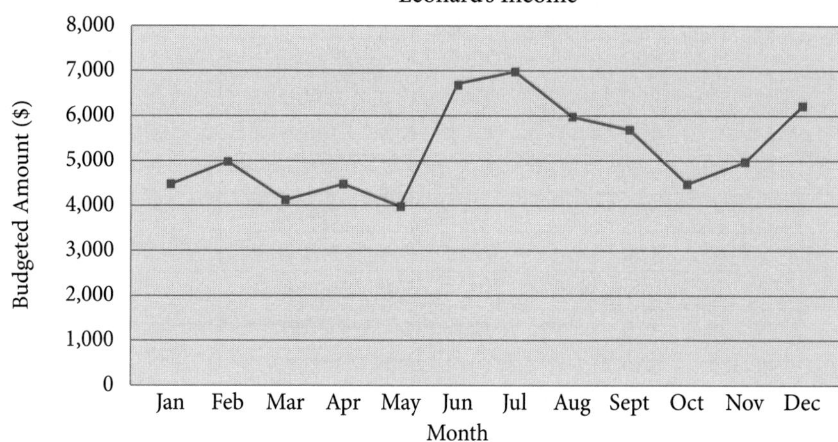

7c.

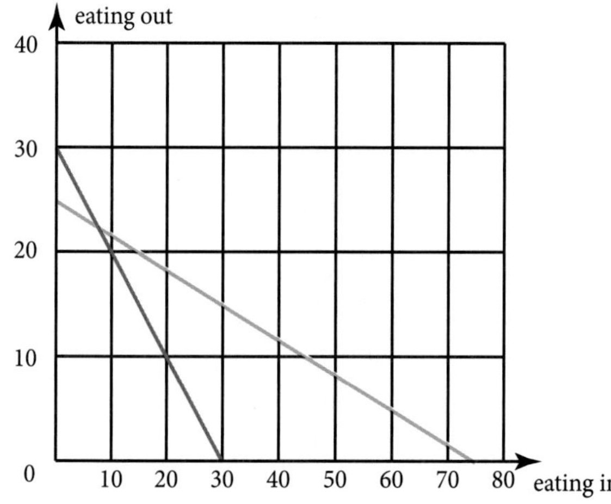

9.

After Tax Income Categories	Income Amounts	Frequency	Annual Amount
Primary Employment	3,500	24	84,000
Secondary Employment	1,000	12	12,000
Interest			
Dividends			
Other Income			
Total Income			**96,000**
Weekly Expenses	**Expense Amounts**		
Food	116	52	6,032
Personal Transportation	70	52	3,640
Public Transportation		52	0
Household		52	0
Childcare		52	0
Dining Out	47	52	2,444
Entertainment	81	52	4,212
Other (contributions)	40	52	2,080
Total Weekly Expenses			**18,408**
Monthly Expenses			
Mortgage	2,800	12	33,600
Utilities	200	12	2,400
Land Line/Cellular Telephone	150	12	1,800
Car Loan	200	12	2,400
Education Loan	200	12	2,400
Personal Loan	100	12	1,200
Car Insurance	90	12	1,080
Homeowner's Insurance	120	12	1,440
Savings	500	12	6,000
Debt Reduction	200	12	2,400
Other	130	12	1,560
Total Monthly Expenses			**58,680**
Other Frequency Expenses			
Medical/Dental	350	2	700
Auto Related	600	1	600
Home Related	250	2	500
Life Insurance	120	3	360
Tuition		2	0
Vacation	1,800	1	1,800
Gifts	300	2	600
Contributions		1	0
Repairs	600	1	600

(*Continued*)

9. (*Continued*)

Taxes	2,500	2	5,000
Other			
Total Other Frequency Expenses			**10,160**
Total Expenses			**84,848**
Annual Surplus Or Deficit			**11,152**